THE LITERARY WORKS OF
LEONARDO DA VINCI

PHAIDON

THE LITERARY WORKS OF

LEONARDO DA VINCI

COMPILED & EDITED

FROM THE ORIGINAL MANUSCRIPTS

BY JEAN PAUL RICHTER

IN TWO VOLUMES   VOLUME II

PHAIDON

ALL RIGHTS RESERVED BY PHAIDON PRESS LTD · 5 CROMWELL PLACE · LONDON SW7

FIRST PUBLISHED 1883

SECOND EDITION (ENLARGED AND REVISED BY JEAN PAUL RICHTER

AND IRMA A. RICHTER) · OXFORD UNIVERSITY PRESS · 1939

THIRD EDITION 1970

PHAIDON PUBLISHERS INC · NEW YORK

DISTRIBUTORS IN THE UNITED STATES: PRAEGER PUBLISHERS INC

111 FOURTH AVENUE · NEW YORK • N.Y. 10003

LIBRARY OF CONGRESS CATALOG CARD NUMBER: 69–19813

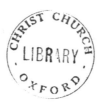

ISBN FOR COMPLETE SET OF TWO VOLUMES: 0 7148 1394 X

ISBN FOR THIS VOLUME: 0 7148 1396 6

MADE IN GREAT BRITAIN

TEXT PRINTED AT THE PITMAN PRESS · BATH

PLATES PRINTED BY CAVENDISH PRESS LTD · LEICESTER

CONTENTS

LIST OF ILLUSTRATIONS

All drawings here reproduced are in pen and ink, unless otherwise stated.

XI

THE NOTES ON SCULPTURE

*T*HERE *had been a project before Lodovico il Moro's accession to erect an equestrian statue in commemoration of Francesco Sforza, the famous Condottiere (d. 1466) who, in the words of Pope Pius the Second, had guided the destinies of Italy from Milan with extraordinary wisdom. At that time the statue of Gattamelata, the Venetian Condottiere, and victor of Milan, which had been set up in an open square in Padua, was regarded almost as a miracle—*non solo fece stupire allora que' che lo videro, ma ogni persona che al presente lo vede—*a view that persisted for centuries (Vasari, ii. 411). Admiration went out to Donatello, the artist from Florence, who had been the first to cast an equestrian statue in bronze like that of Marcus Aurelius.*

Leonardo took it upon himself to propose to Duke Lodovico that the task of making the monument of his ancestor should be entrusted to him. There was no reason why the Duke should not at once accept this proposal, which was submitted in a letter. The honour and glory of his dynasty as well as his own personal ambition were strong inducements. There was, however, in the mind of the artist, when he composed the letter, another motive which he did not express but which could easily be surmised. If the fame of Donatello rested on the statue erected in Padua, why should not another citizen of Florence achieve the same in Milan, and in a way that might excite the astonishment of the world?

No sooner had he finished the model of the horse, without the rider, than it was publicly exhibited. It measured 7·20 metres, i.e. 23 feet, from the top of the horse's head to the base. The total weight was estimated at 200,000 lb. The difficulties that lay in the realization of the plan are mentioned in a report of the Florentine Ambassador in Milan to his master, Lorenzo de Medici: 'Prince Lodovico is planning to erect a worthy monument to his father, and in accordance with his orders Leonardo has been asked to make a model in the form of a large horse in bronze ridden by the Duke Francesco in full armour. As His Highness has in mind something wonderful, the like of which has never been seen, he has directed me to write to you and ask if you would kindly send him one or two Florentine artists who specialize in this kind of work. Moreover, although he has given the commission to Leonardo, it seems to me that he is not confident that he will succeed.'

Among the many chroniclers of Leonardo's work, two of the oldest and most trustworthy Florentine contemporaries, who knew him personally, gave a similar account of the circumstances: Leonardo had modelled a horse in Milan of immense size and seated upon it the figure of Duke Francesco Sforza; when this wonderful model was to be cast in bronze difficulties arose and it was declared to be an impossible undertaking, especially as the intention was to cast the whole in one mould. And that

was the reason why the work failed. The accusation that Leonardo was responsible
for this failure can be answered with documents which have been found in Milan.[1]

It was perhaps natural that partisans of rivals of Leonardo should have made
him the scapegoat for failure in an undertaking which by its very nature was im-
possible. But the judgement of Michelangelo was unexpectedly harsh: 'Tu che
facesti un disegno di uno cavallo per gittarlo di bronzo et non lo potesti gittare
et per vergogna lo lasciasti stare.' *Leonardo never uttered a word in reply when*
Michelangelo taunted him in the streets of Florence amid a crowd of bystanders.
The witness relates that he flushed crimson, probably in anger: it must be remem-
bered that he was twenty years Michelangelo's senior.[2]

The question arises whether the colossal dimensions of the monument were ordered
by the prince or were suggested by Leonardo. The answer is provided in the letter
of the Florentine Ambassador quoted above: 'Il Signor Lodovico . . . ha ordinato
. . . uno grandissimo cavallo di bronzo . . . perchè S. Eccellentia vorrebbe fare
una cosa in superlativo grado.'

The various sketches of the statue which are to be found among his manuscripts
give some indication of Leonardo's plan. They are so numerous that one may
conclude that most of the material is still available. Every conceivable combination
of horse and rider is represented. He gave free rein to his artistic imagination,
much as a musician improvises on his instrument. Generally he worked out his
plans and arrived at a complete conception of the form. The majority of the
sketches would satisfy the standard required for decorative statuettes, and only a
few show a marked monumental conception.[3]

If we may trust the account given by Paolo Govio—about 1527—Leonardo's
horse was represented as 'vehementer incitatus et anhelatus'. *Govio had probably*
seen the model exhibited at Milan; but need we, in fact, infer from this description
that the horse was galloping? Compare Vasari's description of the Gattamelata
monument at Padua: 'Egli [Donatello] vi andò ben volentieri, e fece il cavallo
di bronzo, che è in sulla piazza di Sant' Antonio, nel quale si dimostra lo sbuffa-
mento ed il fremito del cavallo, ed il grande animo e la fierezza vivacissimamente
espressa dall' arte nella figura che lo cavalca.'

These descriptions, it seems, would only serve to mark the difference between the
work of the Middle Ages and that of the Renaissance.

Among the drawings of models of the moulds for casting we find only one which
seems to represent the horse in the act of galloping—No. 713. All the other designs
show the horse as pacing quietly; and as these studies of the horse are accompanied
by copious notes as to the method of casting, the question as to the position of the
horse in the model finally selected seems to be decided by preponderating evidence. 'Il
cavallo dello Sforza'—*C. Boito remarks very appositely in the* Saggio *on page 26,*
'doveva sembrare fratello al cavallo del Colleoni. E si direbbe che questo fosse

[1] Fr. Malaguzzi-Valeri, *La Corte di Lodovico il
Moro: Bramante e Leonardo da Vinci*, pp. 435 ff.

[2] Compare Vasari vii, p. 171, note, for the difficulties experienced by Michelangelo in casting his
statue of Julius II.

[3] Leonardo's numerous drawings of horses have
recently been published in facsimile by the Reale Commissione Vinciana, Disegni. Fascicolo IV. Rome, 1936.
Compare also K. Clark, *Catalogue of Drawings of
L.d.V. at Windsor Castle*, Vol. I, pp. xxxv. sqq.

figlio del cavallo del Gattamelata, il quale pare figlio di uno dei quattro cavalli che stavano forse sull' Arco di Nerone in Roma' (*now at Venice*). *The publication of the* Saggio *also contains the reproduction of a drawing in red chalk, representing a horse walking to the left and supported by a scaffolding, given here on Pl. LXXVI, No. 1. It must remain uncertain whether this represents the model as it stood during the preparations for casting it, or whether—as seems to me highly improbable—this sketch shows the model as it was exhibited in 1493 on the Piazza del Castello in Milan under a triumphal arch, on the occasion of the marriage of the Emperor Maximilian to Bianca Maria Sforza. The only important point here is to prove that strong evidence seems to show that, of the numerous studies for the equestrian statue, only those which represent the horse pacing agree with the schemes of the final plans.*

Nos. 731–40, which treat of casting bronze, have probably only an indirect bearing on the arrangements made for casting the equestrian statue of Francesco Sforza.[1] *Some portions evidently relate to the casting of cannon. We refer to them as giving us some clue to the process of bronze casting at the period.*

'Come si fanno i modelli per fare di bronzo le figure grandi e picciole, e come le forme per buttarle; come si armino di ferri, e come si gettino di metallo &.' *is the title Vasari gave to the fourth chapter of his* Introduzione della Scultura (*ed. Milanesi, vol.* i, *pp.* 158 ff.).

For Leonardo's comparisons between the arts of sculpture and painting see Vol. I, pp. 82–101.

[1] According to Marino Sanudo, *Spedizione di Carlo VIII in Italia*, Venice, 1883, p. 100, the bronze intended for casting the statue was presented by Lodovico il Moro to his father-in-law in November, 1494 and shipped down the Po to Ferrara where it was cast into guns with the help of Giannino Bombardiere. Compare No. 1448, n. 14, and M. Herzfeld, *Zur Geschichte des Sforzadenkmals*, Raccolta Vinciana xiii, p. 83.

DE STATUA

Some practical hints (706–9).

²Se vuoi · fare · vna · figura · di marmo · fa ne · prima vna ³di terra ·, la quale, finita che l'ài, secca e mettila in vna ⁴cassa · che sia · ancora capace ·, dopo la figura tratta ⁵d'esso · loco ·, a ricieuere il marmo · che vuoi scoprir⁶vi dentro la figura · alla · similitudine · di quella · di terra ·; di poi ⁷messa la figura di terra in detta cassa · abbi bacchette ch'ētrino ⁸appūto · per i sua · busi ·, e spingile · dentro · tāto · per ciascuno ⁹buso · che ciascuna bacchetta biāca ·tocca · la figura · in ¹⁰diuersi lochi, e la parte d'esse bacchette, che resta · fori della ¹¹cassa, tigni di nero, e fa il cōtrassegno · alla · bacchetta e al ¹²suo · buso · in modo · che a tua · posta · si scōtrī; ¹³e trai d'essa · cassa · la figura · di terra · e mettivi il tuo ¹⁴pezzo · di marmo, e tāto leua del marmo ·, che tutte le ¹⁵tue · bacchette · si nascondino · sino al loro segnio in detti busi, ¹⁶e per potere questo · meglio fare · fa che tutta · la cassa si po¹⁷ssa · leuare in alto, e 'l fondo · d'essa cassa resti sēpre · sotto ¹⁸il marmo ed a questo modo ne potrai · leuare coi ferri ¹⁹con grā facilità.

OF A STATUE

If you wish to make a figure in marble, first make one of clay, and when you have finished it, let it dry and place it in a case which should be large enough, after the figure is taken out of it, to receive also the marble from which you intend to reveal the figure in imitation of the one in clay. After you have put the clay figure into this said case, have little rods which will exactly slip into the holes in it, and thrust them so far in at each hole that each white rod may touch the figure in different parts of it. And colour the portion of the rod that remains outside black, and mark each rod and each hole with a countersign so that each may fit into its place. Then take the clay figure out if this case and put in your piece of marble, taking off so much of the marble that all your rods may be hidden in the holes as far as their marks; and to be the better able to do this, make the case so that it can be lifted up; but the bottom of it will always remain under the marble and in this way thou canst chisel it with great ease.

W. 19134–19135a] 707

Alcvni àño errato a insegniare alli scultori ²circundare con fili i mēbri · delle loro figure, ³quasi credendo che essi menbri sieno d'equale ⁴rotondità, in qualunque parte da essi fili ⁵circundati sieno.

Some have erred in teaching sculptors to measure the limbs of their figures with threads as if they thought that these limbs were equally round in every part where these threads were wound about them.

A. 1a] 708

MISURE E CŌPARTITIONE DELLA STATUA

²Diuidi la testa in 12 gradi, e ciascuno grado · diuidi in 12 pūti, e ciascuno ³pūto · in 12 minvti ·, e i minvti in minimi, e i minimi ī seminimini.

⁴Grado — punto — minvto — minimo.

MEASUREMENT AND DIVISION OF A STATUTE

Divide the head into 12 degrees, and each degree divide into 12 points, and each point into 12 minutes, and the minutes into minims, and the minims into semi-minims.

Degree—point—minute—minim.

B. N. 2038. 16a] 709

¶ Le figure di rilievo che pajono · ī moto ·, posandole in piè, per ragione deō cadere jnāzi.

Sculptured figures which appear in motion will, in their standing position, actually look as if they were falling forward.

706. 1. desstatua. 2. sevolli. 3. tera .. chellai essecha mettila nvna. 4. chassa chessia anchora [dop atta] "capace". 5. loco .. [chē] schoprir. 7. tera .. chassa . abi bacchette. 8. apūto .. esspignile .. tāto [che]per ciasschuno. 9. ciassuna bacchetta biācha tocha. 10. bachette .. ressta. 11. chassa .. effa .. chōtrassegnio .. bachetta eal. 12. suo buso imodo .. attua .. sisschōtri [ettare lasi]. 13. ettrai .. chassa .. tera. 14. pezo .. ettāto .. chettutte. 15. bachette .. naschōdino .. aloro. 16. chettutta .. chassa. 17. chasa ressti. 18. acquesto .. cho. 19. chon.

707. 1. alchuni .. erato ansegniare. 2. chirchundare. 3. menbr. 4. retondita. 5. circhundati.
708. 1. chōpartitione. 2. 12 [parti e] gradi. 3. minvti iminimi e e. 4. grado [minvto] punto.
709. 1. pajano .. chadere.

709. *figure di rilievo*. Leonardo applies this term exclusively to wholly detached figures, especially to those standing free. This note apparently refers to some particular case, though we have no knowledge of what that may have been. If we suppose it to refer to the first model of the equestrian statue of Francesco

3 Ferri che cingā la forma. ²[Se uolli fare
presti gietti e ³senplici, fagli con vna cassa ⁴di
sabbione di fiume invmidito con ⁵acieto.]

Three braces which bind the mould. [If you
want to make simple casts quickly, make them
in a box of river sand wetted with vinegar.]

Notes on
the casting
of the
Sforza mo-
nument
(710–15).

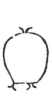
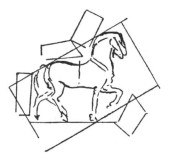
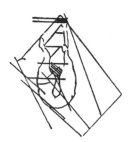

⁶[Quando · tu · avrai · fatto · la ⁷forma · sopra
il cauallo e tu ⁸farai la grossezza del metallo ⁹di
terra.]
¹⁰Nota · nello allegare · quante · ore · vā · per
cētinajo ¹¹[nel gittare ognuno tenga stoppato · il
fornello col ¹²suo · infocato]; ¹³[nel dentro di
tutta la forma · sia inbeuerato olio ¹⁴di lin seme
o di tremētina; e poi sia dato vna mano ¹⁵di
poluere di borrace o di poco greco con acqua vite,
¹⁶e la forma di fori inpeciata, acciochè stādo
sotto ¹⁷terra l'umido non la. . . .
²⁴[Per maneggiare la forma grāde, fa ne
modello della pi²⁵ccola forma; fa una piccola
stātia a proportione;]
²⁶[fa le bocche alla forma, mētre ch'è in sul
cavallo;]
²⁷¶Tieni le corna · in molle ·, e fondile con
colla di pesce¶ ²⁸pesa le parti ²⁹della forma, da
che quātità ³⁰di metallo ella à a essere occupata,
³¹e tāto ne da al fornello, che ³²a quella parte à
a porgere il ³³suo metallo, e questo cognio³⁴scerai
a pesare la terra di quella ³⁵parte della forma,
dove il fornel³⁶lo colla sua quātità à a rispōde-
³⁷re, e questo si fa aciochè 'l ³⁸fornello delle
gābe le ēpia, e che ³⁹dalle gābe non abbia a

[When you shall have made the mould upon
the horse you must make the thickness of the
metal in clay.]
Observe in alloying how many hours are
wanted for each hundredweight. [In casting
each one keep the furnace and its fire well
stopped up.] [Let the inside of all the moulds
be wetted with linseed oil or oil of turpentine,
and then take a handful of powdered borax and
Greek pitch with aqua vitae, and pitch the
mould over outside so that being under ground
the damp may not [damage it?].
[To manage the large mould make a small
mould as a model; make a small room in proportion.]
[Make the vents in the mould while it is on
the horse.]
Hold the hoofs in the tongs, and cast them
with fish glue. Weigh the parts of the mould and
the quantity of metal it will take to fill them, and
give so much to the furnace that it may afford
to each part its amount of metal; and this you
may know by weighing the clay of each part of
the mould to which the quantity in the furnace
must correspond. And this is done in order that
the furnace for the legs when filled may not have

710. *These passages are written in ink and subsequently crossed through with red chalk.* 3. chon. 4. sabiō . . cho. 6. arai . facto. 7. chauallo
ettu. 8. grosseza. 10. hore va . . ciētinaro. 11. hognivno . . stopato . . chol. 12. infochato mādiriano ea ū tenpo di stoppi. 13.
holio. 14. poi dato. 15. grecha chon acq"a". 16. ella . . chesstādo. 17. lomido nolla \\\\\\\\\\\\\\\\\\\\\\\ chose. 18. fatte subito
chella \\\\\\\\\\\\\\\\\\\\\. 19. il sabione di for \\\\\\\\\\\\\\\\\\\\\ azzo cioe di. 20. quello da fforme \\\\\\\\\\\\\\\\\\ chon acieto.
21. e ben \\\\\\\\\\\\\\\. 22. miscia nella forma \\\\\\\\\ uno quadrello. 23. pesto . e cienere cō ciara douo e a ceto. 24. manegiare.
25. cholla . . falle una pichola. 26. falle boche. 27. chorna imole effondile chōlla di pesscie. 28. pensa [la forma] le. 30. ella
essere ochupata. 31. ettāto. 32. acquella parte a porgiere. 33. ecquesto chognio. 34. sscierai . . tera. 35. forne. 36. cholla . .
risspōde. 37. ecquesto. 38. gābe ēpinteche *doubtful*. 39. ale . . abiasschorrer.

Sforza (see the introduction to the notes on Sculpture)
this observation may be regarded as one of his arguments for abandoning the first scheme of the Sforza
monument, in which the horse was to be galloping
(see p. 2). It is also in favour of this theory that
the note is written in a manuscript volume already
completed in 1492.
710. The importance of the notes included under

this number is not diminished by the fact that they
have been lightly crossed out with red chalk. Possibly
they were the first scheme for some fuller observations
which no longer exist; or perhaps they were crossed
out when Leonardo found himself obliged to give up
the idea of casting the equestrian statue. In the
original the first two sketches are above l. 1, and the
third below l. 9.

socorrere ⁴⁰alla testa che sarebbe inpossibile ⁴¹[gitta nel medesimo ⁴²gietto del cavallo ⁴³lo sportello della].

to furnish metal from the legs to help out the head, which would be impossible. [Cast the little door at the same casting as the horse.]

W. 12347]   711

FORMA DEL CAVALLO

²Fa il cavallo sopra gambe di ferro ferme e stabili in bo³no fondamēto, poi lo inseva e fa gli la cappa di sopra, ⁴lasciādo ben seccare a suolo a suolo, e questa ingras⁵serai tre dita ·, di poi arma e ferra secondo il biso⁶gno; oltre a di questo cava la forma, e poi fa la ⁷grossezza, e poi riēpi la forma a mezza a mezza, ⁸e quella integra, poi con sua ferri cierchiala e ⁹cigni e la ricuoci di dētro dove à a toccare il brō¹⁰zo.

THE MOULD FOR THE HORSE

Make the horse on legs of iron, strong and well set on a good foundation; then grease it and cover it with a coating, leaving each coat to dry thoroughly layer by layer; and this will thicken it by the breadth of three fingers. Now fix and bind it with iron as may be necessary. Moreover, take off the mould and then make the thickness. Then fill the mould by degrees and make it good throughout; encircle and bind it with its irons and bake it inside where it has to touch the bronze.

DEL FAR LA FORMA DI PEZZI

¹²Segnia sopra il cavallo finito tutti li pezzi della for¹³ma, di che tu voi vestire tal cavallo, e nello interrare ¹⁴li taglia in ogni interratura, acciochè quādo si è fini¹⁵ta la forma che tu la possi cavare e poi ricōmettere ¹⁶al primo loco colli sua scōtri delli cōtrasegni.

¹⁷*a b* quadretto · starà infra la cappa e 'l maschio, cioè ¹⁸nel uacuo dove à a stare il brōzo liquefatto e questi ¹⁹tali quadretti di brōzo manterrāno li spati della for²⁰ma alla cappa con equal distātia, e per questo tali ²¹quadretti sō di grāde inportantia.

²²¶La terra sia mista ²³cō rena;

²⁴tolli cera, a rēde²⁵re, e pagare la cō²⁶sumata.¶

²⁷Secca la ²⁸a suoli. ²⁹Fa la forma di fori ³⁰di giesso per fugire ³¹il tēpo del seccare, ³²e la spesa di legnie, e cō ³³tal giesso ferma ³⁴li ferri di fori e di ³⁵dentro cō due dita di ³⁶grossezza, fa terra ³⁷cotta.

³⁸E questa tal forma ³⁹farai in un dì; vna mez⁴⁰za navata di giesso ⁴¹ti serue.

⁴²Bono.

⁴³Rītasa cō ⁴⁴colla e terra ⁴⁵over · chiara d'ovo ⁴⁶e mattone e ro⁴⁷ssume.

OF MAKING THE MOULD IN PIECES

Draw upon the horse, when finished, all the pieces of the mould with which you wish to cover the horse, and in laying on the clay cut it in every piece, so that when the mould is finished you can take it off, and then recompose it in its former position with its joins by the countersigns.

The square blocks *a b* will be between the cover and the core, that is, in the hollow where the melted bronze is to be; and these square blocks of bronze will support the intervals between the mould and the cover at an equal distance, and for this reason these squares are of great importance.

The clay should be mixed with sand.

Take wax, to return [what is not used] and to pay for what is used.

[27] Dry it in layers [28].

Make the outside mould of plaster, to save time in drying and the expense in wood; and with this plaster enclose the irons [props] both outside and inside to a thickness of two fingers; make terracotta.

And this mould can be made in one day; half a boat-load of plaster will serve you.

[42] Good.

Dam it up again with glue and clay, or white of egg, and bricks and rubbish.

---

40. chessa rebe inpossib. 42. chavallo. 43. sportello della. *Here the text breaks off.*
711. 2. ghanbe .. esstabile. 3. sondomēto .. effagli la chappa. 4. scechare assuolo assuclo .. ecquesta. 5. efferra sechondo. 6. chava .. falla. 7. grosseza. 8. ecquella . cosua .. ec. 9. ella richuoci .. dove attochare. 11. pezi. 12. pezi. 13. chettu .. vesstire .. chavallo. 14. quādo se fini. 15. chettu .. chavare ricomettere. 16. al p"o" locho cholli .. cōtrassegni. 17. infralla chappa. elmasscio cioe [di]. 18. uachuo dove asstare .. liquefacto ecquesti. 19. lisspati. 20. dallalla chappa chon .. distātia .. quessto 22. tera sie. 27. sechalla soli. 28. assu oli. 31. sechare. 32. espesa. 36. rosseza fatterra. 38. ecquesta. 39. farai nūdi vna me. 43. ritasa. 44. etterra. 47. ssume.

711. See Pl. LXXV. The figure '40' close to the sketch in the middle of the page between ll. 16 and 17 has been added by a collector's hand.

In the original, below l. 21, a square piece of the page has been cut out about 9 centimetres by 7 and a blank piece has been gummed into the place.

Lines 22–24 are written on the margin. Lines 27 and 28 are close to the second marginal sketch. Line 42 is a note written above the third marginal sketch and on the back of this sheet is the text given as No. 642. Compare also No. 802.

C. A. 216b]   712

Tutti · i capi de²lle chiavarde.   All the heads of the large nails.

W. 12349]   713

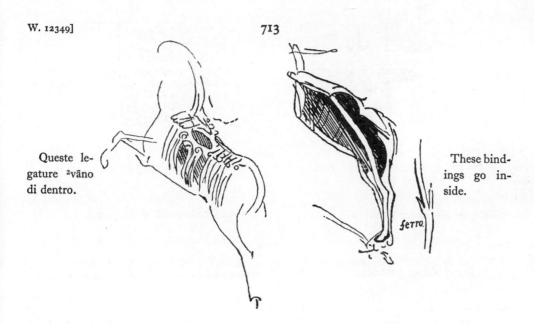

Queste le-
gature ²vāno
di dentro.

These bind-
ings go in-
side.

W.12351   714

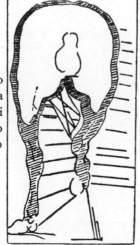

Sale fatto di sterco vmano
bruciato ²e calcinato e fattone liscia
e que³lla distesa al lēto foco, e tutti
li ster⁴chi in simile modo fanno
sale, e quelli ⁵sali destillati · sono
molto penetrāti.

Salt may be made from human
excrements, burnt and calcined,
made into lees and dried slowly at
a fire, and all the excrements produce salt in a similar way and these
salts when distilled are very strong.

712. 1-2 R. 1. tucti i chapi.
714. 1. stercho. 2. chalcinato effatto neliscia ecque. 3. disecha allēto focho ettutti lisster. 4. quali. 5. desstilati.

712. See Pl. LXXVI, No. 1.
714. Vasari repeatedly states, in the fourth chapter of his *Introduzione della Scultura*, that in preparing to cast bronze statues horse-dung was frequently used by sculptors.

W. 12349]   715

MODO DI RICUOCERE

²Questo si potrebbe fare fatto ³il fornello ⁴ferma e pillata.

METHOD OF FOUNDING AGAIN

This may be done when the furnace is made [4] strong and rammed.

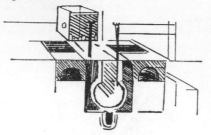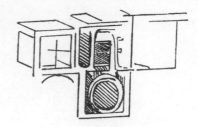

W. 12319]   716

Models for the horse of the Sforza monument (716–18).

Ginnetto · grosso · di messer Galeazzo.

Messer Galeazzo's big genet.

W. 12294]   717

Siciliano di messer Galeazzo.

Messer Galeazzo's Sicilian horse.

C. A. 291b]   718

Misura del siciliano, la ganba dirieto, ²in faccia, alzata e distesa.

Measurement of the Sicilian horse, the leg from behind, seen in front, lifted and extended.

C. A. 391a]   719

Occasional references to the Sforza monument (719–24).

Ancora si potrà dare opera al cauallo di bronzo che sarà gloria īmortale e eterno onore della ²felice memoria del signore vostro patre e della īcljta casa Sforzesca.

Again, the bronze horse may be taken in hand, which is to be the immortal glory and eternal honour of the happy memory of the prince your father, and of the illustrious house of Sforza.

C. 15b (1)]   720

A dì 23 d'aprile 1 · 4 · 90 comīciai questo libro e ricomīciai · il cavallo.

On the 23rd of April 1490 I began this book, and recommenced the horse.

Leic. 9b]   721

Vedesi in nelle montagnie di Parma e Piacētia la moltitudine di nichi e coralli ²intarlati ancora appiccati alli sassi, de' quali, quand' io facevo il grā ³cavallo di Milano, me ne fu portato vn grā sacco ne⁴lla mia fabrica da cierti villani che in tal loco trovati l'aveano.

There is to be seen, in the mountains of Parma and Piacenza, a multitude of shells and corals full of holes, still sticking to the rocks, and when I was at work on the great horse for Milan, a large sackful of them, which were found thereabout, was brought to me into my workshop by certain peasants.

715. 1. richuocere. 2. potre. 4. pilata.
716. 1. gianecto .. galeaz.
717. 1. ciciliano .. meser galeazo.
718. 1. ciciliano. 2. alza
719. 1–2 *written from left to right.* 1. Anchora si potera .. honore dela. 2. S"gre" vost .. dela.
720. chomiciai .. richomīciai.
721. 1. in nelle .. mvltitudine. 2. apichati .. sacho. 3. fabricha.

715. This note in l. 4 is written below the sketches.
716, 717. These notes are by the side of a drawing of a horse with figured measurements. See K. Clark, 12494.
718. There is no sketch belonging to this passage. Galeazzo here probably means the Duke of Milan, or

Galeazzo di San Severino, the famous captain who married Bianca the daughter of Lodovico il Moro. Compare No. 1384.
719. The letter from which this passage is here extracted will be found complete in No. 1340.

C. A. 323*a*]　　　　　　　　　　722

Credetelo a me, Leonardo fiorētino che fa il cauallo del duca Francesco di brōzo che non ne bisognia fare stima, ²perchè à che fare il tenpo di sua vita ·, e dubito che per l'essere si grāde opera, che non la finirà mai.

Believe me, Leonardo the Florentine, who has to do the equestrian bronze statue of the Duke Francesco, that he does not need to care about it, because he has work for all his lifetime, and, being so great a work, I doubt whether he can ever finish it.

C. A. 335*b*]　　　　　　　　　　723

Del cauallo nō dirò niēte perchè cogniosco · i tēpi.

Of the horse I will say nothing because I know the times.

C. A. 277*b*]　　　　　　　　　　724

Del marmo operasi dieci añi; ²io nō vo' aspettare che 'l mio pa³gamēto passi il termine del ⁴fine della opera mia.

During ten years the works on the marbles have been going on; I will not wait for my payment beyond the time when my works are finished.

C. A. 179*b*]　　　　　　　　　　725

SEPULCRO DI MESSER GIOVĀNI JACOMO DA TREVULZO

²Spesa della ³manifattu⁴ra e materi⁵a del cauallo.

⁶Vno corsiero grāde al naturale coll'omo oopra vuole per la spesa del metallo. duc. 500.

⁷E per la spesa del ferramēto che ua in el modello e carboni e legname e la fossa per gittarlo ⁸e per serrare la forma, e col fornello doue si de' gittare . . . duc. 200.

THE MONUMENT TO MESSER GIOVANNI JACOMO DA TREVULZO

[2]Cost of the making and materials for the horse [5].

A courser, as large as life, with the rider, requires for the cost of the metal . duc. 500.

And for cost of the ironwork which is inside the model, and charcoal, and wood, and the pit to cast it in, and for binding the mould, and including the furnace where it is to be cast . . . . duc. 200.

The project of the Trivulzio monument.

722. 1. me saluo [quel] | "lonar fiorētino" cheffa il chauallo . . franc"o" "di brōzo" chēnone. 2. lesere . . nolla.
724. 1. marmoperassi. 2. inōvo. 3. ghamēto. 4. dela.
725. 1. giovāni iacomo da trevlso. 3. manifatu. 7. inel . . ellegrame ella.

722. This passage is quoted from a letter to a committee at Piacenza for whom Leonardo seems to have undertaken to execute some work. The letter is given entire in No. 1346; in it Leonardo remonstrates as to some unreasonable demands.

723. This passage occurs in a rough copy of a letter to Lodovico il Moro, without date (see below, No. 1345, l. 11).

725. In the original, ll. 2–5, 12–14, 33–5, are written on the margin. The simple monument to the great general in San Nazaro Maggiore in Milan consists merely of a sarcophagus placed in recess high on the wall of an octagonal chapel. The figure of the warrior is lying in the sarcophagus, on which his name is inscribed; a piece of sculpture which is certainly not Leonardo's work. Gian Giacomo Trivulzio died at Chartres in 1518, only five months before Leonardo, and it seems improbable that this should have been the date of this sketch; under these circumstances it would have been done under the auspices of Francis I, but the Italian general was certainly not in favour with the French monarch at the time. Gian Giacomo Trivulzio was a sworn foe to Lodovico il Moro, whom he strove for years to overthrow. On September 6, 1499, he marched victorious into Milan at the head of a French army. In a short time, however, he was forced to quit Milan again when Lodovico il Moro bore down upon the city with a force of Swiss troops. On the following 15th of April, after defeating Lodovico at Novara, Trivulzio

once more entered Milan as a conqueror, but his hopes of becoming *Governatore* of the place were soon wrecked by intrigue. This victory and triumph were signalized by acts of vengeance against the dethroned Sforza.

It must have been at this moment that he commissioned the artist to prepare designs for his own monument, which he probably intended should find a place in the Cathedral or in some other church. He, the husband of Margherita di Niccolino Colleoni, would have thought that he had a claim to the same distinction and public homage as his less illustrious connexion had received at the hands of the Venetian republic. It was at this very time that Trivulzio had a medal struck with a bust portrait of himself and the following remarkable inscription on the reverse: DEO FAVENTE · 1499 · DICTVS · IO · IA · EXPVLIT · LVDOVICV̄ · SF · (Sfortiam) DVC · (ducem) MLI (Mediolani) · NOĪE (nomine) · REGIS · FRANCORVM · EODEM · ANN · (anno) RED'T (redit) · LVS (Ludovicus) · SVPERATVS ET CAPTVS · EST · AB · EO. In the Library of the Palazzo Trivulzio there is a MS. of Callimachus Siculus written at the end of the fifteenth or beginning of the sixteenth century. At the beginning of this MS. there is an exquisite illuminated miniature of an equestrian statue with the name of the general on the base; it is, however, very doubtful whether this has any connexion with Leonardo's design.

⁹Per fare il modello di terra e poi di cera . . . . duc. 432.
¹⁰E per li lauorāti che lo netterāno quādo fia gittato . . . . . duc. 450.
¹¹In somma sono . . . . . duc. 1582.
¹²Spesa de' m¹³armi della ¹⁴sepultura.

¹⁵Spesa del marmo secōdo il disegnio; Il pezzo del marmo che ua sotto il cauallo ¹⁶ch'è lungo braccia 4 e largo braccia 2 e oncie 2 e grosso oncie 9, cētinara 58, a L. 4 e S. 10 per cētinaro . . . duc. 58.

¹⁷E per 13 braccia di cornice e ō 6, larga ō 7, e grossa ō 4, cēt. 24 . . duc. 24.

¹⁸E per lo fregio e architrave ch'è lungo br. 4 e ō 6 ·, largo br. 2 e grosso ō 6, cēt 20 . . . . duc. 20.
¹⁹E per li capitelli fatti di metallo, che sono 8, vaño ī tavola ō 5, e grossi ō 2, a prezzo di ²⁰ducati 15 per ciascuno montano . . . . duc. 120.
²¹E per 8 colonne di br. 2 e ō 7, grosse ō 4 e ½ ·, cētinara 20 . . . . . duc. 20.
²²E per 8 base che sono in tauola ō 5 e ½ e alte ō 2, cent. 5 . . . . . duc. 5.
²³E per la pietra dou' è su la sepultura lūga br. 4 e ō 10, larga br. 2 e ō 4 e ½, ²⁴centinara 36 . . . . duc. 36.
²⁵E per 8 piedi di piedistalli che uā lunghi br. 8 e larghi ō 6 e ½ grossi ō 6½, ²⁶centinara 20, mōtano . . . . duc. 20.
²⁷E per la cornice ch'è di sotto, ch'è lūga br. 4 e ō 10, larga br. 2 e ō 5, e grossa ō 4, cēt. 32 . . . . duc. 32.
²⁸E per la pietra di che si fa il morto ch'è lunga br. 3 e ō 8, larga br. uno e ō 6, grossa ō 9, cent. 30 . . . . . duc. 30.

²⁹E per la pietra che ua sotto il morto · ch'è lūga br. 3 e ō 4, larga br. uno e ō 2, grossa ō 4½ . . . . duc. 16.
³⁰E per le tauole del marmo īterposte infra li piedistalli, che sono 8 e son lūghe br. 9, ³¹larghe ō 9, grosse ō 3, cent 8 . duc. 8.
³²In somma sono . . . . . duc. 389.

³³Spesa della ³⁴manifattu³⁵ra ne' marmi.
³⁶Attorno allo inbasamēto del cauallo vā figure 8 di 25 ducati l'una . . . duc. 200.

³⁷E nel medesimo inbasamēto ci vā festoni 8 cō certi altri ornamēti e di questi ³⁸ve n'è 4 a prezzo di ducati 15 per ciascuno, e 4 a prezzo di 8 ducati l'uno . duc. 92.

³⁹E per isquadrare dette pietre . duc. 6.

To make the model in clay and then in wax . . . . duc. 432.
To the labourers for polishing it when it is cast . . . . duc. 450.
              in all . . duc. 1582.
[12] Cost of the marble of the monument [14].
Cost of the marble according to the drawing. The piece of marble under the horse which is 4 braccia long, 2 braccia and 2 inches wide and 9 inches thick, 58 hundredweight, at 4 Lire and 10 Soldi per hundredweight . . . . . . duc. 58.
And for 13 braccia and 6 inches of cornice, 7 in. wide and 4 in. thick, 24 hundredweight . . . . duc. 24.
And for the frieze and architrave, which is 4 br. and 6 in. long, 2 br. wide, and 6 in. thick, 29 hundredweight . . . duc. 20.
And for the capitals made of metal, which are 8, 5 inches in. square and 2 in. thick, at the price of 15 ducats each, will come to . . . . duc. 122.
And for 8 columns of 2 br. 7 in., 4½ in. thick, 20 hundredweight . duc. 20.
And for 8 bases which are 5½ in. square and 2 in. high, 5 hundᵗ . . duc. 5.
And for the slab of the tombstone 4 br. 10 in. long, 2 br. 4½ in. wide, 36 hundredweight . . . . duc. 36.
And for 8 pedestal feet each 8 br. long and 6½ in. wide and 6½ in. thick, 20 hundredweight come to . . . . . duc. 20.
And for the cornice below which is 4 br. and 10 in. long, and 2 br. and 5 in. wide, and 4 in. thick, 32 hundᵗ . . . duc. 32.
And for the stone of which the figure of the deceased is to be made which is 3 br. and 8 in. long, and 1 br. and 6 in. wide, and 9 in. thick, 30 hundᵗ . . . duc. 30.
And for the stone on which the figure lies which is 3 br. and 4 in. long and 1 br. and 2 in. wide and 4½ in. thick. . duc. 16.
And for the squares of marble placed between the pedestals which are 8 and are 9 br. long and 9 in. wide and 3 in. thick, 8 hundredweight . . . . . duc. 8.
              in all . . duc. 389.
[33]Cost of the work in marble [35].
Round the base on which the horse stands there are 8 figures at 25 ducats each . . . . duc. 200.
And on the same base there are 8 festoons with some other ornaments, and of these there are 4 at the price of 15 ducats each, and 4 at the price of 8 ducats each . . . . duc. 92.
And for squaring the stones . . duc. 6.

11. soma. 15. pezo. 16. lungha br 4 ellargho br. 2 e Co egrosso Co 9. 17. 13 br. 18. frego . . lungho . . largho. 19. prezo. 20. ciasscuno. 22. chessono. 25. lungh br. 8. ellarghi. 28. di ce si . . . br ı e ō 6, grosa. 29. larga br ı̄ e ō 2 grosa. 30. infra li piedi di stallo che . . lũgh. 31. larghi. 36. va. 37. li va fessto 8 cō . . queste. 38. ciasscuna . . luna. 39. issguadare.

⁴⁰Ancora pel cornicione che ua sotto lo inbasamēto del cauallo, ch'è br. 13 e ō 6 a duc. 2 per br. . . . . . duc. 27.

Again, for the large cornice which goes below the base on which the horse stands, which is 13 br. and 6 in., at 2 duc. per br. . . . . duc. 27.

⁴¹E per 12 br. di fregio, a ducati 5 per br. . . . . duc. 60.

And for 12 br. of frieze at 5 duc. per br.. . . . . duc. 60.

⁴²E per br. d'architrave, a ducati 1 e ½ per br. . . . . duc. 18.

And for 12 br. of architrave at 1½ duc. per br. . . . . duc. 18.

⁴³E per 3 fioroni che fā soffitta alla sepultura, a 20 ducati per fiorone, . duc. 60.

And for 3 rosettes which will be the soffit of the monument, at 20 ducats each, duc. 60.

⁴⁴E per 8 colonne accanalate, a 8 ducati l'una . . . . duc. 64.

And for 8 fluted columns at 8 ducats each . . . . 64.

⁴⁵E per 8 base, a un ducato l'una . duc. 8.

And for 8 bases at 1 ducat each . duc. 8.

⁴⁶E per 8 piedistalli, de' quali n'è 4 a 10 duc. l'uno, che uā sopra li cātoni, e 4 a 6 duc. l'uno . . . . . duc. 64.

And for 8 pedestals, of which 4 are at 10 duc. each, which go above the angles; and 4 at 6 duc. each. . . . . duc. 64.

⁴⁷E per isquadrare e incorniciare li piedistalli, a due duc. l'uno, che sono 8, duc. 16.

And for squaring and carving the moulding of the pedestals at 2 duc. each, and there are 8 . . . . . duc. 16.

⁴⁸E per 6 tavole con figure e trofei, a 25 ducati l'uno . . . . . . duc. 150.

And for 6 square blocks with figures and trophies, at 25 duc. each . duc. 150.

⁴⁹E per la scorniciatura della pietra che ua sotto il morto . . . . duc. 40.

And for carving the moulding of the stone under the figure of the deceased, duc. 100.

⁵⁰Per la figura del morto a farla bene duc. 100.

For the statue of the deceased, to do it well . . . . duc. 100.

⁵¹Per 6 arpie colli candelieri, a 25 ducati l'una . . . . . . duc. 150.

For 6 harpies with candelabra, at 25 ducats each . . . . . . duc. 150.

⁵²Per isquadrare la pietra dove si posa il morto e sua incorniciatura . . . duc. 20.

For squaring the stone on which the statue lies, and carving the moulding, duc. 20.

⁵³In somma . duc. 1075.

in all . . duc. 1075.

⁵⁴In somma ogni cosa insieme giūta sō duc. 3046.

The sum total of everything added together amounts to . . . . . duc. 3046.

G. 43a] 726

ZECCA DI ROMA

²Puosi ancora fare sanza molla; ³Ma sempre il maschio di sopra debbe ⁴stare congiunto alla parte della gu⁵aina mobile;

⁶Tutte le monete che ⁷non àño jl cierchio ⁸intero, non sieno acci⁹ettate per buone, e a ¹⁰fare la perfectione del lor ¹¹cierchio è neciessario ¹²che in prima le mone¹³te siē tutte di perfetto cir¹⁴colo, e a fare questo ¹⁵e' si debbe in prima fare vna ¹⁶moneta perfetta in peso ¹⁷e in larghezza e grossez¹⁸za, e di questa tal lar¹⁹ghezza e grossezza siē fat²⁰te molte lamine, tira²¹te per una medesima tra²²fila, le quali resterā²³no a modo di righe, e · ²⁴di queste tali righe si ²⁵stanpī fuori le monete ²⁶tōde, a modo

MINT AT ROME

The mint of Rome.

It can also be made without a spring. But the screw above must always be joined to the part of the movable sheath.

All coins which do not have the rim complete are not to be accepted as good; and to secure the perfection of their rim it is requisite that, in the first place, all the coins should be a perfect circle; and to do this a coin must before all be made perfect in weight, and size, and thickness. Therefore have several plates of metal made of the same size and thickness, all drawn through the same gauge so as to come out in strips. And out of [24] these strips you will stamp the coins, quite round, as sieves are made

---

40. cornicone. 41. frego. 46. piedistalle. 47. issguadrare esscornicare lipiedisstallo . . chessono . . luma. 48. trufei. 50. affarla. 52. essa scornicatura. 54. soma ōnicossa . . gūta so duc.
726. 1. zeccha di roma. 2. Puossi anchora. 3. masscio. 4. chom giunto . . ghu. 9. ectate . . eaf. 10. perfectione. 12. prima ne mone 13. perfecto. 14. cholo e affare. 15. e si . . in p"a". 16. perfecta. 18. quessta. 19. sie fac. 24. queste . . sis. 26. chessi.

726. See Pl. LXXVI, No. 2. This passage is taken from a note-book which can be proved to have been used in Rome. Compare Vasari, *Le Vite*, v. 370, note 4.

The text of ll. 31–5 stands parallel to ll. 24–7.

Further evidence of Leonardo's occupations and engagements at Rome under Pope Leo X may be gathered from some rough copies of letters which will be found in this volume.

che si fā²⁷no i criuelli da casta²⁸gnie, e queste
mone²⁹te poi si stanpino nel ³⁰modo sopra detto
ecc.

³¹Il vacuo della stanpa ³²sia più largo da alto
³³che da basso vni³⁴formemente, ³⁵e insēsibile.

³⁶Questo taglia le monete di perfetta ro³⁷ton-
dità e grossezza e peso e ris³⁸parmia l'omo che
taglia e pesa, e ³⁹rispiarmia l'omo che fa le
monete ⁴⁰tonde; adūque sol passa per le mani
⁴¹del trafilatore e dello stanpato⁴²re e fa monete
bellissime.

for sorting chestnuts [27]; and these coins can
then be stamped in the way indicated above; &c.

[31] The hollow of the die must be uniformly
wider above than below, but imperceptibly [35].

This cuts the coins perfectly round and of the
exact thickness and weight; and saves the man
who cuts and weighs, and the man who makes
the coins round. Hence it passes only through
the hands of the gauger and of the stamper, and
the coins are very superior.

C. 15b (1)]   727

POLUERE DA MEDAGLIE

²Stoppini · incombustibili · di fungo ridotto
in poluere, ³stagnio bruciato e tutti i metalli,
⁴allume, scagliuolo, ⁵fumo di fucina da ottone,
On the ⁶e ciascuna cosa inumidisci con acquauite o
ining of
medals maluagia ⁷o acieto · forte di grā uino bianco ·,
(727–8). o di quella prima acqua ⁸di trementina destillata,
o olio, pure che poco sia ⁹invmidità ·, e gitta in
telaroli.

POWDER FOR MEDALS.

The incombustible fibres of mushrooms reduced to powder, burnt tin and all the metals,
alum, isinglass, smoke from a brass forge, each
ingredient to be moistened with aqua vitae or
malmsey or strong vinegar of good white wine
or distilled extract of turpentine, or oil; but
there should be little moisture, and cast in
moulds.

Trn. o']   728

DELLO INPRŌTARE MEDAGLIE

Polta di smeriglio mista con acquavite ²o
scaglia di ferro con aceto ·, o cenere di foglie di
noce ·, o cenere ³di paglia sottilmēte trita.

⁴Il diamante si pesta inuolto in nel piōbo ·,
è battuto con martello ⁵e disteso piv uolte; tal
piōbo è raddoppiato e si tiene inuolto nel⁶la
carta, acciochè tal poluere nō si uersi, e poi fondi
il piōbo e la pol⁷uere viene sopra al pionbo
fonduto, la qual poi sia fregata infra due ⁸piastre
d'acciaio tanto si poluerizi bene, di poi lauala
coll' acqua da partire ⁹e risoluerassi la negrezza
del ferro, e lascierà la poluere netta;

¹⁰Lo smeriglo in pezzi grossi si rompe col
metterlo sopra vn panno in mol¹¹ti doppi, e si
percuote per fianco col martello, e così se ne va;
poi mischia lì ¹²a poco a poco, e poi si pesta cō
facilità, e se tu lo tenessi sopra l'ancu¹³dine,
mai lo rōperesti, essendo così grosso.

¹⁴Chi macina li smalti debbe fare tale esercitio
sopra le pias¹⁵tre d'acciaio tenperato col macina-
tojo da conio, e poi metter¹⁶lo nell' acqva forte,
la qual risolue tutto esso acciaio che si è ¹⁷cōsu-
mato e misto con esso smalto e lo fece nero,
onde poi ¹⁸rimā purificato e netto, e se tu lo
macini sul porfido, esso ¹⁹porfido si consuma e
si mischia collo smalto e lo guasta, ²⁰e l'acqua

OF TAKING CASTS OF MEDALS

A paste of emery mixed with aqua vitae, or
iron filings with vinegar, or ashes of walnut
leaves, or ashes of straw very finely powdered.

The diamond is ground in lead enclosed;
beaten with a hammer and several times extended; the lead is folded and kept wrapped up
in parchment so that the powder may not be
spilt; then melt the lead, and the powder will
be on the top of the melted lead, which must
then be rubbed between two plates of steel till it
is thoroughly pulverized; then wash it with aqua
fortis, and the blackness of the iron will be dissolved, leaving the powder clean.

Emery in large grains may be broken by putting it on a cloth many times doubled, and hit it
sideways with the hammer, when it will break
up; then mix it little by little and it can be
founded with ease; but if you hold it on the
anvil you will never break it when it is large.

Any one who grinds smalt should do it on
plates of tempered steel with a cone-shaped
grinder; then put it in aqua fortis, which melts
away the steel that may have been worked up
and mixed with the smalt, and which makes it
black; it then remains purified and clean; and if
you grind it on porphyry the porphyry will work

28. ecqueste. 29. sisstan pino. 30. decto ele. 31. vachuo. 32. larcho. 33. chedda. 36. Quessto. 37. grosseza eppeso eriss.
38. spiarma . . chettaglia eppesa. 39. rispiarma . . falle. 41. istanpito. 42. effa.
727. 1. stopini inchonbusstibili. 3. brusato ettutti. 4. alume schāgliolo. 6. essciasschuna . . inūmidissci con acq"a". 7 .biancho o di
ella prima acq"a". 8. desstillata o holio.
726. 1. polta di smeriglio . . acq"a". 2. ho cenere. 4. inolto [inp] in . . battutto. 5. radopiato [cre] essitiene. 6. accochettal . . ella
pol. 7. bere vi e. 8. piasstre dacaio . . lauolo chollacq"a". 9. la negredine del ferro ellasscieara. 10. lossmeriglo . . chol . . imol.
11. essi perchote per fianco . . misscagle. 12. a pocho appocho . . essettu. 13. rōperessti . . chosi. 14. lissmalti. 15. chol
macintatoio. 16. accaio chesse. 17. missto . . ello. 18. purifichato ennetto essettullo. 19. essimissca collossmalto ello. 20. ellae
qua dosso [s] perche nō po.

727. The meaning of *scagliuolo* in this passage is doubtful.

da partire mai lo lieva da dosso, perchè nõ può
[21]risoluere tale porfido.

[22]Se volli fare colore bello azzurro risolui lo
smalto, fatto [23]col tartaro, e po' li leva il sal da
dosso.

[24]L'ottone vetrificato fa bello rosso.

up and mix with the smalt and spoil it, and aqua
fortis will never remove it because it cannot dissolve the porphyry.

If you want a fine blue colour dissolve the
smalt made with tartar, and then remove the salt.

Vitrified brass makes a fine red.

G. 75b]   729

STUCCO

[2]Fa stucco sopra il gobbo del . . . di giesso,
[3]il quale sia cõposto di venere e [4]mercurio, e
impasta bene sopra esso gobbo [5]con equal
grossezza di costa di coltello fatta colla [6]sagoma,
e questa copri cõ coperchio di canpa[7]na da
stillare, e riavrai il tuo vmido cõ [8]che inpastasti,
el rimanēte · asciuga bene e poi ī[9]foca e batti
over brunisci cõ buon brunitoio e fa [10]grosso
inverso la costa.

STUCCO

Make stucco over the prominence of the . . . On stucco
which may be composed of Venus and Mercury, (729–30).
and lay it well over that prominence in the thickness of the side of a knife, made with the ruler,
and cover this with the bell of a still, and you will
have again the moisture with which you applied
the paste. The rest you may dry well; afterwards
fire it, and beat it or burnish it with a good
burnisher, and make it thick towards the side.

STUCCO

[12]Poluerizza il vetro · cõ borace e acqua,
in[13]pasta e fa stucco, e poi scalda in modo si
sec[14]chi, e poi vernica con foco in modo che
lustri.

STUCCO

Powder the glass with borax and water to a
paste, and make stucco of it, and then heat it so
that it may dry, and then varnish it, with fire, so
that it shines well.

C. A. 320a]   730

STUCCO DA FORMARE

[2]Togli · butiro parti 6 ·, ciera parti · 2 ·, [3]e
tāta farina volatile · che, messa sopra [4]le cose
strutte ·, le facci · sode a modo [5]di cera · o di
terra · da formare.

STUCCO FOR MOULDING

Take of butter 6 parts, of wax 2 parts, and as
much fine flour as when put with these 2 things
melted will make them as firm as wax or modelling clay.

COLLA

[7]Togli mastice tremētina stillata [8]e biacca.

GLUE

Take mastic, distilled turpentine, and white
lead.

S. K. M. III. 42b]   731

DA GITTARE

[2]Il tartaro bruciato e pol[3]verizzato col giesso
e gitta[4]to fa che esso · giesso si [5]tiene insieme ·
poi ch'è ricot[6]to · e poi · nell' acqua si disfa.

TO CAST

Tartar burnt and powdered with plaster and
cast causes the plaster to hold together when On bronze
it is mixed up again; then it will dissolve in casting
water.   generally
                                               (731–40).

S. K. M. III. 39b]   732

PER GITTARE BRÕZO · IN GIESSO

[2]Togli per ogni 2 scodelle · di giesso una
di [3]corno di bo bruciato e mischia īsieme, [4]e
gitta.

TO CAST BRONZE IN PLASTER

Take to every 2 cups of plaster 1 of ox-horns
burnt, mix them together, and make your cast
with it.

22. azurro . . lossmalto. 24. vetrifichato.

729. 1. stuccho. 2. fasstucho . . ghobb del . a engui di giesso. 3. cõpossto di erenev e. 4. oirucrem e inpassta . . ghobbo. 5. grosseza
. . cholla. 6. saghoma ecquessta . . choperchio. 7. dasstillare erriarai. 8. inpasstassti . . assciugha. 9. focha . . brunissci cõ biõ
brunitoio effa. 10. chossta. 11. stuccho. 12. il ortev cõ ecarob e acq"a" īn. 13. passta effa stucho eppoi scal "d" a. 14. eppoi
vernicha con vocho . . lusstri.

730. 1. stucho. 2. toli bituro parte . . parte. 4. chose. 5. tera. 7. tomastice temetina. 8. biaccha.

731. 2. tartero. 3. verizato chol. 4. hesso . . 5. tiene sieme . . rico. 6. acq"a".

732. 1. giesso ῐ di. 3. bruciata e misscia.

729. In this passage a few words have been written
in a sort of cipher—that is to say, backwards; as in l. 3
erenev for *Venere*, l. 4 *oirucrem* for *Mercurio*, l. 12 *il
ortev cõ ecarob* for *il vetro cõ borace*. The meaning of

the word before '*di giesso*' in l. 1 is unknown; and the
sense in which *sagoma* is used here and in other
passages is obscure.—*Venere* and *Mercurio* may mean
'marble' and 'lime', of which stucco is composed.

S. K. M. II.² 64*b*]   **733**

Quãdo tu voi gittare di ciera, abbrucia la sciuma ²con una candela, e 'l gietto verrà sanza busi.

When you want to take a cast in wax, burn the scum with a candle, and the cast will come out without bubbles.

S. K. M. III. 37*a*]   **734**

[2 õcie di giesso da libbra ²di metallo; ³noce che fa simile alla ⁴curva.]

2 ounces of plaster to a pound of metal;— walnut, which makes it like the curve.

S. K. M. III. 36*b*]   **735**

[Terra asciuta 16 ²libbre, 100 libbre di metallo ³la bagniata terra 20, ⁴di bagniato 100 di metal, ⁵che cresce 4 libbre d'acqua, ⁶una di cera, una libbra di me⁷tallo, alquãto mãco, ⁸cimatura cõ terra, ⁹misura per misura.]

[Dried earth 16 pounds, 100 pounds of metal wet clay 20—of wet 100 of metal which increases 4 lb. of water—1 of wax, 1 lb. of metal, a little less—the clippings of linen with earth, measure for measure.]

H. 100*b*]   **736**

Tal fia il gietto ²qual fia la stãpa.

Such as the mould is, so will the cast be.

Triv. 17*a*]   **737**

COME SI DEBBONO PULIRE I GIETTI

²Farai uno mazzo · di fila · di ferro, grosso · come spaghetto, ³e coll' acqua fregherai, tenẽdo sotto uno tinello, acciò nõ facci ⁴fãgo sotto.

HOW CASTS OUGHT TO BE POLISHED

Make a bunch of iron wire as thick as thread, and scrub them with [this and] water; hold a bowl underneath that it may not make a mud below.

COME SI DE' LEUARE I RICCI DEL BRÕZO

⁶Farai uno · palo di ferro che sia a uso d'uno largo · scarpello, ⁷e cõ quello fregherai · su per quelle · creste · del brõzo, che rimarrãno ⁸sopra · i gietti delle bõbarde, che diriuano dalle schiappature della ⁹forma, · ma fa che 'l palo · pesi · bene ·, e' colpi sieno lũghi e grãdi.

HOW TO REMOVE THE ROUGH EDGES FROM BRONZE

Make an iron rod, after the manner of a large chisel, and with this rub over those seams on the bronze which remain on the casts of the guns, and which are caused by the joins in the mould; but make the tool heavy enough, and let the strokes be long and broad.

FACILITÀ DI FONDERE

¹¹Allega · prima · una parte del metallo alla · manica, di poi lo metti ĩ fornace, ¹²e questo farà prĩcipio · col suo bagnio al fondere del rame.

TO FACILITATE MELTING

First alloy part of the metal in the crucible, then put it in the furnace, and this being in a molten state will assist in beginning to melt the copper.

PER PROVEDERE AL RAME CHE SI FREDDASSE NELLA FORNACE

¹⁴Quando · il rame · si fredasse nella fornace fa · che subito ·, quãdo tu te n'avedi, ¹⁵di tagliarlo cõ frugatoj · mẽtre ch'eli è · ĩ paniccia ·, overo se fusse ¹⁶ĩteramẽte · raffreddato, taglialo, come si fa il piõbo, cõ larghi e grossi scar¹⁷pelli.

TO PREVENT THE COPPER COOLING IN THE FURNACE

When the copper cools in the furnace, be ready, as soon as you perceive it, to cut it with a long stick while it is still in a paste; or if it is quite cold cut it as lead is cut with broad and large chisels.

SE AVESSI A FARE VNO GRÃ GIETTO

¹⁹Se avessi a fare uno gietto di cento mila · libbre, falo cõ · 2 · fornelli con 2000 libbre ²⁰per ciascuno · o ĩsino · in 3000 libbre il piv.

IF YOU HAVE TO MAKE A LARGE CAST

If you have to make a cast of a hundred thousand pounds do it with two furnaces and with 2000 pounds in each, or as much as 3000 pounds at most.

733. 1. abrucia. 2. chandela.
734. 1. libra. 4. cura.
735. 1. assciutta. 2. libre 100 lbbre. 5. cressie. 4 librdacq"a". 6. ℔ di .. ℔ libra.
737. 1. debe. 2. farà ℔ mazo .. spagetto. 3. echollacq"a" frecherai .. ℔ tinello. 6. ℔ palo .. chessia .. largho. 7. chõ .. rimã. 8. isciappature. 9. maffa .. chalpi. 11. ℔ parte .. manicha. 12. ecquesto .. chol .. derame. 13. chessi fredassi. 14. chessubito. 15. chõ .. imẽtre .. overo [mẽte] seffussi. 16. raffredo taglalo chome .. chõ chargi .. schar. 18. affare ℔. 19. affare ℔ .. libre fallo .. cho 2000 libr. 20. ciasschuno .. libr.

734. The second part of this is quite obscure.
735. The translation is given literally, but the meaning is quite obscure.

Triv. 16b]   738

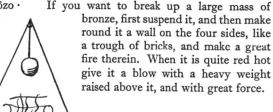

¶ COME SAREBE A RŌPERE VNA GRĀ MASSA DI BRŌZO

²Se volli rōpere · una · grā · massa · di brōzo · sospēdilo · prima, ³poi · lì fa da 4 · lati · uno muro · a vso di truogo · di mattoni, e fa lì grā foco ·, ⁴e quādo è bē rosso, dali · uno colpo con vno ⁵grā peso levato · in alto cō grā forza.

HOW TO PROCEED TO BREAK A LARGE MASS OF BRONZE

If you want to break up a large mass of bronze, first suspend it, and then make round it a wall on the four sides, like a trough of bricks, and make a great fire therein. When it is quite red hot give it a blow with a heavy weight raised above it, and with great force.

Triv. 16a]   739

¶ DEL FARE VNIRE IL PIŌBO CON ALTRO · METALLO

²Se volessi per masseritia · mettere · il piōbo · nel metallo · e per sopire · alla somma ³dello stagnio · che si · richiede · nel metallo ·, allega · prima · il piōbo · collo ⁴stagnio · e poi metti sopra · il rame fōduto.

TO COMBINE LEAD WITH OTHER METAL

If you wish for economy in combining lead with the metal in order to lessen the amount of the tin which is necessary in the metal, first alloy the lead with the tin and then add the molten copper.

¶ COME SI DEBE · FONDERE IN UNO FORNELLO

⁶Il fornello · de’ essere · īfra 4. pilastri bē fōdati.

HOW TO MELT [METAL] IN A FURNACE

The furnace should be between four well-founded pillars.

DELLA GROSSEZZA DELLA CAPPA

⁸La cappa nō debe · prevalicare · la grossezza · di 2 · dita ·, e debesi interrare · ⁹in quatro volte · sopra · la terra · sottile · e poi bene armare, ¹⁰e sia · sola · mēte · ricotta · di dētro · e dato · poi · sottil- mēte · di cenere · bouina.

OF THE THICKNESS OF THE COATING

The coating should not be more than two fingers thick, it should be laid on in four thicknesses over fine clay and then well fixed, and it should be fired only on the inside and then carefully covered with ashes and cow's dung.

DELLA GROSSEZZA DELLA BŌBARDA

¹²La bōbarda · de’ essere da 6oo libbre di ballotta · ī su, cō questa regola; ¹³farai la misura del diametro della · ballotta · e quella · diuidi · ī 6 · parti, ¹⁴e una d’esse parti · fia la grossezza · dināzi e la metà sēpre · piv dirieto, ¹⁵e se la ballotta fia di libbre 7oo, $\frac{1}{7}$ del · diametro della ballotta fia la sua ¹⁶grossezza · dināzi ·, e se la ballotta · fia 8oo ·, l’ottavo del suo diametro ¹⁷dināzi, e se 9oo · $\frac{1}{8}$ e $\frac{1}{2}$ | e se 1ooo $\frac{1}{8}$.

OF THE THICKNESS OF THE GUN

The gun has to be made to carry 6oo lb. of ball and more, by this rule; take the measure of the diameter of the ball and divide it into 6 parts, and one of these parts will be its thickness at the muzzle; but at the breech it must always be half. And if the ball is to be 7oo lb., $\frac{1}{7}$th of the diameter of the ball must be its thickness in front; and if the ball is to be 8oo, the eighth of its diameter in front; and if 9oo, $\frac{1}{8}$th and $\frac{1}{2}$ [$\frac{3}{16}$], and if 1ooo, $\frac{1}{8}$th.

DELLA LŪGHEZZA DELLA TRŌBA DELLA BŌBARDA

¹⁹Se voi · ch’ella · gitti · una ballotta · di pietra · fa la lūghezza della trōba ²⁰in 6 · o insino

OF THE LENGTH OF THE BODY OF THE GUN

If you want to throw a ball of stone, make the length of the gun to be 6, or as much as 7

---

738. 1. be a . . ꝑ grā. 2. ꝑ grā. 3. ꝑ muro . . effa . . focho. 4. ecquādo . . dalli ꝑ colpi chon.
739. 1. chol. 2. e per soperire. 3. chessi . . cholo. 4. eppoi . . arame. 5. fondere ꝑ fornello. 7. grosseza . . chappa. 8. chappa . . prevalichare la grosseza . . debessi. 9. qutro . . soctile. 10. essia . . richotta. 11. grosseza. 12. libr. 13. ba"lo"ta . . diamitro. 14. e ꝑ . . grosseza . . ella. 15. esse . . di br 7oo . . diamitro . . balotta. 16. grosseza . . sella . . diamitro. 17. esse . . | e ese. 18. lūgeza. 19. ꝑ ballotta . . lūgeza. 20. essella . . fussi.

ī 7 ballotte ·, e se la · ballotta · fusse di ferro ·, fa ²¹detta trŏba · īsino in · 12 ballotte ·, e se la ballotta · fusse di ²²piŏbo · farai la insino · in diciotto · ballotte, dico quãdo la bŏbarda ²³avesse · la bocca · atta · a ricieuere · in sé da 600 libr· di ballotta di pietra ī su.

diameters of the ball; and if the ball is to be of iron make it as much as 12 balls, and if the ball is to be of lead, make it as much as 18 balls. I mean when the gun is to have the mouth fitted to receive 600 lb. of stone ball, and more.

DELLA GROSSEZZA DE' PASSA · VOLANTI

²⁵La grossezza dināzi de' passavolanti · nŏ deve passare dalla · metà ²⁶īsino · al terzo del diametro della ballotta; E la lūghezza da 30 īsino ī 36 ²⁷ballotte.

OF THE THICKNESS OF SMALL GUNS

The thickness at the muzzle of small guns should be from a half to one-third of the diameter of the ball, and the length from 30 to 36 balls.

Triv. 15*b*]   **740**

¶ DELLO · ILLOTARE · IL FORNELLO DI DĒTRO

²Il fornello · debbe ināzi · che tu · īforni il metallo · essere · illotato di terra di Valenza, ³e sopra quella · cienere.

OF LUTING THE FURNACE WITHIN

The furnace must be luted, before you put the metal in it, with earth from Valenza, and over that with ashes.

¶ DEL RISTORARE · IL METALLO, QUĀDO · SI VOLESSE FREDDARE

⁵Quãdo · tu · vedi il brŏzo volersi cŏgielare · tolli legnie di salice, schiappate ⁶sottilmēte, e cŏ quelle · fa · foco.

OF RESTORING THE METAL WHEN IT IS BECOMING COOL

When you see that the bronze is congealing, take some willow-wood cut in small chips and make up the fire with it.

¶ LA CAGIONE DEL CŎGIELARSI

⁸Dico · la cagione · d'essa cŏgielatione derivar · spesse volte · da troppo foco ⁹e ancora da legnie · mal secche.

THE CAUSE OF ITS CURDLING

I say that the cause of this congealing often proceeds from too much fire, or from ill-dried wood.

¶ A CONOSCIERE LA DISPOSITIONE DEL FOCO

¹¹Il foco · conoscierai, quãdo fia bono e vtile ·, alle fiame · chiare, e se uedrai ¹²le pūte · d'esse · fiañe turbe e finire cŏ molto · fumo ·, nŏ te ne fidare, e massime ¹³quãdo · avrai il bagnio · quasi · in acqua.

TO KNOW THE CONDITION OF THE FIRE

You may know when the fire is good and fit for your purpose by a clear flame, and if you see the tips of the flames dull and ending in much smoke do not trust it, and particularly when the flux metal is almost fluid.

¶ CHE LEGNIE SONO BONE

¹⁵Le legni · sono · bone · quando fieno di salcio giovane, o non potendo avere salice ¹⁶torai · ontano e ciascuno sia giovane · e ben secho.

WHAT WOOD IS GOOD

Wood is good when of young willow, or if you cannot have willow, take alder and let both be young and very dry.

¶ DELLO ALLEGARE IL METALLO

¹⁸Il metallo · si uole fare vniversalmēte nelle bŏbarde cŏ · 6 · o uisino 8 ¹⁹per ciēto ·, cioè 6 di stagnio · sopra · ciēto · di rame, e quãto meno ve ne metti, ²⁰piv sicura fia · la bŏbarda.

OF ALLOYING THE METAL

Metal for guns must invariably be made with 6 or even 8 per cent., that is, 6 of tin to one hundred of copper, for the less you put in, the stronger will the gun be.

¶ QUĀDO SI DEBE ACCŎPAGNIARE · LO STAGNIO COL RAME

²²Lo stagnio · col rame si debbe · mettere · quãdo · ài il rame cŏdotto in acqua.

WHEN THE TIN SHOULD BE ADDED TO THE COPPER

The tin should be put in with the copper when the copper is reduced to a fluid.

21. essela .. fussi. 23. la bocha. 24. grossezza. 25. grosseza .. debono. 26. diamitro .. lūgeza.
740. 1. ilotare. 2. chetti .. tera di ualēza. 4. uolessi fredare. 5. chŏgielare .. sciapate. 6. chŏ. 8. dicho la chagione .. dirivar. 9. anchora .. seche. 10. focho. 11. conosscierai .. ale .. esse uederai. 12. effinire co. 13. arai .. acq"a". 17. alegare. 18. metalo. 20. sichura. 21. acŏpagniare .. chol. 22. acq"a".

740. l. 2. *Terra di Valenza.*—Valenza is north of Alessandria on the Po.

¶ COME SI DEBE AVMĒTARE IL FONDERE

HOW TO HASTEN THE MELTING

²⁴Il fondere fia da te avmētato · quãdo sarà cõdotto il rame in ⅔ ²⁵in acqua ·, allora · con v̄ legnio di castagnio ispesso rimaneggerai il rima-²⁶nēte del rame ancora ītero · īfra la · parte · fonduta.

24. datte. 25. chastagnio . . rimanerai.

You can hasten the melting when ⅔ of the copper is fluid; you can then, with a stick of chestnut-wood, repeatedly stir what of copper remains entire amidst what is melted.

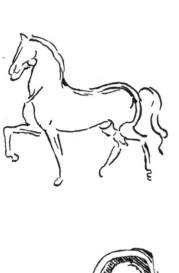

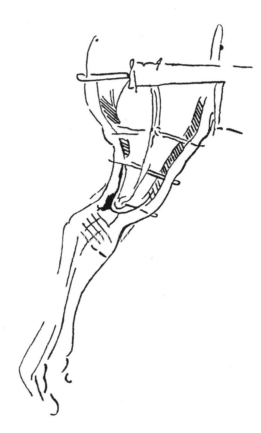

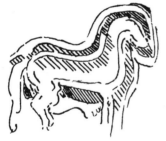

INTRODUCTORY OBSERVATIONS ON THE ARCHITECTURAL DESIGNS (XII) AND WRITINGS ON ARCHITECTURE (XIII)[1]

*N*O *building is known to have been planned and executed by Leonardo,[2] though by some contemporary writers incidental allusion is made to his occupying himself with architecture, and his famous letter to Lodovico il Moro—which has long been a well-known document—in which he offers his service as an architect to that prince, tends to confirm the belief that he was something more than an amateur of the art. This hypothesis is confirmed by certain documents, preserved at Milan, showing that Leonardo was not only employed in preparing plans but that he took an active part, with much credit, as member of a commission on public buildings; his name remains linked with the history of the building of the Cathedral at Pavia and that of the Cathedral at Milan.*

Leonardo's writings on Architecture are dispersed among a large number of manuscripts, and it would be scarcely possible to master their contents without the opportunity of arranging, sorting, and comparing the whole mass of materials, so as to have some comprehensive idea of the whole. The sketches, when isolated and considered by themselves, might appear to be of but little value; it is not till we understand their general purport, from comparing them with each other, that we can form any just estimate of their true worth.

Leonardo seems to have had a project for writing a complete and separate treatise on Architecture, such as his predecessors and contemporaries had composed—Leon Battista Alberti, Filarete, Francesco di Giorgio, and perhaps also Bramante. But, on the other hand, it cannot be denied that possibly no such scheme was connected with the isolated notes and researches, treating on special questions, which are given in this work; that he was merely working at problems in which, for some reason or other, he took a special interest.

A great number of important buildings were constructed in Lombardy during the period between 1472 and 1499, and among them there are several, by unknown architects, of so high an artistic merit, that it is certainly not improbable that either Bramante or Leonardo da Vinci may have been, directly or indirectly, concerned in their erection.

Having been engaged, for now nearly twenty years, in a thorough study of Bramante's life and labours, I have taken a particular interest in detecting the distinguishing marks of his style as compared with Leonardo's. In 1869 I made researches

---

[1] *Henry de Geymüller's account of Leonardo's architectural drawings has served as foundation to subsequent writers who have worked out some of his ideas in greater detail. It is still the most complete general exposition of the subject, and is reproduced, with a few corrections and additions, as it appeared in the first edition. References to recent literature have been embodied in the notes.*

[2] *The church of Santa Maria alla Fontana in Milan was attributed to Leonardo by Diego Sant' Ambrogio, Il Politecnico, Milan, Oct. 1907. This was refuted by Ambrogio Annoni, Dell' Edificio bramantesco di S. Maria alla Fontana in Milano, Rassegna d'arte, 1908.*

about the architectural drawings of the latter in the Codex Atlanticus at Milan, for the purpose of finding out, if possible, the original plans and sketches of the church of Santa Maria delle Grazie at Milan and of the Cathedral at Pavia, which buildings have been supposed to be the work both of Bramante and of Leonardo. Since 1876 I have repeatedly examined Leonardo's architectural studies in the collection of his manuscripts in the Institut de France, and some of these I have already given to the public in my work on Les Projets Primitifs pour la Basilique de St Pierre de Rome, *Pl.* 43. *In* 1879 *I had the opportunity of examining the manuscript in the Palazzo Trivulzio at Milan, and in* 1880 *Dr. Richter showed me in London the manuscripts in the possession of Lord Ashburnham and those in the British Museum. I have thus had opportunities of seeing most of Leonardo's architectural drawings in the original, but of the manuscripts themselves I have deciphered only the notes which accompany the sketches. It is to Dr. Richter's exertions that we owe the collected texts on Architecture which are now published, and while he has undertaken to be responsible for the correct reading of the original texts, he has also made it his task to extract the whole of the materials from the various manuscripts. It has been my task to arrange and elucidate the texts under the heads which have been adopted in this work. MS.* B *at Paris and the* Codex Atlanticus *at Milan are the chief sources of our knowledge of Leonardo as an architect, and I have recently subjected these to a thorough re-investigation expressly with a view to this work.*

A complete reproduction of all Leonardo's architectural sketches has not, indeed, been possible, but as far as the necessarily restricted limits of the work have allowed, the utmost completeness has been aimed at, and no efforts have been spared to include everything that can contribute to a knowledge of Leonardo's style. It would have been very interesting, if it had been possible, to give some general account at least of Leonardo's work and studies in engineering, fortification, canal-making, and the like, and it is only on mature reflection that we have reluctantly abandoned this idea. Leonardo's occupations in these departments have by no means so close a relation to literary work, in the strict sense of the word, as we are fairly justified in attributing to his numerous notes on Architecture.

Leonardo's architectural studies fall naturally under two heads:

I. Those drawings and sketches, often accompanied by short remarks and explanations, which may be regarded as designs for buildings or monuments intended to be built. With these there are occasionally explanatory texts.

II. Theoretical investigations and treatises. A special interest attaches to these because they discuss a variety of questions which are of practical importance to this day. Leonardo's theory as to the origin and progress of cracks in buildings is perhaps to be considered as unique in its way in the literature of Architecture.

HENRY DE GEYMÜLLER.

XII

ARCHITECTURAL DESIGNS

I. PLANS FOR TOWNS

A. Sketches for laying out a new town with a double system of high-level and low-level roadways.

Pl. LXXVII, No. 1 (MS. B 15b). A general view of a town, with the roads outside it sloping up to the high-level ways within.

Pl. LXXVII, No. 3 (MS. B 16a, see No. 741; and MS. B 15b, see No. 742) gives a partial view of the town, with its streets and houses, with explanatory references.

Pl. LXXVII, No. 2 (MS. B 15b; see No. 743). View of a double staircase with two opposite flights of steps.

Pl. LXXVIII, Nos. 2 and 3 (MS. B 37a). Sketches illustrating the connexion of the two levels of roads by means of steps. The lower galleries are lighted by openings in the upper roadway.

B. Notes on removing houses (MS. Br. M. 270b, see No. 744).

B. 16a]   741

Le strade · m · sono · piv · alte · che le strade · p · s · braccia 6 ·, e ciascuna ²strada · de' essere larga braccia 20, e avere ½ braccio di calo dalle stremità ³al mezzo, e in esso mezzo sia a ogni braccio uno braccio di ⁴fessura, largo uno dito, dove l'acqua che pioue debba scolare nelle ca⁵ve fatte al medesimo piano di p · s ·, e da ogni stremità della ⁶larghezza di detta strada · sia · uno · portico di larghezza di braccia 6 ī sul ⁷le colonne, e sappi che, chi volesse andare per tutta la terra per le ⁸strade alte, potrà a suo acconcio usarle, e chi volesse andare ⁹per le basse, ancora il simile; per le strade alte non devono andare ¹⁰carri, nè altre simili cose, anzi siano solamēte per li giēteli o¹¹mini; per le basse deono andare i carri e altre some al uso ¹²e commodità del popolo ·; l'una casa de' volgere le schiene ¹³all' altra ·, lasciādo la strada bassa in mezzo, ed agli usci · n ¹⁴si mettano le vettovaglie, come legnie, vino e simili cose; per le ¹⁵vie sotterrane si de' votare destri, stalle e simili cose fetide ¹⁶dall' uno arco all' altro

The roads *m* are 6 braccia higher than the roads *p s*, and each road must be 20 braccia wide and have ½ braccio slope from the sides towards the middle; and in the middle let there be at every braccio an opening, one braccio long and one finger wide, where the rain-water may run off into hollows made on the same level as *p s*. And on each side at the extremity of the width of the said road let there be an arcade, 6 braccia broad, on columns; and understand that he who would go through the whole place by the high-level streets can use them for this purpose, and he who would go by the low level can do the same. By the high streets no vehicles and similar objects should circulate, but they are exclusively for the use of gentlemen. The carts and burdens for the use and convenience of the inhabitants have to go by the low ones. One house must turn its back to the other, leaving the lower streets between them. Provisions, such as wood, wine, and such things, are carried in by the doors *n*, and privies, stables, and other fetid matter must be emptied away underground, from one arch to the next

B. 15b]   742

de' essere braccia 300, cioè ciascuna via che ricieve il lume dalle fessu²re delle strade di

must be 300 braccia, each street receiving its light through the openings of the upper streets,

741. 1. strade . [m] M . . chelle. 2. largbr . . chalo. 3. mezo [eda esse stremita] einesso mezo . . br unobr. 4. deba. 6. largeza . . I portico di largeza di br · īsu. 7. le colone essapiche . . volessi . . tera. 8. assuo anchoncio . . volessi. 9. no de antare. 10. cari . . simile . . sia. 11. cari. 12. chomodita . . chasa . . lesciene. 13. lassciādo . . imezo edal ussi. 14. mettino le vetto vaglio . . essimili. 15. socterane . . essimile. 16. archo allaltro 5.

742. 1. br . 300 . . ciaschuna . . ilume. 2. ℔ schala.

sopra, e a ogni arco de' essere una scala a luma³ca tõda, perchè ne' cãtoni delle quadre si piscia, e larga, e nella ⁴prima uolta sia vn uscio ch'entri ĩ destri e pisciatoi comuni, e per detta ⁵scala si disciẽda dalla · strada alta · alla bassa, e le strade ⁶alte si comĩcino fori delle porte, e givnte a esse porte abbia⁷no conposto l'altezza di braccia 6; Fia fatta detta terra o presso ⁸a mare o altro fiume grosso, acciocchè le brutture della ⁹città, menate dall' acqua, sieno portate . via.

and at each arch must be a winding stair on a circular plan because the corners of square ones are always fouled; they must be wide, and at the first vault there must be a door entering into public privies; and the said stairs lead from the upper to the lower streets and the high-level streets begin outside the city gates and slope up till at these gates they have attained the height of 6 braccia. Let such a city be built near the sea or a large river in order that the dirt of the city may be carried off by the water.

B. 15b]   743

Modo di scale | le scale · c · d · discendono ȷ f · g ·, e ²similmẽte f · g · ³disciẽde ȷ · h · k.

The construction of the stairs: The stairs c d go down to f g, and in the same way f g goes down to h k.

Br. M. 270b]   744

MUTATIONE DI CASE

²Le case sieno transmutate e messe per ordine, ³e questo cõ facilità si farà, ⁴perchè tali

ON MOVING HOUSES

Let the houses be moved and arranged in order; and this will be done with facility because

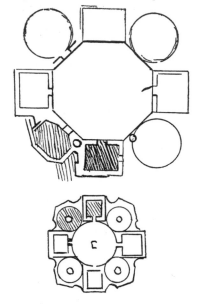

case son prima fatte ⁵di pezzi sopra le piazze, e poi ⁶si cõmettono insieme colli lor ⁷legniami nel sito dove si debbono ⁸stabilire.

⁹Li omini del pae¹⁰se abitino le nuo¹¹ve case in parte, ¹²quando nõ v'è la cor¹³te.

such houses are at first made in pieces on the open places, and can then be fitted together with their timbers in the site where they are to be permanent.

[9] Let the men of the country [of the village] partly inhabit the new houses when the court is absent [12].

3. cãtõ dele . . pisia a elarga. 4. pisciatoi. 5. schala. 6. abbi. 7. chonposte lalteza . . facta decta tera. 8. mere . . acioche le bructure. 9. cicta.
743. 1. disciẽdano . . essimilemẽte.
744. 1. chase. 2. chase. 3. ecquesto cõ facilita (?). 5. eppoi. 6. cõmettano. 11. chase. 12. novela.

743. Pl. LXXVII, No. 2.

744. On the same page we find notes referring to Romolontino and Villafranca with a sketch-map of the course of the 'Sodro' and the '(Lo)era' (both are given in the text farther on). There can hardly be a doubt that the last sentence of the passage given above

refers to the court of Francis I, King of France. Lines 9–13 are written inside the larger sketch, which, in the original, is on the right-hand side of the page by the side of ll. 1–8. The three smaller sketches are below.   J. P. R.

II. PLANS FOR CANALS AND STREETS IN A TOWN

Pl. LXXIX, Nos. 1 and 2 (MS. B 37b, see No. 745, and MS. B 36a, see No. 746).
A Plan for streets and canals inside a town, by which the cellars of the houses are
made accessible in boats. The third text given under No. 747 refers to works
executed by Leonardo in France.

B. 37*b*]   745

La faccia a ²m darà il lume ³alle stā⁴ze; ⁵a · e ·
sarà · braccia 6 ·, a · b fia braccia · 8 ·, b · e fia
braccia 30; acciochè le stanze sotto i portici
siano ⁶luminose ·, c · d · f · fia il loco donde se
vadi a scaricare le navi in nel⁷le case; A volere
che questa cosa · abbia effetto bisogna che la
inondatione ⁸de' fiumi non mādasse l'acqua alle
canove; è neciessario elegiere sito accomodato,
⁹come porsi uicino a vno fiume, il quale ti dia
i canali, che nō si possino nè per ¹⁰inōdatione o
secchezza delle acque dare mutatione alle altezze
d'esse acque, ¹¹e il modo è qui di sotto figurato,
e facciasi eletione di bel fiume che nō intorbidi,
nè ¹²per pioggia, come Tesino, Adda e molti
altri; il modo che l'acque senpre stieno ¹³a un
altezza sarà una cōca, come qui disotto, la quale
fia all' entrare della ¹⁴terra, e meglio alquāto
dētro aciochè nimici nō la disfacciessino.

The front *a m* will give light to the rooms; *a e*
will be 6 braccia—*a b* 8 braccia—*b e* 30 braccia,
in order that the rooms under the porticoes may
be lighted; *c d f* is the place where the boats
come to the house to be unloaded. In order to
render this arrangement practicable, the inundation of the rivers must not penetrate into
the cellars; it is necessary to choose an appropriate situation, such as a spot near a river
which can be diverted into canals in which the
level of the water will not vary either by
inundations or drought. The construction is
shown below; and make choice of a fine river,
which the rains do not render muddy, such as
the Ticino, the Adda, and many others. [12] The
construction to oblige the waters to keep constantly at the same level will be a sort of dock, as
shown below, situated at the entrance of the
town; or, better still, some way within, in order
that the enemy may not destroy it [14].

B. 36*a*]   746

Tanto sia larga la stra²da ·, quanto è la
universale ³altezza delle case.

Let the width of the streets be equal to the
average height of the houses.

Br. M. 270*b*]   747

Il fiume di mezzo ²nō ricieva
acqua ³torbida, ma tale ac⁴qua
vada per li fossi ⁵di fori della terra
⁶con 4 molina nell' ē⁷trata e 4 nella
u⁸scita, e questo si fa⁹rà col ringorgare l'acqua ¹⁰di sopra a
Romolontino;
¹¹Facciāsi fonti ¹²in cia¹³scuna
piazza.

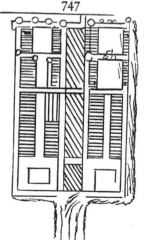

The main underground channel does not receive turbid water,
but that water runs in the ditches
outside the town with four mills at
the entrance and four at the outlet;
and this may be done by damming
the water above Romorantin.
[11] There should be fountains
made in each piazza [13].

745. 2. ilume. 5. br . 6 . . br . 8 . . chelle . .
socto. 6. donde [si dia lum] se . . asscha-
ricare . . ine. 7. cuesta . . abbi effecto bisognia accio chella nōdatione. 8. mādassi
. . achomodato. 9. vissino. 10. rinōdatione
ossecheza . . alteze. 11. el modo . . soto . .
effaci . . nōnintorbidine. 12. per pioigie

745. Lines 1–4 are on the left-hand
side and beside the sketch given on Pl.
LXXIX, No. 1. Then follows, after l.
14, the drawing of a sluice-gate—*conca*
—of which the use is explained in the
text below it.

12. *Tesino, Adda e molti altri*, i.e. rivers coming
from the mountains and flowing through lakes. On
folio 38*a*, which comes next in the original MS., is
the sketch of an oval plan of a town over which is
written 'modo di canali per la città', and through the
longer axis of it 'canale magior' is written with

chome tesino adda . . chellacque. 13.
alteza . . disocto. 14. tera . . sare . .
disfaciesino.
746. 3. alteza . . chase.
747. 1. el . . mezo. 3. mattale. 7. nella vs.
8. ecquesto. 9. ringhorghare. 12. [chome]
in cias. 13. piaza.

'Tesino' on the prolongation of the
canal.

747. In the original this text comes
immediately after the passage given as
No. 744. The remainder of the writing
on the same page refers to the construction of canals
and is given later, in the 'Topographical Notes'.

10. *Romolontino* is Romorantin, south of Orleans
in France.

Lines 1–11 are written to the right of the plan,
ll. 11–13 underneath it.   J. P. R.

III. CASTLES AND VILLAS

A. Castles

Pl. LXXX, No. 1 (P. V. fol. 39b; No. d'ordre 2282). The fortified place here represented is said by Vallardi to be the castello *at Milan, but without any satisfactory reason. The high tower behind the* rivellino, *ravelin, seems to be intended as a watch-tower.*

Pl. LXXX, No. 2 (MS. B 23b). A similarly constructed tower probably intended for the same use.

Pl. LXXX, No. 3 (MS. B 58b). Sketches for corner towers with steps for a citadel.

Pl. LXXX, No. 4 (W. 12552). A cupola crowning a corner tower; an interesting example of decorative fortification.

B. Projects for Palaces

Pl. LXXXI, No. 2 (MS. C. A. 76b; see No. 748). Project for a royal residence at Amboise in France.

Pl. LXXXII, No. 1 (C. A. 315a). A plan for a somewhat extensive residence, and various details; but there is no text to elucidate it; in courts are written the three names:

Sām   cosi   giovā
 (St. Mark)   *(Cosimo)*   *(John),*
arch   mo   nino
  o

C. Plans for small Castles or Villas

The three following sketches greatly resemble each other:

Pl. LXXXII, No. 2 (MS. K³ 36b; see No. 749).

Pl. LXXXII, No. 3 (MS. B 60a; see No. 750).

Pl. LXXXIII (W. 12591a). The text on this sheet refers to Cyprus (see Topographical Notes, No. 1103), but seems to have no direct connexion with the sketches inserted between.

Pl. LXXXVIII, Nos. 6 and 7 (MS. B 12a; see No. 751). A section of a circular pavilion with the plan of a similar building by the side of it. These two drawings have a special historical interest because the text written below mentions the Duke and Duchess of Milan.

The sketch of a villa on a terrace at the end of a garden occurs in C. A. 153a; and in C. A. 78b is another sketch of a villa somewhat resembling the Belvedere *of Pope Innocent VIII, at Rome. In C. A. 63b there is a* Loggia.

Pl. LXXXII, No. 4 (C. A. 395b) is a tower-shaped Loggia *above a fountain. The machinery is very ingeniously screened from view.*

C. A. 76b]   748

[Il palazzo del principe de' auere dināti vna piazza.]

²Le abitationi doue s'abbia a ballare o fare diuersi ³salti o uari movimēti con moltitudine di gente sieno ter⁴rene, perchè già n'ò veduto ruinare colla morte di ⁵molti; E sopra tutto fa che ogni muro, per sottile che ⁶sia, abbia fondamēto in terra o sopra archi bene ⁷fondati.

⁸Sieno il mezzanelli delli abitacoli ⁹diuisi da muri fatti di stretti mat¹⁰toni e sanza legniami per ri¹¹spetto del fuoco.

¹²Tutti li neciessari abbino esalatio¹³ne per le grossezze de' muri, e in ¹⁴modo che spirino per li tetti.

¹⁵Li mezzanelli sieno in volta, le quali ¹⁶sarā tanto più forti quāto e' sarā mi¹⁷nori.

¹⁸Le catene di quercia siē rinchi¹⁹use per li muri acciò nō siē offese ²⁰da foco.

²¹Le stāze d'andare a' destri sieno ²²molte che entrino l'una nell' al²³tra, acciochè il fetore non spiri per ²⁴le abitationi, e tutti li loro usci ²⁵si serrino colli cōtrapesi.

²⁶La massima diuisione della frōte di que²⁷sto palazzo è in due parti, cioè che la larghezza della corte sia la metà di tutta la predetta ²⁹fronte; La 2ª . . .

The palace of the prince must have a piazza in front of it.

Houses intended for dancing or any kind of jumping or any other movements with a multitude of people must be on the ground floor; for I have already witnessed the destruction of some, causing death to many persons, and above all let every wall, be it ever so thin, rest in the ground or on arches with a good foundation.

Let the mezzanines of the dwellings be divided by walls made of very thin bricks, and without wood on account of fire.

Let all the privies have ventilation [by shafts] in the thickness of the walls, so as to exhale by the roofs.

The mezzanines should be vaulted, and the vaults will be stronger in proportion as they are of small size.

The ties of oak must be enclosed in the walls in order to be protected from fire.

The privies must be numerous and going one into the other in order that the stench may not penetrate into the dwellings, and all their doors must shut off themselves with counterpoises.

The main division of the façade of this palace is into two portions, that is to say, the width of the courtyard must be half the whole façade; the 2nd . . .

C. A. 214a]   748 A

La sala della festa vole avere la sua collezione in modo che prima passi dinanti al signore e poi a' convitati: e sia il camino in modo che esso possa venire in sala, in modo non passi dinanzi al popolo più che l'omo si voglia, e sia dall' opposita parte situata a riscontro al signore la entrata della sala, e le scale commode in modo che sieno amplie, in modo che le genti per quelle non abbiano, urtando gl'immascherati, a guastare le loro (f)oggie quando uscissi . . . la turba d'omini, nè con tali immasche(rati) . . . vole tale sala avere due camere per testa, suoi destri doppi . . . di questi un uscio le tiene e uno per li ma(scher)ati.

The banquet-hall should be arranged in such a way that there should be free space for his Lordship and then for the guests: and the disposal of the way should be such that he can enter the hall without passing in front of the people, more than he wants to. And the entrance to the hall should be on the opposite side facing his Lordship. And the stairs should be comfortable, with ample room, so that the people passing through do not spoil their costumes in knocking against the masks, when they go out in crowds . . . such a hall should have two rooms at the head and two double doors, and one of these doors should be kept for them, and the other for the masks.

748. 1. palazo. 2. abitationini . . abballare offare. 3. chomoltitudine. 4. rrene . . cholla. 5. Essopra tucto . . persottile. 6. ossopra arachi. 8. mezanelli . . abitacholi. 9. mac. 10. tono essanza . . ris. 11. fuocho. 12. Tucti. 13. grosseze. 14. chesspirino . . tecti. 15. mezanelli. 18. chatene diquercie. 20. focho. 21. Lesstāze . . adesstri. 23. il ferore non isspiri. 24. li . . ettutti . . vssci. 25. cholli chōtrappesi. 26. ques. 27. chella larghe.

748. The remarks accompanying the plan reproduced on Pl. LXXXI, No. 2, are as follows: Above, to the left: 'in *a* angholo stia la guardia de la sstalla' (in the angle *a* may be the keeper of the stable). Below are the words 'strada dābosa' (road to Amboise), parallel with this 'fossa br 40' (the moat 40 braccia),

fixing the width of the moat. In the large court surrounded by a portico 'stalla in terreno largha br 80 e lūgha br 120'. To the right of the castle is a large basin for aquatic sports with the words 'Giostre colle nave cioè li giostrā ti stieno sopra le nave' (Jousting in boats, that is, the men are to be in boats).

K.³ 116b]   749

Largo per ogni lato br. 30; l'entrata da ²basso   30 braccia wide on each side; the lower en-
è in una sala larga braccia 10 e ³lunga braccia 30   trance leads into a hall 10 braccia wide and 30
e a 4 camere cō sua cami⁴ni.   braccia long with 4 recesses each with a chimney.

B. 60a]   750

Il primo grado sia · tutto ²ripieno.   The first story [or terrace] must be entirely
                                                         solid.

B. 12a]   751

Padiglione del giardino della duchessa ²di   The pavilion in the garden of the Duchess of
Milano.   Milan.
³Fondamēto del padiglione ch'è nel ⁴mezzo   The plan of the pavilion which is in the
del laberinto del duca di Milano.   middle of the labyrinth of the Duke of Milan.

B. 19b]   752

Il terreno · che si cava · dalle · canove ²si   The earth that is dug out from the cellars
debe elevare da cāto tāto · in alto che ³faccia un   must be raised on one side so high as to make a
orto ·, che sia alto quāto la sala, ⁴ma fa che tra 'l   terrace garden as high as the level of the hall;
terreno dell' orto e 'l muro ⁵della casa sia uno ·   but between the earth of the terrace and the wall
intervallo, acciò che ⁶l'umido nō guasti i muri   of the house leave an interval in order that the
maestri.   damp may not spoil the principal walls.

749. 1. Largho .. dab. 2. basso [e ino] e in .. la"r"gha br . 10 el. 3. lungha br 30.
751. 1. zardino. 3. del [z]. 4. mezo.
752. 1. tereno chessi chava delle chanove. 2. ellevare da chāto. 3. chessia. 4. chettral tereno. 5. chasa. 6. maesstri.

749. On each side of the castle, Pl. LXXXII, No. 2, there are drawings of details, to the left 'Camino', a chimney, to the right the central lantern, sketched in red '8 lati', i.e. an octagon.

751. See Pl. LXXXVIII. This passage was first published by Amoretti in *Memorie Storiche*, cap. x: 'Una sua opera da riportarsi a quest' anno fu il bagno fatto per la duchessa Beatrice nel parco o giardino del Castello. Lionardo non solo ne disegnò il piccolo edifizio a foggia di padiglione, nel cod. segnato Q. 3, dandone anche separatarsi la pianta; ma sotto vi scrisse: Padiglione del giardino della duchessa; e sotto la pianta: Fondamento del padiglione ch'è nel mezzo del labirinto del duca di Milano; nessuna data è presso il padiglione, disegnato nella pagina 12, ma poco sopra fra molti circoli intrecciati vedesi—10 Luglio 1492—e nella pagina 2 presso ad alcuni disegni di legumi qualcheduno ha letto Settembre 1482 in vece di 1492, come dovea scriverevi, e probabilmente scrisse Lionardo.'

The original text, however, hardly bears the interpretation put upon it by Amoretti. He is mistaken as to the mark on the MS. as well as in his statements as to the date, for the MS. in question has no date; the date he gives occurs, on the contrary, in another note-book. Finally, it appears to me quite an open question whether Leonardo was the architect who carried out the construction of the dome-like Pavilion here shown in section, or of the ground-plan of the Pavilion drawn by the side of it. Must we, in fact, suppose that 'il duca di Milano' here mentioned was, as has been generally assumed, Lodovico il Moro? He did not hold this title from the Emperor before 1494; till that date he was only called *Governatore*, and Leonardo in speaking of him mentions him generally as 'il Moro' even after 1494. On January 18, 1491, he married Beatrice d'Este, the daughter of Ercole I, Duke of Ferrara. She died on January 2, 1497, and for the reasons I have given it seems improbable that it should be this princess who is here spoken of as the 'duchessa di Milano'. From the style of the handwriting it appears to me to be beyond all doubt that the MS. B, from which this passage is taken, is older than the dated MSS. of 1492 and 1493. In that case the Duke of Milan here mentioned would be Gian Galeazzo (1469–1494) and the Duchess would be his wife Isabella of Aragon, to whom he was married on February 2, 1489. Compare *Raccolta Vinciana*, x. 302.   J. P. R.

IV. ECCLESIASTICAL ARCHITECTURE

A. General Observations[1]

B. 39b]   753

Senpre vno edifitio vole · essere ²spiccato dintorno a volere dimostra³re la sua vera forma.

A building should always be detached on all sides so that its form may be seen.

B. N. 2037. 5b]   754

Qui nō si può nè si debe fare ²cāpanile, anzi debe ³stare separato come à il do⁴mo e Sā Giovanni di Firēze ·, ⁵e così il domo di Pisa · che mo⁶stra il cāpanile per sé dispicca⁷to ī circa e così il domo, e o⁸gnivno per sé può mostrare la sua ⁹perfettione, e chi lo uolesse pure ¹⁰fare colla chiesa, faccia la lā¹¹terna scusare cāpanile ¹²come è la chiesa di Chiaravalle.

Here there cannot and ought not to be any campanile; on the contrary, it must stand apart like that of the Cathedral and of San Giovanni at Florence, and of the Cathedral at Pisa, where the campanile is quite detached as well as the dome. Thus each can display its own perfection. If, however, you wish to join it to the church, make the lantern serve for the campanile as in the church at Chiaravalle.

B. 18b]   755

A nessuna chiesa sta ²bene vedere tetti, āzi ³sia rappianato e per ca⁴nali l'acqua discē⁵da ai condotti fatti nel ⁶fregiō.

It never looks well to see the roofs of a church; they should rather be flat and the water should run off by channels to gutters made in the frieze.

753. 2. ispichato.
754. 1. po nessi. 2. chāpanile. 3. chome. 4. essāgiovani. 6. chāpanile . . displicha. 7. circho e chosi. 8. po. 9. perfettione. 10. colla. 11. schusare chāpanile.
755. 3. rapianato . . cha. 4. la ch . gua dissie. 5. chondotti.

[1] Ludwig H. Heydenreich's Dissertation, *Die Sakralbau-Studien Leonardo da Vinci's*, Leipzig, 1929, describes Leonardo's studies in Dome Architecture in relation to the contemporary works and points out that his style marked the transition from the Early to the High Renaissance. A comprehensive study, by the same author, of Leonardo's architecture and a reconstruction of his planned treatise on the subject is to appear in the series: "Forschungen des Kunsthistorischem Instituts in Florenz, under the title: *L. d. V. als Architekt*. (1940?). Strzygowsky, *Leonardo, Bramante, Vignola im Rahmen vergleichender Kunstforschung, Mitteilungen des Kunsthistorischen Instituts*, Florence, iii, 1919, describes Eastern influences on Leonardo's drawings of domes. C. Baroni, *Elementi Stilistici fiorentini nelli Studi Vinciani di Architettura a Cupola* in Atti del 1° Congresso Nazionale di Storia dell' Architettura, Florence, 1938, describes the Florentine and Eastern influences on Leonardo's designs.

753. The original text is reproduced on Pl. XCII, No. 1, to the left hand at the bottom.

754. This text is written by the side of the plan given on Pl. XCI, No. 2.

12. The Abbey of Chiaravalle, a few miles from Milan, has a central tower on the intersection of the cross as in the Certosa of Pavia, but the style is medieval (A.D. 1330). Leonardo seems here to mean that in a building in which the circular form is strongly conspicuous the campanile must either be separated, or rise from the centre of the building and therefore take the form of a lantern.

755. This text is to the left of the domed church reproduced on Pl. LXXXVII, No. 2.

IV. ECCLESIASTICAL ARCHITECTURE (*cont.*)

B. *The Theory of Dome Architecture*

This subject has been more extensively treated by Leonardo in drawings than in writing. Still, we may fairly assume that it was his purpose ultimately to embody the results of his investigation in a Trattato delle Cupole. *The amount of materials is remarkably extensive.* MS. B *is particularly rich in plans and elevations of churches with one or more domes—from the simplest form to the most complicated that can be imagined. Considering the evident connexion between a great number of these sketches, as well as the impossibility of seeing in them designs or preparatory sketches for any buildings intended to be erected, the conclusion is obvious that they were not designed for any particular monument, but were theoretical and ideal researches, made in order to obtain a clear understanding of the laws which must govern the construction of a great central dome, with smaller ones grouped round it; and with or without the addition of spires, so that each of these parts by itself and in its juxtaposition to the other parts should produce the grandest possible effect.*

In these sketches Leonardo seems to have exhausted every imaginable combination.[1] The results of some of these problems are perhaps not quite satisfactory; still, they cannot be considered to give evidence of a want of taste or of any other defect in Leonardo's architectural capacity. They were no doubt intended exclusively for his own instruction, and, before all, as it seems, to illustrate the features or consequences resulting from a given principle.

I have already, in another place,[2] pointed out the law of construction for buildings crowned by a large dome: namely, that such a dome, to produce the greatest effect possible, should rise either from the centre of a Greek cross, or from the centre of a structure of which the plan has some symmetrical affinity to a circle, this circle being at the same time the centre of the whole plan of the building.

Leonardo's sketches show that he was fully aware, as was to be expected, of this truth. Few of them exhibit the form of a Latin cross, and when this is met with, it generally gives evidence of the determination to assign as prominent a part as possible to the dome in the general effect of the building.

While it is evident, on the one hand, that the greater number of these domes had no particular purpose, not being designed for execution, on the other hand several reasons may be found for Leonardo's perseverance in his studies of the subject.

Besides the theoretical interest of the question for Leonardo and his Trattato *and besides the taste for domes prevailing at that time, it seems likely that the intended erection of some building of the first importance like the Duomos of Pavia and Como, the church of Sta. Maria delle Grazie at Milan, and the construction of a Dome or central Tower (Tiburio) on the cathedral of Milan, may have*

---

[1] *In MS. B 10b (see Pl. CIII, No. 2) we find eight geometrical patterns, each drawn in a square; and in MS. C. A., fol. 87 to 98 form a whole series of patterns done with the same intention.*

[2] Les Projets primitifs pour la Basilique de St Pierre de Rome, par Bramante, Raphael, &c., *vol.* i, *p.* 2.

stimulated Leonardo to undertake a general and thorough investigation of the subject; whilst Leonardo's intercourse with Bramante for ten years or more can hardly have remained without influence in this matter. In fact, now that some of this great architect's studies for St. Peter's at Rome have at last become known, he must be considered henceforth as the greatest master of Dome Architecture that ever existed. His influence, direct or indirect, even on a genius like Leonardo seems the more likely since Leonardo's sketches reveal a style most similar to that of Bramante, whose name, indeed, occurs twice in Leonardo's manuscript notes.[1] It must not be forgotten that Leonardo was a Florentine; the characteristic form of the two principal domes of Florence, Sta. Maria del Fiore and the Battistero, constantly appear as leading features in his sketches.

The church of S. Lorenzo at Milan was at that time still intact. The dome is to this day one of the most wonderful cupolas ever constructed, and with its two smaller domes might well attract the attention and study of a never-resting genius such as Leonardo. A whole class of these sketches betray in fact the direct influence of the church of S. Lorenzo, and this also seems to have suggested the plan of Bramante's dome of St. Peter's at Rome.

In the following pages the various sketches for the construction of domes have been classified and discussed from a general point of view. On two sheets—Pl. LXXXIV (C. A. 362b) and Pl. LXXXV, Nos. 1–11 (B. N. 2037. 3b) we see various dissimilar types, grouped together; thus these two sheets may be regarded as a sort of nomenclature of the different types of which we shall now have to treat.

---

[1] *Leonardo's studies in architecture foreshadow Bramante's Roman period. The plans reproduced on pp. 39, 43 (fig. 1) are related to Bramante's plan for the reconstruction of St. Peter's (1503–4) in the Uffizi. See* L. H. Heydenreich, Zur Genesis des St. Peter's Plans von Bramante, *Forschungen und Fortschritte, Berlin,* Oct. 1934. A. Annoni, *Considerazioni su L. d. V., Architetto. Emporium. Bergamo, April* 1919.

IV. ECCLESIASTICAL ARCHITECTURE (*cont.*)

B. The Theory of Dome Architecture (*cont.*)

I. CHURCHES FORMED ON THE PLAN OF A GREEK CROSS

GROUP I. *Domes rising from a circular base*

The simplest type of central building is a circular edifice.

Pl. LXXXIV, No. 9. Plan of a circular building surrounded by a colonnade.

Pl. LXXXIV, No. 8. Elevation of the former, with a conical roof.

Pl. XC, No. 5. A dodecagon, as most nearly approaching the circle.

Pl. LXXXVI, Nos. 1, 2, 3. Four round chapels are added at the extremities of the two principal axes;—compare this plan with Fig. 1 on p. 31 and Fig. 3 on p. 35 (W. 19134b), where the outer wall is octagonal.

GROUP II. *Domes rising from a square base*

The plan is a square surrounded by a colonnade, and the dome seems to be octagonal.

Pl. LXXXIV. The square plan below the circular building No. 8, and its elevation to the left, above the plan: here the ground-plan is square, the upper story octagonal. A further development of this type is shown in two sketches, C. A. 3a (not reproduced here), and in

Pl. LXXXVI, No. 5 (which possibly belongs to No. 7 on Pl. LXXXIV).

Pl. LXXXV, No. 4, and p. 33, Fig. 3, a Greek cross, is another development of the square central plan.

The remainder of these studies show two different systems; in the first the dome rises from a square plan—in the second from an octagonal base.

GROUP III. *Domes rising from a square base and four pillars*[1]

(a) FIRST TYPE. A Dome resting on four pillars in the centre of a square edifice, with an apse in the middle of each of the four sides. We have eleven variations of this type.

(aa) Pl. LXXXVIII, No. 3.

(bb) Pl. LXXX, No. 5.

(cc) Pl. LXXXV, Nos. 2, 3, 5.

(dd) Pl. LXXXIV, Nos. 1 and 4 beneath.

(ee) Pl. LXXXV, Nos. 1, 7, 10, 11.

(b) SECOND TYPE. This consists in adding aisles to the whole plan of the first type; columns are placed between the apses and the aisles; the plan thus obtained is very nearly identical with that of S. Lorenzo at Milan.

---

[1] *The ancient Capella della Pietà leading out of the left transept of S. Maria presso S. Satiro at Milan is a specimen of this type. It dates back to the ninth century and was renovated soon after 1480, when Bramante was renovating the church.*

Fig. 1 on p. 43 (*MS. B 75a*) *shows the result of this treatment adapted to a peculiar purpose about which we shall have to say a few words later on.*

Pl. XCV, No. 1, shows the same plan but with the addition of a short nave. This plan seems to have been suggested by the general arrangement of S. Sepolcro at Milan.

MS. B 57b (*see the sketch reproduced on p. 39*). *By adding towers in the four outer angles to the last-named plan, we obtain a plan which bears the general features of Bramante's plans for S. Peter's at Rome.*[1]

GROUP IV. *Domes rising from an octagonal base*

This system, developed according to two different schemes, has given rise to two classes with many varieties.

In (a) *on each side of the octagon chapels of equal form are added.*

In (b) *the chapels are dissimilar; those which terminate the principal axes being different in form from those which are added on the diagonal sides of the octagon.*

a. First Class

The Chapel degli Angeli, *at Florence, built only to a height of about 20 feet by Brunellesco, may be considered as the prototype of this group; and, indeed, it probably suggested it. The fact that we see in MS. B 11b (Pl. XCIV, No. 3) by the side of Brunellesco's plan for the Basilica of Sto. Spirito at Florence a plan almost identical with that of the* Capella degli Angeli *confirms this supposition. Only two small differences, or we may say improvements, have been introduced by Leonardo. Firstly the back of the chapels contains a third niche, and each angle of the Octagon a folded pilaster like those in Bramante's* Sagrestia di S. M. presso San Satiro *at Milan, instead of an interval between the two pilasters as seen in the* Battistero *at Florence and in the Sacristy of Sto. Spirito in the same town and also in the above-named chapel by Brunellesco.*

The first set of sketches which come under consideration have at first sight the appearance of mere geometrical studies. They seem to have been suggested by the plan given on p. 32, Fig. 2 (MS. B 55a), in the centre of which is written 'Santa Maria in praticha da Pavia',[2] *at the place marked A on the reproduction.*

(a) (*MS. B 34b, p. 32, Fig. 3*). *In the middle of each side a column is added, and in the axes of the intercolumnar spaces a second row of columns forms an aisle round the octagon. These are placed at the intersection of a system of semicircles, of which sixteen columns on the sides of the octagon are the centres.*

(b) *The preceding diagram is completed and becomes more monumental in style in the sketch next to it (MS. B 35a, see p. 33, Fig. 1). An outer aisle is added by circles, having for radius the distance between the columns in the middle sides of the octagon.*

(c) (*MS. B 96b, see p. 33, Fig. 2*). *Octagon with an aisle round it; the angles of both are formed by columns. The outer sides are formed by 8 niches forming*

See Les Projets primitifs, &c., Pls. 9–12.   [2] *This church was pulled down in* 1815.

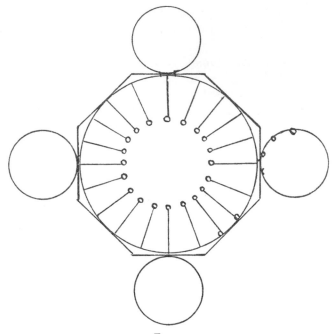

Fig. 1.

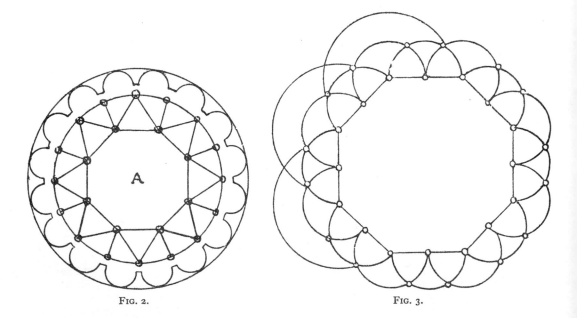

Fig. 2.   Fig. 3.

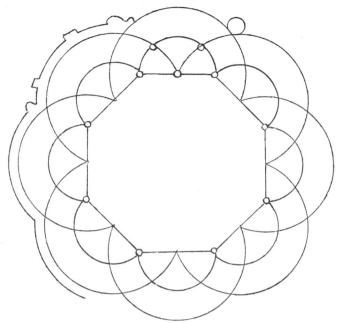

FIG. I.

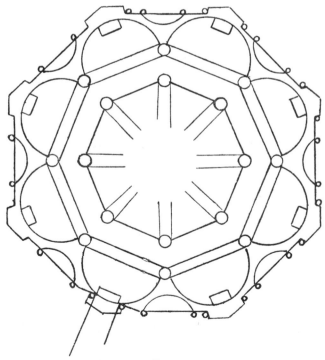

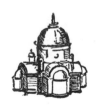

FIG. 3.

FIG. 2.

F

chapels. The exterior is likewise octagonal, with the angles corresponding to the centre of each of the interior chapels.

Pl. XCII, No. 2 (MS. B 96b). Detail and modification of the preceding plan— half-columns against piers—an arrangement by which the chapels of the aisle have the same width of opening as the inner arches between the half-columns. Underneath this sketch the following note occurs: questo vole · avere 12 facce · cō 12 taber-naculi · come · a · b. (*This will have twelve sides with twelve tabernacles as* a b.) *In the remaining sketches of this class the octagon is not formed by columns at the angles.*

The simplest type shows a niche in the middle of each side and is repeated on several sheets, viz.: MS. B 3; MS. C. A. 362b (see Pl. LXXXIV, No. 11), and MS. B N. 2037. 3b; (see Pl. LXXXV, No. 9 and the elevations No. 8; Pl. XCII, No. 3; MS. B. 4b [not reproduced here] and Pl. LXXXIV, No. 2).

Pl. XCII, No. 3 (MS. B 56b) corresponds to a plan like the one in MS. B 35a, in which the niches would be visible outside or, as in the following sketch, with the addition of a niche in the middle of each chapel.

Pl. XC, No. 6. The niches themselves are surrounded by smaller niches (see also No. 1 on the same plate).

Octagon expanded on each side

A. *By a square chapel:*

    MS. B 34b (not reproduced here).

B. *By a square with 3 niches:*

    MS. B 11b (see Pl. XCIV, No. 3).

C. *By octagonal chapels:*

    (a) *MS. B 21b; Pl. LXXXVIII, No. 4.*

    (b) *No. 2 on the same plate. Underneath there is the remark:* 'quest' è come le 8 cappele àno a essere facte' (*this is how the eight chapels are to be executed*).

    (c) *Pl. LXXXVIII, No. 5. Elevation to the plans on the same sheet; it is accompanied by the note:* 'ciasscuno de' 9 tiburi no'uole · passare l'alteza · di · 2 · quadri' (*neither of the 9 domes must exceed the height of two squares*)·

    (d) *Pl. LXXXVIII, No. 1. Inside of the same octagon.*

    MS. B 30a, and 34b; these are three repetitions of parts of the same plan with very slight variations.

D. *By a circular chapel:*

    MS. B 18a (see Fig. 1 on p. 35) gives the plan of this arrangement in which the exterior is square on the ground floor with only four of the chapels projecting, as is explained in the next sketch.

    Pl. LXXXIX, MS. B 17b. Elevation to the preceding plan sketched on the opposite side of the sheet, and also marked A. It is accompanied by the following remark, indicating the theoretical character of these studies: questo · edifitio · anchora · starebbe · bene affarlo dalla linja · a · b · c · d . insù.

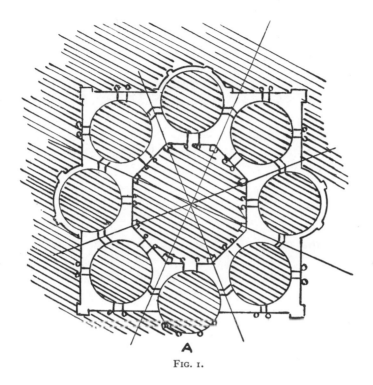

FIG. 1.

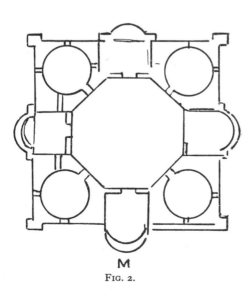

FIG. 2.

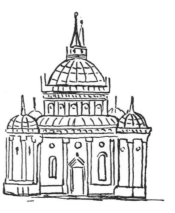

FIG. 3.

(*'This edifice would also produce a good effect if only the part above the lines* a b, c d, *were executed'*).

Pl. LXXXIV, No. 11. *The exterior has the form of an octagon, but the chapels project partly beyond it. On the left side of the sketch they appear larger than on the right side.*

Pl. XC, No. 1. *(MS. B 25b); Repetition of Pl. LXXXIV, No.* 11.

Pl. XC, No. 2. *Elevation to the plan No.* 1, *and also to No.* 6 *of the same sheet.*

E. *By chapels formed by four niches:*

Pl. LXXXIV, No. 7 *(the circular plan on the left below) shows this arrangement in which the central dome has become circular inside and might therefore be classed after this group.*[1]

The sketch on the right-hand side gives most likely the elevation for the last-named plan.

F. *By chapels of still richer combinations, which necessitate an octagon of larger dimensions:*

Pl. XCI, No. 2 *(MS. B. N.* 2037 *5b);*[2] *on this plan the chapels themselves appear to be central buildings formed like the first type of the third group. Pl. LXXXVIII, No.* 3.

Pl. XCI, No. 2, *above; the exterior of the preceding figure, particularly interesting on account of the alternation of apses and niches, the latter containing statues of a gigantic size, in proportion to the dimension of the niches.*

b. Second Class

Composite plans of this class are generally obtained by combining two types of the first class—the one worked out on the principal axes, the other on the diagonal ones.

MS. B 22 *shows an elementary combination, without any additions on the diagonal axes, but with the dimensions of the squares on the two principal axes exceeding those of the sides of the octagon.*

In the drawing W. 19134b *(see p.* 32, *Fig.* 1*) the exterior only of the edifice is octagonal, the interior being formed by a circular colonnade; round chapels are placed against the four sides of the principal axes.*

The elevation, drawn on the same sheet (see p. 35, *Fig.* 3*), shows the whole arrangement which is closely related with the one on Pl. LXXXVI, Nos.* 1, 2.

MS. B 21a *shows:*

(a) *four sides with rectangular chapels crowned by pediments. Pl. LXXXVII, No.* 3 *(plan and elevation);*

(b) *four sides with square chapels crowned by octagonal domes. Pl. LXXXVII, No.* 4; *the plan underneath.*

---

[1] *This plan and some others of this class remind us of the plan of the Mausoleum of Augustus as it is represented for instance by Durand. See* Cab. des Estampes, Bibliothèque Nationale, Paris, Topographie de Rome, V, 6, 82.

[2] *The note accompanying this plan is given under No.* 754.

MS. B 18a shows a variation obtained by replacing the round chapels in the principal axes of the sketch MS. B 18a by square ones, with an apse. Leonardo repeated both ideas for better comparison side by side, see p. 35, Fig. 2.

Pl. LXXXIX (MS. B 17b). Elevation for the preceding figure. The comparison of the drawing marked M with the plan on p. 35, Fig. 2, bearing the same mark, and of the elevation on Pl. LXXXIX below (marked A) with the corresponding plan on p. 35 is highly instructive, as illustrating the spirit in which Leonardo pursued these studies.

Pl. LXXXIV, No. 12 shows the design Pl. LXXXVII, No. 3 combined with apses, with the addition of round chapels on the diagonal sides.

Pl. LXXXIV, No. 13 is a variation of the preceding sketch.

Pl. XC, No. 3. MS. B 25b. The round chapels of the preceding sketch are replaced by octagonal chapels, above which rise campaniles.

Pl. XC, No. 4 is the elevation for the preceding plan.

Pl. XCII, No. 1 (MS. B 39b); the plan below. On the principal as well as on the diagonal axes are diagonal chapels, but the latter are separated from the dome by semicircular recesses. The communication between these eight chapels forms a square aisle round the central dome.

Above this figure is the elevation, showing four campaniles on the angles.[1]

Pl. LXXXIV, No. 3. On the principal axes are square chapels with three niches; on the diagonals octagonal chapels with niches. Cod. Atl. 340b gives a somewhat similar arrangement.

MS. B 30. The principal development is thrown on the diagonal axes by square chapels with three niches; on the principal axes are inner recesses communicating with outer ones.

The plan Pl. XCIII, No. 2 (MS. B 22) differs from this only in so far as the outer semicircles have become circular chapels, projecting from the external square as apses; one of them serves as the entrance by a semicircular portico.

The elevation is drawn on the left side of the plan.

MS. B 19b. A further development of MS. B 18, by employing for the four principal chapels the type Pl. LXXXVIII, No. 3, as we have already seen in Pl. XCI, No. 2; the exterior presents two varieties.

(a) The outer contour follows the inner.[2]

(b) It is semicircular.

Pl. LXXXVII, No. 2 (MS. B. 18b). Elevation to the first variation MS. B 19. If we were not certain that this sketch was by Leonardo, we might feel tempted to take it as a study by Bramante for St. Peter's at Rome.[3]

MS. P. V. 39b. In the principal axes the chapels of MS. B 19, and semicircular niches on the diagonals. The exterior of the whole edifice is also an octagon, concealing the form of the interior chapels, but with its angles on their axes.

---

[1] *The note accompanying this drawing is reproduced under No. 753.*

[2] *These chapels are here sketched in two different sizes; it is the smaller type which is thus formed.*

[3] *See Les Projets primitifs, Pl. 43.*

GROUP V. *Suggested by San Lorenzo at Milan*

*In MS. C. A. 271b there is a plan almost identical with that of San Lorenzo.—
The diagonal sides of the irregular octagon are not indicated. If it could be
proved that the arches which, in the actual church, exist on these sides in the first
story were added in 1574 by Martino Bassi, then this plan and the following
section would be still nearer the original state of San Lorenzo than at present. A
reproduction of this slightly sketched plan has not been possible. It may, however,
be understood from Pl. LXXXVIII, No. 3, by suppressing the four pillars corresponding to the apses.*

*Pl. LXXXVII, No. 1, C. A. 7b, shows the section in elevation corresponding
with the above-named plan. The recessed chapels are decorated with large shells
in the half-domes like the arrangement in San Lorenzo, but with proportions like
those of Bramante's Sacristy of Santa Maria presso S. Satiro.*

*MS. C. A. 271b; a sheet containing three views of exteriors of domes. On the
same sheet there is a plan similar to the one above named but with uninterrupted
aisles and with the addition of round chapels in the axes (compare Pl. XCVII,
No. 3, and p. 32, Fig. 1), perhaps a reminiscence of the two chapels annexed to
San Lorenzo.—Leonardo has here sketched the way of transforming this plan into
a Latin cross by means of a nave with side aisles.*

*Pl. XCI, No. 1. Plan showing a type deprived of aisles and comprised in a square
building which is surrounded by a portico. It is accompanied by the following text:*

B. N. 2037. 4a]   756

Questo edifitio è abitato di sotto · e di sopra
come · è San Sepulcro, [2]ed è sopra come sotto,
saluo che 'l di sopra · à 'l tiburio · *c* · *d* · e 'l di
sotto [3]à 'l tiburio *a* · *b* · e quãdo entri nella chiesa
di sotto, [4]tu cali 10 scalini, e quãdo mõti in
quello di sopra tu sali 20 [5]scalini, che a ⅓ l'uno
fãno 10 braccia, e questo è lo spatio ch' è [6]infra
i piani dell' una e l'altra chiesa.

This edifice is inhabited [accessible] below
and above, like San Sepolcro, and it is the same
above as below, except that the upper story has
the dome *c d*, and the lower has the dome *a b*,
and when you enter into the crypt, you descend
10 steps, and when you mount into the upper
you ascend 20 steps, which, with ⅓ braccio for
each, make 10 braccia, and this is the height
between one floor of the church and the other.

756. 1. socto .. chome .. sansepulchro. 2. chome. 3. a · b · e ecquãdo. nela .. socto. 4. chali 10 schalini. 5. schalini .. 10. br · e
6. ellaltra.

756. The church of San Sepolcro at Milan, founded
in 1030 and repeatedly rebuilt after the middle of the

sixteenth century, still stands over the crypt of the
original structure.

*Above the plan on the same sheet is a view of the exterior. By the aid of these
two figures and the description, sections of the edifice may easily be reconstructed.
But the section drawn on the left side of the building seems not to be in keeping with
the same plan, notwithstanding the explanatory note written underneath it: 'dentro
il difitio di sopra' (interior of the edifice above).*[1]

[1] *The small inner dome corresponds to a b on the
plan—it rises from the lower church into the upper—
above, and larger, rises the dome c d. The aisles above
and below thus correspond ('è di sopra come di sotto,*

*salvochè, &c.'). The only difference is that in the
section Leonardo has not taken the trouble to make the
form octagonal, but has merely sketched circular lines in
perspective.*   J. P. R.

Before leaving this group, it is well to remark that the germ of it seems already indicated by the diagonal lines in the plans Pl. LXXXV, No. 11 and No. 7. We shall find another application of the same type to the Latin cross in Pl. XCVII, No. 3.

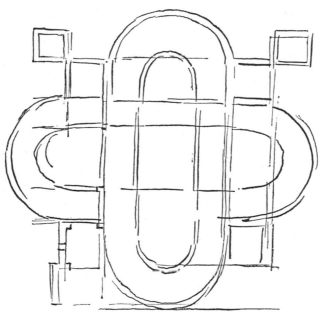

IV. ECCLESIASTICAL ARCHITECTURE (*cont.*)

B. *The Theory of Dome Architecture* (*cont.*)

2. CHURCHES FORMED ON THE PLAN OF A LATIN CROSS

We find among Leonard's studies several sketches for churches on the plan of the Latin cross; we shall begin by describing them, and shall add a few observations.

A. *Studies after existing Monuments*

Pl. XCIV, No. 2 (MS. B 11b). Plan of San Spirito at Florence, a basilica built after the designs of Brunellesco.—Leonardo has added the indication of a portico in front, either his own invention or the reproduction of a now lost design.

Pl. XCV, No. 2. Plan accompanied by the words: 'A è santo sepolcro di milano di sopra' (A *is the upper church of S. Sepolcro at Milan*); *although since Leonardo's time considerably spoilt, it is still the same in plan.*

The second plan with its note: 'B è la sua parte socto tera' (B *is its subterranean part* [*the crypt*]) *still corresponds with the present state of this part of the church as I have ascertained by visiting the crypt with this plan. Excepting the addition of a few insignificant walls, the state of this interesting part of the church still conforms to Leonardo's sketch; but in the Vestibolo the two columns near the entrance of the winding stairs are absent.*

B. *Designs or Studies*

Pl. XCV, No. 1. Plan of a church evidently suggested by that of San Sepolcro at Milan. The central part has been added to on the principle of the second type of Group III. Leonardo has placed the 'coro' (*choir*) *in the centre.*

Pl. XCVI, No. 2. In the plan the dome, as regards its interior, belongs to the First Class of Group IV, and may be grouped with the one in MS. B 35a. The nave seems to be a development of the type represented in Pl. XCV, No. 2, B by adding towers and two lateral porticos.

On the left is a view of the exterior of the preceding plan. It is accompanied by the following note:

B. 24a]   757

Questo · edifitio è abitato di sopra e di sotto; ²di sopra · si va · per li campanili · e uassi sù per lo piano ³dove sono fondati · i · 4 · tiburi, e detto piano ⁴à uno parapetto dinãzi, e di detti tiburi nessuno ⁵ne riesce in chiesa, anzi sono separati ĩ tutto.

This building is inhabited below and above; the way up is by the campaniles, and in going up one has to use the platform, where the drums of the four domes are, and this platform has a parapet in front, and none of these domes communicates with the church, but they are quite separate.

757. 4. a ĩ parapecto. 5. neriessie . . tucto.

C. A. 172*b*]　　　　　　　　757 A

MISURA	MEASURE
San Pagolo di Roma à 5 navi e 8(o) colonne ed è largo dentro alla la(r)gheza delle sue navi br. 130 e dall(e) scale dello altare maggiore alla porta br. 155, e da esse scale al (ul)timo muro di rieto all' altare maggi(o)re br. (7) 70 el portico è lungo br. 130 e largo br. 17 · Fatto alli (?ago)sto 1516.	San Paolo in Rome has 5 naves and 8(o) columns and its width across the naves is 130 braccia, and from the steps of the high altar to the door is br. 155, and from these steps to the farthest wall at the back of the high altar br. 70, and the portico is 130 br. long and 17 br. wide. Taken ? August 1516.

Pl. XCVI, No. 1 (*MS. C. A.* 17*b*). *Perspective view of a church seen from behind; this recalls the Duomo at Florence, but with two campaniles.*

Pl. XCVII, No. 3 (*MS. B* 52*a*). *The central part is a development of S. Lorenzo at Milan, such as was executed at the Duomo of Pavia. There is sufficient analogy between the building actually executed and this sketch to suggest a direct connexion between them. Leonardo accompanied Francesco di Giorgio when the latter was consulted on June* 21, 1490, *as to this church; the fact that the only word accompanying the plan is* 'sagrestia' *seems to confirm our supposition, for the sacristies were added only in* 1492, *i.e. four years after the beginning of the Cathedral which at that time was most likely still sufficiently unfinished to be capable of receiving the form of the present sketch.*

On June 8, 1490, Lodovico il Moro wrote to Bartolomeo Calco that the fabbricieri of the Cathedral of Pavia were in need of the advice of the Sienese architect who was then in Milan in connexion with the cathedral there, and he added as a postscript that also Leonardo and Amadeo should proceed to Pavia: 'Rechedendo ancora maestro Leonardo fiorentino et Magistro Io. Antonio Amadeo operarete che vengano ancora loro.'[1] In that same month Francesco di Giorgio and Leonardo set out together on horseback with a following of 'ingeniarii cum sociis et famulis' for Pavia. They put up at the inn called 'Saracino', where their bill amounting to 'lib. xx' was paid by the Fabbrica del Duomo di Pavia on June 21, it being stated that they both were specially called for a consultation about this building.[2]

Pl. XCVII, No. 2, *shows the exterior of this design. Below is the note:* edifitio al proposito del fōdamēto figurato di socto (*edifice proper for the ground-plan figured below*).

Here we may also mention the plan of a Latin cross drawn in MS. C. A. 271*b* (*see p.* 38).

Pl. XCIV, No. 1 (*MS. L* 15*b*). *External side view of Brunellesco's Florentine basilica San Lorenzo, seen from the North.*

[1] Archivio di Stato, Milano. Carteggio Sforcesco. Published in L. Beltrami, *Documenti e Memorie riguardanti la Vita e le Opere di L. d. V.*, Milan, 1919, p. 30, no. 48.

[2] Reg. Fabbrica, Duomo di Pavia, anno 1488, fol. 30ᵛ, published by E. Motta, *Boll. Stor. della Svizzera Italiana*, 1884, p. 19, and in L. Beltrami, o.c., p. 32, no. 50. For Leonardo at Pavia compare also: Malaspina di Sannazaro, *Memorie Storiche della Fabbrica della Cattedrale di Pavia*, Milan, 1816, p. 10; E. Solmi, *Scritti Vinciani, L. d. V., il Duomo, il Castello e l'Università di Pavia*, Florence, 1924, p. 15; L. Pozzi, *L. d. V. e il disegno del Duomo di Pavia, Boll. d. Soc. Pavese d. Storia Patria*, 1903, anno III, Fasc. III, IV, pp. 390 ff.; Gustavo Uzielli, *Ricerche intorno a L. d. V.*, Turin, 1896, p. 122.

Pl. XCIV, No. 4 (V. A., Frame 27). Principal front of a nave, most likely of a church on the plan of a Latin cross. We notice here not only the principal features which were employed afterwards in Alberti's front of S. Maria Novella, but even details of a more advanced style, such as we are accustomed to meet with only after the year 1520.

In the background of Leonardo's unfinished picture of St. Jerome (Vatican Gallery) a somewhat similar church front is indicated (see the accompanying sketch).

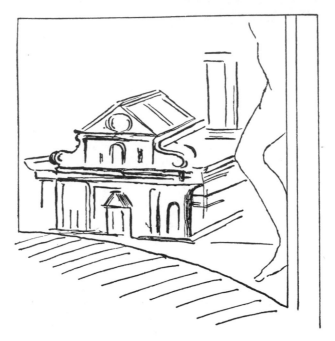

The view of the front of a temple, apparently a dome in the centre of four corinthian porticos bearing pediments (published by Amoretti, Tav. II. B, as being by Leonardo), is taken from a drawing, now at the Ambrosian Gallery. We cannot consider this to be by the hand of the master.

C. Studies for a form of a church most proper for preaching

The problem as to what form of church might answer the requirements of acoustics seems to have engaged Leonardo's very particular attention. The designation of 'teatro' given to some of these sketches clearly shows which plan seemed to him most favourable for hearing the preacher's voice.

Pl. XCVII, No. 1 (MS. B 52). Rectangular edifice divided into three naves with an apse on either side, terminated by a semicircular theatre with rising seats, as in antique buildings. The pulpit is in the centre. Leonardo has written on the left side of the sketch: 'teatro da predicare' (Theatre for preaching).[1]

MS. B 55a (see p. 43, Fig. 1). A domed church after the type of Pl. XCV, No. 1,

---

[1] *The note* teatro de predicar, *on the right side, appears in the handwriting of Pompeo Leoni.*

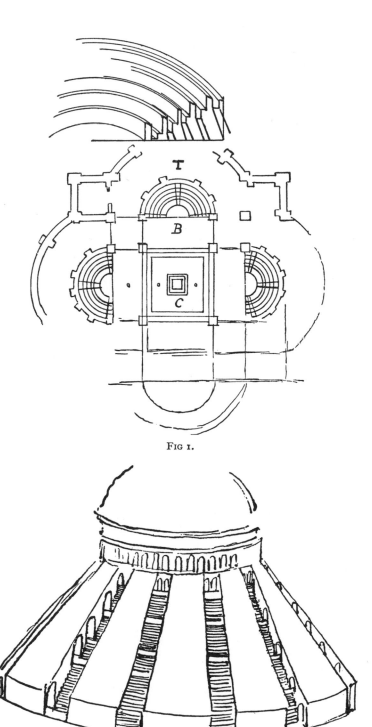

FIG 1.

FIG. 2.

shows four theatres occupying the apses and facing the square 'coro' (choir), which is in the centre between the four pillars of the dome. The rising arrangement of the seats is shown in the sketch p. 43, No. 1. At the place marked B *Leonardo wrote* teatri per uldire messa (*rows of seats to hear mass*), *at* T teatri, *and at* C coro (*choir*).

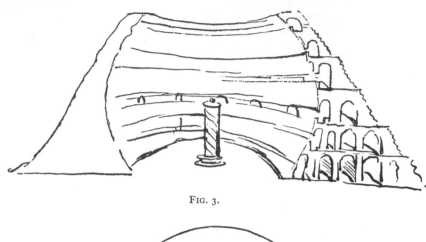

FIG. 3.

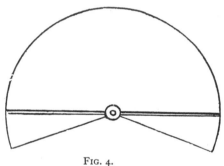

FIG. 4.

In MS. C. A. 264 are slight sketches of two plans for rectangular choirs and two elevations of the altar and pulpit which seem to be in connexion with these plans.

MS. B. N. 2037 5a (see pp. 43 and 44, Figs. 2 and 3). 'Locho dove si predica' (Place for preaching). A most singular plan for a building. The interior is a portion of a sphere, the centre of which is the summit of a column destined to serve as the preacher's pulpit. The inside is somewhat like a modern theatre, whilst the exterior and the galleries and stairs recall the ancient amphitheatres.

Page 44, Fig. 4. A plan accompanying the two preceding drawings. If this gives the complete form Leonardo intended for the edifice, it would have comprised only about two-thirds of the circle. Leonardo wrote in the centre 'fondamento', a word he often employed for plans, and on the left side of the view of the exterior: locho dove si predicha (*a place for preaching in*).

D. Design for a Mausoleum

Pl. XCVIII (P. V. 182. No. d'ordre 2386). In the midst of a hilly landscape rises an artificial mountain in the form of a gigantic cone, crowned by an imposing temple. At two-thirds of the height a terrace is cut out with six doorways forming entrances to galleries, each leading to three sepulchral halls, so constructed as to contain about five hundred funeral urns, disposed in the customary antique style. From two opposite sides steps ascend to the terrace in a single flight and beyond it to the temple above. A large circular opening, like that in the Pantheon, is in the dome above what may be the altar, or perhaps the central monument on the level of the terrace below.

The section of a gallery given in the sketch to the right below shows the roof to be constructed on the principle of superimposed horizontal layers, projecting one beyond the other, and each furnished with a sort of heel, which appears to be undercut, so as to give the appearance of a beam from within. Granite alone would be adequate to the dimensions here given to the key-stone, as the thickness of the layers can hardly be considered to be less than a foot. In taking this as the basis of our calculation for the dimensions of the whole construction, the width of the chamber would be about 25 feet but, judging from the number of urns it contains—and there is no reason to suppose that these urns were larger than usual—it would seem to be no more than about 8 or 10 feet.

The construction of the vaults resembles those in the galleries of some Etruscan tumuli, for instance, the Regolini Galassi tomb at Cervetri and also that of the chamber and passages of the pyramid of Cheops and of the treasury of Atreus at Mycenae.

The upper cone displays not only analogies with the monuments mentioned in the note, but also with Etruscan tumuli, such as the Cocumella tomb at Vulci, and the Regolini Galassi tomb.[1] The whole scheme is one of the most magnificent in the history of Architecture.

It would be difficult to decide as to whether any monument he had seen suggested this idea to Leonardo, but it is worth while to inquire if any monument or group of monuments of an earlier date may be supposed to have done so.[2]

E. Studies for the Central Tower, or Tiburio, of Milan Cathedral

Towards the end of the fifteenth century the Fabbricceria del Duomo *had to settle on the choice of a model for the crowning and central part of this vast building.*

We learn from the accounts of the Works Department that Leonardo was constructing a model for the tiburio in 1487 with the help of the carpenter Bernardo Maggi da Abiate. Payments for this model were entered on July 30, on August 8, 18, and 27, on September 28 and 30, and again on January 11,

[1] *See Fergusson, Handbook of Architecture, i. 291.*

[2] *There are, in Algiers, two Monuments, commonly called 'Le Madracen' and 'Le Madracen' and 'Le Madracen' and 'Le Chré-tienne', which somewhat resemble Leonardo's design. They are known to have served as the Mausolea of the Kings of Mauretania. Pomponius Mela, the geographer of the time of the Emperor Claudius, describes them as having been 'Monumentum commune regiae gentis'. See Le Madracen, Rapport fait par M. le Grand Rabbin Ab. Cahen, Constantine, 1873—Mémoire sur les fouilles exécutées au Madras'en . . . par le Colonel Brunon, Constantine, 1873.—Deux Mausolées afri-*

cains, le Madracen et le tombeau de la Chrétienne par M. J. de Laurière, Tours, 1874.—Le tombeau de la Chrétienne, Mausolée des rois mauritaniens par M. Berbrugger, Alger, 1867. Leonardo's observations on the coast of Africa are given later in this work. The Herodium near Bethlehem in Palestine (Jebel el Fureidîs, the Frank Mountain) was constructed on a very similar plan. Compare K. Humann and Otto Puchstein in Reisen in Kleinasien und Nordsyrien, Berlin, 1890, p. 227, on large and elaborate tumuli in Asia Minor with bases in masonry designed for princely families.

1488.[1] Then the model was submitted to the Works Department, probably with an accompanying letter, for there is a draft for such a letter in the Codice Atlantico (folio 270a, reproduced under No. 1347 A). Other artists who submitted models in that year were Bramante, Luca Paperio (Fancelli), Pietro da Gorgonzola.[2] On May 10, 1490, Leonardo's model was returned at his own request for repair, and he was asked to keep it in readiness.[3] A week later, on May 17, he was paid 12 lire for the construction of a new model, but this seems never to have been delivered, for an entry four years later, in 1494, says that he was still owing that amount.[4] A document entitled 'Bramanti opinio supra domicilium seu templum magnum',[5] and probably written about this time, gives Bramante's views on the tiburio, and begins by enumerating four requisite qualities—strength, conformity with the rest of the building, lightness, and beauty—and then proceeds to criticize the models of the architects Legute, Pietro da Gorgonzola, Giovanni Antonio Amadeo, Antonio Pandino, and Giovanni da Molteno. Leonardo is not mentioned. On June 10, 1490, Bartolomeo Calco, the secretary of the Duke, wrote to Lodovico il Moro that the Sienese architect Francesco di Giorgio Martini was working hard to complete his model and that Leonardo would always be at the Duke's disposal: 'Magister Leonardo Fiorentino me ha dicto sarà sempre aparecchiato omne volte sij richiesto.'[6] There was therefore no model by Leonardo at the consultation which took place at the Castello on June 27, 1490, in the presence of the Duke and the Archbishop. At this meeting four models were under consideration, one by Francesco di Giorgio, the other by Simone da Sturi, the third by Giov. di Battagi, and the fourth was the joint work of Giov. Ant. Amadeo and Giov. Giacomo Dolcebuono. The task of constructing the tiburio was entrusted to the two Lombards last named.

Several sketches by Leonardo refer to this important project:

Pl. XCIX, No. 2 (MS. S. K. III No. 55b), a small plan of the whole edifice.— The projecting chapels in the middle of the transept are wanting here. The nave appears to be shortened and seems to be approached by an inner 'vestibolo'.—

Pl. C, No. 2 (Triv. 11a). Plan of the octagon tower, giving the disposition of the buttress; starting from the eight pillars adjoining the four principal piers and intended to support the eight angles of the Tiburio. These buttresses correspond exactly with those described by Bramante as existing in the model presented by Amadeo.

Pl. C, No. 3 (MS. Triv. 8b). Two plans showing different arrangements of the buttresses, which seem to be formed partly by the intersection of a system of pointed arches such as that seen in

[1] *Archivio della Fabbrica del Duomo, Liber mandatorum,* published in L. Beltrami, L. d. V. negli studi per il tiburio della Cattedrale di Milano, *Milan,* 1903; Documenti e Memorie riguardanti le opere di L. d. V., *Milan,* 1919; Annali della Fabbrica del Duomo di Milano dall' origine sino al presente, *Milan,* 1877 *ff., vol.* iii, *pp.* 38, 41, 57, 60.

[2] *G. L. Calvi,* Notizie sulla vita e sulle opere dei principali architetti, scultori e pittori che fiorirono in Milano, *Part* III, 20. *See also H. de Geymüller,* Les Projets primitifs, &c., i. 37 and 116–19.

[3] *See Beltrami,* Documenti e Memorie riguardanti le opere di L.d.V., *Milan,* 1919, No. 46.

[4] *See ibid.,* Nos. 47 *and* 64.

[5] *First published by G. Mongeri,* Arch. stor. Lomb. 1878, v, *p.* 547.

[6] *Published by Malaguzzi Valeri,* Repertorium für Kunstwissenschaft, xxiv, 1901, *p.* 95.

Pl. C, No. 5 (MS. B 27a), destined to give a broader base to the drum.   The text underneath is given under No. 788.

MS. B 3—three slight sketches of plans in connexion with the preceding ones.

Pl. XCIX, No. 1 (MS. Triv. 8a), contains several small sketches of sections and exterior views of the Dome; some of them show buttress-walls shaped as inverted arches.   Respecting these Leonardo notes:

Triv. 8a]   758

L'arco rivescio è migliore per fare ²spalla che l'ordinario, perchè il rovescio ³trova · sotto · sé · muro resistēte alla sua ⁴debolezza, e l'ordinario nō trova nel suo ⁵debole se non aria.

The inverted arch is better for giving a shoulder than the ordinary one, because the former finds below it a wall resisting its weakness, whilst the latter finds in its weak part nothing but air.

758. 1. larcho. 2. isspalla .. riverscio. 4. deboleza ellordinario.

Three slight sketches of sections on the same leaf—above those reproduced here—are more closely connected with the large drawing in the centre of

Pl. C, No. 4 (MS. Triv. 22b), which shows a section of a very elevated dome, with double vaults, connected by ribs and buttresses ingeniously disposed, so as to bring the weight of the lantern to bear on the base of the dome.

A sketch underneath it shows a round pillar on which is indicated which part of its summit is to bear the weight: 'il pilastro sarà charicho in · a · b.' *(The column will bear the weight at* a b.) *Another note is above on the right side:* Larcho regie tanto sotto asse chome di sopra sé *(The arch supports as much below it [i.e. a hanging weight] as above it).*

Pl. C, No. 1 (C. A. 310a). Larger sketch of half-section of the Dome, with a very complicated system of arches, and a double vault. Each stone is shaped so as to be knit or dovetailed to its neighbour. Thus the inside of the Dome cannot be seen from below.

MS. C. A. 310b. A repetition of the preceding sketch with very slight modifications.

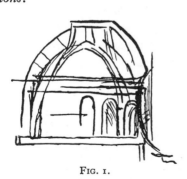

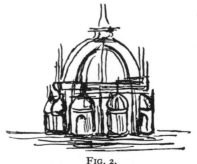

FIG. 1.   FIG. 2.

MS. Triv. 9a (see Figs. 1 and 2). Section of the Dome with reverted buttresses between the windows, above which iron anchors or chains seem to be intended. Below is the sketch of the outside.

Pl. XCIX, No. 3 (*C. A.* 266*a*), *four sketches of the exterior of the Dome.*

C. A. 13*a. Section, showing the points of rupture of a gothic vault, in evident connexion with the sketches described above.*

It deserves to be noticed how easily and apparently without effort Leonardo manages to combine gothic details and structure with the more modern shape of the Dome.

The following notes are on C. A. 310*a*, oni cosa pōderosa, and oni cosa pōderosa desidera de(scendere); *farther below, several multiplications most likely intended to calculate the weight of some parts of the Dome, thus* $16 \times 47 = 720$; $720 \times 800 = 576000$, *next to which is written:* peso del pilastro di 9 teste (*weight of the pillar* 9 *diameters high*).

Below: $576000 \times 8 = 4608000$; *and below:*

Semjliō e se cē 8 Mᵃ il peso del tiburio

(*six millions six hundred* 8 *thousand the weight of the Dome*).

The sketch given at the side shows the arrangement of the second and third socle on the apses of the choir of Sta. Maria delle Grazie; and it is remarkable that these sketches, in MS. S. K. M. II 1. 62*b*, 63*a*, *occur with the passage given in Volume I as Nos.* 665 *and* 666 *referring to the composition of the Last Supper in the Refectory of that church.*

Bossi hazarded the theory that Leonardo might have been the architect who built the church of Sta. Maria delle Grazie, but there is no evidence to support this, either in documents or in Leonardo's manuscripts.[1]

F. The Project for lifting up the Battistero of Florence and setting it on a basement

Among the very few details Vasari gives as to the architectural studies of Leonardo, we read: 'And among these models and designs there was one by way of which he showed several times to many ingenious citizens who then governed Florence, his readiness to lift up, without ruining it, the church of San Giovanni in Florence (the Battistero, opposite the Duomo) in order to place under it the missing basement with steps; he supported his assertions with reasons so persuasive, that while he spoke the undertaking seemed feasible, although every one of his hearers, when he had departed, could see by himself the impossibility of so vast an undertaking.'[2]

---

[1] Leonardo was called 'architetto della cupola della Madonna delle Grazie a Milano' in a copy of Vasari's *Vite,* annotated by an unknown hand (perhaps Sebastiano Resta's) in the 17th century. G. Bossi commenting on this note approved of the suggestion. G. Mongeri, *Postille di un anonimo seicentista alla prima edizione delle Vite dei più eccellenti artefici italiani, scritte da Giorgio Vasari.* Archivio Storicho Lombardo, Milan 1876, p. 103 f.

[2] *This latter statement of Vasari's must be considered to be exaggerated. I may refer here to some data given by* Libri, Histoire des sciences mathématiques en Italie (ii. 216, 217): 'On a cru dans ces derniers temps faire un miracle en mécanique en effectuant ce transport, et cependant dès l'année 1455, Gaspard Nadi et Aristote de Fioravantio avaient transporté, à une distance considérable, la tour de la Magione de Bologne, avec ses fondements, qui avait presque quatre-vingts pieds de haut. Le continuateur de la chronique de Pugliola dit que le trajet fut de 35 pieds et que durant le transport auquel le chroniqueur affirme avoir assisté, il arriva un accident grave qui fit pencher de trois pieds la tour pendant qu'elle était suspendue, mais que cet accident fut promptement réparé (Muratori, Scriptores rer. ital., Tom. XVIII, col. 717, 718). Alidosi a rapporté une note où Nadi rend compte de ce transport avec une rare simplicité. D'après cette note, on voit que les opérations de ce genre n'étaient pas nouvelles.

In the MS. C. A. fol. 298, there are two sketches which possibly might have a bearing on this bold enterprise. We find there a plan of a circular or polygonal edifice surrounded by semicircular arches in an oblique position. These may be taken for the foundation of the steps and of the new platform. In the perspective elevation the same edifice, forming a polygon, is shown as lifted up and resting on a circle of inverted arches which rest on another circle of arches in the ordinary position, but so placed that the inverted arches above rest on the spandrels of the lower range.

What seems to confirm the supposition that the lifting up of a building is here in question is the indication of engines for winding up, such as jacks, and a rack and wheel. As the lifting apparatus represented on this sheet does not seem particularly applicable to an undertaking of such magnitude, we may consider it to be a first sketch or scheme for the engines to be used.

G. Description of an unknown Temple

C. A. 285a]   759

Per dodici gradi di scale al magno tempio si saliva, il quale otto cento braccia circundaua, e con ottāgulare [2]figura era fabricato, e sopra li otto anguli otto gran base si posauano alte un braccio e mezzo, e grosse 3, [3]e lunghe 6 nel suo sodo, coll' angolo in mezzo, sopra delle quali si fondauano 8 grā pilastri: sopra del sodo della basa si le[4]vavā per ispatio di 24 braccia, e nel suo termine erano stabiliti 8 capitelli di 3 braccia l'uno, e largo 6, sopra di questi se[5]guiua architraue fregio e cornice con altezza di 4 braccia e ½, il quale per retta linia [6]dall' un pilastro all'altro s'astendea e così con circuito d'otto cento braccia il tempio circundava infra l'ū [7]pilastro e l'altro; per sostentacolo di tal mēbro erano stabiliti dieci gran coloñe dell' altezza de' pilastri e cō [8]grossezza di 3 braccia sopra le base, le quali erā alte vn braccio e ½.

[9]Salivasi a questo tenpio per 12 gradi di scale, il quale tempio era sopra il dodecimo grado fondato in figura ottan[10]gulare, e sopra ciascuno angulo nasceva vn gran pilastro; e infra li

Twelve flights of steps led up to the great temple, which was eight hundred braccia in circumference and built on an octagonal plan. At the eight corners were eight large plinths, one braccia and a half high, and three wide, and six long at the bottom, with an angle in the middle; on these were eight great pillars, standing on the plinths as a foundation, and twenty-four braccia high. And on the top of these were eight capitals three braccia long and six wide, above which were the architrave frieze and cornice, four braccia and a half high, and this was carried on in a straight line from one pillar to the next and so, continuing for eight hundred braccia, surrounded the whole temple from pillar to pillar. To support this entablature there were ten large columns of the same height as the pillars, three braccia thick above their bases, which were one braccia and a half high.

The ascent of this temple was by twelve flights of steps, and the temple was on the twelfth, of an octagonal form, and at each angle rose a large pillar; and between the pillars were

759. 1. di sala al .. otāgulare. 2. posaua alteiv br e mezo. 3. ellungha .. collangholo imezo .. fondaua. 4. ne di 24 br e .. era stabilito .. di 3 br . luno "elargo 6". 5. alteza di 4 br e ½ [el simile] il quale. 6. pilastra .. circhuito dotto cento br .. infrallū. 7. ellaltro per sostentachulo .. era stabilito .. colone dellalteza. 8. grosseza di 3 br .. vnbr. 9. acquesto .. disscale .. dode | "cimo" .. otta. 10. tangulare [e inf] e sopra .. infralli .. era inframeso.

Celle-ci ne coûta que 150 livres (monnaie d'alors) y compris le cadeau que le Légat fit aux deux mécaniciens. Dans la meme année, Aristote redressa le clocher de Cento, qui penchait de plus de cinq pieds (Alidosi, instruttione, p. 188—Muratori, Scriptores

rer. ital., tom. XXIII, col. 888.—Bossii, chronica Mediol., 1492, in-fol. ad ann. 1455). On ne conçoit pas comment les historiens des beaux-arts ont pu négliger de tels hommes.'   J. P. R.

759. Either this description is incomplete, or, as seems to me highly probable, it refers to some ruin. The enormous dimensions forbid our supposing this to be any temple in Italy or Greece. Syria was the

native land of colossal octagonal buildings, in the early centuries A.D. The Temple of Baalbek and others are even larger than that here described.

                                      J. P. R.

pilastri erano inframessi [11]dieci colonne colla medesima altezza de' pilastri, i quali si levauā sopra del pauimēto · 28 braccia e ½; sopra [12]di questa medesima altezza si posaua architraue fregio e cornice che con lunghezza d'otto cēto braccia, e cingea [13]il tenpio; a vna medesima altezza circuiua dentro a tal circuito sopra il medesimo piano in verso in centro del tempio per spatio di 24 braccia nascono [14]le conrispondentie delli 8 pilastri delli angoli, e delle colonne poste nelle prime faccie, e si [15]leuauano alla medesima altezza sopra detta, e sopra tal pilastri li architraui perpetui [16]ritornavano sopra li primi detti pilastri e colonne.

placed ten columns of the same height as the pillars, rising from the pavement to a height of twenty-eight braccia and a half; and at this height the architrave, frieze, and cornice were placed which surrounded the temple having a length of eight hundred braccia. At the same height, and within the temple at the same level, and all round the centre of the temple at a distance of 24 braccia farther in, are pillars corresponding to the eight pillars in the angles, and columns corresponding to those placed in the outer spaces. These rise to the same height as the former ones, and over these the continuous architrave returns towards the outer row of pillars and columns.

11. cola . . alteza . . 28 br e ½. 12. di queste sta . . alteza . . frego e corice cho collungeza dotto cēto br cigea. 13. alteza . . attal . . piano | "iciero il centro del tenpio per ispatio di 24 br . nasscie. 14. e delle [ottamta] colone . . facce essi. 15. alteza sopra [di que] detta.

V. PALACE ARCHITECTURE

But a small number of Leonardo's drawings refer to the architecture of palaces, and our knowledge is small as to what style Leonardo might have adopted for such buildings.

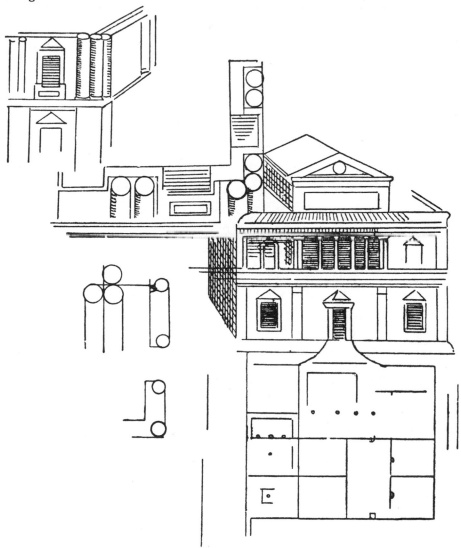

Pl. CII, No. 1 *(W.* 12579b). *A small portion of a façade of a palace in two stories, somewhat resembling Alberti's Palazzo Ruccellai.—Compare with this Bramante's painted front of the Casa Silvestri, and a painting by Montorfano in San Pietro in Gessate at Milan, third chapel on the left-hand side, and also with Bramante's palaces at Rome. The pilasters with arabesques, the rustica between them,*

*and the figures over the window may be painted or in sgraffito. The original is
drawn in red chalk.*

*Pl. LXXXI, No. 1 (MS. Triv. 22 a). Sketch of a palace with battlements and
decorations, most likely graffiti; the details remind us of those in the Castello at
Vigevano.*[1]

*MS. Trn. 0" contains a design for a palace or house with a loggia in the middle
of the first story, over which rises an attic with a pediment reproduced on page 51.*

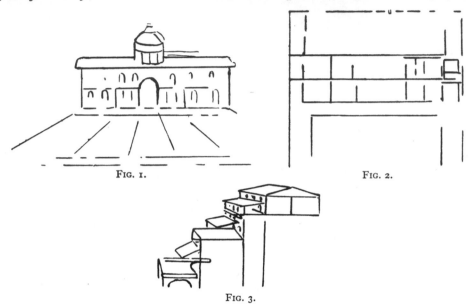

FIG. 1.   FIG. 2.

FIG. 3.

*The details drawn close by on the left seem to indicate an arrangement of coupled
columns against the wall of a first story.*

*Pl. LXXXV, No. 14 (MS. S. K. M. III 15b) contains a very slight sketch in
red chalk, which most probably is intended to represent the façade of a palace. Inside
is the short note 7 he 7 (7 and 7).*

*MS. I 256a (see p. 52, Figs. 1 and 2) contains a view of an unknown palace. Its
plan is indicated at the side.*

*In MS. Br. M. 126a (see Fig. 3 on p. 52) there is a sketch of a house, on which
Leonardo notes:* casa con tre terrazi (*house with three terraces*).

*Pl. CX, No. 4 (MS. L. 36b) represents the front of a fortified building drawn at
Cesena in 1502 (see No. 1040).*

*Here we may also mention the singular building in the allegorical composition
represented on Pl. LVIII in Vol. I. In front of it appears the head of a sphinx or
of a dragon which seems to be carrying the palace away.*

[1] *Count Giulio Porro, in his valuable contribution to
the* Archivio Storico Lombardo, Anno VIII, fasc. iv
(Dec. 31, 1881): L. d. V., Libro di Annotazioni e
Memorie, *refers to this in the following note:* 'Alla
pag. 41 vi è uno schizzo di volta ed accanto scrisse:
"il pilastro sarà charicho in su 6" e potrebbe darsi
che si riferisse alla cupola della chiesa delle Grazie
tanto più che a pag. 42 vi è un disegno che rasso-
miglia assai al basamento che oggi si vede nella
parte esterna del coro di quella chiesa.' *This may,
however, be doubted. The drawing here referred to on
Page 41 of the same manuscript is reproduced on Pl. C,
No. 4, and described on page 47 as being a study for the
cupola of the Duomo of Milan.*

The following texts refer to the construction of palaces and other buildings destined for private use:

W. 1258b] 760

La corte de' auere le parieti ²per l'altezza la metà della sua ³larghezza, cioè se la corte ⁴sarà braccia 40, la casa deve essere ⁵alta 20 nelle parieti di tal ⁶corte, e tal corte vol essere ⁷larga per la metà di tutta la ⁸facciata.

In the courtyard the walls must be half the height of its width, that is, if the court be 40 braccia, the house must be 20 high as regards the walls of the said courtyard; and this courtyard must be half as wide as the whole front.

On the proportions of a courtyard.

B. 39a] 761

PER FARE VNA POLITA STALLA

²Modo · come · si de' · componere · vna · stalla: Dividerai in prima la sua lar³ghezza · in parti · 3 · e la sua lunghezza è libera ·, e le · 3 · dette divisioni ⁴sieno equali e di larghezza di braccia 6 per ciascuna, e alte 10, e la parte di mezzo ⁵sia in uso · de' maestri di stalla ·, le 2 da cāto per i cavagli, de' quali ciascuno ne de' ⁶pigliare per larghezza braccia 3 ·, lūghezza braccia 6, e alte piv dinanti · che dirieto · ½ · braccio ; ⁷la mangiatoia sia alta da terra braccia 2, il principio della rastrelliera ⁸braccia · 3 · o l'ultimo · braccia 4 ·; Ora · a volere atenere · quello ch'io prometto, cioè di ⁹fare detto sito cōtro allo universale vso · pulito e netto · inquāto al · di sopra ¹⁰della stalla ·, cioè dove sta il fieno ·, debe detto loco avere nella sua testa di fori vna ¹¹finestra alta 6 · e larga 6, donde con vn facil modo si cōduca il fieno su detto ¹²solaro, come appare nello strumēto *E* ·, e sia collocata ī un sito di larghez¹³za di braccia 6, e lungo quāto la stalla, come appare in · *k · p* · e l'altre 2 parti ¹⁴che mettano in mezzo · questa, ciascuna sia diuisa in 2 parti, le dua diverso il fieno sia¹⁵no braccia 4 ·, *p. s* ·, solo allo ofitio e andamento de' ministri d'essa stalla, l'altre ¹⁶2 che confinano colle parieti murali · sieno di braccia 2, come appare in *s · r* ·, ¹⁷e queste sieno allo ofitio di dare · il feno alle māgiatoie · per condotti stretti nel ¹⁸principio e larghi sulle māgiatoie, acciò che 'l feno nō si fermi infra via, sieno ¹⁹bene ītonicati e politi, figurati dov' è segnato *4 · f · s* ·; in quanto al dare ²⁰bere siano le māgiatoie di pietra, sopra le quali sia l'acqua, si chè si possino ²¹scoprire le māgiatoie come si scoprono le casse, alzādo i coperchi loro.

FOR MAKING A CLEAN STABLE

The manner in which one must arrange a stable. You must first divide its width in 3 parts, its depth matters not; and let these 3 divisions be equal and 6 braccia broad for each part and 10 high, and the middle part shall be for the use of the stablemasters; the 2 side ones for the horses, each of which must be 3 braccia in width and 6 in length, and be half a braccio higher at the head than behind. Let the manger be at 2 braccia from the ground, to the bottom of the rack, 3 braccia, and the top of it 4 braccia. Now, in order to attain to what I promise, that is, to make this place, contrary to the general custom, clean and neat: as to the upper part of the stable, i.e. where the hay is, that part must have at its outer end a window 6 braccia high and 6 broad, through which by simple means the hay is brought up to the loft, as is shown by the machine *E*; and let this be erected in a place 6 braccia wide, and as long as the stable, as seen at *k p*. The other two parts, which are on either side of this, are again divided; those nearest to the hay-loft are 4 braccia, *p s*, and only for the use and circulation of the servants belonging to the stable; the other two which reach to the outer walls are 2 braccia, as seen at *s r*, and these are made for the purpose of giving hay to the mangers, by means of funnels, narrow at the top and wide over the manger, in order that the hay should not choke them. They must be well plastered and clean and are represented at *4 f s*. As to the giving the horses water, the troughs must be of stone and above them [cisterns of] water. The mangers may be opened as boxes are uncovered by raising the lids.

On the dispositions of a stable.

760. 1. pariete. 2. lalteza. 3. largezza coe sella. 4. br 40 . la casa e essere. 5. altè . . pariete. 6. volerssere. 7. faccata.
761. 2. chome . . chomponere . . isstalla. 3. geza in parte. 3. ella . . lungeza . . decte. 4. largeza di br 6 . . mezo. 6. largeza br . 3 ellūgeza br 6 . . ½ br. 7. la mangiatoria sialta dacterra br . 2 . [larastella era] il . . dela rastelliera. 8. br . 3 . ellultimo br 4 . . attenere . . promecto. 9. decto . . necto. 10. feno . . decto . . nela. 11. feno. 12. apare . . essia colocata . . large. 13. br 6 . . apare in K. p. laltre e laltre. 14. metano imezo . . si diuisa . . feno. 15. no br 4 "p . s" . . ofitio [de mini si ribe] e andamento· 16. 2 che che chonfinano chole pariete . . br 2 . . apare. 17. ecqueste . . māgiatore . per condocti strecti. 18. sule māgiatore acio. 20. le māgiatore . . sia la sichessi. 21. māgiatore chome si schoprano.

760. See Pl. CI, No. 1, and compare the dimensions here given with No. 748, ll. 26–9, and the drawing belonging to it, Pl. LXXXI, No. 2.

761. See Pl. LXXVIII, No. 1.

B. 28b]   762

MODO COME SI FANNO ²L'ARMATURE PER FARE
³ORNAMĒTO ⁴DI EDIFITI

THE WAY TO CONSTRUCT A FRAMEWORK FOR
DECORATING BUILDINGS

Decorations for feasts.

⁵Modo come si debbono ⁶mettere le pertiche ⁷per legare i mazzuoli ⁸de' ginepri sopra esse ⁹pertiche, le quali sono ¹⁰confitte sopra l'ar¹¹matura della vol¹²ta e lega essi ma¹³zzuoli con salci e ¹⁴sù per fare cimerosa ¹⁵colle forbici e la¹⁶vora le cō salci;

¹⁷Sia da l'u¹⁸no all' altro ¹⁹cerchio uno ²⁰½ braccio e 'l gi²¹nepro si de' ²²regiere col²³le cime in giv ²⁴cōmīciādo ²⁵di sotto;

²⁶A questa colonna si lega ²⁷d'intorno 4 pertiche, dintor²⁸no alle quali s'inchioda ²⁹vinchi grossi uno dito · e poi ³⁰si fa da piè e vassi in alto legā³¹do mazzuoli di cime di ³²ginepro colle cime j̄ ba³³sso cioè sotto sopra.

The way in which the poles ought to be placed for tying bunches of juniper on to them. These poles must lie close to the framework of the vaulting, and tie the bunches on with osier withes, so as to clip them even afterwards with shears.

Let the distance from one circle to another be half a braccia; and the juniper [sprigs] must lie top downwards, beginning from below.

Round this column tie four poles to which willows about as thick as a finger must be nailed and then begin from the bottom and work upwards with bunches of juniper sprigs, the tops downwards, that is, upside down.

Br. M. 192a]   763

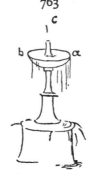

Sia lasciata cadere l'acqua ²in tutto il cerchio di *a · b.*

The water should be allowed to fall from the whole circle *a b.*

762. 1. fa. 2. larmadure. 5. debe. 7. mazoli. 10. chōfitte. 11. madura. 13. coli chon salcie[l]e. 16. cosalci. 19. cierchio. 20. ½ br. 22. cho. 26. acquesta. 28. ale. 29. ĩ dito. 31. mazoli di [gin] cime. 32. cholle.
763. 1. lacq"a". 2. totto il cierchio.

762. See Pl. CII, No. 3. The words here given as the title line, ll. 1–4, are the last in the original MS.— Lines 5–16 are written under Fig. 4.

763. Other drawings of fountains are given on Pl. CI (W. 12690); the original is a pen-and-ink drawing on blue paper; on Pl. CIII (MS. B 70 b) and Pl. LXXXII, No. 4 (C.A. 395b).

VI. STUDIES OF ARCHITECTURAL DETAILS

Several of Leonardo's drawings of architectural details prove that, like other great masters of that period, he had devoted his attention to the study of the proportion of such details. As every organic being in nature has its law of construction and growth, these masters endeavoured, each in his way, to discover and prove a law of proportion in architecture. The following notes in Leonardo's manuscripts refer to this subject.

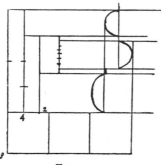

FIG. 1.

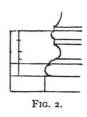

FIG. 2.

MS. S. K. M. III 45a (see Fig. 1). A diagram, indicating the rules as given by Vitruvius and by Leon Battista Alberti for the proportions of the Attic base of a column.

MS. S. K. M. III 37b (see Fig. 2). Diagram showing the same rules.

S.K.M. III. 44*b*]   764

B	toro superiore	.	.	.	.	.	toro superiore
2B	nestroli	.	.	.	.	.	astragali quadre
3B	orbiculo	.	.	.	.	.	troclea
4B	nestroli	.	.	.	.	.	astragali quadre
5B	toro īferiore	.	.	.	.		toro īferiore
6B	latastro	.	.	.	.	.	plintho

L. 19*b*; 20*a*]   765

SCALE D'URBINO

³Il latastro deve ⁴essere largo quā⁵to la grossezza di quā⁶lūque muro dove ⁷tale latastro s'ap⁸poggia.

STEPS OF URBINO

The plinth must be as broad as the thickness of the wall against which the plinth is built.

764. 1. toro superio . . super. 2. nexstroli. 3. torclea. 5. inferior . . iferi. 6. [plato] plinto.
765. 2. [il muro]. 3. illatasstro debbe. 4. [g] largo. 5. grosseza di qu"a". 8. pogga.

764. No explanation can be offered of the meaning of the letter B, which precedes each name. It may be meant for *basa* (base). Perhaps it refers to some author on architecture or an architect (Bramante?) who employed the designations thus marked for the mouldings.

3. *troclea*. Philander: 'Trochlea sive trochalia aut rechanum.'

6. *Laterculus* or *latastrum* is the Latin name for

Plinthus (πλίνθος), but Vitruvius adopted this Greek name and 'latastro' seems to have been little in use. It is to be found besides the text given above, as far as I am aware, only on two drawings of the Uffizi Collection, where, in one instance, it indicates the *abacus* of a Doric capital.

765. See Pl. CX, No. 3. The hasty sketch on the right-hand side illustrates the unsatisfactory effect produced when the plinth is narrower than the wall.

C. A. 325*a*]

766

I nostri antichi architettori . . . comīciando in prima dagli Egitti, i quali secōdo che descrive Diodoro Sicolo [2]furō i primi edificatori e componitori di città grandissime e di castelli ed edifizi publici e privati di forma, grandezza [3]e qualità · per le quali i loro antecedēti riguardevoli con stupefazione e maraviglia [4]le eleuate e grandissime macchine parēdo loro. . . .

[5]La colonna ch'à la sua grossezza nel terzo quivi è atta a rompersi; [6]quella che fusse sottile nel mezzo ronperassi nelle 2 istremità; [7]quella ch'è di pari grossezza e di pari fortezza è migliore pel suo ofizio, [8]seconda di bontà sarà quella ch'à la maggior grossezza dov' ella si cōgivgnie colla [9]basa.

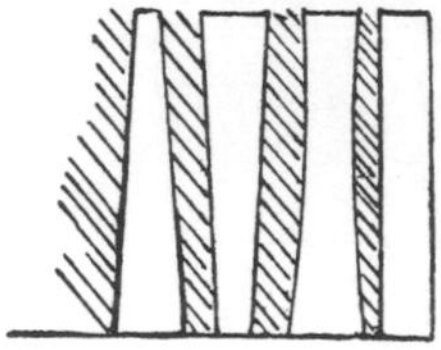

[10]Il capitello à a essere j̄ questa forma; cioè dividi la sua grossezza da capo j̄ 7 e da piè ne metti $\frac{5}{7}$ . . . [11]e fa che sia alto $\frac{5}{7}$ e verrà a essere quadro, dipoi dividi l'altezza j̄ 8, come facesti la colonna, di poi poni $\frac{1}{8}$ l'uovolo [12]e un altro ottavo la grossezza della tavola che sta di sopra al capitello; [13]i corni della tavola del capitello àno a sportare fuori dalla maggior larghezza della cāpana $\frac{2}{7}$ [14]cioè settimi del di sopra della cāpana che tocca a ciascū corno di sporto $\frac{1}{7}$ · [15]e la mozzatura de' corni vuole essere largha quāt' è alta, cioè $\frac{1}{8}$; jl resto degli ornamēti lascio [16]jn libertà degli scultori; [17]ma per tornare alle colonne, e provare la ragione secondo la forma di lor fortezza [18]o debolezza, dico così, che quādo le linie si partiranno dalla sommità della [19]colonna e termineranno nel suo nascimēto e la lor uia e lūghezza sia di pari [20]distanzia o latitudine, dico che questa colonna. . . .

The ancient architects . . . beginning with the Egyptians (?) who, as Diodorus Siculus writes, were the first to build and construct large cities and castles, public and private buildings of fine form, large, and well proportioned, the elevated and big machines of which were regarded with astonishment and wonder by their predecessors, as they seemed to them. . . .

The column, which has its thickness at the third part is liable to break there; the one which would be thinnest in the middle, would break into two; the one which is of equal thickness and of equal strength is better for its function. The second best will be one whose greatest thickness is where it joins with the base.

The capital must be formed in this way. Divide its thickness at the top into 7; at the foot make it $\frac{5}{7}$, and let it be $\frac{5}{7}$ high and you will have a square; afterwards divide the height into 8 parts as you did for the column, and then take $\frac{1}{8}$ for the echinus and another eighth for the thickness of the abacus on the top of the capital. The horns of the abacus of the capital have to project beyond the greatest width of the bell by $\frac{2}{7}$, i.e. sevenths of the top of the bell, so $\frac{1}{7}$ falls to the projection of each horn. The truncated part of the horns must be as broad as it is high, that is $\frac{1}{8}$. I leave the rest of the ornaments to the taste of the sculptors. But to return to the columns and in order to prove the reason of their strength or weakness according to their shape, I say that when the lines starting from the summit of the column and ending at its base and their direction and length are at an equal distance apart; I say that this column. . . .

Firenze Bibl. Laurenziana Trattato of Fr. di Giorgio, 13*b*]

767

Il cilindro d'vn corpo di figura colō[2]nale, e le sua opposite fronti sō due cierchi [3] d'interpositione paralella [4]e infra li lor ciētri s'estēde una linia [5]retta, che passa per il mezzo della grossezza [6]del cilindro e termina nelli ciētri [7]d'essi cierchi, la quale linia [8]dalli antichi è detta axis.

The cylinder of a body columnar in shape and its two opposite ends are two circles enclosed between parallel lines, and through the centre of the cylinder is a straight line, going through the middle of the thickness of the cylinder, ending at the centre of these circles, and called by the ancients the axis.

766. 1–. . *written from left to right* . 1. nosstri . . otalecine chomīciando . . daglitii . . sechōdo . . desscriue . . sicholo. 2. edi . fichatori e chomponitori di cita . . chasstella . . grandeza. 3. anticiedēti [gestupessani che] righuardevoli chonnistupefazione. 4. loro; *here the text breaks off*. 5. cholonna . . groseza . . qui . ve . . arōperse. 6. mezo . . nelle 2 isste mjta. 7. grosseza . . forteza. 8. sechonda . . magior grosseza dovela . . chōgivgnie chola. 10. chapitello . . grosseza da chapo j̄ | 7 | 8 dupie ne me $\frac{5}{7}$. 11. evera . . lalteza . . chome . . cholona . . poni $\frac{1}{8}$ luovolo. 12. grosseza dalla . . chessta . . chapitello. 13. i chorni . . chapitello . . assorportera . . della magior largheza . . chāpana. 14. cio settimi . . chāpana che tocha a ciasschū chorno dissporto $\frac{1}{7}$. 15. mozatura de de chorni . . essre largha . . j̄ resto. 16. ischultori. 17. cholonne . . sechondo . . forteza. 18. deboleza dicho chosi che quādo [che qua] le. 19. cholonna ettermineranno . . nasscimēto ella . . ellūgheza. 20. l disstanzia . . dicho . . cholonna. *Here the text breaks off*.

767. 1. El chilindro . . chorpo . . cholō. 2. elle . . fronte. 3. dinterpositio paralella. 4. e infra li lor ciētri sastēde . . linia pa. 5. mezo . . grossetta. 6. chilindro ottermina. 7. linia e di detta. 8. linia cietrale e dalli . . assis.

766. See Pl. CIII, No. 3, where the sketches belonging to ll. 10–16 are reproduced. The sketch of columns, here reproduced by a wood-cut, stands in the original close to ll. 5–8.

l. 1. Latin translations of the history of Diodorus Siculus appeared in 1471, 1476, 1493; compare Solmi, *Le Fonti*.

767. Leonardo wrote these lines in the margin of a page of the *Trattato* attributed to *Francesco di Giorgio*, with several drawings of columns, as well as a head drawn in profile inside an outline sketch of a capital. See No. 44, note.

H.³ 121b]

768

a · *b* · $\frac{1}{3}$ di · *n* · *m* ·; [2]*m* · *o* $\frac{1}{6}$ di *r o*; [3]l'ovo sporta $\frac{1}{6}$ di *r* · *o*; [4]*s* · *t* $\frac{1}{5}$ di *r* · *o*; [5]*a* · *b* si diuida in 9 e $\frac{1}{2}$; [6]l'abaco è $\frac{3}{9}$; [7]ovo $\frac{4}{9}$; [8]fusaiolo e listello $\frac{2}{9}$ e $\frac{1}{2}$.

a b is $\frac{1}{3}$ of *n m; m o* is $\frac{1}{6}$ of *r o*. The ovolo projects $\frac{1}{6}$ of *r o*; *s t* $\frac{1}{5}$ of *r o*, *a b* is divided into 9$\frac{1}{2}$; the abacus is $\frac{3}{9}$, the ovolo $\frac{4}{9}$, the bead-moulding and the fillet $\frac{2}{9}$ and $\frac{1}{2}$.

768. 1–8 R. 6. labaco he. 7. hovo. 8. fusaulo.

768. See Pl. LXXXV, No. 16. In the original the drawing and writing are both in red chalk.

Pl. LXXXV, No. 6 (*MS. B. N.* 2037 3*b*), *contains a small sketch of a capital with the following note, written in three lines:* I chorni del capitelo deono essere la quarta parte d'uno quadro (*The horns of a capital must measure the fourth part of a square*).

MS. S. K. M. III 22*a contain stwo sketches of ornamentations of windows.*

In MS. C. A. 315*a* (*see Pl. LXXXII, No.* 1) *there are several sketches of columns. One of the two columns on the right is similar to those employed by Bramante at the Canonica di S. Ambrogio. The same columns appear in the sketch underneath the plan of a castle. There they appear coupled, and in two stories one above the other. The archivolts which seem to spring out of the columns are shaped like twisted cords, meant perhaps to be twisted branches. The walls between the columns seem to be formed out of blocks of wood, the pedestals are ornamented with a reticulated pattern. From all this we may suppose that Leonardo here had in mind either some festive decoration, or perhaps a pavilion for some hunting-place or park. The sketch of columns marked '35' gives an example of columns shaped like candelabra, a form often employed at that time, particularly in Milan and the surrounding districts, for instance in the Cortile di Casa Castiglione, now Silvestre, the Porta della Rana, in the Cathedral of Como, &c.*

G. 52*a*]

769

DELLI ARCHITRAVI DI UNO [2]E DI PIÙ PEZZI

[3]L'architrave di più pezzi è più potēte che quel d'ū [4]sol pezzo, essendo essi pezzi colle lor lunghezze situati [5]per inverso il cētro del mōdo; pruovasi perchè [6]le pietre ànno il neruo overo tiglio gienerato per il tra[7]verso, cioè per il uerso delli orizzonti opposti d'un mede[8]simo emisperio, e questo è contrario al tiglio delle [9]piāte le quali ànno. . . .

CONCERNING ARCHITRAVES OF ONE OR SEVERAL PIECES

An architrave of several pieces is stronger than that of one single piece, if those pieces are placed with their length in the direction of the centre of the world. This is proved because stones have their grain or fibre generated in the contrary direction, i.e. in the direction of the opposite horizons of the hemisphere, and this is contrary to fibres of the plants which have . . . .

69. 1. di ī. 2. eddi 4. 3. eppiu . . checquel. 4. pezo . . cholle . . lungheza. 7. orizonti opopositi. 8. ecquesto e chontrario.

769. The text is incomplete in the original.

The Proportions of the stories of a building are indicated by a sketch in MS. S. K. M. II 53*a* (*see Pl. LXXXV, No.* 15). *The measures are written on the left side, as follows:* br 1$\frac{1}{2}$—6$\frac{3}{4}$—br $\frac{1}{12}$—2 br—9 e$\frac{1}{2}$—1$\frac{1}{2}$—br 5—ō 9—ō 3 [*br* = *braccia; ō* = *oncie*].

Pl. LXXXV, No. 13 (*MS. I* ² 110*a*), *and Pl. XCIII, No.* 1 (*MS. B.* 15*a*), *give a few examples of arches supported on piers.*

C. A. 63*b*]   769 A

Lungo braccia 4, largo braccia $2\frac{1}{2}$, grosso braccia $2\frac{1}{4}$. E così sono le pietre che stan nelle fronti del molo che à il porto di Civitavecchia.

Sporto $\frac{1}{2}$ braccio. Fronte del muro del porto di Civita. Fondo lastricato di pulita calcina.

A ☐ è largo 10 e lungo 12 e profondo un mezzo braccio, il quale è murato di calcina e scaglie di tufo tegnente, cioè che sia spugnoso e duro, cioè tenaceo in sé, senza stritolarsi. E la pelle di tale smalto è bene intonacata con perfetta calcina e rena. Di poi el sopra detto mezzo braccio di concavità è riempiuto di ghiara grossa e dura insino alla sua altezza di mezzo braccio, sopra la qual ghiara è fatto un getto di calcina e minuti pezzi di mattoni, e così è fatto con grossezza di un terzo di braccio, sopra il quale è fatto il musaico con vari disegni e fogliami e gruppi di pietre di vari colori; e questi sono li pavimenti delle camere imperiali, fatte sopra il molo del porto, dinanti a le quale camere erā portichi con collone grosse, alle qual si legava le navi e dinanti a esso portico erā nove gradi di scalini insino all' acqua, cioè 3 braccia.

4 braccia long, $2\frac{1}{2}$ braccia wide, $2\frac{1}{4}$ braccia deep. Like this are the stones standing in front of the mole in the harbour of Civitavecchia.

Projection $\frac{1}{2}$ braccio. Front of the wall of the harbour of Civita. The ground of polished mortar.

A ☐ is 10 wide and 12 long and half a braccio deep, built of mortar and flakes of tenacious tufa, spongy and hard, tenacious in itself, without crumbling. And the surface of this cement is well plastered with perfect mortar and sand. The above-mentioned half braccio of concavity is filled with big and hard gravel half a braccio deep, and over this gravel is placed a layer of mortar and minute pieces of brick, and this is a third of a braccio deep, over which the mosaic is laid with various designs of foliage and groups of stones in various colours; and these are the floors of the imperial rooms, built over the mole of the port; in front of these rooms were porticoes with big columns to which the ships were tied. And in front of this portico were nine steps down to the water, that is 3 braccia.

769 A. Leonardo must have visited Civitavecchia during his stay in Rome in 1514. His notes on the ruins of the antique harbour are illustrated by sketches of blocks of stone, and of foundations of antique buildings, which he thought were those of an imperial palace; he reconstructed an elevation in an adjacent sketch and he gives a plan of the harbour on C. A.

271*a* where the position of the supposed palace is marked. L. H. Heydenreich suggests that Leonardo approached these antique ruins as an archaeologist, so to speak, and that his point of view differed from the romantic representations of the antique, prevalent at his time. *Raccolta Vinciana*, xiv, pp. 39 ff.

XIII

THEORETICAL WRITINGS ON ARCHITECTURE

*L*EONARDO'S *original writings on the theory of Architecture have come down to us only in a fragmentary state; still, there seems to be no doubt that he himself did not complete them. It would seem that Leonardo entertained the idea of writing a large and connected book on Architecture; and it is quite evident that the materials we possess, which can be proved to have been written at different periods, were noted down with a more or less definite aim and purpose. They might all be collected under the one title: 'Studies on the Strength of Materials'. Among them the investigations on the subject of fissures in walls are particularly thorough, and very fully reported; these passages are also especially interesting, because Leonardo was certainly the first writer on architecture who ever treated the subject at all. Here, as in all other cases, Leonardo carefully avoids all abstract arguments. His data are not derived from the principles of algebra, but from the laws of mechanics, and his method throughout is strictly experimental.*

Although the conclusions drawn from his investigations may not have that precision which we are accustomed to find in Leonardo's scientific labours, their interest is not lessened. They prove at any rate his deep sagacity and wonderfully clear mind. No one, perhaps, who has studied these questions since Leonardo has combined with a scientific mind anything like the artistic delicacy of perception which gives interest and lucidity to his observations.

I do not assert that the arrangement here adopted for the passages in question is that originally intended by Leonardo; but their distribution into five groups was suggested by the titles, or headings, which Leonardo himself prefixed to most of these notes. Some of the longer sections perhaps should not, to be in strict agreement with this division, have been reproduced in their entirety in the place where they occur. But the comparatively small amount of the materials we possess will render them, even so, sufficiently intelligible to the reader; it did not therefore seem necessary or desirable to subdivide the passages merely for the sake of strict classification.

The small number of chapters given under the fifth class, treating on the centre of gravity in roof-beams, bears no proportion to the number of drawings and studies which refer to the same subject. Only a small selection of these is reproduced in this work, since the majority have no explanatory text.

I

ON FISSURES IN WALLS

Fa prima il trattato delle cause gieneratrici del²le rotture de' muri, e poi il trattato de' rimedi separato.

First write the treatise on the causes of the giving way of walls and then, separately, treat of the remedies.

³Li fessi paralelli sono vniversalmēte gienerati ⁴in quelli edifiti che si edificano in lochi montuosi, li ⁵quali sien cōposti di pietre faldate con obbliquo ⁶faldamēto, e perchè in tale obbliquità spesso penetra ⁷acqua e altra vmidità portatricie di cierta terra ⁸vntuosa e sdrucciolante ·, e perchè tali falde nō sono ⁹continuate insino al fondo delle valli, ¹⁰tali pietre si muovono per la loro obli¹¹quità e mai terminão il moto insin ¹²che discendono al fondo della valle, ¹³portando con seco a vso di barca ¹⁴quella parte dello edifitio che per lo¹⁵ro si separa dal suddetto rimanēte;
¹⁶Il rimedio di questo è il fondare spes¹⁷si pilastri sotto il muro che si move, ¹⁸e con archi dall' uno all' altro e be¹⁹ne abbarbicati, e questi tali ²⁰pilastri sieno funda²¹ti e fermi ²²nelle falde le quali non sieno rotte;
²³Per trovare la parte stabile delle sopra dette falde è neciessario fare vn ²⁴pozzo sotto il piè del muro cō grā profondità infra esse falde ²⁵e di tal pozzo pulirne cō piana superfitie la larghezza d'un palmo ²⁶dalla sōmità insino al fondo da quel lato, donde il mōte discède, ²⁷e in capo d'alquāto tempo questa parte pulita, che si fecie nella pa²⁸riete del pozzo, mostrerà manifesto segnio qual parte del mōte si move.

Parallel fissures constantly occur in buildings which are erected on a hill-side, when the hill is composed of stratified rocks with an oblique stratification, because water and other moisture often penetrates these oblique seams, carrying in greasy and slippery soil; and as the strata are not continuous down to the bottom of the valley, the rocks slide in the direction of the slope, and the motion does not cease till they have reached the bottom of the valley, carrying with them, as though in a boat, that portion of the building which is separated by them from the rest. The remedy for this is always to build thick piers under the wall which is slipping, with arches from one to another, and with a good scarp, and let the piers have a firm foundation in the strata which are not broken up.
In order to find the solid part of these strata, it is necessary to make a shaft at the foot of the wall of great depth through the strata; and in this shaft, on the side from which the hill slopes, smooth and flatten a space one palm wide from the top to the bottom; and after some time this smooth portion made on the side of the shaft will show plainly which part of the hill is moving.

Mai le fessure de' muri ²sarā paralelle, che la ³parte del muro, la qual ⁴si separa dal suo rimanēte, ⁵non discēda.

The cracks in walls will never be parallel unless the part of the wall that separates from the remainder does not slip down.

QUALE REGOLA È QUELLA CHE FA ⁷LI EDIFITI PERMANĒTI

WHAT IS THE LAW BY WHICH BUILDINGS HAVE STABILITY

⁸La permanētia delli edifiti è la regola contra⁹ria alle 2 anteciedēti, cioè che le muraglie ¹⁰sieno eleuate in alto tutte equalmēte con equali ¹¹gradi, che abbraccino l'intera circuitione dello

The stability of buildings is the result of the contrary law to the two former cases. That is to say that the walls must be all built up equally, and by degrees, to equal heights all round the

770. 1. chause. 3. [di] sono. 4. chessi edifichano illochi. 5. chōposti .. chonobbriquo. 8. essdrucciolente. 9. chontinovate. 10. tale .. simovan. 12. cheddisciendano. 13. chonsecho .. barcha. 16. Irimedio .. spe. 17. pilasstri .. chessi. 18. chon. 19. abarbatiati esti. 20. pilasstri. 21. effermi. 22. rutte. 23. per [del]. 24. pozzo [no] sotto .. chō. 25. pozo .. chō .. larcheza. 26. dacquel .. dissciède. 27. chapo dalquāto lento questa .. chessi. 28. mossterra .. mōte si m\\\\\.
771. 2. paralelle chella. 3. par del. 5. dissciēda. 6. reghola ecquella cheffa. 8. edifiti[e] ella reghola. 9. chelle. 10. che qual .. cho quali. 11. abraccino .. circhuitione.

770. See Pl. CIV.
771. Lines 1–5 refer to Pl. CV, No. 2. Line 9 *alle due anteciedēte*, see on the same page. Lines 16–18. The translation of this is doubtful, and the meaning

in any case very obscure. Lines 19–23 are on the right-hand margin close to the two sketches on Pl. C, No. 3.

[12]edifitio colle intere grossezze di qualunque sorte di [13]muri, e ancora che il muro sottile sechi più pre[14]sto che il grosso, e' nõ si avrà a rõpere per il peso che lui [15]possa acquistare dall' una all' altra giornata, perchè, [16]se il suo duplo seccasse in una giornata il dop[17]pio secherà in due o circa, si uerrà ragguagliãdo [18]cõ piccola differẽtia di peso in piccola differẽtia di tẽpo.

[19]Dicie l'aversario [20]che *a* becca[21]tello disciẽde.

[22]E qui dicie l'auersario [23]che *r* disciẽde e non *c*.

building, and the whole thickness at once, whatever kind of walls they may be. And although a thin wall dries more quickly than a thick one, it will not necessarily give way under the added weight day by day and thus, [16] although a thin wall dries more quickly than a thick one, it will not give way under the weight which the latter may acquire from day to day. Because if double the amount of it dries in one day, one of double the thickness will dry in two days or thereabouts; thus the small addition of weight will be balanced by the smaller difference of time [18].

The adversary says that *a*, which projects, slips down.

And here the adversary says that *r* slips and not *c*.

PRONOSTICI DELLE CAVSE [25]DELLE FESSURE DI QUALŨCHE [26]MURO

[27]Quella parte del muro che nõ disciẽde riserua [28]in sé l'obliquità del beccatello, copritricie dell' o[29]bliquità del muro da lei discesa.

HOW TO PROGNOSTICATE THE CAUSES OF CRACKS IN ANY SORT OF WALL

The part of the wall which does not slip is that in which the obliquity projects and overhangs the portion which has parted from it and slipped down.

DE' SITI DE' FONDAMẼTI, E IN QUAL [31]LOCO SÕ CAVSA DELLE RUINE

[32]Quando la fessura del muro è più larga di sopra [33]che di sotto elli è manifesto segnio che la mu[34]raglia à la causa della ruina remota dal perpẽ[35]diculare d'essa fessura.

ON THE SITUATION OF FOUNDATIONS AND IN WHAT PLACES THEY ARE A CAUSE OF RUIN

When the crevice in the wall is wider at the top than at the bottom, it is a manifest sign that the cause of the fissure in the wall is remote from the perpendicular line through the crevice.

Br. M. 138*a*]   772

DELLE FESSURE DE' MURI, LE QUALI SÕ [2]LARGHE DA PIÈ E STRETTE DA CA[3]PO E LOR CAUSA

[4]Quel muro senpre si fende che [5]non si secca vniformemẽte [6]con equal tẽpo;

[7]E quel muro d'uniforme gros[8]sezza nõ si secca con equal [9]tẽpo, il quale non è in cõtat[10]to d'equal mezzo; come se [11]vna parte d'un muro fusse edi[12]ficata in cõtatto d'ũ monte [13]vmido e 'l rimanente restasse [14]in contatto dell' aria, che allo[15]ra il rimanẽte si ristrignie per [16]ciascun verso e l'umido si man[17]tiene nella sua prima grãdezza, [18]e allora · quel che s'asciuga [19]nell' aria, restrignie e diminui[20]scesi, e quel che è inumidito nõ [21]si asciuga, e volentieri si rõ[22]pe il secco dall' umido perchè es[23]so vmido non à tenacità da [24]seguitare il moto di quel che al cõ[25]tinuo si secca.

OF CRACKS IN WALLS, WHICH ARE WIDE AT THE BOTTOM AND NARROW AT THE TOP, AND OF THEIR CAUSES

That wall which does not dry uniformly in an equal time always cracks.

A wall though of equal thickness will not dry in the same time if it is not everywhere in contact with the same medium. Thus, if one side of a wall were in contact with a damp slope and the other were in contact with the air, then this latter side shrinks on every side, while the wet part would remain of the same size as before; that side which dries in the air will shrink or diminish and the side which is kept damp will not dry. And the dry portion will break away readily from the damp portion, because the damp part does not cohere and follow the movement of the part which dries continuously.

---

12. cholle . . qualuche sorte. 13. anchora . . sechi. 14. ara . . chellui. 15. acquisstare. 16. il sudduplo sechassi innuna. 17. sechera . . circha . . ragualgliãdo. 18. cho pichola differẽtia . . pichola diferẽtia. 20. becha. 22. ecqui. 24. chause. 25. delle [mu]. 27. [I] Quella . . nõ [si move] "disciẽde". 28. bechatello dello. 29. delei disciessa. 31. locho sõ chavsa. 32. largha. 33. chella. 34. alla chausa. 35. dichulare.
772. 2. dappiedi esstrtte da cha. 3. ellor chausa. 5. secha. 6. chon. 7. Ecquel . . gro. 8. secha chon. 9. chõta. 10. del qual mezo comesse. 11. fussi. 12. fichato. 13. resstassi. 14. chontatto. 15. sirisstrignie. 16. cias chun . . ellumido. 17. grãdeza. 18. [il] quel chesassciugha. 19. restrignie. 20. ecquel . . înumidito. assciugha. 22. secho. 23. nona tenacita. 24. chõ. 25. secha.

772. The text of this passage is reproduced in facsimile on Pl. CVI to the left. Lines 36–40 are written inside the sketch No. 2. Lines 41–6 are partly written over the sketch No. 3 to which they refer.

DELLI FESSI ARCATI LARGHI DI SOPRA [27]E STRETTI DI SOTTO

[28]Quelli fessi arcati larghi di sopra [29]e stretti di sotto nascono nelle [30]porte rimurate che calã più ne[31]l' altezza che nella larghezza [32]per tanto quãto l'altezza è maggiore [33]che nella larghezza e per quãto le com[34]messure della calcina son piv numerosi [35]in nell' altezza che nella larghezza.

[36]Il fesso diminuisce [37]tanto meno in *r o* [38]che in *m n*, quãto [39]infra *r o* è mẽ ma[40]teria che in *m n*.

[41]Ogni fessura fatta [42]ĩ loco cõcavo è larga [43]di sotto, e stretta di sopra, [44]e questo nascie, come [45]mostra *b c d* da lato figu[46]rato.

[47]pª ¶ Ciò che si inumidi[48]sce cresce per tãto [49]quãto è l'umido ac[50]quistato. ¶

[51]2ª ¶ E ogni cosa umi[52]da si restrignie nel[53]lo asciugare per tã[54]to quanto è l'umido [55]che da lei si diuide. ¶

OF ARCHED CRACKS, WIDE AT THE TOP, AND NARROW BELOW

Arched cracks, wide at the top and narrow below, are found in walled-up doors, which shrink more in their height than in their breadth, and in proportion as their height is greater than their width, and as the joints of the mortar are more numerous in the height than in the width.

The crack diminishes less in *r o* than in *m n*, in proportion as there is less material between *r* and *o* than between *n* and *m*.

Any crack made in a concave wall is wide below and narrow at the top; and this originates, as is here shown at *b c d*, in the side figure.

1. That which gets wet increases in proportion to the moisture it imbibes.

2. And a wet object shrinks, while drying, in proportion to the amount of moisture which evaporates from it.

Br. M. 158a]   **773**

DELLA CAVSA DEL RONPERE DELLI EDIFITI PUBLICI E PRIVATI

[2]Romponsi li muri per fessure, che ànno del diretto e alcune che [3]ànno dello obbliquo; le rotture che ànno del diretto [4]son gienerate dalli muri novi [5]in cõgiũtiõ de' muri vechi diritti o cõ morse giũte alli [6]muri vechi, perchè tali morse, nõ potendo resistere allo [7]insopportabile peso del muro a lor' cõgiũto, è necies[8]sario a quelle ronpersi e dar loco al disciẽso del predet[9]to muro novo, il quale cala vn braccio per ogni 10 braccia, o più [10]o meno, secondo la maggiore o minore soña di calcina [11]interposta infra le pietre murate e cõ calcina più [12]o mẽ liquida; E nota che senpre si debbe ĩprima fare [13]li muri e poi vestirli delle pietre che li ãno a vestire, [14]perchè se così nõ si faciessi, il muro facciẽdo maggiore calo che [15]la crosta di fori, e' sarebbe neciessario che le morse fatte [16]nelli lati de' muri si rõpessino; perchè le pietre che vestono li mu[17]ri, essendo di maggiore grandezza che le pietre da quel[18]le vestite, è neciessario che ricievino minor quãtità di calcina [19]nelle loro coñessure e per cõseguẽza faccino minore calo, [20]il che accadere nõ può, essendo murate tali croste poi ch'el mu[21]ro è secco.

[22]*a b* muro nuo[23]vo, · *c* · è muro vechio [24]che

OF THE CAUSES OF FISSURES IN [THE WALLS OF] PUBLIC AND PRIVATE BUILDINGS

The walls give way in cracks, some of which are more or less vertical and others are oblique. The cracks which are in a vertical direction are caused by the joining of new walls with old walls, whether straight or with indentations fitting on to those of the old wall; for, as these indentations cannot bear the excessive weight of the wall added on to them, it is inevitable that they should break, and give way to the settling of the new wall, which will shrink one braccia in every ten, more or less, according to the greater or smaller quantity of mortar used between the stones of the masonry, and whether this mortar is more or less liquid. And observe that the walls should always be built first and then faced with the stones intended to face them. For if you do not proceed thus, since the wall settles more than the stone facing, the projections left on the sides of the wall must inevitably give way; because the stones used for facing the wall being larger than those over which they are laid, they will necessarily have less mortar laid between the joints, and consequently they settle less; and this cannot happen if the facing is added after

---

26. delli . . archati. 27. esstretti. 28. archati. 29. esstretti . . nasschano. 30. chalã. 31. lalteza . . largheza. 32. magiore. 33. largheza . . lecho. 34. mesurie. 35. larghezza. 36. diminuisscie. 38. quãdo. 41. Õni . . tãtta. 42. locho chõchavo ellargha. 43. esstretta. 44. ecquesto nasscie. 45. dallato fighu. 47. chessi inumidis. 48. scie cresscie. 49. ellumido. 51. chosa. 53. llo assciugrare. 54. ellumido. 55. dallei.

773. 1. chausa . . pubbici. 2. ronpasi . . alchune. 3. rocture. 4. novi [murati in tẽpo brevissimo]. 5. in chõgiũtiõ de muri [no] ve "echi" . . chõ. 7. allor chõgiũto. 8. acquelle . . locho al dissciẽso. 9. chala vn br per ogni 10 br . . oppiu. 10. sechondo . . õminore . . chalcina. 11. interpossta infralle . . chõ chalcina. 12. õmẽ . . chessenpre. 13. eppoi vesstirl. chelli . avesstire. 14. chosi . . faciessi . . magiore chalo chel. 15. lacrossta . . farebe . . chelle. 16. vesstano. 17. esendo . . chelle . . dacque. 18. vesstite . . chalcina. 19. choñessure e per chõseguẽza . . chalo. 20. achadere . . murato tale crosste. 21. essecho. 22. muro [vechio] nuo. 24. affatto il chalo.

già à fatto il calo, ²⁵e lo *a · b* fa il calo poi, ²⁶bēchè *a*, essēdo fonda²⁷to sopra il *c* muro ²⁸vechio, nō si può in nes²⁹sū modo rōpere per ave³⁰re stabile fondamē³¹to sopra tal muro ve³²chio, ma sol si ronpe³³rà il rimanēte del mu³⁴ro nvovo *b* cō³⁵ciò ch'elli è murato di ³⁶sopra dalla sommità del edifitio insino al fondo, ³⁷faciēdo il rimanēte del muro nuovo beccatello ³⁸sopra il muro che disciēde.

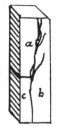

the wall is dry. *a b* is the new wall, *c* the old wall, which has already settled; and the part *a b* settles afterwards, although *a*, being founded on *c*, the old wall, cannot possibly break, having a stable foundation on the old wall. But only the remainder *b* of the new wall will break away, because it is built from top to bottom of the building; and the remainder of the new wall will overhang the gap above the wall that has sunk.

Br. M. 159*b*]   774

Torre nova fondata ²sopra la vechia in parte.

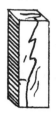

A new tower founded partly on old masonry.

Br. M. 157*b*]   775

DELLE PIETRE CHE SI DIS²GIŪGONO DALLA LOR CALCINA

³Le pietre d'equal numero nella loro altezza, mu⁴rate con equal quātità di calcina, fāno equal ⁵calo nella partita dell' umido che mollifi⁶ca essa calcina.
⁷Per lo passato si prvova che la poca quātità ⁸del muro nuovo interposta infra *a · n* farà po⁹co calo rispetto alla quātità del medesimo mu¹⁰ro che s'interpone infra *c d*, e tal fia la pro¹¹portione che ànno infra loro le raretà delle ¹²dette calcine qual' è la proportiōe delli ¹³nvmeri over delle quātità delle calcine interpo¹⁴ste nelle cōmessure delle pietre murate so¹⁵pra le varie altezze delli muri vechi.

OF STONES WHICH DISJOIN THEMSELVES FROM THEIR MORTAR

Stones laid in regular courses from bottom to top and built up with an equal quantity of mortar settle equally throughout, when the moisture that made the mortar soft evaporates.
By what is said above it is proved that the small extent of the new wall between *a* and *n* will settle but little, in proportion to the extent of the same wall between *c* and *d*. The proportion will in fact be that of the thinness of the mortar in relation to the number of courses or to the quantity of mortar laid between the stones above the different levels of the old wall.

A. 53*a*]   776

Questo · muro · si rōperà · sotto⁰· l'arco *e · f* perchè · i sette · quadrelli ²integri · nō sono · soffitiēti · a sostenere il piè · dell' arco sopra postoli ³e rōperannosi questi · 7 · quadrelli · nel mezzo · apūto come · appare in · *a · b*; ⁴la ragione si è · che il quadrello · *a* · à solamēte · sopra · sé · il peso *a · k* ⁵e l'ultimo · quadrello · sotto · l'arco · à sopra · sé · il peso · *c · d, x · a*; ⁶*c · d* · pare che facci fare · forza · all' arco · verso

This wall will break under the arch *e f*, because the seven whole square bricks are not sufficient to sustain the spring of the arch placed on them. And these seven bricks will give way in their middle exactly as appears in *a b*. The reason is, that the brick *a* has above it only the weight *a k*, whilst the last brick under the arch has above it the weight *c d x a*. *c d* seems to press on the arch towards the abutment at the point *p*

25. ello . . chalo. 34. chō. 35. clo chelli. 37. bechatello. 38. \\|\|\|\| il muro cheddisciēde.
774. 2. sopra il vechio.
775. 1. chessi. 2. giūghano . . chalcina. 3. puetre. 4. chon . . chalcina. 6. cho . . chalcina. 7. la passata . . chella pocha. 9. pocho chalo risspecto. 10. chessinterpone . . ettal. 11. portione [di] che anno infralloro. 12. chalcine. 13. chalcine. 14. chōmesure.
776. 1. Quessto . . larcho [c] e . f. 2. assosstenere . . archo . . posstoli. 3. e rōperanosi quesste . . mezo . . chome apare. 5. larcho.

775. See Pl. CV, No. 1. The top of the tower is wanting in this reproduction, and with it the letter *n* which, in the original, stands above the letter *A* over

the top of the tower, while *c* stands perpendicularly over *d*.

la spalla nel pūto · *p* ·, [7]ma il peso · *p* · *o* · lì fa resistētia ·, õde tutto · il peso · ne va · nella radice dell' arco; [8]adūque fa · la radice delli

but the weight *p o* opposes resistance to it, whence the whole pressure is transmitted to the root of the arch. Therefore the foot of the

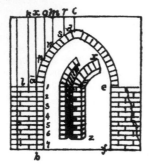
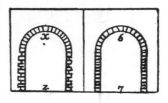

archi · come · 7 · 6, ch'è · più · forte il doppio che · *x* · *z*.

arches acts like 7 6, which is double *x z*.

6. cheffacci . . archo uerlasspalla. 7. archo. 8. chome . . dopio.

II

ON FISSURES IN ARCHES

Br. M. 158a]   777

DELLE ROTTURE DELLI ARCHI

[2]L'arco fatto del semicircolo, il quale fia carico nelli [3]due oppositi terzi della sua curvità, rōperà in [4]cinque lochi della sua curvità; provasi e sieno li pe[5]si *n m*, li quali rompono esso arco *a · b · f ·*, dico per lo [6]passato come *c a* stremi sono equalmēte aggravati dal peso *n*, [7]seguita per la 5ª che l'arco ronperà nella parte più remota dalle [8]due potentie che lo premono, il quale è il mezzo *e ·*, e altre[9]tanto intēdo aver detto dell' arco opposito *d g b*; adū[10]que *n m* pesi vēgono a discēdere, e discēder nō posso[11]no per la 7ª che non si facci più vicini, e avicinar nō si pos[12]sono, che l'arco che infra lor s'interpone non avicini il sua [13]stremi, li quali nō si possono accostare sanza rottura del [14]suo mezzo; adūque l'arco si ronperà in 5 lochi come fu primo [15]posto ecc.

[16]Domāda del peso dato in *a*, che parte ne risponde ī · *n* · [17]*f* linia, e cō che peso s'à a vinciere il peso posto in *f*.

ON FISSURES IN ARCHES

An arch constructed on a semicircle and bearing weights on the two opposite thirds of its curve will give way at five points of the curve. To prove this let the weights be at *n m* which will break the arch *a, b, f*. I say that, by the foregoing, as the extremities *c* and *a* are equally pressed upon by the thrust *n*, it follows, by the 5th, that the arch will give way at the point which is farthest from the two forces acting on it and that is the middle *e*. The same is to be understood of the opposite curve, *d g b*; hence weights *n m* must sink, but they cannot sink, by the 7th, without coming closer together, and they cannot come together unless the extremities of the arch between them come closer, and if these draw together the crown of the arch must break; and thus the arch will give way in five places as was at first said, &c.

I ask, given a weight at *a*, what counteracts it in the direction *n f* and by what weight must the weight at *f* be counteracted.

Br. M. 141b]   778

DELLA DIMINUITIONE DE' CORPI VMIDI [2]DI GROSSEZZA O LARGHEZZA DIFFORME

[3]La finestra *a* è causa della rottura del *b* e questa tal rot[4]tura è aumētata dal peso *n m*, il quale più si ficca ovvero penetra intra la ter[5]ra che riciebe il suo fondamēto, che nō fa la leuità del *b ·*, e ancora il fō[6]damēto vechio che sta sotto *b* à fatto il calo, il che fatto non aveā li pi[7]lastri *n m ·* e la parte *b* non disciēde perpendiculare, anzi si gitta info[8]ri per obbliquo e non si può per l'aversario gittare in dētro,

ON THE SHRINKING OF DAMP BODIES OF DIFFERENT THICKNESS AND WIDTH

The window *a* is the cause of the crack at *b*; and this crack is increased by the pressure of *n* and *m* which sink or penetrate into the soil in which foundations are built more than the lighter portion at *b*. Besides, the old foundation under *b* has already settled, and this the piers *n* and *m* have not yet done. Hence the part *b* does not settle down perpendicularly; on the contrary, it is thrown outwards obliquely, and it

---

777. 1. rocture. 2. semil . . charicho. 3. churvita. 4. churvita prosi essieno. 5. ronpano . . archo . . per la. 6. passata chome ca"stremi" sono ecqualmēte agravati. 7. seguita "per la 5ª chellarcho". 8. chello priemano . . altrec. 9. archo . . addū. 10. vēghano addisscēdere edisscēder nō possa. 12. sano chellarcho che infrallor. 13. achosstare. 14. larcho . . chome fu pr"o". 16. ne rissponde. 17. chō . . possto.
778. 1. chorpi. 2. "ollarghezza". 3. finesstra . . chausa . . roctura . . ecquesta . . roc. 4. ficha over . . intralla. 5. anchora. 6. chessta . . affatto il chalo. 7. lasstri n · m · ella . . disscēde per pēdichulare . . infor. 8. po. 9. eppiu largha . . cheddi dentro [ess] elli.

778. The figure on Pl. CV, No. 4, belongs to the first paragraph of this passage, ll. 1–14; Fig. 5 is sketched by the side of ll. 15 ff. The sketch below of a pomegranate refers to l. 22. The drawing Fig. 6 is, in the original, over l. 37 and Fig. 7 over l. 54.

II   K

perchè tal parte disuni⁹ta dal tutto è più larga di fori che di dentro e li labri del rimanente ¹⁰è della medesima figura, e se tal parte disunita avesse a ētrare in dentro, ¹¹il maggiore entrerebbe nel minore, il che sarebbe inpossibile; adunque ¹²è cōcluso che per necessità la parte di tale emiciclo si disuniscie dal tutto col ¹³gittarsi colla parte inferiore infori e non indētro come vole ¹⁴l'auersario ecc.

¹⁵Quando le tribune intere o mezze ¹⁶sarà di sopra vinte da superchio peso, al¹⁷lora le sue volte si aprirāno ¹⁸cō apritura diminuitiva ¹⁹dalla parte di sopra e larga di sot²⁰to e stretta dalla parte di dentro e ²¹larga di fuori, a similitudine della ²²scorza del pomo ovvero melarācia ²³divisa in molte parti per la sua lūghez²⁴za, che quāto ella sarà premuta dal²⁵le opposite parti della sua lūghezza, ²⁶quella parte delle giūture più si a²⁷prirà, che fia più distāte alla causa ²⁸che la prieme ·; e per questo mai si ²⁹debbono caricare li archi delle volte ³⁰di qualunche emiciclo dalli archi dello ³¹suo edifitio massimo, perchè quel che ³²più pesa più prieme sopra ciò che li è di³³sotto, e più disciende sopra li sua fon³⁴damēti, il che interuenire nō può ³⁵alle cose più lieui come sono li emi³⁶cicli predetti.

³⁷Qual di questi due cubi dimi³⁸nuirà più vniformemēte, o ³⁹il cubo *a* posato sopra il pavi⁴⁰mēto, o 'l cubo *b* sospeso ⁴¹infra l'aria, essēdo l'uno ⁴²e l'altro cubo equali in peso ⁴³e in quantità e di terra mista ⁴⁴con equale vmidità?

⁴⁵Quel cubo che si posa sopra ⁴⁶il pavimēto più diminui⁴⁷scie della sua altezza che per la ⁴⁸sua larghezza, il che ⁴⁹far nō può il cubo ch'è di ⁵⁰sopra e sospeso infra l'aria; ⁵¹pruovasi così; il cubo po⁵²sato sopra questa medesima ⁵³sta meglio qui di sotto.

⁵⁴Il fine delli dua cilindri di ⁵⁵terra fresca cioè *a b* sa⁵⁶rā le figure piramidali di ⁵⁷sotto *c d* || provasi co⁵⁸sì: il cilindro *a*, posato ⁵⁹sopra il suo pavimēto per esse⁶⁰re lui di terra assai mista ⁶¹coll' umido, va calādo me⁶²diante il suo peso che dà di sé ⁶³alla sua basa, e tāto più ca⁶⁴lerà e ingrosserà, quāto e' sa⁶⁵rà colle sua parti più presso ⁶⁶alla sua basa, perchè lì si cari⁶⁷ca il suo tutto ecc.; E si⁶⁸mile farà il peso *b*, il quale pi⁶⁹ù s'astēderà, quāto elli à maggi⁷⁰or peso sotto sé, la qual maggiorità ⁷¹è ne' cōfini del suo sostētaculo.

cannot on the contrary be thrown inwards, because a portion like this, separated from the main wall, is larger outside than inside and the main wall, where it is broken, is of the same shape (and is also larger outside than inside); therefore, if this separate portion were to fall inwards, the larger would have to pass through the smaller—which is impossible. Hence it is evident that the portion of the semicircular wall is disunited from the main wall and will be thrust outwards, and not inwards as our opponent says.

When a dome or a half-dome is crushed from above by an excess of weight the vault will give way, forming a crack which diminishes towards the top and is wide below, narrow on the inner side, and wide outside; as is the case with the outer husk of a pomegranate, divided into many parts lengthwise; for the more it is pressed in the direction of its length, that part of the joints will open most, which is most distant from the cause of the pressure; and for that reason the arches of the vaults of any apse should never be loaded by the arches of the principal building. Because that which weighs most, presses most on the parts below, and they sink into the foundations; but this cannot happen to lighter structures like the said apses.

Which of these two cubes will shrink the more uniformly: the cube *a* resting on the pavement, or the cube *b* suspended in the air, when both cubes are equal in weight and bulk, and of clay mixed with equal quantities of water?

The cube placed on the pavement diminishes more in height than in breadth, which the cube above, hanging in the air, cannot do. Thus it is proved. The cube shown above is better shown here below.

The final result of the two cylinders of damp clay, that is *a* and *b*, will be the pyramidal figures below, *c* and *d*. This is proved thus: The cylinder *a* resting on a block of stone being made of clay mixed with a great deal of water will sink by its weight, which presses on its base, and in proportion as it settles and spreads all the parts will be somewhat nearer to the base because that is charged with the whole weight, &c. And the case will be the same with the weight of *b*, which will stretch lengthwise in proportion as the weight at the bottom is increased, and the greatest tension will be the neighbourhood of the weight which is suspended by it.

---

10. fighura essettal . . avessi. 11. enterrebbe . . addunque. 12. e chōcluso . . disunisscie . . chōl. 13. gittari [dap] cholla . . inferiore [di] inforienone . . chome. 15. trebune . . omeze. 17. apirrāno [chōta]. 18. [tama] chō. 19. ellargha. 20. esstrēta . . dentro el. 21. largha . . assimilitudine. 22. over. 23. imolte parte. 24. sara permuta. 25. parte . . lūgheza. 26. quela. 27. pirra cheffia . . chausa. 28. chella . . quessto. 29. debbe charichare. 32. sopra chilli edi. 33. dissciende. 35. chose . . chome. 36. predecti. 37. quessti . . chubi. 38. ho. 39. chubo. 40. chubo b sosspeso. 41. infrallaria essē luno. 42. ellaltro chub. 43. missta. 44. chon. 45. chubo chessi. 47. alteza. 48. [che] il che. 49. chubo. 50. essossposo. 51. chosi il chubo. 54. chilindri. 55. fressca. 56. ra le. 57. socto . . cho. 58. chilindro. 60. missta. 61. chollumido va chalādo. 63. ettāto piu cha. 64. ēgrossera. 65. cholle . . parte. 66. chari. 67. cha . . Essi. 69. sasstēdera . . magi. 70. laqqual magiorita. 71. enechōfinj . . sostētachulo.

III

ON THE NATURE OF THE ARCH

CHE COSA È ARCO?

[2]Arco non è altro che una fortezza · cavsata da due debolezze, jpero[3]chè l'arco negli edifiti è cōposto di 2 quarti · di circulo, i quali [4]quarti circuli, ciascuno debolissimo per sé, desiderā cadere, e opponē-[5]dosi alla ruina l'uno dell' altro le due debolezze si cōvertono in vni[6]ca fortezza.

WHAT IS AN ARCH?

The arch is nothing else than a force origi-nated by two weaknesses, for the arch in buildings is composed of two segments of a circle, each of which being very weak in itself tends to fall; but as each opposes this tendency in the other, the two weak-nesses combine to form one strength.

DELLA QUALITÀ DEL PESO DELLI ARCHI

[8]Poichè l'arco fia · cōposto ·, quello · rimane in equilibrio, īpero[9]chè tāto spīgie · l'uno · l'altro · quāto l'altro l'uno ·, e se pesa piv l'uno [10]quarto circulo · che l'altro ·, quivi fia leuata e negata la permanēza, [11]imperochè 'l maggiore vicierà · il minore peso.

OF THE KIND OF PRESSURE IN ARCHES

As the arch is a composite force it remains in equilibrium because the thrust is equal from both sides; and if one of the seg-ments weighs more than the other the stability is lost, because the greater pres-sure will outweigh the lesser.

DEL CARICO DATO AGLI ARCHI

[13]Dopo il peso equale de' quarti circuli è neciessario dare loro equale [14]peso di sopra, altremēti si correrebbe nel sopra · detto errore.

OF DISTRIBUTING THE PRESSURE ABOVE AN ARCH

Next to giving the segments of the circle equal weight it is necessary to load them equally, or you will fall into the same defect as before.

DOVE L'ARCO SI RŌPE

[16]L'arco si rōperà j quella · parte che passa · il suo mezzo sotto il ciētro.

WHERE AN ARCH BREAKS

An arch breaks at the part which lies below half-way from the centre.

SECŌDO RŌPIMETO DELL' ARCO

[18]Se 'l superchio · peso · fia posto ī mezzo · l'arco nel pūto · a ·, quello desi[19]dera cadere · in · b ·, e ronpesi ne' $\frac{2}{3}$ della sua altezza in · c · e, [20]e tāto fia più potēte · g · e che e · a · quanto [21]m · o · entra in · m · n.

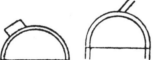

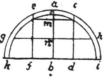

SECOND RUPTURE OF THE ARCH

If the excess of weight is placed in the middle of the arch at the point a, that weight tends to fall towards b, and the arch breaks at $\frac{2}{3}$ of its height at c e; and g e is as many times stronger than e a, as m o goes into m n.

D'UN ALTRA CAGIONE DI RUINA

[23]L'arco verrà · ancora · meno · per essere sospīto da traverso, inpero[24]chè quādo il carico nō si dirizza ai piè de l'arco, [25]l'arco poco dura.

ON ANOTHER CAUSE OF RUIN

The arch will likewise give way under a trans-versal thrust, for when the charge is not thrown directly on the foot of the arch, the arch lasts but a short time.

779. 1. chosa e archo. 2. archo .. ꝉ forteza .. deboleze. 3. larcho .. chōposto .. circhuli. 4. circhuli ciaschuno . debolisimo .. chadere eoponē. 5. deboleze .. chōuertano. 6. cha forteza. 7. dela .. deli. 8. chōposto quelo .. equilibra. 9. chettāto .. esse e pesa. 10. circhulo .. premanēza. 11. magiore. 12. charicho dati ali. 13. circhuli. 14. chorerebe .. erore. 15. larcho. 16. larcho .. mezo [da]. 17. sechōdo .. archo. 18. imezo larcho .. quelo. 19. chadere .. dela .. alteza. 20. [c · in n che in · e] g · e. 22. chagione. 23. larcho vera · anchora .. esserre. 24. charicho .. diriza .. archo. 25. larcho pocho.

A. 50b]　　　　　　　　　780

DELLA FORTEZZA DELL' ARCO

²Il modo di fare l'arco permanēte si è a rienpiere i sua angoli
· di buono ripieno ³insino · al suo
raso overo · culmine.

ON THE STRENGTH OF THE ARCH

The way to give stability to the
arch is to fill the spandrels with
good masonry up to the level of
its summit.

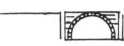

⁴DEL CARICARE SOPRA L'ARCO TŌDO

ON THE LOADING OF ROUND ARCHES

⁵DEL CARICARE L'ARCO · ACUTO BENE

ON THE PROPER MANNER OF LOADING
THE POINTED ARCH

⁶DELLO INCŌVENIĔTE CHE SEGUITA A CARICARE
⁷L'ARCO ACUTO SUL SUO MEZZO

ON THE EVIL EFFECTS OF LOADING THE
POINTED ARCH DIRECTLY ABOVE ITS CROWN

⁸DEL DANNO CHE RICIEVE L'ARCO ACUTO
A ESSERE ⁹CARICATO SOPRA I SUOI FIĀCHI

ON THE DAMAGE DONE TO THE POINTED
ARCH BY THROWING THE PRESSURE ON
THE FLANKS

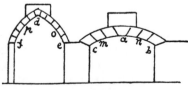
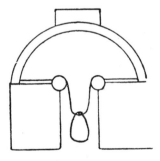
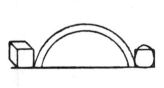
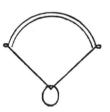

¹⁰L'arco · poco · curvo fia sicuro per sé, ¹¹ma
se fia carico ·, le spalle ·
bisognia ¹²bene · armare;
¹³l'arco d'assai curvità fia
per sé debole, ¹⁴e piv se
fia carico e farà poca noia
¹⁵alle sue spalle ·, e lui · rōperà · in o · p.

An arch of small curve is safe in itself, but if
it be heavily charged, it is
necessary to strengthen the
flanks well. An arch of a very
large curve is weak in itself,
and even more so if it be
charged, and will do little
harm to its abutments, and its
places of giving way are o p.

780. 1. dela forteza delarcho. 2. larcho. 3. chulmine. 4. charichare .. larcho. 5. charichare larcho achuto. 6. delo inchōveniĕte ..
charichare. 7. larcho achuto .. mezo. 8. dano .. larcho achuto. 9. charichato sopra i sua fiāchi. 10. larcho pocho .. sichuro.
11. charicho lesspali. 13. larcho .. churvita. 14. epiv seffia charicho effara. 15. ellui.

780. Inside the large figure on the right is the note: 'Da pesare la forza dell' archo'.

A. 51a]   781

DEL RIPARO A TERREMOTI

[2]L'arco il quale mã[3]derà il peso perpēdicu-[4]lare alle sue radici [5]farà il suo · ofitio per

ON THE REMEDY FOR EARTHQUAKES

The arch which throws its pressure perpendicularly on the abutments will fulfil its

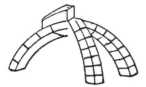
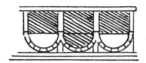

[6]qualūque verso si stia, [7]o rovescio, o a giacere, [8]o ritto.

[9]¶ L'arco · nõ si rõperà · se la · corda de l'arco di fori · nõ toccherà l'arco di dentro ¶ ; [10]Questo · appare per isperiēza, che ogni · volta che la corda · *a · o · n* dell'arco [11]di fori · *n · r · a* · toccherà · l'arco di dentro · *x · b · y* ·, l'arco darà prīcipio a sua [12]debolezza ·, e tãto si farà ·piv · debole · quãto l'arco · di dõtro · rõperà d'essa · corda.

[13]Quell' arco · il quale fia · carico da l'una de' lati, [14]il peso si caricherà · sulla sõmità de l'altro mezzo ·, e pas[15]serà il peso · per īsino · al suo · fondamēto ·, e rõperà · in quella [16]parte che fia · piv · lontana · dai sua · stremi · e dalla sua corda.

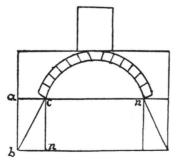

function whatever be its direction, upside down, sideways, or upright.

The arch will not break if the chord of the outer arch does not touch the inner arch. This is manifest by experience, because whenever the chord *a o n* of the outer arch *n r a* approaches the inner arch *x b y* the arch will be weak, and it will be weaker in proportion as the inner arch passes beyond that chord. When an arch is loaded on only one side the thrust will press on the top of the other side and be transmitted to the spring of the arch on that side; and it will break at a point halfway between its two extremes, where it is farthest from the chord.

H.[1] 35b]   782

La quãtità cõtinua, che per forza in arco [2]fia piegata, spīgie per la linia, õde deside[3]ra tornare.

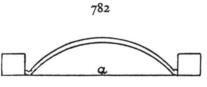

A continuous quantity which has been forcibly bent into an arch, thrusts in the direction of the straight line, which it tends to recover.

H.[1] 36a]   783

L'arco di quãtità discreta fa forza [2]per linia obliqua, cioè il triangulo [3]*c n b* nõ sēte peso.

In an arch judiciously weighted the thrust is oblique, so that the triangle *c n b* has no weight upon it.

781. 2. larcho. 3. perpēdichu. 6. Qulūque "r" so. 7. oadiacere. 9. larcho .. chorda delarcho .. tochera larcho. 10. apare .. chorda .. archo. 11. tochera larcho .. assua. 12. deboleza ettãto .. larcho .. chorda. 13. archo .. charicho. 14. charichera sula somita .. mezo e pa. 15. quela. 16. cheffia .. dala.
782. 1–3 R. 1. archo. 2. fie.
783. 1–3 R. 1. larcho.

S. K. M. II.² 92a]   784

Domando qui che ²pesi fieno quelli ³de' con-
trapesi a fa⁴re resistētia alla ru⁵ina · di ciascun
arco?

I here ask what weight will be needed to
counterpoise and resist the tendency of each of
these arches to give way?

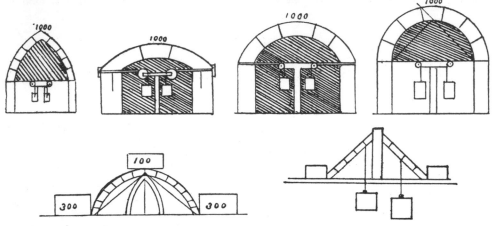

Br. M. 158b]   785

DELLA POTĒTIA DELL' ARCO NELL' ARCHITETTURA

²La permanēza dell' arco fabbricato dallo architetto con³siste nella corda e nelle spalle ſue.

ON THE STRENGTH OF THE ARCH IN ARCHITECTURE

The stability of the arch built by an architect
resides in the tie and in the flanks.

DELLA SITUATIONE DELLA CORDA NEL SOPRA DETTO
ARCO

⁵La situatione della corda à la prima necessità
nel princi⁶pio dell' archo, e nel fine della
rettitudine del pilastro ⁷dove si posa; pruovasi
per la 2ª delli sostētaculi che dicie: ⁸Quella
parte del sostentaculo manco resiste che è più
remota dal fer⁹mamēto del suo tutto; adunque
essendo la ¹⁰sōmità del pilastro vltima remotione dal suo fermamēto, e 'l si¹¹mile accadēdo
nelli oppositi stremi dell' arco, che sono vl¹²tima
distantia dal mezzo, suo vero fermamēto, noi
abbiā con¹³cluso, che tal corda *a b* di neciessità
richiede la situatione delli ¹⁴sua oppositi stremi
infra li 4 oppositi stremi predetti;

¹⁵Dicie l'auersario che tale arco vole essere
più che mezzo ¹⁶tondo, e allora non avrà
bisognio di corda perchè tali stremi ¹⁷nō spigne-
raño infuori, ma indentro, come si di¹⁸mostra
nello ecciesso *a · c · b · d* ; Qui si risponde, tale
¹⁹inventione essere trista per 5 cause, e la prima
è inquanto ²⁰alla fortezza, perchè è provato jl
paralello cir²¹culare, essendo cōposto di due
semicirculi, · sol rōpersi dove ²²tali semicirculi
insieme si congiūgono, come mo²³stra la figura

ON THE POSITION OF THE TIE IN THE ABOVE-
NAMED ARCH

The position of the tie is of the first importance at the beginning of the arch and at the top
of the perpendicular pier on which it rests. This
is proved by the 2nd 'of supports' which says:
That part of a support has least resistance which
is farthest from its solid attachment; hence, as
the top of the pier is farthest from the middle of
its true foundation and the same being the case
at the opposite extremities of the arch which are
the points farthest from the middle, which is
really its [upper] attachment, we have concluded that the tie *a b* requires to be in such a
position that its opposite ends are between
the four above-mentioned extremes.

The adversary says that this arch must be
more than half a circle, and that then it will not
need a tie, because then the ends will not thrust
outwards but inwards, as is seen in the excess at
a c, b d. To this it must be answered that this
would be a very poor device, for five reasons.
The first refers to the strength of the arch, since
it is proved that the circular parallel being composed of two semicircles will only break where

784. 2. hce pesi. 3. affa. 4. resisētia.
785. 1. dellarcho. 2. premanēza dellarcho fabbricato .. architecto ch \\\\\\. 3. chorda. 4. chorda .. archo. 5. chorda allap"a" neciessita.
6. rectitudine del pilasstro. 7. dovessi .. pella .. sostētachuli cheddicie. 8. sostentachulo mā. 9. tucto .. essendo [la somita delli]
la. 10. somita .. pilasstro .. repotione. 11. achadēdo [nellarcho] nelli .. archo chessono .. chon. 13. chluso chettal chorda "a b"
di. 14. infralli .. predecti. 15. chettale archo. 16. ara .. chorda. 17. nō [gitteranno] inspignierāno .. indrēto. 18. mossta ..
rispotale. 19. trissta per "5" [tre] chause ella .. e inq̄. 20. provato [larcho sol] jl. 21. chulare .. chōposto .. semice. 22. semi-
circhuli .. chongiūghano .. mos. 23. fighura .. quessto .. ema.

784. The two lower sketches are taken from the MS. S. K. M. III. 79b; they have there no explanatory text.

n m; oltre a questo seguita, ch'egli è mag[24]giore spatio infra li stremi del semicirculo che infra le pa[25]rieti delli muri; terza è che 'l peso posto per cōtro alla fortezza [26]dell' arco diminuiscie tanto di peso, quāto le poste dell' arco [27]sono più larghe che detto spatio interposto infra li pilastri, (4ª è [28]che) li pilastri indeboliscono per tāto quāto la parte loro *c a* [29]*b d* si piegha indirieto nel ricievere sopra di sé l'arco; la 5ª è [30]che tutta la spesa e 'l peso dell' arco che eccede il mezzo tondo [31]è inutile e dānoso, ed è qui da notare, che il peso [32]sopra posto all' archo rōperà cō più facilità l'arco in *a b* trouā[33]do la curuatura dell' ecciesso che al mezzo circulo s'agiugnie [34]che essendo dirieto il pilastro insino al cōtatto del semicirculo.

L'ARCO IL QUALE È CARICO SOPRA IL SUO MEZZO RŌPERÀ [36]NEL SUO QUARTO DESTRO E SINISTRO

[37]Prouasi per la 7ª di questo che dicie [38]❡ le opposite stremità delli sostētaculi sono equal-mēte agra[39]vate dal peso che per lor si sospēde; adūque il peso dato in *f* si [40]sēte in *b c* cioè mezzo per ciascuno stremo, e per la terza che dioie: [41]Quella parte del sostētacolo d'equal potētia più presto si rompe [42]che è più distantè al suo fermamēto, ōde seguita che . . . [43]per essere *d* equalmente distāte al *f c* ferma . . . .

these semicircles cross each other, as is seen in the figure *n m;* besides this it follows that there is a wider space between the extremes of the semicircle than between the plane of the walls; the third reason is that the weight placed to counterbalance the strength of the arch dimi-nishes in proportion as the piers of the arch are wider than the space between the piers. Fourth-ly, in proportion as the parts at *c a*, *b d* turn outwards, the piers are weaker to support the arch above them. The 5th is that all the material and weight of the arch which are in excess of the semicircle are useless and indeed mischievous; and here it is to be noted that the weight placed above the arch will be more likely to break the arch at *a b*, where the curve of the excess begins that is added to the semicircle, than if the pier were straight up to its junction with the semi-circle [spring of the arch].

AN ARCH LOADED OVER THE CROWN WILL GIVE WAY AT THE LEFT-HAND AND RIGHT-HAND QUARTERS

This is proved by the 7th of this work which says: The opposite ends of the support are equally pressed upon by the weight suspended to them; hence the weight shown at *f* is felt at *b c*, that is half at each extremity; and by the third which says: In a support of equal strength (throughout) that portion will give way soonest which is farthest from its attachment; whence it follows that, *d* being equally distant from *f*, *c* . . . .

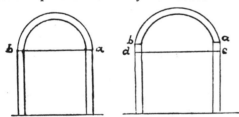
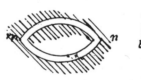

[44]Se l'armadura dell' ar[45]co nō cala insieme [46]col calo dell' arco, la cal[47]cina nel seccarsi restri[48]gnie in sé medesima e [49]si spicca dall' ū de' matto[50]ni, alli quali ella per col[51]legarli è interpo[52]sta, e così li lascia dis[53]legati, per la qual co[54]sa la uolta resta disu[55]nita e le pioggie in brie[56]ve la ruinano.

If the centring of the arch does not settle as the arch settles, the mortar, as it dries, will shrink and detach itself from the bricks between which it was laid to keep them together; and as it thus leaves them disjoined the vault will re-main loosely built, and the rains will soon de-stroy it.

A. 49*b*]　　786

DELLA · FORTEZZA · E QUALITÀ · DELLI ARCHI, E DOVE SONO FORTI [2]O DEBOLI · E COSÌ LE COLONNE

❡[3]Quella · parte dell' arco che fia · piv · piana, farà minore resistētia [4]al peso · sopra · postoli.❡

ON THE STRENGTH AND NATURE OF ARCHES, AND WHERE THEY ARE STRONG OR WEAK; AND THE SAME AS TO COLUMNS

That part of the arch which is nearer to the horizontal offers least resistance to the weight placed on it.

24. infralli . . semics . . infralle. 25. riete . . possto perchōtro. 26. archo diminuisscie . . posste dellarcho. 27. e piu largha . . inter-posto infralli pilasstri \\. 28. \\ elli pilasstri indebolisschano. 29. larcho . . la 5ª he. 30. chettutta . . archo . . eciede. 31. [dellarcho] e innutile. 32. possto . . larcho. 33. churuatura . . mezo circhulo. 34. pilasstro . . chōtatto. 35. larcho . . charicho . . mezo. 36. desstro essinisstro. 37. cheddicie. 38. sosstētachuli seno. 40. ciasscuno. 41. sosstētacholo . . si r\\\\\\\\\\. 42. dis-stante . . seghuita che \\\\\\\\\\\. 43. deq distante al f e ferma \\\\\\\\\\\\\\. 45. cho nō chala. 46. chol chalo dell archo. 47. secharsi. 49. sispicha. 50. chol. 51. legharsi. 52. e chosi. 53. leghati . . qual che. 54. la la . . ressta. 55. elle. 56. ve le.
786. 1. forteza. 2. chosi le cholone. 3. archo cheffia.

[5]Quando · ȷl triãgolo · *a z n* [6]calando caccia indirieto · [7]ȷ $\frac{2}{3}$ di ciascuno $\frac{1}{2}$ arco [8]cioè *a* · *s* · e così *z* · *m*, e la [9]ragiõ si è che *a* · piõba sopra · *b*, [10]e così *z* · sopra *f*.

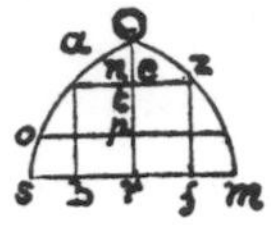

[11]Ciascuno $\frac{1}{2}$ · arco ·, sendo vinto · dal superchio · peso ·, si ronperà ne $\frac{2}{3}$ della [12]sua · altezza ·, la quale · parte · risponde · per perpẽdiculare · linia · sopra · il mezzo della sua [13]basa · come · appare · in · *a* · *b*; E questo accade che 'l peso · desidera cadere [14]e passare pel · pũto · *r* ·; E s'egli desiderasse cõtra sua · natura cade[15]re dal pũto · *s* ·, l'arco · *n* · *s* · si rõperebbe · nel suo · mezzo · appũto [16]e se l'arco · *n* · *s* · fusse d'ũ solo legnio, il peso posto in · *n* · desidereb[17]be cadere in · *m* · e ronperebbesi in mezzo $\frac{1}{2}$ · all' arco *e* · *m* ·, altremẽti si rõperà nel terzo [18]di sopra nel pũto [19]*a* ·, perchè da · *a* · *n* · [20]è l'arco · piv pia[21]no, che non è da [22]*a* · *o* e che no[23]n è da *o* · *s*; [24]e tanto · quãto [25]*p* · *t* · è maggio[26]re che *t* · *n* · [27]tanto fia piv for[28]te · *a* · *o* · che [29]non è *a* · *n* ·; [30]e similmẽte [31]tanto fia piv [32]forte · *s* · *o* · che [33]*o* · *a* · quãto · [34]*r* · *p* · fia maggi[35]ore · che *p t*.

[36]Quel arco · che fia · raddoppiato · nella quadratura della sua · grossezza [37]regierà · quattro · tanti · peso quanto · regieva · lo sciẽpio ·, tanto · piv · [38]quanto · il diamitro della · sua · grossezza · entra · mẽ numero · di uolte nella [39]sua · lunghezza; Cioè · se la · grossezza dell' arco sciẽpio entra · 10 [40]volte nella sua · lũghezza, la grossezza · de l'arco dupplicato · ẽtrerà 5 volte [41]nella · sua · lũghezza ·; Adũque entrãdo la metà meno la grossezza de [42]l'arco · dupplicato · nella sua · lunghezza · che nõ fa quella de[43]l' arco · sciẽpio · nella · sua ·, è ragionevol cosa che regga la metà piv [44]peso che nõ gli tocherebbe, se fusse alla proportione dell' ar[45]co · sciẽpio; Onde essendo quest' arco dupplicato per 4 volte la quã[46]tità de l'arco sciẽpio, parrebbe che dovesse regiere 4 tãti piv peso, [47]e la sopra detta regola dimonstra che ne sostiene · 8 cotãti appũto.

When the triangle *a z n*, by settling, drives backwards the $\frac{2}{3}$ of each $\frac{1}{2}$ circle, that is *a s* and in the same way *z m*, the reason is that *a* is perpendicularly over *b* and so likewise *z* is above *f*.

Either half of an arch, if overweighted, will break at $\frac{2}{3}$ of its height, the point which corresponds to the perpendicular line above the middle of its bases, as is seen at *a b;* and this happens because the weight tends to fall past the point *r*. And if, against its nature, it should tend to fall towards the point *s*, the arch *n s* would break precisely in its middle. If the arch *n s* were of a single piece of timber, if the weight placed at *n* should tend to fall in the line *n m*, the arch would break in the middle of the arch *e m*, otherwise it will break at one-third from the top at the point *a* because from *a* to *n* the arch is nearer to the horizontal than from *a* to *o* and from *o* to *s*. In proportion as *p t* is greater than *t n*, *a o* will be stronger than *a n*, and likewise in proportion as *s o* is stronger than *o a*, *r p* will be greater than *p t*.

The arch which is doubled in quadrature of its thickness will bear four times the weight that the single arch could carry, and more in proportion as the diameter of its thickness goes a smaller number of times into its length. That is to say: if the thickness of the single arch goes ten times into its length, the thickness of the doubled arch will go five times into its length. Hence as the thickness of the double arch goes only half as many times into its length as that of the single arch does, it is reasonable that it should carry half as much more weight than it would have to carry if it were in the said proportion to the single arch. Hence, as this double arch has 4 times the thickness of the single arch, it would seem that it ought to bear 4 times the weight; but by the above rule it is shown that it will bear exactly 8 times as much.

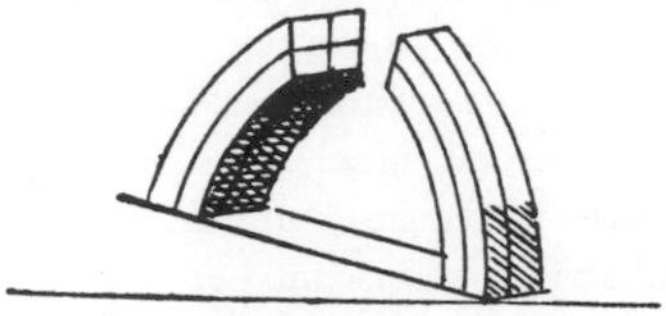

QUEL PILASTRO CHE FIA CARICO DI PIV DISEGUALE PESO VERRÀ PIV [49]PRESTO AL MÃCO

[50]La colonna *c* · *b* · per l'essere carica d'equale · somma fia · piv · permanẽte, [51]e l'altre ·

THAT PIER, WHICH IS CHARGED MOST UNEQUALLY, WILL SOONEST GIVE WAY

The column *c b*, being charged with an equal weight (on each side), will be most durable,

6. chalando chaccia. 7. ciaschuno $\frac{1}{2}$ archo. 8. echosi. 11. ciasschuno $\frac{1}{2}$ · archo. 12. alteza . . risponde perpẽdichulare . . mezo dela. 13. chome apare . . Ecquesto achade . . chadere. 14. Essegli desiderassi . chõtra . . chade. 15. larcho . . rõperebe . . apũto. 16. esselarcho . . [in] fussi . . desidere. 17. be chadere . . eronprrebesi in $\frac{1}{2}$ archo. 20. elarcho. 25. magio. 30. essimilmẽte. 34. magi. 36. archo · cheffia radopiato . . grosseza. 37. lossciẽpio. Ettanto. 38. grosseza. 39. lungeza . . sella grosseza dellarcho . . ẽtera. 40. volte ila . . lũgeza la grosseza . . archo duplichato ẽtera. 41. nela . . lũgeza . . grosseza. 42. larcho duplichato . . lungeza che nõ fa che nõ fa. 43. larcho . . chosa che rega. 44. peso [ap] che . . tocherebe [ali] sefussussi ala. 45. cho . . archo daplichato. 46. archo . . parebe . . dovessi. 47. chotãti apũto. 48. cheffia charicho . . diseghuale . . vera. 49. mãcho. 50. cholona . . cha ricah . . soma premanẽte. 51. ano . . tãdo . . daloro.

2 di fori · àño bisognio di tãto peso dal loro ciẽtro infori ⁵²quãt' è · dal loro · ciẽtro indẽtro · cioè dal ciẽtro della colonna insino a mezzo l'arco.

⁵³Li archi che stano per forza di catene nõ fieno permanẽti.

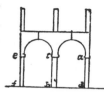

and the other two outward columns require on the part outside of their centre as much pressure as there is inside of their centre, that is, from the centre of the column towards the middle of the arch.

Arches which depend on chains for their support will not be very durable.

L'ARCO · FIA DI PIV LŪGA PERPETUITÀ ·, IL QUALE AVRÀ BONO CONTRARIO AL SUO SPĪGIERE

THAT ARCH WILL BE OF LONGER DURATION WHICH HAS A GOOD ABUTMENT OPPOSED TO ITS THRUST

⁵⁵L'arco per sé desidera cadere, e se l'arco fia 30 braccia e lo ĩteruallo ch' è infra i mvri ⁵⁶che lo sostẽgono sia · 20 ·, noi sappiamo che 30 nõ passerà per 20, se 20 nõ si ⁵⁷fa ancora lui · 30 ·; õde sendo vinto l'arco dal superchio · peso · si dirizza, e i mvri ⁵⁸male resistẽti l'aprono e dãno l'entrata infra loro spatio alla ruina de l'arco; ⁵⁹Ma se tu nõ uolessi mettere all' arco la sua corda di ferro, li debbi fare tali ⁶⁰spalle che facciano · resistẽtia al suo spingiere, la qual cosa · farai così: carica ⁶¹li angoli m · n · di pietre che le linie delle loro givnture se dirizzino al cientro ⁶²del circulo de l'arco; E la ragione, che farà l'arco permanẽte, fia questa; Noi ⁶³sappiamo chiaro che chi carica · l'arco nel quarto suo · a · b di superchio peso ch' el ⁶⁴muro · f · g · fia sospinto, perchè l'arco si uorrà dirizzare; E chi caricasse l'altro quarto ⁶⁵b · c · che li tirerebbe il mvro · f · g · indẽtro, se nõ fusse la linia delle pietre ⁶⁶x y che fa sostegnio.

The arch itself tends to fall. If the arch be 30 braccia and the interval between the walls which carry it be 20, we know that 30 cannot pass through the 20 unless 20 becomes likewise 30. Hence the arch being crushed by the excess of weight, and the walls offering insufficient resistance, part, and afford room between them for the fall of the arch. But if you do not wish to strengthen the arch with an iron tie you must give it such abutments as can resist the thrust; and you can do this thus: fill up the spandrels m n with stones, and direct the lines of the joints between them to the centre of the circle of the arch, and the reason why this makes the arch durable is this: We know very well that if the arch is loaded with an excess of weight above its quarter as a b, the wall f g will be thrust outwards because the arch would yield in that direction; if the other quarter b c were loaded, the wall f g would be thrust inwards, if it were not for the line of stones x y which resists this.

S. K. M. II.² 93a]   787

FONDAMẼTO

²Qui si dimostra · come li archi ³fatti ne' lati dell' ottãgolo spingo⁴no i pilastri delli angoli infori, ⁵come si dimostra nella linia · h · c ⁶e nella linia t d che spingono ⁷il pilastro · m · in fori, cioè si ⁸sforzano cacciarlo dal ciẽtro di tale ⁹ottangolo.

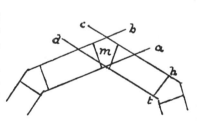

PLAN

Here it is shown how the arches made in the side of the octagon thrust the piers of the angles outwards, as is shown by the line h c and by the line t d which thrust out the pier m; that is they tend to force it away from the centre of such an octagon.

B. 27a]   788

La speriẽza · che vn peso posto sopra vno arco nõ si carica tutto sopra alle sue colon²ne, anzi quãto è maggior peso fraposto sopra l'archi ·, tanto mẽ pesa ³l'arco il peso alle colõne; la sperienza sie questa: sia messo vn

An experiment to show that a weight placed on an arch does not discharge itself entirely on its columns; on the contrary the greater weight placed on the arches, the less the arch transmits the weight to the columns. The experiment is the following. Let a man be placed

52. daloro . . cholona . . mezo. 53. stano . . chatene. 54. larcho . . ara . . chontrario. 55. larcho . . chadere Esselarcho . . 30 br . . iterualo. 56. sostẽgono . . sapiano. 57. anora . . larcho . . diriza. 58. laprano edano . . ala . . archo. 59. Massettu . . archo . . chorda. 60. spale cheffacino . . chosa . . charicha. 61. chelle . . dele . . dirizino. 62. circhulo . . archo . . larcho premanẽte. 63. sapiano . . chariche larcho. 64. larcho si uora dirizare . . charichassi. 65. tirerebe . . fussi. 66. cheffa.
787. 2. dimosstra chome. 8. caciarlo.
788. 1. archo . . carica tu sopra . . colo. 2. magior. 3. larcho el . . cholone . . questa si mezzo.

omo ⁴sopra le stadere in mezzo la trŏba d'uno pozzo; fa dipoi che questo allarghi le mani ⁵e piedi infra le parieti di detto pozzo ·, vedrai questo pesare alla stadera mol⁶to meno ·; dali vno peso alle spalle, uedrai per speriĕza quãto maggior ⁷peso li darai, maggiore forza farà in aprire le braccia e ganbe, e piv pŏ⁸dare nelle parieti, e piv mãcare il pŏdo alle stadere.

on a steelyard in the middle of the shaft of a well, then let him spread out his hands and feet between the walls of the well, and you will see him weigh much less on the steelyard; give him a weight on the shoulders, you will see by experiment that the greater the weight you give him the greater effort he will make in spreading his arms and legs and in pressing against the wall, and the less weight will be thrown on the steelyard.

4. imezo . . pozo.   5. pozo . . ala.   6. spalli . . isperieza . . magior.   7. darai magieor.   8. pariete . . mãchare.

IV

ON FOUNDATIONS, THE NATURE OF THE GROUND, AND SUPPORTS

Br. M. 138a]   789

La prima parte neciessarissima è la loro permanētia.

²Delli fondamēti che ànno le mēbrificationi componi³trici delli tēpli e altri edifiti publici, tal proporti⁴one deve essere da profondità a profondità quale ⁵è da peso a peso che scaricare si deve sopra essi mē⁶bri.

⁷Ogni parte della pro⁸fondità, che à la terra ⁹per alquāto spatio, è ¹⁰fatta a suoli, e o¹¹gni suolo è cōposto di ¹²parti, più grave ¹³e piv leue l'una che l'al¹⁴tra; nel profondarsi è più grave; e questo si prova, ¹⁵perchè questi tali soli sō cō¹⁶posti dalle turbulentie ¹⁷delle acque scaricate ī ¹⁸mare dal corso de' fiumi, ¹⁹che in quello versano, ²⁰delle quali turbulentie ²¹la parte più grave fu ²²quella che prima ²³si scaricò succes-siva²⁴mēte, e questo fa l'ac²⁵qua, dov' ella si ferma, le²⁶vādo prima dove es²⁷sa si move; E di que²⁸sti tali soli di terra ²⁹si manifesta nelli lati ³⁰di fiumi che coi lor con³¹tinui corsi ànno secati ³²e partiti con grā pro³³fondità di tagli l'ū mō³⁴te dall' altro, doue per li ³⁵ghiajosi soli l'acque so³⁶no scolate e per questo ³⁷la materia si è seccata ³⁸e coūertita in dura ³⁹pietra, e massime di ⁴⁰quel fāgo, che era più ⁴¹sottile, e questo ci ⁴²fa cōcludere, che ogni par⁴³te della terrestre superfitie fu ⁴⁴già ciētro della terra e ⁴⁵così de cōverso ecc.

The first and most important thing is stability.

As to the foundations of the component parts of temples and other public buildings, the depths of the foundations must bear the same proportions to each other as the weight of material which is to be placed upon them.

Every part of the depth of earth in a given space is composed of layers, and each layer is composed of heavier or lighter materials, the lowest being the heaviest. And this can be proved, because these layers have been formed by the sediment from water carried down to the sea, by the current of rivers which flow into it. The heaviest part of this sediment was that which was first thrown down, and so on by degrees; and this is the action of water when it becomes stagnant, having first brought down the mud whence it first flowed. And such layers of soil are seen in the banks of rivers, where their constant flow has cut through them and divided one slope from the other to a great depth; where in gravelly strata the waters have run off, the materials have, in consequence, dried and been converted into hard stone, and this happened most in what was the finest mud; whence we conclude that every portion of the surface of the earth was once at the centre of the earth, and vice versa, &c.

A. 50a]   790

¶ Quella parte del fondamēto delli edifiti che piv pesa ²piv si ficca · e lascia in alto il piv leggiero disunito da sé; ¶ ³¶E quel terreno ch'è piv · premvto, sendo poroso ·, piv accon-sente; ¶ ⁴Senpre tu · devi · fare i fondamēti che sportino egualmēte fori del ⁵carico · de' lor mvri e pilastri come appare · in m · a · b ·, e se ⁶farai · come · molti fanno, cioè di fare uno fondamēto d'equale ⁷larghezza · in sino alla superfitie · della terra, e di sopra li danno diseguale ⁸carico come si dimostra in · b · e · e in e · o, la parte del fonda⁹mēto · b · e, perchè è piena dal pilastro del cātone ·, piv pesa e piv

The heaviest part of the foundations of build-ings settles most, and leaves the lighter part above it separated from it.

And the soil which is most pressed, if it be porous, yields most.

You should always make the foundations pro-ject equally beyond the weight of the walls and piers, as shown at m a b. If you do as many do, that is to say if you make a foundation of equal width from the bottom up to the surface of the ground, and charge it above with unequal weights, as shown at b e and at e o, at the part of the foundation at b e, the pier of the angle will

789. 1. ella loro permanentia. 2. chean le mēbrificationi chonponi. 3. pubbici. 4. debbe .. dapprofondita approfondita. 5. dappeso .. chesscaricharе si debbe. 8. alla. 9. spatiotio. 10. factata assuoli. 11. chōpossto. 12. parte .. grave [opi]. 13. eppiv lievi luna chellal. 14. tra "nel-grave" ecquesto si prove. 15. quessti. 16. turbbulentie. 17. scharichate. 21. fuc. 22. prim"a". 23. sisscha-richo. 24. ecquesto fallac. 25. ferme. 29. manifessta. 30. cholor chon. 31. chorsi an seghati. 32. esspartiti. 34. dallaltre. 35. gljarosi. 37. se secha. 38. chōvertita. 40. fāgho. 41. ecquesto. 43. tereste. 45. chosi de chōverso.
790. 1. Quela. 2. ficha · ellasscia .. el .. legieri .. dasse. 3. Ecquel tereno .. achōsēte. 4. debi .. chessportino. 5. pilasstri chome apare .. esse. 6. chome .. ī fondamēto [equi] de quale. 7. largeza .. ala .. delatera .. dano. 8. charicho. 9. chātone.

spīgie ¹⁰in basso il suo fōdamēto che nō fa il muro · *e* · *o* che non occupa ¹¹interamēte il suo fōdamēto, e però meno spegnie e mē si ficca,

weigh most and thrust its foundation downwards, which the wall at *e o* will not do; since it does not cover the whole of its foundation, and

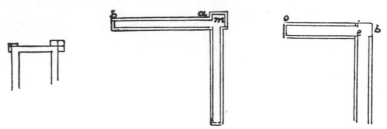

¹²onde ficcādosi il pilastro *b* · *e* · e si diunisce e parte dal mv¹³ro · *e* · *o* · come si uede nel piv delli edifiti che sono spicati ¹⁴intorno · a detti pilastri.

therefore thrusts less heavily and settles less. Hence, the pier *b e* in settling cracks and parts from the wall *e o*. This may be seen in most buildings which are cracked round the piers.

A. 53*a*]   791

La finestra · *a* · sta bene sotto ²la finestra *c* · e la finestra ³· *b* · sta · male · sotto · lo spatio ⁴· *d* ·, perchè detto · spatio · è sanza ⁵sostegnio · e fondamēto, ⁶si chè ricordati di nō rōpere ⁷mai sotto · li spati · delle finestre.

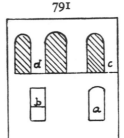

The window *a* is well placed under the window *c*, and the window *b* is badly placed under the pier *d*, because this latter is without support and foundation; mind therefore never to make a break under the piers between the windows.

A. 48*b*]   792

DEL SOSTĒTACULO

²Il pilastro moltiplicato per grossezza · crescierà tanto piv che la sua debita potētia ³quāto · e' māca · della ragionevole altezza.

OF THE SUPPORTS

A pillar of which the thickness is increased will gain more than its due strength, in direct proportion to what it loses in relative height.

ESENPLO

⁵Se uno pilastro · debe · essere · alto · 9 · grossezze ·, cioè · che s'egli · sarà · grosso · uno braccio, la regola ⁶lo pone di · 9 · braccia ·; se ne collegherai · 100 · insieme · per grossezza · fia grosso braccia 10 e alto · 9; ⁷e se il primo pilastro regieva 10000 libbre, perchè questo secōdo non è alto se non è circa ⁸a una grossezza, e mācādoli · 8 parti della lunghezza · e' regierà · piv otto volte, ⁹cioè ogni · pilastro collegato · li toccherà a regiere piv 8 volte che dislegato, cioè ¹⁰che se prima regieva dieci mila libbre ·, adesso ne sosterrà 90 mila.

EXAMPLE

If a pillar should be nine times as high as it is broad—that is to say, if it is one braccio thick, according to rule it should be nine braccia high —then, if you place 100 such pillars together in a mass this will be ten braccia broad and 9 high; and if the first pillar could carry 10,000 pounds, the second, being only about as high as it is wide, and thus lacking 8 parts of its proper length, it, that is to say, each pillar thus united, will bear eight times more than when disconnected; that is to say, that if at first it would carry ten thousand pounds, it would now carry 90 thousand.

---

10. baso . . none ochupa. 11. ficha. 12. fi[g] chādosi . . disunisscie. 13. chome . . chessono spichati. 14. pilasstri.
791. 2. ella. 3. sotto [la finestra] lo spatio. 5. effondamēto. 6. richordati.
792. 1. sosstētachulo. 2. pilasstro mvltiplichato per grosseza cressciera · tanto "piv che". 3. mācha . . alteza. 5. Se l . . grosseze . . chesseli . . l̄ br · [de] la. 6. 9 br . . cholegerai . . grosseza . . br. 10. 7. esse . . lbr . . sechōdo . . circha. 8. al̄ grosseza e māchādoli . . dela lungeza. 9. cholegato . . tochera. 10. chesse . . mila lbr . . sostera.

V

ON THE RESISTANCE OF BEAMS

S. K. M. II² 87b]　　　　　　　　793

[2]Quell' angolo sa[3]rà di piv resistē[4]tia che fia
piv a[5]cuto e 'l piv ottu[6]so fia piv debole.

That angle will offer the greatest resistance
which is most acute, and the most obtuse will be
the weakest.

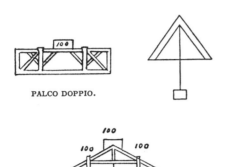

PALCO DOPPIO.

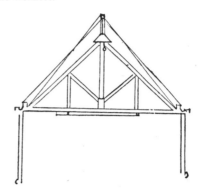

S. K. M. III. 4b]　　　　　　　794

Se i travi e 'l peso *o* fia ·
100 · libre, [2]quãto · peso ·
sarà · in *a* · *b* · a fa[3]re
resistētia · a esso · peso ·
che [4]nõ caggia in basso?

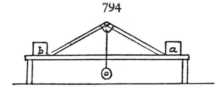

If the beams and the
weight *o* are 100 pounds,
how much weight will be
wanted at *a* and *b* to resist
such a weight, that it may
not fall down?

A. 53a]　　　　　　　795

DELLA LUNGHEZZA DELLE TRAVI

[2]Quella · trave · che fia lūga · piv · che le
20 sua [3]maggiori grossezze, fia poco permanēte
e rõperasi in ½; [4]e ricordati che la parte ch'ētra
nel mvro, sia penetrata [5]di pece calda e fasciata
d'asse di quercia, ācor essa penetrata; [6]Ogni
trave vole passare i sua muri e esser ferma di
là da essi mv[7]ri cõ soffitiēti catene, perchè
spesso si vede per terremoti
le travi usci[8]re de' mvri e
rovinare poi i mvri e solari;
dove, se sono īcatenate,
[9]terranno · i mvri · in ·
sieme fermi, e i mvri fermano · i solari.

[10]Ancora ti ricordo · che tu · nõ faci mai i

ON THE LENGTH OF BEAMS

That beam which is more than 20 times as
long as its greatest thickness will be of brief
duration and will break in half; and remember,
that the part built into the wall should be steeped
in hot pitch and filleted with oak boards likewise
so steeped. Each beam must pass through its
walls and be secured beyond the walls with
sufficient chaining, because
in consequence of earth-
quakes the beams are often
seen to come out of the walls
and bring down the walls
and floors; whilst if they are chained they will
hold the walls strongly together and the walls

793. 4. cheffia. 5. piotu.
794. 1–4 R. 2. affa. 3. resisstētia. 4. chaggio.
795. 1. dela lungeza. 2. cheffia . . pivi · chele [10] 20. 3. magiori grosseze . . pocho. 4. richordoti. 5. chalda . . essa *is wanting*. 7. chõ soffitiēte chatene . . tremoti . . ussci. 8. ichatenate. 9. terano . . e e mvri. 10. Anchora ti richordo chettu.

793. The three smaller sketches accompany the
text in the original, but the larger one is not directly
connected with it. It is to be found on fol. 70b of the
same MS. and there we read in a note, written under-

neath, 'coverchio della perdicha del castello' (roof of
the flagstaff of the castle). Compare also Pl. XCIII,
No. 1.

smalti · sopra legni[11]ame, imperochè nel cresciere e discresciere · che fa il legname [12]per
l'umido · e secco, spesse volte crepano detti
solai e crepa[13]te le loro diuisioni · a poco a poco
si fãno in poluere e fãno [14]brutta evidẽtia.

[15]Ancora ti ricordo nõ facci solari sostenvti
da archi [16]e travi, imperochè col tẽpo il solaro,
ch'è sostenvto dalle tra[17]vi, cala alquãto in nel
suo · mezzo, e quella parte [18]del solaro, ch'è
sostenuta dal arco, resta nel suo loco, onde [19]ȷ
solari che sono sostenvti da 2 varie nature di
sostẽta[20]culi paiono col tẽpo fatti a colli.

will hold the floors. Again I remind you never
to put plaster over timber. Since by expansion
and shrinking of the timber produced by damp
and dryness such floors often crack, and once
cracked their divisions gradually produce dust
and an ugly effect. Again remember not to lay
a floor on beams supported on arches; for, in
time, the floor which is made on beams settles
somewhat in the middle, while that part of the
floor which rests on the arches remains in its
place; hence, floors laid over two kinds of supports look, in time, as if they were made in
hills [19].

11. cressciere e disscressciere cheffa ilegname. 12. essecho . . isspesse . . detti soli e crep. 13. ti le . . apocho apocho .
effano. 15. Anchora ti richordo nõ faci. 16. ettrav . . chol . . dale. 17. chala . . inel . . mezo [che elp] equle parte. 18. sostenta . .
archo . . locho. 19. propositione ȷ solari chessone. 20. ch chili paiano chol . . acholli. *The word* propositione *written on the
margin near line* 19 *has apparently nothing to do with this text, but M. Ravaisson, in his edition of MS. A, has been misled by it to take*
ȷ solari (*line* 19) *for the beginning of a new paragraph.*

795. 19. M. Ravaisson, in his edition of MS. A, gives
a different rendering of this passage, translating it
thus: 'Les planchers qui sont soutenus par deux
différentes natures de supports paraissent avec le
temps faits en voûte [*a cholli*]'.

REMARKS ON THE STYLE OF LEONARDO'S ARCHITECTURE

A few remarks may here be added on the style of Leonardo's architectural studies. However incomplete, however small in scale, they allow us to establish a certain number of facts and probabilities, well worthy of consideration.

When Leonardo began his studies the great name of Brunellesco was still the inspiration of all Florence, and we cannot doubt that Leonardo was open to it, since we find among his sketches the plan of the church of San Spirito[1] and a lateral view of San Lorenzo (Pl. XCIV, No. 1), the beginning of a plan almost identical with the chapel Degli Angeli (Pl. XCIV, No. 3), while among Leonardo's designs for domes several clearly betray the influence of Brunellesco's Cupola and the lantern of Santa Maria del Fiore.[2]

The beginning of the second period of modern Italian architecture falls during the first twenty years of Leonardo's life. However, the new impetus given by Leon Battista Alberti either was not generally understood by his contemporaries, or those who appreciated it had no opportunity of showing that they did so. It was only when taken up by Bramante and developed by him to the highest rank of modern architecture that this new influence was generally felt. Now the peculiar feature of Leonardo's sketches is that, like the works of Bramante, they appear to be the development and continuation of Alberti's.

But a question here occurs which is difficult to answer. Did Leonardo, till he quitted Florence, follow the direction given by the dominant school of Brunellesco, which would then have given rise to his 'first manner', or had he, even before he left Florence, felt Alberti's influence—either through his works (Palazzo Ruccellai and the front of Santa Maria Novella) or through personal intercourse? Or was it not till he went to Milan that Alberti's work began to impress him, through Bramante, who probably had known Alberti at Mantua about 1470 and who not only carried out Alberti's views and ideas but, by his designs for St. Peter's at Rome, proved himself the greatest of modern architects. When Leonardo went to Milan Bramante had already been living there for many years. One of his earliest works in Milan was the church of Santa Maria presso San Satiro, Via del Falcone.

Now we find among Leonardo's studies of Cupolas on Pls. LXXXIV and LXXXV and on Pl. LXXX several sketches which seem to me to have been suggested by Bramante's dome of this church.

The MSS. B and B. N. 2037 contain the plans of S. Sepolcro, the pavilion in the garden of the Duke of Milan, and two churches, evidently inspired by the church of San Lorenzo at Milan.

MS. B contains besides two notes relating to Pavia, one of them a design for the

---

[1] *See Pl. XCIV, No. 2. Then only in course of erection after the designs of Brunellesco, though he was already dead; finished in* 1481.

[2] *A small sketch of the tower of the Palazzo della Signoria (MS. C. A.* 309) *proves that he also studied medieval monuments.*

sacristy of the Cathedral at Pavia, which cannot be supposed to be dated later than 1492, and it has probably some relation to Leonardo's call to Pavia, June 21, 1490.[1] These and other considerations justify us in concluding that Leonardo made his studies of cupolas at Milan, probably between the years 1487 and 1492, in antici- pation of the erection of one of the grandest churches of Italy, the Cathedral of Pavia. This may explain the decidedly Lombardo-Bramantesque tendency in the style of these studies, among which only a few remind us of the forms of the cupolas on S. Maria del Fiore and on the Baptistery of Florence. Thus, although when compared with Bramante's work several of these sketches plainly reveal that master's influence, we find, among the sketches of domes, some which show already Bramante's classic style, of which the Tempietto of San Pietro in Montorio, his first building executed at Rome, is the foremost example.[2]

On Pl. LXXXIV is a sketch of the plan of a similar circular building; and the Mausoleum on Pl. XCVIII, no less than one of the pedestals for the statue of Francesco Sforza (Pl. LXV), is of the same type.

The drawings Pl. LXXXIV, No. 2, Pl. LXXXVI, Nos. 1 and 2, and the ground- floor of the building in the drawing Pl. XCI, No. 2, with the interesting decoration by gigantic statues in large niches, are also, I believe, more in the style Bramante adopted at Rome than in the Lombard style. Are we to conclude from this that Leonardo on his part influenced Bramante in the sense of simplifying his style and rendering it more congenial to antique art? The answer to this important question seems at first difficult to give, for we are here in presence of Bramante, the greatest of modern architects, and with Leonardo, the man comparable with no other. We have no knowledge of any buildings erected by Leonardo, and unless we admit personal intercourse—which seems probable, but of which there is no proof—it would be difficult to understand how Leonardo could have affected Bramante's style. The converse is more easily to be admitted, since Bramante, as we have proved elsewhere, drew and built simultaneously in different manners, and though in Lombardy there is no building by him in his classic style, the use of brick for building, in that part of Italy, may easily account for it.

Bramante's name is incidentally mentioned in Leonardo's manuscripts in two passages (Nos. 1414 and 1448). On each occasion it is only a slight passing allusion, and the nature of the context gives us no adequate information as to any close connexion between the two artists.

It might be supposed, on the ground of Leonardo's relations with the East given in sections XVII and XXI of this volume, that some evidence of oriental influence might be detected in his architectural drawings. I do not, however, think that any such traces can be pointed out with certainty unless, perhaps, the drawings for a Mausoleum, Pl. XCVIII.

Among several studies for the construction of cupolas above a Greek cross there are some in which the forms are decidedly monotonous. These, it is clear, were not

---

[1] *The sketch of the plan of Brunellesco's church of San Spirito at Florence, which occurs in the same MS., may have been done from memory.*

[2] *It may be mentioned here that in 1494 Bramante made a similar design for the lantern of the cupola of the church of Santa Maria delle Grazie.*

designed as models of taste; they must be regarded as the results of certain investigations into the laws of proportion, harmony, and contrast.

The designs for churches on the plan of a Latin cross are evidently intended to depart as little as possible from the form of a Greek cross, and they also show a preference for a nave surrounded with outer porticoes.

The architectural forms preferred by Leonardo are pilasters coupled (Pl. LXXXII, No. 1) or grouped (Pl. LXXX, No. 5, and Pl. XCIV, No. 4), often combined with niches. We often meet with orders superposed, one in each story, or two small orders on one story, in combination with one great order (Pl. XCVI, No. 2).

The drum (tamburo) of these cupolas is generally octagonal, as in the Cathedral of Florence, and with similar round windows in its sides. In Pl. LXXXVII, No. 2, it is circular like the model actually carried out by Michelangelo at St. Peter's.

The cupola itself is either hidden under a pyramidal roof, as in the Baptistery of Florence, San Lorenzo of Milan, and most of the Lombard churches (Pl. XCI, No. 1, and Pl. XCII, No. 1), or it more generally suggests the curve of Sta Maria del Fiore (Pl. LXXXVIII, No. 5; Pl. XC, No. 2; Pl. LXXXIX, M; Pl. XC, No. 4, Pl. XCVI, No. 2). In other cases (Pl. LXXX, No. 4; Pl. LXXXIX; Pl. XC, No. 2) it shows the sides of the octagon crowned by semicircular pediments, as in Brunellesco's lantern of the Cathedral and in the model for the Cathedral of Pavia.

Finally, in some sketches the cupola is either semicircular or, as in Pl. LXXXVII, No. 2, shows the beautiful line adopted sixty years later by Michelangelo for the existing dome of St. Peter's.

It is worth noticing that for all these domes Leonardo is not satisfied to decorate the exterior merely with ascending ribs or mouldings, but employs also a system of horizontal parallels to complete the architectural system. Not the least interesting are the designs for the tiburio *(cupola) of Milan Cathedral. They show some of the forms, just mentioned, adapted to the peculiar gothic style of that monument.*

The few examples of interiors of churches recall the style employed in Lombardy by Bramante, for instance in S. Maria di Canepanuova at Pavia, or by Dolcebuono in the Monastero Maggiore at Milan (see Pl. CI, No. 1 [C. A. 184b]; Pl. LXXXIV, No. 10).

The few indications concerning palaces seem to prove that Leonardo followed Alberti's example of decorating the walls with pilasters and a flat rustica, either in stone or by graffitti (Pl. CII, No. 1, and Pl. LXXXV, No. 14).

By pointing out the analogies between Leonardo's architecture and that of other masters we in no way pretend to depreciate his individual and original inventive power. These are at all events beyond dispute. The project for the Mausoleum (Pl. XCVIII) would alone suffice to rank him among the greatest architects who ever lived. The peculiar shape of the tower (Pl. LXXX), of the churches for preaching (Pl. XCVII, No. 1, and pp. 43 and 44, Figs. 1–4), his curious plan for a city with high- and low-level streets (Pl. LXXVII and Pl. LXXVIII, No. 2 and No. 3), his Loggia with fountains (Pl. LXXXII, No. 4) reveal an originality, a power and facility of invention for almost any given problem, which are quite wonderful.

In addition to all these qualities he probably stood alone in his day in one depart-ment of architectural study—his investigations, namely, as to the resistance of vaults, foundations, walls, and arches.

As an application of these studies the plan of a semicircular vault (Pl. CIII, No. 2)[1] may be mentioned here, disposed so as to produce no thrust on the columns on which it rests: volta ī botte e non ispignie īfori le colone. *Above the geometrical patterns on the same sheet, close to a circle inscribed in a square, is the note:* la ragiō d'una volta quadra cioè del diamitro della sua . . . del tedesco in domo.[2]

There are few data by which to judge of Leonardo's style in the treatment of detail. On Pl. LXXXV, No. 10, and Pl. CIII, No. 3, we find some details of pillars; on Pl. CI, No. 3, slender pillars designed for a fountain, and on Pl. CIII, No. 1, MS. B, is a pen-and-ink drawing of a vase which also seems intended for a fountain. Three handles seem to have been intended to connect the upper parts with the base. There can be no doubt that Leonardo, like Bramante, but unlike Michelangelo, brought infinite delicacy of motive and execution to bear on the details of his work.

---

[1] *Compare the second design on this plate with Pl. C, No. 5.*

[2] *The German architect here mentioned may be Frate J. Mair of Hustorf. Compare No. 1546.*

XIV

ANATOMY, ZOOLOGY, AND PHYSIOLOGY

*L*EONARDO'S *contributions to the sciences of Anatomy and Physiology can now be appreciated owing to the publication of the manuscripts on Anatomy (MSS. A¹ and B, of Windsor, published by Sabachnikoff and Piumati, Paris, 1898, and Turin, 1901; Quaderni d'Anatomia (of Windsor), published by Vangensten, Fonahn, and Hopstock, 6 vols., Christiania, 1911–16²; one sheet at Weimar, published in* Raccolta Vinciana, Supplement to Fasc. XIII, *by Möller, Milan, 1930). In the present work I must limit myself to a general view of these labours, by giving his introductory notes to the various books on anatomical subjects. I have added some extracts and such observations as throw light on his scientific attitude, besides having an interest for a wider circle than that of specialists only. A full description of Leonardo's studies in anatomy and of his contributions to this science is given in J. Mc.Murrich Playfair, L.d.V.* the Anatomist, *with a preface by George Sarton, Baltimore, 1930, published under the auspices of the Carnegie Institution.*

According to Vasari Leonardo studied with Marc Antonio della Torre 'aiutato e scambievolmente aiutando'. This learned Anatomist taught at the universities of Padua and of Pavia (1511), and at Pavia he and Leonardo may have worked and studied together. He was scarcely thirty years old when he died in 1512, and his writings on anatomy have not only never been published, but no manuscript copy of them is known to exist.³

The dissection of dead human bodies for purposes of medical research was practised in Italy since the thirteenth century. Leonardo mentions the treatise of the Bolognese professor Mondino de Luzzi (No. 1494), written in 1316, and first published in Venice in 1478. But, although the author is known to have dissected corpses, his work was chiefly based on the writings of the ancient anatomist Galen and Arab scholars, rather than independent observations of nature. Also Leonardo built to some extent on Galen, whose researches, however, were confined to the dissection of brute animals. (No. 1412). He repeatedly mentions Avicenna, the Arab scholar (Nos. 1434, 1482, 1483, 1494). Other writers on anatomy whose names occur in Leonardo's manuscripts are: Alessandro Benedetti, doctor of Legnago (No. 1421), Egidio Romano (No. 1561), and the Veronese doctor Gabriele Zerbe (No. 1434). The book called Guidone *is probably Guy de Chauliac's* Cirogia *(No. 1469).*

Antonio Beatis, secretary to Cardinal Luigi d'Aragona, saw Leonardo's manuscripts at Cloux and was impressed by the amount of detail and the labour involved in his anatomical studies; and so were Vasari and Lomazzo, who saw the same drawings after they had passed into the possession of Francesco Melzi.⁴

---

¹ Dated 1510; with an instructive introduction by Mathias Duval.
² For details of contents see Bibliography.

³ G. B. De Toni, *Frammenti Vinciani*, Padua, 1900.
⁴ See p. 393.

Only a very small selection from the mass of anatomical drawings has been published here; to appreciate their merit they should be compared with the inadequate figures in books of the early part of the sixteenth century. William Hunter, the great surgeon who in the time of George III saw the originals in the King's Library, said: 'I expected to see little more than such designs in Anatomy as might be useful to a painter in his own profession. But I saw, and indeed with astonishment, that Leonardo had been a general and deep student. When I consider what pains he has taken upon every part of the body, the superiority of his universal genius, his particular excellence in mechanics and hydraulics, and the attention with which such a man would examine and see objects which he has to draw, I am fully persuaded that Leonardo was the best Anatomist, at that time, in the world. . . . Leonardo was certainly the first man we know of, who introduced the practice of making anatomical drawings' (Two introductory letters, London, 1784, pages 37 and 39).

Leonardo not only studied human anatomy but also the structure of animals— of the horse, for instance, which figured so largely in his works of art—and of birds and bats whose wings he scrutinized in order to learn how to fly (No. 1123). It was not only the shape and structure of the body, but primarily the functions of organisms and muscles, that captivated his interest, the heart and the circulation of the blood, the lungs and respiration. The texts Nos. 796 to 799 give the general plan which Leonardo had in mind for his book on Anatomy. It included the study of the growth and development of the human body from the foetus in the mother's womb to the full-grown man. It was to deal with the proportions and the movements of the human figure and with the construction and function of the sense-organs[1] —with Optics, Perspective, &c.—a comprehensive work, foreshadowing that of Vesalius of about a century later. His method consisted in demonstration by means of drawings which showed the anatomical constructions from various points of view (No. 798). The text was merely subsidiary. He wrote down that he dissected ten human bodies (No. 796), and at the end of his life, in his conversation with Cardinal Luigi d' Aragona, the number had increased to thirty. The Anonimo in the Codice Magliabechiano says that many drawings were done in the hospital of Santa Maria Nuova at Florence. From the draft of one of his letters (No. 1352), we learn that he was prevented from pursuing these researches during his stay in Rome by Pope Leo X who was influenced by slanderous and malignant reports. The dissection of corpses was permitted by the Church, but a brief was required.

According to Vasari (vol. vii, pp. 268, 269, 274), Michelangelo in his old age contemplated writing a work on the Anatomy of the Human Figure, having made a thorough study of the subject, but he was deterred by the difficulties involved. Leonardo, however, did not shrink from his tremendous task. But no one with knowledge of his methods of study, and of the dispersal and loss of his manuscripts, will wonder that only mere fragments of his work, as planned, have come down to us.

[1] See Vol. i, pp. 27 sq., 71 sq.

I

ANATOMY

Le cose mentali che non son passate per il senso son vane e nulla verità patoriscano se non danosa; e perchè tal discorsi nascan da povertà di gegnio, pover' son sempre tal discorsori, e se saran nati richi e' moriran poveri nella lor vecheza; perchè pare che la natura si vendichi con quelli che vogliã far miraculi ²abbī mē che li altri o³mini più quieti, e ⁴quelli che vogliono ar⁵ricchirsi in ū dì vivi⁶no lungo tēpo in ⁷grã povertà, co⁸me interviene e ⁹interverrà in etter¹⁰no alli alchimisti, ¹¹cercatori di cre¹²are oro e argēto, ¹³e all' īgegnieri che ¹⁴vogliono che l'a¹⁵cqua morta dia ¹⁶vita motiua ¹⁷a sé medesima ¹⁸con cōtinuo ¹⁹moto, ²⁰e al sōmo stol²¹to negromante ²²e īcantatore.

²³E tu che dici, esser me²⁴glio il uedere fare ²⁵l'anatomia, che uede²⁶re tali disegni, dire²⁷sti bene, se fusse ²⁸possibile vedere tu²⁹tte queste cose che ³⁰in tal disegni si di³¹mostrano in una ³²sola figura, nella ³³quale con tutto il tu³⁴o ingenio nō vedra³⁵si, e nō avrai la no³⁶titia, se nō d'alquã³⁷te poche vene, del³⁸le · quali io, per aver³⁹ne · vera · e piena ⁴⁰notitia, ò disfatti ⁴¹piv di dieci co⁴²rpi vmani, ⁴³distruggendo ogni ⁴⁴altri mēbri, consu⁴⁵mando con minutis-⁴⁶sime particule ⁴⁷tutta la carne che ⁴⁸d'intorno a esse ⁴⁹vene si trovaua, ⁵⁰sanza insangui⁵¹narle, se non d'ī⁵²sensibile insan⁵³guinamēto delle vene capillari; ⁵⁴e vn sol corpo nō ⁵⁵bastava a tanto tēpo, che biso⁵⁶gnava procedere di mano in mano ⁵⁷in tanti corpi, che si finisca la inte⁵⁸ra cognitione; le qual repli⁵⁹cai 2 volte per vedere le differentie.

⁶⁰E se tu avrai l'amore a tal cosa, ⁶¹tu sarai forse inpedito dallo ⁶²stomaco, e se questo nō ti inpedi⁶³sce, tu sarai forse inpedito dal⁶⁴la paura coll' abitare nelli tē⁶⁵pi notturni in cōpagnia di tali ⁶⁶morti squartati e scorticati e ⁶⁷spaventevoli a vederli; e se que⁶⁸sto nō t'ipedisce, forse ti māche⁶⁹rà il disegnio bono, il quale s'appa⁷⁰rtiene a tal figuratione; E ⁷¹se tu avrai il disegnio e' nō sarà ⁷²accōpagnato dalla prospettiva, ⁷³e se sarà accōpagnato ⁷⁴e' ti mācherà l'ordine ⁷⁵delle dimostratiō ⁷⁶geometriche e l'ordine ⁷⁷delle calculation delle ⁷⁸forze e valimēto de' ⁷⁹muscoli; e forse ti ⁸⁰mācherà la

The mental matters which have not passed through the sense are vain, and they produce no other truth than the injurious one; and as such discourses spring from poverty of genius, such discoursers are always poor, and if they are born rich they shall die poor in their old age; because it seems that nature revenges itself on those who wish to work miracles that they shall possess less than other more quiet men; and those who want to grow rich in a day live for a long time in great poverty, as always happens, and to all eternity will happen, to alchemists, the would-be creators of gold and silver, and to engineers who would have dead water stir itself into life and perpetual motion, and to those supreme fools, the necromancer and the enchanter. *A general introduction.*

[23] And you, who say that it would be better to watch an anatomist at work than to see these drawings, you would be right, if it were possible to observe all the things which are demonstrated in such drawings in a single figure, in which you, with all your cleverness, will not see nor obtain knowledge of more than some few veins, to obtain a true and perfect knowledge of which I have dissected more than ten human bodies, destroying all the other members, and removing the very minutest particles of the flesh by which these veins are surrounded, without causing them to bleed, excepting the insensible bleeding of the capillary veins; and as one single body would not last so long, since it was necessary to proceed with several bodies by degrees, until I came to an end and had a complete knowledge; this I repeated twice, to learn the differences [59].

And if you should have a love for such things you might be prevented by loathing, and if that did not prevent you, you might be deterred by the fear of living in the night hours in the company of those corpses, quartered and flayed and horrible to see. And if this did not prevent you, perhaps you might not be able to draw so well as is necessary for such a demonstration; or if you had the skill in drawing, it might not be combined with knowledge of perspective; and if it were so, you might not understand the methods of geometrical demonstration and the method of the calculation of forces and of the strength of

796. 3. quieti ecq. 4. voliano a. 5. richire nūdi. 6. lungho. 9. intervera. 10. archimisti. 14. voglia. 15. cq"a" morta. 17. asse. 20. somo. 23. "e" ettu che di. 27. fussi. 31. mosstrano. 35. e non arai. 37. vene de. 43. destrugendo. 44. consi. 45. minuti. 46. partichule. 53. capillar "e"(?). 54. e [altrettãte] e vn. 55. attanto tēpo che. 56. imano. 57. corpi che si finissimi la inte. 58. cognitione le qual [s] ripri. 59. cai [1] "2" volte .. diferentie. 60. essettu arai. 68. nōtipedisce. 69. qual sapa. 70. attal. 71. settu arai. 72. acōpagnato. 73. esse .. acōpagnato. 76. geometrice. 79. efforse.

patiētia che [81]tu nō sarai diligēte; Delle [82]quali se in me tutte queste [83]cose sono state o no, [84]i cēto 20 libri da me [85]conposti ne darā sentē-[86]tia del sì o del no, nelli [87]quali nō sono stato inpedi[88]to nè d'auaritia o negligētia, [89]ma sol dal tenpo || vale.

the muscles; patience also may be wanting, so that you lack perseverance. As to whether all these things were found in me or not [84], the hundred and twenty books composed by me will give verdict Yes or No. In these I have been hindered neither by avarice nor negligence, but simply by want of time. Farewell [89].

W. 19037*b*]   797

DELL' ORDINE DEL LIBRO

Plans and suggestions for the arrangement of materials (797–802).

[2]Questa · opera · si deve prīcipiare alla · cōciettione · dell' omo ·, e devi descrivere · il modo della matrice, [3]e come il putto · l'abita ·, e in che grado · lui risegga · ī quella ·, e 'l modo · dello vivificarsi e cibarsi, [4] e 'l suo · accrescimēto ·, e che · interuallo · sia · da · uno grado d'accresci-mēto · a · uno · altro, e che cosa lo spigna fori [5]del corpo · della madre ·, e per che · cagione qualche · uolta · lui · uēga fori · dal uētro di sua madre iñāti al debito [6]tēpo.

[7]Poi discriuerai quali mēbra sieno · quelle · che crescono · po · che 'l putto è nato · piv che l'altre, [8]e da la misura d'ū putto · d'un anno.

[9]Poi discrivi l'omo crescivto e la fēmina · e sue · misure · e nature di complessione colore [10]e fisionomie.

[11]Di poi descrivi com' egli è cōposto · di uene ·, nerui ·, muscoli e ossa; Questo farai nell' ultimo del libro; [12]di poi figura · in · 4 storie · quattro vniversali casi delli omini ·, cioè letitia con uari atti di ridere, [13]e figura · la cagiō · del riso ·; piāto in vari modi colla · sua · cagione ·; cōtētione cō uari movi[14]mēti d'uccisione ·, fughe ·, pavre ·, ferocità ·, ardimēti, omicidi · e tutte cose appartenēti a simil casi; [15]di poi figura · vna fatica cō tirare, spiegniere · portare, fermare, sostenere e simili [16]cose;

[17]Di poi discriui attitudine · e movimēto; [18]di poi prospettiva · per l'ofitio dell' ochio e dell' udito—dirai di mvsicha—e descrivi delli altri sēsi.

[19]Di poi discrivi la natura · de' 5 sensi.

OF THE ORDER OF THE BOOK

This work must begin with the conception of man, and describe the nature of the womb and how the foetus lives in it, up to what stage it resides there, and in what way it quickens into life and feeds. Also its growth and what interval there is between one stage of growth and another. What it is that forces it out from the body of the mother, and for what reasons it sometimes comes out of the mother's womb before the due time.

Then I will describe which are the members which, after the boy is born, grow more than the others, and determine the proportions of a boy of one year.

Then describe the fully grown man and woman, with their proportions, and the nature of their complexions, colour, and physiognomy.

Then how they are composed of veins, tendons, muscles, and bones. This I shall do at the end of the book. Then, in four drawings, represent four universal conditions of men. That is, Mirth, with various acts of laughter, and describe the cause of laughter. Weeping in various aspects with its causes. Contention, with various acts of killing; flight, fear, ferocity, boldness, murder, and everything pertaining to such cases. Then represent Labour, with pulling, thrusting, carrying, stopping, supporting, and suchlike things.

Further I would describe attitudes and movements. Then perspective, concerning the functions of the eye; and of hearing—here I will speak of music—and treat of the other senses.

And then describe the nature of the 5 senses.

---

82. seime. 83. onno [lili]. 84. iccēto 20. 86. tia [di] del. 88. negli ētia. 89. del [dalla ve] tenpo.
797. 2. debe . . e disscrivere. 3. chome il pucto . . risega . . uiuicharsi. 4. acresscimēto . . da ī grado da cresscimēto · a · ī · altro . . chosu . . spiga. 5. chorpo . . chagione . . uega . . del. 7. cresscano . . ēnato. 9. ella . . essue . . chōprlessione chollore effiosomie. 11. desscrivi chom eli e chōposto . . musscoli. 12. chasi . . chouari. 13. effigura la chagiō . de riso . . cholla . . chagione · chōte-tione cho. 14. ucisione · fuge . . ettutte chose apartenēti assimil chasi. 15. faticha chō . . sosstenere essimili. 16. chose. 18. lofitio effetti . . della uldito . . musicha . . sesi. 19. de · 2 · "sensi" sensi.

---

796. 84. Leonardo frequently wrote in note-books of a very small size; most of those which have been preserved undivided, contain less than fifty leaves. Thus a considerable number of such volumes must have gone to make up the *Codex Atlanticus* which contains nearly 1200 detached leaves. In the passage under consideration, which was evidently written at a

late period of his life, Leonardo speaks of his manuscript note-books as numbering 120; but we should hardly be justified in concluding that the greater part of his manuscripts were now missing (see *Prolegomena*, vol. i, pp. 108–9).

797. The meaning of the word *nervo* varies in different passages, being sometimes used for tendon.

[20]Questa figura strumētale dell' omo dimostreremo in ... figure, delle [21]quali le 3 prime saranno la ramificatione delle ossa, cioè vna dināzi · che [22]dimostri l'altitudine de' siti e figure delli ossi, la seconda sarà veduta in [23]proffilo e mostrerà la profondità del tutto e delle parti e loro sito; La 3ª [24]figura fia dimostratrice delle ossa dalla parte dirieto; Di poi faremo [25]3 altre figure ne' simili aspetti colle ossa segate, nelle quali si vedranno le lor [26]grossezze e uacuità; 3 altre figure faremo dell' ossa intere e de' nerui che na[27]scono dalla nuca, e in che mēbra ramificano; E 3 altre de' ossa e vene e do[28]ve ramificano, poi 3 con muscoli e 3 con pelle, e figure propor[29]tionate, e 3 della femina per dimostrare la matrice e vene mestruali, [30]che vanno alle poppe.

This mechanism of man we will demonstrate in ... figures; of which the three first will show the ramification of the bones; that is: first one in front-view to show their height and position and shape: the second will be seen in profile and will show the depth of the whole and of the parts, and their position. The third figure will be a demonstration of the bones of the back parts. Then I will make three other figures from the same point of view, with the bones sawn across, in which will be shown their thickness and hollowness. Three other figures of the bones complete, and of the nerves which rise from the nape of the neck, and in what limbs they ramify. And three others of the bones and veins, and where they ramify. Then three figures with the muscles and three with the skin, and their proper proportions; and three of women, to illustrate the womb and the menstrual veins which go to the breasts.

W. 19061a] 798

ORDINE DEL LIBRO

[2]Questa mia figuratione del corpo vmano ti sarà dimostra nō altre[3]menti, che se tu auessi l'omo naturale ināti, e la ragō si è, che se tu vuoi be[4]ne conoscere le parti dell' omo anatomizzato, tu lo volti o lui o l'ochio tuo per di[5]versi aspetti, quello cōsiderando di ootto, e di sopra, e dalli lati, voltando[6]lo e cercando l'origine di ciascū mēbro, e ī tal modo la notomia na[7]turale à soddisfatta alla tua notitia; Ma tu ài a intēdere, che tal noti[8]tia nō ti lascia saddisfatto, cōciosiachè la grādissima confusione che [9]resulta dalla mistione di pañiculi misti cō uene, arterie, nerui, corde, [10]muscoli, ossi, sangue, il quale tignie di sé ogni parte d'un medesimo colo[11]re, e le vene, che di tal sangue si votano non sono conosciute per la lor dimi[12]nutione, e la integrità delli pannicoli, nel cercare le parti che dentro a [13]loro s'includono, si viene a rompere, e la lor trasparētia, tinta di sangue, [14]nō ti lascia conoscere le parti coperte da loro per la similitu[15]dine del lor colore insāguinato, e nō puoi avere la notitia dell' ū che tu [16]nō cōfonda e distrugga l'altro; | adunque è necessario fare più notomie, [17]delle quali 3 te ne bisognia per auere piena notitia delle vene e arterie, [18]distruggēdo con sōma diligentia tutto il rimanēte, e altre 3 per auere la notitia [19]delli pannicoli, e 3 per le corde e muscoli e legamēti, e 3 per li ossi e car[20]tilagini, e 3 per la notomia delle ossa, le quali s'ànno a segare e dimo[21]strare, quale è buso e quale no,

THE ORDER OF THE BOOK

This depicting of mine of the human body will be as clear to you as if you had the natural man before you; and the reason is that if you wish thoroughly to know the parts of man, anatomically, you turn either him, or your eye, to see him from different aspects, considering him from below and from above and from the sides, turning him about and seeking the origin of each member; and in this way the natural anatomy is sufficient for your comprehension. But you must understand that this amount of knowledge will not continue to satisfy you, seeing the very great confusion that must result from the combination of tissues with veins, arteries, nerves, sinews, muscles, bones, and blood which, of itself, tinges every part the same colour. And the veins, which discharge this blood, are not discerned by reason of their smallness. Moreover, integrity of the tissues, in the process of the investigating the parts within them, is inevitably destroyed, and their transparent substance being tinged with blood does not allow you to recognize the parts covered by them, from the similarity of their blood-stained hue; and you cannot know everything of the one without confusing and destroying the other. Hence, some further anatomy drawings become necessary. Of which you want three to give full knowledge of the veins and arteries, everything else being destroyed with the greatest care. And three others to display the tissues; and three for the sinews and muscles and ligaments; and three for the bones and cartilages; and three for the anatomy of the

20. dimōsterreno. 22. effigure .. sechonda. 23. mossterra. 24. delle [ner] ossa .. faren. 25. asspetti .. segate .. uetra le. 26. grosseze e uachuita .. fareno. 27. scā della nucha .. ramifichino. 28. ramifichino .. mvsscoli .. effigure. 29. tionati .. mestruale.
798. 2. Questa. 3. chessettu .. ella .. chessettu. 4. conosscere le parte .. natomizate tu lo voli ollui ollochio. 5. asspetto. 6. eccerchando .. ciasscū. 7. turale ta sadidisfatto .. chettal. 8. lasscia .. cōcosia chella .. chonfusione. 9. della .. pañichuli. 10. musscoli .. dumedesimo. 11. elle .. cognosscute. 12. nuitione ella .. pannichuli nel cierchare le parte .. al. 13. sincludano · si uēgano .. ella .. trassparētia. 14. lasscia cognosscicre le parte [che son sotto a] coperte dalloro per almilitu. 15. poi .. chettu. 16. desstruggha .. natomie. 18. desstruggēdo .. soma. 19. pannichuli .. musscoli ellegamēti e 3 e 3. 20. e [ī] 3 per la natomia .. assegare e dimos. 21. quale he spugn"a".

quale è midolloso, quale è spugno²²so, e quale
è grosso dal fori al dentro, e quale è sottile, e
alcuno à in al²³cuna parte grā sottiglezza, e in
alcuna è grosso, e in alcuna busa, o pieno
²⁴d'osso, o midolloso, o spugnoso; e così tutte
queste cose sarāno alcuna volta tro²⁵vate in un
medesimo osso, e alcuno osso fia che non à
nessuna; e 3 te ne bisog²⁶na fare per la donna,
nella quale è grā misterio, mediante la · matrice
e suo feto; ²⁷Adunque per il mio disegnio ti
fia noto ogni parte e ogni tutto mediante la di-
²⁸mostratione di 3 diuersi aspetti di ciascuna
parte, perchè quando tu avrai vedu²⁹to alcun
mēbro dalla parte dinanzi con qualche neruo,
corda, o vena che ³⁰nasca dalla opposita parte,
ti fia dimostro il medesimo mēbro volto per lato
³¹o dirieto; non altremēti che se tu auessi in
mano il medesimo mēbro e andas³²si lo voltādo
di parte in parte insino a tanto che tu auessi
piena notitia di quel³³lo che tu desideri sapere,
e così similmēte ti fia posto inanti in tre o ³⁴4
dimostrationi di ciascū mēbro per diuersi
aspetti in modo che tu resterai con ³⁵vera e piena
notitia di quello che tu vuoi sapere della figura
dell' omo.

³⁶Adunque qui con 15 figure intere ti sarà
mostrata la cosmografia del minor ³⁷mōdo col
medesimo ordine che ināzi a me fu fatto da
Tolomeo nella sua cosmo³⁸grafia, e così diuiderò
poi quelle in mēbra, come lui diuise il tutto in
provincie; ³⁹e poi dirò l'ufitio delle parti per
ciascū verso, mettēdoti dināti alli ochi la notitia ⁴⁰di tutta la figura e valitudine dell' omo
inquāto a moto locale mediante le sue parti;
⁴¹E così piacesse al nostro autore che io potessi
dimostrare la natura delli omini e lo⁴²ro costumi
nel modo che io descriuo la sua figura.

⁴³E ricordoti che la notomia delli nerui non
ti darà la situatione della loro rami⁴⁴ficatione,
nè in quali muscoli essi si ramificano · mediante
li corpi disfatti in acqua ⁴⁵corrēte, o in acqua di
calcina, perchè, ancorachè ti rimāga la origine
de' lor nascimenti ⁴⁶sanza tale acqua come col-
l'acqua, le ramificationi loro pel corso dell' acqua
si ⁴⁷vengono a vnire, non altremēti che si fascia
il lino o canapa pettinata per filare, ⁴⁸tutto in
vn fascio in modo che inpossibile è a ritrovare
in quali muscoli o cō quale ⁴⁹o cō quāte ramificationi li nerui s'infondino ne' predetti muscoli.

bones, which have to be sawn to show which are
hollow and which are not, which have marrow
and which are spongy, and which are thick from
the outside inwards, and which are thin. And
some are extremely thin in some parts and thick
in others, and in some parts hollow or filled up
with bone, or full of marrow, or spongy. And all
these conditions are sometimes found in one and
the same bone, and in some bones none of them.
And three you must have for the woman, in
which there is much that is mysterious by reason of the womb and the foetus. Therefore by
my drawings every part will be known to you,
and by the demonstration from three different
points of view of each part; for when you
have seen a limb from the front, with any
muscles, sinews, or veins which take their rise
from the opposite side, the same limb will be
shown to you in a side view or from behind,
exactly as if you had that same limb in your hand
and were turning it from side to side until you
had acquired a full comprehension of all you
wished to know. In the same way there will be
put before you three or four demonstrations of
each limb, from various points of view, so that
you will be left with a true and complete knowledge of all you wish to learn of the human
figure [35].

Thus, in fifteen entire figures, you will have set
before you the microcosm on the same plan as,
before me, was adopted by Ptolemy in his cos-
mography; and so I will afterwards divide them
into limbs as he divided the whole world into
provinces; then I will speak of the function of
each part in every direction, putting before your
eyes a description of the whole form and substance of man, as regards his movements from
place to place, by means of his different parts.
And thus, if it please our great Author, I may
demonstrate the nature of men and their customs in the way I describe his figure.

And remember that the anatomy of the nerves
will not give the position of their ramifications,
nor show you which muscles they branch into,
by means of bodies dissected in running water
or in lime water, though indeed their origin and
starting-point may be seen without such water
as well as with it. But their ramifications, when
under running water, cling and unite—just like
flax or hemp carded for spinning—all into a
skein, in a way which makes it impossible to
trace in which muscles or by what ramifications
the nerves are distributed among those muscles.

22. ecqua le he . . essottile . . innal. 23. chuna . . sottiglieza . . alchuna . . alchuna. 24. osspugnosa e chosi . . sarano. 25. nūme-
desimo. 26. essuo. 28. asspetti . . quanto . . arai. 30. parte [tu] eti . . per lalo. 31. chessettu . . imano. 32. attanto chettu. 33. llo
chettu . . possto. 34. asspetti . . chettu. 35. chettu voi. 36. mosstro la cossmografia. 37. fuffatto dattolomeo . . cossmo. 38. imēbra
. . province. 39. ciasscū. 40. lochale . . parte. 41. Eccosi piacessi . . altore . . dimosstrare. 42. cosstumi . . desscrivo. 43. chella
dilora. 44. facione . . musscoli . . ramifichino. 45. corēte o in acq"a" . . rimāgha. 46. tale acq"a" . . ramificatione. 47. vengono
. . chessi facci . . chanapa. 48. fasscio. 49. ramificatione . . mvsscoli.

798. 35. Compare Pl. CVII. The original drawing   figures are slightly washed with indian ink. On the
at Windsor is 28½ × 19½ centimetres. The upper   back of this drawing is the text No. 1140.

W. 19041a]　　　　　　　799

ORDINE DI NOTOMIA

²Fa prima l'ossa come dire le braccia, e poni il motore dalla spalla al ³gomito per tutte le linie; Di poi dal gomito al braccio; Di poi dal ⁴braccio alla mano e dalla mano alli diti.

⁵E nel · braccio porrai li motori de' diti che s'aprono, e ⁶questi nella lor dimostratione porrai soli; nella 2ᵃ dimo⁷stratione vestirai questi muscoli delli secondi motori de' diti, ⁸e così farai a grado a grado per non confondere: ma primo po⁹ni sopra dell' ossa quelli muscoli che con essi ossa si congiungono, ¹⁰sanza altra confusione d'altri muscoli, e con quelli porrai ¹¹li nerui e uene, che li nutriscano, auendo prima fatto l'albero delle ue¹²ne e nerui sopra delle senplici ossa.

THE ARRANGEMENT OF ANATOMY

First draw the bones, let us say, of the arm, and put in the motor muscle from the shoulder to the elbow with all its lines. Then proceed in the same way from the elbow to the wrist. Then from the wrist to the hand and from the hand to the fingers.

And in the arm you will put the motors of the fingers which open, and these you will show separately in their demonstration. In the second demonstration you will clothe these muscles with the secondary motors of the fingers, and so proceed by degrees to avoid confusion. But first lay on the bones those muscles which lie close to the said bones, without confusion of other muscles; and with these you may put the nerves and veins which supply their nourishment, after having first drawn the tree of veins and nerves over the simple bones.

W. 19002a]　　　　　　　800

Comīcia la notomia alla testa e finiscila nella piāta del piede.

Begin the anatomy at the head and finish at the sole of the foot.

W. 19023b]　　　　　　　801

3 · uomini finiti,² 3 con ossa e vene,³ 3 · con ossa e nerui, ⁴3 · con ossa senplici; ⁵Queste sono 12 dimo⁶strationi di figure ī⁷tere.

3 men complete, 3 with bones and veins, 3 with bones and nerves, 3 with the bones only. Here we have 12 demonstrations of entire figures.

W. 19097a]　　　　　　　802

Quādo · tu · ài · finito di ²crescere l'omo · tu ³farai · la statua · cō tu⁴tte · sue misure · ⁵superfitiali.

When you have finished building up the man, you will make the statue with all its superficial measurements.

W. 19003b]　　　　　　　803

Farai tutti li moti dell' ossa ²colle giunture loro dopo ³la dimostratione delle pri⁴me tre figure dell' ossa, e ⁵questo si deve fare nel primo ⁶libro.

You must show all the motions of the bones with their joints to follow the demonstration of the first three figures of the bones, and this should be done in the first book. *Plans for the representation of muscles by drawings (803–9).*

W. 19017a]　　　　　　　804

Ricordoti che per farti certo del nascimento di qualunche muscolo, che tu tiri ²la corda, partorita da esso muscolo, in modo che tu veda

Remember that to be certain of the point of origin of any muscle, you must pull the sinew from which the muscle springs in such a way as

---

799. 2. le br e. 3. al br. 4. br alla. 5. nel br. porrai . . chessaperano. 6. cquesti. 7. musscoli. 9. musscoli . . chon . . chongunghano. 10. musscoli. 11. chelli notrisscano . . p "a" fatto. 12. ennerui.
800. effiniscila.
801. 1. homini. 2. chon. 4. ssenplici. 7. tiere.
802. 2. cressciere . . ettu. 3. lasstatua . chō.
803. 2. gunture. 3. dimosstratione. 4. ecq. 5. defare.
804. 1. nasscimēto . . chettu. 2. corta.

802. *Cresciere l'omo.* This expression can hardly mean anything else than modelling, since the sculptor forms the figure by degrees, by adding wet clay, and the figure consequently increases or grows. *Tu farai*

la statua would then mean: you must work out the figure in marble. Compare vol. i, p. 88.
804. A drawing of the muscles of the foot accompanies this passage. Reproduced by Bodmer, p. 344.

movere esso [3]muscolo e 'l suo nascimēto sopra delle · legature delli ossi.

to see that muscle move, and where it is attached to the ligaments of the bones.

NOTANDO

[5]Tu non farai mai se nō confusione nella di[6]mostratione de' muscoli e lor siti, nascimēti [7]e fini, se prima non fai vna dimostratione di [8]muscoli sottili a uso di fila di refe, e così potrai [9]figurare l'un · sopra dell' altro, come li a situati la [10]natura, e così li potrai nominare secōdo il mēbro [11]al quale lor seruono, cioè il motore della pū[12]ta del dito grosso e del suo osso di mezzo o del primo ecc; [13]e dato che tu ài tale notitia, figurerai allato a [14]questa · la uera forma e quātità e sito di ciascū muscolo; [15]ma ricordati di fare li fili, che insegniano li muscoli, neg[16]li medesimi siti che son le linie centrali di ciascū mu[17]scolo, e così tali fili dimostreranno la figura della ganba [18]e la loro distantia spedita e nota.

[19]Ho spogliato di pelle vno il quale per una mala[20]ttia s'era tanto diminuito che li muscoli erā [21]consumati e restati a uso di pellicola sottile, [22]in modo che le corde in scābio del conuertirsi [23]in muscolo si convertivano in larga pelle, [24]e quādo l'ossa erā uestite di pelle, poco acqui[25]stauā della lor naturale grossezza.

NOTE

You will never get anything but confusion in demonstrating the muscles and their positions, origin, and termination, unless you first make a demonstration of thin muscles after the manner of linen threads; and thus you can represent them, one over another as nature has placed them; and thus, too, you can name them according to the limb they serve; for instance, the motor of the tip of the great toe, of its middle bone, of its first bone, &c. And when you have the knowledge you will draw, by the side of this, the true form and size and position of each muscle. But remember to give the threads which explain the situation of the muscles in the position which corresponds to the central line of each muscle; and so these threads will demonstrate the form of the leg and their distance in a plain and clear manner.

I have removed the skin from a man who was so shrunk by illness that the muscles were worn down and remained in a state like thin membrane, in such a way that the sinews instead of merging in muscles ended in wide membrane; and where the bones were covered by the skin they had very little over their natural size.

W. 19059b]   805

Quale nervo è cagione del moto dell' ochio a fare · che 'l moto dell' un ochio tiri l'altro.

[2]¶ Del chiudere le ciglia, [3]dello alzare le ciglia, [4]dello abbassare le ciglia, ¶ [5]¶ dello chiudere li ochi, [6]dello aprire li ochi, ¶ [7]¶ dello alzare le narici, [8]del aprire le labra cō dēti · serrati,' [9]dello · appūtare · le labra, [10]del ridere, [11]del maravigliarsi.

[12]A discriuere il principio dell' omo quādo elli si cavsa · nella matrice, [13]e perchè uno putto nō uive · d'otto · mesi; [14]che cosa è starnvto, [15]che cosa è sbadiglio, [16]malmaestro, [17]spasimo, [18]paralitico, [19]tremito di freddo, [20]sudore, [21]stāchezza, [22]fame, [23]sonno, [24]sete, [25]lussuria.

[26]¶ Del neruo · ch'è cagione del moto della spalla al gomito, [27]del moto che è dal gomito alla mano, [28]dalla givntura · della · mano · al nascimēto de' diti, [29]dal nascimēto de' diti · al loro · mezzo [30]e dal mezzo all' ultimo nodo. ¶

[31]Del neruo che è cagione del moto della coscia, [32]e dal ginochio al piè, e dalla givntura del piè ai diti [33]e così ai lor mezzi, [34]e del girare d'essa ganba.

Which tendon causes the motion of the eye so that the motion of one eye moves the other?

Of frowning the brows, of raising the brows, of lowering the brows—of closing the eyes, of opening the eyes—of raising the nostrils, of opening the lips, with the teeth shut, of pouting with the lips, of smiling, of astonishment.

Describe the beginning of man when it is caused in the womb and why an eight months' child does not live. What sneezing is. What yawning is. Falling sickness, spasms, paralysis, shivering with cold, sweating, fatigue, hunger, sleepiness, thirst, lust.

Of the tendon which is the cause of movement from the shoulder to the elbow, of the movement from the elbow to the hand, from the joint of the hand to the springing of the fingers. From the springing of the fingers to the middle joints, and from the middle joints to the last.

Of the tendon which causes the movement of the thigh, and from the knee to the foot, and from the joint of the foot to the toes, and then to the middle of the toes, and of the rotary motion of the leg.

---

3. musscolo .. nasscimēto. 6. mosstratione .. musscoli ellor .. nasscimēti. 7. effini .. dimosstratione. 8. musscoli. 10. mēbr. 11. seruano coe .. motore [delluli]. 12. mezo. 13. chettu. 14. cquessta .. essito .. mussolo. 15. musscoli ne. 16. le medesimi .. chesson .. ciasscū. 17. dimosterā. 18. ella .. disstantia .. e note. 19. hosspogliato. 20. chelli musscoli. 21. cresstati. 22. chelle corde niscābio. 23. musscolo .. largha. 24. pocho. 25. grosseza.
805. 1. chagione .. affare. 7. anarise. 8. cho .. serati. 12. [facci] a desscrivere .. chausa. 13. ĺ putto. 14. chosa esstarnuto. 15. chosa essbaviglio. 16. malmaesstro. 18. parleticho. 19. frede. 21. stācheza. 26. chagione .. dalla. 28. nassimēto. 29. nassimēto .. mezo. 30. mezo. 31. chagione .. cosscia. 33. mezi.

F. 95*b*]   **806**

ANATOMIA

²Quali nerui over corde della mano sō ³quelle che accostano e discostano li ⁴diti della mano e de' piedi l'un dall' altro?

ANATOMY

Which nerves or sinews of the hand are those which close and part the fingers and toes laterally?

W. 19143*b*]   **807**

Scuopri a grado a grado tutte le parti dinanti dell' omo ²nel fare la tua notomia, e così insino in sull' osso; ³descritione de' mēbra della vita e lor trauagliamēti.

Remove by degrees all the parts of the front of a man in making your dissection, till you come to the bones. Description of the parts of the bust and of their motions.

K.³ 28*a*]   **808**

Fa la notomia della gā²ba insino al fiāco per ³tutti i versi e per tutti li ⁴atti e in tutte le spoglie, ⁵vene, arterie, nerui, ⁶corde e mvscoli, pel⁷le e ossa, e poi dell' ossa ⁸segate per uedere la gros⁹sezza dell' ossa.

Give the anatomy of the leg up to the hip, in all views and in every action and in every state; veins, arteries, nerves, sinews and muscles, skin and bones; then the bones in sections to show the thickness of the bones.

W. 19044*a*]   **809**

Farai regola e misura di ciascun muscolo, ²e renderai ragione di tutti li loro vfiti, e in che mo³do s'adoperano e che li muove ecc.

⁴Farai prima la spina del dosso, di poi va vestendo ⁵a gradi l'un sopra dell' altro di ciascū di questi musco⁶li, e poni li nervi all' arterie e vene a ciascun ⁷muscolo per sé, e oltre a di questo nota a quā⁸ti spondili si congiūgono, e che intestini sono ⁹loro a riscōtro e che ossi e altri strumēti orga¹⁰nici ecc.

¹¹Le parti più alte de' magri son più alte nelli mu¹²scolosi, e similmēte ne' grassi; Ma la differētia, che è ¹³dalla figura de' muscoli che ànno li grossi a rispetto ¹⁴delli muscolosi, sarà qui di sotto descritta.

Make the rule and give the measurement of each muscle, and give the reasons of all their functions, and in which way they work and what makes them work, &c.

[4] First draw the spine of the back; then clothe it by degrees, one after the other, with each of its muscles, and put in the nerves and arteries and veins to each muscle by itself; and besides these note the vertebrae to which they are attached; which of the intestines come in contact with them, and which bones and other organs, &c.

The most prominent parts of lean people are most prominent in the muscular, and equally so in fat persons. But concerning the difference in the forms of the muscles in fat persons as compared with muscular persons, it shall be described below. On corpulency and leanness (809–11).

W. 12625]   **810**

Descriui quali mu²scoli si perdono nello i³grossare, e nel dimagra⁴re quali muscoli si sco⁵prono.

⁶E nota che quel loco del⁷la superfitie del grasso ⁸che sarà più cōcauata, ⁹quādo si disgrassa fia ¹⁰più eleuato.

¹¹Doue li muscoli ¹²si separano l'ū dal¹³l' altro, farai p¹⁴roffili, e doue s'¹⁵appiccano insieme. . . .

Describe which muscles disappear in growing fat, and which become visible in growing lean.

And observe that that part which on the surface of a fat person is most concave, when he grows lean becomes more prominent.

Where the muscles separate from one another you must give profiles and where they coalesce . . . .

---

806. 1. anotamia. 3. quelle che achostano e disscostano.
807. 1. parte. 3. discretiō de mēbr . . vite ellor.
808. 1–9 R. 2. fiācho. 7. lle. 8. seghate . . gro.
809. 1. reghola . . ciasscū musscolo. 3. he chilli. 4. lasspina . . vavesstendo. 5. hagradi . . ciasscū di quessti. 6. ciasscū. 7. musscholo . . addi quessto . . acquā. 8. chongiūghano . . intesstini. 9. arrisscōtro . . orgha. 11. parte . . mus. 12. scholosi essimilmēte . . Malla diferētia. 13. musscoli che ali . . aris specto. 14. musscholosi . . disocto desscreta.
810. 2. perdano. 4. musscoli. 5. prano. 6. que lochi. 7. lla. 8. chessara. 9. dissgrassa. 11. musscoli. 15. apichano.

808. A straightened leg in profile is sketched by the side of this text.
809. The two drawings given on Pl. CVIII, No. 1, come between ll. 3 and 4. A good and very early copy of this drawing without the written text exists in the collection of drawings belonging to Christ Church, Oxford, where it is attributed to Leonardo.

W. 19142*a*] 811

DE FIGURA VMANA

[2]Qual parte è quella nell' omo che nel suo ingrassa[3]re mai cresce carne?

[4]Quale è quella parte che nel dimagrare dell' omo [5]mai nō dimagra con dimagratiō troppo sēsibile? [6]infra le parti che ingrassano qual' è quella che più [7]ingrassa?

[8]Infra le parti che dimagrano qual' è quella che si fa [9]più magra?

[10]Degli omini potēti in forze quali muscoli son di mag[11]giore grossezza e più eleuati?

[12]Tu ài a figurare nella tua anatomia tutti li gradi [13]delle mēbra dalla creatiō dell' omo insino alla sua [14]morte, e insino alla morte dell' osso, e qual parte d'esso [15]prima si cōsuma e qual più si cōserua.

[16]E similmente dall' ultima magrezza all' ultima grassezza.

OF THE HUMAN FIGURE

Which is the part in man which, as he grows fatter, never gains flesh?

Or which part which as a man grows lean never falls away with a too perceptible diminution? And among the parts which grow fat which is that which grows fattest?

Among those which grow lean which is that which grows leanest?

In very strong men, which are the muscles which are the thickest and most prominent?

In your anatomy you must represent all the stages of the limbs from man's creation to his death, and then till the death of the bone; and which part of him is first decayed and which is preserved the longest.

And in the same way of extreme leanness and extreme fatness.

S. K. M. III. 27*b*] 812

NOTOMIA

[2]I membri semplici · sono · vndici · cioè [3]cartilagine · ossi · nerui · vene, [4]arterie · pannicoli · legamēti e [5]corde, cotica e carne e grasso.

ANATOMY

There are eleven elementary tissues: cartilage, bones, nerves, veins, arteries, fascia, ligament and sinews, skin, muscle, and fat.

The divisions of the head (812–13).

DEL CAPO

[7]Le parti del uaso del capo · sono 10: cioè [8]5 · contenēti · e 5 · cōtenute; le contenēti [9]sono: capegli · cotica · carne [10]muscolosa · panniculo · grosso · e 'l [11]craneo · ‖ le contenvte son queste: du[12]ra madre · pia madre · cieruello | diso[13]tto ritorna la pia e dura madre che dentro [14]a sé rinchiudono il cieruello ·, poi la rete [15]mirabile · poi è l'osso, fondamēto del celabro [16]e donde · nascono li nerui.

OF THE HEAD

The divisions of the head are 10, viz. 5 external and 5 internal; the external are the hair, skin, muscle, fascia, and the skull; the internal are the dura mater, the pia mater, [which enclose] the brain. The pia mater and the dura mater come again underneath and enclose the brain; then the rete mirabile, and the occipital bone, which supports the brain from which the nerves spring.

S. K. M. III. 28*a*] 813

a capelli
n cotica
c carne musculosa
m pañiculo · grosso
[5]*o* craneo cioè osso
b dura madre
d pia · madre
f ciervello
[10]*r* · pia madre · di sotto
t · dura · madre
l · rete mirabile
s · osso fondamēto.

a. hair
n. skin
c. muscle
m. fascia
o. skull, i.e. bone
b. dura mater
d. pia mater
f. brain
r. pia mater, below
t. dura mater
l. rete mirabile
s. the occipital bone.

811. 3. cressce. 4. ecquella. 6. infralle parte. 8. infralle parte .. chessi. 10. musscoli .. di ma. 11. gore grosseza. 12. affigurare. 15. ecqual. 16. essimilmente .. magreza .. graseza.
812. 3. hossi. 4. pannichuli .. he. 5. codigahe. 8. he 5 cōtenute. 9. codiga. 10. musscolosa. 14. asse ringiugano. 15. ellosso. 16. nasscie.
813. 2. codiga. 6. [f cieruello].

813. See Pl. CVIII, No. 3.

W. 19018*b*]   814

Causa dell' alitare, [2]causa del moto del core, [3]causa del uomito, [4]causa del discēdere il [5]cibo dallo stomaco, [6]causa del votare li ī[7]testini;

[8]Causa del moto delle [9]superfluità per li inte[10]stini;
[11]Causa dello inghiottire, [12]causa dello tossire, [13]causa dello sbadigliare, [14]causa dello starnuto, [15]causa dell' adormētamē[16]to di diuerse mēbra;
[17]Causa del perdere il sēso [18]ad alcū mēbro; [19]Causa del solletico;
[20]Causa della lussuria e al[21]tre necessità del corpo, [22]causa dell' orinare, [23]e così di tutte le lotioni natu[24]rali del corpo.

Of the cause of breathing, of the cause of the motion of the heart, of the cause of vomiting, of the cause of the descent of food from the stomach, of the cause of emptying the intestines.
Of the cause of the movement of the super-fluous matter through the intestines.
Of the cause of swallowing, of the cause of coughing, of the cause of yawning, of the cause of sneezing, of the cause of limbs getting asleep.
Of the cause of losing sensibility in any limb.
Of the cause of tickling.
Of the cause of lust and other appetites of the body, of the cause of urine and also of all the natural excretions of the body.

Physio-logical problems (814–15).

W. 19088*a*]   815

Le lagrime [2]vengono dal [3]core e nō dal [4]ceruello.
[5]Difinisci tutte [6]le parti di che si cō[7]pone il corpo, co[8]minciādosi dalla [9]cute colla sua so-[10]praveste, la qual [11]è spesso spiccata [12]mediante il sole.

The tears come from the heart and not from the brain.
Define all the parts of which the body is com-posed, beginning with the skin with its outer cuticle which is often chapped by the influence of the sun.

---

814. 5. dello stomacho. 6. otare le ī. 7. testine. 9. super fruita. 10. stine. 11. delle ingiottire. 13. isbauiglare. 14. isstarnuto. 23. tutte lutioni.
815. 2. vengano. 5. difiniscitute. 6. parte. 8. mincādosi. 9. cutic. 10. pravessta. 11. spicha.

814. By the side of this text stands the pen-and-ink drawing reproduced on Pl. CVIII, No. 4, a skull with indications of the veins in the fleshy covering.

II

ZOOLOGY AND COMPARATIVE ANATOMY

W. 19030a] 816

The divisions of the animal kingdom (816–17).

Uomo | la descritione dell' omo, nella qual si contengono quelli che son qua²si di simile spetie come babbuino, scimmia e simili che sō molti.

³*Leone* | e suoi seguaci come pantieri, leonze, tigri, liopardi, lupi cervie⁴ri, gatti di Spagna, gannetti e gatti comvni e simili.

⁵*Cavallo* e sua seguaci come mulo, asino e simili che ànno dēti sopra e di sotto.

⁶*Toro* | e sua seguaci cornvti e sanza denti di sopra come bufolo, ceruio, daino ⁷capriolo, pecore, capre, stambecchi, mvcheri, camozze, giraffe.

Man. The description of man, which includes that of such creatures as are of almost the same species, as apes, monkeys, and the like, which are many.

The Lion and its kindred, as panthers, wildcats (?), tigers, leopards, lynxes, Spanish cats, common cats, and the like.

The Horse and its kindred, as mule, ass, and the like, with incisor teeth above and below.

The Bull and its allies with horns and without upper incisors, as the buffalo, stag, fallow deer, roebuck, sheep, goat, wild goats, musk-deers, chamois, giraffe.

W. 19054b] 817

Scrivi le varietà ²delli intestini de³lla spetie vma⁴na, scimie e si⁵mili; Di poi in ⁶che si uaria la spe⁷tie leonina, di ⁸poi la bovina, ⁹e vltimo li uccelli, ¹⁰e vsa tal descrit¹¹tione a uso di ¹²discorso.

Describe the various forms of the intestines of the human species, of apes and suchlike. Then, in what way the leonine species differ, and then the bovine, and finally birds; and arrange this description after the manner of a disquisition.

W. 19102a] 818

Miscellaneous notes on the study of Zoology (818–21).

Fa ti dare vna secōdina delli ²vitelli quādo nascono e nota ³la figura de' cotiledoni, se riser⁴vano li cotiledoni mas⁵chi o femminei.

Procure the placenta of a calf when it is born and observe the form of the cotyledons, if their cotyledons are male or female.

W. 19070] 819

Scrivi la lingua del picchio ²e la mascella del cocodrillo.

Describe the tongue of the woodpecker and the jaw of the crocodile.

G. 64b] 820

Volare della 4ª spetie ²di parpaglioni divo-³ratori delle formiche alate; ⁴delle tre principali situationi ⁵che fanno l'ali delli vccielli che discēdono.

Of the flight of the 4th kind of butterflies that consume winged ants. Of the three principal positions of the wings of birds in downward flight.

M. 67a] 821

Che modo fa la coda del pescie a sospin²giere il pescie innāzi, e così l'anguilla, ³biscia e mignatta.

Of the way in which the tail of a fish acts in propelling the fish; as in the eel, snake, and leech.

816. homo la . . contiene . . chesson. 2. essimili. 3. essua seguace . . tigre. 4. essimili. 5. chavallo . . [cervio] essimili cano. 6. essanza. 7. pechore . . stanbeche mvcheri.
817. 2. delli intestini. 4. essi. 7. elonina. 9. ucielli. 10. discrip.
818. 1. fatti. 2. nascano. 3. cotilidoni. 4. cotilidoni mass. 5. ci offeminine.
819. lingha . . pichio. 2. ella masscella.
820. 5. cheffa . . discēda.
821. 1. pesscie assosspī. 2. pesscio . . languila. 3. bisscia e migmatta.

816. 3. *Leonza*—wild cat? 'Secondo alcuni, lo stesso che Leonessa; e secondo altri con più certezza, lo stesso che Pantèra.' Fanfani, *Vocabolario*, p. 858.
820. 4. Compare the observations on this subject

in the introduction to section XVIII.
821. A sketch of a fish swimming upwards is in the original inserted above this text.—Compare No. 1114.

W. 19061a]   822

DELLA MANO DI DENTRO

[2]Farai poi vn discor[3]so delle mani di ciascu[4]n animale per mostrare [5]in che si uariano, come nell' orso che [6]agiugne la legatura de[7]lle corde de' diti del piè [8]sopra il collo d'esso piè.

OF THE PALM OF THE HAND

Then I will discourse of the hands of each animal to show in what they vary; as in the bear, which has the ligatures of the sinews of the toes joined above the instep.

Compara-tive study of the structure of bones and of the action of muscles (822–6).

W. 12631a]   823

Dimostratione secõda [2]interposta infra l'ana-to[3]mia e 'l uiuo.
[4]Figurerai a questo p[5]aragone le gambe de' ra[6]nocchi, le quali ànno gran [7]similitudine colle ganbe [8]dell' omo si nell' ossa come [9]ne' suoi muscoli; di poi [10]seguirai le gãbe dirieto [11]della lepre, le quali son [12]molto muscolose e di [13]muscoli spediti, perchè nõ [14]sono inpedite da grasse[15]zza.

A second demonstration inserted between anatomy and (the treatise on) the living being.
You will represent here for a comparison the legs of a frog, which have a great resemblance to the legs of man, both in the bones and in the muscles. Then, in continuation, the hind legs of the hare, which are very muscular, with strong active muscles, because they are not encumbered with fat.

K.³ 109b]   824

Qui fo ricordo [2]di dimostrare la dif[3]ferentia ch'è dall' o[4]mo al cauallo, e simil[5]mente delli altri ani[6]mali; e prima [7]comincerò all' ossa, e proseguirò [8]tutti li muscoli che sanza corde na[9]scono e finiscono nelle ossa, [10]e poi di quelli che cõ corda na[11]scono e finiscono nell' ossa, e poi di quelle [12]che con una sola corda da v̄ canto.

Here I make a note to demonstrate the differ-ence there is between man and the horse, and in the same way with other animals. And first I will begin with the bones, and then will go on to all the muscles which spring from the bones without tendons and end in the bones, and then to those which begin and end in the bone with a tendon, and then go on to those which start with a single tendon at one end.

E. 16a]   825

Nota delle piegatu[2]re delle giũtu[3]re, e in che mo[4]do cresce la [5]carne sopra di [6]loro nelli [7]lor piegamē[8]ti e stendimē[9]ti; e di questa [10]īportãtis-sima [11]notitia fa uno [12]particulare [13]trattato | nel[14]la descritione [15]de' movimēti [16]delli animali [17]di quattro pi[18]edi, infra li [19]quali è l'omo [20]che ācora lui [21]nella infãtia [22]va cõ 4 piedi.

Note on the bendings of joints and in what way the flesh grows upon them in their flexions or extensions; and of this most important study write a separate treatise: in the description of the movements of animals with four feet; among which is man, who likewise in his infancy crawls on all fours.

C. A. 297a]   826

DELLO · ANDARE DELL' OMO

[2]L'andare dell' omo · è sempre a uso dell' uni-versale andare delli animali di 4 piedi, im-perochè siccome essi [3]movono · i loro · piedi in croce a vso del trotto del cauallo, così l'omo in croce si move le sue 4 · mēbra, cioè [4]se caccia · īnãti il piè destro per caminare, egli caccia inãzi cõ quello il braccio · sinistro, e sempre così seguita.

OF THE WAY OF WALKING IN MAN

The walking of man is always after the uni-versal manner of walking in animals with 4 legs, inasmuch as just as they move their feet cross-wise after the manner of a horse in trotting, so man moves his 4 limbs crosswise; that is, if he puts forward his right foot in walking he puts forward with it his left arm, and vice versa, in-variably.

822. 6. agugne la lecatura.
823. 4. acquessto. 6. nochi. 8. com"e". 9. musscoli. 12. molte.
824. 2. la di. 4. essimil. 6. e p"a". 7. epposseguiro. 8. musscoli. 9. scano effiniscano. 10. eppoi. 11. scano effinisscano . . he poi. 12. [q] che.
825. 1. "nota" delle pieghatu. 4. cressca. 5. charne. 7. pieghamē. 8. esstendimē. 9. quessta. 12. partichulare. 13. tractato. 14. lla desscritione. 18. infralli. 19. ellomo. 20. āchora.
826. 2. essenpre . . inperochessichome. 3. movano illoro . . chauallo . chosi. 4. chaccia . . desstro . . chaminare . . chaccia . . chõ . . sinisstro essepr.

823. This text is written by the side of a drawing in black chalk of a nude male figure, reproduced in Sir K. Clark's Catalogue.
824. See Pl. CVIII, No. 2.

Comparative study of the organs of sense in men and animals.

Ho trovato nella compositione del corpo vmano che, come in tutte ²le compositioni delli animali, esso è di piv ottusi e grossi sentimēti; ³così è composto di strumēto manco ingegnoso e di lochi māco ⁴capaci a ricevere la uirtù de' sensi; ò veduto nella spetie leoni⁵na il senso dell' odorato auere parte della sustantia del celabro, e discē⁶dere le narici, capace ricettaculo contro al senso dello odorato, ⁷il quale entra infra grā nvmero di saccoli cartilaginosi con assai ⁸vie contro all' avenimento del predetto celabro.

⁹Li ochi della spetie leonina ànno gran parte della lor testa per lor ¹⁰ricettacolo, e li nerui ottici immediate congiugonsi col celabro; il che al¹¹li omini si uede in contrario, perchè le casse delli ochi sono vna picco¹²la parte del capo, e li nerui ottici sono sottili e lunghi e deboli, e per debo¹³le operatione si uede di loro il dì, e peggio la notte, e li predetti animali ¹⁴vedono (più) in nella notte che 'l giorno; ¹⁵e 'l segno se ne vede, perchè predano di notte ¹⁶e dormono il giorno come fāno ancora li uccelli notturni.

I have found that in the composition of the human body as compared with the bodies of animals the organs of sense are duller and coarser. Thus it is composed of less ingenious instruments, and of spaces less capacious for receiving the faculties of sense. I have seen in the Lion tribe that the sense of smell is connected with part of the substance of the brain which comes down the nostrils, which form a spacious receptacle for the sense of smell, which enters by a great number of cartilaginous vesicles with several passages leading up to where the brain, as before said, comes down.

The eyes in the Lion tribe have a large part of the head for their sockets and the optic nerves communicate at once with the brain; but the contrary is to be seen in man, for the sockets of the eyes are but a small part of the head, and the optic nerves are very fine and long and weak, and by the weakness of their action we see by day, but badly at night, while these animals can see as well at night as by day. The proof that they can see is that they prowl for prey at night and sleep by day, as nocturnal birds do also.

Advantages in the structure of the eye in certain animals (828–31).

¶Tutte · le cose vedute parrāno ²maggiori · di mezza notte, che · di ³mezzo · dì · e maggiori di mattina che ⁴di mezzodì.¶

⁵Questo · accade · perchè · la pupilla ⁶dell' ochio · è minore · assai di mezzo ⁷dì · che di nessuno · altro tenpo.

⁸Tanto · quāto · è · maggiore · l'ochio ⁹over · pupilla del gufo a proportione ¹⁰dello · animale, che non è · quella · dell' o¹¹mo ·, tanto piv · lume vede di notte che ¹²nō · fa · l'omo; ōde di mezzo · dì nō vede ni¹³ente ·, se lui nō · diminuisce · sua · pupil¹⁴la ·, e similmēte · vede di notte le cose mag¹⁵giori · che di dì.

Every object we see will appear larger at midnight than at midday, and larger in the morning than at midday.

This happens because the pupil of the eye is much smaller at midday than at any other time.

In proportion as the eye or the pupil of the owl is larger in proportion to the animal than that of man, so much the more light can it see at night than man can; hence at midday it can see nothing if its pupil does not diminish; and, in the same way, at night things look larger to it than by day.

DELLI OCHI DELLI ANIMALI

²Li ochi di tutti li animali āno le ³lor popille, le quali per loro medesime cres⁴cono e diminuiscono secōdo il mag⁵giore e minore lume del

OF THE EYES IN ANIMALS

The eyes of all animals have their pupils adapted to dilate and diminish of their own accord in proportion to the greater or less light

---

827. 1. ottrovato .. conpositone .. chome. 3. chosi e conpossto .. mancho .. mancho. 4. chapaci. 5. nel senso .. susstantia del celabro discē. 6. ricettachulo. 7. sachuli chartilaginosi. 9. testta. 10. ricettachulo elli .. ottitti .. congugnersi. 11. lli .. chasse .. picho. 12. elli .. ellunghi. 13. eppeggo .. elli. 14. vegan inela .. gorno. 16. dormano il gorno .. fano .. uccelli.
828. 1. tucte . le chose. 2. magiori .. meza. 3. mezo .. magiori. 4. mezo. 5. acchade. 6. mezo. 8. he magiore. 11. nocte. 12. mezo. 13. diminuisscie .. popi. 14. essimilmēte .. ma. 15. magiore.
829. 1. dell[o]i ochi[o]i. 3. popille le quali pe lor. 4. scano e diminvisschano .. il ma. 5. ēminore.

829. Compare No. 24, ll. 8 ff.

sole o altro [6]chiarore; Ma nelli uccelli fa maggio[7]re differētia, e massima nelli nottur[8]ni, come
gufi, barbagianni, e allochi [9]che son di spetie
di civetta; a questi cresce [10]la popilla in modo
che quasi occupa tut[11]to l'ochio, e diminuisce
insino alla grā[12]dezza d'ū grā di miglio e sempre
osser[13]va figura circulare; Ma la spe[14]tie leonina
come pātere, pardi, [15]leōze, tigri, lupi,
cervieri, gatti di Spa[16]gnia e altri simili
diminuiscono [17]la lucie dal perfetto circulo [18]alla figura biāgolare, cioè questa
[19]è come si dimostra in margine; Ma
l'uomo [20]per avere più debole vista che
nessuno altro a[21]nimale, meno è offeso
dalla superchia luce, [22]e mē s'avmēta nelli
lochi tenebrosi; ma [23]alli ochi delli detti animali
notturni,—al [24]gufo vcciello cornuto, il quale è
'l [25]massimo nella spetie delli vccelli nottur[26]ni:
a questo s'aumēta tanto la uirtù vi[27]siva, che nel
minimo lume notturno (il [28]quale da noi dimā-
dasi tenebre) vede assai cō [29]più vigore che noi
nello splendore del [30]mezzo giorno, nel quale
tali vccielli stā [31]nascosti in lochi tenebrosi; e se
pur [32]sō costretti u[33]scire all' a[34]ria allumina[35]ta
dal sole, elli [36]diminuiscono [37]tāto la lor po-
[38]pilla che la po[39]tentia visiua [40]diminuisce
[41]insieme colla [42]quātità di tale [43]lucie.

[44]Fa notomia [45]di vari ochi, [46]e vedi quali
[47]sō li muscoli [48]ch'aprono e [49]serrano le pre-
[50]dette popille [51]delli ochi del[52]li animali.

of the sun or other luminary. But in birds the
variation is much greater; and particularly in
nocturnal birds, such as horned owls, and in the
eyes of one species of owl; in these the pupil
dilates in such a way as to occupy nearly the
whole eye, or diminishes to the size of a grain of
millet, and always preserves the circular form.
But in the Lion tribe, as panthers, pards,
ounces, tigers, wolves, lynxes, Spanish cats,
and other similar animals, the pupil diminishes from the perfect circle to the figure of
a pointed oval such as is shown in the margin. But man having a weaker sight than
any other animal is less hurt by a very
strong light and his pupil increases but
little in dark places; but in the eyes of these
nocturnal animals, the horned owl—a bird which
is the largest of all nocturnal birds—the power
of vision increases so much that in the faintest
nocturnal light (which we call darkness) it sees
with much more distinctness than we do in the
splendour of noonday, at which time these birds
remain hidden in dark holes; or if indeed they
are compelled to come out into the open air
lighted up by the sun, they contract their pupils
so much that their power of sight diminishes
together with the quantity of light admitted.

Study the anatomy of various eyes and see
which are the muscles which open and close the
said pupils of the eyes of animals.

Br. M. 64b]   830

a b n è il coperchio di sotto che chiude [2]l'ochio
di sotto in sù con coperchio oppaco, [3]c n b
chiude l'ochio dinanzi īdirieto [4]con coperchio
transparēte.

[5]Chiudesi sotto in sù [6]perchè da alto
disciē[7]de.

[8]Quando l'ochio delli uccelli si chiude
[9]colle sue due copriture, esso chiu[10]de
prima la secondina la qual [11]chiude dal
lagrimatoio alla co[12]da d'esso ochio, e la
prima si chi[13]vde da basso in alto, e
que[14]sti due moti intersegati occupano
[15]in prima dal lacrimatoio, perchè già han
veduto che [16]dinanzi e di sotto si sono assicurati,
e sol serba[17]no la parte di sopra per li pericoli
delli uccelli ra[18]paci che discendono di sopra
e dirieto; e sco[19]prano prima il pannicolo di
verso la coda, [20]perchè se 'l nemico viene
dirieto, egli à la como[21]dità del fugire innāzi; E
ancora tiene [22]il pannicolo detto secondino che
è traspa[23]rente, perchè se non avesse tale scudo,
e' nō [24]potrebbe tener li ochi aperti cōtro al

a b n is the membrane which closes the eye
from below, upwards, with an opaque film; c n b
encloses the eye in front and behind with a transparent membrane.

It closes from below, upwards, because it [the eye] comes downwards.

When the eye of a bird closes with its
two lids, the first to close is the nictitating membrane which closes from the
lacrymal duct over to the outer corner
of the eye; and the outer lid closes from
below upwards, and these two intersect-
ing motions begin first from the lacrymatory
duct, because they have already seen that in front
and below they are protected and use only the
upper portion of the eye from fear of birds of
prey which come down from above and behind;
and they uncover first the membrane from the
outer corner, because if the enemy comes from
behind, they have the power of escaping in front;
and they still keep the muscle called the nictitating
membrane which is transparent, because if the eye

---

6. vcielli. 7. diferētia emassime neli. 8. ghufi. 9. chesson . . quessti cresscie. 10. ochupa. 11. diminuissce. 12. essenpre. 13. fighura circulare. M lla. 14. chome. 16. diminuiscano. 17. circhulo. 18. fighura biāghola . . quessta. 19. chome si dimosstra . .
Mallom"o". 20. vissta. 21. luci"e". 23. notturniel. 24. ghufo . . chornuto. 25. vcielli. 26. acquessto. 28. quale noc dimā-
dano . . ve assai chō. 29. vighore. 31. nasscosti inochi . . esseppur. 32. cosstretti vs. 33. allalla. 36. diminuiscā. 38. chella.
40. diminuissie. 41. cholla. 47. musscoli. 48. aprano es.
830. 2. socto . . oppacho. 4. chon choperchio transsparēte. 7. da. 8. vcielli. 9. cholle . . chopriture. 12. ella. 13. di basso . .
ecque. 14. intersegha tiochupano. 15. dalacrimatoio . . giaā ueduto. 16. assichurati. 17. pericholi. 18. dissciendono . . dirieto
essco. 19. panitolo . . choda. 20. nemicho . . diriecto. 22. trāsspa. 23. auessi.

²⁵vĕto che percuote l'ochio nel furo²⁶re del suo velocie volare; E la sua ²⁷popilla crescie e discrescie nel uedere ²⁸minore o maggiore lume cioè splēdore.

had not such a screen, they could not keep it open against the wind which strikes against the eye in the rush of their rapid flight. And the pupil of the eye dilates and contracts as it sees less or more light, that is to say, intense brilliancy.

H.³ *109a*]   831

¶ L'ochio che di notte s'interporrà infra 'l lume e l'ochio ²della gatta, vedrà esso ochio parere di foco. ¶

If at night your eye is placed between the light and the eye of a cat, it will see the eye look like fire.

W. *19115a*]   832

Remarks on the organs of speech (832–3).

La lingua è trouata auere 24 muscoli li quali rispondono alli sei muscoli di che è ²conposta la quātità della lingua che si move per la bocca. . . .

³E quando *a o v* si pronūtiano con ⁴intelligibile e spedita pronūtia, egli è ⁵necessario che nella continua lor ⁶pronūtiatione sanza intermissiō di tēpo, che ⁷l'apritura de' labri si uadi al cōtinuo restri⁸gnendo, cioè larghi sarāno nel dire *a*, pi⁹ù stretti nel dire *o*, e assai piv stretti nel pr¹⁰onuntiare *v*.

¹¹Prouasi come tutte le uo¹²cali son pronūtiate colla ¹³parte ultima del pala¹⁴to mobile, il quale copre l'e¹⁵piglotta. . . .

a	*e*	*i*	*o*	*u*
ba	*be*	*bi*	*bo*	*bu*
ca	*cẹ*	*ci*	*co*	*cu*
dạ	*dẹ*	*dị*	*dọ*	*du*
fạ	*fẹ*	*fị*	*fọ*	*fu*
gạ	*ge*	*gị*	*gọ*	*gu*
lạ	*lẹ*	*lị*	*lọ*	*lu*
mạ	*mẹ*	*mị*	*mọ*	*mu*
nạ	*nẹ*	*ni*	*nọ*	*nu*
pạ	*pe*	*pị*	*pọ*	*pu*
qạ	*qẹ*	*qị*	*qọ*	*qu*
ra	*re*	*ri*	*ro*	*ru*
sạ	*sẹ*	*sị*	*sọ*	*su*
tạ	*tẹ*	*tị*	*tọ*	*tụ*

The tongue is found to have 24 muscles which correspond to the six muscles which compose the portion of the tongue which moves in the mouth.

And when *a o u* are spoken with a clear and rapid pronunciation, it is necessary, in order to pronounce continuously, without any pause between, that the opening of the lips should close by degrees; that is, they are wide apart in saying *a*, closer in saying *o*, and much closer still to pronounce *u*.

It may be shown how all the vowels are pronounced with the farthest portion of the false palate which is above the epiglottis. . . .

Anchora descriverai e fighurerai in che modo l'ufitio del variare e modulare e artichulare la vocie nel chantare è semplice ufitio delli anuli della trachea mossi dalli nervi reversivi e in questo chaso la lingua¹ in alchuna parte non si adopera; E questo resta provato nel avere io prima provato che le channe dell' orghano non si fanno più grave o più achute per la mutatione della fistola (cioè quel locho dove si gienera la vocie) nel farla più largha o più stretta, ma sol per la mutatione della channa in largha o stretta, o in lungha o chorta, chome si vede nell' astenzione o ratractione della tromba torta, e anchora nella channa immobile di larghezza o lunghezza si varia la vocie nel darle il vento chō maggiore o minore inpeto, e questa tal variatione non è nelle cose perchosse cō maggiore o minore percussione, chome si sente nelle campane battute da minimi o massimi perchussori, e il medesimo achade nell' arte le (?) rie simile in larghezza e varie in lunghezza; ma qui la più chorta fa maggiore e più grave strepito che la più lungha, e in questo più nō mi asstendero . . . .

Furthermore you shall describe and figure in what manner the variation, modulation, and articulation of the voice in singing is the simple work of the rings of the trachea moved by the turning of tendons, and in this case the tongue is [1] used in no way.

And this is proved by what I have shown before, that the tone of organ pipes is not made deeper or higher through the mutation of the fistula (i.e. that place where the voice is generated) making it wider or narrower; but only through changing the pipe into a large or narrow one, or into a long or short one, as is done in extending or retracting the trombone; also in the pipe, which is fixed as regards width or length, the voice is varied by introducing air into it with more or less impetus, and such variation is not attainable in things which are struck with greater or smaller percussion, as in bells struck with a very small or a very big hammer, and the same is the case in the . . . (?), similar in width and different in length. But here the shorter one makes a greater and deeper noise than the longer one—and on this I shall not expatiate[2]. . . .

25. perchuote. 26. Ella. 27. cresscie e disscresscie. 28. magiore.
831. 1. ellochio. 2. vedera . . focho.
832. 1. musscole . . risspondano . . musscoli . . boccha. 2. linghua chessi . . perbocha. 4. Essecquando . . cho. 4. esspedita. 7. dellabri . . resstri. 8. coe. 12. chali. 13. lla. 15. piglotto.

832. 1. On the same sheet is a drawing of a human tongue and remarks on the muscles of the tongue and vocal letters.
2. Here follows the passage given under No. 7 B.

Adoperasi la lingua nella pronuntiatione e articulatione delle silabe chomponitrici di tutti i vochaboli. . . .

The tongue is used in the pronunciation and articulation of the syllables, components of all words. . . .

W. 19002a]　　　833

Se tirerai il fiato pel na²so e lo vorrai mādar fori ³per la bocca, tu sentirai il sono ⁴che fa il tramezzo cioè il ⁵pānicolo in . . . .

If you draw in breath by the nose and send it out by the mouth you will hear the sound made by the division, that is the membrane, in [5] . . . .

C. A. 90a]　　　834

DELLA NATURA DEL UEDERE

²Dico · jl uedere · essere operato da tutti li animali · mediāte · la luce; e se alcuno cōtra questo ³allegherà · jl uedere · delli · animali notturni, dirò · questo · medesimamēte essere · sottoposto · a simile · natura; jpero⁴chè · chiaro · si cōprēde ·, j sensi · ricievēdo · le similitudini delle cose · nō mādano · fori di loro alcuna virtù; ⁵anzi mediāte l'aria, che si trova īfra l'obietto e 'l sēso ·, jncorpora · j sé le spetie delle · cose ·, e per lo cōttato, ⁶che à · col sēso, le porgie a quello; Se li obietti o per sono · o per odore mādano le potētie spirituali all' orechio ⁷o al naso ·, qui nōn è neciessario nè si adopera la luce ·; le forme delli obietti non ētrano per similitudine jfra l'aria ⁸se quelli · nō sono · lvminosi ·; essēdo così l'ochio nō la può ricievere da quell' aria che nō l'à e che tocca la sua super-fitie; ⁹Se tu volessi dire di molti animali · j quali predano di notte ·, dico che quando in questi manca la poca luce ¹⁰che basta · alla natura · de' loro · ochi ·, che questi s'aivtano colla · potētia dello · udito · e dello odorato, ¹¹i quali nō sono · īpediti · dalle tenebre ·, e de' quali avāzano di grā lūga · l'omo ·; Se porrai mēte · a una gatta ¹²di giorno · saltare · īfra molte vasellamēti ·, vedrai · quelli rimanere salui, e se farai questo medesimo ¹³di notte, ronperā ne · assai ·; li vccelli notturni · nō volano ·, se nō lucie · tutta o ī parte la luna, āzi si pasco¹⁴no jfra il coricare · del sole · e la · ītera oscurità della notte.

¹⁵Nessuno corpo · si può · cōprendere sāza lume e ōbra; lume e ōbra sono causate dalla luce.

OF THE NATURE OF SIGHT

I say that sight is exercised by all animals, by the medium of light; and if any one adduces, against this, the sight of nocturnal animals, I must say that this in the same way is subject to the very same natural laws. For it will easily be understood that the senses which receive the images of things do not project from themselves any visual virtue [4]. On the contrary, the atmo-spheric medium which exists between the object and the sense incorporates in itself the figure of things, and by its contact with the sense trans-mits the object to it. If the object—whether by sound or by odour—presents its spiritual force to the ear or the nose, then light is not required and does not act. The forms of objects do not send their images into the air if they are not illu-minated [8]; and the eye being thus constituted cannot receive that from the air which the air does not possess, although it touches its surface. If you choose to say that there are many animals that prey at night, I answer that when the little light which suffices the nature of their eyes is wanting, they direct themselves by their strong sense of hearing and of smell, which are not im-peded by the darkness, and in which they are far superior to man. If you make a cat leap, by daylight, among a quantity of jars and crocks, you will see them remain unbroken, but if you do the same at night, many will be broken. Night birds do not fly about unless the moon shines full or in part; rather do they feed be-tween sunset and the total darkness of the night.

On the con-ditions of sight (834-5).

No body can be apprehended without light and shade, and light and shade are caused by light.

G. 90a]　　　835

PERCHÈ NELLI OMINI ATTĒPATI ²IL UEDERE È MEGLIO DISCOSTO

³Il uedere è meglio discosto che da pres⁴so in quelli omini, li quali s'attēpano, ⁵perchè vna

WHY MEN ADVANCED IN AGE SEE BETTER AT A DISTANCE

Sight is better from a distance than near in those men who are advancing in age, because

833. 1. settirarai. 2. ello. 3. bocha tusscutirai. 4. cheffa il tramazzo. 5. pānicholo.
834. 2. operato [mediāte la lu] dattutti . . esse. 3. alegera . . sotto . posti . assimile. 4. cōplēde . . similitudine . . alchuna. 5. ānti . . chessi . . jnchorpora . . chōtatto. 6. chol . . acquelo . . per [romore] "sono" per . . māda . per la. 7. nessi . . lalluce. 8. nolla po. . . dacquell aria "ce nola e" che tocha. 9. che qua|"do" ī . . mancha la pocha. 10. allantatura . . chola . . delo . a[v]uldito. 11. porai mēte · ī̇ · gatta. 12. vedera . . esse. 13. vcielli . . pascā. 14. corichare . . ella. 15. po . chōplēdere . . e chausata.
835. 2. disscosto. 3. disscossto. 5. chosa.

833. 5. Here the text breaks off.　　　834. 4. Compare No. 68. 8. See Nos. 58–67.

medesima cosa ⁶māda di sé minore inpressione nell' oc⁷chio, essendo remota che quādo li è vi⁸cina.

the same object transmits a smaller impression of itself to the eye when it is distant than when it is near.

C. A. 90a]   836

The seat of the Common Sense.

Il sēso comūne è quello · che givdica · le cose · a · lui · date dalli altri sensi; ²Li antichi · speculatori · āno · cōcluso · che quella · parte del giuditio · che è data all' omo, sia causata ³da vno · strumēto ·, al quale referiscono · li altri · 5 · mediāte la īpressiva, e a detto · strumēto · āno posto nome sēso · comvne, ⁴e dicono questo sēso · essere situato · in mezzo · il capo jfra la īpressiva · e la memoria; E questo nome di sēso ⁵comvne dicono solamēte ·, perchè è comvne · judice · delli altri · 5 sēsi, cioè vedere · udire · toccare · gustare e odorare; ⁶Il senso · comvne · si move mediāte la īpressiva ch'è posta · ī mezzo jfra lui e i sēsi; la inpressiua si move ⁷mediāte le similitudini delle cose · a lei date · dalli strumēti · superfitiali cioè sēsi, i quali sono posti ī mezzo ⁸jfra le cose esteriori e la īpressiva ·, e similmēte i sēsi si movono mediāte li obietti; ⁹le · circōstanti · cose · mādano le loro · similitudini · ai sēsi; e i sensi le trāsferiscono alla īpressiva; ¹⁰la īpressiva le māda al sēso comvne ·, e da quello · sono stabilite nella memoria ·, e lì · sono · piv · o meno ¹¹retenute · secōdo la īportātia o potētia della · cosa · data ·; Quello · senso · è piv veloce nel suo ¹²ofitio, jl quale · è piv · uicino · alla · impressiva ·, è l'ochio · superiore · e prīcipe · delli altri ·, ¹³del quale · solo · tratteremo e li altri lascieremo · per nō ci · allūgare · dalla nostra · materia ·; Dice la speriēza ¹⁴che l'ochio · s'astēde · j · 10 · varie nature · d'obietti · cioè · luce · e tenebre, · l'una · cagione dell' altre 9 ·, e l'altra · privatione: ¹⁵colore · e corpo · figura · e sito · remotione · e propīquità · moto e quiete.

The Common Sense is that which judges of things offered to it by the other senses. The ancient speculators have concluded that that part of man which constitutes his judgement is caused by a central organ to which the other five senses refer everything by means of sensation; and to this centre they have given the name Common Sense. And they say that this Sense is situated in the centre of the head between Sensation and Memory. And this name of Common Sense is given to it solely because it is the common judge of all the other five senses, i.e. Seeing, Hearing, Touch, Taste, and Smell. This Common Sense is acted upon by means of Sensation, which is placed as a medium between it and the senses. Sensation is acted upon by means of the images of things presented to it by the external instruments, that is to say, the senses which are the medium between external things and Sensation. In the same way the senses are acted upon by objects. Surrounding things transmit their images to the senses and the senses transfer them to the Sensation. Sensation sends them to the Common Sense, and by it they are stamped upon the memory and are there more or less retained according to the importance or potency of the given thing. That sense is most rapid in its function which is nearest to the sensitive medium, and the eye is the highest, and the chief of the others. Of this then only we will speak, and the others we will leave in order not to make our matter too long. Experience tells us that the eye apprehends ten different natures of things, that is: light and darkness, one being the cause of the perception of the nine others, and the other its absence, colour and substance, form and place, distance and nearness, motion and stillness [15].

W. 19115a]   837

On the origin of the soul.

Ancorachè lo ingiegnio ²vmano faccia īuētioni va³rie, rispōdēdo cō uari ⁴strumēti a ū medesimo ⁵fine, mai esso trove⁶rà inuentione più ⁷bella, nè più facile, nè ⁸più brieue della natu⁹ra, perchè nelle sue in¹⁰venzioni nullo mā¹¹ca e nullo è superflu¹²o, e non va cō contra¹³pesi, quādo essa fa le ¹⁴mēbra atti al moto nel¹⁵li corpi delli animali; ¹⁶Ma ui mette dentro l'a¹⁷nima d'esso

Though human ingenuity may make various inventions which, by the help of various machines, answer the same end, it will never devise any invention more beautiful, nor more simple, nor more to the purpose than Nature does; because in her inventions nothing is wanting and nothing is superfluous, and she needs no counterpoise when she makes limbs proper

836. 1. givdicha . le chose allui . . dali. 2. [j nosstri] li antich[e]i spechulatori . . choncluso checquella . . guditio . . chausata. 3. referischano . . 5. "mediāte la iprēsine" e a . . ano. 4. e dichano . . essere [situato] imezo [il chapo j fralla īpresiua ella . .] Ecquesto. 5. dicano . . chomvne . . deli . . vldire tochare. 6. iprēsiua . . imezo . . inprēsiua. 7. similitudine . . chose . . dali . . sēsiggugali . . mezo. 8. Infralle . . isteriori ella īpressiua essimilemēte . . movano . . obietti le similitudine. 9. delle circhūstanti chose . . similitudine a sēsie sensi . . trāsferischano . . iprēsiua. 10. īprēsiua la . . dacquello . . elli. 11. sechōdo. 12. uisino . ala inprēsiua . . deli. 13. tratereno e laltri lasciereno . . dala. 14. chagne . . ellaltra. 15. chorpo . . essito . . ecquiete.
837. 1. chello. 2. vmano inīuētioni. 5. trover. 11. cha e nulla. 13. fa il. 14. mēbr. 18. coe.

836. 2. See vol. i, p. 24.   15. Compare No. 23 and vol. i, p. 24 sq.

corpo cōpo¹⁸nitore, cioè l'anima del¹⁹la madre che prima ²⁰conpone nella ma²¹trice la figura dell' o²²mo; e al tenpo debito ²³desta l'anima, che di quel ²⁴deve essere abitatore, ²⁵la qual prima restau²⁶a dormētata e in tutela ²⁷del-l'anima della madre, ²⁸la quale la nutrisce e vivifi²⁹ca per la vena ombelica³⁰le, con tutti li sua mē³¹bri spirituali, e così segu³²ita insino che tale ombe³³lico lì è giunto colla se³⁴condina e li cotilido³⁵ni per la quale il figlio³⁶lo si unisce colla madre; ³⁷e questi son causa che v³⁸na volontà, vn sommo desi³⁹derio, vna paura che ⁴⁰abbia la madre, o altro ⁴¹dolor mētale à potēti⁴²a più nel figliolo che nel⁴³la madre, perchè spesse sono ⁴⁴le volte, che il figlio ne per⁴⁵de la vita ecc.

⁴⁶Questo discor⁴⁷so nō ua qui, ⁴⁸ma si r⁴⁹i-chiede ⁵⁰nella cō⁵¹positiō ⁵²delli cor⁵³pi ani-ma⁵⁴ti; E il resto della difinitione dell' anima lascio nel⁵⁵le mēti de' frati, padri de' popoli, li quali per inspira⁵⁶tione sanno tutti li segreti.

⁵⁷Lascio star le lettere incoronate, perchè sō sōma verità.

for motion in the bodies of animals. But she puts into them the soul of the body which forms them, that is, the soul of the mother which first constructs in the womb the form of the man and in due time awakens the soul that is to inhabit it. And this at first lies dormant and under the tutelage of the soul of the mother, who nourishes and vivifies it by the umbilical vein, with all its spiritual parts, and this happens because this umbilicus is joined to the placenta and the cotyledons by which the child is attached to the mother. And these are the reasons why a wish, a strong craving, or a fright or any other mental suffering in the mother has more influence on the child than on the mother; for there are many cases when the child loses its life from them, &c.

This discourse is not in its place here, but will be wanted for the one on the composition of animated bodies—and the rest of the definition of the soul I leave to the imaginations of friars, those fathers of the people who know all secrets by inspiration.

[57] I leave alone the sacred books; for they are supreme truth.

W. 19019a]   838

COME · I · 5 SENSI · SONO · OFITIALI · DELL' ANIMA

HOW THE FIVE SENSES ARE THE MINISTERS OF THE SOUL

²L'anima · pare · risedere · nella parte judi-tiale, · e la · parte · juditiale pare essere ³nel loco · doue · concorrono · tutti i sēsi ·, il quale è detto · senso comvne, e non è tutta ⁴per tutto · il corpo ·, come molti · àno · creduto ·, anzi · tutta in nella · parte ·, imperochè se ella [sc. anima] ⁵fusse · tutta per tutto · e tutta · in ogni · parte ·, non era · necessario · li stru⁶mēti · de' sensi fare infra loro · uno · medesimo cōcorso a uno · solo loco ·, anzi · basta⁷va · che l'ochio operasse · l'ufitio · del sentimēto · sulla · sua superfitie · e nō mandare per la uia ⁸delli nerui · ottici la similitudine · delle cose · vedute · al sēso ·, che l'anima · alla · sopra ⁹detta ragione le poteua comprēdere · in essa · superfitie dell' o-chio ·; ¹⁰E similmēte il sēso · dell' udito · bastaua solamēte · la uoce · risonasse nelle cōcaue porosità ¹¹dell' osso · petroso · che sta · dentro · all' orechio · e nō fare da esso · osso al sēso comune altro ¹²trāsito · dove · essa

The soul seems to reside in the judgement, and the judgement would seem to be seated in that part where all the senses meet; and this is called the Common Sense and is not all-pervading throughout the body, as many have thought. Rather is it entirely in one part. Because if it were all-pervading and the same in every part, there would have been no need to make the instruments of the senses meet in one centre and in one single spot; on the contrary, it would have sufficed that the eye should fulfil the function of its sensation on its surface only, and not transmit the image of the things seen to the sense, by means of the optic nerves, if the soul—for the reason given above—may perceive it in the surface of the eye. In the same way as to the sense of hearing, it would have sufficed if the voice had merely sounded in the porous cavity of the indurated portion of the temporal bone which lies within the ear, without making any farther transit from this bone to the Common

On the relations of the soul to the organs of sense.

---

23. dessa. 24. debbe. 25. resta[ui]. 28. la qual nutrisscie vivifi. 29. cha . . vnbilica. 30. le sua. 32. chettale vnbi. 33. licho. 34. elli. 36. unisscie colla ma. 37. ecquesti. 38. somo. 42. che ne. 43. spesse so. 45. della uita ecc. 54. dellania lasscio ne. 55. le mēte . . ispirita. 56. tatione san. 57. Lascia *doubtful* . . soma.

838. 2. ella. 3. locho . . chonchorano . . chomvne . . ettuta. 4. chorpo chome . . inela . . ssella. 5. fussi tutta [in ogni] per tutto . ettutta . . neciessario · fare li. 6. infralloro · i . . chōchorso a · i . . locho. 7. operassi . . del [suo] sentimēto. 8. ottiti [il] la . . chose . . chellanima. 9. conplēdere. 10. Essimilmēte il . . dellavldito . . risonassi . . chōchaue. 11. chomvne. 12. essaboca · abbia dischorere · al chomune givditio [lodor].

---

837. 57. *lettere incoronate.* By this term Leonardo probably understands not the Bible only, but the works of the early Fathers, and all the books recognized as sacred by the Roman Church.

838. The peculiar use of the words *nervo, muscolo,*

corda, senso comune, which are here literally rendered by nerve, muscle, cord or tendon, and Common Sense, may be understood from ll. 27 and 28.—Compare vol. i, 'Paragone', p. 24.

bocca, abbi a discorrere · al comune givditio; ¹³Il senso dell' odorato · ācora lui si uede · essere dalla neciessità · costretto · a cōcorrere a detto ¹⁴juditio; ¹⁵Il tatto passa · per le corde forate, ed è portato · a esso sēso ·; le quali corde si uanno ¹⁶spargiēdo · con īfinita · ramificatione · in nella pelle · che circūda · le corporee mēbra ¹⁷e visciere ·; ¹⁸Le corde perforate portano il comādamēto · e sentimēto alli mēbri ofitiali, ¹⁹le quali · corde e nerui · infra · i muscoli · e lacierti ²⁰comādano · a quelli · il mouimēto ·; quelli ubidiscono, e tale · obediētia si ²¹mette in atto · collo sgōfiare ·, imperochè 'l gōfiare · raccorta · le loro · lunghezze e tirasi dirieto · i nerui, ²²i quali · si tessono per le particule de' mēbri; essendo infusi nelli · stremi de' diti, ²³portano · al sēso · la cagione del loro · cōttato;

²⁴I nerui · coi loro · muscoli · servono · alle corde · come · i soldati · a cōdottieri ·, e le corde ²⁵seruono · al senso comune · come i cōdottieri al capitano ·, ²⁶e'l senso comune serve all' anima come il capitano serve al suo signore; ²⁷adūque · la givntura delli ossi · obbediscie · al neruo ·, e 'l neruo · al muscolo e 'l muscolo alla corda, ²⁸e la corda al senso comune ·, e 'l sēso comune · è sedia · dell' anima·, e la · memoria è sua ²⁹munitione · e la · impressiva · è sua · referēdaria; ³⁰come il senso · dà · all' anima · e nō l'anima al senso ·, e dove · māca · il senso ofitiale dell' anima ³¹all' anima ·, māca in questa vita · la notizia dell' ufitio · d'esso · sēso, come appare nel ³²mvto e l'orbo nato.

Sense, where the voice confers with and discourses to the common judgement. The sense of smell, again, is compelled by necessity to refer itself to that same judgement. Feeling passes through the perforated cords and is conveyed to this Common Sense. These cords diverge with infinite ramifications into the skin which encloses the members of the body and the viscera. The perforated cords convey volition and sensation to the subordinate limbs. These cords and the nerves direct the motions of the muscles and sinews between which they are placed; these obey, and this obedience takes effect by reducing their thickness; for in swelling their length is reduced, and the nerves shrink which are interwoven among the particles of the limbs; being extended to the tips of the fingers, they transmit to the sense the object which they touch.

The nerves with their muscles obey the tendons as soldiers obey the officers, and the tendons obey the Common [central] Sense as the officers obey the general; and the Common Sense obeys the spirit as the general obeys his master. [27] Thus the joint of the bones obeys the nerve, and the nerve the muscle, and the muscle the tendon and the tendon the Common Sense. And the Common Sense is the seat of the soul [28], and memory is its ammunition, and the impressibility is its referendary, since the sense waits on the soul and not the soul on the sense. And where the sense that ministers to the soul is not at the service of the soul, the functions of that sense are also wanting in that man's life, as is seen in those born mute and blind.

W. 19019b]   839

COME · I NERUI OPERANO QUALCHE UOLTA PER LORO ²SANZA · COMĀDAMĒTO DELLI ALTRI OFITIALI E DELL' ANIMA

HOW THE NERVES SOMETIMES ACT OF THEMSELVES WITHOUT ANY COMMANDS FROM THE OTHER FUNCTIONS AND FROM THE SOUL

On involuntary muscular action. ³Questo · chiaramēte · apparisce ·, inperochè tu · vedrai · movere · ai paraletici e a freddolosi, ⁴e assiderati · le loro · tremāti · mēbra come · testa · e mani · sanza · liciēza · dell' anima ·, la quale ⁵anima cō tutte · sue · forze nō potrà · vietare a essi · menbri · che nō tremino; Questo medesimo ⁶accade nel mal caduco e nelle mēbra tagliate come code di lucierte; ⁷la idea · over imaginatiua · è · timone e briglia de' sensi ·, imperochè la cosa imāginata ⁸move il sēso; ⁹preimaginare · è lo imaginare le cose che saranno; ¹⁰postimaginare è imaginare · le cose passate.

This is most plainly seen; for you will see palsied and shivering persons move, and their trembling limbs, as their head and hands, quake without leave from their soul, and their soul with all its power cannot prevent their members from trembling. The same thing happens in falling-sickness, or in parts that have been cut off, as in the tails of lizards. The idea or imagination is the helm and guiding-rein of the senses, because the thing conceived of moves the sense. Pre-imagining is imagining the things that are to be. Post-imagining is imagining the things that are past.

13. āchora .. chōstretto a chōchorrere. 14. jvditio [il] gusto el tatto. 15. Il tutto nō passa elli per le chorde .. chorde si uano [di]. 16. sprgiēdo chōn .. ramifichatione inella .. circhūda le chorporee. 18. [j nervi] "le corde" .. portano [il sentimento] il chomā-damēto essentimēto. 19. chorde .. musscoli. 20. acquelli .. queli obediscano [chollosco] ettale. 21. chollo schōfiare ipero chel .. rachorta .. lungeze ettirasi. 22. tessano .. partichule. 23. chagione .. chōtatto. 24. choi .. mvsscoli servno .. chorde chome .. chōdottieri · elle chorde. 25. seruano .. chomvne chome i chōdotieri al chapitano. 26. el sēso chomvne serve. 27. [adunque il neruo . serue · al mvssculo el mvsscolo] .. musscholo el mvsscolo .. chorda. 28. ella chorda .. chomvne .. chomvne essedia .. ella .. essua. 29. amvnitione · ella inpresiua essua referēdaria [e il chore essuo]. 30. chome .. de all .. mācha. 31. māchalatotitia .. apare. 32. ellorbo.

839. 1. chome. 2. chomādamēto. 3. apariscie inperro · chettu vederai .. fredollēti. 4. chome. 5. chon .. essi · benbri .. trie mino questo medessi. 6. achade .. mal chaducho .. mēbr .. chome chode. 7. e ētimone .. inpero chella chosa. 9. premaginare .. chose . Chessaranno. 10. posmaginare .. chose.

Triv. 7b]　　　840

4 sono le potentie: memoria · e intelletto, lascibili · e cōcupiscibili, [2]le 2 prime son ragionevoli e l'altre sensuali; [3]I 3 sensi vedere, udire, odorato sono di poca proibitione ·, tatto e gusto [4]no; [5]l'odorato · mena · con seco · il gusto · nel cane e altri · golosi animali.

There are four Powers: memory and intellect, desire and covetousness. The two first are mental and the others sensual. The three senses: sight, hearing, and smell cannot well be prevented; touch and taste not at all. Smell is connected with taste in dogs and other gluttonous animals.

Miscellaneous physiological observations (840–2).

W. 19097b]　　　841

Jo scopro alli omini l'origine [2]della prima · o forse secōda · cagione del loro essere.

I reveal to men the origin of the first, or perhaps second, cause of their existence.

H.[1] 32a]　　　842

Lusåuria è cavsa della gienera[2]tione.

[3]Gola è mātenimēto della vita, [4]pavra over timore è prolūnga[5]mēto di uita, dolo è [6]salvamēto dello strumē[7]to.

Lust is the cause of generation.
Appetite is the support of life. Fear or timidity is the prolongation of life, and fraud the preservation of its instruments.

W. 19045a]　　　843

COME IL CORPO DELL'ANIMALE AL CONTINUO [2]MORE E RINASCIE

[3]Il corpo di qualunche cosa la qual si nutrica, al con[4]tinuo muore e al continuo rinasce, perchè entrare [5]non può nutrimēto se non in quelli luchi, dove il passato [6]nutrimēto è spirato, e s'elli è spirato elli più nō à [7]vita, e se tu nō li rendi nutrimēto equa[8]le al nutrimēto partito, allora la vita manca di su[9]a valetudine, e se tu li leui esso nutrimento, la uita in tut[10]to resta distrutta; Ma se tu ne rēdi tanto quanto se [11]ne distrugge alla giornata, allora tanto rinasce di [12]uita, quanto se ne consuma a similitudine del lume [13]fatto della candela col nutrimēto datoli dall' omore [14]d'essa candela, il quale lume ancora lui al con[15]tinuo con velocissimo soccorso restaura di sotto, [16]quāto di sopra se ne consuma morendo, e di splendi[17]da lucie si converte morēdo in tenebroso fumo, la qual [18]morte è continua, siccome è cōtinuo esso fumo, e la cō[19]tinuità di tal fumo · è equale al cōtinuato nutrimēto, [20]e in instante tutto il lume è morto e tutto rigienerato insie[21]me col moto del nutrimento suo.

HOW THE BODY OF ANIMALS IS CONSTANTLY DYING AND BEING RENEWED

The body of anything whatever that takes nourishment constantly dies and is constantly renewed; because nourishment can only enter into places where the former nourishment has expired, and if it has expired it no longer has life. And if you do not supply nourishment equal to the nourishment which is gone, life will fail in vigour, and if you take away this nourishment, the life is entirely destroyed. But if you restore as much as is destroyed day by day, then as much of the life is renewed as is consumed, just as the flame of the candle is fed by the nourishment afforded by the liquid of this candle, which flame continually with a rapid supply restores to it from below as much as is consumed in dying above: and from a brilliant light is converted in dying into murky smoke; and this death is continuous, as the smoke is continuous; and the continuance of the smoke is equal to the continuance of the nourishment, and in the same instant all the flame is dead and all regenerated, simultaneously with the movement of its own nourishment.

The laws of nutrition and the support of life (843–8).

W. 19084a]　　　844

¶ Come tu ài descritto il rè delli animali—ma io meglio direi dicēdo [2]rè delle bestie · essendo

King of the animals—as thou hast described him—I should rather say king of the beasts, thou

840. 1. lascibili e chōcupiscibili. 2. ellaltre. 3. de [2] 3 sensi .. vldire .. pocha. 5. chōseco .. chane .. golos.
841. 1. schopro. 2. della loro "prima offorse secōdo" sechonda chagione di loro.
842. 1–7 R. 1. chausa. 6. saluamēto.
843. 1. chorpo .. chontinuo. 2. rinasscie. 3. chosa .. nutricha .. chon. 4. chontinuo rinasscie. 5. sēnon. 6. esspirato esselli he . nō[nu]. 7. [trusscie] vita essectu. 8. mancha. 9. valtudine essettulli .. tuc. 10. ressta desstructa Massettu. 11. desstruggie .. rinasscie. 12. chonsuma assimilitudine. 13. chandela chol. 14. chandela .. anchora .. chon. 15. chon velocissimo [vita] "sochorso" .. socto. 16. chonsuma. 17. chonverte .. tenebro. 18. chontinua sichome chontinuo .. ella. 19. chōtinuato. 20. e i ni state .. ettutto. 21. chol.
844. 1. isscritto .. ma i .. dirai. 2. bestie "essendo tu la magore" | perche no li ai uticcoche ti possin.

844. We are led to believe that Leonardo himself was a vegetarian from the following interesting passage in the first of Andrea Corsali's letters to Giuliano de' Medici: 'Alcuni gentili chiamati Guzzarati

tu la maggiore — perchè non li aiuti, acciò che ti possin poi darti [3]li lor figlioli in benifitio della tua gola colla quale tu ài tē[4]tato farti sepultura di tutti li animali, e più oltre direi, se 'l [5]dire il uero mi fusse integramēte lecito; Ma non usciamo [6]delle cose vmane, dicendo vna somma scelerata[7]gine, la qual non accade nelli animali terrestri, [8]inperochè in quelli nō si trovano animali che māgino della loro [9]spetie se nō per mācamēto di celabro (inperochè infra loro, è de ma[10]tti come infra li omini, bēchè nō sieno in tāto numero); [11]e questo non accade se nō nel[12]li animali rapaci, come nella spetie leonina [13]e pardi, pantere, cervieri, gatte e simili, [14]li quali alcuna volta si māgiano i figlioli; ma tu oltre [15]alli figlioli ti māgi il padre, madre, fratelli e amici, e nō [16]ti basta questo, chè tu vai a caccia per le altrui isole, pi[17]gliando li altri omini e quelli mocando il mēbro e li testi-[18]culi fai ingrassare e te li cacci giù per la tua gola; or [19]non produce la natura tāti senplici, che tu ti possa satia[20]re? e se nō ti cōtenti de' senplici, non puoi tu cō la mistiō [21]di quelli fare infiniti conposti, come scrisse il Platina [22]e li altri autori di gola? ¶

being the greatest—because thou doest only help them, in order that they may give thee their children for the benefit of the gullet, of which thou hast attempted to make a sepulchre for all animals; and I would say still more, if I were allowed to speak the entire truth [5]. But we do not go outside human matters in telling of one supreme wickedness, which does not happen among the animals of the earth, inasmuch as among them are found none who eat their own kind, unless through want of sense (as there are fools among them as among men, although they are not in so great number); and this happens only among the rapacious animals, as with the leonine species, and leopards, panthers, lynxes, cats, and the like, who sometimes eat their children; but thou, besides thy children, devourest father, mother, brothers, and friends; nor is this enough for thee, but thou goest to the chase on the islands of others, taking other men and mutilating their membrum virile and testicles thou fattenest, and chasest them down thy own throat [18]; now does not nature produce enough simple (vegetarian food) for thee to satisfy thyself? and if thou art not content with such, canst thou not by the mixture of them make infinite compounds, as Platina wrote [21], and other authors on feeding?

H.[2] 89b]   845

Facciamo nostra vita coll' al[2]trui · morte.
[3]In nella cosa morta rimā vi[4]ta dissensata, la quale ri[5]cōgiūta alli stomachi de' vi[6]ui ripiglia uita sēsitiva [7]e ītellettiva.

Our life is made by the death of others.
In dead matter insensible life remains, which, reunited to the stomachs of living beings, resumes life, both sensual and intellectual.

S. K. M. III. 20b]   846

La natura pare qui in molti [2]o di molti animali stata più pre[3]sto crudele matrignia che ma[4]dre, e d'alcuni nō matrignia [5]ma pietosa madre.

Here nature appears with many animals to have been rather a cruel stepmother than a mother, and with others not a stepmother, but a most tender mother.

    3. figloli . . ai te. 5. fussi . . none vssciā. 6. disscendo . . soma issceleratagi. 7. gine . . soma issceleratagi . . achade . . terresti. 8. trova. 10. numero)e. 11. [alcvna volta] ecquesto none achade . . ne. 12. leonina [che sspessa]. 13. [si māgia che] . . cerveri chatte essimili. 14. māgano i figloli, mattu. 15. figloli. 16. bassta . . chaccia. 18. ettelli caccigu. 19. chettutti. 20. esse nō . . poi. 22. elli . . altori.
845. 1–7 R. 1. faciano nosstra . . choll. 3. jnella. 4. disensata. 5. stomaci. 7. ētellettiva.
846. 1. immolti. 5. piatosa.

non si cibano di cosa alcuna che tenga sangue, nè fra essi loro consentono che si noccia ad alcuna cosa animata, come il nostro Leonardo da Vinci.'
5–18. Amerigo Vespucci, with whom Leonardo was personally acquainted, writes, in his second letter to Pietro Soderini, about the inhabitants of the Canary Islands, after having stayed there in 1503: 'Hanno una scelerata libertà di viuere; . . . . si cibano di carne humana, di maniera che il padre māgia il figliuolo, et all' incontro il figliuolo il padre secondo che a caso e per sorte auiene. Io viddi vn huomo scelleratissimo che si vantaua, et si teneua a non piccola gloria di hauer mangiato più di trecento huomini. Viddi anche vna certa città, nella quale io dimorai forse ventisette giorni, doue le carni humane, hauendole salate, eran

appicate alli traui, si come noi alli traui di cucina appicchiamo le carni di cinghali secche al sole o al fumo, et massimamente salsiccie, et altre simil cose: anzi si marauigliauano grādemēte che noi non māgiassimo della carne de nemici, le quali dicono muouere appetito, et essere di marauiglioso sapore, et le lodano come cibi soaui et delicati' (Lettere due di Amerigo Vespucci Fiorentino drizzate al magnifico Pietro Soderini, Gonfaloniere della eccelsa Republica di Firenze; various editions).
    21. Come scrisse il Platina (Bartolomeo Sacchi, a famous humanist). The Italian edition of his treatise De arte coquinaria was published under the title De la honesta voluptate, e valetudine, Venezia, 1487.

C. A. 76b]

847

L'omo e li animali sono propi trāsito e condotto di cibo, sepoltura · d'animali · albergo de' morti, facciēdo a sé vita ²dell' altrui morte guaina di corrutione!

Man and animals are really the passage and the conduit of food, the sepulchre of animals and resting-place of the dead, making life out of the death of the other, making themselves the covering for corruption.

F. 1a]

848

La morte ne' vecchi sanza febre si causa dalle ²uene che uā dalla milza alla porta del fega³to e s'ingrossan tanto di pelle ch'elle si richi⁴udono e non danno più transito al san⁵gue che li nutrica.

⁶Il continuo corso che fa il sangue per le sue ⁷uene fa che tali vene s'ingrossano e fanno⁸si callose in tal modo che al fine si riserra⁹no e proibiscono il corso al sangue.

Death in old men, when not from fever, is caused by the veins which go from the spleen to the valve of the liver, and which thicken so much in the walls that they become closed up and leave no passage for the blood that nourishes it.

[6] The incessant current of the blood through the veins makes these veins thicken and become callous, so that at last they close up and prevent the passage of the blood.

On the circulation of the blood (848–50).

Leic. 21b]

849

Raggirāsi l'acque con cōtinvo moto dall' infime profondità de' mari alle altissime somità de' mōti, non osseruando ²la natura delle cose graui, e in questo caso fanno come il sangue delli animati che sempre si ³moue dal mare del core e scorre alla sōmità delle loro teste, e che quiui rōpōsi le uene ·, ⁴come si uede una vena rotta nel naso, che tutto il sangue da basso si leua alla altezza della rotta vena; — ⁵Quando l'acqua escie dalla rotta vena della terra essa osserua la natura delle altre cose piv ⁶graui chē l'aria, onde senpre cerca i lochi bassi.

The waters return with constant motion from the lowest depths of the sea to the utmost height of the mountains, not obeying the nature of heavier bodies; and in this they resemble the blood of animated beings which always moves from the sea of the heart and flows towards the top of the head; and here it may burst a vein, as may be seen when a vein bursts in the nose; all the blood rises from below to the level of the burst vein. When the water rushes out from the burst vein in the earth, it obeys the law of other bodies that are heavier than the air, since it always seeks low places.

W. 19082a]

850

Come il sangue che torna indirieto, ²quādo il core si riapre, non è quel che ³riserra le porte del core.

That the blood which returns when the heart opens again is not the same as that which closes the valves of the heart.

Br. M. 147b]

851

Fattevi dare la difinitione e riparo del caso al sancto e all'² · altro · e vedrete che omini son eletti per medici di mala³tie da loro non conosciute.

Make them give you the definition and remedies for the case from the saint and from the other, and you will see that men are selected to be doctors for diseases they do not know.

Some notes on medicine (851–6).

W. 12351a]

852

Medicina da grattature insegniomela l'araldo ²del rè di Frācia: oncie 4 ciera nova, ōcie 4

A remedy for scratches taught me by the Herald to the King of France. 4 ounces of

---

847. 1. elli . . propi "trāsitoe" chondotto . . morti [animali] faciēdo asse. 2. morte [pigliando piacere dellaltri miserie] guaina di chorutione.
848. 1. vechi. 2. miza. 3. to singrossan. 4. vdano . . transitu. 5. chelli nutricha. 6. cheffa. 7. chettali . . effan. 8. risera. 9. proibisscano . . sanghue.
849. 1. Ragirāsi. 2. fa . . animati. 3. move [dal lago] "dal mare" del . . tesste . . echi quiui rōpasi. 4. chettutto . . alteza . . ve"na". 5. esscie. 6. grave chellaria . . cercha.
850. 1. chettorna. 3. de porte.
851. 1. fatevi . . caso al scō e al. 2. laltro evedrete. 3. dallor . . conossciute.

850. Leonardo had a clear conception of the circulation of the blood. His studies on the muscles of the heart are to be found in MS. W. 19071–88. Andreas Caesalpinus (1524–1603) is generally given credit for the earliest statement on the circulation of the blood (*Quest. Peripat.* v. 4). Later this was amplified by

William Harvey (*De motu cordis et sanguinis*, 1628). G. Sarton, differing from the Norwegian editors of the anatomical MSS., asserts that Leonardo was sidetracked by following Galen on this question. *L. d. V. the Anatomist*, Playfair McMurrich, preface.

³pece greca, ōcie 2 inciēso e ogni cosa ⁴stia separata, e fondi la ciera, e poi vi metti den⁵tro l'inciēso, e poi la pece; fa ne pe⁶verada e metti sopr' al male.

virgin wax, 4 ounces of colophony, 2 ounces of incense. Keep each thing separate; and melt the wax, and then put in the incense and then the colophony, make a mixture of it, and put it on the sore place.

Triv. 4a]   853

¶Medicina è ripareggiamēto de' disequali elemēti; ¶²malattia è discordanza d'elemēti īfusi nel uitale corpo.

Medicine is the restoration of discordant elements; sickness is the discord of the elements infused into the living body.

Triv. 18b]   854

A chi dà noia il uomito al nauicare debba bere sugo ²d'assētio.

Those who are annoyed by sickness at sea should drink extract of wormwood.

C. A. 78b]   855

Se vuoi star sano osserva questa norma;
²nō māgiar sanza voglia a cena leve
³mastica bene; e quel che in te ricieve,
⁴sia bē cotto e di semplice forma;
⁵chi medicina piglia mal s'informa.
Guardti dall' ira e fuggi l'aria grieve.
Su dritto sta, quando da mensa levi.
Di mezzo giorno fa che tu non dorma;
E 'l vin sia temprato, poco e spesso,
Non fuor di pasto, nè a stomaco voto,
Non aspettar nè indugiar il cesso,
Se fai esercizio, sia di picciol moto,
Col ventre resupino e col capo depresso
Non star, e sta coperto ben di notte;
E 'l capo ti posa, e tien la mente lieta;
Fuggi lussuria e attienti alla dieta.

To keep in health, this rule is wise:
Eat only when you want and sup light.
Chew thoroughly; and what you take
Have it well cooked, unspiced, and undisguised.
He who takes medicine is ill advised.
Beware of anger and avoid grievous moods.
Do keep standing for a while when you get up from meals.
Do not sleep at midday.
Let your wine be mixed (with water), take little at a time, not between meals, neither on an empty stomach.
Go regularly to stool.
If you take exercise, let it be light.
Do not lie with your belly upwards, or hang your head downwards; be covered well at night.
Rest your head and be cheerful of mind; refrain from wantonness, and observe a strict diet.

W. 19001a]   856

Insegnioti di conse²rvare la sanità ³la qual cosa tanto ⁴più ti riuscirà, ⁵quāto più da fisici ⁶ti guarder⁷ai; ⁸perchè le sue cō⁹positioni sō ¹⁰di spetie d'al¹¹chimia ¹²della ¹³qual ¹⁴non è men ¹⁵numero ¹⁶di libri ch'e¹⁷sista di me¹⁸dicina.

I teach you to preserve your health; and in this you will succeed better in proportion as you shun physicians, because their medicines are of the nature of alchemy about which there are no fewer books than there are about medicine.

852. 4. sta seperata . . metti\\\\\\. 5. effane. 6. mal.
853. 1. ripareggiamēto. 2. dischordanza.
854. 1. al uomito il nauicare deba. 2. dasentio.
855. 1. uoi strasano. 2. voglia ecci\\\\ ellette. 3. masstica . . ecquel. 4. chotto.
856. 1. e ingegniati. 4. riusscira. 9. positione. 10. spetie dar. 12. ella. 13. qual. 14. nonemē. 15. numero. 16. de libri. 17. che sia
    dime. 18. dicina. *The meaning of these short lines 12–18 is doubtful.*

855. In the Municipal Library of Udine is a similar version of this poem.

856. This passage is written on the back of the drawing on Pl. CVIII. Compare also No. 1184.

XV

ASTRONOMY

*E*VER *since the publication by Venturi in 1797 and Libri in 1840 of some few passages of Leonardo's astronomical notes, scientific astronomers have frequently expressed the opinion that they must have been based on very important discoveries, and that the great painter also deserved a conspicuous place in the history of this science. In the passages here printed a connected view is given of his astronomical studies as they lie scattered through the manuscripts which have come down to us. Unlike his other purely scientific labours, Leonardo devotes here a good deal of attention to the opinions of the ancients, though he does not follow the practice universal in his day of relying on them as authorities; he only quotes them, as we shall see, in order to refute their arguments. His researches throughout have the stamp of independent thought. There is nothing in these writings to lead us to suppose that they were merely an epitome of the general learning of the period. The famous words 'e* pur si muove' *reported to have been said by Galilei at his trial by the Inquisition in 1633 were anticipated by Leonardo when he wrote in the corner of a sheet at Windsor* il sole non si muove, *as a proposition occupying his mind. As early as in the fourteenth century there were chairs of astronomy in the universities of Padua and Bologna, but even as late as the end of the sixteenth century Astronomy and Astrology were still closely allied. It may be that Leonardo, when living in Florence, became acquainted in his youth with the doctrines of Paolo Toscanelli, the great astronomer and mathematician (died 1482), of whose influence and teaching but little is now known beyond the fact that he advised and encouraged Columbus to carry out his project of sailing round the world. His name is nowhere mentioned by Leonardo, and from the dates of the manuscripts from which the texts on astronomy are taken, it seems highly probable that Leonardo devoted his attention to astronomical studies less in his youth than in his later years. It was evidently his purpose to treat of Astronomy in a connected form and in a separate work (see the beginning of Nos. 866 and 892; compare also No. 1167). It is quite in accordance with his general scientific thoroughness that he should propose to write a special treatise on Optics as an introduction to Astronomy (see Nos. 867 and 877). Some of the chapters belonging to this section bear the title* 'Prospettiva' *(see Nos. 869 and 870), this being the term universally applied at the time to Optics as well as Perspective (see vol. i, p. 117, note to No. 13, l. 10).*

At the beginning of the sixteenth century the Ptolemaic theory of the universe was still generally accepted as the true one, and Leonardo conceives of the earth as fixed, with the moon and sun revolving round it, as they are represented in the diagram to No. 897. He does not go into any theory of the motions of the planets; with regard to these and the fixed stars he only investigates the phenomena of their luminosity. The spherical form of the earth he takes for granted as an axiom from the first. He anticipates Newton by pointing out the universality of gravitation not merely in the earth but even in the moon. Although his acute research into the nature of the moon's light and the spots on the moon did not bring to light many results of lasting importance beyond making it evident that they were a refutation of the errors of his contemporaries, they contain various explanations of facts which modern science need not modify in any essential point, and discoveries which history has hitherto assigned to a very much later date.

The ingenious theory by which he tries to explain the nature of what is known as earth shine, the reflection of the sun's rays by the earth towards the moon, saying that it is a peculiar refraction, originating in the innumerable curved surfaces of the waves of the sea, may be regarded as absurd; but it must not be forgotten that he had no means of detecting the fundamental error on which he based it, namely, the assumption that the moon was at a relatively short distance from the earth. So long as the motion of the earth round the sun remained unknown, it was of course impossible to form any estimate of the moon's distance from the earth by a calculation of its parallax.

Before the discovery of the telescope accurate astronomical observations were only possible to a very limited extent. It would appear, however, from certain passages in the notes here printed for the first time, that Leonardo was in a position to study the spots in the moon more closely than he could have done with the unaided eye. So far as can be gathered from the mysterious language in which the description of his instrument is wrapped, he made use of magnifying glasses; these do not, however, seem to have been constructed like a telescope—telescopes were first made about 1600. As Libri pointed out (Histoire des sciences mathématiques, iii. 101) *Fracastoro of Verona (1473–1553) succeeded in magnifying the moon's face by an arrangement of lenses (compare No. 910, note), and this gives probability to Leonardo's invention at a not much earlier date.*

Edmondo Solmi gives a connected account of Leonardo's astronomical studies and cognate researches in Atti e Memorie della R. Accademia Virgiliana, *Mantua,* 1905, *pp.* 76–136 *and passim.*

I

THE EARTH AS A PLANET

857

Linia d'equalità, ²linia dell' orizzōte, ³linia giacēte, ⁴linia equigiacēte;
⁵Queste linie sō quelle ⁶che con sua stremi sō ⁷equidistanti al cē⁸tro del mondo.

The equator, the line of the horizon, the ecliptic, the meridian:
These lines are those which in their extremities are equidistant from the centre of the globe.

The earth's place in the universe (857-8).

858

Come la terra non è nel mezzo del cerchio del ²sole, nè nel mezzo del mōdo, ma è ben nel mez³zo de' sua elemēti, conpagni e vniti cō lei, e chi ⁴stesse nella luna, quād' ella insieme col sole ⁵è sotto a noi, questa nostra terra coll' ele-⁶mento dell' acqua parrebbe e farebbe ofitio tal ⁷qual fa la luna a noi.

The earth is not in the centre of the sun's orbit nor at the centre of the universe, but in the centre of its companion elements, and united with them. And any one standing on the moon, when it and the sun are both beneath us, would see this our earth and the element of water upon it just as we see the moon, and the earth would light it as the moon lights us.

859

La forza da carestia · o · douitia · è gienerata; ²questa è figliola del moto · materiale · o nepote ³del moto · spirituale ·, e madre e origine del peso; ⁴e esso peso è finito nell' elemēto dell'acqua e terra, ⁵e essa · forza · è infinita, perchè con essa infiniti ⁶mōdi si mouerebbero ·, se strumēti farsi potessero, ⁷doue essa forza gienerare si potesse.
⁸La forza col moto materiale e 'l peso colla percussione ⁹son le quattro accidētali potētie, colle quali tutte l'opere ¹⁰de' mortali ànno loro essere e lor morte;
¹¹La forza · dal moto · spirituale · à origine; il quale moto, ¹²scorrēdo · per le mēbra degli animali · sensibili ·, ingrossa ¹³i muscoli di quelli ·, onde ingrossati · essi muscoli si uē¹⁴gono a raccortare e trarsi dirieto i nervi che con essi ¹⁵sō cōgiunti ·, e di qui si causa la forza per le mēbra umane.
¹⁶La qualità e quātità delle forze · d'uno uomo potrà · ¹⁷partorire · altra forza ·, la quale sarà proportio ¹⁸nevolmēte tanto maggiore quāto essa sarà di piv ¹⁹lūgo moto, l'una che l'altra.

Force arises from dearth or abundance; it is the child of physical motion, and the grandchild of spiritual motion, and the mother and origin of gravity. Gravity is limited to the elements of water and earth; but this force is unlimited, and by it infinite worlds might be moved if instruments could be made by which the force could be generated.
Force, with physical motion, and gravity, with resistance, are the four external powers on which all actions of mortals depend.
Force has its origin in spiritual motion; and this motion, flowing through the limbs of sentient animals, enlarges their muscles. Being enlarged by this current, the muscles are shrunk in length and contract the tendons which are connected with them, and this is the cause of the force of the limbs in man.
The quality and quantity of the force of a man are able to give birth to other forces, which will be proportionally greater as the motions produced by them last longer.

The fundamental laws of the solar system (859-64).

860

Il peso · o · perchè no resta nel suo sito? ²non resta perchè non à resistētia; e dō³de si moverà?

Why does not the weight o remain in its place? It does not remain because it has no

---

857. 2. dorizōte. 6. che cho. 7. nequidistante.
858. 1. mezo. 2. mezo. 4. stessi. 5. essotto annoi .. nosta. 6. acq"a" parebbe effarebe. 7. annoi.
859. 1. odouitia. 2. effigliola .. enepo. 4. chesso .. heffinito .. ettera. 5. chessa .. he. 6. mouerebbe .. potessi. 7. hessa .. potessi. 9. quatro. 10. ellor. 12. scorēdo. 13. musscoli di quelle .. musscoli. 14. gano aracortare. 16. ecquātita .. homo. 18. magiore. 19. luna cellaltra.

859. Only part of this passage belongs, strictly speaking, to this section. The principle laid down in the second paragraph is more directly connected with the notes given in the preceding section on Physiology.
860. This text and the sketch belonging to it are reproduced on Pl. CXXI.

Moverassi · inverso il ⁴centro; E perchè nõ per altre linie? Perchè ⁵il peso, che non à resistentia, discienderà ⁶in basso per la uia piv brieve, e 'l più bas⁷so sito è il ciẽtro del mondo; E perchè lo sa ⁸così tal peso trovarlo con tanta breuità? ⁹Perchè non va come insensibile prima ¹⁰vagando per diverse linie.

support. Where will it move to? It will move towards the centre [of gravity]. And why by no other line? Because a weight which has no support falls by the shortest road to the lowest point which is the centre of the world. And why does the weight know how to find it by so short a line? Because it does not go like a senseless thing and does not move about in various directions.

F. 22b]   861

Movasi la terra da che parte si voglia, ²mai la superfitie dell' acqua uscirà fori della ³sua spera, ma senpre sarà equidistante al ⁴centro del mondo;

⁵¶ Dato che la terra · si rimovessi dal centro ⁶del mondo, che farebbe l'acqua? ¶

⁷Resterebbe intorno a esso centro ⁸con equal grossezza, ma minore diami⁹tro, che quando ella auea la terra in corpo.

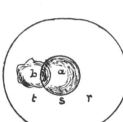

Let the earth turn on which side it may, the surface of the waters will never move from its spherical form, but will always remain equidistant from the centre of the globe.

Granting that the earth might be removed from the centre of the globe, what would happen to the water?

It would remain in a sphere round that centre equally thick, but the sphere would have a smaller diameter than when it enclosed the earth.

F. 11b]   862

Se la terra delli antipodi che sostiene ²l'oceano s'inalzasse e si scoprisse assai ³fori d'esso mare, essendo quasi pia⁴na, in che modo sarebbe poi col tẽpo ⁵a creare li mõti e le valli.

⁶E li sassi di diuerse falde?

Supposing the earth at our antipodes which supports the ocean were to rise and stand uncovered, far out of the sea, but remaining almost level, by what means afterwards, in the course of time, would mountains and valleys be formed?

And the rocks with their various strata?

Triv. 29a]   863

Ogni omo senpre si troua nel mezzo del mõdo e sotto il mezzo ²del suo · emisperio, e sopra il ciẽtro d'esso mõdo.

Each man is always in the middle of the surface of the earth and under the zenith of his own hemisphere, and over the centre of the earth.

Leic. 1a]   864

Ricordo come io ho in prima a dimo²strare la distantia del sole dalla terra, ³e con ũ de' sua razzi passati per ispi⁴racolo in loco oscuro ritrovare ⁵la sua quãtità vera, e oltre a ⁶di questo per lo mezzo della spera del⁷l' acqua ritrovare la grãdezza della terra.¶

⁸Qui si dimostra come, qã⁹do il sole è nel mezzo del nostro ¹⁰emisperio, che li antipodi ¹¹orientali cogli occidentali ue¹²dono in un medesimo tenpo cias¹³cun per sé spechiare il

Mem.: That I must first show the distance of the sun from the earth; and, by means of a ray passing through a small hole into a dark chamber, detect its real size; and besides this, by means of the aqueous sphere calculate the size of the globe . . .

Here it will be shown that when the sun is in the meridian of our hemisphere [10], the antipodes to the east and to the west, alike, and at the same time, see the sun mirrored in their

---

860. 4. cientro he. 8. chon. 9. perche nonva come [in gi] insensibile prima.
861. 2. acq"a" vsscira. 5. chella. 6. cheffarebbe.
862. 1. sella. 2. sinalzassi . . scoprissi essi. 5. elle. 6. elli.
863. 1. mezo . . essotto il mezo.
864. 1. chome . . in p"a" a dimõ. 2. disstantia. 3. razi. 4. rachulo illocho osscuro. 6. mezo. 7. grãdeza. 8. dimostra chome. 9. mezo . . nosstro. 10. emissperio chelli antipodi di. 11. horientali. 12. gano nun. 13. scun.

861. Compare No. 896, ll. 48–64, and No. 936.
864. 10, 11. *Antipodi orientali cogli occidentali.* The word Antipodes does not here bear its literal sense, but—as we may infer from the simultaneous reference

to inhabitants of the north and south—is used as meaning men living at a distance of 90 degrees from the zenith of the horizon of each observer.

sole nelle [14]loro acque, e 'l simile quelli del po[15]lo artico col antartico, se abi[16]tatori ui sono.

waters; and the same is equally true of the arctic and antarctic poles, if indeed they are inhabited.

C. A. 112*b*]   865

Come la terra è una stella.

That the earth is a star.

F. 56*a*]   866

Tu nel tuo discorso ài a cōcludere [2]la terra essere vna stella quasi si[3]mile alla luna, [4]e la nobilità del nostro mōdo.

[5]E così farai vn discorso delle grā[6]dezze di molte stelle, secōdo li autori.

In your discourse you must prove that the earth is a star much like the moon, and the glory of our universe; and then you must treat of the size of various stars, according to the authors.

F. 25*b*]   867

ORDINE DEL PROVARE LA TERRA ESSERE [2]VNA STELLA

THE METHOD OF PROVING THAT THE EARTH IS A STAR

[3]Imprima definisci l'ochio, poi mostra come il bat[4]tere d'alcuna stella viene dall' ochio, e perchè il battere [5]d'esse stelle è più nell' una che nell' altra, e come li [6]razzi delle stelle nascono dall' ochio, e dì, che se 'l batte[7]re delle stelle fusse come pare nelle stelle, che tal bat[8]timēto mostra d'essere di tanta dilatatione, quāt' è [9]il corpo di tale stella; essendo adūque maggiore della ter[10]ra che tal moto fatto in istante sarebbe troppo veloce [11]a raddoppiare la grādezza di tale stella; Di poi pro[12]va come la superfitie dell' aria ne' cōfini del foco, e [13]la superfitie del foco nel suo termine è quel[14]la, nella qual penetrādo li razzi solari portano la [15]similitudine di corpi celesti grāde nel lor leua[16]re, e però è piccola, essendo esse nel mezzo del celo; [17]sia la terra *a* | *n d m* sia [18]la superfitie dell' aria che [19]cofina colla spera del [20]foco; · *h f g* · sia il corso [21]della luna o vuoi del sole; [22]dico che quādo il sole appari[23]sce all' orizzōte *g*, che lì sono ueduti [24]li sua razzi passare per la superfitie [25]dell' aria infra āgoli inequali cioè *o m*, il che non è in *d k*, e ācora [26]passa per maggiore grossezza d'aria; tutto *e m* è aria più spessa.

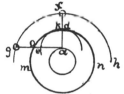 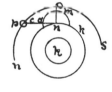 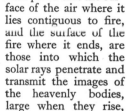

First describe the eye; then show how the twinkling of a star is really in the eye and why one star should twinkle more than another, and how the rays from the stars originate in the eye; and add that if the twinkling of the stars were really in the stars—as it seems to be—that this twinkling appears to be an extension as great as the diameter of the body of the star; therefore, the star being larger than the earth, this motion effected in an instant would be a rapid doubling of the size of the star. Then prove that the surface of the air where it lies contiguous to fire, and the surface of the fire where it ends, are those into which the solar rays penetrate and transmit the images of the heavenly bodies, large when they rise, and small when they are on the meridian. Let *a* be the earth and *n d m* the surface of the air in contact with the sphere of fire; *h f g* is the orbit of the moon or, if you please, of the sun; then I say that when the sun appears on the horizon *g*, its rays are seen passing through the surface of the air at a slanting angle, that is, *o m*; this is not the case at *d k*. And so it passes through a greater mass of air; all of *e m* is a denser atmosphere.

W. 12327 (?)]   868

Infra 'l sole · e noi è tenebre, e però l'aria pare azzurra.

Between the sun and us there is darkness, and so the air appears blue.

E. 15*b*]   869

PROSPETTIVA

PERSPECTIVE

[2]Possibile è fare che l'ochio nō uedrà [3]le cose remote molto diminuite, come fa [4]la prospettiva

It is possible to find means by which the eye shall not see remote objects as much diminished

14. aqcue . . quelgli. 15. articho chol antarticho.

865. R.

866. 1. tutto tuo discorsa a cō cludere. 3. luna [e cosi proverra]. 6. altori.

867. 3. difinissci. 4. piene . . il bat. 6. razi . . nasscā . . e di chessel bate. 7. fussi . . tal ba. 9. magor. 10. istante sare trovo veloce. 11. radopiare la grādeza. 12. foco el. 15. lla superfitie . . focho . . ecquel. 14. razi . . portāta. 16. eppero e pichole . . mezo. 20. foco. 21. della nuna ouoi. 22. apari. 23. orizzōte g chele veduto. 24. razi. 25. coe o m il ce non . . acora. 26. magore grosseza.

868. ettenebre . . azura.

869. 1. prosspettiva. 2. he fare chellochio . . uedera. 3. chome ffa. 4. presspettiva naturale [le spe] le.

868. Compare vol. i, No. 301.

naturale, le quali ⁵diminuiscono mediante la curuità del⁶l' ochio, che è costretto a tagliare sopra di ⁷sé le piramidi di qualunche spetie che viene all' ⁸ochio infra angoli retti sperici; Ma ⁹l'arte, che io insegnio qui in margine, ta¹⁰glia esse piramidi con angoli ret¹¹ti vicino alla superfitie di tal popilla; Ma ¹²la convessa popilla dell' ochio piglia sopra ¹³di sé tutto il nostro emisperio, e que¹⁴sta mostrerà solo una stella; ma doue ¹⁵molte piccole stelle si ricevono per similitu¹⁶dine nella superfitie della popilla, ¹⁷le quali stelle son minime, questa di¹⁸mostrerà vna sola stella, ma fia grāde; ¹⁹E così la luna di maggiore grādezza, e le su²⁰e macule di più nota figura; A questo ²¹nostro ochio si debbe fare v̄ uetro pieno di ²²quell' acqua di che si fa mētione ²³nel 4 del libro 113 delle cose naturali, ²⁴la quale acqua fa parere spogliate di ²⁵vetro quelle cose che son congielate nel²⁶le palle del uetro cristallino.

as in natural perspective, which diminishes them by reason of the convexity of the eye which necessarily intersects, at its surface, the pyramid of every image conveyed to the eye at spherical right angles. But by the method I here teach in the margin [9] these pyramids are intersected at right angles close to the surface of the pupil. The convex pupil of the eye can take in the whole of our hemisphere, while this will show only a single star; but where many small stars transmit their images to the surface of the pupil those stars are extremely small; here only one star is seen but it will be large. And so the moon will be seen larger and its spots of a more defined form [20]. You must place close to the eye a glass filled with the water of which mention is made in number 4 of Book 113 'On natural science' [23]; for this water makes objects which are enclosed in balls of crystalline glass appear free from the glass.

DELL' OCHIO

²⁸Infra li corpi minori della popilla dell'ochio ²⁹quella fia manco nota a essa popilla, ³⁰la quale le sarà più vicina || E con questa ³¹speriētia ci si è fatto noto che la virtù visiva nō ³²si riducie in pūto perchè se la ecc.

³³Leggi ī margine.

³⁴Quella cosa si ³⁵dimostra maggi³⁶ore, che uiene ³⁷all' ochio cō più ³⁸grosso angolo.

³⁹Ma le spetie delli ob⁴⁰bietti, che cōcor⁴¹rono alla popilla ⁴²dell' ochio, si conpar⁴³tono sopra tal popi⁴⁴lla nel medesimo ⁴⁵modo, ch' elle son cō⁴⁶partite infra l'aria; ⁴⁷e la prova di ques⁴⁸to ci è inse⁴⁹gnata quādo noi ⁵⁰riguardiamo il ⁵¹cielo stellato ⁵²sanza por la mi⁵³ra più a una stel⁵⁴la che all' altra, ⁵⁵che allora ci si mo⁵⁶stra il cielo semina⁵⁷to di stelle, e sō pro⁵⁸portionate nell' ochio ⁵⁹siccome lo sono in ⁶⁰cielo, e così li loro ⁶¹spati fanno il simile.

OF THE EYE

Among the smaller objects presented to the pupil of the eye, that which is closest on it will be least appreciable to the eye. And at the same time the experiments here made with the power of sight show that it is not reduced to a point if the &c. [32].

Read in the margin.

[34] Those objects are seen largest which come to the eye at the largest angles.

But the images of the objects conveyed to the pupil of the eye are distributed on the pupil exactly as they are distributed in the air: and the proof of this is shown to us when we look at the starry sky, without sighting more fixedly one star than another; the sky then appears all strewn with stars; and their proportions in the eye are the same as in the sky and likewise the spaces between them [61].

F. 60b]

870

PROSPETTIVA

²Delle cose remosse dall' ochio con equale di³stantia, quella parrà esser mē dimin⁴vita che prima era più.

PERSPECTIVE

Among objects moved from the eye at equal distance, that undergoes least diminution which at first was most remote.

5. le diminuisschano. 6. chosstretta attagliare. 7. piramide . . spetie viene. 8. llochio . . angholi. 10. lia [le] esse piramide chon angholi. 12. delloccio pigli. 13. mostro omissperio ecques. 14. mossterra. 15. pichole . . riciev. 16. popille [qu]. 17. stielle . . quista e di. 18. mossterra . . maffia. 19. chosi . . magiore grādeza elle. 20. machule. 22. acqua [che] di . . mētione [de]. 23. chose. 24. aqua. 25. chose chesson. 26. crissta llino. 28. Infralli chorpi. 29. mancho. 29. a essa [ochu] popilla. 30. chon questa [no]. 31. ci se . . chella. 32. sella. 33. [Quella u]. 34. chosa. 35. dimostra magi. 37. chō. 38. grosse anghole. 39. Malle setie. 40. biecto che chōchor. 41. rano. 42. chonpa"r". 43. tano. 45. chō. 46. infrallari"a". 47. ella. 48. sto [cm] ciē inse. 50. righuardiamo. 52. la ui. 58. ochi"o". 59. si chomelle. 60. chosi.
870. 1. prespectiva. 2. remosse "dallochio" [dellor sito cone] quala di. 4. che p"a" era.

869. 9, 33. *in margine*: ll. 34–61 are, in the original, written on the margin, and above them is the diagram to which Leonardo seems to refer here.

20 ff. Telescopes were not in use till a century later. Compare No. 910 and p. 108.

23. *libro* 113. This is perhaps the number of a

book in some library catalogue. But it may refer, on the other hand, to one of the 120 books mentioned in No. 796, l. 84, or to some work on Natural Science.

32. Compare with this the passage in vol. i, No. 52, written about twenty years earlier.

⁵Delle cose remosse dall' ochio con equal di⁶stantia dal lor primo sito quella mē diminuisce ⁷che prima era più distante da esso ochio; E tal ⁸fia la proportione della diminuitione, qual fù ⁹la proportione delle distantie ch'esse aveā da¹⁰l'ochio auanti il loro moto.

¹¹Come dire il corpo *t* e 'l corpo *e* e ¹²che la proportiō delle lor distantie dall' ochio *a* ¹³è quītupla; io rimovo ciascū dal suo sito ¹⁴e lo fo più distante dall' ochio vno d'essi 5′ in che è

When various objects are removed at equal distances farther from their original position, that which was at first the farthest from the eye will diminish least. And the diminution will be in proportion to the relative distance of the objects from the eye before they were removed.

That is to say, in the object *t* and the object *e* the proportion of their distances from the eye *a* is quintuple. I remove each from its place and

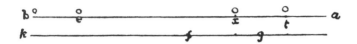

¹⁵diuisa la proportione; accade dūque che il più vicino ¹⁶all' ochio avrà doppiata la distantia, e per la penulti¹⁷ma di questo esso è diminuto la metà del suo tutto, ¹⁸e 'l corpo *e* per lo medesimo moto è diminuito $\frac{1}{5}$ ¹⁹d'esso suo tutto; adūque per la detta penultima ²⁰è vero quel che in questa vltima s'è proposto; ²¹e questo dico per li moti de' corpi celesti ²²in 3500 miglia di distātia che piv essē²³do in oriēte che sopra di noi, non crescono o diminuiscono ²⁴con sensibile dimostratione.

set it farther from the eye by one of the 5 parts into which the proportion is divided. Hence it happens that the nearest to the eye has doubled the distance and, according to the last proposition but one, is diminished by half of its size; and the body *e*, by the same motion, is diminished $\frac{1}{5}$ of its size. Therefore, by that same last proposition but one, that which is said in this last proposition is true; and this I say of the motions of the celestial bodies which are distant 3,500 miles: that, though they (should be) bigger when rising than when overhead, they do not grow or diminish to any sensible degree.

Br. M. 174*b*]   871

a b è lo spiraculo donde ²passa il sole, e se tu po³tessi misurare la grossezza de' ⁴razzi solari in *n m*, tu po⁵tresti por bene le uere linie ⁶del concorso d'essi razzi solari, ⁷stante lo spechio in · *a b*, e ⁸poi fare i razzi reflessi infra ā⁹goli equali inuerso · *n m* · ¹⁰ma poi che tu no li pòi torre in ¹¹*n m* · togli dentro allo spiracu¹²lo in *c d* che si possan misura¹³re nella percussione del razzo solare, ¹⁴e poi poni il tuo spechio nella distā¹⁵tia *a b* ·, e lì fa cadere i razzi *d b, c a*, poi ¹⁶risaltare infra angoli equali in uer¹⁷so *c d* · e questo è il uero modo; ¹⁸ma ti bisognia operare tale spe¹⁹chio nel medesimo mese e medesi²⁰mo dì e ora e pūto, e farà meglio ²¹che di nessū tempo, perchè in tal distantia ²²di sole si causò tal piramide.

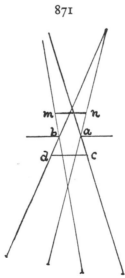

a b is the aperture through which the sun passes, and if you could measure the size of the solar rays at *n m*, you could accurately trace the real lines of the convergence of the solar rays, the mirror being at *a b*, and then show the reflected rays at equal angles to *n m*; but as you cannot take them at *n m*, take them at the inner side of the aperture at *c d*, where they may be measured at the spot where the solar rays fall. Then place your mirror at the distance *a b*, making the rays *d b, c a* fall and then be reflected at equal angles towards *c d*; and this is the best method, but you must use this mirror always in the same month, and the same day and hour and instant, and this will be better than at no fixed time, because when the sun is at a certain distance it produces a certain pyramid of rays.

5. chon . . dis. 6. p"o"sito qualla . . diminuissce. 7. che p"a" . . Ettal. 10. iloro. 11. corpo e che e. 12. chella. 13. ciasscū del. 14. ellolofo . . inche. 15. la pro "ne" achade . . che piu. 16. ara dopiato. 20. preposto. 21. ecquesto. . . celestiche. 22. [1500 m] 3500 . . distātia cheli ā piv. 23. crescano o diminuiscano.
871. 1. ellosspiraculo. 2. essettu. 3. grosseza. 4. razi. 6. razi. 7. losspechio. 8. razi refressi. 10. chettu noli poi. 11 allosspiracu. 12. chessi. 13. razo. 15. elli . . razi; *in the margin*: "d b" c a. 17. ecquesto. 18. matti. 20. effara.

G. 3*b*]   872

In *a* parte del corpo ō²broso *n* vede tutta la pa³rte dell' emisferio *b c d e f* ⁴e nō ui vede parte alcuna ⁵della oscurità della terra; ⁶e 'l simile accade nel punto *o*; adunque lo spatio *a · o · e · d* è ⁷tutto d'una medesima chiarezza, in *s* vede sol 4 gra⁸di dell' emisperio *d e f g k ·*, e vi vede tutta la terra ⁹*s k* che la fa più oscura, quāto darà la calculatione.

a, the side of the body in light and shade *n*, faces the whole portion of the hemisphere *b c d e f*, and does not face any part of the darkness of the earth. And the same occurs at the point *o*; therefore the space *a o e d* is throughout of one and the same brightness, and *s* faces only four degrees of the hemisphere *d e f g k*, and also the whole of the earth is seen from *s k*, which will render it darker; and how much must be demonstrated by calculation.

A. 64*b*]   873

PRUOVA DELL' ACCRESCIMĒTO DEL SOLE ²IN NEL OCCIDĒTE

³Alcuni · matematici · dimostrano · il sole · cresciere nel ponēte ·, perchè l'ochio · sēpre lo uede per aria di maggiore grossezza, ⁴allegādo che le · cose uiste nella · nebbia e nel acqua pajono maggiori: ai quali · io rispōdo di no, inperochè le cose viste īfra la nebbia sō simi⁵li per colore alle lōtane ·, e nōn essendo simili per diminvitione appariscono di maggiore grādezza; Ancora nessuna cosa ⁶crescie · in acqua · piana, e la pruova ne farai a lucidare vn' asse mezza sotta l'acqua; Ma la ragione che 'l sol ⁷crescie · si è che | Ogni corpo luminoso quāto piv s'allōtana, piv pare grāde.

THE REASON OF THE INCREASED SIZE OF THE SUN IN THE WEST

Some mathematicians explain that the sun looks larger as it sets because the eye always sees it through a denser atmosphere, alleging that objects seen through mist or through water appear larger. To these I reply: No; because objects seen through a mist are similar in colour to those at a distance; but not being similarly diminished they appear larger. Again, nothing increases in size in smooth water; and the proof of this may be seen by tracing a board placed half under water. But the reason why the sun looks larger is that every luminous body appears larger in proportion as it is more remote.

F. 94*b*]   874

On the luminosity of the Earth in the universal space (874–8).

Il libro mio s'astēde a mostrare, ²come l'oceā colli altri mari ³fa mediāte il sole splēde⁴re il nostro mōdo a modo ⁵di luna e a più remoti pa⁶re stella e questo provo;

⁷Dimostra prima come ogni lume remoto da⁸ll' ochio fa razzi, li quali pare che accrescino la figu⁹ra di tal corpo luminoso e di questo ne segui¹⁰ta che 2. . . .

¹¹Luna frigida ¹²e vmida.

¹³L'acqua è frigi¹⁴da e vmida; ¹⁵tale influēti¹⁶a da il nostro ¹⁷mare alla lu¹⁸na qual la luna ¹⁹a noi.

In my book I propose to show how the ocean and the other seas must, by means of the sun, make our world shine with the appearance of a moon, and to the remoter worlds it looks like a star; and this I shall prove.

Show first that every light at a distance from the eye throws out rays which appear to increase the size of the luminous body; and from this it follows that 2 . .[10].

[11] The moon is cold and moist.

Water is cold and moist. Thus our seas must appear to the moon as the moon does to us.

872. 1. in a. 5. asscurita. 6. achade . . losspatio a . o . ed. 9. chella . . oscura.
873. 1. dellacrescimēto. 2. inel ocidēte. 3. raria . . maggiore grosseza. 4. alegādo chelle chose . . nebia | "e nel acqª" paro magiore . . llechose . . nebia. 5. le per cholore ale . . esendo simile . . aparischano . . magiore grādeza Anchora nesuna chosa. 6. acqª"a" . . meza . . lacq"a" Malla. 7. cresscie . . chorpo.
874. 1. libro mio (il *is wanting*). 5. e "a" piu. 6. ecquesto. 7. ōni lume. 8. razi. . acresscino. 11. fregida. 13. Lacq"a". 15. infruēti.

872. This passage, which has perhaps a doubtful right to its place in this connexion, stands in the MS. between those given in vol. i as No. 117 and No. 427.

873. Lines 5 and 6 are thus rendered by M. Ravaisson in his edition of MS. A. 'De même, au-

cune chose ne croît dans l'eau plane, et tu en feras l'expérience *en calquant un ais sous l'eau*.'—Compare the diagrams in vol. i, p. 114.

874. 10. Here the text breaks off; ll. 11 ff. are written in the margin.

L'onde dell' acqua crescono il simulacro della cosa che [2]in lor si spechia.

[3]*a* sia il sole, *n m* sia l'acqua inōdata, *b* è 'l simulacro [4]del sole, quando l'acqua nō fusse inondata; *f* sia l'ochio [5]che uede esso simulacro in tutte l'onde che si rinchiudo[6]no nella basa del triangolo *c e f*; adunque il sole [7]che nella superfitie sanza onde occupava l'acqua *c d*, ora [8]nella

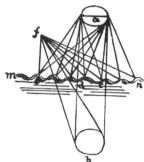

superfitie inondata occupa tutta l'acqua *c e* (come è [9]prouato nel 4 della mia prospettiva), e tanto più occupe[10]rebbe d'acqua quanto esso simulacro fusse più distāte da l'ochio.

[11]¶ Il simulacro del sole si dimostrerà piv lucido nell' onde mi[12]nute che nelle onde grandi ¶; E questo accade perchè le simili[13]tudini over simulacri del sole sono più spesse nell' onde minute [14]che nelle grandi, e li più spessi splendori rendono maggiore [15]lume che li splendori più rari.

[16]L'onde intersegate a uso di scorza di pigna rendono il si[17]mulacro del sole di grandissimo splendore, [18]e questo accade perchè tanto son li simulacri quanto son li gob[19]bi de l'onde

The waves in water magnify the image of an object reflected in it.

Let *a* be the sun, and *n m* the ruffled water, *b* the image of the sun when the water is smooth. Let *f* be the eye which sees the image in all the waves included within the base of the triangle *c e f*. Now the sun reflected in the unruffled surface occupied the space *c d*, while in the ruffled surface it covers all the space on the water *c e* (as is proved in the 4th of my 'Perspective') [9] and it will cover more of the water in proportion as the reflected image is remote from the eye [10].

The image of the sun will be more brightly shown in small waves than in large ones—and this is because the reflections or images of the sun are more numerous in the small waves than in large ones, and the more numerous reflections of its radiance give a larger light than the fewer.

Waves which intersect like the scales of a pine-cone reflect the image of the sun with the greatest splendour; and this is the case because the images are as many as the ridges of the waves on which the sun shines, and the shadows between

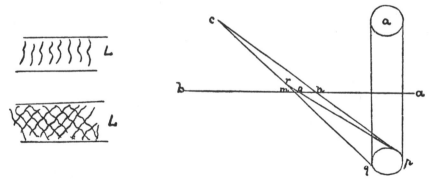

vedute dal sole, e l'onbre che infra esse onde s'inter[20]pongono son piccole e di poca oscurità, e li splendori di tanti [21]simulacri insieme s'in-

these waves are small and not very dark; and the radiance of so many reflections together becomes united in the image which is transmitted

875. 1. aq"a" crescano. 2. sisspechia. 3. lacq"a". 4. lacq"a" .. fussi. 5. chessi rinchiuda. 7. ocupava lacq"a" .. or"a". 8. ochupa. 9. prosspectiva) ettanto .. ochupe. 10. dacq"a" .. fussi. 11. dimosterra. 12. achade chelle. 13. tudine. 14. elli .. rendan magore. 15. chelli. 16. disscorsa di pina rendano [loss] il si. 17. plendore [e chiareza]. 18. ecquesto achade. 19. ellonbre. 20. pongono .. pichole .. pocha ossurita elli. 21. sinfondano .. similitudine.

875. In the original sketch, inside the upper circle in the diagram above, is written *Sole* (sun), and to the right of it *Luna* (moon). Thus either of these heavenly bodies may be supposed to fill that space. Within the lower circle is written *simulacro* (image). In the two next diagrams at the spot here marked *L* the

word *Luna* is written, and in the last *Sole* is written in the top circle at *a*.

9. *Nel quarto della mia prospettiva.* The reflection of the sun in water is also discussed in the theoretical part of the Book on Painting; see vol. i, Nos. 206, 207.

fondono nelle similitudini che di lor [22]viene all' ochio, in modo tale che esse ōbre sono insensibili;¶

[23]Quel simulacro del sole occuperà [24]più lochi nella superfitie dell' acqua, che [25]sarà più distante dall' ochio che lo uede;

[26]a sia il sole, p q è il simulacro d'esso [27]sole, a b è la superfitie dell' acqua doue il sol [28]si spechia, r sia l'ochio che uede esso si[29]mulacro nella superfitie dell' acqua occupare [30]lo spatio o m; c è l'ochio più remoto [31]da essa superfitie dell' acqua, e così dal simulacro, onde esso simulacro [32]occupa maggiore spatio d'acqua,— quāto è lo spatio n o.

to the eye, so that these shadows are imperceptible.

That reflection of the sun will cover most space on the surface of the water which is most remote from the eye which sees it.

Let a be the sun, p q the reflection of the sun; a b is the surface of the water, in which the sun is mirrored, and r the eye which sees this reflection on the surface of the water occupying the space o m. c is the eye at a greater distance from the surface of the water and also from the reflection; hence this reflection covers a larger space of water, larger by the distance n o.

Br. M. 28a]   876

Ɉpossibile è [2]che tan[3]to quāto il sole allumina [4]dello spechio sperico, [5]tāto d'esso spechio ab[6]bia a risplendere, [7]se già esso spechio [8]non fusse ōdāte o globulē[9]to;

[10]Vedi qui il so[11]le allumina[12]re la luna, s[13]pechio speri[14]co, e tan[15]to quāto es[16]so sole ne [17]uede, tāto ne [18]fa splēdere;

[19]Qui si concluderà che ciò che della luna [20]splende è acqua simile a quella deg[21]li nostri mari, e così inōdata, ciò [22]che di lei non splende sone isole e ter[23]ra ferma.

It is impossible that the side of a spherical mirror, illuminated by the sun, should reflect its radiance unless this mirror were undulating or filled with bubbles.

You see here the sun which lights up the moon, a spherical mirror, and all of its surface which faces the sun is rendered radiant.

Whence it may be concluded that what shines in the moon is water like that of our seas, and in waves as that is; and that portion which does not shine consists of islands and *terra firma*.

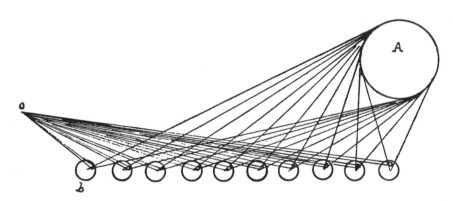

[24]Questa dimostratione di tanti corpi sperici interposti infra l'ochio [25]e 'l sole è fatta per mostrare che, siccome in ciascuno d'essi [26]corpi si uede il simulacro del sole, così si può vedere esso simulacro in cia[27]scuna globosità dell' onde del mare; come in molti di questi sperici si [28]uedono molti soli, così in molte onde si uedono molti lustri, li quali in molta [29]distanzia, ciascū lustro per sé, si fanno grādi all' ochio e,

This diagram of several spherical bodies interposed between the eye and the sun is given to show that, just as the reflection of the sun is seen in each of these bodies, in the same way that image may be seen in each curve of the waves of the sea; and as in these many spheres many reflections of the sun are seen, so in many waves there are many images, each of which at a great distance is much magnified to the eye.

23. sole [se] ochupera. 25. chel uede. 27. ella. 28. sisspechia. 29. acq''a'' ocupare. 30. Losspatio . . elloccio. 32. ochupa magore . . ello.
876. 1. he [chellol spechio]. 2. [consperico possa] chettan. 4. sperico tā. 6. rissplendere. 7. ga. 8. fussi ōdate o globbule. 13. echio. 14. cho ettan. 19. che co che. 20. acqui . . acquella de. 21. ecco. 22. etter. 24. sperichi. 25. sole [nō] effatta per mosstrare [come] che si come in ciasscuno. 26. po . . in ca. 27. globbosita . . mare c. me. 28. uede . . uede . . lusstri. 29. ciasscū lusstro . . fa grande

876. In the original, at letter A in the diagram *Sole* (the sun) is written, and at o ochio (the eye).

così faciēdo ciascu[30]na onda, si uengono a con-
sumare gli spati interposti infra l'onde, [31]e per
questa tal cagione e' pare tutto vn sole conti-
nuato nelli molti soli [32]spechiati nelle molte
onde, e le parti onbrose miste colle spetie
luminose [33]fan che tale splendore non è lucido
come quel del sole in esse ōde spechia[34]to.

And as this happens with each wave, the spaces
interposed between the waves are concealed;
and, for this reason, it looks as though the many
suns mirrored in the many waves were but one
continuous sun; and the shadows, mixed up
with the luminous images, render this radiance
less brilliant than that of the sun mirrored in
these waves.

F. 77*b*]   877

Questa avrà ināzi a sé il trattato de' [2]onbra
e lumi.

This will have before it the treatise on light
and shade.

[3]Li stremi della luna
sarā più alluminati e si
dimostre[4]ran più luminosi, perchè in quelli non
appare se nō le sō[5]mità
dell' ōde delle sue acque.

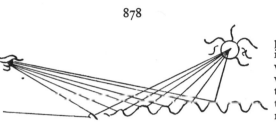

The edges in the moon
will be most strongly
lighted and reflect most
light because, there, no-
thing will be visible but
the tops of the waves of
the water [5].

W. 12350]   878

Il sole parirà mag-
giore nell' acqua
movente e ōdeg-
giāte [2]che nella fer-
ma: esemplo del
lume visto sopra le
corde [3]del mono-
cordo.

The sun will ap-
pear larger in mov-
ing water or on
waves than in still
water; an example is
the light reflected on
the strings of a mo-
nochord.

.. ciasscu. 30. lesspati .. infrallonde. 31. cagone. 32. elle parte onbro. 33. chettale .. none e .. in ese.
877. 1. ara .. asse. 2. ellumi. 3. dimoste. 4. apare.
878. 1. magiore .. ōdegiato. 2. essenplo .. chorde.

877. 5. I have not reproduced the detailed explanation of the theory of reflection on waves contained in
the passage which follows this.

II

THE SUN

LAUDE DEL SOLE

IN PRAISE OF THE SUN

The true and the apparent size of the sun (879–84)

[2]Se guarderai le stelle sanza razzi (come si fa a veder[3]le per un piccolo foro fatto colla strema pūta da[4]la sottile aguglia, e questo posto quasi a toccare l'ochio), [5]tu uedrai esse stelle essere tanto minime che nul[6]la cosa pare essere minore, e ueramēte la lūga di[7]stātia le fa ragionevolmente diminuire, ancoraché [8]molte vi sono che son moltissime volte maggiori che la [9]stella cioè la terra coll' acqua ·; ora pensa quel che par[10]rebbe essa nostra stella in tāta distantia, e conside[11]ra poi, quāte stelle si metterebbero e per longitudine e la[12]titudine infra esse stelle, le quali sono semina[13]te per esso spatio tenebroso; mai nō posso fare [14]ch'io non biasimi molti di quelli antichi, li quali disse[15]ro che 'l sole non avea altra grādezza che quella che [16]mostra, īfra quali fu Epicuro, e credo che caua[17]si tale ragione da vn lume posto in questa nostra a[18]ria, equidistāte al cētro; chi lo uede, non lo uede mai di[19]minuito di grādezza in nessuna distātia; e le ragi-

If you look at the stars, cutting off the rays (as may be done by looking through a very small hole made with the extreme point of a very fine needle, placed so as almost to touch the eye), you will see those stars so minute that it would seem as though nothing could be smaller; it is in fact their great distance which is the reason of their diminution, for many of them are very many times larger than the star which is the earth with the water. Now reflect what this our star must look like at such a distance, and then consider how many stars might be added—both in longitude and latitude—between those stars which are scattered over the darkened sky. But I cannot forbear to condemn many of the ancients, who said that the sun was no larger than it appears; among these was Epicurus, and I believe that he founded his reason on the effects of a light placed in our atmosphere equidistant from the centre (of the earth?). Any one looking at it never sees it diminished in size at whatever distance; and the reasons of its size and power I

oni della sua grandezza e virtù le riseruo nel [2]4° libro; ma bē mi maraviglio che Socrate biasi[3]masse questo tal corpo, e che dicesse quello esse[4]re a similitudine di pietra infocata, e certo, chi [5]l'oppose di tal errore poco peccò; Ma io vorrei [6]avere vocabuli che mi seruissero a biasimare quel[7]li che vogliono laudare più lo adorare li omini che [8]tal sole, nō uedēdo nell' uniuerso corpo [9]di maggiore magnitudine e virtù di quello; e 'l

shall reserve for Book 4. But I wonder greatly that Socrates [2] should have depreciated that solar body, saying that it was of the nature of incandescent stone, and the one who opposed him as to that error was not far wrong. But I only wish I had words to serve me to blame those who are fain to extol the worship of men more than that of the sun; for in the whole universe there is nowhere to be seen a body of

879. 1. lalde. 2. razi. 3. picholo. 4. acuchia ecque posto .. attocare. 6. lūgha dis. 7. stātia dalloro ragionevole diminuitione anchora che. 8. magore chella. 9. coe .. aq"a" .. che pa. 11. metterebbe e per .. ella. 14. quali diso. 15. no chel sole .. grādeza. 16. mostra [alla] īfra. 18. noluede. 19. minuto .. grādeza inessuna .. elle.
880. 1. grandeza. 3. massi .. dicessi. 4. assimilitudine. 5. loponi .. erore .. pecho. 6. seruissino abbiasimare que. 7. che vollō laldare. magore.

879–83. What Leonardo says of Epicurus he probably derived from Diogenes Laertius, *Vitae Philosophorum*, of which a free Italian version appeared in Venice in 1480. (Comp. No. 1485, n.)

880. 2. *Socrates*: Leonardo here quotes Diogenes Laertius, loc. cit. p. 9. Plato's Socrates declares on more than one occasion that in his youth he had turned his mind to the study of celestial phenomena (Μετέωρα). Here and there in Plato's writings we find incidental notes on the sun and other heavenly bodies. Leonardo may very well have known of these, since the Latin version by Ficinus was printed as early as 1491; indeed an undated edition exists which may very likely

have appeared between 1480 and 1490.

There is but one passage in Plato, *Epinomis* (983), where he speaks of the physical properties of the sun and says that it is larger than the earth.

Aristotle, who goes very fully into the subject, says the same. A complete edition of Aristotle's works was first printed in Venice in 1496 (Comp. No. 1481, n.). Leonardo could also study Aristotle's views in the works of scholastic writers such as Albertus of Saxony (No. 1496c), whom he also calls Albertuccio (No. 1421); he quotes from his work *Quaestiones in Aristotelis de coelo et mundo* (Nos. 903–4).

[10]suo lume allumina tutti li corpi celesti che per l'u[11]niverso si cōpartono; tutte l'anime discēdono da lui, [12]perchè il caldo ch'è in nelli animali viui viē dall' ani[13]me, e nessuno altro caldo nè lume è nell' u[14]niverso, come mostrerò nel 4º libro, e cier[15]to costoro che ànno voluto adorare uomini per i dei [16]come Giove Saturno Marte e simili ànno fatto grā[17]dissimo errore, vedēdo che ancorachè l'omo fus[18]se grande quāto il nostro mōdo, che parrebbe simi[19]le a vna minima stella, la qual pare vn pūto nell' uni[20]verso, e ancora vedendo essi omini mortali e [21]putridi e corruttibili nelle lor sepolture.

[22]La Spera [23]e Marullo [24]lauda cō m[25]olti altri [26]esso sole.

greater magnitude and power than the sun. Its light gives light to all the celestial bodies which are distributed throughout the universe; and from it descends all vital force, for the heat that is in living beings comes from the soul [vital spark]; and there is no other centre of heat and light in the universe, as will be shown in Book 4; and certainly those who have chosen to worship men as gods—as Jove, Saturn, Mars, and the like—have fallen into the gravest error, seeing that even if a man were as large as our earth, he would look no bigger than a little star which appears but as a speck in the universe; and seeing again that these men are mortal, and putrid and corrupt in their sepulchres.

The 'Spera' and Marullus [23] and many others praise the sun.

F. 6a]   881

Forse Epicuro vide le ōbre delle colonne ripercosse nelli an[2]tiposti muri essere equali al diametro della colōna [3]donde si partì a tale ōbra; essendo adunque il cōco[4]rso dell' ōbre paralello dall' suo nascimēto al suo fine, [5]li parue da giudicare che 'l sole an[6]cora lui fusse frōte di tal paralel[7]lo, e per cōsegueza non essere piv gros[8]so di tal colonna, e nō s'avvide che tal

Epicurus perhaps saw the shadows cast by columns on the walls in front of them equal in diameter to the columns from which the shadows were cast; and the breadth of the shadows being parallel from beginning to end, he thought he might infer that the sun also was directly opposite to this parallel and that consequently its breadth was not greater than that of the column; not perceiving that the diminution in the shadow

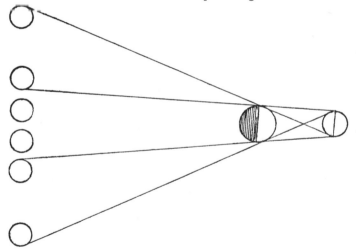

[9]diminuitione d'ōbra era insēsibile [10]per la lunga distantia del sole; [11]se 'l sole fusse minore della terra, le stelle [12]di grā parte del nostro emisperio sarebbero sā[13]za lume; cōtro a Epicuro che dice, tāto è [14]grāde il sole, quāto e' pare.

was insensibly slight by reason of the remoteness of the sun. If the sun were smaller than the earth, the stars on a great portion of our hemisphere would have no light; against Epicurus, who says the sun is only as large as it appears.

22. *Spera*, a book on Leonardo's list No. 1469, identified by Solmi with *La Spera* of Goro Dati, Florence, 1482.

23. Marullus, poet of Byzantine extraction (see Gaspary, *Gesch. der it. Lit.*, ii. 225). His hymn on the

sun was published in M. Tarcaniota's *Hymni et epigrammata*, Florence, 1487.

881. In the original the writing is across the diagram.

F. 8b]   882

Dice Epicuro il sole essere tāto quāto esso si dimostra; a²dunque e' pare essere vn piè, e così l'abbiamo a tenere; ³seguirebbe che la luna quād' ella fa oscurare il sole, il so⁴le non l'avāzerebbe di grādezza come e' fa, onde, sendo ⁵la luna minor del sole, essa luna sarebbe meno d'un piede, ⁶e per conseguēza quando il nostro mōdo fa oscurare la lu⁷na, sarebbe minore a un dito del piedi, conciò sia se 'l so⁸le è un piede, e la nostra terra fa onbra piramidale in⁹verso la luna, egli è necessario che sia maggiore il lumi¹⁰noso, causa della piramide ōbrosa, che l'opaco, causa d'essa ¹¹piramide.

Epicurus says the sun is the size it looks. Hence as it looks about a foot across we must consider that to be its size; it would follow that when the moon eclipses the sun, the sun ought not to appear the larger, as it does. Then, the moon being smaller than the sun, the moon must be less than a foot, and consequently when our world eclipses the moon, it must be less than a foot by a finger's breadth; inasmuch as if the sun is a foot across, and our earth casts a conical shadow on the moon, it is inevitable that the luminous cause of the cone of shadow must be larger than the opaque body which casts the cone of shadow.

F. 10a]   883

Misura quāti soli si metterebbero ²nel corso suo di 24 ore.

³Fa vn circulo e voltalo a mezzodì, come sō ⁴li orilogi da sole, e metti vna bachetta in ⁵mezzo, in modo che la sua lūghezza si di⁶rizzi al cētro di tal cerchio, e nota l'on⁷bra che fa il sole d'essa bacchetta sopra la ⁸circūferentia di tale cerchio, che sarà ⁹l'onbra larga, diciamo tutto a n; ora ¹⁰misura quante volte tale ōbra entra in ¹¹tale circūferētia di cerchio, e tāte vol¹²te fia il numero che 'l corpo solare entrerà nel ¹³corso suo in 24 ore; e qui si potrà ¹⁴vedere, se Epicuro disse, che 'l sole era ¹⁵tanto grande quāto esso parea | che, pa-¹⁶rendo il diametro del sole vna misura ¹⁷pedale, e che esso sole entrasse mille ¹⁸volte nel suo corso di 24 ore, egli avre¹⁹bbe corso mille piedi, cioè 300 braccia che ²⁰è vn sesto di miglio; ora ecco che 'l cor²¹so del sole infra dì e notte sarebbe ²²la sesta parte d'ū miglio, ²³e questa venerabile lumaca del sole av²⁴rebbe caminato 25 braccia per ora.

To measure how many times the diameter of the sun will go into its course in 24 hours.

Make a circle and place it to face the south, after the manner of a sun-dial, and place a rod in the middle in such a way that its length points to the centre of this circle, and mark the shadow cast in the sunshine by this rod on the circumference of the circle, and this shadow will be—let us say—as broad as from a to n. Now measure how many times this shadow will go into this circumference of a circle, and that will give you the number of times that the solar body will go into its orbit in 24 hours. Thus you may see whether Epicurus was [right in] saying that the sun was only as large as it looked; for, as the apparent diameter of the sun is about a foot, and as that sun would go a thousand times into the length of its course in 24 hours, it would have gone a thousand feet, that is, 300 braccia, which is the sixth of a mile. Whence it would follow that the course of the sun during the day would be the sixth part of a mile and that this venerable snail, the sun, will have travelled 25 braccia an hour.

F. 0″]   884

Possidonius cōpose libri della grādezza del sole.

Poseidonius composed books on the size of the sun.

882. 2. labiamo attenere. 3. seguirebe chella. 4. nollauāzerebbe . . grādeza chome. 5. medun piedi. 6. chonsequēza . . osscurar. 7. concosia. 8. piedi ella. 9. luna "la" egli . . magore. 10. caua della.
883. 1. metterebbe. 3. mezodi. 4. dassole . . bachetta. 5. mezo . . chella. 5. lūgeza. 6. rizi. 7. cheffa. 8. cercio chessara. 9. largha. 11. ettāte. 12. il n"o" chel . . entera. 13. ecqui. 16. diamitro. 17. entrassi. 18. egliare. 19. coe 300 br . che. 20. miglo ora e che chel corso. 21. serebbela. 22. minato la sesta. 23. che questa . . lumacha del sole a. 24. rebe . . 25. br per.

884. Poseidonius of Apamea, commonly called the Rhodian, because he taught in Rhodes, was a Stoic philosopher, a contemporary and friend of Cicero's, and the author of numerous works on natural science, among them: Φυσικὸς λόγος, περὶ κόσμου, περὶ μετεώρων.

Strabo quotes no doubt from one of his works, when he says that Poseidonius explained how it was that the sun looked larger when it was rising or setting than during the rest of its course (iii, p. 135). Kleomedes, a later Greek Naturalist, also mentions this

observation of Poseidonius' without naming the title of his work; however, as Kleomedes' *Cyclica Theorica* was not printed till 1535, Leonardo must have derived his quotation from Strabo. He probably wrote this note in 1508, and as the original Greek was first printed in Venice in 1516, we must suppose him to quote here from the translation by Guarinus Veronensis, which was printed as early as 1471, also at Venice (H. Müller-Strübing).

G. 34*a*]   885

DELLA PROVA CHE 'L SOLE È CAL²DO PER NATURA
E NŌ PER VIRTÙ

³Che 'l sol sia in sé caldo per natura e nō per vir⁴tù, si dimostra manifestamēte per ⁵lo splendore del corpo solare, nel ⁶qual nō si può fermare l'ochio vmano, ⁷e oltre a di questo manifestissima⁸mēte lo dimostrano li sua razzi refle⁹ssi dalli spechi concavi, li quali, quā¹⁰do la lor percussione sarà di tāto sp¹¹lendore, che l'ochio non lo possa soppo¹²rtare, allora essa percussione ¹³avrà splendore simile al sole nel ¹⁴suo propio sito; e che sia vero, pro¹⁵vo che se tale spechio à la sua ¹⁶cōcavità tal qual si richiede alla ¹⁷generatione di tale razzo, allora ¹⁸nessuna cosa creata reggerà ¹⁹alla caldezza di tale percussione ²⁰di razzo reflesso d'alcuno spechio; ²¹e se tu dirai che lo spechio anco²²ra lui è freddo e gitta i razzi caldi, io ²³ti rispondo, che 'l razzo viē dal sole ed va passando per lo spechio a assomigliarsi alla sua causa e passi per che mezzo passar si voglia il razzo dello spechio concavo, passato a traverso della finestra delle fornace dove son fonduti i . . . (?) non a gran caldezza ne anchor biagza.

OF THE PROOF THAT THE SUN IS HOT BY NATURE
AND NOT BY VIRTUE

That the heat of the sun resides in its nature and not in its virtue [or mode of action] is abundantly proved by the radiance of the solar body on which the human eye cannot dwell, and besides this no less manifestly by the rays reflected from a concave mirror, which—when they strike the eye with such splendour that the eye cannot bear them—have a brilliancy equal to the sun in its own place. And that this is true I prove by the fact that if the mirror has its concavity formed exactly as is requisite for the collecting and reflecting of these rays, no created being could endure the heat that strikes from the reflected rays of such a mirror. And if you argue that the mirror itself is cold and yet sends forth hot rays, I should reply that the ray comes really from the sun and in passing through the mirror remains like its cause, through whatever medium it is made to pass. The ray of the concave mirror passing through the window of a furnace where are melted . . . (?) has neither great heat nor brightness.

Of the nature of sunlight.

W. 12669*a*]   886

Il sole nō si move.

The sun does not move.

Considerations as to the size of the sun (886–91).

B. N. 2038. 16*b*]   887

PRUOVA · COME QUĀTO PIV · SARAI PRESSO ALLA
CAGI²ONE · DE' RAZZI DEL SOLE ·, PIV TI PARRÀ
MAGGIORE IL SOLE ³SPECHIATO SUL MARE

⁴Se il sole adopera il suo splendore col suo ciētro ⁵a fortificare la potētia di tutto il corpo, è ne⁶ciessario · che i sua razzi, quāto piv · s'alontanano da lui, piv si uadino ⁷aprēdo: se così è, tu che sei col ochio presso all' acqua · che spechia il sole, ⁸vedi una minima parte de' razzi del sole portare sulla superfitie ⁹de l'acqua la forma d'esso sole spechiato ·, e se tu sarai presso al sole, ¹⁰come sarebbe quādo il sole è ī mezzodì e 'l mare sia per ponēte, ved¹¹rai il sole spechiarsi su detto mare di grādissima forma, perchè, ¹²essēdo tu più presso al sole ·, l'ochio tuo, pigliādo i razzi presso al

PROOF THAT THE NEARER YOU ARE TO THE SOURCE
OF THE SOLAR RAYS, THE LARGER WILL THE REFLEC-
TION OF THE SUN FROM THE SEA APPEAR TO YOU

[4] If it is from the centre that the sun employs its radiance to intensify the power of its whole mass, it is evident that the farther its rays extend, the more widely they will be divided; and this being so, you, whose eye is near the water that mirrors the sun, see but a small portion of the rays of the sun strike the surface of the water, and reflecting the form of the sun. But if you were near to the sun—as would be the case when the sun is on the meridian and the sea to the westward—you would see the sun, mirrored in the sea, of a very great size; because as you are nearer to the sun, your eye taking in the rays

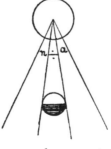

---

885. 1–47 R. 4. manifestamēti. 5. sprendore. 6. po. 8. razi refre. 9. delli. 11. eldore chellochio nol possa sopo. 12. percussione ar.
13. ara. 15. va chesse tale . . alla. 17. razo. 18. regiera. 20. refresso. 21. essettu . . chello. 22. fredo . . razi. 23. razo.
886. El sol.
887. 2. razi . . para magiore. 4. splendre. 5. a forzifichato dala . . chorpo. 6. razi. 7. che se chol . . preso. 8. vedi ĩ . . parte [del sole]
de razi . . sula. 9. esse tussarai. 10. sarebe . . mezodi . . vede. 12. razi.

886. This sentence occurs incidentally among mathematical notes, and is written in unusually large letters.

887. Lines 4 ff. Compare vol. i, Nos. 130, 131.

pūto, ¹³ne piglia piv, e perciò ne resulta mag-giore splēdore, e per questa ca¹⁴gione si po-trebbe provare la luna essere un' altro mondo simile ¹⁵al nostro, e quella parte d'essa che risplende essere mare che spe¹⁶chia · il sole ·, e quello che nō risplēde fia terra.

nearer to the point of radiation takes more of them in, and a great splendour is the result. And in this way it can be proved that the moon is another world similar to ours, and the part of her which shines is sea reflecting the sun, and the parts which do not shine are land.

Br. M. 78b]   888

[Togli la misura ²del sole in solstitio ³a mezzo ⁴giugnio.]

Take the measure of the sun at the solstice in mid-June.

A. 64a]   889

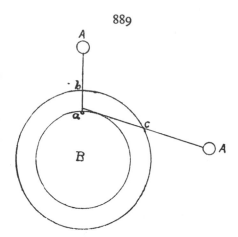

PERCHÈ · IL SOLE · PARE MAGGIORE NEL TRA²MŌ-TARE · CHE DI MEZZO GIORNO CHE CI È PRESSO

³Ogni corpo ch'è visto per curvo mezzo ⁴ap-parisce di maggiore for-ma, che non è.

WHY THE SUN APPEARS LARGER WHEN SETTING THAN AT NOON, WHEN IT IS NEAR TO US

Every object seen through a curved me-dium seems to be of lar-ger size than it is.

C. A. 237a]   890

Perchè l'ochio è piccolo, esso non può vedere ²il sole in simvlacro, se nō piccolo; ³Se l'occhio fusse equale al sole, esso vedrebbe ⁴nell' acque, dato che le fussī ⁵piane, il simulacro del sole equa⁶le al uero corpo del sole.

Because the eye is small it can only see the image of the sun as of a small size. If the eye were as large as the sun it would see the image of the sun in the water of the same size as the real body of the sun, so long as the water is smooth.

Triv. 6b]   891

MODO DI VEDERE · IL SOLE ECLISSATO SANZA · PASSIONE · DELL' OCHIO

²Tolli · vna carta · e falle busi con una agu-chia, e per es³si busi · riguarda il · sole.

A METHOD OF SEEING THE SUN ECLIPSED WITHOUT PAIN TO THE EYE

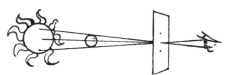

Take a piece of paper and pierce holes in it with a needle, and look at the sun through these holes.

13. perco . . magiore. 14. potrebe. 15. ecquela.
888. 1. to la. 2. sostitio. 3. stiuo [a mezo]. 4. gugnio.
889. 1. magiore. 2. megogorno checepresso. 3. chorpo . . churvo mezo. 4. aparisscie di magiore.
890. 1. picholo . . po. 2. dere il . . picholo. 3. Sellochio fussi. 4. aque . . chelle.
891. 1. da vedere. 2. charta . . chonaguchia epere.

889. At A is written *sole* (the sun), at B *terra* (the earth).

III

THE MOON

DELLA LUNA

[2]Volendo io trattare della essentia della luna · è neciessario in prima [3]descriuere la prospettiva delli spechi piani, cōcaui e cōuessi; [4]e prima che cosa è razzo luminoso, e come si piega per varie nature [5]di mezzi; Dipoi dove il razzo riflesso è più potēte, o nell' esser

OF THE MOON

As I propose to treat of the nature of the moon, it is necessary that first I should describe the perspective of mirrors, whether plane, concave, or convex; and first what is meant by a luminous ray, and how it is refracted by various kinds of media; then, when a reflected ray is

On the luminosity of the moon (892–901).

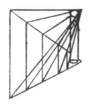
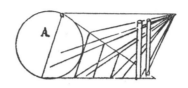

lato [6]della incidentia acuto retto o ottuso, o nelle cōuessità o piano o [7]cōcavità, o da corpo dēso e trasparēte; Oltre a di questo, [8]come li razzi solari, che percuotono l'onde marine, si dimostrano al[9]l' ochio in tanta larghezza nell' āgolo dell' ochio quanto nell' ultima somma [10]dell' ōde all' orizzōte, e per questo nō māca che tale splendore solare ri[11]flesso dall' ōde marittime nō sia di figura piramidale e per conseguē[12]za in ogni grado di distātia non acquisti gradi di larghezza ācorachè [13]inquāto al nostro vedere si dimostri paralello.

[14]1[1a] ¶ Nessū lievissimo [15]è opaco; ¶

[16]2[2a] ¶ Nessū più lieve sta [17]sotto al mē lieve; ¶

[18]3[3a] ¶ Se la luna à sito [19]in mezzo alli sua ele[20]mēti o no;

[21]e s'ella non à sito [22]particulare co[23]me la terra nelli sua [24]elemēti, perchè nō ca[25]de al cientro de' nostri [26]elemēnti?

[27]E se la luna non è [28]in mezzo alli sua elemē[29]ti e nō discēde, [30]adūque ella è più [31]lieve che altro elemē[32]to;

[33]E se la luna è più lie[34]ve che altro elemēto, per[35]chè è solida e nō traspare.

[36] ¶ Delle cose di varie grādezze che, poste in

most powerful, whether when the angle of incidence is acute, right, or obtuse, or from a convex, a plane, or a concave surface; or from an opaque or a transparent body. Besides this, how it is that the solar rays which fall on the waves of the sea are seen by the eye of the same width at the angle nearest to the eye as at the highest line of the waves on the horizon; but notwithstanding this the solar rays reflected from the waves of the sea assume the pyramidal form and, consequently, at each degree of distance increase proportionally in size, although to our sight they appear as parallel.

1[stly]. Nothing that has very little weight is opaque.

2[dly]. Nothing that is light can remain beneath that which is heavier.

3[dly]. As to whether the moon is situated in the centre of its elements or not.

And if it has no proper place of its own, like the earth, in the midst of its elements, why does it not fall to the centre of our elements [26]?

And if the moon is not in the centre of its own elements and yet does not fall, it must then be lighter than any other element.

And if the moon is lighter than the other elements, why is it opaque and not transparent?

When objects of various sizes, being placed at

---

892. 2. tractare. 3. desscriuere .. presspectiva .. cōchaui e chōuissi [e che]. 4. chosa errazzo .. chome .. piegha. 5. mezi .. refresso eppiu potēte o nell esser lato. 6. achuta retta o hottusa ho .. pioni ho. 7. chōchavita adda chorpo .. ettrasparete .. addiquesto. 8. chome li razi .. perchotano. 9. llochio .. largheza .. āghol .. soma. 10. orizōte .. mācha chettale. 11. fresso .. fighura .. chosseghuē. 12. disstātia .. largheza āchora. 13. nosstro .. dimosstri parallela. 15. he oppacho. 18. sella .. assito. 20. onno. 21. essella. 22. partichulare cho. 24. cha. 25. nosstri. 27. essella. 28. imezzo. 29. disscēde. 30. eppiu. 33. essella .. eppiu. 35. solita .. trasspare. 36. delle chose .. grādezze [chessendo] posste.

892. In the diagram Leonardo wrote *sole* at the place marked *A*.
26. The problem here propounded by Leonardo

was not satisfactorily answered till Newton in 1682 formulated the law of universal attraction and gravitation. Compare No. 902, ll. 5–15.

varie distātie, [37]si mostrano equali, tal proportione fia da distātia a distā[38]tia, qual fia da
magnitudine a magnitudine. ¶

various distances, look of equal size, there must
be the same relative proportion in the distances
as in the magnitudes of the objects.

F. 93a]   893

DELLA LUNA E SE ELLA È PULITA E SPERICA

[2]Il simulacro del sole in lei è potētemen[3]te
luminoso ed è in piccola parte della su[4]a superfitie; E la prova vedrai a tor[5]re vna palla d'oro
brunito, posta nel[6]le tenebre, con vn lume da
lei remoto, [7]il quale ancorachè esso allumini
circa [8]la metà d'essa palla, l'ochio non lo uede,
se nō [9]in piccola parte della sua superfitie, e
tut[10]to il resto di tal superfitie spechia le tenebre
[11]che la circūdano, e per questo in lei solo
appa[12]risce il simulacro del lume e tutto il
re[13]sto rimane invisibile, stando l'ochio remo[14]to
da tal palla; Questo medesimo interue[15]rrebbe
nella superfitie della luna, essendo po[16]lita,
lustra e densa, come son corpi che spe[17]chiano;

[18]Prova tu [19]come, se tu [20]stessi nella [21]luna
o in una [22]stella, [23]la nostra [24]terra ti par[25]rà far
l'u[26]fitio col so[27]le che fa la [28]luna;

[29]E prova [30]come in nel si[31]mulacro [32]del sole
nel [33]mare nō [34]può parere [35]vn sole co[36]me
pare in u[37]no spechio pi[38]ano.

OF THE MOON AND WHETHER IT IS POLISHED AND SPHERICAL

The image of the sun in the moon is power-
fully luminous, and is only on a small portion of
its surface. And the proof may be seen by taking
a ball of burnished gold and placing it in the
dark with a light at some distance from it; and
then, although it will illuminate about half of
the ball, the eye will perceive its reflection only
in a small part of its surface, and all the rest of
the surface reflects the darkness which surrounds it; so that it is only in that spot that the
image of the light is seen, and all the rest remains invisible, the eye being at a distance from
the ball. The same thing would happen on the
surface of the moon if it were polished, lustrous,
and opaque, like all bodies with a reflecting surface.

Show how, if you were standing on the moon
or on a star, our earth would seem to reflect the
sun as the moon does.

And show that the image of the sun in the sea
cannot appear one and undivided, as it appears
in a perfectly plane mirror.

B. N. 2038. 16b]   894

Come l'onbre si cōfondono per lūnga distātia,
[2]si prvova nel' ōbra della luna che mai [3]si
vede.

How shadows are lost at great distances, as is
shown by the shadow side of the moon which is
never seen.

Br. M. 28a]   895

O la luna à lume da sé [2]o no; s'ell' à lume
da sé, per[3]chè non risplende sanza [4]l'aiuto del
sole? e s'ella [5]non à lume da sé, necies[6]sità
la fa spechio sperico; [7]e se ella è spechio,
non è prova[8]to in prospettiua ¶ che 'l sim[9]u-
lacro d'uno obbietto lumi[10]noso nō sarà mai
equale alla [11]parte di quello spechio che da
esso luminoso è [12]alluminato? ¶ e se così è,
come [13]mostra qui la figura in r s, dō[14]de

Either the moon has intrinsic luminosity or
not. If it has, why does it not shine without the
aid of the sun? But if it has not any light in
itself it must of necessity be a spherical mirror;
and if it is a mirror, is it not proved in Perspective that the image of a luminous object
will never be equal to the extent of surface
of the reflecting body that it illuminates? And
if it be thus [13], as is here shown at r s in the

---

37. disstātia adisstā.
893. 1. esselle. 2. illei. 3. pichola. 4. attor. 6. dallei. 8. noluede. 9. pichola .. ettu. 11. chella circūda .. illei .. apa. 12. ettutto.
14. dattal. 15. rebe. 16. lusstra .. chesspe. 19. settu. 21. onni. 24. pa. 27. cheffa. 30. col inel si. 34. po. 35. vnsole. 36. pare
nū. 37. no spechio. 38. anano.
894. 1. chōfondono. 2. dela.
895. 1. Olla .. allume dasse. 2. onno. 3. risplde. 4. essella. 5. dasse. 7. essello spechio. 8. prosspectiva. 11. parte "di quello spechio"
che .. he. 12. esse.

894. Compare also vol. i, Nos. 175–9.
895. 13. At A, in the diagram, Leonardo wrote

'sole' (the sun), and at B 'luna o noi terra' (the moon
or our earth). Compare also the text of No. 876.

uiē tanta quantità di splendo[15]re che à il plenilunio, che noi ve[16]diamo nella quinta decima
della [17]luna?

figure, whence comes so great an extent of
radiance as that of the full moon as we see it,
at the fifteenth day of the moon?

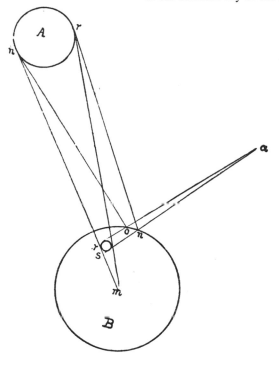

Br. M. 94b]   896

DELLA LUNA

[2]La luna non à lume da sé, se nō quāto ne
vede il sole tanto l'alumina, [3]della qual luminosità tanto ne vediamo quāto è quella che vede
noi; [4]E la sua notte riceve tanto di splēdore,
quāto è quello che li pre[5]stano le nostre acque
nel refletterli il simulacro del sole, che in [6]tutte
quelle che vedono il sole e la luna, si spechia;
[7]La pelle over superfitie dell' acqua, di che si
cōpone il mare della luna e il [8]mare della nostra
terra, è senpre rugoso, [9]o poco o assai, o più
o meno, e tale rugosità è cavsa di dila[10]tare
l'innumerabili simulacri del sole, che nei colli
e cōcavità e la[11]ti e frōti delle innumerabili
rughe si spechiano, cioè in tāti vari siti di
ciascuna [12]ruga quāto son vari li siti che ànno
li ochi che le vedono, jl che ac[13]cadere nō
potrebbe, se la spera dell' acqua, che ī grā parte
di sé veste la [14]luna fusse d'uniforme spericità,
perchè allora il simulacro del [15]sole sarebbe uno
a ciascuno ochio, e la sua reflessione sarebbe
particu[16]lare e senpre sarebbe splēdore sperico,

OF THE MOON

The moon has no light in itself; but so much
of it as faces the sun is illuminated, and of that
illumined portion we see so much as faces the
earth. And the moon's night receives just as
much light as is lent it by our waters as they
reflect the image of the sun, which is mirrored
in all those waters which are on the side towards the sun and the moon. The outside or
surface of the waters forming the seas of the
moon and of the seas of our globe is always
ruffled little or much, or more or less—and this
roughness causes an extension of the numberless
images of the sun which are repeated in the ridges
and hollows, the sides and fronts of the innumerable waves; that is to say, in as many different
spots on each wave as our eyes find different
positions to view them from. This could not
happen if the aqueous sphere which covers a great
part of the moon were uniformly spherical, for
then the images of the sun would be one to each
spectator, and its reflections would be separate

896. 2. dasse.   3. vedano . . ecquella.   4. Ella . . chelli pres.   5. nosstre acque . . refretterli.   6. vedano . . elluna si sspechia.
7. dichessi . . luna edel.   8. [la nostra luna] mare . . nosstra . . essenpre rughoso.   9. oppocho . . oppiu ōmeno ettale rughosita
e chausa. 10. ine cholli e chōchavita ellati. 11. ti effrote "delle inumerabili" rughe sisspechiano . . ciasscuna. 12. rugha . . che
āli . . chelle vedano. 13. chadere . . sella . . achq"a" . . vesste. 14. luno fussi. 15. uno "acciascuno ochio" ella . . refressione . .
partichu. 16. essenpre . . spericho chome.

come manifestamē[17]te ci assegnano le palle dorate, poste nelle sommità delli alti edifiti; Ma [18]se tali palle dorate fussino rugose o globulēti come son le mo[19]re, frutti neri conposti di minute globosità rotonde, allora ciascuna delle parti d'essa [20]globosità, vedute dal sole e dall' ochio, mostrerà a esso ochio il lustro [21]gienerato dal simulacro d'esso sole; e così in ū medesimo corpo si ue[22]drebbero molti minimi soli, li quali spesse sō le volte che per lunga distātia [23]si uniscono e paiono cōtinuati; E 'l lustro della luna nuova è più lucido e più [24]potēte che quādo è in plenilunio, e questo si ca[25]vsa perchè l'angolo della incidētia è molto più ottuso nella luna nuo[26]va che nella vechia, doue tali angoli sono acutissimi; e l'onde della [27]luna spechiano il sole così nelle lor ualli come nelli colli, e li lati [28]restano oscuri ·; ma ne' lati della luna li fondi dell' onde non [29]vedono il sole, ma solo uedono le cime d'esse ōde, e per questo li simu[30]lacri son più rari e più misti coll' ombre delle valli, e tal mistione [31]delle spetie ōbrose e luminose, così insieme infuse, vengono all' o[32]chio cō poco splēdore, e nelli stremi sarā piv oscure per essere [33]la curuità 'de' lati di tale ōde insuffitiēte a riflettere all' ochio li ri[34]cievuti razzi; La luna nova per natura riflette li [35]razzi solari più inverso l'ochio

and its radiance would always appear circular; as is plainly to be seen in the gilt balls placed on the tops of high buildings. But if those gilt balls were rugged or composed of several little balls like mulberries, which are a black fruit composed of minute round globules, then each portion of these little balls, when seen in the sun, would display to the eye the lustre resulting from the reflection of the sun; and thus, in one and the same body many tiny suns would be seen; and these often combine at a long distance and appear as one. The lustre of the new moon is brighter and stronger than when the moon is full; and the reason of this is that the angle of incidence is more obtuse in the new than in the full moon, in which the angles [of incidence and reflection] are highly acute. The waves of the moon therefore mirror the sun in their hollows as well as on the ridges, and the sides remain in shadow. But at the sides of the moon the hollows of the waves do not catch the sunlight, but only their crests; and thus the images are fewer and more mixed up with the shadows in the hollows; and this intermingling of the shaded and illuminated spots comes to the eye with a mitigated splendour, so that the edges will be darker, because the curves of the sides of the waves are insufficient to reflect to the eye the rays that fall upon them. Now the new moon naturally reflects the solar rays more directly towards the eye from the crests of the waves than

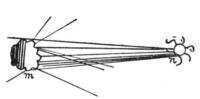

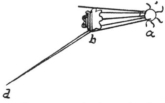

per tali ōde streme, [36]che per nessuno altro loco, come mostra la figura della luna che [37]percuotēdo con razzi a nell' onda b riflette in b d, dou' è situa[38]to l'ochio d; E questo accadere nō può nel plenilunio dove [39]il razzo solare, stando all' occidēte, percuote l'onde streme della [40]luna all' oriēte dal n in m, e non riflette inverso l'oc[41]chio occidētale, ma risalta all' oriēte, poco piegādo la rettitu[42]dine d'esso razzo solare, e così l'angolo della incidētia è grossissimo.

[43]La luna è corpo opa[44]co e solido, e se per lo a[45]versario ella fusse trāspa[46]rente, ella nō ricieverebbe [47]il lume del sole.

[48]Il rossume over tuorlo dell' o[49]vo sta [50]in

from any other part, as is shown by the form of the moon, whose rays a strike the waves b and are reflected in the line b d, the eye being situated at d. This cannot happen at the full moon, when the solar rays, being in the west, fall on the extreme waters of the moon to the east from n to m, and are not reflected to the eye in the west, but are thrown back eastwards, with but slight deflection from the straight course of the solar ray; and thus the angle of incidence is very wide indeed.

The moon is an opaque and solid body and if, on the contrary, it were transparent, it would not receive the light of the sun.

The yellow or yolk of an egg remains in the

17. asegnia. 18. ssettali .. rughose o globbulēti chome. 19. "neri" chonposti .. "rotonde" allora ciasscuna "delle parte". 20. globbosita .. mossterra. 21. chosi nūn .. chorpo. 22. derebbe .. lungha disstātia. 23. vnisschono e ppaiano chōtinuati .. eppiu cido epiu. 24. pleniunnio ecquesto .. cha. 25. langholo. 26. vechia .. tale angholi .. achutissimi ellonde. 27. chosi .. chome .. cholli elli. 28. resstano osschuri. 29. vedano .. massolo vede .. quessto. 30. choll .. ettal. 31. elluminose chosi .. infussi venghano. 32. chō pocho .. osschure. 33. churuita .. arefrettere. 34. razza da qual chosa la luna .. refrette. 35. razi .. tale. 36. locho .. mosstra la fighura. 37. percho tendo cho razi .. b e rēfrette. 38. Ecquesto achadere .. dove || o. 39. razo solare [que] perchote stando allocidēte perchote lonte. 40. refrette. 41. pocho pieghādo. 42. chosi langholo. 43. chorpo. 44. cho essolido esse. 45. e fussi. 46. enō. 49. sta [in in al piu delle]. 50. [volte] in.

896. 48–64. Compare No. 861.

mezzo al suo al[51]bume sanza discēdere [52]d'alcuna parte, ed è pi[53]v lieve o più grave o equale d'esso [54]albume; e s'elli è più li[55]eve egli dovrebbe surgie[56]re sopra tutto l'albume e [57]fermarsi in cōtatto del[58]la scorza d'es[59]so uovo, e s'elli è più [60]grave dovrebbe di-[61]sciēdere, e s'egli è equa[62]le così potrebbe stare [63]nell' v̄ delli stremi, co[64]me in mezzo o disotto;

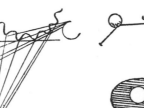

[65]L'īnvmerabili simulacri [66]che dalle innumerabili onde del ma[67]re reflettono li sola[68]ri razzi, in esse onde percos[69]si, son causa di rē[70]dere cōtinuato e larghissi[71]mo splēdore sopra la superfitie [72]del mare.

middle of the albumen, without moving on either side; now it is either lighter or heavier than this albumen, or equal to it; if it is lighter, it ought to rise above all the albumen and stop in contact with the shell of the egg; and if it is heavier, it ought to sink, and if it is equal, it might just as well be at one of the ends as in the middle or below [54].

The innumerable images of the solar rays reflected from the innumerable waves of the sea, as they fall upon those waves, are what cause us to see the very broad and continuous radiance on the surface of the sea.

Br. M. 104a]　　　　　　　　　　897

[Come nō si può specchiare il sole nel corpo [2]della luna, essendo spechio colmo, in mo[3]do

That the sun could not be mirrored in the body of the moon, which is a convex mirror, in

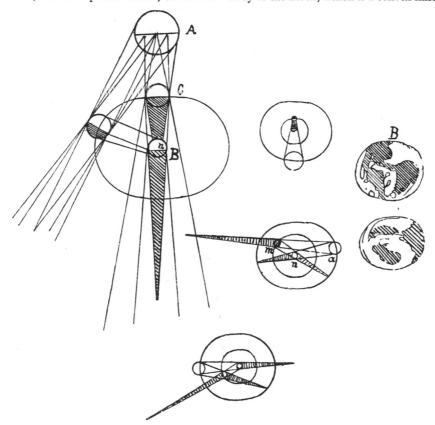

897. In the original diagrams *sole* is written at the place marked *A*; *luna* at *C*, and *terra* at the two spots marked *B*.

che tanto quanto esso sol ne alumina, [4]tanto essa luna ne spechia, se già tal luna [5]non avesse la superfitie atta a spechiare, [6]che fusse rugosa, a vso di superfitie di mare, [7]quando in parte è mossa dal uento.]

[8]L'onde dell' acqua crescono [9]il simulacro della cosa [10]in lei spechiata.

[11][Quest' onde si fanno per o[12]gni linia a similitu[13]dine della spoglia del[14]la pina.]

[15]Queste son 2 figure sichè [16]farai le l'una disperse dall' altra, [17]cioè l'acqua [18]ondeggiante dall' acqua piana.

[19]Inpossibil' è [20]che per alcuna distantia il [21]simulacro del sole, [22]fatto nella superfitie [23]del corpo sperico, occupi [24]la metà d'esso sperico;

[25]Qui tu ài a provare, come la terra fa tutti [26]quelli medesimi ofiti inverso la luna che [27]la luna inverso la terra;

[28]Nō luce la luna col suo lume riflesso come [29]fa il sole, perchè il lume della luna non piglia [30]il lume del sole continuo in nel[31]la superfitie, ma in su colmi e cavi del[32]le onde delle acque, e per esser tal sole nella [33]luna cōfusamente spechiato per le mi[34]stioni delle onbre, che sono infra [35]l'onde che lustrano, perciò non è [36]il suo lume lucido e chiaro [37]com' è 'l sole.

[38]Terra infra la luna in quīta decima e il sole; [39]Qui il sole è nel ponente e la luna in levante in quīta decima; [40]luna infra la terra in quīta decima e il sole; [41]Qui è la luna che à il sole per levāte e la terra per ponēte.

such a way that so much of its surface as is illuminated by the sun should reflect the sun unless the moon had a surface adapted to reflect it—in waves and ridges, like the surface of the sea when its surface is moved by the wind.

The waves in water multiply the image of the object reflected in it.

These waves are, each by its own line, as the surface of the fir cone [14].

These are 2 figures, make them one dispersed by the other; the one with undulating water by the other with smooth water.

It is impossible that at any distance the image of the sun cast on the surface of a spherical body should occupy half of the sphere.

Here you must prove that the earth produces all the same effects with regard to the moon as the moon with regard to the earth.

The moon, with its reflected light, does not shine like the sun, because the light of the moon is not a continuous reflection of that of the sun on its whole surface, but only on the crests and hollows of the waves of its waters; and thus the sun being confusedly reflected, from the admixture of the shadows that lie between the lustrous waves, its light is not pure and clear as the sun is.

[38] The earth between the moon on the fifteenth day and the sun. [39] Here the sun is in the west and the moon on the fifteenth day in the east. [40] The moon on the fifteenth [day] between the earth and the sun. [41] Here it is the moon which has the sun to the east and the earth to the west.

A. 64a]   898

CHE COSA · È LA LUNA

WHAT SORT OF THING THE MOON IS

[2]La luna non è · luminosa · per sé, ma bene è atta · a ricievere la natura · della · luce [3]a similitudine · dello · spechio · e dell'acqua · o altro · corpo · lucido ·, e crescie nell' oriēte [4]e occidēte · come · il sole · e gli altri pianeti ·; E la ragione · si è · che ogni · corpo · luminoso [5]quāto piv · s'allontana · piv cresce ·; Chiaro · si può · cōprēdere · che · ogni pianeta e stel[6]la · è piv lontano · da noi nel ponēte che quādo · ci è · sopra · capo ·, circa · 3500, per la pruova se[7]gniata · da parte ·, e se uedi spechiare · il sole o la luna nell' acqua che ti sia · vicina, [8]paratti in detta acqua della grādezza che ti · pare · in cielo; E se t'al-

The moon is not of itself luminous, but is highly fitted to assimilate the character of light after the manner of a mirror, or of water, or of any other reflecting body; and it grows larger in the east and in the west, like the sun and the other planets. And the reason is that every luminous body looks larger in proportion as it is remote. It is easy to understand that every planet and star is farther from us when in the west than when it is overhead, by about 3,500 miles, as is proved on the margin [7], and if you see the sun or moon mirrored in the water near to you, it looks to you of the same size in the water as in the sky. But if you recede to the

---

4. nesspechi. 5. avessi la superfitie che atta asspechiare. 6. cheffussi. 7. emmosso daluencto. 8. acq"a" cresscano. 10. illei. 12. assimilitu. 13. spoglia de siche. 16. fara le luna disspersi. 17. acqua [ondosa]. 18. ondegiante dallacq"a". 21. simularcro. 23. ochupi. 28. refresso. 32. acq"e". 34. chessono. 35. lusstrano pero. 38. infralla .. decima il sole. 39. Ogni el .. "po"nente ella luna illeuante. 40. infralla .. decima il sole. 41. ella .. perleuāte ella terra per ponēte.
898. 1. chosa ella. 2. nōne. 3. assimilitudine .. acq"a" .. cho"r"po .. ecresscie. 4. chome .. chorpo. 5. cresscie Chiaro .. chōplēdere .. esste. 6. da "noi" .. chapo . circha. 7. esse .. oluna .. chetti. 8. acq"a" .. grādeza chetti .. Essettalontanera.

14. See the diagram, p. 115.
38. This refers to the small diagram placed between *B* and *B*.—39. See the diagram below the one referred to in the preceding note.
40, 41. Refers to the diagram below the others.

898. This text has been published by Libri, *Histoire des sciences*, iii, pp. 224, 225.
Line 7 refers to the first diagram. A = *sole* (the sun), B = *terra* (the earth), C = *luna* (the moon).

lontanerai · vno [9]miglio · parrà maggiore 100 volte, e se lo vedrai spechiare · ī mare [10]nel tramōtare · il sole · spechiato · ti · parrà grāde · piv di · 10 · miglia, per[11]chè occuperà · in detta spechiatione · piv · di 10 miglia · di marina ·, e se tu fussi [12]dov' è la luna · parrebbe ti · esso · sole spechiarsi · in tāto · mare · quāto egli [13]n'allumina · alla giornata ·, e la terra · parrebbe infra detta · acqua come pajono · le [14]macchie scure che sono · in nella · luna ·, la quale stādo in terra · si dimostra ta[15]le agli omini, qual farebbe agli omini che abitassino · nella luna il nostro [16]mondo · appūto.

distance of a mile, it will look 100 times larger; and if you see the sun reflected in the sea at sunset, its image would look to you more than 10 miles long; because that reflected image extends over more than 10 miles of sea. And if you could stand where the moon is, the sun would look to you as if it were reflected from all the sea that it illuminates by day; and the land amid the water would appear just like the dark spots that are on the moon, which, when looked at from our earth, appears to men the same as our earth would appear to any men who might dwell in the moon.

DELLA QUALITÀ · DELLA · LUNA

[18]La luna quādo · è tutta · luminata · al nostro vedere, noi vediamo tutto il suo [19]giorno, e allora per riflessione de' razzi del sole, percossi in lei e risaltati a noi, [20]l'ocieano · suo · ci gitta · meno vmidità, e quāto mē è luce piv noce.

OF THE NATURE OF THE MOON

When the moon is entirely lighted up to our sight, we see its full daylight; and at that time, owing to the reflection of the solar rays which fall on it and are thrown off towards us, its ocean casts off less moisture towards us; and the less light it gives the more injurious it is.

Leic. 30a]   **899**

DELLA LUNA

[2]Dico che non avendo la luna lume da sé, essendo luminosa, egl' è necessario che tale lume [3]sia causato da altri.

OF THE MOON

I say that as the moon has no light in itself and yet is luminous, it is inevitable but that its light is caused by some other body.

Leic. 36b]   **900**

DELLA LUNA

Tutte le cōtraditiō dell' auersario a dir che nella luna non sia acqua.

OF THE MOON

All my opponent's arguments to say that there is no water in the moon.

Leic. 1b]   **901**

Risposta a maestro Andrea da Imola,

Risposta a maestro Andrea da Imola, che disse come li razzi solari riflessi dal corpo dello spechio convesso si confondono [2]e si consumano in brieue spatio, e che per questo si negaua al tutto la parte luminosa della luna non essere di natu[3]ra di

Answer to Maestro Andrea da Imola,

Answer to Maestro Andrea da Imola, who said that the solar rays reflected from a convex mirror are mingled and lost at a short distance; whereby it is altogether denied that the luminous side of the moon is of the nature of a mirror, and that

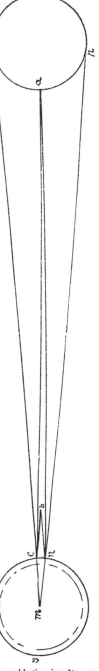

9. parira magiore .. essello vederai .. mare [il sole]. 10. [spe] nel .. para. 11. ochopera .. essettu. 12. parebbeti .. inquāto. 13. nalumina .. ellatera parebe .. achva chome pare. 14. mache schure chessono inella .. qual. 15. farebe alla. 16. acpūto. 19. refressione .. razi .. perchossi illei.
899. 2. dicho .. dasse .. chettale. 3. sie chausato.
901. 1. razi .. refressi .. chonvesso .. confondeano. 2. essi.

900. 2. acqu"a".

900. The objections are noted down in detail in the manuscript, but they hardly seem to have a place here.

901. The large diagram on the margin of this page belongs to this chapter.

spechio, e per consequenza non essere nato tale lume dalla innvmerabile moltitudine dell' onde di quel ⁴mare, il quale io proponeuo essere quella parte della luna che s'alluminava per li razzi solari.

⁵*o p* · sia il corpo del sole, *c n s* sia la luna, *b* sia l'ochio, che in su la basa *c n* del cateto *c n m* vede spechia⁶re il corpo del sole infra li equali angoli *c n*, e 'l simile fa remouendosi l'ochio da *b* in *a*.

consequently the light is not produced by the innumerable multitude of the waves of that sea which I declared to be the portion of the moon which is illuminated by the solar rays.

Let *o p* be the body of the sun, *c n s* the moon, and *b* the eye which, above the base *c n* of the cathetus *c n m*, sees the body of the sun reflected at equal angles *c n*; and the same again on moving the eye from *b* to *a*.

Leic. 2a]   902

DELLA LUNA

Explanation of the lumen cinereum *in the moon.*

¶ ²Nessun denso è piv lieue che l'aria.

³Avendo noi provato come la parte della luna che risplende è acqua, che spechia il corpo del sole, ⁴la quale ci riflette lo splendore da lui ricevuto; E come, se tale acqua fusse sanza ōde, ch'ella ⁵piccola si dimostrerebbe, ma di splendore quasi simile al sole; Al presente bisognia provare, se essa ⁶luna è corpo grave o lieve: inperochè se fusse grave, — confessando che dalla terra in sù in ogni grado d'altez⁷za s'acquista gradi di leuità, cōciosiachè l'acqua è più lieue che la terra, e l'aria che l'acqua, e'l foco che l'aria, e così ⁸seguitando successiuamēte, — e' parrebbe che, se la luna auesse densità com' ella à, ch'ella auesse gravità, e avēdo ⁹gravità che lo spatio, ove essa si troua, non la potesse sostenere, e per conseguēza avesse a discendere ¹⁰inverso il centro dell' universo, e congiugnersi colla terra, e se nō lei, al māco le sue acque aues¹¹sino a cadere e spogliarla di sé e cadere inverso il cētro e lasciar di sé la luna spogliata e sanza lu¹²stro; ōde, nō seguitando quel che di lei la ragione ci promette, egli è manifesto segno che tal luna è vestita de' sua ¹³elemēti, cioè acqua, aria e foco, e così in sé, per sé si sostenga in quello spatio come fa la nostra ter¹⁴ra coi sua elemēti in quest' altro spatio, e che tale ofitio faccino le cose gravi ne' sua elemē¹⁵ti, qual fanno l'altre cose gravi nelli elemēti nostri.

¹⁶Quando l'ochio in oriēte vede la luna in occidente vicina al tramōtato sole, esso la vede ¹⁷colla sua parte onbrosa circundata da parte luminosa, del quale lume la parte laterale ¹⁸e superiore deriua dal sole, e la parte inferiore deriva dallo oceano occidentale, il qual ¹⁹ancora

OF THE MOON

No solid body is less heavy than the atmosphere.

Having proved that the part of the moon that shines consists of water which mirrors the body of the sun and reflects the radiance it receives from it; and that, if these waters were devoid of waves, it would appear small, but of a radiance almost like the sun;—[5] It must now be shown whether the moon is a heavy or a light body: for if it were a heavy body—admitting that at every grade of distance from the earth greater levity must prevail, so that water is lighter than the earth, and air than water, and fire than air, and so on successively—it would seem that if the moon had density as it really has, it would have weight, and having weight, that it could not be sustained in the space where it is, and consequently that it would fall towards the centre of the universe and become united to the earth; or if not the moon itself, at least its waters would fall away and be lost from it, and descend towards the centre, leaving the moon without any and so devoid of lustre. But as this does not happen, as might in reason be expected, it is a manifest sign that the moon is surrounded by its own elements: that is to say, water, air, and fire; and thus is, of itself and by itself, suspended in that part of space, as our earth with its elements is in this part of space; and that heavy bodies act in the midst of its elements just as other heavy bodies do in ours [15].

When the eye is in the east and sees the moon in the west near to the setting sun, it sees it with its shaded portion surrounded by luminous portions; and the lateral and upper portion of this light is derived from the sun, and the lower portion from the ocean in the

3. disspechio e per chonseguenza .. inumerabile. 4. chessalumjnava .. razi. 6. lochio di.
902. 2. chellaria. 3. chome .. rissplende. 4. refrette .. dallui ricevuti .. ssettale acq"a" fussi .. chel. 5. pichola .. dimoster"r"ebbe. 6. ollieve .. fussi .. dalte. 7. concosiachellacq"a" .. piv .. chella .. chellacq"a" .. focho chellaria. 8. eparebe chessella auessi .. chomella chella auessi .. avdo. 9. chello .. ouessa .. nolla potessi sosstenere .. chon .. auessi a disscendere. 10. congugnersi .. esse .. macho. 11. chadere .. ellasscia .. spoglata .. essanza lus. 12. ragon .. "segno" chettal. 13. coe .. effocho echosi .. sostengha. 14. rra cosua .. chettale .. grave. 15. nosstri. 16. ochidento .. vede [la luna]. 17. circhundata .. luminoso. 18. essuperiore .. ella. 19. razi .. elli refrette.

902. 1. On the margin are the words *tola romantina, tola = ferro stagnato* (tinned iron); *romantina* is some special kind of sheet-iron no longer known by that name.

15–29. This passage would certainly seem to establish Leonardo's claim to be regarded as the original discoverer of the cause of the ashy colour of the new moon (*lumen cinereum*). His observations,

lui riceue li razzi solari e li riflette nelli inferiori mari della luna, e ancora per [20]tutta la parte ōbrosa · della luna dà tanto di splendore, qual' è quel che dà la luna alla terra nella mez[21]zanotte, e perciò nō resta integralmēte scura, e di qui à alcuno creduto, che la [22]luna abbia in parte lume da sé oltre a quel che gli è dato dal sole, il quale lume diriua dalla āti[23]detta causa delli nostri mari alluminati dal sole.

[24]Ancora si potrebbe dire che 'l cerchio dello splendore che fa la luna, quand' el' è col sole in [25]occidente, dirivasse dal sole integralmente ·, quando essa col sole e coll'ochıo è situata nel [26]modo che qui disopra si dimostra.

[27]Alcuni potrebbono dire che l'aria, elemēto della luna, pigliando il lume del sole, come fa la no[28]stra spera dell' aria, fusse quella che finisce il cerchio luminoso al corpo della luna.

[29]Alcuni àn creduto che la luna abbia alquanto di lume da sé, la quale ope[30]nione è falsa, perchè l'ànno fondata sopra quel chiarore che si uede in mezzo a li [31]corni quando la luna è nova, la quale alli confini dello splendore pare oscura, [32]e al confine della oscurità · del campo pare si chiara, che molti credono essere [33]vn cerchio di nouo splendore, che finisca di circundare, doue le punte de' corni

west, which receives the solar rays and reflects them on the lower waters of the moon, and indeed affords the part of the moon that is in shadow as much radiance as the moon gives the earth at midnight. Therefore it is not totally dark, and hence some have believed that the moon must in parts have a light of its own besides that which is given it by the sun; and this light is due to the above-mentioned cause—our seas illuminated by the sun.

Again, it might be said that the circle of radiance shown by the moon when it and the sun are both in the west is wholly borrowed from the sun, when it and the sun and the eye are situated as is shown above.

Some might say that the air surrounding the moon as an element catches the light of the sun as our atmosphere does, and that it is this which completes the luminous circle on the body of the moon.

Some have thought that the moon has a light of its own, but this opinion is false, because they have founded it on that dim light seen between the horns of the new moon, which looks dark where it is close to the bright part, while against the darkness of the background it looks so light that many have taken it to be a ring of new radiance completing the circle

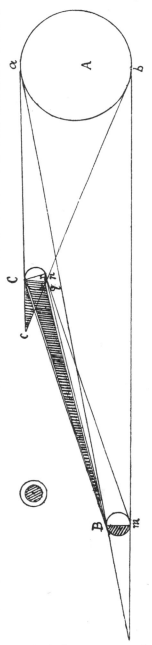

20. dissplendore . . nella me. 21. perco . . integralmēte [luminosa e di] "[onb]os" osscura . . alchuna . . chella. 22. parte di lume dasse . . accquel chelle. 23. chavsa nosstri. 24. Anchora si p"r"otrebbe . . cheff. 25. noccidente . . dirivassi . . choll ochio essituato. 26. dimosstra. 27. Achuni potrebono . . chellaria . . piglando ilume. 28. fussi . . finissi 29. alchuni . . chella . . dasse. 30. effalsa . . fondato . . chessi . . mezo. 31. quandella . . il quale alli . . osscuro. 32. osscurita . . molte credano. 33. finissca di circhundare.

however, having hitherto remained unknown to astronomers, Moestlin and Kepler have been credited with the discoveries which they made independently a century later.

Some disconnected notes treat of the same subject in MS. C. A. 243b: 'Perchè la luna cinta dalla parte alluminata del sole in ponente, à maggior splendore in mezzo a tal cerchio, che quando essa eclissava il sole. Questo accade perchè nell' eclissare il sole ella ombrava il nostro oceano, il qual caso non accade

essendo in ponente, quando il sole alluma esso oceano.' The editors of the Saggio who first published this passage (page 12) add another short one about the seasons in the moon which I have not seen in the original MS.: 'La luna ha ogni mese un verno e una state, e ha maggiori freddi e maggiori caldi, e i suoi equinozii son più freddi de' nostri.'

23, 24. The larger of the two diagrams reproduced above stands between these two lines, and the smaller one is sketched in the margin. At the spot marked A

[34]alluminati dal sole terminano il loro splendore; e questa varietà di campo nasce [35]perchè quella parte d'esso campo, che termina colla parte luminosa della luna, per tal [36]paragone di splendore si dimonstra piv oscura che non è, e quella parte di sopra, doue [37]pare vn pezzo di cerchio luminoso d'uniforme larghezza, nasce che quiui la luna, essendo più chiara che [38]il mezzo over il campo, oue essa si troua, pel paragō di tale oscurità si dimostra in tale confine piv lu[39]minosa che non è, la qual luminosità in tal tenpo nasce dal nostro oceano colli mediterrani [40]che in quel tēpo è alluminato dal sole che già è tramōtato, in modo che il mare allora fa tale ofitio alla [41]parte oscura della luna, qual fa la luna in quīta decima a noi, quando il sol' è tramōtato, e tal propor[42]tione è da quel poco lume che à la parte oscura della luna alla chiarezza della parte alluminata, qual è dalla . . . .

[43]Se uoi vedere [44]quanto la parte [45]onbrosa della luna [46]sia più chiara che 'l [47]canpo, ove tal luna si [48]truova, occupa col[49]la mano, o con altro [50]obietto più distāte occu[51]pi all' ochio, la parte lu[52]minosa della luna.

where the tips of the horns illuminated by the sun cease to shine [34]. And this difference of background arises from the fact that the portion of that background which is conterminous with the bright part of the moon, by comparison with that brightness looks darker than it is; while at the upper part, where a portion of the luminous circle is to be seen of uniform width, the result is that the moon, being brighter there than the medium or background on which it is seen, by comparison with that darkness looks more luminous at that edge than it is. And that brightness at such a time is derived from our ocean and other inland seas. These are, at that time, illuminated by the sun which is already setting in such a way that the sea then fulfils the same function to the dark side of the moon as the moon at its fifteenth day does to us when the sun is set. And the small amount of light which the dark side of the moon receives bears the same proportion to the light of that side which is illuminated, as that . . . [42].

If you want to see how much brighter the shaded portion of the moon is than the background on which it is seen, conceal the luminous portion of the moon with your hand or with some other more distant object.

F. 84a]   903

MACULE DELLA LUNA

On the spots on the moon (903–7).

[2]Alcuni dissero leuarsi da essa vapori a modo di [3]nugoli e interporrsi infra la luna e li ochi no[4]stri; il che, se così fusse, mai tali macule sare[5]bbero stabili nè di siti nè di figura, e vedendo la [6]luna in diuersi aspetti, ancor che tal macule [7]nō fossero variate, esse muterebbero figura come [8]fa quella cosa che si vede per più versi.

THE SPOTS ON THE MOON

Some have said that vapours rise from the moon, after the manner of clouds, and are interposed between the moon and our eyes. But if this were the case, these spots would never be permanent, either as to position or form; and, seeing the moon from various aspects, even if these spots did not move they would change in form, as objects do which are seen from different sides.

F. 84b]   904

DELLE MACHIE DELLA LUNA

[2]Altri dissero che la luna era conposta di parti più [3]o mē transparenti, come se una parte fusse a modo [4]d'alabastro, e alcuna altra a modo di cristallo o vetro, [5]che ne seguirebbe che 'l sole, ferēdo colli sua razzi [6]nella parte mē transparēte, il lume rimarrebbe in [7]superfitie, e così la parte più densa resterebbe allu[8]minata, e la parte transparēte mostrerebbe le [9]onbre delle profondità sue oscure, e così si cōpo[10]ne

OF THE SPOTS ON THE MOON

Others say that the moon is composed of more or less transparent parts; as though one part were something like alabaster and others like crystal or glass. It would follow from this that the sun casting its rays on the less transparent portions, the light would remain on the surface, and so the denser part would be illuminated, and the transparent portions would display the shadow of their darker depths; and this is their account of the structure and nature of the moon.

34. ecquesta . . canpo nassce. 35. chettermina. 36. hosscura . . nonne ecquella. 37. pezo . . largeza nassce. 38. mezo over chanpo. 39. nassce . . occeano coli . . mediterani. 40. ga. 41. osscura . . annoi quādel . . ettal. 42. dacquel pocho . . alla . . osscura . . ciareza. 48. ochupi. 49. chon. 50. distāte ochu. 51. pi all.
903. 2. disse. 3. interprsi infralla . . elli . . nos. 4. fussi . . tal. 5. bon stabili. 6. chettal. 7. fusi variate . . muterebō. 8. chessi.
904. 2. chella . . parte. 3. transsparenti . . fussi. 5. cēne . . coli. 6. rimarebbe. 7. resterebbe. 8. ella . . mosterrebbe. 9. osscure. 10. ecquesto openione.

Leonardo wrote *corpo solare* (solar body) in the larger diagram and *Sole* (sun) in the smaller one. At *C luna* (moon) is written and at *B terra* (the earth).

903, 904. Compare Albertus of Saxony, *Quaestiones in Aristotelis de coelo et mundo*, Lib. II, Quaestio

XVIII, XVI, quoted in Solmi, *Le Fonti*. See No. 880, n.

34. See Pl. CVIII, No. 5.

42. Here the text breaks off; ll. 43–52 are written on the margin.

la qualità della luna; e questa opinione è [11]piaciuta a molti filosofi, e massime a Aristotele, e [12]pure ella è falsa opinione, perchè ne' di[13]versi aspetti, che si trovano spesso la luna e il so[14]le alli nostri ochi, noi vedremmo variare tal ma[15]cule, e quando si farebbono oscure, e quãdo chi[16]are; scure si farebbono, quãdo il sole è in oc[17]cidēte e la luna nel mezzo del celo, che allora le [18]cõcauità transparēti piglierebbono l'onbre in[19]sino alle sommità de' labbri di tal cõcauità trãs[20]parēti, perchè il sole nõ potrebbe penetrare li [21]sua razzi dentro alle boche di tali cõcauità, [22]le quali parrebbono chiare nel plenilunio, [23]doue la luna in oriēte guarda il sole all' occide[24]te; allora il sole alluminerebbe insino ne' fõ[25]di di tali transparētie, e, così, nõ generãdosi [26]onbre, la luna non ci mostrerebbe in tal tenpo [27]le predette machie, e così ora piv ora meno, [28]secondo le mutatiõ del sol dalla luna e della lu[29]na da li ochi nostri, come di sopra dissi.

And this opinion has found favour with many philosophers, and particularly with Aristotle, and yet it is a false view—for, in the various phases and frequent changes of the moon and sun to our eyes, we should see these spots vary, at one time looking dark and at another light: they would be dark when the sun is in the west and the moon in the middle of the sky; for then the transparent hollows would be in shadow as far as the tops of the edges of those transparent hollows, because the sun could not then fling his rays into the mouth of the hollows, which, however, at full moon, would be seen in bright light, at which time the moon is in the east and faces the sun in the west; then the sun would illuminate even the lowest depths of these transparent places and thus, as there would be no shadows cast, the moon at these times would not show us the spots in question; and so it would be, now more and now less, according to the changes in the position of the sun to the moon, and of the moon to our eyes, as I have said above.

F. 85a]   905

DELLE MACULE DELLA LUNA

[2]Si è detto che le macule della luna son create in essa luna, [3]da essere in sé di uaria rarità e dēsità, il che so cosi fusse, [4]nell' eclissi della luna i razzi solari penetrebbono per [5]alcuna parte della predetta rarità, e, nõ si ueden[6]do tale effetto, detta opinione è falsa;

[7]Altri dicono che la superfitie della luna, essendo tersa [8]e pulita, che essa, a similitudine di spechio, riceue in [9]sé la similitudine della terra; Questa openione [10]è falsa, conciosiachè la terra, scoperta dall' acqua, per diuer[11]si aspetti à diuerse figure; adunque, quando la luna [12]è all' oriēte, essa specchierebbe altre machie, che quã[13]do essa ci è di sopra, o quãdo essa è in occidēte; però [14]le machie della luna, come si uede nel plenilunio, [15]mai si uariano nel moto da lei fatto nel nostro emi[16]sperio; 2ª ragione è, che la cosa specchia[17]ta nella convessità piglia piccola parte d'es[18]so spechio, com' è provato in prospettiua; 3ª ragione [19]li è, che nel plenilunio la luna vede solo il mezzo [20]della spera della terra alluminata, nella quale [21]l'oceano colle altre acque risplendono, e la terra [22]fa macule in esso splendore, e così si

OF THE SPOTS ON THE MOON

It has been asserted that the spots on the moon result from the moon being of varying thinness or density; but if this were so, when there is an eclipse of the moon the solar rays would pierce through the portions which were thin as is alleged [5]. But as we do not see this effect the opinion must be false.

Others say that the surface of the moon is smooth and polished and that, like a mirror, it reflects in itself the image of our earth. This view is also false, inasmuch as the land, where it is not covered with water, presents various aspects and forms. Hence when the moon is in the east it would reflect different spots from those it would show when it is above us or in the west;

now the spots on the moon, as they are seen at full moon, never vary in the course of its motion over our hemisphere. A second reason is that an object reflected in a convex body takes up but a small portion of that body, as is proved in perspective [18]. The third reason is that when the moon is full, it only faces half the hemisphere of the illuminated earth, on which only the ocean and other waters reflect bright

11. piacuta..massime aristotie e. 12. puere..oppennione perche inne de. 13. asspetti trauãno..esso. 14. vederem. 15. ecquando..farebono osscure ecquando. 16. in o. 17. ella..mezo. 18. transparēte piglierebono. 19. somita delabri. 21. razi. 22. parebono. 23. ocidē. 24. alora. 26. mosterebbe. 28. ella lu.
905. 2. Essi detto chelle. 3. rareta..chosi fussi. 4. razi..peneterrebono. 5. rareta il ce nõ. 6. to tale..oppenione effalsa. 7. dicano chella. 8. assimilitudine disspechio. 10. concosiache..acq"a". 11. asspecti. 12. spechierebe. 13. ocquãdo..ocidēte il che. 14. plenilunio che. 16. he chella..spechi. 17. pichola..che. 18. ragone. 19. mezo. 21. locean..rsplendano ella.

905. 3–5. *Eclissi.* This word, as it seems to me, here means eclipses of the sun; and the sense of the passage, as I understand it, is that by the foregoing hypothesis the moon, when it comes between the sun

and the earth, must appear as if pierced—we may say 'like a sieve'.
18. *com' è provato.* This alludes to the accompanying diagram.

uedrebbe ²³la metà della nostra terra cinta dallo splendo²⁴re del mare alluminato dal sole, e nella luna tal ²⁵similitudine sarebbe minima parte d'essa luna; ²⁶4ª è che la cosa splendida non si spechia nell' al²⁷tra splendida; adunque il mare, pigliando splendo²⁸re dal sole, siccome fa la luna, e' nō si potrebbe in lei spe²⁹chiare tal terra, che ancora specchiar non vi si vedesse ³⁰particularmēte il corpo del sole e di ciascuna stel³¹la a lei opposta.

light, while the land makes spots on that brightness; thus half of our earth would be seen girt round with the brightness of the sea lighted up by the sun, and in the moon this reflection would be the smallest part of that moon. Fourthly, a radiant body cannot be reflected from another equally radiant; therefore the sea, since it borrows its brightness from the sun—as the moon does—could not cause the earth to be reflected in it, nor indeed could the body of the sun be seen reflected in it, nor indeed any star opposite to it.

Br. M. 19a]   906

Se terrai osseruate le particule delle machie della luna, ²tu troverai in quelle spesse uolte gran varietà, e di questo ³ò fatto pruova io medesimo disegnādole; E questo nasce da nuvo⁴li che si leuano dall' acque d'essa luna, li quali s'interpongo⁵no infra 'l sole e essa acqua, e colla loro onbra tolgo⁶no i razzi del sole a tale acqua, onde essa acqua viene a ri⁷manere oscura, per non potere spechiàre il corpo solare.

If you keep the details of the spots of the moon under observation you will often find great variation in them, and this I myself have proved by drawing them. And this is caused by the clouds that rise from the waters in the moon, which come between the sun and those waters, and by their shadow deprive these waters of the sun's rays. Thus those waters remain dark, not being able to reflect the solar body.

Leic. 5a]   907

Come le mac²chie della luna ³son variate da ⁴quel che già fu⁵rō, per causa del ⁶corso delle sue ⁷acque.

How the spots on the moon must have varied from what they formerly were, by reason of the course of its waters.

C. A. 349b]   908

DE' CIERCHI DELLA LUNA

OF HALOES ROUND THE MOON

On the moon's halo.

²Jo · truouo · che quelli · cierchi ·, li quali · par che di notte circūdino la luna · di uarie grādezze e grossezze, ³sono · causati da uarie · qualità di grossezze d'umori, i quali in varie altezze infra la luna e li ochi ⁴nostri sono situati ·; E quel cierchio maggiore è mē rosso · ed è nella prima parte più bassa di detti ⁵umori, il secondo minore è piv alto, e pare piv rosso, perch' è visto per 2 umori ·; e così quanto ⁶piv alti sieno, minori e piv rossi appariràno, perchè infra l'ochio e quello fiā piv solidi umori, ⁷e per questo si pruova che doue apparisce maggiore rossore · lì è piv somma d'umori.

I have found that the circles which at night seem to surround the moon, of various sizes and degrees of density, are caused by various gradations in the densities of the vapours which exist at different altitudes between the moon and our eyes. And of these haloes the largest is least red and is caused by the lowest of these vapours; the second, smaller one, is higher up, and looks redder because it is seen through two vapours. And so on, as they are higher they will appear smaller and redder, because between the eye and them there is thicker vapour. Whence it is proved that where they are seen to be reddest the vapours are highest.

W. 12326]   909

On instruments for observing the moon (909-10).

Come tu vuoi prouare, la luna mostrarsi ²maggiore che essa non è, giugnendo all' orizzonte; ³tu torrai vn ochiale colmo da una

If you want to prove why the moon appears larger than it is when it reaches the horizon; take a lens which is highly convex on one sur-

24. aluminato. 25. luna c. 26. 4ª he chella .. splendita no si. 27. splendita .. piglando. 28. si come fa laluna enō .. illei. 29. speciar .. vedessi. 30. sole di ciascuna. 31. allei opposita.

906. 1. Setterrai. 2. troverrai. 3. offatto .. "disegnādole" Ecquesto nassce da nugho. 4. chessi .. sinterponga. 5. cholla .. tolgho. 6. razi .. attale .. arri. 7. osscura.

907. 4. ga.

908. 2. circhūdino .. grādeze e rosseza. 3. chausati .. grosseze domori .. alteze infralla .. elli. 4. nosstri .. Ecquel .. magiore .. edella prima. 5. omori .. sechondo .. vissto .. omori e chosi. 6. infrallochio ecquello .. solidomori. 7. apariscie magiore .. domori.

909. 1 .volli. .mosstrare. 2. magore .. gngnendo.

superfitie ⁴e concauo dalla superfitie opposita, e tieni ⁵l'ochio dal concavo, e guarda l'obbietto fori ⁶della superfitie conuessa, e così ⁷avrai fatto vn vero simile ⁸all' aria, che si include in⁹fra la spera del foco e de¹⁰lla acqua, la quale aria è ¹¹concaua diuerso la terra e ¹²conuessa diuerso il foco.

face and concave on the opposite, and place the concave side next the eye, and look at the object beyond the convex surface; by this means you will have produced an exact imitation of the atmosphere included between the sphere of fire and that of water; for this atmosphere is concave on the side next the earth and convex towards the fire.

C. A. 190a]   910

Fa ochiali da vedere ²la luna grande.

Construct glasses to see the moon magnified.

4. conchauo . . ettieni. 6. chonuessa e chosi. 7. arai. 8. chessi. 9. fralla . . focho chede. 12. focho.

910. See the Introduction, p. 108. Fracastoro says in his work *Homocentres*: 'Per dua specilla ocularia si quis perspiciat, alteri altero superposito, majora multo et propinquiora videbit omnia. Quin imo quaedam specilla ocularia fiunt tantae densitatis, ut si per ea quis aut lunam, aut aliud siderum spectet, adeo propinqua illa iudicet, ut ne turres ipsas excedant' (sect. ii, c. 8, and sect. iii, c. 23).

VI

THE STARS

F. 5*b*]   911

On the light
of the stars
(911–13).

Veggonsi le stelle di notte e nō di dì, per esser noi sotto [2]la grossezza dell' aria, la quale è piena d'infinite particu[3]le d'umidità, le quali, ciascuna per sé quãdo è percossa [4]dalli razzi del sole, rendono splendore, e così l'in[5]nvmerabili splēdori occupano esse stelle, e se [6]tale aria nō fusse, il celo senpre ci mostrerebbe [7]le stelle nelle sua tenebre.

The stars are visible by night and not by day, because we are beneath the dense atmosphere, which is full of innumerable particles of moisture, each of which independently, when the rays of the sun fall upon it, reflects a radiance, and so these numberless bright particles conceal the stars; and if it were not for this atmosphere the sky would always display the stars against its darkness.

F. 57*a*]   912

SE LE STELLE ÀNNO LUME DAL SOLE O DA SÉ

[2]Dicono di auere il lume da sé, allegando [3]che se Venere e Mercurio non avessino [4]il lume da sé, quãdo essa s'interpone infra [5]l'ochio nostro e 'l sole, esse oscurerebberō tan[6]to d'esso sole, quãto esse ne coprono a l'ochio [7]nostro; E quest' è falso, perch'è prouato [8]come l'onbroso, posto nel luminoso, è cinto e coper[9]to tutto da razzi laterali del rimanēte di tal lu[10]minoso, e così resta inuisibile, come si di[11]mostra: quando il sole è veduto per la ra[12]mificazione delle piãte sanza foglie in lūga di[13]stantia, essi rami non occupano parte al[14]cuna d'esso sole alli ochi nostri; jl simile [15]accade a' predetti pianeti, li quali ancora [16]che da sé sieno sanza luce, eglino non oc[17]cupano, com' è detto, parte alcuna del sole [18]all' ochio nostro.

WHETHER THE STARS HAVE THEIR LIGHT FROM THE SUN OR IN THEMSELVES

Some say that they shine of themselves, alleging that if Venus and Mercury had not a light of their own, when they come between our eye and the sun they would darken so much of the sun as they could cover from our eye. But this is false, for it is proved that a dark object against a luminous body is enveloped and entirely concealed by the lateral rays of the rest of that luminous body and so remains invisible. As may be seen when the sun is seen through the boughs of trees bare of their leaves, at some distance the branches do not conceal any portion of the sun from our eye. The same thing happens with the above-mentioned planets, which, though they have no light of their own, do not—as has been said—conceal any part of the sun from our eye [18].

SECONDA [20]PROVA

[21]Dicono le stelle nella notte parere lucidissime [22]quãto più ci sō superiori, e che, se esse nō auessino lume [23]da sé, che l'ombra che fa la terra, che s'interpone [24]fra loro e 'l sole, verrebbe a scurarle, non vedē[25]do esse, nè sēdo vedute dal corpo solare; Ma [26]questi non ànno considerato, che l'onbra piramidale de[27]lla terra non aggiugne infra troppe stelle, e in [28]quelle ch'ella aggiugne, la piramide è tanto dimi[29]nuita, che poco occupa del corpo della stella; e 'l ri[30]manēte è alluminato dal sole.

SECOND ARGUMENT

Some say that the stars appear most brilliant at night in proportion as they are higher up; and that if they had no light of their own, the shadow of the earth which comes between them and the sun would darken them, since they would not face nor be faced by the solar body. But those persons have not considered that the conical shadow of the earth cannot reach many of the stars; and even as to those it does reach, the cone is so much diminished that it covers very little of the star's mass, and all the rest is illuminated by the sun.

---

911. I. vegãsi lesselle. 2. grosseza. 3. ciasscuna. 4. rende .. cossi. 5. ochupano .. esse. 6. fussi .. mosterrebbe. 7. lesstelle.
912. I. ã lume. 2. dicano di havere .. dasse. 3. uenere e merchurio nōn auessi. 4. illume dasse .. infral. 5. oscurerebō. 6. coprano. 9. razi. 12. ilūga. 13. ochupano. 15. acade. 16. esieno .. non o. 18. nosstro. *Lines 19 and 20 are written on the margin.* 20. pruoua. 21. Dicano. 22. superiore e chesselle nō auesino. 23. chelobra cheffa .. chessinterpone. 24. le verebe asscurare. 25. nessēdo. 26. nōnã .. chellonbra. 27. nōnagugne .. stelle ege. 28. chellagugnie .. ettanto. 29. ochupa. 30. aluminato.

911. See vol. i, No. 296, which also refers to star-light.
912. From this and other remarks (see No. 902,

l. 34, &c.) it is clear that Leonardo was familiar with the phenomena of irradiation. In the diagram A stands for *sole*, B for *terra*, c for *luna*, s for *stella*.

F. 60a]　　　　　　　913

Perchè li pianeti appariscono maggiori ²in oriēte che sopra di noi, che dovrebbe ³essere il contrario, essendo ⁴3500 miglia più vicini a noi, essendo ⁵nel mezzo del celo, che essendo all' o-⁶rizzōte.

⁷Tutti li gradi delli elemēti, donde passa-⁸no le spetie de' corpi celesti, ⁹che vengono all' ochio, sono ¹⁰equali, e li angoli, ¹¹donde li penetra ¹²la linia cē-trale di tali spetie, sono ¹³inequali, e la distantia è ¹⁴maggiore, come mostra l'eccesso *a b* so¹⁵pra *a d*, e per la 9ª del 7° la grandezza ¹⁶d'essi corpi celesti nel-l'orizzonte è provata.

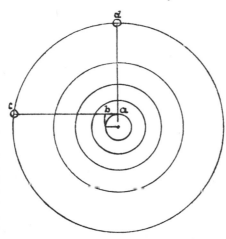

Why the planets appear larger in the east than they do overhead, whereas the contrary should be the case, as they are 3,500 miles nearer to us when in mid-sky than when on the horizon.

All the degrees of the elements, through which the images of the celestial bodies pass to reach the eye, are equal curves, and the angles by which the central line of those images passes through them are unequal angles, and the distance is greater, as is shown by the excess of *a b* beyond *a d*; and the enlargement of these celestial bodies on the horizon is shown by the 9th of the 7th.

Br. M. 279b]　　　　　914

Per uedere la natura delli pi²aneti apri il tetto e mo³stra alla basa vn sol pia⁴nieta, e 'l moto reflesso da ⁵tale basa dirà la comples-⁶sione del predetto pianeta, ⁷ma fa che tal basa nō ne ⁸veda più d'uno per uolta.

To see the real nature of the planets open the covering and note at the base [4] one single planet, and the reflected movement of this base will show the nature of the said planet; but arrange that the base may face only one at the time.

Observations on the stars.

E. o']　　　　　915

Tullius de Diuinatione ²ait Astrologiam fuisse ³adinuentā ante trojanum ⁴bellū Quingentis septua⁵ginta milibus añorum.

57000.

Cicero says in [his book] De Divinatione that Astrology has been practised five hundred seventy thousand years before the Trojan war.

57000.

On history of astronomy.

Br. M. 173b]　　　　　916

Benchè il tenpo · sia annumerato infra le con-tinue ²quātità, esso, per essere inuisibile e sanza corpo, non cade integralmēte sotto la ³geo-

Although time is included in the class of con-tinuous quantities, being indivisible and im-material, it does not come entirely under the

Of time and its divisions (916–18).

---

913. 1. apariscā magori. 2. douerebbe. 5. mezo. 6. rizōte. 7. gradi | "delli elemēti". 9. vengano. 10. cului elli angoli [della luna]. 11. [contra le di] donde li. 12. tale. 13. nequali ella. 14. magore . . ecesso. 15. grandeza. 16. orizonte.
914. 4. refresso. 5. compless. 8. duna.
915. *Six lines written from right to left.*
916. 1. anvmerato infralle. 3. geometricha | "potentia" . . diuida . . chorpi difinita.

914. 4. *basa.* This probably alludes to some instru-ment, perhaps the Camera obscura.

915. The statement that Cicero, *De Divin.*, ascribes the discovery of astrology to a period 57000 years before the Trojan war I believe to be quite erroneous. According to Ernesti, *Clavis Ciceroniana*, Ch. G. Schulz (*Lexic. Cicer.*), and the edition of *De Divin.* by Giese, the word 'Astrologia' occurs only twice in Cicero: *De Divin.* ii. 42.87. 'Ad Chaldaeorum monstra veniamus, de quibus Eudoxus, Platonis auditor, in astrologia judicio doctissimorum hominum facile princeps, sic opinatur (id quod scriptum reliquit): Chaldaeis in praedictione et in notatione cujusque

vitae ex natali die minime esse credendum.' He then quotes the condemnatory verdict of other philosophers as to the teaching of the Chaldaeans but says nothing as to the antiquity and origin of astronomy. Cicero further notes (*De Oratore*, i. 16) that Aratus was 'ignarus astrologiae', but that is all. So far as I know the word occurs nowhere else in Cicero; and the word 'Astronomia' he does not seem to have used at all. (H. Müller-Strübing.)

916. This passage is repeated word for word on page 190b of the same manuscript, and this is accounted for by the text in vol. i, No. 4. Compare also No. 1216.

metrica potentia, la quale lo diuide per figure e corpi d'infinita varietà, [4]come continuo nelle cose uisibili e corporee far si uede; Ma sol co' sua primi [5]principi si cōuiene ·, cioè col punto e colla linia ·; jl punto nel tempo è da [6]essere equiparato · al suo instante, e la linia à similitudine colla lūghez[7]za d'una quantità d'un tempo, e siccome i pūti sō principio e fine della predet[8]ta linia ·, così li instanti sō termine e principio di qualūche dato spatio di tempo; E se [9]la linia è diuisibile in īfinito, lo spatio d'ū tenpo di tal diuisione non è alieno, [10]e se le parti diuise della linia sono proportionabili infra sé, ancora le parti del tenpo [11]saraño proportionabili infra loro.

head of Geometry, which represents its divisions by means of figures and bodies of infinite variety, such as are seen to be continuous in their visible and material properties. But only with its first principle does it agree, that is with the point and the line; the point may be compared to an instant of time, and the line may be likened to the length of a certain quantity of time, and just as a line begins and terminates in a point, so such a space of time begins and terminates in an instant. And whereas a line is infinitely divisible, the divisibility of a space of time is of the same nature; and as the divisions of the line may bear a certain proportion to each other, so may the divisions of time.

Br. M. 176a]   917

Scriui la qualità del [2]tenpo, separata dalla [3]geometrica.

Describe the nature of time as distinguished from the geometrical definitions.

Br. M. 191a]   918

Fa che vn ora sia diui[2]sa in 3000 parti, e [3]questo farai coll' oriolo [4]alleggerēdo o aggravādo [5]il cōtrapeso.

Divide an hour into 3,000 parts, and this you can do with a clock by making the pendulum lighter or heavier.

4. uisibile . . farsi e uede Massol.   5. coe . . cholla.   6. Ella . . "a" . . cholla lūggez.   7. "duna quantita" dun . . essicome . . effine.   8. instanct . . prcipio . . Esse.   10. esselle parte.   11. infralloro.
917. 2. seperata.   3. geometricha.
918. 3. cquesto.   4. allegerēdo o agravādo.

XVI

PHYSICAL GEOGRAPHY

*L*EONARDO'S *researches on the structure of the earth and sea were made at a time when the extended voyages of the Spaniards and Portuguese had excited a special interest in geographical questions in Italy, and particularly in Tuscany. Still, it need scarcely surprise us to find that in deeper questions, as to the structure of the globe, the primitive state of the earth's surface, and the like, he was far in advance of his time.*

The number of passages which treat of such matters is relatively considerable; like almost all Leonardo's scientific notes they deal partly with theoretical and partly with practical questions. Some of his theoretical views of the motion of water were transcribed in 1643 in a manuscript volume by the Dominican Fra Luigi Maria Arconati. This copy, now in the Vatican Library (Barberini 4332), was published under the title: De moto e misura dell' acqua, Bologna, 1828, 1923 (see bibliography). Texts are arranged under the following titles: Libr. I. Della spera dell' acqua; Libr. II. Del moto dell' acqua; Libr. III. Dell' onda dell' acqua; Libr. IV. Dei retrosi d'acqua; Libr. V. Dell' acqua cadente; Libr. VI. Delle rotture fatte dall' acqua; Libr. VII. Delle cose portate dall' acqua; Libr. VIII. Dell' oncia dell' acqua e delle canne; Libr. IX. De molini e d'altri ordigni d'acqua.

The large number of isolated observations scattered through the manuscripts accounts for our frequently finding notes of new schemes for the arrangement of those relating to water and its motions, particularly in the Codex Atlanticus*: I have printed several of these plans as an introduction to the Physical Geography, and I have actually arranged the texts in accordance with the clue afforded by one of them which is undoubtedly one of the latest notes referring to the subject (No. 920). The text given as No. 930, which is also taken from a late note-book of Leonardo's, served as a basis for the arrangement of the first of the seven books—or sections—bearing the title: 'Of the Nature of Water' (Dell' acque in sé).*

As I have not made it any part of this undertaking to print the passages which refer to purely physical principles, it has also been necessary to exclude those practical researches which, in accordance with indications given in No. 920, ought to come in as Books 13, 14, and 15.[1] I can only incidentally mention here that Leonardo— as it seems to me, especially in his youth—devoted a great deal of attention to the construction of mills. This is proved by a number of drawings of very careful and minute execution, which are to be found in the Codex Atlanticus*. Nor was it possible to include his considerations on the regulation of rivers, the making of canals, and so forth (No. 920, Books 10, 11, and 12); but those passages in which the structure of a canal is directly connected with notices of particular places will be*

---

[1] *Recent researches by Nando de Toni, L'Idraulica in L. d. V., Brescia, 1934 and 1935.*

found duly inserted under section XVII (Topographical Notes). In Vol. I, No. 5, the text refers to canal-making in general.

On one point only can the collection of passages included under the general heading of 'Physical Geography' claim to be complete. When comparing and sorting the materials for this work I took particular care not to exclude or omit any text in which a geographical name was mentioned even incidentally, since in all such researches the chief interest, as it appeared to me, attached to the question whether these observations on the various local characteristics of mountains, rivers, or seas had been made by Leonardo himself, and on the spot. It is self-evident that the few general and somewhat superficial observations on the Rhine and the Danube, on England and Flanders, must have been obtained from maps or from some informants, and in the case of Flanders Leonardo himself acknowledges this (see No. 1008). But that most of the other and more exact observations were made, on the spot, by Leonardo himself may be safely assumed from their method and the style in which he writes of them; and we should bear in mind that in all investigations, of whatever kind, experience is always spoken of as the only basis on which he relies. In No. 984 Leonardo points to the absence of literary evidence on the subject.

The Leicester Codex contains the most important texts on geological problems. Leonardo tried to reconstruct the geological history of the earth from first-hand observations made in the Valsassina and other mountain valleys. He pointed out the absurdity of the hypothesis of a universal flood, and argued that the surface of the earth was being gradually transformed mainly by the action of water. He explained the origin of fossils, of salt in sea-water, and he proved that the greater part of surface strata were sediments. Compare W. Salomon, Geologische Beobachtungen des L.d.V., *Sitzungsberichte der Heidelberger Akademie der Wissenschaften, Berlin, 1928, and G. de Lorenzo, L. d. V. e la Geologia, Bologna, 1920.*

I

INTRODUCTION

Schemes for the arrangement of the materials (919–28).

Leic. 5*a*]   919

Questi libri contēgono in ne' primi ²della natura dell' acqua in sé ne' ³sua moti, li altri contēgono delle ⁴cose fatte dai sua corsi, ⁵che mv⁶tano il mondo di centro e di figura.

These books contain in the beginning: Of the nature of water itself in its motions; the others treat of the effects of its currents, which change the world in its centre and its shape.

Leic. 15*b*]   920

DIUISIŌ DEL LIBRO

Libro pº dell' acque in sé,
libro 2º del mare,
libro 3º delle uene,
⁵libro 4º de' fiumi;
libro 5º delle nature de' fōdi,
libro 6ºdelli obbietti,
libro 7ºdelle ghiaje,
libro 8º della superfitie de l'acqua,
¹⁰libro 9ºdelle cose che in quella son mosse;
libro 10º de' ripari de' fiumi,
libro 11º delli condotti,
libro 12 de' canali,
libro 13 delli strumēti volti dall' acqua,
¹⁵libro 14 del far mōtare l'acque,
libro 15 delle cose cōsumate dall' acque.

DIVISIONS OF THE BOOK

Book 1 of water in itself.
Book 2 of the sea.
Book 3 of subterranean rivers.
Book 4 of rivers.
Book 5 of the nature of the abyss.
Book 6 of the obstacles.
Book 7 of gravels.
Book 8 of the surface of water.
Book 9 of the things moved therein.
Book 10 of the repairing of rivers.
Book 11 of conduits.
Book 12 of canals.
Book 13 of machines turned by water.
Book 14 of raising water.
Book 15 of matters worn away by water.

Leic. 9*a*]   921

Farai prima un libro ²che tratti de' lochi ³occupati dall' acque ⁴dolci, e 'l 2º dal⁵l' acque salse, e 'l ⁶3º come, per la par⁷tita di quelle, queste ⁸nostre parti son ⁹fatte piv lieui, e ¹⁰per consequēza piv ¹¹remosse dal cen¹²tro del mōdo.

First you shall make a book treating of places occupied by fresh waters, and the second by salt waters, and the third, how by the disappearance of these, our parts of the world were made lighter and in consequence more remote from the centre of the world.

F. 87*b*]   922

Descriui in prima tutta l'acqua in ciascuno suo moto, di poi ²descriui tutti li sua fondi e le lor materie, senpre al³legando le propositioni delle predette acque, e fia bu⁴ono ordine, che altrimēti l'opera sarebbe cōfusa.
⁵Descriui tutte le figure che fa l'acqua dalla sua ⁶maggiore alla sua minore onda e le lor cause.

First write of all water, in each of its motions; then describe all its bottoms and their various materials, always referring to the propositions concerning the said waters; and let the order be good, for otherwise the work will be confused.
Describe all the forms taken by water from its greatest to its smallest wave, and their causes.

F. 88*a*]   923

Libro 9 de' surgimenti accidentali dell' acqua.

Book 9, of accidental risings of water.

F. 90*b*]   924

ORDINE DEL LIBRO

²Poni nel principio ciò che può fare vn fiume.

THE ORDER OF THE BOOK

Place at the beginning what a river can effect.

919. 1. cōtēgano. 3. cōtēgano. 4. dae sua.
920. 8. giare. 9. delle . . acq"a". 10. quelle. 16. dell cose . . acq"e".
921. 1. p"a" vn libr. 3. ochupati. 7. quele. 8. parte.
922. 1. scriui in p"a" . . lacq"a" . . ciasscuno. 2. desscriui . . elle. 4. altremēti 5. cheffa lacq"a". 6. magore . . elle.
923. acq"a".
924. 2. co che po.

Br. M. 35a]   925

Libro d'abbattere li eserciti · col' impeto de' diluui fatti dall' acque disgorgate,

²Libro da allagare li eserciti colli seramenti delle boche delle valli,

³Libro che l'acque cōducino a saluamento li legniami tagliati ne' mōti,

⁴Libro delle barche condotte contro all' inpeto de' fiumi,

⁵Libro dell' alzare li gran ponti col senplice accrescimēto dell' acque,

⁶Libro del riparare all' inpeto de' fiumi che le città da quelli nō siē percosse.

A book of driving back armies by the force of a flood made by releasing waters.

A book of inundating armies by closing the mouths of valleys.

A book showing how the waters safely bring down timber cut in the mountains.

A book of boats driven against the impetus of rivers.

A book of raising large bridges higher, simply by the swelling of the waters.

A book of guarding against the impetus of rivers so that towns may not be damaged by them.

Br. M. 35b]   926

[Libro della dispositiō de' fiumi a cōseruatiō dell' argine sue,

²Libro delli monti, che si spianerāno, e fiā la terra sotto il nostro emisperio scoperta dall' acqua.

³Libro del terreno portato da l'acqua a riēpiere la grā profondità de' pelaghi,

⁴Libro de' modi che la fortuna per sé netti li riēpiuti porti del mare,

⁵Libro dell' argine de' fiumi e lor permanentia,

⁶Libro del fare che li fiumi con lor corso tēgin netti li fondi loro per le città dōde passano,

⁷Libro del fare o rifondare li ponti sopra li fiumi,

⁸Libro di ripari che farsi debbō alli muri e argini de' fiumi percossi dall' acqua,

⁹Libro del generare li colli dall' arena o ghiaja sopra le gran profondità dell' acque.]

A book of the ordering of rivers so as to preserve their banks.

A book of the mountains, which level down and become land, if our hemisphere were to be uncovered by the water.

A book of the earth carried down by the waters to fill up the great abyss of the seas.

A book of the ways in which a tempest may of itself clear out filled-up sea-ports.

A book of the shores of rivers and of their permanency.

A book of how to deal with rivers, so that they may keep their bottom scoured by their own flow near the cities they pass.

A book of how to make or to repair the foundations for bridges over the rivers.

A book of the repairs which ought to be made in walls and banks of rivers where the water strikes them.

A book of the formation of hills of sand or gravel at great depths in water.

Br. M. 122a]   927

[L'acqua dà principio al moto suo,

²Libro liuellamenti d'acque per diuersi modi,

³Libro del discostare li fiumi dai lochi da loro offesi,

⁴Libro del dirizzar li fiumi che occupano superchio terreno,

⁵Libro del diuidere li fiumi in molti rami e farli guadabili,

⁶Libro dell' acque che cō diuersi moti passā pe' pelaghi loro,

⁷Libro del profondare li letti alli fiumi cō uari corsi d'acque,

⁸Libro di disporre li fiumi ī modo che li piccoli prīcipj de' sua danni non accrescino,

Water gives the first impetus to its motion.

A book of the levelling of waters by various means.

A book of diverting rivers from places where they do mischief.

A book of guiding rivers which occupy too much ground.

A book of parting rivers into several branches and making them fordable.

A book of the waters which with various currents pass through seas.

A book of deepening the beds of rivers by means of currents of water.

A book of controlling rivers so that the little beginnings of mischief, caused by them, may not increase.

925. *The head of each line is marked by the letter* d *which is crossed out.* 1. dabatter . . chol inpito . . dilumi . . dellacq"a" discorghate. 3. chellacque . . assaluamento. 5. acresscimēto. 6. chelle cita dacquelli . . percossi.

926. 2. chessi spich[a] erāno effia la terra "sotto il nostro emisperio" scoperta dellacqua. 3. terē. 4. perse nettili riēpiuti porta del mare. 5. ellor premanentia. 6. chelli . . collor . . tēginetti . . fondi "lor". 7. orrifondare. 8. cheffarsi. 9. ghiara . . acq"e".

927. 1. \\\\\\\\\\\\\\\\\\\\ grado dobbliquita Lacq"a".   2–13. *Each line is headed by an* L, *meaning* Libro.   3. discosstare . . dalloro. 4. dirizar . . ce ochupan. 5. effarli. 6. chō. 7. chō . . chorsi. 8. di sporre . . chelli picholi . . accresscino.

⁹Libro de' uari moti dell' acque che passan per diuerse figure di canali,

¹⁰Libro del fare che li piccoli fiumi non pieghino il maggiore percosso dalle loro acque,

¹¹Libro della maggior bassezza che trouar si possa nella corrēte della superfitie de' fiumi,

¹²Libro dell' origine de' fiumi che versā per l'alte cime de' monti,

¹³Libro della uarietà de' moti dell' acque ne' lor fiumi.]

A book of the various movements of waters passing through channels of different forms.

A book of preventing small rivers from diverting the larger one into which their waters run.

A book of the lower level which can be found in the current of the surface of rivers.

A book of the origin of rivers which flow from the high tops of mountains.

A book of the various motions of waters in their rivers.

Br. M. 45a] 928

[1] Della inequalità della concauità del nauilio,

²[1] Libro della inequalità della curuità de' lati de' nauili,

³[1] Libro della inequalità del sito del timone,

⁴[1] Libro della inequalità della carena de' nauili,

⁵[2] Libro della uarietà delli spiraculi donde l'acqua si uersa,

⁶[3] Libro dell' acqua inclusa ne' vasi insieme coll' aria e sua moti,

⁷[4] Libro del moto dell' acqua per le cicognole,

⁸[5] Libro delli scontri e concorsi dell' acque venute da diuersi aspetti,

⁹[6] Libro delle varie figure delli argini traversati dalli fiumi,

¹⁰[7] Libro delle uarie secche generate sotto le chiuse de' fiumi,

¹¹[8] Libro delle torture e pieghamēti delle corrēti de' fiumi,

¹²[9] Libro de' uari siti donde si de' trar l'acqua de' fiumi,

¹³[10] Libro delle figure dell' argini de' fiumi e lor permanētia,

¹⁴[11] Libro dell' acqua cadente perpēdicularmente sopra diuersi obbietti,

¹⁵[12] Libro del corso dell' acqua inpedito in diuersi siti,

¹⁶[12] Libro delle uarie figure delli obbietti che impediscono il corso del acque,

¹⁷[13] Libro delle concauità e globosità fatte dal fondo ītorno a vari obbietti,

¹⁸[14] Libro del condurre li canali navigabili sopra o sotto li fiumi che l'ītersegano,

¹⁹[15] Libro delli terreni che beono le acque de' canali e lor ripari,

²⁰[16] Libro della creatiō de' corsi de' fiumi che votano il letto de' fiumi riēpiuti di terreno.

[1] Of inequality in the concavity of a ship [1].

[1] A book of the inequality in the curve of the sides of ships.

[1] A book of the inequality in the position of the tiller.

[1] A book of the inequality in the keel of ships.

[2] A book of various forms of apertures by which water flows out.

[3] A book of water contained in vessels with air, and of its movements.

[4] A book of the motion of water through a syphon.

[5] A book of the meetings and union of waters coming from different directions.

[6] A book of the various forms of the banks through which rivers pass.

[7] A book of the various forms of shoals formed under the sluices of rivers.

[8] A book of the windings and meanderings of the currents of rivers.

[9] A book of the various places whence the waters of rivers are derived.

[10] A book of the configuration of the shores of rivers and of their permanency.

[11] A book of the perpendicular fall of water on various objects.

[12] A book of the course of water when it is impeded in various places.

[12] A book of the various forms of the obstacles which impede the course of waters.

[13] A book of the concavity and globosity formed round various objects at the bottom.

[14] A book of conducting navigable canals above or beneath the rivers which intersect them.

[15] A book of the soils which absorb water in canals and of repairing them.

[16] A book of creating currents for rivers, which quit their beds, [and] for rivers choked with soil.

9. acq"e" .. chanali. 10. chelli picholi .. magore perchosso. 11. dalla maggor basseza .. corēte. 12. pellalte.
928. 4. charena. 5. spirachuli .. lacq"a". 6. essua. 7. cicognuole. 8. acq"e" .. di .. asspetti. 9. delle .. traversate alli. 10. secche [fatte sotto] generate. 11. chorrēti. 12. lacque. 13. fighure dellargine .. ellor premanētia. 14. chadende perpēdichulare. 15. acq"a". 16. chenpedisscano .. acq"e". 17. globbosita. 18. condure .. navichabili .. ossotto .. chellitersegano. 19. beano . chanali ellor.

928. 1. The first line of this passage was added subsequently, evidently as a correction of the following line. 7. *cicognole*, see No. 966. 11, 17.

A. 55*b*]   929

COMĪCIAMĒTO DEL TRATTATO DE L'ACQUA

THE BEGINNING OF THE TREATISE ON WATER

General introduction.

[2]L'omo è detto · da li antiqui · mōdo minore ·, e cierto la ditione · d'esso · nome è bene collocata, [3]impero · chè, siccome · l'omo · è cōposto · di terra ·, acqua ·, aria · e foco ·, questo corpo · della · terra [4]è il simiglante ·; se l'omo · à in sé · ossi, sostenitori e armadura · della carne ·, jl mōdo à i sassi, [5]sostenitori della · terra ; se l'omo à in sé il lago · del sangue, doue crescie · e discrescie il polmo[6]ne · nello · alitare ·, jl corpo della terra à il suo oceano mare ·, il quale ancora · lui crescie [7]e discrescie ogni · sei · ore · per lo alitare · del mōdo ·; se dal detto · lago di sangue · diriuano ve[8]ne ·, che si vanno ramificādo · per lo corpo · vmano ·, similmēte il mare oceano enpie [9]il corpo della terra · d'infinite vene d'acqua ; mancano al corpo della terra · i nerui, i quali nō ui [10]sono ·, perchè i nervi sono fatti al proposito · del movimēto ·, e il mōdo sendo di perpetua stabilità, [11]non accade movimēto e, nō accadēdo movimēto, · i nervi · nō ui sono · neciessari; Ma ī tutte [12]l'altre · cose · sono · molto simili.

By the ancients man has been called the world in miniature; and certainly this name is well bestowed, because, inasmuch as man is composed of earth, water, air, and fire, his body resembles that of the earth; and as man has in him bones, the supports and framework of his flesh, the world has its rocks, the supports of the earth; as man has in him a pool of blood in which the lungs rise and fall in breathing, so the body of the earth has its ocean tide which likewise rises and falls every six hours, as if the world breathed; as in that pool of blood veins have their origin, which ramify all over the human body, so likewise the ocean sea fills the body of the earth with infinite springs of water. The body of the earth lacks sinews, and this is because the sinews are made expressly for movements and, the world being perpetually stable, no movement takes place, and, no movement taking place, muscles are not necessary. But in all other points they are much alike.

929. 1. acq"a". 2. cholochata. 3. impero · chessi · chome . . chōposto di tera · acq"a" . . effocho . . chorpo . . tera. 4. sellomo . . osso . . charne. 5. ssisotenitori . . lacho. 6. tera . . occicano . . anchora . . cresscie. 7. diriua ve. 8. chessi vano ramifichādo . . chorpo . . [C] similmēte . . occieano. 9. dacq"a" mancha . . tera. 11. achade . . achadēdo. 12. chose.

I

ON THE NATURE OF WATER

ORDINE DEL PRIMO LIBRO DELLE ACQUE

[2]Difinisci prima che cosa è altezza e bassezza || anzi come sō situati [3]li elemēti l'ū dentro all' altro; Di poi che cosa è gravità dē[4]sa e che è gravità liquida, ma prima che cosa è in sé gravi[5]tà e leuità ·; Di poi descrivi perchè l'acqua si move e perchè ter[6]mina il moto suo, poi perchè si fa più tarda o velocie, oltre [7]a di questo come ella senpre disciède, essendo in cōfine d'ari[8]a più bassa di lei | E come l'acqua si leua in aria mediante [9]il calore del sole e poi · ricade in pioggia ·; ancora perchè l'acqua [10]surgie dalle cime de' monti | e se l'acqua di nessuna vena più alta [11]che l'oceano mare può versare acqua più alta che la superfitie [12]d'esso · oceano ·; E come tutta · l'acqua che torna all' oceano è più alta [13]della spera dell' acqua | e come l'acqua delli mari equinotiali è più alta [14]che le acque settōtrionali, ed è più alta sotto il corpo del sole [15]che in nessuna parte del circulo equinotiale | come si speri[16]mēta sotto il calore dello stizzo infocato, l'acqua che mediā[17]te tale stizzo bolle e l'acqua circustāte al ciētro di tal bol[18]lore senpre disciende con onda circulare e come l'acque [19]settētrionali son piv basse che li altri mari e tāto più, quā[20]to esse son piv fredde, insin che si convertono in ghiaccio.

THE ORDER OF THE FIRST BOOK ON WATER

The ar-rangement of Book I.

Define first what is meant by height and depth; rather how the elements are situated one inside another. Then what is meant by solid weight and by liquid weight; but first what weight and lightness are in themselves. Then describe why water moves, and why its motion ceases; then why it becomes slower or more rapid; besides this, how it always falls, being in contact with the air but lower than the air. And how water rises in the air by means of the heat of the sun, and then falls again in rain; again, why water springs forth from the tops of mountains; and if the water of any spring higher than the ocean can pour forth water higher than the surface of that ocean. And how all the water that returns to the ocean is higher than the sphere of water. And how the waters of the equatorial seas are higher than the waters of the north, and higher beneath the body of the sun than in any part of the equatorial circle; for experiment shows that under the heat of a burning brand the water near the brand boils, and the water surrounding this ebullition always sinks with a circular eddy. And how the waters of the north are lower than the other seas, and more so as they become colder, until they are converted into ice.

CHE COSA È ACQUA

[2]Acqua è infra i quatro elemēti il secōdo mē grave e di seconda volubilità. . . .

Tutti li elementi fori del loro naturale sito desiderano a esso sito ritornare.

OF WHAT IS WATER

Definitions (931–2).

Among the four elements water is the second both in weight and in instability. . . .

All the elements which are out of their natural place desire to return to that place.

PRINCIPIO DEL LIBRO DELL' ACQUE

[2]Pelago è detto quello, il quale à figura larga [3]e profōda; [4]nel quale l'acque stanno con poco moto.

THE BEGINNING OF THE BOOK ON WATER

Sea is the name given to that water which is wide and deep, in which the waters have not much motion.

---

930. 1. p"o" libro. 2. p"a" che chosa he .. ebbasseza. 3. chosa. 4. chosan. 5. elleuita. 7. addi questo chomella .. cōfino. 8. chome. 9. chalore .. eppoi richade .. anchora. 10. delle cime .. essellacqua. 11. chellocciceano .. chella. 12. occieano .. chome .. chettorna .. occieano eppiu. 13. [desso] della .. chome .. ecquinotiali eppiu. 14. chelle. 15. inessuna .. circhulo .. sissperi. 16. chalore .. infochato. 17. talle .. ellacqua circhustāte. 18. dissciende .. circhulare e chome. 19. chelli .. ettāto. 20. chessi chonvertano in diaccio.
931. 1. chosa. 2. sechōdo .. grieve .. sechonda.
932. 2. pellago .. affigura.

931. Only three lines of this passage are here given.
932. Only the beginning of this passage is here

given; the remainder consists of definitions which have no direct bearing on the subject.

II   U

Leic. 34b]

933

Of the surface of the water in relation to the globe (933–6).

Li centri della spericità dell' acqua sono due: l'uno è della vniuersale acqua, l'altro è particulare; [2]l'vniuersale è quello, il quale serue a tutte l'acque sanza moto, che sono in sé in grā quātità, [3]come canali, fossi, viuai, fonti, pozzi, fiumi morti, laghi, paduli stagni e mari, li quali, ancorachè sieno di uarie altezze ciascuno per sé, àno li termini delle lor superfitie equi[4]distanti al centro del mondo, come sono i laghi posti nelle cime delli alti mōti come sopra [5]Pietra Pana e lago della Sibilla a Norcia, e tutti li laghi che dā principio a grandi fiumi, come Tesino [6]dal lago Maggiore, Adda dal lago di Como, Mincio dal lago di Garda e Reno dal lago di Costan[7]tia | e di Coira e dal lago di Lucerne, e come Trigon, il quale passa per la Minore Africa, il quale ne porta [8]con seco l'acqua di 3 paduli, l'un dopo l'altro, di uarie altezze, de' quali il piv alto è Munace, el mezzano è Pallas [9]e 'l più basso è Triton; ancora el Nilo diriua da 3 altissimi paduli in Etiopia.

The centres of the sphere of water are two, one universal and common to all water, the other particular. The universal one is that which is common to all waters not in motion, which exist in great quantities. As canals, ditches, ponds, fountains, wells, dead rivers, lakes, stagnant pools, and seas, which, although they are at various levels, have each in itself the limits of their superficies equally distant from the centre of the earth, such as lakes placed at the tops of high mountains; as the lake near [5] Pietra Pana and the lake of the Sybil near Norcia; and all the lakes that give rise to great rivers, as the Ticino from Lago Maggiore, the Adda from the lake of Como, the Mincio from the lake of Garda, the Rhine from the lakes of Constance and of Chur, and from the lake of Lucerne, like the Trigon which passes through Minor Africa, carrying with it the waters of three lakes, one above the other at different heights, of which the highest is Munace, the middle one Pallas, and the lowest Triton; the Nile again flows from three very high marshes in Ethiopia.

A. 58b]

934

DEL CIĒTRO DELL' OCIEANO · MARE

[2]Il ciētro della spera · dell' acqua · è il centro · vero · della rotōdità del nostro mōdo, · il quale si cōpone [3]infra · acqua e terra · in forma · rotōda ·; Ma se tu · volessi trovare · il ciētro dello · elemēto della [4]terra ·, questo · è cōtenuto · per equidistāte · spatio · dalla superfitie · dell' oceano · mare ·, e nō dalla [5]equidistante · superfitie · della · terra ·, perchè chiaro · si comprende · questa palla · della · terra non [6]avere · niente · di perfetta · rotōdità ·, se non è · in quella · parte dou' è mare · o paduli o altre acque mor[7]te, · e qualunque · parte · d'essa · terra che escie · fori · d'esso mare, s'allontana · dal suo · ciētro.

OF THE CENTRE OF THE OCEAN

The centre of the sphere of waters is the true centre of the globe of our world, which is composed of water and earth, having the shape of a sphere. But if you want to find the centre of the element of the earth, this is placed at a point equidistant from the surface of the ocean, and not equidistant from the surface of the earth; for it is evident that this globe of earth has nowhere any perfect rotundity, excepting in places where the sea is, or marshes or other still waters. And every part of the earth that rises above the water is farther from the centre.

E. 4b]

935

DEL MARE CHE MUTA [2]IL PESO DELLA TERRA

[3]Li nichi, ostrighe e altri simili animali, [4]che nascono nelli fanghi marini, ci testifi[5]cano la mutatiō della terra intorno al [6]ciētro de' nostri elemēti; pruovasi così: [7]Li fiumi reali senpre

OF THE SEA WHICH CHANGES THE WEIGHT OF THE EARTH

The shells, oysters, and other similar animals which originate in sea-mud, bear witness to the changes of the earth round the centre of our elements. This is proved thus: Great rivers

933. 1. Lli centri . . acq"a" . . partichulare. 2. deluniuersale . . attutte lacque . . chessono. 3. cannali fossi "viuai fonti pozi" fiumi . . quali "ancorche sieno di uarie alteze ciascun per se" ano. 4. distante . . illaghi. 5. pietra pana ellago . . sibilla a norca ettutti. 6. [adda da] dal . . magore . . lagho . . como [adice] "menzo" dal lagho . . erreno . . gostan. 7. curio lacho . . Trigon . . minore africha il quane ne. 8. consecholacq"a" . . alteze . . mezano he. 9. di.

934. 1. occieano. 2. dellacq"a" . . retōdita . . nosstro . . qualle . . chōpone. 3. acq"a" ecterra . . retōda Massettu . . ellemēto. 4. quessto e chōtenuto . . equidisstante . . occieano. 5. equidisstante . . chonplende quessta . . nōna. 6. retōdita. 7. ecqualumque . . terra esscie.

935. 3. osstrighe. 4. nasschano . . tessti. 5. chano. 6. nosstri. 7. senpre [stanno] corā.

933. 5. *Pietra Pana*, a mountain near Florence. Near Norcia, the Nursia of Roman time, are the Monti Sibilline. The plain of Norcia, surrounded by

high mountains, was at one time a lake without an outlet. 7. About Trigon compare No. 1095.

corrono torbidi [8]mediăte la terra, che per lor
si leua mediăte la cŏ[9]fregatiŏ delle sue acque
sopra il fondo e nelle sue [10]riue, e tal cŏsuma-
tione scopre le fronti de' gradi [11]fatti a' suoli
di quelli nichi, che stan nella superfitie [12]del
fango marino, li quali in tal sito nascieron,
quă[13]do l'acque salse li coprivano, e questi tali
gradi erano ri[14]coperti di tenpo in tenpo dalli
fanghi di uarie grossez[15]ze o condotti al mare
dalli fiumi cŏ diluvi di diverse gră[16]dezze; e così
tali nichi resstavano murati e morti [17]sotto
tali făghi composti in tăta altezza, che dal
fondo si [18]scopriua all' aria; Ora questi tali
fondi sono in tăta [19]altezza che son fatti colli,
o alti mŏti, e li fiumi, [20]consuma[21]tori de' lati
[22]d'essi monti, [23]scoprono [24]li gradi d'es[25]si nichi,
e co[26]sì il levi[27]ficato lato [28]della terra [29]al cŏti-
nuo [30]s'Inalza, e [31]li antipo[32]di s'accosta[33]no più
al [34]ciètro del [35]mondo, [36]e li anti[37]chi fondi del
[38]mare son fatti [39]gioghi di monti.

always run turbid, owing to the earth, which is
stirred by the friction of their waters at the
bottom and on their shores; and this wearing
disturbs the face of the strata made by the layers
of shells, which lie on the surface of the marine
mud, and which were produced there when the
salt waters covered them; and these strata were
covered over again from time to time with mud
of various thickness, or carried down to the sea
by the rivers and floods of more or less extent;
and thus these shells remained walled in and
dead underneath these layers of mud raised to
such a height that they came up from the
bottom to the air. At the present time these
bottoms are so high that they form hills or high
mountains, and the rivers, which wear away the
sides of these mountains, uncover the strata of
these shells, and thus the softened side of the
earth continually rises and the antipodes sink
closer to the centre of the earth, and the ancient
bottoms of the seas have become mountain
ridges.

Leic. 10b]   936

Faccia mutatiŏ la terra colla sua gravezza,
quăte farsi [2]voglia, che mai la superfitie della
spera dell' acqua nŏ si partirà dalla sua equi-
distătia col centro del mŏdo.

Let the earth make whatever changes it may
in its weight, the surface of the sphere of waters
can never vary in its equal distance from the
centre of the world.

Leic. 35b]   937

SE LA TERRA È MĒ CHE L'ACQUA

[2]Dicono alcuni esser vero, che la terra, ch'è
scoperta dalle acque, sia molto minore
che quella che da esse acqu' è coperta;
[3]Ma che considerando la grossezza di
7000 miglia di diametro, che à · essa
terra, e' si può concludere l'acqua
essere di [4]poca profondità.

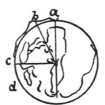

WHETHER THE EARTH IS LESS THAN THE WATER

Some assert that it is true that the earth
which is not covered by water is much
less than that covered by water. But
considering the size of 7,000 miles in
diameter which is that of this earth, we
may conclude the water to be of small
depth.

Of the pro-
portion of
the mass of
water to that
of the earth
(937–8).

Leic. 36a]   938

DELLA TERRA IN SÉ

[2]L'alzarsi tanto le cime de' monti sopra la
spera dell' acqua può esser diriuato, perchè il
loco grandissimo [3]della terra, il quale era ripieno

OF THE EARTH

The great elevations of the peaks of the mountains above the sphere of the water may have
resulted from the fact that a very large portion

8. medinte la terra. 9. freghatiŏ .. accque .. nelle sine. 10. rive ettal .. sconpre .. fronte. 11. assuoli .. chesstan. 12. fangho ..
nasscicrono. 13. ecquessti .. era ri. 14. grosse. 15. indotti. 17. făghi conpossti .. alteza. 18. quessti. 19. alteza .. elli fiumi.
23. scoprano. 25. echo. 26. si [I] illeui. 27. fichato. 32. sacosstă. *Lines 20–39 are written on the margin.*
936. 1. facia .. graveza. 2. dellacq"a".
937. 1. Sella .. chellacq"a". 2. dicano .. chella. 3. groseza .. diamitro .. po con chludere lacqua per essere. 4. pocha.
938. 2. lasspera .. ilocho. 3. coe.

938. The small sketch p. 148 on the left is placed in the original close to the text referring to the Dead Sea.

d'acqua, cioè la grandissima cauerna, douette caderne ⁴assai della sua volta inuerso il centro del mondo, trovandosi ispiccata mediante il corso de⁵lle uene che al continuo consumano il loco donde passano. . . .

of the earth which was filled with water, that is to say, the vast cavern inside the earth, may have fallen in a vast part of its vault towards the centre of the earth, being pierced by means of the course of the springs which continually wear away the place where they pass. . . .

⁶Profondamēto di paesi ⁷come nel Mare Morto di So⁸ria cioè Sodoma e Gomorra.

Sinking in of countries like the Dead Sea in Syria, that is, Sodom and Gomorrah.

⁹È necessario che l'acqua sia più che la terra, e la parte scoperta del mare nō lo dimostra, onde bisognia che ¹⁰molta acqua sia dentro alla terra, sanza quella ch'è infusa nella bassa aria e che scorre ¹¹per li fiumi e uene.

It is of necessity that there should be more water than land, and the visible portion of the sea does not show this; so that there must be a great deal of water inside the earth, besides that which rises into the lower air and which flows through rivers and springs.

F. 27a]   939

FIGURA D'ELEMĒTI

The theory of Plato.

²Della figura delli elemēti, e prima contro a chi nega ³l'opinione di Platone, che dicono che se essi elemēti vestis⁴sero l'un l'altro, colle figure che mette Platone, che si ca⁵vserebbe vacuo infra l'uno e l'altro; e non è vero, e ⁶qui lo provo, ma prima bisogna proporre alcuna cō⁷clusione; Non è neciessario che nessuno ele⁸mento, che veste l'ū l'altro, sia d'equal grossezza in tu⁹tta la sua quantità infra la parte che ueste e quel¹⁰la ch'è uestita; Noi uediamo la spera dell' acqua ma-¹¹nifestamēte essere di uarie grossezze dalla sua ¹²superfitie al fondo, e che, nō che essa vestisse ¹³la terra quando fusse di figura cuba cioè di 8 angoli come ¹⁴vole Platone, essa veste la terra che à innumerabili ¹⁵angoli di scogli coperti dall' acqua e varie globosità e cō¹⁶cavità, e non si genera vacuo infra l'acqua e la terra; Ancora l'aria veste la spera dell' acqua ¹⁷insieme colli monti e valli che superano essa spera, e nō ¹⁸rimane vacuo infra la terra e l'aria, sicchè, chi disse¹⁹generarsi vacuo, ebbe tristo discorso.

²⁰A Platō si rispōde che la superfitie ²¹delle figure che avrebbero li elemēti, ²²che lui pone, non potrebbero sta²³re.

THE FIGURES OF THE ELEMENTS

Of the figures of the elements; and first as against those who deny the opinions of Plato, and who say that if the elements include one another in the forms attributed to them by Plato they would cause a vacuum one within the other. I say it is not true, and I here prove it, but first I desire to propound some conclusions. It is not necessary that the elements which include each other should be of corresponding magnitude in all the parts, of that which includes and of that which is included. We see that the sphere of the waters varies conspicuously in mass from the surface to the bottom, and that, far from investing the earth when that was in the form of a cube, that is, of 8 angles as Plato will have it, that it invests the earth which has innumerable angles of rock covered by the water and various prominences and concavities, and yet no vacuum is generated between the earth and water; again, the air invests the sphere of waters together with the mountains and valleys which rise above that sphere, and no vacuum remains between the earth and the air, so that any one who says a vacuum is generated speaks foolishly.

But to Plato I would reply that the surface of the figures which according to him the elements would have could not exist.

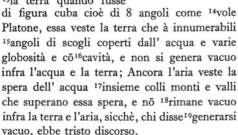

---

4. isspichata. 5. iloco. 8. coe soddoma e gamor. 9. chellacq"a" . . chella terra ella . . dell . . dimosstra.
939. 2. p"a" contro . . niegha. 3. lopēnione . . dicano chesse . . vessti. 4. sin lūlaltro cholle. 5. vserebe . . ellaltro ilenone vere. 6. p"a". 8. grosseza. 9. infralla . . ecquel. 10. lasspera dellacq"a". 11. grosseze. 12. vestissi [il cubo]. 13. quande fussi . . cubo "coe di 8 angoli" come. 14. esse . . inunbili. 15. acq"a". 16. cavita "e non sigenera vacuo infra lacqua ell aterra" Ancora laria che veste. 17. cholli. 18. ellaria siche. 20. chella. 21. arebō. 22. chellui . . potrebono.

A. 58*b*] 940

PRUOVA · COME · LA TERRA · NON È · TŌDA, ²E NON ESSENDO TŌDA, NŌ PUÒ AVER COMVNE · CĒTRO

PROVES HOW THE EARTH IS NOT GLOBULAR, AND NOT BEING GLOBULAR CANNOT HAVE A COMMON CENTRE

³Noi · vediamo · il Nilo · partirsi dalle · meridiane · regioni · e rigare · diuerse provincie, corrēdo ⁴inverso · settentrione · per ispatio · di 3000 · miglia e versare nelle mediterrane ōde ai liti d'Egitto, e se noi · vogliamo · dare a questo · di calo quelle ⁵dieci · braccia per miglio ·, le quali comvnalmēte · si concede · alla · vniversalità · del corso · de' fiumi, ⁶noi troveremo · il Nilo · avere il suo · fine piv basso · che 'l prīcipio · miglia dieci ·; ⁷Ancora · vediamo il Reno, Rodano e Danvbio · partirsi dalle Germaniche · parti, quasi ciētro ⁸d'Evropa ·, e l'uno a oriēte, l'altro a settētrione ·, e l'ultimo · a meridiani mari fa suo corso; ⁹se tu cōsiderai · bene tutto, vedrai le pianvre d'Europa fare vno cōcorso molto ¹⁰piv· elevato ·, che nō sono · l'alte cime de' marittimi mōti; or pēsa, quāto le loro cime ¹¹si trovano · piv· alte · che liti marini.

We see the Nile come from southern regions and traverse various provinces, running towards the north for a distance of 3,000 miles, and flow into the Mediterranean by the shores of Egypt; and if we will give this a fall of ten braccia a mile, as is usually allowed to the course of rivers in general, we shall find that the Nile must have its mouth ten miles lower down than its source. Again, we see the Rhine, the Rhône, and the Danube starting from the German parts, almost the centre of Europe, and having a course one to the east, the other to the north, and the last to southern seas. And if you consider all this you will see that the plains of Europe in their aggregate are much higher than the high peaks of the maritime mountains; think then how much their tops must be above the sea-shores.

That the flow of rivers proves the slope of the land.

A. 55*b*] 941

DEL CALDO CHE NEL MŌDO · È

OF THE HEAT THAT IS IN THE WORLD

²Dov' è · vita lì è calore ·, e dou' è · calore · vitale, quiui è mouimēto · d'umori; ³Questo · si pruova, · inperochè si uede · per effetto · che il caldo · dello elemēto · del foco · senpre · tira · a sé ⁴li umidi · vapori · e folte nebbie e spessi · nuvoli ·, i quali · spiccano da' mari e altri · paduli · e fiumi e vmide ⁵valli, e quelle tirādo · a poco a poco · insino · alla · fredda · regione, quella prima parte si ferma, ⁶perchè · il caldo · e vmido nō si affà · col freddo · e secco; onde · ferma la prima parte lì assetta l'altre ⁷parti, e così, aggiugniēdosi parte cō parte ·, si fa · spesse · e oscure nvbole ·; e spesso sono ⁸remosse e portate da vēti d'una · in altra regione; dove per la densità loro fanno sì spessa gravezza, ⁹che cadono · cō spessa · pioggia ·; e se 'l caldo · del sole s'aggivgne · alla potētia dello elemēto ¹⁰del foco ·, i nvuoli fieno tirati piv · alti e trovano · piv freddo, in nel quale si ghiacciano e cavsasi ¹¹tēpestosa · grādine ·; Ora · quel medesimo · caldo ·, che tiene · sì grā peso · d'acqua ·, come si uede ¹²piovere de' nvvoli, sveglie di basso · in alto · dalle base delle mōtagnie, e cōduciele, e tienle ¹³dētro · alle · cime delle mōtagnie, le quali, trovādo qualche fessura, al · continuo vsciēdo, ¹⁴causā i fiumi.

Where there is life there is heat, and where vital heat is, there is movement of vapour. This is proved inasmuch as we see that the element of fire by its heat always draws to itself damp vapours and thick mists as opaque clouds, which it raises from seas as well as lakes and rivers and damp valleys; and these being drawn by degrees as far as the cold region, the first portion stops, because heat and moisture cannot exist with cold and dryness; and where the first portion stops the rest settle, and thus one portion after another being added, thick and dark clouds are formed. They are often wafted about and borne by the winds from one region to another, where by their density they become so heavy that they fall in thick rain; and if the heat of the sun is added to the power of the element of fire, the clouds are drawn up higher still and find a greater degree of cold, in which they form ice and fall in storms of hail. Now the same heat which holds up so great a weight of water as is seen to rain from the clouds, draws them from below upwards, from the foot of the mountains, and leads and holds them within the summits of the mountains, and these, finding some fissure, issue continuously and cause rivers.

Theory of the elevation of water within the mountains.

940. 1. chome . . tera. 2. po avr chomune. 3. vedemo . . delle . . chorēdo. 4. settantrione . . isspatio . . miglia "e vessare nelle mediterane ōde a liti degitto e se . . acquessto di chalo qualle. 5. dieci br . . quale chomvnemēte . . chonciede. 6. no trovrremo . . prēcipio . . . diecip. 7. vedemo . . delle. 8. elluno . . assettātrione . . chorso. 9. settu chōsiderai . be . . verai [levr] le . . deropia . . chōchorso. 10. cime.
941. 1. chalda. 2. vita | "li" e chalore . . quiue . . domori [Essel chaldo move lumido "il fredo lo ferma".] 3. chaldo . . focho . . asse. 4. effolte nebie esspessi nuboli . . spicha de . . effiumi. 5. quele . . apocho apocho . . freda regione [i] e. 6. chaldo . . chol . . essecho . . li assetta laltre. 7. chosi agiugnēdo . . chō . . oscure . . esspesso sono [portale]. 8. fano . . graueza. 9. chadano chō-ispessa piogia esselchaldo . . sagivgne. 10. focho . . fredo inel . . diacciano e chavsasi. 11. chaldo chettiene . . chome. 12. nvboli [tiene] disuelle . . delle mōtagnie e chōducie le ettielle. 13. mōtagnie lequali . . li chontinui vssciēdo. 14. chausano ifiumi.

F. 73a]   942

DEL MARE CHE A MOLTI ²SENPLICI PAR PIÙ ALTO ³CHE LA TERRA CHE GLI FA LITI

OF THE SEA, WHICH TO MANY FOOLS APPEARS TO BE HIGHER THAN THE EARTH WHICH FORMS ITS SHORE

The relative height of the surface of the sea to that of the land (942-5).

⁴*b d* è vna pianvra, donde corre ⁵vn fiume al mare, la qual pianu⁶ra à per termine esso mare; e per⁷chè in vero essa terra scoperta nõ ⁸è nel sito dell' equalità — perchè, se co⁹sì fusse, il fiume non avrebbe mo¹⁰to — onde, movendosi, questo sito ¹¹à piutosto da essere detto spiagg¹²ia che pianvra; e così essa pia¹³nura *d b* termina in tal modo ¹⁴colla spera dell' acqua che, chi la produ¹⁵cesse in continua rettitudine in *b a*, ¹⁶essa entrerebbe sotto il mare, e ¹⁷di qui nasce che 'l mar *a c b* pare più alto che la terra discoperta.

¹⁸Naturalmẽte nes¹⁹suna parte della ²⁰terra discoperta da ²¹l'acqua fia mai ²²più bassa che la ²³superfitie della ²⁴spera d'essa acqua.

b d is a plain through which a river flows to the sea; this plain ends at the sea, and since in fact the dry land that is uncovered is not perfectly level—for, if it were, the river would have no motion—as the river does move, this place is a slope rather than a plain; hence this plain *d b* so ends where the sphere of water begins that if it were extended in a continuous line to *b a* it would go down beneath the sea, whence it follows that the sea *a c b* looks higher than the dry land.

Obviously no portions of dry land left uncovered by water can ever be lower than the surface of the sphere of this water.

A. 58b]   943

D'ALCUNI CHE DICONO · L'ACQUA ESSERE · PIV · ALTA · CHE LA TERRA · SCOPERTA

OF CERTAIN PERSONS WHO SAY THE WATERS WERE HIGHER THAN THE DRY LAND

²Cierto · non poca · ammiratione · mi da · la comvne · opinione fatta cõtro · al uero dallo vniversale ³cõcorso · de' givditi · delli omini ·, e questo · è che tutti · s'accordano · che la superfitie · del mare ⁴sia · piv · alta · che l'altissime · cime delle · mõtagnie ·, allegãdo molte · vane e puerili · ragioni, ⁵cõtro ai quali · io n'allegherò · solo · vna · senplie e brieve ragione ·; Noi vediamo chiaro, che ⁶se si toglie · via · l'argine · al mare ·, che lui · vestirà · la terra e faralla di perfetta rotõdità; ⁷or cõsidera · quãta · terra si leuerebbe a fare che l'õde marine coprissino ⁸il mõdo; adũque ciò, che si leuasse, sarebbe piv · alto · che la riua del mare.

Certainly I wonder not a little at the common opinion which is contrary to truth, but held by the universal consent of the judgement of men. And this is that all are agreed that the surface of the sea is higher than the highest peaks of the mountains; and they allege many vain and childish reasons, against which I will allege only one simple and short reason: We see plainly that if we could remove the shores of the sea, it would invest the whole earth and make it a perfect sphere. Now, consider how much earth would be carried away to enable the waves of the sea to cover the world; therefore that which would be carried away must be higher than the sea-shore.

A. 56a]   944

OPINIONE D'ALCUNI · CHE DICONO · CHE L'ACQUA D'ALCUNI ²MARI È PIV ALTA CHE LE PIV ALTE SOMMITÀ DE' MÕTI, ³E PERÒ · SIA SOSPĪTA L'ACQUA · A ESSE SÕMITÀ

THE OPINION OF SOME PERSONS WHO SAY THAT THE WATER OF SOME SEAS IS HIGHER THAN THE HIGHEST SUMMITS OF MOUNTAINS; AND NEVERTHELESS THE WATER WAS FORCED UP TO THESE SUMMITS

⁴L'acqua nõ si moverà · da loco a loco · se la bassezza · non la tira; E per corso ⁵naturale · nõ potrà · mai · ritornare · a altezza · simile · al

Water would not move from place to place if it were not that it seeks the lowest level, and by a natural consequence it never can return to a

---

2. 2. senpici par pu. 3. chella..chelli. 4. a d e vna. 5. lacqual. 6. essesso. 9. fussi..arebbe. 14. dellacq"a". 15. cessi. 16. enterebbe. 17. nassce. *On the margin is written:* cella tera
di scoperta.
Lines 18-24 are also written on the margin. 18. ne. 22. chella. 24. acq"a".

943. 1. dichano lacq"a" . . chella. 2. pocha amiratione . . chomvne oppenione fatto chõtra. 3. chõchorso . . ecquesto e chettutti sachordano chella. 4. chellaltissime . . ragione. 5. nalegero . . vedemo. 6. tolglie . . chellui vesstira . . effaralla . . retõdita. 7. chõsidera [vn pocho] . . affare chellõde . . choprissino. 8. chessi leuassi . . chella.

944. 1. Openione dalchuni che dichano chellacqua dalchuni. 2. alta [che alchu] chelle . . somita. 4. Lacq"a" . . dalocho allocho sella bassezza . . chorso. 5. alteza . . locho.

primo loco, do⁶ve nel uscire
de' mõti si mostrò · al cielo ·; E
quella · parte del mare ·, che ⁷cõ
falsa · imaginatione · tu · diciesti
· essere si alta ·, che uersaua ·
per le cime · de ⁸li alti · mõti, ·
per tãti seculi · sarebbe · cõsu-
mata · e uersata per l'uscita
d'esse ⁹mõtagnie; Tu puoi bene
pēsare · che tãto tēpo che Tigris
ed Eufrates

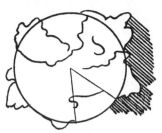

height like that of the place
where it first on issuing from the
mountain came to light. And
that portion of the sea which, in
your vain imagining, you say was
so high that it flowed over the
summits of the high mountains,
for so many centuries would be
swallowed up and poured out
again through the issue from
these mountains. You can well
imagine that all the time that Tigris and
Euphrates

A. 56b]   945

ànno · versato · per le · sommità de' mõti ·
Armeni ·, che si può · credere · che tutta
l'acqua dell' ocieano ²sia · moltissime · volte ·
passata · per dette · bocche ·; or non credi tu
che 'l Nilo · abbi messo · piv ³acqua · ī mare ·
che non è · al presente tutto lo elemēto ·
dell' acqua ·? cierto · sì; · e se detta · acqua
⁴fusse · caduta fori di questo · corpo · della
terra ·, questa machina · sarebbe già lūgo tēpo
⁵stata sãza acqua; sichè si può cõcludere · che
l'acqua vadi dai fiumi al mare e dal mare ⁶ai
fivmi, senpre così ragirãdo e voltãdoui, e che
tutto · il mare · e i fivmi sieno passati per la
bocca del Nilo infinite volte.

have flowed from the summits of the mountains
of Armenia, it must be believed that all the
water of the ocean has passed very many times
through these mouths. And do you not believe
that the Nile must have sent more water into the
sea than at present exists of all the element of
water? Undoubtedly, yes. And if all this water
had fallen away from this body of the earth, this
terrestrial machine would long since have been
without water. Whence we may conclude that
the water goes from the rivers to the sea, and
from the sea to the rivers, thus constantly cir-
culating and returning, and that all the sea and
the rivers have passed through the mouth of the
Nile an infinite number of times.

6. usscire . . Ecquella. 7. chõ . . dicievi. 8. tãte sechuli sarebe chõ sumata . . lusscita. 9. mõtãgnia . . chettãto . . chettigris.
945. 1. mõti ermini che si po . . che | "tutta"llacq"a". 2. boche . . abi. 3. imare . . e "al presēte" tutto . . esse. 4. fussi chaduta . .
chorpo . . tera . . sarebe. 5. chõchiudere. 6. ragirãdo . . chettutto . . sia pasato . . bocha; *the last two words* infinite volte *are
written on the margin.*

945. *Mõti Armeni, Ermini* in the original, in M.
Ravaisson's transcript 'monti ernini [le loro ruine?]'.
He renders this 'Le Tigre et l'Euphrate se sont dé-
versés par les sommets des montagnes [avec leurs
eaux destructives?]; on peut croire', &c. Leonardo
always writes *Ermini, Erminia,* for *Armeni, Armenia.*

PERCHÈ L'ACQUA È SALSA

Refutation of Pliny's theory as to the saltness of the sea (946–7).

²Dicie Plinio nel 2⁰ suo libro, al 103 ca³pitolo, che l'acqua del mare è salata perchè ⁴l'ardore del sole secca l'umi⁵do e quello succia, e questo al mare, che ⁶molto s'allarga, dà sapore di sale; ⁷Ma questo nō si cōciede, perchè se la salsedine ⁸del mare avesse cavsa dallo ardore del sole, ⁹e' non è dubbio che tanto maggiormente li laghi, stagni e paduli ¹⁰sarebbono più insalati, quāto ¹¹le loro acque son manco mobili e di ¹²minore profondità, e la esperiēzia ci mo¹³stra il contrario; tali paduli ci mostrā ¹⁴le loro acque essere al tutto private di sal¹⁵sedine; Ancora s'assegnia da Plinio nel medesimo ¹⁶capitolo che tal salsedine ¹⁷potrebbe nasciere, perchè, leuatone ogni ¹⁸dolce e sottile ¹⁹parte, la qual facilmēte il caldo a sé ti²⁰ra, rimane la parte più aspra e più ²¹grossa, e per questo l'acqua, che è nella su²²perfitie, è più dolcie che nel fōdo; ²³a questa si cōtradice colle medesime ²⁴sopradette ragioni, cioè che il medesimo ac²⁵caderebbe alli paduli e altre acque che per il cal²⁶do s'asciugano; Ācora fu detto che ²⁷la salsedine del mare è sudore della terra; ²⁸a questo si rispōde che tutte le uene dell' acque ²⁹che penetrano la terra, sarebbono insalate; Ma ³⁰si cōclude la salsedine del mare esser nata ³¹dalle molte vene d'acqua le quali nel ³⁴penetrare la ter³⁵ra trovano ³⁶le mini³⁷ere del sale, e ³⁸quelle in parte ³⁹si soluono e por⁴⁰tā seco all' o⁴¹cieano e li altri ⁴²mari, d'ō⁴³de mai ¶ li nuvo⁴⁴li, seminatori ⁴⁵d'elli fiumi ¶ ⁴⁶lo leuano; ed e' sarebbe ⁴⁷più salato il ma⁴⁸re alli nostri tē⁴⁹pi che mai per ⁵⁰alcun altro tē⁵¹po fusse, e se per ⁵²l'auersario

WHY WATER IS SALT

Pliny says in his second book, chapter 103, that the water of the sea is salt because the heat of the sun dries up the moisture and sucks it up; and this gives to the wide stretching sea the savour of salt. But this cannot be admitted, because if the saltness of the sea were caused by the heat of the sun, there can be no doubt that lakes, pools, and marshes would be so much the more salt, as their waters have less motion and are of less depth; but experience shows us, on the contrary, that these lakes have their waters quite free from salt. Again it is stated by Pliny in the same chapter that this saltness might originate because, all the sweet and subtle portions which the heat attracts easily being taken away, the more bitter and coarser part will remain, and thus the water on the surface is fresher than at the bottom [22]; but this is contradicted by the same reason given above, which is, that the same thing would happen in marshes and other waters, which are dried up by the heat. Again, it has been said that the saltness of the sea is the sweat of the earth; to this it may be answered that all the springs of water which penetrate through the earth would then be salt. But the conclusion is that the saltness of the sea must proceed from the many springs of water which, as they penetrate into the earth, find mines of salt, and these they dissolve in part and carry with them to the ocean and the other seas, whence the clouds, the begetters of rivers, never carry it up. And the sea would be more salt in our times than it ever was at any time; and if the adversary were to say that in infinite time the

946. 1. essalsa. 2. a 103 capitoli. 3. chellacqua .. essalata. 4. [li razi solari] Lardore .. secha "abrōzre e (?)" lumi. 5. ecquello .. ecquesto. 6. sallargha .. sale | [qui]. 7. Macquesto .. sella. 8. avessi chausa dello. 9. chelli "tanto magiormente" laghi. 10. [dove [nel me]. sarebbono. 11. [le] le .. mancho .. eddi. 12. ella .. mos. 13. in chontrario .. mosstrā. 14. tucto. 15. Ācora sasegnia lacque] sarebbono. 16. chapitolo chettal. 17. nassciere .. leuato | "ne ogni" parte. 18. dolcie [dellacq"a" ressta lasspra] essottile. 19. chaldo asseti. 20. asspra. 22. fōdo || contro. 23. acquessta si cōtraddicie cholle. 25. chaderebbe .. chal. 26. sassciughano Āchora fuddetto. 27. essudore. 28. acquessto .. chettutte. Lines 32–66 are written on the margin. 32. ¶ finiscie quel che. 33. mācha di socto.¶ 35. trovano [le ve]. 36. [ne del 5] le. 40. secho alloc. 41. elli. 42. mari [dove] dō. 43. de mai (li nuvo. 45. delli fiumi) mai. 46. nō leuano ede "sare". 48. nosstri. 50. alchū. 51. fussi esse.

946. Pliny, Hist. Nat. II, ciii [c]: 'Itaque Solis ardore siccatur liquor: et hoc esse masculum sidus accepimus, torrens cuncta sorbensque. (cp. civ.) Sic mari late patenti saporem incoqui salis, aut quia exhausto inde dulci tenuique, quod facillime trahat vis ignea, omne asperius crassiusque linquatur: ideo summa aequorum aqua dulciorem profundam; hanc esse veriorem causam asperi saporis, quam quod mare terrae sudor sit aeternus: aut quia plurimum ex arido misceatur illi vapore: aut quia terrae natura sicut medicatas aquas inficiat .. (cp. cv): altissimum mare XV

stadiorum Fabianus tradit. Alii in Ponto coadverso Coraxorum gentis (vocant Βαθέα Ponti) trecentis fere a continenti stadiis immensam altitudinem maris tradunt, vadis nunquam repertis. (cp. cvi [ciii]) Mirabilius id faciunt aquae dulces, juxta mare, ut fistulis emicantes. Nam nec aquarum natura a miraculis cessat. Dulces mari invehuntur, leviores haud dubie. Ideo et marinae, quarum natura gravior, magis invecta sustinent. Quaedam vero et dulces inter se supermeant alias.'

22. Compare No. 948.

si di⁵³cesse, che il tenpo ⁵⁴infinito secchereb⁵⁵be over cōgielereb⁵⁶be il mare in sa⁵⁷le, a questo ⁵⁸si risponde, che ⁵⁹tal sale si rē⁶⁰de alla terra ⁶¹colla liberatione ⁶²d'essa terra, che ⁶³s'inalza col suo ⁶⁴acquistato sale, ⁶⁵e li fiumi lo rendo-⁶⁶no alla sōmersa terra.

sea would dry up or congeal into salt, to this I answer that this salt is restored to the earth by the setting free of that part of the earth which rises out of the sea with the salt it has acquired, and the rivers return it to the earth under the sea.

G. 49a]   947

Terza e vlti²ma ragione di³remo, il sale ⁴essere in tutte ⁵le cose create, ⁶e questo c'ī⁷segniano ⁸le acque passa⁹te per tutte le ci¹⁰eneri e calci¹¹ni delle cose ¹²bruciate, e le ¹³orine di qua¹⁴lūche anima¹⁵le e le super¹⁶fluità uscit¹⁷e de' lor cor¹⁸pi e le terre, ¹⁹nelle quali si ²⁰cōuertono ²¹le corrutioni ²²di tutte le cose.

²³Ma a dire meglio, essendo dato il mōdo eterno, egli è neciessario ²⁴che li sua popoli sieno ācora loro eterni; ōde ²⁵eternalmēte fu e sarebbe la spetie vmana cōsu²⁶matricie del sale; e se tutta la massa della terra fas²⁷si sale, non basterebbe alli cibi vmani, per la qual ²⁸cosa ci bisognia confessare, o che la spetie del sale ²⁹sia eterna īsieme col mōdo, o che quella ³⁰mora e rinasca insieme cogli omini d'essa di³¹voratori; Ma se la esperiēza c'insegnia quel ³²non avere morte come per il foco si manife³³sta, il qual non la cōsuma, e pei l'acqua che di tūto oi ³⁴oala di quāto ella in sé ne risolue, evaporādo l'a³⁵qua, sempre il sale resta nella prima quātità, ³⁶deve passare per li corpi vmani che in orina, ³⁷o sudore, o altre superfluità fia ritrovato, e ques³⁸to è il sale che ogni anno si porta alle città; adūque ³⁹cavasi il sale de' lochi, dov' è piscia;—li porci e li vēti marini sō salati;—

⁴⁰Diremo che la ⁴¹pioggia pene⁴²tratrice della ⁴³terra sia que⁴⁴lla, ch'è sotto ⁴⁵alli fonda⁴⁶mēti delle cit⁴⁷tà e popoli, ⁴⁸e sia quella che ⁴⁹per li meati del⁵⁰la terra rē⁵¹da la salsedi⁵²ne leuata dal ⁵³mare, e che ⁵⁴la mutatiō ⁵⁵del mare, sta⁵⁶to sopra tutti ⁵⁷li monti, lo la⁵⁸sci per le minie⁵⁹re ritrovate ⁶⁰in essi monti ecc.

For the third and last reason we will say that salt is in all created things; and this we learn from water passed through the ashes and cinders of burnt things; and the urine of every animal, and the superfluities issuing from their bodies, and the earth into which all things are converted by corruption.

But—to put it better—given that the world is everlasting, it must be admitted that its population will also be eternal; hence the human species has eternally been and would be consumers of salt; and if all the mass of the earth were to be turned into salt, it would not suffice for all human food; whence we are forced to admit either that the species of salt must be everlasting like the world, or that it dies and is born again like the men who devour it. But as experience teaches us that it does not die, as is evident by fire, which does not consume it, and by water, which becomes salt in proportion to the quantity dissolved in it—and when it is evaporated the salt always remains in the original quantity—it must pass through the bodies of men either in the urine or the sweat or other excretions where it is found again; and this salt is carried every year into towns; therefore salt is dug in places where there is urine.—Sea hogs and sea winds are salt.

We will say that the rain which penetrates the earth is that which is under the foundations of cities with their inhabitants, and which restores through the internal passages of the earth the saltness taken from the sea; and that the change in the place of the sea, which had been over all the mountains, caused it to be left there in the mines found in those mountains, &c.

Leic. 21b]   948

L'acque de' mari salati son dolci nelle sua grā profondità.

The waters of the salt sea are fresh at the greatest depths.   The characteristics of sea-water (948–9).

G. 38a]   949

COME L'OCEANO NŌ PE²NETRA INFRA LA TERRA

THAT THE OCEAN DOES NOT PENETRATE UNDER THE EARTH

³L'oceano nō penetra infra la terra, e que⁴sto c'insegniano le molte e varie vene d'acque dol⁵ci,

The ocean does not penetrate under the earth, and this we learn from the many and various

53. ciessi. 54. sechere. 55. cōgielere. 57. acquesto. 59. sare. 61. cholla. 65. elli .. rēda. 66. somersa.
947. 3. direno .. sale es. 5. chose. 6. ecquessto. 7. segnia [lecho]. 10. enere e chalci. 11. ne. 12. elle. 15. elle. 16. fruita vssci. 17. de de. 18. elle. 19. nelle. 20. cōuertano. Lines 1–27 are written on the margin along the text no. 1201, under which is the text of lines 23–39, parallel with the lines 40–60. 23. essendo | "dato" il mōdo "etterno" egli. 24. chelli .. āchora .. ecterni. 25. etternalmēte .. essarebbe lasspetie .. cōsu. 26. essettutta. 27. bassterebbe. 28. chonfessare || o chella. 29. etterna .. chol .. checquella. 30. rinascca .. chogli. 31. Massella essperiēza. 32. focho. 33. nolla. 35. sepre .. ressta. 36. ne vale passare. 37. ritrorato ecq"a". 38. ōni. 39. pisscia. 40. direno chelle. 41. piogie. 42. tratrici. 43. sien. 44. lla. 46. delli ci. 48. sie quella che. 49. de. 60. nessi.
949. 1. loccieano. 2. infralla. 3. loccieano .. infralla .. ecques. 4. cinsegnia .. euuarie. 5. occieano "pe" nene.

le quali in diuersi lochi d'esso oceano pene-
⁶trano dal fondo alla sua superfitie; Ancora il
me⁷desimo dimostrano li pozzi fatti dopo lo
spa⁸tio d'ū miglio remoti dal detto ocieano, ⁹li
quali s'enpiano d'acqua dolcie, e questo ac¹⁰cade
perchè l'acqua dolcie è più sottile che l'ac¹¹qua
salata, e per cōseguēza più penetra¹²tiva.

¹³Qual pesa più, ¹⁴o l'acqua ghiac¹⁵ciata o la
nō ¹⁶ghiacciata?

PIÙ PENETRA L'ACQUA DOLCE CŌTRO ¹⁸ALL' ACQUA
SALSA, CHE LA SALSA CŌTRO AL¹⁹LA DOLCIE

²⁰Che l'acqua dolcie penetri più cōtro all' ac-
²¹qua salsa, che essa salsa cōtro alla dolcie, ci
²²lo manifesta vna sottil tela ascuitta e ²³vechia,
pendente con equal bassezza ²⁴colli sua oppositi
stremi nelle due varie ²⁵acque, delle quali le lor
superfitie siē ²⁶d'equal bassezza, e allor si vedrà
elevar²⁷si in alto infra essa pezza tanto più
l'acqua ²⁸dolcie, che la salsa, quanto la dolcie è
più ²⁹lieve che essa salsa.

springs of fresh water which in many parts of
the ocean make their way up from the bottom to
the surface. The same thing is further proved
by wells dug beyond the distance of a mile from
the said ocean, which fill with fresh water; and
this happens because the fresh water is lighter
than salt water and consequently more penetrating.

Which weighs most, water when frozen or
when not frozen?

FRESH WATER PENETRATES MORE AGAINST SALT
WATER THAN SALT WATER AGAINST FRESH WATER

That fresh water penetrates more against salt
water than salt water against fresh is proved by
a thin cloth, dry and old, hanging with the two
opposite ends equally low in the two different
waters, the surfaces of which are at an equal
level; and it will then be seen how much higher
the fresh water will rise in this piece of linen
than the salt: by so much is the fresh lighter than
the salt.

C. A. 160b]   950

On the for-
mation of
gulfs
(950–1).

Tutti li mari mediterrani e li ²golfi d'essi mari
sō fatti da fi³vmi che versano in mare.

All inland seas and the gulfs of those seas are
made by rivers which flow into the sea.

C. A. 84b]   951

QUI SI RENDE RAGIONE DELLI EFFETTI FATTI
DALLE ACQUE NEL PREPOSTO SITO

²Tutti li laghi e tutti li golfi del mare e tutti
li mari mediterrani nascono dalli fiumi, che in
quelli spā³dono le loro acque, e dalli impedimēti
della loro declinatione ⁴nel Mare Mediterrano,
diuisore d'Africa dall' Europa, e dell' Europa
dall' Asia, mediāte il Nilo e Tanai che in ⁵lui
versano le loro acque; Si domāda, quale inpedi-
mēto è maggiore a proibire il corso delle sue
acque, che nō si renda all' oceano.

HERE THE REASON IS GIVEN OF THE EFFECTS PRO-
DUCED BY THE WATERS IN THE ABOVE-MENTIONED
PLACE

All the lakes and all the gulfs of the sea and all
inland seas are due to rivers which distribute
their waters into them, and from impediments
in their downfall into the Mediterranean—
which divides Africa from Europe and Europe
from Asia by means of the Nile and the Don
which pour their waters into it. It is asked what
impediment is great enough to stop the course
of the waters that they do not reach the ocean.

Firenze Bibl. Laurenziana. *Trattato di
Francesco di Giorgio*]   952

DE ONDA

On the en-
croach-
ments of the
sea on the
land and
vice versa
(952–4).

²L'onda del mare
senpre ruina ³dinanti
alla sua basa, e quella
par⁴te del colmo si tro-
verà più bassa che ⁵pri-
ma era più alta.

OF WAVES

A wave of the sea
always breaks in front of
its base, and that portion
of the crest will then be
lowest which before was
highest.

7. dimosstrano li pozi . . losspa. 8. miglio [li quali] remōti. 9. ecquessto. 10. chade . . chellac. 11. piu [soct] penetra. *Lines
13–16 are written on the margin.* 14. diac. 15. olla. 16. diacciata. 17. dole. 18. chella. 20. chellacqua . . chōtro. 21. dolcie cie.
22. assciuta eo. 23. pendente [cholli] chon. 24. cholli. 26. vedra mē eleua "r". 27. si [eleua] in . . tantu. 28. chella . . he piu.
950. 1. elli. 2. gholfi.
951. 1. effecti . . delle. 2. ettuttili gholfi . . etti ttutti . . nasschano. 3. dano le . . ed dalli la pedimēti. 4. mediterano . . ettanai che
il. 5. domāde . . occieano.
952. 2. Londa [delle] del. 3. ecquella. 4. cholmo. 5. alta sara poi piu bas.

952. The page of the *Trattato* attributed to Francesco di Giorgio on which Leonardo has written this
remark, contains some notes on the construction of
dams, harbours, &c. See No. 44, note.

Leic. 20a]

953

Come le riue del ma²re al continvo acquistano terreno inuerso il mezzo del mare; Come li scogli e promontori ³de' mari al continvo ruinano e si consumano; Come i mediterrani scopriranno i lor fondi all' aria e sol ri⁴serberanno il canale al maggior fiume, che dentro vi metta, il quale correrà all' oceano e iui uerse⁵rà le sue acque insieme con quelle di tutti i fiumi, che cō seco s'accōpagnano.

That the shores of the sea constantly acquire more soil towards the middle of the sea; that the rocks and promontories of the sea are constantly being ruined and worn away; that the Mediterranean seas will in time discover their bottom to the air, and all that will be left will be the channel of the greatest river that enters it; and this will run to the ocean and pour its waters into that with those of all the rivers that are its tributaries.

Leic. 27b]

954

Come il fiume del Po in brĭeve tenpo secca il mare Adriano nel ²medesimo modo ch'elli asseccò grā parte di Lonbardia.

How the river Po in a short time might dry up the Adriatic sea in the same way as it has dried up a large part of Lombardy.

C. A. 165b]

955

¶ Dove è maggior quātità d'acqua, ²quivi è maggior flusso e riflusso; e 'l ³contrario fa nelle acque strette. ¶

⁴Guarda se 'l mare è nella som̃a cresciē⁵te quādo la luna è nel mezzo del tuo emi⁶spero.

Where there is a larger quantity of water, there is a greater flow and ebb, but the contrary in narrow waters.
Look whether the sea is at its greatest flow when the moon is half-way over our hemisphere [on the meridian].

The ebb and flow of the tide (955–60).

Leic. 17b]

956

Se 'l flusso e riflusso nasce dalla luna o sole, overo è l'ali²tare di questa terrestre machina; Come il flusso e riflusso è vario in diuersi paesi e mari.

Whether the flow and ebb are caused by the moon or the sun, or are the breathing of this terrestrial machine. That the flow and ebb are different in different countries and seas.

Leic. 5a]

957

Libro 9° delli scontri de' fiumi e lor flusso e riflusso; e la medesima ²causa lo crea nel mare per causa dello stretto di Gibiltar, e ancora accade per le uoragini.

Book 9 of the meeting of rivers and their flow and ebb. The cause is the same in the sea, where it is caused by the straits of Gibraltar. And again it is caused by whirlpools.

Leic. 6b]

958

DEL FLUSSO E RIFLUSSO

²Tutti li mari ànno il lor flusso e riflusso in v̄ medesimo tempo, ma pare variarsi, perchè li giorni nō co³minciano in vn medesimo tenpo in tutto l'universo, cōciosiachè, quādo nel nostro emisperio è mezzo ⁴giorno, nell' opposito emisperio è mezzanotte ·, e nelle congiuntioni oriētali dell' uno e de l'altro emispe⁵rio comincia la notte che corre dirieto al giorno, e nelle congiūtioni occidentali d'essi emisperi comincia ⁶il giorno che seguita la notte dalla sua opposita

OF THE FLOW AND EBB

All seas have their flow and ebb in the same period, but they seem to vary because the days do not begin at the same time throughout the universe; in such wise that when it is midday in our hemisphere, it is midnight in the opposite hemisphere; and at the eastern boundary of the two hemispheres the night begins which follows on the day, and at the western boundary of these hemispheres begins the day, which follows the night from the opposite side. Hence it is to

953. 2. acquisstano .. mezo .. liscogli. 3. essi chonsum̃ano Come e .. scopiranno .. essol. 4. magor. 5. cōsecho sacōpagnano.
954. 1. secha. 2. assecho.
955. 1. he magior. 2. frusso e refrusso. 4. gharda. 5. mezo.
956. 1. frusso e refrusso nascce. 2. tereste .. frusso e refrusso.
957. 1. isscontri .. ellor frusso e refrusso ella. 2. chausa .. strett[i] o di gibiltar .. achade .. voragine.
958. 1. frusso e refrusso. 2. frusso e refrusso nv̄ .. gorni nō cho. 3. mincano .. concosia .. nosstro .. mez. 4. gorno .. oposito .. mezanotte .. congiuntioni .. emisspe. 5. cominca .. gorno .. congūtioni ocidentali .. comica. 6. gorno .. oposita. 7. acres-

956. Several passages in various manuscripts treat of the ebb and flow. In collecting them I have been guided by the rule only to transcribe those which

named some particular place.

957. For continuation see No. 971.

parte ·; adunque è conchiuso che, ancora che 'l [7]detto accrescimēto e diminvitione delle altezze de' mari sien fatte in vn [8]medesimo tenpo, essi mostrano variarsi per le già dette cagioni; sono adunque sōmerse le acque [9]nelle uene partite dai fondi de' mari, le quali ramificano dentro al corpo della terra, e rispondono [10]al nascimento de' fiumi ·, i quali al continvo tolgono del fondo, e il mare al mare àn dato e tolto; innvme-[11]rabili volte nella superfizie il mare al mare; E se tu volessi, che la luna, apparendo all' orientale parte [12]del Mare Mediterrano, comīciasse ad attrarre a sé l'acque del mare, ne seguirebbe che inmediate [13]se ne vedrebbe la speriēza al fine oriētale di tal mare predetto; Ancora essendo il Mar Medi[14]terrano circa alla ottava parte della circūferenza della spera dell' acqua, per essere lui [15]lungo 3 mila miglia, e 'l flusso e riflusso nō fa se nō 4 volte in 24 ore, e' nō s'accorderebbe tale [16]effetto col tenpo d'esse 24 ore, se esso Mare Mediterrā nō fusse lungo semila miglia, perchè [17]se lo spogliamēto di tanto mare avesse a passare per lo stretto di Gibiltar nel correr dietro [18]alla luna, e' sarebbe si grāde il corso delle acque per tale stretto, e s'alzerebbe in tāta altezza, [19]che dopo esso stretto farebbe tal corso, che per molte miglia infra l'oceano farebbe inōdatione e bolli[20]menti grandissimi, per la qual cosa sarebbe inpossibile passarui, e dopo questo · subito l'ocea[21]no rēderebbe colla medesima furia l'acque ricevute, donde esso le riceve; ecco che adūque mai si [22]passerebbe per tale stretto ·, e la speriēza mostra che d'ogni ora vi si passa, saluo che quādo il uento [23]viē per la linia della corrēte, allora il riflusso forte s'aumēta ·; Il mare non alza l'acqua nelli [24]stretti che ànno vscita ma ben s'ingorga e si ritarda dināti a quelli ·, onde con furioso moto [25]poi ristora il tempo del suo ritardamēto insino al fin del suo moto riflesso.

be inferred that the above-mentioned swelling and diminution in the height of the seas, although they take place in one and the same space of time, are seen to vary from the above-mentioned causes. The waters are then withdrawn into the fissures which start from the depths of the sea and which ramify inside the body of the earth, corresponding to the sources of rivers, which are constantly taking from the bottom of the sea the water which has flowed into it. A sea of water is incessantly being drawn off from the surface of the sea. And if you should think that the moon, rising at the Eastern end of the Mediterranean sea, must there begin to attract to herself the waters of the sea, it would follow that we must at once see the effect of it at the eastern end of that sea. Again, as the Mediterranean sea is about the eighth part of the circumference of the aqueous sphere, being 3,000 miles long, while the flow and ebb only occur 4 times in 24 hours, these results would not agree with the time of 24 hours, unless this Mediterranean sea were six thousand miles in length; because if such a superabundance of water had to pass through the straits of Gibraltar in running behind the moon, the rush of the water through that strait would be so great, and would rise to such a height, that beyond the straits it would for many miles rush so violently into the ocean as to cause floods and tremendous seething, so that it would be impossible to pass through. This agitated ocean would afterwards return the waters it had received with equal fury to the place they had come from, so that no one ever could pass through those straits. Now experience shows that at every hour they are passed in safety, but when the wind sets in the same direction as the current, the strong ebb increases [23]. The sea does not raise the water that has issued from the straits, but it checks them, and this retards the tide; then it makes up with furious haste for the time it has lost until the end of the ebb movement.

Leic. 13a]   959

Come jl flusso e riflusso non è generale, perchè [2]in riuiera di Genova non fa niēte, a Vinegia due braccia, tra la Inghilterra e Fiandra

That the flow and ebb are not general; for on the shore at Genoa there is none, at Venice two braccia, between England and Flanders 18

scimēto . . dellellaltezze de mari ancora chelle . . nvn. 8. mostra . . chagoni . . somerse. 9. defondi . . ramifichano . . rispondano. 10. nasscimento De . . tolgano "del fondo" [e rendano] il . . andato "e tolto" invmerabili volte "nella superfitie" umare . . Essettu . . chella . . aparendo. 12. mediterano comjcassi . . asse. 13. lassperiēza . . mare "predetto". 14. terano circha . . acqu"a". 15. lungho . . frusso e refrusso . . sacorderebe. 16. mediterā fussi lungho. 17. sello . . avessi . . dirie. 18. sarebe . . essalzerebe. 19. hesso . . infrall . . ebbolli. 21. rederebbe . . riceve . . echoche. 22. passerebe . . ella . . ora usi passa. 23. refrusso . . lacq"a". 24. vsscita [ne in quelli] ma ben siningorgha "essiritarda . . acquelli onde poi con. 25. tenpo [cheche] del . . refresso. 959. 1. frusso e refrusso. 2. genva . . uinegia due br tralla ingilterra . . 18 br. 3. cicilia lacorēte. 4. adriatico.

959. A few more recent data may be given here to facilitate comparison. In the Adriatic the tide rises 2½ feet, at Terracina 1¼. In the English channel between Calais and Kent it rises from 18 to 20 feet. In the straits of Messina it rises no more than 2½ feet, and that only in stormy weather, but the current is all the stronger. When Leonardo accounts for this

by the southward flow of all the Italian rivers along the coasts, the explanation is at least based on a correct observation; namely, that a steady current flows southwards along the coast of Calabria and another northwards, along the shores of Sicily; he seems to infer, from the direction of the first, that the tide in the Adriatic is caused by it.

fa 18 braccia; [3]Come per lo stretto di Sicilia la corrēte è grādissima, perchè di lì passā tutte l'acque de' fiumi che uersā [4]nel Mare Adriatico.

braccia. That in the straits of Sicily the current is very strong because all the waters from the rivers that flow into the Adriatic pass there.

Leic. 35a]   960

Nelle parti occidentali·, appresso alla Fiandra, il mare cresce e māca ogni 6 ore circa 20 braccia, [2]e 22 quādo la luna è in suo fauore, ma le 20 braccia è il suo ordinario, il quale ordinario manifestamēte si uede [3]non essere per cavsa della luna; Questa varietà del crescere e discrescere del mare ogni 6· ore può [4]accadere per le ringorgationi delle acque, le quali son condotte nel Mare Mediterrano da quella quantità de' fiu[5]mi dell' Africa, Asia ed Evropa, che in esso mare versano le loro acque, le quali per lo stretto di Gibiltar infra Abila e Calpe [6]promōtori rende all' occeano le acque che da essi fiumi li son date, jl quale oceano, astendendosi [7]infra le isole d'Inghilterra e l'altre più settētrionali, si uiene a ringorgare e tenere in collo per diuersi golfi, [8]li quali, essendo tali mari discostatisi colla lor superfitie dal centro del mōdo·, ànno acquistato peso, il quale, [9]poichè supera la potentia dell' avenimēto delle acque che lo cavsauano, essa acqua ripiglia im[10]peto in contrario al suo avenimēto, e fa impeto contro alli stretti, che li davano l'acque e massime fa [11]contra lo stretto di Gibiltar, il quale per alquātò spatio di tenpo rimā ringorgato e viene a riseruarsi tut[12]te l'acque che di novo in tal tenpo li sō date dalli già detti fiumi, e questa mi pare una delle ragioni che [13]si potrebbe assegnare della causa d'esso flusso e riflusso, come nella 21ª del 4ª della mia teori[14]ca è provato.

In the West, near to Flanders, the sea rises and decreases every 6 hours about 20 braccia, and 22 when the moon is in its favour; but 20 braccia is the general rule, and this rule, as it is evident, cannot have the moon for its cause. This variation in the increase and decrease of the sea every 6 hours may arise from the damming up of the waters, which are poured into the Mediterranean by the quantity of rivers from Africa, Asia, and Europe which flow into that sea, and the waters which are given to it by those rivers; it pours them to the ocean through the straits of Gibraltar, between Abila and Calpe [5]. That ocean extends to the island of England and others farther north, and it becomes dammed up and kept high in various gulfs. These, being seas of which the surface is remote from the centre of the earth, have acquired a weight which, as it is greater than the force of the incoming waters which cause it, gives this water an impetus in the contrary direction to that in which it came, and it is borne back to meet the waters coming out of the straits; and this it does most against the straits of Gibraltar; these, so long as this goes on, remain dammed up, and all the water which is poured out meanwhile by the aforementioned rivers is pent up [in the Mediterranean]; and this might be assigned as the cause of its flow and ebb, as is shown in the 21st of the 4th of my theory.

960. 1. parte hoccidentale .. cressce "e mācha .. circha 20 bra. 2. 20 br quale "ordinario". 3. chavsa .. cressciere e discresscere .. ore po. 4. achadere .. mediterano da "quella". 5. africha .. versano "le loro acque" le .. abile e calpe. 6. asstendendosi. 7. infralle isola digilterra ellaltre .. settātrionali .. ettenere. 8. cholla .. del mō . ano. 9. chello .. ripiglia ē. 10. pito .. inpit. .. chelli. 12. ta lacq"a" .. ga detti .. ecquesti. 13. chausa .. frusso e refrusso comi. 14. cha e.

960. 5. *Abila*, Lat. *Abyla*, Gr. Ἀβύλη, now *Sierra Ximiera* near Ceuta; *Calpe*, Lat. *Calpe*, Gr. Κάλπη, now Gibraltar. Leonardo here uses the ancient names of the rocks, which were known as the Pillars of Hercules.

III
SUBTERRANEAN WATERCOURSES

C. A. 160*b*]   961

Theory of
the circula-
tion of the
waters
(961-2).

Grādissimi fiumi corrono ²sotto terra.

Very large rivers flow underground.

Leic. 31*a*]   962

Qui s'à a īmagina²re la terra ³segata pel mez⁴zo, e vedrannosi ⁵le profondità ⁶del mare e della ⁷terra; ⁸le uene si partono ⁹da' fondi de' ma¹⁰ri e tessono la ¹¹terra, e si leua¹²no alla sommità ¹³de' mõti, e riuer¹⁴sano per li fiumi e ¹⁵ritornano al ma¹⁶re.

This is meant to represent the earth cut through in the middle, showing the depths of the sea and of the earth; the waters start from the bottom of the seas, and ramifying through the earth they rise to the summits of the mountains, flowing back by the rivers and returning to the sea.

Leic. 21*b*]   963

Observa-
tions in
support of
the hypo-
thesis
(963-9).

Raggirāsi l'acque con cõtinvo moto dall' infime profondità de' mari alle altissime somità de' mõti, non osseruando ²la natura delle cose graui, e in questo caso fanno come il sangue delli animali, che sempre si ³moue dal mare del core e scorre alla sõmità delle loro teste, e chi quiui rõpesi le uene, come si uede ⁴una vena rotta nel naso, che tutto il sangue da basso si leua alla altezza della rotta vena; ⁵Quando l'acqua escie della rotta vena della terra, essa osserua la natura dell' altre cose piv gravi ⁶che l'aria, onde senpre cerca i lochi bassi. . . . ⁷Vaño ⁸le uene scorrēdo con īfinita ramificatione pel corpo della terra.

The waters circulate with constant motion from the utmost depths of the sea to the highest summits of the mountains, not obeying the nature of heavy matter; and in this case they act as does the blood of animals which is always moving from the sea of the heart and flows to the top of their heads; and he who here bursts veins— as one may see when a vein bursts in the nose, that all the blood from below rises to the level of the burst vein. When the water rushes out of a burst vein in the earth it obeys the nature of other things heavier than the air, whence it always seeks the lowest places. . . . [7] These waters traverse the body of the earth with infinite ramifications.

Br. M. 233*b*]   964

Quella cavsa, che move li umori in tutte le spetie de' corpi · animati e che cõ quelle soccorre a ogni lesione, ²move l'acqua dall' infima profõdità del mare alla soma altezza de' mõti, ³e come l'acqua si leua dalle ⁴inferiori parti della vite all' alte tagliature. . . .

The same cause which stirs the humours in every species of animate body and by which every injury is repaired also moves the waters from the utmost depth of the sea to the greatest heights and just as the water (sap) rises from the inferior parts of the vine to the cuts higher up. . . .

Br. M. 236*b*]   965

L'acqua è proprio quella che per vitale umore ²di questa · arida terra · è dedicata ·, e ³quella cavsa che la move · per le sue rami-

It is the property of water that it constitutes the vital humour of this arid earth; and the cause which moves it through its ramified veins,

961. 1. corã.
962. 4. uedrassi. 7. [e come]. 8. partã. 10. ettessano. 11. essi.
963. 1. Rogirāsi. 2. fa .. animati. 3. move [dal lago] "dal mare" del .. tesste. 4. chettutto .. alteza .. ve "ne". 5. esscie .. grave. 6. chellaria .. cercha.
964. 1. socore. 2. frofõdita .. alteza. 3. come [il sangue] lacq"a". 4. tagliature de. *here the text breaks off.*
965. 1. lacq"a" .. omore. 2. quessta .. dedichata.

963. The greater part of this passage has been given as No. 849 in the section on Anatomy.

[4]ficate vene · cōtro al natural corso del[5]le cose gravi ·, è proprio quella che mo[6]ve · li umori · in tutte le spetie de' corpi [7]animati; E quella, che con sōma āmi[8]ratiō de' sua contemplanti, è che dall' infima pro[9]fondità del mare · all' altissime somità [10]de' mōti si leua, e per le rotte · vene ver[11]sando · al basso mare · ritorna, · e di novo [12]con celerità · sormōta, e all' ātidetto de[13]sceso · ritorna ·, così dalle parti intrī[14]siche · all' esteriori ·, così dalle infime alle [15]superiori voltādo · quādo con naturale cor[16]so ruina ·, così insieme cōgiunta, cō [17]cōtinua revolutione, [18]per li terrestri meati si ua raggirādo.

against the natural course of heavy matters, is the same property which moves the humours in every species of animate body. And that which crowns our wonder in contemplating it is that it rises from the utmost depths of the sea to the highest tops of the mountains, and flowing from the opened veins returns to the low seas; then once more, and with extreme swiftness, it mounts again and returns by the same descent, thus rising from the inside to the outside, and going round from the lowest to the highest, from whence it rushes down in a natural course. Thus by these two movements combined in a constant circulation it travels through the veins of the earth.

C. A. 171a]   965 A

Quella causa che move li omori in tucte le spezie de' corpi animati contra 'l natural corso della lor gravezza, è proprio quella, che per le terrestre vene move l'acqua dentro a esse inclusa, e pe' sottili meati la distingue, e come il basso sangue in alto surge, e per le rocte vene della fronte versa, e come dalla inferiore parte della vite l'acqua surmonta a sua tagliati rami, così dall' infima profondità del mare l'acqua s'inalza alle sommità de' monti, dove trovando le sue vene rocte per quelle cade, e al basso mare ritorna. Così dentro e di fori si va variando, quando con accidental moto consurge, e quando con natural libera discende. Così insieme congiunta con continua revoluzione si va girando, così di qua, di là, di su, di giù, scorrendo nulla quiete la riposa mai, non che nel corso, ma nella sua natura,[1] nessuna cosa à da sè, ma tutto piglia e 'n tante varie nature si transmuta, quanto son vari i lochi donde passa; facendo proprio come fa lo specchio che tante similitudine in sé piglia, quanto son le cose che dinanzi li passano; così questa sempre si varia, quando di sito, e quando di colore, quando novi odori o sapori dentro a sè include, quando nuove sustanzie o qualità ritiene, quando mortale o salutifera si pruova, alcuna volta coll' aria si mista o da caldo in alto si lascia tirare, e quando giugne alla fredda regione dove il caldo sua guida con quella si restrigne. E come la man sott' acqua prieme la spugna, onde l'acqua che

The same cause which moves the humours in every species of animate bodies against the natural law of gravity also propels the water through the veins of the earth wherein it is enclosed and distributes it through small passages. And as the blood rises from below and pours out through the broken veins of the forehead, as the water rises from the lowest part of the vine to the branches that are cut, so from the lowest depth of the sea the water rises to the summits of mountains, where, finding the veins broken, it pours out and returns to the bottom of the sea. Thus the movement of the water inside and outside varies in turn, now it is compelled to rise, then it descends in natural freedom. Thus joined together it goes round and round in continuous rotation, hither and thither from above and from below, it never rests in quiet, not from its course, but from its nature. It has nothing of its own but takes everything, changing into as many different natures as there are different places on its course, acting just like the mirror, which takes in as many images as there are things passing in front of it. So it changes continually, now as regards place, now as regards colour, now it absorbs new smells or tastes, now it detains new substances or qualities, now it brings death, now health, sometimes it mixes with air or lets itself be drawn on high by heat, and on reaching the cold region, the heat that guided it upward is squeezed by the cold. And as the hand presses the sponge under water whence the water flowing out makes an in-

---

4. chōtro . de. 5. chose. 6. omori . . lesspetie. 7. che chōsōma ami. 8. contenplanti | "e che" dall. 10. rocte. 12. cono celerita . . dis. 13. scienso. 15. cho. 17. revoluitione siua [ragirādo]. 18. teresti . . ragirādo.

965A. [1] These lines recall Dante's description of the wind in the *Inferno*:

   Di qua, di là, di su, di giù li mena,

nulla speranza li conforta mai,
non che di posa ma di minor pena. (v. 43 ff.)

di quella fugge, fra l'altra acqua fa ondazione, tal fa l'aria che tra l'acqua era mista, quando quella dal freddo è premuta, con furia fugge, e l'altra aria scaccia, così questa del vento è causa.

undation into the other water, so the cold presses the air that is mixed with water, making it flee in great haste and drive away the other air, which thus causes the wind.

G. 70a]   966

SE L'ACQUA PUÒ MŌTARE DAL MARE ²ALLE CIME DELLI MONTI

³Il mare oceano nō può penetrare ⁴dalle radici alle cime de' mōti che con lui ⁵confinano, ma solo si leua quādo la secchità ⁶del mōte ne tira; E se per l'aversario la ⁷pioggia, che penetra dalla cima del monte ⁸alle radici sua, che col mare confinano, discē⁹de e mollifica la spiaggia opposta del me¹⁰desimo monte e tira al continuo, si come ¹¹fa la cicogniola che versa per il suo lato più lū¹²go, fusse quella che tira in alto l'acqua del ¹³mare; come se *s n* fusse la pelle del ma¹⁴re, e la pioggia discende dalla cima del mō¹⁵te *a* allo *n* da vn lato e dall' altro lato di¹⁶scēde da *a* allo *m*, sanza dubbio que¹⁷sto sarebbe il modo dello stillare a feltro o ¹⁸come si fa per la canna detta cico¹⁹gniola, e senpre l'acqua che à mollificato ²⁰il monte per la gran pioggia, che discende dal²¹li due oppositi lati, tirerebbe a sé al lato ²²più lūgo la pioggia *a n* insieme coll' acqua ²³del mare perpetuamēte, se il lato del mōte ²⁴*a m* fusse più lūgo che l'altro *a n*, il che essere ²⁵nō può, perchè nessuna parte di terra che nō ²⁶sia sōmersa dall' oceano sarà più bassa ²⁷d'esso oceano ecc.

WHETHER WATER RISES FROM THE SEA TO THE TOPS OF MOUNTAINS

The water of the ocean cannot make its way from the bases to the tops of the mountains which bound it, but only so much rises as the dryness of the mountain attracts. And if, on the contrary, the rain, which penetrates from the summit of the mountain to the base, which is the boundary of the sea, descends and softens the slope opposite to the said mountain and constantly draws the water, like a syphon [11] which pours through its longest side, it must be this which draws up the water of the sea; thus if *s n* were the surface of the sea, and the rain descends from the top of the mountain *a* to *n* on one side, and on the other side it descends from *a* to *m*, without a doubt this would occur after the manner of distilling through felt, or as happens through the tubes called syphons [17]. And at all times the water which has softened the mountain, by the great rain which runs down the two opposite sides, would constantly attract the rain *a n* on its longest side together with the water from the sea, if that side of the mountain *a m* were longer than the other *a n*; but this cannot be, because no part of the earth which is not submerged by the ocean can be lower than that ocean.

A. 55b]   967

DELLE VENE DE L'ACQUA SOPRA · LE CIME DELLE MŌTAGNIE

²Chiaro · apparisce · che tutta la · superfitie dell' ocieano ·, quādo non à fortuna ·, è di pari distātia ³al ciētro · della · terra ·, e che le cime delle mōtagnie sono tanto piv lontane · da esso ⁴ciētro · quāto · elle s'alzano · sopra alla superfitie d'esso · mare ·; Adūque se 'l corpo della ⁵terra non avesse similitudine · coll' omo, sarebbe · inpossibile, · che l'acqua · del mare, essendo tāto ⁶piv · bassa · che le mōtagnie ·,

OF SPRINGS OF WATER ON THE TOPS OF MOUNTAINS

It is quite evident that the whole surface of the ocean—when there is no storm—is at an equal distance from the centre of the earth, and that the tops of the mountains are farther from this centre in proportion as they rise above the surface of that sea; therefore if the body of the earth were not like that of man, it would be impossible that the waters of the sea—being so much lower than the mountains—could by their

966. 1. sellacq"a".. mōtare. 3. occieano. 4. radicie.. collui. 5. sul si leua quato la seccita. 6. Esse. 7. cheppienetra. 8. chol.. chonfina dissciē. 9. mollifiche. 10. ettira. 12. gho fussi.. chettira. 13. chome.. fusse. 14. ella.. disciende alla. 15. da ullato. 16. disciēde.. dubbio che. 17. affeltro. 18. chome.. lla channa [decta]. 19. essenpre.. mollifichato. 20. cheddissciēde. 21. asse illato. 22. lūgho.. chollacq"a". 23. sellatto. 24. fussi.. lūgho chellaltro. 26. occieano. 27. occieano.

967. 1. acq"a". 2. aparisscie.. chella "tutta". 3. tera e chelle.. mōtagni "e".. esso [mare]. 4. sopa.. chorpo. 5. tera.. avessi.. choll.. chellacqua.

966. 11, 17. *Cicognola*, Syphon. See vol. i, Pl. XXIV, No. 1. It has been pointed out that the works on hydrostatics by Heron of Alexandria must have been an inspiration to Leonardo, who cites his name in the C.A. (see No. 1496B). On folios 40b and 48a of MS. G are drawings and notes on syphons which recall Heron, *Pneumaticorum Libri*, I, 13 and 4, 5

(ed. Teubner). W. Schmidt, L.d.V. und Heron von Alexandria, *Bibliotheca Mathematica*, Leipzig, 1902.

967, 968. This conception of the rising of the blood, which has given rise to the comparison, was recognized as erroneous by Leonardo himself at a later period. It must be remembered that the MS.

ch'ella potesse · di sua natura · salire · alle · sommità · d'esse mōtagnie; ⁷Onde · è da credere · che quella · cagione ·, che tiene il sangue · nella · sōmità della · testa · dell' omo, ⁸quella · medesima · tenga l'acqua · nella · sommità · de' monti.

nature rise up to the summits of these mountains. Hence it is to be believed that the same cause which keeps the blood at the top of the head in man keeps the water at the summits of the mountains.

A. 56a]   968

DELLA CŌFERMATIONE PERCHÈ L'ACQUA È NELLE · SŌMITÀ DE' MŌTI

IN CONFIRMATION OF WHY THE WATER GOES TO THE TOPS OF MOUNTAINS

²Dico · che siccome · il naturale · calore · tiene il sāgue nelle uene · alla sommità dell' omo, ³e quādo lo · omo · è morto, esso sangue · freddo · si riduce ⁴ne' lochi · bassi ·, e, quādo · il sole · riscalda · la testa all' omo, ⁵moltiplica · e sopraviene tāto sangue con omori ·, che forzādo · le uene ⁶gienera · spesso · dolori · di testa ·, similemēte le uene ·, che vanno ramificādo ⁷per il · corpo · della · terra · e per lo · naturale · calore, · ch'è sparso per tutto · il cōti⁸nēte · corpo ·, l'acqua · sta · per le uene · eleuate · all' alte cime de' mōti; E que⁹lla · acqua ·, che passasi · per uno · condotto mvrato · nel corpo d'essa · mōtagnia, ¹⁰come · cosa · morta · non uscirà · dalla · sua · prima · bassezza ·, perchè non è ¹¹riscaldata · dal uitale · calore della · prima · vena ·; ancora · il calore ¹²dell' elemēto del fuoco · e, il giorno · il caldo del sole ·, ànno potētia di sueglere ¹³l'umidità · de' bassi lochi · de' mōti e tirare in alto · nel medesimo · modo ch'ella ¹⁴tira · i nvvoli · e sueglie · la loro · vmidità · del letto del mare.

I say that just as the natural heat of the blood in the veins keeps it in the head of man—for when the man is dead the cold blood sinks to the lower parts—and when the sun is hot on the head of a man the blood increases and rises so much, with other humours, that by pressure in the veins pains in the head are often caused; in the same way veins ramify through the body of the earth, and by the natural heat which is distributed throughout the containing body, the water is raised through the veins to the tops of mountains. And this water, which passes through a closed conduit inside the body of the mountain like a dead thing, cannot come forth from its low place unless it is warmed by the vital heat of the first vein. Again, the heat of the element of fire and, by day, the heat of the sun, have power to draw forth the moisture of the low parts of the mountains and to draw them up, in the same way as it draws the clouds and collects their moisture from the bed of the sea.

Leic. 11b]   969

Come molte vene d'acqua salata si trovano fortemēte distanti dal ²mare, e questo potrebbe accadere, perchè tal uena passasi per qualche miniera di sale come quella d'Ungheria, che si caua ³il sale per le grandissime cave, come qua si cavano le pietre.

That many springs of salt water are found at great distances from the sea; this might happen because such springs pass through some mine of salt, like that in Hungary, where salt is hewn out of vast caverns, just as stone is hewn here.

7. checquella chagione . chettiene . . somita. 8. lacq"a".
968. 1. chōfermatione . . lacq"a". 2. dicho chessichome . . chalore tie "il sāgue" leuene . ala somita. 3. [cho] e quādo [esso] "lo" omo . . fredo. 4. bassi [chosi] echauado il . . risschalda [il n] la. 5. molti pricha essopraviene . . chon . . chefforzādo. 6. vano ramifichādo. 7. lochorpo . . tera . . chalori chessparso . . chōti. 8. chorpo . elleuate . . Ecque. 9. per î chondotto . . chorpo. 10. chome chosa . . vsscira della . . basseza . . nōne. 11. rischaldata . . chalore . . anchora il chalore. 12. focho . . chaldo . sole a . . dissueglere. 13. lochi "de mōti" ettirare. 14. nvuoli essueglie . . delletto.
969. 1. trova . . distante da. 2. ecquesto . . achadere . . passasi . . chessi. 3. quasi caua.

A, from which these passages are taken, was written about twenty years earlier than the MS. Leic. (Nos. 963 and 849).

There is, in the original, a sketch with No. 968 which is not reproduced. It represents a hill of the same shape as that shown at No. 982. There are veins, or branched streams, on the side of the hill, like those

on the skull, Pl. CVIII, No. 4.

969. The great mine of Wieliczka in Galicia, out of which 60,000 tons of rock-salt are annually dug extends for 2½ miles from west to east, and 1,050 yards south. The depth reaches 983 feet.—The mine is composed of chambers and passages which Leonardo calls caverns.

IV

OF RIVERS

DELLE DIRIUATIONI DE' FIUMI

On the way in which the sources of rivers are fed.

[2]Il corpo della terra, a similitudine de' corpi de li animali, è tessuto di ramificationi di uene, le quali son tutte insieme cōgiunte, [3]e son constituite a nvtrimento e viuificatione d'essa terra e de' sua creati ·; partono dalle profondità del mare, e a quelle dopo molta revolutio[4]ne ànno a tornare per li fiumi creati dalle alte rotture d'esse uene; e se tu volessi dire, le pio[5]ve il uerno o la resolutione della neue l'estate essere causa del nascimento de' fiumi, e' si ti potrebbe allegare [6]li fiumi, che ànno origine ne' paesi focosi dell' Africa, nella quale non piove e meno nevica, perchè il superchio [7]caldo senpre risolue in aria tutti li nuvoli, che da uēti in là son sospinti; e se tu dicessi che tali fiumi, che uē[8]gono grossi il Luglio e 'l Agosto, son delle nevi che si risoluono il Maggio e 'l Giugnio per l'appressamēto del sole alle ne[9]ui delle montagnie di Scitia, e che tali resolutioni si riducono in certe valli e fanno laghi, doue poi entrano per le [10]vene e caue sotterane, le quali riescono poi all' origine del Nilo, questo è falso, inperochè è piv bassa la [11]Scitia che l'origine del Nilo, conciosiachè la Scitia è presso al mare di Pōto a 400 miglia, e l'origine del Nilo è [12]remoto 3000 miglia dal mare d'Egitto, ove versa le sue acque.

OF THE ORIGIN OF RIVERS

The body of the earth, like the bodies of animals, is intersected with ramifications of veins which are all in connexion and are constituted to give nutriment and life to the earth and to its creatures. These come from the depth of the sea and, after many revolutions, have to return by the rivers created by the bursting of these veins high up; and if you choose to say that the rains of winter or the melting of the snows in summer were the cause of the birth of rivers, I could mention the rivers which originate in the torrid countries of Africa, where it never rains—and still less snows—because the intense heat always melts into air all the clouds which are borne thither by the winds. And if you choose to say that such rivers as increase in July and August come from the snows which melt in May and June from the sun's approach to the snows on the mountains of Scythia [9], and that such meltings come down into certain valleys and form lakes by which they enter into veins and subterranean caves to issue forth again at the sources of the Nile, this is false; because Scythia is lower than the sources of the Nile, and, besides, Scythia is only 400 miles from the Black Sea, and the sources of the Nile are 3,000 miles distant from the sea of Egypt into which its waters flow.

The tide in estuaries.

Libro 9° delli scontri de' fiumi e lor flusso e riflusso, e la medesima [2]causa lo crea nel mare per causa dello stretto di Gibilterra, e ancora accade per le uoragini;

[3]Se due fiumi insieme si scontrano per vna medesima linia, la qual sia retta, e poi infra 2 angoli retti [4]pigliano insieme lor corso, e' seguirà il flusso e riflusso · ora a l'uno fiume, ora all' altro, avanti [5]che sieno · vniti e massime, se l'uscita nella loro vnitione nō sarà piv veloce, che quād' erā disuniti; [6]Qui accadono 4 casi.

Book 9, of the meeting of rivers and of their ebb and flow. The cause is the same in the sea, where it is caused by the straits of Gibraltar; and again it is caused by whirlpools.

[3] If two rivers meet together to form a straight line, and then two right angles take their course together, the flow and ebb will happen now in one river and now in the other above their confluence, and principally if the outlet for their united volume is no swifter than when they were separate. Here occur 4 instances.

---

970. 2. assimi . . ettessudi di ramifichatione . . cōgunte. 3. consstituite "a nvtrimento" e viuifichatione . . terra | "e de sua creati" essi partano delle . . acquele. 4. ano attornare . . essettu. 5. olla . . lastate . . chausa . . nasscimento . . portrebbe. 6. fochosi africha . . nevicha. 7. chaldo . . nvoli . . illa . . sosspinte essettu . . chettali. 8. gano . . ellagosto . . chessi . . mago . . gugnio . . lapressamēto. 9. disscitia . . riduchano . . effano lagh. 10. riescano . . effalso inperochelle . . las. 11. chellorigine . . concosia chella.

971. 1. isscontri . . ellor frusso e refrusso alta. 2. chausa . . strett[i] di gibiltar . . achade . . uoragine. 3. retta e poi. 4. piglino . . refrusso. 5. chessieno . . lusscita nedella. 6. achade 4 chasi.

970. 9. Scythia means here, as in ancient geography, the whole of the northern part of Asia as far as India.

971. The first two lines of this passage have already been given as No. 957. In the margin, near line 3 of this passage, the text given as No. 919 is written.

Leic. 15a]   972

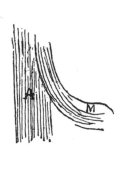

Quando il fiume minore versa le sue acque nel maggiore, il quale maggiore corra dall' opposita ²riua, allora il corso del fiume minore piegherà il suo corso inverso l'auenimēto del fiume ³maggiore; e questo accade perchè, quando esso maggiore fiume enpie d'acqua tutto il suo letto, e' ⁴gli viene a fare ritroso sotto la bocca di tal fiume, e così spingnie cō seco l'acqua versata dal fi⁵vme minore; Quando il fiume minore versa le sue acque nel fiume maggiore, il quale ⁶abbia la corrente alla foce del minore, allora le sue acque si piegheranno inverso la fu⁷ga del fiume maggiore.

When a smaller river pours its waters into a larger one, and that larger one flows from the opposite direction, the course of the smaller river will bend up against the approach of the larger river; and this happens because, when the larger river fills up all its bed with water, it makes an eddy in front of the mouth of the other river, and so carries the water poured in by the smaller river with its own. When the smaller river pours its waters into the larger one, which runs across the current at the mouth of the smaller river, its waters will bend with the downward movement of the larger river.

On the alterations caused in the courses of rivers by their confluence (972–4).

Leic. 16b]   973

Quando le piene de' fiumi sō ²diminuite ·, allor li angoli acuti, che si generā nelle congiuntioni de' sua rami, si fanno piv cor³ti nelli lor lati e più grossi nelle lor punte, come sia la corrente *a n*, e la corrente *d n*, ⁴le quali si congiunghino insieme in · *n*, quando il fiume è nelle sue gran piene; dico che, quando sia ⁵nella predetta dispositione ·, che se *d n* avanti la piena era piv basso che *a n*, che nel tempo della piena, ⁶*d n* sarà piē di rena e fango, il quale nel calare delle acque *d n* porterà uia il fango e rimar⁷rà col fondo basso, e 'l canale *a n*, trovandosi alto, scolerà le sue acque nel basso *d n* e consumerà tutta ⁸la punta del renaio *b c n*, e così rimarrà l'angolo *a c d* piv grosso che l'angolo *a n d*, e di lati più corti, come ⁹prima dissi.

When the fullness of rivers is diminished, then the acute angles formed at the junction of their branches become shorter at the sides and wider at the point; like the current *a n* and the current *d n*, which unite in *n* when the river is at its greatest fullness. I say that when it is in this condition if, before the fullest time, *d n* was lower than *a n*, at the time of fullness *d n* will be full of sand and mud. When the water *d n* falls, it will carry away the mud and remain with a lower bottom, and the channel *a n*, finding itself the higher, will fling its waters into the lower, *d n*, and will wash away all the point of the sand-spit *b n c*, and thus the angle *a c d* will remain larger than the angle *a n d* and the sides shorter, as I said before.

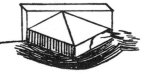

972. 1. magore il cqual "magore" corra "dall oposita riua" [remoto dalla sua]. 2. piegera. 3. magore ecquesto acchade .. magor .. letto el. 4. affare retroso .. bocha. 5. magore. 6. minor [fiume] allora .. piegeranno. 7. magore.

973. 2. congiuntione. 3. corente .. ella corente. 4. congunghino .. dicho. 5. predecta disspositione chesse. 6. effango .. rima. 8. cori rimara lanolo .. groso.

972. In the original sketches the word *Arno* is written at the spot here marked *A*, at *R Rifredi*, and at *M Mugnone*.

973. Above the first sketch we find, in the original,

this note: *Sopra il pōte rubaconte alla torricella*; and by the second, which represents a pier of a bridge, *Sotto l'ospedal del ceppo*.

G. 48a]   **974**

AQUA

DEL MOTO D'Ū SUBITO ENPITO FATTO ³DA UN FIUME SOPRA IL SUO LETTO ASCIUTTO

⁴Tanto è più tardo o velocie il corso dell' acqua, ⁵data dallo isboccato lago al secco fivme, quā⁶to esso fiume fia più largo o piv stretto, over ⁷più piano o cupo in un loco che in un' altro, ⁸per quel che è proposto; il flusso e ri⁹flusso del mare che dallo oceano entra nel Me¹⁰diterraneo Mare e de' fiumi, che giostrano ¹¹con lui, alzano tanto più o meno le loro acque, ¹²quanto tal mare è piv o meno stretto.

WATER

OF THE MOVEMENT OF A SUDDEN RUSH MADE BY A RIVER IN ITS BED PREVIOUSLY DRY

In proportion as the current of the water given forth by the draining of the lake is slow or rapid in the dry river-bed, so will this river be wider or narrower, or shallower or deeper in one place than another, according to this proposition: the flow and ebb of the sea which enters the Mediterranean from the ocean, and of the rivers which meet and struggle with it, will raise their waters more or less in proportion as the sea is wider or narrower.

C. A. 370b]   **975**

Whirlpools. Voragine, cioè caverne, ²cioè residui d'acque p:e³cipitose.

Whirlpools, that is to say, caverns; that is to say, places left by precipitated waters.

G. 49b]   **976**

DELLA VIBRATIONE DELLA TERRA

On the alterations in the channels of rivers. ²Li corsi sotterranei ³delle acque, sicome quelli che son fatti infra ⁴l'aria e la terra, son quelli che al continuo ⁵cōsumano e profondano li letti del⁶li lor corsi.

OF THE VIBRATION OF THE EARTH

The subterranean channels of waters, like those which exist between the air and the earth, are those which unceasingly wear away and deepen the beds of their currents.

Leic. 6b]   **977**

The origin of the sand in rivers (977–8). Il fiume che esce de' mōti pone gran quātità di sassi grossi in nel suo ghiareto, i quali sassi sono ancora ²con parte de' sua angoli e lati, e nel processo del corso conduce pietre minori con angoli piv cōsumati, cioè le grā ³pietre fa minori, e piv oltre pō ghiaia · grossa, e poi minvta ·, e seguita rena grossa, e poi minvta ·; dipoi procede ⁴litta grossa, e poi piv sottile, e così seguēdo giugne al mare l'acqua turba di rena e di litta; la rena scarica sopra de' ⁵liti marini per il rigurgitamēto dell' ōde salse, e segue la litta di tanta sottilità che par di natura d'acqua, la qual non si fer⁶ma sopra de' marī liti, ma ritorna indirieto coll' o(nda) per la sua leuità, perch' è nata di foglie marcie e d'altre cose leuissime, si ⁷che, essendo quasi, com' è detto, di natura d'acqua, essa poi in tenpo di bonaccia si scarica e si ferma sopra del ⁸fondo del mare, ove per la sua sottilità si condensa e resiste all' onde che sopra vi passano per la sua lubricità, e ⁹qui stanno i nichi e quest' è terra bianca da far boccali.

A river that flows from mountains deposits a great quantity of large stones in its bed, which still have some of their angles and sides, and in the course of its flow it carries down smaller stones with the angles more worn; that is to say, the large stones become smaller. And farther on it deposits coarse gravel and then smaller, and as it proceeds this becomes coarse sand and then finer, and going on thus the water, turbid with sand and gravel, joins the sea; and the sand settles on the sea-shores, being cast up by the salt waves; and there results the sand of so fine a nature as to seem almost like water, and it will not stop on the sea-shores but returns with the wave by reason of its lightness, because it was formed of rotten leaves and other very light things. Still, being almost—as was said—of the nature of water itself, it afterwards, when the weather is calm, settles and becomes solid at the bottom of the sea, where by its fineness it becomes compact and by its smoothness resists the waves which glide over it; and in this shells are found; and this is white earth, fit for pottery.

974. 3. da u .. assciucto. 4. eppiu .. chorso .. acq"a". 5. isbochato lagho .. secho. 6. largho .. strecto. 7. ochupo nū locho che inu. 8. propossto .. e re. 9. frusso .. dello occieno. 10. mediterano .. giosstrano. 11. chō. 12. eppiu .. strecto.
975. 2. coe residii. 3. cipitosa.
976. 1. viberatio. 2. supterrani [e super accquelli]. 3. so fatti infral. 4. ella. 6. chorsi.
977. 1. essce .. inel. 2. ellati .. agoli .. coe. 3. grosa e po .. grosa .. prociede. 4. lita .. gugne .. lita .. scaricha. 5. per e . ricitramēto .. lita .. dachq"a". 6. indirieta collo per .. marce. 7. bonacca .. scaricha essi. 9. ecquest .. biancha daffar bochali.

974. In the margin is a sketch of a river which winds so as to form islands.

Tutte l'uscite dell' acque dal monte nel mare portā cō seco li sassi del monte in es²so mare, e per la inōdatione dell' acque marine contro alli sua monti, esse pietre erā ributta³te inverso il mōte, e nell' ādare e nel ritornare indietro delle acque al mare, le pietre insieme cō quel⁴la tornavano, e nel ritornare li angoli loro insieme si percuoteano, e come parte men ⁵resistente alle percosse si cōsumavano e facean le pietre sanza angoli, in figu⁶ra rotonda ·, come ne' liti dell' Elba si dimostra, e quelle rimanevā piv grosse, che manco sarā remosse ⁷dal lor nascimēto; e così quella si facea minore, che piv si rimouea dal predet⁸to loco, in modo che nel procedere ella si cōuerte in ghiaja minvta, e poi in rena ⁹e in vltimo in fango ·; dipoi che 'l mare si discosta dalli predetti monti ·, la salsedine lascia¹⁰ta dal mare con altro umore della terra à fatta vna collegatione a essa ghiaja e rena, che la ¹¹ghiaja in sasso e la rena in tufo s'è convertita; E di questo si uede l'esenplo ¹²in Adda all' uscire de' monti di Como e in Tesino, Adige, Oglio e Adriano dall' alpi de' Tedeschi, e il si¹³mile d'Arno dal monte Albano intorno a Mōte Lupo e Capraia, doue li sassi grandissimi oon tutti ¹⁴di ghiaia cōgelata di diuersc pietre e colori.

All the torrents of water flowing from the mountains to the sea carry with them the stones from the hills to the sea, and by the influx of the sea-water towards the mountains, these stones were thrown back towards the mountains, and as the waters rose and retired, the stones were tossed about by it and in rolling their angles hit together; then, as the parts which least resisted the blows were worn off, the stones ceased to be angular and became round in form, as may be seen on the shores of Elba. And those remained larger which were less removed from their native spot; and they became smaller, the farther they were carried from that place, so that in the process they were converted into small pebbles and then into sand and at last into mud. After the sea had receded from the mountains the brine left by the sea with other humours of the earth made a concretion of these pebbles and this sand, so that the pebbles were converted into rock and the sand into tufa. And of this we see an example in the Adda where it issues from the mountains of Como, and in the Ticino, the Adige, the Oglio and Adria from the German Alps, and in the Arno at Monte Albano [13], near Monte Lupo and Capraia, where the rocks, which are very large, are all of conglomerated pebbles of various kinds and colours.

978. 1. lusscite dellacq"e" .. secho .. in e. 2. rebutta. 3. mōde "e nellādare" e .. indirieto. 4. toravano .. perchoteano. 5. perchose .. effacean. 6. ritonda "come ne liti dellelba si dimosstra" ecquella rimanē .. mancho. 7. nasscimēto. 8. locho .. procedere in si .. giara. 9. fangho .. disscosste .. lasscia. 10. ta del .. altromore .. affatto .. giara errena chella. 11. giara .. ella .. chonvertita. 12. inada .. adice oglio eadriano dell alpi .. tedesci el si. 13. darno del. 14. cholori.

978. 13. At the foot of Monte Albano lies Vinci, the birth-place of Leonardo. Opposite, on the other bank of the Arno, is Monte Lupo.

V

ON MOUNTAINS

The forma-
tion of
mountains
(979–83).

979

¶Li mõti son fatti dalli cor²si de' fiumi;¶
³¶Li mõti son disfatti dalle pi⁴oggie e dalli
fiumi.¶

Mountains are made by the currents of rivers.
Mountains are destroyed by rains and rivers.

980

Come le ²radici settentrionali di qualunche
alpe · non sono ancora petrificate; e questo si
vede ma³nifestamente doue i fiumi, che le
tagliano, corrano inverso settentrione, li quali
tagliã ⁴nell' altezze de' mõti le falde delle pietre
viue, e nell' congiugniersi colle pianure le predette falde ⁵son tutte di terra da fare boccali ·,
come si dimostra in Val di Lamona al fiume
Lamona nel⁶l' uscire del Mõte Appenino fargli
le predette cose nelle sue rive;

Come li fiumi ànno tutti segati ⁷e diuisi li
menbri delle grand' alpi l'uno dall' altro, e
questo si manifesta per lo ordine delle ⁸pietre
faldate, chè dalla sommità del monte insino al
fiume si vedono le corrispõdenze delle falde
essere ⁹così da l'un de' lati del fiume come
dall' altro; Come le pietre faldate de' monti ·
son tutti i gradi ¹⁰de' fanghi posati l'un sopra
l'altro per le inõdationi de' fiumi; Come le
diuerse grossezze delle falde del¹¹le pietre son
create da diuerse inondationi de' fiumi, cioè
maggiore ondatione o minore.

That the northern bases of some Alps are not
yet petrified. And this is plainly to be seen
where the rivers which cut through them flow
towards the north; where they cut through the
strata in the living stone in the higher parts of
the mountains, and where they join the plains,
these strata are all of potter's clay; as is to be
seen in the valley of Lamona, where the river
Lamona, as it issues from the Appenines, does
these things on its banks.

That the rivers have all cut and divided the
mountains of the great Alps one from the other.
This is visible in the order of the stratified rocks,
because from the summits of the banks down
to the river the correspondence of the strata in
the rocks is visible on either side of the river.
That the stratified stones of the mountains are
all layers of clay, deposited one above the other
by the various floods of the rivers. That the
different size of the strata is caused by the difference in the floods—that is to say, greater or
lesser floods.

981

Le sommità de' monti per ²lungo tempo
senpre s'i³nalzano;

⁴I lati opposti de' mõ⁵ti senpre
s'auicinano; ⁶le profondità delle
ualli, ⁷le quali son sopra la ⁸spera
dell' acqua, per lungo ⁹tenpo senpre
¹⁰s'appropinquano al cẽ¹¹tro del
mondo;

¹²In equal tẽpo molto pi¹³v si
profondano le ual¹⁴li che non s'alzano i mõ¹⁵ti;

¹⁶Le base de' monti senpre ¹⁷si
fanno piv strette;

¹⁸Quanto ¹⁹la ualle piv si pro-
²⁰fonda, piv si consu²¹ma de sua lati in ²²più
brieue tenpo.

The summits of mountains in the course of
time rise constantly.

The opposite sides of the mountains always approach each other;
the depths of the valleys which
are above the sphere of the waters
are in the course of time constantly
getting nearer to the centre of the
earth.

In an equal period, the valleys
sink much more than the mountains rise.

The bases of the mountains always come closer together.

In proportion as the valleys become deeper,
the more quickly are the sides worn away.

979. 1. facti .. chor.
980. 2. radice .. petrifichàte ecquesto. 3. chelle .. chorrane .. settantrione. 4. alteze .. congungnersi cholle. 5. daffare bochali ..
lumona fare al. 6. lusscire .. farli .. fiumi an. 7. alpe .. ecquesto. 8. somita .. vede .. conrisspõdenze. 9. tutti e gradi. 10.
grosseze. 11. coe magore .. õminorj.
981. 1. somita. 7. la 5. 8. acq"a". 9. senpre [sabb]. 17. strecte. 20. consũ. 21. ma desua.

979. Compare No. 789.

Br. M. 30*b*]

982

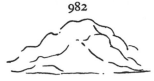

In ogni concauità delle cime de' monti senpre si trover²anno li piegamēti delle falde delle pietre.

In every concavity at the summit of the mountains we shall always find the divisions of the strata in the rocks.

C. A. 126*b*]

983

DEL MARE CHE CIGNE LA TERRA

²Jo truovo il sito della terra essere ab antico · nelle sue pianure tutto ³occupato e coperto dall' acque salse . . . .

OF THE SEA WHICH ENCIRCLES THE EARTH

I find that of old the state of the earth was that its plains were all covered up and hidden by salt water . . . .

Leic. 31*a*]

984

Perchè molto sō ²piv antiche le ³cose che le lette⁴re, non è maravi⁵glia, se alli nostri ⁶giorni non appari⁷sce scrittura de⁸lli predetti ma⁹ri essere occupa¹⁰tori di tanti pa¹¹esi; ¹²e se pure alcuna ¹³scrittura aparia, ¹⁴le guerre, l'incēdi, li diluvi dell' acque, ¹⁵le mutationi delle ¹⁶lingue e delle leggi ¹⁷ànno cōsumato ¹⁸ogni antichità, ma ¹⁹a noi bastano le testi²⁰monianze delle co-²¹se nate nelle acque ²²salse ritrouarsi ²³nelli alti mōti, ²⁴lontani dalli mari ²⁵d'allora.

Since things are much more ancient than letters, it is no marvel if, in our day, no records exist of these seas having covered so many countries; and if, moreover, some records had existed, war and conflagrations, the deluge of waters, the changes of languages and of laws have consumed everything ancient. But sufficient for us is the testimony of things created in the salt waters and found again in high mountains far from the seas of to-day.

The authorities for the study of the structure of the earth.

982. 2. ra li.
983. 1. ce cignie. 2. abbantiahe . . tuste. 9. ochupato e choperto
984. 3. chelle. 6. gorni non áparis. 7. sciptura del. 9. ocupa. 11. [esi essetto]. 12. cose. 14. "li diluui dellaeque". 15. le mutationi
16. legi. 19. basta. 20. monātie. 25. talor.

VI
GEOLOGICAL PROBLEMS

Leic. 3a]   985

In questa tua opera tu ài jn prima a provare, come li nichi in mille braccia d'altura nō ui furō [2]portati dal diluuio, perchè si uedono a ū medesimo liuello, e si vedono auāzare assai mōti sopra [3]esso liuello, e a dimādare se 'l diluvio fù per piogga o per ringorgamēto di mare; e poi ài [4]a mostrare, che nè per pioggia che ingrossi i fiumi, nè per rigonfiamēto d'esso mare, li nichi, come cosa [5]grave, non sono sospinti dal mare alli mōti, nè tirati a sé dalli fiumi cōtro al corso delle [6]loro acque.

In this work you have first to prove that the shells at a thousand braccia of elevation were not carried there by the deluge, because they are seen to be all at one level, and many mountains are seen to be above that level; and to inquire whether the deluge was caused by rain or by the swelling of the sea; and then you must show how, neither by rain which makes the rivers swell, nor by the overflow of this sea, could the shells —being heavy objects—be floated up the mountains by the sea, nor have been carried there by the rivers against the course of their waters.

C. A. 155a]   986

DUBITATIONE

Doubts about the deluge. [2]Mouesi qui vn dubbio e questo è, se 'l [3]diluvio, venuto al tenpo di Noè, fù vni[4]versale o no; E qui parrà di no, per le [5]ragioni che si assegnieranno; Noi abbiamo nella bibbia, [6]che il predetto diluvio fù conposto di 40 [7]dì e 40 notti di continua e vniversa piog[8]gia, e che tal pioggia alzò dieci [9]gomiti sopra al più alto mōte dell' univer[10]so; E se così fù, che la pioggia fusse vniver[11]sale, ella vestì di sé la nostra ter[12]ra di figura sperica; E la superfi[13]tie sperica in ogni sua parte equalmen[14]te distante dal ciètro della sva spe[15]ra, onde la spera de l'acqua, trovandosi [16]nel modo della detta conditione, elli è [17]inpossibile, che l'acqua sopra di lei si mova, [18]perchè l'acqua in sé non si move, s'ella non [19]disciède; addunque l'acqua di tanto dilu[20]vio come si partì, se qui è provato, non a[21]ver moto? e s'ella si partì, come si mosse, [22]se ella non ādava allo insù? e qui ne mācano[23] le ragiō naturali, ōde bisognia per soccor[24]so di tal dvbitatione chiamare il mira[25]colo per aiuto, o dire che [26]tale acqua fu vaporata dal calore del sole.

A DOUBTFUL POINT

Here a doubt arises, and that is: whether the deluge which happened at the time of Noah was universal or not. And it would seem not, for the reasons now to be given: We have it in the Bible that this deluge lasted 40 days and 40 nights of incessant and universal rain, and that this rain rose to ten cubits above the highest mountain in the world. And if it had been that the rain was universal, it would have covered our globe which is spherical in shape. And this spherical surface is equally distant, in every part, from the centre of its sphere; hence the sphere of the waters being under the same conditions, it is impossible that the water upon it should move, because water does not move of its own accord unless to descend; therefore how could the waters of such a deluge depart, if it is proved that it has no motion? and if it departed, how could it move unless it went upwards? Here, then, natural reasons are wanting; hence to remove this doubt it is necessary to call in a miracle to aid us, or else to say that all this water was evaporated by the heat of the sun.

Leic. 8b]   987

DEL DILUUIO E DE' NICHI MARINI

That marine shells could not go up the mountains. [2]Se tu dirai che li nichi, che per li confini d'Italia lontano dalli mari in tāta altezza si

OF THE DELUGE AND OF MARINE SHELLS

If you were to say that the shells which are to be seen within the confines of Italy now, in our

985. 1. quessta .. br daltura. 2. perchessi uedano .. e uedesi. 4. mosstrare .. piogga chengrossi .. chome. 5. sosspinti .. asse .. chorso. 6. accq"e".
986. 2. ecquesso. 4. onno. 5. chessi .. abbian "nella bibbia". 6. chonpossto. 7. nocte .. pio. 8. chettal piogg. 9. ghomiti. 10. chosi .. chella piggia fussi. 12. fighura spericha Ella. 13. spericha nogni. 14. disstante al. 16. chonditione. 17. chellacqua .. mov"a". 20. chome. 21. essella .. chome. 22. ecquimāca. 23. sochor. 25. cholo [per sochorso] per .. oddire. 26. chalor.
987. 1. 8 del. 2. settu .. chelli .. luntano dali .. alteza si uegghano.

985. Some preliminary notes on the subject are to be found in MS. F 80a and 80b; but as compared with the fuller treatment here given they are, it seems to me, of secondary interest. They contain nothing that is not repeated here more clearly and fully. Libri, *Histoire des sciences mathématiques*, iii, pp. 218–21,

has printed the text of F 80a and 80b.

987. Ovid has anticipated Leonardo's observations in *Met.* xv. 257 ff.:

Vidi ego, quod fuerat quondam solidissima tellus
Esse fretum; vidi factas ex aequore terras,
Et procul a pelago conchae iacuere marinae . . .

168

ueggono ³alli nostri tempi, siano stati per causa del diluuio che lì li lasciò, io ti rispōdo che, credendo tu che ⁴tal diluvio superasse il piv alto monte 7 cubiti, come scrisse chi li misurò, tali nichi che senpre ⁵stanno vicini ai liti del mare, e' doueano restare sopra tali mōtagnie, e nō si poco sopra le radi⁶ci de' monti per tutto a vna medesima altezza a suoli a suoli; E se tu dirai che, essendo tali ⁷nichi vaghi di stare vicini alli liti marini e che, crescēdo in tāta altezza, che li nichi si ⁸partirono da esso lor primo sito e seguitarono l'accresscimēto delle acque insino alla lor ⁹som̄a altezza, Qui si risponde che, sendo il nichio anima¹⁰le di non più veloce moto, che si sia la lumaca, fori dell' acqua, e qualche cosa più tarda perchè nō nota, ā¹¹zi si fa vn solco per l'arena mediante i lati di tal solco ove s'appoggia, caminerà il dì dalle 3 alle 4 · braccia; ¹²adunque questo cō tale moto nō sarà caminato dal mare Adriano insino in Mōferrato di Lon-¹³bardia, chè v'è 250 miglia di distantia, in 40 giorni, come disse chi tenne cōto d'esso tenpo; e se tu dici che ¹⁴l'onde ve li portarono, essi per la lor gravezza non si reggono, se nō sopra il suo fondo ·; e se questo nō mi¹⁵concedi, cōfessami al meno ch' elli aueano a rimanere nelle cime de' piv alti mōti e ne' laghi che in ¹⁶fra li mōti si serrano, come lago di Lario e 'l Maggiore, e di Como, e di Fiesole, e di Perugia e simili;

¹⁷E se tu dirai che li nichi son ¹⁸portati dall' onde, essēdo voti e morti, io dico che, dove andauano li morti, poco si rimoveuano da' uiui, e in que¹⁹ste montagnie sono trovati tutti i uiui che si cognoscono che sono colli gusci appaiati, e sono ²⁰in vn filo doue non è nessun de' morti, e poco piv alto è trovato doue eran gittati dall' ō²¹de tutti li morti colle loro scorze separate; Apresso a dove li fiumi casca-vano in ²²mare in grā profondità; come Arno, che cadea dalla Gonfolina apresso a ²³Mōte Lupo e quiui lasciaua la ghiaja, la quale ancor si uede, che si è insieme ricōgielata e di pie²⁴tre di uari paesi, nature e colori e durezze se n'è fatto vna sola congelatione, e poco più oltre la congelatione dell' are²⁵na s'è fatta tufo, dou' ella

days, far from the sea and at such heights, had been brought there by the deluge which left them there, I should answer that if you believe that this deluge rose 7 cubits above the highest mountains—as he who measured it has written—these shells, which always live near the sea-shore, should have been left on the mountains and not such a little way from the foot of the mountains; nor all at one level, nor in layers upon layers. And if you were to say that these shells are desirous of remaining near to the margin of the sea, and that, as it rose in height, the shells quitted their first home, and followed the increase of the waters up to their highest level; to this I answer that the cockle is an animal of not more rapid movement than the snail is out of water, or even somewhat slower, because it does not swim, on the contrary, it makes a furrow in the sand; by leaning against the sides of this furrow it will travel each day from 3 to 4 braccia; therefore this creature, with so slow a motion, could not have travelled from the Adriatic sea as far as Monferrato in Lombardy [13], a distance of 250 miles, in 40 days; which he has said who took account of the time. And if you say that the waves carried them there, by their gravity they could not move, excepting at the bottom. And if you will not grant me this, confess at least that they would have to stay at the summits of the highest mountains, and in the lakes enclosed among the mountains, like the lakes of Lario, and il Maggiore [16], and of Como, and of Fiesole, and of Perugia, and others.

And if you should say that the shells were carried by the waves, being empty and dead, I say that where the dead went they were not far removed from the living; for in these mountains living ones are found, which are recognizable by the shells being in pairs; and they are in a layer where there are no dead ones; and a little higher up they are found, where they were thrown by the waves, all the dead ones with their shells separated, near to where the rivers fell into the sea, to a great depth; like the Arno which fell from the Gonfolina near to Monte Lupo[23] where it left a deposit of gravel which may still be seen, and which has agglomerated; and of stones of various districts, natures, and colours, and hardness, making one single conglomerate.

3. nosstri tenpi sia stato . . chausa . . lasscio . . rispōde. 4. diluio superassi . . chessenpre. 5. aliti del mare doueano . . pocho . . li radi. 6. ce de . . assuoli assuoli Essettu. 7. cresscēdo . . alteza chelli. 8. partirano . . lor pᵘ'o' sito esseguitorno lacresscimēto. 9. alteza . . chessendo. 10. chessi . . lumacha . . ecqualche . . tarde. 11. solcho . . sapogia chaminera . . 4 br. 12. chaminato . . i mōferato. 13. gorni . . tene . . essettu di che. 14. portorono . . regano. 15. cedi. 16. fralli . . magore . . peruga. 17. Esse tu dirai dirai chelle. 18. dicho . . andaua . . pocho. 19. cognoscano . . cholli gussci . . essono. 20. in vnn . . pocho. 21. cholle . . chasscavano. 22. gra . . chadea della Golfolina. 23. giara . . chesse insieme . . ricōgielata. 24. nari "paesi" nature "ecolori e dureze" se ne fatto . . gongelatione . . pocho. 25. seffatto . . invero chastel . . scharichava il fangho.

987. 13. *Monferrato di Lombardia.* The range of hills of Monferrato is in Piedmont, and Casale di Monferrato belonged, in Leonardo's time, to the Marchese di Mantova.

16. *Lago di Lario.* Lacus Larius was the name given by the Romans to the Lake of Como. It is evident that it is here a slip of the pen, since the words

in the MS. are: 'Come Lago di Lario e 'l Magore e di Como.' In the MS. after line 16 we come upon a digression treating of the weight of water; this has here been omitted. It is 11 lines long.

23. *Monte Lupo* (compare No. 978. 13) lies between Empoli and Florence.

s'agiraua inverso Castel Fiorētino, più oltre si scaricava il fango, [26]nel quale abitavano i nichi, il quale s'inalzava a gradi, secondo che le piene d'Arno torbido [27]in quel mare versauano, e di tempo in tenpo s'inalzaua il fondo al mare, jl quale a gradi [28]producea essi nichi, come si mostra nel taglio di Colle Gonzoli, dirupato dal fiume d'Arno, [29]che il suo piede consuma, nel qual taglio si uedono manifestamēte li predetti gradi de' nichi in [30]fango azzureggiante, e ui si trova di uarie cose marine; E si è alzata la terra del nostro [31]emisperio per tanto più che nō solea, per quāto ella si fece più lieue delle acque, che le manca[32]rono per il taglio di Calpe e d'Abila, e altrettanto piv s'è alzata, perchè il peso dell' acque, che di qui mā[33]carono, s'aggiunsero · alla terra volta all' altro emisperio; E se li nichi fussero stati [34]portati dal torbido diluuio, essi si sarebbero misti, separatamente l'un da l'altro, infra 'l fango e non [35]con ordinati gradi a suoli, come alli nostri tenpi si vede.

And a little beyond the sandstone conglomerate a tufa has been formed, where it turned towards Castel Florentino; farther on the mud was deposited in which the shells lived, and which rose in layers according to the levels at which the turbid Arno flowed into that sea. And from time to time the bottom of the sea was raised, depositing these shells in layers, as may be seen in the cutting at Colle Gonzoli, laid open by the Arno which is wearing away the base of it; in which cutting the said layers of shells are very plainly to be seen in clay of a bluish colour, and various marine objects are found there. And if the earth of our hemisphere is indeed raised by so much higher than it used to be, it must have become by so much lighter by the waters which it lost through the rift between Gibraltar and Ceuta; and all the more the higher it rose, because the weight of the waters which were thus lost would be added to the earth in the other hemisphere. And if the shells had been carried by the muddy deluge they would have been mixed up and separated from each other amidst the mud, and not in regular steps and layers—as we see them now in our time.

Leic. 9a]   988

The marine shells were not produced away from the sea.

Di quelli che dicono che i nichi sono per molto spatio e nati remoti dalli mari · per la natura del sito e de' cieli, [2]che dispone e influiscie tal loco a simile creatione d'animali ·; a costor si risponderà che tale influētia [3]d'animali nō potrebbe accadere in vna sola linia, se nō animali di medesima sorte e età, e non il uechio col gio[4]vane, e nō alcun col coperchio e l'altro essere sanza sua copritura, e nō l'uno esser rotto e l'altro intero, [5]e nō l'uno ripieno di rena marina e rottame minvto e grosso d'altri nichi dentro alli nichi [6]interi, che lì son rimasti aperti, e nō le boche de' granchi sanza il rimanēte del suo tutto, e non li ni[7]chi d'altre spetie appiccati con loro in forma d'animale che sopra di quelli si mouesse, perchè ancora resta [8]il uestigio del suo andamento sopra la scorza che lui già, a uso di tarlo sopra il legname, andò cōsumādo; [9]nō si troverebbero infra loro ossa e denti di pescie, li quali alcuni dimandano saette e altri lingue di ser[10]penti, e nō si troverebbero tanti mēbri di diuersi animali insieme vniti se lì da liti marini gittati nō fussino, [11]e 'l diluuio lì nō gli avrebbe portati, perchè le cose gravi più del' acqua nō stanno a galla sopra l'acqua, e le cose pre[12]dette

As to those who say that shells existed for a long time and were born at a distance from the sea, from the nature of the place and of the cycles, which can influence a place to produce such creatures—to them it may be answered: such an influence could not place the animals all on one line, except those of the same sort and age; and not the old with the young, nor some with an operculum and others without their operculum, nor some broken and others whole, nor some filled with sea-sand and large and small fragments of other shells inside the whole shells which remained open; nor the claws of crabs without the rest of their bodies; nor the shells of other species stuck on to them like animals which have moved about on them; since the traces of their track still remain, on the outside, after the manner of worms in the wood which they consume. Nor would there be found among them the bones and teeth of fish which some call arrows and others serpents' tongues, nor would so many portions of various animals be found all together if they had not been thrown on the sea-shore. And the deluge cannot have carried them there, because things that are heavier than water do not float on the water. But these things

26. abitava . . chelle piane. 27. quell . . versaua. 28. deripato. 29. piedi . . taglo si vede. 30. fangho azuregante . . Essi alzato . . nosstro. 31. emissperio . . mancho. 32. perl . . calpe dattile . . perche[la] il. 33. chorono sagunsono . . emissperio Esselli . . futtino. 34. portadi . . essi saren misti . . fangho ennō. 35. assuoli.
988. 1. dicano che nichi. 2. infruisscie . . locho assimile . . risodera chesse . . infruētia. 3. po achadere . . enone il . . col go. 4. ellaltro esere colla sua . . ellaltro. 6. chelli . . rimassti . . rimanē dal . . e none. 7. colloro apichati . . mouessi. 8. lasscorza chellui ga. 9. troverra infrallaro . . pesscie. 10. troverra. 11. auebe . . stano . . elle cose. 12. sarieno . . alteza . . ga a noto . . inposi.

988. 1. Scilla argued against this hypothesis, which was still accepted in his days; see: *La vana Speculazione*, Napoli, 1670.

nõ sarieno in tanta altezza, se già a nuoto ivi sopra dell' acque portate non furono, la qual cosa è inpossi[13]bile per la lor graveza; Dove le uallate non ricievono le acque salse del mare, quiui i nichi mai non si [14]vedono, come manifesto si uede nella gran valle d'Arno di sopra alla Gonfolina, sasso per antico vnito [15]con Monte Albano in forma d'altissimo argine, il quale tenea ringorgato tal fiume in modo che prima che versasse nel mare, [16]il quale era dopo ai piedi di tal sasso, conponea 2 grandi laghi, de' quali il primo è, dove oggi si uede fiorire la città di Fiorẽ[17]ze insieme con Prato e Pistoia; e Monte Albano seguiva il resto dell' argine insin doue oggi è posto Serravalle ·; dal Val d'Arno [18]di sopra insino Arezzo si creava vno secondo lago, il quale nell' ãtidetto lago versaua le sue acque, [19]chiuso circa dove oggi si uede Girone, e occupaua tutta la detta valle di sopra per ispatio di 40 miglia [20]di lũghezza; questa valle riceue sopra il suo fondo tutta la terra portata dall' acqua da quella intorbidata, la quale [21]ancora si uede a' piedi di Prato Magno restare altissima, doue li fiumi nõ l'ãnno consumata, e infra essa terra si uedono le pro[22]fonde segature de' fiumi che quiui son passati, li quali discedono dal grã mõte di Prato Magno, nelle quali [23]segature nõ si uede vestigio alcuno di nichi e di terra marina; questo lago si congiugnea col lago di Perugia;

[24]Gran somma di nichi si uede doue li fiumi versano in mare, perchè in tali siti l'acque non so[25]no tanto salse per la mistion dell' acque dolci che con quelle s'uniscono ·, e 'l segnio di ciò si vede doue per antico li Mo[26]nti Appenini versauano li lor fiumi nel mare Adriano, li quali in gran parte mostrano infra li mõti grã [27]somma di nichi insieme coll azzurigno terreno di mare, e tutti li sassi, che di tal loco si cauano, son pieni di nichi; [28]Il medesimo si conoscie auere fatto Arno, quando cadea dal sasso della Gonfolina nel mare, [29]che dopo quella non troppo basso si trovaua, perchè a quelli tempi superaua l'altezza di San Miniato al Tedesco, [30]perchè nelle somme altezze di quello si uedono le ripe piene di nichi e ostriche dentro alle sue mvra; non si distesero li ni[31]chi inverso Val di Nievole, perchè l'acque dolci d'Arno in là non si astendeano;

Come li nichi nõ si [32]partirono dal mare per diluuio, perchè l'acque, che di uerso la terra veniuano, ãcora che esse tirassino il mare [33]inverso la terra, esse erã quelle che percuoteano il suo fondo, perchè l'acqua, che viene diuerso

could not be at so great a height if they had not been carried there by the water, such a thing being impossible from their weight. In places where the valleys have not been filled with salt sea-water shells are never to be seen; as is plainly visible in the great valley of the Arno above Gonfolina, a rock formerly united to Monte Albano, in the form of a very high bank which kept the river pent up, so that before it could flow into the sea, which was then at its foot, it formed two great lakes; of which the first was where we now see the flourishing city of Florence together with Prato and Pistoia. And Monte Albano followed the rest of its bank as far as where Serravalle now stands. From the Val d'Arno upwards, as far as Arezzo, another lake was formed, which discharged its waters into the former lake. It was closed at about the spot where now we see Girone, and occupied the whole of that valley above for a distance of 40 miles in length. This valley received on its bottom all the soil brought down by the turbid waters. And this is still to be seen at the foot of Prato Magno; there it lies very high where the rivers have not worn it away. Across this land are to be seen the deep cuts of the rivers that have passed there, falling from the great mountain of Prato Magno; in these cuts there are no vestiges of any shells or of marine soil. This lake was joined with that of Perugia [23].

A great quantity of shells are to be seen when the rivers flow into the sea, because on such shores the waters are not so salt owing to the admixture of the fresh water which is poured into it. Evidence of this is to be seen where, of old, the Apennines poured their rivers into the Adriatic Sea; for there in most places great quantities of shells are to be found, among the mountains, together with bluish marine clay; and all the rocks which are quarried in such places are full of shells. The same may be observed to have been done by the Arno when it fell from the rock of Gonfolina into the sea, which was not so very far below; for at that time it was higher than the top of San Miniato al Tedesco, since at the highest summit of this the shores may be seen full of shells and oysters within its flanks. The shells did not extend towards Val di Nievole, because the fresh waters of the Arno did not extend so far.

That the shells were not carried away from the sea by the deluge, because the waters which came from the earth, although they drew the sea towards the earth, were those which struck its

---

13. graveza. 14. vidone..vale. 15. "con monte albano" in forma daltissima argine [il quale] tene..versassi nel ma. 16. apiedi.. il p"o"e dove ogi si uide "fruire" la. 17. ze "insieme con" prato .. il re"sto" .. ogi .. ualdarno. 18. arezo .. lagho .. ati detto. 19. chircha .. ochupaua. 20. di lũglza .. tera porta dallacque di. 21. acora .. al "tissima" .. nõ lan .. si uede. 22. disscedano. 23. alchuno..terra [azurigma come] "marina" questo..congugnea collacho di peruga. 24. soma. 25. suniscano..dicosi..anticho. 26 nti. appenini .. moti. 27. chollazurigno terẽ .. ettutti. 28. conosscie .. fatto [il ual darno] arno .. chadea del .. golfolina. 29. tropo .. acquelli tenpi .. lalteza di saminiato. 30. some alteze .. uede .. osstrighe .. distesono. 31. nievole per lacque.. asstendeano. 32. partirõ del .. lache che diuerso terra veniuano al mare ancora e esse. 33. inverso terra .. peroteano .. vie diuerso tera | a.

23. See Pl. CXIII. Compare K. Clark, *Windsor Drawings*, No. 12278.

la terra, à ³⁴più corso che quella del mare, e per cōseguenza è piv potente, entra sotto l'altra acqua del mare ³⁵e rimove il fondo e accompagnia con seco tutte le cose mobili che in quella trova, come son i predetti ³⁶nichi e altre simili cose, e quanto l'acqua, che viē di terra, è piv torbida che quella del mare, tā³⁷to piv si fa potente e grave che quella; adunque io nō ci vedo modo di tirare i predetti nichi tanto in³⁸fra terra, se quiui nati nō fussino; se tu mi dicessi, il fiume Loira, che passa per la Francia, ³⁹nell' accrescimēto del mare si copre piv di ottanta miglia di paese, perchè è loco di grā pia-⁴⁰nvra, e 'l mare s'alza circa braccia 20, e nichi si uengono a trovare in tal pianvra, disco⁴¹sta dal mare essa 80 miglia, qui si rispōde che 'l flusso e reflusso ne' nostri mediterrani ⁴²mari nō fanno tanta varietà, perchè in Genovese nō uaria nvlla, a Vinegia poco, in A⁴³frica poco, e dove poco varia, poco occupa di paese;

Senpre la corrēte dell' acqua de' fiumi ⁴⁴s'inōda sopra del loco doue li è inpedito il corso ·; ancora doue essa si ristrignie per passare sotto ⁴⁵li archi de' ponti.

depths; because the water which goes down from the earth has a stronger current than that of the sea, and in consequence is more powerful, and enters beneath the sea-water and stirs the depths and carries with it all sorts of movable objects which are to be found in the earth, such as the above-mentioned shells and other similar things. And in proportion as the water which comes from the land is muddier than sea-water it is stronger and heavier than this; therefore I see no way of getting the said shells so far inland, unless they had been born there. If you were to tell me that the river Loire [38], which traverses France, covers when the sea rises more than eighty miles of country, because it is a district of vast plains, and the sea rises about 20 braccia, and shells are found in this plain at the distance of 80 miles from the sea; here I answer that the flow and ebb in our Mediterranean Sea does not vary so much; for at Genoa it does not rise at all, and at Venice but little, and little in Africa; and where it varies little it covers but little of the country.

The course of the water of a river always rises higher in a place where the current is impeded; it behaves as it does where it is reduced in width to pass under the arches of a bridge.

Leic. 9*b*]   989

CONFUTATIONE CH' È CONTRO COLOR CHE DICONO, I NICHI ESSER PORTATI PER MOLTE GIORNATE DISTANTI DALLI MARI PER CAUSA DEL DILUUIO

A CONFUTATION OF THOSE WHO SAY THAT SHELLS MAY HAVE BEEN CARRIED TO A DISTANCE OF MANY DAYS' JOURNEY FROM THE SEA BY THE DELUGE

Further researches (989–91).

²Dico che il diluuio non potè portare le cose nate dal mare alli mōti, se già il mare gonfiando nō creasse inōdazione ³tant' alto che superasse tale altezza ⁴insino alli lochi sopradetti, la qual gonfiatione accadere nō può perchè si darebbe vacuo, e se tu diciessi l'aria quiui ⁵riempierebbe ·, noi abbiamo concluso il grave non si sostenere sopra il lieue, onde per neciessità si cō⁶clude, esso diluuio essere cavsato dall' acque piovane, e se così è, tutte esse acque corrono al mare, ⁷e nō corre il mare alle montagnie, e se elle corrono al mare, esse spingono li nichi del lito nel mare, e nō le ⁸tirano a sé; E se tu dicessi, che poichè 'l mare alzò per l'acque piovane, portò essi nichi a tale altezza, ⁹già abbiamo detto che le cose piv gravi dell' acqua nō notā sopra di lei, ma stāno nei fondi, dalle quali nō si ¹⁰rimovono, se nō per cavsa di percussiō d'onda ·; E se tu dirai che l'onde le portassino in tali lochi alti, noi abbiamo ¹¹prouato che l'onde nelle grā profondità tornano in

I say that the deluge could not carry objects native to the sea up to the mountains, unless the sea had already increased so as to create inundations as high up as to be above those heights and reach as far as those places; and this increase could not have occurred because it would cause a vacuum; and if you were to say that the air would rush in there, we have already concluded that what is heavy cannot remain above what is light, whence of necessity we must conclude that this deluge was caused by rain-water, so that all these waters ran to the sea, and the sea did not run up the mountains; and as they ran into the sea, they thrust the shells from the shore of the sea and did not draw them towards themselves. And if you were to say that the sea, raised by the rain-water, had carried these shells to such a height, we have already said that things heavier than water cannot rise upon it, but remain at the bottom of it, and do not move unless by the impact of the waves. And if you

34. checquella . . acq"a". 35. aconpagnia consecho . . mobile . . son e prede. 36. ecquanto . . checquella. 37. adunque i nō ci vego . . e predetti. 38. fratterra . . settu . . era . . franca. 39. acresscimēto . . ellocho. 40. cricha br 20 e . . uengano attrorare . . discos. 41. sto dal . . esse . . risspōde . . frusso e refrusso . . medi terani. 42. nola . . pocho. 43. pocho . . pocho . . pocho schupa . . correte. 44. locho douele . . corso | anchora.
989. 1. dicano . . gornate . . chausa. 2. Dicho che diluuio no po | "te" . . cose "nate" del . . creassi. 3. tantalta . . superassi. 4. achadere . . po . . dare vachuo. 5. rienpierebe . . abiā . . greve. 6. esse chosi . . corrano. 7. esselle corrano. 8. asse Esse . . attale alteza. 9. abiā . . chelle . . grav . . stano in fondo delle. 10. removano . . . Essettu . . abiā. 11. chellonde . . provondita.

38. Leonardo has written 'Era' instead of 'Loera' or 'Loira'—perhaps under the mistaken idea that *Lo* was an article.

contrario nel fondo al moto di sopra, la qual cosa ¹²si manifesta per lo intorbidare del mare dal terreno tolto vicino alli liti; Muouesi la cosa piv lieue che l'¹³acqua insieme colla sua onda, ed è lasciata nel piv alto sito della riva dalla piv alta onda; Muouesi la cosa ¹⁴più grave che l'acqua ·, sospinta dalla sua ōda nella superfitie e dal fondo suo ‖ e per queste due conclusioni, che ai lochi ¹⁵sua · sarā provate a pieno, noi concludiamo che l'onda superfitiale nō può portare nichi, per essere più grievi che l'¹⁶acqua ....

¹⁷Quando il diluuio auesse avto a portare li nichi trecento e quattro cento mi¹⁸glia distanti dalli mari, esso li avrebbe portati misti con diuerse nature insieme ammontati, e noi vediamo in ¹⁹tal distantie l'ostriche tutte insieme, e le conchilie, e li pesci calamai, e tutti li altri nichi, che stanno insieme a congre²⁰gatione, essere trovati tutti insieme morti, e li nichi soletari trovarsi distanti l'uno dall' altro, come ne' liti marittimi ²¹tutto il giorno vediamo; E se noi troviamo l'ostriche insieme apparētate grādissime, infra le quali assai vedi quelle ²²che ànno ancora il coperchio congiunto, a significare che qui furono lasciate dal mare, che ancor viveano quando fù ²³tagliato lo stretto di Gibilterra; Vedesi in nelle montagnie di Parma e Piacētia le moltitudini di nichi e coralli ²⁴intarlati, ancora appiccati alli sassi, de' quali, quand' io facevo il grā cavallo di Milano, me ne fù portato vn grā sacco ne²⁵lla mia fabbrica da certi villani, che in tal loco furō trovati, fralli quali ve n'era assai delli conseruati nella prima bōtà;

²⁶Truovāsi sotto terra e sotto li profondi cavamenti de' lastroni li legniami delle traui lauorati, fatti già neri, li qua²⁷li furō trovati a mio tenpo in quel di Castel Fiorētino ·, e questi in tal loco profondo v'erano prima che la litta gittata ²⁸dall' Arno nel mare, che quiui copriva, fusse abbandonata in tant' altezza, e che le pianvre del Casentino fussī tanto abbassate ²⁹dal terrē che Arno al continuo di lì sgombra;

³⁰E se tu dicessi, tali ³¹nichi essere crea³²ti e creano a cō³³tinvo in simili lochi per ³⁴la natura del ³⁵sito e de' cieli, che qui³⁶vi influisce, questa ³⁷tale openione non ³⁸sta in cervelli di trop³⁹po discorso, perchè qui⁴⁰vi s'envmerā li anni ⁴¹del

were to say that the waves had carried them to such high spots, we have proved that the waves in a great depth move in a contrary direction at the bottom to the motion at the top, and this is shown by the turbidity of the sea from the earth washed down near its shores. Anything which is lighter than the water moves with the waves, and is left on the highest level of the highest margin of the waves. Anything which is heavier than the water moves, suspended in it, between the surface and the bottom; and from these two conclusions, which will be amply proved in their place, we infer that the waves of the surface cannot convey shells, since they are heavier than water. ...

If the deluge had to carry shells three hundred and four hundred miles from the sea, it would have carried them mixed with various other natural objects heaped together; and we see at such distances oysters all together, and sea-snails and cuttlefish, and all the other shells which congregate together, all to be found together and dead; and the solitary shells are found wide apart from each other, as we may see them on sea-shores every day. And if we find oysters of very large shells joined together and among them very many which still have the covering attached, indicating that they were left here by the sea, and still living when the strait of Gibraltar was cut through; there are to be seen, in the mountains of Parma and Piacenza, a multitude of shells and corals, full of holes, and still sticking to the rocks there. When I was making the great horse for Milan, a large sack full was brought to me in my workshop by certain peasants; these were found in that place and among them were many preserved in their first freshness.

Underground, and under the foundations of buildings, timbers are found of wrought beams and already black. Such were found in my time in those diggings at Castel Fiorentino. And these had been in that deep place before the sand carried by the Arno into the sea, then covering the plain, had been raised to such a height; and before the plains of Casentino had been so much lowered, by the earth which the Arno constantly carries down from them.

[30] And if you were to say that these shells were created, and were continually being created in such places by the nature of the spot and of the heavens which might have some influence there, such an opinion cannot exist in a brain of much reason; because here are the years of their growth, numbered on their shells, and there are

---

12. del terē .. chella. 13. acq"a" .. lassciata. 14. chellacqua . sospinte .. e del. 15. chellonda .. po. 17. auessi. 18. disstanti .. arebbe .. chon .. amōtati. 19. losstriche .. elli conchili elli .. chalamai ettutti. 20. elli ..trovare .. l unoall. 21. gorno .. Esse .. losstriche .. aparētadi grādissimi infralle quale. 22. anchora .. congunto .. assignificare .. lassciate .. ancorauveano. 23. losstretto di gibiltar .. inelle .. moltitudine de. 24. apichati .. ne nefu . sachone. 25. fabricha .. nella p"a" bōta. 26. essotto .. ga neri. 27. ecquesti .. profondor "o"no .. chella lita gitta. 28. copria fussi abondata .. alteza e chelle .. tante abassate. 29. del .. sgonbera. 30. essettu. 31. niche. 33. nvo. 36. infruisscie. 37. none. 38. di tro. 41. deloro acresscimento.

989. 30–47. These lines are written in the margin.

loro accrescimento [42]sulle loro scorze, e se ne [43]vedono piccoli e grādi, [44]i quali sanza cibo nō cre[45]scerebbero e non si cibarebbero sā[46]za moto, e quivi mouere nō si po[47]teano.

large and small ones to be seen which could not have grown without food, and could not have fed without motion—and here they could not move [47].

Leic. 10a]   990

Come [2]nelle falde, infra l'una e l'altra si trovano ancora li andamēti delli lonbrici, che caminavano infra esse [3]quādo non erano ancora asciutte; Come tutti li fanghi marini ritengono ancora de' nichi [4]ed è petrificato il nichio insieme col fango; della stoltitia e senplicità di quelli, che uogliono che ta[5]li animali fussino alli lochi distanti dai mari portati dal diluvio; Come altra setta d'ignoranti [6]affermano la natura, o i celi auerli in tali lochi creati · per īflussi celesti, come in quelli [7]nō si trovassino l'ossa de' pesci cresciuti cō lūghezza di tenpo, come nelle scorze de' nichi e lumache nō si potesse [8]annvmerare li anni o i mesi della lor uita, come nelle corna de' buoi e de' castroni e nella ramificatione de[9]lle piante, che nō furō mai tagliate in alcuna parte; E auendo con tali segni dimostrato e la lunghezza della lor uita [10]essere manifesta, ecco bisognia confessare, che tali animali nō uiuino sanza moto per cercare [11]il loro cibo e in loro non si uede strumēto da penetrare la terra e 'l sasso, ove si trovano rinchiusi ·; [12]Ma in che modo si potrebbe trovare in vna grā lumaca i rottami e parte di molt' altre sorti di nichi di uarie na[13]ture, se ad essa, sopra de' liti marini già morta, non li fussino state gittate dalle onde del mare, come dentro al[14]tre cose lieui, che esso gitta a terra? Perchè si truoua tanto rottame e nichi interi fra falda e falda di pie[15]tra, se già quella sopra del lito nō fusse stata ricoperta da una terra rigittata dal mare, la qual poi si uenne pe[16]trificando? E se 'l diluvio predetto li auesse in tali siti dal mare portato, tu troveresti essi nichi in nel termi[17]ne d'una sola falda, e non al termine di molte; deuonsi poi annvmerare le uernate delli ā[18]ni, che 'l mare mvltiplicaua le falde dell' arena e fango, portatoli da fiumi vicini, e ch'elli scaricava in sui liti sua, e se [19]tu volessi dire, che piv diluui fussino stati a produrre tali falde e nichi infra loro, e' bisognierebbe, [20]che ancora tu affermassi ogni āno essere vn tal diluuio accaduto; Ancora infra li rot[21]tami di tal nichi si prosume in tal sito essere spiaggia di mare, doue tutti i nichi son gittati rotti e diuisi e nō

That in the drifts, among one and another, there are still to be found the traces of the worms which crawled upon them when they were not yet dry. And all marine clays still contain shells, and the shells are petrified together with the clay. Of the silliness and stupidity of those who will have it that these animals were carried up to places remote from the sea by the deluge. Another sect of ignorant persons declare that Nature or Heaven created them in these places by celestial influences, as if in these places we did not also find the bones of fishes which have taken a long time to grow; and as if we could not count, in the shells of cockles and snails, the years and months of their life, as we do in the horns of bulls and oxen, and in the branches of plants that have never been cut in any part. And having proved by these signs the length of their lives, it is evident, and it must be admitted, that these animals could not live without moving to fetch their food; and we find in them no instrument for penetrating the earth or the rock where we find them enclosed. But how could we find in a large snail-shell the fragments and portions of many other sorts of shells, of various sorts, if they had not been thrown in when dead, by the waves of the sea like the other light objects which it throws on the earth? Why do we find so many fragments and whole shells between layer and layer of stone, if this had not formerly been covered on the shore by a layer of earth thrown up by the sea, and which was afterwards petrified? And if the before-mentioned deluge had carried them to these parts of the sea, you might find these shells at the boundary of one drift but not at the boundary between many drifts. We must also account for the winters of the years during which the sea multiplied the drifts of sand and mud brought down by the neighbouring rivers, by washing down the shores; and if you choose to say that there were several deluges to produce these rifts and the shells among them, you would also have to affirm that such a deluge took place every year. Again, among the fragments of these shells, it must be presumed that in those places there were sea-coasts where all the shells were thrown up, broken, and divided, and never in pairs, since they are found alive in the sea, with two valves,

42. sule. 43. vede picoli. 45. bono e non si ciborō. 47. trono.
990. 2. infralluna allaltra . . trova anchora. 3. neuera . . asscutta . . fangh . . ritengano. 4. essenplicita . . uogliano chettal. 5. fossi inali . . diluio. 6. i frussi. 7. trovassi . . cressciuti . . lugeza . . pote. 8. anvmerare . . casstroni . . del. 9. signi dimostro o la lungeza. 10. ecci bisognia . . chettali.· 11. illor . . nosi. 12. nvna gra lumacha . . altre sotte. 13. ture e essa sopa de . . morta nolli . . comellā. 14. essa . . atterra. 15. fussi. 16. trifichando Essel diluio . . auessi . . troverresti hessi . . inel. 17. nōne . . di [qualunche falda] "di molte" deunsi po anvmerare [li ani] le uernate. 18. del [fango] "larena effangho" portatoli . . insuliti . . esset. 19. ennichi infralloro. 20. ongni . . tatal . . acaduto [e che tenessi] Ancora infralli. 21. spiagia.

²²mai appaiati, come infra 'l mare viui si trovano con due gusci, che fan coperchio l'uno all' altro; E infra ²³le falde della riuiera e de' liti marittimi son trovati de' rottami; E dentro alli termini delle pietre son trovati ²⁴rari e appaiati de' gusci, come quelli che furō lasciati dal mare sotterrati viui dentro al fango, il qual ²⁵poi si seccò e col tenpo petrificò.

each serving as a lid to the other; and in the drifts of rivers and on the shores of the sea they are found in fragments. And within the limits of the separate strata of rocks they are found, separated and in pairs like those which were left by the sea, buried alive in the mud, which subsequently dried up and, in time, was petrified.

Leic. 10b]   991

E se tu vuoi dire che tale diluuio fu quello che portò tali nichi fuor de' mari cētinaia di miglia ·, questo nō può acca²dere, essendo stato esso diluuio per cause di pioggie, perchè naturalmente le pioggie spingono i fiumi insieme colle cose da loro ³portate inuerso il mare, e nō tirano inverso de' mōti le cose morte dai liti marittimi ·, e se tu dicessi che 'l diluvio poi s'al⁴zò colle sue acque sopra de' mōti, il moto del mare fù si tardo col camino suo contro al corso de' fiumi, che non avrebbe ⁵sopra di sé tenvto a noto le cose piv gravi di lui, e se pur l'auesse sostenute, esso nel calare l'avrebbe lasciate in diversi ⁶lochi seminate; Ma come accomoderemo noi li coralli, li quali inverso Mōte Ferrato di Lonbardia essersi tutto ⁷dì trovati intarlati appiccati alli scogli, scoperti dalle corrēti de' fiumi? e li detti scogli sono tutti coperti di parentadi ⁸e famiglie d'ostriche, le quali noi sappiamo che nō si movono, ma stā senpre appiccate col' ū de' gusci al sasso, e l'altro apro⁹no per cibarsi d'animaluzzi, che notā per lacque, li quali, credendo trovar bona pastura, diuentano cibo del predetto nichio; non si ¹⁰trova egli l'arena mista coll' aliga marina essersi petrificata, poichè l'aliga, che la ramezzaua, venne meno; e di questo ¹¹scopre tutto il giorno il Po nelle ruine delle sue ripe.

And if you choose to say that it was the deluge which carried these shells away from the sea for hundreds of miles, this cannot have happened, since that deluge was caused by rain; because rain naturally forces the rivers to rush towards the sea with all the things they carry with them, and not to bear the dead things of the sea-shores to the mountains. And if you choose to say that the deluge afterwards rose with its waters above the mountains, the movement of the sea must have been so sluggish in its rise against the currents of the rivers, that it could not have carried, floating upon it, things heavier than itself; and even if it had supported them, in its receding it would have left them strewn about in various spots. But how are we to account for the corals which are found every day towards Monte Ferrato in Lombardy, with the holes of the worms in them, sticking to rocks left uncovered by the currents of rivers? These rocks are all covered with stocks and families of oysters which, as we know, never move, but always remain with one of their halves stuck to a rock, and the other they open to feed themselves on the animalcules that swim in the water, which, hoping to find good feeding-ground, become the food of these shells. Does he not find that the sand mixed with seaweed has been petrified, because the weed which was mingled with it has shrunk away. And this the Po shows us every day in the debris of its banks.

Leic. 20a]   992

Perchè sono trovate l'ossa ²de' grā pesci e le ostriche e coralli e altri diuersi nichi e chiocciole sopra l'alte cime de' mōti ma³rittimi nel medesimo modo che si trovā ne' bassi mari?

Why do we find the bones of great fishes and oysters and corals and various other shells and sea-snails on the high summits of mountains by the sea, just as we find them in low seas? Other problems (992–4).

Leic. 36a]   993

Tu ài ora a provare come li nichi nō nascono, se nō in acque salse, quasi tutte le sorte, e come ²li nichi di Lonbardia ànno 4 liuelli, e così è per tutti, li quali sono fatti in piv tēpi, e questi ³sono per tutte le ualli che sboccano alli mari.

You now have to prove that the shells cannot have originated if not in salt water, almost all being of that sort; and that the shells in Lombardy are at four levels, and thus it is everywhere, having been made at various times. And they all occur in valleys that open towards the seas.

---

22. apaiati . . gussci cheffan . . infralle. 24. apaiati di gussci . . lassciati . . sollerati. 25. secho . . petrificho.
991. 1. Essettu volli . . chettale . . for . . po acha. 2. chause di piogie . . piogie spingano . . dallor. 3. morte de liti . . esse . . diluui. 4. sittardo . . arebe [te]. 5. esse . . lauesi sosstenvte . . larebe lassciate. 6. acomodereno. 7. ildi . . "intarlati" apichati alli scolgli . . elli . . scolgli . . parendadi e. 8. sapiano . . movano . . apichate cholū degussci . . apra. 9. danimaluzi . . diuenta. 10. cholla . . poichellaliga chella framezaua. 11. gorno.
992. 2. pessci elle osstriche . . cioccole.
993. 1. nasscano. 3. chessabochano.

Br. M. 156*b*]   **994**

Per le 2 linie de' nichi bisognia dire che la terra per sdegno ²s'attufasse sotto il mare, e fece il primo suolo, poi il diluuio ³fece il secondo.

From the two lines of shells we are forced to say that the earth indignantly submerged under the sea and so the first layer was made; and then the deluge made the second.

C. A. 92*b*]   **994 A**

Fatti disegnare dove sono li nicchi a Monte Mari.

Let them show you where are the shells on Monte Mario.

994. 1. nicch . . chellatera. 2. sattu fassi sottollmare effe. 3. fe il sechondo.

994. This note is in the early writing of about 1470–80. On the same sheet are the passages Nos. 1217 and 1219. Compare also No. 1339. All the foregoing chapters are from manuscripts of about 1510. This explains the want of connexion and the contradiction between this and the foregoing texts.

VII

ON THE ATMOSPHERE

Leic. 20a]

995

Come la chiarezza dell' aria na²scie dall' acqua che in quella s'è resoluta e fattasi in īsēsibili graniculi, li quali, preso il lume del sole dall' op-³posita parte, rēdono la chiarezza che in essa aria si dimonstra, e l'azzurro, che in quella apparisce, nascie ⁴dalle tenebre, che dopo essa aria si nascondono.

That the brightness of the air is occasioned by the water which has dissolved itself in it into imperceptible molecules. These, being lighted by the sun from the opposite side, create the brightness which is visible in the air; and the azure which is seen in it is caused by the darkness that is hidden beyond the air.[4]

Constituents of the atmosphere.

Leic. 22b]

996

Come i retrosi de' uēti a certe ²boche di ualli percuotino sopra delle acque e quelle concauino cō grā cauamēto, e portino ³l'acqua in aria in forma colunnale in color di nugola, e il mede-simo vid' io già fare sopra ⁴uno renaio d'Arno, nel quale fu concauato l'arena più d'una statura d'uomo, e ⁵di quella fu remossa la ghiaja e gittata in disparte per lūgo spatio, e parea per l'aria in forma ⁶di grādissimo canpanile, e cres-ceva la sommità come ⁊ rami di gian pino, e ŏı piegaua ⁷poi nel contatto del retto uēto che passaua sopra li mōti.

That the return eddies of wind at the mouth of certain valleys strike upon the waters and scoop them out in a great hollow, whirl the water into the air in the form of a column, and of the colour of a cloud. And I saw this thing happen on a sand-bank in the Arno, where the sand was hollowed out to a greater depth than the height of a man; and with it the gravel was whirled round and flung about for a great space; it appeared in the air in the form of a great bell-tower; and the top spread like the branches of a pine-tree, and then it bent at the contact of the direct wind which passed over from the mountains.

On the motion of air (996–9).

Leic. 23a]

997

L'onda dell' aria fa il me²desimo vfitio infra l'elemēto del fuoco ·, che fa l'onda dell' acqua infra l'aria, o l'onda dell' a³rena, cioè terra, infra l'acqua, e sono i lor moti in tal proportione qual è quella de' lor mo⁴tori infra loro.

The element of fire acts upon a wave of air in the same way as the air does on water, or as water does on a mass of sand—that is, earth; and their motions are in the same proportions as those of the motors acting upon them.

S. K. M. II.¹ 46a]

998

DE MOTO

Domādo, se 'l uero moto ²de' nuvoli si può conosciere ³per lo moto delle sua ombre, ⁴e similemēte del moto ⁵del sole.

OF MOTION

I ask whether the true motion of the clouds can be known by the motion of their shadows; and in like manner of the motion of the sun.

H.³ 100a]

999

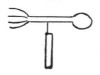

Per cognosciere ²meglio i vēti.

To know better the direction of the winds.

---

995. 1. chiareza. 2. sscie .. effattasi .. presi. 3. rēdano la ciareza .. dimonsstra ellazurro .. apparissce nasscie. 4. nasscondano.
996. 1. accerte. 2. percotino . ecquelle .. chauamēto. 3. colunale .. vidio cia. 4. duome he. 5. giara e gittatta. 6. ecresscieva lasomita .. rāmi di girapino essi.
997. 2. infrallelemēto .. focho . cheffa. 3. coe .. infrallacqua essono .. quele quella delor.
998. 2. nvvoli spo. 3. obre. 4. essimilemēte.
999. 1–2 R. 1. cōgnosciere. 2. e vēti.

995. 4. Compare vol. i, No. 300. Compare also No. 1021 (on cloud effects).

999. In connexion with this text I may here mention a hygrometer drawn and probably invented by Leonardo. A facsimile of this is given on Pl. XXXIIIв

with the note: 'Modi di pesare l'arie eddi sapere quando s'à arrompere il tēpo' (Mode of weighing the air and of knowing when the weather will change); by the sponge '*Spugna*' is written.

II   A a

Leic. 34a]   1000

The globe an organism. Nessuna cosa nasce in loco doue nõ sia vita sensitiua, vegetatiua e rationale; nascono le penne sopra li uccelli, e si mvtano ogni anno; nascono ²li peli sopra li animali, e ogni anno si mvtano, saluo alcuna parte, come li peli delle barbe de' lioni e gatte e simi³li; nascono l'erbe sopra li prati e le foglie sopra li alberi, e ogn' āno in grā parte si rinovano; adunque potremo dire, ⁴la terra avere anima vegetatiua, e che la sua carne sia la terra, li sua ossi sieno li ordini delle collegationi de' sas⁵si, di che si compongono le mōtagnie, il suo tenerume sono li tufi, il suo sangue sono le uene delle acque, il lago ⁶del sangue, che sta dintorno al core, è il mare oceano, il suo alitare e 'l crescere e discrescere del sangue ⁷pelli polsi, e così nella terra è il flusso e riflusso del mare, e 'l caldo dell' anima del mondo è il fuoco, ⁸ch'è infuso per la terra, e la residenza dell' anima vegetativa sono li fochi, che per diuersi lochi della ⁹terra spirano in bagni, e in miniere di solfi, e in vulcani, e Mõ Gibello di Sicilia, e altri lochi assai.

Nothing originates in a spot where there is no sentient, vegetable, and rational life; feathers grow upon birds and are changed every year; hairs grow upon animals and are changed every year, excepting some parts, like the hairs of the beard in lions, cats, and their like. The grass grows in the fields, and the leaves on the trees, and every year they are, in great part, renewed. So that we might say that the earth has a spirit of growth; that its flesh is the soil, its bones the arrangement and connexion of the rocks of which the mountains are composed, its cartilage the tufa, and its blood the springs of water. The pool of blood which lies round the heart is the ocean, and its breathing, and the increase and decrease of the blood in the pulses, is represented in the earth by the flow and ebb of the sea; and the heat of the spirit of the world is the fire which pervades the earth, and the seat of the vegetative soul is in the fires, which in many parts of the earth find vent in baths and mines of sulphur, and in volcanoes, and at Mount Ætna in Sicily, and in many other places.

C. A. 260a]   1000 A

Adunque la terra à polmone, nervi e muscoli e cartilagine dentro a sé.

Therefore the earth has inside lung, nerves, muscles, and cartilage.

1000. 1. nassce .. locho .. vita "sensitiua [intellettiva] vigitatiua erationall nassce le pene .. essi .. nassce.   2. alchuna .. essimi.   3. nassce .. elle .. potren.   4. vigitatiua e chella .. collegatione.   5. comogano.   6. occeano .. cresscere e disscresscere.   7. frusso e refrusso .. focho.   8. ella reside dell .. vigitativa.   9. in vulgano .. cicilia.

XVII

TOPOGRAPHICAL NOTES

*A*LARGE *part of the texts published in this section might perhaps have found their proper place in connexion with the foregoing chapters on Physical Geography. But these observations on Physical Geography, of whatever kind they may be, as soon as they are localized acquire a special interest and impor- tance and particularly as bearing on the question whether Leonardo himself made the observations recorded at the places mentioned or merely noted the statements from hearsay. In a few instances he himself tells us that he writes at second hand. In some cases again (though, as it seems to me, these cases are not very numerous) the style and expressions used make it seem highly probable that he has derived his information from others; we find, however, among these Topographical Notes a great number of observations about which it is extremely difficult to form a decided opinion. Of what the Master's life and travels may have been throughout his sixty-seven years of life we know comparatively little; between the years 1481 and 1487 there are unexplained gaps in the chronology. It seems likely that he travelled about and even visited foreign lands. Thus, from a biographical point of view a very great interest attaches to some of the Topographical Notes, and for this reason it seemed that it would add to their value to arrange them in a group by themselves. Leonardo's intimate knowledge of places, some of which were certainly remote from his native home, is of importance as contributing to decide the still open question as to the extent of Leonardo's travels. We shall find in these notes a confirmation of the view that the manuscripts in which the Topographical Notes occur are in only a few instances such diaries as may have been in use during a journey. These notes are mostly found in the manuscript books of his later and quieter years, and it is certainly remarkable that Leonardo is very reticent as to the authorities from whom he quotes his facts and observations: for instance, as to the Straits of Gibraltar, the Nile, the Taurus Mountains, and the Tigris and Euphrates. Is it likely that he who declared that in all scientific research his own experience should be the foundation of his statements (see XIX, 'Philosophy', Nos. 1148–61) should here have made an exception to this rule without mentioning it? As, for instance, in the discussion as to the equilibrium of the mass of water in the Mediter- ranean Sea—a subject which, it may be observed, had at that time attracted the interest and study of hardly any other observer. The observations, in Nos. 985–94, on the presence of shells at the tops of mountains suffice to prove that it was not in his nature to allow himself to be drawn into wide generalizations extending beyond the limits of his own investigations.*

Most of these Topographical Notes, though suggesting very careful and thorough research, do not afford indisputable evidence that that research was Leonardo's own. But it must be granted that in more than one instance probability is in favour of it.

Among the passages which treat of the topography of Eastern places, the most interesting is a description of the Taurus Mountains; as this text is written in the style of a formal report and is associated with letters which give the history of its origin, it will be found under No. XXI (Letters).

Florence and its neighbourhood is mentioned in connexion with the projects for canals which occupied his attention for some short time during the first ten years of the sixteenth century. The various passages relating to the construction of canals in Tuscany, which are put together at the beginning, are immediately followed by those which deal with schemes for canals in Lombardy; and after these come notes on the city and vicinity of Milan as well as on the lakes of North Italy.

The notes on some towns of Central Italy which Leonardo visited in 1502, when in the service of Cesare Borgia, are reproduced here in the same order as in the notebook used during these travels (MS. L, Institut de France). The maps of the districts drawn by Leonardo at the time are of special interest (see No. 1054, note). The names on these maps are not written from right to left, but in the usual manner, and we may infer that they were made in obedience to some command, possibly for the use of Cesare Borgia himself; the fact that they remained nevertheless in Leonardo's hands is not surprising when we remember the sudden political changes and warlike events of the period. There can be no doubt that these maps are drawn from observations of the places themselves; this is proved by the fact that we find among his manuscripts the rough sketches and studies for them. But Leonardo must have referred to contemporary maps for parts which he could not study first hand, since in some cases, on the map of Tuscany (Pl. CXII) f.i., he repeats some of their errors. His method of procedure seems to have been first to chart the river systems and determine the locality of the towns, and then to insert mountains in the watersheds: the result is very suggestive of the nature of the terrain. These maps are individual in conception and constitute a step in advance of contemporary cartography.[1] It was the custom of the time to employ artists for making plans and maps. Compare Vasari (vi. 62) on Tribolo's plan of Florence, and on Niccolò Giolfino's Veronese plans and maps Gerola, Madonna Verona, iii. 1, p. 43 f., Verona, 1909.

The interesting map of the world, so far as it was then known, which is among the Leonardo MSS. at Windsor (published in the 'Archaeologia', vol. xi) cannot be attributed to the Master, as the Marchese Girolamo d'Adda has sufficiently proved; it has not therefore been reproduced here.

Such of Leonardo's observations on places in Italy as were made before or after his travels as military engineer to Cesare Borgia have been arranged in alphabetical order, under Nos. 1034–54. The most interesting are those which relate to the Alps and the Apennines, Nos. 1057–68.

Leonardo's notes on the Mediterranean show his interest in the countries of the Near East. There is no mention in the manuscripts of Christopher Columbus and his discoveries.

---

[1] Mario Baratta, *L. d. V. e la Cartografia*, Voghera, 1912; *Sopra le fonti cartografiche di L. d. V.*, Florence, 1923.

I

ITALY

CANALE DI FIRĒZE

²Facciasi alle Chiane d'Arezzo · tali · cateratte che, mācando · acqua l'estate in Arno ·, il canale nō rimāga · arido; ³e facciasi esso canale · largo · in fōdo braccia 20 ·, e 30 in bocca, e braccia 2 · sempre qua o 4 ·, perchè dua d'esse braccia serva ⁴alli mvlini e li prati ·; questo · bonificherà il paese ·, e Prato, Pistoia e Pisa insieme cō Firēze, faranno l'anno di meglio ⁵dugiēto mila ducati ·, e porgieranno le mani e spesa a esso · aivtorio, e i Lucchesi il simile, perchè il lago di Sesto fia navicabile; ⁶fo lo · fare · la uia di Prato · e Pistoia e tagliare Serravalle · e uscire nel lago ·, perchè nō bisognia conche o sostegni i qua⁷li · nō sono · eterni, anzi senpre si sta in esercitio · a operarli e mantenerli.

⁸E sappi che se, cauādo · il canale ·, doue esso è profondo · 4 braccia, si · dā 4 dinari per braccio quadro, in doppia profondità · si ⁹dā · 6 dinari, se fai 4 ¹⁰braccia e sono solamēte · 2 · banchi ·, cioè · vno dal fondo · del fosso · alla superfitie de' labri del fosso ·, e l'altro da essi labri ¹¹alla · somità del mōte · della · terra che d'in sulla · riva · dell' argine · si leua ·; e se fusse di doppia profondità ·, esso argine ¹²cresce solo · uno · banco, cioè braccia · 4 ·, che crescie · la metà della · prima spesa, cioè che, dove prima in 2 banchi · si da¹³va · dinari · 4, · in 3 si viene a dare · sei · a 2 dinari · per banco, essendo il fosso in fondo braccia · 16; ancora se 'l fosso fusse largo braccia 16 ¹⁴e profōdo · 4 ·, venēdo · a · 4 soldi · per opera ·, dinari 4 · Milanesi · il braccio quadro ·; il fosso · che in fondo sarà braccia ¹⁵32, verrà a stare dinari · 8 il · braccio quadro.

CANAL OF FLORENCE

Sluices should be made in the valley of la Chiana at Arezzo, so that when, in the summer, the Arno lacks water, the canal may not remain dry: and let this canal be 20 braccia wide at the bottom, and at the top 30, and 2 braccia deep, or 4, so that two of these braccia may flow to the mills and the meadows, which will benefit the country; and Prato, Pistoia, and Pisa, as well as Florence, will gain two hundred thousand ducats a year, and will lend a hand and money to this useful work; and the Lucchese the same, for the lake of Sesto will be navigable; I shall direct it to Prato and Pistoia, and cut through Serravalle and make an issue into the lake; for there will be no need of locks or supports, which are not lasting and so will always be giving trouble in working at them and keeping them up.

And know that in digging this canal where it is 4 braccia deep, it will cost 4 dinari the square braccio; for twice the depth 6 dinari, if you are making 4 braccia and there are but 2 banks; that is to say, one from the bottom of the trench to the surface of the edges of it, and the other from these edges to the top of the ridge of earth which will be raised on the margin of the bank. And if this bank were of double the depth only the first bank will be increased, that is, 4 braccia increased by half the first cost; that is to say, that at first 4 dinari were paid for 2 banks, for 3 it would come to 6, at 2 dinari the bank, if the trench measured 16 braccia at the bottom; again, if the trench were 16 braccia wide and 4 deep, coming to 4 soldi for the work, 4 Milan dinari the square braccio a trench which was 32 braccia at the bottom would come to 8 dinari the square braccio.

Canals in connexion with the Arno (1001–8).

Dal muro d'Arno della ²Giustitia all' argine d'Ar³no di Sardigna, dove sono ⁴i muri alle mulina, è braccia ⁵7400, cioè migla 2 ⁶e braccia 1400, ⁷e 'l di là d'Arno è braccia 5500.

From the wall of the Arno at (the gate of) la Giustizia to the bank of the Arno at Sardigna where the walls are, to the mills, is 7,400 braccia, that is, 2 miles and 1,400 braccia, and beyond the Arno is 5,500 braccia.

1001. 2. alle chiane darezo .. chateratte .. māchando .. acqua \ lastate innarno. 3. effacciasi .. br. 20 .. boccha e br. 2 . sen per qua .. dua desse br. serua. 4. elli .. quessto .. pisstoia .. chō .. fia lano dimeglio. 5. porgierano le mani "esspesa" .. sessto. 6. folli fare .. ettagliare .. esscire. 7. etterni . *Lines* 8–15 br. *stands always for* braccia. 8. Essapi chesse chauādo il chanale .. dopia. 9. dinari [onsi in . 7 . si da il doppio . perche . quelle . sechonde 4 br. il tereno e giassmosso e poi perche] seffai 4. 10. dellabri .. ellaltro. 11. esse fussi. 12. cresse solo . İ . bancho .. cresscie. 13. viene dinari sei .. bancho "essendo il fosso in fondo braccia 16" anchora .. fusi largho. 14. [e al] e profōdo. 15. verra dinari.
1002. 2. gusstitia. 4. e br. 5. [8000] 7400 coe. 6. br. 7. br.

1001. This passage is illustrated by a map, on which these places are indicated from west to east: Pisa, Luccha, Lago, Seravalle, Pistoja, Prato, Firenze.

1002. 2. *Giustizia.* By this the Porta della Giustizia seems to be meant; from the fifteenth to the

sixteenth centuries it was also commonly known as Porta Guelfa, Porta San Francesco del Renaio, Porta Nuova, and Porta Reale. It was close to the Arno, opposite to the Porta San Niccolò, which still exists.

C. A. 289*a*]   1003

Dirizzare Arno [2]di sotto e di sopra; [3]s'auan-
zerà vn tesoro, [4]a tanto per stajoro [5]a chi lo
vole.

By guiding the Arno above and below, a
treasure will be found in each acre of ground by
whomsoever will.

Br. M. 273*b*]   1004

Il muro dalle [2]casaccie si [3]dirizza alla por[4]ta
di San Niccolò.

The wall of the old houses runs towards the
gate of San Nicolo.

Br. M. 274*a*]   1005

640 braccia è il muro rotto, [2]e 150 è il muro
rimanête [3]col mulino, [4]300 braccia à rotto dal
Bisarno in 4 anni.

The ruined wall is 640 braccia; 150 is the
wall remaining with the mill; 300 braccia were
broken in 4 years by Bisarno.

W. 12279]   1006

Nõ sanno, perchè Arno [2]non starà mai in
ca[3]nale; perchè [4]i fiumi che vi mettono, [5]nella
loro entrata põ[6]gono terreno, e dalla oppo[7]sita
parte leuano e [8]pieganvi il fiume; [9]6 miglia si
fa per Ar[10]no dalla Caprona a Li[11]vorno, e 12 si
fa per li [12]stagni che s'avãzano 32 [13]miglia, e
16 dalla Caprona [14]in sù, che fã 48 [15]per Arno
da Firenze, [16]avanzasi 16 miglia; a Vico miglia
16, [17]e 'l canale à 5; [18]da Firenze a Fucechio
miglia 40 per [19]acqua d'Arno.

[20]Miglia 56 · per Arno [21]da Firêze a Vico,
[22]e pel canale di Pistoia [23]è miglia 44 · adũ[24]que
è piv corta 12 [25]miglia per canale che per Arno.

They do not know why the Arno will never
remain in a channel. It is because the rivers
which flow into it deposit earth where they
enter, and wear it away on the opposite side,
bending the river in that direction. The Arno
flows for 6 miles between la Caprona and Leg-
horn; and for 12 through the marshes, which
extend 32 miles, and 16 from La Caprona up the
river, which makes 48; by the Arno from Florence beyond 16 miles; to Vico 16 miles, and the
canal is 5; from Florence to Fucechio it is 40
miles by the river Arno.

56 miles by the Arno from Florence to Vico;
by the Pistoia canal it is 44 miles. Thus it is
12 miles shorter by the canal than by the Arno.

1003. 1. dirizare arnno. 4. attanto perisstaioro.
1004. 1. mro delle. 2. casace [con]. 3. diriza. 4. nicolo.
1005. 1. 6400 bre. 2. moro.
1006. 2. nõnistara. 4. mettano. 6. gã terreno e dallopo. 10. caprona alli. 12. savãza. 17. ecanale. 19. acq"a". 24. chorta.

1004. By the side of this text there is an indistinct
sketch, resembling that given under No. 973. On the
bank is written the word *Casace*. There then follows
in the original a passage of 12 lines in which the consequences of the windings of the river are discussed.
A larger diagram on the same page represents the
shores of the Arno inside Florence as in two parallel
lines. Four horizontal lines indicate the bridges. By
the side these measures are stated in figures: 1. (at
the Ponte alla Carraja): 230—*largho br. 12 e 2 di
spõda e 14 di pile e a 4 pilastri*; 2. (at the Ponte S.
Trinità): 188—*largho br. 15 e 2 di spõde he 28 di
pilastri for delle spõde e pilastri sõ 2*; 3. (at the Ponte
Vecchio): *põte lung br. 152 e largo*; 4. (at the Ponte
alle Grazie): 290 *ellargo 12 e 2 di spõde e 6 di pili*.
   There is, in MS. W. 12681, a sketched plan of
Florence, with the following names of gates: *Nicholo
—Saminiato—Giorgo—Ghanolini—Porta San Fredian
—Prato—Faenza—Ghallo¹—Pinti—Giustitia* (written
from left to right).
   1006. This passage is written by the side of a map,
washed in indian ink, of the course of the Arno; it is
evidently a sketch for a completer map.
   These investigations may possibly be connected
with the following documents: *Francesco Guiducci
alla Balìa di Firenze. Dal Campo contro Pisa 24
Luglio* 1503 (Archivio di Stato, Firenze, *Lettere alla
Balìa*; published by J. Gaye, *Carteggio inedito
d'Artisti*, Firenze, 1840, Tom. ii, p. 62): Ex Castris,

Franciscus Ghuiduccius, 24. Jul. 1503. 'Appresso fu
qui hieri con una di V. Signoria Alexandro degli
Albizzi insieme con Leonardo da Vinci et certi altri, et
veduto el disegno insieme con el ghovernatore, doppo
molte discussioni et dubii conclusesi che l'opera
fussi molto al proposito, o si veramente Arno volgersi
qui, o restarvi con un canale, che almeno vieterebbe
che le colline da nemici non potrebbono essere
offese; come tucto referiranno loro a bocha V. S.'
   And, 'Archivio di Stato, Firenze, *Libro d'Entrata
e Uscita di cassa de' Magnifici Signori di luglio e
agosto* 1503 a 51 T.: Andata di Leonardo al Campo
sotto Pisa. 'Spese extraordinarie dieno dare a dì
XXVI di luglio L. LVI sol. XIII per loro a Giovanni
Piffero; e sono per tanti, asegnia avere spexi in vetture
di sei chavalli a spese di vitto per andare chon Lionardo
da Vinci a livellare Arno in quello di Pisa per levallo
del lito suo.' (Published by Milanesi, *Archivio Storico
Italiano*, Serie III, tom. xvi.) Vasari asserts: '(Leonardo) fu il primo ancora, che giovanetto discorrese
sopra il fiume d'Arno per metterlo in canale da Pisa a
Fiorenza' (ed. Milanesi, iv. 20).' Compare K. Clark,
Windsor Catalogue 12279 and 12683; M. Baratta, *L.
d. V. negli studi per la navigazione dell' Arno*, Bolletino
della Società Geografica Italiana, Rome 1905; E.
Solmi, *L. d. V. alla Sollevazione d'Arezzo*, Archivio
Storico Italiano XLIX, 1912, p. 122.
   The passage above is in some degree illustrated by
the map on Pl. CXII.

Leic. 18b]   **1007**

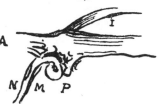

Cōcauità fatta da Mēsola, **A**
quādo Arno è basso e Mēsola
grossa.

The eddy made by the Mensola, when the Arno is low and the Mensola full.

Leic. 13a]   **1008**

Come il fiume, che s'à a piegare d'uno in altro loco, debbe essere lusin²gato e nō con uiolenza aspreggiato, e a questo fare si de' cauare infra 'l fiume alquāto ³di pescaia, e poi di sotto gittarne vna piv ināti, e così si faccia colla 3ᵃ 4ᵃ e 5ᵃ, in modo che 'l ⁴fiume inbocchi col canale datoli, o che per tal mezzo si scosti dal loco da lui danneggiato, come ⁵fu fatto in Fiādra, dettomi da Niccolò di Forzore;

Come si de' vestire di riparo vn argine percosso ⁶dal' acqua, come sotto l'isola de' Cocomeri.

That the river which is to be turned from one place to another must be coaxed and not treated roughly or with violence; and to do this a sort of flood-gate should be made in the river, and then lower down one in front of it and in like manner a third, fourth, and fifth, so that the river may discharge itself into the channel given to it, or that by this means it may be diverted from the place it has damaged, as was done in Flanders— as I was told by Niccolò di Forzore.

How to protect and repair the banks washed by the water, as below the island of Cocomeri.

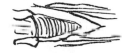

FIG. 1.

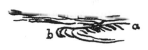

FIG. 3.

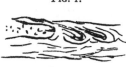

FIG. 4.

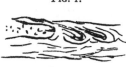

FIG. 2.

⁷Pōte Rubaconte (Fig. 1); ⁸sotto il Bisticci ⁹e Canigiani (Fig. 2); ¹⁰sopra la pescaia de¹¹lla Givstitia (Fig. 3); ¹²a b è vna secca ¹³a riscōtro doue fi¹⁴nisce l'isola de' Coco¹⁵meri in mezzo d'Ar¹⁶no (Fig. 4).

Ponte Rubaconte (Fig. 1); below [the palaces] Bisticci and Canigiani (Fig. 2). Above the flood-gate of la Giustizia (Fig. 3); a b is a sand-bank opposite the end of the island of Cocomeri in the middle of the Arno (Fig. 4).

C. A. 395a]   **1009**

Navilio di San Cristoforo di Milano fatto a dì 3 di maggio 1509.

The canal of San Cristofano at Milan, made May 3rd, 1509.

F. 76b]   **1010**

DEL CANALE DI MARTESANA

OF THE CANAL OF MARTESANA

²Facēdo il canale di Martesana e' si diminuisce ³l'acqua all' Adda, la qual è destribuita

By making the canal of Martesana the water of the Adda is greatly diminished by its distribution

Canals in the Milanese and Piemontese (1009–13).

1008. 1. chessa . . locho. 2. asspreggato e acquessto. 4. inbochi . . mezo si scossti dal locho dallui damegato. 5. nicholo . . percossa. 8. besticci. 9. camigagani. 10. pesscaja. 11. giosstitia. 15. imezo.
1009. crisstofano . . facto addi . . maggo.
1010. 1. martigana. 2. martigana . . diminuissce. 3. imol.

1007. *Mensola* is a mountain stream which falls into the Arno about a mile and a half above Florence.
A = Arno, I = Isola, M = Mvgone, P = Pesa, N = Mesola.

1008. The course of the river Arno is also discussed in Nos. 987 and 988.

5. Leonardo had this meeting with *Niccolò di Forzore Spinelli*, the Florentine engraver and medallist

(1430–1514), in 1505. See Racc. Vinc. vii, p. 138.

1009. This observation is written above a coloured pen-and-ink drawing.

1010. *el navilio di Martigana* is also mentioned in a note written in red chalk, MS. H² 65a. Leonardo has, as it seems, little to do with Lodovico il Moro's scheme to render this canal navigable. The canal had

in mol⁴ti paesi al seruitio de' prati; Ecco vn rime⁵dio, e questo è di fare molti fontanili, chè q⁶uell' acqua, che è bevuta dalla terra nō fa ser⁷uitio a nessuno, nè ancora danno, perchè a ⁸nessuno è tolta, e facēdo tali fontanili, l'acqua, ⁹che prima era perduta, ritorna di nouo a rifa¹⁰re seruitio e vtile alli omini.

over many districts for the irrigation of the fields. A remedy for this would be to make several little channels, since the water drunk up by the earth is of no more use to any one, nor mischief either, because it is taken from no one; and by making these channels the water which before was lost returns again and is once more serviceable and useful to men.

Leic. 18a]

Nessuno canale, che esca fori de' fiumi, sarà durabile, se l'acqua del fiume, donde ²nascie, non è integralmēte rinchiusa come il canal di Martisana quel ch'escie di Tesino.

1011

No canal which is fed by a river can be permanent if the river whence it originates is not wholly closed up, like the canal of Martesana which is fed by the Ticino.

C. A. 141b]

Dal principio del navilio al mo-²lino.
³Dal prīcipio del navilio di Briuio al ⁴molino del Travaglia è trabochi 2794, ⁵cioè · braccia 11176, che son più di 3 miglia ⁶e due terzi, e quiui truovo più alto il ⁷navilio che la pelle dell' acqua di Adda · braccia 57, ⁸a

1012

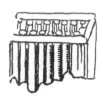

From the beginning of the canal to the mill.
From the beginning of the canal of Brivio to the mill of Travaglia is 2,794 trabochi, that is, 11,176 braccia, which is more than 3 miles and two-thirds; and here the canal is 57 braccia higher than the surface of the water of the

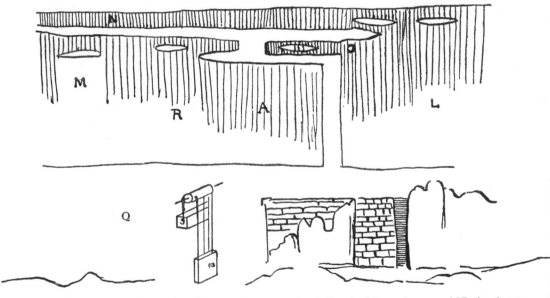

4. Ecci. 5. ecquesto . . checq. 6. beuta datta terra. 8. nessono ettolta effacēdo . . lacq"a". 9. primo. 10. omini E . *there the text breaks off.*
1011. 1. chanale . . essca . . sellacqua. 2. nasscie . . rinciusa . . martigana ecquel . . esscie .. tessino.
1012. 5. br. 11176. 6. ecqui. 7. chella . . dellacq"a" . . br. 57. 8. chalo .

been conceived by Bertola da Novate in 1457. Il Moro issued his decree in 1493, but Leonardo's notes about this canal were, with the exception of one (No. 1343), written about sixteen years later.

1012. The following are written on the sketches: At the place marked *N: navilio da dacquiue* (canal of running water); at *M: molin del Travaglia* (Mill of Travaglia); at *R: rochetta ssanta maria* (small rock of Santa Maria); at *A · Adda*; at *L: Lagho di Lecho*

ringorgato alli 3 corni in Adda,—Concha perpetua (lake of Lecco overflowing at Tre Corni in the Adda—a permanent sluice). Near the second sketch, referring to the sluice near *Q: qui la chatena ttalie d'ū peso* (here the chain is in one piece). At *M* in the lower sketch: *mol del travaglia, nel cavare la concha il tereno ara chōtrapeso cō cassa d'acqua* (Mill of Travaglia, in digging out the sluice the soil will have as a counterpoise a vessel of water).

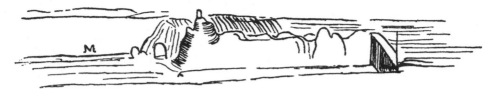

dare due ōcie di calo per ogni cēto trabochi, [9]e in tal sito disegniamo torre la bocha [10]del nostro navilio.

Adda, giving a fall of two inches in every hundred trabochi; and at that spot we propose to take the opening of our canal.

C. A. 236a]   1013

¶Se nō si dà fama che questo sia canale pu[2]blico, e' sarà necessario pagare il terreno, [3]e lo pagherà il rè col lasciare li dazi d'un āno.

If it be not reported there that this is to be a public canal, it will be necessary to pay for the land; and the king will pay it by remitting the taxes for a year.

C. A .211v]   1013 A

Navilio d'Ivrea, facto dal fiume della Doira; Montagnie d'Ivrea nella sua parte silvagia, produce di verso tramontana.

The canal of Ivrea fed by the river Dora; the mountains of Ivrea have a wild part, and a fertile one towards the north.

H.ª 91a]   1014

NAVILIO

[2]Jl navilio · che sia · largo in fōdo [3]braccia 16 · e in bocca · 20 ·, si potrà dire [4]in soma · tutto · largo braccia 18 ·, e se sarà [5]profondo · 4 · braccia ·, a 4 · dinari il quadretto ·, [6]costerà · il miglio · cavatura · sola [7]duc · 900 ·, essendo · i quadretti · di [8]comune · braccio, ma se le · braccia saranno [9]a vso · di misura · di terra ·, che ogni [10]4 · son 4 · e ½, e se il miglio s'i[11]tēde di tre mila braccia comuni, a tornar · [12]in braccia · di · terra · le sua 3000 · braccia tor[13]nano · māco ¼, che restano · braccia · [14]2250, che a 4 dinari il · braccio, mōta [15]il miglio ducati 675; a 3 dina[16]ri il quadretto mōta il miglio ducati [17]506¼, che la cavatura di 30 mi[18]glia di navilio mōta ducati 15187 · ½.

CANAL

The canal, which may be 16 braccia wide at the bottom and 20 at the top, we may say is on the average 18 braccia wide, and if it is 4 braccia deep, at 4 dinari the square braccia, it will only cost 900 ducats to excavate by the mile, if the square braccio is calculated in ordinary braccia; but if the braccia are those used in measuring land, of which every 4 are equal to 4½, and if by the mile we understand three thousand ordinary braccia; turned into land braccia, these 3,000 braccia will lack ¼; there remain 2,250 braccia, which at 4 dinari the braccio will amount to 675 ducats a mile. At 3 dinari the square braccio, the mile will amount to 506¼ ducats, so that the excavation of 30 miles of the canal will amount to 15,187½ ducats.

Estimates and preparatory studies for canals (1014-15).

Br. M. 149a]   1015

Per fare il grā [2]canale, fa prima [3]il piccolo e dalli [4]l'acqua, che colla [5]rota farà il grāde.

To make the great canal, first make the smaller one and conduct into it the waters, which by a wheel will help to fill the great one.

1013. 2. necesario. 3. ello pagera .. lidati.
1014. 2. chessia. 3. br. 16 .. boccha .. portra di. 4. tucto .. br. 18 essessara. 5. 4 br. a 4 . di. 6. chosstera. 7. quadrecti. 8. br. massellebr. sarano. 10. ⅓ M sseil. 11. mila br. 12. br. di .. comunitornar. 12. 3000 br. 13. restaño br. 14. il [br. 16. duc. 17. chella. 18. colasciare duc.
1015. 1-5 R. 3. picholo. 4. lachq"a" che cholla.

1013. 3. *il rè.* Louis XII or Francis I of France. The canals here spoken of were probably intended to be in the Milanese. Compare the draft of a letter to the *Presidente dell' Ufficio regolatore dell' acqua* on

No. 1350. See also the note to No. 745, l. 12.
1013 A. A drawing of a bridge and notes on the displacement of water are on the same page.

C. A. 73b]   **1016**

¶Poni il uero mezzo di Milano.¶   Indicate the centre of Milan.

Notes on buildings at Milan (1016–19). Mōforte—porta rēsa—porta nova—strada nova—navilio—porta cumana—barco—porta giovia—porta vercellina—porta sco Anbrogio—porta Tesinese—torre dell' Imperatore—porta Lodovica—acqua.

I.¹ 32b]   **1017**

A

Rifosso di Mila²no;   The moat of Milan.

³Canale ⁴largo 2 ⁵braccia;   Canal 2 braccia wide.

⁶Castello ⁷con fossi ingorgati;   The castle with the moats full.

⁸Ingorgatione ⁹de' fossi del ¹⁰castello di Milā.   The filling of the moats of the Castle of Milan.

I.¹ 34a]   **1018**

BAGNO   THE BATH

²Per iscaldare l'acqua della stufa della ³duchessa torrai 3 parti d'acqua cal⁴da sopra 4 parti d'acqua fredda.   To heat the water for the stove of the Duchess take four parts of cold water to three parts of hot water.

L. 15a]   **1019**

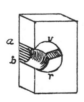
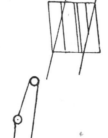

In domo alla carru-co²la del chiodo della croce;   In the Cathedral at the pulley of the nail of the cross.

³item.   Item.

⁴Da mettere il ⁵corpo *v r* ⁶pello . . . .   To place the mass *v r* through the . . . .

1016. 1. mezo;—barcho—tore delomperatore—porta lodovicha.
1018. 2. lacq"a". 3. torai . . parte dacq"a" chal. 4. dacq"a".
1019. 1. charucho. 2. ciodo. 6. pello s *here the text breaks off.*

1016. See Pl. CIX. The original sketch is reduced to about half its size. The gates are named, beginning on the right and following the curved line. Measurements are inserted. For a comparison between this map and one at Windsor (19115), see L. Beltrami, *Un altro contributo di L. d. V. alla cartografia Milanese*, Milan, 1918. In the bird's eye view of Milan below, the cathedral is in the middle; to the right is the tower of San Gottardo; on the left the buildings of the

Castello. On the margin of the Plan of Florence (see No. 1004, note) are the names of gates of Milan: Vercellina—Ticinese—Ludovica—Romana—Orientale—Nova—Beatrice—Cumana.—Compare too No. 1448, ll. 5, 12.

1018. *Duchessa di Milano*, Beatrice d'Este, wife of Lodovico il Moro, to whom she was married in 1491. She died in June 1497.

1019. The 'Santo chiodo', the nail believed to be

E. 1a]　　　　　　　　　　　　1020

DELLA POTENTIA DEL UACUO ²GIENERATO IN ISTĀTE	OF THE FORCE OF THE VACUUM FORMED IN A MOMENT

³Vidi a Milano v̄a saetta percuotere la ⁴torre della Credenza da quella parte ⁵che risguarda tramōtana e disciese ⁶con tardo moto per esso lato, e inmediate ⁷si divise da essa torre, e portò seco; ⁸e si ualse d'esso ⁹muro uno spa¹⁰tio di 3 braccia per o¹¹gniv̄o e pro¹²fondo due, e ¹³questo muro ¹⁴era grosso 4 braccia, ¹⁵ed era mura¹⁶to di sottili e ¹⁷minuti matto¹⁸ni antichi, ¹⁹e questo fu ti²⁰rato dal uacu²¹o, che la ²²fiāma della ²³saetta lasciò ²⁴di sé ecc.

I saw, at Milan, a thunderbolt fall on the tower della Credenza on its northern side, and it descended with a slow motion down that side, and then at once parted from that tower and carried with it and tore away from that wall a space of 3 braccia wide and two deep; and this wall was 4 braccia thick and was built of thin and small old bricks; and this was dragged out by the vacuum which the flame of the thunderbolt had caused, &c.

Leic. 28a]　　　　　　　　　　1021

Io sono già stato a vedere tal mvltiplicatione (di nuvole) e già ²sopra a Milano inverso lago Maggiore vidi vna nvuola in forma di grandissima mōtagnia, piena di scogli ³infocati, perchè li razzi del sole, che già era all' orizzonte che rosseggiava, la tigneano del suo colore, e questa tal nugola ⁴attraeva a sé tutti li nvgoli piccoli che intorno li stavano, e la nugola grāde nō si mouea di suo loco, anzi ri⁵seruò nella sua sommità il lume del sole insino a una ora e mezzo di notte, tant' era la sua immēsa grādezza; ⁶e infra due ore di notte gienerò si gran vēto che fu cosa stupēda e inavdita.

I have once seen such a conglomeration of clouds. And lately over Milan towards Lago Maggiore I saw a cloud in the form of an immense mountain full of rifts of glowing light, because the rays of the sun, which was already close to the horizon and red, tinged the cloud with their own hue. And this cloud attracted to it all the little clouds that were near while the large one did not move from its place; thus it retained on its summit the reflection of the sunlight till an hour and a half after sunset, so immensely large was it; and about two hours after sunset such a violent wind arose that it was really tremendous and unheard of.

Remarks on natural phenomena in and near Milan (1021–2).

W. 12416]　　　　　　　　　　1022

A dì 10 di diciembre a ore 15 ²fu appicato il fuoco;
³A dì 18 di dicembre 1511 a ore 15 fu fatto questo ⁴secondo incendio da Suizzeri a Milano ⁵al luogo detto DCXC.

On the 10th day of December at 9 o'clock a.m. fire was set to the place.
On the 18th day of December 1511 at 9 o'clock a.m. this second fire was kindled by the Swiss at Milan at the place called DCXC.

1020. 1. uachuo. 2. istāte. 3. perchotere. 4. dacquella. 5. rissghuarda mōtana e dissciesse. 7. torre e porto chonsecho. 8. essiulse. 10. 3. br. 13. cquesto. 14. 4 br. 18. antichi ec. 19. ecquessto. 20. uachu. 21. chella. 23. lasscio.
1021. 1. mvltiplicatione e ga. 2. magore .. mōtaggnia .. scoli. 3. infochati .. razi .. ga .. orizonte .. rossegaua .. ecquesta. 4. asse .. picholi .. locho. 5. somita .. mezo .. imēsu grādeza. 6. stupēte inavldita.
1022. 1–5 (R). 2. apicato .. fuocho. 3. Lore. 4. suizeri. 5. alloguo dicto.

of the cross, one of the precious relics of Milan Cathedral, kept in the vaulting of the nave. Leonardo supplied a device for lowering it on special occasions (see Ramussi, *Il Duomo di Milano*, Milano, 1927, p. 72). Compare Amoretti, *Memorie Storiche*, chap. ix: 'Nell' anno stesso lo veggiamo formare un congegno di carucole e di corde, con cui trasportare in più venerabile e più sicuro luogo, cioè nell' ultima arcata della nave di mezzo della metropolitana, la sacra reliquia del Santo Chiodo, che ivi ancor si venera. Al fol. 15 del codice segnato Q. R. in 16, egli ci ha lasciata di tal congegno una doppia figura, cioè una di quattro carucole, e una di tre colle rispettive corde, soggiugnendovi: in Domo alla carucola del Chiodo della Croce.'

1020. 4. Torre di Credenza, so called because it was at the head-quarters of the Credenza di Sant' Ambrogio, a governing body founded in 1198, is no longer in existence. See G. Giulini, *Memorie di Milano*, 1760, vol. vii, p. 140 f., for a detailed account. The sketch-map of the town of Milan on Pl. CIX contains probably a view of it. (Comp. No. 1046, n.).

1021. *di nuvole* is wanting in the original but may safely be inserted in the context, as the formation of clouds is under discussion before this text.

1022. With these two texts (ll. 1–2 and ll. 3–5 are in the original side by side) there are sketches of smoke wreaths in red chalk. The handwriting is perhaps not by Leonardo (cf. Kenneth Clark, *Catalogue*, p. 55).

B. 58a]

1023

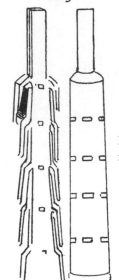

Note on Pavia.

Camini del castello di Pauia, ²àño 6 gradi di busi; è dall' uno ³all' altro uno braccio.

The chimneys of the castle of Pavia have 6 rows of openings and from each to the other is one braccio.

H.² 65b]

1024

Notes on the Sforzesca near Vigevano (1024–8).

A dì 2 di febraro 1494 alla ²Sforzesca ritrassi scalini 25 ³di ⅔ di braccio l'uno, larghe braccia 8.

On the 2nd day of February 1494. At the Sforzesca I drew twenty-five steps, ⅔ braccia to each, and 8 braccia wide.

H.¹ 38a]

1025

Vignie di Vigevano ²a dì 20 di marzo 1494.

The vineyards of Vigevano on the 20th day of March 1494.

H.¹ 1a]

1026

Da serrare in chiave vno · īcastro ²a Vigevano.

To lock up a casing at Vigevano.

Leic. 21a]

1027

Ancora se la infima parte dell' argine trauersalmēte opposto al cor²so delle acque sarà fatto in potenti e larghi gradi a uso di scala, l'acque ³che nell' abassamento del lor corso sogliono perpendicularmente cadere dal ter⁴mine di tale loco in infima sua bassezza e scalzare i fondamēti d'esso argine, non po⁵tran più discendere con colpo di troppa valitudine; e lo esenpio dico fu a me quella ⁶scala, onde cadea l'acqua de' prati della Sforzesca di Vigeuano, sulla quale ui cadea ⁷l'acqua corrēte in 50 braccia d'altezza.

Again, if the lowest part of the bank which lies across the current of the waters is made in deep and wide steps, after the manner of stairs, the waters which in their course usually fall perpendicularly from the top of such a place to the bottom, and wear away the foundations of this bank, can no longer descend with a blow of too great a force; and I found the example of this in the stairs down which the water falls in the fields at Sforzesca at Vigevano, over which the running water falls for a height of 50 braccia.

1023. 2. buse. 3. ł br.
1024. 1–3 R. 1. allas. 2. sforzesscha . . schalini. 3. di br . . large br.
1025. 1–2 R. 1. vigievine.
1026. 1–2 R. 1. asserare. 2. avigievine.
1027. 1. sella pare . . oposto.   2. fatti . . ellarghi . . disscala lacqua.   3. delor . . soglian . . chadere.   4. tale infima . . basseza e dissalzare . . desse.   5. dissciendere . . tropa . . ello . . foame colla.   6. pradi . . sforzessca di uigieuine la qual ui cadea su.   7. corēte . . br. daltezza.

1024. See Pl. CX, No. 2. The rest of the notes on this page refer to the motion of water. On the lower sketch we read: 4 *br.* (four braccia) and *giara* (for *ghiaja*, sand, gravel).

1025. On one side there is an effaced sketch in red chalk.

Leic. 32a]   1028

Scala di Vigevano ²sotto la Sforzesca di 130 ³scaglioni, alti ¼ e lar⁴ghi ½ braccio, per la qual ⁵cade l'acqua e non ⁶con-suma niēte nell' ul⁷tima percus-sione, e per ⁸tale scala è disceso ⁹tanto terreno che a¹⁰sseccò vn padule, cio¹¹è riempì, e se n'è fat¹²to praterie da padu¹³le di grā profondità.

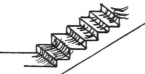

Stair of Vigevano below La Sforzesca, 130 steps, ¼ braccio high and ½ braccio wide, down which the water falls, so as not to wear away anything at the end of its fall; by these steps so much soil has come down that it has dried up a pool; that is to say, it has filled it up and a pool of great depth has been turned into meadows.

Leic. 11b]   1029

Come in molti lochi si trovano ve²ne d'acqua che sei ore crescono e sei ore calano, e io per me n'ò veduto vna in sul lago di Como, detta fonte Pli³niana, la quale fa il predetto crescere e diminuire in modo che, quando uersa, macina due mulini, e quãdo māca, ⁴cala sì ch'egli è come guardare l'acqua in vn profondo pozzo.

In many places there are streams of water which swell for six hours and ebb for six hours; and I, for my part, have seen one above the Lake of Como called Fonte Pliniana, which increases and ebbs, as I have said, in such a way as to turn the stones of two mills when it pours; and when it fails it falls so low that it is like looking at water in a deep pit.

Notes on the North Italian lakes (1029–33).

C. A. 214a]   1030

LAGO DI COMO · ²VAL DI CHIAUENNA

³Sù pel lago di Como, diuerso la Magnia, è valle Chiauenna doue la Mera fiume mette in esso ⁴lago; qui si truovano mõtagnie · sterili e altissime · con grādi scogli ·; ĵ queste mõtagnie ⁵li uccielli · d'acqua sono detti maragoni; qui nascono abeti, larici e pini ·, daini, stābecchi, camoz⁶zi · e terribili · orsi ·; nõ ci si può mõtare ·, se non è a 4 piedi ·; vannoci · i villani a' tēpo delle ⁷nevi cõ grādi · ingegni · per fare traboccare gli orsi giv · per esse · ripe; queste ⁸mõtagnie strette mettono in mezzo · il fiume ·, sono a destra e a sinistra per spatio ⁹di miglia 20 · tutte a detto modo ·; truovāsi di miglio in miglio bone · osterie ·; su¹⁰per detto fiume · si truovano · cadute · d'acqua di 400 braccia, le quale fanno bel vedere; ¹¹e c'è bõ uiuere · a 4 soldi per scotto ·; per esso fiume si cõduce assai · legniame.

LAKE OF COMO. VALLEY OF CHIAVENNA

Above the Lake of Como towards Germany is the valley of Chiavenna where the river Mera flows into this lake. Here are barren and very high mountains with huge rocks. Among these mountains are to be found the water-birds called gulls. Here grow fir-trees, larches, and pines; deer, wild goats, chamois, and terrible bears. It is impossible to climb them without using hands and feet. The peasants go there at the time of the snows with great devices to make the bears fall down these rocks. These mountains, which very closely approach each other, are parted by the river. They are to the right and left for the distance of 20 miles throughout of the same nature. From mile to mile there are good inns. Above on the said river there are waterfalls of 400 braccia in height, which are fine to see; and there is good living at 4 soldi the reckoning. This river brings down a great deal of timber.

VAL SASINA

¹³Val Sasina · viene diuerso · la Italia ·; questa è quasi di simile forma e natura; ¹⁴nascie vi assai mappello ·, e ci sono grā ruine e cadute d'acque.

VAL SASINA

Val Sasina runs down towards Italy; this is almost the same form and character. There grow here many *mappello* and there are great ruins and falls of water.

1028. 1. schala di uigeuine. 2. sforzessa di [100] 130. 3. ellar. 4. ½ br .. 5. chade. 7. perchussione. 8. dissceso. 10. secho .. co. 11. rienpivto essene. 12. di padu.

1029. 1. imolti .. trova. 2. cresscano essei .. chalano .. veduta .. sulago di chomo .. fonte pri. 3. cresciere macina piv mulina .. mācha. 4. chalisi .. lacqua non .. pozo.

1030. 2. ciauenna. 3. super .. diuer .. ciauenna .. "fiume" mette. 4. truova mõtagni .. chon. 5. dacqua dette .. nasscie .. larice eppini .. stā buche chamo. 6. ze .. teribili .. po .. delli. 7. chõ grāde ingiēgni .. trabochare. 8. metano .. mezo .. desstra e assinistra .. isspatio. 9. imiglio. 10. truova chadute .. br. le quale. 11. uci bõ .. ischotto per ess .. chõduce. 14. nasscievi .. ecci grā .. ecchadute.

1029. 2. Leonardo can hardly have known what Pliny the Elder wrote: 'In Comensi juxta Larium lacum fons largus horis singulis semper intumescit ac residet' (*Nat. Hist.* ii. 232). Pliny the Younger in a letter to a friend, a scientist, gives a detailed descrip-tion of the phenomenon and asks for an explana-tion of the miracle—'tantum miraculum' (*Ep.* iv. 30). His description, however, differs essentially from that of Leonardo.—The Villa Pliniana is near Torno on the eastern shore. Compare No. 1031.

VALLE D'INTROZZO

¹⁶Questa valle · produce assai abeti pini e larici ·, è doue Anbrogio Fereri fa ¹⁷venire · il suo legniame ·; in testa · della Valtellina sono le mōtagnie di Bormio, ¹⁸terribili · e piene sēpre di neve; qui nascono ermellini.

A BELLAGGIO

²⁰A riscontro · a Bellaggio · castello è il fiume Latte ·, el quale · cade da alto ²¹piv che braccia · 100 dalla vena ·, donde nascie, a piōbo nel lago · cō inestimabile strepito ²²e romore ·; questa vena versa solamēte agosto e settēbre.

VALTELLINA

²⁴Valtellina ·, com' è detto, valle circūdata d'alti e terribili · mōti, fa ²⁵vini potēti · e assai ·, e fa tanto bestiame · che da paesani · è concluso · nascierui ²⁶piv latte che uino ·; questa è la ualle · doue passa Adda, la quale prima corre ²⁷piv che 40 miglia per la Magnia ·; questo fiume fa il pescie temolo, il quale ²⁸vive d'argiēto ·, del quale · se ne truova · assai per la sua rena; ²⁹j̄ questo paese ognivno · può vēdere pane · e vino, e 'l uino vale al piv uno soldo ³⁰il boccale · e la libbra della uitella uno soldo, e 'l sale 10 dinari, e 'l simile il burro, ³¹ed è la loro libbra 30 ōcie e l'oua uno soldo la soldata.

VALLEY OF INTROZZO

This valley produces a great quantity of firs, pines, and larches; and from here Ambrogio Fereri has his timber brought down; at the head of the Valtellina are the mountains of Bormio, terrible and always covered with snow; marmots (?) are found there.

BELLAGGIO

Opposite the castle Bellaggio there is the river Latte, which falls from a height of more than 100 braccia from the source whence it springs, perpendicularly, into the lake with an inconceivable roar and noise. This spring flows only in August and September.

VALTELLINA

Valtellina, as it is called, is a valley enclosed in high and terrible mountains; it produces much strong wine, and there is so much cattle that the natives conclude that more milk than wine grows there. This is the valley through which the Adda passes, which first runs more than 40 miles through Germany; this river breeds the fish *temolo* which live on silver, of which much is to be found in its sands. In this country every one can sell bread and wine, and the wine is worth at most one soldo the bottle and a pound of veal one soldo, and salt ten dinari and butter the same, and their pound is 30 ounces, and eggs are one soldo the lot.

C. A. 214*b*]   1031

A BORMIO

²A Bormio sono · i bagni ·;—sopra Como otto miglia · è la Pliniana, ³la quale · crescie e discrescie ogni 6 · ore, e 'l suo crescire fa ⁴acqua per 2 mvlina e n'avanza, e 'l suo calare fa asciugare la fonte; ⁵più su 2 miglia · è Nesso · terra, dove cade uno fiume cō grāde ⁶enpito per una grādissima fessura di mōte ·; Queste gite sō da ⁷fare nel mese di maggio; E i maggior sassi scoperti che si truovano ⁸in questi paesi · sono le mōtagnie di Mādello, vicine alle mō- tagnie di ⁹Lecco e di Gravidona inverso Bellin- zona, a 30 miglia da Lecco, ¹⁰e quelle di ualle Chiavenna ·, ma la maggiore è quella di Mā- dello, ¹¹la quale · à nella · sua basa vna buca diuerso il lago, la quale va sotto ¹²200 scalini ·, e qui d'ogni tēpo è ghiaccio · e vēto.

AT BORMIO

At Bormio are the baths;—about eight miles above Como is the Pliniana, which increases and ebbs every six hours, and its swell supplies water for two mills; and its ebbing makes the spring dry up; two miles higher up there is Nesso, a place where a river falls with great violence into a vast rift in the mountain. These excursions are to be made in the month of May. And the largest bare rocks that are to be found in this part of the country are the mountains of Man- dello near to those of Lecco, and of Gravidona towards Bellinzona, 30 miles from Lecco, and those of the valley of Chiavenna; but the largest of all is that of Mandello, which has at its base an opening towards the lake, which goes down 200 steps, and there at all times is ice and wind.

15. valle ditrozzo. 16. ellarici. 17. tessta .. Voltolina elle .. leorme. 18. sepre .. nascie. 19. abbellagio. 20. arischontro abbel- lagio . chastello .. fiume lacci"o" el. 21. nascie a piōbo ne gallo chō inistimabile strepido. 22. erromore. 23. valtolina. 24. chome .. circhūdata .. etteribili. 25. vni .. effa .. besstiame .. paessani .. nasscier ui. 26. ella .. ada .. chore. 27. pesscio temere il. 29. po .. ī soldo. 30. bochale ella .. ī soldo ell .. burlo. 31. lbra .. elloua.
1031. abormi. 2. abormi .. ella priniana. 3. cresscie e disseresscie ōgni .. cresscire. 4. assciugare. 5. piussu .. tera .. ī fiume chō 7. del .. magio .. magior .. schoperti chessi truovno. 8. visine. 9. leche e di gravidonia .. mglia allecho. 10. ecquelle .. ciavenna malla magiore ecquella. 11. busa. 12. schalini .. diaccio.

1031. Compare No. 1029.

IN VALSASINA

[14]İ Valsasina infra · Vimognio et · Introbbio ·, a man destra entrādo per uia di [15]Lecco, si trova la Troggia fiume ·, che cade da uno sasso · altissimo e cadēdo entra [16]sotto terra · e lì finisce · il fiume ·; 3 · miglia · piv là si truovano li edifiti [17]della · vena · del rame · e dello argēto ·, presso a una terra · detta Prato Santo Pietro, [18]e vene di ferro, e cose fantastiche ·; la Grignia è piv alta · mōtagnia ch'abbino [19]questi paesi ed è pelata.

IN VAL SASINA

In Val Sasina, between Vimognio and Introbbio, to the right hand, going in by the road to Lecco, is the river Troggia which falls from a very high rock, and as it falls it goes underground and the river ends there. 3 miles farther we find the buildings of the mines of copper and silver near a place called Pra' Santo Pietro, and mines of iron and curious things. La Grigna is the highest mountain there is in this part, and it is quite bare.

C. A. 275a]   1032

Il lago di Pusiano [2]versa in nel lago [3]di Alserio e d'Annone [4]e di Sala; [5]Il lago d'Anōne ha 22 braccia più alta la pelle [6]della sua acqua che la pelle dell' acqua [7]del lago di Lecco, e 20 braccia è più alto [8]il lago di Pusiano che 'l lago d'Añone, [9]le quali, giūte colle braccia 22 dette, fan braccia 42, [10]e quest è la maggiore altezza che abbia la pe[11]lle del lago di Pusiā sopra la pelle del la[12]go di Lecco.

The lake of Pusiano flows into the lake of Alserio and of Annone and of Sala. The lake of Annone is 22 braccia higher at the surface of its water than the surface of the water of the lake of Lecco, and the lake of Pusiano is 20 braccia higher than the lake of Annone, which added to the aforesaid 22 braccia make 42 braccia, and this is the greatest height of the surface of the lake of Pusiano above the surface of the lake of Lecco.

G. 1a]   1033

A Santa Maria Hoé nella valle [2]di Rovagnate ne' mōti Briātia sō le pertiche [3]di castagne di 9 braccia e di 14 l'u[4]no in 100.

[5]A Varallo di Ponbia presso a Sesto [6]sopra Tesino sono li cotogni biāchi grā[7]di e duri.

At Santa Maria Hoé in the Valley of Rovagnate in the mountains of Brianza are the rods of chestnuts of 9 braccia, and one out of an average of 100 will be 14 braccia.

At Varallo di Pombia near to Sesto on the Ticino the quinces are white, large, and hard.

L. 6a]   1034

Colōbaia a Urbino a dì 30 [2]di luglio 1502.

Pigeon-house at Urbino, the 30th day of July 1502.

Notes on places in Central Italy, visited in 1502 (1034–54).

L. 6b]   1035

Fatta al mare di Piōbino.

Made by the sea at Piombino.

---

14. ualsasina ifra . . desstra. 15. leccho . . trosa . . chade . . da ĩ . . chadēdo. 16. elli finissce . . pivlla si truova. 17. arzēto . . prascto petro. 18. fero . . chabbi. 19. edie.
1032. 1. ilago di pusiā. 2. inel lagho. 3. di serio e danō. 5. lagho danō . . br . . alto. 6. chella. 7. lagho . . br. eppiu. 8. he il lagho. 8. pustā . . danō br. 20. 9. gute . . br. 22 . . br. 42. 10. ecqueste la magore alteza . . la pel . . Pusiā. 12. gho di lecho.
1033. 1. maria \\\\ o nella. 2. di ranvagnā . . briātia. 3. 9 br. e di 14 [et] 7 (?) lu. 4. re (? = no)in 100 di 9 br. 5. a voral di ponbio presso assesto. 6. licotani. 7. edduri.
1034. 1. du vrbino. 2. luglio 1402.

1032. This text has in the original a sketch to illustrate it.

1033. 2. *Rovagnate* in the Brianza is between Oggiono and Brivio, south of the Lake of Lecco.

5. Varallo di Pombia, about nine miles south of Sesto Calende.

1034. An indistinct sketch is introduced with this text, in the original, in which the word *Scolatoro* (conduit) is written.

1035. Below the sketch there are eleven lines of text referring to the motion of waves.

L. 10*b*]

1036

Acquapendente è a Oruieto.

Acquapendente is near Orvieto.

L. 15*b*]

1037

Rocca di Cesena.

The rock of Cesena.

L. 19*b*]

1038

Siena ^2a b braccia ^{34}, ^4a c braccia ^{510}; ^{6}Scale d'Urbino.

Siena, a b 4 braccia, a c 10 braccia. Steps at [the castle of] Urbino.

L. 33*b*]

1039

Campana · di Siena, cioè ^{2}il modo del suo moto ^{3}e sito della dinodatura ^{4}del battaglio suo.

The bell of Siena, that is, the manner of its movement, and the place of the attachment of the clapper.

L. 36*b*]

1040

El dì di Sāta Maria mezz' agosto ^{2}a Cesena 1502.

On St. Mary's day in the middle of August, at Cesena, 1502.

L. 40*a*]

1041

Scale del cōte d'Urbino, saluatiche.

Stairs of the [palace of the] Count of Urbino —rough.

L. 46*b*]

1042

Alla fiera di Scō ^{2}Lorenzo a Cesena, ^{3}1502.

At the fair of San Lorenzo at Cesena, 1502.

L. 47*a*]

1043

Finestre da Cesena.

Windows at Cesena.

L. 66*b*]

1044

Porto Cesenatico a dì 6 di set^{2}tenbre 1502, a ore 15;
^{3}In che modo debbono ^{4}uscire bastioni fori delle ^{5}mura delle terre per potere ^{6}difendere l'argini di fori, ^{7}aciò nō sieno battuti coll' artiglieria.

At Porto Cesenatico, on the 6th of September, 1502, at 9 o'clock a.m.
The way in which bastions ought to project beyond the walls of earth to defend the outer talus; so that they may not be beaten by artillery.

L. 67*a*]

1045

La rocca del porto di Cesena sta a Ce^{2}sena per la 4^a di libeccio.

The fort of the harbour of Cesena is four points towards the south-west from Cesena.

L. 72*a*]

1046

In Romagnia, capo d'ogni grossezza ^{2}d'ingegno, vsano i carri di 4 rote, de qua^{3}li ○ n'àño 2 dinanzi basse e due alte ^{4}dirieto, la qual cosa è in gran dis^{5}fauore di moto, perchè in sulle ^{6}rote dinanzi si scarica piv peso, che ^{7}in su quelle dirieto, come mostrai ^{8}nella prima del 5° delli elemēti.

In Romagna, the realm of all stupidity, vehicles with four wheels are used, of which ○ the two in front are small and two high ones are behind; an arrangement which is very unfavourable to the motion, because on the fore wheels more weight is discharged than on those behind, as I showed in the first of the 5th on 'Elements'.

1036. Aquapendente. **1037.** rocha. **1038.** 2. br. 3. br. **1039.** 1. coe. 3. essito. **1040.** 1. mezagossto. 2. [4] 502.
1044. 4. vsscire basstioni. **1045.** 1. rocha. 2. pla . . libecco. **1046.** 1. grosseza. 2. rote equa. 7. mostai.

1038. See Pl. CX, No. 3; compare also No. 765.
1039. The text is accompanied by an indistinct sketch.
1040. See Pl. CX, No. 4.
1041. The text is accompanied by a slight sketch.

1043. There are four more lines of text which refer to a slightly sketched diagram.
1044. An indistinct sketch accompanies this passage.

L. 77a]   1047

Uve portate ²a Ciesena;	Thus grapes are carried at Cesena.
³Il numero de' cavatori ⁴de' fossi è piramidale.	The number of the diggers of the ditches is [arranged] pyramidically.

L. 78a]   1048

¶Fassi vn armonia colle diuerse cadute ²d'acqua, come vedesti alla fonte di ³Rimini; come vedesti a dì 8 d'agosto ⁴1502.¶

There might be a harmony of the different falls of water as you saw them at the fountain of Rimini on the 8th day of August, 1502.

L. 78b]   1049

Fortezza d'Urbino.   The fortress at Urbino.

L. 88b]   1050

Imola vede Bologna a ⅝ di ponente inverso ²maestro con ispatio di 20 miglia;

³Castel San Piero è ueduto da Imola in ¼ ⁴infra ponente e maestro · con ispatio di ⁵7 miglia;

⁶Faenza sta con Imola tra leuãte e scirocco ⁷in mezzo giusto a 10 miglia di spatio; ⁸Forlì sta cõ Faenza infra scirocco e levã⁹te in mezzo giusto con ispatio di 25 miglia ¹⁰da Imola e 10 da Faēza;

¹¹Forlimpopoli fa il simile a 25 mi¹²glia da Imola;

¹³Bertinoro sta con Imola a ⅝ infra levã¹⁴te e scirocco a 27 miglia.

Imola, as regards Bologna, is five points from the west, towards the north-west, at a distance of 20 miles.

Castel San Piero is seen from Imola at four points from the west towards the north-west, at a distance of 7 miles.

Faenza stands with regard to Imola exactly between east and south-east at a distance of ten miles. Forlì stands with regard to Faenza exactly between south-east and east at a distance of 25 miles from Imola and 10 from Faenza.

Forlimpopoli lies in the same direction at 25 miles from Imola.

Bertinoro, as regards Imola, is five points from the east towards the south-east, at 27 miles.

W. 12284]   1051

Imola uede Bologna a ⅝ di po²nente · inuerso maestro con di³stantia · di miglia · 20;

⁴Castel · San Piero · è veduto · da Imo⁵la in mezzo infra ponente e mae⁶stro · in distantia di miglia · 7.

Imola as regards Bologna is five points from the west towards the north-west at a distance of 20 miles.

Castel San Pietro lies exactly north-west of Imola, at a distance of 7 miles.

1047. 1. vue.   1048. 1. chadute. 3. addi.   1049. forteza.
1050. 1. inver. 2. maesstro conisspatio .. migla. 4. maesstro. 6. faenta .. esscirocho. 7. mezo gùsto .. disspatio. 8. furli .. scirocho alleuã. 9. mezo gussto. 11. furinpopoli. 13. bertonora. 14. esscirocho.
1051. *written from left to right.* 1. blogna. 2. inuer maesstro con dis. 4. Chastel. 5. mezo .. emaes. 6. indisstantia .. migla.

1047. A sketch, representing a hook on which two bunches of grapes are hanging, refers to these first two lines. Cesena is mentioned again, Fol. 82a: *Carro da Cesena* (a cart from Cesena).

1049. In the original the text is written inside the sketch in the place here marked *n*.

1051. Leonardo inserted this passage on the margin of the circular plan, in water-colour, of Imola—see Pl. CXI, No. 1.—In the original the fields surrounding the town are light green; the moat, which surrounds the fortifications, and the windings of the river Santerno are light blue. The parts close to the river

II   C C

[7]Faenza · è veduto da Imola infra leuante [8]e scirocco in mezzo apunto in distantia [9]di migla · 10, e 'l simile fa · Forlì con Imo[10]la con distantia di miglia · 20, e Forlimpo[11]poli · fa il simile con Forlì con distantia di [12]miglia 25;

[13]Bertinoro si uede da Imola a ⅜ di leuante [14]inverso scirocco con distantia di 27 miglia.

Faenza as regards Imola lies exactly half-way between the east and south-east at a distance of 10 miles; and Forlì lies in the same direction from Imola at a distance of 20 miles; and Forlimpopolo lies in the same direction from Forlì at a distance of 25 miles.

Bertinoro is seen from Imola two points from the east towards the south-east at a distance of 27 miles.

L. 94b]   **1052**

Da Bōcon[2]vento alla [3]Casa Nova [4]miglia 10, [5]dalla Casa No[6]va a Chiusi [7]miglia · 9 ·, [8]da Chiusi a Pe[9]rugia miglia 12[10]da Peru[11]gia a Santa [12]Maria degli [13]Angeli, e poi [14]a Fuligno.

From Bonconvento to Casa Nova are 10 miles, from Casa Nova to Chiusi 9 miles, from Chiusi to Perugia, 12 miles from Perugia to Santa Maria degli Angeli, and then to Fuligno.

L. 0″]   **1053**

Dì primo d'agosto 1502 [2]in Pesaro la libreria.

On the first of August 1502, the library at Pesaro.

L. 21a]   **1054**

PICTURA

[2]Scorta sulle sommità e in su' lati [3]de' colli le figure de' terreni e le sue [4]diuisioni, e nelle cose uolte a te [5]fale in propria forma.

OF PAINTING

On the tops and sides of hills foreshorten the shape of the ground and its divisions, but give its proper shape to what is turned towards you.

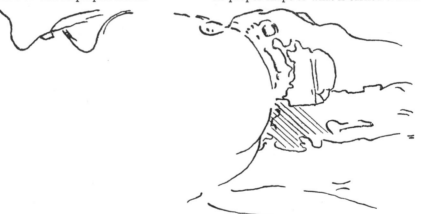

7. veduta. 8. esscirrocho in mezo appunto in disstantia. 9. furli. 10. chon disstantia di migla . . furlinpo. 11. furli . . disstantia. 12. migla. 13. Bernotoro. 14. inver scilocho . . disstantia . . migla.
1052. 1. bōchon. 8. aper. 11. assanta.   **1053.** 1. di p"o".   **1054.** 3. essue. 4. atte. 5. falle.

are yellow ochre. The dark groups of houses inside the town are red. At the four points of the compass drawn in the middle of the town Leonardo has written (from right to left): *Mezzodì* (south) at the top; to the left *Scirocho* (south-east), *Levante* (east), *Greco* (north-east), *Septantrione* (north), *Maesstro* (north-west), *Ponente* (west), *Libecco* (south-west). The circle in which the plan is drawn is, in the original, 42 centimetres across.

At the beginning of October 1502 Cesare Borgia was shut up in Imola by a sudden revolt of the Condottieri, and it was some weeks before he could release himself from this state of siege (see Gregorovius, *Geschichte der Stadt Rom im Mittelalter*, vol. vii, book xiii. 5. 5).

Besides this incident Imola plays no important part in the history of the time. I therefore think myself justified in connecting this map with the siege of 1502 and with Leonardo's engagements in the service of Cesare Borgia; a comparison of texts Nos. 1050 and 1051 raises the hypothesis to a certainty. Compare K. Clark, *Windsor Catalogue* and Mario Baratta, *La pianta d'Imola di L. d. V.*, Bollettino della Società Geografica Italiana, Rome, 1911, pp. 945–67.

1052. Most of the places here described lie within the district shown in the maps on Pl. CXIII.

1054. This passage evidently refers to the making of maps, such as Pl. CXII, CXIII, and CXIV.

By the side of this text we find, in the original, a very indistinct sketch, perhaps a plan of a position. Instead of this drawing I have here inserted a much clearer sketch of a position from the same MS., L. 82b and 83a. They are the only drawings of landscape, it may be noted, which occur at all in that MS.

Leic. 9b]   **1055**

In Candia di Lonbardia · presso Alessandria della Paglia, facendosi per ²messer Gualtieri di Candia vno pozzo, fu trovato vno principio di navilio grandissimo sotto terra, circa a braccia 10, e perchè ³il legname era nero e bello, parue a esso messer Gualtieri di fare allungare tal bocca di pozzo in forma che i termini ⁴di tal navilio si scoprissino.

At Candia in Lombardy, near Alessandria della Paglia, in making a well for Messer Gualtieri of Candia, the skeleton of a very large boat was found about 10 braccia underground; and as the timber was black and fine, it seemed good to the said Messer Gualtieri to have the mouth of the well lengthened in such a way that the ends of the boat should be uncovered.

Alessandria in Piedmont (1055-6).

Leic. 10b]   **1056**

Alessandria della Paglia in Lombardia non à altre pietre ²da far calcina, se nō miste con infinite cose nate in mare, la quale oggi è remota dal mare piv di 200 miglia.

At Alessandria della Paglia in Lombardy there are no stones for making lime of, but such as are mixed up with an infinite variety of things native to the sea, which is now more than 200 miles away.

G. 1b]   **1057**

Monbracco, sopra Saluzzo — ²sopra la Certosa vn miglo, al piè di mō Viso — ³à vna miniera di pietra ⁴faldata, la quale è biāca ⁵come marmo di Carrara, sanza ⁶macvle, ch'è della durez⁷za del porfido o più; ⁸della quale il conpare ⁹mio, maestro Benedet¹⁰to scultore, à in pro¹¹messo mandarmene una ¹²tavoletta per li colori, ¹³a di 2 di genaro 1511.

At Monbracco, above Saluzzo—a mile above the Certosa, at the foot of Monte Viso, there is a quarry of flaky stone, which is as white as Carrara marble, without a spot, and as hard as porphyry or even harder; of which my friend Master Benedetto the sculptor has promised to send me a small slab, for the colours, the 2nd day of January 1511.

The Alps (1057-62).

Leic. 11b]   **1058**

Come son uene che per terremoti o altri accidenti subito nasco²no e subito mācano; E questo accade in vna mōtagnia in Sauoia, doue certi boschi sprofondarono e lasciarono vno ³baratro profondissimo · e lontano circa 4 miglia di lì s'aperse il terreno in certa spiaggia di mōte, e gittò vna ⁴subita inōdatione grossissima d'acqua, la quale nettò tutta vna vallata di terreni lauoratiui, vignie e case, e fece ⁵grādissimo danno ovunque discorse.

That there are springs which suddenly break forth in earthquakes or other convulsions and suddenly fail; and this happened in a mountain in Savoy where certain forests sank in and left a very deep gap, and about four miles from here the earth opened itself like a gulf in the mountain, and threw out a sudden and immense flood of water which scoured the whole of a little valley of the tilled soil, vineyards, and houses, and did the greatest mischief, wherever it overflowed.

C. A. 87b]   **1059**

Riuiera d'Arua presso a Ginevra 2¼ di miglio in Sauoia, doue si fa la fiera ³in San Giovanni nel uillaggio di San Gervagio.

The river Arve, a quarter of a mile from Geneva in Savoy, where the fair is held on midsummer day in the village of Saint Gervais.

1055. 2. pozo . . circha a br. 3. ebbello . . meser . . bocha di pozo. 4. navili si scoprissi.
1056. Alesandria . . illonbardia. 2. mista . . il quale.
1057. *Lines* 1, 3–13 R. 1. monbracho . . saluzo. 2. a pie . . uiso. 4. biācha. 5. carra"ra"sa. 6. machvle . . dure. 7. obpiu. 8. delle quali. 9. maesstro benedec. 11. messo madarmene.
1058. 1. nasca. 2. essubito . . Ecquesto acade nvna . . bosci profondorono ellasciorono. 3. baladro . . circha . . spiagga. 4. terē . . effece. 5. ovunche.
1059. 2. miglo. 3. batte in san govanni . . uilago . . cervagio.

1055. Candia, now Candia Lomellina, situated between Alessandria and Vercelli.

2. *Messer Gualtieri*, the same probably as is mentioned in Nos. 672 and 1344.

1057. 9, 10. *Maestro Benedetto scultore*: probably

Benedetto Briosco of Pavia.

1059. An indistinct sketch is to be seen by the text. Town and country of Geneva became Swiss after Leonardo's time. St. Gervais, now St. Gervais les Bains, is at the foot of the Mont Blanc.

Leic. 4a]   1060

E questo vedrà come vid' io, chi ādrà so²pra Mōboso, giogo dell' Alpi che diuidono la Francia dalla Italia, la qual montagnia a la sua basa che parturisce ³li 4 fiumi che rigā per 4 aspetti contrari tutta l'Europa, e nessuna montagnia à le sue base in simile al⁴tezza; questa si leua in tanta altura che quasi passa tutti li nuuoli e rare volte vi cade neve, ma sol grādi⁵ne d'istate quando li nvvoli sono nella maggiore altezza, e questa grandine vi si cōserua in modo, che se nō ⁶fusse la (ra)retà del caderui e del montarui nvuoli, che non accade 2 volte in vna estate, egli ui sarebbe altissima quātità di ghiaccio inalzato da li gradi della grādine, il qua⁷le di mezzo luglio vi trouai grossissimo ·, e vidi l'aria sopra di me tenebrosa e 'l sole che percotea la mōta⁸gnia essere piv luminoso quiui assai che nelle basse pianure, perchè minor grossezza d'aria s'interpone in⁹fra la cima d'esso monte e 'l sole.

And this may be seen, as I saw it, by any one going up [5] Monbroso, a peak of the Alps which divide France from Italy. The base of this mountain gives birth to the 4 rivers which flow in four different directions through the whole of Europe. And no mountain has its base at so great a height as this, which lifts itself above almost all the clouds; and snow seldom falls there, but only hail in the summer, when the clouds are highest. And this hail lies [unmelted] there, so that if it were not for the absorption of the rising and falling clouds, which does not happen twice in a life-time, an enormous mass of ice would be piled up there by the layers of hail, and in the middle of July I found it very considerable; and I saw the sky above me quite dark, and the sun as it fell on the mountain was far brighter here than in the plains below, because a smaller extent of atmosphere lay between the summit of the mountain and the sun.

Leic. 9b]   1061

Truouasi nelle montagnie di Verona la sua pietra rossa mista tutta di nichi convertiti ²in essa pietra ·, dalli quali, per la loro bocca, era gommata la materia d'essa pietra, ed erano in alcuna parte restati ³separati dall' altra massa del sasso che li circundaua; perchè la scorza del nichio s'era interposta, e nō li auea ⁴lasciati congiugniere; E in alcun altra parte tal gomma auea petrificate le invecchiate e guaste la scorza.

In the mountains of Verona the red marble is found all mixed with cockle shells turned into stone; some of them have been filled at the mouth with the cement which is the substance of the stone; and in some parts they have remained separate from the mass of the rock which enclosed them, because the outer covering of the shell had interposed and had not allowed them to unite with it; while in other places this cement had petrified those which were old and destroyed the outer skin.

C. A. 234b]   1062

Ponte di Goritia ²Vilpago.

Bridge of Gorizia—Wippach.

Leic. 10a]   1063

The Apennines (1063–8)
Quella parte della terra s'è piv alienata dal centro ²del mōdo, la qual s'è fatta piv lieve ·; E quella parte della terra s'è fatta piv lieve, per la quale ³è passato maggior concorso · d'acque, E si è adūque fatta piv lieue quella parte, donde sco⁴la piv numero di fiumi, come l'alpi, che diuidono la Magnia e la Francia dalla Italia,

That part of the earth which was lightest remained farthest from the centre of the world; and that part of the earth became the lightest through which the greatest quantity of water flowed. And therefore that part became lightest where the greatest number of rivers flow; like the Alps which divide Germany and France from Italy;

1060. 1. ecquesto. 2. gogo . . diuitano la franca . . alla . . parturissce. 3. alle. 4. nvuoli . . chade. 5. magore . . ecquesta . . īmodo chesse. 6. fussi "la reta del caderui e del montarui nvuoli" che non achade [del s] . . eta e. 7. mezo . . grossimo . . tenenebrosa ellsole. 8. luminosi . . grosseza.
1061. 2. delli . . era gornata . . edera. 3. masa . . chelli circhundava . . lasscorza. 4. lassciati congugniere . . goma . . petrificata le invegiate e guasi scorzo.
1062. 2. vilpagho.
1063. 2. lequella . . seffatta. 3. magor choncorso . . Essi adūque. 4. diuidano . . ella franca . . della qual.

1060. I have vainly inquired of every available authority for a solution of the mystery as to what mountain is intended by the name Momboso (cf. vol. i, Nos. 300 and 301). It seems most obvious to refer it to Monte Rosa. *Rosa* is derived from the Keltic *ros* which survives in Breton and in Gaelic, meaning, in its first sense, a mountain spur, but which also—like *Horn*—means a very high peak; thus Monte Rosa would mean literally the High Peak. Compare

G. Uzielli, *L. d. V. e le Alpi*, Torino, 1890, pp. 14, 17, 26.

1062. There is a slight sketch with this text; Leonardo seems to have intended to suggest, with a few pen-strokes, the course of the Isonzo and of the Wippach in the vicinity of Gorizia. He himself says in another place that he had been in Friuli (see No. 1077, l. 19).

delle quali ⁵escie il Rodano a mezzodì, e il Reno a tramōtana ·, jl Danubio over Tanoia a greco, e 'l Po a leuā⁶te con īnvmerabili fiumi che con loro s'accōpagnano, i quali senpre corrono torbidi, dalla terra ⁷da loro portata al mare;

Mouōsi al continvo i liti marittimi inverso il mezzo del mare e lo ⁸scacciā dal suo primo sito; Riseruerassi la piv bassa parte del Mediterrano per letto e cor⁹so del Nilo, fiume massimo, che versa in esso mare; E con lui s'accompagnieranno tutti li fiumi sua ¹⁰aderēti, che prima in esso mare le loro acque versar soleano, come far si uede al Po colli aderēti ¹¹sua, li quali prima versauā nel mare · che infra l'Appennino e le Germaniche alpi si era vnito ¹²col Mare Adriatico;

Come le alpi galliche son la piv alta parte dell' Evropa.

whence issue the Rhône flowing southwards, and the Rhine to the north. The Danube or Tanoia towards the north-east, and the Po to the east, with innumerable rivers which join them, and which always run turbid with the soil carried by them to the sea.

The shores of the sea are constantly moving towards the middle of the sea and displace it from its original position. The lowest portion of the Mediterranean will be reserved for the bed and current of the Nile, the largest river that flows into that sea. And with it are grouped all its tributaries, which at first fell into the sea; as may be seen with the Po and its tributaries, which first fell into that sea, which between the Apennines and the German Alps was united to the Adriatic Sea.

That the Gallic Alps are the highest part of Europe.

E. 1a]   1064

E di questi ò ri²trovato nelli ³sassi dell' alto ⁴Appenino e ⁵massime nel ⁶sasso della Ver⁷nia.

And of these I found some in the rocks of the high Apennines and mostly at the rock of La Vernia.

E. 80a]   1065

A Parma alla ²Cāpana a dì 25 ³di settēbre 1514.

At Parma, at 'La Campana' on the 25th of October, 1514.

C. A. 139a]   1066

Modo di seccare il padule ²di Pionbino.

A method for drying the marsh of Piombino.

K.¹ 2a]   1067

Fanno li pastori ²in quel di Roma³gnia nelle radici ⁴dell' Appēnino certe ⁵gran concauità ne⁶l monte a uso di cor⁷no e da parte commet⁸tono vn corno, e q⁹uello piccol corno di¹⁰uēta vn medesimo col¹¹la già fatta concauità, ō¹²de fa grādissimo suono.

The shepherds in the Romagna at the foot of the Apennines make peculiar large cavities in the mountains in the form of a horn, and on one side they fasten a horn. This little horn becomes one and the same with the said cavity and thus they produce by blowing into it a very loud noise.

Leic. 31b]   1068

Vedesi vna vena surgere in Sicilia, la ²quale a certi tehpi dell' anno versa foglie di castagno in moltitudine, e in Sicilia nō na³scono castagnie, è adūque necessario che tal uena esca d'alcū pelago dell' Italia e va⁴da poi sotto il mare e sbocchi poi in Sicilia.

A spring may be seen to rise in Sicily which at certain times of the year throws out chestnut-leaves in quantities; but in Sicily chestnuts do not grow, hence it is evident that that spring must issue from some abyss in Italy and then flow beneath the sea to break forth in Sicily.

5. attramōtana . . danubbio . . tanoia a grecho . . alleu. 6. chon . . cholloro sacōpagniano . . corrā. 7. dallo portata . . movāsi . . mezo . . ello. 8. scaccā del . . mediterano. 9. ineso . . sachonpagniera. 10. solano . . colli aderē. 11. apenino elle . . serava. 12. chol . . adriaticho . . le alpe le . . pivolta.
1064. 1. quessti. 2. trovati. 7. nia.   1066. 1. sachare.
1067. 3. radice. 4. apēnino. 5. chonchauita. 7. pare come. 8. tano vn chorno ecq. 9. pichol. 10. chol. 11. ga. 12. sono.
1068. 1. cicilia. 2. accerti . . ano . . chasstagno . . moltitudile. 3. scie chastagnie . . chettal . . esscha dalchū pellagho. 4. dia poi . . essbochi . . cicilia.

1064. 6. *Sasso della Vernia.* The frowning rock between the sources of the Arno and the Tiber, as Dante describes the mountain, 1,269 metres in height. This note is written by the side of No. 1020.

1065. 2. *Cāpana*, an inn. A note on fossils near Parma will be found under No. 989.

1066. There is a slight sketch with this text in the original.—Piombino is also mentioned in Nos. 609, ll. 55-8 (compare Pl. XXXV, No. 3, below). Also in No. 1035. On his return from Lombardy to Tus-

cany Leonardo was interested in the draining of the marshes at Piombino, and in the Val di Chiana (Pl. CXII). A map of the region of the Pontine Marshes (Pl. CXIV) suggests a scheme for draining these, which may have been of interest to Giuliano de Medici, and Pope Leo X. Comp. M. Baratta, *L. d. V. e la Val di Chiana*, La Geografia, Novara, 1927; and *L. d. V. e le Paludi Pontine*, ibid., 1928.

1067. For Romagna see also No. 1046.

II

FRANCE

1069

ALEMAGNIA	FRANCIA	GERMANY	FRANCE
[2]a. Austria,	a. Picardia,	a. Austria.	a. Picardy.
[3]b. Sassonia,	b. Normandia,	b. Saxony.	b. Normandy.
[4]c. Norimberga,	c. Delfinato;	c. Nuremberg.	c. Dauphiné.
[5]d. Fiandra;	d.	d. Flanders.	

SPAGNIA	SPAIN
[7]a. Biscaglia,	a. Biscay.
[8]b. Castiglia,	b. Castille.
[9]c. Galitia,	c. Galicia.
[10]d. Portogallo,	d. Portugal.
[11]e. Tarragona,	e. Taragona.
[12]f. Granada.	f. Granada.

C. A. 367b] 1070

Perpigniana;	Perpignan.
[2]Roana,	Roanne.
[3]Lione,	Lyons.
[4]Anvers,	Antwerp.
[5]Parigi,	Paris.
[6]Guāto,	Ghent.
[7]Brugia,	Bruges.
[8]Olanda.	Holland.

Leic. 27b] 1071

Come in Bordea presso a Guascognia alza il mare circa a 40 braccia pel suo reflus[2]so, e 'l suo fiume ringorga l'acque salze piv di cento cinquāta miglia, e li nauili, che [3]si debbono calafatare, restano alti sopra un' alto colle sopra dello abassato mare.

At Bordeaux in Gascony the sea rises about 40 braccia before its ebb, and the river there is filled with salt water for more than a hundred and fifty miles; and the vessels which are repaired there rest high and dry on a high hill above the sea at low tide.

Leic. 34b] 1072

El Rodano esce dal lago di Ginevra e corre prima [2]a ponente, e poi a mezzodì, con corso di 400 miglia, e versa le sue acque nel mare mediterrano.

The Rhône issues from the Lake of Geneva and flows first to the west and then to the south, with a course of 400 miles, and pours its waters into the Mediterranean.

1069. *In the original the three columns are parallel.* 1. alamania franca—spognia. 4. nolinberg—dalfinato. 5. flandra. 7. bisscaglia. 8. casstiglia. 11. taragona. 12. granata.
1070. 3. liōne.
1071. 1. guasscogna . . circha a 40 br . . refru. 2. elli. 3. deano . . chollo.
1072. 1. essce del lagho. 2. mezodi . . mediterano.

1069. Two slightly sketched maps, one of Europe, the other of Spain, are at the side of these notes.
1070. *Roana,* Roanne, a wealthy town on the upper course of the Loire, probably of interest to Leonardo because its distance from the Rhône at Lyons is only

13 miles. See note to No. 1078.
1071. 2. This is obviously an exaggeration founded on inaccurate information. Half of 150 miles would be nearer the mark.

K.³ 100a]   1073

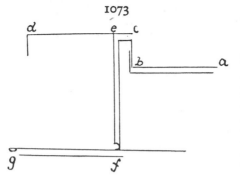

c d giardino di Bles;
²*a b* è il cŏdotto di Bles,
fatto ī ³Frācia da Fra
Giocŏdo, *b c* è il ⁴māca-
mēto dell' altezza di tal
cŏ⁵dotto, *c d* è l'altezza
del giar⁶dino di Bles,
e f è la caduta ⁷della cicognola, *b c, e f, f g* ⁸è
dove tal cicognola versa
nel ⁹fiume.

c d is the garden at
Blois; *a b* is the conduit
of Blois, made in France
by Fra Giocondo, *b c* is
what is wanting in the
height of that conduit,
c d is the height of the
garden at Blois, *e f* is the
siphon of the conduit,
b c, e f, f g is where the
siphon discharges into
the river.

Br. M. 269a]   1074

Loira fiume ²d'Ambosa.
³Il fiume è più ⁴alto dentro al⁵l' argine *b d* che
⁶fuori d'esso ar⁷gine;

The river Loire at Amboise.
The river is higher within the bank *b d* than
outside that bank.

1073. 1. gardino. 3. gocŏdo. 4. alteza. 5. ellalteza del gar. 6. ella.   **1074.** 1. Loera. 2. dā[n]bosa. 3. eppiu.

1073. The tenor of this note (see ll. 2 and 3) seems to me to indicate that this passage was not written in France, but was written from oral information. We have no evidence as to when this note may have been written beyond the circumstance that Fra Giocondo, the Veronese architect, left France not before the year 1505. The greater part of the magnificent Château of Blois has now disappeared. Whether this note was made for a special purpose is uncertain. The original form and extent of the Château is shown in Androvet, *Les Plus Excellents Bastiments de France*, Paris, MDCVII, and it may be observed that there is in the middle of the garden something somewhat similar to that shown on Pl. LXXXVIII, No. 7.

See S. de la Saussaye, *Histoire du Château de Blois*, 4ème édition, Blois et Paris, p. 175: 'En mariant sa fille aînée à François, comte d'Angoulême, Louis XII lui avait constitué en dot les comtés de Blois, d'Asti, de Coucy, de Montfort, d'Étampes et de Vertus. Une ordonnance de François Ier lui laissa en 1516 l'administration du comté de Blois.

'Le roi fit commencer, dans la même année, les travaux de cette belle partie du château, connue sous le nom d'aile de François Ier et dont nous avons donné la description au commencement de ce livre. Nous trouvons en effet, dans les archives du Baron de Joursanvault, une pièce qui en fixe parfaitement la date. On y lit: "Je, Baymon Philippeaux, commis par le Roy à tenir le compte et fair le payement des bastiments, ediffices et reparacions que le dit seigneur fait faire en son chastu de Blois, confesse avoir eu et reçeu ... la somme de trois mille livres tournois .... le cinquième jour de juillet, l'an mil cinq cent et seize." [P. 24] Les jardins avaient été decorés avec beaucoup de luxe par les différents possesseurs du château. Il ne reste de tous les bâtiments qu'ils y élevèrent que ceux des officiers chargés de l'administration et de la culture des jardins, et un pavillon carré en pierre et en brique flanqué de terrasses à chacun de ses angles. Quoique défiguré par des mesures élevées sur les terrasses, cet édifice est très-digne d'intérêt par l'originalité du plan, la décoration architecturale et le souvenir d'Anne de Bretagne qui le fit construire.' Félibien describes the garden as follows: 'Le jardin haut était fort bien dressé par grands compartimens de toutes sortes de figures, avec des allées de meuriers blancs et des palissades de coudriers. Deux grands berceaux de charpenterie séparoient toute la longueur et la largeur du jardin, et dans les quatres angles des allées, où ces berceaux se croissent, il y auoit 4 cabinets, de mesme charpenterie... Il y a pas longtemps qu'il y auoit dans ce mesme jardin, à l'endroit où se croisent les allées du milieu, un édifice de figure octogone, de plus de 7 thoises de diamètre et de plus de neuf thoises de haut; avec 4 enfoncements en forme de niches dans les 4 angles des allées. Ce bastiment ... estoit de charpente mais d'un extraordinairement bien travaillé. On y voyait particulièrement la cordilière qui régnait tout autour en forme de cordon. Car la Reyne affectait de la mettre non seulement à ses armes et à ses chiffres mais de la faire représenter en diverses manières dans tous les ouvrages qu'on lui faisait pour elle ... le bastiment estoit couvert en forme de dôme qui dans son milieu avait encore un plus petit dôme, ou lanterne vitrée au-dessus de laquelle estait une figure dorée représentant Saint Michel. Les deux dômes estoient proprement couverts d'ardoise et de plomb doré par dehors; par dedans ils estoient lambrissez d'une menuiserie très délicate. Au milieu de ce Salon il y avait un grand bassin octogone de marbre blanc, dont toutes les faces estoient enrichies de différentes sculptures, avec les armes et les chiffres du Roy Louis XII et de la Reine Anne. Dans ce bassin il y en avait un autre posé sur un piédestal lequel auoit sept piedz de diamètre. Il estoit de figure ronde à godrons, avec des masques et d'autres ornements très sçauamment taillés. Du milieu de ce deuxiesme bassin s'y levoit un autre petit piédestal qui portait un troisiesme bassin de trois pieds de diamètre, aussy parfaitement bien taillé; c'estoit de ce dernier bassin que jallissoit l'eau qui se répendoit en suitte dans les deux autres bassins. Les beaux ouvrages faits d'un marbre esgalement blanc et poli, furent brisez par la pesanteur de tout l'édifice, que les injures de l'air renversèrent de fond en comble.'

1074. See Pl. CXV. Lines 1–7 are above, ll. 8–10 in the middle of the large island and the word *Isola* is written above *d* in the smaller island; *a* is written

[8]Isola dove è [9]vna parte [10]d'Anbuosa.

[11]Il fiume Loira che passa per Anbosa passa per *a b, c d*, e poichè è passato il pōte, [12]ritorna contro al suo avenimento per il canale *d e, b f* in contatto dell' argine [13]che si interpone infra li due moti contrari del predetto fiume *a b, c d, d e, b f*; [14]di poi si riuolta in giù per il canale *f l, g h, n m*, e si ricongiugnie col fiume dōde [15]prima si diuise, che passa per *k n*, che fa *k m, r t*; ma quãdo il fiume è [16]grosso, allora elli corre tutto per uno solo verso, passãdo l'argine *b d*.

The island where there is a part of Amboise.

The river Loire which passes through Amboise; it passes at *a b, c d*, and when it has passed the bridge it turns back, against the original current, by the channel *d e, b f*, in contact with the bank which lies between the two contrary currents of the said river, *a b, c d*, and *d e, b f*. It then turns down again by the channel *f l, g h, n m*, and reunites with the river from which it was at first separated, which passes by *k n*, which makes *k m, r t*. But when the river is very full it flows all in one channel passing over the bank *b d*.

Br. M. 270*b*]   1075

L'acque sieno rin[2]gorgate sopra [3]il termine di Ro[4]morontino in tã[5]ta altezza, ch'elle [6]faccino poi nel [7]loro discieso mol[8]te molina;

[9]Il fiume di Villa[10]franca sia cō[11]dotto a Romorō[12]tino, e sia fatto dal suo [13]popolo, e li legni[14]ami, che conpō[15]gono le lor case, [16]siē per barche cō[17]dotte a Romorō[18]tino; e 'l fiume [19]sia ringorga[20]to in tãta altez[21]za, che l'acqua [22]si possa cō co[23]modo discie[24]so riduciere [25]a Romorōtino.

The water may be dammed up above the level of Romorantin to such a height that in its fall it may be used for numerous mills.

The river at Villefranche may be conducted to Romorantin, which may be done by the inhabitants; and the timber of which their houses are built may be carried in boats to Romorantin [18]. The river may de dammed up at such a height that the waters may be brought back to Romorantin with a convenient fall.

Br. M. 269*b*]   1076

S'elli è meglio che l'acqua [2]vada tutta in alto in una so[3]la volta, o veramēte in due?

[4]Rispōdesi che in vna sola vol[5]ta la rota nō potreb[6]be sostenere tutta l'acqua [7]ch'ella leua in due volte, per[8]chè nella mezza volta della [9]rota leverebbe 100 libbre, [10]e nō più, e s'ell' auesse a leua[11]re le 200 libbre la uolta inte[12]re, non le leverebbe, se [13]tal rota nō raddoppiasse il dia[14]metro, e raddoppiando tal [15]diametro raddoppiereb[16]be il tenpo; adūque è meglio [17]e più comodità di spesa a fare [18]tal rota sub 2[a] che 2 la ecc.

[19]Il descieso del mozzo non s'ab[20]bassa insino alla pelle dell' acqua, [21]perchè toccãdo l'acqua diminuireb[22]be il peso suo. . . .

[23]E se per l'aversario [24]s'ingrossasse il [25]fugatore dell' ac[26]qua dieci tan[27]ti più, che la [28]canna dell' [29]acqua fuggiē[30]te, [31]dieci tanti [32]men moto [33]che a questo, [34]che vfitio sareb[35]be il suo? Ri[36]spōdesi per la [37]9[a] di questo [38]che dice, che l'acqua [39]s'alzerebbe [40]la decima parte di quel che prima s'alza [41]nell' altezza di quella canna donde prima surgieua.

As to whether it is better that the water should all be raised in a single turn or in two?

The answer is that in one single turn the wheel could not support all the water that it can raise in two turns, because at the half turn of the wheel it would be raising 100 pounds and no more; and if it had to raise the whole 200 pounds in one turn, it could not raise them unless the wheel were of double the diameter, and if the diameter were doubled, the time of its revolution would be doubled; therefore it is better and a greater advantage in expense to make such a wheel of half the size (?), &c.

The going down of the nave of the wheel must not be so low as to touch the surface of the water, because by touching the water its momentum will be lessened. . . .

And if on the contrary the conduit for the water were ten times the size of the pipe for the water escaping from it, and if it had ten times less motion, what would be its office? This is answered by the 9th of this which says that the water would rise in the pipe whence it first flows, to a tenth part of its original height.

---

11. fiume era che. 13. chessi . . infralli . . controri . . predecto. 14. ess richongiugnie. 15. diuise [eppa] che . . cheffa.
1075. 1. Lacqua sia rio. 2. ghorghata. 5. alteza. 7. suo disscieso. 9. uilla. 10. francha. 11. docto a romolō. 12. del. 13. elli. 14. conpo. 15. ghano. 17. aremolō. 19. ringhorgha. 21. chellacqua. 23. dissciē. 25. romolōtino.
1076. 1. selli . . chellacq"a". 2. alto nuna. 4. nvna. 6. bono sosstenere . . lacq"a". 7. chella. 8. meza. 10. essellauessi alleua. 12. nolle leverebbe [se el] se. 13. raddopiassi. 14. mitro [e in] e. 15. [tempo] diamitro radoppiereb. 17. affare. 19. disscièso . . nossab. 20. acqu"a". 21. tochãdo lacqu"a". 23. Esse. 24. singrossassi. 25. fughatore. 27. chella. 28. channa della. 30. te dessi se li. 31. tanta. 33. che acque sto. 35. Ris. 37. quessto. 38. chellacqua. 40. che p"a". 41. channa donde p"a" sue. 42. giena.

in the margin on the bank of the river above l. 1; in the reproduction it is not visible. As may be seen from the last sentence, the observation was made after long study of the river's course, when Leonardo had resided for some time at, or near, Amboise.

1075. 18. Compare No. 744.

1076. The topographical interest of this passage arises from the circumstance that it is written on the reverse of the sheet on which we find the text relating to Romorantin, No. 1074.

Br. M. 270*b*]   1077

Se 'l fiume *m n*, ramo del fiume Loira, si manda nel ²fiume di Romorontino colle sua acque torbide, esso ī³grasserà le canpagnie sopra le quali esso adaque⁴rà, e rēderà il paese fertile da nutrire li a⁵bitatori, e farà canale navicabile e mercātile.

⁶Modo che 'l fiume ⁷col suo corso ⁸netti il fondo del ⁹fiume.

¹⁰Per la nona del 3°; ¹¹Quello ch'è più velo¹²cie, più cōsuma il ¹³suo fondo, e per la cō¹⁴versa: l'acqua ch'è più ¹⁵tarda piv lascia ¹⁶di quel che la intorbi¹⁷da;

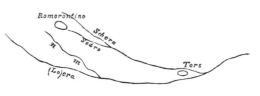

¹⁸Addunque nelli diluui de' fiumi si debbono aprire le cate¹⁹ratte de' molini, acciochè tutto il corso del fiume si renda per ca²⁰teratta in ciascū molino; sieno molte, acciochè . . . s'apra e ²¹si faccia maggiore īpeto, e così netterà tutto il fondo; ²²e facciasi il serraglio mobile, che io or²³dinai nel Friuli, del quale, aperto vna cate²⁴rat²ᵃta, l'acqua che di quella vsciva cauò il fondo; ²⁵e infra le due poste de' moli²⁶ni sia vna delle dette caterat²⁷te; sia vna d'esse poste di tal cate²⁸ratte mobile infra l'uno e l'al²⁹tro molino.

If the river *m n*, an affluant of the river Loire, were turned with its turbid waters into the river of Romorantin, this would fatten the land which it would water and would render the country fertile to supply food to the inhabitants, and would make navigable canals for mercantile purposes.

The way in which the river in its flow should scour its own channel.

By the ninth of the third; the more rapid it is, the more it wears away its channel; and by the converse proposition, the slower the water the more it deposits that which renders it turbid.

Therefore when the rivers are flooded, the sluices of the mills ought to be opened in order that it opens and the whole course of the river may pass through falls to each mill; there should be many in order to give a greater impetus, and so all the bottom will be scoured. And let the sluice be movable like the one I arranged in Friuli [23], where when one sluice was opened the water which passed through it dug out the bottom. And between the site of each of the two mills there may be one of the said sluice falls; one of them may be placed between each mill.

C. A. 336*b*]   1078

Vno trabocco è quattro braccia e vno miglio è tre mila d'esse braccia; E 'l braccio si diuide in 12 ōcie; ²e l'acqua de' canali à di calo in ogni cēto trabocchi 2 delle dette oncie; adūque 14 oncie ³di calo son neciessarie a due mila ottocēto braccia di moto ne' detti canali; seguita che 15 oncie ⁴di calo danno debito moto alli corsi dell' acque dei predetti canali, cioè uno braccio e ½ ⁵per miglio; E per questo cōcluderemo che l'acqua che si toglie dal fiume di Villa Franca e si ⁶presta al fiume di Romorontino vuole.   Dove l'ū fiume mediante la sua bassezza nō ⁷può entrare nell' altro, è neciessario

A trabocco is four braccia, and one mile is three thousand of the said braccia. Each braccio is divided into 12 inches; and the water in the canals has a fall in every hundred trabocchi of two of these inches; therefore 14 inches of fall are necessary in two thousand eight hundred braccia of flow in these canals; it follows that 15 inches of fall give the required momentum to the currents of the waters in the said canals, that is, one braccio and a half in the mile. And from this it may be concluded that the water taken from the river of Villefranche and lent to the river of Romorantin will. . . . Where one river

1077. 1. fiume [era] Era | si. 2. romolontino . . torbite. 3. essesso. 5. effara chanale navichabile e merchātile. 11. Quella. 14. cheppiu. 15. lasscia. 16. chella. *Lines 6–17 are written in the margin.* 18. si debbe apr\\\\\\\\\\\\\\. 19. ratte demolini . . del fiume si\\\\\\\\\\\\\\\\. 20. ciasscū . . . accioche \\\\\\\\\\\\\. 21. sapra effacci magiore . . tutto if\\\\\\\\\\\\. 22. effaciasi. 23. nel frigholi. 24. lacq"a"che . . vssciva cav"o". 25. infralle . . posste. 27. posste. 28. rate molini infralluna ellal. *Lines 25–9 stand in the original above line 18.*

1078. 1. traboccho.. br. e ī . . El br. [s] si . . ōcie\\\\\\. 2. ellacqua . . addi chalo . . trabochi .. 14 ō di. 3. di chalo . . adumila . . br. di moto [de de] ne .. 15 ō di. 4. di chalo . . corsi [de detti o] dell . . de . . cioe ī br. 5. quesso cōcludereno chellacqua chessi . . francha essi. 6. pressta . . remolontino vole . . mediante [la ba] la sua.

1077. 23. From this passage it appears that Leonardo visited Friuli and stayed there for some time. Compare No. 1062.

1078. Lines 6–18 are partly reproduced in the facsimile on p. 202, and the whole of ll. 19–25.

The following names are written along the rivers on the larger sketch: *era f* (the Loire), *scier f* (the Cher), three times. *Pōte Sodro* (bridge of the Soudre). *Villa francha* (Villefranche), *banco* (sand-bank), *Sodro* (Sou-

dre). The circle below shows the position of Romorantin. The words '*orologio del sole*' written below do not refer to the map of the rivers. The following names are written by the side of the smaller sketch-map: *tors* (Tours), *Ābosa* (Amboise), *bres*—for Bles (Blois), *mō rica* \\\\ (Montrichard), *Lione* (Lyons). This map was also published in the 'Saggio' (Milan, 1872), Pl. XXII, and the editors remark: 'Forse la linia retta che va da Amboise a Romorantin segna

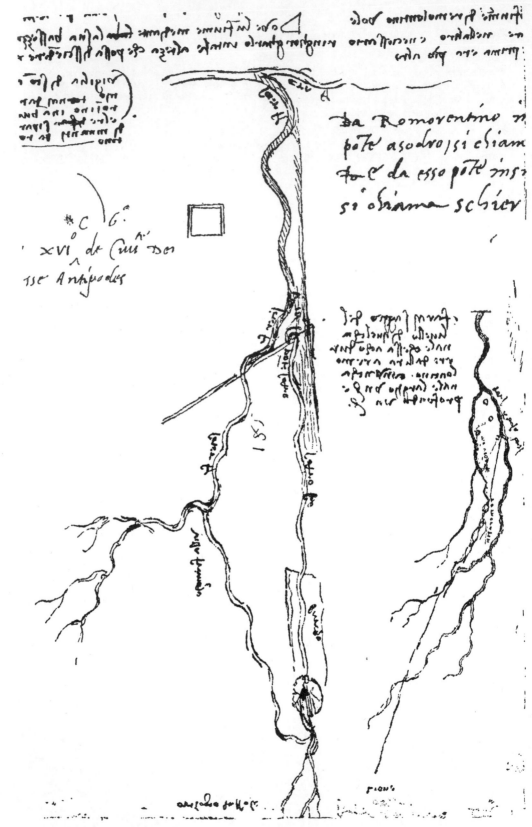

da Romorentino n
potte asodro,si chiam
to e da esso potte insi
si chiama schier

ringorgarlo in tale altezza che possa disciĕdere [8]in quel che prima era piv alto.

[9]¶Vigilia di Sc̄o Anto[10]nio tornai da Romo-[11]rōtino in Ābuosa,¶ [12]e 'l rè si partì due [13]dì innanti da Romorō[14]tino.

[15]Da Romorontino insino al [16]pōte a Sodro | si chiama Soudro; [17]e da esso pōte insino a Tours [18]si chiama Schier.

[19]Farai saggio del [20]liuello di quel ca[21]nale che si à a cōdur[22]re dalla Loira a Remo[23]lontino con vn ca[24]nale largo vn braccio e [25]profondo vn braccio.

by reason of its low level cannot flow into the other, it will be necessary to dam it up, so that it may acquire a fall into the other, which was previously the higher.

The eve of Saint Antony I returned from Romorantin to Amboise, and the King went away two days before from Romorantin.

From Romorantin as far as the bridge at Saudre it is called the Saudre, and from that bridge as far as Tours it is called the Cher.

I would test the level of that channel which is to lead from the Loire to Romorantin, with a channel one braccio wide and one braccio deep.

Br. M. 263*b*]　　　　　1079

STRADA D'ORLEANS

[2]Alla quarta di mezzodì verso scirocco; [3]alla terza di mezzodì verso scirocco; [4]alla quarta di mezzodì verso scirocco; [5]alla quinta di mezzodì verso scirocco; [6]Tra libeccio e mezzodì [7]a leuante participando di mezzodì; [8]tra mezzo giorno verso leuante $\frac{1}{8}$; [9]Da poi verso ponente; [10]tra mezzodì e libeccio; [11]a mezzodì.

THE ROAD TO ORLEANS

At $\frac{1}{4}$ from the south to the south-east. At $\frac{1}{3}$ from the south to the south-east. At $\frac{1}{4}$ from the south to the south-east. At $\frac{1}{5}$ from the south to the south-east. Between the south-west and south, to the east bearing to the south; from the south towards the east $\frac{1}{8}$; thence to the west, between the south and south-west; at the south.

B. 61*a*]　　　　　1080

Modo come i Tedeschi ingarbugliano e tessano, serãdosi īsieme, [2]le loro lancie lunghe cōtro a nemici ·, abassandosi e mettēdo [3]vna delle teste a terra, tenēdo il resto · in mano.

The way in which the Germans, closing up together, cross and interweave their long spears against the enemy, stooping down and putting one of the ends on the ground while they hold the rest in their hand. _{On the Germans (1080-1).}

B. 63*b*]　　　　　1081

Vsano i Germani · annegare · castellani cō fumo di pivma, solfo [2]e risagallo ·, e fanno durare detti fumi 7 e 8 ore; ācora la [3]pula del frumēto fa assai e durabil fumo; e letame secco ancor lui, [4]ma fa sia mischiato colla sãsa, cioè vliue tratte nel' olio, o vuoi morchia [5]d'olio.

The Germans are wont to annoy a garrison with the smoke of feathers, sulphur, and realgar, and they make this smoke last 7 or 8 hours. Likewise the husks of wheat make a great and lasting smoke; and also dry dung; but this must be mixed with olive husks, that is, olives pressed for oil and from which the oil has been extracted.

---

7. ringhorgharlo. . alteza . . disscièdere \\\\\\. 12. el re [di fran] si. *Lines 15–18 are written from left to right.* 15. Romorentino. 17. [po] e da. 20. cha. 21. chessa a chōdur. 22. rre dalleraa remo. 23. cha. 24. largho vn br. 25. vn br. **1079.** *Written from left to right:* 1. dorléons. 2. de mezo syroccho. 3. de mezo . . syroccho. 4. mezo . . syrocco. 5. mezo . . syrocco. 6. lybeccio e mezodi. 6. mezo. 7. mezo. 9. ponte. 10. mezo . . lybeccio. 11. mezo. **1080.** 2. chome i tedesci ingarigliano ettessano. 2. lange lunge. 3. dele . . attera . . imano. **1081.** 1. anegare chastelani. 2. risalgallo effano. 3. elletame secho. 4. ovoi morcha.

l'andamento proposto d'un Canale, che poi sembra prolungarsi in giù fin dove sta scritto Lione.' M. Ravaisson has enlarged on this idea in the *Gazette des Beaux-Arts* (1881, p. 530): 'Les traces de Léonard permettent d'entrevoir que le canal commençant soit auprès de Tours, soit auprès de Blois et passant par Romorantin, avec port d'embarquement à Villefranche, devait, au delà de Bourges, traverser l'Allier au-dessous des affluents de la Dore et de la Sioule, aller par Moulins jusqu' à Digoin; enfin, sur l'autre

rive de la Loire, dépasser les monts du Charolais et rejoindre la Saône auprès de Mâcon.'

g. Jan. 16, 1518. Between 1516 and 1519 the court passed 11 months at Amboise.

1079. Not in Leonardo's hand (?). Compare No. 744.

1080. Above the text is a sketch of a few lines crossing each other and the words *de ponderibus*. The meaning of the passage is obscure.

1081. There is with this passage a sketch of a round tower shrouded in smoke.

Leic. 1b]   1082

The Danube.

Come le ualli furō già coperte in grā parte da laghi, no perchè senpre il suo terreno fece argine a fiumi, e da mari, i quali poi colla perseueratione de' fiumi . . . ²segarono li monti, e li fiumi coi lor vagabundi corsi portarono via le altre pianvre incluse dalli mōti, e le segature de' mōti so³no note per le falde delle pietre, che si corrispondono nelle lor tagliature fatte dalli detti corsi de' fiumi; ⁴Il Monte Emus che riga la Tratia e la Dardanja e si congiugne per ponente col Monte Sardonius, el quale, seguendo ⁵a ponēte, muta il nome di Sardus in | Rebi nel toccare la Dalmatia, poi seguendo a ponēte riga li Illirici ⁶oggi detta Schiavonia, e mvta nome di | Rebi in | Albanus, e seguendo pure a ponēte si muta nel Mōte Ocra ⁷a tramōtana, e a mezzodì sopra all' Istria si nomina | Caruancas e si congiugne a ponēte sopra l'Italia col Mōte Adula, ⁸doue nascie il Danubio, il quale s'astende a leuante con corso di 1500 miglia, e la sua linia breuissima è circa ⁹mille miglia, e altrettanto o circa è 'l ramo del Monte Adula mutato ne' predetti nomi di mōti; sta a tramon¹⁰tana il monte | Carpatus, il quale termina la larghezza della valle del Danubio, la qual, come dissi, s'astende ¹¹a leuāte cō lunghezza di circa mille miglia, ed è larga doue 200 e doue 300 miglia; questa si mette pel ¹²mezzo il Danvbio, primo fiume d'Europa per magnitudine, il qual Danvbio si lascia per mezzo di ¹³Austria e Albania e per tramōtana Bauaria, Polonia, Ungheria, Valachia e Bosnia; versaua adunque il Danubio | over | Da¹⁴noia nel mare di Ponto, il quale s'astendea insino vicino all' Austria e occupaua tutta la pianvra che oggi ¹⁵discorre esso Danvbio, e 'l segno dico ne mostrano l'ostriche e li nichi e bovoli e cappe e ossa di grā pesci, che an¹⁶cora in molti lochi si trouano nell' alte coste de' predetti mōti; ed era tale mare fatto per la ringorgatione delli ra¹⁷mi del Monte Adula, che s'astendeano a leuante e si congiugneano colli rami del Mōte Tauro, che s'astendono a po¹⁸nēte, e circa alla Bitinia versauā l'acque d'esso Mare di Pōto nel Propontico, cadendo nel Mare Egeo cioè ¹⁹Mar Mediterrano, doue poi il lungo corso spiccò li rami

That the valleys were formerly in great part covered by lakes, the soil of which always forms the banks of rivers—and by seas, which afterwards, by the persistent wearing of the rivers, cut through the mountains, and the wandering courses of the rivers carried away the other plains enclosed by the mountains; and the cutting away of the mountains is evident from the strata in the rocks, which correspond in their sections as made by the courses of the rivers [4]. The Hæmus mountains which go along Thrace and Dardania and towards the west join the Sardonius mountains which, going on westward, change their name from Sardus to Rebi, as they near Dalmatia; then turning to the west cross Illyria, now called Sclavonia, changing the name of Rebi to Albanus, and going on still to the west, they change to Mount Ocra in the North; and to the south above Istria they are named Caruancas; and to the west above Italy they join the Adula, where the Danube rises [8], which stretches to the east and has a course of 1,500 miles; its shortest line is about 1,000 miles, and the same or about the same is that branch of the Adula mountains changed as to their name, as before mentioned. To the north are the Carpathians, closing in the breadth of the valley of the Danube, which, as I have said, extends eastward, with a length of about 1,000 miles, and is sometimes 200 and in some places 300 miles wide; and in the midst flows the Danube, the principal river of Europe as to size. The said Danube runs through the middle of Austria and Albania and northwards through Bavaria, Poland, Hungary, Wallachia, and Bosnia and then the Danube or Donau flows into the Black Sea, which formerly extended almost to Austria and occupied the plains through which the Danube now courses; and the evidence of this is in the oysters and cockle shells and scollops and bones of great fishes which are still to be found in many places on the sides of those mountains; and this sea was formed by the filling up of the spurs of the Adula mountains which then extended to the east, joining the spurs of the Taurus which extend to the west. And near Bithynia the waters of this Black Sea poured into the Propontis [Marmora], falling into the Aegean Sea, that is, the Mediterranean, where, after a long course, the spurs of the Adula mountains became separated from those of the Taurus. The

---

1082. 1. laghi "noperche senpre il suo terreno fece argine afiumi" e da mari. 2. segorono . . elli fiumi co . . portorono . . mōti elle. 3. chessi conrisspondano. 4. enjus . . tratia ella dardaria essi congvgne . . monte [scardus] sardonius. 5. nel cottare la. 6. sciavonia . . ponente [segue] si muta. 7. attramōtana e mezodi . . isstria . . essi congugne. 8. nasscie il reno il quale . . alleuante conchorso. . . ella . . circha. 9. circha . . attramon. 10. largeza. 11. alleuāte cō lungeza . . largha [dalle do] doue. 12. mezo . . danvbbio . . danvbbio si lasscia per mezo. 13. vngeria . . ebboxnia . . danubbio over da. 14. sasstendea . . ochupaua. 15. disscorre . . losstriche elli . . e chappe . . pessci. 17. chessastendeano alleuante essi congugneano . . taruro chessastendanoal. 18. circha allabetti ma . . proponticho chadendo . . egeocoe. 19. mediterano . . spicho.

1082. 4. *Emus*, the Balkan; *Dardania*, now Jugoslavia as we may infer from *come dissi*, l. 10, &c.

8. *Danubio*, in the original *Reno*; evidently a mistake.

del Mõte Adula dalli rami del Mõte Tauro; el Mare [20]di Põto s'abassò e scoperse la val di Danubio colle prenominate provincie, e tutta l'Asia Minore di là dal monte Ta[21]vro per tramõtana e la pianvra ch'è da Mõte Caucasso al mare di Ponto per ponẽte, e la pianura del Ta[22]nai dentro alli monti Rifiei cioè a' piedi loro; Ecco che 'l mare di Ponto abbassò circa a braccia 1000 [23]nello scoprire di tanta pianura.

Black Sea sank lower and laid bare the valley of the Danube with the above-named countries, and the whole of Asia Minor beyond the Taurus range to the north, and the plains from mount Caucasus to the Black Sea to the west, and the plains of the Don this side—that is to say, at the foot of the Ural Mountains. And thus the Black Sea must have sunk about 1,000 braccia to uncover such vast plains.

20. esscoperse la ual di danv | "bbio" . . province ettutta . . minore dala dal. 21. ella . . chavcaso . . ella. 22. coe . . Ecchoche . . circha a br. 1000. 23. isscoprire.

THE COUNTRIES OF THE WESTERN END OF THE MEDITERRANEAN

A. 57a]   1083

PERCHÈ IL MARE FA LA CORRÈTE NELLO STRETTO DI SPAGNIA PIV CH'ALTROVE

The Straits of Gibraltar (1083–5).
²¶Il fiume · d'equal profondità · avrà · tanto · piv · fuga · nella · minore · larghezza ³che nella · maggiore ·, quanto · la maggiore · larghezza · avanza · la minore; ¶

⁴Questa · propositione · si pruova · chiaramēte per ragione cōferma ⁵dalla sperienza ·, jnperochè, quando · per uno canale · d'uno miglio · di larghezza passe⁶rà uno miglio · di lūghezza d'acqua, dove · il fiume · fia · largo 5 migli, ciascuno ⁷de 5 migli quadri metterà $\frac{1}{5}$ · di sé · per ristaurare il mi⁸glio · quadro d'acqua mācato · nello pelago, ⁹e dove il fivme · fia · lar¹⁰go · 3 · miglia ·, ciascu¹¹no · d'essi migli quadri ¹²metterà di sé lo terzo ¹³di sua quātità per lo mā¹⁴care che fecie il mi¹⁵glio quadro dello stret¹⁶to ·, come si dimo¹⁷stra · in · f · g · h ¹⁸per lo miglio · n.

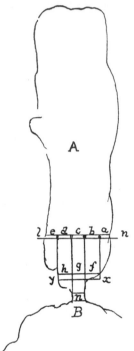

WHY THE SEA MAKES A STRONGER CURRENT IN THE STRAITS OF SPAIN THAN ELSEWHERE

A river of equal depth runs with greater speed in a narrow space than in a wide one, in proportion to the difference between the wider and the narrower one.

This proposition is clearly proved by reason confirmed by experiment. Supposing that through a channel one mile wide there flows one mile in length of water; where the river is five miles wide each of the 5 square miles will require $\frac{1}{5}$ of itself to be equal to the square mile of water required in the sea, and where the river is 3 miles wide each of these square miles will require the third of its volume to make up the amount of the square mile of the narrow part; as is demonstrated in $f g h$ at the mile marked n.

C. A. 215b]   1084

PERCHÈ È MAGGIORE SĒPRE LA CORRĒTE DI SPAGNIA INVERSO PONĒTE · CHE PER LEUĀTE

²La ragiō si è ·, che se tu · metterai · insieme · le boche · de' fiumi · che mettono · in questo · Mare Mediterrano, tu tro³verai · essere · maggiore · soma d'acqua · che · quella · che uersa · esso · mare per lo stretto in nell' oceano mare; ⁴tu vedi · l'Africa scaricare · i sua fiumi · che corrono · a tramōtana in esso mare īfra i quali ⁵è · il Nilo ·, che riga · 3000 miglia dell' Africa ·,

WHY THE CURRENT OF GIBRALTAR IS ALWAYS GREATER TO THE WEST THAN TO THE EAST

The reason is that if you put together the mouths of the rivers which discharge into the Mediterranean Sea, you would find the sum of water to be larger than that which this sea pours through the straits into the ocean. You see Africa discharging its rivers that run northwards into this sea, and among them the Nile, which runs through 3,000 miles of Africa; there is also the Bagrada river and the Schelif and others.

1083. 1. chorète .. chaltro"ve". 2. ara .. fugha .. larigheza. 3. chenella .. quancto .. larigheza. 4. [perissperienza] per .. chōferma. 5. dallissperienza .. per ī chanale. 6. ra ī miglio di lūgezza dacq"a" .. ciaschuno. 7. ciasscun "de 5" migli[o] quadr[o] i mettera [per ristaurare il mā] $\frac{1}{5}$. di se. 8. dacq "a" māchato .. pelago *4.* 9. ⊤e dove. 10. gho .. ciaschu. 14. chare cheffecie. 15. stre. 16. chome. *Lines 9–18 are written in the margin.*
1084. magiore .. chorēte .. inver. 2. settu .. mettano. 3. magiore .. dacq"a" .. inell. 4. lafricha scharichare .. chorano attramōtana .. equali. 5. dellafricha . euj . il fiume bragada.

1083. In the place marked A in the diagram *Mare Mediterano* (Mediterranean Sea) is written in the original. And at B, *stretto di Spagna* (straits of Spain, i.e. Gibraltar). Compare No. 960.

e vi è · il · fiume Bagrada, · e 'l Mavretano, e altri simili; ⁶l'Europa vi versa il Tanai e 'l Danvbio ·, il Po e 'l Rodano, Arno e Teuere, sich' è chiaro questi fivmi insieme co⁷n ĩfiniti fivmi di minor fama · fanno · maggiore · larghezza e profõdità · e corso ·, e non è il mare stretto 18 miglia ⁸che nel ultima terra di ponēte · diuide · l'Europa dal' Africa.

Likewise Europe pours into it the Don and the Danube, the Po, the Rhône, the Arno, and the Tiber, so that evidently these rivers, with an infinite number of others of less fame, make its greater breadth and depth and current; and the sea is not wider than 18 miles at the most westerly point of land where it divides Europe from Africa.

Leic. 10b]　　　　　　1085

Il ²seno mediterrano come pelago ricevea l'acque regali de l'Africa, Asia ed Europa, che a esso erano volte, ³e le sue acque veniano alle piaggie de' monti, che le circũdavano, e lì faceano argine, e le cime ⁴dello Apennino stauano in esso mare in forma d'isole, circũdate dalle acque salse, ⁵e ancora l'Africa dentro al suo Mõte Atalante non mostraua al celo scoperta la terra delle sue grã pianvre cõ circa ⁶a 3000 miglia di lunghezza, e Mẽfi risedeua in sul lito di tal mare, e sopra le pianvre della Italia, doue oggi ⁷volã li ucielli a turme, soleano discorrere i pesci a grãdi squadre.

The gulf of the Mediterranean, as an inland sea, received the principal waters of Africa, Asia, and Europe that flowed towards it; and its waters came up to the foot of the mountains that surrounded it and closed them in. And the summits of the Apennines stood up out of this sea like islands, surrounded by salt water. Africa again, behind its Atlas Mountains, did not expose uncovered to the sky the surface of its vast plains about 3,000 miles in length, and Memphis [6] was on the shores of this sea, and above the plains of Italy, where now birds fly in flocks, fish were wont to wander in large shoals.

Leic. 27b]　　　　　　1086

Co²me sopra Tunisi è il maggior riflusso che faccia il Mare Mediterrano che son circa 2 braccia ³e ½, e a Venezia cala 2 braccia; e in tutto il resto di tal Mare Mediterrano cala poco o ni⁴ente.

The greatest ebb made anywhere by the Mediterranean is above Tunis, being about two and a half braccia, and at Venice it falls two braccia. In all the rest of the Mediterranean Sea the fall is little or none. _Tunis._

F. 61a]　　　　　　1087

Descriui li mõti de' flessibili aridi, cioè della ²creatione dell' onde della rena portate dal uẽ³to, e de' sua mõti e colli, come accade nella Li⁴bia; l'esenplo ne vedrai sulli grã renaj ⁵di Po o di Tesino o altri grã fiumi.

Describe the mountains of shifting deserts; that is to say, the formation of waves of sand borne by the wind, and of its mountains and hills, such as occur in Libya. Examples may be seen on the wide sands of the Po and the Ticino, and other large rivers. _Libya._

B. 82b]　　　　　　1088

Circũfulgore · è vna macchina navale ·, fu invẽtione di quelli di Majolica.

Circumfulgore is a naval machine. It was an invention of the men of Majorca. _Majorca._

B. N. 2037. 9a]　　　　　1089

Alcuni · nel Mare Tirreno · vsarono questo modo, cioè ²appiccauano vn ãcora a l'una delle

Some at the Tyrrhene Sea employed this method; that is to say, they fastened an anchor _The Tyrrhene Sea._

6. levropia .. siche ciaro .. cho. 7. fano magiore largeza .. chorso .. moglia. 8. nelũtimatera .. leeropa .. africha.
1085. 1. nel. 2. seno [mediterano] mediterano il quale come pelagho .. regali [di circha 300 fiumi regali] "delafrica asia edeuropa, che acso erano volte". 3. e cholle .. acque veniano ale piagge .. chello .. elli faceano .. elle cime. 4. apennino [in forma di sole] stauano in eso .. circhũdate. 5. lafricha [non mos] dentro .. attalante no mostraua .. celo "scoperta la terra de" le sue .. circha. 6. lungeza e mẽfi .. sulito .. mare "e sopra" le. 7. [disorã] volã .. atturme solea .. pessci a grãde.
1086. 2. tuniti .. magor refrusso .. mediterano .. circha 2 br. 3. vinegia chala .. meditera .. pocho.
1087. 1. desscriui .. fressibili. 3. cholli. 4. esenpro .. [rena] grã.
1088. maccina .. maiolica.
1089. 1. tireno. 2. apichauano nãcora [chorda che ĩbaso sapienvavãcora] "aluna delle stremita dellatēna".

1084. 5. _Bagrada_ (Leonardo writes 'Bragada') in Tunis, now Medscherda; _Mavretano_, now Schelif.
　1085. 6. _Mẽfi._ Leonardo can only mean here the citadel of Cairo on the Mokattam hills.

1088. The machine is fully described in the MS. and shown in a sketch.
　1089. This text is illustrated in the original by a pen-and-ink sketch.

stremità dell' ātēna, [3]e dall' altra vna · corda che
ī baso s'appiccava a vn ācora, [4]e nel pugniare
attacavano detta · ācora ai remeggi dell' o[5]po-
sito navilio, e per forza d'argano quello māda-
vano alla bāda [6]e gittavano sapon tenero e stoppa
īpeciata e īfocata sulla [7]prima bāda dou' era
l'ācora attaccata, acciochè, per fugir detto [8]foco,
i difenditori d'esso navilio avessino a fugire da
l'op[9]posita bāda, e faciēdo così facievano avmēto
· allo spugnia[10]tore, perchè la galera piv facilmēte per lo cōtrapeso [11]andava alla bāda.

to one end of the yard, and to the other a cord,
of which the lower end was fastened to an
anchor; and in battle they flung this anchor on
to the oars of the opponent's boat and by the use
of a capstan drew it to the side; and threw soft
soap and tow, daubed with pitch and set ablaze,
on to that side where the anchor hung; so that
in order to escape that fire, the defenders of that
ship had to fly to the opposite side; and in doing
this they aided the attack, because the galley
was more easily drawn to the side by reason of
the counterpoise.

3. chorda . . sapicava.   4. decta āchora ai remigi.   5. ala.   6. stopa ipegolata . . sula.   7. bōda . . lācoratachata acio.   8. affugire
dallo.   9. effaciēdo.   10. galea.

IV

THE LEVANT

Truovāsi nelle riue del Mare Mediterrano versare fiumi 300, [2]e porti 40 mila 200, e esso mare è di lunghezza miglia 3000; Molte volte s'è accozza[3]to l'accrescimēto de' mari del riflusso suo e 'l soffiare delli venti occidē[4]tali al diluuio dei Nilo, e delli fiumi che uersā dal mare di Pōto, vennere alzato tanto li mari che sō [5]cō grādissimi diluui discorsi per molti paesi, · e questi diluui accadono nel tenpo, che 'l sole [6]distrugie le neui delli alti mōti d'Etiopia che si leuano alla fredda regiō dell' aria, e si[7]mil-mēte fa l'appressamēto del sole alli mōti della Sarmatia Asiatica e quella d'Europa, [8]in modo che l'accozzamēto di queste 3 dette cose sono, e sono state cagione di grā[9]dissimi diluui, cioè il riflusso del mare, e li uenti occidentali, e la distrutiō delle neui; è ogni cooa [10]ringorgata nella Siria, Samaria, la Giudea infra Sinai e il Libano, e 'l resto della Siria infra [11]il Libano e Mōte Tauro, e la Cilicia dentro alli mōti Armeni e la Pamfilia e Licia dentro alli mōti Celeni [12]e l'Egitto insino al mōte Atlante; Il seno di Persia, che già fu lago grādissimo del Tigris e cade[13]a nel mare d'India, ora à consumato il mōte · che li facea argine, e si è ragguagliato coll' altezza [14]dello Oceano Indico; E se 'l Mare Mediterrano sequiva il moto suo nel sē d'Arabia, ācor facieva il simile, [15]cioè che si ragguagliava l'altezza Mediterranea colla altezza d'esso Mare Indico.

On the shores of the Mediterranean 300 rivers flow, and there are 40,200 ports. And this sea is 3,000 miles long. Many times has the increase of waters, heaped by their backward flow and the blowing of the west winds, caused the overflow of the Nile and of the rivers which flow from the Black Sea, and has so much raised the seas that they have spread with vast floods over many countries. And these floods take place at the time when the sun melts the snows on the high mountains of Ethiopia that rise up into the cold regions of the air; and in the same way the approach of the sun acts on the mountains of Sarmatia in Asia and on those in Europe [7]; so that the gathering together of these three things are, and always have been, the cause of tremendous floods: that is, the return flow of the sea, the west wind, and the melting of the snows. So every river will overflow in Syria, in Samaria, in Judea between Sinai and the Lebanon, and in the rest of Syria between the Lebanon and the Taurus Mountains, and in Cilicia, in the Armenian Mountains, and in Pamphylia and in Lycia, in the mountains of Celaene, and in Egypt as far as the Atlas Mountains. The gulf of Persia, which was formerly a vast lake of the Tigris and discharged into the Indian Sea, has now worn away the mountains which enclosed it and laid them even with the level of the Indian Ocean. And if the Mediterranean had continued its flow through the gulf of Arabia, it would have done the same, that is to say, would have reduced the level of the Mediterranean to that of the Indian Sea.

The Mediterranean.

Versò l'acqua Mediterrana lungamente pel Mare Rosso, el quale è [2]largo cento miglia e lungo mille cinque cento; è tutto pieno di scogli,

For a long time the water of the Mediterranean flowed out through the Red Sea, which is 100 miles wide and 1,500 long, and full of

The Red Sea (1091-2).

1090. 1. mediterano. 2. porti [5] 40 mila 200 .. langeza .. seacoza. 3. lacresscimēto .. refrusso. 4. del mare .. ponto ve nere. 5. luui disscorsi .. ecquesti .. achagiano. 6. le neue .. chessi .. freda .. essi. 7. lapressamēto .. asiaticha ecquella. 8. chellacogamēto .. chagione. 9. coe il refrusso .. ocidentali ella. 10. soria someria la gudea .. sinai e e libano .. soria. 11. elibano .. ella cilicia .. mōtermini ella .. litia dentrali. 12. ellegitto .. attalante .. lagho .. chade. 13. chelli .. argine edessi ragualgliato .. alteza. 14. indicho Esse .. mediterano. 15. coe chesi racualgliaua lalteza mediterranea .. alteza .. indicho.
1091. 1. mediterana lunghamente. 2. largho .. ellungho .. cinquecento tutto.

1090. 2. *Porti* 40 *mila* 200. An extravagant statement, to be accounted for as a mistake in copying figures written as customary in high ancient classical writings. In these number 500 is written IↃ, called 'apostrophus'. When multiplied by 40 a new apostrophus is to be added: IↃↃ = 20,000. And also when multiplying five hundred there have to be written as many C in front of the apostrophus as there are behind it: CIↃ = 1,000. For one thousand stands the sign ∞.

Incorrectness in writing high numbers may occasionally have happened where so highly unpractical a system prevailed, at last superseded by the introduction of the Arabic numerals in the tenth century.

7. After the time of Augustus Sarmatia was generally the name of the country east of the Carpathians and of the Vistula. Leonardo, however, follows the geographer Ptolemaeus (about A.D. 150), who distinguishes between European and Asiatic Sarmatia.

e à consumato li la³ti del Mõte Sinai, la qual cosa testifica, nõ da inõdatione del Mar d'India, che in tali liti percuo⁴tesse, ma da una ruina d'acqua, la qual portaua con seco tutti li fiumi che soprabbon⁵dauano al Mare Mediterrano, e oltre a questo il riflusso del mare; ⁶e poi, essendo tagliato nel ponente, 3 mila miglia remoto da questo loco, il mõte Calpe è s⁷piccato dal Mõte Abila, e fu tal taglio fatto bassissimo nelle pianure che si trouauã infra Abila ⁸e l'oceano a piè del monte in loco basso, aiutato dal concauamẽto di qualche vallata fatta ⁹da alcun fiume che quiui passasse; venne Ercole ad aprire il mare nel ponẽte, e allora ¹⁰l'acque marine cominciarono a uersare nell' oceano occidentale, e per la grã bassezza, il Mare ¹¹Rosso rimase piv alto, onde l'acque ànno abbandonato il corso di quiui; senpre ànno poi versa¹²to l'acque per lo Stretto di Spagna.

reefs; and it has worn away the sides of Mount Sinai, a fact which testifies, not to an inundation from the Indian Sea beating on these coasts, but to a deluge of water which carried with it all the rivers which abound round the Mediterranean, and besides this there is the reflux of the sea; and then, a cutting being made to the west 3,000 miles away from this place, Gibraltar was separated from Ceuta, which had been joined to it. And this passage was cut very low down, in the plains between Gibraltar and the ocean at the foot of the mountain, in the low part, aided by the hollowing out of some valleys made by certain rivers, which might have flowed here. Hercules came to open the sea to the westward and then the sea waters began to pour into the Western Ocean; and in consequence of this great fall, the Red Sea remained the higher; whence the water, abandoning its course here, ever after poured away through the Straits of Spain.

C. A. 328*b*]   1092

La superfitie del Mare Rosso è in liuello coll' oceano . . . .

²Può esser caduta vna mõtagnia e, serrato la bocca ³del Mare Rosso, e proibito l'esito al Mediterrano, e co⁴sì rīgorgato tal mare abbia per esito il trãsito ī⁵fra li gioghi Gadetani, perchè il simile abbiã ⁶veduto alli nostri tẽpi cadere v̄ monte di sette ⁷miglia e serrare vna valle e farne lago, e così sõ ⁸fatti la maggior parte de' laghi da mõti come Lago di ⁹Garda' di Como e Lugano, e 'l Lago Maggiore; ¹⁰il Mediterrano poco s'abbassò per il taglio Gaditano ne¹¹li cõfini della Siria e assai in esso taglio, perchè pri¹²ma che tal taglio si creassi, esso mare versaua per scirocco, ¹³e poi s'ebbe a fare la calata, che corresse al taglio Gaditano.

¹⁴In *a* cadea l'acqua ¹⁵del Mediterraneo nel oce¹⁶ano.

¹⁷¶Tutte le pianure che son ¹⁸dalli mari · alli mõti sono ¹⁹già state coperte dall' acque salse;¶

²⁰¶Ogni valle è fatta dal suo fiu²¹me e tal

The surface of the Red Sea is on a level with the ocean . . . .

A mountain may have fallen and closed the mouth of the Red Sea and prevented the outlet of the Mediterranean, and the Mediterranean Sea thus overfilled had for outlet the passage between the mountains of Gades; for in our own times a similar thing has been seen; a mountain fell seven miles across a valley and closed it up and made a lake. And thus most lakes have been made by mountains, as the Lake of Garda, the Lakes of Como and Lugano, and the Lago Maggiore. The Mediterranean fell but little on the confines of Syria, in consequence of the Straits of Gibraltar, but a great deal in this passage, because before this cutting was made the Mediterranean Sea flowed to the south-east, and then the fall had to be made so that it ran through the Straits of Gibraltar.

At *a* the water of the Mediterranean fell into the ocean.

All the plains which lie between the sea and mountains were formerly covered with salt water.

Every valley has been made by its own river;

3. de mõti sinai .. percho.   4. tessi .. consecho .. soprabon.   5. dauono .. mediterano e oltre adiquesto il refrusso.   6. chalpe es.   7. pichato .. abile effu .. chessi trouaua .. abile.   8. ellocceano .. locho .. chonchauamẽto.   9. passassi .. erchole.   10. comincorono .. occeano .. perlla .. bassezza.   11. lacque anbandonato.

1092. 1. mare [so] rosso e illiuello.   2. chaduta .. esserrato [el] la bocha.   3. mediterano.   4. rīghorghato.   5. fralli .. ghadetani .. 6. veduta.   7. serare .. effarne lagho.   8. magiore . laghi de mõti .. lagho.   9. gharda [lac] di como ellughano ellagho magiore. 10. mediterano pocho sabasso .. ghaditano.   11. soria.   12. chettal .. scirocho.   13. affare .. choressi .. Gadetano.   14. chadea. 15. mediteraneo.   17. chesson.   19. dallacq.   20. effatta.   21. ettal pro"ne".

1091. 6, 7. Κάλπη ὄρος, Pliny, III chap. 2, § 4. 9. Leonardo seems here to mention Hercules half-jestingly and only in order to suggest to the reader an allusion to the legend of the Pillars of Hercules.
1092. See Pl. CXI, No. 2, a sketch of the shores of the Mediterranean Sea, where ll. 10–16 may be seen.

The large figures 158 are not in Leonardo's writing. The character of the writing leads us to conclude that this text was written later than the fore-going. A slight sketch of the Mediterranean is also to be found in MS. I. 47*a*.

proportione è da valle a val[22]le, quale è da fiume a fiume;¶

[23]¶Il massimo fiume del nostro mõdo è [24]il Mediterrano fatto fiume,¶

[25]¶che si move dal principio [26]del Nilo all' Oceano occidē[27]tale,¶

[28]e la sua suprema altezza [29]è nella Mavretania este[30]riore, e à di corso 10 mila [31]miglia, prima che si ripatri [32]col suo Oceano, padre del[33]le acque,

[34]Cioè 3000 il Mediterrano, 3000 [35]il Nilo scoperto, e 3000 il Nilo [36]che corre a oriēte ecc.

and the proportion between valleys is the same as that between river and river.

The greatest river in our world is the Mediterranean river,

which moves from the sources of the Nile to the western ocean.

And its greatest height is in Western Morocco and it has a course of ten thousand miles before it reunites with its ocean, the father of the waters:

That is, 3,000 miles for the Mediterranean, 3,000 for the Nile [35], as far as discovered, and 3,000 for the Nile which flows to the East, &c.

C. A. 95b]	1093

[4]Adūque cõcluderemo quelle · mõtagnie · essere di maggiore altura, [5]sopra · delle · quali · fioccando · l'origine · del Nilo · dai nuvoli · casca.

Therefore we must conclude those mountains to be of the greatest height, above which the clouds falling in snow give rise to the Nile.

The Nile (1093–8).

B. 61b]	1094

Gli Egiziani, gli Etiopi · e gli Arabi · nel passare il Nilo vsano ai cameli [2]appiccare ai lati del busto 2 baghe cioè otri ī questa forma di sotto.

[3]In queste 4 maglie di rette mettono i piè i cameli [5]di carriaggi.

The Egyptians, the Ethiopians, and the Arabs, in crossing the Nile with camels, are accustomed to attach two bags on the sides of the camels' bodies, that is, skins in the form shown underneath.

In these four meshes of the net the camels for baggage place their feet.

Leic. 34b]	1095

Come Trigon il quale passa per l'Africa Minore, il quale ne porta [2]con seco l'acqua di 3 paduli, l'un dopo l'altro di uarie altezze, de' quali il piv alto è Munace, e 'l mezzano è Pallas, [3]e 'l più basso è Triton; ancora el Nilo diriua di 3 altissimi paduli in Etiopia, il quale cor[4]re a tramõtana e versa nel mare d'Egitto con corso di 4000 miglia, e la sua breuissima e diritta linia [5]è 3000 miglia; di quel che s'à notitia escie de' mõti della luna con diuersi e incogniti prīcipi, e tro[6]vāsi li detti laghi alti sopra la spera dell' acqua circa a 4000 braccia cioè vn miglio e ⅓, a dare [7]vn braccio di caduta al Nilo per ogni miglio.

Like the Trigon which passes through Africa Minor and brings with it the water of three lakes, one after the other, of various elevations; the first being Munace and the middle Pallas and the lowest Triton. And the Nile again springs from three very high lakes in Ethiopia, and runs northwards towards the Sea of Egypt with a course of 4,000 miles, and by the shortest and straightest line it is 3,000 miles. It is said that it issues from the Mountains of the Moon, and has various unknown sources. The said lakes are about 4,000 braccia above the surface of the sphere of water, that is, 1⅓ miles, giving to the Nile a fall of 1 braccio in every mile.

22. he daffiume affiume. 23. del "nostro" mõde he. 24. mediterano [fatto] fiume. 25. [di] chessi. 26. occieano. 28. ella . . supprema. 29. he . . esste. 32. occieano. 34. mediterano. 36. chorre [da] a oriēte.

1093. 1. [adūque chõcluderemo quelle mõtagnie essere di magiore altura]. 2. [sopra delle quali lorigine del nilo dai nvvoli fiochando cade]. 3. sopra delle quali | "fiochando l'origine del nilo . dai nvvoli . cade". 4. chõcuderano . . magiore. 5. fiochando . . nvuoli casscha.

1094. 1. egiti. 2. apichare . . bage. 4. mettano. 5. cariagi.

1095. 1. la minore africha il quane ne. 2. consecho lacq"a" . . alteze . . mezano. 4. attramõtana . . ella sua . . ediritti. 5. he 3000 . . quel chessa notitio esscie. 6. vasi . . soppra lasspera dellacq"a" circha 4000 br. coe. 7. vn br. di.

35. Compare Nos. 970, 1063, 1084, 1095–8.

1094. Unfortunately both the sketches which accompany this passage are too much effaced to be reproduced. The upper represents the two sacks joined by ropes, as here described, the other shows four camels with riders swimming through a river.

1095. Africa Minor, the Mauretania of the ancients.

The lakes Munace, Pallas, and Triton are called by Ptolemy (IV. iii. 19) Libye, Pallas, and Tritonitis. The river Trigon connected these lakes with the Gulf of Gabes (Syrtis Minor). According to an old legend Pallas Athene was born here. The reading of this passage differs from that in the first edition. Compare No. 933.

Leic. 21b]   1096

Moltissime volte il Nilo e gli altri fiumi di grā ma²gnitudine ànno · versato tutto l'elemēto dell' acqua · e rēduto al mare.

Very many times the Nile and other very large rivers have poured out the whole element of water and restored it to the sea.

Leic. 22a]   1097

Perchè il Nilo inōda l'estate e viē da paesi focosi?

Why does the inundation of the Nile occur in the summer, coming from torrid countries?

Leic. 32b]   1098

Nō si nega che 'l ²Nilo al continvo ³non ētri torbido ⁴nel mare d'Egitto, ⁵e che tal turbu-lē⁶tia non sia ca⁷vsata dal terrē, ⁸che esso fiume le⁹ua al continvo da' ¹⁰lochi, onde passa, ¹¹il qual terrē ¹²mai ritorna in¹³dirieto nel ma¹⁴re che lo ricieue, ¹⁵se nō lo ributta al¹⁶li sua liti; vedi ¹⁷il mare areno¹⁸so dirieto al mō¹⁹te Atlante, doue già ²⁰fu coperto d'acqua ²¹salsa.

It is not denied that the Nile is constantly muddy in entering the Egyptian Sea and that its turbidity is caused by soil that this river is continually bringing from the places it passes; which soil never returns in the sea which receives it, unless it throws it on its shores. You see the sandy desert beyond Mount Atlas where formerly it was covered with salt water.

B. 61b]   1099

Customs of Asiatic nations (1099–1100).

Gli Assiri e quelli di Evbea vsano ai loro cavalli ²portare sacchi da potere a lor posta · ēpiere di uēto, ³i quali portano in scābio di bandella della sella di sopra ⁴e d'accanto, e bene è coperta di piastre di corame cotto, ⁵accio-chè 'l saettame non le fora, si che non àno in cvore la ⁶fuga sicura che la uittoria īcierta; vno cavallo ⁷così fatto passa 4 e 5 omini a v̄ bisognio.

The Assyrians and the people of Euboea accustom their horses to carry sacks which they can at pleasure fill with air, and which in case of need they carry instead of the girth of the saddle above and at the side, and they are well covered with plates of *cuir bouilli*, in order that they may not be perforated by flights of arrows. Thus they have not on their minds their security in flight, when the victory is uncertain; a horse thus equipped enables four or five men to cross over at need.

B. 62b]   1100

NAVICULA

²Le navicule · apresso · a li Assiri furono fatte di uirghe sottili di salice ³e tessute sopra per-tiche pur di salice, ridotte ī forma di barchetta, ilotate ⁴di poluere sottile inbeuerata d'olio, o di tremētina · ridotta ī natura ⁵di fango, la qual facieva resistētia a l'acqua, e per colpi non is-sedea perchè ⁶senpre stava fresca; Cesare vestì detta sorte di navicule · di pelle bouine ⁷nel passare Sicuris ·, fiume di Spagnia, secōdo ne testifica Lucano;

⁸L'Ispani ·, li Sciti · e li Arabi ·, quādo vogliono fare vn subito pōte, ⁹alligano · li gra-ticci fatti di salice sopra le baghe overo otri di pelli bouine, ¹⁰e così passā sicuramente.

SMALL BOATS

The small boats used by the Assyrians were made of thin laths of willow plaited over rods also of willow, and bent into the form of a boat. They were daubed with fine mud soaked with oil or with turpentine, and reduced to a kind of mud which resisted the water and was not displaced by blows; for it always remained fresh; Caesar covered this sort of boats with the skins of oxen in safely crossing the river Sicuris of Spain, as is reported by Lucan [7].

The Spaniards, the Scythians, and the Arabs, when they want to make a bridge in haste, fix hurdlework of willows on bags of ox-hide, and so cross in safety.

1097. lastade .. dipaesi.
1098. 1. negha. 5. chettal. 6. cha. 9. de. 11. equal. 14. re lo. 15. nollo rebutta. 19. attalante. 20. dacq"a".
1099. 1. ecquelli .. cavagli. 3. schābio. 4. dacanto. 5. acciochel saettumel .. fora si che non ano inēcare (?) la. 6. uettoria.
1100. 1. navichula. 2. navichula .. sali \\\\\\\. 3. ettessute. 4. o di tue mētina ridotta. 5. alacqua e pechel pinōnis fede aper. 6. fresca
    .. di pele bouine. 8. lissciti elli .. voliono. 9. aligano li grātici .. bage ovrotri .. pelle. 10. passa.

1100. 7. See Lucan's *Pharsalia*, iv. 130:
    Utque habuit ripas Sicoris camposque reliquit,
    Primum cana salix madefacto vimine parvam
    Texitur in puppim, caesoque inducta juvenco
    Vectoris patiens tumidum superenatat amnem.
    Sic Venetus stagnante Pado, fusoque Britannus
    Navigat oceano, sic cum tenet omnia Nilus,
    Conseritur bibula Memphitis cumba papyro.

His ratibus trajecta manus festinat utrimque
Succisam curvare nemus, &c.

Caesar (*De bello civ.* i. 54) has the same remark about the Britanni (confirmed by Pliny, *Hist. Nat.* iv. 15, Chap. 30), which Leonardo here makes about the Assyrians. This and the foregoing text are illustrated by slight sketches.

Leic. 10b]   **1101**

Nello ottanta 9 fu vno terremoto nel mar di Atalia presso a Rodi, il quale aperse il mare cioè il fondo, ²nella qual apritura si sommerse tanto diluuio d'acque, che per piv di 3 · ore si scoperse il fondo del mare dall' acque, che ³di quiui si spogliarono, e poi si richiuse al primo grado.

In [fourteen hundred and] eighty-nine there was an earthquake in the sea of Atalia near Rhodes, which opened the sea—that is, its bottom—and into this opening such a torrent of water poured that for more than three hours the bottom of the sea was uncovered by reason of the water which was lost in it, and then it closed to the former level. Rhodes [1101-2].

L. 0]   **1102**

Rodi à dētro 5000 case.

Rhodes has in it 5,000 houses.

W. 12591a]   **1103**

PEL SITO DI VENERE

²Farai le scale da 4 faccie, per le quali si pervenga a un prato fatto dalla natura sopra vn sasso, ³il quale sia fatto vuoto e sostenvto dinanzi con pilastri, e sotto traforato con magno portico, nel⁴li quali uada l'acqua in diuersi vasi di graniti porfidi e serpētini, dentro a emicicli,

FOR THE SEAT OF VENUS

You must make steps on four sides, by which to mount to a meadow formed by nature at the top of a rock which may be hollowed out and supported in front by pilasters and open underneath in a large portico, in which the water may fall into various vases of granite, porphyry, and serpentine, within semicircular recesses; and the Cyprus [1103-4].

1101. 1. mare disatalia preso .. aperse "il mare co" el fondo [del mare]. 2. somerse tane diluuio .. mare dellacqua. 3. spogliorono.
1103. 2. lesscale .. pervena .. prato [for] fatto [sopr] dalla. 3. voto essoslenvta .. pilasstri essotto .. conmagnio porticho ne. 4. vada lacque in diuersi [5] vasi .. esspā.

1101. *Nello ottanta 9.* It is scarcely likely that Leonardo should here mean A.D. 89. Dr. H. Müller-Strübing writes to me as follows on this subject: 'With reference to Rhodes, Ross says (*Reise auf den Griechischen Inseln*, iii. 70 ff., 1840) that ancient history affords instances of severe earthquakes at Rhodes, among others one in the second year of the 138th Olympiad = 270 B.C.; a remarkably violent one under Antoninus Pius (A.D. 138–61) and again under Constantine and later. But Leonardo expressly speaks of an earthquake 'nel mar di Atalia presso a Rodi', which is singular. The town of Attalia, founded by Attalus, which is what he no doubt means, was in Pamphylia and more than 150 English miles east of Rhodes in a straight line. Leake and most other geographers identify it with the present town of Adalia. Attalia is rarely mentioned by the ancients, indeed only by Strabo and Pliny, and no earthquake is spoken of. I think therefore you are justified in assuming that Leonardo means "1489".' In the elaborate catalogue of earthquakes in the east by Selale Dshelal eddin Sayouthy (an unpublished Arabic MS. in the possession of Prof. Schefer, Membre de l'Institut, Paris) mention is made of a terrible earthquake in the year 867 of the Mohammedan Era corresponding to the year 1489, and it is there stated that a hundred persons were killed by it in the fortress of Kerak. There are three places of this name: Kerak on the sea of Tiberias, Kerak near Tahle on the Lebanon, which I visited in the summer of 1876—but neither of these is the place alluded to. Possibly it may be the strongly fortified town of Kerak = Kir Moab, to the west of the Dead Sea. There is no notice about this in Alexis Percy, *Mémoire sur les tremblements de terre ressentis dans la péninsule turco-hellénique et en Syrie* (Mémoires couronnés et mémoires des savants étrangers, Académie Royale de Belgique, tome xxiii).

1103. See Pl. LXXXIII. Compare also p. 24 of this volume. The standing male figure at the side is evidently suggested by Michelangelo's David. Compare Vasari, vii. 153. On the same place a slight sketch of horses seems to have been drawn first; there is no reason for assuming that the text and this sketch, which have no connexion with each other, are of the same date.

Sito di Venere. Cyprus was conquered in 1191 by Richard I of England, who gave it in fee to the French knight Lusignan. Two centuries later a Lusignan of Cyprus married the Venetian gentlewoman Catarina Cornaro, who after his death inherited his possessions and became head of the government of Cyprus. In 1489 Venice forced her to abdicate and the island became a Venetian dependency. Such was the state of affairs in Cyprus at the time of Leonardo.

Cyprus is the Kypris of Homer and was considered by the ancients to be the home and birth-place of Aphrodite. In the imagination of men of the Renaissance Cyprus was suggestive of inspiration; Leonardo, too, had visions of this island, as shown by these notes.

The author Giovanni Gherardi of Prato preceded Leonardo in his enthusiasm. In the first book of his novel *Paradiso degli Alberti* Cyprus is chosen as the scene of a vision of allegorical figures placed in a beautiful landscape.

Vasari in his life of Perino del Vaga relates (v. 597): 'Essendo in questo tempo (1516) l'arcivescovo di Cipri [Aldobrandini, a Florentine] in Roma, uomo molto amatore delle virtù, ma particolarmente della pittura; ed avendo egli una casa ... con un giardinetto con alcune statue ... fece chiamare Perino', &c. In short, with the help of this pupil of Raphael, the archbishop's garden was turned into an imaginary pagan paradise decorated with 'storie di baccanti, di satiri, e di fauni, e di cose salvagge'.

e spā⁵da l'acqua in sé medesimi, e dintorno a tal portico inverso tramōtana sia un lago · con vna isoletta ⁶in mezzo, nella quale sia vn folto e ōbroso bosco; l'acque in testa ai pilastri siē uersate in uasi ai piè ⁷de' sua inbasamēti chollochati, de' quali si spargano piccoli riuetti.

⁸Partendosi dalla ⁹riviera di Cilitia inverso meridio si scopre ¹⁰la bellezza dell' isola di Cipri.

water may overflow from these. And round this portico towards the north there should be a lake with a little island, in the midst of which should be a thick and shady wood; the waters at the top of the pilasters should pour into vases placed at their base, from whence they should flow in little channels.

Starting from the shore of Cilicia towards the south you discover the beauties of the island of Cyprus.

W. 12591b]   1104

Dalli meridionali lidi di Cilitia si uede per australe la bell' isola ²di Cipri, la qual fu regnio della dea Venere, e molti incitati dalla sua bellezza ³ànno rotte li loro navili e sarte infra li scogli circundati dalle vertiginose ōde; ⁴quiui la bellezza del dolce colle invita i vagabundi navicanti a re⁵crearsi infra le sue fiorite verdure, fralle quali i uēti ragirādosi enpiono l'i⁶sola e 'l circūstante mare di suaui odori; o quāte naui quiui già son sommerse! o quanti ⁷navili rotti negli scogli! quiui si potrebbero vedere invmerabili navili; chi è rotto e mezzo ⁸coperto dall' arena, chi si mostra da poppa, e chi da prua, chi da carena e chi da costa, e parà ⁹a similtitudine d'un giudizio, che voglia risucitare navili morti; tant' è la somma di quelli, che ¹⁰copre tutto il lito settentrionale; quiui i uenti d'aquilone resonādo fan uari e paurosi ¹¹soniti.

From the shore of the southern coast of Cilicia may be seen to the south the beautiful island of Cyprus, which was the realm of the goddess Venus, and many navigators, being attracted by her beauty, had their ships and rigging broken amidst the reefs, surrounded by the whirling waters. Here the beauty of delightful hills tempts wandering mariners to refresh themselves amidst their flowery verdure, where the winds are tempered and fill the island and the surrounding seas with fragrant odours. Ah! how many a ship has here been sunk. Ah! how many a vessel broken on these rocks. Here might be seen barks without number, some wrecked and half covered by the sand; others showing the poop and another the prow, here a keel and there the ribs; and it seems like a day of judgement when there should be a resurrection of dead ships, so great is the number of them covering all the northern shore; and while the north gale makes various and fearful noises there.

The Caspian Sea (1105–6). C. A. 260a]   1105

Scriui a Bartolomeo turco del flusso e ²riflusso del mar di Ponto, e che intenda, ³se tal flusso e riflusso è nel Mare Ircano ⁴over Mare Caspio.

Write to Bartolomeo the Turk as to the flow and ebb of the Black Sea, and whether he is aware if there be such a flow and ebb in the Hyrcanean or Caspian Sea.

F. 50a]   1106

PERCHÈ L'ACQUA ²È IN SÙ MŌ³TI

⁴Dallo stretto di Gibilterra al Tanai è migli⁵a 3500, edè alto vn miglio e ⅙, dando vn braccio ⁶per miglio di calo a ogni acqua che si move me⁷diocremēte, e il Mar Caspio è assai più al⁸to; e nessū de' mōti d'Europa si leua vn ⁹miglio sopra la pelle delli nostri mari; adū¹⁰que si potrebbe dire, che l'acqua ch'è nelle ¹¹cime de' nostri mōti, venisse dall' altezza d'essi ¹²mari e de' fiumi che vi versano, che sō più alti.

WHY WATER IS FOUND AT THE TOP OF MOUNTAINS

From the Straits of Gibraltar to the Don is 3,500 miles, that is, 1⅙ miles up, giving a fall of one braccio in a mile to any water that moves gently. The Caspian Sea is a great deal higher; and none of the mountains of Europe rise a mile above the surface of our seas; therefore it might be said that the water which is on the summits of our mountains might come from the height of those seas, and of the rivers which flow into them, and which are still higher.

5. attal .. si lago. 6. mezo .. testa a pilastri .. uasi a pie. 7. sparga pichole riuetti. 8. dalla riuiera [di lic di cilitia] partendosi. 9. cilitia [si scopr] inver meridio si co. 10. beleza .. cipri la qua.
1104. 1. dalla riuiera dalli. 2. della sa belleza. 3. an rotte lor navili essarte .. delle ruertinali ōde. 4. belleza del del dolce callo invita [invita] i. 5. infralle .. fral .. enpiano. 6. adori .. ga son somerse. 7. roti nelgli .. potrebe .. roto e mezo. 8. arena [altri] chissi .. popa .. charena e qui. 9. assimilitudine .. volglia .. nvavili .. tantella soma. 10. chopre .. settantirone [sopra].
1105. 1. turcho .. frusso. 2. refrusso. 3. settal frusso e refrusso. 4. casspio.
1106. 1. lacq"a". 5. 3500 coen on miglio .. vn br. 6. acq"a" chessi. 7. e mar casspio. 9. pele. 10. chellacqua. 11. venissi .. alteza.

1105. Bartolomeo Turco, probably the traveller and geographer, author of a book of sonnets, entitled Isolario, on the Aegean islands.

F. 68a]　　　　　　　　　　1107

Qui seguita che 'l Mare della Tana, che ²confina col Tanai, è la più alta parte ³che abbia il Mare Mediterrano, il qua⁴le è remoto dallo Stretto di Gibilterra ⁵3500 miglia, come mostra la carta da ⁶nauicare; e à di calo 3500 braccia, cioè uno ⁷miglio e ⅛; e è più alto adunque que⁸sto mare che mōte che abbia l'occidēte.

Hence it follows that the Sea of Azov which ends with the Don is the highest part of the Mediterranean Sea, being at a distance of 3,500 miles from the Straits of Gibraltar, as is shown by the map for navigation; and it has 3,500 braccia of descent, that is, one mile and ⅛; therefore it is higher than any mountains which exist in the west.

The sea of Azov.

Leic. 31b]　　　　　　　　　1108

In nello stretto di Tratia il Mare di Pō²to senpre versa nel Mare Egeo, e mai l'Egeo in lui, e questo diriua, che 'l Mare Caspio, che cō 400 miglia sta per leuāte colli ³fiumi che ī lui versano, senpre versa per cave sotterrane in esso Mar di Pōto; e 'l simile fa il Tanai ⁴col Danvbio, in modo che senpre esse acque Pōtiche son piv alte che quelle dello Egeo, ⁵e per ciò le piv alte senpre discendono nelle basse, e nō mai le basse nelle alte.

In the Bosphorus the Black Sea flows always into the Aegean Sea, and the Aegean Sea never flows into it. And this is because the Caspian, which is 400 miles to the east, with the rivers which pour into it, always flows through subterranean caves into this sea of Pontus; and the Don does the same as well as the Danube, so that the waters of the Pontus are always higher than those of the Aegean; for the higher always fall towards the lower, and never the lower towards the higher.

The Dardanelles.

L. 66a]　　　　　　　　　　1109

Ponte da Pera a Costantinopoli · largo ²40 braccia, alto dall' acqua braccia 70, lungo ³braccia 600, cioè 400 sopra del mare, e 200 ⁴posa in terra, faciendo di sé spalle a sé ⁵medesimo.

The bridge of Pera at Constantinople, 40 braccia wide, 70 braccia high above the water, 600 braccia long; that is, 400 over the sea and 200 on the land, thus making its own abutments.

Constantinople.

Leic. 28a]　　　　　　　　　1110

Se si volterà il fiu²me alla rottura del ³terremoto, il fiume ⁴non correrà piv ⁵ināti, mai ritorne⁶rà nel corpo della ⁷terra, come fa l'Eu-⁸frate fiume, e co⁹sì faccia, a chi a Bo¹⁰lognia rīcresce li ¹¹sua fiumi.

If the river will turn to the rift of the earthquake, it will not run farther; it will never return to its bed, as the Euphrates does, and this may happen in Bologna to the one who is disappointed in its rivers.

The Euphrates.

C. A. 95b]　　　　　　　　　1111

Mons Caucasus · Comedorum · e Paropanisi insieme cōgiṽti, ²che tra Batriana e India nascono Oxus fiume ·, che in essi mōti nascie ³e

Mounts Caucasus, Comedorum, and Paropemisidae are joined together between Bactria and India, and give birth to the river Oxus

Central Asia.

1107. 2. ella. 3. mediterano. 6. navicare che . . 3500 br. coe l. 7. e ⅛ che e piu.
1108. 2. ecquesto . . caspio "che cō [3] 400 (?) mili sta per leuāte" colli. 3. cave socterrane. 4. danvbbio . . chessenpre. 5. perco le . . dissēdano.
1109. 1. gostantinopoli. 2. 40 br . . br. 70. 3. br. 600 coe. 4. spalle asse.
1111. 1. mō caucassus comedorū. 2. nasscano [oduss] oxus . . nasscie.

1107. The passage before this, in the original, treats of the exit of the waters from lakes.

1109. Leonardo's plan of the bridge must have been made about 1502. In that year ambassadors of Sultan Bajazet II to Pope Alexander VI (Borgia) were in Rome, and they may have looked out for Italian engineers to replace the bridge of pontoons over the Golden Horn by a permanent structure. (In 1453, by order of Sultan Muhamet II. the Golden Horn was crossed by a pontoon bridge laid on barrels: Joh. Dukas's *History of the Byzantine Empire*, xxxviii. 279.) See Pl. CX, No. 1, and compare Vasari (ed. Milanesi, vii. 168) in his *Life* of Michelangelo: 'Michelangelo, veduto questa furia del papa, dubitando di lui, ebbe, secondo che si dice, voglia di andarsene in Gostantinopoli a servire il Turco, per mezzo di certi frati di San Francesco, che desideravan di averlo per fare un ponte che passassi

da Gostantinopoli a Pera.' Michelangelo, so Condivi confirms (*Vita*, chap. 30), 'vedendosi condotto a questo, temendo dell' ira del papa, pensò andarsen' in Levante, massimamente essendo stato dal Turco ricercato con grandissime promesse per mezzo di certi frati di San Francesco, per volersene servire per fare un ponte da Gostantinopoli a Pera ed in altri affari.' Compare Seidlitz, i. p. 396, and Solmi in *Arch. Stor. Lomb.*, 1908, p. 353.

1110. Compare Vasari, vii. 106, for the regulation of the river at Bologna.

1111. Leonardo's notes on Central Asia are transcribed from the Latin translation of Cl. Ptolemaei *Geographia*, which appeared in print in numerous editions during the second half of the fifteenth century, and later with maps. First edition 1462. Described by I. L. Heiberg, *Hermes*, xlv (1910), pp. 57 ff., and xlvi (1911), pp. 206 ff.

corre 500 miglia a tramõtana e altrettãte a ponẽte e versa le sue acque nel Mare Ircano [4]e cõ seco s'accõpagnia · Osus ·, Dragodos ·, Arthamis ·, Xariaspis, Dragamaim ·, Ocus ·, Margus, [5]fiumi grãdissimi ·; dall' opposita parte uerso mezzodì · nasce · jl grã fiume · Indo · il quale di[6]rizza le sue õde per 600 miglia · inverso meridio, e per questa linia s'accõpagnia cõ seco i fiumi Zaradrus ·, Bibasis ·, [7]Vadris ·, Vandabal ·, Bilaspus · per leuãte ·, Suastus · e cioè per ponẽte ·, e incorporati tali fiumi colle [8]sue acque si uolta · corrẽdo miglia 800 per ponẽte ·, e ribattẽdosi ne' Mõti Arbeti fa li uno gomito, e si volta [9]a mezzodì, per la quale linia · infra 500 miglia truova il mare d'India doue per sette · rami · in quello si sommergie.

[10]Nell' aspetto del medesimo mõte nascie il magnio [11]Gãgie, il quale fiume corre per mezzodì miglia 500 [12]e per scirocco · mille · e · Sarabus · Diamvna e Soas [13]e Scilo · con gran unda · li faño cõpagnia; [14]versa in mare Indo per molte bocche.

which takes its rise in these mountains and flows 500 miles towards the north and as many towards the west, and discharges its waters into the Caspian Sea; and is accompanied by the Oxus, Dargados, Arthamis, Xariaspes, Dragamaim, Ocus, and Margus, all very large rivers. From the opposite side towards the south rises the great river Indus which sends its waters for 600 miles southwards and receives as tributaries in this course the rivers Xaradrus, Hyphasis, Vadris, Vandabal, Bilaspus to the east, Suastus to the west, uniting with these rivers, and with their waters it flows 800 miles to the west; then, turning back by the Arbiti mountains makes an elbow and turns southwards, where after a course of about 500 miles it finds the Indian Sea, in which it pours itself by seven branches. On the side of the same mountains rises the great Ganges, which river flows southwards for 500 miles and to the south-west a thousand and Sarabus, Diamuna, Soas, and Scilo, with big waves are its tributaries. It flows into the Indian Sea by many mouths.

C. A. 393*b*]

On the natives of hot countries.

1112

Li omini nati in [2]paesi caldi amano [3]la notte, perchè li rifre[4]sca, e àño in odio la [5]luce, perchè li riscal[6]da, e però sono del co[7]lore della notte cio[8]è neri | e ne' paesi [9]freddi ogni cosa è [10]per l'opposito.

Men born in hot countries love the night because it refreshes them, and have a horror of light because it burns them; and therefore they are of the colour of night, that is, black. And in cold countries it is just the contrary.

3. attramõtana.   4. e chõsecho sacõpagnia.   5. dalloposita parte [nass] uer mezodi nasscie.   6. riza . . inver . . sachõpagnia.   7. biilasspus . . suasstus hecoe per . . inchoporate.   8. chorrendo . . arbeti [assali] î gomito.   9. mezodi . . somergie.   10. nasscie.   11. mezodi.   12. sscirocho . . he sarabas e so as.   13. esscilo.   14. mare | "indo" per molte boche.
1112. 2. chaldi amaño.   3. perche le.   6. perosino.   9. cosa he.

1112. The sketch here inserted is in MS. H.[3] 103*b*.

XVIII

DYNAMICS. NAVAL WARFARE. AVIATION. MECHANICAL APPLIANCES. MUSICAL INSTRUMENTS

*S*UCH *theoretical questions as are contained in Sections XVI and XVII were prominent in Leonardo's studies of the sea. A few passages have been collected at the beginning of this section which prove that he had turned his mind to the practical problems of navigation, and more especially of naval warfare. What we know for certain of his life gives us no data, it is true, as to when or where these matters came under his consideration; but the fact remains certain both from these notes in his manuscripts, and from the well-known letter to Lodovico il Moro (No. 1340), in which he expressly states that he is as capable as any man in this very department.*

Leonardo's theories on statics and dynamics and his experiments and inquiries in these fields are outside the scope of this work. Full justice to them has been done by Roberto Marcolongo in 'La Meccanica di Leonardo da Vinci', in Atti della R. Accademia delle scienze fisiche e matematiche, vol. xix, Naples, 1933, containing a systematic exposition of Leonardo's sources and of the contributions he has made to these sciences. He intended writing a treatise on mechanics the contents of which were to be arranged under five headings. See vol. I, 8b, note; also Pierre Maurice Duhem, Les Origines de la statique, 2 vols., Paris, 1905 and 1906; Léonard de Vinci, Ceux qu'il a lus et ceux qui l'ont lu, 3 vols., Paris, 1906–14. We give but two excerpts here, one on gravitation and another showing Leonardo's spiritual conception of force (1113A and B).

The numerous notes as to the laws and rationale of the flight of birds are scattered through several note-books.

The purpose of these investigations was his desire to construct a flying-machine. His study of the nature and origin of the winds served the same purpose (K. Clark, Windsor Catalogue, 12671–2). A passage in MS. E (fol. 54b) affirms that the science of winds is a preparatory study to the 'scienza del moto degli uccelli infra l'aria'.—His notes and drawings reveal different types of flying-machines. Some require the aviator to lie in a horizontal position (MS. B. 73b, 74b, 75a, 79a; Cod. Atl. 276a, 302a and b); others show him standing erect (C.A. 314 a, 308a, 276b). On fol. 381b C. A. is a drawing of a parachute (1126); fol. 74a G. deals with gliding. His famous saying about the grande uccello (No. 1428) shows that he was at one time considering a trial-flight over Florence, starting off from Monte Ceceri.

Leonardo's notes on these subjects are scattered and his drawings represent but parts of machinery at a time. Attempts have recently been made to reconstruct

II   F f

his schemes by the aeronautical engineer Raffaelle Giacomelli in Gli scritti di L. d.
V. sul volo, *Roma,* 1936 *(see* Raccolta Vinciana, *vol. xiii, pp.* 156 *ff. and vol. xiv.
pp.* 278 *ff.).   At the Mostra della Storia e della Scienza of* 1929 *in the Istituto
Nazionale di Firenze various models were shown designed by Giuseppe Schneider
purporting to be founded on Leonardo's conceptions, and in the same year Mr. Paul
Garber presented his model of Leonardo's flying-machine to the aeronautical exhi-
bition at New York.   Reconstructions of Leonardo's models are to be seen in the
Science Museum, London.   See* Aeronautics *Handbook,* 1935.

In this publication we can give but a few texts bearing on the subject: Nos.
1122–6.

Only notes on musical instruments and acoustics are given here (Nos. 1129 *and*
1130). *Leonardo's views on Music are to be found in the* 'Paragone', *where he
compares it with Painting and Poetry (see vol. i, pp.* 76 *ff.).   His great reputation
as a musician is described by Vasari* (iv. 28): *see vol. I, p.* 69.

*We find many drawings and descriptions of machinery and mechanical appli-
ances in Leonardo's MSS.: especially in the Codex Atlanticus.   They include
pumps (F.* 13*a), augers (B.* 65*a; C.A.* 9*b), saw-mills (I.* 48*b), file-cutter (C.A.* 6*a),
rolling mills (C.A.* 2*a; G.* 70*b), windmills (L.* 35*b), cogwheels (C.A.* 8*b), printing-
press (C.A.* 14*a), instrument for measuring the velocity of the wind (No.* 1125A,
C.A. 249*b), hygrometer (ibid.; Plate XXXIII B., No.* 999, *n.), proportional
compasses (C.A.* 375*a,* 248*a), compass (C.A.* 316*a), magnet (A.* 20*b), spinning
machine (C.A.* 393*b), cloth shearing machine (C.A.* 397*a), revolving bridge
(C.A.* 312*a), diving suit (C.A.* 333*b,* 386*a; Leic.* 22*b; B.* 18*a), revolving chimney
cowl (C.A.* 394*b), cannon (C.A.* 3*b,* 19*a,* 26*b,* 34*a,* 56*b,* 399*a,* 340*a), etc.   See*
F. M. Feldhaus, Leonardo der Techniker und Erfinder, *second edition, Jena,*
1922.

III3 A

Ogni grave che libero disciende al cientro del mondo si diriza e quel che più pesa più presto discende, e quanto più disciende, più si fa veloce.

Every weight that descends and is free takes the direction to the centre of the earth, and that which weighs more will descend the quicker, and the longer its descent, the greater its velocity. On gravitation and force.

C. A. 302a] III3 B

La forza è tutta per tutta sé medesima, ed è tutta in ogni parte di sé.

Forza è una virtù spirituale, una potenza invisibile, la quale è infusa, per accidental violenza, in tutti i corpi stanti fori della naturale inclinazione.

Forza non è altro che una virtù spirituale, una potenza invisibile, (infusa) la quale è creata e infusa, per accidental violenza, da corpi sensibili nelli insensibili, dando a essi corpi similitudine di vita; la qual vita è di maravigliosa operazione, costrignendo e stramutando di sito e di forma tutte le create cose, corre con furia a sua disfazione, e vassi diversificando mediante le cagioni.

Tardità la fa grande, e prestezza la fa debole.

Vive per violenza, e more per libertà.

(È atta a) Trasmuta e costrigne (re) ogni corpo a mutazione di sito e di forma.

Gran potenza le dà gran desiderio di morte.

Sca(ch)ccia con furia ciò che s'oppone a sua ruina.

Trasmutatrice di varie forme.

Sempre vive con disagio di chi la tiene.

Sempre si contrapone ai naturali desideri.

Da piccola con tardità s'amplifica, e fassi d'una orribile e maravigliosa potenza.

E costrignendo sé (ogni cosa) stessa, ogni cosa costrigne.

. . . abita ne' corpi stati fori de lor naturale corso e uso.

. . . volentieri consuma sé stessa.

. . . forza è tutta in tutto, e tutta per tutto il corpo dov' è causata.

. . . nza è (un) solo un desiderio di fuga.

(Se)mpre desidera farsi debole e spegnersi.

. . . o costretta, ogni corpo costrigne.

(Ne)ssuna cosa sanza lei si move.

(Ne)ssuno sono o voce sanza lei si sente.

. . . sua vera semenza sta ne' (l vivi corpi) sensibili corpi.

Il peso è tutto in tutta sua perpendiculare opposizione, ed è tutto in ogni parte di quella.

Se la oppositione obliqua, contra posta al peso, fia dislegata e libera, non farà resistenza alcuna (a quello) a esso peso, anzi, con ruina, discenderà con quello.

Il peso trapassa per natura al suo desiderato sito.

Force is the same throughout and the whole is in every part of it.

Force is a spiritual power, an invisible energy which is imparted by violence from without to all bodies out of their natural balance.

Force is nothing but a spiritual power, an invisible energy which is created and communicated, through violence from without, by animated bodies to inanimated bodies, giving to these the similarity of life, and this life works in a marvellous way, compelling all created things from their places, and changing their shapes.

It speeds in fury to its undoing, and continues to modify according to the occasion.

Retardation strengthens, and speed weakens it.

It lives by violence and dies through liberty.

It transmutes and compels all bodies to a change of form and place.

Great power gives it great desire for death.

It drives away in its fury whatever stands in the way to its ruin.

Transmuter of various forms.

Wherever it is held, it is always ill at ease.

It is always opposing forces of nature.

It grows slowly from small beginnings to terrible and marvellous energy, and by compression of itself, compels all things.

. . . it lives in bodies which are out of their natural course and state.

. . . it likes to consume itself.

Force is the same throughout, and the whole of it is in the body where it is generated.

Force is but a desire to flight.

It always wants to weaken and extinguish itself.

. . . when compressed it compels all bodies.

Without it nothing moves.

No sound or voice is heard without it.

Its true source is in living bodies.

Weight is transmitted to the full by perpendicular resistance, and it is all in every part of the resistance.

If an oblique resistance opposed to the weight be loosened and freed, it will make no resistance to the weight; on the contrary, it will descend with it to ruin.

It is in the nature of weight to transmit itself of its own accord to the desired place.

III3 B. Marcolongo (see p. 217) quotes a very fine similar passage from MS. A.

Ogni parte d'essa forza contiene il tutto contrario al peso.

E spesso sono vincitori l'uno de l'altro.

Sono nel priemere di (pari potenzia, e 'l
maggiore) simile natura, e 'l più potente supera
il minore.

Il peso mal volentieri si muta, e la forza
sempre sta in fuggire.

Il peso è corporeo, e la forza incorporea.

Il peso è materiale, e la forza ispirituale.

Se l'una desidera di sé fuga (e disfazione) e
morte, quell' altra vuole stabilità e permanenza.

Sono spesso generatori l'uno dell' altro.

S'il peso partorisce la forza, e la forza il peso.

S'il peso vince la forza, e la forza il peso.

E, se sono di pari tempera, fanno lunga com-
pagnia.

Se l'uno è eterno, quell' altro è mortale.

Every part of force contains the whole—contrary to weight.

Often they are victors one over the other.

They are of similar nature as regards pressure
and the stronger overpowers the weaker.

Weight does not change of its own accord,
while force is always fugitive.

Weight has body, force has none.

Weight is material, force is spiritual.

One desires flight and death, the other seeks
stability and permanence.

Often one generates the other.

If weight creates force, force is weight.

If weight conquers force, force is weight.

And if they are of equal strength they will
keep in company for a long time.

If one is eternal, the other is mortal.

G. 54a]   1113

DEL MOTO DEL MOBILE—[2]DEL COGNOSCERE
QUĀTO [3]IL NAVILIO SI MOVE PER ORA

ON MOVEMENTS—TO KNOW HOW MUCH A SHIP
ADVANCES IN AN HOUR

[4]Ànno li nostri antichi vsato diuersi in[5]giegni
per vedere che viaggio faccia v̄ navilio per ci[6]as-
cuna ora, infra li quali Vitruvio ne po[7]ne vno
nella sua opera d'Architettura, il qua[8]le modo è
fallace insieme cogli altri; e que[9]sto è vna rota
da mulino tocca dall' onde [10]marine nelle sue
stremità, e mediante le [11]intere sue revolutioni
si descrive vna linia [12]retta che rappresenta la
linia circūferē[13]tiale di tal rota ridotta in rettitudine; [14]Ma questa tale inventione non è
valida, [15]se nō nelle superfitie piane e immobili
de' [16]laghi; Ma se l'acqua si move insieme col
[17]navilio con equal moto, allora tal rota re[18]sta
inmobile, e se l'acqua è di moto più o mē
[19]velocie che 'l moto del nauilio, ancora tal
ro[20]ta non à moto equale a quel del navilio,
[21]modo che tale inventione è di poca valitudine;
[22]Ecco vn altro modo fatto colla speriētia d'uno
[23]spatio noto da una isola a vn altra, e questo si
[24]fa con un asse lieua percossa dal uēto, che si
fa tanto piv o meno obbliqua quanto il vento,
che la percuote è più o [25]men velocie, e questo
è in Battista Alberti;

[26]Il modo di Battista [27]Alberti è fat[28]to sopra
la speri[29]entia d'uno spa[30]tio noto da vn[31]a isola
a un altra; [32]Ma tale inventi[33]one nō riesce, [34]se
nō a vn navi[35]lio simile a quel [36]dove è fatto tale
[37]speriētia, ma [38]bisognia che sia [39]col medesimo [40]carico, e me[41]desima vela, [42]e medesima

The ancients used various devices to ascertain
the distance gone by a ship each hour, among
which Vitruvius [6] gives one in his work on
Architecture which is just as fallacious as all the
others; and this is a mill-wheel which touches
the waves of the sea at their tips and in each complete revolution describes a straight line which
represents the circumference of the wheel extended to straightness. But this invention is of
no worth excepting on the smooth and motionless surface of lakes. But if the water moves together with the ship at an equal rate, then the
wheel remains motionless; and if the motion of
the water is more or less rapid than that of the
ship, then the wheel has neither the same motion
as the ship, so that this invention is of but little
use. There is another method tried by experiment with a known distance between one island
and another; and this is done by a board under
the pressure of wind which is more or less
oblique according as the wind strikes on it
with more or less swiftness. This is in Battista
Alberti [25].

Battista Alberti's method is made by experiment on a known distance between one island
and another. But such an invention does not
succeed excepting on a ship like the one on
which the experiment was made, and it must be
of the same burden and have the same sails, and

The ship's
logs of Vi-
truvius, of
Alberti, and
of Leonardo.

1113. 2. cogniossciere. 4. nosstri. 6. asscuna . . infralli . . vetruvio. 7. darchitectura. 8. effallacie . . ecque. 9. tocha dallonde. 11.
desscrive. 12. circhūferē. 13. diridotta. 14. Macquessta. 15. inmobile. 16. Massellacqua. 17. rota res. 18. essellacqua.
19. anchora. 20. nona . . acquel. 21. chettale . . pocha. 22. Ecci . . cholla. 23. ecquesto. 24. fa vasse lieva perchossa . . chella
perchote eppiuō. 25. ecquesto . . batissta albrti. 26. batissta. 27. albertiche effat. 28. lassperi. 31. issola. 32. Mattale. 33.
riesscie. 35. acquel. 36. effatto. 37. essperiētia. 38. chessia. 39. chol. 40. charicho.

1113. 6. See Vitruvius, *De Architectura lib.* x, ix.
25. Leon Battista Alberti, *De Architectura lib. v.*,
c. 12, treats 'de le navi e parti loro', but there is no
reference to the machine mentioned by Leonardo.
Alberti says here: 'Noi abbiamo trattato lungamente

in altro luogo de' modi de le navi, ma in questo luogo
ne abbiamo detto quel tanto che si bisogna.' This
refers to a treatise entitled *Liber navis* still extant
in the sixteenth century, but now lost. See Suida in
Thieme Becker's *K.L.*, vol. i, p. 210.

situ⁴³atiō di vela, e ⁴⁴medesime grã⁴⁵dezze
d'onde; ma ⁴⁶il mio modo ser⁴⁷ve a ogni navi-
⁴⁸lio, sì di remi co⁴⁹me vela, e sia pi⁵⁰ccolo o
grãde, stret⁵¹to lūgo o alto, ⁵²o basso, sēpre
serve.

the sails in the same places, and the size of the
waves must be the same. But my method will
serve for any ship, whether with oars or sails;
and whether it be small or large, narrow or long,
or high or low, it always serves [52].

Leic. 22b]

1114

Come con otricoli l'esercito debbe pas²sare i
fiumi a noto; ... Del modo del notare de' pesci;
del modo ³del lor saltare fori delle acque, come
far si uede a' delfini, che par cosa marauigliosa
for⁴mare salto sopra la cosa che non aspetta,
anzi si fugge; Del notare delli animali di lū⁵ga
figura, come anguille e simili; Del modo del
notar contro alle corēti e grã ⁶cadute de' fiumi;
Del modo come notino li pesci di retōda figura;
Come li animali ⁷che non ànno lunga fessa non
sã notare; Come tutti li altri animali naturalmente sã⁸no notare, auendo li piedi colle dita,
saluo che l'omo; In che modo l'omo debbe in-
para⁹re a notare; Del modo del riposarsi sopra
delle acque; Come l'omo si debbe difen¹⁰dere
dalle revertigini over retrosi delle acque che lo
tirano in fondo; Come l'omo ti¹¹rato in fondo
abbia a cercare del moto riflesso, che lo gitti
fori della profondità; Co¹²me si debo passeg-
giare colle · braccia; come si debbe notare
riverscio; Come, e come non ¹³si può star sotto
l'acque ·, se non quando si può ritenere lo
alitare; Come molti stie¹⁴no con istrumēto
alquāto sotto l'acque; Come e perchè io non
scrivo il mio modo di ¹⁵star sotto l'acqua, quāto
io posso star sanza mangiare, e questo nō publico
o diuolgo per le ma¹⁶le nature delli omini, li quali
vserebbero li assasinamēti ne' fondi de' mari
col ronpere ¹⁷i nauili in fondo, e sommergierli
insieme colli omini che ui son dentro, e bēchè
io insegni ¹⁸delli altri, quelli nō son di pericolo,
perchè di sopra all' acqua apparisce la bocca
della canna, ¹⁹onde alitano, posta sopra li otri
o sughero.

How an army ought to cross rivers by swimming with air-bags. ... How fishes swim [2]; of
the way in which they jump out of the water, as
may be seen with dolphins; and it seems a
wonderful thing to make a leap from a thing
which does not resist but slips away. Of the
swimming of animals of a long form, such as
eels and the like. Of the mode of swimming
against currents and in the rapid falls of rivers.
Of the mode of swimming of fishes of a round
form. How it is that animals which have not
long hind quarters cannot swim. How it is that
all other animals which have feet with toes
know by nature how to swim, excepting man.
In what way man ought to learn to swim. Of
the way in which man may rest on the water.
How man may protect himself against whirlpools or eddies in the water which drag him
down. How a man dragged to the bottom must
seek the reflux which will throw him up from
the depths. How he ought to move his arms.
How to swim on his back. How he can and how
he cannot stay under water unless he can hold
his breath [13]. How by means of a certain
machine many people may stay some time under
water. How and why I do not describe my
method of remaining under water, or how long
I can stay without eating; and I do not publish
or divulge these by reason of the evil nature of
men, who would use them as means of destruction at the bottom of the sea, by piercing a hole
in the bottom, and sinking them with the men
in them. And although I will impart others,
there is no danger in them; because the mouth
of the tube by which you breathe is above
the water, supported on bags or corks [19].

Methods of
staying and
moving in
water and
air.

C. A. 308b]

1114 A

Essendo tutti i prencipi delle cose spesse volte
causa di grandi momenti, come noi vediamo un
piccol moto, quasi insensibile, del timone avere
potenzia di voltare una nave di maravigliosa
grandezza, carica di grandissimo peso, e in fra
tanto pondo d'acqua, che da ogni banda la
grava, e contro alli corsi delli 'mpetuosi venti,

Inasmuch as all beginnings of things are often
the cause of great results, so we may see a small
almost imperceptible movement of the rudder
to have power to turn a ship of marvellous size
and loaded with a very heavy cargo and amid
such a weight of water which presses on it from
all directions and against the impetuous winds,

---

45. deze .. M"a". 47. a "o"gni. 48. cho. 49. essia. 50. c"j"colo ogrande strec. 51. to ollūgho. 52. obbasso.
1114. 1. otricolli lessercito .. pa. 2. pescci. 3. adalfini. 4. fuge. 5. essimili De. 6. pescci. 7. nonã. 8. cõlle .. chellomo riposarsi
lomo sopra. 10. delle revertigini .. chelli tirano. 11. refresso .. che gitti. 12. passegare colle br .. Come e non. 13. si postar ..
quanto si po. 14. isscrivo. 15. quāto iposso .. magare ecquesto. 16. vserebono. 17. sonmergierli .. ebēce. 18. aparisce la
bocha. 19. ossugero.

52. Leonardo does not reveal the method invented
by him.

1114. 2. Compare No. 821.
Lines 13–19 will also be found in vol. i, No. 1.

coll' abbracciamento di sì gran vele. Adunque noi possiamo essere certi, con piccol moto d'alia o di coda da entrare sotto o sopra il vento, per quelli uccelli, che sopra al corso de' venti sanza battimento d'alie si sostengano, sia atto e soffiziente a proibire il discenso de' predetti uccelli.

which are embracing its mighty sails. Therefore we may be certain in the case of those birds which can support themselves above the course of the winds without beating their wings that the slight movement of the wing or tail which will serve them to enter either below or above the wind will suffice to prevent the fall of the said bird.

C. A. 66a]

1114 B

Il notare sopra dell' acqua insegna alli uomini come fanno li uccelli sopra dell' aria.

Swimming on water teaches men what birds do in the air.

B. N. 2037.1b]

1115

On naval warfare (1115–16).

Se sarā in pugnia · naui · e · galee ·, essendo vincitori le naui per le loro alte gaggie, ²si de' tirare l'antēna · per īsino quasi alla sommità dell' albero, ³e abbi nella stremità di detta ātēna, cioè quella ch'è sporta sopra ⁴il nemico, appiccato v̄a gaggietta fasciata, e di sotto e dītorno uno ⁵grosso materasso pieno di bābagia, acciò nō sia offesa dalle bō-

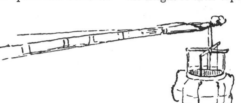

Supposing in a battle between ships and galleys that the ships are victorious by reason of the height of their tops, you must haul the yard up almost to the top of the mast, and at the extremity of the yard, that is, the end which is turned towards the enemy, have a small cage fastened, wrapped up below and all round it a great mattress full of cotton so that it may

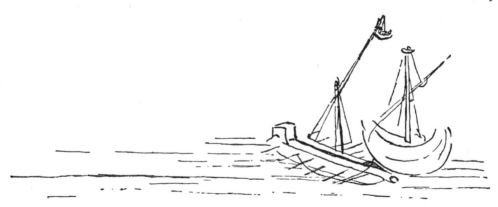

bardelle, ⁶poi tira col' argano ī basso l'opposita parte d'essa antēna, e la gaggia ⁷opposita andrà tāto · in alto ·, ch'ella di grā lūga avāzerà la gaggia del⁸la nave, e potrassi facilmēte cacciare li omini che dētro ui sono; ⁹ma bisognia che gli omini che sono nella galea · vadino dall' opposita banda, ¹⁰acciò · faccino · contrapeso al carico delli omini posti dētro · alla gaggia ¹¹della antēna.

not be injured by the bombs; then, with the capstan, haul down the opposite end of this yard, and the top on the opposite side will go up so high that it will be far above the round-top of the ship, and you will easily drive out the men that are in it. But it is necessary that the men who are in the galley should go to the opposite side of it so as to afford a counterpoise to the weight of the men placed inside the cage on the yard.

1115. 1. sara .. gagie. 2. si de [mettere] tirare .. somita. 3. abi .. ītena .. che [apichata] sporta. 4. apichato va gagietta fassciatta .. ditorno dino. 6. chol .. ella gagia. 7. oposita andera .. gagia de. 8. chaciare. 9. chessono .. ghalea .. daloposita. 10. chontrapeso .. charicho .. gagia. 11. antena.

B. N. 2037. 3a]   **1116**

Se vuoli fare vna · armata marittima, vsa di
questi navili per sfondare le navi, ²cioè fa
navili · di 100 piè, e larghi piedi 8, ma fa che
i remi sinistri abino i loro ³motori nel lato
destro del navilio, e così
i destri nel sinistro come
appare in M, acciochè lo
lieve de' remi ⁴sia piv
lūgo ·, e detto navilio sia
grosso piè uno e ½ ·
cioè fatto di travi fermi

If you want to build an armada for the sea,
employ these ships to ram in the enemy's ships.
That is, make ships 100 feet long and 8 feet
wide, but arranged so that the left-hand rowers
may have their oars to the
right side of the ship, and
the right-hand ones to the
left side, as is shown at M,
so that the leverage of the
oars may be longer. And
the said ship may be one

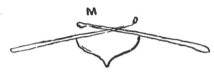

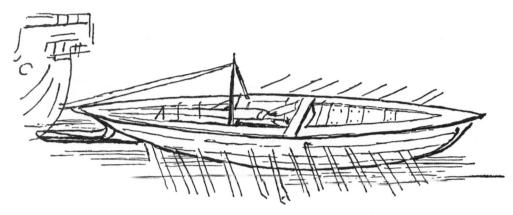

di ⁵fuori e di dētro con asse con cōtrari linia-
mēti; e questo navilio avrà, sotto ⁶l'acqua vn

foot and a half thick, that is, made with cross
beams within and without, with planks in con-

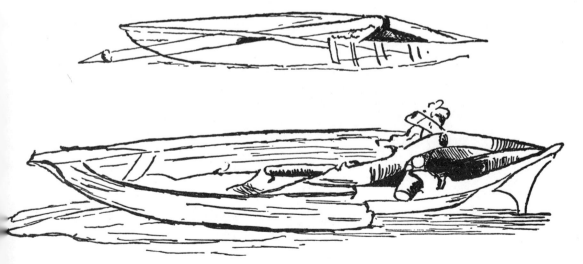

piede, appiccato vno spūtone ferrato di peso e
grossezza d'un ācudi⁷ne · e questo per forza di

trary directions. And this ship must have
attached to it, a foot below the water, an iron-

1116. 1. isfondare. 2. cheremi . . ilor. 3. nelato . . sinistro "come apare in M" aciochello. 4. sieno piv lūge . . pie 1 e . . facto di trav.
5. fori . . chon asse chō cōtrari . . navilio avc. 6. lacq"a" vn piedi apuchato . . ferato adi peso . . grosseza. 7. ecferm.

remi potrà, dato il primo colpo, tornare īdirietro, ⁸e cõ furia ricacciarsi ināti e dare il colpo secõdo, e poi il terzo, e tāti che rõpa detto navilio.

shod spike of about the weight and size of an anvil; and this, by force of oars, may, after it has given the first blow, be drawn back, and driven forward again with fury give a second blow, and then a third, and so many as to destroy the other ship.

B. 81b]   1117

MODO DI SALUARSI · IN VNA · TĒPESTA E NAVFRAGIO · MARITTIMO

A METHOD OF ESCAPING IN A TEMPEST AND SHIPWRECK AT SEA

The use of swimming belts.

Bisognia · avere v̄a vesta ²di corame ch'abbi doppio i labri del petto per spatio d'vno · dito, e così sia doppio ³dalla cītura īsino al ginocchio ·, e sia corame sicuro dallo · esalare ·; E quādo ⁴bisognasse saltare ī mare ·, sgō̄fia · per li labri del petto le code del tuo vestito, ⁵e salta in mare ·, e lasciati guidare all' onde · ; quādo nõ vedi vicina riva, ⁶ne abbi notitia · del mare ·, e tieni sempre · ī bocca la canna dell' aria che va nel vestito, ⁷e quādo per una volta o 2 ti bisognasse trare dell' aria comvne, e la schiuma t'inpedisce, ⁸tira per bocca di quella del vestito.

Have a coat made of leather, which should have the part over the breast with two layers, a finger's breadth apart; and in the same way it must be double from the waist to the knee; and the leather must be quite air-tight. When you have to leap into the sea, blow out the skirt of your coat through the double layers of the breast; and jump into the sea, and allow yourself to be carried by the waves; when you see no shore near, give your attention to the sea you are in, and always keep in your mouth the air-tube which leads down into the coat; and if now and again you require to take a breath of fresh air, and the foam prevents you, you may draw a breath of the air within the coat.

S. K. M. III. 66a]   1118

On the gravity of water.

Se 'l mare si pesa sul suo fondo, ²vn omo, che giacesse sopra esso ³fondo e avesse 1000 braccia d'acqua ⁴a dosso, n'avrebbe a scoppiare.

If the weight of the sea bears on its bottom, a man, lying on that bottom and having 1,000 braccia of water on his back, would be crushed.

S. K. M. II.² 65b]   1118 A

Tanto pesa l'acqua che ssi parte del suo sito per causa della nave, quanto il peso propio d'essa nave apunto.

The weight of the water displaced by a ship is precisely the same as the weight of that ship. . . .

C. A. 7a]   1119

Diving apparatus and skating (1119-21).

D'andar sotto acqua; ²Modo di caminare ³sopr' acqua.

Of walking under water. Method of walking on water.

B. N. 2037. 2b]   1120

Siccome per lo fivme ghiacciato uno omo corre ²sanza mvtatione di piedi ·, così vn carro fia ³possibile fare che corra per sé.

Just as on a frozen river a man may run without moving his feet, so a car might be made that would slide by itself.

questo . . forza adi remi . . īdirieto. 8. richaciarsi.

1117. 2. dopio . . peto perispatio dono . . dopio. 3. aginochio essia . . sicuro dello. 4. biscognassi . . schõfia. 5. essalta imare ellassciati . . visina. 6. abi . . ettieni . . bocha la cana. 7. per ỉ . . bisognassi trare dellaria *partly indistinct*; sciuma tĩpedissi. 8. boca.

1118. 2. diaciessi. 3. avessi 1000 br dacu. 4. asscopiare.   **1119.** 2. chomin. 3. sop acq"a".

1120. 1. sichome . . diacciato ī omo core. 2. chosi vn charo. 3. possiuile . . chora.

1118A. This note is accompanied by the sketch of a boat with indication of water-line.
1119. Two sketches illustrate this passage.

1120. The drawings of carts by the side of this text have no direct connexion with the problem as stated in words.—Compare No. 1448, l. 16.

S. K. M. III. 46a]   **1121**

Difiniscimi perchè vno ²che sdrucciola sopra il ghiaccio ³nõ cade.

Define why a man who slides on ice does not fall.

Trn. (Mz.) 6a]   **1122**

L'uomo ne' volatili à a stare libero dalla cintura insù ²per potersi bilicare, come fa in barca acciò che 'l cē³tro della grauità di lui e dello strumēto si possa ⁴bilicare e trasmutarsi, dove necessità il dimāda ⁵alla mutatione del centro della sua resistētia.

Man when flying must stand free from On flying-
the waist upwards so as to be able to machines
balance himself as he does in a boat, so (1122–6).
that the centre of gravity in himself and in the machine may counterbalance each other, and be shifted as necessity demands for the changes of its centre of resistance.

C. A. 45a]   **1122 A**

Se l'ucciel non batte in basso le sue alie con più velocità che non sarebbe il suo discenso naturale, colla medesima astensione e situazione di tale alie, allora il suo moto sarà allo ingiù. Ma se tal moto d'alie sarà più velocie che 'l predetto natural discienso, allora tal moto sarà allo insù, con tanta maggiore velocità, quanto il discenso di tale alie sarà più veloce.

L'ucciello disciende da quella parte, donde lo stremo dell' alia è più vicino al cientro della sua grauità. Farai l'anatomia dell' alie d'uno ucciello, insieme colli muscoli del petto motori d'esse alie. El simile farai dell' omo, per mostrare la possibilità che è nell' omo a volersi sostenere infra l'aria con battimenti d'alie.

If the bird does not strike its wings downwards with greater velocity than would be its descent in the course of nature, with both its wings spread out equally and in the same position, then its motion will be downwards. But if the movement of the wings is faster than the aforesaid natural descent, then the bird's motion will be upwards; and its velocity will be greater according as the downward strokes of the wings are faster.

The bird descends on the side where the tip of the wing is nearer to its centre of gravity.

You must study the anatomy of the wing of a bird together with the muscles of the chest which cause these wings to move; and you must study the same in man in order to show the potential faculty in man to sustain himself in the air by the flapping of wings.

Trn. (Mz.) 16a]   **1123**

Ricordati siccome jl tuo vccello non debbe imitare ²altro che 'l pipistrello per cavsa che i pannicoli fāno ³armadura over collegatione alle armadure, cioè ma⁴estre delle ali;

Remember that your flying-machine must imitate no other than the bat, because the membranes serve as framework, or rather the connexion of the framework, i.e. that which commands the wings.

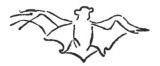

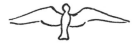

⁵E se tu imitassi l'alie delli vccelli pennvti, esse ⁶son di piv potēte osse e nervatura, per essere esse ⁷traforate; cioè che le lor penne sõ disunite e passa⁸te dall' aria; Ma il pipistrello è aivtato dal panni⁹culo che lega il tutto, e non è traforato.

If you imitate the wings of feathered birds, you will find a much stronger structure, because they are penetrable; that is, their feathers are separate and the air passes through them. But the bat is aided by the membrane that connects the whole and is not penetrated by the air.

1121. 2. strusi . . diaccio.
1122. 1. volatili asstare. 2. barcha. 4. bilichare e strassmutarsi. 5. ressistētia.
1123. 1. sichome. 2. pipisstrello . . chavsa che panichuli. 3. chollegacione . . coe. 4. esstre . . alie. 5. essettu. 6. enervatura. 7. coe chelle. .eppassa. 9. chulo chellega.

1121. A sketch accompanies the passage in the original.

1122A. For illustrations of artificially constructed

wings see C. A. 307–9, 311, 313, 314, etc., and MS. B 73, 74, 77, etc.

F. 41b]   1123 A

Notomizza il pipistrello e a questo t'attieni e di questo ordina lo strumento.

Dissect the bat, and keep to this study, and on this model arrange the machine.

Trn. (Mz.) 17a]   1123 B

Persuasione alla 'mpresa che leva l'obbiezioni.

Se tu dirai che li nerbi e muscoli dell' uccello, sanza comparazione esser di magior potenza che quelli dell' omo, con ciò sia che tutta la carnosità di tanti muscoli e polpe del petto essere fatti a benefizio e aumento del moto delle alie, con quello osso d'un pezzo nel petto, che aparechia potenza grandissima all' uccello, coll'alie tutte tessute di grossi nervi e altri fortissimi legamenti di cartilagini e pelle fortissima con vari muscoli; qui si risponde che tanta forteza è aparechiata per potere, oltre all' ordinario suo sostenimento delle alie, gli bisogna, a sua posta, radopiare e triplicare il moto, per fugire dal suo predatore, o seguitare la preda sua; onde in tale effetto, li bisognia radopiare o triplicare la forza sua, e oltre a di questo, portare tanto peso ne' sua piedi, per l'aria, quanto è il peso di sé medesimo; come si vede al falcon portare l'anitra e all' aquila la lepre, per la qual cosa assai bene si dimostra dove tal superchia forza si stribuisce; ma poca forza li bisogna a sostener sé medesimo, e bilicarsi sulle sue alie e ventilarle sopra del corso de' venti e dirizzare il temone alli sua cammini e poco moto d'alie basta, e tanto di più tardo moto, quanto l'uccello è magiore.

A plea for the undertaking that disposes of the objections.

You will perhaps say that the sinews and muscles of a bird are incomparably more powerful than those of man, because all the strength of so many muscles and fleshy parts of the breast goes to aid and increase the movement of the wings, while the bone in the breast is all in one piece and consequently affords the bird very great power, the tissue of the wings consisting of thick sinews and other very strong ligaments of cartilage and the skin being very thick with various muscles. The reply to this is that such great strength is given as a reserve of power beyond what it ordinarily uses to support itself on its wings, since it is necessary for it whenever it may desire either to double or treble its motion in order to escape from its pursuer or to follow its prey. Consequently in such a case it becomes necessary for it to put forth double or treble the amount of effort, and in addition to this to carry through the air in its talons a weight corresponding to its own weight; so one sees a falcon carrying a duck, and an eagle carrying a hare; which circumstance shows well enough where the excess of strength is spent; for they need but little force in order to sustain themselves and to balance themselves on their wings and flap them in the pathway of the wind; and to steer their ways a slight movement of the wings is sufficient, and the movement will be slower in proportion as the bird is greater in size.

Trn. (Mz.) 13b]   1124

PER FUGIRE IL PERICOLO DELLA RUINA

[2]Può accadere la ruina di tali strumēti per · 2 · modi, de' quali [3]il primo · è del ronpersi lo strumēto; secondario fia quā[4]do lo strumento si uoltasse per taglio o vicino a esso taglio, [5]perchè senpre debbe discendere per grande obbliquità e quasi [6]per la linia dell' equalità; In quanto al riparo, [7]del ronpersi lo strumēto, si riparerà col farlo di somma for[8]tezza, per qualunche linia esso si potesse voltare. . . .

TO ESCAPE THE PERIL OF DESTRUCTION

Destruction to such a machine may occur in two ways; of which the first is the breaking of the machine. The second would be when the machine should turn on its edge or nearly on its edge, because it ought always to descend in a highly oblique direction, and almost exactly balanced on its centre. As regards the repair— the breaking of the machine—that may be prevented by making it as strong as possible in whichever direction it may tend to turn over. . . .

1124. 1. pericholo. 2. achadere .. tale. 3. sechondario. 4. losstrumento si uoltassi .. vicico. 5. disscendere. 7. losstrumēto. 8. teza. 8. potessi.

1124. Compare No. 1428.

Trn. (Mz.) 8*a*]   1124 A

Il predetto uccello si debbe coll' aiuto del vento levare in grande alteza e questa fia la sua sicurtà: perchè ancora che l'intervenissi tutte le antidette revoluzioni, esso ha tempo a ritornare nel sito dell' equalità, perchè le sue menbra sieno di grande resistenzia a ciò che possin sicuramente resistere al furore e inpeto del discenso, colli antidetti ripari, e le sue giunture di forti mascherecci e li sua nervi di corde di seta cruda fortissima; e non s'inpacci alcuno con ferramenti, perchè presto si schiantano nelle lor torture o si consumano; per la qual cosa non è da 'mpacciarsi con loro.

The bird I have described ought by the help of the wind to rise to a great height, and this will be its safety: since even if all the above-mentioned revolutions were to befall it it would still have time to regain a condition of equilibrium, provided that its parts have a great resistance; so that they can safely withstand the fury and impetus of the descent, by aid of the defences which I have mentioned, and of its joints of strong leather treated with alum and its rigging made of cords of very strong raw silk; and let no one encumber himself with iron bands, for these are very soon broken in twisting, or they become worn out; and for this reason it is well not to encumber oneself with them.

Trn. (Mz.) 17*a*]   1125

Baghe dove l'omo in 6 braccia [2]d'altezza cadendo nō si faccia male, [3]cadendo così in acqua come [4]in terra; e queste baghe le[5]gate a vso di paternostri s'avol[6]gino altrui addosso.

Bags by which a man falling from a height of 6 braccia may avoid hurting himself, by a fall whether into water or on the ground; and these bags, strung together like a rosary, are to be fixed on one's back.

C. A. 249*b*]   1125 A

Qui bisogna un orilogio, che mostri l'ore punti e minutii a misurare quanta via si vada per ora, col corso d'un vento.

A cognoscere le qualità e grossezze dell' aria e quando à a piovere.

Here we need a clock to show the hours, minutes, and seconds to measure what distance per hour one travels with the course of the wind.

To know the quality and density of the air and when it has to rain.

C. A. 381*b*]   1126

Tāta forza si fa colla cosa īcōtro all' aria, quāto l'aria contro alla cosa; [2]Vedi l'alie percosse cōtro all' aria fanno sostenere la pesante aquila sulla suprema sottile aria [3]vicina all' elemēto del fuoco; Ancora vedi la mossa aria sopr' al mare ripercossa [4]nelle gōfiate vele far correr la carica e pesāte nave; sichè per queste demostra[5]tive e assegnate ragioni potrai conosciere l'uomo colle sua cōgiegniate e grādi ale, [6]facciēdo forza cōtro alla resistēte aria, vincēdo poterla soggiogare a le[7]varsi sopra di lei.

Se uno uomo ha un padiglione di pannolino intasato che sia 12 braccia per faccia e alto 12, potrà gittarsi d'ogni grande altezza sanza danno di sé.

A substance offers as much resistance to the air as the air does to the substance. See how the beating of its wings against the air supports a heavy eagle in the highly rarefied air, close to the sphere of elemental fire. Observe also how the air in motion over the sea fills the swelling sails and drives heavily laden ships. From these instances, and the reasons given, a man with wings large enough and duly attached might learn to overcome the resistance of the air, and conquering it, succeed in subjugating it and raise himself upon it.

If a man has a tent 12 braccia wide and 12 high covered with cloth he can throw himself down from any great height without hurting himself.

L. 59*b*]   1126 A

Sono alcuni uccelli i quali usano movere con più velocità le loro alie nel calare che nello alzare, e questo si vede ne' colombi e simili.

There are some birds which are in the habit of moving their wings more swiftly when they lower them than when they raise them, and this

1125. 1. 6 br. 2. dalteza . facca. 3. chedendo. 4. ecqueste. 5. paternosstri savol. 6. glino . . adosso.
1126. 1. [vo] tāta . . cholla chosa ī chōtro . . chosa. 2. perchosse chōtro . . fassosstenere . . sulla "supplema" sottile. 3. fuocho Anchora . . riperchossa. 4. ghōfiate . . chorrer la charicha . . qsste [asse] demosstra. 5. chonossciere . . cholle . . chōgiegniate. 6. chōtro . . resisstēte aria [potersi e] e vincēdo poterla sogiogare alle.

1125 A. These texts are accompanied by drawings of instruments.

1126. This first project for a parachute is accompanied by a drawing of a man suspended in the air, hanging by ropes to a hollow quadrangular pyramid.

Altri sono che il loro calare d'ali sono di più tardità che la loro elevazione, e questo si vede nelle cornacchie e altri simili uccelli.

Usano li uccelli i quali volano velocemente con equale altezza da terra di battere le loro alie allo 'ngiù e allo indirieto: allo ingiù quanto basta al resistere al discenso del volatile, allo indirieto quanto esso vole con più velocità andare innanzi. La velocità delli uccelli è ritardata dallo aprimento e allargamento della lor coda.

is seen to be the case with doves and suchlike birds. There are others which lower their wings more slowly than they raise them, and this is seen with crows and other similar birds.

The birds which fly swiftly, keeping at the same distance above the ground, are in the habit of beating their wings downwards and behind them: downwards to the extent needed to prevent the bird from descending, backwards according as it wishes to advance with greater speed.

The speed of the birds is checked by the opening and spreading out of their tail.

C. A. 308*b*]   1126 B

Ha la natura dato che tutti li grandi uccelli stieno in tanta altura che 'l vento che aumenta il lor volare sia di retto corso e potente, perchè il lor volare basso infralle montagne, dove il vento s'aggira, e sta sempre pieno di retrosi e moti revertiginosi, dove non potessi, per la furia del condensato vento per le gole delli monti, a sua posta schermirsi e governarsi colle sua grande alie, allo scifare le percussioni delle spiagge e alti scogli e alberi, non avessi qualche volta a essere causa della lor distruzione; onde nelle grande alture, quando, per qualche accidente il vento l'avesse a voltare per qualunque modo, sempre esso ha tempo a ridirizzarsi, e ritemprare sicuramente il suo volare, il quale sempre sarà per tutto spedito; ma passi sempre sopra li nugoli, acciò scifi il bagnamento delle sua piume.

Nature has so provided that all the large birds can stay at so great an elevation that the wind which increases their flight may be of straight course and powerful. For if their flight were low among mountains where the wind goes round and is perpetually full of eddies and whirls, and where they cannot find, in the fury of the wind compressed in the hollows of the mountains, any spot of shelter nor so guide themselves with their great wings as to avoid being dashed upon the cliffs and the high rocks and trees, would not this sometimes be the cause of their destruction? Whereas at great altitudes whenever through some accident the wind turns in any way, the bird has always time to redirect its course and in safety adjust its flight which will always proceed through everything, and it can always pass above clouds in order to avoid wetting its wings.

Trn. (Mz.) 6*b*]   1126 C

Il nibbio e li altri uccelli, che battan poco le alie, vanno cercando il corso del vento, e quando il vento regnia in alto, allora essi fieno veduti in grande altura, e se regnia basso essi stanno bassi.

Quando il vento non regnia nell' aria, allora il nibbio batte più volte l'alie nel suo volare, in modo tale, ch'esso si leva in alto e acquista inpeto, col quale inpeto, esso poi declinando alquanto, va lungo spazio sanza battere alie; e quando è calato esso di novo fa il simile, e così segue successivamente; e questo calare sanza battere alie, li scusa un modo di riposarsi per l'aria dopo la fatica del predetto battimento d'alie.

The kite and the other birds which move their wings only a little way go in search of the current of the wind; and when the wind is blowing at a height they may be seen at a great elevation, but if it is blowing low they remain low.

When there is no wind in the air, then the kite beats its wings more often in its flight, in such a way that it raises itself on high and acquires an impetus, with which impetus, dropping then gradually, it can travel for a great distance without beating its wings; and when it has descended it does the same over again and so continues in succession; this descent without beating the wings serves it as a means of resting in the air after the fatigue of the above-mentioned beating of the wings.

C. A. 161*a*]   1126 D

L'uccello è strumento oprante per legge matematica, il quale strumento è in potestà dell' omo poterlo fare con tutti li sua moti, ma non con tanta potenzia; ma solo s'astende i nella potenzia del bilicarsi. Adunque diren che tale strumento composto per l'omo non li manca se non

A bird is an instrument working according to mathematical law, which instrument it is in the capacity of man to reproduce with all its movements but not with as much strength; though it is deficient only in the power of maintaining equilibrium. We may therefore say that such an

l'anima dell' uccello, la quale anima bisogna che sia contrafatta dall' anima dell' omo. L'anima alle membra delli uccelli sanza dubbio obbidirà meglio a' bisogni di quelle che a quelle non farebbe l'anima dell' omo da esse separato, e massimamente ne' moti di quasi insensibili bilicazioni. Ma, poichè alle molte sensibile varietà di moti noi vediamo l'uccello provvedere, noi possiamo per tale esperienza giudicare, che le forte sensibili potranno essere note alla cognizione dell' omo, e che esso largamente potrà provvedere alla ruina di quello strumento, del quale lui s'è fatto anima e guida.

instrument constructed by man is lacking in nothing except the life of the bird, and this life must needs be imitated by the life of man. The life which resides in the birds' members will without doubt better obey their needs than will that of man which is separated from them and especially in the almost imperceptible movements which preserve equilibrium. But since we see that the bird is equipped for many sensitive varieties of movements we are able from this experience to deduce that the most obvious of these movements will be capable of being comprehended by man's understanding, and that he will to a great extent be able to provide against the destruction of that instrument of which he has made himself life and guide.

B. N. 2037. 1a]   1127

Se tu · vuoi sapere · doue · una caua faccia suo · corso, metti vno tāburo [2]in tutti quelli lochi, dove tu sospetti si facci la cava ·, e sopra detto tābu[3]ro · metti vno pajo di dadi ·, e quãdo sarai apresso · al loco dove si caua, i dadi risal[4]teranno alquãto sopra del tāburo · per lo colpo che si dà sotto terra nel cavare del tereno.

If you want to know where a mine runs, place a drum over all the places where you suspect that it is being made, and upon this drum put a couple of dice, and when you are over the spot where they are mining, the dice will jump a little on the drum at every blow which is given underground in the mining. Of mining.

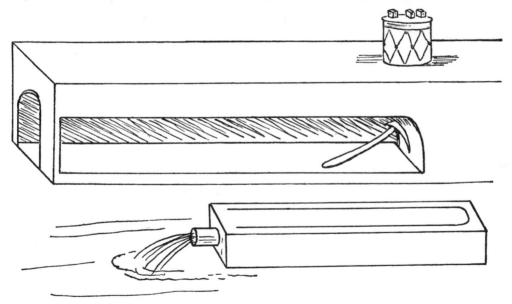

[5]Sono alcuni che per auere comodità d'ū fiume o di padule [6]alle lor terre, ànno fatto apresso di quel loco, doue sospettano si faccia [7]la cava, vno grã riserbo d'aqua, e cauato · in cõtra il nemi[8]co e, quel trouato, ànno sboccato il bottino e annegato nella [9]cava grã popolo.

There are persons who, having the convenience of a river or a lake in their lands, have made, close to the place where they suspect that a mine is being made, a great reservoir of water, and have countermined the enemy, and having found them, have turned the water upon them and destroyed a great number in the mine.

1127. 1. settu vuoli . . ꝑ cha faccia . . chorso. 2. tussosspetti . . essopra. 3. vno pa di. 4. terano . . chessi da . . tera. 5. chomodita. 6. tere . . facci. 7. riserbo daq"a" e chauato. 8. ano isboccato . . anegatti.

Triv. 19a]   1128

FUOCO GRECO

Of Greek fire.

²Tolli · carbon di salcio, e sale nitro, e acqua-vite, e sulfore, ³pegola con īciēso, e cãfora, e lana etiopica e fa bollire ⁴ogni cosa īsieme; questo fuoco · è di tanto desiderio di bru⁵ciare, che seguita il legniame sin sotto l'acque; ⁶e se aggivgnierai in essa conpositione vernice liquida, ⁷e olio petrolio, e tremētina, e acieto forte, mischia ⁸ogni cosa īsieme, e seccai al sole o nel forno quãdo n'è trat⁹to 'l pane, e poi volta intorno alla stoppa di canapa o altra, ¹⁰riduciē-dola in forma rotonda, e ficcati da ogni pa¹¹rte i chiodi acutissimi, solamēte lascia ī detta palla vn ¹²buco come razzo; poi la copri di colofonio e di solfo;

¹³Ancora questo foco appiccato in som-mità d'una lunga asta, ¹⁴la quale abbi uno braccio di pūta di ferro acciò nõ sia bru-ciata da det¹⁵to foco, è bono per evitare e proibire īfra le naui ostili, per ¹⁶non essere soprafatti da īpito;

¹⁷Ācora gittate vasi di uetro pieni di pegola sopra ¹⁸li aversi navili, — ītendi li omini di quelli alla battaglia — ¹⁹e poi gittate dirieto simili palle accese ànno potēza a brucia²⁰re ogni navilio.

GREEK FIRE

Take charcoal of willow, and saltpetre, and sulphuric acid, and sulphur, and pitch, with frankincense and camphor, and Ethiopian wool, and boil them all together. This fire is so ready to burn that it clings to the timbers even under water. And add to this composition liquid var-nish, and bituminous oil, and turpentine and strong vinegar, and mix all together and dry it in the sun, or in an oven when the bread is taken out; and then stick it round hempen or other tow, moulding it into a round form, and stud-ding it all over with very sharp nails. You must leave in this ball an opening to serve as a fusee, and cover it with rosin and sulphur.

Again, this fire, stuck at the top of a long plank which has one braccio length of the end pointed with iron that it may not be burnt by the said fire, is good for avoiding and keeping off the ships, so as not to be overwhelmed by their onset.

Again, throw vessels of glass full of pitch on to the enemy's ships. I mean on the men engaged in the battle; and then by throwing similar burning balls upon them you have it in your power to burn all their ships.

Br. M. 175a]   1129

Of music (1129–30).

Tanburo di tacche, fregate ²da rote di molle;

³Tanburo quadro, dal quale ⁴si tira e allenta la sua car⁵ta colla lieua *a b*;

A drum with cogs working by wheels with springs [2].

A square drum of which the parchment may be drawn tight or slackened by the lever *a b* [5].

1128. 1. fuocho grecho. 2. charbon di salco essale . . essulfore. 3. chãfera elana etiopicha effa. 4. onichosa . . focho . . dessiderio. 5. sare che seghuita ilegniame . . lacq"e". 6. esse agivg . . chonpositione. 7. emiscia. 8. oni . . essecha . . ne forno quãdo ne tra. 9. e po volta . . ala stopa. 10. retonda effichati da ongni. 11. achutissimi . . lassa īdetta balla. 12. buso chomaraza . . colofonia. 13. quesso . . appichato in somita . . asste. 14. abi ī br di . . fero acio . . brusata da de. 15. oviare . . ne nave. 17. gittate. 18. ītenti . . queli ala. 19. gitato . . simile . . acese ano potēza a brusa. 20. õni.   **1129.** 5. cholla.

1128. J. B. Venturi has given another short text about the Greek fire in a French translation (*Essai*, § xiv). He adds that the original text is to be found in MS. B. (Here Callimachus is mentioned as its in-ventor. Compare No. 1381). Libri speaks of it in a note as follows (*Histoire des mathématiques en Italie*, vol. II, p. 129): 'La composition du feu grégeois est une des choses qui ont été les plus cherchées et qui sont encore les plus douteuses. On dit qu'il fut inventé au septième siècle de l'ère chrétienne par l'architecte Callinique (*Constantini Porphyrogennetae opera*, Lugd.-Batav. 1617, in-8ᵛᵒ, p. 172, *de admin. imper.* cap. 48), et il se trouve souvent mentionné par les historiens byzantins. Tantôt on le lançait avec des machines, comme on lancerait une bombe, tantôt on le soufflait avec de longs tubes, comme on soufflerait un gaz ou un liquide enflammé (*Annae Comnenae Alexias*, p. 336, lib. xi.—*Aeliani et Leonis impera-toris tactica*, Lugd.-Bat. 1613, in-4°. part. 2a, p. 322, *Leonis tact.* cap. 19.—Joinville, *Histoire de Saint Louis*, collect. Petitot, tom. ii, p. 235). Les écrivains contemporains disent que l'eau ne pouvait pas éteindre ce feu, mais qu'avec du vinaigre et du sable on y parvenait. Suivant quelques historiens le feu

grégeois était composé de soufre et de résine. Marcus Graecus (*Liber ignium*, Paris, 1804, in-4°) donne plusieurs manières de le faire qui ne sont pas très intelligibles, mais parmi lesquelles on trouve la com-position de la poudre à canon. Léonard de Vinci (MSS. de Léonard de Vinci, vol. B, f. 30) dit qu'on le faisait avec du charbon de saule, du salpêtre, de l'eau de vie, de la résine, du soufre, de la poix et du camphre. Mais il est probable que nous ne savons pas quelle était sa composition, surtout à cause du secret qu'en faisaient les Grecs. En effet, l'empereur Con-stantin Porphyrogénète recommande à son fils de ne jamais en donner aux Barbares, et de leur répondre, s'ils en demandaient, qu'il avait été apporté du ciel par un ange et que le secret en avait été confié aux Chrétiens (*Constantini Porphyrogennetae opera*, pp. 26–7, *De admin. imper.*, cap. 12).

1129. This chapter consists of explanations of the sketches shown on Pl. CXXI. Lines 1 and 2 of the text are to be seen at the top at the left-hand side of the first sketch of a drum. E. Solmi says of this sketch: 'Un disegno importantissimo che preannunzia quella che poi si chiamerà "ruota dello Stewart" [Savart?] rappresentando uno strumento destinato all' analisi

6Tanburo a cōsonāza;

7Vna tabella a cōsonā8za, cioè 3 tabelle insieme;

9Siccome vn medesimo 10tanburo fa voci 11graui e acute, 12secondo le carte più o mē 13tirate, così queste carte, 14variamente tirate sopra 15vn medesimo corpo di tā16buro, farà uarie uoci;

17Tasti stretti, e sarano buchi di grā distātie infra loro, 18e sono al proposito della tronba prossima di sopra in *a b*;

19*a* entri in loco dell' ordinarie posite 20che ànno i pratici ne' lor busi de' zufoli.

A drum for harmony [6].

[7] A clapper for harmony; that is, three clappers together.

[9] Just as one and the same drum makes a deep or acute sound according as the parchments are more or less tightened, so these parchments variously tightened on one and the same drum will make various sounds [16].

Keys narrow and holes will be far apart; these will be right for the trumpet shown above at *a b*.

a must enter in the place of the ordinary keys which have the . . . in their openings which are like those of a flute.

A. 22*b*]   1129 A

Il colpo nella champana lascia dopo sé la sua similitudine inpressa come il sol nell' ochio o ll'odore innell' aria. . . .

Il colpo dato nella campana risponderà e moverà alquanto un altra campana simile a ssé, e lla corda sonata d'un liuto risponderà e moverà una altra simile corda di simile voce in un altro liuto; ecquesto vederai col porre una paglia sopra la corda oimile alla sonata.

The stroke in a bell will leave behind its likeness impressed just as the sun in the eye or the smell in the air. . . .

The stroke on a bell will be responded to and will move somewhat another bell similar to it. And the string of a lute will be responded to and will move another similar string of like voice in another lute. And this you will see by placing a straw on the string similar to the one that is played.

Br. M. 136*a*]   1130

Tanpani sona2ti come il mo3nacordo 4o voi dolze5mele;

6Qui si fa una rota di canne a vso 7di tabelle con vn circulo mvsicale det8to canone, che si canta a quattro e 9ciascū cantore canta tutta la rota, e però 10fo io qui vna rota cō 4 denti che ogni 11dente per sé fa l'ofitio d'un cantore.

Tymbals to be played like the monochord, or the soft flute.

[6] Here there is to be a cylinder of cane after the manner of clappers with a musical round called a canon, which is sung in four parts; each singer singing the whole round. Therefore I here make a wheel with 4 teeth so that each tooth takes by itself the part of a singer.

A. 61*a*]   1130 A

Benchè le voci che penetrano quest' aria si partino con circolari movimenti dalle lor cagioni, niente di meno i circuli mossi da diversi principi si scontrano insieme sanza alcuno

Although the voices penetrating the air spread in circular motion from their sources, there is no impediment when the circles from different centres meet, and they penetrate and pass into

Acoustics (1130 A–C).

8. coe.   9. sicome.   10. fa boce.   13. quesste.   16. uoce.   17. tassti . . esserrano bichi di grā disstātie infrallo.   19. illoco . . posste.
1130.   6. channe.   7. chon. . circul.   8. chessi . . acquattro he.

dei suoni e composto di un disco di tamburo sulla cui faccia anteriore è una sega a denti acuti che rende vari suoni secondo la maggiore o minore velocità di una rota a molle vibranti ('Il Trattato di L. d. V. sul linguaggio *De Vocie*', *Arch. Stor. Lomb.*, an. xxxiii, 1906, vol. vi, p. 82). Lines 3–5 refer to the sketch immediately below this. Line 6 is written at the side of the seventh sketch, and ll. 7 and 8 at the side of the eighth. Lines 9–16 are at the bottom in the middle.

The remainder of the text is at the side of the drawing at the bottom.

1130. In the original there are some more sketches, to which the text, from l. 6, refers. They are studies for a contrivance exactly like the cylinder in our musical boxes.

1130 A. Compare Vitruvius, *De Architectura*, v, c. iii. 6–8, and sketch of building on page 43 of vol. ii. Compare also Helmholtz, 'Über die physiologischen

impedimento e penetrano, e passano l'uno nel-
l' altro, mantenendosi sempre per centro le lor
cagioni. Perchè in tutti casi del moto l'acqua à
gran conformità coll' aria.

Io l'alegerò per esempio alla sopra detta propositione. Io dico: se tu gitterai 'n un medesimo
tempo 2 picciole pietre, alquanto distanti l'una
dall' altra, sopra un pelago d'acqua sanza moto,
tu vederai causare, intorno alle due dette percussioni, 2 separate quantità di circuli, le quali
quantità acressciendo, vengano a scontrarsi insieme, e poi a 'ncorporarsi, intersegandosi l'un
circulo coll' altro, sempre mantenendosi per
cientro i lochi percossi dalle pietre. E la ragion
si è che benchè li apparisca qualche dimostra-
zion di movimento, l'acqua non si parte dal suo
sito, perchè l'apertura fattale dalle pietre subito
si richiuse, e quel moto fatto dal subito aprire e
serrare dell' acqua fa in lei un cierto riscoti-
mento, che si pò più tosto dimandare tremore,
che movimento. E quel ch'io dico ti si facci
più manifesto: poni mente a quelle festuche,
che per lor leggerezza stanno sopra l'acqua,
che per l'onda fatta sotto loro dall' avenimento
de' circuli, non si partano però dal loro primo
sito. Essendo adunque questo tal risentimento
d'acqua piuttosto tremore che movimento, non
possan per riscontrarsi, rompere l'un l'altro,
perchè avendo l'acqua tutte le sue parti d'una
medesima qualità, è neciessario che le parti
appichino esso tremor l'una all' altra, sanza
mutarsi di lor loco: perchè stando l'acqua nel
suo sito, facilmente pò pigliare esso tremore
dalle parti vicine, e porgierle all' altre vicine,
sempre diminuendo sua potentia insino al fine.

one another, keeping to the centres from which
they spring. Because in all cases of motion there
is great likeness between water and air.

I shall cite an example for the above proposition. I say: If you throw two small stones at the
same time on a sheet of motionless water at some
distance from one another, you will observe that
around the two percussions quantities of separate
circles are formed which will meet as they increase in size and then penetrate and intersect
one another, while all the time maintaining as
their respective centres the spots hit by the
stones. And the reason for this is that the water,
although apparently moving, does not leave its
original position, because the opening made by
the stone closed again immediately. Therefore
the motion produced by the quick opening and
reclosing of the water caused but a shock which
may be described as tremor rather than movement. In order to understand better what I
mean, watch the blades of straw that because of
their lightness are floating on the water, and
observe how they do not depart from their
original position in spite of the waves underneath them caused by the arrival of the circles.
The impression on the water being (in the nature
of) tremor rather than movement, (the circles)
cannot break one another on meeting, and as
the water is of the same quality all through, its
parts transmit the tremor to one another without change of position. Thus the water, although
remaining in its position, can easily transmit the
tremor to the adjacent parts and these to other
adjacent parts while gradually diminishing in
force until the end.

C. 16a]   1130 B

La voce d'eco dico essere refressa dalla percussione all' orechio come all' ochio le percussioni fatte nelli spechi dalle spezie delli
obbietti; e si come la similitudine è cadente
dalla cosa allo spechio e dallo spechio all' ochio
infra equali angoli, così infra equali angoli
caderà e risalterà la voce nella concavità dalla
prima percussione all' orechio.

I say that the sound of the echo is reflected to
the ear from the percussion, just as the shapes
of the objects are reflected from the mirror into
the eye. And as the likeness is reflected from
the object into the mirror and from the mirror
to the eye at equal angles, so sound will also fall
and be reflected at equal angles as it passes from
the original percussion into the concavity and
travels out to meet the ear.

Ursachen der musikalischen Harmonie', *Vorträge
und Reden*, 1896, p. 129: 'Wenn wir einen Punkt in
einer ruhenden Wasserfläche in Erschütterung verset-
zen, z. B. einen Stein hineinwerfen, so pflanzt sich die
Bewegung, welche wir hervorgerufen haben, in Form
kreisförmig sich verbreitender Wellen über die Oberfläche des Wassers fort. . . . Während die Welle über
die Oberfläche der Flüssigkeit hinläuft, bewegen sich
nicht etwa die Wassertheilchen, aus denen sie besteht,
mit ihr fort. Wir können dies leicht erkennen, wenn
ein Hälmchen auf dem Wasser schwimmt. Die

Wellen, welche es erreichen, heben es und senken es,
aber wenn sie vorüber gezogen sind, ist das Hälmchen
nicht merklich von seiner Stelle gerückt. . . . Um nun
von den Wasserwellen auf die Schallwellen zurückzu-
kommen, denken Sie sich statt des Wassers eine
zusammendrückbare elastische Flüssigkeit. . . .'
Compare also No. 69.

1130 B. Leonardo points out that the laws of reflection of sound are identical with those of the reflection
of light: that the angles of incidence and reflection
are equal.

C. A. 382b]

La musica ha due malattie, delle quali l'una è mortale, l'altra è decrepitudinale: la mortale è sempre congiunta allo instante sequente a quel della sua creazione; la decrepitudinale la fa odiosa e vile nella sua replicazione.

1130 C

Music has two ills, one of which is mortal, and the other subjects it to deterioration. The mortal is ever linked to the instant which follows its creation, while the deterioration lies in its repetition making it hateful and vile.

B. 4a]

Pañi biāchi e cielesti, ²tessuti a scacchi ³per fare uno apparecchio;

⁴Pañi tirati ⁵in $a \cdot b \cdot c \cdot d \cdot e \cdot f \cdot g \cdot h \cdot i \cdot k \cdot$, ⁶da fa⁷re uno ciclo a uno ap-⁸parecchio.

1131

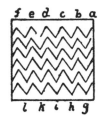

White and sky-blue cloths, woven in checks to make a decoration.

Cloths with the threads drawn at $a\,b\,c\,d\,e\,f\,g\,h\,i\,k$, to go round the decoration.

Of decorations.

1131. 1.Cielestri. 2. schachi. 3. Í aparechio. 6. daffa. 7. re Í cielo a Í a. 8. parechio.

XIX

PHILOSOPHICAL MAXIMS. MORALS. POLEMICS AND SPECULATION

*T*HE *passages here classed under the head 'Morals' reveal Leonardo to us as a man whose life and conduct were unfailingly governed by lofty principles and aims. He could scarcely have recorded his stern reprobation and un-measured contempt for men who do nothing useful and strive only for riches, if his own life and ambitions had been such as they have so often been misrepresented.*

At a period when superstition still exercised unlimited dominion over the minds not merely of the illiterate crowd but of the cultivated and learned classes, it was very natural that Leonardo's views as to Alchemy, Ghosts, Magicians, and the like should have been met with stern reprobation whenever and wherever he expressed them; this accounts for the argumentative tone of all his utterances on such subjects in Subdivision III of this section. To these are added some passages which throw light on Leonardo's personal views on the Universe. They are, without exception, characterized by a broad spirit of naturalism of which the principles are more strictly applied in his essays on Astronomy, and still more on Physical Geography.

To avoid repetition, only such notes on Philosophy, Morals, and Polemics have been included in this section as occur as independent texts in the original manuscripts. Several moral reflections have already been given in vol. I, in the section 'Allegorical Representations, Mottoes, and Emblems'. Others will be found in the following section. Nos. 9–12, vol. I, are also passages of an argumentative character. It did not seem requisite to repeat these and similar passages here, since their direct connexion with the context in places where they have appeared already is far closer than it would be here.

The incredible and demonstrably fictitious legend of Leonardo's death in the arms of Francis the First is given, with others, by Vasari and further embellished by this odious comment: Mostrava tuttavia quanto avea offeso Dio e gli uomini del mondo, non avendo operato nell' arte come si conveniva. *This last accusation is evidence of the superficial character of the information which Vasari was in a position to give about Leonardo. It seems to imply that Leonardo was disdainful of diligent labour. With regard to the second, referring to Leonardo's morality and dealings with his fellow men, Vasari himself contradicts it by asserting the very contrary in several passages. A further refutation may be found in the following sentence from the letter in which Melzi, the young Milanese nobleman, announces the Master's death to Leonardo's brothers:* Credo siate certificati della morte di Maestro Lionardo fratello vostro, e mio quanto optimo padre, per la cui morte sarebbe impossibile che io potesse esprimere il dolore che io ho preso; e in mentre che queste mia membra si sosterranno insieme, io possederò una per-petua infelicità, e meritamente perchè sviscerato et ardentissimo amore mi portava giornalmente. È dolto ad ognuno la perdita di tal uomo, quale non è più in podestà della natura, &c.

It is true that, in April 1476, we find the names of Leonardo and Verrocchio entered in the Libro degli Uffiziali di notte e de' Monasteri *as breaking the laws; but we immediately afterwards find the note* Absoluti cum condizione ut retamburentur (*Tamburini* (cf. *Vasari, ii.* 637) *was the name given to the warrant cases of the night police*). *The acquittal, therefore, did not exclude the possibility of a repetition of the charge. It was in fact repeated, two months later, and on this occasion the Master and his pupil were again fully acquitted. Verrocchio was at this time forty and Leonardo four-and-twenty. The documents referring to this affair are in the State Archives of Florence.*

I

PHILOSOPHICAL MAXIMS

S. K. M. III. 29a]   **1132**

Io t'ubidisco, Signore, prima per l'a²more che ragionevolmente portare ³ti debo, secōdariamente chè tu sai ⁴abbreviare o prolungare le uite ⁵a li omini.

I obey Thee, Lord, first for the love I ought, in all reason, to bear Thee; secondly for that Thou canst shorten or prolong the lives of men.

Prayers to God (1132–3).

W. 12642b]   **1133**

¶ORATIO

²Tu o Iddio ci vendi ³tutti li beni per prez⁴zo di fatica. ¶

A PRAYER

Thou, O God, dost sell us all good things at the price of labour.

A. 24a]   **1134**

O mirabile givstitia di te, primo motore, · tu ·non ài · voluto · mācare · a nessuna ²potētia l'ordine e qualità de' sua · neciessari effetti.

O admirable impartiality of Thine, Thou first Mover; Thou hast not permitted that any force should fail of the order or quality of its necessary effects.

The powers of Nature (1134–9).

S. K. M. III. 43b]   **1135**

La neciessità · è · maestra ²e tutrice · della · natura;
³La neciessità è tema e in⁴ventrice · della natura ⁵e freno e regola e tema.

Necessity is the mistress and guide of nature.
Necessity is the theme and the inventress of nature, the curb and law and theme.

Triv. 39a]   **1136**

Molte volte una medesima cosa · è tirata da 2 violētie, ²cioè · neciessità · e potentia ·; l'acqua piove, la terra l'assorbisce, ³per neciessità d'omore ·, e 'l sole la soleva nō per neciessità, ma per potētia.

In many cases one and the same thing is attracted by two strong forces, namely, Necessity and Potency. Water falls in rain; the earth absorbs it from the necessity for moisture; and the sun raises it, not from necessity, but by its power.

S. K. M. II.² 116b]   **1137**

La gravità, la forza · · e 'l moto · accidentale · insieme col²la percussione · son · le quatro · accidentali · potentie, ³colle · quali · tutte · l'euidenti · opere de' mortali ⁴ànno · loro · essere · e loro morte.

Weight, force, and casual impulse, together with resistance, are the four external powers in which all the visible actions of mortals have their being and their end.

1132. 3. sechondaria. 4. abrieviere.
1133. 2. "tu" | o idio [che] ci vende. 3. per pre. 4. faticha.
1134. 1. māchare a nessuna [creata chosa]. 2. "equalita" de sua.
1135. 1. he maesstra. 2. ettutrice. 3. ettema. 5. effrno.
1136. 1. volte va medesima chosa ettirata. 2. losorbisscie. 3. sole lassuele.
1137. 1. chol. 3. cholli . . tucte. 4. elloro.

1133. Horace says: 'Life gave nothing to mortals without hard work' (*Sat.*, Lib. I. ix. 59–60):

> Nil sine magno
> Vita labore dedit mortalibus.

This is a Latin version of a Greek oracle, given in Apollo's name by the Branchidae at Didyma near Miletus.

οὐδὲν ἄνευ καμάτου πέλει ἀνδράσιν εὐπετὲς ἔργον

(Kiessling's commentary on Horace, *Sat.* I. viii, ad loc., Berlin, 1910).

Triv. 36b]   1138

¶ Il corpo nostro è sottoposto al cielo, e lo cielo è sottoposto allo spirito. ¶

Our body is dependent on heaven and heaven on the Spirit.

H.³ 141a]   1139

Il moto è causa d'ogni vita.

The motive power is the cause of all life.

W. 19001a]   1140

Psychology (1140–7).

E tu uomo, che consideri in questa ²mia fatica l'opere mirabili della ³natura, se giudicherai essere cosa ⁴nefanda il distruggerla, or pēsa ⁵essere cosa nefandissima il torre la ⁶vita all' omo, del quale, se questa ⁷sua cōpositione ti pare di marauiglio⁸so artifitio, pensa questa essere ⁹nulla rispetto all' anima che in ¹⁰tale architettura abita, e vera¹¹mente, quale · essa si sia, ella è ¹²cosa diuina, sicchè lascia ¹³la abitare nella sua opera a suo be¹⁴neplacito, e nō volere che la tua ¹⁵ira o malignità distrugga ¹⁶una tāta vita, chè ve¹⁷ramēte, chi non la ¹⁸stima, non la ¹⁹merita.

And you, O Man, who will discern in this work of mine the wonderful works of Nature, if you think it would be a criminal thing to destroy it, reflect how much more criminal it is to take the life of a man; and if this, his external form, appears to thee marvellously constructed, remember that it is nothing as compared with the soul that dwells in that structure; for that, indeed, be it what it may, is a thing divine. Leave it then to dwell in its work at its good will and pleasure, and let not your rage or malice destroy a life—for indeed, he who does not value it, does not himself deserve it [19].

Triv. 40b]   1141

L'anima mai si può corrōpere · nella corruttiō del corpo, ma fa nel corpo ²a similitudine del uēto che cavsa il suono del organo, ³che guastādosi vna canna, nō resultava per quella del uēto ⁴buono effetto.

The soul can never be corrupted with the corruption of the body, but is in the body as it were the air which causes the sound of the organ, where, when a pipe bursts, the wind would cease to have any good effect.

C. A. 59a]   1142

Ogni parte à inclinatiō ²di ricōgiugnersi al suo ³tutto per fugire dalla ⁴sua inperfectione; ⁵L'anima desidera stare ⁶col suo corpo, perchè sanza ⁷li strumēti organici di tal ⁸corpo nulla può operare ⁹nè sētire.

The part always has a tendency to reunite with its whole in order to escape from its imperfection. The spirit desires to remain with its body, because, without the organic instruments of that body, it can neither act nor feel anything.

C. A. 76a]   1143

Chi vuole vedere come l'anima abita nel suo ²corpo, guardi come esso corpo vsa la ³sua cotidiana abitatione, cioè se quella ⁴è sanza ordine e confusa, disordina⁵to e cōfuso fia il corpo tenvto dalla su' anima.

Whoever would see how the soul dwells within its body, let him observe how this body uses its daily habitation; that is to say, if this is devoid of order and confused, the body will be kept in disorder and confusion by its soul.

Br. M. 278b]   1144

Perchè vede piv certa la cosa l'ochio ne' sogni ²che colla imaginatione, stando desto?

Why does the eye see a thing more clearly in dreams than with the imagination awake?

1138. 1. essottoposto. 2. ello . . essottoposto.
1139. R. chausa.
1140. 1. questta. 3. gudicherai. 4. desstrugerla. 7. sua cō[sa]positione. 12. diuina [sig] che [si] lasscia. 13. assuo. 14. chella. 15. distrugha. 17. chi nolla. *The last seven lines are very indistinct.* 20. poiche. 21. cosi. 22. mal. 23. vole. 24. tie. 25. ri si parte dal. 26. corpo eben. 27. credo chel su. 28. o pianto e do. 29. lore non sia. 30. sanza ca. 31. one.
1141. 1. chorrōpere . . curuttiō . . maffa. 2. assimilitudine . . chavsa del sono. 3. guasstādosi . . chana.
1142. 3. tutto [fa] per. 6. chol. 7. orghanjci.
1143. 1. vole . . chome. 2. chorpo . . chome esso chorpo. 3. chotidiana . . secquella. 4. chonfusa. 5. chōfuso . . chorpo.
1144. 2. dessto.

1140. This text is on the back of the drawings reproduced on Pl. CVII. Compare No. 798. 35, note on p. 88. Compare also Nos. 837 and 838.

19. In MS. I¹ 15a is the note: 'chi nō stima la vita, non la merita.'

1141. Compare No. 845.

Triv. 33a]   **1145**

I sensi sono terrestri, la ragione sta ²fuor di quelli, quãdo cõtenpla.

The senses are of the earth; Reason stands apart from them in contemplation.

Triv. 36b]   **1146**

Ogni attione bisognia che s'esercita ²per moto;
³ ¶ Cogniosciere e volere sõ 2 operationi ⁴vmane. ¶
⁵Discernere, givdicare, cõsigliare ⁶sono atti vmani.

Every action needs to be prompted by a motive.
To know and to will are two operations of the human mind.
Discerning, judging, deliberating are acts of the human mind.

Triv. 20b]   **1147**

Ogni nostra cognitione prĩcipia da sentimẽti.

All our knowledge has its origin in our perceptions.

Triv. 17b]   **1148**

Sciẽtia — notitia delle cose che sono possibili, presẽti e preterite; ²presciẽtia — notitia delle cose che possĩ uenire.

Science is the observation of things possible, whether present or past; prescience is the knowledge of things which may come to pass.

Science: its principles and rules (1148–61).

E. 55a]   **1148 A**

Ma prima farò alcuna esperienza avanti ch'io più oltre proceda, perchè mia intenzione è allegare prima la sperienza e poi colla ragione dimostrare perchè tale esperienza è constretta in tal modo ad operare.
E questa è la vera regola come li speculatori delli effetti naturali hanno a procedere. E ancora che la natura cominci dalla ragione e termini nella sperienzia, a noi bisogna seguitare in contᵽario, cioè cominciando (come sopra dissi), dalla sperienza, e con quella investicare la ragione.

But first I shall test by experiment before I proceed further, because my intention is to consult experience first and then with reasoning show why such experience is bound to operate in such a way.
And this is the true rule by which those who analyse the effects of nature must proceed; and although nature begins with the cause and ends with the experience, we must follow the opposite course, namely (as I said before), begin with the experience and by means of it investigate the cause.

C. A. 147b]   **1148 B**

Nessuno effetto è in natura sanza ragione; intendi la ragione e non ti bisogna sperienza.

In nature there is no effect without cause; once the cause is understood there is no need to test it by experience.

F. 59 a]   **1148 C**

... L'altra prova che dette Platone a que' di Delo non è geometrica perchè si va con l'istrumento di seste e di riga, e la sperienza noi lo mostra; ma questa è tutta mentale e per conseguenza geometrica.

The other proof which Plato gave to those of Delos is not geometrical because you proceed by the instrument of compasses and of ruler, and experience shows it to us. But this is exclusively an occupation of the mind, therefore geometry.

1145. 1. teresti. 2. for di queli . . chõtempla.
1146. 1. chessesercita. 3. cogniossciere . . operatione. 5. dissciernere . . chõsigliare.
1147. 1. prẽcipia.
1148. 1. notiti delle . . chessono possibile presente. 2. cose che pesiuine che posĩ uenire.

1145. Compare No. 842.
1148C. This passage follows on a geometric problem dealing with the duplication of the cube. Solmi,

Fonti, p. 233; he reads *non* instead of *noi* in the above passage.

C. A. 86a]   1149

La speriĕza, ²interprete infra ³l'artifitiosa natu⁴ra e la umana spe⁵tie, ne insegnia ciò ⁶che essa natura infra ⁷mortali adopera, ⁸da neciessità co⁹stretta non altri¹⁰mĕti operarsi po¹¹ssa · che la ragiō, suo timone, ¹²operare le 'nse¹³gni.

Experience, the interpreter between formative nature and the human race, teaches how that nature acts among mortals; and being constrained by necessity cannot act otherwise than as reason, which is its helm, requires it to act.

S. K. M. III. 14a]   1150

La sapiĕtia è figliola della ²speriĕtia.

Wisdom is the daughter of experience.

I.¹ 18a]   1151

La natura è piena d'infinite ragioni ²che nō furō mai in isperiĕtia.

Nature is full of infinite causes that have never occurred in experience.

M. 58b]   1152

¶ La verità fu sola fi²gliola del tenpo. ¶

Truth was the only daughter of Time.

C. A. 154a]   1153

La speriĕza nō falla mai, ma sol fallano i vostri giuditi, promettendosi di quella ²efetto · tale che ne' uostri esperimĕti causati nō sono;

Perchè dato un princi³pio è necessario che ciò che seguita di quello è vera consequenza di tal princi⁴pio, se già non fussi impedito; e se pur seguita alcuno impedimento, l'effetto che doveva ⁵seguire del predetto principio partecipa tanto più o meno del detto impedimento quan⁶to esso impedimento è più o men potente del già detto principio.

⁷La speriĕza nō falla ·, ma sol fallano i vostri giuditi, promettēdosi di lei cose, che nō ⁸sono in sua potestà; ⁹a torto si lamentano li omini della speriĕza, la quale cō somme rampogne quella ¹⁰accusano esser fallace, ¹¹ma lasciano stare essa speriĕtia, ¹²e voltate tale lamentatione contro alla vostra ignoranza, la quale ui ¹³fa trascorrere con uostri vani e stolti desideri a inprometterui di quella cose che nō sono ¹⁴in sua potĕtia, ¹⁵dicendo quella esser fallace; ¹⁶a torto si lamĕtan li omini della innocente sperientia ·, quella spesso accusando ¹⁷di fallacia e di bugiarde ¹⁸dimostrationi.

Experience never errs; it is only your judgements that err by promising themselves effects such as are not caused by your experiments.

Because what follows from a given cause must necessarily be its true consequence unless there is an impediment; but should there be an impediment, the effect of the aforesaid cause will partake of the impediment in proportion as it is more or less powerful than the aforesaid cause.

Experience does not err; only your judgements err by expecting from her what is not in her power. Men wrongly complain of Experience; with great abuse they accuse her of leading them astray. Let experience alone, and turn your complaints against your ignorance, which causes you to be carried away by vain and foolish desires as to expect from it things that are not in her power; saying that she is fallacious. Men are unjust in complaining of innocent Experience, constantly accusing her of error and of false evidence.

A. 47a]   1153 A

. . . ma innanzi che tu facci di questo caso regola generale pruovalo 2 o tre volte, e guarda se le pruove fanno simili effetti.

. . . But before you found a law on this case test it two or three times and see whether the experiments produce the same effects.

1149. 1. lassperiĕza. 4. ella. 5. ninsegna. 8. cō. 11. chella ragiō "suotimōe". 12. hoperare lense. 13. gnj.
1150. 1. dela. 2. speriĕtia la quale speri. 3. ēza. *here the text breaks off.*
1152. 1. verita sola fu fi. 2. glola.
1153. 1. vosstri guditi. 2. [tale] effetto | "tale" che ine uosstri . . chausati. 7. essperiĕza . . m̦assol . . vosstrigiuditi [i quali sa] prometa "desi". 9. attorto si lamenta . . della "innocēte" isspierieza la quale cō some ranpogne. 11. Ma lasciāno. 12. evoltati talle. 13. transcorrere co uosstre "vani e" in stolti . . "di quella" chose. 14. in "sua" potĕtia. 16. attorto . . della "inocente" essperientia . . achusando. 17. bugarde. 18. dimōstrationj. Ma. *here the text breaks off.*

1150. See Dante, *Paradiso,* ii. 94–6.
1152. A. Gellius, *Noctes Atticae* 12, 11, 2: 'Veritas filia temporis'.

Trn. (Mz.) 3a] 1154

¶La scientia strumentale over machinale ²è nobilissima e sopra tutte l'altre vtilissima, ³cōciosiachè mediante quella tutti li corpi ani⁴mati, che ànno moto, fanno tutte loro operationi, i quali moti ⁵nascono dal centro della lor grauità che è posto ⁶in mezzo a parte di pesi disequali, e à questo ⁷carestia e dovitia di muscoli, ed etiā lie⁸va e contralieua. ¶

Instrumental or mechanical science is of all the noblest and the most useful, seeing that by means of this all animated bodies that have movement perform all their actions; and these movements are based on the centre of gravity which is placed in the middle dividing unequal weights, and it has dearth and wealth of muscles and also lever and counter-lever.

E. 8b] 1155

DELLA MECCANICA

²La meccanica è il paradiso delle sciētie matema³tiche, perchè cō quella si viene al frutto matematico.

ON MECHANICS

Mechanics are the Paradise of mathematical science, because here we come to the fruits of mathematics.

Br. M. 191a] 1156

A ciascuno strumēto si richiede ²esser fatto colla speriēza.

Every instrument requires to be made by experience.

W. 19084a] 1157

Chi biasima la soma certezza delle ²matematiche, si pasce di confusione ³e mai porrà silentio ⁴alle contraditioni delle soffi⁵stiche sciētie, colle quali ⁶s'inpara vno eterno gridone.

The man who blames the supreme certainty of mathematics feeds on confusion, and can never silence the contradictions of sophistical sciences which lead to an eternal quackery.

G. 96b] 1158

Nessuna certezza delle sciētie è, do²ve nō si può applicare ³vna delle sciētie matema⁴tiche over che non sono v⁵nite con esse matematiche.

There is no certainty in sciences where one of the mathematical sciences cannot be applied, or which are not in relation with these mathematics.

C. A. 76a] 1159

Chi disputa allegādo l'autorità, non adopera ²lo ingiegno, ma pivtosto · la memoria; ³le buone · lettere son nate da vn bono naturale, ⁴e perchè si de' piv laudare la cagiō che l'effetto, ⁵piv lauderai vn buon naturale sanza lettere, ⁶che vn bon letterato sanza naturale.

Any one who in discussion relies upon authority uses, not his understanding, but rather his memory. Good culture is born of a good disposition; and since the cause is more to be praised than the effect, you will rather praise a good disposition without culture, than good culture without the disposition.

I.² 130a] 1160

La sciētia è il capitano, e la pratica sono i soldati.

Science is the captain, and practice the soldiers.

G. 8a] 1161

DELL' ERRORE DI QUELLI CHE VSANO ²LA PRATICA SANZA SCIĒTIA

³Quelli che s'inamorā di pratica ⁴sāza sciētia sō come 'l nocchiere che ē⁵tra navilio sanza timone e bussola, ⁶che mai à certezza dove si vada.

ON THE ERRORS OF THOSE WHO DEPEND ON PRACTICE WITHOUT SCIENCE

Those who fall in love with practice without science are like a sailor who enters a ship without a helm or a compass, and who never can be certain whither he is going.

1154. 1. Lasscientia. 2. essopra. 3. conco sia che. 4. mati "che annomoto" fanno . . ecquali. 5. nasscano . . possto. 6. mezo aparte . . acquesto. 7. charesstia e dovitia di mvsscoli.
1155. 1. dela mechanicha. 2. mechanicha. 3. perchche chō . . matema"ticho".
1156. 1. ciasscuno. 2. cholla essperiēza.
1157. 1. certeza delle. 2. matematiche si passce. 3. [e mati] e mai.
1158. 1. certezza "dele sciētie" e do. 2. po applichare.
1159. 1. lalturita. 2. longiegno. 3. sonate. 4. laldare la chagiō chelle fetto. 5. lalderai vn bo. 6. literato.
1160. 1. ella pratica.
1161. 1–6 R. 1. erore. 2. praticha. 3. chessinnamorā di praticha. 4. nochieri. 5. ebbussola. 6. cierteza.

1155. Compare No. 660, ll. 19–22 (vol. i, p. 372).

MORALS

What is life?
(1162–3).

Or vedi la sperāza e 'l desiderio del ripatriarsi ²e ritornare nel primo chaos fa a similitudine della farfalla al lume, e l'uomo ³che cō cōtinvi desideri sēpre cō festa aspetta la nvova ⁴primavera, sempre la nvova state, sempre e' nvovi mesi, ⁵e' nvovi anni, parēdogli che le desiderate cose, venēdo, ⁶sieno troppo tarde, e non s'avede che desidera la sua disfazi⁷one; ma questo desiderio è ne quella quītessenza spirito degli ele-⁸menti, che trovādosi rīchivsa pro anima dello vmano corpo ⁹desidera senpre ritornare al suo mandatario; ¹⁰E uo' che sappi che questo medesimo desiderio è quella quītessēza, ¹¹cōpagnia della natura, e l'uomo è modello dello mōdo.

Now you see that the hope and the desire of returning to the first state of chaos is like the moth to the light, and that the man who with constant longing awaits with joy each new spring-time, each new summer, each new month and new year—deeming that the things he longs for are ever too late in coming—does not perceive that he is longing for his own destruction. But this desire is the very quintessence, the spirit of the elements, which finding itself imprisoned with the soul is ever longing to return from the human body to its giver. And you must know that this same longing is that quintessence, inseparable from nature, and that man is the image of the world.

O tēpo, consumatore delle cose, ²e o invidiosa antichità, tu distruggi tutte le cose, ³e consumi tutte le cose da duri dēti ⁴della vecchiezza a poco a poco cō lēta ⁵morte! Elena quando si specchiaua, vedēdo ⁶le vizze grinze del suo viso, fatte per la vecchi⁷ezza, piagnie e pēsa seco, perchè fu rapita ⁸due volte.

⁹O tēpo consumatore delle · cose ·, e o invidiosa · antichi¹⁰tà, per la quale tutte ¹e cose sono consumate!

O Time, consumer of all things! O envious age! Thou dost destroy all things and devour all things with the hard teeth of years, little by little in a slow death. Helen, when she looked in her mirror, seeing the withered wrinkles made in her face by old age, wept and wondered why she had twice been carried away.

O Time, consumer of all things! And O envious age by which all things are consumed!

Se di diletto la tua mente pasce . . . .

If you feed your mind with delight . . . .

Death.

Ogni danno lascia dispiacere ²nella ricordatione, saluo ³che 'l sommo dāno, cioè la morte, che ⁴uccide essa ricordatione īsieme ⁵colla vita.

Every evil leaves behind a grief in our memory, except the supreme evil, that is death, which destroys this memory together with life.

How to spend life
(1165–79).

¶O dormiēte · che cosa · è sonno? jl sōno à similitudine · colla morte; O perchè non fai ·

O thou that sleepest, what is sleep? Sleep resembles death. Ah, why then dost thou not

---

1162. 1. *On the margin:* pro *meaning probably* propositione . . lassperāza [del suo] el desidero.   2. chas"o" . . assimilitudine "dela farfalla alume" dell' uomo.   3. chō chōtinvi . . chō fessta asspetta.   5. chose.   6. dissfazi.   7. desidero e ne i [q] la quīte essenza.   8. chorpo.   10. chessapi . . quīta esēza.   11. chōpagnia . . elluomo.
1163. 1. chonsumatore . . chose.   2. disstruggi . . chose.   3. consumate . . chose.   4. vecchieza appocho appocho chō.   5. elena . . sisspecchiaua.   6. leuzze grinze.   7. eppēsa secho.   8. da volte.   9. chonsumatore . . chose.   10. lesono chonsumate.
1164. 1. dāv lasscia disspiacere.   3. somo.   4. ucide.
1165. 1. chosa . . assimilitudine cholla.

1163. Compare Ovid, *Metamorphoses*, xv. 228–33. On the same page, but not in Leonardo's handwriting: 'Lionardo mio, non avete d . . . Lionardo,

perchè tanto penate?' See 1555 A.
1165. Compare No. 676, vol. i, p. 385.

adunque tale opera, che dopo la morte ²tu abbi similitudine di perfetto viuo, che uiuendo · farti col sonno simile ai tristi morti?¶

work in such wise that after death thou mayst retain a resemblance to perfect life, rather than during life make thyself like the hapless dead by sleeping?

C. A. 12*b*]   1165 A

. . . nè modi di compartire e misurare . . . giorni ne' quali ci doviamo affaticare di non trapassarli . . . la misera vita non trapassi sanza lasciare di noi alcuna memoria nelle menti de' mortali.

. . . da . . . do in saperlo spendere . . . difendere e contastare . . . li el più delle volte son cagione . . . questa nostra misera vita.

Piombo · cuojo. Un peso di piombo, spingnendo e calcando un sacchetto di cuoio pieno d'aria, nel suo calare ti potrà ancor mostrare l'ore, [non ci manca modi nè vie di compartire e misurare questi nostri miseri giorni, i quali ci debba ancor piacere di non ispenderli e trapassarli indarno e sanza alcuna loda, e sanza lasciare di sé alcuna memoria nelle menti de' mortali].

Acciochè questo nostro misero corso non trapassi indarno . . . .

. . . no ways to divide and measure . . . days when we must toil in order not to pass them . . . the miserable life should not pass without leaving some memory of ourselves in the minds of mortals . . . knowing how to spend it . . . defend and contest . . . and more often they are the cause . . . this our miserable life.

Lead: leather, a weight of lead pressing forwards and backwards a little bag of leather filled with air, the descent will show you the hour. We do not lack ways and means to divide and measure these our miserable days which it should be our pleasure not to spend and pass away in vain and without praise, and without leaving record of themselves in the mind of mortals . . . so that this our miserable course should not be sped in vain . . . .

G. 89*a*]   1166

L'un caccia l'al²tro.
³Per questi quadretti ⁴s'intende la uita ⁵e li stati umani.

One pushes down the other.
By these square-blocks are meant the life and the states of men.

C. A. 373*b*]   1167

¶La cognitiõ del tēpo preterito ²e del sito della terra è orna³mēto e cibo delle mēti vmane.¶

The knowledge of past times and of the places on the earth is both ornament and nutriment to the human mind.

Trn. (Mz.) 12*a*]   1168

È di tāto vilipēdio la bugia, che s'ella dicesse bene gran ²cose di Dio, ella toglie gratia a sua deità, ed è di tāta eccellē³tia la uerità, che s'ella laudasse cose minime elle si faño nobili;

⁴Sanza dubbio tal proportione è dalla verità alla bugia, qual è ⁵dalla luce alle tenebre, ed è essa verità in sé di tanta eccellē⁶tia che, ancora ch'ella s'estenda sopra vmili e basse materie, ⁷sanza comparatione ella eccede le incertezze e bugie estese so⁸pra li magni e altissimi discorsi, perchè la mē⁹te nostra, ancora ch'ell' abbia la bugia pel quīto elemēto, ¹⁰non resta però che la verità delle cose nõ sia di sommo no¹¹trimento delli intelletti fini, ma non di uaga¹²bundi ingegni;

¹³Ma tu che ¹⁴viui di sogni, ¹⁵ti piacciono più le ¹⁶ragioni soffistiche ¹⁷e barerie de' ¹⁸pallaji nelle ¹⁹cose grādi ²⁰e incerte, che ²¹le certe ²²naturali e ²³nõ di tāta al²⁴tura.

To lie is so vile, that even if it were speaking well of godly things it would take off something from God's grace; and truth is so excellent, that if it praises but small things they become noble.

Beyond a doubt truth bears the same relation to falsehood as light to darkness; and this truth is in itself so excellent that, even when it dwells on humble and lowly matters, it is still infinitely above uncertainty and lies on high and lofty matters; because in our minds, even if lying should be their fifth element, this does not prevent that the truth of things is the chief nutriment of superior intellects, though not of wandering wits.

But you who live in dreams are better pleased by the sophistical reasons and frauds of wits in great and uncertain things, than by those reasons which are certain and natural and not so exalted.

2. abi . . chol sono.   1166. 5. elli.   1167. 1. chognitiõ. 3. eccibo . . vma"ne".
1168. 1. ede di . . chessella dicessi. 2. dio ella to di gratia assua. 3. chessella laldassi. 5. verita "in se" di. 6. anchora sastende.
7. comperatione ellaccede . . esstese. 8. pra [le altissime] li . . disscorsi. 9. nosstra anchora. 10. no resta . . chella . . chose . .
some. 12. ingegni ingegni. 13. mattu. 15. piace. 16. ragõ soffistice. 18. palari. 21. delle certe.

S. K. M. III. 55a]   **1169**

Fuggi quello · studio · del quale ²la resultante opera more insie³me coll' operante d'essa.

Avoid studies of which the result dies with the worker.

C. A. 76a]   **1170**

A torto si lamētā li omini della fuga del tenpo, ²incolpando quello di troppa velocità, nō s'accorgiēdo ³quello essere di bastevole trāsito, ma (la) bona me⁴moria ·, di che la natura ci à dotati, ci fa che ⁵ogni cosa lungamēte passata ci pare essere presente.

Wrongly do men lament the flight of time, accusing it of being too swift, and not perceiving that it is sufficient as it passes; but good memory, with which nature has endowed us, causes everything long past to seem present.

C. A. 112a]   **1171**

Acquista cosa nella tua giovētù ²che ristori il danno della tua ve³cchiezza; ⁴e se tu intēdi ⁵la vecchiezza aver per suo cibo la sa⁶piētia, adoperati in tal modo in giovē⁷tù che tal uecchiezza nō māchi di nu⁸trimēto.

Acquire learning in youth which restores the damage of old age; and if you understand that old age has wisdom for its food, you will so conduct yourself in youth that your old age will not lack sustenance.

C. A. 226b]   **1172**

¶L'acquisto di qualūche cognitione ²è sēpre vtile allo intelletto, perchè potrà ³scacciare da sé le cose inutili e riserva⁴re le buone; ¶

⁵¶Perchè nessuna cosa si può amare nè odiare, ⁶se prima nō si à cognitiō di quella.¶

The acquisition of any knowledge is always of use to the intellect, because it may thus drive out useless things and retain the good.

For nothing can be loved or hated unless it is first known.

Triv. 27a]   **1173**

¶Siccome · vna · giornata · bene spesa dà lieto dormire, così vna vita · bene · vsata · dà lieto morire. ¶

As a day well spent brings happy sleep, so a life well used brings happy death.

Triv. 34a]   **1174**

L'acqua che tochi de' fivmi, è l'ulti²ma di quella · che ādò, e la prima ³di quelle · che viene; così il tēpo ⁴presēte;

⁵La vita bene spesa lunga è.

The water you touch in a river is the last of that which has passed, and the first of that which is coming. Thus it is with time present.

Life, if well spent, is long.

W. 12349a]   **1175**

Siccome māgiare · sanza voglia si cōuerte ²ī fastidioso · notrimento ·, così lo studio sā³za desiderio · guasta la ⁴memoria, col ⁵nō ritenere cosa ch'ella pigli.

Just as food eaten without caring for it is turned into loathsome nourishment, so study without a taste for it spoils memory, causing it to retain nothing which it has taken in.

B. N. 2038. 34a]   **1176**

Siccome il mangiare · sanza · voglia fia dañoso · alla salute, ²così lo studio sanza · desiderio guasta · la memoria, e nō ritiē cosa · ch'ella pigli.

Just as eating against one's will is injurious to health, so study without a liking for it spoils the memory, and it retains nothing it takes in.

1169. 3. choll.
1170. 2. incholpando . . tropa . . sachorgiēdo. 4. ci fa [parere] "che". 5. chosa.
1171. 1. chosa . . goventu. 2. cherestorj il. 3. chieza [ovr o chettu ttransstulli la tu]. 4. [a vechieza]—essettu. 6. govē. 7. chettal vecheza . . māchi il.
1172. 1. chognitione. 3. schacciare dasse le chose inutile. 5. chosa. 6. chognitiō.
1173. 1. sicchome . . dallieto.
1174. 1. chettochi. 2. ādo ella. 3. quella.
1175. 1. sichome . . chōuerte. 2. losstudio. 3. za [disspositione] desiderio quassta. 4. memoria [chol nō pigliare alchuna]. 5. e nō ritenere chosa chella.
1176. 1. sichome . . voglia [da danno] fia. 2. chosi losstudio . . chosa.

C. A. 289b]   1177

Ti ghiacciano le parole · in bocca, ²e faresti gielatina ī Mōgibello;

³Siccome il fero s'arruginiscie sanza ⁴esercitio, e l'acqua si putrefa o nel freddo ⁵s'agghiaccia ·, così l'ingiegnio sanza e⁶sercitio si guasta;

⁷Mal fai se lodi ·, e peggio se tu riprēdi ⁸la cosa·, quādo bene · tu nō la intēdi;

⁹Quādo fortuna viē, prēdi l'a mā salua ¹⁰dināti dico, perchè direto · è · calua.

On Mount Etna the words freeze in your mouth and you may make ice of them.

Just as iron rusts from disuse, and stagnant water putrifies or, in cold, turns to ice, so our intellect spoils unless it is kept in use.

You do ill if you praise, and still worse if you reprove, in a matter you do not understand.

When Fortune comes, seize her in front with a sure hand, because behind she is bald.

W. 19038b]   1178

Nō mi | pare che li omini grossi e di ²tristi costumi e di poco discorso meritino si bello stru³mēto, nè tanta varietà di machinamēti quanto li omini speculatiui e ⁴di grā discorsi, ma solo vn sacco doue si riceua il cibo, e donde esso ⁵esca, chè in vero altro che un transito di cibo non sō da essere giudicati, ⁶perchè niente mi pare che essi participino di spetie vmana altro, che la voce ⁷e la figvra, e tutto il resto è assai manco che bestia.

It seems to me that men of coarse and clumsy habits and of small knowledge do not deserve such fine instruments or so great a variety of natural mechanism as men of speculation and of great knowledge; but merely a sack in which their food may be stowed and whence it may issue, since they cannot be judged to be anything else than vehicles for food; for it seems to me they have nothing about them of the human species but the voice and the figure, and for all the rest are much below beasts.

S. K. M. III. 74b]   1179

Ecco alcuni che non altamente che tra²sito di cibo e avmētatori di ster³co e rienpitori di destri chiamarsi debono, perchè per ⁴loro non altro nel mōdo apare, alcuna virtù in opera si ⁵mette, perchè di loro altro ⁶che pieni destri non resta.

Some there are who are nothing else than a passage for food and augmentors of excrement and fillers of privies, because through them no other things in the world, nor any good effects, are produced, since nothing but full privies results from them.

C. A. 156b]   1180

Il massimo ingāno delli omini ²è nella loro opinione.

The greatest deception men suffer is from their own opinions.

<small>On foolish-'
ness and
ignorance
(1180–2).</small>

Triv. 14b]   1181

La stoltitia è scudo della vergognia, come la imprōtitudine ²della povertà.

Folly is the shield of shame, as unreadiness is that of poverty.

Trn. 17b]   1182

La ciecca igniorāza così ci cōduce ²cō effetto de' lascivi sollazzi

³⟮per nō conosciere la uera luce.
⁴⟮per nō conosciere qual sia la uera luce.

⁵E 'l uano splendor ci toglie l'esser ⁶. . .;
⁷¶ vedi che per lo splendor nel fuoco andiamo,
⁸come ciecca jgnorāza ci cōduce.
¹⁰O miseri mortali aprite li occhi.

Blind ignorance misleads us thus and delights with the results of lascivious joys
⟮Because it does not know the true light.
⟮because it does not know what is the true light.
Vain splendour takes from us the power of being . . . behold how owing to the glare of the fire we walk where blind ignorance leads us.
O wretched mortals, open your eyes.

1177. 1. diaciano . . bocha. 2. effaresti. 3. si chome il fero sa . ruginissce. 4. ellacq"a" . . fredo. 5. sagiacia chosi. 7. pegio istu. 8. nolantēdi.

1178. 1. chelli . . grosi. 2. trissti chorstumi "e di pocho disscorso" meritino. 3. nettanta . . spechulatiui e di. 4. disscorsi . . sacho [da cibo] doue. 5. essca . . gudicati. 6. chella voce. 7. ella . . ettutto erresto . . mancho che besstia.

1179. 1. ecci . . che altro chettrā. 3. cho | "e rienpitori di desstri" chiamarsi. 4. loro | "altro nel mōdo" . . alchuna. 6. pieni e desstr.

1180. 2. he nelloro oppennione.

1181. 1. esschudo . . chome.

1182. 1. ciecha . . chosi ci chōduce. 2. e chō . . lasscivi. 3. chonossciere. 4. chonosciere. 6. b \\\\ ¶ vedi fucho andiano. 7. ¶ ciecha ignorāza . . intal modo chōduce. 8. coe chome ciecha jgnorāza ci chōduce. 9. che.

1182. Written beside a sketch of butterflies fluttering round a flame.

B. N. 2038. 34*b*]   1183

*On riches
(1183–7).*
Nō si dimāda · richezza · quello che si può perdere; ²la uirtù · è vero · nostro · bene ed è vero premio ³del suo · possessore ·; lei nō si può · perdere ·, lei ⁴nō ci abandona ·, se prima la uita nō ci lascia; ⁵le robe e le esterne diuitie · senpre le tieni ⁶cō timore; spesso lasciano · con scorno ⁷e sbeffato · il loro possessore perdēdo lor possessione.

That is not riches, which may be lost; virtue is our true good and the true reward of its possessor. That cannot be lost; that never deserts us, but when life leaves us. As to property and external riches, hold them with trembling; they often leave their possessor in contempt, and mocked at for having lost them.

Ox. A. 32*b*]   1183 A

Prima fia il corpo sanza l'ombra che la virtù sanza Invidia.

A body may sooner be without its shadow than virtue be without envy.

F. 96*b*]   1184

Ogni omo desidera far capitale per ²dare a medici destruttori di uite, adūque debono essere richi;
³L'uomo à grande discorso, del quale la più parte ⁴è vana e falsa, li animali l'ànno piccolo, ma è vti⁵le e vero, e meglio è la piccola certezza che la grā ⁶bugia.

Every man wishes to make money to give it to the doctors, destroyers of life; they then ought to be rich [2].
Man has much power of discourse which for the most part is vain and false; animals have but little, but it is useful and true, and a small truth is better than a great lie.

C. A. 109*b*]   1185

Chi piv possiede piv debbe ²temere di nō perdere.

He who possesses most must be most afraid of loss.

W. 12351*a*]   1186

Chi uole essere ricco in v̄ dì ²e impiccato in vn anno.

He who wishes to be rich in a day will be hanged in a year.

S. K. M. III. 17*b*]   1187

E questo uomo à vna somma ²pazzia cioè che sēpre stēta per ³non stētare, e la uita se li ⁴fugie sotto sperāza di gode⁵re i beni con somma fatica ac⁶quistati.

That man is of supreme folly who always wants for fear of wanting: and his life flies away while he is still hoping to enjoy the good things which he has with extreme labour acquired.

B. 3*b*]   1188

*Rules of
life (1188–1202).*
Se tu · avessi · il corpo secōdo la virtù ·, tu · nō cuperesti ²in questo mōdo;
³Tu cresci ī reputatione come il pane ī mano a' putti.

If you governed your body by the rules of virtue you would have no desires in this world.
You grow in reputation like bread in the hands of a child.

Triv. 1*b*]   1189

Saluatico è quel che si salua.

Savage he is who saves himself.

1183. 1. richeza . . chessi. 4. lasscia. 5. elle essterne. 6. isspeso lassciano choniscorno. 7. essbeffato iloro.
1184. 2. medici "destruttori di uite" . . esse. 4. pichole. 5. verso . . ella pichola certeza.
1185. 1. ci piv posiede.
1186. 1. richo n̄vdi. 2. empichato nvn.
1187. 1. omo . . soma. 2. pazia . . chessēpre. 3. istētare ella uita. 5. soma fatica a. 6. quisstati.
1188. 1. settu . . cupresti. 3. cressi.

1183 A. This note is written above a drawing of a winged figure pursuing a figure with bow and arrow; underneath is written 'virtu' and 'Invidia'.
1184. 2. Compare No. 856.

1189. A play on words: *Selvatico* means 'savage', 'unsociable'. *Salvaticus* is the name of a noble Milanese family. Compare No. 1554 A.

E. 31b]　　　　　　　　　　　　1190

Non si debbe desiderare lo inpossibile.　　　We ought not to desire the impossible.

H.³ 118b]　　　　　　　　　　　1191

Dimāda cōsiglio a chi bē si corregge;　　　Ask counsel of him who governs himself well.
²Givstitia vuol potētia, intelligē³tia e volontà,　Justice requires power, insight, and will; and
e si assomi⁴glia al rè delle api;　　　　it resembles the queen-bee.
⁵Chi nō puniscie il male, co⁶māda che si　He who does not punish evil commands it to
facci;　　　　　　　　　　　be done.
⁷Chi piglia la biscia per la coda ⁸quella poi　He who takes the snake by the tail will pre-
lo morde;　　　　　　　　　sently be bitten by it.
⁹Chi cava la fossa, quella ¹⁰gli ruina adosso.　The grave will fall in upon him who digs it.

H.³ 119a]　　　　　　　　　　1192

¹Chi nō rafrena la uoluttà ·, colle bestie　The man who does not restrain wantonness,
²s'acōpagni;　　　　　　　　allies himself with beasts.
³Nō si può avere maggior nè minor signio⁴ria　You can have no dominion greater or less
che quella di sé medesimo;　　　　than that over yourself.
⁵Chi poco pēsa, molto erra;　　　　He who thinks little, errs much.
⁶Più facilmēte si cōtesta al prīcipio, ⁷che al　It is easier to contend with evil at the first
fine;　　　　　　　　　　than at the last.
⁸Nessuno cōsiglio è piv leale che ⁹quello che　No counsel is more loyal than that given on
si dà alle navi che so¹⁰no in pericolo; ¹¹Aspetti　ships which are in peril: He may expect loss
danno quel che si regie per ¹²giovane scon-　who acts on the advice of an inexperienced
sigliato.　　　　　　　　　youth.

Triv. 23b]　　　　　　　　　　1193

Dov' è piv sentimēto, lì è piv martirio; grā　Where there is most feeling, there is the
martire.　　　　　　　　　greatest martyrdom; a great martyr.

H. 16b]　　　　　　　　　　　1194

La memoria de' benifitj apres²so l'īgratitudine　The memory of benefits is a frail defence
è fragile;　　　　　　　　against ingratitude.
³Reprēdi l'amico ī segre⁴to, e laudalo ī　Reprove your friend in secret and praise him
paleso;　　　　　　　　　openly.
⁵Chi teme i · pericoli, non perisscie ⁶per quegli.　He who fears the dangers, does not perish
⁷Non essere bugiardo del ⁸preterito.　　through them.
　　　　　　　　　　　　Be not false about the past.

C. A. 117b]　　　　　　　　　1195

CŌPERATIONE DELLA PATIĒTIA　　　A SIMILE FOR PATIENCE

²La patiētia fa cōtra alle ingiurie non altra-　Patience serves us against insults precisely as
mēti che si faccino i panni ³contra del freddo,　clothes do against cold. For if you put on more

1190. 1. debba.
1191. 1–10 R. 1. ach bē si corege. 2. vol. 3. essi. 4. gia are delleave. 5. punisscie. 9. cicava. 10. glruina.
1192. 1–12 R. 1. cholle. 3. po .. magior. 5. ci poco. 6. a prīcipio. 8. nesuno chōsiglio. 9. chessi da dalle. 10. pericholo. 11. dano.
　12. scōsiglo.
1193. piv ne martiri.
1194. 1–6 R. 1. benifiti apre. 4. ellaldalo.
1195. 2. allengiurie .. altremēti .. chessi. 3. fredo jnpero chessetti .. sechondo.

1190. The writing of this note, which is exceedingly minute, is reproduced in facsimile on Pl. XLI, No. 5, above the first diagram.

jnperochè se ti mvltiplicherai li pañi secondo la mvl⁴tiplicatione · del freddo ·, esso freddo · nocere nō · potrà ·; similmēte alle ⁵grādi ingivrie · cresci la patiētia, · e esse ingiurie offendere nō ti po⁶tranno la tua mēte.

garments as the cold increases, that cold cannot hurt you; in the same way increase your patience under great offences, and they cannot vex your mind.

S. K. M. II.¹ 41b]   1196

Tanto è a dire bē d'ū tristo, ²quanto a dire male d'ū bono.

To speak well of a base man is much the same as speaking ill of a good man.

H.² 60b]   1197

La invidia offēde colla fitta ²infamia, cioè col detrarre, ³la qual cosa spavēta la virtù.

Envy wounds with false accusations, that is with detraction, a thing which scares virtue.

L. 0″]   1198

Decipimur votis et tempore fallimur et mors ²deridet curas; anxia vita nihil.

We are deceived by promises; time disappoints us; death derides our cares; life's anxieties are naught.

L. 90b]   1199

¶ La pavra nascie piv tosto ²che altra cosa. ¶

Fear arises sooner than anything else.

C. A. 76b]   1200

Siccome l'animosità è pericolo di uita · così la paura · è sicurità di quella;
²Le minaccie sol sono ³arme dello minacciato;
⁴¶ Dov' entra la uētura, la invidia · vi pone lo assedio e la cōbatte, e dond' ella si parte, vi lascia il dolore e pētimēto;
⁵¶ Raro cade chi ben camina;
⁶¶ Mal' è se laudi e peggio se riprēdi la cosa, dico se bene tu non la intēdi;

⁷¶ Mal fai se laudi e peggio se tu riprēdi ‖ la cosa quādo bene tu non la intendi.

Just as courage imperils life, fear protects it.

Threats alone are the weapons of the threatened man.
Wherever good fortune enters, envy lays siege to the place and attacks it; and when it departs, sorrow and repentance remain behind.
He who walks straight rarely falls.
It is bad if you praise, and worse if you reprove, a thing—I mean, if you do not understand the matter well.
It is ill to praise, and worse to reprimand, matters that you do not understand.

G. 49a]   1201

Senpre le parole che nō soddisfaño all' orechio dello ²auditore, li danno tedio over rincrescimēto, e'l segnio di ³ciò vedrai, spesse uolte tali auditori essere ⁴copiosi di sbadigli; addūque che parli dināti a omini ⁵di chi tu · cierchi benivolētia, quādo tu vedi · tali pro⁶digi di rīcrescimēto, abreuia il tuo parlare, o tu mu⁷ta ragionamēto, e se tu altramēti farai, allora in lo⁸co della desiderata gratia tu acquisterai odio ⁹e nimicitia;
¹⁰E se vuoi vedere di quel che vn si diletta

Words which do not satisfy the ear of the hearer weary him or vex him, and the symptoms of this you will often see in such hearers in their frequent yawns; you therefore, who speak before men whose goodwill you desire, when you see such an excess of fatigue, abridge your speech, or change your discourse; and if you do otherwise, then instead of the favour you desire you will get dislike and hostility.
And if you would see in what a man takes

4. esso fredo. 5. grāde . . cressci.
1196. 1. trissto.
1197. 1–3 R. 1. lanvidia . . cholla. 2. chol.
1198. 1. et mos. 2. nhil.
1199. 1–2 R. 1. nasscie. 2. chosa.
1200. 1. sichome . . pericholo . . chosi . . sichurta. 3. iminacciato. 4. lanvidia . . essedio ello chōbatte E . . lasscia il "dolore he" piētimēto. 5. chade . . chamina. 6. laldi e pegio . . chosa dicho . . tu nolla. 7. laldi e pegio is tu . . tu nollātēdi.
1201. 1. saddisfāno. 2. alditore . . rincresscimēto. 3. uolte [alli] ttali vlditore. 4. chopiosi di sbavigli. 6. rīcresscimēto . . ottu. 7. essettu altremēti . . allora illo. 8. cho. 9. ennimicitia. 10. Esse voi . . sanza vl.

1198. This elegiac distichon, found in books of Latin inscriptions, occurs also on epitaphs; it is of

unknown origin, but was frequently used. Compare W. v. Seidlitz, *Leonardo*, i. 96.

sanza u¹¹dirlo parlare, parla a lui mutãdo diuersi ragio¹²namẽti, e quel dove tu lo vedi stare intẽto sanza ¹³sbadigliamẽti o storcimẽti di ciglia o altre varie ¹⁴azione, sia cierto che quella cosa, di che si parla, ¹⁵è quella di che lui si diletta, ecc.

pleasure, without hearing him speak, change the subject of your discourse in talking to him, and when you presently see him intent, without yawning or wrinkling his brow or other actions of various kinds, you may be certain that the matter of which you are speaking is such as is agreeable to him, &c.

Triv. 6a]   1202

SUGIETTO CHOLLA FORMA

Mvouesi l'amante per la cosa amata come il senso · e lo sensibile, e cõ seco s'uniscie ²e fassi vna cosa medesima; ³l'opera è la prima cosa che nasce dall' unione; ⁴se la cosa amata è vile ·, l'amãte si fa vile;

⁵Quando · la cosa vnita è cõueniẽte al suo ⁶vnitore ·, li seguita · dilettatione · e piacere e soddisfatione;

⁷Quãdo l'amãte è gĩvto all' amato, lì si riposa; ⁸quãdo · il peso · è posato · lì si riposa.

THE SUBJECT WITH ITS FORM

The lover is moved by the beloved object as the senses are by sensible objects; and they unite and become one and the same thing. The work is the first thing born of this union; if the thing loved is base the lover becomes base.

When the thing taken into union is perfectly adapted to that which receives it, the result is delight and pleasure and satisfaction.

When that which loves is united to the thing beloved it can rest there; when the burden is laid down it finds rest there.

C. A. 65b]   1203

La prima fama si fa etterna insieme colli abitatori ²della città da lui edificata o accresciuta;

³Tutti i popoli · obbediscono e sõ mossi da lor magniati ·, e essi magniati · si collegano e costringono co' signori ⁴per 2 · vie: o per sanguinità ·, o per roba: sanguinità, quãdo · i lor figlioli sono a similitudine ⁵di statichi, sicurtà e pegnio della lor dubitata · fede; roba, quãdo · tu farai a ciascũ d'essi ⁶murare vna casa o 2 dentro alla tua città, della quale lui ne tragga qual⁷ch' entrate · e trarrà da 10 città · cinque mila · case · cõ trenta ⁸mila abitationi ·, e digregerai tanta cõgregatione di popolo che a similitudine di capre l'ũ ⁹adosso all' altro stanno, ẽpiẽdo ogni parte di fetore si fanno semẽza di pestilẽte ¹⁰morte!

¹¹E la città si fa di bellezza cõpagnia del suo nome e a te vtile di dati e fama etterna del suo crescimẽto.

There will be eternal fame also for the inhabitants of that town, constructed and enlarged by him. *Politics (1203–4).*

All communities obey and are led by their magnates, and these magnates ally themselves with the lords and subjugate them in two ways: either by consanguinity, or by fortune; by consanguinity, when their children are, as it were, hostages, and a security and pledge of their suspected fidelity; by property, when you make each of these build a house or two inside your city which may yield some revenue, and he shall have from 10 towns five thousand houses with thirty thousand inhabitants, and you will disperse this great congregation of people which stand like goats one behind the other, filling every place with fetid smells and sowing seeds of pestilence and death!

And the city will gain beauty worthy of its name and to you it will be useful by its revenues, and the eternal fame of its aggrandizement.

B. N. 2037. 10a]   1204

Per mãtenere il dono prĩcipal ²di natura cioè libertà, trovo modo ³da offẽdere e difẽdere stãte assediati ⁴da li ãbitiosi tirãni, e prima dirò del si⁵to mvrale, e ãcora per che i popoli possino ⁶mãtenere i loro boni e giusti signiori.

To preserve Nature's chiefest boon, that is, freedom, I can find means of offence and defence, when it is assailed by ambitious tyrants, and first I will speak of the situation of the walls, and also I shall show how communities can maintain their good and just lords.

---

11. allui. 12. ecquel . . tullo. 13. sbavigliamẽti osstorcimeti. 14. di chessi. 15. ecquella . . lui si di che lui si diletta.
1202. 1. lamata per la cosamato . . senso colla sensibbile e chõsecho. 2. effassi. 3. ella . . chosa . . nasscie dell. 4. sella. 5. chosa . . chõueniẽte . . essadisfatione. 8. li si riposato. 9. la cosasa chogni usscivta chol nostro intelletto.
1203. 2. dallui . . acressciuta. 3. obbedisscano esso mossi . . collogano co signiori "e costringano." 4. sagvinita . . roba sanguinata sanguinita . . assimilitudine. 5. tuffarai aciasscũ. 6. casa [de] o 2 . . traga. 7. ettrarra 1 br 10 citta . . mila casse. 8. edigregierai tanto . . assimilitudine. 9. allalstano . . oni . . fetore si fano . . pessilẽte. 11. ella . . atte . . dati effama . . cresscimẽto.
1204. 1. istãdo assediati.

1203. These notes were possibly written in preparation for a letter.
1204. Compare No. 1266.

III

POLEMICS. SPECULATION

G. 47a]   1205

Against speculators (1205-6).

O speculatore del²le cose, nõ ti laudare ³di conosciere le cose ⁴che ordinariamē⁵te per sé medesima la ⁶natura ⁷conduce; ⁸Ma rallegrati di co⁹nosciere il fine ¹⁰di quelle cose che ¹¹son disegniate dalla ¹²mēte tua.

Oh! speculators on things, boast not of knowing the things that nature ordinarily brings about; but rejoice if you know the end of those things which you yourself devise.

W. 19115a]   1205 A

Ancora che lo ingiegno umano in inventioni varie rispondendo con vari strumenti e un medesimo fine, mai esso troverà invention nè più bella nè più facile nè più brieve della natura, perchè nelle sue invenzioni nulla mancha e nulla è superfluo.

Though human genius in its various inventions with various instruments may answer the same end, it will never find an invention more beautiful or more simple or direct than nature, because in her inventions nothing is lacking and nothing superfluous.

S. K. M. II. 292b]   1206

O speculatori · dello continvo moto, quã²ti vani disegni in simile cerca avete creati! ³accõpagniatevi colli cercatori dell' oro.

Oh! speculators on perpetual motion, how many vain projects in this search you have created! Go and be the companions of the searchers for gold.

C. A. 76b]   1207

Against alchemists (1207-8).

J bugiardi · interpreti di natura · affermano l'argiēto viuo · essere comvne semēza a tutti i metalli ·, nõ si ricordãdo che la ²natura varia le semēze · secõdo la diuersità delle cose che essa vole produrre al mõdo.

The false interpreters of nature declare that quicksilver is the common seed of every metal, not remembering that nature varies the seed according to the variety of the things she desires to produce in the world.

F. 5b]   1208

E molti ²fecero bot³tega cõn ī⁴ganni e ⁵miraculi ⁶finti, ingan⁷nãdo la sto⁸lta molti⁹tudine.

And many have made a trade of delusions and false miracles, deceiving the stupid multitude.

Triv. 34a]   1209

Against friars.

¶ Farisei ·, frati · santi vol dire. ¶

Pharisees—that is to say, holy friars.

W. 19084a]   1210

Against writers of epitomes.

I abbreuiatori delle opere · fanno ingiuria ²alla cognitione e allo amore, ³conciosiachè

Abbreviators do harm to knowledge and to love, seeing that the love of anything is the off-

---

1205. 1. hosspechulatori. 2. chose .. laldare. 3. conossciere. 6. per sua [natu] "[ordine]". 7. [ralmēte] chonducie. 8. dicho. 9. nossciere. 10. chose.
1206. 1. spechulatori. 2. ciercha ave creati. 3. acõpagniatevi .. cierchator.
1207. 1. interpetri .. chomvne .. attutti .. richordãdo chella. 2. sechõdo .. chose .. produre.
1208. 2. fecē bot. 6. inga. 10. esse nesun siscopria cognoscitore de loro ingãni essigli poniano.
1210. 1. abreuiatori .. opre . f . fanno ingiuia. 2. cognitione [concosia che] e allo. 3. concosia chellamore .. effilol.

1206. Another passage in MS. I, 102a, referring also to speculators, is given by Libri (*Hist. des sciences math.* iii. 228): 'Sicchè voi speculatori non vi fidate delli autori che ànno sol col immaginatione voluto farsi interpreti tra la natura e l'omo, ma sol di quelli che non coi cienni della natura, ma cogli effetti delle sue esperienze ànno esercitati i loro ingegni.'

1209. Compare No. 837, ll. 54-7, No. 1296 (pp. 101 and 301), and No. 1305 (p. 306).

l'amore di qualūche cosa è figliuolo ⁴d'essa cognitione; e l'amore ⁵è tanto più feruēte, quanto la ⁶cognitione è più certa, la qual ⁷certezza nascie dalla cognitione ⁸integrale di tutte quelle par⁹ti le quali, essendo insieme vnite, ¹⁰conpongono il tutto di quelle co¹¹se che debbono essere amate; ¹²che vale a quel, che per abbreuiare ¹³le parti di quelle cose che lui fa ¹⁴professione di darne integral no¹⁵titia, che lui lascia indietro la ¹⁶maggior parte delle cose, di che il tutto ¹⁷è cōposto? egli è vero che la inpa¹⁸tientia, madre della stoltitia, è que¹⁹lla che lauda la breuità; come se ²⁰questi tali non avessino tāto di uita, ²¹che li seruisse a potere avere vna ²²intera notitia d'un sol particulare co²³me è vn corpo vmano! e poi vogli²⁴ono abbracciare la mēte di dio nella ²⁵quale s'include l'universo, cara²⁶ctando e minuzzando quella in īfinite ²⁷parti, come se l'avessino anatomizzate;

²⁸O stoltitia vmana nō ²⁹t'avedi tu che tu sei stato con teco ³⁰tutta la tua età, e non ài ancora ³¹notitia di quella cosa che tu più possie³²di, cioè della tua pazzia? e vuoi po³³i colla moltitudine de' soffistichi ingannare ³⁴te e altri, sprezzando le matematiche sciē³⁵zie, nelle qual si contiene la vera no³⁶titia delle cose che in lor si cōtēgono; e vuoi ³⁷poi scorrere ne' miracoli e scrivere e dar ³⁸notitia di quelle cose, di che la mēte vmana ³⁹non è capace, e non si possono dimostrare per ne⁴⁰ssuno esenplo naturale, e ti pare avere ⁴¹fatto miraculi, quādo tu ài guastato vna ⁴²opera d'alcuno ingegnio speculativo, e nō ⁴³t'avedi che tu cadi nel medesimo errore, ⁴⁴che fa quello che denuda la piāta dell' orna⁴⁵mento de' sua rami, pieni di fronde, miste co⁴⁶li odoriferi fiori o frutti, sopra, dimostra in quella pianta esser da fare di inude tavole ⁴⁸come fece Giv⁴⁹stino, abbreuiatore delle storie scritte da Trogo ⁵⁰Pōpeo, il quale scrisse ornatamente tutti ⁵¹li eccellēti fatti delli sua antichi, li quali e⁵²rā pieni di mirabilissimi ornamēti; e così ⁵³conpose vna cosa ignuda, ma sol degna d'in⁵⁴gegni inpatiēti, li quali pare lor perder ⁵⁵tanto di tenpo, quāt' è quello che è adoperato vtil⁵⁶mēte, cioè nelli studi delle opere di nature e delle ⁵⁷cose vmane; Ma stieno questi tali in conpa⁵⁸gnia delle bestie; e li lor cortigiani sieno cani e ⁵⁹i altri animali piē di rapina e accompagniansi ⁶⁰collor correndo sempre dietro a chi fuge, seguitan⁶¹do l'inocēti animali che cō la fame alli tem⁶²pi delle grā nevi ti uengono alle case, dimandā⁶³toti limosina come lor tutore. . . .

spring of this knowledge, the love being the more fervent in proportion as the knowledge is more certain. And this certainty is born of a complete knowledge of all the parts, which, when combined, compose the totality of the thing which ought to be loved. Of what use then is he who abridges the details of those matters of which he professes to give thorough information, while he leaves behind the chief part of the things of which the whole is composed? It is true that impatience, the mother of stupidity, praises brevity, as if such persons had not life long enough to serve them to acquire a complete knowledge of one single subject, such as the human body; and then they want to comprehend the mind of God in which the universe is included, weighing it minutely and mincing it into infinite parts, as if they had to dissect it!

Oh! human stupidity, do you not perceive that you have spent your whole life with yourself and yet have no knowledge of the thing you chiefly possess, that is, of your folly? and then, with the crowd of sophists, you deceive yourselves and others, despising the mathematical sciences in which dwells the true knowledge of the things included in them. And then you occupy yourself with miracles, and write and give information of those things of which the human mind is incapable and which cannot be proved by any instance from nature. And you fancy you have wrought miracles when you spoil a work of some speculative mind, and do not perceive that you are falling into the same error as that of a man who strips a tree of the ornament of its branches covered with leaves mingled with the scented blossoms or fruit thereon and demonstrates that out of this plant naked boards are to be made [48] as Justinus did, in abridging the histories written by Trogus Pompeius, who had written in an ornate style all the worthy deeds of his forefathers, full of the most admirable and ornamental passages; and so composed a bald work worthy only of those impatient spirits, who fancy they are losing time when they are engaged in the useful study of the works of nature and the deeds of men. But these may remain in company of beasts; among their associates should be dogs and other animals full of rapine, and they may hunt with them after those which flee and follow helpless beasts, which in time of great snows come near to your houses asking alms as from their master. . . .

4. ella [cogni] more. 5. ettanto. 7. feruēde certeza nasscie. 8. i integrale . . pa. 9. te le. 10. conpongano . . quella. 11. sa che 12. abreuiare. 13. parte. 15. chellui lassci indirieto. 16. magor. 17. chella. 19. chellalda . . chomesse. 21. chelli seruissi. 22. da "sol" particulare. 24. ano abracciare . . nelle. 26. minvzando. 27. parte . . lavessino anatomizare. 28. [e delle chose che] o. 29. tu [chett] chettu se. 31. chettu. 32. coe . . pazzia [vole] e volli. 33. i conlla . . inganare. 34. splezando. 35. ze nella. 36. cōtēgano e voi. 39. posso. 40. naturale letti. 41. tu guasto. 42. spechulativo. 43. chettu. 44. cheffa. 45. misto. 46. offrutti sopra dimostar. 48. di [molte] lun se tavole come fece givs. 49. abreuiatore . . da troc. 50. pō peo il . . tuti. 51. eceletti. 53. inuda . . degnia di. 55. quelloche. 56. coe . . dele. 57. quessti. 58. cortigani sie. 59. a altri . . rap ina eaconpagniasi. 60. senpre dirieto ach fuge. 61. alli ten. 62. uengano . . casi. 63. lor tutore essnull. *here the text breaks off.*

1210. 48. *Givstino*, Marcus Junianus Justinus, a Roman historian of the second century, compiler of an epitome from the general history written by Trogus Pompeius, who lived in the time of Augustus. The work was published at Venice in 1477. Compare No. 1469.

C. A. 190*b*]　　　　　　　　　1211

On spirits
(1211-15).

O matematici fate lume a tale er²rore!
³Lo spirito non à voce, perchè dov' è voce ⁴è
corpo, e dove è corpo è occupatiõ di lo⁵co, il
quale inpediscie all' ochio il ue⁶dere delle cose
poste dopo tale loco; ⁷adunque tal corpo enpie
di sé tutta ⁸la circustante aria, cioè colla sua
s⁹petie.

O mathematicians, shed light on this error.
The spirit has no voice, because where there is
a voice there is a body, and where there is a
body space is occupied, and this prevents the
eye from seeing what is placed behind that
space; hence the surrounding air is filled by the
body, that is by its image.

B. 4*b*]　　　　　　　　　　　1212

Nõ può essere voce, dove non è movimēto e
percussione d'aria; ²nõ può essere percussione
d'essa aria, doue non è strumēto; ³nõ può essere
strumēto incorporeo; essē⁴do così, vno spirito nõ
può avere nè voce nè forma nè forza, ⁵e se piglierà
corpo, non potrà penetrare nè ⁶entrare doue li
usci sono serrati; ⁷e se alcuno diciesse: per aria
cõgregata ⁸e ristretta īsieme lo spirito piglia i
corpi ⁹di uarie · forme ·, e per quello strumēto
parla ¹⁰e move cõ forza, a questa parte dico,
¹¹che doue non sono nerui e ossa, non può
esse¹²re forza · operata in nessuno movimēto
¹³fatto dagl' imaginati spiriti;

¹⁴fuggi i precetti · di quelli · speculatori, chè
le loro ¹⁵ragioni · nõ son · confermate · dalla ·
speriēza.

There can be no voice where there is no
motion or percussion of the air; there can be no
percussion of the air where there is no instrument; there can be no instrument without a
body; and this being so, a spirit can have neither
voice, nor form, nor strength. And if it were to
assume a body it could not penetrate nor enter
where the passages are closed. And if any one
should say that by air, compressed and com-
pacted together, a spirit may take bodies of
various forms and by this means speak and move
with strength—to him I reply that when there
are neither nerves nor bones there can be no
force exercised in any kind of movement made
by such imaginary spirits.

Beware of the teaching of these speculators,
because their reasoning is not confirmed by experience.

W. 19048*b*]　　　　　　　　　1213

Delli discorsi vmani stoltissimo è da essere
riputato quello, il qual s'astēde al²la credulità
della negromātia, sorella della alchimia, partori-
tricie del³le cose senplici e naturali; Ma è tanto
più degnia di riprensio⁴ne che l'alchimia, quāto
ella non partorisce alcuna cosa se nõ simile a sé,
⁵cioè bugie; il che non interviene nella alchimia,
la quale è ministra⁶tricie de' senplici prodotti
della natura, il quale vfitio fatto esser nõ può
⁷da essa natura, perchè in lei non sono strumēti
organici colli quali essa possa operare quel ⁸che
adopera l'uomo mediante le mani, che in tale
vfitio ⁹à fatti i vetri ecc.; ma essa negromātia,
stendardo ovvero bandiera ¹⁰volante, mossa dal
uēto, guidatricie della stolta moltitudine, la
quale ¹¹al continuo è testimonia collo abbaiamēto
d'infiniti effetti di tale ¹²arte; e n'hanno ēpiuti i
libri, affermando che l'incāti e spiriti adoperino
¹³e sanza lingua parlino, e sanza strumēti organici, sāza i quali ¹⁴parlar nõ si può, parlino, e
portino gravissimi pesi, facino tēpestare ¹⁵e

Of all human opinions that is to be reputed
the most foolish which deals with the belief in
Necromancy, the sister of Alchemy, which gives
birth to simple and natural things. But it is all
the more worthy of reprehension than Alchemy,
because it brings forth nothing but what is like
itself, that is, lies; this does not happen in
Alchemy which deals with simple products of
nature and whose function cannot be exercised
by nature itself, because it has no organic instruments with which it can work, as men do by
means of their hands, who have produced, for
instance, glass, &c., but this Necromancy, the
flag and flying banner, blown by the winds,
the guide of the stupid crowd which is constantly witness to the dazzling and endless effects
of this art; and there are books full, declaring
that enchantments and spirits can work and
speak without tongues and without organic instruments—without which it is impossible to
speak—and can carry the heaviest weights and

1211. 1. attale. 4. e do e corpo e ochupatiõ. 5. cho. 6. posste .. locho. 7. dal. 8. coe.
1212. 1. nõ po. 2. nõ po. 3. nõ po. 4. nõ po .. voce "| ne forma" ne forza. 5. esse. 6. sera "ti". 7. esse .. diciessi perr. 8. chorpi.
　9. quelo. 10. Acquesta .. dicho. 11. none nerui e ossa non po. 12. operrata inessuno. 14. fugi. 15. isperiēza.
1213. *Above the text is the note*: seguita quel che mācha dirieto alla facia del pie. 1. Ma dalli disscorsi .. essere [tenuto] "re putato"
　.. sasstēde. 2. archimia. 3. lle chose [naturali] senplici .. ettanto .. ripresi. 4. chellarchimia .. partorissce .. chosa .. asse.
　5. [parole] "cioe bugia" il che noñe .. archimia .. e [vfit] ministra. 6. dalla. 7. illei none .. orghanici [da poter] "cholli quali"
　essa. 8. lomo [il quale] mediante. 9. affatti e vetri .. stendar "do" over. 10. uēto guidatricie. 11. chontinuo e tesstimonia chollo.
　12. ēpiute .. chellinchāti esspiriti. 13. essanza .. essanza .. saza. 14. po .. tēpesstare. 15. chelli .. ghatte.

piovere, e che li omini si cōvertino in gatte, lupi e altre bestie, [16]benchè in bestia prima ētrā quelli che tal cosa affermano;

[17]E cierto, se tale negromātia fusse in essere, come dalli bassi ingiegni è creduto, [18]nessuna cosa è sopra la terra che al danno e seruitio dell' omo fusse di tanta valitudine, perchè se fus[19]se vero, che in tale arte si avesse potētia di far turbare la trāquilla serenità dell' ari[20]a, convertendo quella in notturn aspetto, e far le corruscationi e venti con spa[21]vētevoli toni e folgori scorrēti infra le tenebre, e con īpetuosi venti ruinare [22]li alti edifiti, e diradicare le selue, e con quelle percuotere li eserciti, e quelli [23]ronpēdo e atterrādo, e oltr' a questo le dannose tenpeste, privando li cultori [24]del premio delle lor fatiche,—o qual modo di guerra può essere, che con tanto dan[25]no possa offendere il suo nemico di aver potestà di privarlo delle sue raccolte? qual bat[26]taglia marittima può essere che si assomigli a quella di colui che comāda alli vēti [27]e fa le fortune ruvinose e sommergitrici di qualunche armata?—cierto quel che [28]commāda a tali inpetuose potētie sarà signore delli popoli, e nessuno vma[29]no ingiegnio potrà reoiotere alle sue dannose forze; Li occulti tesori e [30]giemme, riposte nel corpo della terra, fieno a costui tutti manifesti; nessun [31]serrame o fortezze inespugnabili sarā quelle che saluar possino al[32]cuno sanza la voglia di tal negromāte; Questo si farà portare per l'aria dal[33]l' oriente all' occidēte e per tutti li oppositi aspetti dell' universo; Ma per[34]chè mi vo io più oltre astendendo? quale è quella cosa che per ta[35]le arteficie far nō si possa? quasi nessuna, eccietto il levarsi la morte; ad[36]dunque è concluso in parte il danno e la vtilità che in tale arte si contiene, essē[37]do vera; e s'ella è vera, perchè non è restata infra li omini che tanto la deside[38]rano, non avēdo riguardo a nessuna deità? e so, che infiniti ce n'è, che per soddisfare [39]a vn suo appetito, ruinerebbero Iddio cō tutto l'universo; e s'ella non è rimasta infra [40]li omini, essendo a lui tanto neciessaria, essa nō fu mai, nè mai è per dovere essere, [41]per la difinitiō dello spirito, il quale è invisibile incorporeo; e dentro alli elemē[42]ti non sono cose incorporee, perchè doue non è corpo, è vacuo, e il uacuo nō si dà dē[43]tro alli elemēti, perchè subito sarebbe dall' elemēto riēpiuto; || volta carta.

raise storms and rain; and that men can be turned into cats and wolves and other beasts, although indeed it is those who affirm these things who first become beasts.

And surely if this necromancy did exist, as is believed by small wits, there is nothing on the earth that would be of so much importance alike for the detriment and service of men, if it were true that there were in such an art a power to disturb the calm serenity of the air, converting it into darkness, and to make coruscations or winds, with terrific thunder and lightnings rushing through the darkness, and with violent storms to overthrow high buildings and to root up forests; and thus to oppose armies, crushing and annihilating them; and, besides these, frightful storms which should deprive the peasants of the reward of their labours. Now what kind of warfare is there to hurt the enemy so much as to deprive him of the harvest? What naval warfare could be compared with that of the man who has power to command the winds and to make ruinous gales by which any fleet may be submerged? Surely a man who could command such violent forces would be lord of the nations, and no human ingenuity could resist his crushing force. The hidden treasures and gems reposing in the body of the earth would all be made manifest to him. No lock or fortress, though impregnable, would be able to save any one against the will of the necromancer. He would have himself carried through the air from east to west and through all the opposite sides of the universe. But why should I enlarge further upon this? What is there that could not be done by such a craftsman? Almost nothing, except to escape death. Hereby I have explained in part the mischief and the usefulness contained in this art, if it is real; and if it is real, why has it not remained among men who desire it so much, having nothing to do with any deity? For I know that there are numberless people who would, to satisfy a whim, destroy God and all the universe; and if this necromancy, being, as it were, so necessary to men, has not been left among them, it can never have existed, nor will it ever exist according to the definition of the spirit, which is invisible, for within the elements there are no incorporeal things, because where there is no body, there is a vacuum; and no vacuum can exist in the elements because it would be immediately filled up. Turn over.

---

16. che dattal chosa. 17. eccierto settale .. fussi .. chome. 18. chosa essopra .. al "danno e" seruitio .. fussi .. tanta [vtilita] 'valitudine' perchesse fu. 19. si .. arte [fussi] si avessi .. turbare [laria] la. 20. chonvertendo .. inotturnasspetto effarle corrusscati oni .. chon isspa. 21. effolgo"ri" .. infralle .. e chonni petuosi. 22. diradichare le piante "selue" e chon .. perchotere .. ecquelli. 23. oltradiquesto .. tenpesste .. chultori. 24. ghuerra po .. chon. 25. nemicho aver potessta .. richolte .. ba. 26. po .. chessi .. acquella dicho .. chomāda. 27. effa .. essomergitrici. 28. chomāda attali. 29. resissttere .. ocholti. 30. gieme .. chorpo .. achosstu .. nessu. 31. fortezza [chef] inepugnabili .. chessalvar. 32. chuno. 33. lloriente .. oposti asspetti. 34. mi voio piu oltre asstendendo .. chosa che pera. 36. choncluso "inparte" il .. ella .. chontiene. 37. essella .. nonee resstata infralli .. chetta deside. 38. essol che infiniti ciene .. saddisfare. 39. ruinerebono .. chō .. essella 40. allui tanta (?) .. mai nemmai. 41. chorpo. 42. none chose inchorporee .. chorpo e vachuo .. vachuo.

DELLI SPIRITI

[2]Abiāo insin qui dirieto a questa faccia detto, [3]comè la difinitiō dello spirito [4]è vna potentia congiunta al corpo, perchè per sé medesimo [5]reggiere nō si può, nè pigliare alcuna sorte di moto locale, [6]e se tu dirai che per sé si regga, questo essere non può [7]dentro alli elemēti, perchè se lo spirito è quātità incor[8]porea, questa tal quantità è detta vacuo, e il ua[9]cuo non si dà in natura; e dato che si desse, subito sa[10]rebbe riempiuto dalla ruina di quello elemento nel [11]qual tal uacuo si gienerasse; adunque per la difinition del pe[12]so che dicie, la grauità è vna potētia accidentale creata [13]dall' uno elemento tirato o sospinto nell' altro, seguita, che [14]nessuno elemēto, non pesando nel medesimo elemēto, e' pe[15]sa nell' elemēto superiore ch'è più lieve di lui; come si uede [16]la parte dell' acqua non à gravità o leuità nell' altra [17]acqua, ma se tu la tirerai nell' aria, allora ella acqui[18]sterà gravezza, e se tu tirerai l'aria [19]sotto l'acqua, allora l'acqua, che si trova sopra tale [20]aria, acquista gravezza, la qual gravezza per sé sostener [21]non si può, onde lì è neciessario la ruina, e così cade infra [22]l'acqua in quel loco ch'è vacuo d'essa acqua; tale ac[23]caderebbe nello spirito, stando infra li elemēti, che al [24]continuo gienererebbe vacuo in quel tale elemēto, dove [25]lui si trovasse, per la qual cosa gli sarebbe neciessario la con[26]tinua fuga inverso il cielo, insinche vscito fusse di tali [27]elemēti.

SE LO SPIRITO TIENE CORPO INFRA LI [29]ELEMĒNTI

[30]Abbiā provato, come lo spirito non può per sé stare infra li [31]elementi sanza corpo, nè per sé si può mouere per moto vo[32]lontario, se non è allo in sù; Ma al presente diremo co[33]me, pigliando corpo d'aria tale spirito, è necies[34]sario che s'infonda infra essa aria, perchè, s'elli stesse vnito, [35]e' sarebbe separato e caderebbe alla gieneratiō del uacuo, [36]come di sopra è detto; addunque è neciessario che, a volere [37]restare infra l'aria, che esso s'infonda in una quātità d'aria; e [38]se si mista coll' aria, elli seguita due inconvenienti, cioè [39]che elli leuifica quella quātità dell' aria dove esso si mista, [40]per la qual cosa l'aria leuificata per sé uola in alto, e non resta [41]infra l'aria più grossa

OF SPIRITS

We have said, on the other side of this page, that the definition of a spirit is a power conjoined to a body; because it cannot move of its own accord, nor can it have any kind of motion in space; and if you were to say that it moves itself, this cannot be within the elements. For if the spirit is an incorporeal quantity, this quantity is called a vacuum, and a vacuum does not exist in nature; and granting that one were formed, it would be immediately filled up by the rushing in of the element in which the vacuum had been generated. Therefore, from the definition of weight, which is this—gravity is an accidental power, created by one element being drawn to or suspended in another—it follows that an element, not weighing anything compared with itself, has weight in the element above it and lighter than it; as we see that the parts of water have no gravity or levity compared with other water, but if you draw it up into the air, then it would acquire weight, and if you were to draw the air beneath the water, then the water which remains above this air would acquire weight, which weight could not sustain itself by itself, whence collapse is inevitable. And this happens in water; wherever the vacuum may be in this water it will fall in; and this would happen with a spirit amid the elements, where it would continuously generate a vacuum in whatever element it might find itself, whence it would be inevitable that it should be constantly flying towards the sky until it had quitted these elements.

AS TO WHETHER A SPIRIT HAS A BODY AMID THE ELEMENTS

We have proved that a spirit cannot exist of itself amid the elements without a body, nor can it move of itself by voluntary motion unless it be to rise upwards. But now we will say how such a spirit taking an aerial body would be inevitably melted into air; because if it remained united, it would be separated and fall to form a vacuum, as is said above; therefore it is inevitable, if it is to be able to remain suspended in the air, that it should absorb a certain quantity of air; and if it were mingled with the air, two difficulties arise; that is to say: it must rarefy that portion of the air with which it mingles; and for this cause the rarefied air must fly up of itself and will not remain among the air that is heavier than itself;

1214. 2. acquesta . . decto. 3. chome . . spirito [e vn ome nōch]. 4. chongiunta. 5. alchuna . . lochale. 6. essettu . . reggha . . po. 7. perchessello . . inchor. 8. quantita [se] e decta vachuo. 9. chuo . . dato che se dessi subita. 10. reimpiuto . . ellemento. 11. uachuo si gienerassi. 13. ossosspinto. 14. ellemēto. 15. chome. 16. olleuita ellaltra. 17. massetti. 18. essettu. 19. chessi. 20. sosstener. 21. po onde le neciessuro . . chosi chade. 22. locho. 23. chaderebbe . . infralli. 24. chontinuo gienerrebbe. 25. trovassi . . chosa . . chon. 26. fugha . . vsscito fussi. 27. [adunque di reno]. 28. sello . . chorpo infralli. 30. losspirito . . infralli. 31. chorpo . . po. 32. sennon . . direno cho. 33. chorpo daria chettale. 34. chessinfonda . . perchesselli. 35. seperato e chadrebbe . . uachuo. 36. Chome . . decto. 37. resstare . . nuna. 38. ssesi . . chollaria . . coe. 39. leuificha . . missta. 40. chosa . . leuifichata . . ressta. 41. infrallaria . . a di questo.

di lei; e oltre a di questo tal uirtù [42]spirituale sparsa si disunisci e altera sua natura, per la qual [43]cosa esso māca della prima virtù; aggiugnesi vn 3º incō[44]veniente, e questo è, che tal corpo d'aria, preso dallo spirito, è [45]sottoposto alla penetratiō de' venti, li quali al continuo disu[46]niscono e stracciano le parti vnite dell' aria, quelle rivolgiē[47]do e raggirando infra l'altra aria; adunque lo spirito, in tale

and besides this the subtle spiritual essence disunites itself, and its nature is modified, by which that nature loses some of its first virtue. Added to these there is a third difficulty, and this is that such a body formed of air assumed by the spirits is exposed to the penetrating winds, which are incessantly sundering and dispersing the united portions of the air, revolving and whirling them amidst the rest of the atmosphere; therefore the spirit which is infused in this

W. 19047b]   1215

aria infuso, sarebbe smēbrato overo sbranato e [2]rotto insieme collo sbranamēto dell' aria, nella qual s'infuse.

air would be dismembered or rent and broken up with the rending of the air into which it was incorporated.

SE LO SPIRITO, AVĒDO PRESO CORPO [4]D'ARIA, SI PUÒ PER SÉ MOVERE O NO

[5]Inpossibile è che lo spirito, infuso 'n una quātità d'aria, [6]possa movere essa aria; e questo si manifesta per la passa[7]ta dove dice ¶lo spirito leuifica quella quātità dell' aria, [8]nella quale esso s'infonde; adunque tale aria [9]si leuerà in alto sopra l'altra aria, e sarà moto fatto dall' a[10]ria per la sua leuità e nō per moto volontario dello spirito, e [11]se tale aria si scontra nel ueto per la 3ª di questo, essa [12]aria sarà mossa dal uēto e nō dallo spirito in lei infuso.

AS TO WHETHER THE SPIRIT, HAVING TAKEN THIS BODY OF AIR, CAN MOVE OF ITSELF OR NOT

It is impossible that the spirit infused into a certain quantity of air should move this air; and this is proved by the above passage where it is said: the spirit rarefies that portion of the air in which it incorporates itself; therefore this air will rise high above the other air and there will be a motion of the air caused by its lightness and not by a voluntary movement of the spirit, and if this air is encountered by the wind, according to the 3rd of this, the air will be moved by the wind and not by the spirit incorporated in it.

SE LO SPIRITO PUÒ PARLARE O NO

[14]Volendo mostrare, se lo spirito può parlare o no, è necies[15]sario in prima difinire che cosa e uocie, e come si giene[16]ra; e diremo in questo modo: la vocie è movimē[17]to d'aria confricata in corpo denso, o 'l corpo denso [18]confricato nell' aria che è il medesimo, la qual cō[19]fricatione di denso con raro condensa il raro e fassi resis[20]tētia, o ancora il uelocie raro nel tardo raro si condensa[21]no l'uno e l'altro ne' contatti, e fanno suono o grandissimo [22]strepito; è il suono ovvero mormorio fatto dal raro [23]che si move nel raro cō mediocre movimēto, come [24]la grā fiamma gieneratricie di suono infra l'aria; e 'l grandissi[25]mo strepito fatto di raro cō raro, è quando il uelocie ra[26]ro penetra lo immobile raro, come la fiāma del foco vsci[27]ta dalla bōbarda, e percossa infra l'aria, e ancora la fiamma [28]vscita dal nuvolo percuote l'aria nella· gieneratiō delle saette; [29]Addunque diremo che lo spirito non possa gienerar vocie sanza [30]movimento d'aria, e aria

AS TO WHETHER THE SPIRIT CAN SPEAK OR NOT

In order to prove whether a spirit can speak or not, it is necessary in the first place to define what a voice is and how it is generated; and we will say that the voice is the movement of air in friction against a dense body, or a dense body in friction against the air—which is the same thing. And this friction of the dense and the rare condenses the rare and causes resistance; again, the rare, when in swift motion, and the rare in slow motion condense each other when they come in contact and make a noise or very great uproar; and the sound or murmur made by the rare moving through the rare with only moderate swiftness, like a great flame generating noises in the air; and the tremendous uproar made by the rare mingling with the rare, is when that air which is both swift and rare rushes into that which is itself rare and motionless, like the flame of fire which issues from a big gun and strikes against the air; and again when a flame issues from the cloud, there is a concussion in the air as the bolt is generated.

42. disunisscie. 43. chosa .. mācha .. a giugnecisi. 44. ecquesto he chettal. 45. sottopossto .. venetratiō .. chontinuo. 46. nisscano esstracciano le parte. 47. ragirando infrallaltra .. losspirito in tale '/.
1215. 1. issmēbrato .. sbranato er. 2. chollassbranamēto. 3. sello .. avēdo .. chorpo. 4. po per .. onno. 5. Inpossibile che chello. 6. ecquesto. 7. losspirito leuificha. 9. essara. 11. essettale .. quessto. 13. sello sspirito po .. onno. 14. mosstrare sello. 15. chosa .. chome. 16. quessto modo. 17. confrighata in chorpo .. chorpo. 18. chonfrighato. 19. freghatio .. chon .. chondensa .. effassi. 20. stēti e anchora. 21. ellatro .. chontatti effanno sono. 22. sono over .. facto .. raro [nel ra]. 23. [ro] chessi .. chō .. chome. 24. fiama .. soni infrallaria. 25. rarro cō raro ecquando. 26. chome .. focho vssci. 27. della .. perchossa infrallaria e anchora la fiama. 28. vsscita del nughulo e perchote. 29. direno chello. 30. nella puo chaccia ra dasse.

in lui non è, nè la può cacciare da sé [31]se elli nō l'à, e se vuol movere quella, nella quale lui è infuso, [32]egli è neciessario che lo spirito multiplichi, e multiplicar nō [33]pvò se lui non à quātità; e per la 4ª che dicie: nessuno raro [34]si move se non à loco stabile, donde lui pigli il movimēto, e [35]massimamēte auendosi a mouere lo elemento nello elemēto [36]il quale nō si move da sé, se nō per vaporatione vniforme al ciētro della [37]cosa vaporata, come accade nella spugnia ristretta [38]in nella mano che sta sotto l'acqua, dalla qual l'acqua fuggie per qua[39]lunche verso con equal movimēto per le fessure interposte infra [40]le dita della man che dentro a sé la strignie;

[41]Se lo spirito à vocie articulata, [42]e se lo spirito può essere udito, [43]e che cosa è udire e vedere; e come [44]l'ōda della vocie va [45]per l'aria e come le spetie delli [46]obbietti vanno all' ochio.

Therefore we may say that the spirit cannot produce a voice without movement of the air, and air in it there is none, nor can it emit what it has not; and if it desires to move that air in which it is incorporated, it is necessary that the spirit should multiply itself, and that cannot multiply which has no quantity. And in the 4th place it is said that no rare body can move, if it has not a stable spot whence it may take its motion; much more is it so when an element has to move in an element, which does not move of itself, excepting by uniform evaporation at the centre of the thing evaporated; as occurs in a sponge squeezed in the hand held under water; the water escapes in every direction with equal movement through the openings between the fingers of the hand in which it is squeezed.

As to whether the spirit has an articulate voice, and whether the spirit can be heard, and what hearing is, and seeing; how the wave of the voice passes through the air and how the images of objects pass to the eye.

Br. M. 131a]　　　　　　　　　　　　1216

Nonentity.　[Ogni quātità continva intellettualmē[2]te è diuisibile in infinito;]

[3][Infra le · grandezze · delle · cose · che sono infra noi [4]l'essere · del nulla tiene · il principato ·, e 'l suo · ofitio [5]s'estende · infra le · cose · che non àño · l'essere ·, e la sua [6]essentia · risiede · apresso · del tenpo · infra 'l preterito [7]e 'l futuro, e nulla possiede del presente; Questo nulla [8]à la · sua · parte equale · al tutto ·, e 'l tutto · alla parte, [9]e 'l diuisibile · allo indiuisibile ·; e tal somma · produce nella [10]sua partitione come nella multiplicatione, [11]e nel suo sommare · quanto nel sottrarre, come si dimostra [12]apresso delli aritmetici dello suo 10º carattere che rap[13]presenta esso nvllo; E la podestà sua non si estende infra [14]le cose di natura.]

[15][Quello che è · detto · niēte, · si ritrova solo nel tenpo · e nelle [16]parole; nel tenpo si trova · infra 'l preterito · e 'l futuro, [17]e nulla ritiene del presente ·, e così infra le · parole delle co[18]se che si dicono · che non sono · o che sono impossibili.]

[19][Apresso · del tenpo il nulla · risiede infra 'l preterito e 'l futuro, [20]e niente possiede del presente, e apresso di natura e' s'ac[21]conpagnia infra le cose inpossibili ·, onde per quel ch'è [22]detto · e' non à l'essere; [23]Inperochè doue fusse [24]il nvlla, sarebbe dato il uacuo.]

[Every quantity is intellectually conceivable as infinitely divisible.]

[Amid the vastness of the things among which we live, the existence of nothingness holds the first place; its function extends over all things that have no existence, and its essence, as regards time, lies precisely between the past and the future, and has nothing in the present. This nothingness has the part equal to the whole, and the whole to the part, the divisible to the indivisible; and the product of the sum is the same whether we divide or multiply, and in addition as in subtraction; as is proved by arithmeticians by their tenth figure which represents zero; and its power has no extension among the things of Nature.]

[What is called nothingness is to be found only in time and in speech. In time it stands between the past and future and has no existence in the present; and thus in speech it is one of the things of which we say: They are not, or they are impossible.]

[With regard to time, nothingness lies between the past and the future, and has nothing to do with the present, and with regard to Nature it is to be classed among things impossible: hence, from what has been said, it has no existence; because where there is nothing there would necessarily be a vacuum.]

31. esse uol. 32. chello. 33. sellui . . nessuna. 34. locho. 36. move dasse se. 37. chome acondo nella . . risstretta. 38. inella . . chessta . . lacq"a" della. 39. chon . . interpossste. 40. della ma che . . asse lasstrignie. 41. sello . . artichulata. 42. essello . . po . . vldito. 43. chosa. 44. e [chon] lōda. 45. echome.

1216. 3. Infralle grandeze . . chose chessono infrannoi. 5. sastende infralle chose . . ella. 8. alla sua. 9. soma. 11. somare . . sottrare. 12. arismetrici della sua 10a caratta che ra. 13. Ella . . nosastende. 15. Quello chche. 16. preterito hel. 17. infralle. 18. chessi dicano . . chessono inpossibile. 20. posiede . . apresso. 21. infralle . . inpossibile. 23. fussi.

1216. Compare No. 916.

C. A. 131a]　　　　　　　　　　1216 A

Qual è quella chosa che non si dà, e s'ella si dessi non sarebbe? Egli è lo infinito, il quale se si potesse dare, e' sarebbe terminato e finito, perchè ciò che si pò dare, à termine colla cosa che la circuisce ne' sua stremi, e ciò che non si pò dare è quella cosa che non à termini.

Which is the proposition which cannot be granted? and, if granted, would have no sense? It is the infinite, which thereby would become circumscribed and limited. For what the proposition assumes is of necessity bounded by something that surrounds it, and that which cannot be granted is that which has no limits.

Br. M. 156a]　　　　　　　　　　1217

ESEMPLO DELLA SAETTA FRA NUVOLI

[²O potēte e già anjmato strumēto dell' artificiosa natura, ³a te nō valēdo le tue grā forze ti cōuiene abādonare la trāquilla vita obbedire alla legie, ⁴che Dio e 'l tēpo die alla gienitrice natura. A te nō valse] ⁵le ramute e gagliarde ischiere colle quali tu sequitādo la tua ⁶preda solcavi co' petto aprendo con tempesta le salse ōde. ⁷O quāte volte furono vedute le īpavrite schiere ⁸de' delfini e de grā tonni fugire da l'inpia tua furia, ⁹e tu co' veloci e ramute ali e colla forcielluta coda ¹⁰fulminado gienerasti nel mare nibia, subita tēpesta con grā busso e sommersione di navili cō grā¹¹de ōdamēto, ēpievi gli scoperti liti degli īpavriti e sbigo¹²ttiti pesci, e togliēdosi a te per lasciato mare rimasi in secco divenivano soperchia e ¹³abbondante preda de' vicini popoli;

¹⁴O tempo consumatore delle cose, in te rivolgendo ¹⁵dai alle tratte vite nuove e varie abitazioni.

¹⁶O tempo, velocie predatore ¹⁷delle create cose, quāti re, quāti popoli ài tu disfatti, e quā¹⁸te mutazioni di stati e vari casi sono seguite dopo che la mara¹⁹vigliosa forma di questo pescie qui morì ²⁰per le cavernose e ritorte interiora; ²¹ora disfatto dal tēpo patiēte diaci ī questo chiuso loco, colle ispogliate, spolpate e igniude ossa ²²ài fatto armadura e sostegnio al sopra posto mōte.

EXAMPLE OF THE LIGHTNING IN CLOUDS

[O mighty and once living instrument of formative nature. Incapable of availing thyself of thy vast strength thou hast to abandon thy tranquil life and to obey the law which God and time gave to creative nature. To thee availed not] the branching, sturdy, dorsal fins wherewith pursuing thy prey thou wast wont to plough thy way tempestuously tearing open the briny waves with thy breast.

Reflections on Nature (1217–19).

Ah how many a time the terrified shoals of dolphins and big tunny-fish were seen to flee before thy insensate fury, and thou lashing with swift, branching fins, and forked tail, didst create in the sea mist and sudden tempest with buffeting and foundering of ships; with great waves thou didst heap up the uncovered shores with terrified and desperate fishes which fled from thee, and were left high and dry when the sea abandoned them and became the plentious and abundant spoil of the people in the neighbourhood.

O time, consumer of things, by turning them into thyself thou givest to the taken lives new and different abitations.

O time, swift despoiler of all created things, how many kings, how many nations hast thou undone, and how many changes of states and of circumstance have followed since the wondrous forms of this fish perished here in this cavernous and winding recess. Now destroyed by time thou liest patiently in this confined space with bones stripped and bare, serving as a support and prop for the mountain placed above thee.

Br. M. 155b]　　　　　　　　　　1218

Rimaso lo elemēto dell' acqua rīchiuso īfra li crescivti argini de' fiumi e rive del mare ²īfra l'acrescivta terra ³converrà che la circundatricie

The watery element was left enclosed between the raised banks of the rivers and the sea-shores; and it will come to pass that between the uplifted

1217. 1. essēplo . . nvuolli. 3. chōuene "abādonare la trāquila vita" obidire. 4. chel che . . natura a tette nō ualse. 5. e ha ghagliardre schiere cholle quali tu seghuitādo la tua. 6. pleda aprivis sol chavi "chonvetro" aprendo chō tē pes. 8. dalfini . . tua | "tua" furia e cchupare. 9. ettu che chol veloce tramvre lalie cholla forci elluti choda. 10. fuminando gieneravi nel . . chō . . somersione . . chō. 11. schoperti . . essbigho. 12. pessci . . atte . . seccho . . divenivano supercha. 13. bodante pleda. 14. o tēpo chonsumatore delle chose āteri volgiēdole. 15. dai [lo] alle tratte vite nvuove e varie abitazioni [o quante]. 16. tēpo [vīcitore] velocie pledatore. 17. chleate chose . . dissfatti. 18. disstati e vari chasi sono seghuite poche la mara. 19. vgliosa forma di questo pesscie qui mori. 20. per lechavernole. 21. ora "dsifato dal tēpo" pazēte . . locho chole jsspogliate "spolpate" . . possto. 22. sosstegnio . . possto.
1218. 1. dela acq"a" . . cresscivte argine. 2. jnfralla cressciuta tera. 3. chotra che la chichīatricie . . affassciare e circho.

1217–19. The character of the handwriting points to an early period of Leonardo's life. It has become very indistinct, and is at present exceedingly difficult to decipher. Some passages remain doubtful.

1217, 1218. Compare No. 1339, written on the same sheet.

aria, avēdo a fasciare e circon[4]scrivere la molti-
plicata machina della terra, e la sua [5]grossezza, che
staua fra l'acqua e lo elemēto del fuoco, [6]rimāga
molto ristretta e privata dalla bisogniosa acqua;
i fivmi [7]rimarrāno senza le loro acque, la fertile
terra nō māderà piv le giermoglianti [8]frōde, nō
fieno piv i cāpi adorniti dalle ricascāti biade; tutti
[9]li animali nō trovādo da pasciere le fresche erbe,
morranno, e mā[10]cherà il cibo ai rapaci lioni e
lupi e altri animali che vivono [11]di ratto, e agli
omini dopo molti ripari cōverrà abādonare [12]la
loro vita, e mācherà la gienerazione vmana; E a
questo modo la fertile e fruttuosa terra [13]aban-
donata rimarrà arida e sterile e per rīchivso
omo[14]re dell' acqua, rīchivsa nel suo ventre,
e per la vivace natura osserve[15]rà alquāto dello
suo accrescimēto, tāto che passata la fredda e
so[16]ttile aria fia costretta a terminare collo elemēto del fuoco; [17]allora la sua superfice rimarrà
in riarsa cienere, e questo fia il termine [18]della
terrestre natura.

earth and the surrounding air which has to
envelop and enclose the increased machine of
the earth, and whose mass, standing between the
water and the element of fire, was left much
restricted and deprived of its indispensable
moisture, the rivers will be deprived of their
waters, the fruitful earth will no more put forth
garlands of leaves; the fields will no more be
decked with waving corn; all the animals, finding
no fresh grass for pasture, will die, and food
will then be lacking to the lions and wolves and
other beasts of prey and to men, who after many
efforts will be compelled to abandon their life,
and the human race will die out. In this way the
fertile and fruitful earth will remain deserted,
arid, and sterile from the water being shut up in
its interior, and from the activity of nature it will
continue a little time to increase until the cold
and subtle air being gone, it will be forced to
end with the element of fire; and then its surface
will be left burnt up to cinder and this will be
the end of all terrestrial nature.

Br. M. 156b]   1219

Perchè la natura non ordinò che l'uno animale
nō uivesse [2]dalla morte dell' altro? [3]La natura,
essēdo vaga e pigliādo piacere del creare e fare
cōtin[4]ue vite e forme, perchè cogni[5]oscie che
sono accrescimēto della sua terrestre materia,
[6]è volonterosa e piv presta col suo creare che 'l
tēpo col cō[7]sumare; e però à ordinato che molti
animali sieno cibo l'uno del[8]l' altro; e nō soddis-
faciēdo questo a simile desiderio, e' spesso [9]māda
fuora cierti avelenati e pestilēti vapori e continua
peste sopra le grā moltipli[10]cazioni e cōgregazioni
d'animali, e massime sopra gli omini, che fanno
[11]grāde accrescimēto, perchè altri animali [12]nō
si cibano di loro, e tolte via le cagioni mācheran-
no li effetti; [13]adūque questa terra cierca di
mācare di sua vita, desiderādo [14]la continva
moltiplicazione per la tua assegniata e demonstrata [15]ragione; spesso li effetti sommigliano le
loro cagioni; gli animali so[16]no esēplo della vita
mōdiale.

Why did nature not ordain that one animal
should not live by the death of another? Nature,
being inconstant and taking pleasure in creating
and making constantly new lives and forms, because she knows that her terrestrial materials
become thereby augmented, is more ready and
more swift in her creating than time in his destruction; and so she has ordained that many
animals shall be food for others. Nay, this not
satisfying her desire, to the same end she
frequently sends forth certain poisonous and
pestilential vapours and frequent plagues upon
the vast increase and congregation of animals;
and most of all upon men, who increase vastly
because other animals do not feed upon them;
and, the causes being removed, the effects would
cease. This earth therefore seeks to lose its
life, desiring only continual reproduction as you
bring forward and demonstrate by argument;
like effects always follow like causes, animals are
a type of the life of the world.

H.² 60a]   1219 A

Se la natura a ordinato la doglia nell' anime
vigitative col moto per conservatione degl' instrumenti quali per moto si potrebbono diminuire e guastare, l'anime vigitative sanza moto
nō hanno a percotere ne contra sé posti obietti;
onde la doglia non è necessaria nelle piante,
onde rompendole non sentono dolore come
quelle dell' animali.

If nature has ordained that animals, having
motion, should experience pain in order to con-
serve those parts which by their motion might
diminish or waste, the plants, being without
motion, do not strike against any objects placed
in their way; the feeling of pain is not required
in plants and therefore they do not feel pain
when they are broken, as animals do.

4. moltifichata .. terra chella.   5. grosseza chesstaua .. fralla aqua .. fuocho.   6. rimāgha .. dela .. aqua.   7. rimarāno .. acq.
8. chāpi adorni delle richasschati biade tuti.   9. morano.   10. cher il cibo a .. ellupe .. vano.   11. rato .. chō prvra.
12. vita | "e māchera la gieneraziode vmana" a .. modo [la tera] fertile e frutuosa tera.   13. rimara alida essterile.   14. "acq" ..
per la la.   15. fredda esso.   16. chosstretta .. cholo .. fuocho.   17. rimara inriarsa (*) cienere.   18. teresstre.
1219.   1. chō ❡ perche .. chelluno .. uivessi.   3. pro ❡ la .. vagha .. del "creare e fare" "[fare]" chōtinv.   4. efforme [mette piv vite
sopra la terra che] perche.   5. osscie chessono accrescimēto.   6. pressta chol .. chol chō.   8. sosdisfaciēdo qussto assimile ..
esspesso.   9. vapori "e pestilētie chontinva pessta" sopra.   10. chazioni e chō greghazioni .. fano.   11. accrescimēto .. altr.
12. chagione.   13. chō ❡ adūque .. ciercha .. māchare.   14. chontinva moltiplichazione .. emosstra.   15. somigliano ..
chagioni.   16. dela.

XX

FANTASTIC TALES AND 'PROFETIE'

*J*UST *as Michelangelo's occasional poems reflect his private life as well as the general disposition of his mind, we may find in the writings collected in this section the transcript of Leonardo's fanciful nature, and we should probably not be far wrong in assuming that he himself had recited these fables in the company of his friends or at the court festivals of princes and patrons.* Era tanto piacevole nella conversazione—*so relates Vasari*—che tirava a sè gli animi delle genti. *And Paolo Giovio says in his short biography of the artist:* Fuit in ingenio valde comi, nitido, liberali, vultu autem longe venustissimo, et cum elegantiae omnis delitiarumque maxime theatralium mirificus inventor ac arbiter esset, ad lyramque scite caneret, cunctis per omnem aetatem Principibus mire placuit.

The sources of Leonardo's observations on animals were Pliny's H. N. *and books which go by the name of* Physiologus (*i.e. one well versed in Physiology*). *These were 'Bestiaries' with moralizing tales of animals much in vogue during the Middle Ages in eastern as well as in western countries. The compilation dates back to the third century* A.D. *and was probably made by Didymus of Alexandria; later additions were made by Isidore of Seville, Bede, and others.*

Part I. The first forty-three paragraphs, Nos. 1220 *to* 1263, *are all from MS. H, and have been transcribed in exactly the order in which they were written. E. Solmi has shown that most of these were extracts made by Leonardo from three different works, all mentioned in his list of books on fol.* 210a *of the Codice Atlantico, No.* 1469.[1] *Nos.* 1220 *to* 1234 *and Nos.* 1263, 1264 *are taken from* Fiore di Virtù, *published in* 1488 *at Venice (Solmi, Fonti, pp.* 155–69). *Nos.* 1235–1241 *are taken from* L'Acerba, *by Cecco d'Ascoli (No.* 1469, *note* 6, *and Solmi, pp.* 115–20). *Nos.* 1245–1262 *are taken from Pliny,* H.N. (*Solmi, pp.* 235–46).

Part II (Nos. 1265 *to* 1279) *contains Fables, as the headlines indicate in most instances. Solmi asserts (Fonti, p.* 147), *'per profondo convincimento e lunghe ricerche', that these are really original. Leonardo here competes with Aesop.*

In No. 1293 *there is a scheme for grouping the Prophecies, comprising riddles, but the texts are not so numerous as to render the suggested classification useful to the reader. We have, however, regarded Leonardo's scheme for the classification of the Prophecies as available for that of the Fables and Jests, and have adhered to it as far as possible.*

Among the Miscellanea, *Part V, we might perhaps have included the* Rebuses *of which there are several at Windsor; it seems unlikely that many of them could be solved at the present day. The Rebus reproduced on Pl. LXIV is accompanied by a text, No.* 688, *vol. I, which explains its meaning.*

---

[1] See also G. Calvi, *Il MS. H di L. d. V.* Arch. Stor. Lomb. xxv, 1898.

Nor did we feel justified in including in Leonardo's Literary Works his caricatures of human faces. One only has been given, Pl. CXXII, which is generally accepted as the most important of all. The notes on the back of the sheet No. 1355 (W. 12495) possibly refer to the drawing. It seems that no satisfactory interpretation of this group of abnormal heads has as yet been published. One may doubt whether it was really his intention to produce caricatures of the human features with the purpose of defacing them, of rendering them ridiculous. A psychologist of standing has advanced a more convincing explanation. He suggested that the crowned head in the centre is a personification of megalomania; the profile head of a woman with protruding lower lip is a typical example of dementia paralytica; *the woman's head on the left suggests mental imbecility; the head with open mouth above, raving lunacy; the corresponding full-face head on the right, obstinacy. If this interpretation is correct, we must revise our judgements and appreciations of Leonardo's caricatures.*

The maxims and morals in verse which have been ascribed to Leonardo are not to be found in his manuscripts. Prof. G. Uzielli has proved that they cannot be by him. But poetry is not the monopoly of writers in verse. In its more comprehensive meaning the term 'poetry' may surely be said to apply to many of his writings, such as his imaginative descriptions of landscapes, of the deluge, the battles, the giant, and his fables and aphorisms.

I

BESTIARY: PHYSIOLOGUS

AMORE DI UIRTÙ

²Calendrino · è · vno · vcciello · jl quale ³si dice · che, essendo · esso · portato · dinanzi ⁴a vno · infermo · che, se 'l detto · infermo · de⁵be morire, questo · ucciello · li uolta · la te⁶sta per lo · cōtrario · e mai · lo riguarda ·, e se ⁷esso infermo · debe · scampare ·, questo ⁸vcciello · mai · l'abandona · di uista, anzi ⁹è causa · di leuarli · ogni · malattia;

¹⁰Similmēte è · l'amore · di uirtù ·; nō guar¹¹da · mai · cosa · vile ·, nè trista; anzi di¹²mora · senpre · in cose oneste · e uirtuo¹³se ·, e ripatria in cor giētile a si¹⁴militudine degli uccielli nelle uerdi selue ¹⁵sopra · i fioriti rami · ; e si dimostra piv ¹⁶esso amore nelle auersità che nelle prosperi¹⁷tà, faciēdo come il lume che piv risplēde ¹⁸doue truoua piv tenebroso · sito.

THE LOVE OF VIRTUE

The calander is a bird of which it is related that, when it is carried into the presence of a sick person, if the sick man is going to die, the bird turns away its head and never looks at him; but if the sick man is to recover the bird never loses sight of him but is the cause of curing him of all his sickness.

Like unto this is the love of virtue. It never looks at any vile or base thing, but rather clings always to pure and virtuous things and takes up its abode in a noble heart; as the birds do in green woods on flowery branches. And this love shows itself more in adversity than in prosperity; as light does, which shines most where the place is darkest.

INVIDIA

²Del nibbio · si leggie ·, che quādo esso uede ³i sua figlioli nel nido esser di troppa gra⁴ssezza, che per invidia egli becca loro le coste e tiē⁵gli sanza māgiare.

ENVY

We read of the kite that, when it sees its young ones growing too big in the nest, out of envy it pecks their sides, and keeps them without food.

ALLEGREZZA

⁷L'allegrezza · è appropriata · al gallo · che ⁸d'ogni piccola · cosa · si rallegra e cā⁹ta · con vari e scherzāti mouimēti.

CHEERFULNESS

Cheerfulness is proper to the cock, which rejoices over every little thing, and crows with varied and lively movements.

TRISTEZZA

¹¹La tristezza · s'assomiglia al corbo, il quale, ¹²quādo uede i sua nati figlioli esser biā¹³chi, che per lo grāde dolore si parte cō tristo ¹⁴rammarichio, gl' abādona e nō gli pascie · ¹⁵īsino che non gli vede alquāte poche pēne ¹⁶nere.

SADNESS

Sadness resembles the raven, which, when it sees its young ones born white, departs in great grief, and abandons them with doleful lamentations, and does not feed them until it sees in them some few black feathers.

PACE

²Del castoro si legge che, quādo è perse-³guitato ·, cōnosciēdo · essere · per la virtù ⁴de' sua medicinali · testiculi, esso nō po⁵tēdo piv fuggire, si ferma, e per auere ⁶pace coi cacciatori coi sua tagliēti ⁷dēti si spicca i testiculi e li lascia a sua ⁸nimici.

PEACE

We read of the beaver that when it is pursued, knowing that it is for the virtue [contained] in its medicinal testicles and not being able to escape, it stops; and to be at peace with its pursuers, it bites off its testicles with its sharp teeth, and leaves them to its enemies.

1220. 4. chessel. 5. quessto. 6. esse. 7. isschanpare quessto. 9. chausa .. hogni. 11. trissta. 12. honesste he. 13. ripatria [senpre] in .. assi. 15. essi. 16. prossperi. 17. comelume .. rissplēde.

1221. 2. nibio si legie. 4. sseza che "per inuidia" egli gli becha .. cosste ettiē. 6. allegreza. 7. lalegreza e apropriata. 8. pichola chosa .. echā. 9. cōuari esscerzāti. 10. tristeza. 11. tristeza sasomiglia al corb. 14. ramarichio. 15. nogli .. poce.

1222. 2. he. 3. cōnossciēdo. 5. fugire. 7. sisspicha .. elli lasscia assua.

IRA

¹⁰Dell' orso si dice che · quãdo va alle case ¹¹delle api per torre loro il mele, esse ¹²api comĩncian a pũgierlo, onde lui lasci¹³a il mele e corre alla vendetta, e volē¹⁴dosi cõ tutte quelle che lo mordono vē¹⁵dicare, cõ nessuna si uēdica, in modo che la ¹⁶sua ira si cõuerte in rabbia, e gittatosi ¹⁷in terra colle mani e coi piedi innaspando ¹⁸indarno da quelle si difende.

RAGE

It is said of the bear that when it goes to the haunts of bees to take their honey, the bees having begun to sting him he leaves the honey and rushes to revenge himself. And as he seeks to be revenged on all those that sting him, he is revenged on none; in such wise that his rage is turned to madness, and he flings himself on the ground, vainly exasperating, by his hands and feet, the foes against which he is defending himself.

H.¹ 6b]   1223

GRATITUDINE

²La virtù · della gratitudine si dice ³essere piv nelli uccielli detti upupa, ⁴i quali, conosciēdo il benificio della ⁵ricievuta vita e nvtrimēto dal pa⁶dre e dalla lor madre, quãdo li uedo⁷no vechi fanno loro vno nido e li ⁸covano e li nutriscono, e cavã loro ⁹col becco le vechie e triste penne, e ¹⁰cõ cierte erbe li rēdano la uista, ¹¹in modo che ritornano in prospertà.

GRATITUDE

The virtue of gratitude is said to be more (developed) in the birds called hoopoes which, knowing the benefits of life and food they have received from their father and their mother, when they see them grow old, make a nest for them and brood over them and feed them, and with their beaks pull out their old and shabby feathers; and then, with certain herbs, restore their sight so that they return to a prosperous state.

AVARITIA

¹³Il rospo si pascie di terra e senpre ¹⁴sta macro, perchè nõ si satia; tant 'è ¹⁵il timore che essa terra nõ li manchi.

AVARICE

The toad feeds on earth and always remains lean, because it never fills itself—it is so afraid lest it should be without earth.

H.¹ 7a]   1224

INGRATITUDINE

²I colonbi sono assimigliati alla ³ingratitudine, inperochè quãdo ⁴sono in età che non abbino piv biso⁵gnio d'essere cibati, cominciano a ⁶cõbattere col padre; e nõ finisce ⁷essa pugnia insino a tãto che ⁸caccia il padre e togli la moglie ⁹faciendose la sua.

INGRATITUDE

Pigeons are a symbol of ingratitude; for when they are old enough no longer to need to be fed, they begin to fight with their father, and this struggle does not end until the young one drives the father out and takes the hen and makes her his own.

CRUDELTÀ

¹¹Il basilisco · è di tanta crudeltà che, ¹²quãdo colla sua venenosa vista nõ può ¹³occidere li animali, si volta all' erbe ¹⁴e le piãte, e fermãdo in quelle la sua ¹⁵vista le fa seccare.

CRUELTY

The basilisk is so utterly cruel that when it cannot kill animals by its baleful gaze, it turns upon herbs and plants, and fixing its gaze on them withers them up.

H.¹ 7b]   1225

LIBERALITÀ

²Dell' aquila si dice che non à mai sì grã ³fame ·, che non lasci parte della sua ⁴preda · a quelli vcciegli che gli son ⁵dintorno ·, i quali, nõ potēdosi per sé ⁶pasciere, è neciessario che sieno cor⁷teggiatori d'essa aquila, perchè in tal ⁸modo si cibano.

GENEROSITY

It is said of the eagle that it is never so hungry but that it will leave a part of its prey for the birds that are round it, which, being unable to provide their own food, are necessarily dependent on the eagle, since it is thus that they obtain food.

---

11. ave. 12. ave lo . . a pũgiere . . lassci. 13. core. 14. chello mordano. 15. imodo chella. 17. tera cholle mani eco . . inaspãdo. 18. dacquelle.
1223. 1. [misericordia] over graditudine. 3. detti upica. 4. conossciēdo. 5. nvtrimēdo. 6. ueda. 7. fano . . elli. 8. elli notrisscano 9. becho . . trisste. 10. chõ. 11. imodo. 13. rosspo si passcie . . essenpre.
1224. 4. abino. 6. finissce. 7. attãto. 8. cacia . . toli. 9. rafaciendosela. 11. basalisscio. 12. vissta nõpo. 14. elle. . effermãdo . . lassua. 15. sechare.
1225. 3. nollassci. 4. acquelli . . chelle. 6. passciere . . chessieno. 7. tegiatori.

CORETTIONE

[10]Quãdo il lupo · va asentito intorno [11]a qualche stallo di bestiame, e che per caso [12]esso põga il piede in fallo in modo facci [13]strepito, egli si morde il piè per correg[14]giere sé da tale errore.

DISCIPLINE

When the wolf goes cunningly round some stable of cattle, and by accident makes a false step, so that he makes a noise, he bites his foot off to punish himself for his folly.

H.[1] 8a]   1226

LUSINGHE OVER SOIE

[2]La sirena sì dolcemēte cāta [3]che adormēta i marinari, e essi [4]mõta sopra i navili e occide li a[5]dormētati marinari.

FLATTERERS, OR ADULATION

The siren sings so sweetly that she lulls the mariners to sleep; then she climbs upon the ships and kills the sleeping mariners.

PRUDĒTIA

[7]La formica per naturale cõsiglio [8]provede la 'state per lo uerno, uccidē[9]do le racolte semēze, perchè nõ ri[10]nascino, e di quelle al tenpo si pascono.

PRUDENCE

The ant, by her natural foresight, provides in the summer for the winter, killing the seeds she harvests that they may not germinate, and on them in due time she feeds.

PAZZIA

[12]Il bo saluatico avēdo in odio il co[13]lore rosso, i cacciatori vestono di rosso [14]il pedal d'una piāta, e esso bo corre a [15]quella e cõ gran furia v'inchioda le cor[16]na, õde i cacciatori l'uccidono.

FOLLY

The wild bull having a dislike of red colour, the hunters dress up the trunk of a tree with red and the bull runs at this with great frenzy, thus fixing his horns, and forthwith the hunters kill him there.

H.[1] 8b]   1227

GIVSTITIA

[1]E' si può · assimigliare la uirtù della giusti[3]tia allo rè delle api, il quale ordina [4]e dispone ogni cosa cõ ragione, impero[5]chè alcune api sono ordinate anda[6]re per fiori, altre ordinate a lavora[7]re, altre a cõbattere colle vespe, [8]altre a leuare le sporcitie, altre [9]a accõpagniare e corteggiare il loro rè; e quã[10]do è vecchio e sāza ali, esse lo portano, [11]e se ui vna mãca di suo ofitio, sāza [12]alcuna remissione è punita.

JUSTICE

We may liken the virtue of justice to the king of the bees which orders and arranges everything with judgement. For some bees are ordered to go to the flowers, others are ordered to labour, others to fight with the wasps, others to clear away all dirt, others to accompany and escort the king; and when he is old and has no wings they carry him. And if one of them fails in his duty, he is punished without reprieve.

VERITÀ

[14]Benchè le pernici rubino l'oua l'una al-l'al[15]tra, nõdimeno i figlioli nati d'esse ova [16]senpre ritornano alla lor uera madre.

TRUTH

Although partridges steal each other's eggs, nevertheless the young born of these eggs always return to their true mother.

H.[1] 9a]   1228

FEDELTÀ OVER LEALTÀ

[2]Le grù son tanto fedeli e leali al loro rè [3]che la notte, quãdo lui dorme, alcune vã[4]no dintorno al prato per guardare da lū[5]ga ·; altre ne stanno dapresso e tengono [6]vno sasso ciascuna in piè, che se 'l son[7]no le uincesse, essa pietra caderebbe e fa[8]rebbe tal romore, che si ridesterebbero; e [9]altre vi sono che insieme intorno al rè dor-[10]mono, e ciò fanno ogni notte scãbiãdosi, [11]acciò che loro rè nõ uogliono mãcare.

FIDELITY, OR LOYALTY

The cranes are so faithful and loyal to their king that at night, when he is sleeping, some of them go round the field to keep watch at a distance; others remain near, each holding a stone in his foot, so that if sleep should overcome them, this stone would fall and make so much noise that they would wake up again. And there are others which sleep together round the king; and this they do every night, changing in turn so that their king may never find them wanting.

10. assentito. 11. acqualche. 12. imodo faci. 13. strepido . . percore. 14. tatale.
1226. 1. lusinge oversoie. 8. vcidē. 9. semēza. 13. caciatori vesta. 14. core. 15. cho gra . . vīciodale cor. 16. iccaciatori loccidano.
1227. 2. delagusti. 3. ave. 4. chosa . . ipero. 5. alchuna ave. 6. allauora. 7. chõbottere cholle vesspe. 8. spurcitie. 9. acõpagnare e corteggiare loree. 10. essāza. 11. esse . . mãcha. 14. benchelle.
1228. 1. lialta. 2. allorre. 3. chella. 5. ettengano. 6. sasso [per] ciascuna . . chesselso. 7. vinciessi . . chaderebe effa. 8. rebe . . chess i ridesterebono. 9. chensieme . . are. 10. mano . . fano. 11. acio chollorore nõ uē gli mãchare.

FALSITÀ

[13]La uolpe quãdo vede alcuna torma di gaz[14]ze o taccole o simili uccielli, subito si gitta in ter[15]ra in modo colla bocca aperta che par morta, [16]e essi uccielli le uogliono beccare la lingua, e essa [17]gli piglia la testa.

FALSEHOOD

The fox when it sees a flock of jackdaws or magpies or birds of that kind, suddenly flings himself on the ground with his mouth open to look as if he were dead; and these birds want to peck at his tongue, and he bites off their heads.

H.[1] 9b]   1229

BUGIA

[2]La talpa · à li ochi molto · piccoli ·, e senpre [3]sta · sotto · terra · e tanto · viue ·, quanto essa [4]sta occulta ·, e come · viene alla luce [5]subito · more · perchè si fa nota; così la bugia.

LIES

The mole has very small eyes and it always lives underground; and it lives as long as it is in the dark, but when it comes into the light it dies immediately, because it becomes known. So it is with lies.

FORTEZZA

[7]Il lione · mai · teme ·, anzi · cõ forte animo [8]pugna cõ fiera battaglia contra la mol[9]titudine de' cacciatori ·, senpre ciercãdo [10]offendere · il primo · che l'offese.

VALOUR

The lion is never afraid, but rather fights with a bold spirit and savage onslaught against a multitude of hunters, always seeking to injure the first that injures him.

TIMORE OVER UILTÀ

[12]La lepre senpre teme ·, e le foglie che ca[13]dono dalle piãte · per autunno senpre la tẽ[14]gono in timore, e 'l piv delle volte in fuga.

FEAR, OR COWARDICE

The hare is always frightened; and the leaves that fall from the trees in autumn always keep him in terror and generally put him to flight.

H.[1] 10a]   1230

MAGNIANIMITÀ

[2]Il falcone nõ preda · mai ·, se non uccelli [3]grossi ·, e prima si lascierebbe morire che [4]si cibasse de' piccoli, o che mangiasse car[5]ne fetida.

MAGNANIMITY

The falcon never preys but on large birds; and it will let itself die rather than feed on little ones, or eat stinking meat.

VANA GLORIA

[7]In questo vitio si legge del pavone esser[8]li più che altro animale sottoposto, [9]perchè senpre contempla in nella bellezza [10]della sua coda, quella allargãdo in for[11]ma di rota e col suo grido trae a sé [12]la uista de' circustãti animali; [13]E questo · è l'ultimo vitio che si possa [14]vinciere.

VAINGLORY

As regards this vice, we read that the peacock is more guilty of it than any other animal. For it is always contemplating the beauty of its tail, which it spreads in the form of a wheel, and by its cries attracts to itself the gaze of the creatures that surround it.

And this is the last vice to be conquered.

H.[1] 10b]   1231

CONSTANTIA

[2]Alla costantia · s'assimiglia · la fenice, [3]la quale intẽdẽdo per natura la sua re[4]novatione ·, è costante a sostenere le cuocenti [5]fiamme · le quali la cõsumano, e poi [6]di novo rinascie.

CONSTANCY

Constancy may be symbolized by the phoenix which, knowing that by nature it must be resuscitated, has the constancy to endure the burning flames which consume it, and then it rises anew.

INCÕSTANTIA

[8]Il rondone si mette per la incostantia, [9]il quale senpre sta in moto · per nõ sopporta[10]re alcuno minimo disagio.

INCONSTANCY

The swallow may serve for inconstancy, for it is always in movement, since it cannot endure the smallest discomfort.

---

13. torma dissga. 14. ze . . tacole ossimili . . sibito . . inte. 15. imodo . . bocha. 16. occielli . . uoglia becare . . e ess.
1229. 1. busia. 2. picioli essenpre. 3. ettanto. 4. occhulta e chome. 6. forteza. 7. ilione . . chõ. 8. puglia. 9. caciatori. 10. chelloffese. 12. elle . . che cha. 13. giano delle . . altunno. 14. gano.
1230. 2. senone ucielli. 3. lasscierebe. 4. chessicibassi de picholi. 6. groria. 7. legie del pagone. 9. chontenpra inella belleza. 11. chol . . asse.
1231. 2. sasimiglia. 4. sosstene lecocẽ. 5. ti fiame. 6. rinasscie. 8. incosstantia. 9. imoto . . soporta.

TĒPERĀZA

¹²Il camello è il piv · lussurioso animale ¹³che sia, e andrebbe mille miglia dirieto a vna ¹⁴camella ·, e se vsasse cōtinvo cō la madre o so-¹⁵relle, mai le tocca; tāto si sa bē tēperare.

CONTINENCE

The camel is the most lustful animal there is, and will follow the female for a thousand miles. But if you keep it constantly with its mother or sister it will leave them alone, so temperate is its nature.

H.¹ 11a] 1232

INTĒPERANZA

²Il liocorno overo vnicorno · per la sua intē³perāza e nō sapersi uīciere per lo diletto che à ⁴delle donzelle · dimētica la sua ferocità ⁵e saluatichezza; ponēdo da cāto ogni sospetto ⁶va alla sedente donzella e se le adormē⁷ta · in grēbo ·, e i cacciatori in tal modo ⁸lo pigliano.

INCONTINENCE

The unicorn, through its intemperance and not knowing how to control itself, for the love it bears to fair maidens forgets its ferocity and wildness; and laying aside all fear it will go up to a seated damsel and go to sleep in her lap, and thus the hunters take it.

VMILITÀ

¹⁰Dell' umilità si uede somma speriētia nello ¹¹agnello, il quale si sottomette a ogni ani-¹²male; e quādo per cibo son dati ai incarcerati ¹³leoni ·, a quelli si sottomettono come alla ¹⁴propria madre, in modo che spesse volte ¹⁵si è visto i lioni non li volere occidere.

HUMILITY

We see the most striking example of humility in the lamb, which will submit to any animal; and when they are given for food to imprisoned lions they are as gentle to them as to their own mother, so that very often it has been seen that the lions forbear to kill them.

H.¹ 11b] 1233

SUPERBIA

²Il falcone per la sua alterigia e superbia ³vole signioreggiare · e soprafare tutti li al⁴tri vccielli · che sono di rapina, e sempre ⁵desidera · essere solo, e spesse volte si è ⁶veduto il falcone assaltare l'aquila, ⁷regina delli vccielli.

PRIDE

The falcon, by reason of its haughtiness and pride, is fain to lord and rule over all the other birds of prey, and longs to be sole and supreme; and very often the falcon has been seen to assault the eagle, the queen of birds.

ASTINENTIA

⁹Il saluatico · asino · quādo · va alla ¹⁰fonte · per bere · e trova · l'acqua intor¹¹bidata, non avrà mai si grā sete, che nō ¹²s'astēga di bere, e aspetti ch'essa acqua ¹³si rischiari.

ABSTINENCE

The wild ass, when it goes to the well to drink, and finds the water troubled, is never so thirsty but that it will abstain from drinking, and wait till the water is clear again.

GOLA

¹⁵Il vulture · è tanto sottoposto alla gola ¹⁶che andrebbe mille miglia per māgiare ¹⁷d'una carognia, e per questo seguita li eserciti.

GLUTTONY

The vulture is so addicted to gluttony that it will go a thousand miles to eat a carrion [carcass]; that is why it follows armies.

H.¹ 12a] 1234

CASTITÀ

²La tortora nō fa mai fallo al suo cōpagnio, ³e se l'uno more, l'altro osserua perpetua ca⁴stità e non si posa mai su ramo verde e nō ⁵beue mai acqua chiara.

CHASTITY

The turtle-dove is never false to its mate; and if one dies the other preserves perpetual chastity, and never again sits on a green bough, nor ever again drinks of clear water.

LUSSURIA

⁷Il pipistrello per la sua sfrenata lussu⁸ria non osserua alcuno vniversale mo⁹do di lussuria, anzi maschio cō maschio, ¹⁰femina cō femina, siccome a caso si tro¹¹vano insieme, vsano il lor coito.

UNCHASTITY

The bat, owing to unbridled lust, observes no universal rule in pairing, but males with males and females with females pair promiscuously, as it may happen.

13. chessia e ādebe. 14. esse vsassi . . osso. 15. tocha . . teprare.
1232. 2. lalicorno. 4. dimēticha. 5. saluaticheza . . sospeto. 6. essele. 7. chaciatori. 10. soma. 12. dati [ai dimessti] alincarcerati. 13. cileoni . . sottomettano. 14. imodo chesspesse. 15. se visto . . noli.
1233. 2. essuperbia. 3. signioregiare essopra. 4. chessō di rapina essē. 5. esspesse voltese. 8. asstinentia. 9. assino. 10. ettruova. 11. non ara . . sede. 12. asspetti . . acqa. 13. sirissciari. 15. la voltore ettanto sotto possto. 16. andrebe mile miglia [all] per. 17. per que seguita.
1234. 1. casstita. 3. esselluno. 7. palpisstrello . . isfrenata. 9. masscio cō masscio. 10. sichome achaso.
1232. Compare drawings by Leonardo of maiden with unicorn at the British Museum and at the Ashmolean Museum, Oxford.

MODERANZA

[13]L'ermellino per la sua moderātia nõ māgia [14]se non vna sola volta il dì, e prima si lascia pi[15]gliare dai cacciatori che volere fugire [16]nella infangata tana, [17]per nõ maculare la sua giētilezza.

MODERATION

The ermine out of moderation never eats but once in the day; it will rather let itself be taken by the hunters than take refuge in a dirty lair, in order not to stain its purity.

H.[1] 12b]   1235

AQUILA

[2]L'aquila, quādo è vechia, vola tāto [3]in alto, che abbrucia le sue penne, e na[4]tura cõsente che si rinoui in giovētù, [5]cadendo nella poca acqua;

[6]E se i sua nati nõ possono tenere la uista [7]nel sole—; nõ li pascie di nessuno uccello, [8]che nõ uole morire; non s'accostano al suo [9]nido gli animali che forte la tema[10]no, ma essa a lor nõ noce, senpre [11]lascia il rimanēte della sua preda.

THE EAGLE

The eagle when it is old flies so high that it scorches its feathers, and Nature allowing that it should renew its youth, it falls into shallow water [5]. And if its young ones cannot bear to gaze on the sun [6]—; it does not feed them with any bird that does not wish to die. Animals which much fear it do not approach its nest, although it does not hurt them. It always leaves part of its prey uneaten.

LUMERPA—FAMA

[13]Questa nascie nell' Asia Maggiore, e splē[14]de si forte che toglie le sue õbre, e morendo [15]nõ perde esso lume, e mai li cadono giù le [16]penne, e la penna che si spicca piv nõ [17]luce.

LUMERPA—FAME

This is found in Asia Major, and shines so brightly that it absorbs its own shadow, and when it dies it does not lose this light, and its feathers never fall out, but a feather pulled out shines no longer.

H.[1] 13a]   1236

PELICANO

[2]Questo porta grāde amore a sua nati, [3]e trouādo quelli nel nido morti dal [4]serpēte, si pūgie a riscõtro al core e, col [5]suo piovente sangue bagniādoli, li tor[6]na in vita.

THE PELICAN

This bird has a great love for its young; and when it finds them in its nest dead from a serpent's bite, it pierces itself to the heart, and with its blood it bathes them till they return to life.

SALAMĀDRA

[8]Questo · non à mēbra passive, e nõ si [9]cura d'altro cibo che di foco, e spesso in [10]quello rinova la sua scorza.

[11]La salamādra nel foco [12]rafina la sua scorza —[13]per la [14]vir[15]tù.

THE SALAMANDER

This has no digestive organs, and gets no food but from the fire in which it constantly renews its scaly skin.

The salamander, which refines its scaly skin in the fire—for virtue.

CAMELEÕ

[16]Questo viue d'aria, e ī quella sta su[17]bietto a tutti li uccielli, e per stare piv [18]saluo vola sopra le nvvole; e truoua [19]aria tāto sottile, che nõ può sostenere [20]vcciello che lo seguiti.

[21]A questa altezza nõ va, se nõ a chi da cieli [22]è dato, cioè dove vola il cameleone.

THE CHAMELEON

This lives on air, and there it is the prey of all the birds; so in order to be safer it flies above the clouds and finds an air so rarefied that it cannot support the bird that follows it.

At that height nothing can go unless it has a gift from Heaven, and that is where the chameleon flies.

H.[1] 13b]   1237

ALEPO PESCIE

[2]Alepo nõ uive fori dell' acqua.

THE ALEPO, A FISH

The fish *alepo* does not live out of water.

---

14. senvna .. lasscia. 15. gliare a caciatori. 17. giētileza.
1235. 3. abrucia .. pene. 4. chessi. 5. cadē. 6. esse .. nõ posso tene. 7. pascie nessuno vciel. 8. morire nossacosti. 9. chefforte. 11. lasscia. 12. P. fama—lumerpa fama (?). 13. nasscie .. magiore essplē. 14. chettoglie. 15. li cade piv le. 16. ella pena chessi spicha.
1236. 4. risscõtro. 9. espesso. 17. bietta attutti .. istare. 18. nvbe. 19. po. 20. chello. 21. acquesta. *Lines 11-15 are written on the margin near the title-line.*   **1237.** 1. alep[o] pesscie.

1234. Compare drawing in the collection of Miss Clarke, London.

STRUZZO
⁴Questo cōuerte il ferro in suo ⁵nutrimēto; cova l'uova colla vista; ⁶¶ per l'arme nutrimēto ⁷de' capitani.¶

CIGNO
⁹Cignio è candido sanza alcuna ¹⁰macchia, e dolcemēte canta nel mo¹¹rire, il qual cāto termina · la uita.

CICOGNIA
¹³Questa, beuēdo la salsa acqua, ¹⁴caccia da sé il male; se truova la cō¹⁵pagnia in fallo, l'abandona; e quādo ¹⁶è vechia, i sua figlioli la curano e pa¹⁷scono, infinchè more.

THE OSTRICH
This bird converts iron into nourishment, and hatches its eggs by its gaze—Armies as nourishment of commanders.

THE SWAN
The swan is white without any spot, and it sings sweetly as it dies, its life ending with that song.

THE STORK
This bird, by drinking salt water, purges itself of distempers. If the male finds his mate unfaithful, he abandons her; and when it grows old its young ones brood over it, and feed it till it dies.

H.¹ 14a]   1238

CICALA
²Questa col suo canto fa tacere ³il cucco, more nell' olio, e resucita ⁴nello aceto, cāta per li ardēti caldi.

PIPISTRELLO
⁶Questo dov' è piv luce piv si fa ⁷orbo, e come piv guarda il sole ⁸più s'acciecca; ⁹pel uitio che nō può ¹⁰stare do¹¹v' è la vir¹²tù.

PERNICE
¹⁴Questa si trasmuta di femina i maschio, ¹⁵e dimētica il primo sesso, e fura per īuidia ¹⁶l'oua a l'altre, e le coua, ma i nati segui¹⁷tano la uera madre.

RŌDINE
¹⁹Questa colla celidonia lumina i sua ²⁰ciechi nati.

THE GRASSHOPPER
This silences the cuckoo with its song. It dies in oil and revives in vinegar. It sings in the greatest heats.

THE BAT
The more light there is the blinder this creature becomes; as those who gaze most at the sun become most dazzled—For Vice, that cannot remain where Virtue appears.

THE PARTRIDGE
This bird changes from the female into the male and forgets its former sex; and out of envy it steals the eggs from others and hatches them, but the young ones follow the true mother.

THE SWALLOW
This bird gives sight to its blind young ones by means of celandine.

H.¹ 14b]   1239

OSTRIGA—PEL TRADIMĒTO
²Questa, quādo la luna è piena, s'apre tutta, ³e quādo il grācio la vede, dētro le gietta ⁴qualche sasso o festuca, e questa nō si ⁵può riserrare, ōde è cibo d'esso grāchio; ⁶così fa, chi apre la bocca a dire il suo segreto, ⁷che si fa preda dello indiscreto auditore.

BARALISSIO—CRUDELTÀ
⁹Questo è fugito da tutti i serpēti; la don¹⁰nola per lo mezzo della ruta cōbatte con essi ¹¹e così l'uccide.

L'ASPIDO
¹⁴Questo porta ne' dēti la subita morte ¹⁵e per nō sentire l'incāti, colla coda si ¹⁶stoppa li orechi.

THE OYSTER—FOR TREACHERY
This creature, when the moon is full, opens itself wide, and when the crab looks in he throws in a stone or seaweed and the oyster cannot close again, whereby it serves for food to that crab. This is what happens to him who opens his mouth to tell his secret. He becomes the prey of the treacherous hearer.

THE BASILISK—CRUELTY.
All snakes fly from this creature; but the weasel attacks it by means of rue and kills it.

THE ASP
This carries instantaneous death in its fangs; and, that it may not hear the charmer, it stops its ears with its tail.

4. suo "nutrimēto".   5. cova lava. *Lines 6 and 7 are written on the margin near the title-line.*   8. cingno.   14. cacia dasse. 15. ecquādo. 16. issua. 17. scano.
1238. 1. cichala. 3. cucho. 5. palpistrello. 8. saciecha. 9. po. 14. trassmuta .. masscio. 15. iprimo. 16. elle cova. 20. cieci.
1239. 1. hosstriga. 2. quasta. 3. ecquādo. 4. qualchessasso offistuca ecquesta. 5. po riserare. 6. faciaprla bocha .. sigreto. 7. chessi .. vlditore. 8. bavalisscio. 9. effugito dettutti .. la do. 10. mezo. 11. essi. 12. ¶ rua per la virtu¶. 16. stopa.

H.¹ 15a]   1240

DRAGO

²Questo lega le gābe al liofante ³e quel li cade adosso, e l'uno e l'al⁴tro more, e morēdo fa sua vēdetta.

THE DRAGON

This creature entangles itself in the legs of the elephant, which falls upon it, and so both die, and in its death it is avenged.

VIPERA

⁶Questa nel suo accoppiare apre la bocca, e nel fine ⁷strīgnie dēti e amazza il marito, poi ⁸i figlioli in corpo crescivti straccia⁹no il uētre e occidono la madre.

THE VIPER

She, in pairing, opens her mouth and at last clenches her teeth and kills her husband. Then the young ones, growing within her body, rend her open and kill their mother.

SCORPIONE

¹¹La saliua sputa a digivno · sopra dello scor¹²pione e l'occide; a similitudine dell' a-¹³stinētia della gola, che togle via e cura ¹⁴le malatie che da essa gola dipēdono, e a¹⁵pre la strada alle virtù.

THE SCORPION

Saliva, spit out when fasting, will kill a scorpion. This may be likened to abstinence from greediness, which removes and heals the ills which result from that gluttony, and opens the path of virtue.

H.¹ 17a]   1241

COCCODRILLO. IPOCRESIA

²Questo · animale piglia l'o³mo e subito l'uccide poichè l'à morso ⁴con lamētevole voce e molte lacrime ⁵lo piāge ·, e finito il lamēto crudel⁶mēte lo diuora ·; così fa l'ipocrito ⁷che per ogni lieue cosa s'enpie il uiso ⁸di lagrime; mostrādo un cor di tigro e ral⁹legrasi nel core dell' altrui male cō ¹⁰piātoso volto.

THE CROCODILE—HYPOCRISY

This animal catches a man and straightway kills him; after he is dead, it weeps for him with a lamentable voice and many tears. Then, having done lamenting, it cruelly devours him. It is thus with the hypocrite, who, for the smallest matter, has his face bathed with tears, but shows the heart of a tiger and rejoices in his heart at the woes of others, while wearing a pitiful face.

BOTTA

¹²La botta fugie la luce del sole, e se pure ¹³per forza v'è tenvta, si gōfia tāta, che s'ascon-¹⁴de la testa in basso, e privasi d'essi razzi; ¹⁵così fa chi è nimico della chiara e luciē¹⁶te virtù, che nō può se nō con gōfiato ¹⁷animo forzata-mēte starle davāti.

THE TOAD

The toad flies from the light of the sun, and if it is held there by force it puffs itself out so much as to hide its head below and shield itself from the rays. Thus does the foe of clear and radiant virtue, who can only be constrainedly brought to face it with puffed-up courage.

H.¹ 17b]   1242

BRUCO—²DELLA VIRTÙ IN GIENERALE

³Il bruco ·, che mediante l'esercitato studio ⁴di tessere con mirabile artifitio e sottile lauoro ⁵intorno a sé fa la nova abitatione, escie ⁶poi fori di quella colle dipinte e belle ⁷ali, cō quelle leuādosi inverso il cielo.

THE CATERPILLAR—FOR VIRTUE IN GENERAL

The caterpillar, which by means of assiduous care is able to weave round itself a new dwelling-place with marvellous artifice and fine workmanship, comes out of it afterwards with painted and lovely wings, with which it rises towards Heaven.

RAGNIO

⁹Il ragnio · partoriscie fori di sé l'ar¹⁰tifitiosa e maestrevole tela, la quale ¹¹gli rēde per benifitio la presa preda.

THE SPIDER

The spider brings forth out of herself the delicate and ingenious web, which makes her a return by the prey it takes.

1240. 3. delluno ellal. 6. suo coperbocha. 7. amaza. 8. cresscivti. 11. la sciliua . . dellosschor. 12. pione locide assimilitudine. 13. chettole via e ocide. 14. l \\\\ mal \\\\\\\\\ che \\\ a. *Lines 14 and 15 are very indistinct and nearly effaced.*
1241. 1. cocodrillo. 2. animale [offende]. 3. poichella morto. 4. collamētevole. 8. mostrādo icor di tigro e ra. 12. esse. 13. scōfia . . chessasco. 14. baso. 15. cosi facie nemico . . ciara. 16. po . . con\\\\\\. 17. \\\\ animo . . stale.
1242. 4. comirabile | "artificio" essottile. 5. asse la . . esscie. 6. chelle dipinte . . lauādosi. 10. maesstre vole tella. 11. rēdende.

1242. Two notes are underneath this text. The first, 'nessuna chosa e da ttemere piu che lla sozza fama', is a repetition of the first line of the text given in vol. i, No. 695.

The second, 'faticha fugga cholla fama in braccio quasi ochultata c', is written in red chalk and is evidently an incomplete sentence.

H,¹ 18a]   1243

LIONE

²Questo animale col suo tonãte grido ³desta
i sua figlioli dopo il terzo giorno ⁴nati, aprẽdo
a quelli tutti li adormẽta⁵ti sẽsi, e tutte le fiere,
che ⁶nella selua sono, fuggono.

⁷Puossi assimigliare a figlioli della ⁸virtù ·,
che mediãte il grido delle lode ⁹si suegliano · e
crescono per li studi onorevoli ¹⁰che senpre piv
gli inalza, e tutti i tristi ¹¹a esso grido fuggono
ciessãdosi dai ¹²vertuosi.

¹³Ancora il leone copre le sue pedate, ¹⁴perchè
nõ s'intenda il suo viaggio ¹⁵per i nimici; questo
sta bene al capitano ¹⁶a cielare i segreti del suo
animo, acciochè ¹⁷il nimico nõ cogniosca i sua
tratti.

THE LION

This animal, with his thundering roar, rouses
his young the third day after they are born,
teaching them the use of all their dormant senses
and all the wild things which are in the wood
flee away.

This may be compared to the children of
Virtue who are roused by the sound of praise
and grow up in honourable studies, by which
they are more and more elevated; while all that
is base flies at the sound, shunning those who
are virtuous.

Again, the lion covers over its foot-tracks, so
that the way it has gone may not be known to
its enemies. Thus it beseems a captain to conceal the secrets of his mind so that the enemy
may not know his purpose.

H.¹ 18b]   1244

TARÃTA

²Il morso della tarãta mãtiene l'omo ³nel suo
proponimẽto, cioè quello che ⁴pensava quãdo
fu morso.

THE TARANTULA

The bite of the tarantula fixes a man's mind
on one idea; that is, on the thing he was thinking
of when he was bitten.

DUGO E CIVETTA

⁶Questi gastigano i loro schernitori ⁷privãdoli
di uista, chè così à ordina⁸to la natura, perchè
si cibino.

THE SCREECH-OWL AND THE OWL

These punish those who are scoffing at them
by pecking out their eyes; for nature has so
ordered it that they may thus be fed.

H.¹ 19a]   1245

LEOFANTE

²Il grãde elefante · à per natura quel ³che raro
negli omini si truova, cioè ⁴probità, prudẽtia,
equità e osser⁵vãtia e religione, inperochè, quãdo
⁶la luna · si rinova ·, questi vanno ai fi⁷vmi e
quivi purgãdosi solennemẽte ⁸si lauano, e così
salutato il pianeta ⁹ritornano alle selue; E quãdo
¹⁰sono ammalati, stando supini, gitta¹¹no l'erbe
verso il cielo, quasi com' esse ¹²sacrificare volessino; ¶sotterrano li dẽ¹³ti quãdo per vecchiezza
gli cadono; ¶ de' ¹⁴sua due dẽti l'uno adopera
a cauare ¹⁵le radici per cibarsi; all' altro cõserua
¹⁶la pũta per cõbattere; Quãdo sono ¹⁷superati
da cacciatori, e chè la stãchezza ¹⁸gli uĩcie per-
cotesi li dẽti l'elefanti, quelle ¹⁹trattesi, con esse
si ricomprano.

THE ELEPHANT

The huge elephant has by nature what is
rarely found in man; that is, Honesty, Prudence,
Justice, and the Observance of Religion; inasmuch as when the moon is new, these beasts go
down to the rivers, and there, solemnly cleans-
ing themselves, they bathe, and so, having
saluted the planet, return to the woods. And
when they are ill, being laid down, they fling up
plants towards Heaven as though they would
offer sacrifice.—They bury their tusks when
they fall out from old age.—Of these two tusks
they use one to dig up roots for food; but they
save the point of the other for fighting with;
when they are taken by hunters, worn out by
fatigue, they strike off their tusks and having
drawn them out ransom themselves therewith.

H.¹ 19b]   1246

Sono clementi e conoscono i pericoli; ²¶e
se esso trova · l'omo solo e smarito, ³piacievol-
mẽte lo rimette nella perduta ⁴strada; se truova
le pedate dell' omo ⁵prima che veda l'omo,

They are merciful, and know the dangers,
and if one finds a man alone and lost, it kindly
puts him back in the road he has missed. If it
finds the footprints of the man before the man

1243. 4. aprẽda acquelli. 5. ettutti [li anima] le. 6. sona. 8. delle lalde. 9. sissuegliano e crescono li studi. 10. chessenpre piv glinalza
ettutti. 11. esse . . fugano. 13. ileoni co. 14. viagio. 15. ai capitani.
1244. 4. pesava. 5. duco. 7. diuita. 8. to natura.
1245. 2. ellefante. 4. he equita e osser. 6. quessti vano. 9. Ecquãdo. 10. amalati . . suppini. 12. volessino (sotterra. 13. uechieza gli
cagiano (de. 16. Quã sono. 17. caciatori e chella stãcheza. 18. dẽti le lepãte ecquele (?). 19. trattosi \\\\\\ nessosiricõprano.
These two last lines are much effaced.   1246. 1. sono elemẽti e conosschano. 2. esse . . sole essmarito.

⁶¶esso teme tradimēto, ōde si ferma ⁷e soffia, mostrādolo a li altri elefanti, ⁸e fanno schiera e vanno assentitamēte.

⁹Questi vanno senpre a schiere, e 'l più ¹⁰vechio va ināzi, e 'l secōdo d'età resta ¹¹l'ultimo, e così chiudono la schiera; ¹²temono vergogna, non vsano il co¹³ito se nō di notte di nascosto, e nō tor¹⁴nano dopo il coito alli armēti, se prima ¹⁵nō si lauano nel fiume; nō cōbattono ¹⁶mai femine, come gli altri animali; ¹⁷¶ed è tāto clemēte, che mal uolōtieri per na¹⁸tura nō noce ai mē potenti di sé, e scō¹⁹trādosi nella mandria o greggi delle pecore

himself, it dreads betrayal, so it stops and blows, pointing it out to the other elephants who form in a troop and go warily.

These beasts always go in troops, and the oldest goes in front and the second in age remains the last, and thus they enclose the troop. Out of shame they pair only at night and secretly, nor do they then rejoin the herd but first bathe in the river. They never fight with females as other animals do; and it is so merciful that it is most unwilling by nature ever to hurt those weaker than itself. And if it meets a drove or flock of sheep

---

H.¹ 20a]   1247

colla sua mano le pone da parte ²per non le pestare coi piedi, nè mai noce ³se nō sono provocati; quādo son ca⁴duti nella fossa, gli altri cō rami, ⁵terra e sassi riēpiono la fossa, ⁶in modo che alzano il fondo, che esso facil⁷mēte riman libero; temono forte ⁸lo stridore de' porci e fugono indiri⁹eto; e nō fa māco danno poi coi piedi a sua ¹⁰che a nimici; dilettāsi de' fiumi, ¹¹e sempre vāno vagabūdi intorno ¹²quelli, ¶e per lo grā peso nō possono ¹³notare; diuorano le pietre, e trō¹⁴chi delli alberi sono loro gratissimo cibo; ¹⁵ànno in odio i ratti; le mosche si dilettano ¹⁶del suo odore e posādosi li adosso, quello ¹⁷arraspa la pelle, e ficca le pieghe strette, e l'uccide.

it puts them aside with its trunk, so as not to trample them under foot; and it never hurts anything except when provoked. When one has fallen into a pit the others fill up the pit with branches, earth, and stones, thus raising the bottom that he may easily get out. They greatly dread the noise of swine and fly in confusion, doing no less harm then, with their feet, to their own kind than to the enemy. They delight in rivers and are always wandering about near them, though on account of their great weight they cannot swim. They devour stones, and the trunks of trees are their favourite food. They have a horror of rats. Flies delight in their smell and settle on their back, and the beast scrapes its skin, making its folds deep and tight and kills them.

H.¹ 20b]   1248

Quādo passano i fiumi, mādano ²i figlioli diuerso il calar dell' acqua, ³e stando loro inverso l'erta ronpono ⁴il rapido corso dell' acqua, aciochè 'l cor⁵so non le menasse via; il drago ⁶se li gitta sotto il corpo, colla ⁷coda l'annoda le gābe, coll' alie ⁸e colle branche anche li strignie le coste ⁹e coi denti lo scanna, el liofante ¹⁰li cade adosso e il drago scoppia, ¹¹e così colla sua morte del nemico ¹²si uēdica.

When they cross rivers they send their young ones down the stream of the water; thus, being set towards the current, they break the united current of the water so that the current does not carry them away. The dragon flings itself under the elephant's body, and with its tail it ties its legs; with its wings and with its claws it also squeezes its ribs and cuts its throat with its teeth, and the elephant falls upon it and the dragon is burst. Thus, in its death, it is revenged on its foe.

IL DRAGONE

¹⁴Questi s'accōpagniano insieme e si tessa¹⁵no a uso di radici, e colla testa leuata ¹⁶passano i paduli, e notano dove trouano ¹⁷migliore pastura, e se così non si vnissero,

THE DRAGON

These go in companies together, and they twine themselves after the manner of roots, and with their heads raised they cross lakes, and swim to where they find better pasture; and if they did not thus combine

---

7. essoffia mosstrādola. 8. effano sciera e vano. 9. vano .. assciere. 11. civdano lassciera. 12. temano. 13. nasscosto. 15. nocōbattano. 16. me femine. 18. esscō. 19. "gregi".
1247. 1. cholla .. pone de parte. 2. per nolle pestare co. 5. essassi riēpiano. 6. imolalzano .. cheso. 7. rimō\\\\\\\ temano. 9. dano poico piedi. 10. diletāsi .. fiuvmi. 11. essēpre .. intorna. 12. quelgli .. possā. 14. soloro. 15. ano. 17. arapa .. efficale piege strette lucide.
1248. 4. lunito (?) corso dellacua. 5. nolle menasse via | li. 6. chola. 7. lanoda .. chollalie. 8. cholle .. cignie. 9. e cho denti. 10. drago sciopa. 14. sacōpagnian .. essi. 15. ratici. 16. troua. 17. essecosino si vnisser.

H.¹ 21a]　　　　　　　　　　　1249

annegherebbero; così fa la unitione.

they would be drowned, therefore they combine.

SERPĒTE

³Il serpēte, grādissimo animale, ⁴quādo vede alcuno ucciello per l'aria, ⁵tira a sé si forte il fiato, che si tira ⁶gli uccielli in bocca; Marco ⁷Regulo, consule dello esercito Roma⁸no, fu col suo esercito da un simile ⁹animale assalito e quasi rotto, il qua¹⁰le animale, essēdo morto per una machina ¹¹mvrale, fu misurato 123 piedi, cio¹²è 64 braccia e ½; avāzava colla testa tutte ¹³le piāte d'una selua.

THE SERPENT

The serpent is a very large animal. When it sees a bird in the air it draws in its breath so strongly that it draws the birds into its mouth too. Marcus Regulus, the consul of the Roman army, was attacked, with his army, by such an animal and almost defeated. And this animal, being killed by a catapult, measured 123 feet, that is, 64½ braccia, and its head was high above all the trees in a wood.

BOIE

¹⁵Questa e grā biscia, la quale cō sé mede-¹⁶sima si aggruppa alle ganbe della vacca in mo-¹⁷do nō si mova, poi la tetta in modo che quasi ¹⁸la dissecca; di questa spetie a tēpo di Claudio ¹⁹iperatore nel mōte Vaticano ne fu una morta

THE BOA

This is a very large snake which entangles itself round the legs of the cow so that it cannot move and then sucks it, in such wise that it almost dries up. In the time of Claudius, the Emperor, one was killed, on the Vatican Hill,

H.¹ 21b]　　　　　　　　　　　1250

che avea vno putto intero in corpo ²il quale avea trāghiottito.

which had inside it a boy, entire, that it had swallowed.

MACLI. ❡PEL SONNO È GIŪTO

⁴Questa bestia nascie in Scādinavia isola; ⁵à forma di grā cavallo, se nō che la ⁶grā lūghezza dello collo e delli orechi lo vari⁷ano; pascie l'erba allo indietro, perchè à sì ⁸lūgo il labro di sopra che pasciēdo inā⁹zi coprirebbe l'erba; à le gābe d'ū pezzo; ¹⁰per questo, quādo vuol dormire s'appoggia ¹¹a vno albero, e i cacciatori, ātivedēdo ¹²il loco vsato a dormire, segā quasi tutta ¹³la piāta, e quādo questo poi vi s'appoggia ¹⁴nel dormire ·, per lo sonno cade, e i cacciato¹⁵ri così lo piglano, e ogni altro modo di pi¹⁶glarlo è vano, perchè è d'incredibile velocità ¹⁷nel correre.

THE MACLI—CAUGHT IN SLEEP

This beast is born in Scandinavia. It has the shape of a great horse, excepting that the great length of its neck and of its ears makes a difference. It feeds on grass, going backwards, for it has so long an upper lip that if it went forwards it would cover up the grass. Its legs are all in one piece; for this reason when it wants to sleep it leans against a tree, and the hunters, spying out the place where it is wont to sleep, saw the tree almost through, and then, when it leans against it to sleep, in its sleep it falls, and thus the hunters take it. And every other mode of taking it is in vain, because it is incredibly swift in running.

H.¹ 22a]　　　　　　　　　　　1251

BONASO NOCE COLLA FUGA

²Questo nascie · in Peonia; à collo ³cō crini simile al cauallo, in tutte ⁴l'altre parti è simile · al toro, saluo ⁵che le sue corna sono in modo piegate ⁶indētro, che nō può cozzare, e per questo ⁷non à altro scanpo · che la fuga ·, nella ⁸quale · getta sterco per spatio di 400 ⁹braccia del suo corso ·, il quale, dove to¹⁰cca, abbrucia come foco.

THE WILD OX WHICH DOES INJURY IN ITS FLIGHT

This beast is a native of Paeonia and has a neck with a mane like a horse. In all its other parts it is like a bull, excepting that its horns are in a way bent inwards so that it cannot butt; hence it has no safety but in flight, in which it flings out its excrement to a distance of 400 braccia in its course, and this burns like fire wherever it touches.

LEONI, PARDI, PĀTERE, TIGRI

¹²Questi tēgono · l'ūgie nella guaina, e mai ¹³le sfoderanno, se non è adosso alla preda o ne¹⁴mico.

LIONS, PARDS, PANTHERS, TIGERS

These keep their claws in the sheath, and never put them out unless they are on the back of their prey or their enemy.

1249. 1. anegerebono. 3. grādisimo. 5. asse .. chessi. 6. bocha. 7. cūsulo. 8. ma fu chol .. da vsimili. 10. macin"a". 12. e 64 bre ½. 15. bisscie. 16. sagluppa .. della vecha imo. 17. imodo. 18. ladiseza. 19. īperadore.

1250. 2. trāgiottito. 4. iniscandinavia. 5. chella. 6. lūgeza. 7. passie .. allōdirieto .. assi. 8. passciēdo. 9. ci copirebe .. ha le .. pezo. 10. vol .. sapogia. 11. eichaciatori. 13. sapogia. 14. ecaciato.

1251. 2. nasscie. 4. essimile. 5. chelle sie .. imodo. 6. pocozare. 7. chella. 8. gita stercho per ispatio. 9. bracia. 10. tocha abrucia. 12. tēgano. 13. lessfoderano.

LEONESSA

[16]Quãdo la leonessa difēde i figli[17]oli dalle mã de' cacciatori, per nõ si spauē[18]tare dalli spiedi, abbassa li ochi a terra [19]acciochè per la sua fuga i figli nõ sieno [20]prigioni.

THE LIONESS

When the lioness defends her young from the hand of the hunter, in order not to be frightened by the spears she keeps her eyes on the ground, to the end that she may not by her flight leave her young ones prisoners.

H.[1] 22b]   1252

LEONE

[2]Questo · si terribile animale niēte teme [3]piv che lo strepido delle vuote carrette [4]e simile · il cãto de' galli, · e teme a[5]ssai nel uederli e con pauroso a[6]spetto riguarda la sua cresta; [7]e forte invilisce, quãdo à coper[8]to · il uolto.

THE LION

This animal, which is so terrible, fears nothing more than the noise of empty carts, and likewise the crowing of cocks. And it is much terrified at the sight of one, and looks at its comb with a frightened aspect, and is strangely alarmed when its face is covered.

PÃTERE IN AFRICA

[10]Questo à forma di leonessa, ma è [11]piv alta di gãbe, e piv sottile, e lũga; [12]è tutta biãca e punteggiata di ma[13]chie nere a modo di rosette, e di que[14]sta si dilettano · tutti li animali di [15]vedere ·, e senpre le starebbero dintorno, [16]se nõ fusse la terribilità · del suo viso,

THE PANTHER IN AFRICA

This has the form of the lioness but it is taller on its legs and slimmer and long-bodied; and it is all white and marked with black spots after the manner of rosettes; and all animals delight to look upon these rosettes, and they would always be standing round it if it were not for the terror of its face;

H.[1] 23a]   1253

onde essa, questo conosciēdo, ascõ[2]de il uiso, e li animali circũstãti [3]s'assicurano e fannosi vicini per me[4]glio potere fruire tãta bellezza, õ[5]de questa subito piglia il piv uici[6]no e subito lo diuora.

therefore knowing this, it hides its face, and the surrounding animals grow bold and come close, the better to enjoy the sight of so much beauty; when suddenly it seizes the nearest and at once devours it.

CAMELLI

[8]Quegli Battriani ànno 2 gobbi, [9]gli Arabi uno; sono veloci in battaglia [10]e vtilissimi a portare le some; [11]questo animale à regole e misura [12]oseruãtissima, perchè nõ si move se à [13]piv carico che l'usato, e se fa piv [14]uiaggio fa il simile, subito si ferma, [15]õde lì bisognia a mercatãti allog[16]giare.

CAMELS

The Bactrian have two humps; the Arabian one only. They are swift in battle and most useful to carry burdens. This animal is extremely observant of rule and measure, for it will not move if it has a greater weight than it is used to, and if it is taken too far it does the same, and suddenly stops, and so the merchants are obliged to lodge there.

H.[1] 23b]   1254

TIGRO

[2]Questa nascie in Ircania, la qua[3]le è simile alquãto alla pãtera per le [4]diuerse machie della sua pelle, ed è ani[5]male di spauētevole velocità; il caccia[6]tore quãdo truova i sua figli, [7]li rapiscie subito, ponēdo spechi nel [8]loco donde li leua, e subito sopra [9]veloce cauallo si fugie; la pantera tor[10]nãdo truova li spechi fermi in terra, ne [11]quali vedēdosi, li pare vedere li sua fi[12]glioli, e raspãdo

THE TIGER

This beast is a native of Hyrcania, and it is something like the panther from the various spots on its skin. It is an animal of terrible swiftness; the hunter when he finds its young ones carries them off hastily, placing mirrors in the place whence he takes them, and at once escapes on a swift horse. The panther returning finds the mirrors fixed on the ground and looking into them believes it sees its young; then

---

17. caciatori.   19. acciochè | "per"ella . . nõ siē"o".
1252. 2. teribile.   3. chello . . vote carette.   4. essimile . . etteme.   6. cressta.   7. efforte invilissce.   11. ellũga.   12. ettutta biãcha e punegiata.   15. starebõ ditorno.   16. fussi . . teribilita.
1253. 1. conossciēdo asscõ.   2. elli.   3. sasicurano e fanosi.   4. belleza.   8. batriani.   9. arabi î.   13. chellusato esse.   14. uiagio . . sibito.   15. alo.   16. ciare.
1254. 2. nasscie.   3. lehe simile.   5. cacia.   6. truova [la sua ta] i sua.   8. leva [ecque] essubito.   10. tera.

colle zāpe scuopre ¹³l'inganno, ōde mediāte l'odore de' figli ¹⁴seguita il cacciatore, e quādo esso caccia¹⁵tore vede la tigra, lascia vno de' figlioli, ¹⁶e questa lo piglia, e portalo al nido; ¹⁷subito rigivgne esso cacciatore, e fa

scratching with its paws it discovers the cheat. Forthwith, by means of the scent of its young, it follows the hunter, and when this hunter sees the tigress he drops one of the young ones and she takes it, and having carried it to the den she immediately returns to the hunter and does

il simile insino a tāto ch'esso mōta ²in barca.

the same till he gets into his boat.

CATOPLEA

⁴Questa nascie · in Etiopia · vicino al fonte ⁵Nigricapo; è animale nō troppo · grande ·, è ⁶pigra · in tutte le mēbra ·, e à 'l capo di tāta grā⁷dezza · che malagievolmēte · lo porta ·, in modo che ⁸senpre · sta · chinato · inverso · la terra ·, altri⁹menti · sarebbe · di soͫa · peste · alli omini, ¹⁰perchè chiunque è veduta da sua · ochi ¹¹subito · more.

CATOBLEPAS

It is found in Ethiopia near to the source Nigricapo. It is not a very large animal, is sluggish in all its parts, and its head is so large that it carries it with difficulty, in such wise that it always droops towards the ground; otherwise it would be a great pest to man, for any one on whom it fixes its eyes dies immediately.

BASILISCO

¹³Questo · nascie · nella provincia · Cirenaica ¹⁴e nō è · maggiore · che · 12 · dita e à · in capo ¹⁵vna machia bianca a similitudine di diadema; ¹⁶col fischo · caccia · ogni serpēte ·; à similitudi¹⁷ne di serpe, ma nō si move cō torture, anzi ¹⁸man ritto · dal mezzo · innāzi ·, diciesi che vno

THE BASILISK

This is found in the province of Cyrenaica and is not more than 12 fingers long. It has on its head a white spot after the fashion of a diadem. It scares all serpents with its whistling. It resembles a snake, but does not move by wriggling but from the centre forwards to the right. It is said that one

di questi, essendo · morto · con vn aste da vno che ²era · a cavallo, che 'l suo veneno discorrendo ³super l'aste ·, e nō che l'omo · ma il cavallo morì; ⁴guasta · le biāde e nō solamēte quelle ⁵che tocca ·, ma quelle · doue · soffia ·; secca l'er⁶be, spezza · i sassi.

of these, being killed with a spear by one who was on horseback, and its venom flowing on the spear, not only the man but the horse also died. It spoils the wheat, and not only that which it touches, but where it breathes the grass dries and the stones are split.

DONNOLA OVER BELLULA

⁸Questa · trovādo · la tana · del basilisco, coll' o⁹dore della · sua · sparsa · orina l'uccide; l'o¹⁰dore della quale orina · ācora spesse volte ¹¹essa donola occide.

THE WEASEL

This beast finding the lair of the basilisk kills it by the smell of its urine, and this smell, indeed, often kills the weasel itself.

CERASTE

¹³Queste · ànno quattro · piccoli corni mobili; ¹⁴onde quādo si uogliono · cibare, nascōda¹⁵no sotto · le foglie tutta la persona, sal¹⁶vo · esse cornicina ·, le quali movēdo pare ¹⁷agli ucielli quelli essere piccoli uermini ¹⁸che scherzino, ōde subito si calano per beccar¹⁹li; e questa subito s'avviluppa loro in cie²⁰rchio, e esse lì diuora.

THE CERASTES

This has four movable little horns; so, when it wants to feed, it hides under leaves all of its body except these little horns which, as they move, seem to the birds to be small worms at play. Then they immediately swoop down to pick them and the Cerastes suddenly twines round them and encircles and devours them.

---

12. cholle . . schuopre. 13. longano. 14. essocacia. 15. lasscia. 17. r | givgnieso caciatore effa.
1255. 1. imile . . attāto. 4. nasscie. 6. tucte. 7. deza . . imodo. 8. altre. 9. pesste. 10. he veduta. 13. nasscie. 14. magiore . . he a in. 16. fisscio . . assimilitudi. 18. marito dal mezo.
1256. 2. chavallo. 2. discorendo. 3. chellomo. 4. [colio] guassta. 5. chettoccha macquelle . . secha. 7. donola . . belola. 8. basilissco. 12. cerasste. 13. pichorni mobili. 14. uogliano. 14. nasscōda. 17. picoli. 18. cescerzino . . becar. 19. ecquesta . . sauilupa. 20. cio esseli diuora.

H.¹ 25a]   1257

AMPHESIBENE

²Questa · à · due teste ·, l'una nel suo loco, l'al³tra nella · coda ·, come se nō bastasse che ⁴da uno solo loco gittasse il ueneno.

IACULO

⁶Questa · sta sopra · le piāte ·, e si lancia · come ⁷dardo; e passa a trauerso le fere, e l'uccide.

ASPIDO

⁹Il morso · di questo · animale · non à · rimedio, ¹⁰se nō di subito · tagliare · le parti morse; Questo ¹¹si pestifero · animale · à tale affetione nella ¹²sua cōpagnia · che sempre vanno accōpagniati, ¹³chè se per disgratia · l'uno di loro è morto ·, l'al¹⁴tro con incredibile velocità seguita l'ucci¹⁵ditore, ed è tāto attēto e sollecito alla vēdetta, ¹⁶che vīcie · ogni difficultà ·; passando ogni eser¹⁷cito, solo il suo nemico cierca · offendere; ¹⁸e passa ogni spatio, e nō si può schifarlo, se nō ¹⁹col passare l'acque · e cō velocissima fuga; ²⁰à li ochi ī dētro e grādi orechi, e piv lo move l'udito che 'l uedere.

THE AMPHISBOENA

This has two heads, one in its proper place, the other at the tail; as if one place were not enough from which to fling its venom.

THE IACULUS

This lies on trees, and flings itself down like a dart, and pierces through the wild beasts and kills them.

THE ASP

The bite of this animal cannot be cured unless by immediately cutting out the bitten part. This pestilential animal has such a love for its mate that they always go in company. And if, by mishap, one of them is killed the other, with incredible swiftness, follows him who has killed it; and it is so determined and eager for vengeance that it overcomes every difficulty, surmounting every effort it seeks to hurt none but its enemy. And it will travel any distance, and it is impossible to avoid it unless by crossing water and by very swift flight. It has its eyes turned inwards, and large ears, and it hears better than it sees.

H.¹ 25b]   1258

ICNEUMONE

²Questo · animale · è mortale nemico all'aspido; ³nascie · in Egitto ·, e quādo · vede presso al ⁴suo · sito alcuno · aspido ·, subito corre ⁵alla litta over fango · del Nilo, e cō quello ⁶tutto · s'infanga, e poi, risecco dal sole, di no⁷vo di fango s'inbratta; e così seguitando l'ū do⁸po l'altro si fa tre o 4 veste a similitudine ⁹di corazza ·, e dipoi assalta l'aspido, e bē cō¹⁰testa cō quello in modo che, tolto il tēpo, ¹¹se li caccia in · gola e l'annega.

CROCODILLO

¹³Questo nascie nel Nilo, à 4 piedi, vi¹⁴ve in terra e in acqua, nè altro terrestre ¹⁵animale si truova sanza lingua che questo; ¹⁶e solo morde movēdo la mascella di sopra; ¹⁷crescie insino in 40 piedi, è unghiato, ¹⁸armato di corame, atto a ogni colpo; el dì ¹⁹sta in terra, e la notte in acqua; questo, ²⁰cibato di pesci, s'adormēta sulla riua del ²¹Nilo colla bocca aperta e l'ucciello detto

THE ICHNEUMON

This animal is the mortal enemy of the asp. It is a native of Egypt and when it sees an asp near its place, it runs at once to the sand or mud of the Nile and with this makes itself muddy all over, then it dries itself in the sun, smears itself again with mud, and thus, drying one after the other, it makes itself three or four coatings like a coat of mail. Then it attacks the asp, and fights well with him, so that, taking its time, it catches him in the throat and destroys him.

THE CROCODILE

This is found in the Nile, it has four feet, and lives on land and in water. No other terrestrial creature but this is found to have no tongue, and it only bites by moving its upper jaw. It grows to a length of forty feet and has claws and is armed with a hide that will take any blow. By day it is on land and at night in the water. It feeds on fishes, and going to sleep on the bank of the Nile with its mouth open, a bird called

H.¹ 26a]   1259

trochilo, piccolissimo vcciello ·, subito li ²corre alla bocca e, saltatoli fra denti ³dentro ·, e' fora · leva beccando il rimaso ⁴cibo ·; e così stuzzicādolo cō dilettevole ⁵voluttà lo inuita aprire tutta

trochilus, a very small bird, runs at once to its mouth and hops among its teeth and goes pecking out the remains of the food, and so inciting it with voluptuous delight tempts it to open the

1257. 2. tesste. 3. basstassi. 4. da ī solo locho. 6. essi. 7. attrauero le fiere elluccide. 11. attale. 12. ce senpre .. acōpagniati. 13. chesseper. 14. luci. 15. essollecito. 16. dificulta. 18. scifarlo. 20. laldito.
1258. 1. ichneumone. 3. nasscie. 4. asspido. 5. lita .. echō. 6. risecchio. 7. cosi sēchāda lū. 8. assimilitudine. 9. coraza .. lasspido. 10. tasta .. imodo chettolto. 11. cacia .. ella niega. 13. nasscie .. piedi nvc vi. 14. ce in terra e in acq"a" [e sua] ne .. tereste. 15. checquesto. 16. massciella. 17. cresscie .. vngliato. 18. [vestito] "armato" di .. atto ogni. 19. ella notte. 20. pessci. 21. bocha .. elluciello.
1259. 1. trocilo picholissimo vciello. 2. bocha essaltatoli. 3. effora liva bechando. 4. cibo e e cosi stuzicādolo. 5. lonuita .. boccha.

la bocca, [6]e così s'adormēta; questo veduto [7]dal icneumone · subito si li slācia · in bocca, [8]e foratoli lo stomaco e le budelle finalmēte [9]l'uccide.

whole of its mouth, and so it sleeps. This being observed by the ichneumon it flings itself into its mouth and perforates its stomach and bowels, and finally kills it.

DELFINI

[11]La natura à dato tal cognitione alli · ani[12]mali che, oltre allo conosciere la lor co[13]modità, conoscono · la incomodità del ni[14]mico ·; onde intēde il delfino · quāto [15]vaglia · il taglio delle sue · penne, posteli [16]sulla schiena, e quāto sia tenera la pācia [17]del cocodrillo ·; onde nel lor cōbattere se li [18]caccia sotto e tagliali la pācia, e così [19]l'uccide.

[20]Il cocodrillo è terrible a chi fuggie, e vilis[21]simo a chi lo caccia.

THE DOLPHIN

Nature has given such knowledge to animals that besides the consciousness of their own advantages they know the disadvantages of their foes. Thus the dolphin understands what strength lies in a cut from the fins placed on his chine, and how tender is the belly of the crocodile; hence in fighting with him it thrusts at him from beneath and rips up his belly and so kills him.

The crocodile is a terror to those that flee, and a base coward to those that pursue him.

H.[1] 26b]   1260

IPPOPOTAMO

[2]Questo · quando si sente aggravato · va [3]ciercando le spine, o dove siā i rimanē[4]ti de' tagliati cannetti, e lì tāto frega vna ve[5]na che la taglia, e cauato il sangue, che li [6]bisognia, colla litta s'infanga, e risalta alla [7]piaggia; à forma quasi come cavallo; l'ūgia [8]fessa, coda torta, e dēti di cīghiale; collo co [9]crinī; la pelle nō si può passare ·, se nō si ba[10]gnia ·; pasciesi di biade ne' cāpi, entravi [11]allo dirieto, acciochè pare ne sia uscito.

THE HIPPOPOTAMUS

This beast when it feels itself over-full goes about seeking thorns, or where there may be the remains of canes that have been split, and it rubs against them till a vein is opened; then when the blood has flowed as much as he needs, he plasters himself with mud and walks up again to the shore. In form he is almost like a horse with hooves cloven, twisted tail, and teeth of a wild boar; his neck has a mane; the skin cannot be pierced, unless he is bathing; he feeds on oats in the fields and enters them backwards that it may seem as though he had come out.

IBIS

[13]Questo à similitudine colla cicognia, e quan[14]do si sente ammalato, ēpie il gozzo d'acqua, [15]e col becco si fa vn clistero.

THE IBIS

This bird resembles a stork, and when it feels itself ill it fills its craw with water, and with its beak makes an injection of it.

CIERUI

[17]Questo quando si sente morso dal ragno [18]detto falangio · māgia de' grāchi, e si libera [19]di tale veneno.

THE STAG

These creatures, when they feel themselves bitten by the spider called phalangium, eat crabs and free themselves of the venom.

H.[1] 27a]   1261

LUCERTE

[2]Questa quādo cōbatte colle serpi [3]mangia la cicierbita; e sō libere.

THE LIZARD

This, when fighting with serpents, eats the sow-thistle and is immune.

RONDINE

[5]Questa rende il uedere alli orbiti [6]figlioli col sugo della celidonia.

THE SWALLOW

This [bird] gives sight to its blind young ones with the juice of the celandine.

BELLULA

[8]Questa quando caccia ai ratti, māgia [9]prima · della · ruta.

THE WEASEL

This, when chasing rats, first eats of rue.

---

7. daleleumone . . si linācia in bocch.a. 8. elle. 9. luccide [essimile al ramarro vergezzo]. 12. alo nassciere. 13. cogniosscano. 15. pene. 16. sula sciena . . pāca. 17. nellor. 18. ettagliali. 20. etteribile acci fuggie e vili. 21. accilo.
1260. 1. hippotamo. 2. agravato. 3. cierchando . . sia. 4. caneti elli. 5. chauato . . chelli. 6. cola lita . . risaldala. 8. cīglare. 9. si po pasare. 10. passciesi . . biāde. 11. vsscito. 13. assimilitudine . . ciguognia ecq"ā". 14. amalato . . il cozo dacque. 15. e chol becho . . cristero. 18. falange . . grāci essi.
1261. 2. colle [lucerte] serp. 3. essō. 5. alli unorbiti. 6. chol. 7. belola.

CINGHIALE
[11]Questo medica · i sua · mali mangiãdo [12]della edera.

THE WILD BOAR
This beast cures its sickness by eating of ivy.

SERPE
[14]Questa quãdo si uol renovare, gitta il [15]vechio scoglio, comĩciãdosi dalla testa; [16]mvtasi in vn dì e vna notte.

THE SNAKE
This creature when it wants to renew itself casts its old skin, beginning with the head, and changing in one day and one night.

PANTERA
[18]Questa, poichè le sono · uscite l'interiora, [19]ancora conbatte coi cani e cacciatori.

THE PANTHER
This beast after its bowels have fallen out will still fight with the dogs and hunters.

H.[1] 27*b*]   1262

CAMELEONTE
[2]Questo · piglia · senpre il colore della cosa [3]dove si posa ·; onde insieme colle frõdi [4]dove si posano, spesso da li elefanti sõ diuorati.

THE CHAMELEON
This creature always takes the colour of the thing on which it is resting, whence it is often devoured together with the leaves on which the elephant feeds.

CORBO
[6]Questo quando à ucciso el cameleonte [7]si purga coll' alloro.

THE RAVEN
When it has killed the chameleon it takes laurel as a purge.

H.[1] 48*b*]   1263

¶Moderanza raffrena tutti i vitj.
[2]L'ermelino prima vol morire che imbrat-[3]tarsi.

Moderation checks all the vices.
The ermine will die rather than besmirch itself.

DELL' ANTIUEDERE
[5]Il gallo nõ cãta, se prima 3 volte nõ batte [6]l'alie; il papagalo nel mutarsi pe' rami [7]nõ mette i piè, doue non à prima [8]messo il becco; [9]¶il uoto nascie quãdo la sperãza more.

[10]Il moto seguita il ciĕtro del peso.

OF FORESIGHT
The cock does not crow till it has thrice flapped its wings; the parrot in moving among boughs never puts its feet excepting where it has first put its beak. Vows are not made till Hope is dead.

Motion tends towards the centre of gravity.

H.[3] 101*a*]   1264

MAGNANIMITÀ
Il falcone nõ pi[2]glia se nõ vccelli grossi, e prima more [3]che mãgiare carne di nõ bono odore.

MAGNANIMITY
The falcon never seizes any but large birds and will sooner die than eat [tainted] meat of bad savour.

N.Y.]   1264 A

Il ramarro, fedele all' omo, vedendo quello adormentato, combatte colla biscia e sse vede no lla poter vincere corre sopra il volto dell' omo e lo desta acciochè essa biscia non offenda lo adormentato homo.

The lizard is faithful to man, and when it sees that he is asleep it will fight the snake, and when it realizes that it cannot conquer it will run across the face of the man and wake him so that the snake should not hurt him while asleep.

16. mvtasi nvndi . . nocte. 18. poichelle sono vsscite lenteriora.
1262. 6. quessto . . cameleont. 7. pugra choll alloro.
1263. 2. chĕbra. 8. becho. 9. nasscie.
1264. 2. vcielli. 3. chane.

1263. Compare No. 1234.   **1264.** An illustration accompanies this text.

FABLES

1265

FAVOLA

²Sendo l'ostrica insieme colli altri ³pesci in casa del pescatore scarica⁴ta vicino al mare ·, priega il ratto, ⁵che al mare la cōduca; il ratto fatto ⁶disegnio di māgiarla la fa aprire, ⁷e mordēdola questa li serra la testa ⁸e si lo ferma; viene la gatta e l'uccide.

A FABLE

An oyster being turned out together with other fish in the house of a fisherman near the sea, he entreated a rat to take him to the sea. The rat purposing to eat him bid him open; but as he bit him the oyster squeezed his head and closed; and the cat came and killed him.

Fables on animals (1265–70).

1266

FAVOLA

²I tordi si rallegrarono forte, vedēdo che l'omo prese la ciuetta ³e le tolse la libertà, quella legando con forti legami ai sua piedi; la ⁴qual ciuetta fu poi mediante il uischio causa nō di far perdere ⁵la libertà · ai tordi, ma la loro propia vita ·; detta per quelle ⁶terre che si rallegrā di uedere perdere la libertà ai loro maggio⁷ri, mediante i quali poi perdono il soccorso, e rimāgono lega⁸ti in potētia del loro nemico ·, lasciādo la libertà e spesse volte la uita.

A FABLE

The thrushes rejoiced greatly at seeing a man take the owl and deprive her of liberty, tying her feet with strong bonds. But this owl was afterwards by means of bird-lime the cause of the thrushes losing not only their liberty, but their life. This is said for those countries which rejoice in seeing their governors lose their liberty, when by that means they themselves lose all succour, and remain in bondage in the power of their enemies, losing their liberty and often their life.

1267

FAVOLA

²Dormēdo · il cane · sopra la pelle · d'un castrone, vna delle sua ³pulci ·, sentēdo · l'odore · della vnta · lana ·, givdicò quello ⁴dovesse essere · loco di migliore · vita e piv sicura da denti e unghie del cane, che pascier⁵si del cane ·; e sanza altri pensieri abbandonò il cane, e entrata ⁶infra la folta lana ·, cominciò cō somma fatica · a volere ⁷trapassare alle radici de' peli ·; la quale inpresa dopo molto ⁸sudore trovò esser uana ·, perchè tali peli erano tanto spessi che ⁹quasi si toccavano, e nō u'era spatio dove la pulcie potesse saggiare ¹⁰tal pelle ·; ōde · dopo lūgo travaglio e fatica cominciò a vole¹¹re ritornare al suo cane ·, il quale essendo già partito, fu ¹²costretta dopo lūgo pētimēto e amari piāti a morirsi di fame.

A FABLE

A dog lying asleep on the fur of a sheep, one of his fleas, perceiving the odour of the greasy wool, judged that this must be a land of better living, and also more secure from the teeth and nails of the dog than where he fed on the dog; and without further reflection he left the dog and went into the thick wool. There he began with great labour to try to pass to the roots of the hairs; but after much sweating had to give up the task as vain, because these hairs were so close that they almost touched each other, and there was no space where fleas could taste the skin. Hence, after much labour and fatigue, he began to wish to return to his dog, who, however, had already departed; so he was constrained, after long repentance and bitter tears, to die of hunger.

1268

FAVOLA

²Non si cōtentando · il uano · e vagabūdo parpaglione ³di potere · comodamēte · volare · per l'aria, ⁴vinto · dalla dilettevole · fiamma ·

A FABLE

The vain and wandering butterfly, not content with being able to fly at its ease through the air, overcome by the tempting flame of the

---

1265. 2. lostriga . . colli al. 5. ce al māre . . fato. 7. sera. 8. essilo . . ellucide.
1266. 2. rallegrorono . . chellomo. 3. elle . . choforti. 4. uiscio · chausa . . far perde. 5. malla. 6. chessi ralegrā . . mgai. 7. perdano il sochorso. 8. nemicho . . esspesse.
1267. 2. chastrone. 4. dovessi . . locho . . sichura "da denti e vnglia del cane" che passcier. 5. essanza . . abandono. 6. infralla . . soma faticha. 7. molta [fa]. 9. tochauano . . potessi sagiare. 10. faticha cōmincio. 12. pētimēto amari.
1268. 2. chōtentando. 3. chomodamēte . . laria [dilibero dischore]. 4. revintᵒ . . fiama . . chādela dili. 5. giochōdo.

della cādela, deli⁵berò · volare in quella ·; e 'l suo · giocōdo · movimē⁶to · fu cagione di subita · tristitia ·, inperochè in detto ⁷lume si consumarono · le sottili ali · e 'l parpa⁸glione · misero caduto · tutto bruciato a piè del ⁹candeliere ·; dopo · molto · pianto e pētimē¹⁰to · si rascivgò · le lagrime dai bagniati ochi, ¹¹e levato · il uiso in alto · disse ·: o falsa luce, ¹²quāti · come me debi tu · avere · ne passa¹³ti tenpi · avere miserabilmēte · ingañati! o se ¹⁴pure volevo · vedere · la luce ·, nō doveu' · io cono¹⁵sciere il sole · dal falso · lume dello spurco sevo?

candle, decided to fly into it; but its sportive impulse was the cause of a sudden woe, for its delicate wings were burnt in the flame. And the hapless butterfly having dropped, all scorched, at the foot of the candlestick, after much lamentation and repentance, dried the tears from its swimming eyes, and raising its face exclaimed: 'O false light! how many must thou have miserably deceived in the past, like me; or, if I must indeed see light so near, ought I not to have known the sun from the false glare of dirty tallow?'

FAVOLA

¹⁷Trovando la scimia vno nidio di piccoli ¹⁸vccelli ·, tutta · allegra · appressatasi a quelli, e quali essē¹⁹do già da volare, ne potè solo pigliare il minore; essē²⁰do pieno d'allegrezza con esso · in mano, se n'ādò al suo ²¹ricetto; e comīciato a cōsiderare questo vccelletto, ²²lo comīciò a baciare; e per lo sviscerato · amore tanto ²³lo baciò, e rivolse, e strinse · ch'ella gli tolse la uita; ²⁴È detta per quelli che per nō gastigare i figlioli capita²⁵no male.

A FABLE

The monkey, finding a nest of small birds, went up to it greatly delighted. But they being already fledged, he could only succeed in taking the smallest; greatly delighted he took it in his hand and went to his abode; and having begun to look at the little bird he took to kissing it, and from excess of love he kissed it so much and turned it about and squeezed it till he killed it. This is said for those who by not punishing their children let them come to mischief.

C. A. 67b] 1269

FAVOLA

²Stando il topo assediato · in vna piccola sua abitatione ³dalla donnola ·, la quale cō cōtinva vigilantia attēdea ⁴alla sua disfatione, · e' per uno · piccolo spiraculo riguarda⁵va il suo grā pericolo; infrattanto · venne la gatta, ⁶e subito prese essa donnola, e imediate l'ebbe diuorata; ⁷allora il ratto ·, fatto sacrificio a Giove d'alquāte sue noc⁸ciole ·, ringratiò sommamēte la sua deità, e uscito fori dalla ⁹sua buca a possedere la già persa libertà, della quale subito in¹⁰sieme colla vita fu dalle feroci unghie e denti della ¹¹gatta privato.

A FABLE

A rat being besieged in his little dwelling by a weasel which with unwearied vigilance awaited his surrender, was watching his imminent peril through a little hole. Meanwhile the cat came by and suddenly seized the weasel and forthwith devoured it. Then the rat offered up a sacrifice to Jove of some of his store of nuts, humbly thanking his providence, and came out of his hole to enjoy his lately lost liberty. But he was instantly deprived of it, together with his life, by the cruel claws and teeth of the cat.

C. A. 67b] 1270

FAUOLA

²La formica · trovato vno · grano di ³miglio ·, jl grano sētendosi preso da quel⁴la gridò: se mi fai tāto piacere di ⁵lasciarmi fruire il mio desiderio del ⁶nasciere ·, io ti rēderò · ciēto me medesimi; ⁷e così fu fatto.

⁸Trovato il ragnio vno grappolo · d'uue, ⁹il quale per la sua dolcezza era · molto · visitato · da avi e diuerse ¹⁰qualità · di mosche ·, li parue · avere trouato ¹¹loco · molto · comodo · al suo · inganno ·; e cala¹²tosi giù · per lo suo · sottile · filo, e ētrato · nella no¹³va · abitatione · lì ogni · giorno ¹⁴faciēdosi alli spiraculi ·, fatti dalli ¹⁵interualli · de' grani · dell' uue ·, assaltaua

A FABLE

The ant found a grain of millet. The seed feeling itself taken prisoner cried out to her: 'If you will do me the kindness to allow me to accomplish my function of reproduction, I will give you a hundred such as I am.' And so it was.

A spider found a bunch of grapes which for its sweetness was much resorted to by bees and divers kinds of flies. It seemed to her that she had found a most convenient spot to spread her snare, and having settled herself on it with her delicate web, and entered into her new habitation, there, every day placing herself in the openings made by the spaces between the grapes,

6. chagione . . inperochēdetto. 7. chonsumorono . . sottile ali . [ch]el. 8. brusato. 9. chandelieri. 11. dise. 12. chome . . pasa. 13. ossi. 14. chono. 17. scimia [inp] vno . . di [lusi] di picioli. 18. vcielli . . apressatasi a queli. 20. dalegreza chon eso imano. 21. ricieto e chomīciato a chōsiderare . . vcielletto. 22. issuecerato. 23. esstrinse chellagli tolsi.
1269. 2. stanto . . pichola. 3. della donora. 4. per l picholo spirachulo raguarda. 5. perichulo . . vene. 6. donola. 7. dalquāte sue no. 8. rigratio somamente . . vsscito . . della. 9. busa . . dela. 10. ungha. 11. privata.
1270. 2. formicha. 4. lagrodo. 5. lassciarmi. 6. nasscciere . . redero. 9. il quale "per la sua dolceza" era. 10. mossche. 11. locho . . chomodo . . cholla. 12. gu. 13. giorno [con ingani]. 14. [chonduci] faciēdosi. 15. chome.

come ¹⁶ladrone i miseri animali · che da lui non
si ¹⁷guardauano; e passati · alquanti · giorni il ·
¹⁸uendemiatore · colse · essa uva e, messa col-
l'al¹⁹tre · insieme, con quelle · fu pigiata ·; e così
²⁰l'uva · fu laccio e inganno · dello ingañatore
²¹ragnio ·, come · delle · ingannate mosche.

²²Addormētatosi · l'asino · sopra il ghiaccio
²³d'ū profondo · lago ·, il suo · calore dissolue
²⁴esso ghiaccio ·, e l'asino · sott' acqua a mal suo
²⁵danno si destò · e subito · annegò.

²⁶Il falcone ·, nō potendo sopportare cō
patiētia ²⁷il nascōdere che fa l'anitra, fugiēdo sé
le dināzi ²⁸e entrādo sotto · acqua · volle, come
quelle, sott' acqua ²⁹seguitare, e bagniatosi le
penne rimase in essa ³⁰acqua; e l'anitra, leuatasi
in aria ·, scherne ³¹il falcone che annegaua.

³²Il ragno ·, volendo · pigliare · la mosca cō
sue ³³false · reti ·, fu sopra · quelle · dal cala-
brone ³⁴crudelmēte morto.

³⁵Volendo · l'aquila · schernire · il gufo,
rimase ³⁶coll' alie · inpaniata ·, e fu dall' omo ·
presa e morta.

she fell like a thief on the wretched creatures
which were not aware of her. But, after a few
days had passed, the vintager came, and cut
away the bunch of grapes and put it with others,
with which it was trodden; and thus the grapes
were a snare and pitfall both for the treacherous
spider and the betrayed flies.

An ass having gone to sleep on the ice over a
deep lake, his heat dissolved the ice and the ass
awoke under water to his great grief, and was
forthwith drowned.

A falcon, unable to endure with patience the
disappearance of a duck which, flying before
him, had plunged under water, wished to follow
it under water, and having soaked his feathers
had to remain in the water while the duck, rising
in the air, mocked at the falcon as he drowned.

The spider, wishing to take flies in her
treacherous net, was cruelly killed in it by the
hornet.

An eagle wanting to mock at the owl was
caught by the wings in bird-lime and was taken
and killed by a man.

S. K. M. III. 2a]　　　　　　　1271

Trovandosi l'acqua nel superbo mare, suo
elemē²to, le veñe voglia di mōtare sopra ³l'aria,
e cōfortata dal foco elemēto, eleuatasi ī sottile
vapore, ⁴quasi parea della sottigliezza dell' aria; ⁵e
mōtata in alto givnse īfra l'a⁶ria piv sottile e
fredda, dove fu abādona⁷ta dal foco, e i piccoli
granicoli, ⁸sendo ristretti, già s'uniscono e
fā⁹nosi pesanti, ove cadēdo la superbia ¹⁰si
cōuerte in fuga, e cade dal cielo, ¹¹ōde poi fu
bevuta dalla secca terra, ¹²dove lūgo tēpo in-
carcerata ¹³fece penitētia del suo peccato.

The water finding itself in its element, the **Fables on
inanimate
objects**
(1271–4).
lordly ocean, was seized with a desire to rise
above the air, and being encouraged by the
element of fire and rising as a very subtle vapour,
it seemed as though it were really as thin as air.
But having risen very high, it reached the air
that was still more rare and cold, where the fire
forsook it, and the minute particles, being
brought together, united and became heavy;
whence its haughtiness deserting it, it betook itself to flight and it fell from the sky, and was
drunk up by the dry earth, where, being imprisoned for a long time, it did penance for its sin.

C. A. 175b]　　　　　　　　　1272

FAUOLA

²Vsciendo vn giorno il rasojo · di quel manico,
col quale si fa gvaina a sé medesimo, ³e postosi
al sole ·, vide il sole spechiarsi nel suo corpo;
della qual cosa prese somma gloria, ⁴e rivolto col
pensiero · indirieto · cominciò cō seco medesimo
· a dire: Or tornerò io ⁵piv a quella bottega della
quale novamēte uscito · sono ·? cierto · no ·;
nō piaccia alli Dei che ⁶si splendida bellezza
caggia in tāta viltà d'animo! che pazzia sarebbe
quella, la qual mi cō⁷ducesse a radere le insapo-
nate barbe de' rustici villani · e fare sì mecaniche
operationi! ⁸Or è questo corpo da simili eserciti?
Cierto no; Io mi voglio nascondere in qualche

A FABLE

The razor having one day come forth from
the handle which serves as its sheath and having
placed himself in the sun, saw the sun reflected
in his body, which filled him with great pride.
And turning it over in his thoughts he began to
say to himself: 'And shall I return again to that
shop from which I have just come? Certainly
not; such splendid beauty shall not, please God,
be turned to such base uses. What folly it would
be that could lead me to shave the lathered
beards of rustic peasants and perform such
menial service! Is this body destined for such
work? Certainly not. I will hide myself in some

---

16. dallui.　18. colta . . vua e messe.　20. laccio ēnganno.　21. chome . . mossche.　22. adormentatosi . . diaccio.　23. disolue.
24. diaccio ellasino sottacqa.　25. dessto.　26. soportare chō.　27. nasschōdere cheffallanitra.　28. sottacqa.　29. pene.　30. ellanitra
. . schernia.　31. anegaua.　32. cosua.　33. rete.　35. schenire.　36. inpaniate eff.
1271. 1. lacq"a" . . superbo "mare" suo.　3. laria "e cōfortata dal foco elemēto" eleuatosi.　4. sittiglieza.　5. infralla.　6. sottile "effreda"
dove.　7. focho e picoli.　8. restretti . . suniscano effā.　9. la superb.　10. del cielo.　11. bevute . . sechatera.　13. fe . . pechato.
1272. 2. vssciendo . . rasoro . . manicho chol . . giaina asse.　3. isspechiarsi . . chorpo . . chosa . . soma groria.　4. chol . . chomincio
chōsecho.　5. acquella . . vsscito . . piacia alli de · la e.　6. belleza chagia . . pazia sarebe . . michō.　7. duciessi . . russtrichi vilani
effare smechaniche operatione.　8. or questo orpo da . . vogli naschondere.

[9]oculto loco, e lì cō trāquillo riposo passare mia vita ·; E così nascosto per alquāti mesi, [10]vn giorno ritornato all' aria e uscito fori della sua guaina, vide sé essere fatto a si[11]militudine d'una rugginēte sega, e la sua superfitie non ui spechiare piv lo splendiēte sole; [12]cō vano pētimēto indarno piāse lo inriparabile danno, con seco diciēdo: o quanto [13]meglio era esercitare col barbiere il mio perduto taglio di tāta sottilità; dov' è la lustrante [14]superfitie? cierto la fastidiosa e brutta ruggine l'à consumata!

[15]Questo medesimo · accade nelli ingiegni · che in scābio dello esercitio si danno · all' otio; [16]I quali · a similitudine del sopradetto · rasojo · perdono la tagliente sua sottilità, [17]e la rugine della ignioranza guasta la sua forma.

retired spot and there pass my life in tranquil repose.' And having thus remained hidden for some months, one day he came out into the air, and issuing from his sheath, saw himself turned to the similitude of a rusty saw while his surface no longer reflected the resplendent sun. With useless repentance he vainly deplored the irreparable mischief, saying to himself: 'Oh! how far better was it to employ at the barbers my lost edge of such exquisite keenness! Where is that lustrous surface? It has been consumed by this vexatious and unsightly rust.'

The same thing happens to those minds which instead of exercise give themselves up to sloth. They are like the razor here spoken of, and lose the keenness of their edge, while the rust of ignorance spoils their form.

FAUOLA

[19]Vna · pietra novamēte per l'acque scoperta di bella grādezza si staua sopra vn cierto loco rilevata, [20]dove terminava un dilettevole boschetto sopra vna sassosa strada in cō[21]pagnia d'erbe, di uari fiori di diuersi colori ornate, e vedea [22]la grā somma delle pietre che nella a sé sotto[23]posta strada collocate · erano ·; le uenne · desiderio di là giv lasciarsi ca[24]dere, diciēdo · cō seco: che fo io qui · cō queste erbe? io voglio cō que[25]ste mie sorelle in cōpagnia abitare; e giv lasciatosi cadere infra [26]le desiderate cōpagnie finì suo volubile corso ·; e stata alquāto co-[27]mīciò a essere dalle rote de' carri ·, dai piè de' ferrati cavalli, e de [28]viandāti · a essere in continvo travaglio ·; chi la volta, quello la pesta-[29]va; alcuna volta si leuava alcuno pezzo, quādo stava coperta da fā[30]go o sterco di qualche animale ·, e in vano riguardava il loco dō[31]de partita s'era in nel loco della solletaria e trāquilla pace;

[32]Così accade a quelli che dalla vita soletaria cōtenplativa voglio[33]no venir abitare nelle città infra i popoli pieni d'infiniti mali.

A FABLE

A stone of some size recently uncovered by the water lay on a certain spot somewhat raised, and just where a delightful grove ended above a stony road; here it was surrounded by plants decorated by various flowers of divers colours. And as it saw the great quantity of stones collected together in the roadway below, it began to wish it could let itself fall down there, saying to itself: 'What have I to do here with these plants? I want to live in the company of those, my sisters.' And letting itself fall, its rapid course ended among these longed-for companions. When it had been there some time it began to find itself in constant travail under the wheels of the carts, the iron-shod feet of horses and of travellers. This one rolled it over, that one trod upon it; sometimes it lifted itself a little and then it was covered with mud or the dung of some animal, and it was in vain that it looked at the spot whence it had come as a place of solitude and tranquil peace.

Thus it happens to those who choose to leave a life of solitary contemplation, and come to live in cities among people full of infinite evil.

C. A. 67a]   **1273**

[2]Le fiamme · già · uno mese durato nella fornace [3]de' bichieri, e veduto a sé avicinarsi vna [4]candela in vn bello e lustrante cādeliere, con gran deside[5]rio si forzauano · accostarsi a quella; infra le qua[6]li vna, lasciato el suo naturale [7]corso e tiratasi dentro · a vno · voto stizzo, dove [8]si pascieva · e vsscita da l'opposito fori d'una piccola fessura [9]alla cādela, che vicina l'era, si

Some flames had already lasted a month in the furnace of a glass-blower, when they saw a candle approaching in a beautiful and glittering candlestick. With ardent longing they strove to reach it; and one of them, quitting its natural course, writhed up to an unburnt brand on which it fed and passed at the opposite end out by a narrow chink to the candle which was near. It

9. ochulto locho elli chō .. chosi naschosto.   10. gorno .. vsscito .. fatto assi.   11. ruginēte .. ella .. noui spechiare.   12. cho .. dano cho secho .. o qua.   13. chol .. il mi .. lusstrante.   14. fasstidiosa .. rugine.   15. chenisschābio.   16. assimilitudine .. decto rasoro perde .. suttilita.   17. ella .. guassta.   19. pietra | "novamēte per lacque scoperta" di bella grādeza .. locho.   20. vdi lettevole bosschetto .. ichō.   21. derbetedi uari .. cholori ornata.   22. soma .. asse.   23. chollochate .. uene .. lassciarsi cha.   24. chōsecho .. chō .. chō.   25. sorele .. chōpagnia .. lassatosi chadere.   26. chōpagnie .. cho.   27. dale .. charri .. defferati chavalli.   28. chontinvo .. quale la.   29. alchuna .. alchuno pezo .. choperta.   30. osstercho .. locho.   31. partata .. inel locho.   32. acade acquelli che della .. chōtenplativa voglia.
1273. 1. [lo ingordo fochosapiglia nelle legnie].   2. [il focho] "le fiame" gia vno .. me.   3. de bichieri .. asse.   4. chandela .. bello chandelliere "ellusstrante" chon gra.   5. achostarsi a chuella infralle.   6. vna [falcara] laciato.   7. stizo.   8. vsscita | "dal oposito" fori.   9. [alume che lara] alla cādella.   10. chō soma .. ingordigia [di] quella.

¹⁰gittò · e cō somma · golosità · e ingordigia quella ¹¹diuorando · quasi · al fine la condusse ·; e volendo ripa¹²rare · al prolungamēto · della sua vita, indar¹³no tētō tornare alla fornace ·, donde partita s'era, ¹⁴perchè fu costretta · morire, e mancare insieme ¹⁵colla cādela, ōde al fine cō piāto e pētimēto ¹⁶ · in fastidioso fumo si convertì, lasciādo ¹⁷tutte le sorelle in splendente e lūga vita e bellezza.

flung itself upon it, and with fierce jealousy and greediness it devoured it, having almost finished it, and, wishing to procure the prolongation of its life, it tried to return to the furnace whence it had come. But in vain, for it was compelled to die, perishing together with the candle, being at last converted, with lamentation and repentance, into foul smoke, while leaving all its sisters in brilliant and enduring life and beauty.

C. A. 67b]

1274

Trovandosi · alquanta · poca neve ²appiccata alla sommità · d'un sasso, il quale ³era collocato sopra la strema · al⁴tezza d'una · altissima · mōtagnia, · e raccol⁵to · in sé · la imaginatione, comīciò · con quella ⁶a considerare e infra sé · dire: Or nō son io ⁷da essere · givdicata · altera · e superba, avere ⁸me piccola · dramma · di neve · posto · in sì al⁹to loco? e sopportare che tanta quātità di neve, ¹⁰quanta · di qui · per me · essere veduta può, stia ¹¹piv bassa di me? cierto · la mia poca quāti¹²tà non merita · questa · altezza, chè bene posso per ¹³testimonāza · della mia · piccola · figura conoscie¹⁴re quello che 'l sole fecie · icri alle mia con¹⁵pagnie, · le quali in poche · ore · dal sole furo¹⁶no · disfatte ·; e questo interuenne per essersi ¹⁷posto piv alto · che a loro nō si richiedea ·; io vo¹⁸glio fugire · l'ira · del sole, e abbassarmi, e trovare ¹⁹loco · cōueniēte · alla mia parua quātità; ²⁰e gittatasi in basso e comīciata a disciēdere rottādo ²¹dall'alte spiaggie · su per l'altra neve, quāto piv ciercò ²²loco · basso ·, piv · crebbe · sua · quātità in modo ²³che, terminato · il suo · corso sopra · uno colle, si trouò ²⁴di nō quasi minor grādezza · che 'l colle che essa sostenea; ²⁵e fu · l'ultima · che in quella · 'state · dal sole disfatta ²⁶fusse ·; detto · per quelli · che s'umiliano, son esaltati.

A small patch of snow finding itself clinging to the top of a rock which was lying on the topmost height of a very high mountain, and being left to its own imaginings, it began to reflect in this way, saying to itself: 'Now, shall not I be thought vain and proud for having placed myself—such a small patch of snow—in so lofty a spot, and for allowing that so large a quantity of snow as I can see here around me should take a place lower than mine? Certainly my small dimensions by no means merit this elevation. How easily may I, in proof of my insignificance, experience the same fate as that which the sun brought about yesterday to my companions, who were all, in a few hours, destroyed by the sun. And this happened from their having placed themselves higher than became them. I will flee from the wrath of the sun, and humble myself and find a place befitting my small importance.' Thus, flinging itself down, it began to descend, hurrying from its high home on to the other snow; but the more it sought a low place the more its bulk increased, so that when at last its course was ended on a hill, it found itself no less in size than the hill which supported it; and it was the last of the snow which was destroyed that summer by the sun. This is said for those who, humbling themselves, become exalted.

C. A. 76a]

1275

Avēdo jl ciedro desiderio di fare uno bello e grāde frutto ²in nella sommità · di sé lo mise in essecutione cō tutte le ³forze del suo omore ·; jl quale frutto cresciuto · fu cagione ⁴di fare declinare la eleuata e diritta cima.

⁵Il persico avēdo · jvidia alla grā quātità de' fru⁶tti visti fare al noce suo vicino, deliberato fare ⁷jl simile ·, si caricò de' sua in modo tale che 'l peso ⁸di detti frutti lo tirò diradicato e rotto alla piana ⁹terra.

The citron, being desirous of producing a fine and noble fruit at its summit, set to work to form it with all the strength of its sap. But this fruit, when grown, was the cause of the tall and upright tree-top being bent over.

The peach, being envious of the vast quantity of fruit which she saw borne on the nut-tree, her neighbour, determined to do the same, and loaded herself with her own in such a way that the weight of the fruit pulled her up by the roots and broke her down to the ground.

Fables on plants (1275-9).

11. fine chō . . e volento. 13. tonare. 14. chostretta . . le mācare. 15. cholla . . chō. 16. [si cō uerti] in . . lassciā. 17. issplendevole ellūga . . belleza.
1274. 1. pocha. 2. apichata . . somita. 3. chollochato soprapra lasstrema. 4. teza . . rachol. 5. lamaginatione chomīcio chon. 6. chonsiderare. 7. givdichata. 8. picciola drama. 9. locho essoportare che tante. 10. quanto . . veduta po stia. 11. pocha. 12. nomerta questa alteza. 13. pichola . . chonosscie. 14. chon. 16. disfacte ecquesto interuene. 19. chōueniēte. 20. chomīciata . . rotāto. 21. dell . . spiagie . . quato. 22. imodo. 23. sopra ī cole. 24. grādeza. 25. effu. 26. chessa umiliani.
1275. 2. inella somita . . mise aseguitione chō tuttalla. 3. frutto "crescivto" fu chagione. 5. persicho. 6. diliberato. 7. charicho . . imodo. 8. diradichato. 9. tere.

[10]Il noce mostrādo sé per vna strada ai viā-danti [11]la richezza de' sua frutti, ogni omo lo lapidaua.

[12]Il fico stādo sanza frutti, nessuno lo riguar-dava; [13]volendo col fare essi frutti essere laudato dali o[14]mini ·, fu da quelli piegato · e rotto.

The nut-tree stood always by a road-side dis-displaying the wealth of its fruit to the passers-by, and every one cast stones at it.

The fig-tree having no fruit, no one looked at it; then, wishing to produce fruits that it might be praised by men, it was bent and broken down by them.

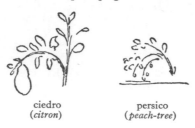

ciedro   persico   noce   fico   fico   olmo
(*citron*)   (*peach-tree*)   (*nut-tree*)   (*fig-tree*)   (*fig-tree*)   (*elm-tree*)

[15]Stando il fico vicino all' olmo ·, e riguardan-do i sua [16]rami essere · sanza frutti e avere ardimēto [17]di tenere il sole · a sua · acerbi fichi cō rā[18]pognie gli disse : o olmo ·, non ài tu vergognia a [19]starmi dināzi? ma aspetta · che mia figlioli sieno [20]in matura · età, e vedrai dove ti troverai! i quali [21]figlioli poi maturati, capi-tādovi una squadra [22]di soldati, fu da quelli per torre i sua fichi tutto lacera[23]to · e diramato e rotto; il quale stādo poi così [24]storpiato delle sue mēbra ·, l'olmo lo dimādò diciē[25]do: o fico quāto era il meglio a stare sanza figlioli [26]che per quelli venire in sì miserabile stato!

The fig-tree, standing by the side of the elm and seeing that its boughs were bare of fruit, yet that it had the audacity to keep the sun from its own unripe figs said to it reprovingly: 'O elm, are you not ashamed to stand in front of me? But wait till my offspring are fully grown and you will see where you are!' But when her offspring were mature, a troop of soldiers coming by fell upon the fig-tree and her figs were all torn off her, and her boughs cut away and broken. Then, when she was thus maimed in all her limbs, the elm asked her, saying: 'O fig-tree, how much better was it to be without offspring, than to be brought by them into so miserable a plight?'

S. K. M. III. 47*b*]   1276

La piāta si dole del palo [2]secco e vechio che se l'era [3]posto al lato e de' pali [4]secchi che la circūdano;
[5]L'ū lo mātiene diritto, [6]l'altro lo guarda dalla [7]triste cōpagnia.

The plant complains of the old and dry stick which stands by its side and of the dry stakes that surround it.

One keeps it upright, the other keeps it from low company.

C. A. 67*a*]   1277

FAVOLA

[2]Trovādosi la noce essere della cornacchia [3]portata · sopra vn alto · campanile, e' per [4]vna fessura, doue cadde, fu liberata · dal mortale [5]suo becco; pregò · esso muro · [6] per quella · gratia che Dio li aveva dato · del essere tanto [7]eminēte · e magnio · e ricco di si belle cāpane e di tā[8]to · onorevole · suono · che la douesse soccorrere; perchè [9]poi ch'ella non avea potuta cadere sotto [10]i verdi rami del suo vechio · padre ·, e essere nella gras[11]sa terra, ricoperta dalle sue ca-dēti foglie ·, che non la [12]volesse lui abandonare ·,

A FABLE

A nut, having been carried by a crow to the top of a tall campanile and released by falling into a chink from the mortal grip of its beak, it prayed the wall by the grace bestowed on it by God in allowing it to be so high and thick, and to own such fine bells and of so noble a tone, that it would succour it, and that, as it had not been able to fall under the verdurous boughs of its venerable father and lie in the fat earth covered up by his fallen leaves, it would not abandon it; because, finding itself in the beak

10. mostādo.   11. richeza . . frutto.   12. ficho.   13. chol . . frutte . . laudato.   15. ficho.   17. acerbi [fra] fichi chō.   18. dise hoholmo . . ha.   19. aaspetta.   20. imatura . . vederai.   21. chapitādovi . . sguadra.   22. queli pertore i sua.   23. chosi. 25. do h''o'' ficho.   26. queli.
1276. 2. secho.   3. ede pa\\\\\\.   4. sechi chello.
1277. 2. della chornachia.   3. [essere] portato . . chanpanile.   4. chade.   5. [becho] suo becho prego . . mvro [chella ricieta].   7. richo . . chāpane.   8. honorevole sono . . douessi sochorere.   9. poichela non era pututa chadere.   10. nella gra.   11. tera richoperto delle . . chadēti . . nola.   12. volessi.

jnperoch' ella, trovădosi [13]nel fiero becco della · fiera cornacchia, [14]votò, che scappădo da essa voleua finire la ui[15]ta · sua · in un piccolo buco; Alle quali parole [16]il mvro ·, mosso · a cōpassione, · fu cōtento riciettar[17]la nel loco ov' era caduta ·; e infra poco tēpo [18]la noce cominciò aprirsi e mettere le radici infra [19]le fessure delle pietre ·, e quelle allargare, e gitta[20]re i rami fori della sua · caverna ·; e quegli [21]in brieve leuati sopra lo edifitio, e ingrossate le [22]ritorte radici, cominciò aprire i mvri e ca[23]cciare le antiche pietre de' loro · uechi lochi; allo[24]ra il muro · tardi e indarno pianse · la cagione del suo danno; [25]e in breve aperto, rovinò grā parte delle sua mēbre.

of the cruel crow, it had there made a vow that if it escaped from her it would end its life in a little hole. At these words the wall, moved to compassion, was content to shelter it in the spot where it had fallen; and after a short time the nut began to split open and put forth roots between the rifts of the stones and push them apart, and to throw out shoots from its hollow shell; and, after a short time, these rose above the building, and the twisted roots, growing thicker, began to thrust the walls apart and tear out the ancient stones from their old places. Then the wall too late and in vain bewailed the cause of its destruction, and thrust apart in a short time, it wrought the ruin of a great part of it.

C. A. 67a]   1278

FAVOLA

[2]Il rovistico ·, sendo stimolato nelli sua sottili · rami ripieni di novelli [3]frutti dai pugnēti artigli e becco · delle inportune merle, si do[4]leva cō pietoso · ramarichio · īuerso essa · merla, pregando quella [5]che, poichè lei li toglieva · e sua diletti · frutti, il meno non le privasse [6]delle foglie, le quali lo difendevano · dai cociēti · razzi del sole, e che coll' a[7]cute vnghie non la scortīcasse e suestisse della · sua renera · pelle; [8]Alla quale la merla con villane rāpognie rispose: o taci salua[9]tico · sterpo ·! nō sai che la natura t'à fatto produrre · questi frutti [10]per mio notrimēto? nō uedi che sei al mōdo per servirmi di tale cibo? [11]nō sai, vilano ·, che tu · farai in nella prossima īuernata notri[12]mēto e cibo del fuoco · ? le quali parole ascoltate da l'albero [13]patiētemēte, nō sanza lacrime ·, jnfra poco tenpo, il merlo preso [14]dalla ragnia, e colti de' rami per fare gabbia per īcarcerare esso merlo [15]toccò infra l'altri rami al sottile rovistrico a fare legni vinimi [16]della gabbia, le quali vedēdo essere causa della persa libertà del merlo, [17]rallegratasi mosse tale parole: O merlo · io sono qui non ācora [18]consumata, come dicievi, dal foco; prima vedrò te prigione, che tu me brusiata.

A FABLE

The privet, feeling its tender boughs, loaded with young fruit, pricked by the sharp claws and beak of the insolent blackbird, complained to the blackbird with piteous remonstrance entreating it that since she stole its delicious fruits it should at least not deprive it of the leaves with which it preserved them from the burning rays of the sun, and that she should not divest it of its tender bark by scratching it with her sharp claws. To which the blackbird replied with angry upbraiding: 'O, be silent, uncultured shrub! Do you not know that Nature made you produce these fruits for my nourishment; do you not see that you are in the world [only] to serve me as food; do you not know, base creature, that next winter you will be food and prey for the fire?' To which words the tree listened patiently, and not without tears. After a short time the blackbird was taken in a net and boughs were cut to make a cage in which to imprison her. Branches were cut, among others, from the pliant privet, to serve for the plaited twigs of the cage; and seeing herself to be the cause of the blackbird's loss of liberty it rejoiced and spoke as follows: 'O blackbird, I am here, and not yet burnt by fire as you said. I shall see you in prison before you see me burnt.'

FAVOLA

[20]Vedendo ·il lavro · e mirto · tagliare il pero ·, con alta voce [21]gridarono: O pero ·, ove vai · tu? ov' è la superbia che aveui quādo [22]avevi · i tua · maturi · frutti? ora nō ci farai · tu ōbra [23]colle tue · folte chiome ·; Allora · il pero · rispose: io ne vo [24]coll' agricola che mi taglia e mi porterà alla bottega d'ottimo [25]scultore, il quale mi farà con

A FABLE

The laurel and the myrtle seeing the pear-tree cut down cried out with a loud voice: 'O pear-tree! Whither are you going? Where is the pride you had when you were covered with ripe fruits? Now you will no longer shade us with your mass of leaves.' Then the pear-tree replied: 'I am going with the husbandman who has cut

13. becho .. chorna chia chella si.   14. boto [v] che schāpado.   15. nvn piciolo buso.   16. chōpassione .. chōtento.   17. nelocho .. chaduta .. pocho.   18. chomīcio.   19. ecquelle.   20. chaverna.   21. ingrosate.   24. tardi | ''e indarno'' pianse .. dano. 25. brieve apero rovino.
1278. Irovisstrice.   3. pugiēti .. becho.   4. chō .. ramarichio.   5. poichellei .. meno nolle [togliessi] privasse.   6. dele .. razi .. cholla. 7. chute .. non ischortichasse dissuestissi .. pella.   8. Ala .. chon vilani rāgognie.   9. tichostrepo .. fatti produre.   10. chesse. 11. inela.   12. foco .. quali [dopo pi] parole ascholdate.   13. pocho.   14. dala .. cholti .. gabia .. ichacierare.   15. stocho .. rouisericho affare lenimini.   16. dela gabia .. chaua.   17. ralegratasi .. i sono .. āchora.   18. chonsumata chome .. focho .. vedero. . chettu.   20. chon.   22. hora.   23. chole .. focie.   24. cholagrichola.   25. chon.

su' arte pigliare la forma [26]di Giove · Idio , e sarò dedicato nel tenpio · e dagli omini [27]adorato · invece di Giove; e tu ti metti ī pūto a rimanere [28]spesso storpiata · e pelata de' tua rami, i quali mi sieno [29]da li omini per onorarmi poste d'intorno.

me down and who will take me to the workshop of a good sculptor who by his art will make me take the form of Jove the god; and I shall be dedicated in a temple and adored by men in the place of Jove, while you are bound always to remain maimed and stripped of your boughs, which will be placed round me to do me honour.

FAVOLA

[31]Vedēdo jl castagnio · l'vomo · sopra · il fico, il quale piegava [32]inverso sé i sua rami e di quelli spiccava · i maturi frutti · i quali mette[33]va nell'aperta bocca difaciēdoli e disertādoli coi duri dēti, crollā[34]do · i lunghi rami, e' cō tumultevole mormorio disse: [35]O fico · quāto sei tu mē di me obbligato alla natura ·! vedi come [36]in me ordinò · serrati · i mia dolci figlioli ·, prima vestiti di sottile ca[37]micia, sopra la quale è posta la dura e foderata pelle ·, e nō cō[38]tētandosi di tanto benificarmi · ch'ell' à fatto loro la forte abi[39]tatione, e sopra quella fondò acute · e folte · spine ·, aciochè le [40]mani dell' omo · nō mi possino nvocere ·; Allora il fico comī[41]ciò insieme coi sua figlioli a ridere, e ferme le risa disse: [42]conosci l'omo essere di tale ingiegnio che lui ti sappi col[43]le pertiche e pietre e sterpi, tratti infra i tua rami, farti povero [44]de' tua frutti, e quelli caduti posta coi piedi o coi sassi, in modo [45]che i frutti tua escino stracciati e storpiati fora dell' armata [46]casa; e io sono cō diligiēza tocco dalle mani, e nō come te da bastoni e da sassi e ....

A FABLE

The chestnut, seeing a man upon the fig-tree, bending its boughs down and pulling off the ripe fruits, which he put into his open mouth, destroying and crushing them with his hard teeth, it tossed its long boughs and with a noisy rustle exclaimed: 'O fig! How much less are you protected by nature than I. See how in me my sweet offspring are set in close array; first clothed in soft wrappers over which is the hard but softly lined husk; and not content with taking this care of me, and having given them so strong a shelter, on this she has placed sharp and close-set spines so that the hand of man cannot hurt me.' Then the fig-tree and her offspring began to laugh and having laughed she said: 'You know man to be of such ingenuity that with rods and stones and stakes flung up among your branches he will bereave you of your fruits; and when they are fallen, he will trample them with his feet or with stones, so that your offspring will come out of their armour crushed and maimed; while I am touched carefully by their hands, and not like you with sticks and stones and . . . .'

C. A. 67a]   1279

Il misero · salice trovādosi nō potere fruire [2]il piacere di uedere i sua · sottili · rami · fare over [3]cōdurre · alla · desiderata · grandezza e dirizzarsi al cielo per cagione · della [4]vite · e di qualunche piāta · li era uicina ·, senpre elli [5]era · storpiato · e diramato; e guasto; e raccolte · in sé tutti li spiri[6]ti · e' con quelli apre e spalanca · le porte alla [7]imaginatione ·; e stando · in cōtinva · cogitatione ·, e ricier[8]cando · con quella · l'universo · delle piāte, cō quale [9]di quelle · esso collegare · si potesse che · non avesse biso[10]gnio · dell' aivto · de' sua · legami; e stando · alquanto · in questa [11]nutritiva · imaginatione ·, cō subito assa[12]limēto li corse · nel pensiero · la zucca ·, e crollato tutti i ra[13]mi · per grāde · allegrezza · pare li · avere trovato cōpa[14]gnia · al suo · desiato · proposito, imperochè quella è piv atta [15]a legare · altri che

The hapless willow, finding that she could not enjoy the pleasure of seeing her slender branches grow or attain to the height she wished, or point to the sky, because, for the sake of the vine and any trees that grew near, she was always maimed and lopped and spoiled, brought all her spirits together and by this means opened wide the portals of her imagination and remaining in continual meditation and seeking, in the world of plants, for one wherewith to ally herself which had no need of the help of her withes. Having stood for some time in this prolific imagination, with a sudden flash the gourd presented itself to her thoughts, and tossing all her branches with extreme delight, it seemed to her that she had found the companion suited to her purpose, because the gourd is more apt to bind others than to need binding; having

---

26. essaro dedichato. 27. ettu. 28. ispeso. 31. chastagno . . ficho. 32. "in verso se" i sua . . isspichava . . frutti quelli i quali. 33. bocha . . choi. 34. chōtemultevole. 35. ficho . . settu · obrigato . . chome. 36. ime . . serati . . cha. 37. chō. 38. benificharmi . . la [spinosa] abi. 39. achute effolte . . aciochelle. 40. aloro il ficho chomī. 41. choi . . dise. 42. cho chonosci . . sapicho. 44. queli chaduti posta cho . . chosassi. 45. chefrutti . . straciati. 46. chasa . . chō . . tocho . . chome te "da bastoni e".

1279. 1. trovādosi [ognino] nō. 3. condure . . grandeza | "e dirizarsi al cielo" per chagione. 4. vite ·[d]e . . visina. 5. diramato | "e guasto" e racholte . . lisspi. 6. chon . . esspalancha. 7. chōtinva. 8. chando chon . . chō. 9. di qule . . chollegare si potessi [la quale] "che" non avessi. 10. gni . . esta "do" alquanto. 11. [imaginatione] notritiva. 12. zucha e chrollato. 13. allegreza . . chōpa. 14. disiato . . iperochecquella. 15. allegare . . legata [e per ato la sschaza].

essere · legata; [16]e fatta tal diliberatione rizzò i sua rami in uerso il cielo aspettando [17]qualche amiche-vole · vcciello, che li fusse a tal disiderio mezzano; [18]jfra quali · veduta · a sé vicina · la sgazza disse inverso [19]di quella: o giētile vcciello ·, per quello · soccorso [20]che a questi giorni da mattina · ne' mia rami trovasti, [21]quādo · l'affamato, crudele e rapace falcone ti voleva diuorare, [22]e pcr quelli · riposi che sopra me spesso ài [23]vsato · quādo · [24]l'ali tue · a te · riposo chiedeano ·, e per quelli piacie[25]ri che infra detti mia rami scherzādo colle tue cōpagnie [26]ne' · tua · amori già ài vsato, jo ti priego · che tu truovi [27]la zucca ·, e inpetri da quella alquāte delle sue semēze; [28]e dì a quelle · che, nate · ch' elle · fieno ·, ch'io le tratterò no[29]n altramēte · che se del mio corpo · gienerate l'auessi; [30]e similmēte vsa tutte quelle parole, che di simile intē[31]tione persuasiue · sieno, benchè a te, maestra de' linguag[32]gi, insegniare · non biso-gnia ·; e se questo [33]farai, io sono · cōtēta di ricie-uere il tuo nidio sopra [34]il nascimēto de' mia · rami · insieme colla tua fa[35]miglia sanza paga-mēto d'alcū fitto ·; Allora la sgaz[36]za · fatto · e fermato alquāti capitoli di novo col salice, e mas[37]sima che biscie o faine sopra sé mai non accettasse, [38]alzato la coda e bassato · la testa e gittatasi dal ramo [39]rēde il suo · peso · all' ali, e quelle battēdo sopra [40]la fugitiva · aria ·, ora qua, ora in là curiosamēte col timō della coda [41]dirizzādosi ·, peruēñe · a vna zucca, e cō bel saluto [42]e alquāte bone parole inpetrò le dimand-date semēze; [43]e condottele al salice fu con lieta ciera ricevuta; [44]e raspato alquāto coi piè il terreno vicino al salicie, [45]col becco in cierchio a esso essi · grani · piātò ·, li quali [46]in brieve tēpo · cresciēdo · comīciarono collo accresci-mēto · e aprimēto de' sua [47]rami · a occupare · tutti · i rami del salice, e colle sue [48]grā foglie · a toglierle · la bellezza del sole e del cielo ·; e nō [49]bastādo · tāto male, seguēdo le zucche comī-ciarono, per discō[50]scio peso, a tirare le cime de' teneri rami inverso la te[51]rra con strane tor-ture e disagio di quelli.

[52]Allora scuotēdosi, e indarno crollandosi per fare da sé esse zuche cadere, e indarno [53]vaneg-giando alquāti giorni · in simile inganno ·, perchè la bona e forte collegatione tal [54]pēsieri

come to this conclusion she straightened her branches towards heaven, awaiting some friendly bird who should be the mediator of her wishes. Among the rest seeing near to her the magpie she said to him: 'O gentle bird! By the refuge which you found during these days in the morning among my branches, when the hungry, cruel, and rapacious falcon wanted to devour you, and by that repose which you have always found in me when your wings craved rest, and by the pleasure you have enjoyed among my boughs, when playing with your companions while making love—I entreat you to find the gourd and obtain from her some of her seeds, and tell her that those that are born of them I will treat exactly as though they were my own offspring; and in this way use all such words as are of the same persuasive purport; though, indeed, since you are a master of language, there is no need for me to teach you. And if you will do me this service I shall be happy to have your nest in the fork of my boughs, and all your family without payment of any rent.' Then the magpie, having made and confirmed certain new stipulations with the willow—and principally that she should never admit upon her any snake or polecat, cocked his tail, and put down his head, and flung himself from the bough, throwing his weight upon his wings; and these beating the fleeting air, now here, now there, bearing about inquisitively, while his tail served as a rudder to steer him, he came to a gourd; then with a handsome bow and a few polite words, he obtained the required seeds, and carried them to the willow, who received him with cheerful looks. And when he had scraped away with his foot the earth near the willow, he planted the grains round about her in a circle with his beak. These in a short time began to grow, and the branches by increasing and opening out began to take up all the boughs of the willow, while their broad leaves deprived it of the beauty of the sun and sky. And not content with so much evil, the gourds next began, by their rude weight, to drag the ends of the tender shoots down towards the earth, with strange twisting and discomfort.

Then, being much annoyed, she shook herself in vain to throw off the gourd. After raving for some days in such plans vainly, because the

16. [chelli piāti di] effatte .. diliberatione | "rizo isua rami iuerso il cielo" attēde asspettare. 17. chelli fussi .. mezano. 18. asse .. lassgaza disse iver. 19. vciello [jo ti priego] per .. sochorso. 20. acquessti .. ine. 21. lafamato falchone | "crudele he." 22. [etti priego] "e" per .. sopra [inparani] speso. 23. quādo [i nervi "motori delle tue" istāchi nō poteano piv menare]. 24. [le tue alie] lalie | "tue" atte. 25. re che .. cholle .. chōpagnie. 26. amorigia .. chettu. 27. zucha .. inpretri dacquella. 28. ediacquelle .. lettrattero. 29. altremēti chesse .. chorpo .. lauessi [essi]. 30. essimilmēte. 31. atte .. lingua. 32. ne bisognia essecquesto [seruitio ni]. 33. chōtēta. 34. nasscimēto .. cholla. 35. lassga. 36. fatto "effermi" alquāti .. novo \\\ chol .. e ma. 37. bissie offaine .. acciettassi. 38. del rarmo. 39. ecquelle. 40. ora illa "curiosamēte" cho. 41. dirizādosi .. zucha echo .. dimadate. 43. chondottele .. cho lieto ciera. 44. rasspato .. copie il tereno. 45. chol becho iciercho [al salice ¶ esse] "a esso" grani .. le. 46. cresciēdo .. chollo "accresscimēto he a" primēto. 47. ochupare .. cholle. 48. attorle la belleza. 49. bastādo .. zuche comīcie per discō. 50. attirare .. inver la. 51. chon istrane. Lines 52-4 are written on the margin. 52. scon tēdossi .. crollados̄i .. dasse .. chadere. 53. vanegiādo .. ingano .. efforte chollegatione. 54. acquello .. ecquello.

negava, vedēdo passare il uēto ·, a quello raco-
mādādosi, e quello soffiò forte; Allora s'a[55]perse
il uechio e voto gābo del salice in 2 parti insino
[56]alle sue radici; e caduto in 2 parti indarno
pianse sé me[57]desimo, e conobbe che era nato
per non aver mai bene.

grasp of the gourds was so sure and firm as
to forbid such thoughts, seeing the wind come
by it commended itself to him. The wind blew
hard and opened the old and hollow stem of the
willow in two down to the roots, so that it fell
into two parts. In vain did it bewail itself,
recognizing that it was born to no good end.

56. radice.   57. conobe.

III

JESTS AND TALES

1280

FACIETIA

[2]Andãdo vn prete per la sua parrochia il sabato santo, dãdo [3]come vsanza l'acqua bene-detta per le case, capitò nella stãza [4]d'ũ pittore, doue spargiẽdo essa acqua sopra alcuna sua pittu[5]ra esso pittore voltosi indirieto, alquãto crucciato; dis[6]se perchè faciesse tale spargimẽto sopra le sue pitture; allora [7]il prete disse, essere così vsanza, e ch'era suo debito il fare [8]così, e che facieva bene, e chi fa bene debbe aspettare be[9]ne e meglio, che così promettea Dio, e che d'ogni bene, che si [10]facieva in terra, se n'avrebbe di sopra per ogni vn 100; allora [11]il pittore, aspettato ch'egli uscisse fori, se li fecie di sopra [12]alla finestra, e gittò vn grã sechione d'acqua adosso a esso [13]prete, diciẽdo: ecco che di sopra ti uiene per ogni v̄ 100, come [14]tu diciesti ·, che accaderebbe del bene che mi facievi colla [15]tua acqua santa, colla quale m'ài guasto mezze le mie [16]pitture.

A JEST

A priest, making the rounds of his parish on Easter Eve, and sprinkling holy water in the houses as is customary, came to a painter's room, where he sprinkled the water on some of his pictures. The painter turned round, somewhat angered, and asked him why this sprinkling had been bestowed on his pictures; then said the priest that it was the custom and his duty to do so, and that he was doing good; and that he who did good might look for good in return, and indeed, for better, since God had promised that every good deed that was done on earth should be rewarded a hundredfold from above. Then the painter, waiting till he went out, went to an upper window and flung a large pail of water on the priest's back, saying: 'Here is the reward a hundredfold from above, which you said would come from the good you had done me with your holy water, by which you have damaged half my pictures.'

1281

[Il uino cõsumato dallo [2]ubriaco, esso vino col beuitore si vẽdica.]

When wine is drunk by a drunkard, that wine is revenged on the drinker.

1282

[8]Trovãdosi il uino, divino licore dell' uua, in vna [9]avrea · e ricca tazza sopra la tavola di Ma[10]vmetto, e mõtato · in gloria di tã[11]to onore, subito fu assaltato · da vna · cõtraria [12]cogita-tione · diciẽdo · a sé · medesimo: che foi' ? Di che [13]mi rallegro · io? Non m'avvedo · essere vicino alla [14]mia morte? E lasciare l'aurea abitazione de[15]lla tazza · e entrare in nelle brutte e fetide caverne [16]del corpo vmano · e lì trasmv-tarmi di odorife[17]ro e suave · licore · in brutta e trista orina? E nõ [18]bastãdo tãto male · ch'io ancora deba si lũga[19]mẽte · giacere · ne' brutti ricettacoli coll' altra [20]fetida e corrotta materia, vscita dalle vmane inte[21]riora? Gridò inverso · il cielo, chiedẽdo [22]vẽdetta di tanto danno,

Wine, the divine juice of the grape, finding it-self in a golden and richly wrought cup on the table of Mahomet, was puffed up with pride at so much honour; when suddenly it was struck by a contrary reflection, saying to itself: 'What am I about, that I should rejoice, and not per-ceive that I am now near to my death and shall leave my golden abode in this cup to enter into the foul and fetid caverns of the human body, and to be transmuted from a fragrant and delicious liquor into foul and base urine. Nay, and as though so much evil as this were not enough, I must for a long time lie in hideous receptacles, together with other fetid and cor-rupt matter, cast out from human intestines.'

1280. 4. hessa acq. 5. scrucciato di. 6. faciessi. 8. asspettare. 9. chessi. 10. narebbe. 11. asspettato chelli vsscissi. 13. echo. 14. acaderebbe. 15. cholla .. meze.
1281. 1. chõsumato. 2. ibriaco .. chol .. vendicha.
1282. 1. [Il uino vedendosi "nelle partimaumettane" ogni giorno · dai beuitori. 2. essere messo inelle fasstidiose brudella e chõuer. 3. tito in urina e diaciere "lu gamẽte" poi nei brutti e pu. 4. zolenti lochi · dilibero adoperare [i sua spiriti]. 5. [u] ogni sua forza [ara] al riparo di tãta. 6. nefanda vilta . e trovãdosi sopra la tavola di. 7. mavmetto nvna richa e bella]. 8. trovãdosi [il] il uino. 9. richacha taza. 10. groria. 11. honore. 12. cheffo i di che. 13. nomavedo. 14. ellasciare. 15. taza .. inelle .. effetide chaverne. 16. ellisstrassmvtarmi. 17. essuave .. ettrista. 18. basstãdo .. anchora. 19. diasiere ine .. riciettacholi choll. 20. fitidae chor"o"tta .. vsscita delle. 22. danno [allora giove fecie].

²³e che si ponesse ora mai fine a tāto dispregio, ²⁴che, poichè quello paese producea le piv belle ²⁵e migliori · uve di tutto · l'altro mōdo, che al meno ²⁶esse non fussino · in vino cōdotte; allora Giove fece ²⁷che 'l bevuto · vino · da Mavmetto eleuò l'anima sua ²⁸inverso · il cielabro ·, e quello · in modo cōtaminò che ²⁹lo fecie · matto ·, e partorì tanti errori che, torna³⁰to in sé, fecie legge che nessuno · Asiatico bevesse ³¹vino ·; e furono lasciate poi libere le uiti coi sua frutti.

³²Già il uino, ³³entrato nel³⁴lo stomaco, co-³⁵mincia a bo³⁶llire e sgōfia³⁷re; già l'ani³⁸ma di quello ³⁹comincia a abā⁴⁰donare il cor⁴¹po; già si volta ⁴²inverso il cie⁴³lo; trova il cie⁴⁴labro ·, cagione ⁴⁵della diuisione ⁴⁶dal suo corpo; ⁴⁷già lo comincia ⁴⁸a cōtaminare ⁴⁹e farlo furia⁵⁰re a modo di ma⁵¹tto; già fa in⁵²riparabili erro⁵³ri, ammazzādo i su⁵⁴a amici.

And it cried to Heaven, imploring vengeance for so much insult, and that an end might henceforth be put to such contempt; and that, since that country produced the finest and best grapes in the whole world, at least they should not be turned into wine. Then Jove made that wine drunk by Mahomet to rise in spirit to his brain; and that in so deleterious a manner that it made him mad, and gave birth to so many follies that when he had recovered himself, he made a law that no Asiatic should drink wine, and henceforth the vine and its fruit were left free.

As soon as wine has entered the stomach it begins to ferment and swell; then the spirit of that man begins to abandon his body, rising as it were skywards, and the brain finds itself parting from the body. Then it begins to degrade him, and make him rave like a madman, and then he does irreparable evil, killing his friends.

S. K. M. III. 34b]   1283

Vno · artigiano andando ²spesso a visitare vno signiore ³sanza · altro · proposito dimādare ⁴al quale, jl signore domandò ⁵quello · che · andava faciēdo? ⁶questo · disse che veniua lì ⁷per avere · de' piacieri che lui ⁸aver nō potea; perrò che lui ⁹volentieri vedeua omi¹⁰ni piv potenti di lui, come ¹¹fanno i popolani, ma che 'l si¹²gnore non potea · vedere se ¹³non omini di mē possa di lui; ¹⁴per questo i signori māca¹⁵vano d'esso piacere.

An artisan often going to visit a great gentleman without any definite purpose, the gentleman asked him what he did this for. The other said that he came there to have a pleasure which his lordship could not have; since to him it was a satisfaction to see men greater than himself, as is the way with the populace; while the gentleman could only see men of less consequence than himself; and so lords and great men were deprived of that pleasure.

C. A. 150b]   1284

Vsano i frati minori a cierti tempi alcune loro quaresime, nelle quali essi non māgiano carne ne' lor cōuēti, ²ma in viaggio, perchè essi viuono di limosine ·, ànno liciētia di māgiare · ciò che è posto loro innāzi; ōde abattē³dosi in detti viaggi una coppia d'essi frati a vn' osteria · in cōpagnia d'ū cierto · mercantuolo ·, il quale essendo ⁴a vna medesima mēsa, alla quale · nō fu portato per la pouertà dell' osteria altro che vn pollastro cotto; ōde es⁵so mercātuolo, vedendo questo essere poco per lui, si uolse a essi frati e disse: se io ho bē ⁶di ricordo ·, voi nō māgiate in tali dì ne' vostri cōuēti · d'alcuna maniera di carne; alle quali parole i fra⁷ti furono costretti per la regola sanza altre cavillationi · a dire ciò essere la uerità ·; ōde il mercā-tetto ⁸ebbe il suo desiderio, e così si māgiò essa pollastra, e i frati fecero il meglio poterono ·; ora dopo tale desinare ⁹questi cōmēsari si partirono tutti e 3 di conpagnia ·, e dopo alquanto di uiagio, trovati vn fiume di bona

Franciscan begging friars are wont, at certain times, to keep fasts, when they do not eat meat in their convents. But on journeys, as they live on charity, they have licence to eat whatever is set before them. Now a couple of these friars on their travels stopped at an inn, in company with a certain merchant, and sat down with him at the same table, where, from the poverty of the inn, nothing was served to them but a small roast chicken. The merchant, seeing this to be but little even for himself, turned to the friars and said: 'If my memory serves me, you do not eat any kind of flesh in your convents at this season.' At these words the friars were compelled by their rule to admit, without cavil, that this was the truth; so the merchant had his wish and ate the chicken, and the friars did the best they could. After dinner the messmates departed, all three together, and after travelling some distance they came to a river of some width and depth. All three being on foot—the friars

---

23. ponessi . . attāto disspregio. 24. paesse. 25. migliore . . il meno. 26. elle non . . chōdotte. 27. beuto. 28. ecquello imodo. 29. chettorna. 30. legie . . assiaticho beessi. 31. effunassciato . . libere . . cosua. 34. o stomaco. 36. esscōfia. 47. cia lo comincia a. 49. effarlo. 52. ero. 53. amazādo.
1283. 6. quessto. 7. chellui. 8. perochello. 9. ivollentieri. 11. fano.
1284. 1. tenpi. 2. uiagio . . uiuano . . che he posto. 3. viagi una "copia" dessi . . mecantuolo. 4. polostro . . ōdehe. 5. merchantuolo. 5. hessere pocho. 7. alte gavillationi a direco essere. 8. ebe . . chosisi . . frati feciono il meglio poterone · ore dopo. 9. chonpagnia.

[10]larghezza e profondità ·, essendo tutti 3 a piedi, i frati per pouertà e l'altro per auaritia ·, fu neciessario per l'uso [11]della cōpagnia che vno de' frati, essendo scalzi ·, passasse sopra i sua omeri esso mercātuolo ·; onde datoli [12]il frate al servo i zoccoli, si caricò di tale uomo; onde accade, che trovandosi esso frate in mezzo del [13]fiume ·, esso ancora si ricordò della sua · regola ·, e fermatosi a vso di San Cristoforo alzò la testa [14]inverso quello che l'aggravava, e disse: dimi vn poco ·, ài tu nessū dinari adosso? bē sai, rispose que[15]sto; come credete voi ch'a mia pari mercatāte andasse altramēti attorno ·? oimè, disse il frate, la nostra [16]regola vieta che noi nō possiano portare danari adosso ·! e subito lo gittò nell' acqua; la qual cosa conosciuta [17]dal mercatāte facetamēte la già fatta ingiuria essere vēdicata ·, cō piacievole uiso pacificamēte, [18]mezzo arossito per vergognia, la uēdetta sopportò.

by reason of their poverty, and the other from avarice—it was necessary by the custom of company that one of the friars, being barefoot, should carry the merchant on his shoulders: so having given his wooden shoes into his keeping, he took up his man. But it so happened that when the friar had got to the middle of the river, he again remembered a rule of his order, and stopping short, he looked up, like Saint Christopher, to the burden on his back and said: 'Tell me, have you any money about you?'—'You know I have,' answered the other, 'How do you suppose that a merchant like me should go about otherwise?' 'Alack!' cried the friar, 'our rules forbid us to carry any money on our persons,' and forthwith he dropped him into the water, which the merchant perceived was a facetious way of being revenged on the indignity he had done them; so, with a smiling face, and blushing somewhat with shame, he peaceably endured the revenge.

M. 58b]   **1285**

FACETIA

[2]Vno volendo provare coll' autorità [3]di Pitagora, come altre volte lui era [4]stato al mōdo, e vno nō li lasciava [5]finire il suo ragionamēto, allor costui [6]disse a questo tale: è per tale segniale che [7]io altre volte ci fussi stato, io mi ricor[8]do che tu eri mvlinaro; allora costui [9]sentēdosi mordere colle parole gli [10]confermò essere vero, che per questo cō[11]trassegnio lui si ricordava che questo [12]tale era stato l'asino che gli portava la [13]farina.

A JEST

A man wishing to prove, by the authority of Pythagoras, that he had formerly been in the world, while another would not let him finish his argument, the first speaker said to the second: 'It is by this token that I was formerly here: I remember that you were a miller.' The other one, feeling himself stung by these words, agreed that it was true, and that by the same token he remembered that the speaker had been the ass that carried the flour.

FACETIA

[15]Fu dimādato vn pittore perchè, facciēdo [16]lui de' figure sì belle che erā cose morte, [17]per che causa esso avesse fatti i figlioli [18]sì brutti; allora il pittore rispose che le [19]pitture le fecie di dì, e i figlioli di notte.

A JEST

A painter was asked why, since he made such beautiful figures, which were but dead things, his children were so ugly; to which the painter replied that he made his pictures by day, and his children by night.

C. A. 13a]   **1286**

Vno · vede vna grāde · spada al lato · a vn altro, e dice: o poverello ell' è grā tēpo ch'io [2]t'ò veduto · legato a questa · arme ·, perchè ·

A man saw a large sword which another one wore at his side. Said he: 'Poor fellow, for a long time I have seen you tied to that weapon; why

---

10. largeza .. tutte .. ellaltro.   11. discalzi passassi.   12. asserbo izocholi .. charicho .. homo .. imezo.   13. hesso .. richordo dela .. effermatosi .. cristofano. 14. chellagravava .. pocho .. risspose. 15. merchatāte andassi altre. 16. chenōj .. conossciuta. 17. merchatate facietamēte .. vīdichata .. pacifichamēte. 18. mezo .. soporto.
1285. 2. cholla alturita. 3. pictagora. 4. lassciava. 5. chostui. 6. acquesto. 7. ciffussi. 8. chettu .. chosstui. 9. cholle. 11. richordaua. 12. chelli. 15. pictore. 17. chausa .. auessi. 18. risspose chelle. 19. figlio.
1286. 2. acquesta .. disslegi [e sta liber] avēdo .. dissciolte.

1285. 15. This witty saying has its prototype in Macrobius, *Saturnalia* (ii. 2, p. 129, ed. Byssenhardt), accessible at Leonardo's time in its first edition, Venice, 1472. When in ancient Rome a stranger called on Lucius Mallius, painter of repute, he saw the painter's children: 'non similiter inquit—so Macrobius reports—Malli, fingis et pingis, et Mallius: in tenebris enim fingo, luce pingo.' The

story, as copied by Leonardo from Macrobius, evidently spread about, and has also been taken up by Michelangelo, whose jest about Francia's son is reported by Vasari (vii. 170). At the Renaissance time the artist's profession ranked much below that of literary men who claimed the monopoly for the revival of classical Roman culture. Therefore artists liked to show that they too had connexions there.

nõ ti disleghi, avēdo le māni disciolte, ³e possiedi libertà? la qual · costui rispose: questa è cosa · nõ tua, anzi · è vecchia; ⁴questo sentēdosi mordere ·rispose: io · ti conosco · sapere si poche cose in questo ⁵mõdo · ch'io credevo · che ogni divulgata · cosa · a te · fusse · per nova.

do you not release yourself as your hands are untied, and set yourself free?' To which the other replied: 'This is none of yours, on the contrary, it is an old story.' The former speaker, feeling stung, replied: 'I know that you are acquainted with so few things in this world that I thought any notorious thing would be new to you.'

C. A. 306b]   1287

Vno lasciò lo usare con uno · suo · amico, ²perchè · quello · spesso · li dicieva · male · delli ³amici · sua ·; Il quale · lasciato · amico · ⁴vn dì dolendosi collo amico e dopo il molto ⁵dolersi lo pregò, ch'elli · dicesse quale fusse ⁶la cagione, che lo auesse · fatto dimēticare · ⁷tanta amicitia; al quale esso · rispose: jo ⁸non voglio più usare · con teco per ⁹ch'io · ti uoglio bene ·, e non uoglio che, diciē¹⁰do tu male ad altri di me ·, tuo amico ·, che al¹¹tri abbiano, come me, a fare trista impressione ¹²di te ·, diciendo tu a quelli male di me, tuo amico; ¹³õde, non vsando noi piv insieme, parrà che noi ¹⁴siamo fatti nimici, e il dire tu male di me, com' è ¹⁵tua vsanza ·, non sarai tanto da essere biasi¹⁶mato ·, come se noi usassimo · insieme.

A man gave up his intimacy with one of his friends because he often spoke ill of his other friends. The neglected friend one day lamenting to this former friend, after much complaining, entreated him to say what might be the cause that had made him forget so much friendship. To which he answered: 'I will no longer be intimate with you because I love you, and I do not choose that you, by speaking ill of me, your friend, to others, should produce in others, as in me, a bad impression of yourself, by speaking evil to them of me, your friend. Therefore, being no longer intimate together, it will seem as though we had become enemies; and in speaking evil of me, as is your wont, you will not be blamed so much as if we continued intimate.

C. A. 76b]   1288

Vno disputãdo e vantãdosi · di sapere fare molti vari · e belli · giochi ·, vn altro de' circonstanti · disse: Io so fare ²vno gioco · il quale · farà · trarre le brache · a chi a me parirà; il primo vantatore, trovandosi sanza brache, ³disse · che a me non le farai trarre e vadane vn pajo di calze; il proponitore d'esso gioco accettato ⁴lo invito · inpromuti piv paja di brache, e trassele nel uolto · al mettitore delle calze, e vinse il pegnio.

⁵Vno disse a vn suo conosciēte: tu ài · tutti · li ochi · trasmutati · in strano · colore; Quello · li ripose interuenirli ⁶spesso, ma tu nõ ci ài posto cura;—e quãdo t'addiviē questo?—rispose l'altro: ogni volta, che mia · ochi vedono jl tuo viso ⁷strano ·, per la violenza riceuuta da si grã dispiaciere · subito s'impallidiscono · e mvtano in istrã colore;

⁸Vno disse a un altro: tu ài tutti li ochi mutati in istrã colore; Quello li rispose egli è perchè i mia ochi vedono ⁹il tuo viso strano.

¹⁰Vno disse che in suo paese · nascievano le piv strane cose del mõdo ·; l'altro rispose : tu che vi sei na¹¹to, confermi ciò esser uero · per la stranezza della tua brutta presenza.

A man was arguing and boasting that he knew many and various tricks. Another among the bystanders said: 'I know how to play a trick which will make whomsoever I like pull off his breeches.' The first man—the boaster, being without breeches—said: 'You won't make me pull off mine, and I bet you a pair of hose on it.' He who proposed the game, having accepted the offer, produced breeches and drew them across the face of him who bet the pair of hose and won the bet.

A man said to an acquaintance: 'Your eyes are changed to a strange colour.' The other replied: 'It often happens, but you have not noticed it.' 'When does it happen?' said the former. 'Every time that my eyes see your ugly face, from the shock of so unpleasing a sight they suddenly turn pale and change to a strange colour.'

A man said to another: 'Your eyes are changed to a strange colour.' The other replied: 'It is because my eyes behold your strange ugly face.'

A man said that in his country were the strangest things in the world. Another answered: 'You, who were born there, confirm this as true, by the strangeness of your ugly face.'

3. cosstui risspose. 4. rispuose . . conossco . . chose . . quessto. 5. chosa atte fussi.
1287. 1. lasscio . . amicho. 2. isspesso. 3. lassciato amicho [si do]. 4. cholla amicho. 5. diciessi . . fussi. 6. chagione chello auessi . . dimētichare. 7. risspose. 8. no . . chontecho. 9. nõno. 10. amicho. 11. abbia chome me affare trissta. 12. acquegli. 13. noi | "piv" insieme para. 14. siano . . tire tu . . chome. 15. tu. 16. chome.
1288. 1. dissputãdo . . circhustanti. 2. giocho . . trare. 3. che no disse . . nole sarai . . parodi chalze . . giocho aciettato. 4. ettrassele . . chalze. 5. chonossciēte . . trassmutati in insstrano cholore. 6. chura ecquãdo . . oni . . vegano. 7. sinpalidiscano . . cholore. 8. ellgie . . vegano. 10. nasscieva . . chose . . ui sena. 11. chonfermi . . straneza.

Triv. 40b]   1289

Dispreggiādo uno vecchio publicamēte vn giovane mostrādo auda²cemēte nō temer quello, onde il giovane li rispuose che la ³sua lūga età li facieva migliore scudo che la lingua ⁴o la forza.

An old man was publicly casting contempt on a young one, and boldly showing that he did not fear him; on which the young man replied that his advanced age served him as a better shield than either his tongue or his strength.

S. K. M. II.¹ 30b]   1290

FACIETIA

²Sendo uno infermo in articulo ³di morte, esso sentì battere la porta, ⁴e domādato vno de' sua serui chi era ⁵che batteva l'uscio, esso seruo rispose ⁶esser vna che si chiamava madoña ⁷Bona; allora l'infermo alzato le ⁸braccia al cielo ringraziò Dio con al⁹ta voce; poi disse ai serui che lasci¹⁰assino venire presto questa, accio¹¹chè potesse vedere vna donna ¹²bona iñazi che esso morisse, ¹³imperochè in sua vita mai ne vide nessuna.

A JEST

A sick man finding himself in *articulo mortis* heard a knock at the door, and asking one of his servants who was knocking, the servant went out, and answered that it was a woman calling herself Madonna Bona. Then the sick man, lifting his arms to Heaven, thanked God with a loud voice, and told the servants that they were to let her come in at once, so that he might see one good woman before he died, since in all his life he had never yet seen one.

S. K. M. II.¹ 31a]   1291

FACIETIA

²Fu detto a vno che si levasse ³dal letto, perchè già era leva⁴to il sole; E lui rispose: se ⁵io avessi a fare tanto viaggio ⁶e facende quanto lui, ancora io sarei ⁷già levato, e però avendo a fa⁸re si poco camino, ancora non ⁹mi voglio levare.

A JEST

A man was desired to rise from his bed, because the sun was already risen. To which he replied: 'If I had as far to go, and as much to do as he has, I should be risen by now; but having but a little way to go, I shall not rise yet.'

F.o]   1292

Vno vedendo vna femina parata a tener ta²vola in giostra guardò il tavolaccio e gridò ³vedendo la sua lancia: oimè quest' è troppo pic⁴col lavorante a si grā bottega.

A man, seeing a woman ready to hold up the target for a jousting-match, exclaimed, looking at the shield, and considering his spear: 'Alack! this is too small a workman for so great a business.'

1289. 1. dispregiādo l̄ vecchio .. mostrādo alda. 3. schudo chella linghua.
1290. 5. lusscie .. risspose. 6. eser .. chessi chiamav. 8. rigrazio. 9. chellasci. 11. potessi. 12. hessomorissi. 13. iperoche .. ma ne.
1291. 2. chessi levassi. 3. del .. hera. 4. Ellui. 5. affare .. viago. 6. "e facende" quanto. 7. av̄do affa. 8. anchora no. 9. mi vo levare.
1292. 2. ingostra .. tavolacco. 3. lassua .. tropo pi. 4. assi .. botteghua.

IV

PROPHECIES

C. A. 145*a*]   1293

DIUISIONE DELLA PROFETIA

²Prima delle cose degli animali razionali; secōda delli ³irrationali; 3ᵃ delle piāte, quarta delle cerimonie; ⁴quīta de' costumi; sesta delli casi overo editti, over qui⁵stioni; settima de' casi che nō possono stare ⁶in natura, come dire: di quella cosa, quāto piv ne le⁷vi piv crescie; e riserua i grādi casi ⁸inverso il fine, e deboli dà dal principio, ⁹e mostra prima i mali, e poi le punitioni ¹⁰delle cose filosofiche.

⟦Delle formiche.⟧

¹²Molti popoli fien quelli che nascōderā sé ¹³e sua figlioli, vettovaglie dentro alle oscure caverne, ¹⁴e lì nelli lochi tenebrosi ciberā sé e sua ¹⁵famiglia per molti mesi sanza altro lume accidentale o naturale.

⟦Dell' api⟧

¹⁷E a molti altri sarā tolte le mvnitioni e lor cibi, ¹⁸e crudelmēte da giēte sanza ragione saranno ¹⁹sommerse e annegate; o giustitia di Dio ²⁰perchè nō ti desti a vedere così malmenare e tua ²¹creati?

⟦Delle pecore vacche ²³e capre e simili⟧

²⁴A innumerabili saran tolti i loro piccoli figlio²⁵li e quelli scarnati ²⁶e crudelissimamēti squartati.

⟦Delle noci e vliue e ghiā²⁸de e castagnie e simili⟧

²⁹Molti figlioli da spietate bastona³⁰te fieno tolti dalle propie braccia delle lor ³¹madri e gittati in terra e poi lacerati.

⟦De' fanciulli che stanno ³³legati nelle fascie⟧

³⁴O città marine, io vedo in uoi i uostri citta-³⁵dini così femine come maschi stret³⁶tamente dai forti legami colle braccia e ganbe esser le³⁷gati da geńte che non ītenderanno i uostri

THE DIVISION OF THE PROPHECIES

First, of things relating to reasoning animals; secondly, of irrational creatures; thirdly of plants; fourthly, of ceremonies; fifthly, of manners; sixthly, of cases or edicts or disputes; seventhly, of cases that are contrary to nature, as, for instance, of those things which, the more is taken from them, the more they grow. And reserve the great matters till the end, and the small matters give at the beginning. And first show the evils and then the punishments, of philosophical things.

⟦Of Ants⟧

These will form many communities, which will hide themselves and their young ones and victuals in dark caverns, and they will feed themselves and their families in dark places for many months without any light, either artificial or natural.

⟦Of Bees⟧

And many others will be deprived of their store and their food, and will be cruelly submerged and drowned by folks devoid of reason. Oh Justice of God! Why dost thou not wake and behold thy creatures thus ill used?

⟦Of Sheep, Cows, Goats, and the like⟧

Endless multitudes of these will have their little children taken from them, ripped open and flayed, and most barbarously quartered.

⟦Of Nuts, and Olives, and Acorns, and Chestnuts, and suchlike⟧

Many offspring shall be snatched by cruel thrashing from the very arms of their mothers, and flung on the ground, and crushed.

⟦Of Children wrapped in swaddling bands⟧

O cities of the Sea! In you I see your citizens —both females and males—tightly bound, arms and legs, with strong withes by folks who will not understand your language. And you will

1293. 3. inrationali . . cirimonie. 4. sessta. 5. chasi. 6. inatura. 7. cresscie . . chasi. 9. emali. 12. queli . . nasscōderā. 13. e sue "figloli" e . . dēntro alle "osscure" caverne. 14. elli nelli. 15. famiglia "per molti mesi" sanza . . acidentale. 16. ape. 17. e amolti | "[era]" altri . . toltolte la. 18. ragone sarano. 19. gustitia. 20. dessti. 22. vache. 23. essimili. 24. invmerabili . . elloro picholi. 25. ecquelli [crudelissimamēte] scannati [essqua]. 28. essimili. 29. disspietate. 30. fietolti delle. 32. fanculli chesstano. 33. fasscie. 34. veggho . . uosstri. 35. dini [esse] cossi . . massci essere isstre. 36. dei . . cole br.

1293. Lines 1–51 are in the original written in one column, beginning with the text of l. 11. At the end of the column is the programme for the arrangement of the prophecies, placed here at the head: ll. 56–79 form a second column, ll. 80–97 a third one (see the reproduction of the text on the facsimile, Pl. CXVIII).

li³⁸guaggi, e sol ui potrete sfogare li vostri dolori e la per³⁹duta libertà mediante i lagrimosi piā⁴⁰ti e li sospiri e lamentatione infra uoi mede⁴¹simi, chè chi vi lega, non v'intenderà, nè voi loro in⁴²tenderete.

⟦Delle gatte che māgiano i topi⟧

⁴⁴A voi città dell' Africa si uedrà i uostri nati essere ⁴⁵squarciati nelle propie case da crudelissimi e ra⁴⁶paci animali del paese vostro.

⟦Delli asini bastonati⟧

⁴⁸O natura trascurata, perchè ti sei fatta ⁵⁰partiale, facciēdoti ai tua figli d'alcuna pietosa ⁵⁰e benignia madre, ad' altri crudelissima e spieta⁵¹ta matrignia? io vedo i tua figlioli esser dati in al⁵²trui seruitù sanza mai benifitio alcuno, e in lo⁵³co di remuneratione de' fatti benifitj esser pagati ⁵⁴di grādissimi martiri, e spēdere senpre la lo⁵⁵r vita in benifitio del suo malefattore.

⟦Delli omini che dormono nell' asse d'albero⟧

⁵⁷Li omini dormiranno e māgieranno e abiterāno ⁵⁸infra li alberi nelle selue e cāpagnie.

⟦Del sogniare⟧

⁶⁰Alli omini parrà vedere nel cielo nove rui⁶¹ne; parrā in quello leuarsi a uolo, e di quello fuggi⁶²re cō paura le fiamme che di lui discē⁶³dono; sentirā parlare li animali di qua⁶⁴lūche sorte in linguaggio vmano; scorre⁶⁵ranno inmediate colla lor persona ⁶⁶in diverse parti del mōdo sanza mo⁶⁷to; vedrāno nelle tenebre grādissimi ⁶⁸splēdori; o maraviglia della vmana ⁶⁹spetie qual frenesia t'à sì condotto! ⁷⁰parlerai cogli animali di qualūche spetie, ⁷¹e quelli cō teco in linguaggio vmano, ⁷²vedrati cadere di grande alture san⁷³za tuo danno; i torrēti t'accompa⁷⁴gneranno e miste ... col lor rapido corso ....

⟦De' cristiani⟧

⁸¹Molti che tengono la fede del figlio⁸²lo e sol fan tenpli nel nome ⁸³della madre.

⟦Del cibo stato animato⟧

⁸⁴Gran parte de' corpi animati ⁸⁵passerà pe' corpi degli altri animali, ⁸⁶cioè le case disabitate passerā ⁸⁷in pezzi per le case abitate, dan⁸⁸do a quella vtile, e portā⁸⁹do cō seco i sua danni; ⁹⁰cioè la uita dell' omo si fa dalle cose ⁹¹māgiate ·, le quali portā con se⁹²co la parte dell' omo ch'è morta ....

only be able to assuage your sorrows and lost liberty by means of tearful complaints and sighing and lamentation among yourselves; for those who will bind you will not understand you, nor will you understand them.

⟦Of Cats that eat Rats⟧

In you, O cities of Africa, your children will be seen quartered in their own houses by most cruel and rapacious beasts of your country.

⟦Of Asses that are beaten⟧

O indifferent Nature! Wherefore art thou so partial, being to some of thy children a tender and benignant mother, and to others a most cruel and pitiless stepmother? I see thy children given up to slavery to others, without any sort of advantage, and instead of remuneration for the good they do, they are paid with the severest suffering, and spend their whole life in benefiting their oppressor.

⟦Of Men who sleep on planks from Trees⟧

Men shall sleep, and eat, and dwell among trees, in the forests and open country.

⟦Of Dreaming⟧

Men will seem to see new destructions in the sky. The flames that fall from it will seem to rise in it and to fly from it with terror. They will hear animals of every kind speak in human language. They will instantaneously run in person in various parts of the world, without movement. They will see the greatest splendour in the midst of darkness. O! marvel of the human race! What frenzy has led you thus! You will speak with animals of every species and they with you in human speech. You will see yourself fall from great heights without any harm, and torrents will accompany you, and will mingle in their rapid course. ...

⟦Of Christians⟧

Many who hold the faith of the Son only build temples in the name of the Mother.

⟦Of Food which has been alive⟧

[84] A great portion of bodies that have been alive will pass into the bodies of other animals; that is, the deserted tenements will pass piecemeal into the inhabited ones, ministering to their needs, and carrying with them what is waste. That is to say, the life of man is formed from things eaten, and these carry with them that part of man which is dead. ...

38. essol . . issfogare li uosstri "dolori e" eper. 39. mediante [i gran pian] i lagrimosi. 40. elle i sosspiri ellamentatione. 43. māgano e topi. 44. uosstri. 46. vosstro. 47. basstonati. 48. O natura [sanza] in stacchurata perchetti seffatta. 49. dalchuna. 50. disspieta. 51. vegho. 52. alchuno eillo. 53. cho. 54. da [ere] di grādissime [bastonate] "martiri" esspēder. 56. dormā nellasse. 57. māgierano. 60. para. 61. parā . . fugi. 62. pauvra . . fiame . . disscē. 63. dano. 64. ilinguaggio. 66. parte. 68. sprēdori . . delle vmane. 69. tasi chondotto. 71. ecqueli cōtecho . . liguagio vmano [cha]. 72. chadere. 73. tataconpa. 74. gnierano e miscerate chollor rapido corso. 75. \\\\ sera car \\\\\\\\\\\\\\\\\ madressore. 76. \\\\\\\\\\\\\\\\\ erai cholli a. 77. \\\\\\\\\\\\\ ādis. 78. \\\\\\\\\\\\\\\\\\\\\\\ anime. 79. \\\\\\\\\\\\\\\\\\\\\\\ le penne. 80. crisstiani. 81. chettengo. 82. essol. 86. coe. 87. pezi . . chase. 88. acquella vntile. 89. cōsecho . . danni queste. 90. coe . . delle. 91. māgate [e] le . . chon se. 92. cho. 93. \\\\\\\\\\\\\\\\\\\\\\\ te cō ponitu. 94. \\\\\\\\\\\\\\\\\\\\\\\ elle māgano. 95. \\\\\\\\\\\\\\\\\\\\\\\\\ morte rifara. 96. \\\\\\\\\\\\\\\\\\\\\\\ ma nōne. 97. \\\\\\\\\\\\\\\\\\\\\\ [case].

l. 48 and following. Compare No. 846.

C. A. 145*b*]   1294

⟦Delli ufitj funerali ²e prociessioni e lumi ³e cãpane e cõpagnia⟧

⁴Agli omini saran fatti grandissimi ⁵onori e ponpe sanza lor saputa.

⟦Of Funeral Rites, and Processions, and Lights, and Bells, and Followers⟧

The greatest honours and ceremonies will be paid to men, without their knowledge.

C. A. 370*a*]   1295

⟦Dell' auaro⟧

²Molti fieno quelli che con ogni studio e sollecitudine seguiranno ³con furia quella cosa che senpre li à spauẽtati, nõ conosciendo la sua ⁴malignità.

⟦Of the Avaricious⟧

There will be many who will eagerly and with great care and solicitude pursue furiously that which has always terrified them, not knowing its evil nature.

⟦Delli omini che, quãto piv inuechiano, piv ⁶si fanno avari, chè auẽdosi a star poco dovrebbero farsi liberali⟧

⁷Vedansi a quelli, che son giudicati di piv speriẽtia e giuditio, quanto ⁸egli ànǹo mẽ bisognio delle cose, cõ piv auidità cercarle e riseruarle.

⟦Of men who, the older they grow, the more avaricious they become, whereas, having but little time to stay, they should become more liberal⟧

We see those who are regarded as being most experienced and judicious, when they least need a thing, seek and cherish it with more avidity.

⟦Della fossa⟧

¹¹Starã molti occupati in esercitio a leuare di quella cosa che tanto crescierà, quan¹²to se ne leuò.

⟦Of the Ditch⟧

Many will be busied in taking away from a thing, which will grow in proportion as it is diminished.

⟦Del peso posto sul piumaccio⟧

¹⁴E a molti corpi nel vedere da lor leuar la testa, si uedrà manifesta¹⁵mente crescere, e rendendo loro la leuata testa · immediatamente ¹⁶diminviścono la grãdezza.

⟦Of a Weight placed on a Feather-pillow⟧

And it will be seen in many bodies that by raising the head they swell visibly; and by laying the raised head down again, their size will immediately be diminished.

⟦Del pigliare de' pidocchi⟧

¹⁸E saran molti cacciatori d'animali che, quanto piv ne piglierãno ¹⁹mãco n'avranno, e così de conuerso piv n'avrã, quãto men ne piglie²⁰ranno.

⟦Of catching Lice⟧

And many will be hunters of animals, which, the fewer there are the more will be taken; and conversely, the more there are, the fewer will be taken.

⟦Del attignere l'acqua colle 2 sechie a vna sola corda⟧

²²E rimaranno occupati molti che quãto piv ²³tirerãno in giù la cosa, essa piv se ne fugirà in contrario ²⁴modo.

⟦Of Drawing Water in two Buckets with a single Rope⟧

And many will be busily occupied, though the more of the thing they draw up, the more will escape at the other end.

⟦Le lingue de' porci e vitelli nelle budelle⟧

²⁸O cosa spurca, che si vedrà l'uno animale aver la lingua ²⁹in culo all' altro.

⟦Of the Tongues of Pigs and Calves in Sausage-skins⟧

Oh! how foul a thing, that we should see the tongue of one animal in the guts of another.

1294. 2. ellumi. 4. sara.
1295. 2. fien"o" .. essollecitudine seguirano. 3. chessenpre. 6. fano .. asstar .. doberebõ. 7. vedanssi acquelli chesson gudichati .. guditio. 9. della fossa ⟦ della informa di frenesia o farnetico. 10. dinsania di ceruello.⟦ 11. molti "ochupati" in .. alleua"r" di .. chosa .. cresscier. 12. ta se ne leuo [ecquãto piv se ne pone piv gressere diminissce]. 13. piumacco. 14. moti corpi .. dallor .. manit \\\\\\\. 15. cresscicre .. imediate. 16. diminvissean. 17. pidochi. 18. essaran. 19. naranno .. narã. 21. dellottignier lacq"a". 22. ochupati .. piv [tirerano]. 23. trireroña in gu. 25. la salsiccia che mu nelle budelle. 26. molti si farã casa "e abiterano nelle" delle propie. 27. linguie de porci "e vitelli" nelle. 28. spurcha.

1294. A facsimile of this text is on Pl. CXVI below on the right; the writing is larger than the other notes on the same sheet and of a somewhat different style. The ink is also of a different hue, as may be seen on the original sheet at Milan.

⟦De' crivelli fatti di pelle d'animali⟧

[31]Vedrassi il cibo degli animali passar dentro alle [32]lor pelli per ogni parte salvo che per la bocca, e penetra[33]re dall' opposita parte insino alla piana terra.

⟦Delle lanterna⟧

[35]Le feroci corna de' possenti tori difenderan-[36]no la luce notturna dall' inpetuoso furor de' uĕti.

⟦Delle piume ne' letti⟧

[38]Li animali volatili sosterrā l'omini colle lor propie [39]penne.

⟦Li omini che uā sopra li alberi, ādando in zoccoli⟧

[41]Sarā si grāde i fanghi che li omini andranno sopra l'al[42]beri de' lor paesi.

⟦Delle sola delle scarpe che son di bue⟧

[44]E si uedrā in gran parte del paese caminare sopra le pelli [45]delli grandi animali.

⟦Del nauicare⟧

[47]Saranno gran venti, per li quali le cose oriĕtali si faranno occiden[48]tali, e quelli di mezzodì in grā parte miste col corso de' uĕ[49]ti seguirānolo per lunghi paesi.

⟦Delle pitture de' santi adorati⟧

[51]Parleranno li omini alli omini che non sentiranno; avrā gli (occhi) [52]aperti e nō uedranno; parleranno a quelli e nō fia loro risposta; [53]chiederā gratie a chi avrā orecchi e non ode; farā lume a chi [54]è orbo . . . .

⟦De' segatori⟧

[59]Saranno molti che si moverā l'uno [60]contra dell' altro, tenendo in mano il tagliente ferro; Questi nō si [61]faranno infra loro altro nocimĕto che di stāchezza, perchè quā[62]to l'uno si caccierà inanti, tanto l'altro si ritirerà indirieto; [63]ma trist' a chi s'inframetterà in mezzo, perchè al fine rimarrà ta[64]gliato in pezzi.

⟦Il filatoio da seta⟧

[66]Sentirassi le dolenti grida, le alte strida, [67]le rauce e infoccate vocie di quei che fieno con tormento spogliati e al fine [68]lasciati ignudi e sanza moto; e questo fia per cavsa del motore che tutto volge.

⟦Of Sieves made of the Hair of Animals⟧

We shall see the food of animals pass through their skin every way excepting through their mouths, and penetrate from the outside downwards to the ground.

⟦Of Lanterns⟧

[35] The cruel horns of powerful bulls will screen the lights of night against the wild fury of the winds.

⟦Of Feather-beds⟧

Flying creatures will give their very feathers to support men.

⟦Of Men which walk on Trees—wearing wooden Shoes⟧

The mire will be so great that men will walk on the trees of their country.

⟦Of the Soles of Shoes, which are made from the Ox⟧

And in many parts of the country men will be seen walking on the skins of large beasts.

⟦Of Sailing in Ships⟧

There will be great winds by reason of which things of the East will become things of the West; and those of the South, being involved in the course of the winds, will follow them to distant lands.

⟦Of Worshipping the Pictures of Saints⟧

Men will speak to men who hear not; having their eyes open, they will not see; they will speak to these, and they will not be answered. They will implore favours of those who have ears and hear not; they will make light for the blind . . . .

⟦Of Sawyers⟧

There will be many men who will move one against another, holding in their hands a cutting tool. But these will not do each other any injury beyond tiring each other; for when one pushes forward the other will draw back. But woe to him who comes between them! For he will end by being cut in pieces.

⟦Silk-spinning⟧

Dismal cries will be heard loud, shrieking with anguish, and the hoarse and smothered tones of those who will be despoiled, and at last left naked and motionless; and this by reason of the mover, which makes everything turn round.

---

32. bocha. 33. oposita. 35. feroce . . difendera. 38. voltatili. 40. zocholi. 41. chelli. 45. delli "grandi" animali. 47. sara . . occi \\\\. 48. ecquelle dimezodi. 51. parlerano . . ali . . sentirano . . arā gli \\\\\\. 52. nō fie lor riss. 53. aciara orechi . . lume e \\\\\\\. 54. he orbo parlerà color di cō gra \\\\\\\\\\\\\\\ ore. 55. pronossticho. 56. metti per ordine e mesi elle cirimonie chessusano e cosi fa del. 57. gorno e della notte. 59. molti [chessanza moto di piedi] si moverà [cholle br lur.] "[in altie cholle teste]". 60. chontra . . itagliente. 61. infralloro. 62. chachiera inati. 63. tristo chessinfra mezo . . rimara. 64. innpezzi. 65. dasseta. 66. dolenti grida [fatti chon diuerse voci] le. 67. rave e infiochate . . cheffieno | "con tormento" ispogliati. 68. lassciati ignudi | "e sanza moto" ecquesto . . chausa . . chettutto.

1295. 35. Lanterns were in Italy formerly made of horn.

For ll. 55–7 'Pronostico' see unrevised text at the bottom of the page.

⟦Del mettere e trarre il pan dalla bocca del forno⟧

⁷⁰Per tutte le città e terre e castelli, ville e case si uedrà, per desiderio di māgiare, trarre il ⁷¹propio cibo di bocca l'uno all' altro sanza poter fare difesa alcuna.

⟦Of putting Bread into the Mouth of the Oven and taking it out again⟧

In every city, land, castle, villa, and house, men shall be seen who for want of food will take it out of the mouths of others, who will not be able to resist in any way.

⟦Le terre lauorate⟧

⁷³Vedrassi voltare la terra sotto sopra e risguardare l'opositi ⁷⁴emisperii e scoprire le spelonche a ferocissimi animali.

⟦Of tilled Land⟧

The Earth will be seen turned upside down and facing the opposite hemispheres, uncovering the lurking holes of the fiercest animals.

⟦Del seminare⟧

⁷⁶Allora in grā parte delli omini, che resterā uiui, gitterā ⁷⁷fori delle lor case le serbate vettovaglie in libera preda delli ⁷⁸vcelli e animali terrestri sanza curarsi d'essi in parte alcuna.

⟦Of Sowing Seed⟧

Then many of the men who will remain alive will throw the victuals they have preserved out of their houses, a free prey to the birds and beasts of the earth, without taking any care of them at all.

⟦Delle pioggie che fanno che fiumi intorbidati ⁸⁰portan via le terre⟧

⁸¹Verrà diuerso il cielo chi trasmuterà gran parte dell' Africa ⁸²che si mostra a esso cielo inverso l'Europa, e quella di Euro⁸³pa inverso l'Africa ·, e quelle delle provincie Scitiche si mischieranno in⁸⁴sieme con grā revolutione.

⟦Of the Rains, which, by making the Rivers muddy, wash away the Land⟧

[81] Something will fall from the sky which will transport a large part of Africa which lies under that sky towards Europe, and that of Europe towards Africa, and that of the Scythian countries will meet with tremendous revolutions [84].

⟦De legniami che bruciano⟧

⁸⁷Li alberi e arbusti delle grā selue si convertiranno in cenere.

⟦Of Wood that burns⟧

The trees and shrubs in the great forests will be converted into cinder.

⟦Delle fornaci di mattoni e calcina⟧

⁸⁹Al fine la terra si farà rossa per lo infocamēto di molti giorni, ⁹⁰e le pietre si convertiranno in cenere.

⟦Of Kilns for Bricks and Lime⟧

Finally the earth will turn red from a conflagration of many days, and the stones will be turned to cinders.

⟦I pesci lessi⟧

⁹²Li animali d'acqua moriranno nelle bollenti acque.

⟦Of boiled Fish⟧

The natives of the waters will die in the boiling flood.

⟦L'uliue che cadono dagli uliui dannoci l'olio che fa lume⟧

⁹⁴Discenderà con furia diuerso la terra, chi ci darà notrimēto e luce.

⟦Of the Olives which fall from the Olive-trees, shedding oil which makes light⟧

And things will fall with great force from above, which will give us nourishment and light.

⟦Delle ciuette e gufi; con che s'uccella alla pania⟧

⁹⁶Molti periranno · di fracassamento di testa e salteranno loro li ochi in grā par⁹⁷te della testa · per causa · d'animali pavrosi vsciti dalle tenebre.

⟦Of Owls and Screech Owls and what will trap them⟧

Many will perish of dashing their heads in pieces, and the eyes of many will jump out of their heads by reason of fearful creatures come out of the darkness.

---

69. ettrarre . . della bocha. 70. etterre e chastelle . . e chase "per desiderio di māgiare" trarre. 71. [cibo] propio . . bocha "luno all' altro" sanza . . alchuna. 73. rissguardare. 74. esschoprire . . spilonche. 76. allor [li omini] in. 77. chase. 78. terresti . . churarsi. 79. piove chenfanche. 81. africha. 82. chessi mosstra a . . ecquella di. 83. lafricha . ecquelle . . simichieranno. 84. chon . . revolutione [al fine si fermeranno e mvterano na. 85. tura di novi frutti]. *Lines 86–8 come in the original after lines 89 and 93, but Leonardo directs us to invert the order by writing 2ᵃ at the beginning of the former passage and 1ᵃ at the head of the latter one.* 86. bruca no. 87. albusti . . convertirano. 89. gorni. 90. elle . . convertiranno [in polvere] "in cenere". 91. epessci. 92. morirano . . acq"e". 93. che chagiō deli uliui eda noci lolio. 94. diuerso il celo chicci . . elluce. 95. guficōchessuecella alla pania. 96. tessta essaltera . . li ochin. 97. tessta . . danimali [vsscti delle] pavrosi vsscti delle.

81–4. Compare No. 945.

❡⟦Del lino che fa la cura de' cenci⟧

[99]Sarā reveriti e onorati e cō reuerētia e amore ascoltati li sua precetti [100]di chi prima fu splezzato, stratiato o martorizato da molte e diuerse battiture.

❡⟦De' libri che insegnano precetti⟧

[102]I corpi sanz' anima ci daranno con lor sententie precietti vtili al ben morire.

❡⟦De' battuti e scoreggiati⟧

[104]Li omini si nasconderanno · sotto le scorze delle scorticate erbe, e quiui gri[105]dando si darā martiri con battimēti di menbra a sé medesimi.

❡⟦Delle maniche de' coltegli fatte di corna [111]di castrone⟧

[112]Nelle corna delli animali si vedranno tagliēti [113]ferri colli quali si torrà la uita a molti della loro [114]spetie.

❡⟦Della notte che nō si conosce [116]alcun colore⟧

[117]Verrà a tanto che non si conoscierà diferenza infra [118]colori, anzi si faran tutti di nera qualità.

❡⟦Delle spade e lance che per sé [120]mai nuoconò a nessuno⟧

[121]Chi per sé è māsueto e sanza alcuna offensione, si farà [122]spauentevole e feroce mediante le triste cōpa[123]gnie, e torrà la vita crudelissimamēte [124]a molte genti; e piv n'ucciderebbe, se corpi sā[125]z' anima e usciti dalle spelonche non li difendessino, [126]cioè le corazze di ferro.

❡⟦De' laccioli e trappole⟧

[128]Molti morti si moverā con furia e piglierāño e legheranno [129]i vivi, e serviranno gli a lor nemici cercar [130]la lor morte e distrutione.

❡⟦De' metalli⟧

[132]Uscirà dalle oscure e tenebrose [133]spelonche che metterà tutta l'umana spe[134]tie in grandi affanni, pericoli e mor[135]te · ; a molti segua[136]ci lor, dopo molti affanni, darà [137]diletto; ma chi nō fia suo partigiano morrà [138]con stento e calamità; questo commette[139]rà infiniti tradimēti, questo avmēte[140]rà e persuaderà li omini tristi alli assassinamēti [141]e latrocini · e le ser-

❡⟦Of flax which works the cure of rags⟧

That which was at first despised, cast out, and rent by many and various blows, will be respected and honoured, and its precepts will be listened to with reverence and love.

❡⟦Of Books which teach Precepts⟧

Bodies without souls will, by their statements, give us precepts by which to die well.

❡⟦Of Flagellants⟧

Men will hide themselves under the bark of trees, and, screaming, they will make themselves martyrs by striking their own limbs.

❡⟦Of the Handles of Knives made of Rams' Horns⟧

We shall see the horns of certain beasts fitted to sharp irons, which will take the lives of many of their kind.

❡⟦Of Night when no Colour can be distinguished⟧

There will come a time when no difference can be discerned between colours, on the contrary, everything will be black in hue.

❡⟦Of Swords and Spears which of themselves never hurt any one⟧

One who by himself is gentle and void of all offence will become terrible and fierce by being in bad company, and will most cruelly take the life of many men, and would kill many more if it were not hindered by bodies having no soul, that have come out of pits, that is, cuirasses of iron.

❡⟦Of Snares and Traps⟧

Many dead things will move furiously, and will take and bind the living, and will ensnare them for the enemies who seek their death and destruction.

❡⟦Of Metals⟧

There shall come forth out of dark and obscure caves that which will put the whole human race in great anxiety, peril, and death. To many that seek it, after many sorrows it will give delight, and to those who are not in its company, death with want and misfortune. This will lead to the commission of endless crimes; this will increase the number of bad men and encourage them to assassinations, robberies, and enslavement,

98. cheffa . . de cēci. 99. reverita e onorata . . asscoltata. 100. diuerse battitare. 101. chensegnā. 103. scoregiati. 104. lesscōze delle isscorticate. 105. asse. 106. della lusuria. 107. essinfurieranno dellecose piu belle "a cercare" possedere e operarele parte lor piv brutte. 108. doue poi con danno e penitentia ritornati nellorsentimento narā grāde amira. 109. tiō di se stessi. 111. chastrone. 112. uedra. 113. feri cholli. 115. cognosscie. 117. vera attanto . . cognossciera. 119. ellance. 120. nocano añessuno. 121. perse | "he mā sueto" e . . alchuna. 122. si far aspauentevole "e feroce" mediante le trisste. 123. ettorra. 124. nucciderebe. 125. vssciti delle spliIonche noli. 126. coe le corraze. 127. lacioli. 128. chon furia "e piglierano" e legerano. 129. e vivi esserberā . . cercha. 132. vsscira delle . . ettenebrose. 134. pericholi. 135. molti [al sin darano piacere] segua. 136. ci lor [darā diletto] dopo. 137. partigano. 138. chonisstento e chalamita . . comette. 139. infinita. 140. omini "tristi" alli. 141. elle seruita questa terra in.

For ll. 106–9 'of sensuality' see unrevised text at the bottom of this page.

vitù ·; questa darà [142]sospetto · i sua parti-
giani ·; questo torrà [143]lo stato alle città libere;
questo torrà [144]la uita a molti; questo travaglierà
[145]li omini infra loro con molte fraudi, [146]inganni
e tradimēti; O animal mo[147]struoso! quāto sa
rebbe meglio per li omini [148]che tutti tornassero
nell' inferno! per costui [149]rimarrā diserte le grā
selue delle lor [150]piāte; per costui infiniti animali
perderanno la ui[151]ta.

⟦Del fuoco⟧

[153]Nascierà di piccolo principio, [154]chi si farà
cō prestezza grande; que[155]sto non stimerà alcuna creata [156]cosa, anzi colla sua potētia [157]quasi
il tutto avrà in potentia [158]di transformare di
suo essere [159]in vn altro.

⟦De' navili che annegano⟧

[161]Vedrassi grandissimi [162]corpi sanza vita
por[163]tare con furia moltitu[164]dine d'omini alla
distrutti[165]one di lor uita.

⟦De' boi che si māgiano⟧

[167]Māgieranno i padrō delle posses[168]sioni i
lor propi lauoratori.

⟦De' battere il letto per rifarlo⟧

[170]Verranno li omini in tanta ingratitudine,
[171]che, chi darà loro albergo sanza alcū prezzo,
[172]sarà carico di bastonate, in modo che [173]gran
parte delle interiora si spiccherā[174]no dal loco
loro e s'andranno rivoltando pel [175]suo corpo.

⟦Delle cose che si māgiano [177]che prima s'uccidono⟧

[178]Sarà morto da loro il loro nutritore e fra-
[179]gellato cō spietata morte.

⟦Dello spechiare le mura [181]delle città nel-l'acqua de' lor fossi⟧

[182]Vedrannosi l'alte mvra delle grā città sotto
sopra ne' lo[183]ro fossi.

⟦Dell' acqua che corre torbida [185]e mista cō terra, e della polue[186]re e nebbia mista col-l'aria, e del [187]foco misto col suo caldo cō ciascūo⟧

[188]Vedrassi tutti li elementi insieme misti con
grā re[189]volutione trascorrerre ora inverso il
centro del mō[190]do, ora inverso il celo, e quādo
dalle parti meri[191]dionali scorreran cō furia
inverso il fred[192]do settentrione, alcuna volta
dall' oriēte inverso [193]l'occidente, e così di questo
in quell' altro emisperio.

and by reason of it each will be suspicious of his
partner. This will deprive free cities of their
happy condition; this will take away the lives of
many; this will make men torment each other
with many artifices, deceptions, and treasons. O
monstrous creature! How much better would it
be for men that everything should return to
Hell! For this the vast forests will be devastated
of their trees; for this an infinite number of
animals will lose their lives.

⟦Of Fire⟧

One shall be born from small beginnings
which will rapidly become great. This will respect no created thing, rather will it, by its
power, transform almost everything from its
own nature into another.

⟦Of Sinking Ships⟧

Huge bodies will be seen, devoid of life,
carrying with fierce speed a multitude of men
to the destruction of their lives.

⟦Of Oxen which are eaten⟧

The masters of estates will eat their own
labourers.

⟦Of beating Beds to renew them⟧

Men will be seen so deeply ungrateful that
they will turn upon that which has harboured
them, without any price; they will so load it with
blows that a great part of its inside will come out
of its place, and will be turned over and over in
its body.

⟦Of Things which are eaten and which first are killed⟧

Those who nourish them will be killed by
them and afflicted by merciless deaths.

⟦Of the Reflection of Walls of Cities in the Water of their Ditches⟧

The high walls of great cities will be seen upside down in their ditches.

⟦Of Water, which flows turbid and mixed with Soil and Dust; and of Mist, which is mixed with the Air; and of Fire, which is mixed by its heat with each⟧

All the elements will be seen mixed together
in a great whirling mass, now borne towards the
centre of the world, now towards the sky; and
now furiously rushing from the south towards
the frozen north, and sometimes from the east
towards the west, and then again from this
hemisphere to the other.

142. partigani. 145. lor comolte [f] balde ingan. 146. ingani. 147. sare meglio. 148. chettutti tornassi . . cosstui. 149. rimarā.
150. perda laui. 152. fuocho. 153. nassciera di picholo. 154. presteza. 155. isstimera. 156. sua potē. 157. tutto fara in. 160.
navili canegano. 162. chorpi. 166. chessimāgano. 167. e padrō . . prezo. 168. e lor. 171. che che . . prezo. 172. charicho
di basstonate. 173. spigerā. 174. del locho . . essandrano. 175. chorpo. 176. chose chessi. 177. succidano. 178. sarmorto
dalloro . . effra. 179. disspietata. 182. vederassi. 187. chol suo e alticōciascūo. 189. trans [mutarsi] "correre" ora. 190. delle
parte. 191. scorerā . . il fre. 192. to settantrione acūa. 193. emissperio.

❡In ogni punto si può fare diuisio[195]ne de' 2 emisperi❩

[196]Li omini tutti scābieranno emisperio immediate.

❡In ogni pūto è diuisione da o[198]riente a occidente❩

[199]Moverannosi tutti li animali da oriēte a occidente, e così [200]da aquilone a meriggio scanbievolmēte, e così de' cōuerso.

❡Del moto dell' acque che portano [202]i legniami che son morti❩

[203]Corpi sanz' anima · per sé medesimi si moveranno e porterā [204]cō seco innumerabile generatione di morti, toglien[205]do le richezze a circūstanti viuēti.

❡Dell' oua che sendo māgiate nō possono [207]fare e pulcini❩

[208]O quanti fiē quegli, ai quali sarà proibito il nascere!

❡De' pesci che si māgiano ovati❩

[210]Infinita gieneratione si perderà per la morte delle grauide.

❡Del piāto fatto il venerdì santo❩

[220]In tutte le parti d'Europa sarà piāto da grā popoli per la morte d'u [221]solo omo morto in oriēte.

❡Del sogniare❩

[223]Andranno li omini e nō si moveranno, [224]parleranno cō chi nō si trova, senti[225]rāo chi nō parla.

❡Dell' onbra che si move coll' uomo❩

[227]Vedrannosi forme e figure d'uomini [228]e d'animali, che seguiranno essi ani[229]mali e omini dovunque fugiranno; [230]e tal fia il moto dell' un quant' è del[231]l'altro, ma parrà cosa mirabile delle [232]varie grandezze in che essi si tras[233]mutano.

❡❡Dell' ombra del sole e dello spechiarsi [235]nell' acqua in un medesimo tēpo❡❩

[236]Vedrassi molte volte l'uno uomo [237]diuentare 3, e tutti lo seguo[238]no, e spesso l'uno, il piv certo, l'abandona.

❡Delle casse che riseruano [240]molti tesori❩

[241]Troverrassi dentro a de' noci e de li alberi [242]e altre piante tesori grādissimi, i quali [243]lì stanno occulti e ben guardati.

❡The World may be divided into two Hemispheres at any Point❩

All men will suddenly be transferred into opposite hemispheres.

❡The division of the East from the West may be made at any point❩

All living creatures will be moved from the east to the west; and in the same way from north to south, and vice versa.

❡Of the Motion of Water which carries wood, which is dead❩

Bodies devoid of life will move by themselves and carry with them endless generations of the dead, taking wealth from the living standing around them.

❡Of Eggs which being eaten cannot form Chickens❩

Oh! how many will they be that never come to birth!

❡Of Fishes which are eaten with roe❩

Endless generations will be lost by the death of the pregnant.

❡Of the Lamentation on Good Friday❩

Throughout Europe there will be a lamentation of great nations over the death of one man who died in the East.

❡Of Dreaming❩

Men will walk and not stir, they will talk to those who are not present, and hear those who do not speak.

❡Of a Man's Shadow which moves with him❩

Shapes and figures of men and animals will be seen following these animals and men wherever they flee. And exactly as the one moves the other moves; but what seems so wonderful is the variety of height they assume.

❡Of our Shadow cast by the Sun, and our Reflection in the Water at one and the same time❩

Many a time will one man be seen as three and all three move together, and often the most real one quits him.

❡Of wooden Chests which contain great Treasures❩

Within walnuts and trees and other plants vast treasures will be found, which lie hidden there and well guarded.

194. po. 196. inmediate. 199. moverōsi. 200. meridio. 201. acqua. 202. e legniami chesson. 204. invmerabile .. morti [dondo et] toglē. 206. chessendo māgiata .. possā. 208. nassciere. 209. pessci chessi māgano. 211. delli animali che si castrano. 212. a gran parte della spetie masculina pell esser tolti loro e tes. 213. tichuli fia proibito el generare. 214. delle bestie cheffano il caco. 215. illate fia tolto ai pichuli figlioli. 216. delle som mate fatte delle troie. 217. a grā parte delle femine latine fia tolto ettagliato lor le tette. 218. insieme cholla vita [elle avendo ipichuli figloletti in corpo]. 219. venerdi scō. 220. popoli la. 221. homo. 224. chō. 226. chessi .. chollomo. 227. vedrassi .. effigure. 228. chesse guiranno. 229. dunche. 230. ettal .. dellui quate del. 231. para. 232. grandeze .. trans. 234. delleobr. 235. nvn. 237. ettutti. 238. esspesso luno piu. 243. ochulti .. guarda.

For ll. 211–18: 'of castrated animals'; 'of animals that make cheese'; 'of sows', see unrevised text at the bottom of this page.

❬Dello spegnere el lume a chi ²⁴⁵va al letto❭

²⁴⁶Molti per mandare fori il fiato ²⁴⁷con troppa prestezza perderanno il ue²⁴⁸dere e in brieue tutti i sentimēti.

❬Delle canpanelle de' muli ²⁵⁰che stanno presso ai loro orechi❭

²⁵¹Sentirassi in molte parti dell' Europa · stru²⁵²mēti di uarie magnitudini far diuerse ²⁵³armonie con grandissime fatiche di chi ²⁵⁴piv presso l'ode.

❬Delli asini❭

²⁵⁶Le molte fatiche saran remvnerate di ²⁵⁷fame, di sete, di disagio, e di mazzate, e di pū²⁵⁸ture, [e bestem̃ie, e grā uillanie.]

❬De' soldati a cauallo❭

²⁶⁰Molti sarā veduti portati da grādi ani²⁶¹mali con veloce corso alla ruina della sua ²⁶²vita e prestissima morte.
²⁶³Per l'aria e per la terra saranno veduti ani²⁶⁴mali di diuersi colori portarne cō fu²⁶⁵rore li omini alla destrutione di lor vita.

❬Delle stelle delli sproni❭

²⁶⁷Per causa delle stelle · si uedranno li omini ²⁶⁸esser velocissimi al pari di qualūche ²⁶⁹animal ueloce.

❬Il bastone ch' è morto❭

²⁷¹Il movimēto de' morti farà fugire ²⁷²cō dolore e piāto e cō grida molti viui.

❬Dell' esca❭

²⁷⁴Cō pietra e con ferro si rende²⁷⁵ranno visibili le cose che prima nō ²⁷⁶si vedeano.

❬Of putting out the Light when going to Bed❭

Many persons, puffing out a breath with too much haste, will thereby lose their sight, and soon after all consciousness.

❬Of the Bells of Mules, which are close to their Ears❭

In many parts of Europe instruments of various sizes will be heard making divers harmonies, to the great annoyance of those who hear them most closely.

❬Of Asses❭

The severest labour will be repaid with hunger and thirst, and discomfort, and blows, and goadings, and curses, and great abuse.

❬Of Soldiers on horseback❭

Many men will be seen carried by large animals, swift of pace, to the loss of their lives and immediate death.
In the air and on earth animals will be seen of divers colours furiously carrying men to the destruction of their lives.

❬Of the Stars of Spurs❭

By the aid of the stars men will be seen who will be as swift as any swift animal.

❬Of a Stick, which is dead❭

The motions of a dead thing will make many living ones flee with pain and lamentation and cries.

❬Of Tinder❭

With a stone and with iron things will be made visible which before were not seen.

C. A. 370b]　　　　1296

❬Del navicare❭

²Vedrassi li alberi delle grā selue di Tavrus, ³e di Sinai, Apenino, e Atlante scorrere per l'aria ⁴da oriēte a occidēte, da aquilone a meridi⁵e, e portarne per l'aria grā moltitudine ⁶d'omini; o quāti voti! o quāti mor⁷ti! o quanta separatiō d'amici e di parēti! o quā⁸ti fiē quelli che nō rivedranno piv le lor pro⁹vincie nè le lor patrie, e che moriranno sanza se¹⁰poltura colle lor ossa sparse in diuersi ¹¹siti del mōdo!

❬Of Sailing in Ships❭

We shall see the trees of the great forests of Taurus and of Sinai and of the Apennines and others rush by means of the air, from east to west and from north to south; and carry, by means of the air, great multitudes of men. Oh! how many vows! Oh! how many deaths! Oh! how many partings of friends and relations! Oh! how many will those be who will never again see their own country or their native land, and who will die unburied, with their bones strewn in various parts of the world!

〖Dello sgomberare l'Ognisanti〗

13Molti · abandoneranno le propie abitationi, e por14terā cō seco tutti e sua valsenti, e andran15no abitare in altri paesi.

〖Of moving on All Saints' Day〗

Many will forsake their own dwellings and carry with them all their belongings and will go to live in other parts.

〖Del dì de' morti〗

17E quāti fiē quelli che piāgeranno i lor 18antichi morti portādo lumi a quelli.

〖Of All Souls' Day〗

How many will they be who will bewail their deceased forefathers, carrying lights to them.

〖De' frati che spēdendo parole 20riceuono di grā ricchezze e danno 21il paradiso〗

24¶ Le invisibili monete farā triōfare molti spē25ditori di quelle. ¶

〖Of Friars, who, spending nothing but Words, receive great Gifts and bestow Paradise〗

Invisible money will procure the triumph of many who will spend it.

〖Degli archi fatti 27colli corni de' boi〗

28Molti fiē quelli che per causa delle bouine cor29na moriranno di dolente morte.

〖Of Bows made of the Horns of Oxen〗

Many will there be who will die a painful death by means of the horns of cattle.

〖Dello scriver lettere da vn 31paese a vn altro〗

32Parleransi li uomini di remotissimi paesi l'uno all' altro e rispōderāsi.

〖Of writing Letters from one Country to another〗

Men will speak with each other from the most remote countries, and reply.

〖Degli emisperi che sono infiniti 34e da infinite linie son diuisi, in mo35do che senpre ciascuno uomo n'à 36vna d'esse linie infra l'ū de' piedi e l'altro〗

37Parleransi e toccheransi e abbraccieransi li omini stanti dall' uno all'38altro emisperio, e tenderansi i loro linguaggi.

〖Of Hemispheres, which are infinite; and which are divided by an infinite Number of Lines, so that every Man always has one of these Lines between his Feet〗

Men standing in different hemispheres will converse and touch each other and embrace each other, and understand each other's language.

〖De' preti che dicono messe〗

40Molti fien quelli che per esercitare la lor arte si uestirā richissi41mamente e questo parrà esser fatto secōdo l'uso de grēbiali.

〖Of Priests who say Mass〗

There will be many men who, when they go to their labour, will put on the richest clothes, and these will be made after the fashion of aprons [petticoats].

〖De' frati che confessano〗

43Le suēturate donne di propia volontà 44andranno a palesare agli omini 45tutti le loro lussurie e opere 46vergognose e segretissime.

〖Of Friars who are Confessors〗

And unhappy women will, of their own free will, reveal to men all their sins and shameful and most secret deeds.

〖Delle chiese e abitatiō de' frati〗

53Assai saranno che lascieranno 54li eserciti e le fatiche 55e povertà di uita e di roba, e andranno abitare nelle 56richezze e triōfanti edifiti mostrando questo esser 57il mezzo di farsi amico a Dio.

〖Of Churches and the Habitations of Friars〗

Many will there be who will give up work and labour and poverty of life and goods, and will go to live among wealth in splendid buildings, declaring that this is the way to make themselves acceptable to God.

---

12. issgonbrare. 14. chōsecho .. andra. 17. i lor[parē]. 18. acquelli. 20. riceuano .. richeze e dano. 22. [vadrassi gradissima turba i quali acquisterā grā]. 23. [dissime richeze chō prezodinvisibile monete]. 24. invisibile. 28. chausa. 33. chessono. 35. ciasscuno homo. 36. infralli lun piedi. 37. tocherano e abracieransi. 38. ilor. 39. dicā. 41. ecquesto .. grēbivli. 42. chonfessore. *Lines 43–6 are written on the margin parallel to lines 47–51*. 44. andrano [a dire] "palesare" ali omini [dalor]. 47. [assai fien quelli che vorranno sapere co che ffanole le femmi. 48. ne nelle lor lussurie chon se e cogli altri omini elle messcine. 49. cōverra che palesino tutte le loro ochulte opere vergognose. 50. e premiare li asscoltatori di lor miserie e [infamie sce]. 51. [lerate infamie]. 53. sarano [chea] lasscieranno "le" [la lor povera vita]. 54. elle. 56. ettriō fanti .. mosstrando quessto. 57. il mezo [di seruire] di farsi addio [effarsi allui benivolo].

For ll. 22–3 and 47–51 see unrevised text at the bottom of this page.

❰Del uendere il paradiso❱

[61]Infinita moltitudine venderanno publica-mente e pacificamēte [62]cose di grandissimo prezzo sanza licenza del padrone di quelle, [63]e che mai nō furō loro nè in lor potestà, e a questo nō prove[64]drà la giustitia vmana.

❰De' morti che si uanno a sotterrare❱

[66]I senplici popoli porterā gran quantità di lumi per far lumi [67]ne' viaggi a tutti quelli che integralmente ànno perso la uirtù [68]visiua.

❰Delle dote delle fanciulle❱

[71]E doue prima la gioventù feminina nō si potea difendere dal[72]la lussuria e rapina de' maschi, nè per guardie di parenti nè fortezze di mvra, [73]verrà tenpo che bisognierà che padri e parēti d'esse fanciulle [74]paghino di grā prezzi chi voglia dormire con loro, ancorachè es[75]se sien ricche, nobili, e bellissime; Cierto è, par qui che la [76]natura voglia spegniere la umana spetie come cosa invtile al mondo, [77]e guastatrice di tutte le cose create.

❰Della crudeltà dell' omo❱

[79]Vedrannosi animali sopra della terra, i quali senpre conbatteranno infra [80]loro e con danni grandissimi e spesso morte di ciascuna delle [81]parti; questi non avrà termine nelle lor malignità; per le fiere mē[82]bra di questi uer-ranno a terra grā parte delli alberi delle gran selue dell' u[83]niverso, e poi ch'essi avranno pasciuto, il nutrimēto de' loro desideri sa[84]rà, di dar morte e affanno e fatiche e paure e fuga a qualūche cosa animata; e per la loro smisurata superbia questi si vor[85]ranno leuare inverso il cielo, ma la superchia gravezza delle lor membra gli terrà [86]in basso; nulla cosa resterà sopra la terra o sotto la terra e l'acqua che nō [87]sia perse-guitata ·, remossa o guasta ·, e quella dell' ū paese remossa nell' altro; [88]e 'l corpo di questi si farà sepultura e transito di tutti i già da lor morti cor[89]pi animati; O mōdo, come è che nō t'apri a precipitarlo nell' alte fessure de' tua [90]grā balatri e spelonche, e non mostrare più al cielo si crudele e spie[91]tato mōstro!

❰Of Selling Paradise❱

An infinite number of men will sell publicly and unhindered things of the very highest price, without leave from the Master of them, while they never were theirs nor in their power; and human justice will not prevent it.

❰Of the Dead which are carried to be buried❱

The simple folks will carry vast quantities of lights to light up the road for those who have entirely lost the power of sight.

❰Of Dowries for Maidens❱

And whereas, at first, maidens could not be protected against the lust and violence of Men, neither by the watchfulness of parents nor by the strength of walls, the time will come when it will be necessary for the fathers and parents of those girls to pay a large price to whoever is willing to marry them, even if they are rich, noble, and most handsome. Certainly this seems as though nature wished to eradicate the human race as being useless to the world, and as spoiling all created things.

❰Of the Cruelty of Man❱

Animals will be seen on the earth who will always be fighting against each other with the greatest loss and frequent deaths on each side. And there will be no end to their malice; by their strong limbs we shall see a great portion of the trees of the vast forests laid low throughout the universe; and when they are filled with food, the satisfaction of their desires will be to deal death and grief and labour and fears and flight to every living thing; and from their immoderate pride they will desire to rise towards heaven, but the excessive weight of their limbs will keep them down. Nothing will remain on earth, or under the earth, or in the waters, which will not be persecuted, disturbed, and spoiled, and those of one country removed into another. And their bodies will become the tomb and means of transit of all the living bodies they have killed.

O Earth, why dost thou not open and engulf them in the fissures of thy vast abyss and caverns, and no longer display in the sight of heaven so cruel and horrible a monster?

Br. M. 42*b*]   1297

PROFETIE

[2]Molte fien quelle che cresce[3]rā nelle lor ruine.

❰La palla della neue [5]rotolādo sopra la [6]neue.❱

PROPHECIES

There will be many which will increase in their destruction.

❰The Ball of Snow rolling over Snow.❱

59. [infinita moltitudine venderanno publichamēte "chosa di grādissima valuta" quel che. 60. mai nō fu loro ne i lor podesta eancho]. 61. publica e pacifichamēte. 62. chose .. prezo. 63. illor .. acquesto. 64. dera. 65. chessiuanno assotterrare. 67. quelli cintera "gralm" mēte an. 68. visiua o uma ne sciochezze o viue pazze questedue e. 69. piteti vanno nel prīcipio della propositione. 70. fanculle. 72. lla .. massci .. guardie |"di parenti" ne. 73. vera .. fanculle. 74. paghi .. plezzi .. colloro. 75. sien [belli] riche .. chella. 77. guasstatrice .. chose. 79. vedrassi. 80. chon .. esspesso .. ciasscuna. 81. parte .. arā. 82. atterra. 83. poi-chessarā passcuti .. dellor. 84. affanno "e fatiche .. effuge" accqualūche cossa animata "e per la loro issisurata superbia". 85. malla. . graveza "delle lor menbra". 86. resstera .. ossotto .. ellacqua. 87. guassta ecquella. 88. ettransito .. iga da. 89. chome me nō tapri e precipita nellaltre fessure. 90. palatri esspelonche e no .. disspia.
1297. 2. cresscce.

For ll. 59–60 and 68–9 see unrevised text at the bottom of this page.

⁷Molta turba fie quella ⁸che, dimēticato loro esse⁹re e nome, staran come ¹⁰morti sopra le spoglie ¹¹deli altri morti.

❲Il dormire sopra ¹³le piume dell' uccielli.❳

There will be many who, forgetting their existence and their name, will lie as dead on the spoils of other dead creatures.

❲Sleeping on the Feathers of Birds.❳

¹⁴Vedrannosi le parti oriēta¹⁵li discorrere¹⁶nell' occidentali e le me¹⁷ridionali in settentri¹⁸one, avviluppando¹⁹si per l'universo con grande ²⁰strepito e tremore o furore.

❲Il uento d'oriēte che ²²scorreua in ponente.❳

The east will be seen to rush to the west and the south to the north in confusion round and about the universe, with great noise and trembling or fury.

❲In the east wind which rushes to the west.❳

²³I razzi solari accende²⁴rāno il foco in te²⁵rra coll' quale s'in²⁶focherà ciò ch' è sotto ²⁷il cielo, e ripercossi ²⁸nel suo inpedimē²⁹to ritorneranno ³⁰in basso.

❲Lo spechio cavo ³²acciēde il foco, col ³³quale si scalda il ³⁴forno che à il fō³⁵do che sta sotto il suo ³⁶cielo.❳

The solar rays will kindle fire on the earth, by which a thing that is under the sky will be set on fire, and, being reflected by some obstacle, they will bend downwards.

❲The Concave Mirror kindles a Fire, with which we heat the oven, and this has its foundation that stands beneath its roof.❳

³⁷Gran parte del mare ³⁸si fuggirà inverso il ³⁹cielo e per molto tēpo nō fa⁴⁰rà ritorno; ❲Cioè pe' nuvoli.❳

A great part of the sea will fly towards heaven and for a long time will not return. ❲That is, in Clouds.❳

⁴¹Restaci · il moto che separa ⁴²il motore dal mobile.

There remains the motion which divides the mover from the thing moved.

⁴³Sarà annegato chi fa il lume ⁴⁴al culto diuino. ‖ ❲Le ape che ⁴⁵faño la cera delle candele.❳

Those who give light for divine service will be destroyed. ❲The Bees which make the Wax for Candles.❳

⁴⁶I morti uscirāno di sotto terra ⁴⁷e coi loro fieri mouimēti cac⁴⁸cieranno dal mondo · innumera⁴⁹bili creature umane.

❲Il ferro uscito di sot⁵¹to terra è morto, ⁵²e se ne fa l'arme che ⁵³ammorti tanti uomini.❳

The dead will come from underground and by their fierce movements will send numberless human beings out of the world.

❲Iron, which comes from underground, is dead, but the Weapons are made of it which kill so many Men.❳

⁵⁴Le grandissime montagnie ⁵⁶ācorachè sieno remo⁵⁷te da marini liti, scaccieraño ⁵⁸il mare dal suo sito.

❲Questo sono li fiumi ⁶⁰che portanno le terre, ⁶¹da loro leuate dalle mō⁶²tagnie, e le scarica⁶³no ai marini · liti, ⁶⁴e doue entra ⁶⁵la terra si fuggie il ⁶⁶mare.❳

The greatest mountains, even though they are remote from the sea-shore, will drive the sea from its place.

❲This is by Rivers which carry the Earth they wash away from the Mountains and bear it to the Sea-shore; and where the Earth comes the Sea retires.❳

⁶⁷L'acqua caduta dai nuvoli ancora in moto sopra le spiaggie de' mōti si ferme⁶⁸rà per lūgo spatio di tempo sanza ⁶⁹fare alcū moto, e questo accade⁷⁰rà in molte e diuerse provincie.

❲La neve che fiocca ⁷²che è acqua.❳

The water dropped from the clouds still in motion on the flanks of mountains will lie still for a long period of time without any motion whatever; and this will happen in many and divers lands.

❲Snow, which falls in Flakes and is Water.❳

10. lesspoglie de. 13. dellucie. 14. vedrassi le parte. 15. li [trans] discorrere. 16. ochidentallelle me. 17. settantri. 18. siavilupando. 19. cogra. 20. strepido e tremore "o furore". 23. razi. 25. si. 26. coche. 27. riperchossi. 29. nto ritorneran. 31. pechio. 32. aciēde. 35. soto. 36. celo. 38. o si fugira. 39. celo. 40. rtorno coe pe nvgoli. 41. Resstaci .. chessepera. 43. anegato chiffa ilume. 46. vsscirāno. 47. hecholoro .. ca. 48. del .. invmera. 50. usscito diso. 51. momorto. 52. esse. 53. amorti. 54. montagnie per. 55. [lunga remotione fia an]. 56. anchorachessieno che sieno. 58. del. 61. dallor .. delle. 62. elle scarica. 63. noa. 67. de nvgoli ‖ "ancora in moto sopra le spiage de mōti sua natura che" si ferme. 69. acade. 70. imolte .. prouince. 71. fiocha.

⁷³I gran sassi de' monti gitterã ⁷⁴fuoco tale che brucieranno il le⁷⁵gname di molte e grãdissime selue ⁷⁶e molte fere saluatiche e dimestiche.

⟨La pietra del fucile, ⁷⁸che fa foco che consu⁷⁹ma tutte le some del⁸⁰le legnie con che si ⁸¹disfã le selve; ⁸²E cuocierassi con esse ⁸³la carne delle bestie.⟩

⁸⁴O quanti grandi edifitj fieno ruinati ⁸⁵per causa del fuoco!

⟨Del fuoco delle bonbarde.⟩

⁸⁷I buoi fieno in gran parte cavsa delle ruine ⁸⁸delle città, e similmẽte cavalli e bufoli.

⟨Tirã le bonbarde.⟩

The great rocks of the mountains will throw out fire; so that they will burn the timber of many vast forests, and many beasts both wild and tame.

⟨The Flint in the Tinder-box which makes a Fire that consumes all the Loads of Wood of which the Forests are despoiled, and with this the Flesh of Beasts is cooked.⟩

Oh! how many great buildings will be ruined by reason of Fire.

⟨The Fire of great Guns.⟩

Oxen will be to a great extent the cause of the destruction of cities, and in the same way horses and buffaloes.

⟨By drawing Guns.⟩

I.² 63a]   1298

⟨Vedrassi la spetie leonina · colle unghiate ²branche aprire la terra · e nelle fatte ³spelonche · seppellire · sé insieme col⁴li altri animali a sé sottoposti.⟩

⟨⁵Usciranno dalla terra · animali · vestiti di tenebre, ⁶i quali con maravigliosi assalti ⁷assaliranno l'umana generatione, e quella ⁸da feroci morsi · fia con confusion di sã⁹gue da essi · diuorata.⟩

¹⁰Ãcora scorrerà per l'aria · la nefãda spetie volatile, ¹¹la quale · assalirà · li omini e li a¹²nimali, e di quelli si ciberanno cõ grã ¹³gridore; empierãno i loro vẽtri di vermiglio sangue.

The Lion tribe will be seen tearing open the earth with their clawed paws and, in the caves thus made, burying themselves together with the other animals that are beneath them.

Animals will come forth from the earth in gloomy vesture, which will attack the human species with astonishing assaults, and which will devour them by their ferocious bites will make confusion of blood.

There shall also hurtle through the air a tribe of dreadful winged creatures who will assail men and beasts and feed upon them with loud cries, filling their bellies with scarlet blood.

I.² 63b]   1299

Vedrassi il sangue uscire dalle · stracciate carni, ²rigare le superfitiali parti delli omini;

⟨³Verrà alli omini · tal crudele mala⁴tia, che colle propie vnghie · si strac⁵cieranno le loro carni ‖ ⟨sarà la rognia.⟩⟨

⟨⁶Vedrannosi le piãte rimanere sanza foglie, ⁷e i fiumi fermare i loro corsi.⟩

⟨⁸L'acqua del mare si leuerà sopra l'alte cime de' mõti ⁹verso il cielo, e ricaderà sopra alle a¹⁰bitationi delli omini ‖ ⟨cioè per nuvoli.⟩⟨

⟨¹¹Vedrannosi i maggiori alberi delle selue essere ¹²portati dal furor de' venti dall' oriẽte ¹³all' occidente ‖‖ ⟨cioè per mare.⟩⟨

⟨¹⁴Li omini gitterão via le propie vetto-vaglie ⟨¹⁵cioè seminãdo.⟩⟨

Blood will be seen issuing from the torn flesh of men, and trickling down the surface.

Men will have such cruel maladies that they will tear their flesh with their own nails. ⟨The Itch.⟩

Plants will be seen left without leaves, and the rivers standing still in their channels.

The waters of the sea will rise above the high peaks of the mountains towards heaven and fall again on to the dwellings of men. ⟨That is, in Clouds.⟩

The largest trees of the forest will be seen carried by the fury of the winds from east to west. ⟨That is, across the Sea.⟩

Men will cast away their own victuals. ⟨That is, in Sowing.⟩

---

73. gra. 74. focho . . ile. 76. fiere. 79. some de. 81. disfa. 82. e cocierassicon eso. 83. della bestie. 85. chausa del focho. 86. focho. 87. boi. 88. essimilmẽte cavgli. 83. tira.

1298. 1. vederassi . . colle vngliate. 2. b\\\\ache. 3. secho . . cho. 4. asse sottopossti. 5. vsscira della . . animali "vestitidi tenebr[oso]" di osscuro. 6. [colore] i quali cho. 7. gienerationa ecq. 8. quela da . . fia confusion. 10. laria [vcielli] "la nefãda specie volati". 11. assaliranno . . ellia. 13. enperãno . . sange.

1299. 1. usscire delle. 4. cholle . . si stra. 6. vedrassi. 8. leuera "sopra lalte cime de mõti" [molte miglia]. 10. bitatione . . nvgoli. 11. vedera . . magiori. 13. coe.

I.² 64a]   1300

¶Verrà a tale la gieneratione vmana ²che nõ si intēderà il parlare · l'uno dell' altro; ³cioè un tedesco con un turco.¶

¶⁴Vedrassi ai padri donare le lor figliole ⁵a lussuria delli omini e premiare e abbādonare ogni ⁶passata guardia ‖ ⊄quādo si maritano le putte.⊅¶

¶⁷Uscirāno li omini dalle sepulture cõuertiti ⁸in vccelli ·, e assaliranno li altri omini togliendo ⁹loro il cibo dalle propie mani e mēse ‖ ⊄le mosche.⊅¶

¶¹⁰Molti fien quegli che scorticādo la madre li arrove¹¹scieranno la sua pelle · adosso; ‖ ⊄i lavoratori della terra.⊅¶

¶ ¹²Felici fiē quelli che presterāno orechi alle parole de' morti; | ⊄leggere ¹³le bone opere e osseruarle.⊅¶

The generation of men shall come to such a pass as not to understand each other's speech; that is, a German with a Turk.

Fathers will be seen giving their daughters into the power of man and giving up all their former care in guarding them. ⊄When Girls are married.⊅

Men will come out of their graves turned into flying creatures; and they will attack other men, taking their food from their very hands or tables. ⊄As Flies.⊅

Many will there be who, flaying their mother, will turn the skin on her back. ⊄Husbandmen tilling the Earth.⊅

Happy will they be who lend ear to the words of the Dead. ⊄Who read good Works and obey them.⊅

I.² 64b]   1301

¶Le penne leuerāno li omini siccome gli uccielli inverso il cielo; ²| ⊄cioè per le lettere · fatte da esse pēne.⊅¶

³¶ L'umane opere fieno cagione di lor morte; | ⊄le spade e lācie.⊅

¶⁴Li omini perseguiraño quella cosa della qual piv temono,¶ ⁵cioè | ⊄sarā miseri per nõ venire ī miseria.⊅¶

¶⁶Le cose disunite · s'unirāno · e ricieverāno in sé ⁷tal uirtù, che rēderanno la persa memoria alli omi⁸ni ·, cioè i papiri · che sõ fatti di peli disuniti ⁹e tēgono memoria delle cose e fatti delli omini.¶

¶¹⁰Vedrannosi l'ossa de' morti cõ veloce moto tratta¹¹re la fortuna del suo motore; ⊅i dadi.⊅¶

¶ ¹²I buoi colle lor corna difenderā¹³no il foco dalla · sua · morte; ‖ ⊄la lāterna.⊅¶

¶¹⁴Le selue partorirāno figlioli che fiano causa della ¹⁵lor morte; ‖ ⊄il manico della scura.⊅¶

Feathers will raise men, as they do birds, towards heaven. ⊄That is, by the letters which are written with their Quills.⊅

The works of men's hands will occasion their death. ⊄Swords and Spears.⊅

Men out of fear will cling to the thing they most fear. ⊄That is, they will be miserable lest they should fall into Misery.⊅

Things that are separate shall be united and acquire such virtue that they will restore to man his lost memory; that is, papyrus (sheets) which are made of separate strips and have preserved the memory of the things and acts of men.

The bones of the dead will be seen by their rapid movement to govern the fortunes of their mover. ⊄By Dice.⊅

Cattle with their horns protect the flame from its death. ⊄In a Lantern [13].⊅

The forests will bring forth young which will be the cause of their death. ⊄The Handle of the Hatchet.⊅

I.² 65a]   1302

¶Li omini batteranno aspramēte · chi fia causa ²di lor uita; ‖ ⊄batteraño · il grano.⊅¶

¶³Le pelli delli animali · removerāno li omini con gran ⁴gridori e bestemie dal lor silentio; | ⊄le balle da giuocare.⊅¶

⁵Molte volte la cosa disunita fia causa di grāde unitione; ⁶⊄cioè il pettine fatto dalla disunita canna unisce · le ⁷fila · nella tela.⊅

Men will deal bitter blows to that which is the cause of their life. ⊄In thrashing Grain.⊅

The skins of animals will rouse men from their silence with great outcries and curses. ⊄Balls for playing Games.⊅

Very often a thing that is severed is the occasion of much union. ⊄That is, the comb made of split cane which unites the threads of cloth.⊅

1300. 1. verano attale. 3. vtedesco con v̄ turco. 5. ebādonare "e premiare" ogni. 7. vsscirāno . . delle. 8. vcielli e assalirano . . tolendo. 9. delle . . le mosche [ecc]. 10. arove. 11. scierano. 12. quelli [che osseruerano] "che presterāno orechi" | le . . legere.
1301. 1. sichome. 2. faete. 3. lesspade he lāce. 4. chosa . . temano. 7. rēderaūno. 8. palpiri chessõ. 9. tēgano . . cosse effatti. 10. vederassi . . chõ. 12. [le corna delle] i boi. 14. cheffia chausa.
1302. 1. batterano asspramēte cheffia chausa. 3. pelle . . con gā. 4. besstemie . . giucare. 5. chausa. 6. della . . vnisscie.

1301. 13. See note, p. 295.

¶ ⁸Il uēto passato per le pelli delli animali farà saltare ⁹li omini; || ℂcioè la piva che fa ballare.𝔇¶

The wind passing through the skins of animals will make men leap. ℂThat is, the Bagpipe, which makes People dance.𝔇

I.² 65b]   1303

ℂDe' noci battuti𝔇

²Quelli che avranno · fatto meglio, saranno ³piv battuti e i sua figlioli tolti ⁴e scorticati overo spogliati e rotte e fra⁵cassate le sue ossa.

ℂOf Walnut-trees, that are beaten𝔇

Those which have done best will be most beaten, and their offspring taken and flayed or peeled, and their bones broken or crushed.

ℂDelle scolture𝔇

⁷Oimè, che vedo il saluatore di novo crocifisso.

ℂOf Sculpture𝔇

Alas! whom do I see? The Saviour crucified anew.

ℂDella bocca dell' omo ch'è sepoltura𝔇

⁹Usciranno grā romori dalle sepolture di ¹⁰quelli che sō finiti da cattiva e uiolēte morte.

ℂOf the Mouth of Man, which is a Sepulchre𝔇

Great noise will issue from the sepulchres of those who died evil and violent deaths.

ℂDelle pelli delli animali ¹²che tengono il senso del tatto ¹³che v'è sulle scritture.𝔇

¹⁴Quāto piv si parlerà · colle pelli, veste del ¹⁵sentimento, tanto piv s'acquisterà sapiētia.

ℂOf the Skins of Animals which have the sense of Feeling what is in the Things written𝔇

The more you converse with skins covered with sentiments, the more wisdom will you acquire.

ℂDe' preti che tengono l'ostia ¹⁷in corpo.𝔇

¹⁸Allora tutti quasi i tabernaculi dove sta il ¹⁹corpus domini si vedraño manifestamēte ²⁰per sé stessi andare per diuerse strade del mōdo.

ℂOf Priests who bear the Host in their Bodies𝔇

Then almost all the tabernacles where dwells the Corpus Domini will be plainly seen walking about of themselves on the various roads of the world.

I.² 66a]   1304

¶ E quelli che pascono l'aria ²farā della notte ³giorno; ||| ℂsevo.𝔇¶

¶ ⁴E molti terrestri e acquatici ⁵animali mōterāno fralle ⁶stelle; | ℂcioè pianeti.𝔇¶

¶ ⁷Vedrassi i morti portare ⁸i vivi in diuerse parti.𝔇; || ℂi carri ⁹e navi ¶

¹⁰A molti fia tolto il cibo di bocca; ℂAi forni.𝔇

¶ ¹²E quelli che si inbocheranno, per l'altrui ¹³mani fia lor tolto il cibo di bo¹⁴cca; ℂil forno.𝔇¶

And those who feed on air will turn night into day ℂTallow.𝔇

And many creatures of land and water will go up among the stars ℂThat is, Planets.𝔇

The dead will be seen carrying the living in various places. ℂIn Carts and Ships𝔇

Food shall be taken out of the mouth of many ℂFrom Ovens.𝔇

And those which will have their food in their mouths will be deprived of it by the hands of others ℂThe Oven.𝔇

I.² 66b]   1305

ℂDe' crocifissi vēduti𝔇

²Io vedo di novo vēduto e crocifisso Cristo ³e marterizzare i sua sāti.

ℂOf Crucifixes which are sold𝔇

I see Christ sold and crucified afresh, and His Saints suffering martyrdom.

ℂI medici che uiuono de' malati𝔇

⁵Verrāno li omini in tanta viltà, che avrà di gra⁶tia, che altri triōfino sopra i loro mali ⁷ovvero della perduta lor uera ricchezza, cioè la sanità.

ℂOf Physicians, who live upon the Sick𝔇

Men will come into so wretched a plight that they will be glad that others will derive profit from their sufferings or from the loss of their real wealth, that is, health.

9. cheffa \\\\\\\ are.
1303. 2. aranno. 3. e e sua. 4. esscorticha . . effra. 5. chassate. 7. ome . . saluadore. 8. dela bocha. 9. vsscira . . delle . . de. 10. queli chesso finiti de. 11. belle. 12. tengano. 13. che vesule. 14. cholle pelleveste del. 16. chettengano. 19. vederano.
1304. 1–14 R. 1. ecqueli che pascā lere. 2. [cholla] farā. 4. teresti e aquatici. 6. stelle e pianeti. 8. i carri. 10. amoli fia . . bocha. 11. a. 12. ecque chessi. 14. bocha.
1305. 2. i vedo. 3. marterizare. 4. uiuā. 5. verāno . . arā. 6. triōfi . . ilor. 7. ovedella . . richeza coe.

1305. See No. 1184 on physicians.

⟦Della religione de' frati ⁹che vivono per li loro sā¹⁰ti, morti per assai tēpo⟧

¹¹Quelli che saranno morti dopo mille anni ¹²fien quelli che daranno le spese a molti ¹³vivi.

⟦De' sassi cōvertiti in calcina, ¹⁵de' quali si murano le prigioni.⟧

¹⁶Molti che fieno disfatti dal fuoco ¹⁷innāzi a questo tenpo, torrāno la libertà a mol¹⁸ti uomini.

I.² 67a]   1306

⟦De' putti che tettano⟧

²Molti Francescani, Domenicani, e Bene-³dettini mangieranno quel che da altri ⁴altre volte vicinamēte è stato māgia⁵to, che staranno molti mesi avanti ⁶che possino parlare.

⟦De' nichi e chiocciole che sono rebuttati ⁸dal mare che marciscono dētro ai lor gusci⟧

⁹O quanti fien quelli che, poichè fiē morti, mar¹⁰ciranno nelle lor propie case, ēpiēdo le ¹¹circūstāte parti piene di fetulēte puzzo!

L. 91a]   1307

⟦De' mvli che portano le ricche some ²doll' argiēto e oro⟧

³Molti tesori e grā ricchezze · saranno appre⁴sso alli animali di 4 piedi, i quali le por-⁵teranno in diversi lochi.

K.² 50b]   1308

⟦Dell' onbra che fa l'omo di not²te col lume⟧

³Appariranno grandissime figure in forma ⁴vmana, le quali quanto piv le ti fa⁵rai vicine, più diminuiranno la ⁶loro immensa magnitudine.

C. A. 129b]   1309

⟦Delle biscie portate dalle cicognie⟧

²Vedrannosi in grandissima altezza dell' aria lūghissimi serpenti ³conbattere colli uccielli.

⟦Delle bōbarde ch'escono dalla fossa e dalla forma⟧

⁵Uscirà di sotto terra chi con spauētevoli grida stordirà ⁶i circonstanti vicini e col suo fiato farà morire li omini ⁷e ruinare le città e castella.

⟦Of the Religion of Friars, who live by their Saints who have been dead a great while⟧

Those who are dead will, after a thousand years, be those who will give a livelihood to many who are living.

⟦Of Stones converted into Lime, with which Prison Walls are made⟧

Many things that have been before that time destroyed by fire will deprive many men of liberty.

⟦Of Children who are suckled⟧

Many Franciscans, Dominicans, and Benedictines will eat that which at other times was eaten by others, who for some months to come will not be able to speak.

⟦Of Cockles and Sea Snails which are thrown up by the Sea and which rot inside their Shells⟧

How many will there be who, after they are dead, will putrefy inside their own houses, filling all the surrounding air with a fetid smell.

⟦Of Mules which have on them rich Burdens of Silver and Gold⟧

Much treasure and great riches will be laid upon four-footed beasts, which will convey them to divers places.

⟦Of the Shadow cast by a Man at Night with a Light⟧

Huge figures will appear in human shape, and the nearer you get to them, the more will their immense size diminish.

⟦Of Snakes, carried by Storks⟧

Serpents of great length will be seen at a great height in the air, fighting with birds.

⟦Of great Guns, which come out of a Pit and a Mould⟧

Creatures will come from underground which with their terrific noise will stun all who are near; and with their breath will kill men and destroy cities and castles.

---

8. delle religiō. 9. vivano. 11. chessarano. 15. mure. 16. cheffieno .. foco [dopo molti]. 17. ināzi acquesto. 18. homini.
1306. 1. chettattaño. 2. franciessci domenichi. 3. detta mangierano. 7. chesson. 8. marciscano .. a lor. 10. cirano. 11. puzo.
1307. 1. riche. 2. he oro. 3. recheze .. apre. 5. terano.
1308. 1. dino. 2. chol. 4. sitifa. 5. ra vicino .. diminvirano. 6. inmensa.
1309. 1. bissce. 2. vedrassi .. alteza .. lūgisimi serpe. 3. conbatere. 4. escan della .. della. 5. vsscira .. conispauēteuoli. 6. circu-stanti.

1307. It seems to me probable that this note, which occurs in the note-book used in 1502, when Leonardo, in the service of Cesare Borgia, visited Urbino, was suggested by the pillage of the palace of Guidobaldo, whose treasures Cesare Borgia had carried to Cesena (see Gregorovius, *Geschichte der Stadt Rom im Mittelalter*, xiii. 5, 4).

Br. M. 212b]   1310

⟦Del grāo e altre semēze⟧

²Gitteranno li omini fori delle lor propie case quelle uettovalglie, le quali ³erā dedicate a sostētare la lor uita.

⟦Delli alberi che nutriscono linnesti⟧

⁵Vedrannosi i padri e le madri fare molto piv giovamento ai figliastri che ai lor ueri ⁶figlioli.

⟦Del turibolo dell' incēso⟧

⁸Quelli che cō uestimēti bianchi andranno con arrogante movimēto minacciā⁹do con metallo e fuoco, che nō facieva lor detrimēto alcuno.

⟦Of Grain and other Seeds⟧

Men will fling out of their houses those victuals which were intended to sustain their life.

⟦Of Trees, which nourish grafted shoots⟧

Fathers and mothers will be seen to take much more delight in their stepchildren than in their own children.

⟦Of the Censer⟧

Some will go about in white garments with arrogant gestures threatening others with metal and fire which will do no harm at all to them.

S. K. M. II.1; 34a]   1311

⟦Del segare dell' erbe⟧

²Spegnieransi innumerabili vite ³e farassi sopra la terra innumera⁴bili busi.

⟦Della vita delli omini ⁶che ogni 10 āni si mv⁷tano di carne⟧

⁸Li omini passerā morti per le ⁹sue propie budelle. . . .

⟦Of mowing Grass⟧

Innumerable lives will be destroyed and innumerable vacant spaces will be made on the earth.

⟦Of the Life of Men, who every ten Years change their bodily Substance⟧

Men will pass dead through their own bowels.

S. K. M. II.1; 61b]   1312

⟦I calzolari⟧

²Li omini vedranno cō piacere ³disfare e rōpere l'opere loro.

⟦Shoemakers⟧

Men will take pleasure in seeing their own work destroyed and injured.

S. K. M. II.1; 9b]   1313

⟦De capretti⟧

²Ritornerà ³il tēpo d'Erode, perchè ⁴l'innocēti figliuoli sarā ⁵tolti alle loro ⁶balie, e da cru⁷deli omini di gran ferite moriranno.

⟦Of Kids⟧

The time of Herod will come again, for the little innocent children will be taken from their nurses, and will die of terrible wounds inflicted by cruel men.

1310. 2. chase. 3. assosstētare. 4. notriscano e nesti. 5. vedrassi . . elle . . govamento . . figliasstri. 7. tuibile. 8. uestimēte biāche . . arogante . . minaciā. 9. cōmetallo effoco chi.
1311. 2. spēgineransi inumerabili. 3. invmera. 8. paserā. 10. de vai. 11. [molti animali].
1312. 1–3 R. 2. vederā chō. 3. diffare.
1313. 2. [sarāno tolti] ritornera. 3. perche [essi]. 4. li nocēti figlioli. 7. gra.

V

MISCELLANEA

1314

FAUOLA

²El granchio stā³do sotto il sasso per piglia⁴re pesci che sotto a quel⁵lo entrauano, vene la pi⁶ena con rovinoso precipita⁷mento di sassi, e col loro rotolare ⁸si fraciellò tal grāchio.

QUEL MEDESIMO

¹⁰Il ragnio, stante infra ¹¹l'uue, pigliaua le mosche ¹²che in su tali uve si pasci¹³evano; venne la vēdemmi¹⁴a e fu pestato, il ragno in¹⁵sieme coll' uue.

¹⁶La uite invecchiata sopra l'al¹⁷bero vecchio · cade insi¹⁸eme colla ruina d'esso al¹⁹bero, e fu per la trista conpa²⁰gnia a mancare insieme ²¹con quella.

²²Il torrēte portò tanto ²³di terra e pietre nel ²⁴suo letto, che fu costre²⁵tto a mutar sito.

²⁶La rete che soleua pigliare ²⁷li pesci fu presa e portata ²⁸via dal furor de' pesci.

²⁹La palla della neue quan³⁰to pìv rotolando disciese ³¹dalle mōtagnie della neue ³²tāto pìv multiplicò la sua ³³magnitudine.

³⁴Il salice che per li sua lun³⁵ghi giermi à a mente e uol ³⁶cresciere da superare ciascuna ³⁷altra piāta, per avere fatto ³⁸cōpagnia colla vite che o³⁹gni anno si potta, fu ancora ⁴⁰lui senpre storpiato.

A FABLE

The crab standing under the rock to catch the fish which crept under it, it came to pass that the rock fell with a ruinous downfall of stones, and by their rush the crab was crushed.

Schemes for fables, &c. (1314–23).

THE SAME

The spider, being among the grapes, caught the flies which were feeding on those grapes. Then came the vintage, and the spider was trampled with the grapes.

The vine that has grown old on an old tree falls with the ruin of that tree, and through that bad companionship must perish with it.

The torrent carried so much earth and stones into its bed that it was then constrained to change its course.

The net that was wont to take the fish was seized and carried away by the rush of fish.

The ball of snow when, as it rolls, it descends from the snowy mountains, increases in size as it falls.

The willow, which by its long shoots hopes as it grows to outstrip every other plant, from having associated itself with the vine which is pruned every year was always crippled.

1315

Fauola della lingua morsa dai dēti.

²Il ciedro insuperbito dalla sua bellezza ³dubita delle piāte che li sō dītorno, e fat⁴tole si torre dinanzi, il uēto poi non essē⁵do interrotto ·, lo gittò per terra · diradicato.

⁶La uitalba · non stādo cōtēta nella sua ⁷siepe ·, commiciò · a passare co' sua · rami la ⁸comvne strada · e appicarsi all' opposita siepe; ⁹onde da uiādanti · poi · fu · rotta.

Fable of the tongue bitten by the teeth.

The citron, puffed up with pride of its beauty, separated itself from the trees around it and in so doing it turned away towards the wind, which not being broken in its fury, flung it uprooted on the earth.

The traveller's joy, not content in its hedge, began to fling its branches out over the high road, and to cling to the opposite hedge, and for this it was broken away by the passers-by.

1316

Il calderugio dà il titimalo(?) ²ai figliuoli ingabbiati;—pri³ma morte che perdere libertà.

The goldfinch gives a poisonous herb to its caged young. Death rather than loss of liberty.

1314. 2. El . . stando stā. 4. pessci chessotto acquel. 6. chon. 7. colloro tala. 8. siffracielloro tal. 10. infral. 12. suttale vue . . sipassi. 13. eva . . uedemi. 14. a effu pesto. 16. uite [cresscuta] "iuechiata" sopr lal. 17. vechio chade. 19. effu. 23. eppietre. 24. pochōstre. 27. pessci. 28. pessci. 30. dissciese. 31. delle. 35. gierminamenti eul. 36. cresscie perare ciascuna. 38. cholla. 39. ano si pota fu.
1315. 2. della . . belleza. 3. chelli . . effa. 4. tore. 5. interotto. 5. pertera . . diradichato. 6. istādo. 7. comīcio . . cosua. 8. apicharsi . . oposita.
1316. 1. calderigio dal il tortomalio. 2. a figlioli ingabiati.

1316. Above this text is another note, also referring to liberty; see No. 694.

S. K. M. II.1; 52b]   **1317**

〖Delle baghe〗

²Le capre cōdur³raño il uino alle ⁴città.

〖Of Bags〗

Goats will convey the wine to the city.

I.¹ 39b]   **1318**

Tutte le cose che nel uerno fiē ²nascoste sotto la neve rimaranno sco³perte e palesi nell' estate; 〖detta per la ⁴bugia che nō può stare occulta.〗

All those things which in winter are hidden under the snow, will be uncovered and laid bare in summer. 〖For Falsehood, which cannot remain hidden.〗

H.¹ 44a]   **1319**

FAVOLA

²Il giglio si pose sopra la ripa di Tesino, ³e la corrēte tirò la ripa īsieme col lilio.

A FABLE

The lily set itself down by the shores of the Ticino, and the current carried away the bank and the lily with it.

H.² 62b]   **1320**

FACETIA

²Perchè li Ungheri tēgono la croce ‡ doppia.

A JEST

Why Hungarian ducats have a double cross on them.

Triv. 38a]   **1321**

CŌPARATIONE

¶ ²Vn vaso crudo rotto si può riformare, ³ma il cotto no. ¶

A SIMILE

A broken vase of unbaked clay may be remoulded, but not a baked one.

S. K. M. III. 27a]   **1322**

Vedēdosi la carta tutta macchiata ²dalla oscura negrezza dell' īchiostro, ³di quello si duole; il quale mostra a essa ⁴che per le parole ch'esso sopra lei cōpone ⁵essere cagione della cōnseruatione di ⁶quella.

The paper, beholding itself all spotted with the deep blackness of ink, laments it; but the ink proves to it that the words which it composes upon it were the cause of its being preserved.

L. o]   **1323**

¶Neciessaria cōpagnia à la penna col tenperatoio, ²e similemēte vtile cōpagnia, perchè l'ū sanza l'altro nō ³vale troppo. ¶

The pen must necessarily have the penknife for a companion, and it is a useful companionship, for one is not good for much without the other.

S. K. M. III. 44b]   **1324**

Schemes for prophecies (1324–9).

Il coltello, accidētale armatura, caccia dall' omo le sua ²unghie, armatura naturale;

³Lo spechio si grona forte tenē⁴do · dentro · a sé spechiata la re⁵gina · , e partita quella le spe⁶chio riman in le . . . .

The knife, which is an artificial weapon, deprives man of his nails, his natural weapons.

The mirror conducts itself haughtily, holding mirrored in itself the Queen. When she departs the mirror remains there . . . .

1317. 1. bage. 2. chapre cōdu. 3. ale.
1318. 1. chose. 3. palese nella state. 4. ochulta.
1319. 2. iligio. 3. ella corēte.
1320. 1–2 R. 2. perchelli ūgeri tēgā.
1321. 2. rotto crudorottosi po.
1322. 1. charta . . machiata. 2. osscura negreza. 3. dole el . . mostra a ess. 4. parolle. 5. chagione.
1323. 1. ha la. 2. essimilemēte.
1324. 1. coltello | "accidētale armatura" cacia. 2. ungie. 3. losspechio. 4. asse. 5. losspe. 6. rimāinle.

L. 72*b*] 1325

El lino è dedicato a morte e cor²rutione de' mortali, a morte pe' lac³ciuoli delli vccelli, ⁴animali e pesci, ⁵a corrutione per le tele line dove s'in⁶volgono i morti, che si sotterrano, ⁷quali si corrōpono in tali tele; ⁸E ancora esso lino nō si spicca dal suo ⁹festuco, se esso nō comīcia a macerar¹⁰si e coronpersi, e questo è quello ¹¹collo quale si debbe incoronare e or¹²nare li ufiti funerali.

Flax is dedicated to death, and to the corruption of mortals. To death, by being used for snares and nets for birds, animals, and fish; to corruption, by the flaxen sheets in which the dead are wrapped when they are buried, who become corrupt in these winding-sheets.— And again, this flax does not separate its fibre till it has begun to steep and putrefy, and this is the flower with which garlands and decorations for funerals should be made.

I.² 139*a*] 1326

〖De' villani in camicia che lavorano〗

²Verranno tenebre diuerso · l'oriēte, le qua³li con tāta oscurità tignieranno il ⁴cielo che copre l'Italia.

〖De' barbieri〗

⁶Tvtti li omini si fuggiranno in Africa.

〖Of Peasants who work in Shirts〗

Shadows will come from the east which will blacken with great darkness the sky that covers Italy.

〖Of the Barbers〗

All men will take refuge in Africa.

G. 89*a*] 1327

Per il pannilino che si ²tiē colla mano nel co³rso dell' acqua corrē⁴te, nella quale acqua ⁵il panno lascia ⁶tutte le sue bruttu⁷re, significa ⁸quello ecc.

⁹Per lo spino inserito¹⁰li sopra boni fru¹¹tti significa que¹²llo che per sé non e¹³ra disposto a vir¹⁴tù, ma median¹⁵te l'aiuto dei pr¹⁶ecettori dà di sé ¹⁷utilissime vi¹⁸rtù.

The cloth which is held in the hand in the current of a running stream, in the waters of which the cloth leaves all its dirt, is meant to signify this, &c.

The thorn whereon is grafted good fruit signifies those natures which of themselves were not disposed towards virtue, but by the aid of their preceptors they produce most useful deeds.

C. A. 37*b*] 1328

USO COMUNE

²Vn meschino sarà soiato e essi soiatori ³senpre sien sua ingannatori e rubatori ⁴e assassini d'esso meschino.

⁵La percussione della spera del sole ⁶apparirà cosa che, chi la crederà coprire, sa⁷rà coperto da lei.

〖De' danari e oro〗

⁹Uscirà dalle cavernose spelonche, chi farà ¹⁰con sudore affaticare tutti i popoli del mōdo, ¹¹cō grādi affanni, ansieta, sudori per essere ¹²aivtato da lui.

〖Della paura della pouertà〗

¹⁴La cosa maluagia e spauēteuole darà di sé tāto ¹⁵timore appresso a delli omini che quasi come ¹⁶matti, credendo fugirla, concorreranno cō ¹⁷veloce moto alle sue smisurate forze.

A COMMON THING

A wretched person will be flattered, and these flatterers are always the deceivers, robbers, and murderers of the wretched person.

The image of the sun where it falls appears as a thing which covers the person who attempts to cover it.

〖Money and Gold〗

Out of cavernous pits a thing shall come forth which will make all the nations of the world toil and sweat with the greatest torments, anxiety, and labour, that they may gain its aid.

〖Of the Dread of Poverty〗

The malicious and terrible (monster) will cause so much terror of itself in men that they, with rapid motion, almost like madmen, thinking they are escaping her, will rush together towards her boundless force.

1325. 1. morte e cu. 2. pela. 3. vcielli. 4. pessci. 5. currutione pe le. 6. volgano .. chessi. 7. corrōpano. 8. spicha. 10. choronpersi ecquesto ecquello. 11. colla.
1326. 1–6 R. 1. camica chellavorano. 2. verra tienbre. 3. codioscurita tignierano.
1327. 1–18 R. 1. panolino chessi. 3. acq"a". 5. pano lasscia. 7. significha. 9. losspino insidito. 11. significha. 13. dissposto. 15. ti laiuto del. 17. vnlissimme.
1328. 1. vcomune. 2. mescino. 4. messcino. 5. percusione. 6. aparira .. crederra. 7. dallei. 9. vsscira delle. 10. effattichare .. pololi. 11. affani. 12. dallui. 14. la maluagia esspauēteuole. 15. apresso a delli omini che cquasi. 16. cocoreranno. 17. moto le le sua isspermisurate.

⟦Del consiglio⟧

[19]E colui che sarà piv neciessario a chi avrà bi[20]sogno di lui sarà sconosciuto, e conosciuto piv sprezzato.

⟦Of Advice⟧

The man who may be most necessary to him who needs him will be unknown, and when known greatly contemned.

W. 12587a]   1329

⟦Delle ape⟧

[2]Vivono a popoli insieme, [3]sono annegate per torli il mele; [4]molti e grandissimi popoli sarā [5]annegati nelle lor propie (case).

⟦Of Bees⟧

They live together in communities, they are destroyed that we may take the honey from them. Many and very great nations will be destroyed in their own dwellings.

F. 47a]   1330

PERCHÈ LI CANI ODORĀ VOLENTIERI IL CULO L'UNO AL[2]L' ALTRO

Questo animale à in odio i po[3]veri, perchè e' māgiano tristi cibi, e ama li richi, [4]perchè essi àn' bone vivāde e massime di car[5]ne; E lo sterco delli animali senpre ri[6]tiene della virtù della sua origine, come mo[7]strano le feccie . . . .

[10]Ora i cani ànno sì sottilissimo odo[11]rato che col naso sentono la uirtù rima[12]sta in tali feccie; e che sie uero, se le trovā [13]per le strade odorano, e se vi sentono dentro [14]vi[1]rtù di carne o d'altro, essi le pigliano, e [15]se no, le lasciano; e per tornare al quesito di[16]co, che se conoscono il cane mediante tali [17]odori essere ben pasciuto, essi lo riguar[18]dano, perchè stimano quello avere potēte e ricco pa[19]drone, e se nō sentono tale odore cō uirtù, essi sti[20]mano tal cane essere da poco, e avere povero [21]e tristo padrone, e però mordono tali cani come fare[22]bbero il suo padrone.

WHY DOGS TAKE PLEASURE IN SMELLING AT EACH OTHER

This animal has a horror of the poor, because they eat poor food, and it loves the rich, because they have good living and especially meat. And the excrement of animals always retains some virtue of its origin, as is shown by the faeces. . . .

Now dogs have so keen a sense of smell that they can discern by their nose the virtue remaining in these faeces, and if they find them in the streets, smell them, and if they smell in them the virtue of meat or of other things, they take them, and if not, they leave them. And to return to the question, I say that if by means of this smell they know that dog to be well fed, they respect him, because they judge that he has a powerful and rich master; and if they discover no such smell with the virtue (of meat), they judge that dog to be of small account and to have a poor and humble master, and therefore they bite that dog as they would his master.

C. A. 69b]   1331

Sono li moti della terra [2]circulari assai vtili, [3]cōciosiachè mai li o[4]mini si fermano; e fa[5]si in piv modi, de' qua[6]li nell' uno li omini por[7]tano la terra in spal[8]la, l'altro, colle bare[9]lle, e altri col carret[10]to; Quel che la porta [11]in spalla si fa prima [12]enpiere il uassoio in ter[13]ra ·, e perde tēpo a metterselo [14]in spalla; Quel della barel[15]la non perde tenpo.

The circular plans of carrying earth are very useful, inasmuch as men never stop in their work; and it is done in many ways. By one of these ways men carry the earth on their shoulders, by another in chests, and others on wheelbarrows. The man who carries it on his shoulders first fills the tub on the ground, and he loses time in hoisting it on to his shoulders. He with the chests loses no time.

Irony (1332).

Triv. 1b]   1332

Se 'l Petrarca amò si forte il lauro, [2]fu perch' egli è buon fralla salsiccia e tor(do); [3]io nō posso di lor ciancie far tesauro.

If Petrarch was so fond of bay, it was because it is of a good taste with sausages and thrush; I cannot put any value on their foolery.

19. cholui . . ara. 20. sara isconosciuto ecognoscuto piv sprezato.
1329. 2. vivano apopoli ensieme. 3. anegate. 5. [no] gati nelle lororo propie. \\\\ 6. [si some] sarà se.
1330. 1. adorā. 5. Ello stercho. 7. stra leuetie miseraice strebute insin ne. 8. le ultima basseza delle intestine. 9. per trarre asse desse fecce la uirtu cheue. 10. rimasa ora i cani ā si. 11. sentano. 12. sa in tale fecce. 13. strade [elle] odorano esse uisentā dentro. 14. esse le. 15. lassciano. 16. cognoscano. 17. odore . . passiuto. 18. richo. 19. esse nō setā. 21. mordā. 22. bono.
1331. 3. cōcosia. 4. effa. 6. po"r". 7. inispal. 8. collebare. 9. le e . . carre. 10. chella. 11. inispalla. 14. inispalla.
1332. 1. petrarcha . . ilaur \\\\. 2. percheglie bō . . e tor \\\\\. 3. i nō . . giāce.

1331. The subject of this text has apparently no connexion with the other texts of this section.

1332. Petrarch affirms (*Son.* xliii and *Sest.* II. v. 4, l. 5) that he does not aspire to laurel for the sake

Br. M. 129*b*]   **1333**

Noi siamo due fratelli, che ciascuno di noi ²à vn fratello; qui il modo del dire páre che ³2 fratelli diuētino 4.

We are two brothers, each of us has a brother. Here the way of saying it makes it appear that the two brothers have become four. Tricks (1333-5).

C. 19*b*]   **1334**

GIOCHI DI PARTITO

²Mettiti in 2 mani equali numeri ·; metti 4 della mā ³destra nella sinistra || gitta via il rimanēte || gitta via altrettā⁴to della man sinistra || metti vi sopra · 5 ·; ora tu ti trovi ⁵in quella mano 13 || cioè io vi ti feci mettere 4 dalla destra nel⁶la sinistra, e gittar uia il rimanēte; ora qui la mā destra à piv 4 che là ⁷nō sonovi; io ti fo poi gittare via altrettanto dalla destra quāto tu ⁸gittasti dalla sinistra, che gittando dalle 2 mani due quātità e⁹quali, il rimanente fia equale; ora e' ti resta 4 e 4, che fa 8, ¹⁰e perchè il giocco nō sia conosciuto io vi ti feci mettere sopra 5 ¹¹che fece · 13.

TRICKS OF DIVIDING

Take in each hand an equal number; put 4 from the right hand into the left; cast away the remainder; cast away an equal number from the left hand; add 5, and now you will find 13 in this [left] hand; that is—I made you put 4 from the right hand into the left, and cast away the remainder; now your right hand has 4 more; then I make you throw away as many from the right as you threw away from the left; so, throwing from each hand a quantity of which the remainder may be equal, you now have 4 and 4, which make 8, and that the trick may not be detected I made you put 5 more, which made 13.

GIOCHI DI PARTITO

¹³Togli da 12 in giù che numero ti piace; togli poi tāti de' mia che ¹⁴tu finisca il numero di 12 ·, e quel che rimane a me è ¹⁵il numero che tu aveui prima; perchè quādo io ti dissi to¹⁶gli da 12 in giù qual numero ti piace, io mi missi in mano ¹⁷12, e di questo mio 12 tu togliesti tale numero, che tu ¹⁸faciesti il tuo numero 12; ecco che tu cresciesti al tuo nu¹⁹mero che tu togliesti al mio; cioè che se tu aveui 8, a andare insino ²⁰in 12, tu togliesti del mio 12 vn · 4; onde quel 4 trasmu²¹tato da me a te fa che 'l mio 12 resta 8, e 'l tuo 8 si fa 12; ²²adunque il mio 8 è equale al tuo 8 innāzi che lo facesse 12.

Take any number less than 12 that you please; then take of mine enough to make up the number 12, and that which remains to me is the number which you at first had; because when I said, take any number less than 12 as you please, I took 12 into my hand, and of that 12 you took such a number as made up your number of 12; and what you added to your number, you took from mine; that is, if you had 8 to go as far as to 12, you took of my 12, 4; hence this 4 transferred from me to you reduced my 12 to a remainder of 8, and your 8 became 12; so that my 8 is equal to your 8, before it was made 12.

C. A. 76*b*]   **1335**

Se tu vuoi insegnia²re a vno · vna cosa ³che tu · nō sappia, falli ⁴misurare la lunghezza ⁵d'una cosa a te incogni⁶ta ·, e lui saprà la mi⁷sura che tu prima nō sa⁸peui — maestro Gi⁹ovanni da Lodi.

If you want to teach some one a subject you do not know yourself, let him measure the length of an object unknown to you, and he will learn the measure you did not know before—Master Giovanni da Lodi.

1333. 1. nosiamo . . ciasscu. 2. qui el.
1334. 3. desstra. 4. tutti trovi. 5. coe . . della desstra. 6. chella. 7. soneva . . desstra. 8. gittassti . . sinisstra. 9. ressta . . cheffa. 10. gocho . . cognossciuto . . fesi. 11. cheffece. 12. givochi di part "to". 13. potāti. 14. ttu finissca . . ecquel . . anmehe. 15. chettu . . prima tu. 16. ingu. 17. quessto mi 12 tu togliessti . . chettu. 18. faciessti . . chettu cressciessti. 19. mero tu togliessti . . coe chessetu . . andare. 20. togliessti. 21. atte . . ressta. 22. e he quale . . chello facessi.
1335. 1. settu volli insegni. 3. chettu . . sapia. 4. lungeza. 5. atte. 6. ellui. 7. chettu. 8. maesstro. 9. dallodi.

of glory but as a medicine. In *Archivio Stor. Lombardo*, IX. 600, Count Porro writes, commenting on this passage: 'Pare che allo stesso modo ch'egli amava di disegnare caricature gli piacesse di scherzare e lo arguisco dalle sequenti linee che lessi a pag. 2 (del. MS. Trivulzi): Se'l Petrarca amò si forte . . .'. G. Calvi attributes these lines to Bellincioni. *Archivio Storico*

Lombardo, XLIII, p. 452.

1334. G. Govi says in the *Saggio*, p. 22: 'Si dilettò Leonardo di giuochi de prestigi e molti ne descrisse, che si leggono poi riportati dal Pacioli nel suo libro: *de Viribus Quantitatis*, e che, se non tutti, sono certo in gran parte invenzioni del Vinci.'

XXI

LETTERS. PERSONAL RECORDS. DATED NOTES

*W*HEN *we consider how superficial and imperfect are the accounts of Leonardo's life written some time after his death by Vasari and others, any notes or letters which can throw more light on his life, his movements, his engagements must occupy a foremost place as authentic information.*

The drafts of letters written in Rome, Nos. 1351–1353, furnish a strange aspect of Leonardo's activities in the palace of the Vatican where Raphael and Michelangelo were at the time occupied, the former with paintings al fresco—the famous Disputa, the School of Athens, the Heliodorus, &c.—while the latter, after completing the paintings on the ceiling of the Sistine chapel, was entrusted with other work. What a contrast, what an irony of fate: Leonardo's activities in the same palace and at the same time: he, the painter of the Last Supper at Milan, of the Battle of Anghiari at Florence, and of the Mona Lisa! Moreover, he was then in the service of a proud Medici, Giuliano, Duke of Nemours, who by contemporaries has been described as gran spenditore, *the only surviving brother of Pope Leo X. Truly a strange world.*

At the beginning of Section XXI have been placed Leonardo's drafts of a report on earthquakes and floods in Armenia, on social unrest, and strange professions of faith suggesting apostasy. The report is addressed to a high official in Egypt, and its authenticity cannot be questioned, since it is written in Leonardo's own hand. It has been suggested by modern critics that Leonardo was here collecting material for a fantastic tale—such as the stories by Boccaccio, Ariosto, Bandello. But this hypothesis has a serious defect. These drafts of letters to an Eastern official in high position betray exasperation on the part of the writer, who seems to have been at pains to find the proper submissive terms. No other drafts of letters by Leonardo show so much hesitation, and one wonders why he should feel so troubled over a mere fanciful tale.

Moreover, his seemingly fantastic stories are corroborated in the Diaries of Marin Sanuto, in which are quoted official reports sent from Egypt to the Doge and Signoria of Venice, giving information which substantiates Leonardo's account of recent events in the East. E. Solmi, author of Le Fonti dei manoscritti di Leonardo da Vinci *(Turin, 1908), in quoting Marin Sanuto does not hesitate to conclude:* il famoso viaggio in Oriente Leonardesco ha in sé la sua verità. *And:* Ecco un nuovo filo conduttore per risolvere la tanto dibattuta questione del viaggio in Oriente del Vinci.

When naming places in the East, in Egypt and Mauretania, Leonardo habitually used Ptolemy's maps, which were then in general use. Several editions were published in Rome and elsewhere in Italy in 1462, 1477, 1478, &c. These maps of the Alexandrian geographer of the second century before Christ were much superior to any maps of the Middle Ages and more recent times.

The drafts of letters to Lodovico il Moro are very remarkable. Leonardo and this prince were certainly far less closely connected than has hitherto been supposed. It is impossible that Leonardo can have remained so long in the service of this prince because the salary was good, as is commonly stated. On the contrary, it would seem that what kept him there, in spite of his sore need of the money owed him by the prince, was the hope of some day being able to carry out the project of casting the gran cavallo.

AL DIODARIO DI SIRIA LOCOTENĒTE DEL SACRO SOLTANO ²DI BABILONIA

³Il nvouo accidēte accaduto in queste nostre parti settentrionali, il quale sō certo che nō solamēte a te ma a tutto l'universo farà ⁴terrore; il quale successiuamente ti sarà detto per ordine mostrando primo l'effetto e poi la causa . . . .

⁵Ritrovandomi · io in queste parti d'Erminia

TO THE DEFTERDAR OF SYRIA, LIEUTENANT OF THE SACRED SULTAN OF BABYLON

[3] The recent disaster in our northern parts which I am certain will terrify not you alone but the whole world, which shall be related to you in due order, showing first the effect and then the cause [4] . . . .

Drafts of Letters and Reports referring to Armenia (1336–7)

Finding myself in this part of Armenia [5] to

1336. 1. soria. 3. [eaca n] "duto" [vono] "il nvouo" accidēte | "achaduto" in queste . . parte settantrionali [le quali so] "il quale [ere] sō cierto" che . . atte mattuto . . dara. 4. terrore [e ca] il . . causa [e du]. 5. dare | "con amore essollecitudine" opera acquello

1336. Lines 1–52 are reproduced in facsimile on Pl. CXVI.

1. *Diodario.* This word is not to be found in any Italian dictionary, and for a long time I vainly sought an explanation of it. The chief town of each Turkish vilayet, or province, was the residence of a Defterdar, who presides over the financial affairs of the province. *Defterdar hane* was, in former times, the name given to the Ministry of Finance at Constantinople; the Minister of Finance to the Porte was then known as the *Maliye Naziri* and the *Defterdars* were his subordinates. A *Defterdar* was merely the head of the finance department in each provincial district. With regard to my suggestion that Leonardo's *Diodario* might be identical with the Defterdar of former times, the late M. C. Defrémerie, Arabic Professor and Membre de l'Institut de France, wrote to me as follows: 'Votre conjecture est parfaitement fondée; diodario est l'équivalent de dévadar ou plus exactement dévâtdâr, titre d'une importante dignité en Égypte, sous les Mamlouks.'

The word, however, is not of Turkish, but of Perso-Arabic derivation. دواتدار, دفتردار literally *Daftar*, *dāwātdar*, Arab. for 'parchment', 'inkstand'; and *dar* a Persian termination. The compound word means the holder of an office. During the Mameluke supremacy over Syria, which corresponded in date with Leonardo's time, the office of Defterdar was the third in importance in the state.

Soltano di Babilonia. The name of Babylon was commonly applied to Cairo in the Middle Ages. For instance, Breidenbach, *Itinerarium Hierosolyma*, p. 218, says: 'At last we reached Babylon. But this is not that Babylon which stood on the further shore of the river Chober, but that which is called the Egyptian Babylon. It is close by Cairo and the twain are but one and not two towns; one half is called Cairo and the other Babylon, whence they are called together Cairo-Babylon; originally the town is said to have been named Memphis and then Babylon, but now it is called Cairo.' Compare No. 1085, l. 6.

Egypt was governed from 1382 till 1517 by the Borgite or Tcherkessian dynasty of the Mameluke Sultans. One of the most famous of these, Sultan Kaït Bey, ruled from 1468 to 1496, during whose reign the tomb mosque of Kaït Bey was erected in Cairo, which preserves his name to this day. Under the rule of this great and wise prince many foreigners, particularly Italians, found occupation in Egypt, as may be seen in the 'Viaggio di Josaphat Barbaro', among other travellers. 'Next to Leonardo (so I learned from Jacob Burckhardt of Basle) Kaït Bey's most helpful engineer was a German who in about 1487 superintended the construction of the Mole at Alexandria. Felix Fabri knew him and mentions him in his *Historia Suevorum*, written in 1488.'

4. The text here breaks off. The following lines are a fresh beginning written afterwards. The corrections and amendments amply prove that the writer was particularly anxious to choose such words and phrases as might best suit the occasion.

5. *Parti d'Erminia.* See No. 945, note. The extent of Armenia in Leonardo's time is only approximately known. In the fifteenth century the Persians governed the eastern and the Arabs the southern portions. Arabic authors—as, for instance, Abu'l-Fidā—include Cilicia and a part of Cappadocia in Armenia, and Armenia Maior was the tract of that country known later as Turcomania, while Armenia Minor was the territory between Cappadocia and the Euphrates. It was not till 1522, or even 1574, that the whole country came under the dominion of the Ottoman Turks, in the reign of Selim I.

The Mameluke Sultans of Egypt seem to have taken a particular interest in this, the most northern, province of their empire, which was even then in danger of being conquered by the Turks. In the autumn of 1477 Sultan Kaït Bey made a journey of inspection, visiting Antioch and the valleys of the Tigris and Euphrates with a numerous and brilliant escort. This tour is briefly alluded to by Mujīr-ad-Dīn, p. 561; and by Weil, *Geschichte der Abbasiden*, v, p. 358. An anonymous member of the suite wrote a diary of the expedition in Arabic, which has been published by R. V. Lonzone (*Viaggio in Palestina e Soria di Kaid Ba XVIII sultano della II dinastia mamelucca, fatto nel 1477. Testo arabo. Turin*, 1878, without notes or commentary). Compare the critique on this edition by J. Gildemeister in *Zeitschrift des Deutschen Palaestina Vereins* (vol. iii, pp. 246–9). Lanzone's edition seems to be no more than an abridged copy of the original. I owe to Professor Schéfer, Membre de l'Institut, the information that he was in possession of a manuscript in which the text is fuller, and more correctly given. The Mameluke dynasty was, as is well known, of Circassian origin, and a large proportion of the Egyptian Army was recruited in Circassia even as late as the fifteenth century. That was a period of political storms in

· a dare con amore e sollecitudine opera a quello
vfitio, pel quale tu mi mădasti, e nel ⁶dare principio in quelle parti che a me pareano esser · piv
al proposito nostro ·, entrai nella ⁷città · di
Calindra, vicina ai nostri confini; questa città
è posta nelle spiaggie di quel⁸la parte del mõte
Tavro, che è diuisa dall' Eufrates e riguarda i
corni del grã Mõte Tav⁹ro per ponẽte ·; Questi
corni · son di tanta altura che par che tocchino
il cielo, che nell' universo non è parte terre¹⁰stre
piv alta della sua cima ·; e senpre 4 ore inanzi
dì è percossa dai razzi del sole ¹¹in oriẽte ·; e per

carry into effect with due love and care the task
for which you sent me [6]; and to make a beginning in a place which seemed to me to be most
to our purpose, I entered into the city of Calindra [7], near to our frontiers. This city is
situated at the base of that part of the Taurus
Mountains which is divided from the Euphrates
and looks towards the peaks of the great Mount
Taurus [8] to the west [9]. These peaks are of
such a height that they seem to touch the sky,
and in all the world there is no part of the earth
higher than its summit [10], and the rays of the

[pe] vfitio . . mădassti. 6. parte [chontingne ne a noi] che . . pareano | "esser" piv . . nosstro. 7. cita di chalindra . . confini [e]
questa . . ispiegge [del m] di quel. 8. diuisa [dal lago] dalleufrates [essa per le] e riguarda i [grã] corni del "grã". 9. altura [che
lo per me non credo] "che par chettochino il celo" che nell universo [sia] "none" parte. 10. ste piv al della . . essenpre . . di
[allu] e perchossa . . sole [che allei si mostra].

Syria and Asia Minor, and it is easy to suppose that
the Sultan's minister, to whom Leonardo addresses
his report as his superior, had a special interest in the
welfare of those frontier provinces. Only to mention
a few historical events of Sultan Kaït Bey's reign, we
find that in 1488 he assisted the Circassians to resist the
encroachments of 'Alā'ud-Daulat, an Asiatic prince
who had allied himself with the Osmanli to threaten
the province; the consequence was a war in Cilicia
by sea and land, which broke out in the following
year between the contending powers. Only a few
years earlier the same province had been the scene of
the so-called Caramenian war in which the united
Venetian, Neapolitan, and Slavonic fleets had been
engaged (see Coriolano Cippico, *Della guerra dei
Veneziani nell' Asia dal 1469–74*, Venice, 1796, p.
54), and we learn incidentally that a certain Leonardo
Boldo—as his name would indicate, of Italian birth—
Governor of Scutari under Sultan Maḥmūd played
an important part in the negotiations for peace.

5. *Ritrovandomi io* . . . . Opening words of a report.
The writer is particular in the choice of his words, and
there is an unusual amount of corrections; he was evidently preparing an important document. G. Govi
and G. Calvi thought that these writings were either
on the level of modern novel-writers, the novel to be
illustrated by views of fanciful landscapes, or that,
possibly, they were copies of somebody else's observations on the effects of an earthquake in Armenia.

tu mi mandasti. Such colloquial addressing of a
high official is, I believe, only intelligible on the
hypothesis that the two were on the most intimate
terms, that the Defterdar had been one of the many
Italian renegades in the Sultan's service. Compare
ll. 54 and 55.

7. *Città de Calindra* (*Chalindra*). The position of
this city is so exactly determined, between the valley
of the Euphrates and the Taurus range, that it ought
to be possible to identify it. But it can hardly be the
same as the seaport of Cilicia with a somewhat similar
name—Celenderis, Kelandria, Celendria, Kilindria,
now the Turkish Gulnar. In two Catalonian Portulans
in the Bibliothèque Nationale in Paris—one dating
from the fifteenth century, by Wilhelm von Soler,
the other by Olivez de Majorca, in 1584—I find this
place called Calandra. But Leonardo's Calindra must
have lain more to the north-west, probably somewhere
in Kurdistan. The fact that the geographical position
is so carefully determined by Leonardo seems to prove
that it was a place of no great importance and little

known. It is singular that the words first written in
l. 8 were *divisa dal lago* (Lake Van?), altered afterwards to *dall' Eufrates*.

Nostri confini, and in l. 6 *proposito nostro*. These
refer to the frontier and to the affairs of the Mameluke Sultan. Lines 65 and 66 throw some light on the
purpose of the reporter's mission.

8. *I corni del gran monte Tauro* (Pls. CXVI–
CXVIII). W. M. Ramsay and Dr. Plüchmann think
that Leonardo speaks here of the 'Alā Dāgh (*Sit-
zungsber. der Berliner Akademie der Wissenschaften*,
1883). Strabo places the Euphrates in the neighbourhood, by mistake. Prof. Govi wrote:

'Quanto alle notizie sul monte Tauro, sull' Armenia
e sull' Asia Minore che si contengono negli altri
frammenti, esse vennero prese da qualche geografo
o viaggiatore contemporaneo. Dall' indice imperfetto
che accompagna quei frammenti, si potrebbe dedurre
che Leonardo volesse farne un libro, che poi non
venne compiuto. A ogni modo, non è possibile di
trovare in questi brani nessun indizio di un viaggio
di Leonardo in oriente, nè della sua conversione alla
religione di Maometto, come qualcuno pretenderebbe.
Leonardo amava con passione gli studi geografici, e
ne' suoi scritti s'incontran spesso itinerarî, indica-
zioni o descrizioni di luoghi, schizzi di carte e abbozzi
topografici di varie regioni, non è quindi strano che
egli, abile narratore com' era, si fosse proposto di
scrivere una specie di romanzo in forma epistolare
svolgendone l'intreccio nell' Asia Minore, intorna alla
quale i libri d'allora, e forse qualche viaggiatore amico
suo, gli avevano somministrato alcuni elementi più o
meno fantastici. (See *Transunti della Reale Accademia
dei Lincei*, vol. v, Ser. 3).

For further discussion on the subject compare G.
Calvi, *I Manoscritti di L. d. V.* (Bologna, 1925), pp.
62–4; v. Seidlitz, *Leonardo*, i, pp. 93–5, 396.

Lines 9–10. Aristotle (*Meteorol.*, lib. 1, cap. 13)
states that the highest peak of the Caucasus remains
illuminated by the sun for four hours after the sun has
set in the valley below. The ancients had an exaggerated idea of the heights of mountains (compare
Pliny, *N.H.* ii. 65). Observations on the Lake of
Geneva show that Mont Blanc retains the rays
of the sun only 29 minutes longer than the shore of
the lake. *4 ore inanzi* seems to mean four hours
before the sun's rays penetrate to the bottom of the
valleys.

11. *Pietra bianchissima.* The Taurus Mountains
consist in great part of limestone.

essere lei di pietra biāchissima, essa forte risplende, e fa l'ufitio a questi Ermini come farebbe vn bel lume [12]di luna · nel mezzo delle tenebre; e per la sua grande altura essa passa la somma altezza de' nuvoli per spatio di 4 miglia per linia retta; [13]Questa cima è ueduta di grā parte dell' occidente alluminata dal sole dopo il suo tramontare [14]insino alla 3ª parte della notte; ed è quella che appresso di voi ne' tempi sereni abbiamo già giudicato essere vna cometa, e pare a noi nelle [15]tenebre della notte mvtarsi varie figure, e quādo diuidersi in due o in 3 parti, e quādo lūga e quādo corta; e questo nascie per li [16]nuvoli che ne l'orizzonte del cielo s'interpongono infra parte d'esso monte e il sole, e per tagliare loro essi raz[17]zi solari ·, il lume del monte è interrotto con vari spati di nvvoli, e però è di figvra uaria[18]bile nel suo splendore.

sun always fall upon it on its east side, four hours before daytime; and being of the whitest stone [11] it shines resplendently and fulfils the function to these Armenians which a bright moonlight would in the midst of the darkness; and by its great height it outreaches the utmost level of the clouds by a space of four miles in a straight line. This peak is seen in many places towards the west, illuminated by the sun after its setting, the third part of the night. This it is which with you [14] we formerly in calm weather had supposed to be a comet, and which appears to us in the darkness of night to change its form, being sometimes divided in two or three parts, and sometimes long and sometimes short. And this is caused by the clouds on the horizon of the sky which interpose between part of this mountain and the sun, and by cutting off the solar rays the light on the mountain is intercepted by various intervals of clouds, and therefore varies in the form of its brightness.

DIVISIONE DEL LIBRO

[20]La predica e persuasione di fede;

[21]¶ La subita inōdatione insin al [22]fine suo; ¶

[23]¶ La ruina della città;

[24]¶ La morte del popolo [25]e disperatione; ¶

[26]La caccia del predica[27]tore e la sua liberatione e benivo[28]lentia; ¶

[29]¶ Descritione della cavsa di tal [30]ruina del mōte; ¶

[31]¶ Il danno ch'ella fece;

[32]¶ Ruina di neve;

[33]¶ Trovata del profeta;

[34]¶ La profetia sua;

[35]¶ Allagamēto delle parti basse [36]di || Erminia occidentale, [37]li scolamēti delle quali era[38]no per la tagliata di mōte Tav[39]ro; ¶

[40]Come il novo profeta mostra che [41]questa ruina è fatta [42]al suo proposito;

THE DIVISIONS OF THE BOOK [19]

Sermon and conversion to the faith [20].

The sudden inundation, to its end.

[23] The destruction of the city.

[24] The death of the people and their despair.

The hunt for the preacher, his release and benevolence [28].

Description of the cause of this fall of the mountain [30].

The mischief it did.

[32] Destruction by snow.

The finding of the prophet [33].

His prophecy.

[35] The inundation of the lower portion of Eastern Armenia, the draining of which was effected by the cutting through the Taurus Mountains.

How the new prophet showed [40] that this destruction had happened as he had foretold.

---

11. lesere .. petra biāchissima [essa] "essa forte rissplende e" fa .. acquesti .. chome. 12. luna "nel mezzo delle tenebre" e per .. le [magnie] somme alteza de nugoli per [piv di 4 miglia] "per isspatio di 4 miglia" a [p]. 13. ueduta [prima per] di .. dell ochcidente [pi] allumi. 14. e "jnsino alla 3 parte della notte" de cquella che apresso div[n]oi .. tenpi .. abiā ga gudicato .. cumeta .. annoi. 15. ecquādo .. parti "e equādo lūga ecquādo corta" ecquesto nasscie. 16. nvoli .. orizonte .. celo sinterpongano .. elsole .. essira. 17. ellume .. monte he .. varri [e] spati .. nvgoli. 24. popolo [el suo piāto]. 26. la [cōfermatio] la cerca. 27. ella .. venivo. 35. alagamēto .. parte. 40. profeta [mostra]; che *is wanting*. 41. [disc] questa .. effatta.

19. The next 33 lines are evidently the contents of a connected report of which we possess no trace.

20. *Persuasione di fede*—of the Christian or the Mohammedan faith? We must suppose the latter, at the beginning of a document addressed to so high a Mohammedan official. *Predica* probably stands as an abbreviation for *predicazione* (Lat. *praedicatio*) in the sense of praise or glorification; very probably it may mean some such initial doxology as we find in Mohammedan works. (Compare l. 40.)

26, 28. The phraseology of this is too general for any conjecture as to its meaning to be worth hazarding.

30. *Ruina del monte*. In a catalogue of earthquakes, entitled *kashf as-salsabīl wa-waṣf az-zalzala*, and written by Jalālu'd-Din Siyūṭī, the following statement occurs: 'In the year 889 (1484 A.D.) there were

six shocks of earthquake at Aleppo. They were excessively violent and threw the inhabitants into consternation.' I owe this communication to Prof. Ch. Schéfer, Membre de l'Institut, to whom this unpublished Arabic MS. belongs. Other entries refer to two earthquakes in Cairo, in 1476 and 1481.

36. *Tagliata di Monte Tauro*. The Euphrates flows through the Taurus range near the influx of the Kura Shai; it rushes through a rift in the wildest cliffs from 2,000 to 3,000 feet high and runs on for 90 miles in 300 falls or rapids till it reaches Telek, near which at a spot called Gleikash, or the Hart's Leap, it measures only 35 paces across. Compare the map on Pl. CXIX and the explanation of it on p. 321.

40. *Novo profeta*, l. 33, *profeta*. Mohammed. Leonardo here refers to the Koran:

[43]Descritione del mōte Tavro [44]e del fiume Evfrates;

[45]Perchè il monte risplende nella sua cima [46]la metà o 'l 3° della notte, e pare vna [47]cometa a quelli di ponente dopo la [48]sera, e ināti dì a quelli di leuāte.

[49]Perchè essa cometa par di uariabile [50]figura in modo che ora è tonda or [51]lunga e or diuisa in 2 or in 3 parti, e [52]ora vnita, e quando si perde, e quādo si riuede.

FIGURA DEL MŌTE TAVRO

[54]Non sono, o Diodario, da essere da te inputato di pigritia come le tue rāpogne · par che accennino ·, ma lo isfrenato amore, [55]il quale ha creato il benifitio ch'io posseggo da te, è quello, che mi à costretto cō somma [56]sollecitudine a cercare e cō diligiētia a investigare la cavsa di sì grāde e stupēdo effetto ·; la qual cosa [57]nō sanza tēpo à potuto avere effetto; ora, per farti ben satisfatto della causa di sì grande effetto, è neciessario ch'io ti mostri [58]la forma del sito, e poi verrò allo effetto col quale credo rimarrai satisfatto;

[59]Nō ti dolere, o Diodario, del mio tardare · a dar risposta alla tua desiderosa richiesta, perchè queste cose, di che tu mi richie[60]desti, son di natura che nō sanza processo di tenpo si possono bene esprimere, e massime perchè, a voler mostrare la causa di [61]sì grande effetto, bisognia descrivere cō bona forma la natura del sito, e mediante quella tu potrai poi cō [62]facilità satisfarti della predetta richiesta;

[63]Jo lascierò indietro la descritione della forma dell' Asia Minore, e che mari o terre sien quelle che terminono [64]la figura della sua quātità, perchè so che la diligentia e sollecitudine de' tua studi non t'ànno di tal notitia [65]privato; e verrò a denotare la vera figura di Tavrus Mōte, il quale è quello ch'è cavsatore di sì stupenda e dannosa maraviglia, il quale · serue alla espeditione del nostro pro[66]posito; Questo monte Tavro è quello che appresso di molti è detto essere il giogo del Monte Cavcaso, ma, avēdo [67]voluto ben chiarirmi ·, ò voluto parlare con alquanti di quelli che abitano sopra del Mar Caspio, i quali mostrano che

Description of the Taurus Mountains [43] and the river Euphrates.

Why the mountain shines at the top, from half to a third of the night, and looks like a comet to the inhabitants of the West after the sunset, and before day to those of the East.

Why this comet appears of variable forms, so that it is now round and now long, and now again divided into two or three parts, and now in one piece, and when it is lost and when to be seen again.

OF THE SHAPE OF THE TAURUS MOUNTAINS [53]

I am not to be accused, Oh Defterdar, of idleness, as your chidings seem to hint; but your excessive love for me, which gave rise to the benefits you have conferred on me [55], is that which has also compelled me to the utmost painstaking in seeking out and diligently investigating the cause of so great and stupendous an effect. And this could not be done without time; now, in order to satisfy you fully as to the cause of so great an effect, it is requisite that I should explain to you the form of the place, and then I will proceed to the effect, by which I believe you will be amply satisfied.

[59] Do not be aggrieved, O Defterdar, by my delay in responding to your pressing request, for those things which you require of me are of such a nature that they cannot be well expressed without some lapse of time; particularly because, in order to explain the cause of so great an effect, it is necessary to describe with accuracy the nature of the place; and by this means I can afterwards easily satisfy your above-mentioned request [62].

I will pass over any description of the form of Asia Minor, or as to what seas or lands form the limits of its outline and extent, because I know that by your own diligence and carefulness in your studies you have not remained in ignorance of these matters [65]; and I will go on to describe the true form of the Taurus Mountain which is the cause of this stupendous and harmful marvel, and which will serve to advance us in our purpose [66]. This Taurus is that mountain which, by many people, is said to be the ridge of

---

45. rissplende. 47. cometa [in] acquelli di. 48. acquelli. 50. ettondo. 51. lungho . . diuiso. 54. ho diodaro . . datte . . piegritia chome . . lo [tuo] isfrenato. 55. datte ecquello che [apv "a" chavoluto] che ma cōstretto chō somma [dieligiētia] . . 56. [cerchare ei] sollecitudine a cerchare . . anvesstighare la chavsa . . stupēte. 57. hora . . sodisfatto di si grande "della causa [effetto] e . . mosstri. 58. la [cavsa ella] forma . . rimarai sadisfatto. 59. risspossta tua . . "desiderosa" richiessta . . queste [son cho] chose di che. 60. possano "bene" esspriemere . . mosstrare. 61. disscrivere. 62. sadisfarti. 63. lasscriero [sta] indirieto la desscriptione . . etterre . . chetterminino. 64. chella [tua] diligentia [de tua] essollecitudine . . notanno. 65. mōte | "il quel equello che chavsatore di si stupenta e danosa maraviglia" la quale . . espeditione . . nostro. 66. ecquello . . gogo . . cavcasso ma avē . . chasspio . . mosstrano.

'In the name of the most merciful God.—When the earth shall be shaken by an earthquake; and the earth shall cast forth her burdens; and a man shall say, what aileth her? On that day the earth shall declare her tidings, for that thy Lord will inspire her. On that day men shall go forward in distinct classes, that they may behold their works. And whoever shall have wrought good of the weight of an ant, shall behold the same.' (*The Koran*, translated by G. Sale, chap.

xcix, p. 452).

53–94. The facsimile of this passage is given on Pl. CXVII.

54–62. Here begin two drafts for letters, the second (ll. 59–62) being an improvement of the first. The purport of both is essentially the same, but the first is pitched in a key of ill-disguised annoyance which is absent from the second.

[68]che, benchè i mõti loro abbino il medesimo nome, questi son di maggiore altura, e però cõfermano, quel sia il uero Mõte Caucaso, perchè Caucaso in lingua Scitica vuol dire somma altezza ·, e in vero non ci è noti[69]tia che l'oriēte nè l'occidente abbia monte di si grande altura ·; e la pruova, che così sia ·, è che li abitatori de' pae[70]si, che gli stanno per ponēte, vedono i razzi del sole che allumina insino alla 4ª parte delle maggior notti grã [71]parte della sua cima ·, e 'l simile fa a quelli paesi che gli stanno per oriēte.

Mount Caucasus; but wishing to be very clear about it, I desired to speak to some of the inhabitants of the shores of the Caspian Sea, who give evidence that though their mountains bear the same name, yet these are higher; and confirm that this must be the true Caucasus, for in the Scythian tongue, Caucasus means a very high [68] peak, and in fact we have no information of there being, in the east or in the west, any mountain so high. And the proof of this is that the inhabitants of the countries to the west see the rays of the sun illuminating a great part of its summit for as much as a quarter of the longest night. And in the same way, in those countries which lie to the east.

QUALITÀ E QUĀTITÀ DEL MÕTE TAVRO

[73]L'ombra di questo giogo del Tauro è di tanta altura che, quãdo di mezzo giugno il sole è a mezzo giorno, la sua õbra s'a[74]stende insino al principio della Sarmatia, che sõ giornate · 12, e a mezzo dicembre s'astē[75]de insino ai mõti Iperborei, che è viaggio d'un mese inverso tramontana; E senpre la sua parte opposita al uē[76]to che soffia è piena di nuvoli e nebbie, perchè il uento, che s'apre nella percussione del sasso, dopo esso sasso si uiene a richi[77]vdere, e in tal modo porta con oeco i nvvoli da ogni parte, e lasciali nella lor percussione; e senpre è piena di percussione di saette per la grã moltitudine di nvvoli che lì sõ ricettati, onde il sasso è tutto fracassato e pien di grã ruine; Questa nelle [78]sua radici è abitata da richissimi popoli, ed è piena di bellissimi fonti e fiumi; è fer[79]tile e abondante d'ogni bene e massime nelle parti che riguardano a mezzo giorno; — [80]ma quando se n'è

OF THE STRUCTURE AND SIZE OF MOUNT TAURUS

[73] The shadow of this ridge of the Taurus is of such a height that when, in the middle of June, the sun is at its meridian, its shadow extends as far as the borders of Sarmatia, twelve days off; and in the middle of December it extends as far as the Hyperborean Mountains, which are at a month's journey to the north [75]. And the side which faces the wind is always full of clouds and mists, because the wind, which is parted in beating on the rock, closes again on the farther side of that rock, and in its motion carries with it the clouds from all quarters and leaves them where it strikes. And it is always full of thunderbolts from the great quantity of clouds which accumulate there, whence the rock is all riven and full of huge debris [77]. This mountain, at its base, is inhabited by a very rich population and is full of most beautiful springs and rivers, and is fertile and abounding in all

68. "che beche i moti loro abbino il medesimo nome e questi sondi magorealtura e pero cõfermano" caucasso perche [a] cavcasso illingua isciticha vol .. alteza. 69. nelloccidente .. ella .. chosi .. he chelli. 70. chelli .. veggano i razi .. magor notto. 71.acquelli .. chelli. 73. gogho .. mezo gugnio .. he a mezo gorno. 74. insino [alla sarmatia] al .. chessõgornate .. mezo di[s]. cenbre sasste. 75. he viaggio .. Essenpre .. oposita. 76. chessoffia .. nvuoli ennebbie .. chessi .. perchussione. 77. vedere [perche] e in .. nvuoli .. parte [e ne] ellasscia .. perchussione. *The text bettwen the words* perchussione *and* Questa *has subsequently been added and is written on the margin in* 13 *short lines.* nugoli chelli .. ettutto frachassato. 78. effiumi. 79. mezo gorno. 80. montata circha .. comica attrovare.

68. Caucasus; Herodotus. Καύκασις; Arm. Kaukaz.
77. Sudden storms are equally common on the heights of Ararat. It is hardly necessary to observe that Ararat cannot be meant here. Its summit is formed like the crater of Vesuvius. The peaks sketched on Pls. CXVI–CXVIII are probably views of the same mountain, taken from different sides. Near the solitary peak, Pl. CXVII, these three names are written : *goba*, *arnigasar*, *carūda*, names most likely of different peaks. Pls. CXVI and CXVII are in the original on a single sheet folded down the middle, 30 centimetres high and 43½ wide. On the reverse of one half of the sheet are notes on *peso* and *bilancia* (weight and balance), on the other are the 'prophecies' printed under Nos. 1293 and 1294. It is evident from the arrangement that these were written subsequently, on the space which had been left blank. These pages are reproduced on Pl. CXVIII. In Pls. CXVI–CXVIII the size is smaller than in the original; the map of Armenia, Pl. CXVIII, is on Pl. CXIX slightly enlarged. On this map we find the following names, beginning from the right hand at the top: *pariardes*

mō (for Paryadres Mons, Arm. Parchar, now Barchal or Kolai Dagh; Trebizond is on its slope). *Aquilone*— North; *Antitaurus Antitaurus \\\\ psis mō* (probably meant for Thospitis = Lake Van, Arm. Dgov Vanai, Tospoi, and the mountain range to the south); *Gordis mō* (Mountains of Gordyaea), the birthplace of the Tigris; *Oriente*—East; *Tigris*, and then, to the left, *Eufrates*. Then, above to the left, *Argeo mō* (now Erdshigas, an extinct volcano, 12,000 feet high); *Celeno mō* (no doubt Sultan Dagh in Pisidia). Celeno is the Greek town of Κελαιναί (now the ruins of Dineir); *oriente*—East; *africo libezco* (for libeccio —South-west). In the middle of the Euphrates river on this small map we see a shaded portion surrounded by mountains, perhaps to indicate the inundation mentioned in l. 35. The affluent to the Euphrates, shown as coming with many windings from the high land of 'Argeo' on the west, is the Tochma Su, which joins the main river at Malatie. Here may be mentioned the Catalonian Portulan of Olivez de Majorca, executed in 1584;. it is less correct than Leonardo's.

II T t

montato circa 3 miglia, si comīcia a trovare le selue de' grā[81]di abeti, pini e faggi e altri simili alberi; dopo questi per spatio di 3 al[82]tre miglia si trovano praterie e grādissime pasture, e tutto il resto, insino [83]al nascimēto del Monte Tavro, sono nevi eterne che mai per alcū tenpo si par-[84]tono, che s'astendono all' altezza di circa 14 miglia in tutto; da questo na[85]scimēto del Tavro insino all' altezza d'vn miglio non passano mai i nuvoli; [86]che qui abbiamo 15 miglia, che sono circa a 5 · miglia d'altezza per linia retta, [87]e altrettanto o circa troviamo essere la cima delli corni del Tauro, [88]ne' quali dal mezzo in su si comincia a trovare aria che riscalda e nō [89]vi si sente soffiamēti de' uēti, ma nessuna cosa ci può troppo vivere; [90]quiui nō nascie cosa alcuna, saluo alcuni vccelli rapaci che [91]covano nell' alte fessure del Tavro, e disciēdono poi sotto i nuvoli [92]a fare le lor prede sopra i monti erbosi; Questo è tutto sasso senplice, [93]cioè da' nuvoli insù, ed è sasso candidissimo · e in sulla alta cima nō [94]si può andare per l'aspra e pericolosa sua salita.

good produce, particularly in those parts which face to the south. But after mounting about three miles we begin to find forests of great fir-trees, and beech and other similar trees; after this, for a space of three more miles, there are meadows and vast pastures; and all the rest, as far as the beginning of the Taurus, is eternal snows which never disappear at any time, and extend to a height of about fourteen miles in all. From this beginning of the Taurus up to the height of a mile the clouds never pass away; thus we have fifteen miles, that is, a height of about five miles in a straight line; and the summit of the peaks of the Taurus are as much, or about that. There, half-way up, we begin to find a scorching air and never feel a breath of wind; but nothing can live long there; there nothing is brought forth save a few birds of prey which breed in the high fissures of Taurus and descend below the clouds to seek their prey on the wooded hills; there all is bare rock, that is, from the clouds upwards; and the rock is the purest white. And it is impossible to walk to the high summit on account of the rough and perilous ascent.

C. A. 214*b*]   1337

[Avēdoti · io più volte fatto · con mia lettere partecipe · delle cose che di qua · sono · accadute ·, no m'è paruto tacere a [2]vna novità· accaduta · ne' giorni passati · la quale . . . .

[3]Avēdoti io piv volte . . . .]

[4]Essendomi io più volte con lettere rallegrato · teco della tua prospera fortuna ·, al presente so che come amico ti cōtristerai · con meco [5]del misero · stato nel quale mi trovo; ¶e questo è che ne' giorni · passati · sono stato · in tāti affanni, [6]pavre, pericoli e danno · insieme con questi miseri paesani, che avevamo d'avere invidia ai morti, e cierto · io nō credo · [7]che, poichè gli elemēti con lor separatione · disfeciono · il grā caos, ch'elli riunissino · lor forza, anzi rabbia ·, a fare tanto nocimēto alli omini [8]quāto al presente da noi · s'è veduto · e provato, in modo ch'io nō posso imaginare · [che cosa si possin [9]piv accresciere a tanto male, il quale noi provammo in spatio di dieci ore]; In

[Having often made you, by my letters, acquainted with the things which have happened, I think I ought not to be silent as to the events of the last few days, which [2] . . . .

Having several times . . . .]

Having many times rejoiced with you by letters over your prosperous fortunes, I know now that as a friend you will be sad with me over the miserable state in which I find myself; and this is, that during the last few days I have been in so much trouble, fear, peril, and loss, besides the miseries of the people here, that we have been envious of the dead; and certainly I do not believe that since the elements by their separation reduced the vast chaos to order, they have ever combined their force and fury to do so much mischief to man. As far as regards us here, what we have seen and gone through is such [that I could not imagine that things could ever rise to such an amount of mischief as we

81. effaggi .. alberi [infrallo] dopo questo .. isspatio. 82. trova .. passture ettutto il retto. 83. nasscimēto .. neve etterne. 84. tano chessastedano all alteza .. circha .. da cquesto. 85. alteza .. mai e nvuoli. 86. abiamo .. chessono circha .. dalteza. 87. circha troviano. 88. cominca attrovare .. risscalda. 89. cipo. 90. nasscie chosa. 91. disciēdano .. nvgoli. 92. affare .. Quessto ettutto. 93. coe .. nvgoli .. chandidissimo. 94. si po .. lasspra e pericholosa.
1337. 1. avēdoti "io" piu .. commia .. participe .. che didi qua .. achadute. 2. achaduta. 4. chollettere .. techo .. so "che chome amico" ti .. comecho. 5. ecquesto he. 6. pericholi .. chō .. avno | "davere" invidia .. inō credo. 7. collor .. che el rivnissino .. rabie affare. 8. dannoi .. imodo .. chosa. 9. accressciere attanto male "il quale" noi prevamo .. ore [Nori abbiamo] jn ..

1337. On comparing this commencement of a letter, ll. 1–2, with that in ll. 3 and 4 of No. 1336 it is quite evident that both refer to the same event. (Compare also No. 1337, ll. 10–12 and 17, with No. 1336, ll. 23, 24, and 32.) But the text No. 1336, including the fragment ll. 3–4, was obviously written later than the draft here reproduced. The person addressed is not known.

prima fummo assaliti e comba[10]ttuti dall' impeto · e furore de' vēti e a questo s'aggiunsero le ruine delli grā mõti di neve, i quali ànno ripieno tutte questi valli [11]e cõquassato grā parte della nostra città; E nõ si cõtentãdo di questo, la fortuna [12]cõ subiti diluvi d'acque ebbe a sommergere tutta la parte bassa di questa città; oltre a di questo s'aggiunse vna subita piog[13]gia ·, anzi ruinosa tēpesta piena d'acqua, sabbia, fango e pietre, insieme avviluppati cõ radici, sterpi e ciocchi di uarie piāte; [14]e ogni cosa scorrendo per l'aria discēdea sopra di noi ·; e in vltimo vno inciēdio di fuoco il qual parea cõdotto nõ che da vēti ma da 30 milia diavoli, che 'l portassino, il quale à abbruciato e disfatto tutto questo [15]paese, e ancora non è cessato; E que' pochi, che siamo restati, siamo rimasti · cõ tanto sbigottimēto [16]e tãta pavra che appena come balordi abbiamo ardire di parlare · l'uno coll' altro ·; avēdo · abbãdonato ogni · nostra cura, ci stiamo insieme vniti [17]jn cierte ruine di chiese insieme misti maschi e femine, piccoli e grãdi, a modo di [18]torme di capre; ¶ i vicini per pietà ci ànno soccorso di uettovaglie, i quali erã prima nostri nimici; ¶ e se nõ fussero cierti popoli che ci ànno soccorso di uettovaglia, tutti saremmo morti di fame, Ora vedi come ci [19]troviamo ·; E tutti questi mali son niēte · a cõparatione di quelli che in breve tēpo ne son promessi;

[20]So che come amico ti cõtristerai del mio · male · come già con lettere ti mostrai con effetto rallegrarmi del tuo bene . . . .

experienced in the space of ten hours.] In the first place we were assailed and attacked by the violence and fury of the winds [10]; to this was added the falling of great mountains of snow which filled up all this valley, thus destroying a great part of our city [11]. And not content with this the tempest sent a sudden flood of water to submerge all the low part of this city [12]; added to which there came a sudden rain, or rather a ruinous torrent and flood of water, sand, mud, and stones, entangled with roots and stems and fragments of various trees; and every kind of thing flying through the air fell upon us; finally a great fire broke out, not brought by the wind, but carried, as it would seem, by 30 thousand devils, which completely burnt up all this neighbourhood, and it has not yet ceased. And those few who remain unhurt are in such dejection and such terror that we hardly have courage to speak to each other, as if we were stunned. Having abandoned all our business, we stay here together in the ruins of some churches, men and women mingled together, small and great [17], just like herds of goats. The neighbours out of pity succoured us with victuals, and they had previously been our enemies. And if it had not been for certain people who succoured us with victuals, all would have died of hunger. Now you see the state we are in. And all these evils are as nothing compared with those which are promised to us shortly.

I know that as a friend you will grieve for my misfortunes, as I, in former letters, have shown my joy at your prosperity . . . .

F. 37b]   1338

LIBRO 43 DEL MOTO DELL' ARIA INCLUSA SOTTO L'ACQUA

. . . Ho veduto mov[3]imēti d'aria tanto furiosi, che ànno ac[4]conpagniati e misti col corso suo li [5]grandissimi alberi delle selue e li tetti in[6]teri de grā palazzi, e questa medesima [7]furia fare vna buca con moto reuer[8]tiginoso e cavare vn ghiareto e portare ghi[9]ara, rena, acqua più d'ū mezzo miglio in [10]aria.

BOOK 43 OF THE MOVEMENT OF AIR ENCLOSED IN WATER

I have seen motions of the air so furious that they have carried, mixed up in their course, the largest trees of the forest and whole roofs of great palaces, and I have seen the same fury bore a hole with a whirling movement, digging out a gravel-pit, and carrying gravel, sand, and water more than half a mile through the air.

Notes about events observed abroad (1338-9).

furno "assaliti". 10. tutti . . effurore . . vēti [e in breue] acquesto sagivnse . . neve i quli ano ripieno . . valle. 11. parte [di questa] "della nostra" citta [e morte molte giēte] E nõ si cõtentã di. 12. dilui . . assomergiere . . questa [terra] citta . . sagivnse . . pio. 13. dacq "a" sabia . . avilupati cõ radici "sterpi" ezzochi. 14. cosa | "scorendo per laria" discēdea . . focho il quala [a disfatto e] "parea cõdotto nõ che da vēti ma da 30 milia diavoli chel portassin" a abruciato e disfatto. 15. ancora [nõ da fine al suo cõsumare] "none cessato" E que . . chessiano . . si ano rimasi . . esbigottimēto. 16. appena | "come balordi" abiamo advre . . abandonato. 17. ciese . . massci effemine picoli. *The text between the words* capre *and* Ora *is written on the margin. The words:* i vicini . . nostri nimici *are written in six short lines on the right side and the following words* esse nõ . . di fame *are written in eleven lines on the opposite side:* i vicini | "per pieta" ci à sochorso . . esse nõ fussi socorso di uttovaglia . . saremo. 19. Ettitti . . chē brieve . . ne promesso. 20. chome . . cõtrisserai . . chome . . collettere timosstra . . ralegrarmi.
1338. 1. lacq"a". 3. anno a. 5. elli. 6. palazi ecquesta. 7. bucha. 8. giareto e portare gia. 9. mezo miglo. 10. naria.

17. *Certe ruine di chiese.* Either of Armenian churches or of mosques, which it was not unusual to speak of as churches.

Maschi e femme insieme unite implies an infringement of the usually strict rule of the separation of the sexes.

18. *I vicini, nostri nimici.* The town must then have stood quite close to the frontier of the country. Com-

pare No. 1336, l. 7, *vicini ai nostri confini.* The designation of the population of the country round a city as 'the enemy' (*nemici*) is not appropriate to Italy in the time of Leonardo.

1338. The first sixteen lines of this passage, which treat of the subject as indicated on the title-line, have no place in this connexion and have been omitted.

2. *Ho veduto movimenti,* &c. The descriptions of the

Br. M. 155*a*]   1339

A similitudine d'uno ritrosito vento che scorra in una ²renosa e cavata valle che pel suo velocie corso scac³cia al cētro tutte quelle cose che s'oppōgono al suo furi⁴oso corso

⁵Non altrimēti il settētrionale aquilone ripercuote ⁶colla sua tēpesta

⁷Nō fa sì grā mugghio il tēpestoso mare, ⁸quādo il settētrionale aquilone ⁹lo ripercuote colle scivmose onde fra Scilla e Cariddi, nè Stronboli o Mō¹⁰gibello, quando le solfure fiāme, essendo rīchiuse, ¹¹per forza ronpēdo e aprēdo il grā mōte, fulminādo ¹²per l'aria pietra terra īsieme coll' uscita e vomitata fiāma . . . .

¹³Nè quādo le infocate caverne di Mōgibello rivomitādo il male tenuto elemēto, spigniendolo ¹⁴alla sua regione, cō furia cacciādo īnāzi qualūche ostacolo ¹⁵s'interpone alla sua īpetuosa furia

¹⁶E tirato dalla mia bramosa voglia, vago di uedere la gran copia ¹⁷delle varie e strane forme fatte dalla artifiziosa natura, ragiratomi ¹⁸alquāto jfra gli ōbrosi scogli pervenni all' ētrata d'una ¹⁹grā caverna dinanzi alla quale restato alquāto ²⁰stupefatto e jgniorante di tal cosa; piegato le mie rene ²¹in arco e ferma la stāca mano sopra il ginocchio e colla destra mi feci tenebre ²²alle abbassate e chivse ciglia; e spesso piegādomi in qua e in là per ve²³dere dētro vi discernessi alcuna cosa, e questo vietatomi per ²⁴la grāde oscurità, che là entro era, e stato alquāto, subito s'alse ²⁵in me 2 cose, pavra e desiderio; paura · per la minaccio²⁶sa oscura spilonca, desiderio per vedere se là ētro fusse alcuna ²⁷miracolosa cosa . . . .

Like a whirling wind which rushes down a sandy and hollow valley, and which, in its hasty course, drives to its centre everything that opposes its furious course . . . .

No otherwise does the northern blast whirl round in its tempestuous progress . . . .

Nor does the tempestuous sea bellow so loud, when the northern blast dashes it, with its foaming waves, between Scylla and Charybdis; nor Stromboli, nor Mount Etna, when their sulphurous flames, having been forcibly confined, rend and burst open the mountain, fulminating stones and earth through the air together with the flames they vomit. . . .

Nor when the inflamed caverns of Mount Etna, rejecting the ill-restrained element, vomit it forth, back to its own region, driving furiously before it every obstacle that comes in the way of its impetuous rage . . . .

Unable to resist my eager desire and wanting to see the great multitude of the various and strange shapes made by formative nature, and having wandered some distance among gloomy rocks, I came to the entrance of a great cavern, in front of which I stood some time, astonished and unaware of such a thing. Bending my back into an arch I rested my tired hand on my knee and held my right hand over my downcast and contracted eyebrows: often bending first one way and then the other, to see whether I could discover anything inside, and this being forbidden by the deep darkness within, and after having remained there some time, two contrary emotions arose in me, fear and desire—fear of the threatening dark cavern, desire to see whether there were any marvellous thing within it . . . .

1339. 1. chesschorranuna. 2. chavata . . chorso scha. 3. qlle chose chessoppōghono. 4. chorso. 5. altremēti . . settātrione . . riperchuote. 6. cholla. 7. mvglia il [settantrionale] tēpesstoso. 8. [mosso chō grā furia da] quādo . . settātrionale. 9. riperchuote "chole scivmose onde" frassilla echariddi nesstronboli. 10. zolfure. 12. chollusscita "e vomitata" fiāma. 13. lēfochate chaverne "di mōgibello" . . "rēdaje il mal tenuto elemento" spigniendolo. 14. chō . . chacciāci . . osstacholo. 16. vagho . . la grā cho\\\\\. 17. varie "e strane" forme . . ragiratom\\\\. 18. schogli pervenni [alla b] all. 19. chaverna [nella quale] dinanzi . . resstato. 20. chosa [chomīciaj] pieghato . . ren\\\. 21. archo [e colla] "e ferma la" stācha mano [su] "sopra il" ginocchio e cholla desstra . . feci ten\\\\. 22. ecchiuse . . esspesso pieghādomii n qua e illa per\\\\\. 23. vdissciernessi alchuna chosa . . vietatom\\\\\. 24. osschuria . . esstato alquāto subitosa. 25. se īme 2 [chōstrarie] chose . . la mina. 26. te esscura spiloncha . . alchu\\\. 27. miracholosa chosa . *6*.

Deluge, vol. i, Nos. 607–11, and that of the fall of a mountain, No. 610, ll. 17–30, may have been inspired by vivid impressions derived from personal experience. Compare also Pls. XXXIV–XL.

1339. It may be inferred from the character of the writing, which is in the style of the note on Plate XXXIII B, that this passage was written between 1470 and 1480. As the figure *6* at the end of the text indicates, it was continued on another page, but I have searched in vain for it. No. 1379 also refers to Leonardo's journeys in Southern Italy.

 · 13. *Mongibello* is a name commonly given to Mount Etna (from *Djebel*, Arab. = mountain). Fr. Ferrara,

Descrizione dell' Etna con la storia delle eruzioni (Palermo, 1818, p. 88), tells us, on the authority of the *Cronaca del Monastero Benedettino di Licordia*, of an eruption of the volcano with a great flow of lava on Sept. 21, 1447. The next records of the mountain are from the years 1533 and 1536. A. Percy does not mention eruptions of Etna during the years to which this note must probably refer (*Mémoire des tremblements de terre de la péninsule italique*, vol. xxii of the *Mémoires couronnées et Mémoires des savants étrangers*, Académie Royale de Belgique). In Vasari, vi. 349, Mongibello is coupled with the Inferno for its terror.

C. A. 391*a*]　　　　　　　　　1340

Auēdo, signore mio illustrissimo, uisto e considerato oramai a sufficiētia le proue di tutti
quelli · che si ²reputano maestri e compositori
di instrumēti bellici ·, et che la inuētione e
operatione di detti ³instrumēti nō sono niente

Most Illustrious Lord, Having now sufficiently
considered the specimens of all those who
proclaim themselves skilled contrivers of instruments of war, and that the invention and operation of the said instruments are nothing different

Drafts of
letters to
Lodovico il
Moro
(1340–5).

aliene dal commune vso: Mi forzerò, nō dero-
gando a nessuno altro, ⁴farmi ītendere da Vostra
Eccellentia, aprēdo a quella li secreti · mei ·, e
appresso offerendoli ad ogni suo piacimento ⁵ī
tempi opportuni operare con effetto circa tutte
quelle cose · che sub breuità in parte saranno
qui disotto ⁶notate.

　1. ⁷Ho modi di ponti leggierissimi e forti,
e atti ad portare facilissimamēte, et cō quelli
seguire ⁸e alcuna uolta fuggire li inimici, e altri
securi e īoffensibili da foco ⁹e battaglia ·, facili

from those in common use: I shall endeavour,
without prejudice to any one else, to explain myself to your Excellency, showing your Lordship
my secrets, and then offering them to your best
pleasure and approbation to work with effect at
opportune moments on all those things which,
in part, shall be briefly noted below.

　(1) I have a sort of extremely light and strong
bridges, adapted to be most easily carried, and
with them you may pursue, and at any time flee
from the enemy; and others, secure and inde-

1340. 1–36 *written from left to right.* 1. Hauēdo S"re" mio jll. . . horamai ad. 2. che le . . di dicti. 3. alieni dal cōe . . exforzero . . altº.
4. ītende"re" da v. ex"tia" . . qlla . . appsso . . ad ōi . . piacimͭo.　5. oportuni . . cū . . breuita "ī pāte" saranno.　6. notate
[e anchora ī molte piu secōdo le occurretie de diuēsi casi s]. 7. acti . . qlli. 8. uolta [secondo le occurrētie] fuggire. 9. de ādē . .

1340. The numerous corrections, the alterations in
the figures (l. 18), indicate that this is a draft of a letter
to Lodovico il Moro. It is one of the very few MSS.
which are written from left to right—see the facsimile
of the beginning as here reproduced. Leonardo no
doubt very rarely wrote so, and this is probably the
reason of the conspicuous dissimilarity in the handwriting when he did. (Compare Pl. XXXVIII.) It
is noteworthy too that here the orthography and
abbreviations are also exceptional. But such superficial peculiarities are not enough to stamp the document as altogether spurious. It is neither a forgery
nor the production of any artist but Leonardo himself. As to this point the contents leave us no doubt
as to its authenticity, particularly l. 32 (see No. 719,
where this passage is repeated). But whether the

fragment, as we here see it, was written from Leonardo's dictation—a theory favoured by the orthography, the erasures and corrections—or whether it
may be a copy made for or by Melzi or Mazenta is
comparatively unimportant. There are in the Codex
Atlanticus a few other documents not written by
Leonardo himself, but the notes in his own hand
found on the reverse pages of these leaves amply prove
that they were certainly in Leonardo's possession.
This mark of ownership is wanting in the text in
question, but the compilers of the Codex Atlanticus,
at any rate, accepted it as a genuine document.
　Compare G. Calvi, *I Manoscritti di L. d. V.* (Bologna,
1925), p. 65 f., and Beltrami, *La destra mano di
L. d. V.*; Calvi, 'Contributi alla biografia di L.d.V.',
Archivio Stor. Lomb. xliii (1916), p. 437.

e cōmodi da leuare e ponere · ; Et modi di ardere e disfare quelli de l'inimico.

[10]2. So ī la ossidione di una terra togliere uia l'acqua de' fossi · ; e fare īfiniti pōti: gatti e scale [11]e altri īstrumenti pertinēti a detta speditione.

[12]3. Itē se per altezza di argine o per · fortezza di loco e di sito nō si potesse ī la ossidione di [13]vna terra usare l'officio delle bombarde: ho modi di ruinare omni rocca o altra fortezza, [14]se già nō fusse fondata ī su el sasso ecc.

[15]4. Ho ancora modi di bombarde cōmodissime e facili a portare: Et con quelle buttare minuti sassi [16]a similitudine quasi di tempesta · ; E con il fumo di quella dando grāde spauēto al' inimico [17]con graue suo danno e confusione.

[18]9. E quādo accadesse essere ī mare, ho modi di molti īstrumenti attissimi da offendere e difendere: [19]et nauili che faranno resistentia al trarre di omni grossissima bōbarda: e poluere e fumi.

[20]5. Itē ho modi: per caue e uie secrete distorte fatte senza alcuno strepito per uenire e disegnato [21]. . . ancora che bisogniasse passare sotto fossi o alcuno fiume.

[22]6. Item farò carri coperti sicuri e īoffensibili · , i quali ētrādo ītra li inimici con sue artiglierie:, nō è si grāde multi[23]tudine di gente d'arme che nō rompessino: E dietro a questi potranno seguire fāterie assai illesi e sēza [24]alcuno īpedimēto.

[25]7. Item occorrendo di bisogno, farò bōbarde, mortari et passauolanti di bellissime e utili forme fuori del comune uso;

[26]8. Doue mācasse la operatione · delle bōbarde comporrò briccole, māgani | trabuchi e altri īstrumenti di mirabile [27]efficacia e fuori de l'usato: Et ī sōma secondo la uarietà de' casi cōporrò uarie e īfinite cose da offēdere e di . . . .

[28]10. Jn tēpo di pace credo di soddisfare benissimo al paragone di ogni altro in architettura, ī compositione di edifitii e publici [29]e priuati: e ī cōdurre acqua da uno loco ad uno altro.

[30]Jtē cōdurrò ī scultura, di marmore, di bronzo e di terra: similiter ī pictura ciò che si possa fare [31]a paragone di ogni altro e sia chi uole.

[32]Ancora si potrà dare opera al cauallo di

structible by fire and battle, easy and convenient to lift and place. Also methods of burning and destroying those of the enemy.

(2) I know how, when a place is besieged, to take the water out of the trenches, and make endless variety of bridges, and covered ways and ladders, and other machines pertaining to such expeditions.

(3) Item. If, by reason of the height of the banks, or the strength of the place and its position, it is impossible, when besieging a place, to avail oneself of the plan of bombardment, I have methods for destroying every rock or other fortress, even if it were founded on a rock, &c.

(4) Again, I have kinds of mortars; most convenient and easy to carry; and with these I can fling small stones almost resembling a storm; and with the smoke of these cause great terror to the enemy, to his great detriment and confusion.

(9) [8] And if the fight should be at sea I have kinds of many machines most efficient for offence and defence; and vessels which will resist the attack of the largest guns and powder and fumes.

(5) Item. I have means by secret and tortuous mines and ways, made without noise, to reach a designated [spot], even if it were needed to pass under a trench or a river.

(6) Item. I will make covered chariots, safe and unattackable, which, entering among the enemy with their artillery, there is no body of men so great but they would break them. And behind these, infantry could follow quite unhurt and without any hindrance.

(7) Item. In case of need I will make big guns, mortars, and light ordnance of fine and useful forms, out of the common type.

(8) Where the operation of bombardment might fail, I would contrive catapults, mangonels, *trabocchi*, and other machines of marvellous efficacy and not in common use. And in short, according to the variety of cases, I can contrive various and endless means of offence and defence.

(10) In time of peace I believe I can give perfect satisfaction and to the equal of any other in architecture and the composition of buildings public and private; and in guiding water from one place to another.

Item. I can carry out sculpture in marble, bronze, or clay, and also I can do in painting whatever may be done, as well as any other, be he who he may.

[32] Again, the bronze horse may be taken in

qlli. 10. obsidione de . . toglie"r" uia laqua et . . ghatti. 11. ad dicta expeditione. 12. de āgine . . de loco . . pottesse . . obsidione de. 13. dele . . omni [forte] o | "rocca" (?) altra. 14. saxo. 15. anchora . . de bombāde . . facile ad . . Et cū q̃lle . . minuti [saxi]. 16. a [disimilitudine quasi] di . . cũel . . q̃lla. 17. cū. 18. accadessi de . . īstrumti actissimi . . offendē e defendē. 19. de . . g"o"ssissima . . polue. 20. facte . . uenire [ad uno ce"r"to] e diseg"a"to. 21. \|\|\|\|\|\|\| anchora. 22. coperti "e sicuri" e . . cq"a"li ītrādo ītra [in] li inimica cū . . si [grosso] grande. 23. Et . . poteranno tlesi. 24. alchuno. 25. occurendo di bisoğ . . mōtari . . utile forma fora del cõe. 26. mācassi . . de le componero . . māgliani. 27. fora . . sēdo . . cōpoñro . . ed \|\|\|\|\|. 28. credo satisfare . . ŏ. edifitii e p. 29. et pvati . . cōducē aqua . . alto [acto ad offendē e defendē.] 30. cōducero. 31. ad . . deõni . . uole. 32. Anchora si potera . . honore dela.

bronzo, che sarà gloria īmortale e eterno onore della 33felice memoria del signore vostro padre e dela īcljta casa Sforzesca;

34E se alcuna delle sopradette cose a alcuno paressino īpossibili e īfattibili, mi offro 35paratissimo a farne esperimento ī parco uostro, o ī qual loco piacerà a vostra Excellenza, al36la quale umilmente quanto più posso, mi raccomando.

hand, which is to be to the immortal glory and eternal honour of the prince your father of happy memory, and of the illustrious house of Sforza.

And if any of the above-named things seem to any one to be impossible or not feasible, I am most ready to make the experiment in your park, or in whatever place may please your Excellency —to whom I commend myself with the utmost humility, &c.

S. K. M. III. 62*b*]   **1341**

Al mio Illustrissimo Signore Lodouico,
  Duca di Bari·/.
Leonardo Da · Vinci
  Fiorentino ·
  5Leonardo.

To my illustrious Lord, Lodovico,
  Duke of Bari,
Leonardo da Vinci
  of Florence—
  Leonardo.

S. K. M. III. 68*a*]   **1342**

Vi piace vedere uno · modello · del quale 2risulterà · vtile · a uoi e a me ·, e vtili3tà · a quelli che fieno · cagione · di no4stra vtilità.

Does it please you to see a model which will prove useful to you and to me, also it will be of use to those who will be the cause of our usefulness.

S. K. M. III. 15*a*]   **1343**

Ecco · oignor · molti · giētil omini 2che faranno infra loro · questa · spesa, 3lasciādo loro · godere l'entrata dell' acque, 4mvlina e passaggio di navili, e quādo 5e' sarà rēduto · loro il prezzo loro rēderā6no il navilio di Martigiana . . . .

There are here, my Lord, many gentlemen who will undertake this expense among them, if they are allowed to enjoy the use of admission to the waters, the mills, and the passage of vessels, and when it is sold to them the price will be repaid to them by the canal of Martesana . . . .

C. A. 315*b*]   **1344**

Assai mi rincrescie d'essere ī neciessità ·, ma piv mi dole 2che quella · sia causa · dello interrōpere il desiderio mio, il 3quale · è senpre disposto a vbidir uostra Eccellentia; 4forse che uostra Eccellēntia 5nō commise altro a messer Gual6tieri, credēdo che io avessi dina7ri . . . .

8E mi rincrescie assai che tu m'abbi ri9trovato in neciessità, e che l'auere io 10a guadagniare il uitto, · m'abbi 11a interronpere . . . .

12Assai mi rincresce che l'auere a guadagnia13re il uitto · m'abbia forzato interrōpere

I am greatly vexed to be in necessity, but I still more regret that this should be the cause of the hindrance of my wish which is always disposed to obey your Excellency.

Perhaps your Excellency did not give further orders to Messer Gualtieri, believing that I had money enough . . . .

I am greatly annoyed that you should have found me in necessity, and that my having to earn my living should have hindered me. . . .

[12] It vexes me greatly that having to earn my living has forced me to interrupt the work

---

33. s"r"vost"o" patre e dela. 34. Et se alchuno dele sop"r" dicte . . alchuno . . īpossible e infactibile me offer. 35. ad farene experimento . . q"al" . . vost ex"tia" ad. 36. humilr̄īte . . me recomādo de.
1341. *Written from left to right.* 1. Ill"mo" Sig"re". 2. bari.
1342. 1. vedere ī modello. 2. mme. 3. acquelli cheffieno chagione.
1343. 1. Ecci. 2. fa rano infralloro. 3. lassciādo. 4. passagio. 5. prezo lor rēdenā.
1344. 1. rincrescie. 2. chausa . . interōpere . . il q. 3. ecellentia. 5. chomise altro [al] meser qual. 8. rineresscie . . chettu mabbi ri\\\\\\. 9. echellauere. 10. guadagnare [il pane] il uicto mabi. 11. anteronpere. 12. rincrescce chellauere. 13. uicto mabia

---

1341. Evidently a note of the superscription of a letter to the Duke, and written, like the foregoing, from left to right. The MS. containing it is of the year 1493. Lodovico was not proclaimed and styled Duke of Milan till September 1494. The Dukedom of Bari belonged to the Sforzas till 1499.

1342, 1343. These two notes occur in the same

note-book as No. 1341, and it is possible that they are fragments of the same letter. The *Modello* is probably that of the monument of Francesco Sforza, the equestrian statue publicly exhibited in this very year, 1493, on the occasion of the marriage of the Emperor Maximilian with Bianca Maria Sforza.

[l'opera e di soddis[14]fare ad alcuni piccoli],– il seguitare l'o[15]pera che già vostra Signoria mi commise; Ma spero in bre[16]ue avere guadagniato · tanto che potrò · soddisfare [17]ad animo riposato · a vostra Eccellenza, alla quale [18]mi raccomãdo, e se uostra Signoria credesse ch'io [19]avessi · dinari, quella s'ingannerebbe perchè ò tenvto · 6 · boche 36 mesi, e ò avuto 50 ducati.

and to attend to small matters, instead of following up the work which your Lordship entrusted to me. But I hope in a short time to have earned so much that I may carry it out quietly to the satisfaction of your Excellency, to whom I commend myself; and if your Lordship thought that I had money, your Lordship was deceived because I had to feed 6 men for 36 months, and have had 50 ducats.

C. A. 335*b*]   1345

E se mi dato piv alcuna commissione d'alcuna . . .
[2]del premio del mio seruitio ·, perchè nõ sõ da essere da . . .
[3]cose assegniationi, perchè loro ànno intrate di pe . . .
[4]tie che bene possono assettare piv di me . . .
[5]nõ la mia arte, la quale voglio mvtare ed . . .
[6]dato qualche vestimẽto si oso vna somma . . . .
[7]Signiore ·, conosciẽdo · io · la mẽte · di uostra · Ecciellentia · essere · occupa . . .
[8]il ricordare · a vostra Signioria · le mie piccole e l'arti messe in silẽtio . . .
[9]che 'l mio · taciere fusse causa · di fare · isdegniare vostra Signori . . .
[10]la mia vita ai uostri seruiti · mi tiẽ continvamẽte parato · a vbidire . . .
[11]del cauallo nõ dirò niẽte, perchè cogniosco · i tẽpi . . .
[12]a vostra Signoria com' io restai avere · il salario di 2 · anni · del . . .
[13]cõ due · maestri · i quali cõtinvo · stettero · a mio salario e spesa . . .
[14]che al fine mi trovai · avanzato di tal opera · circa 15 lire · M . . .
[15]opere di fama per le quali io potessi mostrare a quelli che ueranno ch'io sono sta . . .
[16]fa per tutto · ma io nõ so, doue io potessi spẽdere le mia opere a per . . .
[17]l'auere io · atteso a guadagniarmi la uita . . .
[18]per non essere informata in che essere io mi trovo . . .
[19]si ricorda · della commissione del dipigniere · i camerini . . .
[20]portavo a vostra Signoria · solo richiedẽdo a quella . . . .

And if any other commission is given me by any . . .
of the reward of my service. Because I am not [able] to be . . .
things assigned because meanwhile they have. . . to them . . .
. . . which they well may settle rather than I . . .
not my art which I wish to change and . . .
given some clothing if I dare a sum . . .
My Lord, I knowing your Excellency's mind to be occupied . . .
to remind your Lordship of my small matters and the arts put to silence . . .
that my silence may be the cause of making your Lordship scorn . . .
my life in your service. I hold myself ever in readiness to obey . . .
[11] Of the horse I will say nothing because I know the times [are bad] . . .
to your Lordship how I had still to receive two years' salary of the . . .
with the two skilled workmen who were constantly in my pay and at my cost . . .
that at last I found myself advanced this sum about 15 lire . . .
works of fame by which I could show to those who shall see it that I have been . . .
everywhere, but I do not know where I could bestow my work [more] . . .
[17] I, having been working to gain my living . . .
I not having been informed what it is, I find myself . . .
[19] remember the commission to paint the rooms . . .
I conveyed to your Lordship only requesting you . . . .

---

interõpere [lopera de il sadis].   14. fare ad alcuni piciolo de il seguitare [aluna] lo.   15. smi chomisse.   16. podro sadisfare. 17. eccieleza. 18. \\\\\\\\ racomãdo esse uostra S si. 19. \\\\\\\\ ssi dinari quella quella singanerebe.
1345. 1. esse . . comesione. 3. tante di pe. 4. possano. 6. sioso vna soma. 7. uosstra . . ochupa. 8. vosstra . . mi | "pichol ellarejmesse. 9. fussi chausa. 11. [ta di rare an]. 12. chomio . . ave"re" el. 13. maessti . . cõtinovo stettono . . salario esspe. 14. avnzato ditta . . circha. 15. opere | "di fama" per elle . . acqelli che uerano. 16. opere [in piv] a per. 18. trovo [come e mi]. 19. richorda della comessione. 20. acquella.

1345. The paper on which this is written is torn down the middle; about half of each line remains.
    11. See No. 723, where this passage is repeated.
    17. See No. 1344, l. 12.

    19. In April 1498 Leonardo was engaged in painting the Saletta Nigra of the Castello at Milan. (See G. Mongeri, *L'Arte in Milano*, 1872, p. 417.)

C. A. 323*a*]   1346

Magnifici · fabbricieri ·, intēdendo io vostre magni²ficēze avere · preso · partito · di fare cierte · magnie opere di bronzo; delle quali · io vi ³darò · alcuno · ricordo · prima · che voi nō siate · tanto · veloci · e tanto · presti a fare essa allocatione ⁴che per essa cielerità sia tolto · la uia del potere · fare bona eletione d'opera, e maestro; qualche omo che pe.⸍ la · sua · insofficiētia abbia apresso a vostri ⁵successori · a vituperare, sé · e la vostra · età ... givdicādo che questa · età fusse mal fornita d'omini ⁶di bon givditio · che di boni · maestri, vedendo le altre città, e massime la città de' Fiorentini, · quasi ne' medesimi tēpi, essere ⁷dotata di si belle e magnie opere di bronzo, intra le quali le porte del loro Battistero ·; la qual Fiorētia ·, si come Piaciētia, ⁸è terra di passo · doue · cōcorrono assai forestieri., i quali vedendo le opere belle o bone, d'elle fanno a sé ⁹medesimi inpressione: quella città · essere fornita di degni abitatori, vedendo l'opere testimonie d'essa opinione; e per lo contrario di¹⁰co, vedendo · tanta spesa di metallo operata si tristamēte, che mē uergognia alla città ¹¹sarebbe che esse porte fussino di senplice legniame ·, perchè la poca spesa della materia ¹²nō parebbe meriteuole di grāde · spesa di magisterio ·, ode che ....

¹³La principale parte che per le città · si ricierchi · si sono · i domi, ai quali appressatisi, le prime · cose, ¹⁴che all' ochio appariscono, · sono · le porte donde in esse chiese passare si possa.

¹⁵Guardate ·, signiori · fabbricieri ·, che la · troppa celerità del uolere voi con tāta ¹⁶prestezza · dare · speditione alla locatione · di tanta magnia opera, quanto io sento che per uoi ¹⁷s'è ordinata, non sia cagione che quello ·, che per onore · di dio · e delli omini si fa ·, non torni in grā ¹⁸disonore de' uostri giuditi e della vostra città, doue, per essere terra degnia e di passo, è concorso · d'innumera¹⁹bili forestieri ·; e questo disonore accaderebbe ·, quādo per le · uostre · indiligiētie ²⁰voi prestasti · fede · a qualche vantatore che per le · sue frasche o per fauore ·, che di qua · dato li fusse, ²¹da uoi auesse a inpetrare · simile opera ·, per la quale · a

Magnificent Commissioners of Buildings, I, understanding that your Magnificencies have made up your minds to make certain great works in bronze, will remind you of certain things: first that you should not be so hasty or so quick to give the commission, lest by this haste it should become impossible to select a good model and a good master; some man may be chosen, who by his insufficiency may cause himself and this age to be abused by your descendants, judging that this age was but ill supplied with men of good counsel and with good masters; seeing that other cities, and chiefly the city of the Florentines, has been, as it were in these very days, endowed with beautiful and grand works in bronze; among which are the doors of their Baptistery. And this town of Florence, like Piacenza, is a place of intercourse, through which many foreigners pass; who, seeing that the works are fine and of good quality, carry away a good impression, and will say that that city is well filled with worthy inhabitants, seeing the works which bear witness to their opinion; and on the other hand, I say, seeing so much metal expended and so badly wrought, it were less shame to the city if the doors had been of plain wood; because the material, costing so little, would not seem to merit any great outlay of skill. ...

Draft of letter to be sent to Piacenza (1346-7).

Now the principal parts which are sought for in cities are their cathedrals, and of these the first things which strike the eye are the doors by which one passes into these churches.

Beware, gentlemen of the Commission, lest too great speed in your determination, and so much haste to expedite the entrusting of so great a work as that which I hear you have ordered, be the cause that that which was intended for the honour of God and of men should be turned to great dishonour of your judgements, and of your city, which, being a place of mark, is the resort and gathering-place of innumerable foreigners. And this dishonour would result if by your lack of diligence you were to put your trust in some vaunter, who by his tricks·or by favour shown to him here should obtain such work from you, by which lasting and very great shame would result to him and to you. Thus

---

1346. 1. [venerabili] e m*a*gnifici fabricieri [parēdo amme fare in parte]. 2. ficēze [volere] avere. 3. richordo .. ettanto presst a "affare essa allocatione" [pigliare partito]. 4. tolto "la uia del potere fare bona elletione dopere e maesstro" qualche homo [di picho] | che .. abia .. vosstri.   5. suciessori .. ella vosstra eta "perche italia sia finicie di boni igiegni"\\\\\\\\ jvdicādo .. heta fussi. 6. maesstri vedendo | "nellaltre cita e massime" nella cita.   7. magnie | "opere di bronzo intrall quali le" porte .. batissterio. 8. he tera .. cōcorre .. fano asse. *On the margin near line 1 is the note*: piaciētia he terra di passo come fiorenza. 9. essere [ben] fornita .. abitatori | "vedendo lopere testimonie desso oppenione" e per lo contra di.   10. ovedendo .. trisstamēte.11. sarebe .. perchella pocha.   12. parebe.   13. la principale "parti" [chosa delle citta per] che .. domi di quelle delle quali apresatosi le .. chose.   14. porte [per le quali] "donde" in ese ciese.   15. chella .. ciclerita [e pressteza] del .. chon. 16. pressteza .. isspeditione. 17. omini "si fa" non.   18. "disonore de uostri iuditi e" della vosstra cita .. chonchorso dinumera. 19. foresstieri ecquesto .. achaderebe .. perlle uosstre. 20. presstassi .. acqualche vantato .. frape . fussi. 21. auessi .. asse e auoi auessi appartorire.

1346, 1347. Piacenza belonged to the Duchy of Milan. The Lord spoken of in this letter is no doubt Lodovico il Moro. One may infer from the concluding sentence (No. 1346, ll. 33, 34, and No. 1347) that

Leonardo, who no doubt compiled this letter, did not forward it to Piacenza himself, but gave it to some influential patron, under whose name and signature a copy of it was sent to the Commission.

sé e a uoi avesse a partorire lunga [22]e grādissima infamia ·; Chè non posso · fare · che io non mi crucci · a ripensare quali omini [23]sieno quelli che con me abbino · conferito · volere · in simile inpresa ētra[24]re sanza pensare alla loro sofitiēzia, sanza dirne altro ·; chi è maestro · di boccali ·, chi di corazze, chi canpanaro, alcuno [25]sonagliere, E insino a bonbardiere, fra i quali vno del signiore s'è uātato · che tra l'essere [26]lui compare de Messere · Anbrosio Ferere—che à qualche commissione—dal quale lui à buone promessioni ·; e se quello nō basterà [27]che mōterà · a cavallo · e andrà dal signiore e impetrerà tali lettere, [28]che per uoi mai simile opera nō gli sarà dinegata ·; o guardate dove i miseri studiosi, [29]atti a simili opere, sono ridotti quādo con simili omini ànno a gareggiare; [30]aprite li ochi · e vogliate bē uedere che i vostri dinari nō si spēdino [31]in conprare · le uostre · vergognie ·; jo vi so annvntiare che di questa terra voi nō [32]trarete se non · opere di forte e di vili e grossi magisteri; nō ci è uomo che vaglia; [33]e credetelo a me, saluo Leonardo Fiorētino, che fa il cauallo del duca Frācesco di brōzo, che non ne bisogna fare stima, [34]perchè à che fare il tenpo di sua vita ·, e dubito che per l'essere si grāde opera che non la finirà mai.

[35]I miseri [36]studiosi . . . [41]con che spe[42]ranza e' posso[43]no aspettare pre[44]mio di lor virtù?

I cannot help being angry when I consider what men those are who have conferred with me as wishing to undertake this great work without thinking of their sufficiency for it, not to say more. This one is a potter, that one a maker of cuirasses, this one is a bell-founder, another a bell-ringer, and one is even a bombardier; and among them one in his Lordship's service, who boasted that he was the gossip of Messer Ambrosio Ferere [26], who has some power and who has made him some promises; and if this were not enough he would mount on horseback, and go to his Lord and obtain such letters that you could never refuse [to give] him the work. But consider where poor students fit for such work are brought when they have to compete with such men as these. Open your eyes and look carefully lest your money should be spent in buying your own disgrace. I can declare to you that from that place you will procure none but average works of inferior and coarse masters. There is no capable man—[33] and you may believe me—except Leonardo the Florentine, who is making the equestrian statue in bronze of the Duke Francesco and who has no need to bring himself into notice, because he has work for all his lifetime; and I doubt whether, being so great a work, he will ever finish it [34].

The miserable painstakers . . . with what hope may they expect a reward of their merit?

C. A. 323b]   1347

[Ecco vno il quale il signiore ·, per fare questa sua opera à tratto di Firenze [2]che è degnio maestro, ma à tāta faciēda che non la finirà mai; [3]e credete voi che differētia · sia a vedere vna cosa bella da una brutta; [4]allega Plinio.]

There is one whom his Lordship invited from Florence to do this work and who is a worthy master, but with so very much business he will never finish it; and you may imagine what a difference there is to be seen between a beautiful object and an ugly one. Quote Pliny.

C. A. 270a]   1347 A

Signori padri diputati, si come ai medici, tutori, curatori de li ammalati [corpi] bisogna intendere che cosa è omo, che cosa è vita, che cosa è sanità [e inte] e in che modo una parità,

Sirs, Father Deputies, Just as doctors, guardians, nurses should understand what is man, what is life, what is health, and how it is maintained by a balance and an agreement of

---

22. grādissima [vergognia] infamia . . nomi isscrucci a "ri" | pēsare quali | "[sieno li] [quelgli]" omini.   23. quelli [dai quali io sia] ce ōme [cho] abbino chonferito.   24. sanza | "sanza pensare alla loro sofitiēzia" dir ne . . maessro . . bochali . . coraze . . chanpanaro.   25. sonaglieri [insino] E insino [a un]a bonbardiere | "frai quali vno del" del . . trallessere.   26. ferere "ce a qualce comessione" dal . . essi.   27. che [vel fara] mōtera a cchavallo e andra [attrovare] del signiore [che vi portera] e "inpetera" tale.   28. gli sa dinegata mo . . dove [i maesstri dibono ingiegnio].   29. asimile . . garegiare.   30. voliate . . uedere [in] che [modo] i vosstri dinari [si debbono spendere] nō . . le uosstre le uosstre vergogni . . anvntiare . . tera.   32. none hopere di forte [e vili e dib] e di vile . . homo.   33. saluo [quel] "lonar fiorētino" cheffa il chauallo . . frāc° "di brōzo" che.   34. lesere.   nolla.   36. studiosi dif–.   37. [li uirtu che cō].   38. [tanti studi sono].   39. [venvti in qual].   40. [ce grado di dise].   41. [gnio] chon che spe.   42. possa.   43. asspettare.
1347. 1. Eci . . attratto di firenze.   2. tāta faciēda nolla.   3. diferētia da ǐ brutta.

1346. 26. Messer Ambrogio Ferere was Farmer of the Customs under the Duke. Compare No. 1030, l. 16.

1347. Compare Müller-Walde, *Berliner Jahrbuch*, 1897, p. 99. However, Nos. 1346 and 1347 are written on the same sheet and therefore, probably, supplement each other.

1347 A. The letter of which this is the draft was probably sent in to the Works Department of the

Cathedral of Milan together with Leonardo's model of the Tiburio; see p. 45. Francesco di Giorgio Martini (*Trattato di Architettura civile e militare*, lib. iv, c. 4) also draws comparisons between an ailing body and a dilapidated building, and so does Filarete (*Trattato d'Architettura*, lib. 1). For comparison between architect and doctor see L. B. Alberti, *De Re Aedificatoria*, lib. X. c. 1. *Filarete*, lib. xv.

una concordanza d'elementi la mantiene, e così una discordanza di quelli la ruina e disfà; e conosciuto ben le sopra dette nature, potrà meglio riparare che chi n'è privato.

[Si come la medicina è atta a contrastare a la malattia] voi sapete le medicine [esser] essendo bene adoperate, rendon sanità ai malati, questo bene adoperate sarà, quando il medico, con lo intendere la lor natura, intenderà che cosa è omo, che cosa è vita, che cosa è complessione e così sanità. Conosciute ben queste, ben conoscerà il suo contrario, [e così] essendo così, ben si saprà riparare.

Voi sapete le medicine, essendo bene adoperate, rendon sanità ai malati. [la persa sanità] e quello che bene le conosce, ben l'adopererà, quando ancora lui conoscerà che cosa è omo, che cosa è vita e complessione, che cosa è sanità; conoscendo queste bene conoscierà i sua contrari; essendo così piu visino sarà al riparo ch'alcun altro. Questo medesimo bisogna al malato [edifizio] domo, cioè uno medico architetto, che 'ntenda bene che cosa è edifizio, e da che regole il retto edificare diriva; e donde dette regole sono tratte e 'n quante parti sieno divise, e quale sieno le cagione, che tengono lo edifizio insieme, e che lo fanno permanente, e che natura sia quella del peso, e quale sia il desiderio de la forza, e in che modo si debbono contessere e collegare insieme, e, congiunte che effetto partoriscino; Chi di queste sopra dette cose avrà vera cognitione vi lascierà di sua rason e opera sadisfatto. . . .

Onde per questo io m'ingegnerò non ditraendo, non . . . infamando alcuno . . . di soddisfare in parte con ragioni e in parte coll' opere, alcuna volta dimostrando li effetti per le cagioni, alcuna volta affermando ragioni colle sperienze . . . queste accomodando alcuna alturità di li architetti antichi, le pruove de li edifizi fatti e quali sieno . . . le cagioni di lor ruina e di loro permanenzia &c.

E con quelle dimonstrare qual è [qual è la cagione] prima del carico e quale e quante sieno le cagioni che danno ruina a li edifizi, e quale è il modo della loro stabilità e permanenza.

Ma per non essere prolisso a vostre eccellenze, dirò prima la invenzione del primo architetto del domo e chiaramente vi dimosterò qual fussi sua intenzione, affermando quella collo principiato edifizio, e . . . faciendovi questo intendere, chiaramente potrete conoscere il modello da me fatto avere in sé quella simetria, quella corrispondenzia, quella conformità, quale s'appartiene al principiato edifizio.

Che cosa è edifizio, e donde le regole del retto edificare ànno dirivazione, e quante e quali siano le parte appartenente a quelle.

O io, o altri che lo dimostri me' di me, pigliatelo, mettete da canto ogni passione.

elements, while a disagreement is its ruin and undoing; and one with a good knowledge of the order of things mentioned above will be better able to repair than one without it.

[Just as medicine is for fighting illness] You know that medicines properly used restore health to the patients; and they are properly used when the doctor, understanding their nature, also knows what is man, what is life, what is the constitution of the body, and thus what is health. Understanding these well he will also well understand the opposite, and this being so, he will know well how to repair.

You know that when medicines are rightly used they restore health to the invalid, and that he who knows them well makes the right use of them if he also understands what man is, and what life is, and the constitution of the body, and what health is. He who knows these things well will also know their opposite, and he will then be nearer a cure than any one else. The case of the invalid cathedral is similar. It also requires a doctor architect who understands the edifice well, and knows the rules of good building from their origin, and knows into how many parts they are divided, what are the causes that keep together an edifice and make it last, what is the nature of weight and of energy in force, and in what manner they should be combined and related to one another and what effect they will produce when combined. He who has true knowledge of these things, will plan the work to your satisfaction.

Therefore I shall try, without detracting and without . . . abusing any one . . . to convince you, partly by reasoning and partly by my works, sometimes showing the effects by their causes, sometimes sustaining my argument by experiment . . . and bringing in the authority of ancient architects and the proofs afforded by edifices that have been constructed and show the causes of their ruin or their survival, &c.

And thereby to show what is the weight and how many and what are the causes that ruin buildings, and what causes their stability and permanence. But so as not to prolong unduly this discourse to your Excellencies, I shall begin by explaining the plan of the first architect of the cathedral, and show clearly what was his intention, as revealed by the edifice begun by him, and having understood this, you will see clearly that the model which I have made embodies the symmetry, the correspondence, the conformity which appertained to the edifice from the beginning.

What is an edifice and wherefrom do the rules of correct building derive, and into what parts are they divided.

Either I, or others who can do better, choose him, and put aside all passions.

1348

Illmo ac Rm̃o Dñỡ Meo Unico.
D. Hip. Car.—li Estensi D. meo Colm̃o.
Ferrarie.

Illm̃ ac R. me D. ne mi hu. co. men.

Letter to the Cardinal Ippolito d'Este. Pochi giorni sono ch'io venni da Milano, et trovando che uno mio fratello maggiore non mi vuol servare uno testamento facto da 3 anni in qua che è morto nostro padre; ancor che la ragione sia per me, non dimeno per non mancare a me medesimo in una cosa che io stimo assai, non ho voluto ommettere di richiedere la R. ma V. S. di una l. ra commendatizia et di favore, qui a el Sor. Raphaello Jheronymo, che è al presente uno de n.ri excelsi Sig.ri, ne quali questa mia causa si agita et particularmente è suta dal Ex.tia del gonfaloniere rimessa nel pren.to S.or Raphaello et sua S.ia la ha a decidere et terminare prima venga la festa di tutti e sancti. Et però Mons.or mio io prego quanto più so e posso V. R. S. che scriva una l.ra qui al decto S.or Raphaello in quel dextro et affettuoso modo che lei saprà, raccomandandoli Leonardo Vincio svisceratissimo Ser.re suo, come mi appello, et sempre voglio essere: ricercandolo, e gravandolo mi voglia fare non solo ragione, ma expeditione favorevole, et io non dubito punto per molte relationi mi son facte che, sendo el S.or Raphaello a V. S. Affectionatissimo, la cosa mi succederà ad votū. Il che attribuirò a la l.ra di V. R. S. a la quale iterum mi racomando. Et bene valeat.

Florentie XVIII.ª 7bris 1507
E. V. R. D.
S.tor Humil.
Leonardus Vincius pictor.

Most Illustrious and most Reverend Lord.
The Lord Ippolito, Cardinal of Este at
Ferrara.

Most Illustrious and most Reverend Lord.

I arrived from Milan but a few days since, and finding that my elder brother refuses to carry into effect a will made three years ago when my father died—as also, and no less, because I would not fail in a matter I esteem most important—I cannot forbear to crave of your most Reverend Highness a letter of recommendation and favour to Ser Raphaello Hieronymo, at present one of the illustrious members of the Signoria before whom my cause is being argued; and more particularly it has been laid by his Excellency the Gonfaloniere into the hands of the said Ser Raphaello, that his Worship may have to decide and end it before the festival of All Saints. And therefore, my Lord, I entreat you, as urgently as I know how and am able, that your Highness will write a letter to the said Ser Raphaello in that admirable and pressing manner which your Highness can use, recommending to him Leonardo Vincio, your most humble servant as I am, and shall always be; requesting him and pressing him not only to do me justice but to do so with dispatch; and I have not the least doubt, from many things that I hear, that, Ser Raphaello being most affectionately devoted to your Highness, the matter will issue *ad votum*. And this I shall attribute to your most Reverend Highness's letter, to whom I once more humbly commend myself. *Et bene valeat.*

Florence XVIIIª 7bris 1507.
E. V. R. D.

your humble servant
Leonardus Vincius, pictor.

1348. *Written from left to right.*

1348. This letter addressed to the Cardinal Ippolito d'Este is here given from Marchese G. Campori's publication, 'Nuovi documenti per la Vita di L.d.V.', *Atti e Memorie delle R. R. Deputazioni di Storia patria per le provincie modenosi e parmenesi,* vol. iii. The discoverer of this letter—the only letter from Leonardo hitherto known as having been delivered —adds these interesting remarks: 'Codesto Cardinale nato ad Ercole I. nel 1470, arcivescovo di Strigonia a sette anni, poi d'Agra, aveva conseguito nel 1497 la pingue ed ambita cattedra di Milano, là dove avrà conosciuto il Vinci, sebbene il poco amore ch'ei professava alle arti lasci credere che le proteste di servitù di Leonardo più che a gratitudine per favori ricevuti e per opere a lui allogate, accennino a speranza per un favore che si aspetta. Notabile è ancora in questo prezioso documento la ripetuta signatura del grande artista che si scrive Vincio e Vincius, non da Vinci come si tiene communemente, sebbene l'una e l'altra possano valere a significare così il casato come il paese; restando a sapere se il nome del paese di

Vinci fosse assunto a cognome della famiglia di Leonardo nel qual supposto più propriamente avrebbe a chiamarsi Leonardo Vinci, o Vincio (latinamente Vincius) com'egli stesso amò segnarsi in questa lettera, e come scrissero parecchi contemporanei di lui, il Casio, il Cesariano, Geoffroy Tory, il Gaurico, il Bandello, Raffaelle Maffei, il Paciolo. Per ultimo non lascerò d'avvertire come la lettera del Vinci è assai ben conservata, di nitida e larga scrittura in forma pienemente corrispondente a quella dei suoi manoscritti, vergata all' uso comune da sinistra a destra, anzichè contrariamente come fu suo costume; ma indubbiamente autentica e fornita della menzione e del suggello che fresca ancora conserva l'impronta di una testa di profilo da un picciolo antico cammeo.' (Compare No. 1368, note.)

A facsimile of this letter is in Malaguzzi Valeri, 'La Corte di Lodovico il Moro', *Bramante e Leonardo da Vinci*, fig. 694, p. 644 (Milan, 1915). Compare Calvi, *Archivio Stor. lomb.* XLIII (1916), 'Contributi alla Biografia di L. d. V.'

C. A. 317a] 1349

Jo ho sospetto che la poca mia remuneratione de' gran benifiti che io ho riceuuti da uostra Eccelẽtia ²non l'abbino alquãto fatto sdegniare con meco, e questo è che da tante lettere che io ho scritte a uostra ³Signoria io non ò mai auuto risposta; hora io mando costì Salai per fare intendere a uostra Signoria ⁴come io sono quasi al fine del mio letigio che io ho · co' mia fratelli, come io credo trouarmi costì in questa ⁵pasqua e portare con meco due quadri di due nostre donne di uarie grandezze, le quali son fatte ⁶pel cristianissimo nostro rè, o per chi a uostra Signoria piacerà, jo avrei ben caro di sapere alla mia ⁷tornata di costà, doue io auessi a stare per stanza, perchè non uorrei dare più noia a uostra Signoria, e ⁸ancora, auendo io lauorato pel cristianissimo rè, se la mia prouisione è per correre o no; jo scriuo ⁹al presidente di quella acqua che mi donò il · rè ·, della quale non fui messo in possessione, perchè in quel tẽpo u'era ¹⁰carestia nel nauilio per causa de' gran secchi, e perchè i sua bocchelli non erano moderati; ma bẽ mi promise che, ¹¹fatta tal moderatione, io ne sarei messo in possessione; sicchè io prego uostra Signoria · che non le incresca, ¹²che ora che tali bochelli son moderati, di fare ricordare al presidente la mia espeditione cioè di darne la ¹³possessione d'essa acqua, perchè alla uenuta mia spero farui su strumẽti e cose che sarà di grã piacere al ¹⁴nostro cristianissimo rè; Altro non mi accade; sono senpre a uostri comandi.

I am afraid lest the small return I have made for the great benefits I have received from your Excellency has not made you somewhat angry with me, and that this is why to so many letters which I have written to your Lordship I have never had an answer. I now send Salai to explain to your Lordship that I am almost at an end of the litigation I had with my brothers; that I hope to find myself with you this Easter, and to carry with me two pictures of two Madonnas of different sizes. These were done for our most Christian King, or for whomsoever your Lordship may please. I should be very glad to know on my return thence where I may have to reside, for I would not give any more trouble to your Lordship. Also, as I have worked for the most Christian King, whether my salary is to continue or not. I wrote to the President as to that water which the king granted me, and which I was not put in possession of because at that time there was a dearth in the canal by reason of the great droughts and because [10] its outlets were not regulated; but he certainly promised me that when this was done I should be put in possession. Thus I pray your Lordship that you will take so much trouble, now that these outlets are regulated, as to remind the President of my matter; that is, to give me possession of this water, because on my return I hope to make there instruments and other things which will greatly please our most Christian King. Nothing else occurs to me. I am always yours to command.

Draft of letter to the Governor of Milan.

C. A. 372b] 1350

Magnifico presidẽte, io mando costì Salai mio discepolo, il quale ²di questa sia aportatore e da lui intenderete a bocca la causa del mio tanto sopra . . . .

³Magnifico presidẽte io ò.

⁴Magnifico presidente, essendomi io piv volte ricordato delle proferte fattemi da uostra Eccel-lẽtia più volte, ò preso sicurtà ⁵di scriuere e di

Magnificent President, I am sending thither Salai, my pupil, who is the bearer of this, and from him you will hear by word of mouth the cause of my . . . .

Magnificent President, I have . . . .

Magnificent President:—Having ofttimes remembered the proposals made many times to me by your Excellency, I take the liberty of

Drafts of letters to the Superintendent of Canals and to Fr. Melzi.

1349. 1. sosspecto chella poche .. uostra. 2. nonabbino .. isdegnare conmecho ecquesto .. uostra [ecci]. 3. auto risspossta .. cossti .. uostra. 4. lettigio .. fratelgi .. cossti in quessta. 5. passqua epportare conmecho .. nosstre .. quale. 6. crisstianissimo .. uostra .. arei. 7. cossta .. asstare per isstanza .. uosstra .. he. 8. re sella .. he per .. onno. 9. possessione. 10. sechi .. bochelli non era .. promisse. 11. possessione siche io priegho uosstra .. nolle incressca. 12. expeditione coe di. 13. posessione .. isspero .. chessarà. 14. nomi acade.
1350. 1. Magni"co" presidẽte [questa sol per ricordare a u] io .. quale [di questa sia]. 2. [la porta] di questa .. abocha. 3. Magni"co" [mio] presidẽte [avẽ] io. 4. presidẽde esendomi .. uostra [se] ecellẽtia. 5. [a vostra signoria] "acquesta" la .. fattomi [alla

1349. Charles d'Amboise, Maréchal de Chaumont, was Governor of Milan under Louis XII. Leonardo was in personal communication with him as early as 1503. The Maréchal was absent from Milan in the autumn of 1506 and from October 1510—when he besieged Pope Julius II in Bologna—till his death, which took place at Correggio, February 11, 1511. Francesco Vinci, Leonardo's uncle, died—as Amoretti tells us—in the winter of 1510-11 (or according

to Uzielli, in 1506?), and Leonardo remained in Florence for business connected with his estate. The letter written with reference to this affair, No. 1348, is undoubtedly earlier than the letters Nos. 1349 and 1350.

10. Compare Nos. 1009 and 1010.

1350. Compare Calvi, *I Manoscritti di L. d. V.*, pp. 264 ff. This letter is addressed to Geoffroy Carles, Président du Dauphiné.

ricordare a quella la promessa fattami a l'ultima partita, cioè la possessione di quel[6]le 12 once d'acqua donatemi dal cristianissimo rè; vostra Signoria sa che io non ētrai in essa possessione, perchè in quel [7]tempo, ch'ella mi fu donata, era carestia d'acqua nel navilio, si pel grā secco come pel non essere ancora moderati li sua bochelli; ma [8]mi fu promesso da uostra Eccellentia che fatta tal moderatione io avrei l'attento mio; di poi, intendendo essere acconcio il navilio, io scrissi più volte a vo[9]stra signoria e a Messer Girolamo da Cusano, che à apresso di sé la carta di tal donazione, e così scrissi al Corigero, e [10]mai ebbi risposta; Ora io mādo costì Salai, mio discepolo, aportatore di questa, al quale vostra Signoria potrà [11]dire a bocca tutto quel ch'è seguito, della qual cosa io prego vostra Eccellenza; [12]Jo credo esser costì in questa pasqua per esser presso al fine del mio piateggiare, e porterò cō meco due quadri di nostra [13]donna che io ò commīciate, e ò le ne' tempi, che mi sono avāzati, condotte in assai bō porto; Altro nō mi accade.

[14]Magnifico Signore mio, l'amore che uostra Eccellētia m'à senpre dimostro, e' benefiti ch'io ò riceuuti da quella al continuo [15]mi sō dināzi ....

[16]Io ò sospetto che la poca remuneratiō de' grā benifiti ch'io ho riceuuto da uostra Eccellentia non l'abbi[17]no fatto alquāto turbare con meco, e questo è che di piv lettere che io ò scritte a vostra Eccellentia io non ò mai [18]avuta risposta ·, ora io mando costì Salai per fare intendere a vostra signoria, come io son quasi al fine del mio [19]letigio coi mia fratelli, e come io credo essere costì in questa pasqua e portare con meco due quadri doue sono [20]due Nostre Donne di varie grādezze, le quali io ò comīciato pel cristianissimo rè, o per chi a uoi piacerà; avrei ben caro di sa[21]pere alla mia tornata di costà, dove io ò a stare per stanza, perchè nō uorrei dare più noia a uostra Signoria, e ā[22]cora, auendo io lauorato pel cristianissimo Rè, se la mia prouisione è per correre o no; io scriuo al presidē[23]te di quell' acqua che mi donò il rè, della quale nō fui messo in possessione per esserne carestia nel navilio per ca[24]usa de' grā secchi, e perchè i sua bocchegli non erā moderati; ma bē mi promise che, fatta tal moderatione, i' ne sarei [25]messo in possessione, sichè io vi prego che, scontrandosi in esso presidente, nō

writing to remind your Lordship of the promise made to me at my last departure, that is, the possession of the twelve inches of water granted to me by the most Christian King. Your Lordship knows that I did not enter into possession, because at that time when it was given to me there was a dearth of water in the canal, as well by reason of the great drought as also because the outlets were not regulated; but your Excellency promised me that as soon as this was done, I should have my rights. Afterwards hearing that the canal was complete, I wrote several times to your Lordship and to Messer Girolamo da Cusano, who has in his keeping the deed of this gift; and so also I wrote to Corigero and never had a reply. I now send thither Salai, my pupil, the bearer of this, to whom your Lordship may tell by word of mouth all that happened in the matter about which I petition your Excellency. I expect to go thither this Easter since I am nearly at the end of my lawsuit, and I will take with me two pictures of our Lady which I have begun, and at the present time have brought them on to a very good end; nothing else occurs to me.

My Lord, the love which your Excellency has always shown me and the benefits that I have constantly received from you I have hitherto ....

I am fearful lest the small return I have made for the great benefits I have received from your Excellency may not have made you somewhat annoyed with me. And this is why to many letters which I have written to your Excellency I have never had an answer. I now send to you Salai to explain to your Excellency that I am almost at the end of my litigation with my brothers, and that I hope to be with you this Easter and carry with me two pictures on which are two Madonnas of different sizes which I began for the most Christian King, or for whomsoever you please. I should be very glad to know where, on my return from this place, I shall have to reside, because I do not wish to give more trouble to your Lordship; and then, having worked for the most Christian King, whether my salary is to be continued or not. I write to the President as to the water that the king granted me, of which I had not been put in possession by reason of the dearth in the canal, caused by the great drought and because its outlets were not regulated; but he promised me certainly that as soon as the regulation was made, I should be put in possession of it; I therefore pray you that, if you should meet the said President, you would be good enough, now that the

partita mia di costa] a . . coe "la posessione" di. 6. dacq"a" donatomi . . crisstianissimo . . posesione. 7. tenpo "che la mi fa donata" era . . dacq"a" . . secho. 7. moderato. 8. ecellentia cheffatta . . arei lattento . . poi | "intendendo esser a conco il navilio" io. 9. donagone. 10. bocha . . quel . . ipriegho vosstra. 12. passqua . . piategare. 13. commicate e olle acade poe. 14. M"o"signore [antonio maria] "mio" lamore "laben" che uostra [signoria] "ecellētia" ma senpre di . . chio o"chi" . . riceuuti dacquella mi al. 16. ossosspetto . . pocha remuneratiō [de benifitich] de . . abi. 17. conmecho ecquesto . . osscritte avosstra . . inōno. 18. vta rissposta hora . . vosstra. 19. letigo comia . . cossti . . passqua . . comecho . . doue su. 20. grādeze . . comicate . . arei. 21. asstare . . istantia . . uorei [piu] . . uosstra. 22. crisstianisimo . . sella . . onno. 23. acq"a" . . re [la qua] della . . caresstia. 24. sechi . . bochelgli . . promisse. 25. priegho chesscontrandosi.

ui incresca che ora, che tali bochelli sõ ²⁶moderati, di ricordare a detto presidente di farmi dare la possessione d'essa acqua, che mi parue intēdere che in grã par²⁷te staua a lui; altro non mi accade; sono senpre a uostri comādi.

²⁸Buõ dì, messer Francesco ·, può lo fare Iddio che di tante lettere ch'io v'ò scritte · che mai voi non m'abbiate risposto; Or aspettate ²⁹ch'io venga costà, per Dio, ch'io vi farò tanto scrivere che forse vi rincrescerà.

³⁰Caro mio, messer Francesco, io mādo costì Salai per intendere dalla magnificentia del presidente che fine à avuta quella ³¹moderatione dell' acque che alla mia partita fu ordinata per li bochelli del navilio, perchè el magnifico presidēte mi promi³²se che subito fatta tal moderatione, io sarei spedito; Ora egli è più tenpo che io intesi che il nauilio s'accõ³³ciaua, e similmente i sua bochelli, e inmediate scrissi al presidente e a uoi, e poi replicai, e mai ebbi ³⁴risposta; adūque voi degnerete di rispōdermi quel ch'è seguito, e non essendo per spedirsi nō u'īcresca per mio a³⁵more di sollecitarne vn poco il presidente e così messer Girolamo da Cusano, al quale uoi mi racomādere³⁶te e offeriretemi a sua magnihcētia.

outlets are regulated, to remind the said President to cause me to be put in possession of that water, since I understand it is in great measure in his power. Nothing else occurs to me; always yours to command.

Good day to you, Messer Francesco. Why, in God's name, of all the letters I have written to you, have you never answered one. Now wait till I come, by God, and I shall make you write so much that perhaps you will become sick of it.

Dear Messer Francesco. I am sending thither Salai to learn from His Magnificence the President to what end the regulation of the water has come, since at my departure this regulation of the outlets of the canal had been ordered, because His Magnificence the President promised me that as soon as this was done I should be satisfied. It is now some time since I heard that the canal was in order, as also its outlets, and I immediately wrote to the President and to you, and then I repeated it, and never had an answer. So you will have the goodness to answer me as to that which happened, and as I am not to hurry the matter, would you take the trouble, for the love of me, to urge the President a little, and also Messer Girolamo Cusano, to whom you will commend me and offer my duty to his Magnificence.

C. A. 93a]   1350 A

Se si dice che manca 72 ducati al rè d'entrata, tollendo tale acqua a Sancto Cristofano.

Questo Sua Maestà sa che quel che dà a me ei lo toglie a sé. Ma qui non si to' niente al rè, ma tosi a chi n'à rubata perchè nel moderare le [se dicano] bocche, che ànno allargate li rubatori dell' acqua. . . .

Se si dice che questo [impedisce la sua] è in danno di molti, questo non è altro che ritorre alli ladri quello che ànno a restituire.

La qual cosa il magistrato al continuo ritoglie sanza mia cagione, e avanza più di 500 once d'acqua, e a me n'è stabilita sol 12 once.

Se si dice questa mia acqua valere assai l'anno, qui s'affitta l'oncia, in tal bassezza di canale, sol 7 ducati, di 4 lire l'uno, per oncia l'anno, che son 70.

Se dicano questo impedire la navicazione, questo non è vero perchè (l'acqua che serve alla) le bocche che servano a tal (navicazione son) adacquamento, son da la navicazione in su.

If it is said that by taking this water at Santo Cristofano the King loses 72 ducats.

His Majesty knows that whatever he gives to me, of that he deprives himself. But in this case the King is not deprived of anything, but it is taken away from those who have stolen it by altering the so-called mouths, which were enlarged by the thieves of the water. . . .

If it is said that this [impedes] is to the disadvantage of many, it only is taking back from the thieves what they should restore.

The magistrate does this constantly of his own accord, taking more than 500 ounces of water, while the quantity agreed upon for me is only 12 ounces.

If it is said that this water of mine is of considerable value per year, here, where the canal is at such a low level, the ounce is hired at only 7 ducats, of 4 lire each, per year, that is, 70.

If they say that this hinders the navigation it is not true, because the mouths supplying this water are above the navigation.

26. posesione . . acq"a". 27. allui . . nomi achade [se nõ di racoman]. 28. meser . . puollo . . idio . . vosscritte . . nomabiate rissposto. 29. vengha . . chefforse vi rincrescera. 30. charo . . meser francesco . . cheffine a uta. 31. della cq"a" . . partia. 32. che nauilio sacõ. 33. caua essimilmente . . scrissi [io auoi e] al . . ripricai. 34. rissposta . . risspodermi . . isspedirsi. 35. pocho. 36. offerrete assua mgnifcētia.

1350. 28–36. Draft of a letter to Francesco Melzi, born 1493—a youth therefore of about 17 in 1510. Leonardo addresses his young friend as 'Messer', being the son of a noble house. Melzi practised art under Leonardo as a dilettante.

C. A. 247*b*]   1351

Drafts of a letter to Giuliano de' Medici (1351–2).

[Jllustrissimo mio Signore, ²Assai mi rallegro, illustrissimo mio signiore ·, del uostro].

³Tanto mi son rallegrato, o illustrissimo mio signore, del desiderato acquisto di vostra sanità che io quasi ho [riavuto la sanità mia]—[sono all' ultimo del mio male]—e'l male mio da me s'è fuggito della quasi reintegrata sanità di vostra Eccellenza; ⁴Ma assai mi rincrescie il nõ auere io potuto integralmẽte satisfare alli desideri di uostra Ecciellentia mediã⁵te la malignità di cotesto ingannatore, al quale non ò lasciato indirieto cosa alcuna colle quale ⁶io li abbia potuto giovare che per me non li sia stata fatta; e prima la sua provisione inanzi al tẽpo immediate li era pagata, la quale io credo che volentieri ⁷negherebbe, se io non avessi la scritta attestata di man dello interprete, e vedendo io che per me nõ si lauorava, se nõ quãdo ⁸i lavori d'altri li mãcavano, de' quali lui era sollecito investigatore, jo lo pregai che dovesse mangia⁹re con meco, e lauorare di lime appresso di me, perchè oltre al conto . . . elli acquisterebbe il linguaggio italiano; [lui senpre lo promise e mai lo volle fare]; E questo facevo ancora, perchè quel giovã tedesco che fa li spechi ogni dì lì era in bottega, e volleua vedere e intendere ciò che si facieva e publicava per la terra biasimando quel che lui non intendea; e questo facevo perchè lui mãgiava cõ que' ¹⁰della guardia del papa, e poi se n'ãdava

[Most illustrious Lord. I greatly rejoice, most Illustrious Lord, at your . . .]

I was so greatly rejoiced, most Illustrious Lord, by the desired restoration of your health that it almost had the effect that [my own health recovered]—[I have got through my illness]—my own illness left me——of your Excellency's almost restored health. But I am extremely vexed that I have not been able completely to satisfy the wishes of your Excellency, by reason of the wickedness of that deceiver, for whom I left nothing undone which could be done for him by me and by which I might be of use to him; and in the first place his allowances were paid to him before the time, which I believe he would willingly deny, if I had not the writing signed by myself and the interpreter. And I, seeing that he did not work for me unless he had no work to do for others, which he was very careful in soliciting, invited him to eat with me, and to work afterwards near me, because, besides saving of expense, he would acquire the Italian language. [He always promised, but would never do so.] And this I did also, because that young German who makes the mirrors, was there always in the workshop, and wanted to see and to know all that was being done there and made it known outside blaming what he did not understand and because he dined with those of the Pope's

1351. 1. Illusimo permio signiore Aven. 2. rallegro [della] illusttrissimo. 3. del [famoso] desiderato . . uosstra . .che ĩ quasi [il io haffatto] "[riavta la sanita mia]" "[son sono allultimo del mio male]" "el mal mio dame se fuggito" [del grãde acquisto] della . . reîntegrata . . uosstra eccielltia. 4. [chel mia . . rincresscie [della malignità] il . . auere | "io" potuto "integralmẽte" saddisfare . . uosstra 5. te la malignita [de] di cotessto . . lassciato indirieto [nessuna] cosa "alcuna" colle. 6. giovare | "che per me non li sia stata fatta" e . . li sua [danari] provisione "inanzi al tẽpo" immediate . . paghata. 7. negherebbe "neghata" se . . avesi lasscritta. 8. daltri [erã finiti] "si mãcavano" de . . sollecito [cierchatore] "investighatore" jo [lo uolsi e lo feci] "lo" pregha "i" che do"ve" ssi. 9. comecho "ellauorare di limi apresso di me perche oltre alcõto .\·—*Here on the margin is the note in three lines* .\· bẽ lopere elli acquisterebbe i linghagio italiano . . lui senpre [lo promisse e mai lo volle fare] .\· Ecque"sto" facievo ||. *On the margin in twelve short lines:* || ecquesto facievo ancora perche que . . ongni . . ibottegha . . cio chessi e publicava per la tera biasimando quel che none itendeva. *Here ends the note on the margin.* perche lui mãgiava [colli tedesschi che so] cõ quel. 10. nãdava "in conpagnia" cholli schopietti.

1351, 1353. Writings addressed to Giuliano de' Medici, Leonardo's patron while in Rome, 1513–15. Giuliano was the third son of Lorenzo il Magnifico and brother of Pope Leo X whom he joined in Rome, where he settled. A medal struck in his honour bears the words MAG. IVLIAN. MEDICES. Leonardo too uses 'Magnifico' in his address. Compare also No. 1377.

Gino Capponi (*Storia della Repubblica di Firenze*, vol. iii, p. 139) thus describes the character of Giuliano de' Medici, who died in 1516: 'Era il migliore della famiglia, di vita placida, grande spenditore, tenendo intorno a sè uomini ingegnosi, ed ogni nuova cosa voleva provare.'

Giuliano lived in the Vatican, and it may be safely inferred from No. 1352, l. 2, and No. 1353, l. 4, that Leonardo worked there. Accounts for work done in Leonardo's rooms in the Belvedere are entered in a book entitled *Libretto di ricordi 1513*, now in the archives of the Fabbrica di San Pietro. These include the alterations of windows, a table for grinding colours, &c. See Mario Cermenati, 'Leonardo a Roma nel periodo Leoniano', *Nuova Antologia*, 16 Maggio 1919.

The following notice in the Vatican archives, to which Eug. Müntz drew my attention, gives colour to Leonardo's account of Giorgio Tedesco:

'Nota delle provisione (sic) a da pagare per me in nome del nostro ill. S. Bernardo Bini e chompᵃ di Roma, e prima della illᵐᵃ sua chonsorte ogni mese d. 800.

'A Lᵈᵒ da Vinci per sua provisione d. XXXIII, e più d. VII al detto per la provisione di Giorgio tedescho, che sono in tutto d. 40.'

From this we learn that seven ducats formed the German's monthly wages, but according to No. 1353, l. 7, he pretended that eight ducats had been agreed upon.

The names of seventy Germans, mostly servants or in humble situations, occur in the 'Rotulus familiae Leonis X', discovered at the Vatican Library in 1895. See 'Il ruolo della corte di Leone X (1514–1516),' by Alessandro Ferrajoli, *Archivio della R. Società Romana di Storia Patria*, vol. xxxiv, 1911; also 'Ein rotulus familiae Papst Leo's X', by Walter Friedenburg, in *Quellen und Forschungen aus italienischen Archiven und Bibliotheken*, Königl. preuss. historisches Institut in Rom, vol. vi, part I, pp. 55–71, 1903.

in conpagnia colli scoppietti, amazādo vccielli per queste anticaglie e così seguitava da dopo desinare a sera; E se io mandavo Lorēzo [11]a sollecitarli il lavoro lui si cruciava e dicieva che nō volea tanti maestri sopra capo, e che il lauorar suo era [12]per la guardaroba di vostra Ecciellētia, e passò dua mesi e così seguitava e un dì, trovādo Gianicolò della [13]guardaroba, domādailo s'el tedesco avea finito l'opere del Magnifico, e lui mi disse non esser vero, ma che so[14]lamēte li avea dato a nettar dua scoppiette; di poi faciēdolo io sollecitare lui lasciò la bottega, e comīciò a lavorare ī came[15]ra, e perde assai tēpo nel fare vn' altra morsa e lime e altri strumēti a vite; e quiui lavorava mulinelli da torcere seta, [16]li quali nascōdeva, quādo nessun de' mia v'ētrava, e con mille bestemie e rimbrotti, in modo che nessū de' mia voleva piv entrare.

[17]Tanto mi sō rallegrato, jllustrissimo mio Signore, del desiderato acquisto di vostra sanità che quasi il male mio da me [18]s'è fugito; Ma assai mi rincrescie il non avere io potuto integralmēte satisfare alli desideri di uostra Eccellenza [19]mediante la malignità di cotesto ingānatore tedesco, per il quale non ò lasciato indirieto cosa alcuna, [20]colla quale io abbia creduto tarli piaciere; e prima invitarlo ad abitare e vivere con meco, per la qual cosa io ve[21]drei al continuo l'opera che lui faciesse, e cō facilità ricorreggierei li errori ·; e oltre a di questo inparerebbe la lingua italiana, [22]mediante la quale lui cō facilità potrebbe parlare sanza interprete; e prima li sua danari li furò [23]sēpre dati ināzi al tēpo ·; Dipoi la richiesta di costui fu di avere li modelli [24]finiti di legniame, com' ellino aveano a essere di ferro, e quali volea portare nel suo paese; La qual cosa io li negai diciē[25]doli ch'io li darei in disegnio la larghezza, lunghezza e grossezza e figura di ciò ch'elli avesse a fare, e così restammo mal volētieri.

[26]La secōda cosa fu, che si fecie vn' altra bottega e morse e strumenti, dove dormiua, e quivi lavorava per altri, dipoi andava a desi-[27]nare coi Suizzeri della guardia, dove sta giēte sfacciēdata, della qual cosa lui tutti li uīcieva; di lì se ne usciva e 'l piv [28]delle volte se n'andauano due o tre di loro, colli scoppietti ammazzādo vccielli per le anticaglie, e questo durava insino a sera;

guard, and then they went out with guns killing birds among the ruins; and this went on from after dinner till the evening; and when I sent Lorenzo to urge him to work he said that he would not have so many masters over him, and that his work was for Your Excellency's Wardrobe; and thus two months passed and so it went on; and one day finding Gian Niccolò of the Wardrobe and asking whether the German had finished the work for your Magnificence, he told me this was not true, but only that he had given him two guns to clean. Afterwards, when I had urged him further, he left the workshop and began to work in his room, and lost much time in making another pair of pincers and files and other tools with screws; and there he worked at reels for twisting silk which he hid when any one of my people went in, and with a thousand oaths and mutterings, so that none of them would go there any more.

I was so greatly rejoiced, most Illustrious Lord, by the desired restoration of your health that my own illness almost left me. But I am greatly vexed at not having been able to completely satisfy your Excellency's wishes by reason of the wickedness of that German deceiver, for whom I left nothing undone by which I could have hope to please him; and first I invited him to lodge and board with me, by which means I should constantly see the work he was doing and with greater ease correct his errors, while, besides this, he would learn the Italian tongue, by means of which he could with more ease talk without an interpreter; first his moneys were always given him in advance of the time when due. Afterwards he wanted to have the models finished in wood, just as they were to be in iron, and wished to carry them away to his own country. But this I refused him, telling him that I would give him, in drawing, the breadth, length, height, and form of what he had to do; and so we remained in ill will.

The next thing was that he made himself another workshop and pincers and tools in his room where he slept, and there he worked for others; afterwards he went to dine with the Swiss of the guard, where there are idle fellows, in which he beat them all; from here he went out and most times they went in two or three with guns, to shoot birds among the ruins, and this went on till evening.

. . antichaglie "ecosi segutava da dopo desinare assera" Esse. 11. [a richordarli] a solecitarli . . lui "si scruciava e" dicieva . . maesstri . . chapo echese [la] cche se [la] e i lauorare. 12. ghuardaroba [del s] di . . e [chosi] passo . . seghuita ve [se no] e vndi [li] trovādo. 13. ghuardaroba [del s] domādalo selli [ave] sel tedessco . . magnificho ellui . . Mace. 14. solecitare . . lassio . . bottegha e comōcio allavorare. 15. ellime . . llavorava mulenelli dattorciere. 16. loi quali nascōdeva . . nesū de mia vēdrava . . comile . . rinbrotti . . nesū. 17. vosstra . . che | "quasi" il [mio] male. 18. rincrescie . . sadifare . . uosstra. 19. ingānatore [tedesco il quale] tedesco . . lassciato . . chosa. 20. cholle . . e "p" prima | "secondariamente" invitarlo . . vi"ve"re comecho. 21. chellui faciessi. 22. ricoregiere . . oltre a di questo . . taliana . . interprete [e oltre a di questo] "e prima" li sua. 23. ināzi [al mese] al tēpo alltuttofu Di . . riciessta . . modelli [finiti di legniane]. 24. fin [iti di pūto] di . . chomelli . . neghai. 25. darei [di] in . . luneza e grosseza . . avessi affare . . restamo. 26. bottegha "emvro (?) e morse esstrumēti" [nella camera] dove. 27. nare [colla ghuardi] co suizeri . . ghardia . . uīcieva disene vssciva e piv. 28. senadaua . . ottre . . amazādo . . antichaglie

[29]Al fine ò trovato come [30]questo maestro Giovā[31]ni delli spechi è quello [32]che à fatto il tutto per [33]due cagioni; e la prima [34]perchè lui à avuto a dire che [35]la venuta mia qui [36]li à tolto la cõuersa[37]tione e 'l favore di uostra [38]Signoria, che senpre ve . . .; [39]L'altra è [40]che la stãtia [41]di questo ferreri [42]disse cõuenirsi a lui per [43]lavorare li spechi, e [44]di questo n'à fatto dimostra-[45]tione che, oltre al farmi [46]costui nimico, li à fatto vē[47]dere ogni suo e lasciare [48]a lui la sua bot[49]tega, nella qual lavora [50]cõ molti lavorãti assai spe[51]chi per mãdare alle fiere.

At last I found how this master Giovanni the mirror-maker was he who had done it all, for two reasons: the first because he had said that my coming here had deprived him of the countenance and favour of Your Lordship which always . . . The other is that he said that his iron-workers' rooms suited him for working at his mirrors, and of this he gave proof; for besides making him my enemy, he made him sell all he had and leave his workshop to him, where he works with a number of workmen making numerous mirrors to send to the fairs.

C. A. 283a]   1352

Tanto mi son rallegrato, illustrissimo mio signiore, del desiderato acquisto di uostra sanità, che quasi il male mio da me [2]s'è fuggito; di che iddio ne sia laudato; Ma assai mi rincresce il non avere io potuto integralmēte satisfare alli desideri di uostra Eccellenza [3]mediante la malignità di cotesto ingānatore tedesco, per il quale non ò lasciato indirieto cosa alcuna, [4]colla quale io abbia creduto farli piacere; E prima li sua danari li furono inte[5]gramente pagati innanzi al . . . del mese, nel qual correr dovea la sua provesione e secondariamente invitarlo ad abitare e vivere con meco, per la qual [6]cosa io farei piantare vn desco a' piedi d'una di queste finestre, dove lui potesse lauorar di lima, e finire le cose di sotto fabbricate, e così io vedrei al continuo l'opera che lui facessi e con facilità si ricorreggierebbe. E oltre a di questo, imparerebbe la lingua taliana mediante la quale lui con facilità parlare potrebbe sanza interprete.

I am so greatly rejoiced, most Illustrious Lord, by the wished-for recovery of your health, that my own ills have almost left me; and I say God be praised for it. But it vexes me greatly that I have not been able completely to satisfy your Excellency's wishes by reason of the wickedness of that German deceiver, for whom I left nothing undone by which I could hope to please him; first he was paid in full before the (beginning of the) appointed month, and secondly I invited him to lodge and board with me, for which purpose I would have a table fixed at the foot of one of these windows, where he could work with the file and finish the things made below; and so I should constantly see the work he was doing, and it could be corrected with greater ease. And besides, he would learn the Italian language and be able to speak with ease without an interpreter.

C. A. 182b]   1353

Draft of letter written at Rome.

Quest' altro m'à īpedito l'anatomia [2]col papa biasiamãdola, e così all' o[3]spedale, e ēpie di botteghe da spechi [4]tutto questo Beluedere o lavorā[5]ti; e così à fatto nella stãtia di ma-[6]estro Giorzio; . . . [7]disse che otto du[8]cati li furon promes[9]si ogni mese, comī[10]ciãdo il primo dì [11]che si mise in via, [12]o il più tardo quã[13]do e' ui parlò, e che [14]voi l'acciettaste;

[15]Vedēdo io costui rare volte sta[16]re a bottega e che cōsumava assai, io [17]li feci dire che se li piacea che io farei [18]con lui mercato di ciascuna cosa che [19]lui facesse, e a stima tãto li darei [20]quãto noi fussimo d'accordo; elli [21]si cōsigliò col uicino e lasciò lì la stã[22]tia, vendendo ogni cosa, e venne a trovare . . . .

This other hindered me in anatomy, blaming it before the Pope; and likewise at the hospital; and he has filled [4] this whole Belvedere with workshops for mirrors or with workmen; and he did the same thing in Maestro Giorgio's room. . . . He said that he had been promised [7] eight ducats every month, beginning with the first day, when he set out, or at latest when he spoke with you; and that you agreed.

Seeing that he seldom stayed in the workshop, and that he ate a great deal, I sent him word that if he liked I could make a bargain with him separately for each thing that he might make, and would give him what we might agree to be a fair valuation. He took counsel with his neighbour and gave up his room, selling everything, and went to find . . . .

ecquesto . . assera. 30. maesstro. 33. ella. 34. lui avuto. 35. mia [ari] qui. 36. tolto [il s] la. 37. uosstra. 38. Signoria. 39. [nēdo] Laltra. 40. [faciendoli] chella. 41. di questo [mini] fereri. 42. disscie cõnuenirsi allui. 43. lisspechi. 47. ellassciare. 48. allui . . boc. 49. tecca. 51. chi pe.
1352. 2. seffuggito "dicho idio ne sia laldato" Ma . . rincre. *Here the text breaks off.* 2. *The text from lines* 1-4: Ma assai &c. *to* ad piacere *is an exact copy of lines* 18-20, No. 1349. 5. al [tempo cheliavessi meritati] del . . . comecho . . chosa. 6. io vedrei.\'. *Here follow six short lines on the margin:* farei piantare vn dessco . . questse . . potessi . . di sot fabbricare e chosi. *The marginal note ends here.* faciessi e chõ.
1353. 2. chosi. 3. dasspechi. 4. ollavrã. 5. affatto. 6. esstro giorzo. 8. fu. 9. sa. 11. misse. 16. abottegha . . asai. 17. chesseli piacca che i farei. 18. collui merchato . . ciasscuna. 19. faciessi e asstima ettãto. 20. dacchordo. 21. ellasciolli. 22. vendēda ogni cosa e vene attrovare.

C. A. 92*a*]

1353 A

Sommi accertificato che esso lavora a tutti, e che fa bottega per il popolo: per la qual cosa io non voglio che lavori per me a provvisione, ma che e' si paghi de' lavori che fa per me; e per ch' egli ha bottega e casa del Magnifico, che sia tenuto a mandare i lavori del Magnifico innanzi a tutti.

I have ascertained that he works for everybody and that his workshop is open to anybody; for this reason I do not want him to work for me on account, but that what he works for me should be paid there and then, and since his workshop and lodging have been granted him by the Magnifico he should be bound to expedite works for the Magnifico before those of everybody else.

C.A. 96 *b*]

Stalla del Magnifico dalla parte di sopra lunga braccia 110 e larga braccia 40 . . . . Stalla del Magnifico dal lato di sotto . . . è capace di cento venti otto cavalli.

The stables of the Magnifico in the upper part 110 br. long and 40 br. wide. . . . The stables of the Magnifico in the lower part . . . can accomodate 128 horses.

C. A. 311*a*]

1354

Caro Benedetto Dei (?)

Per darti nuove de le cose qua [2]di levante, [3]sappi come [4]del mese [5]di Giugno [6]è apparito [7]un gigante che vien di [8]la diserta Libia. [9]Questo gigante era nato nel mont' Atalante, ed era [10]nero, ed ebbe contro Artaserse cogli Egiti e Arabi, [11]Medi e Persi; viveva in mare delle bale[12]ne, (de') gran capidogli e de' navili. [13]Caduto il fier gigante per la cagione della insanguinata [14]e fangosa terra, parve che cadesse vna montagnia; [15]onde la campagnia a guisa di terremoto, con ispavento [16]a Plutone infernale; e per la gran percossa ristette [17]su la piana terra alquanto stordito; onde subito [18]il popolo, credendo fusse morto di qualche saetta . . . [19]e per la gran caduta parve la provincia [20]tutta tremasse. . . . Marte, temendo della vita, [21]s'era fugito sotto il let[22]to di Giove. . . . [23]tornando la gran barba, a guisa di formiche che scorrono [24][furiando per] a furia, quando per il corpo del caduto rogero (?) . . . [25]a similitudine de le [26]formiche che sfurian[27]do or qua or là, su pel rogero [28]abbattuto da la scure del [29]rigido villano così questi [30]scorrendo per l'ampie membra, e traversando con ispesse [31]ferite; onde risentito il gigante, e sentendosi [32]quasi coperto da la moltitudine, subito sentesi cuo[33]cere per le punture; mise un mugghio che parve [34]fussi vno spaventoso tono, e posto le mani in [35]terra, e levatosi il pavroso volto, e postosi [36]una delle mani in capo trovòselo [37]pieno [38]di uomini appiccati a cape[39]gli, a similitudine

Dear Benedetto Dei,

To give you news of things here in the East, you should know that in the Month of June there appeared a giant who comes from the Desert Libia. This giant was born on Mount Atlas; he was black and had to fight with Artaxerxes, Egyptians, Arabs, Medes, and Persians; he lived in the sea on whales, grampuses, and ships. When the proud giant fell because of the bloody and miry state of the ground it was as though a mountain had fallen, so that the country shook as with an earthquake, and terror fell on Pluto in Hell, and from the violence of the shock he (the giant) lay somewhat stunned on the level ground. Suddenly the people seeing him as if killed by a thunderbolt and it seemed as though the whole province quaked at the great fall—and Mars, fearing for his life, took refuge under the bed of Jove; turning the big beard like ants running wildly over the trunk of the fallen oak—like ants rushing here and there over the oak struck down by the axe of the strong peasant—thus they rushed over his ample limbs, piercing him with many wounds. Then this giant, being roused and feeling himself almost covered by the multitude, suddenly felt the smarting of the stabs; he sent forth a roar which sounded like a terrific clap of thunder; and placing his hands on the ground he raised his terrible face and having lifted one hand to his head he found it full of men sticking to it like the minute creatures which not infrequently are

Miscellaneous records (1354–5).

1354. 1. benedetto de per tarti. 3. sapi. 4. de lme se. 7. vgigāte ce viē dila. 9. mõ ta ta lāte e dera. 10. cotrõ atassese. 13. dela. 14. tera . . cadessi. 15. gujsa di tere moto. 16. plutone ifernale eper la grã percosa. 17. sula . . tera . . stordito . . on sobito. 18. popo gerededo fusi. 23. lagrã . . scorano. 24. per olcorpo delcaduto vogore | 27. do orqa or la super lorego. 33. umuglio. 34. fusi u nos paventoso. 35. te ra. 36. dele. 37. pieno [di mj nvti anjmali]. 38. apicati acape. 42. ode scotēdo jlca p glio.

1354. A piece of raillery. Perhaps Leonardo had the Giant Antaeus in his mind. Of him the myth relates that he was a son of Gê, that he fed on lions; that he hunted in Libya and killed the inhabitants. He enjoyed the peculiarity of renewing his strength whenever he fell and came in contact with his mother earth; but Hercules lifted him up and so conquered and strangled him. Lucan gives a full account of the struggle *Pharsalia*, iv, 617. Compare the description of Giants in Dante, *Inf.* xxi and xxii. See also E. Solmi, *Le Fonti*, p. 249. Benedetto Dei is the author of a diary describing a journey made in the interests of the Florentine merchants Portinari (see No. 1448) in 1476 through France, the Netherlands, and Switzerland (Bibl. Riccardiana, Florence).

de' mi[40]nvti animali, che fra que[41]gli sogliono nascere; [42]onde scuotendo il capo, gli [43]omini facevano non altrementi per l'aria che si faccia [44]la grandine, quando va con furor di venti; e trovossi molti [45]di questi vomini esser morti da quegli che gli tempestavano adosso; [46]po' ritto coi piedi calpestando [47]e tenendosi a capegli e 'ngegnandosi nascondere fra quegli, facevano [48]a similitudine de' marinai quand' àn fortuna, che corrono su per le corde [49]per abbassar la vela a poco vento.

found there. Then shaking his head he sends the men through the air just as hail does when driven by the fury of the winds, and many of the men who had been treading on him were found dead. Then he straightened himself and stamped with his feet and they clinging to his hair and striving to hide in it behaved like sailors in a storm who run up the ropes to lower the sails to lessen the force of the wind.

W. 12495b]   **1355**

Il quale spirito ritrova · il cerebro, dõde partito s'era ·, con alta vocie cõ tali parole mosse . . . .

[2]E se alcuno uomo bēchè abbi discretione o bõtà . . . ., dalli altri omini . . . [3] . . . . e peggio se da esso son remote.

[4]O felice, o avēturato spirito, dõde partisti! jo ho questo uomo a male mio grado bē cono-[5]scivto ·; Questo è ricietto · di villania ·, questo è propio · ammonitione di somma ingratitudine, [6]in cõpagnia di tutti i viti ·; ma che mi vo io cõ parole indarno affaticãdomi? la somma de' pec-cati [7]solo in lui trovati sono; E se alcuno infra loro si trova, che alcuna bontà possegga, non altri[8]mēti come che me dalli altri uomini trat-tati sono ·, e in effetto io ho questa cõclusione ch'è [9]male s'eli sono nimici e peggio s'eli son amici.

This spirit returns to the brain whence it had departed, with a loud voice and with these words it moved . . . .

And if any man though he may have wisdom or goodness . . . from other people . . . and worse if they are removed from him.

O blessed and happy spirit, whence comest thou? Well have I known this man, much against my will. This one is a receptacle of villainy; he is a perfect heap of the utmost ingratitude combined with every vice. But of what use is it to fatigue myself with vain words? Nothing is to be found in him but every form of sin. . . . And if there should be found among them any that possess any good, they will not be treated differently from myself by other men; and in fine, I come to the conclusion that it is bad if they are hostile, and worse if they are friendly.

H.³ 137a]   **1356**

Miscella-neous drafts of letters and personal records (1356–68).

Tutti i mali che sono [2]e che furono, [6]essēdo messi in opera da costui [7]nõ satisfarebbero al deside[8]rio del suo iniquo animo; [9]io nõ potrei con lunghezza di tēpo [10]descriverui la natura di costu[11]i, ma bē cõchivdo che . . . .

All the ills that are or ever were, if they could be set to work by him, would not satisfy the desires of his iniquitous soul; and I could not in any length of time describe his nature to you, but I conclude . . . .

C. A. 297b]   **1356 A**

M. ca d. Cecilia—Amantissima mia Diva. Lecta la tua suaviss.a . . . .

Cecilia—My dearest Goddess, having read your most gracious . . . .

C. A. 389b]   **1357**

[Io ho uno · che per auersi di me promesso cose assai · mē che debite, [2]essendo rimasto ingañato del suo prosontuoso desiderio, à tē[3]tato di tormi tutti li amici e perchè li à trouati saui e non

[I know one who, having promised himself of me much less than my due, being disappointed of his presumptuous desires, has tried to deprive me of all my friends; and as he has found them wise

46. porito co pie di.   47. e a te nēdosi acapegli   49. pe rabasar.
1355. 1. E. quale . . cierbio . . chon . . vo cie [ne] cotali.   2. alchuno homo . . bota di nolmē li che me dalli altri omini tr\\\\\\\so\\\\\\\\. 3. la settu\\\\\\\\   4. spiritoche dõde me partisti joho . . homo"a"male . . chono.   5. uilania . . amv nitione.   6. chõpagnia . . voi chõ . . affatichãdomi lassoma de pechati.   7. solo nello trovati sono Esse alchuno . . alchuna . . possega.   8. chome . . omini . . effetti . . chõclusione.   9. male seli sonimiche e pegio seli son irattatiamicho.
1356. 1. chessono.   2. furono [nõ sadisfare].   3. [bono al de a esser pre messi].   4. [in opera allo iniquo desiderio].   5. [di questo homo]. 7. nõ sadissfarebono.   9. inõ . . collungeza dite.   11. cõciudo.
1357. 1. huno . . promesse chose.   2. desiderio attē.   3. sauieno legi.

1355. The writing, very difficult to decipher, is on the reverse of a drawing at Windsor, Pl. CXXII, which possibly has some connexion with it. The drawing is slightly reduced in this reproduction, the original being 26 cm. high by 20·5 cm. wide. Ancient

copies of it are in the Louvre and at Weimar.

1356 A. Written from left to right. Leonardo is known to have painted the portrait of Cecilia Gal-lerani, mistress of Lodovico il Moro. She said of him: 'Credo non se ne trova a lui un paro'.

leggi[4]eri al suo volere mi à minacciato che trouate le annūtiationi [5]che mi torrà i bene-fattori; ōde io ho di questo informato [6]vostra Signoria accio che, velendo questo seminare li usati [7]scādoli, non troui terreno atto a seminare pensieri e li [8]atti della sua mala natura; [9]che, tentādo lui fare di uostra signoria strumēto · della sua iniqua e maluagia natura [10]rimāga ingannato di suo desiderio.]

and not pliable to his will, he has menaced me that, having found means of denouncing me, he would deprive me of my benefactors. Hence I have informed Your Lordship of this, to the end [that this man who wishes to sow the usual scandals may find no soil fit for sowing the thoughts and deeds of his evil nature] so that he, trying to make your Lordship the instrument of his iniquitous and malicious nature, may be disappointed of his desire.]

C. A. 202b]   1357 A

Amatissimo mio fratello, solo questa per auisarti come ne dì passati io ricevetti una tua, per la quale io intesi tu avere auuto erete, della quale cosa intendo (tu) come ai fatto strema ale-greza, il che (conosc) stimando io tu essere (savio) prudente al tutto son chiaro, come i' sono tanto alieno da l'auere bono giuditio quanto tu dalla prudenza, conciosiachè tu ti se' rallegrato d'auerti creato un sollecito nemico, il quale con tutti li sua sudori disidererà libertà, la quale non sarà sanza tua morte.

My dearest brother, this is only to inform you that some days ago I received yours, from which I hear that you have an heir, and that you are extremely pleased about it. Thinking that you are prudent—I am quite sure that I am as far from having good judgement as you are from prudence, since you are pleased at having created an enemy intent on his liberty, which he will not have before your death.

W. 19084a]   1358

E in questo caso io so che io ne acquisterò pochi nomici, conciosia[2]chè nessū crederà ch'io possa dire di lui, perchè pochi son quelli [3]a chi i sua viti dispiacino; anzi solamente a quelli omini li dispiacio[4]no che son di natura cōtraria a tali uitj; e molti odiano li [5]padri e guastan le amicitie, reprēsori de' sua viti e non [6]vale esenpli contrari a essi, nè nessuno vmā consiglio.

And in this case I know that I shall make not a few enemies, seeing that no one will believe what I can say of him; for they are but few whom their vices disgust, nay, they are dis-pleasing only to those men whose natures are contrary to those vices. And many hate their fathers, and break off friendship with those who reprove their vices; and they will not permit any examples against them, nor any human advice.

[7]E se alcuno se ne trova virtuoso e bono, non lo scacciate [8]da voi; fatteli onore, acciò che non abbia a fugirsi da [9]voi e ridursi neli eremi, o spelonche, o altri lochi soleta[10]ri, per fugirsi dalle vostre insidie, e se alcun di questi [11]tali si trova, fatteli onore, perchè questi sono li uostri Iddei [12]terrestri, questi meritā da uoi le statue, simulacri e li onori; ma [13]bē ui ricordo che li lor simulacri nō siē da uoi mā[14]giati come achade in alcuna regione del India; [15]chè quādo li lor simulacri operano alcuno mi[16]raculo secondo

If you meet with any one who is virtuous, do not drive him from you; do him honour, so that he may not have to flee from you and betake himself to hermitages, or caves, or other solitary places to escape from your treachery; if there is such a one among you do him honour, for these are our saints upon earth; these are they who deserve statues from us, images and honours; but remember that their images are not to be eaten by you, as is done in some parts of India [15], where, when the images have according to

4. nia minaccato .. trouata le anutione.   5. torra e benifactori.   6. vosstra .. le usate.   7. chādali .. tereno .. assemi-nare "[aricievere]" in pēsieri elli.   9. [accioche nō ui faccia] "che tentādo lui fare di uosstr asignoria [ecciellencia] strumēti.
1358.   1. chaso iso .. acquistero pochi .. concosia.   2. crederra .. poci.   3. disspiacino .. sol queli .. dispiaca.   4. attali .. odiano.   6. vale .. esse.   7. esse .. vertuoso .. nollo scaccia de.   8. da voi[m] fatteli .. abia | affugirsi.   9. ermi .. saleta.   10. vosstre .. esse.   11. fate onore che "perche" questi.   12. statue elli onori "simulacri" ma.   13. chelli.   14. gati chome.   16. lo tagliano .. pezi esse.

1358. Below this text we read *gusstino* = Giustino, and in another passage on the same page Justin is quoted (No. 1210, l. 48). The two have, however, no real connexion.

15. In explanation of this passage I have received the following communication from Dr. G. W. Leitner of Lahore: 'So far as Indian customs are known to us, this practice spoken of by Leonardo as 'still existing in some parts of India' is perfectly unknown; and it is

equally opposed to the spirit of Hinduism, Moham-medanism and Sikhism. In central Tibet the ashes of the dead, when burnt, are mixed with dough, and small figures—usually of Buddha—are stamped out of them and some are laid in the grave while others are distributed among the relations. The custom spoken of by Leonardo may have prevailed there but I never heard of it.'

loro, li sacerdoti li tagliano in pezzi, essen[17]do di legno, e ne danno a tutti quelli del paese e nõ [18]sanza premio, e ciascũ raspa sottilmẽte la sua parte [19]e mette sopra la prima vivanda che mãgiano; e così tẽ[20]gono per fede aversi mãgiato il suo santo, e credono che luï li [21]guardi poi da tutti li pericoli || che ti pare, uomo, qui della [22]tua spetie? sei tu così sauio, come tu ti tieni? son [23]queste cose da esser fatte da omini?

them performed some miracle, the priests cut them in pieces, being of wood, and give them to all the people of the country, not without payment; and each one grates his portion very fine, and puts it upon the first food he eats; and thus believes that by faith he has eaten his saint who then preserves him from all perils. What do you think here, man, of your own species? Are you so wise as you believe yourselves to be? Are these things to be done by men?

C. A. 4*b*]   1359

Come io vi dissi ne' dì passati, voi sapete [2]che io sono sanza alcuno . . . degli amici.
[3]Francesco d'Antonio [4]Bernardo di Maestro Jacopo.

As I told you in past days, you know that I am without any . . . of my friends.
Francesco d'Antonio.
Bernardo di Maestro Jacopo.

C. A. 39*b*]   1360

Dimmi come le cose sono passate.

Tell me how the things happened.

C. A. 18*b*]   1361

J̄ lorẽzo\\ [2]inbiadali\\\ [3]inferri de\\\ [4]in lorẽzo\\\ [5][inno abuil]\\\ [6]in acõcatu\\\ [7]per la sella\\\ [8]colte di lor\\\ [9]v̄ cavallott\\\ [10]el uiagg\\\ [11]al\\\ [12]a lurẽz\\\ [13]in biada\\\ [14]inferri\\\ [15]abusso\\\ [16]in viagg\\\ [17]alorẽz\\\\

C. A. 66*b*]   1363

Questo scriuersi distintamẽte del nibbio [2]par che sia mio destino, perchè nella prima [3]ricordatione della mia infantia e' mi [4]parea che, essendo io in culla, che vn [5]nibbio venisse a me e mi aprisse la [6]bocca colla sua coda, e molte volte [7]mi percuotesse cõ tal coda dentro alle [8]labra.

W. 19030(?)]   1362

E così piacesse al nostro autore che io potessi dimostrare la natura delli omini [2]e loro costumi nel modo che io descrivo la sua figura.

And so may it please our great Author that I may demonstrate the nature of man and his customs, in the way I describe his figure.

This writing distinctly about the kite seems to be my destiny, because among the first recollections of my infancy, it seemed to me that, as I was in my cradle, a kite came to me and opened my mouth with its tail, and struck me several times with its tail inside my lips.

C. A. 252*a*]   1364

[Quãdo io feci Domeniddio putto, voi mi mettesti in prigione, [2]ora s'io lo fo grãde, voi mi farete peggio.]

[When I made a Christ Child you put me in prison. Now if I represent Him grown up, you will treat me worse.]

17. attutti . . paese [il qa]. 18. rasspa. 19. viuada che mãgano. 20. gã per fede avrsimãgato . . credã. 21. dattutti pericoli || chettitti pare omo. 22. settu . . tuttiti eni.
1359. 1–4. *Written from left to right.* 1. Chome io vidj si. 2. alchuno. 3. [franco dantonio]. 4. [brn brnado di m"o" iachopo].
1360. 1. chome le chosse.
1362. 1. piacessi . . altore. 2. desscrivo.
1363. 1. nibio. 2. nela. 5. venissin me e mi aprissi. 6. bocha chola. 7. perchotessi.
1364. 1. feci domene dio putto. 2. forãde . . pegio.

1361. This seems to be the beginning of a letter, but only the first words of the lines have been preserved, the leaf being torn down the middle. No translation is possible.
1362. A preparatory note for the passage given as No. 798, ll. 41–2.
1363. This note probably refers to the text No. 1221.
1364. This statement must refer to an unpleasant

incident in his life in connexion with a painting of the Infant Christ. Various drawings by Leonardo at Windsor (12564) and at the British Museum represent Christ fondling a cat, preliminary sketches for a picture now lost. Such subjects would have been considered strange and irreverent by the Church authorities and have brought him in collision with the Inquisition.

Br. M. 251b]

1365

Dimmi se mai fu fatto alcuna cosa.

Tell me if anything was ever done.

Br. M. 253a]

1366

Dimmi · se mai fece ²cosa che mi di . . . .

Tell me if ever he did a thing which me. . . .

S. K. M. III. 10b]

1367

¶Non iscoprire se libertà ²t'è cara, che 'l uolto mio ³è carciere d'amore. ¶

Do not reveal, if liberty is precious to you; my face is the prison of love.

C. A. 191b]

1368

Maestro Leonardo Fiorentino.

Maestro Leonardo of Florence.

C. A. 159a]

1368 A

Li Medici mi creorono ²e destrussono.

The Medicis made me and ruined me.

Flor. Uff.]

1369

Dì di Sca Maria della Neve, ²a dì 2 d'agosto 1473.

The day of Santa Maria *della Neve* [of the Snows], August the 2nd 1473. _{Notes bea ing dates (1369–78).}

W. 19059a]

1370

A dì 2 d'aprile 1489 libro titolato de figura vmana.

On the 2nd of April 1489, book entitled 'Of the human figure'.

C. A. 76b]

1370 A

A dì 23 d'aprile 1490.

On the 23rd of April 1490.

C. A. 318b]

1370 B

Domattina, a dì 2 Gennaro 1496 farai fare la soatta e pruova.

To-morrow, on the 2nd of January 1496, you will have the leather strap made and the test.

1365. P. — di mi semmai . . facto alchuna chosa.
1366. 1. semmai. 2. chosa chemmi di.
1367. 1. nonisscoprire selliberta. 2. te chara. 3. charciere.
1368. m"o".
1369. 2. addi 2 daggossto.
1370. 1489 [del] libro.

1368. So Leonardo writes his name on a sheet with sundry short notes, evidently to try a pen. Compare the signature with those in Nos. 1341, 1348, and 1374 (see also No. 1346, l. 33). The form 'Lionardo' does not occur in the autographs. The supposed Portrait of the Master in the Royal Library at Turin, which is reproduced—slightly diminished—on Pl. L, has in the original two lines of writing underneath; one in red chalk of two or three words is partly effaced: *lionardo it . . . lm* (or *lai?*); the second written in pencil is as follows: *fatto da lui stesso assai vecchio*. In both of these the writing is very like the Master's, but is certainly only an imitation.

1369. This date is on a drawing of a rocky landscape. See *Chronique des arts*, 1881, no. 23: 'Léonard de Vinci a-t-il été au Righi le 5 août 1473 ?', letter by H. de Geymüller. The next following date in the MSS. is 1478 (see No. 663).

1370. While the letters in the MS. notes of 1473 and 1478 are very ornate, this note and the texts on anatomy on the same sheet (for instance, No. 805) are in the same simple hand we see on Pls. CXVI and

CXIX. No. 1370 is the only dated note of the years between 1480 and 1489, and the characters are in all essential points identical with those that we see in the latest MSS. written in France (compare the facsimiles on Pl. CXV and p. 202), so that it is hardly possible to determine exactly the date of a MS. from the style of the handwriting, if it does not betray the peculiarities of style as displayed in the few notes dated previous to 1480.—Compare the facsimile of the manuscripts from 1479 on Pl. LXII, No. 2; No. 664, note, vol. i, p. 379. This shows already a marked simplicity as compared with the calligraphy of 1478.

The text No. 720 belongs to the year 1490; No. 1510 to the year 1492; No. 1459, No. 1384, and No. 1460 to the year 1493; No. 1463, No. 1517, Nos. 1024, 1025, and 1461 to the year 1494; Nos. 1523 and 1524 to the year 1497.

1370. The book *De Figura Umana* may be the same as the one mentioned by Luca Paciolo, *De Divina Proportione*, chap. i, where he states: 'havendo già (Leonardo da Vinci) con tutta diligentia al degno libro de pictura e movimenti humani posto fine'.

C. A. 2*a*]   1370 C

La verga del ferro che si debbe trafilare . . . .

Il ferro trafilato da una ruina fatta di una parte del molo di Genova, fu trafilato da minor potentia di questa.

Iron that is to be drawn out into the shape of a rod . . . .

In the ruined part of the breakwater at Genoa the iron was drawn out into rods by less power than this.

C. A. 104*a*]   1371

A dì primo d'agosto 1499 · scrissi qui de moto · e peso.

On the 1st of August 1499 I wrote here of motion and of weight.

Br. M. 272*a*]   1372

A dì 9 di luglio 1504, mercoledì a ore 7 morì Ser ²Piero da Vinci, notaio al Palazzo del Podestà, mio padre, ³a ore 7; era d'età d'anni 80, lasciò 10 figlioli ma⁴schi e 2 femmine.

On the 9th of July 1504, Wednesday, at seven o'clock, died Ser Piero da Vinci, notary at the Palazzo del Podestà, my father,—at seven o'clock, being eighty years old, leaving behind ten sons and two daughters.

C. A. 62*b*]   1373 A

Padre carissimo, A l'ultimo del passato ebbi la lettera mi scrivesti, la quale in brieve spazio mi dette piacere e tristizia: piacere in quanto che per quella intesi voi essere sano di che ne rendo grazie a Dio; ebbi dispiacere intendendo il disagio vostro.

Dearest father. On the last day of last month I got the letter you wrote me which gave me pleasure and pain at the same time: pleasure in so far as by it I learned that you are well, for which I thank God: but I was pained to hear of your troubles.

C. A. 71*b*]   1373

Mercoledì a ore 7 ²morì Ser Piero da Vinci a dì 9 ³di luglio 1504.

On Wednesday at seven o'clock died Ser Piero da Vinci, on the 9th of July 1504.

1371. adi p"o" dagosto.
1372. *Written from left to right:* 1. addi . . luglio 1504 in mercheledi.   2. palago.   3. lasco.   4. sci.
1373. 3. luglio.

1370 C. This note suggests that Leonardo may have accompanied Duke Lodovico il Moro to Genoa on March 17, 1498, when part of the breakwater was destroyed by a tempest. The Duke, who visited the port the next day, gave orders that it should be repaired. E. Solmi, 'Su una probabile gita di L. d. V. in Genova il 17 marzo 1498 per visitare quel porto', *Arch. Stor. Lomb.*, 1910, vol. xiv, pp. 439 ff.

1371. *Scrissi qui.* Leonardo does not say where; still we may assume that it was not in Milan. The next date is 1502; to this year belong Nos. 1034, 1040, 1042, 1048, and 1053. The note No. 1525 belongs to the year 1503.

1372. This statement of Ser Piero's age contradicts that of the *Riassunto della portata di Antonio da Vinci* (Leonardo's grandfather), who speaks of Ser Piero as being thirty years old in 1457; and that of the *Riassunto della portata di Ser Piero e Francesco*, sons of Antonio da Vinci, where Ser Piero is mentioned as being forty in 1469. These documents were published by G. Uzielli, *Ricerche intorno a L. d. V.*, Florence, 1872, pp. 144 and 146. Leonardo was, as is well known, a natural son. His mother was married in 1457

to Acattabriga di Piero di Luca da Vinci. She died in 1519. Leonardo never mentions her in the MSS. In the year of Leonardo's birth Ser Piero married Albiera di Giovanni Amadoci, and after her death at the age of thirty-eight he again married, Francesca, daughter of Ser Giovanni Lanfredi, then only fifteen. Their children were Leonardo's half-brothers, Antonio (b. 1476), Ser Giuliano (b. 1479), Lorenzo (b. 1484), a girl, Violante (b. 1485), and another boy, Domenico (b. 1486); Domenico's descendants still exist as a family. Ser Piero married for the third time Lucrezia di Guglielmo Cortigiani, by whom he had six children: Margherita (b. 1491), Benedetto (b. 1492), Pandolfo (b. 1494), Guglielmo (b. 1496), Bartolommeo (b. 1497), and Giovanni (date of birth unknown). Pierino da Vinci the sculptor (about 1520–54) was the son of Bartolommeo, the fifth of these children. The dates of their deaths are not known, but we may infer from the above passage that they were all still living in 1505.

1373 A. This valuable fragment (written from left to right) was discovered on the reverse side of sheet 62*a*, heretofore covered up. It testifies to fine filial sentiment.

S. K. M. I. 3b]　　　　　　　　　　**1374**

Principiato da me Leonardo ²da Vīci a dì 12 di luglio 1505.

Begun by me, Leonardo da Vinci, on the 12th of July 1505.

Trn. 18b]　　　　　　　　　　**1374 A**

Come il cortone uccello di rapina ch'io vidi andando a Fiesole sopra il locho di Barbiga nel 5 (1505) addì 14 di Marzo.

Like the . . . bird of prey which I saw above the place Barbiga on my way to Fiesole on the 14th of March, 1505.

F. 1a]　　　　　　　　　　**1375**

Comīciato a Milano a dì 12 di settēbre 1508.

Begun at Milan on the 12th of September 1508.

W. 19016]　　　　　　　　　　**1376**

In questa vernata del mille 510 credo spedire tutta tal notomia.

In the winter of this year 1510 I expect to complete all this anatomy.

W. 19077b]　　　　　　　　　　**1376 A**

Addì 9 di giennaro 1513.

On the 9th of January 1513.

C. A. 90b]　　　　　　　　　　**1376 B**

Finita a dì 7 di Luglio (1514) a ore 23 a Belvedere nello studio fattomi dal Magnifico.

Finished to-day July 7th (1514) an hour before midnight in the studio granted me by the Magnifico at the Belvedere.

G. 0']　　　　　　　　　　**1377**

Partissi il magnifico Giuliano de' ²Medici a dì 9 di giennaio 1515 ³in sull' aurora da Roma per ādare ⁴a sposare la moglie in Savoia; ⁵e in tal dì ci fu la morte del rè di Francia.

The Magnifico Giuliano de' Medici left Rome on the 9th of January 1515, just at daybreak, to take a wife in Savoy; and on the same day fell the death of the king of France.

C. A. 230b]　　　　　　　　　　**1377 A**

Addì 3 di marzo 1516.

On the 3rd of March, 1516.

C. A. 103a]　　　　　　　　　　**1377 B**

Il dì dell' Ascensione in Ambosa 1517 di Maggio nel clu.

Ascension Day at Amboise 1517 in May at Cloux.

C. A. 249a]　　　　　　　　　　**1378**

A 24 di giugnio il dì di san Giovanni ²1518 in Ābosa nel palazzo del clu.

On the 24th of June, St. John's day, 1518, at Amboise, in the palace of Cloux.

1374. 2. uīci addi.
1375. comīcato . . addi.
1376. e cquesta.
1377. 1. magnificho. 2. addi. 3. darroma. 4. assposare. 5. dere.
1378. 2. clu.

1374. The title is on the foregoing coversheet (3a) as follows: *Libro titolato disstrafformatione coe* (cioè) *d'un corpo nvn* (in un) *altro sanza diminuitione o acrescimento di materia.*
1375. No. 1528 and No. 1529 belong to the same year. The text vol. i, No. 4 belongs to the following year 1509 (1508 old style); so also does No. 1009.—Nos. 1022, 1057, and 1464 belong to 1511.
1376. A. No. 1465 belongs to the same year; No. 1065 to the next year 1514.
1376 B. C. Amoretti copied the following note from one of the missing folios of MS. E: Sulla riva del Po vicino a S. Angelo, nel 1514, addì 27 settembre. *Memorie Storiche*, Milan, 1804, p. 113.

1377. Giuliano de Medici, brother to Pope Leo X; see note to Nos. 1351–3. In February 1515 he was married to Filiberta, daughter of Filippo, Duke of Savoy, and aunt to Francis I, Louis XII's successor on the throne of France. Louis XII died on Jan. 1st, and not on Jan. 9th as is here stated. For the next dated note, August 1516, see No. 757 A; soon afterwards Leonardo must have left for France.

For a co-ordination of these dated notes with dated entries in documents referring to Leonardo's life and work see Ettore Verga, *Racc. Vinc.* ii, iii, viii, x, and L. Beltrami, *Documenti e Memorie riguardanti la Vita e le Opere di L.d.V.*, Milan, 1919.

XXII

MISCELLANEOUS NOTES

*T*HE *incidental memoranda scattered here and there throughout the manu-*
scripts can have been for the most part intelligible to the writer only; in some
cases their meaning and connexion are all the more obscure because we are in
ignorance about the persons with whom Leonardo used to converse, nor can we say
what part he may have played in the various events of his time. Vasari and other
early biographers give us a very superficial and far from accurate picture of Leo-
nardo's private life. Though his own memoranda refer for the most part to more or
less trivial matters about his pupils, his housekeeping, about various known and
unknown personages,[1] they are nevertheless of importance as helping to throw light
on his private life and giving clues for dating his notes.

I have endeavoured to make these 'Miscellaneous Notes' as complete as possible,
for in many cases an incidental memorandum will help to explain the meaning of some
other note of a similar kind. The first portion of these notes (Nos. 1379–1457), as
well as those referring to his pupils and to other artists and artificers who lived in his
house (1458–68), are arranged in chronological order. A considerable proportion of
these notes belong to the period between 1490 and 1500, when Leonardo was living
at Milan under the patronage of Lodovico il Moro, a time concerning which we have
otherwise only very scanty information.

There is nothing surprising in the fact that the notes regarding his pupils are few
and meagre. Excepting for the record of money transactions only very exceptional
circumstances would have prompted him to make any written observations on the
persons with whom he was in daily intercourse, among whom, of course, were his
pupils. Of them all none is so frequently mentioned as Salai.

Leonardo's quotations from books and his lists of titles supply nothing more than
a hint as to his occasional literary studies or recreations. It was evidently no part of
his ambition to be deeply read (see Nos. 10, 11, 1159), and he more than once ex-
pressly states (in various passages which will be found in the foregoing sections) that
he did not recognize the authority of the Ancients on scientific questions, which in
his day was held paramount. Archimedes is the sole exception, and Leonardo frankly
owns his admiration for the illustrious Greek to whose genius his own was so much
akin (see No. 1476). Compare Vol. I, pp. 41 ff. To his notes on various authors
(1469–1508) the editions which were available at that time have been added in the
footnotes.

The passages next in order contain accounts and inventories principally of house-
hold property. The publication of these—often very trivial entries—is only justi-
fiable as proving that the wealth, the splendid mode of life, and lavish expenditure

---

[1] For a complete list of the names which occur in Leonardo's MSS. see Nando de Toni, *Frammenti Vinciani I*, Racc. Vinc. xiv.

which have been attributed to Leonardo are altogether mythical; unless we put forward the very improbable hypothesis that these notes as to money in hand, outlay, and receipts, refer throughout to an exceptional state of his affairs, viz. when he was short of money.

The memoranda collected at the end (Nos. 1505–65) are, in the original, in the usual writing, from left to right. Besides, the style of the handwriting is at variance with what we should expect it to be if really Leonardo himself had written these notes. Most of them are to be found in juxtaposition with undoubtedly authentic writing of his. But this may be easily explained if we take into account the fact that Leonardo frequently wrote on loose sheets. He may therefore have occasionally used paper on which others had made short memoranda, for the most part, as it would seem, for his use. At the end of all I have given Leonardo's will from the copy of it formerly preserved in the Melzi Library. It is not known what has become of the original document.

Truova ingil e digli che tu l'aspetti amor a e che tu andrai cō seco ilopan a; [2]fatti fare enoiganod al; e tolli il libro di Vitolone, e le misure · delli edifiti [3]publici ·; fa fare 2 casse coperte da mvlattiere, ma meglio fia · le coperte da letto, che [4]son 3, delle quali lascierai una a Vinci; togli le fochere (?) delle gratie, to' da Gio-[5]vā Lonbardo il teatro di Verona ·; cōpra delle tovaglie · e mātili berretti, scarpini, [6]calze 4 para, vn giubbone di camoza e pelle per farne de' novi; il tornio d'Ales[7]sandro ·; vendi quel che nō si può portare; piglia da Gian di Paris il modo de colorire [8]a secco ·, e 'l modo del sale bianco e del fare le carte inpastate; soli e in mol[9]ti doppi; e la sua cassetta de' colori; inpara la tempera delle carnage, inpara [10]a disoluere la lacca gomma, tolli del seme de fotteragi e delle gniffe biāche, [11]delli algli da Piacētia, togli 'De Pōderibus'; tolli l'opere di Leonardo Cremo[12]nese; leua il fornello [13]di Giannino. To' della [14]semēza de ligli [15]e dell' erba stella, [16]delle zuche marine, [17]vedi l'asse della sosta, [18]fatti dare la fochera [19]a chi la rubò, pi[20]glia il liuellare, [21]quāto terreno può [22]cauare l'omo 'n un dì.

Find Ligny and tell him that you wait for him at Rome for going with him to Naples; have the donation paid [2] and take the book by Vitolone, and the measurements of the public buildings.[3] Have two covered boxes made to be carried on mules, but bed-covers will be best; they are three, of which you will leave one at Vinci.[4] Obtain the . . . of the grating; take from Giovanni Lombardo the theatre of Verona. Buy handkerchiefs and towels, caps and shoes, 4 pairs of hose, a jerkin of chamois and skins to make new ones; the lathe of Alessandro.[7] Sell what you cannot take with you. Get from Jean de Paris the method of colouring *a secco* and the way of white salt, and how to make tinted paper; single and many double ones; and his box of colours; learn to work flesh colours in tempera, learn to dissolve gum shellac, take . . . the seed of the fodder (?) and of the turnips, of the garlic of Piacenza; take *de Ponderibus*; take the works of Leonardo of Cremona. Remove the small furnace of Giannino, take the seed of lilies and of . . . . Sell the boards of the support. Make him who stole it give you the . . . take what is required for levelling, and how much soil a man can dig out in a day.

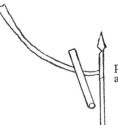

Questo fecie Lione in piazza [2]di castello con v̄ vincolo e vna [3]saetta.

This was done by Leone in the piazza of the castle with a chain and an arrow.

1379. 1. truova ingol edilli chettu . . chettu . . ilopana. 2. fare la eno iganodal ettolli . . elle. 3. faffare . . dalletto. 4. lascierai ł a uinci . . le fochere delle gratieto doglio. 6. gubbone di ci moza . . tornio dale. 7. si po . . piglia dāgandiparis. 8. assecho . . folie in mol. 9. ti doppi ella sua . . cornage. 10. lacha. 11. leonardo chermo. 13. diganni noto della. 14. semēza deli gli. 21. tereno po. 20. lomo nūdi.

1380. 1. questa . . piaza. 2. casstello chon v̄ uīcho e vna.

1379. A note apparently to himself. The words, distinctly written, in line 1: *ingil, amor a, ilopan a*, and on line 2: *enoiganod al*, are obviously in cipher and the solution is a simple one; by reading them backwards we find for *ingil*: *ligni*: evidently: *Ligny*; for *amor a*: *a Roma*, for *ilopan a*: *a Napoli, for enoiganod al*: *la donagione*. Leonardo has done the same in two passages on secrets of his art, Nos. 641 and 729, the only other places where this cipher is employed; we may conclude that it was for the sake of secrecy that he used it. The Comte de Ligny accompanied his cousin Charles VIII on his expedition to Italy in 1494–5 and took part in the operations against Naples.

There can be no doubt, from the tenor of this passage, that Leonardo projected a secret excursion to Naples. G. Calvi has shown (*Raccolta Vinc.* iii.

99 ff.) that Leonardo had made some agreement with the French Prince Ligny (about 1499) to accompany him to Naples. See also *ibid.* viii. 79.

2. *Libro di Vitolone*: see No. 1506, note.

7. Jean de Paris is the French painter Jean Péréal who accompanied Louis XII on his expeditions against Italy. See *Racc. Vinc.* xi. 62 f.; comp. No. 1412.

11. *De Ponderibus.* A large number of Leonardo's notes bear this superscription. Compare No. 1436, 3.

Leonardo Mainardi Cremonense, active 1404–38, author of *Artis metrice pratice compilatio*, pub. in Atti del R. Istituto Veneto, 1904, vol. 63, and of other mathematical treatises, as yet unpublished, preserved in codex 5437, coll. Mazarin, Bibl. Nat. See Solmi, *Fonti*, p. 196 sq.

1380. Probably at Milan.

B. 50b]　　　　　　　　　　　　1381

NOMI D'ĪGIEGNIERI

[2]Callias Rodiano, [3]Epimaco Ateniense, [4]Diogine filosofo Rodano, [5]Calcedonio di Tracia, [6]Febar di Tiria, [7]Callimaco architetto, maestro di fochi.

NAMES OF ENGINEERS

Callias of Rhodes, Epimachus the Athenian, Diogenes, a philosopher, of Rhodes, Calcedonius of Thrace, Febar of Tyre, Callimachus the architect, a master of fires.

B. N. 2037, 10b]　　　　　　　　1382

A maestro Lodovico chiedi li condotti d'acqua el fornello le sta il moto continuo · i mantaci i soffioni.

Ask maestro Lodovico for the conduits of water and the little stove. In it is to be found the perpetual motion. The large and the small bellows.

Fl. Uff.]　　　　　　　　　　　1383

. . . ĵ Pistoja; [2]Fiorauante di Domenico ĵ Firenze è cōpare [3]amantissimo, quant' è mio . . . .

. . . at Pistoja, Fioravante di Domenico at Florence is my most beloved friend, as though he were my [brother].

S. K. M. III. 88a]　　　　　　　1384

A dì 16 di luglio.
[2]Caterina venne a dì 16 [3]di luglio 1493.
[4]Morel Fiorētino di meser Mariolo, cavallo [5]grosso à bel collo e assai bella testa.
[6]Rōzone biāco del falconiere à belle cosscie, [7]dirieto sta in Porta Comasina.
[8]Cauallo grosso del Chermonino del signor Givlio.

On the 16th day of July.
Caterina came on the 16th day of July, 1493.
Messer Mariolo's Morel the Florentine is a big horse with a fine neck and a beautiful head.
The white stallion belonging to the falconer has fine hind quarters; it is behind the Comasina Gate.
The big horse of Cermonino, of Signor Giulio.

S. K. M. III. 61b]　　　　　　　1385

DELLO STRUMĒTO

[2]Chiūque spēde uno ducato per paro [3]pigli lo strumēto, e non spē[4]derà · se non v̄ mezzo per premi[5]nētia allo invētore dello strum[6]ēto, e vno grosso per l'operatore [7]ma non uoglio sottovfiti [8]ale.

OF THE INSTRUMENT

Any one who spends one ducat the pair may take the instrument; and he will not pay more than half a ducat as a premium to the inventor of the instrument and one grosso to the workman but I do not want sub-officials.

S. K. M. III. 37b]　　　　　　　1386

Maestro Givliano da Mar[2]liano a v̄ bello erbolaro; [3]sta a riscōtro alli Strami [4]legnamieri.

Maestro Giuliano da Marliano has a fine herbal. He lives opposite to Strami the Carpenters.

1381. 3. acte niense. 4. filosafo. 7. challimacho architecto.
1382. 1. mastro lodovicho ciedi . . dacq"a".
1383. 1. \\\ e echopa ĵ pisstoja. 2. domenicho . . cōpere. 3. mio jjrsuiosssam (?). 4. jnde nom. 5. amante quanto mjo.
1384. 2. catelina. 4. R. chaval. 5. chollo eassa. 6. rōzino. 8. chaual.
1385. 2. R. chiūq spēde ī ducato . . pano. 3. lustrumēto . . ispē. 4. mezo. 6. e ī groso.
1386. 4. legiamieri.

1381. Callias, architect of Rhodes, mentioned by Vitruvius (x. 16, 4). Epimachus, of Athens, invented a battering-engine for Demetrius Poliorketes (Vitruvius, x. 16, 4). Callimachus, the inventor of the Corinthian capital (Vitr. iv. 1, 10), and of the method of boring marble (Paus. i. 26, 7), was also famous for his casts in bronze (Plin. xxxiv. 19, §35). He invented a lamp for the temple of Athene Polias, on the Acropolis of Athens (Paus. i. 26, 7). In a note to fol. 19r. of the Trivulzi MS. Beltrami suggests that Callimaco stands here for Callinico—Leonardo probably quoted these names from Valturio De Re Militari. See Solmi, Fonti, p. 288.

1382. Here follows an inscription in strange characters, perhaps a secret. Mastro Lodovico may be Giovan Lodovico de Raufi, who took part in the deliberations on the tiburio of Milan Cathedral. Calvi, I Manoscritti, p. 87; Annali del Duomo di Milano, iii, p. 39.

1383. On the same sheet is the text No. 663.

1384. Compare Nos. 1522 and 1517. Caterina seems to have been his housekeeper.

4. Mariolo de' Guiscardi, attendant at Lodovico Sforza's court, brother of Gianni Antonio da Mariolo mentioned on C.A. 311b. Both brothers took part in the tournament of 1491. See No. 1458, n. 9, and No. 1406.

5. Compare Malaguzzi Valleri, Bramante e Leonardo, p. 441.

1385. Refers perhaps to the regulation of the water in the canals.

1386. Giuliano da Marliano, appointed physician to the court of Lodovico il Moro. Compare No. 616, note. 4. legnamiere (Milanese dialect) = legnajuolo. For Strami compare No. 1415.

S. K. M. III. 1*b*]　　　　　　　　　　1387

Cristofano da Castiglio²ne sta alla Pietà, à bona ³testa.

Christofano da Castiglione who lives at the Pietà has a fine head.

A. C. 1*a*]　　　　　　　　　　1388 A

Barbara Stampa.

C. A. 335*a*]　　　　　　　　　　1388

Opera di . . . ²della stalla di G³aleazzo; ⁴per la via di Brera; ⁵benefitio dello Stangha; bene⁶fitio della por⁷ta nova; ⁸benefitio di Mon⁹sa—¹⁰errore dell' Inta¹¹co—¹²dì prima li benefitj; ¹³e poi l'opere e poi ¹⁴le ingratudini ¹⁵e poi le īdegne la¹⁶mētationi e poi . . .

Work of . . . of the stable of Galeazzo; by the road of Brera [4]; benefice of Stangha [5]; benefice of Porta Nuova; benefice of Monza; Indaco's mistake; give first the benefices; then the works; then ingratitude, indignity, and lamentations, and then . . .

H.³ 95*b*]　　　　　　　　　　1389

Chiliarco, capo di mille, ²Prefetti—capitani; ³Legione, semila 63.

Chiliarch—captain of 1,000. Prefects—captains.
A legion, six thousand and sixty-three men.

H.² 62*b*]　　　　　　　　　　1390

Vna monica sta alla Colōba ²in Cremona che lavora bē ³cordoni di paglia, e vno frate ⁴di Scō Francesco.

A nun lives at La Colomba at Cremona; she works good straw plait, and a friar of Saint Francis.

H.² 94*a*]　　　　　　　　　　1391

Aguglia — Niccolao — ²refe — ³Ferrādo — ⁴iacopo ādrea — ⁵tela — ⁶pietra — ⁷colori — ⁸penelli — ⁹tavoletta da colori — ¹⁰spūga — ¹¹tavola del Duca.

Needle — Niccolao — thread — Ferrando — Iacopo Andrea — canvas — stone — colours — brushes — pallet — sponge — the panel of the Duke.

S. K. M. II. 1. 57*b*]　　　　　　　　　　1392

Messer Giā Domenico ²Mezzabarba, e messer ³Giovā Francesco Mezzabarba, ⁴al lato a messer Piero da Galera.

Messer Gian Domenico Mezzabarba and Messer Giovanni Franceso Mezzabarba. By the side of Messer Piero da Galera.

S. K. M. II. 1. 57*a*]　　　　　　　　　　1393

Cōte Francesco Torello.

Conte Francesco Torello.

S. K. M. II. 1. 52*b*]　　　　　　　　　　1394

Givliā Trōbetta—²Antonio di Ferrara.

Giuliano Trombetta — Antonio di Ferrara.

S. K. M. II. 1. 45*b*]　　　　　　　　　　1395

Pagolo fu ratto in cielo.

Paul was snatched up to heaven.

1387. 1. cristofano da chasstiglio. 3. tessta.
1388. 1. Opera di ronca. 2. digh. 5. benjfitio . . benj. 8. benjfitio. 9. cia. 10. erore. 11. cho. 12. benifiti. 14. ingratitudine.
1390. 1–4 R. 2. chermona chellavora. 3. chordoni. 4. franc"o".
1391. 1–11 R. 1. agugia niccholao. 3. ferādo.
1392. 1. domenicho. 2. meza . . meser. 3. franc"o" meza. 4. Piero dagale. 5. ra sotto il coperto debe lacq"a".
1394. 1. trobebetta. 3. olio da bolo.

1388 A. *Barbara* Crivelli, wife of Pietro Martire Stampa, was lady-in-waiting to Bianca Maria Sforza. See Racc. Vinc. x, p. 127.

1388. This note is dated 1510 by Calvi, *I Manoscritti di L.d.V.*, pp. 300–2. 4. *Brera*, see No. 1448, 11, 13; 5. *Stanghe*, see No. 1509.

1390. *La Colomba* is to this day the name of a small house at Cremona, decorated with frescoes.

1391. 3. *Ferrando*; a Magistro Ferrando was at work in the Castello at Milan in 1495 at the same time as Leonardo. See Calvi, l.c., p. 154.

1392. *G. D. Mezzabarba*, ambassador of Lodovico Sforza to Ercole I of Ferrara, see Calvi, l.c., p. 176.

1395. This note is shown on Pl. XXIII, No. 2.

S. K. M. II. 1. 43*b*]   **1396**

Givliã da Mariã, medico ²à vn mazaro sãza mano.

Giuliano da Marian, physician, has a steward without a hand.

S. K. M. II. 1. 38*b*]   **1397**

Fatti mãdare spighe di ²grã grosso da Firēze.

Have some ears of corn of large size sent from Florence.

S. K. M. II. 1. 25*a*]   **1398**

Vedi la lettiera a Scã Maria; ²Segreta.

See the bedstead at Santa Maria. Secret.

S. K. M. II. 1. 24*b*]   **1399**

¶Arrigo de' avere ²ducati 11 d'oro;¶ ³Arrigo de' avere ⁴ducati 4 d'oro ⁵a mezzo Agosto.

Arrigo is to have 11 gold ducats. Arrigo is to have 4 gold ducats in the middle of August.

S. K. M. II. 1. 15*b*]   **1400**

Dà al patrone lo esēplo ²del capitano, che nõ lui vī³cie, ma li soldati mediãte ⁴il suo cõsilio, e pur merita il saldo.

Give to the master the instance of a captain who does not himself win the victory, but the soldiers do by his counsels; and so he still deserves the reward.

S. K. M. II. 1. 10*a*]   **1401**

Messer Pier Antonio.

Messer Pier Antonio.

S. K. M. II. 1. 9*b*]   **1402**

Olĩo — ²giallo — ³Ambrosio — ⁴la bocca — ⁵la masseria.

Oil — yellow — Ambrosio — the mouth — the farmhouse.

S. K. M. II. 1. 6*a*]   **1403**

Alessandro Carissimo, ²da Parma per la mã di xpo.

Alessandro Carissimo of Parma, for the hand of Christ.

S. K. M. II. 1. 3*a*]   **1404**

Giovannina, viso fantastico, ²sta a Scã Caterina, all' ospedale.

Giovannina has a fantastic face, is at Santa Caterina, at the hospital.

I.² 59*a*]   **1405**

24 tavole fanno una pertica; ²4 trabochi fanno una tavola; ³4 braccia e mezzo fanno uno trabocco; ⁴vna pertica è 1936 braccia □, ⁵ovvero 1944.

24 tavole make 1 perch. 4 trabochi make 1 tavola. 4 braccia and a half make a trabocco. A perch contains 1,936 square braccia, or 1,944.

1396. R. 2. avmasaro.
1397. R. 1. spige.
1399. R. 1. arigo. 3. arigo. 5. mezo.   **1400.** 1. padrone.   **1401.** R. meser pier ātõ chodi. 2. diga.
1402. R. 3. abrosio. 4. bocha. 5. masera.   **1403.** R. 1. charissimo. 2. [si] da . . mã di[l]p.
1404. R. 1. fantasticho. 2. chaterina.
1405. 1–5. R. 1. fã ĩ perticha. 2. fa ĩ. 3. br e mezo fa ĩ trabocho. 4. perticha he . . br. 5. ovr.

1403. See *Raccolta Vinc.* x. 307. Compare the text in the same MS., No. 667, about a model suitable for the figure of Christ.

1405. These and related calculations on folios 50*b*, 51*a*, 58*b* of MS. I, on folio 91*b* of MS. L, and on folios 158*a* and 393*a* of C.A. refer to Leonardo's vineyard. See Calvi, *I Manoscritti di L.d.V.*, pp. 164 sqq., No. 1406, note, and p. 389, note.

I.² 118*b*]   **1406**

La strada di messer Mariolo è braccia 13¼,
²la casa di Vãgelista è 75;
³Entra braccia 7 e ½ ⁴nella casa di Mariolo.

The road of Messer Mariolo is 13¼ braccia
wide; the House of Evangelista is 75.
It enters 7½ braccia in the house of Mariolo.

I.² 120*b*]   **1407**

Domando in che parte del suo moto curvo
²la cavsa, che move, lascierà la cosa mossa ³e
mobile.

I ask at what part of its curved motion the
moving cause will leave the thing moved and
movable.

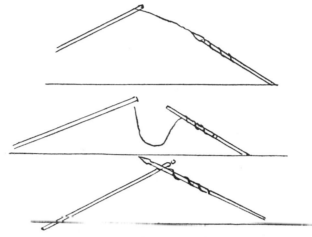

⁴Parla cõ Pietro Mõti di questi tali ⁵modi di
trarre i dardi.

Speak to Pietro Monti of these methods of
throwing spears.

I.² 135*a*]   **1408**

Antonio de' Risi sta al cõ²siglio di Givstitia.

Antonio de' Risi is at the council of Justice.

I.¹ 28*a*]   **1409**

Disse Paolo che nessuno strumento ²che move
vn altro . . . .

Paolo said that no machine that moves another . . . .

W. 19136–19139]   **1410**

Caravaggio.

Caravaggio.

W. 19106*b*]   **1411**

Carrucole — ²chiodi — ³corda — ⁴mercurio —
⁵tela — ⁶lunedì — ī domo adj.

Pulleys — nails — rope — mercury — cloth —
Monday — in the dome on the day.

W. 19019*a*]   **1412**

RICORDO

²Maghino Speculus di maestro Giovanni
Frãcese; ³Galieno de vtilità.

MEMORANDUM

Maghino, Speculus of Master Giovanni the
Frenchman; Galenus on Utility.

1406. 1. meser . . he br. 2. vãgelissta he. 3. br 7 e ½.
1410. carovagio.
1412. 1. richordo. 2. maghino spechulus di m"o". . frãcioso.

1409. 1. pagolo.
1411. 1. carruchole. 4. merchurio. 7. idomoodi (?).

1406. On this and the following page are diagrams
of streets with measurements of allotments. On 119*a*
are the following notes: 'dal ponte detto al cientro
della porta è br. 31 / comincio br. 1 presso al ponte /
e da esso ponte al chantone della strada 23 1/2 . . .
pordiaco e 5° pilastro della ciesa (probably the church
of S. Gerolamo) / la tua strada (Leonardo's street?)
fia 30/ volte lunga la sua largeza'. On folio 43*b* are
calculations with the note 'la strada del marchese'.

Calvi has proved that all these notes are connected
with Leonardo's vineyard. Comp. No. 1405, note.
4. The house of Mariolo was situated near this
vineyard. Comp. No. 1384, note.
1410. *Caravaggio*, a village between Milan and
Brescia. This note is given on Pl. XIII, No. 1.
1412. Galeni *Opera—Therapeuticorum libri XIV*,
Venice, 1490, 1502, 1511, etc.

W. 12350]   **1413**

Presso al Corduso · sta Pier Antonio da Fossano ²e Serafino · suo fratello.

Near to Cordusio is Pier Antonio da Fossano and his brother Serafino.

L. o']   **1414**

Memoranda after 1500 1414–34).

Paolo di Vannoccio in Siena. Domenico Chiavajo.
³La saletta di sopra per li apostoli;
⁴Edifiti di Bramāte;
⁵Il castellano fatto prigione;
⁶Il Visconte strascinato e poi morto il figliuolo;
⁷Gian della Rosa toltoli i danari;
⁸Borgonzo principiò e nol volle, e però fuggì le fortune;
⁹Il duca perso lo stato e la roba e libertà, ¹⁰e nessuna sua opera si finì per lui.

Paul of Vannochio at Siena, Domenicus Chiavajo.
The upper chamber for the apostles.
[4] Buildings by Bramante.
The governor of the castle made a prisoner.
[6] Visconti carried away and his son killed.
Giovanni della Rosa deprived of his money.
[8] Borgonzio began and did not want it; and therefore he escaped from fortune.
The Duke lost the state, property, and liberty, and none of his enterprises was carried out by him.[10].

L. 1a]   **1415**

²1 Ābrosio Preti — ³6 Scō Marco — ⁴4 asse per la finestra — ⁵2 Guaspari Strame — ⁶3 i sāti di capella — ⁷5 a casa li Gienovesi.

1 Ambrogio de Predis, 6 St. Mark, 4 boards for the window, 2 Gaspar Strame, 3 the saints of chapels, 5 the Genoese at home.

L. 1b]   **1416**

Panno d'arazzo — ²seste — ³libro di Maso — ⁴libro di Giovanni Bēcj — ⁵cassa in dogana — ⁶tagliare la vesta — ⁷cintura della spada — ⁸rinpedulare li stivaletti — ⁹cappello legieri — ¹⁰canne delle casaccie — ¹¹il debito della touagla — ¹²bata da notare — ¹³libro di carte bianche per disegnare — ¹⁴carboni. ¹⁵ ¶ quāto è uno fiorino ¹⁶di sugello? ¶ ¹⁷¶vn guarda¹⁸cuore di pelle. ¶

Piece of tapestry — pair of compasses — Tommaso's book — the book of Giovanni Benci — the box in the custom-house — to cut the cloth — the sword-belt — to sole the boots — a light hat — the cane from the ruined houses — the debt for the table-linen — swimming-belt — a book of white paper for drawing — charcoal.— How much is a florin . . . a leather bodice.

L. 2a]   **1417**

Borges ti farà avere Archimede del ²vescouo di Padova, e Vitellozzo quello ³dal Borgo a San Sepolcro.

Borges shall get for you the Archimedes from the Bishop of Padua, and Vitellozzo the one from Borgo a San Sepolcro.

1413. 1. chorduso . . daffossano. 2. essera fino.
1414. 1. pagolo di uannocco. 2. codi rōcho—domenico. 5. prigone. 6. bisscote .. el figlolo. 7. gan della rosa tollto li e danari. 8. pro. 9. ella roba elliberta.
1415. 1. equria (?). 7. chasa legienovesi.
1416. 1. darazo. 6. taglare lavessta. 8. lissti valetti. 10. dalle cassacce. 15. e ï fi. 18. core.   **1417.** 2. vesscovo. 2. vitellozo.

1413. This note is written between ll. 23 and 24 of the text No. 710. Corduso, Cordusio (*curia ducis*) = Cordus in the Milanese dialect, is the name of a Piazza between the Via del Broletto and the Piazza de' Mercanti at Milan. In the time of il Moro it was the centre of the town. The persons here named were members of the noble Milanese family de' Fossani; Ambrogio da Fossano, the contemporary painter, had no connexion with them.

1414. 4–10. This passage evidently refers to events in Milan at the time of the overthrow of Lodovico il Moro. Amoretti published it in the *Memorie Storiche* and added copious notes.

6. *Visconte.* 'Chi fosse quel Visconte non sapremmo indovinare fra tanti di questo nome. Arluno narra che allora atterrate furono le case de' Visconti, de' Castiglioni, de' Sanseverini, e de' Botta e non è improbabile che ne fossero insultati e morti i padroni. Molti Visconti annovera lo stesso Cronista che per essersi rallegrati del ritorno del duca in Milano furono

da' Francesi arrestati, e strascinati in Francia come prigionieri di stato; e fra questi Messer Francesco Visconti, e suo figliuolo Battista.' (Amoretti, *Mem. Stor.* xix.)

8. 'Borgonzio o Brugonzio Botta fu regolatore delle ducali entrate sotto il Moro, alla cui fuga la casa sua fu pur messa a sacco da' partitanti francesi.' (Amoretti, loc. cit.)

1415. 5. *Strame.* Compare No. 1386. 'Gaspart Stremit' was entrusted with the repair of the gates and bridges of Milan under French rule. See Gerolamo Calvi, *Raccolta Vinciana* iii, p. 108; and *Chroniques de Louis XII par Jean d'Auton*, ed. Maulde la Clavierè, Paris, 1889. II, p. 363.

1417. *Borges.* Boyer Antonio, Archbishop of Bourges. See Solmi, *Fonti*, p. 20.

2. Probably Pietro Barozzi, Bishop of Padua 1488–1507, distinguished for his learning. *Vitellozzo*, condottiere serving under Cesare Borgia and murdered by him December, 1502.

L. 30b]   1418

Tabella di marzocco.   Panel of the painted lion.

L. 0″]   1419

Marcello sta in casa di Giacomo da Mē-   Marcello lives in the house of Giacomo da
²gardino.   Mengardino.

Br. M. 202b]   1420

Dou' è Valentino? — ²stiuali — ³casse in   Where is Valentino?—boots—boxes in the
dogana — ⁴falleri — ⁵frate del Carmine —   custom-house . . .—[5] the monk at the Car-
⁶squadre — ⁷Piero Martelli — ⁸Salui Bor-   mine—squares—[7] Piero Martelli — [8]
gherini — ⁹rimanda le saca — ¹⁰sostētaculo   Salvi Borgherini—send back the bags—a
delli ochiali — ¹¹lo igniudo del Sangallo — ¹²la   support for the spectacles—[11] the nude study
cappa.   of San Gallo—the cloak.
   ¹³Porfido — ¹⁴gruppi — ¹⁵squadra —   Porphyry — groups — square — [16] Pandol-
¹⁶Pandolfino.   fino.

F. 0]   1421

¶Spechi cōcavi;   ¶filosofia d'Aristotile,   Concave mirrors; philosophy of Aristotle;
²¶libri da Venezia; ¶messer Ottauiā Palaui-   [2] the books from Venice; Messer Ottaviano
³¶vocabolista vul- cino pel suo Vetruuio;¶   Italian and Latin vocabu- Palavicino for his
⁴gare e latino.¶   lary;   Vitruvius [3].
⁵¶Coltelli di Boemia; ¶Va ogni sabato alla   Bohemian knives;   Go every Saturday
⁶Vetruuio;¶   stufa e vedrai delli   Vitruvius; [6]   to the hot bath
                  nudi;¶   where you will see
                                                                   naked men;

⁷¶Meteora;   'Meteora' [7].
⁸¶Archimede, de cē- ¶Fa gōfiare il polmō   Archimedes, on the centre   Inflate the lungs
⁹tro grauitatis.¶   d'ū porco, e guarda   of gravity; [9]   of a pig and ob-
¹⁰¶Anotomia, Alessā- se cresce in larghezza   anatomy [10] Alessandro   serve whether they
¹¹dro Benedetto;¶   e ī lūghezza, over in   Benedetto;   increase in width
                  larghezza e māco in   and in length, or
                  lūghezza.¶   in width diminish-
¹²¶Il Dāte di Niccolò   The Dante of Niccolò   ing in length.
del¹³la Croce.¶   della Croce.
¹⁴Albertuccio, il Marliano de calculatione,   Albertuccio [14] Marliano, on Calculation,
¹⁵Alberto de celo e mūdo · [da fra Bernardino];   Albertus, on heaven and earth [15], [from the
¹⁶Oratio scrisse della velocità del cielo.   monk Bernardino]. Horace has written on the
                                        movements of the heavens.

1418. marzoccho.   **1419.** 1. chasa diachomo .. mō(?).   **1420.** 8. borgerini. 11. lognudo.
1421. 2. dauinega atta.   3. vocabolissta — sino pel. 4. ellatino.   5. buemia.   6. vederai.   7. meteura.   9. trugrauitatis — dū porcho.
   10. alesā — cresse in largeza.   11. lūgeza .. largeza.   12. nicolo de — e mācha in lūgeza.   14. bertucco.   16. oratio .. del celo.
   These six words are written in four short lines on the margin near lines 1–4.

1420. *Valentino.* Cesare Borgia is probably meant.   7. *Meteora.* See No. 1448, 25.
After being made Archbishop of Valence by Alex-   8. The works of Archimedes were not printed
ander VI he was commonly called Valentinus or   during Leonardo's lifetime.
Valentino. With reference to Leonardo's engage-   10. *Alessandro Benedetti* of Legnago, author of
ments by him see pp. 180 and 194, note.   *Historia corporis humani sive Anatomice,* libri v,
   5. *Carmine.* The Carmelite church and monastery   Venice 1495, 1502.
at Florence.   12. *Nicolò della Croce.* A Lombard noble favoured
   7, 8. *Martelli, Borgherini.* Names of Florentine   by Lodovico il Moro. Cf. Solmi, *Fonti,* pp. 128, 134.
families. See No. 4.   14. *Johannes Marliano sua etate philosophorum et*
   11. *San Gallo.* Possibly Giuliano da San Gallo, the   *medicorum principis et ducalis phisic. primi de propor-*
Florentine architect.   *tione motuum velocitate questio subtilissima incipit ex*
   16. *Pandolfini.* See No. 1444, note.   *ejusdem Marliani originali feliciter extracta,* M(ilano)
   1421. *Filosofia d'Aristotile.* See No. 1481, note.   1482. Another work by him has the title: *Probatio*
   2. *The Pallavicini* were supporters of the French in   *cujusdam sententiae calculatoris de motu locali,* Pavia,
Lombardy.   1482.
   3, 6. *Vitruvius.* See vol. i, No. 343, note.   *Albertuccio* stands for Albert of Saxony, philosopher
   5. Vasari, vii. 13 (ed. Milanesi): 'si diede Fran-   (d. 1390); taught at the Sorbonne, Paris. Leonardo
cesco (Salviati) a studiare ignudi di naturale, e Giorgio   mentions him again, No. 1496. c. Cf. Solmi, *Fonti,*
(Vasari) con esso lui, in una stufa qui vicina; e dopo   p. 49.
faciono in campo santo alcune notomie.'   15. See Nos. 1469, l. 7, and 1477.

F. 27*b*]   1422

De' 5 corpi regolari cōtro alcū comēta²tori che biasimā li ātichi īvētori dōde naquero le gramatiche e le scientie, e fansi cavalieri contro alli morti inventori, e perchè essi non han trovato da farsi inventori, per la pigritia et comoditate de' libri, attendono al continuo con falsi argomenti a riprendere li lor maestri . . . .

Of the five regular bodies as opposed to some commentators who disparage the Ancients, who were the originators of grammar and the sciences, and they set themselves up as knights to fight deceased inventors, and not having succeeded in becoming inventors themselves on account of their sloth, being bookworms, they spend time in reproving their masters with unsound arguments.

W. 19077*b*]   1423

Camera de²lla Torre da ³Vaneri.

The room in the tower of Vaneri.

W. 19076*a*]   1424

Riserua all' ultimo dell' ōbre le figure ²che apariano nello scrittoio di Gerar³do miniatore a Sā Marco in Firēze.
⁴[Va per il Melso, ⁵e allo Ambasciatore ⁶e a maestro Bernardo.]

Reserve those figures for the last book on shadows which were to be seen in the study of Gerardo the illuminator at San Marco at Florence.
[Go to see Melzo, and the Ambassador, and Maestro Bernardo].

M. o']   1425

Ermete ²filosofo.

Hermes the philosopher.

M. 8*a*]   1426

De moto lochale ²Suisset cioè calculatore — ³Tisber — ⁴Angelo Fossabron — ⁵Alberto.

De motu locale Suisset, viz. calculator—Tisber —Angelo Fossabron—Alberto.

M. 53*b*]   1427

Modo del pōte leuatojo che mi mostrò Donnino, ²e perchè $c \cdot e\ d$ spingano in basso. . . .

The structure of the drawbridge shown me by Donnino, and why c and d thrust downwards.

Trn. M2 o'']   1428

Piglerà il primo volo il grāde vccello sopra del dosso del suo ²magno Cecero, empiēdo l'universo di stupore, em³piēdo di sua fama tutte le scritture e gloria etterna al loco ⁴dove nacque.

The first flight of the great bird from the summit of Monte Ceceri will fill the universe with wonder; all writings will be full of its fame, bringing eternal glory to the place of its origin.

1423. 1. chamera.
1424. serua. 2. scriptoio [del] di giera. 3. marcho. 5. ïbassciatore. 6. maesstro.
1425. 2. filosofo.   **1426.** 2. coe chalculatore.   **1427.** 1. leuato i che. 2. c he d spingano.
1428. 1. il p''o'' volto [leverassi delge] il. 2. magnio cecero c enpiēdo. 3. groria . . alaido. 4. [dore] doue.

1423. This note is written inside the sketch of a plan of a house. On the same page is the date 1513 (see No. 1376).

1424. Lines 1–3 are in the original written between ll. 3 and 4 of No. 292. But the sense is not clear in this connexion. It is scarcely possible to divine the meaning of the following sentence.

2, 3. *Gherardo* Miniatore, a famous illuminator, 1445–97, to whom Vasari dedicated a section of his *Lives* (vol. ii, pp. 237–43, ed. Milanesi, 1879).

6. *Bernardo*, possibly the painter Bernardo Zenale.

1425. Hermes Trismegistus. In the Biblioteca Sforzesca at the Castle of Pavia Leonardo may have seen a book entitled *Albertus de mineralibus cum hermete*

de alchimia. Vebere de collectione secretorum nature et aliis pluribus, numbered DCCCCXXXVIII.

1426. Suisset and Tisber stand for Swineshead and Heytesburg (Latin Heuliberus), of Oxford; cp. Marcolongo, *La Meccanica di L. d. V.*, Naples, 1933, p. 29. Fossabrone wrote *De motu locale.*

1427. The sketch on the same page as this text represents two poles one across the other. At the ends of the longest are the letters, *c* and *d*. Donnino, that is, 'dear Donato', Bramante's Christian name. Mentioned also C. A. 118*b* and MS. I, 63*a*.

1428. *Magno Cecero* (translated 'great swan' in the first edition) is the name of a mountain above Fiesole and Florence.

Trn. Mz. 18*b*]   **1428 A**

Del monte che tiene il nome del grande uccello
piglierà il volo il famoso uccello ch'enpiera il
mondo di sua gran fama.

From the mountain which is named after the
great bird, the famous bird, which will fill the
world with its great fame, will start on its flight.

Triv. 11*b*]   **1429**

Questo inganno fu vsato dai Ga²lli · contro ·
a' Romani, e seguì³ne tal mortalità che tutta
⁴Roma · si vestì · a bruno.

This stratagem was used by the Gauls against
the Romans, and so great a mortality ensued
that all Rome was dressed in mourning.

K.² 75*b*]   **1430**

Alberto da Imola—²algebra cioè dimostratione come ³una cosa s'agguaglia a un' altra.

Alberto da Imola—Algebra, that is, the
demonstration of the equality of one thing to
another.

K.³ 128*b*]   **1431**

Joannes Rupicissa e Robbia.

Johannes Rupicissa e Robbia.

W. 19101*a*]   **1432**

Dimāda la moglie di Bia²gin Crivelli come il
cappone ³allieva e cova l'oua della ⁴gallina,
essendo lui inbri⁵acato.

Ask the wife of Biagino Crivelli how the
capon nurtures and hatches the eggs of the
hen, he being drunk.

W. 19102*b*]   **1433**

Libro dell' acque a messer Marco Antonio.

The Book on Water to Messer Marco Antonio.

W. 19076*b*]   **1434**

Fa tradurre Avicenna: de' giovamēti—²ochiali
col cartone, ³acciajuolo e forchetta e . . . gamaut
— ⁴carbone, asse e fogli e lapis e biāchetto e cera
— ⁵tanagle e topo da vetri, sega da osso di sottil
dētatura, scarpello, ⁶calamaro tenperatoio, Zerbe
e Agnol Benedetto, ⁷fa d'avere vn teschio, noce,
mostada;
⁸Stivali — guāti — ⁹calcetti — ¹⁰pettine papiri
—¹¹ . . . . — ¹²camisce . . . — ¹³stringhe
carboni — ¹⁴scarpe — ¹⁵tēperatoio — ¹⁶penne —
¹⁷vna pelle al petto.

Have Avicenna translated: on the utilities,
spectacles with the case, steel and fork and bis-
toury, charcoal, boards, and paper, and chalk
and pipeclay and wax; thongs and glass breaker,
a saw for bones with fine teeth, a chisel, inkstand, penknife, Zerbe [6], and Agnolo Benedetto. Get a skull, nutmeg.
Boots—gloves, socks, comb, papers, towel,
shirts . . . shoe-laces — . . . shoes, penknife,
pens. A skin for the chest.

W. 19092*a*]   **1435**

Libro di Piero Crescēzio — ²i nvdi di
Giouañj Ambrosio — ³compasso — ⁴libro di
Gian Jacomo. . . .

The book of Piero Crescenzo—studies from
the nude by Giovanni Ambrosio — compasses
—the book of Giovanni Giacomo. . . .

Undated
memoranda
(1435-57).

1429. 2. chontro . . essegui. 3. chettutta. 4. vessti.
1430. 2. alcibra coe mostra come. 3. n"o" e cosa sagualglia alla cosa.
1431. 1. ioanēs "erobbia" rupicissa.
1432. 2. gi cri velli . . cuppone. 4. ghallina.
1433. 1. dellacq"e" . . marcho ant.
1434. 1. avicena di govamēti. 3. accarolo. 4. ellapis e biāchetto. 5. tanaglie "e topo da vetri" segha "da osso" di. 6. calimaro
    7. tesscio. 10. palpiri. 11. scugaco da scarto. 12. camisce cci.
1435. 1. cressciēzo.

1429. Leonardo perhaps alludes to the Gauls
under Brennus, who laid his sword in the scale when
the tribute was weighed.

1431. Rupicissa is Jean de la Roquetaillade, author
of *Liber Lucis* of which the Biblioteca Civica of Padua
possesses a part of the manuscript.

1432. Biagino Crivelli, favourite of Duke Lodovico
and head of his crossbowmen. See Solmi, *Le Fonti*,
p. 127.

1433. Possibly Marc Antonio della Torre; see p. 83.

1434. 1. See No. 1482, note.

4. *Lapis.* Compare Condivi, *Vita di Michelagnolo
Buonarotti*, chap. xviii: 'Ma egli [Michelangelo] non
avendo che mostrare, prese una penna (perciochè in
quel tempo il lapis non era in uso) e con tal leggiadria
gli dipinse una mano ecc.' The incident is of the year
1496. *Lapis* means 'pencil', and 'chalk' (*matita*).

6. Zerbe, author of *Liber anatomie corporis ʰ ʷani et
singulorum membrorum illius*, editus per excellentissimum philosophum ac medicum D. Gabrielem da
Zerbis, Veronensem, Venice 1502.
Between ll. 7 and 8 are the texts Nos. 819 and 7.

W. 19092b]   1436

RICORDO	MEMORANDUM
²Andare in provisione per il mio giardino — ³Giordano 'de pŏderibus' — ⁴el cŏciliatore, de flusso e reflusso del mare — ⁵far fare due casse da soma — ⁶vedi il tornio del Beltraffio e falli trarre vna pietra — ⁷Lascia il libro a messere Andrea tedesco, ⁸fa vna bilancia d'una freccia e pesa la cosa ĩfocata e poi la ripesa fredda; ⁹Lo spechio di maestro Luigi — ¹⁰olio, petrolio *a b* flusso e reflusso dell' acque, provato al molino di Vaprio — ¹¹beretta.	To make some provision for my garden— Giordano, *De Ponderibus* [3]—the conciliator, the flow and ebb of the sea—have two baggage trunks made, look to Beltraffio's [6] lathe and have the stone taken—leave the book belonging to Messer Andrea the German—make a balance with a cock and weigh the substance when hot and again when cold. The mirror of Master Luigi; oil, rock-oil; *a b* the flow and ebb of the water is shown at the mill of Vaprio—a cap.

W. 12676]   1437

Giovanni Fabre — ²Lazaro del Volpe — ³comune, ⁴Ser Piero. —	Giovanni Fabre—Lazaro del Volpe—the common—Ser Piero.

W. 12673b]   1438

[Lattantio] ²[libro di Benozzo], ³gruppi — ⁴legare il libro — ⁵lucerne — ⁶Ser Pecantino — ⁷Pandolfino — ⁸[Rosso] — ⁹squadra — ¹⁰coltellini — ¹¹caneze — ¹²stregghia ¹³[tavaglino] — ¹⁴tazza.	[Lactantius], [the book of Benozzo], groups, —to bind the book—a lantern—Ser Pecantino — Pandolfino — [Rosso] — a square — small knives — carriages — curry-combs — cup.

C. A. 12b]   1439

Quadrāte di Carlo Marmocchi — ²messer Francesco Araldo — ³Ser Benedetto de' Cieperello — ⁴Benedetto de l'abbaco — ⁵maestro Pagolo medico — ⁶Domenico di Michelino — ⁷el Caluo de li Alberti — ⁸messer Giovanni Argiropolo.	Quadrant of Carlo Marmocchi—Messer Francesco Araldo — Ser Benedetto de Cieperello—Benedetto on arithmetic—Maestro Paulo, physician—Domenico di Michelino— Calvo of the Alberti—Messer Giovanni Argiropolo.

C. A. 20b]   1440

Colore — ²formulario — ³Archimede — ⁶Marcanto⁷nio; ⁸Ferro stagnato—⁹ferro traforato.	Colours, formula—Archimedes—Marcantonio. Tinned iron—pierced iron.

1436. 1. Richordo. 2. provitione. 4. frusso e refrusso. 5. dassoma. 6. effalli. 7. lasscia . . messere andrea tedesscho. 8. ifochata eppoi. 9. losspechio. 10. frusso e refrusso . . di uavrio.
1437. 1. govanni. 2. lazero elulpe.
1438. 11. caneze. 12. streglia.
1439. 1. charlo. 2. franc"o". 3. benedetto daccieperello. 4. abbacho. 5. maesstro pagholo medicho. 6. domenicho. 7. chaluo. 8. meser.
1440. 4. cechino. 5. a 10 ditti.

1436. 3. *Giordano*. Jordanus Nemorarius, a mathematician of the beginning of the thirteenth century. No particulars of his life are known. The title of his principal work is: *Arithmetica decem libris demonstrata*, first published at Paris in 1496. In 1523 appeared at Nuremberg: *Liber Jordani Nemorarii de ponderibus, propositiones XIII et earundem demonstrationes, multarumque rerum rationes sane pulcherrimas complectens, nunc in lucem editus.*

6. *Beltraffio*, see No. 1465, note 2.
There are sketches by the side of ll. 8 and 10.
1437. These names are inserted on a plan of plots

of land adjoining the Arno.

1439. About the persons here named see *Raccolta Vinciana*, x. 301. *Carlo Marmocchi*, geographer and astronomer; *Ser Benedetto de' Cieperello*, notary; *Benedetto del abbaco*, Benedetto Aritmetico, the celebrated Florentine mathematician; *Maestro Pagolo, Medico*, Paolo dal Pozzo Toscanelli (1397–1482), the famous scientist and physician; *Domenico di Michelino*, (1417–1491) painter, pupil of Giov. da Fiesole; *Giov. Argiropolo* was herald to the Signoria in Florence, *circa* 1478.

C. A. 28a]　　　　**1441**

Vedi la bottega che fu di ²Bartolomeo cartolaio.

See the shop that was formerly Barto-lommeo's, the stationer.

C. A. 71a]　　　　**1442**

Questo libro è di Michele di Francesco Bernabini e di sua discendenza.

This book is by Michele di Franceso Bernabini and his descendants.

C. A. 114a]　　　　**1443**

Messer Francesco, medico Lucchese . . . al cantone apresso il Cardinale Farnese.

Messer Francesco, physician of Lucca . . . in the quarter near the Cardinal Farnese.

C. A. 120a]　　　　**1444**

Libro del Pandolfino — ²coltelli — ³penna da rigare — ⁴tignere la uesta — ⁵libreria di Scō Marco — ⁶libreria di Scō Spirito — ⁷Lattantio de' Daldi — ⁸Antonio Couoni — ⁹libro di maestro Paolo infermieri — ¹⁰stiualetti, scarpe e calze — ¹¹lacca — ¹²garzone che mi facci il modello — ¹³Guantiera di Lorenzo de' Medici — ¹⁴Giouanni del Sodo — ¹⁵Sansouino — ¹⁶riga — ¹⁷coltello sottilissimo — ¹⁸occhiali — ¹⁹rotti fisici — ²⁰rifare l'abernucco — ²¹libro di Maso — ²²catenuzza di Michelagnolo — ²³¶impara la multiplicatione ²⁴delle radici da maestro Luca¶ ²⁵el mio mappamōdo che à Giovanni Bēci, ²⁶calcetti — ²⁷veeta dal gabellottu — ²⁸cordovano rosso — ²⁹mappamōdo di Giovanni Benci — ³⁰paese di Milano in istāpa — ³¹libri di mercato — de arco e corda — tanaglino — moncatto.

Pandolfino's book [1]—knives—a pen for ruling—to have the vest dyed—The library at St. Mark's—The library at Santo Spirito—Lactantius of the Daldi [7]—Antonio Covoni —A book by Maestro Paolo Infermieri—Boots, shoes, and hose—(Shell)lac—An apprentice to do the model for me—glove-case of Lorenzo de' Medici — Giovanni del Sodo — Sansovino [15] —a ruler—a very sharp knife—spectacles— fractions — repair the mantle — Tomaso's book—Michelagnolo's little chain; learn the multiplication of roots from Maestro Luca— my map of the world which Giovanni Benci has [25] — socks — clothes from the custom-house officer — red Cordova leather — the map of the world, of Giovanni Benci　a print, the districts about Milan—market book—arch and cord—pincers . . .

C. A. 147a]　　　　**1445**

¶ Di quel di Pavia si lauda · piv · il movimēto · che nessun altra cosa;

¶ ²L'imitatione · delle cose · antiche · è piv laudabile · che quella delle · moderne;

¶ ³Nō può essere bellezza · e vtilità · come appare nelle fortezze ⁴e nelli omini; ¶

¶ ⁵Il trotto · è quasi di qualità di cavallo libero;

⁶Doue · manca · la uiuacità naturale, bisognia farne una accidētale. ¶

In that at Pavia the movement is more to be admired than anything else.

The imitation of antique work is better than that of the modern things.

Beauty and utility cannot exist together, as seen in fortresses and in men.

The trot is almost the nature of the free horse.

Where natural vivacity is lacking it must be supplied by art.

C. A. 179b]　　　　**1446**

Saluadore materassaio ²sta in sulla piazza di Scō An³drea; entra da pellicciai . . . .

Salvadore, the mattress-maker, lives on the Piazza di Sant' Andrea, you enter by the furrier's.

1441. 1. bottegha cheffu. 2. bartol.
1442. q"o" libro . . franc"o" eddi sua disciē.
1444. 2. coltegli. 3. darrigare. 5. marcho. 9. palogo. 17. sotillssimo. 22. catenuza. 23. ipara. 24. radice . . maesstro. 27. vesta di gā bellotto 29. govanni.
1445. 1. lalda . . chosa. 2. chose . . laldabile chelle. 3. nopo belleza . . chome apare. 5. trocto . . chavallo. 6. mancha . . fare ĩ accidētale.
1446. 2. piaza di sco\\\\\\. 3. pelliccai\\\\\\. 4. dedare a francº paio\\\\\\. 5. ĩ di lenzola e s.50\\\\\\.

1441. 6. *Marc Antonio.* See No. 1433.

1443. *Alessandro Farnese,* afterwards Pope Paul III, was created in 1493 Cardinal di San Cosmo e San Damiano, by Alexander VI. Not in Leonardo's hand.

1444. 1. *Pandolfino, Francesco.* Florentine ambassador at Milan.

7. The works of Lactantius were often published in Italy during Leonardo's lifetime. The first edition published in 1465 'in monastero sublacensi' was also

the first book printed in Italy.

15. *Sansovino, Andrea.* The sculptor; 1460–1529.

24. Fra Luca Pacioli.

1445. *Quel di Pavia.* Gisulf (?), king of the Goths, known as Regisole, from Ravenna moved to Pavia; destroyed at the time of the French Revolution. Compare W. von Seidlitz, *Leonardo,* i, p. 182.

2. See No. 487, note. Vol. i, p. 303.

C. A. 188*b*]   **1447**

Mōsignor de' Pazzi — ²ser Ātonio Pacini.   Monsignore de' Pazzi—Ser Antonio Pacini.

C. A. 225*a*]   **1448**

Algibra ch' è apresso i Marliani fatta dal loro   An algebra, which the Marliani have, written
padre—   by their father [1]—
²Dell' osso, de' Marliani,   On the bone, by the Marliani—
³Dell' osso che fora, Gian Giacomo da Bellin-   On the bone which penetrates, Gian Gia-
zona, e tirare fori il chiodo cō facilità—   como of Bellinzona, to draw out the nail with
                                                      facility—
⁴Misura di Boccalino—   The measurement of Boccalino—
⁵Misura di Milano e borghi—   The measurement of Milan and the suburbs
                                                      [5]—
⁶Libro che tratta di Milano e sua chiese, che   A book, treating of Milan and its churches
à l'ultimo cartolaio īuerso il Corduso—   which is to be had at the last stationer's on the
                                                      way to Corduso [6]—
⁷Misure della corte vechia—   The measurement of the Corte Vecchia—
⁸Misure del castello—   The measurement of the Castle—
⁹Fatti mostrare al maestro · d'abbaco ·   Get the master of arithmetic to show you how
riquadrare · uno triangolo . . .   to square a triangle—
¹⁰Fatti mostrare a messer Fatio 'di propor-   Get Messer Fazio to show you [the book] on
tione'—   proportion—
¹¹Fatti mostrare · al frate di Brera 'de   Get the Friar di Brera to show you [the book]
pōnderibus'—   *de Ponderibus* [11]—
¹²Della misura di Sco Lorenzo—   Of the measurement of San Lorenzo—
¹³A fra Filippo di Brera prestai · cierti   I lent certain groups to Fra Filippo de Brera
gruppi—   [13]—
¹⁴Ricorda a Giannino Bombardieri · del   Memorandum: to ask Giannino Bombardieri
modo, come si mvrò la torre di Ferrara · sāza   as to the mode in which the tower of Ferrara
buche—   is walled without loopholes—
¹⁵Dimāda · maestro Antonio, come · si piantā   Ask Maestro Antonio how mortars are placed
bōbarde e bastioni di dì o di notte—   on bastions by day or by night—
¹⁶Domanda Benedetto Portinari in che modo   Ask Benedetto Portinari how the people go on
si corre per lo ghiaccio · in Fiādra—   the ice in Flanders—
¹⁷Le proportioni · d'Alchino colle cōsidera-   On proportions, by Alchino, with notes by
tioni del Marliano da messer Fatio—   Marliano, from Messer Fazio—
¹⁸La misura del sole promessami da maestro   The measurement of the sun, promised me
Giovanni frāzese—   by Maestro Giovanni, the Frenchman—
¹⁹Balestra di maestro Gianetto—   The crossbow of Maestro Gianetto—
²⁰Il libro di Giovanni Taverna che · à · messer   The book by Giovanni Taverna that Messer
Fatio—   Fazio—
²¹Ritrai Milano—   You will draw Milan [21]—
²²Misura di navilio, conche e sostegni e   The measurement of the canal, locks and
barche maggiori e spesa—   supports, and large boats; and the expense—

1447. 1. pazi.
1448. 1. alcibra. 3. cheffora giaiachomo da belinchona ettirān .. ciodo chō. 4. bochalino. 6. chettratta .. essa .. chartolaio .. chorduso.
7. chorte. 8. chastello. 9. dabbacho .. riquadrare ī. 13. fraffillippo. 14. richorda .. chome .. tore di ferara. 15. chome.
16. chore .. diacio di fiādra. 17. cholle chōsideratione. 18. promissami. 22. chōche esso stegnio .. magiori esspesa.

1448. 1, 2. *Girolamo Marliani*, author of *Algebra*,   12. *Sco Lorenzo.* A church at Milan; see pp. 29
celebrated physician; so were his sons.   and 38.
    5, 21. See Pl. CIX and No. 1016.   13, 24. *Gruppi.* See vol. i, p. 387, No. 680, note 9.
    6. *Corduso*, see No. 1413, note.   14. *Giannino Bombardiere*, a well-known metal-
    10. Fazio Cardano, father of the scientist Girolamo founder of Ferrara. See Uzielli, *Ricerche*, 1896, pp.
Cardano; see vol. i, pp. 125 and 243.   513–16.
    11, 13. *Brera*, now Palazzo delle Scienze ed Arti.   16. The *Portinari* were one of the great merchant
Until 1571 it was the monastery of the order of the families of Florence.
Umiliati and afterwards of the Jesuits.   17. *Alchino*, the Arab philosopher Alkindi. See
    De ponderibus: compare No. 1436, l. 3.   vol. i, p. 243, and Solmi, *Fonti*, pp. 58, 112.

²³Milano ī fondamēto—
²⁴Gruppi di Bramāte—
²⁵Meteora d'Aristotile vulgare—

²⁶Fa d'avere Vitolone ch'è nella libreria di
Pauia che tratta della matematica—²⁷truova
uno maestro d'acqua, e fatti dire i riparo d'essa,
e quello che costa ²⁸vn riparo, e una · conca ·,
e uno navilio, e uno molino alla lonbarda;

²⁹Un nipote · di Gian Āgelo · dipītore à uno
libro d'acque che fu del padre;
³⁰Paolino Scarpellino ·, detto Assiolo ·, è bono
· maestro d'acque.

Plan of Milan [23]—
Groups by Bramante [24]—
The book on celestial phenomena by Aris-
totle, in Italian [25]—
Try to get Vitolone, which is in the library
at Pavia [26] and which treats of Mathematics
—Find a master [learned] in waterworks, and
get him to explain the repair and the costs of a
repair and a lock and a canal and a mill in the
Lombard fashion.
A grandson of Gian Angelo's, the painter, has
a book on water which was his father's.
Paolino Scarpellino, called Assiolo, has great
knowledge of waterworks.

C. A. 320b]   1449

Francesco d'Antonio j Firenze.

Francesco d'Antonio at Florence.

C. A. 367b]   1450

Givliano Gōdi — ²Tomaso Ridolfi —
³Tomaso · Capponi — Gerardo · Paganelli —
⁴Niccolò · del Nero — ⁵Simō · Zati — ⁶Nasi —
⁷erede di Lionardo Manelli — ⁸Guglielmo di
Ser Martino — ⁹Bartolomeo · del Tovaglia —
¹⁰Andrea · Airrgucci — ¹¹Niccolo · Capponi —
¹²Giovan Portinari.

Giuliano Gondi [1] — Tomaso Ridolfi —
Tomaso Capponi — Gerando Paganelli —
Niccolò del Nero — Simone Zati — Nasi — the
heir of Lionardo Manelli—Guglielmo di Ser
Martino—Bartolomeo del Tovaglia —Andrea
Arrigucci — Niccolò Capponi — Giovanni
Portinari.

Br. M. 48a]   1451

Pandolfino.

Pandolfino.

Br. M. 132b]   1452

Il Vespuccio mi vol dare un libro di geo-
metria.

Vespuccio will give me a book of Geometry.

Br. M. 150b]   1453

Marcantonio Colonna ²in Scō Appostolo.

Marcantonio Colonna at Santi Apostoli.

26. tratte delle matematice.   27. ī maestro dacq"a" effatti . . ecquelo che chosta.   26. e ī choncha e ī . . e ī.   29. vnipote . .
giānāgelo . . a ī libro.   30. pagolino scharpellino.
1449. 1. franc"o" dant"o" jffirence (*early writing*).
1450. 1–12 R. 4. nicholo. 5. zasti. 7. rede di. 11. nicholo.
1452. 1. el vespucco . . dare ī libro di gieometria.
1453. marchātonio cholonna.

23. *Fondamento* is commonly used by Leonardo to
mean ground-plan. See, e.g., p. 41.
25. *Meteora.* By this Leonardo means no doubt
the four books τὰ μετεωρολογικά. He must refer here
to a MS. translation, as no Italian translation is known
to have been published.
26. *Vitolone.* See No. 1506, note.
Libreria di Pavia. One of the most famous of Italian
libraries. After the victory of Novara in April 1500,
Louis XII had it conveyed to France, 'come trofeo di
vittoria'.
1450. 1. *Guiliano Gondi.* Ser Piero da Vinci, Leonardo's father, lived till 1480 in a house belonging to
Giuliano Gondi. In 1498 this was pulled down to
make room for the fine Palazzo built on the Piazza San
Firenze by Giuliano di San Gallo, which still exists.
In the *Riassunto del Catasto di Ser Piero da Vinci*,
1480, Leonardo is not mentioned; it is evident, therefore, that he was living elsewhere. In the *Catasto di
Giuliano Gondi* of the same year the following mention is made of his four eldest sons:
Lionardo mio figliuolo d'età d'anni 29, non fa nulla,

Giovambatista d'età d'anni 28 in Ghostantinopoli,
Billichozo d'età d'anni 24 a Napoli,
Simone d'età d'anni 23 in Ungheria.
He himself was a merchant of gold filigree ('facciamo lavorare una bottegha d'arte di seta . . . facciamo
un pocho di trafico a Napoli'). As he was 59 years old
in 1480, he certainly would not have been alive at the
time of Leonardo's death. But Leonardo must have
been on intimate terms with the family till the end of
his life, for in a letter dated June 1, 1519, in which
Fr. Melzi, writing from Amboise, announces Leonardo's death to Giuliano da Vinci at Florence (see
p. 235), he says at the end 'Datemene risposta per i
Gondi' (see Uzielli, *Ricerche*, passim).
Most of the other names on the list are those of
well-known Florentine families.
12. *Giov. Portinari* represented the Medici bank at
Milan.
1452. See No. 844, note, p. 104.
1453. In July 1506 Pope Julius II gave Donna
Lucrezia della Rovere, the daughter of his sister

Br. M. 190b–191a]   1454

Cassa,	gabbia—	A box,	a cage—
[2]Liuello,	far l'uccello—	A square,	to make the bird [2]—
[3]Libro del Pandolfino,	grassellino—	Pandolfino's book,	mortar [?]—
[4]Coltellini,	Renieri per la	Small knives,	Renieri for the
[5]Penna da rigare,	pietra—stella—	Pen for ruling,	stone—star—
[6]Tignere la uesta,	la tazza d'Alfieri—	To have the vest dyed,	Alfieri's tazza—
[7]Librerie,	la Meteora—	The Libraries,	the book on celestial phenomena[7]—
[8]Lattantio Tedaldi,	va a casa de' Pazzi—	Lactantius Tebaldi,	go to the house of the Pazzi,
[9]Libro di maestro Paolo Infermieri	cassetta—	Book from Maestro Paolo Infermieri—	small box—
[10]Stiualetti, calze e scarpe,	suchiellino—	Boots, shoes and hose,	small gimlet—
[11]Lacca,	. . . .	Lac,	. . . . —
[12]Garzone pe' modelli,	. . . .	An apprentice for models,	. . . . . —
[13]Gramatica di Lorēzo de' Medici—	la valuta del botro	Grammar of Lorenzo de' Medici,	the amount of the . . .
[14]Giouanni del Sodo per rotti fisici . . .	. . . .	Giovanni del Sodo . . . —for the broken	. . . . .
[15]Sansauino,	valuta del tafetta	Sansovino,	the amount of material
[16]Pier di Cosimo,	per l'alie—	Piero di Cosimo [16],	for the wings—

[17]Filippo e Lorenzo — [18]riga — [19]ochiali — [20]rifare labernucco . . .—[21]libro di Maso—[22]catena di Michelagnolo—[23]mvltiplicatione di radici — [24]di corda e arco—[25]mappamōdo de' Benci — [26]calcetti — [27]vesta dal gabellotto—[28]cordovano—[29]libri di mercato—[30]acque del Cronaca—[31]acque del Tanaglino — [32]. . .—[33]le berrette —[34]spechio del Rosso vederlo fare—[35]$\frac{1}{3}$ di che no. $\frac{5}{8}$—[36]Meteora d'Aristotele—[37]casse di Lorēzo di Pier Francesco—[38]maestro Piero dal Borgo —[39]legare il mio libro—[40]¶ mostra al Serigatto il libro—[41]e fatti dare la regola dell' orilogio, anello ¶ — [42]noce muscato —[43]gomma —[44]squadra—[45]Giovā Batista a la piazza de' Mozzi—[46]Giovanni Benci il libro mio, e' diaspri, [47]ottone per li ochiali.

Filippo and Lorenzo [17] — a ruler — spectacles—to remake the cloak—Tomaso's book, —Michelagnolo's chain — the multiplication of roots — of the bow and string — the map of the world from Benci — socks — the clothes from the custom-house officer — Cordova leather — market-books — waters of Cronaca — waters of Tanaglino . . . — the caps — Rosso's mirror; to see him make it — $\frac{1}{3}$ of what number $\frac{5}{8}$ — on the celestial phenomena, by Aristotle [36]—boxes of Lorenzo di Pier Francesco [37] — Maestro Piero of the Borgo — to have my book bound—show the book to Serigatto—and get the rule of the clock [41] — ring — nutmeg — gum—the square—Giovan' Batista at the piazza de' Mozzi—Giovanni Benci has my book and jaspers—Brass for the spectacles.

1454. 1. chassa. 4. pella. 5. darrigare. 7. metaura. 8. casa e pazi. 9. maesstro pa"lo". 10. esscarpe. 11. lacha—trai 2 aguti. 12. dalli antellessi. 14. vatro. 15. del ca. 16. fetta per lalie. 24. archo. 25. mapamōdo. 27. di ganbelletto. 30. clonica. 32. moncatto. 35. n"o". 36. metaura. 38. maesstro. 41. effatti. 42. moscade. 45. govā batissta . . piaza de mozi. 46. govanni . . ellibro mio e diasspri.

Lucchina, in marriage to the youthful Marcantonio Colonna, who, like his brothers Prospero and Fabrizio, became one of the most famous Captains of his family. He gave to him Frascati and made him a present of the palazzo he had built, when Cardinal, near the church of Santi Apostoli, which is now known as the Palazzo Colonna (see Gregorovius, *Gesch. der Stadt Rom*, vol. viii, book xiv. 1, 3. And Coppi, *Mem. Colonnesi*, p. 251).

1454. Much of No. 1444 is repeated in this memorandum.

2. Vasari states that Leonardo invented mechanical birds which moved through the air. Compare No. 703.

7, 36. *Meteora.* See No. 1448, 25.

16. *Pier di Cosimo*, the well-known Florentine painter, 1462–1521. See Vasari, *Vite* (vol. iv, p. 134, ed. Milanesi, 1880), about Leonardo's influence on Piero di Cosimo's style of painting.

17. *Filippo e Lorenzo.* Probably the painters Filippino Lippi and Lorenzo di Credi. L. di Credi's pictures and Vasari's history of that painter bear ample evidence to his intimate relations with Leonardo.

37. *Lorenzo di Pier Francesco* and his brother *Giovanni* were a lateral branch of the Medici family and changed their name to Popolani.

41. Possibly this refers to the clock on the tower of the Palazzo Vecchio at Florence. In February 1512 it had been repaired, and so arranged as to indicate the hours after the French manner (twelve hours a.m. and as many p.m.).

Br. M. 192*b*]   **1455**

Cerca in Firenze della Ramondina.   Search in Florence for the Ramondina.

Mi. Ambrosiana]   **1456**

Bernardo da Pōte . . .²Val di Lugā al fiē disce   Bernardo da Ponte . . . Val di Lugano . . .
. . .³e questo e mostr . . . ⁴molte vene per   many veins for anatomical demonstration.
l'anotomia.

Br. M. P. 1875–6–12–17]   **1457**

Paolo da Tavechia, per ²vedere le machie   Paolo of Tavechia, to see the marks in the
de³lle pietre tedesche.   German stones.

C. 15*b* (1)]   **1458**

Jacomo venne a stare · con meco jl dì della   Giacomo came to live with me on St. Mary <small>Notes on</small>
Maddalena nel mille 490, d'età d'anni 10;   Magdalen's [1] day, 1490, aged 10 years. The <small>pupils and assistants</small>
²Il secondo dì li feci tagliare 2 camicie, uno   second day I had two shirts cut out for him, a <small>(1458–68).</small>
pajo di calze e vn giubbone, e quãdo mi posi i   pair of hose, and a jerkin, and when I put aside
dinari al lato per pagare dette cose lui mi rubò   some money to pay for these things he stole
                                    lire 4   4 *lire*
³detti dinari dalla scarsella, e mai fu possibile   the money out of the purse; and I could never
farli le confessare, bench' io n'avessi vera cier-   make him confess, though I was quite certain
tezza—ladro, bugiardo, ostinato, ghiotto.—   of the fact. Thief, liar, obstinate, glutton.
⁴Il dì seguente andai a ciena con Iacomo   The day after, I went to sup with Giacomo
Andrea, e detto Iacomo · cienò per 2 e   Andrea, and the said Giacomo supped for two
fece male per 4, inperochè rupe 3 ampolline,   and did mischief for four; for he brake 3 cruets,
⁵versò il uino, e dopo questo venne a ciena doue   spilled the wine, and after this came to sup
me . . . .   where I . . . .
⁶Itē a dì 7 di settēbre · rubò uno grafio di   Item. On the 7th day of September he stole
valuta di 22 soldi a Marco che staua con meco,   a silver point of the value of 22 soldi from
jl quale era   Marco [6], who was living with me, this being
⁷d'argiēto e tolseglilo dal suo studiolo, e poi   of silver; and he took it from his studio, and
che detto Marco n'ebbe assai ciercato, lo trovò   when the said Marco had searched for it a long
na⁸scosto in nella cassa di detto Iacomo   while he found it hidden in the said Giacomo's
                                  lire 1 s(oldi)   box.
⁹Item a dì 26 di gienaro seguēte, essendo io in   *l. su*
casa di messer Galeazzo da San Severino a   Item. On the 26th January following, I, being
ordinare la festa ¹⁰della sua giostra, e spogliandosi   in the house of Messer Galeazzo da San Severino
cierti staffieri per prouarsi alcune vesti d'omini   [9], was arranging the festival for his jousting,
saluatici ch'a detta   and certain footmen having undressed to try on
¹¹festa accadeano, Giacomo s'accostò alla   some costumes of wild men for the said festival,
scarsella d'uno di loro, la qual era ī sul letto con   Giacomo went to the purse of one of them which
altri panni, ¹²e tolse quelli dinari che dētro vi   lay on the bed with other clothes, 2 *lire* 4 *S*,
trovò.   *lire* 2 *S* 4   and took out such money as was in it.

1455. 1. cercha . . dellaramōdina.
1456. 1. pōte\\\\\. 2. al fiē dis\\\\\\. 3. ecquesto e mostr\\\\. 4. la not\\\\\\. 5. paroffa di sā posā\\\\\.
1457. 1. pagol. 3. tedessce.
1458. 1. Iachomo vene . . chomecho . . madalena . . dani. 2. sechondo . . chamice ! paro di chalze . . gibone ecquãdo . . chose. 3. della
scharsella . . farlie le chonfessare . . cierteza . . ladro—ghiotto *these four words are written on the margin.* 4. chon iachomo . .
3 amole. 5. vene.   6. graffio . . ualluta . . marcho . . chomecho . . era [di ua].   7. [luto di] dargiēto ettolse glielo del . . marcho
[glielebe] nebe assai cierco lo tro na. 8. schosto inella chassa . . iachomo. 9. Ite adi . . esendo . . chasa . . galeazo dassanseverino
ardinare la. 10. alchune veste . . saluatichi. 11. achadeano iachomo sachosto allasscharsella . . chon.

1456. This fragmentary note is written on the   he left the master shortly after this, his term of study
margin of a drawing of three legs.   having perhaps expired.
1458. *Giacomo* is probably Giacomo Salai. See G.   9. *Galeazzo.* See No. 717, note, and G. Calvi,
Calvi, *Il vero nome di un' allievo di Leonardo* (Gian   'Contributi alla Biografia di L. d. V.', *Archivio Storico*
Giacomo Caprotti), Rassegna d'Arte, 1919, vol. I,   *Lombardo*, xliii, p. 479 f., for details of the tournament
p. 138. *Il dì della Maddalena.* July 22.   as described by Tristano Calco in *Nuptiae Medio-*
    4. *Jacomo Andrea* of Ferrare, Milanese architect   *lanensium et Estensium Principum scilicet Ludovici*
and engineer.   *Mariae cum Beatrice, Alphonsi cum Anna, Ludovici*
    6. *Marco*, probably Leonardo's pupil Marco d'Og-   *nepte, in Residua e biblioteca Patricij Nobilissimi Lucii*
gionno; born *c.* 1475, died 1530.   *Hadriani Cottae*, Milan, 1644, pp. 94–5. This note
    Che stava con meco. We may infer from this that   can therefore be dated 1491.

[13]Itē essendomi da maestro Agostino da Pauia donato in detta casa una pelle turchesca da fare uno [14]pajo di stiualetti ·, esso Giacomo infra uno mese me la rubò, e vendè la a uno conciatore di [15]scarpe per 20 soldi, de' quali danari secondo che lui propio mi cōfessò, ne cōprò anici cōfetti; *lire 2.*

[16]Itē ancora a dì 2 d'aprile, lasciādo Giā Ātonio uno grafio d'argiēto sopra uno suo disegnio, [17]esso Giacomo gli lo rubò, il qual era di ualuta di soldi 24 *lira 1[a] S 4.*

[18]Il primo [19]anno
[20]v̄ mātello, *lire 2*
[21]camicie 6, *lire 4*
[22]3 givboni, *lire 6*
[23]4 paja di calze, *lire 7 S 8*
[24]vestito foderato, *lire 5*
[25]24 paja di scarpe, *lire 6 · S 5*
[26]vna baretta, *lire 1*
[27]strīghe, *lire 1.*

Item. When I was in the same house, Maestro Agostino da Pavia gave to me a Turkish hide to have a pair of short boots made of it; this Giacomo stole it of me within a month and sold it to a cobbler for 20 soldi, with which money, by his own confession, he bought anise comfits. *2 lire.*

Item. Again, on the 2nd April, Giovan Antonio [16] having left a silver point on a drawing of his, Giacomo stole it, and this was of the value of 24 soldi *1 lira 4 S.*

The first year—
A cloak, *2 lire,*
6 shirts, *4 lire,*
3 jerkins, *6 lire,*
4 pairs of hose, *7 lire 8 soldi,*
1 lined doublet, *5 lire,*
24 pairs of shoes, *6 lire 5 soldi,*
A cap, *1 lira,*
laces, *1 lira.*

S. K. M. III 88b] 1459

A dì penvltimo di febraio;
[2]giobia, a dì 27 di settēbre, [3]tornò maestro Tōmaso, [4]lavorò per sé insino a dì penvltimo di febraio; [5]a dì 18 di marzo 1493 [6]venne Iulio tedesco [7]a stare meco; Antonio, Bartolomeo, Lucia—Piero—Lionard.
[9]A dì 6 d'ottobre.

On the last day but one of February;
Thursday the 27th day of September Maestro Tommaso came back and worked for himself until the last day but one of February. On the 18th day of March, 1493, Giulio, a German, came to live with me—Antonio, Bartolomeo, Lucia, Piero, Leonardo.
On the 6th day of October.

H.[1] 106b] 1460

1493
[2]A dì primo di novēbre facemmo [3]cōto; Givlio restava a rimettere mesi [4]4 || e maestro Tōmaso mesi 9; [5]maestro Tōmaso fece di poi 6 cādellie[6]ri ·, dì 10 ·; Givlio in cierte molli [7]dì 15; Giulio lavorò poi per sé in[8]sino a dì 27 di maggio, e lavorò [9]per me uno martinello insino a dì 18 [10]di luglio, poi per sé insino a dì 7 [11]d'agosto, e questo uno mezzo dì per una donna; [12]di poi per me in 2 serrature [13]insino a dì · 20 d'agosto.

1493.
On the 1st day of November we settled accounts. Giulio had to pay 4 months; and Maestro Tommaso 9 months; Maestro Tommaso afterwards made 6 candlesticks, 10 days' work; Giulio some fire-tongs, 15 days' work. Then he worked for himself till the 27th of May, and worked for me at a lever till the 18th of July; then for himself till the 7th of August, and for half a day, on the fifteenth, for a lady. Then again for me at 2 locks until the 20th of August.

H.[1] 41a] 1461

¶A dì 23 d'agosto lire 12 da Pulisena;
¶ [2]a dì 14 di marzo 1494 [3]venne Galeazzo a stare con meco [4]cō patto di dare 5 lire il mese [5]per le sue spese, pagādo ogni 14 [6]dì de' mesi.
[7]Dettemi suo padre fiorini 2 di Reno;
[8]A dì 14 di luglio ebbi da Galeazzo fio[9]rini 2 di Reno.

On the 23rd day of August, 12 lire from Pulisena. On the 14th of March 1494, Galeazzo came to live with me, agreeing to pay 5 lire a month for his cost, paying on the 14th day of each month.
His father gave me 2 Rhenish florins.
On the 14th of July I had from Galeazzo 2 Rhenish florins.

---

13. chasa. 14. paro . . iachomo infra ī mese. 15. de qua dinari sechondo . . chōfessone chōpro . . chōfetti. 16. anchora . . lassciādo . . ātonio ī graffio. 17. iachomo gliele. 18–27. R. 23. para di chalze. li 5. 25. para . . scarpeli. 27. incīti strige.
1459. 1. R. 3. maesstro. 4. addi. 6. tedessco. 7. asstare mecho. 9. R. *The words* lucia piero lionard *are written on the margin.*
1460. 1–13 R. 2. facemo. 8. magio. 9. me ī. 11. mezo ī dì per ī dona. 13. addi 20.
1461. 1–7 R. 3. galeazo asstare comecho. 4. chō pacto. 7. padre f. 2 di rē. 8. galeazo.

16. *Giovan Antonio,* probably Beltraffio, 1467–1516.

H.³ 105*a*]   **1462**

A dì 15 di ²settēbre Gi³vlio comī⁴ciò la serratu⁵ra del mio ⁶studiolo 14⁷94.

On the 15th day of September Giulio began the lock of my studio; 1494.

Br. M. 271*b*]   **1463**

Sabato mattina a dì 3 d'agosto · 1504 venne Iacopo ²tedesco a stare con meco in casa; convennesi con me³co che io li facessi le spese per uno carlino ⁴il dì.

Saturday morning the 3ʳᵈ of August 1504 Jacopo the German came to live with me in the house, and agreed with me that I should charge him a carlino a day.

G. 0⁷]   **1464**

1510

A dì 26 di settēbre Antonio ²si rupe la gāba, à a stare 40 dì.

1510

On the 26ᵗʰ of September Antonio broke his leg; he must rest 40 days.

E. 1*a*]   **1465**

Partì da Milano per Roma a dì 24 ²di settēbre 1513 cō Giovā, Francesco ³de' Melsi, Salai, Lorēzo e il Fāfoia.

I left Milan for Rome on the 24ᵗʰ day of September, 1513, with Giovanni [2], Francesco di Melzi [3], Salai, Lorenzo, and il Fanfoia.

C. A. 68*a*]   **1466**

A dì 3 di gienajo.

²Benedetto veñe a 17 d'ottobre a ducati 4 el mese; ³è stato con meco due mesi e 13 dì ⁴dell' anno passato, nel qual tēpo à me⁵ritato li 38 e S 18 di 8; ⁶ne à avuto lire 26 e S 8, resta a ⁷avere per l'anno passato lire 12 S 10.

⁸Ioditti venne · a dì 8 di settēbre ⁹a 4 ducati al mese, è stato con me ¹⁰mesi · 3 e dì 24; à meritato · li. ¹¹59 S 14 di · 8, ne à avuto li¹²re 43 S 4; ¹³restà auere lire 16 ¹⁴10 di 8.

¹⁵Benedetto grosoni 24.

On the 3ʳᵈ day of January.

Benedetto came on the 17ᵗʰ of October at 4 ducats a month; he stayed with me two months and 13 days of last year [4], in which time he earned 38 lire 18 soldi and 8 dinari; he had of this 26 lire and 8 soldi, and there remains to be paid for the past year 12 lire 10 soldi.

Joditti came on the 8ᵗʰ day of September, at 4 ducats a month, and stayed with me 3 month and 24 days, and earned 59 lire 14 soldi and 8 dinari; he has had 43 lire, 4 soldi, there remains to pay 16 lire 10 soldi and 8 dinari.

Benedetto, 24 grosoni.

1462. 1–7 R.
1463. *Written from left to right.* 1. addi . . iachopo. 2. tedesscho asstare chome cho in chasa chonvennesi chome. 3. choche . . lesspese . . charlino.
1464. 1. addi . . setēbre. 2. ruppe.
1465. 1. addi. 2. sectēbe . . frāciesscho.
1466. *Written from left to right.* 1. gienaro.   2. dottobre a di 4 elm.   3. cho mecho.   4. dellano. 6 anneauto.   8. Io di ttj venne . . settēbr. 9. stato come. 11. ane auto li. 14. [e ½].

1463. Compare No. 1527, note.
1464. This note refers possibly to Beltraffio.
1465. 1. The transfer of Leonardo's establishment from Milan to Rome in company of four persons may have taken place in connexion with his engagement by Giuliano de' Medici; see note, Nos. 1351, 1353.

2. *Giovan.* It is not likely that Leonardo should have called Giovan' Antonio Beltraffio at one time Giovanni, as in this note, and another time Antonio, as in No. 1464, while in No. 1458, l. 16, we find *Giovan' Antonio*, and in No. 1436, l. 6, *Beltraffio*. Possibly the Giovanni here spoken of is Leonardo's less known pupil Giovan Pietrino (see No. 1467, 5).

2, 3. *Francesco de' Melzi* is often mentioned. See No. 1350.

3. *Salai.* See No. 1519, note. See Suida, *Leonardo u. sein Kreis* (Munich, 1929), pp. 227 ff.

4. *Lorenzo.* See No. 1351, l. 10 (p. 337). Amoretti gives the following note in *Mem. Stor.* xxiii. 1505:

'Martedi–sera a dì 14 d'aprile. Venne Lorenzo a stare con mecho: disse essere d'età d'anni 17 . . a di 15 del detto aprile ebbi scudi 25 d'oro dal chamer-lingo di Santa Maria nuova.' This, he asserts, is derived from a MS. marked S, in quarto (now in Turin, see No. 1530 A). Amoretti himself had not seen it, but copied from a selection of extracts made by Oltrocchi before the Leonardo MSS. were conveyed to Paris on the responsibility of the first French Republic. Lorenzo, by this, must have been born in 1487. Amoretti was mistaken in suggesting the Venetian Lorenzo Lotto.

Il Fāfoia, perhaps a nickname. Cesare da Sesto, Leonardo's pupil, seems to have been in Rome in these years, as we learn from a drawing by him in the Louvre.

1466. This seems to be an account for two assistants. The name of the second is not clear. The year is not given. The note is nevertheless of chronological

C A. 264*a*]

   ³Giã Maria 4
   ⁴Benedetto 4
   ⁵Gian Pietro 3
   ⁶Salai 3
   ⁷Bartolomeo 3
   Girardo 4.

1467

Gian Maria 4,
Benedetto 4,
Gian Pietro [5] 3,
Salai 3,
Bartolomeo 3,
Gherardo 4.

C. A. 284*a*]

   Salai lire 20
   ²Bonifacio lire 2
   ³Bartolomeo lire 4
   ⁴Arrigo lire 15.

1468

Salai, 20 lire,
Bonifacio, 2 lire,
Bartolomeo, 4 lire,
Arrigo [Harry], 15 lire.

C. A. 210*a*]

L'Abbaco,   Fiore di Virtù,

Quotations ²Plinio,   Vita de' Filosofi,
and notes
on books
and authors ³Bibbia,   Lapidario,
(1469–
1508).

1469

Book on Arithmetic, [1]   'Flowers of Virtue',
Pliny, [2]   'Lives of the Philo-
                          sophers',
The Bible, [3]   'Lapidary',

1467. 1. \\\\\nco. 2. \\\\\\\iberdo. 5. gian petro.
1468. 2. prefacio. 4. arigo.
1469. 1–25 R. 1. dabacho. 2. filosafi. 3. bibia.

value. The first line tells us the date when the note was registered, January 3rd, and the observations that follow refer to the events of the previous month 'of last year' (*dell' anno passato*). Leonardo cannot therefore have written thus in Florence, where the year was, at that period, calculated as beginning in the month of March (see vol. i, No. 4, note 2). He must then have been in Milan. What is more important is that we thus learn how to date the beginning of the year in all the notes written at Milan. This clears up Uzielli's doubts: 'A Milano facevasi cominciar l'anno ab incarnatione, cioè il 25 Marzo e a nativitate, cioè il 25 Decembre. Ci sembra probabile che Leonardo dovesse prescegliere lo stile che era in uso a Firenze' (*Ricerche*, p. 84, note).

1467. 5. See No. 1465, l. 2, and Calvi, *I Manoscritti*, p. 154, note.

1469. The late Marchese Girolamo d'Adda published a disquisition on this passage under the title *L.d.V. e la sua Libreria, note di un bibliofilo* (*Milano* 1873); privately printed. In the autumn of 1880 he showed me a considerable mass of additional notes prepared for a second edition. This, as he then intended, was to come out after the publication of this work of mine. After the death of the elder Marchese, his son, the Marchese Gioachino d'Adda, was so liberal as to place these MS. materials at my disposal for the present work, through the kind intervention of Signor Gustavo Frizzoni. The following passages, with the initials G. d'A., are prints from the notes in that publication; the MS. additions I have marked.* I did not, however, reproduce here the observations on the contents of the books here enumerated.

1. '*La nobel opera de arithmethica ne la qual se tracta tute cosse amercantia pertinente facta & compilata per Piero borgi da Veniesia*', *in*-4°. In fine: '*Nela inclita cita di Venetia a çorni . 2 augusto . 1484 . fu imposto fine ala presente opera*'. *Segn. a–p . quaderni. V'ha però un' altra opera simile di Filippo Calandro*, 1491. *È da consultarsi su quest' ultimo, Federici: Memorie Trevigiane*. (G.d'A.) Or: *Arte de labbacho*, Treviso, 1478,

or a work in manuscript such as the *Trattato d'abbaco, d'astronomia e di segreti naturali e medicinali* by Paolo Dagomari, called Paolo del Abbaco (1281–1374). *Fiore di virtù: pag. 73. 'Libricciuolo composto di bello stile verso il 1320 e più volte impresso nel secolo XV'* (*ristampato poi anche più tardi*). *Gli accademici della Crusca lo ammettono nella serie dei testi di lingua. Vedasi Gamba, Razzolini, Panzer, Brunet, Lechi, ecc.* (G. d'A.) A collection of moralizing tales from animal life written by the friar Tommaso Gozzadini of Bologna, who lived in the thirteenth century; in the fourteenth century the book was rewritten in the standard Florentine Italian and became for centuries a favourite of the people. Printed in Venice in 1488.

2. '*Historia naturale di C. Plinio Secondo, tradocta di lingua latina in fiorentina per Christophoro Landino & Opus Nicolai Jansonis gallici imp. anno salutis M.CCCC.LXXVI . Venetiis' in-fol.—Diogene Laertio. Incomincia: 'El libro de la vita de philosophi etc.: Impressum Venetiis per Bernardinum Celerium de Luere, 1480', in-4°.* (G. d'A.)

3. '*La Bibia volgare historiata (per Nicolò di Mallermi) Venecia . . . . M.CCCC.LXXI in kalende di Augusto (per Vindelino de Spira)' 2 vol. in-fol. a 2 col. di 50 lin.; od altra ediz. della stessa versione del Mallermi, Venetia 1471, e sempre: 'Venecia per Gabriel de Piero 1477', in-fol.; 2 vol.; Ottavio Scotto da Modoetia 1481', 'Venetia 1487 per Joan Rosso Vercellese', '1490 Giovanni Ragazo di Monteferato a instantia di Luchanthonio di Giunta, ecc.'—Lapidario Teofrasto? Mandeville: 'Le grand lapidaire', versione italiana ms.? forse Alberto Magno: de mineralibus.* Potrebbe essere una traduzione del poema latino (*Liber lapidum seu de gemmis*) di Marbodio vescovo di Rennes (*morto nel 1123*) *da lui stesso tradotto in francese dal greco di Evao rè d'Arabia celebre medico che l'aveva composto per l'imperatore Tiberio. Marbodio scrisse il suo prima per Filippo Augusto rè di Francia. Vi sono anche traduzioni in prosa. 'Il lapidario o la forza e la virtù delle pietre preziose, delle Erbe e degli Animali.'* (G. d'A.)

⁴De re militari,	Pistole del Filelfo,	'On warfare' [4]	'Epistles of Filelfo',
⁵Deca prima,	Della cõseruatiõ della sanità,	The first decade, [5]	'On the preservation of health',
⁶Deca terza,	Ciecco d'Ascoli,	The third decade, [6]	Ciecho d'Ascoli,
⁷Deca quarta,	Alberto Magno,	The fourth decade, [7]	Albertus Magnus,
⁸Guidone,	Retorica nova,	Guido, [8]	New treatise on rhetorics,
⁹Piero Cresciẽtio,	Cibaldone,	Piero Crescentio, [9]	Cibaldone,
¹⁰Quadriregio,	Esopo,	'Quadriregio', [10]	Æsop,

5. decha. 6. decha — ciecho dasscholi. 7. decha — magnio. gidone — rettoricha. 9. cibdone. 10. de 4 regi — isopo.

4. *Il Vegezio? . . . Il Frontino? . . . Il Cornazzano? . . . Noi crediamo piuttosto il Valturio. Questo libro doveva essere uno de' favoriti di Leonardo poichè libro di scienza e d'arte nel tempo stesso.*—See No. 1492, note. *Le edizioni a stampa sono le seguenti: La prima: 'Roberti Valturii de re militari, libri XII ad Sigismundum Pandulfum Malatestam . . . Johannes ex Verona oriundus: Nicolai cyrugiae medici filius: Artis impressorie magister: hunc de re militari librum elegantissimum; litteris, & figuratis signis sua in patria primus impressit. An. M.CCCCLXXII.' in-fol. senza numerazione. La seconda edizione è di Bologna, 1483, ristampata a Parigi nel 1532, e poi nuovamente nel 1533. Paolo Ramusio la volgeva in italiano e la pubblicava di nuovo in Verona col tipi del Paganino, sempre in-fol., 1483 (le stampe di formato più piccolo), e Luigi Meigret la traduceva in lingua francese nel 1555 a Parigi.*

Pistole del Felelfo. 'Mediolani per Leon. Pachel & Ulric. Scizenzeler 1484', in-4°.

5-7. Several editions of Livy's *Decades* appeared in the fifteenth century; the Italian version by maestro Antonio da Bologna, Venice, 1478, in three volumes: I. Deca prima e seconda, II. Deca terza, III. Deca quarta, corresponds to Leonardo's note.

5. *'Arnaldi de Villanova & Johannis Mediolanensis Regimen sanitatis Salernitanum, 1480', in-4°, ovvero 'Tractato utilissimo circa la conservatione de la sanitade, ecc. composto per il clarissimo ed excellente philosopho & doctore di medicina messer Ugo Benzo di Siena, ecc.', in-4°, caratteri gotici senza numeri e senza nome di tipografo. In fine: 'Exactum est hoc opus Mli (Mediolani) cura & diligentia Petri de Corneno Mediolanensis, 1481. pridie kalendas Junias . Johanne Galeatio Sforcia Vicecomite principe nostro invictissimo dominante.' V. Sassi-Argelati. Parte I, vol. I, p. DLXXV.* (G. d'A.)

6. *L'Acerba (da acervus, cumulo), di Francesco Stabili (Cecco d'Ascoli), astrologo nemico dell' Alighieri. Numerose edizioni del secolo XV e XVI. È una vera enciclopedia in versi, ripiena di idee arditissime e che valsero all' infelice pensatore il rogo nel 1347. In questo poema trovansi delineate le origini di molti trovati moderni, ed in particolare della circolazione del sangue, due secoli prima del Michele Serveto. Della prima edizione di Brescia Ferrandus s. a. in-fol. non si conosce che un solo esemplare nella Spenceriana. V. Dibdin.* (G. d'A.)

7. *'Incomenza el libro chiamato della vita ecc., cõposto per Alberto magno filosofo excellentissimo ecc. Neapoli Bernardini de gerardinis de Amelia, 1478,' in-4°. Altra edizione di 'Bologna per Bazalino di Bazaliero, 1493', in-4° got.* (G. d'A.). Or, more likely one of the following works: *De generatione et cor-*

ruptione, 1495; *De metheoris*, 1488, 1494; *De mineralibus*, 1476, 1491, 1495; *De rerum proprietatibus*, 1478, 1479, 1495; *De animalibus*, 1478. Comp. Nos. 1477, 1421, l. 15.

8. Forse 'Guido dalle Colonne' detto anche 'da Cauliaco'. *'Guidonis de Cauliaco Cyrurgia. Turra de Castello recepta atque balnei de Porecta ecc. Venetiis mandato & expensis Octaviani Scoti cura & arte Boneti Locatelli, 1498', in-fol. got.: rarissimo trattato di chirurgia. Ebbe traduzioni francesi parecchie e nel secolo XV anche una versione italiana s. l. n. a. ed un' altra in lingua castigliana nel 1498. Vedi: Brunet, Panzer, Hain e Mendez.*—L. Guil. de Saona *rhetorica nova, S. Albano, in-4°·1480 (Laurentius Guilelmus). È libro de' più rari (Brunet, Tomo V, col. 137).* S. Albans, Albani Villa, Vorulantium, Burgo ingleso nella contea di Hertfordshire, la patria di Bacone Francesco. (G. d'A.). Or, more likely: *Retorica nova*, compiled by Guidotto da Bologna about 1260 and printed in Venice 1473, Modena 1475.

9. *De agricultura. 'Il libro della agricultura di Pietro Crescentio', prima edizione di questa versione italiana scritta nel trecento e testo di lingua citato dall' Accademia della Crusca. 'Florentie per me Nicholaum Laurentii alemanum diocesis uratislaviensis anno M.CCCC.L.XXVIII.', in-fol.* (G. d'A.). *Cibaldone*, meaning 'miscellanea', is the title of a small popular treatise in verse on the conservation of health of which eight to nine editions appeared in the fifteenth century. It was a free translation, from the Latin version, of the third book of *Ad Almansorem libri X* by the Arab physician Rhazes, the dedicatee being al-Mansūr, prince of Khurāsān.

10. *Quadriregio (libro chiamato il) di Federigo Frezzi domenicano. È poema religioso-morale-scientifico in terzine. Fra gli imitatori della Divina Comedia è dei migliori 'non indegno di gir dietro a Dante' dice il Quadrio. Questo poema è in oggi ingiustamente negletto e quasi sconosciuto, ancorchè in tempi da noi lontani fosse stato nobilmente stampato più volte. Ebbe almeno sette edizioni dal 1481 al 1515, e contiene bellezze di primo ordine. *L'edizione che con molta probabilità era fra i libri di Leonardo riteniamo quello di Milano 1488 Zaroto. Un' esemplare all' Ambrosiana fra i quattrocentisti donati da G. Porro;—forse più rara che molte altre.*

'Fabulae de Esopo historiate', in-4° fig. senza nota di tempo e di luogo; o l'edizione di Venezia per Manfredo da Monferrato, in-4° fig., 1481 e 1490; od anche: 'Brescia per Boninum de Boninis 1487', in-4° con 67 belle figure silografiche; 'Roma, Silber 1483,' Venetia Manfredo Bonello da Streno, 1497, in-4°, ecc., o più probabilmente: 'Aesopi' vita & fabulæ latine cum

11Donato,	Salmi,	Donato, [11]	Psalms,
12Ivstino,	De Immortalità d'a-nima,	Justinus, [12]	'On the immortality of the soul',
13Guidone,	Burchiello,	Guido [13]	Burchiello,
14Dottrinale,	Driadeo,	'Doctrinale' [14]	Driadeo,
15Morgãte,	Petrarca,	Morgante [15]	Petrarch.
16Giovã di Mãdiuilla,		John de Mandeville [16]	
17De onesta voluttà,		'On honest recreation' [17]	
18Mãganello,		Manganello, [18]	
19Cronica d'Isidoro,		The Chronicle of Isidoro, [19]	
20Pistole d'Ouidio,		The Epistles of Ovid, [20]	
21Pistole del Filelfo,		Epistles of Filelfo, [21]	
22Spera,		Sphere, [22]	
23Facetie di Poggio,		The Jests of Poggio [23]	

12. imortalita. 15. petrarcha. 17. [deg] de. 19. desidero. 23. pogio.

versione italica & allegoriis Fr. Tuppi impressæ, Napoli, 1483,' in-fol., rara edizione ornata di belle vignette incise in legno. Questo Esopo è anche libro di novelle. Nel Catalogo Cicognara abbiamo una minuta descrizione di questo rarissimo volume. (G. d'A.)

11. *'Donatus latine & italice: Impressum Venetiis pensis Johannis Baptistae de Sessa anno 1499, in-4°'. 'El Psalterio de David in lingua volgare (da Malermi Venetia nel M.CCCC.LXXVI,' in-fol. s. n.* (G. d'A.)

12. *Compare No. 1210, 48.—La versione di Girolamo Squarzafico: 'Il libro di Justino posto diligentemente in materna lingua. Venetia ale spese (sic) di Johane de Colonia & Johane Gheretze . . . 1477,' in-fol. —'Marsilii Ficini Theologia platonica, sive de animarum immortalitate, Florentine, per Ant. Misconimum 1482,' in-fol., ovvero qualche versione italiana di questo stesso libro ms.* (G. d'A.) *Or rather Fr. Filelfo's Dialogo, Cosenza, 1478.* (Solmi, *Fonti*, pp. 153 f.)

13. *Forse 'la Historia Trojana Guidonis', od il 'manipulus' di 'Guido da Monterocherii', ma più probabilmente 'Guido d'Arezzo,' il di cui libro: 'Micrologus, seu disciplina artis musicae' poteva da Leonardo aversi ms.; di questi ne esistono in molte biblioteche, e fu poi impresso nel 1784 dal Gerbert.* Solmi (*Fonti*, p. 105), suggests Guido Bonatti's treatise on Antronomy, Venice, 1506 etc.

Molte sono le edizione dei sonetti di Burchiello Fiorentino, impresse nel secolo XV. La prima e più rara e ricercata: 'Incominciano li sonetti, ecc.(per Christoforo Arnaldo)', in-4° senza numeri, richiami o segnature, del 1475, e fors' anche del 1472, secondo Morelli e Dibdin, ecc. (G. d'A.)

14. *Versione italiana del 'Doctrinal de Sapience' di Guy de Roy, e fors' anche l'originale in lingua francese.— 'Il Driadeo composto in rima octava per Lucio Pulci,' 'Florentiae 1479', in-4°. Altre ediz. del secolo XV, 'Florentie Miscomini 1481, in-4°, Firenze, apud S. Jacob. de Ripoli, 1483,' in-4° e 'Antoni de Francesco, 487,' in-4° e Francesco di Jacopo 1489, in-4° ed altre ancora di Venezia e senza alcuna nota ecc.* (G. d'A.)

15. *Una delle edizioni del Morgante impresse nel secolo XV, di Luigi Pulci. Quale delle opere di Francesco Petrarca, sarebbe malagevole l'indovinare, ma probabilmente il Canzoniere.* (G. d'A.)

16. *Sono i viaggi del cavaliere 'Mandeville,' gentiluomo inglese. Scrisse il suo libro in lingua francese. Fu stampato replicamente nel secolo XV in francese, in inglese ed in italiano, *ed in tedesco; del secolo XV ne*

annoverano forse più di 27 edizioni, di cui ne conosciamo otto in francese, quattro in latino, sei in tedesco e molte altre in volgare. (G. d'A.)

17. *Il Platina (Bartolomeo Sacchi) la versione italiana 'de la honesta voluptate, & valetudine (& de li obsonnii) Venezia (senza nome di tipografo) 1487,' piccolo in-4° gotico.* (G. d'A.)—Compare No. 844, 21.

18. *Il Manganello: Satira eccessivamente vivace contro le donne ad imitazione della Sesta di Giovenale. Manganello non è soltanto il titolo del libricino, ma anche il nome dell' autore ch'era un 'milanese'. Di questo libercolo rarissimo, che sembra impresso a Venezia dallo Zoppino (detto il Nicolo d'Aristotile), senza data, ma dei primissimi anni del secolo XVI, e forse più antico, come vedremo in appresso, non se ne conoscono fra biblioteche pubbliche e private che due soli esemplari in Europa.* (G. d'A.)

19. *'Cronica desidero', sembra si deggia leggere piuttosto 'cronico disidoro'; ed in questo caso s'intenderebbe la 'cronica d'Isidoro' tanto in voga a quel tempo. 'Comenza la Cronica di Sancto Isidoro menore con alchune additione cavate del testo & istorie de la Bibia & del libro di Paulo Oroso . . . . Impresso in Ascoli in casa del reverendo miser Pascale . . . . . per mano di Guglielmo de Linis de Alamania M.CCCC.LXXVII', in-4° di 157 ff. È il primo libro impresso ad Ascoli e l'edizione principe di questa cronica in oggi assai rara. Non lo è meno l'edizione di Cividal del Friuli, 1480, e quella ben anche di Aquila, 1482, sempre in-4°. Vedasi Panzer, Hain, Brunet e P. Dechamps.* (G. d'A.)

20. *'Le pistole di Ovidio tradotte in prosa. Napoli Sixt. Riessinger', in-4°, oppure: 'Epistole volgarizzate 1489', in-4° a due col. 'impresse ne la cita (sic) di Bressa per pre: Baptista de Farfengo,' (in ottavo) o: 'El libro dele Epistole di Ovidio in rima volgare per messere Dominico de Monticelli toschano. Brescia Farfengo,' in-4° got. (in rima volgare), 1491, ed anche la versione di Luca Pulci. Firenze, Mischomini, 1481, in-4°.* (G. d'A.)

21. *See l. 4.*

22. *'Jo: de Sacrobusto', o 'Goro Dati,' o 'Tolosano da Colle' di cui molteplici edizioni del secolo XV.* (G. d'A.)

23. *Tre edizioni delle facezie del Poggio abbiamo in lingua italiana della fine del secolo XV, tutte senza data. 'Facetie de Poggio fiorentino traducte de latino in vulgare ornatissimo', in-4°, segn. a–e in caratteri romani; l'altra: 'Facetie traducte de latino in vulgare', in-4°, caratteri gotici, ecc.* (G. d'A.)

²⁴De chiromãtia.
²⁵Formulario di pistole.

Chiromancy [24].
Formulary of letters [25].

S. K. M. III. 8*a*]   **1470**

[Nonio Marciello, ²Festo Pōpeo, ³Marco Varrone.]

[Nonius Marcellus, Festus Pompeius, Marcus Varro.]

F. o″]   **1471**

Piãta d'Elefante d'India che à Antonello Merciaio. Cerca di Vetruvio fra cartolaj.

Map of Elephanta in India which Antonello Merciaio has. Inquire at the stationers' about Vitruvius.

F. o′]   **1471 A**

Da maestro Mafeo, perchè 7 anni l'Adige alza e 7 abbassa.

From maestro Maffeo, why for seven years the Adige rises and for 7 it sinks.

Leic. 13*a*]   **1472**

Vedi de naui messer Battista ²e Frontino de' aquidotti.

See Messer Battista *On Ships*, and Frontinus *On Aqueducts* [2].

C. A. 385*b*]   **1473**

Anasagora; ²ogni cosa viē da ogni cosa — ed ogni cosa si fa ogni cosa, ³e ogni cosa torna in ogni cosa, perchè ciò ch' è nelli elemē'ti è fatto da essi elemēti.

Anaxagoras: Everything proceeds from everything, and everything becomes everything, and everything can be turned into everything else, because that which exists in the elements is composed of those elements.

L. 94*b*]   **1474**

Archimede del uescouo ²di Padoua.

The Archimedes belonging to the Bishop of Padua.

1470. R. 3. marcho.
1472. 1. meser batista.
1473. 1. anasaghora. 2. chosa viē. 3. chogni .. ogni chosa. 4. effatto.
1474. 1. uesscouo.

1471. dellefan\\\\ dindia chella.

24. **Die Kunst Cyromantia etc. in tedesco. 26 ff. di testo e figure il tutte esquito sù tavole di legno verso la fine del secolo XV da Giorgio Schapff.' Dibdin, Heinecken, Sotheby e Chatto ne diedero una lunga descrizione; i primi tre accompagnati da facsimili. La data 1448 che si legge alla fine del titolo si riferisce al periodo della composizione del testo, non a quello della stampa del volume benchè tabellario. Altri molti libri di Chiromanzia si conoscono di quel tempo e sarebbe opera vana il citarli tutti.* (G. d'A.)

Or rather: Chyromantica scientia naturalis, Padue per mgrm matheū Cerdonis de vuindischgrecz mgri Erhardi radolt instrumentis, 1484. Solmi, *Fonti*, p. 123.

25. *Miniatore Bartolomeo:* 'Formulario de epistole vulgare missive e responsive, & altri flori de ornati parlamenti al principe Hercule d'Este ecc. composto ecc. Bologna per Ugo di Rugerii,' *in-4°, del secolo XV. Altra edizione di* 'Venetia Bernardino di Novara, 1487' *e* 'Milano per Joanne Angelo Scinzenzeler 1500,' *in-4°.* (G. d'A.)

Five books out of this list are noted by Leonardo in another MS. (Triv. 2*a*): *donato — lapidario — plinio — abacho — morgante.*

1470. Nonius Marcellus and Sextus Pompeius Festus were Roman grammarians of about the third century A.D. Early publications of the works of Marcellus are: *De proprietate sermonis, Romae* (about 1470), and 1471 (place of publication unknown). *Compendiosa doctrina, ad filium, de proprietate sermonum,* Venice, 1476. Brunet, *Manuel du libraire* (iv, p. 97), notes: 'Le texte de cet ancien grammairien a été réimprimé plusieurs fois à la fin du XVᵉ siècle, avec ceux de Pomponius Festus et de Terentius Varro. La plus ancienne édition qui réunisse ces trois auteurs est celle de Parme, 1480.... Celles de Venise, 1483, 1490, 1498, et de Milan, 1500, toutes in-fol., ont peu de valeur.'

1471 A. *Mafeo,* probably Gerolamo Maffei, editor of Mondino de Luzzi's anatomy. See No. 1494, note.

1472. 1. Compare No. 1113, l. 25.

2. *Frontinus, De aquis urbis Romae.* There were several editions extant: Rome, 1490, Venice, 1494.

1490. Leonardo's notes on Anaxagoras are derived from Lucretius, *De rerum natura* I. 830 ff. Latin editions appeared at Verona in 1484, in Venice in 1495 and 1500.

1474. See No. 1421, ll. 3, 6, and vol. i, No. 343.

II

3 B

W. 12280*a*]   **1475**

Archimede à dato la ²☐ra d'una figura late³rata e ⁴nõ del cerchio; ¶⁵adunque Ar⁶chimede non ⁷quadrò mai figu⁸ra di lato curuo; ¶ ⁹e io quadro il cer¹⁰chio meno una portio¹¹ne tanto minima quã¹²to lo intelletto possa immaginare, cioè quanto il pũto visibile.

Archimedes gave the quadrature of a polygonal figure, but not of the circle. Hence Archimedes never squared any figure with curved sides; and I square the circle minus the smallest portion that the intellect can conceive, that is, the smallest point visible.

Br. M. 279*b*]   **1476**

Chi auesse trovato l'ultima vali²tudine della bõbarda in tutte ³sua varietà, e presẽtato tale ⁴segreto alli Romani, cõ ⁵qual prestezza avrebbero conquista⁶to ogni terra e superato ogni ese⁷rcito, e qual premio era, ⁸che potesse equipararsi a tanto ⁹benifitio! Archimenide ã¹⁰corachè lui auesse grãdemẽte dan¹¹neggiati li Romani alla spugna¹²tione di Siracusa, nõ li fu mai ¹³mãcato l'offerta di grãdissimi pre¹⁴mi da essi Romani, e nella pre¹⁵sa di Siracusa fu cercato diligẽ¹⁶temẽte d'esso Archimenide, e tro¹⁷vato morto, ne fu fatto maggiore ¹⁸lamẽtatione nel senato e ¹⁹popolo Romano, che s'egli auessi²⁰no perso tutto il loro esercito, e non ²¹mancarono d'onorarlo di sepoltu²²ra e di statua, della quale fu capo ²³Marco Marcello; e dopo la seconda ²⁴ruina di Siracusa fu ritrouato ²⁵da Catone la sepoltura d'esso Archi²⁶mede nel²⁷le ruine d'un tenpio; onde Catone fe²⁸cie rifare il tẽpio e la sepoltura ²⁹onoratissimamente . . . ³⁰e di questo si scriue ³¹auere detto Catone ³²non si gloriar di ³³nessuna cosa tan³⁴to, quanto d'auere ³⁵onorato esso Archi³⁶mede d'esso orna³⁷mẽto.

If any man could have discovered the utmost powers of the cannon, in all its various forms, and have given such a secret to the Romans, with what rapidity would they have conquered every country and have vanquished every army, and what reward could have been great enough for such a service! Archimedes indeed, although he had greatly damaged the Romans in the siege of Syracuse, nevertheless did not fail of being offered great rewards from these very Romans; and when Syracuse was taken, diligent search was made for Archimedes; and he being found dead greater lamentation was made for him by the Senate and people of Rome than if they had lost all their army; and they did not fail to honour him with burial and with a statue. At their head was Marcus Marcellus. And after the second destruction of Syracuse, the sepulchre of Archimedes was found again by Cato [25], in the ruins of a temple. So Cato had the temple restored and the sepulchre he so highly honoured. . . . Whence it is written that Cato said that he was not so proud of anything he had done as of having paid such honour to Archimedes.

I.² 130*b*]   **1477**

Aristotile 3° della fisica, e Alberto e Tomaso, ²e li altri de risaltatione, j̄ 7ᵃ della fisica, ³de cielo e mv̄do.

Aristotle, Book 3 of the Physics, and Albertus Magnus, and Thomas Aquinas and the others on the rebound of bodies, in the 7th on Physics, on heaven and earth.

M. 62*a*]   **1478**

Dice Aristotile che se vna potentia move v̄ ²¶corpo vn tanto spatio in tanto tẽpo, la me³desima potentia moverà la metà di quel ⁴corpo due tanti di spatio nel medesimo tẽpo.¶

Aristotle says that if a force can move a body a given distance in a given time, the same force will move half the same body twice as far in the same time.

1475. 1. data. 3. rato. 6. chimenide. 10. cio meno ỉ. 11. tanta. 12. inmaginare coe q"u"to.
1476. 1. auessi trovata. 4. romani [qual] cõ. 5. presteza arebõ. 7. ecqual. 8. potessi . . attanto. 10. chellui auessi grãdemẽte da. 11. negati . . allasspugna. 12. serausa. 13. lo fere li grãdissimi. 15. serausa fu cerco. 17. magore. 18. nel [po] senato. 19. romane chessegli. 20. e no. 21. mancarono. 22. distaua. 23. dopo la 2ᵃ. 24. seragosa. 26. mede e [esso catone la retro] ne. 28. ella. 29. onoratissiman\\\\\. 30. scriun\\\\\. 31. cat\\\\\. 32. sigroriar\\\\\. 33. cosa t\\\\\. 34. daue\\\\\. 35. ar\\\\\. 36. orn\\\\.
1477. 1. fisicha. 2. elli . . fisicha.   **1478.** 1. chesse. 4. dua tanti spatio.

1475. Compare No. 1504.
1476. Where Leonardo found the statement that Cato had found and restored the tomb of Archimedes, I do not know. It is a merit that Cicero claims as his own (Tusc. v. 23) and certainly with a full right to it. It is evidently a slip of the memory on Leonardo's part. Besides, according to the passage in Cicero, the grave was not found *nelle ruine d'un tempio*—which is highly improbable as relating to a Greek—but in

an open spot (H. Müller-Strübing).
Leonardo says in MS. B fol. 33*a*: *Architronito è una macchina di fino rame, invenzione d'Archimede* (see Solmi, *Fonti*, p. 64).
1477. Probably Albertus Magnus, *Commentarium in libros physicorum*, and Thomas Aquinas, *Expositio super octo libros physicorum*, or *Interpretamenta in libros de celo et mundo*. See Solmi, *Fonti*, pp. 44, 273.

C. A. 289*b*]   1479

Aristotile nel terzo dell' etica: ²l'uomo · è degnio di lode e di uituperio solo in quelle · cose · che sono ꞵ sua potestà ⁴di fare e di nō fare.

Aristotle in Book 3 of the Ethics: Man merits praise or blame solely in such matters as lie within his power to do or not to do.

C. A. 123*a*]   1480

Dicie · Aristotile · che ogni cosa desidera mātenere la sua natura.

Aristotle says that every body tends to maintain its nature.

K.² 52*b*]   1481

De incremēto ²Nili, opera d'Ari³stotile piccola.

On the increase of the Nile, a small book by Aristotle.

W. 19097*b*]   1482

Avicenna vole ²che l'anima partorisca ³l'anima, e 'l corpo il corpo, ⁴e ogni mēbro per rata.

Avicenna will have it that soul gives birth to soul as body to body, and each member in proportion.

F. o″]   1483

Avicenna de' liquidi.

Avicenna on fluids.

Br. M. 71*b*]   1484

Rugiero Bacone fatto in isstanpa.

Roger Bacon, done in print.

C. A. 141*b*]   1485

Cleomete filosofo.

Cleomedes the philosopher.

Triv. 2*b*]   1486

CORNELIO CELSO

²Il somo · bene · è la sapiēza ·; il somo male · è il dolore · del corpo; jmperochè, essēdo ³noi conposti · di 2 cose, cioè · d'anima · e di corpo, ⁴delle quali la prima · è migliore ·, la peggiore · è il corpo; la sapiētia è ⁵della miglior parte ·; il sommo male è della peggior parte e pessima; Ottima cosa è nell' animo la sapiēza, così è pessima ⁶cosa nel corpo il dolore; ⁷adūque,

CORNELIUS CELSUS

The highest good is wisdom, the chief evil is suffering in the body. Because, as we are composed of two things, that is, soul and body, of which the first is the better, the body is the inferior; wisdom belongs to the better part, and the chief evil belongs to the worse part and is the worst of all. As the best thing of all in the soul is wisdom, so the worst in the body is suf-

1479. 1. eticha. 3. i mquelle chose chessono.
1480. 2. la gravita per essere ecc.   **1481.** 3. pichola.
1483. 1. avicena.
1484. 1. Rugieri bachō.   **1485.** 1. filosafo.
1486. 2. ella sapiēza . . iperoche. 3. corp\\\ [lanima e meliore cel corpo]. 4. pegiore . . chorpo. 5. somo . . pegior. 7. somo . . choporal . . chosi.

1482. 1. aviciena. 2. chellanima partorischa.

1479. Quoted in Dante's *Convivio* (Trat. III, c. 4), which was published by Francesco Bonaccorsi at Florence in 1490.

1481. *De inundatione Nili* is quoted here and by others as a work of Aristotle. The Greek original is lost, but a Latin version of the beginning exists (Arist. Opp. iv, p. 213, ed. Did. Par.).

In his quotations from Aristotle Leonardo possibly refers to one of the following editions: *Aristotelis de philosophia naturali interprete Georgio Valla*, Venice, 1482; *Aristotelis opera Georgio Valla interprete*, Venice, 1496; *Aristotelis libri IV de coelo et mundo; de anima libri III; libri VIII physicorum; de generatione et corruptione; de sensu et sensato . . . omnia latine, interprete Averroe.* Venice, 1483. There is also a separate edition of the *Liber de coelo et mundo*, dated 1473.

1482. *Avicenna* (980–1037), Arab philosopher. There were many Latin editions of his works on philosophy and medicine extant in Leonardo's time.

The above is a reference to the treatise *De Anima*.

1483. Reference to Avicenna's study of the fluids in the body, such as the blood and the bile, in his canon of medicine.

1484. A note put down for inquiry, as it seems; because none of R. B.'s works had as yet been printed in Leonardo's lifetime.

1485. *Cleomede.* A Greek mathematician of the fourth century B.C. There is a cyclic theory of Meteorica by him. A Latin version appeared in Venice in 1498.

1486. *Aulus Cornelius Celsus,* a Roman physician, known as the Roman Hippocrates, probably contemporary with Augustus. Only his eight Books 'De Medicina', are preserved. The earliest editions are: *Cornelius Celsus, de medicina libr. VIII*, Milan, 1481; Venice, 1493 and 1497. This is one of Leonardo's numerous quotations from Valturio.

sicome il sommo male è 'l corporal dolore, così la sapiētia è dell' animo ⁸il somo bene, cioè dell'uomo sagio, e nissvna altra cosa è da cōparare a questa.

fering. Therefore just as bodily pain is the chief evil, wisdom is the chief good of the soul, that is, with the wise man; and nothing else can be compared with it.

Trív. 14b]   1487

Demetrio solea dire non essere differētia · dalle parole e voci dell' inperiti igniorāti, ²che sia da suoni e strepiti · cavsati dal ventre ripieno di superfluo vēto; ³e questo nō senza cagiō dicea, īperochè lui nō reputava esser differētia da qual parte ⁴costoro mādassino · fuora la voce, o dalle parti īferiori o dalla bocca, ⁵che l'una e l'altra era di pari valimēto e sustātia.

Demetrius was wont to say that there was no difference between the speech and words of the foolish and ignorant, and the noises and rumblings of the wind in an inflated stomach. Nor did he say so without reason, for he saw no difference between the parts whence the noise issued; whether their lower parts or their mouth, since one and the other were of equal use and importance.

S. K. M. III. 2b]   1488

[Maestro Stefano ²Caponi, medico, ³sta alla piscina, ⁴à Euclide 'de pō⁵deribus'.]

[Maestro Stefano Caponi, a physician, lives at the piscina, and has Euclid *De Ponderibus*.]

K.² 51a]   1489

5° Euclide. ²Prima definitione ¶parte è quantità di quantità ³minore della maggiore, cōciosia⁴chè la minore numeri la mag⁵giore;

⁶Parte propriamēte detta è quella ⁷ch'è moltiplicatiua, cioè che, multi⁸plicata per alcuno numero, ricōpo⁹ne il suo tutto con precisione;

¹⁰Parte comune aggregatiua è que¹¹lla, la quale, quantunche volte si pi¹²glia più o meno del suo tutto, ¹³ond' è necessario che coll' ajuto d'al¹⁴tra quantità diuersa rifaccia il suo ¹⁵tutto, e perciò è detta aggregatiua.

¹⁶Seconda definitione. ¶La multiplicità è maggiore della mi¹⁷nore, quando la minore misura qu¹⁸ella;

¹⁹Di sopra difinimmo il minore estremo, ²⁰e qui si difinisce il maggiore; La parte

5th Book of Euclid. First definition: a part is a quantity less than the greater when the less is contained in the greater.

A part properly speaking is that which may be multiplied, that is, when, being multiplied by a certain number, it forms exactly the whole. A common aggregate part is that which, however many times it is taken, makes either more or less than its whole, wherefore it is called aggregate . . .

Second definition. A greater magnitude is said to be a multiple of a less, when the greater is measured by the less.

By the first we define the lesser [magnitude] and by the second the greater is defined. A part is spoken

K.² 51b]   1490

relatiuamente è detta al tutto, ²e in questi due estremi sta tutta ³la relatione di quegli, e chiamā⁴si mvltiplici.

of in relation to the whole; and all their relations lie between these two extremes, and are called multiples.

S. K. M. III. 75a]   1491

Dice Ippocrate che la origine della ²nostra semenza diriva dal cielabro · e dal ³polmone · e testiculi di nostri gie⁴nitori ·, dove si fa l'ultima decotione; ⁵e tutti li altri mēbri porgono · per sudatio⁶ne la loro sustātia a esso seme, per⁷chè non si dimostra alcuna via, ⁸che a essa semēza peruenire possino.

Hippocrates says that the origin of men's sperm derives from the brain, and from the lungs and testicles of our parents, where the final decocture is made, and all the other limbs transmit their substance to this sperm by means of transpiration, because there are no channels through which they might come to the sperm.

8. delonsagio eñivna . . chosa e da a questa cōparare.
1487. 1. diferētia . . evoce. 2. chessia da soni e strepidi. 3. ecquesto. 3. īperochellui . . diferētia. 4. parte . . bocha. 5. chelluna ellaltra.
1488. R. 3. pesccina. 4. a heuclide.
1489. 2. pᵃ difinitione *is written on the margin*. 3. magore concosia. 4. chella. 5. gore. 6. ditta ecque. 7. che moltiplichatiua coe. 10. cumune agreghatiua cqu"e". 12. plia [ma fa] piu . . tutt"o". 13. chollaiuto. 14. rifacca. 15. pero e detto agregatiua. 16. 2ᵃ difinitione *is written on the margin*. La multipli e magore. 19. difinimo . . extremo. 20. ecqui si difinissce il maggiore.
1490. 2. quessti duextremi.
1491. R. 1. ipocrate chella. 2. nosstra senza. 3. ettestichuli di nosstri. 4. dovessi . . dechotione. 5. ettutti . . porgano. 6. susstātia. 7. dimosstra alchuna.

1487. Compare vol. i, No. 10. Quotation from Valturio, *De re militari*.
1491. There were various editions of the works of Hippocrates at the end of the fifteenth century, notably one published at Venice in 1487. Leonardo here refers to Book IV, c. 1–32, of Περὶ νούσων.

B. N. 2037. 8*b*.]　　　**1492**

Lucretio nel terzo · delle cose · naturali ‖ le mani, vnghie e dēti furono ²le armi · de li ātichi (165);

³Ācora vsano per stēdardo · di vno fasciculo d'erba · legato a vna pertica (167).

Lucretius in his third [book] *De Rerum Natura*. The hands, nails, and teeth were the weapons of ancient man (165).

They also use for a standard a bunch of grass tied to a pole (167).

Triv. 1*b*]　　　**1493**

Ammiano Marcellino afferma, essere abbruciati ²7 cēto mila volumi di libri nella pugnia Alessādrina ³al tēpo di Givlio Cesare.

Ammianus Marcellinus asserts that seven hundred thousand volumes of books were burnt during the siege of Alexandria in the time of Julius Caesar.

W. 19017*a*]　　　**1494**

Dice Mōdino che li muscoli che alza²no li diti del piede stanno nella parte ³siluestra della coscia, e poi soggiugne ⁴che 'l dosso del piede non à muscoli, ⁵perchè la natura li volle fare legieri ac⁶ciochè fussino facili al movimēto, per⁷chè se fussino carnosi, sarebbero più ⁸gravi; e qui la speriētia mostra . . . .

Mondino says that the muscles which raise the toes are in the outward side of the thigh, and he adds that there are no muscles in the back [upper side] of the feet, because nature desired to make them light, so as to move with ease; and if they had been fleshy they would be heavier; and here experience shows . . . .

G. 8*a*]　　　**1495**

Del error di quelli che voano ⁴la pratica sanza sciētia; ³vedi primo ⁴la poetica ⁵d'Oratio.

Of the error of those who practise without knowledge; [3] See first the *Ars poetica* of Horace [5].

S. K. M. III. 86*a*]　　　**1496**

¶Eredi di maestro Giovā ²Ghirīgello ànno opere del Pe³lacano.¶

The heirs of Maestro Giovanni Ghiringhello have the works of Pelacano.

1492. 1. naturale. 3. istēdare diono.
1493. 1. amiano . . abrusiati. 2. 7 cēto M"a" [di] volumi . . nela [spu] pugnia. 3. ivlio.
1494. 1. chelli musscoli. 2. piedi. 3. cosscia . . sogugne. 4. piedi . . musscoli. 5. lo volle . . legeri a. 6. coche fussi facile. 7. fussi carnoso sarebbe. 8. grave.
1495. 1–5 R. 1. eror. 4. poetria.
1496. R. 1. maesstro jovā. 2. ghirīgello ano. 3. lachano.

1492, 1493. Quotations from Valturio, *De re militari*. See No. 1469, note 4. G. Calvi, *I Manoscritti di L.d.V.*, pp. 100 ff., E. Solmi, *Fonti*, pp. 277 ff., and G. B. de Toni, *Frammenti Vinciani, III*, Padua, 1900.

1494. 'Mondino de Luzzi, Anathomia. Mundini praestantissimorum doctorum almi studii ticinensis cura diligentissime emendata. Impressa Papiae per magistrum Antonium de Carcano 1478,' in-fol.; ristampata: 'Bononiae Johan. de Noerdlingen, 1482,' in-fol.; 'Padova per Mattheum Cerdonis de Vuindischgretz, 1484,' emendata per excellentissimum artis et medicinae doctorem magistrum Hieronymum de Mafeis de Verona, in-4°; 'Lipsiae, 1493,' in-4°; 'Venezia, 1494,' in-4° e ivi '1498,' con fig. Queste figure per altro non sono, come si è preteso, le prime che fossero introdotte in un trattato di Notomia. Nel 'fasciculus Medicinae' di Giovanni Ketham, che riproduce l'"Anatomia' del Mundinus, impresso pure a Venezia da J. e G. de Gregoriis, 1491, in-fol., contengonsi intagli in legno (si vogliono disegnati non già incisi da Andrea Mantegna) di grande dimensione, e che furono più volte riprodotti negli anni successivi. Quest' edizione del 'fasciculus' del 1491, sta fra nostri libri e potrebbe benissimo essere il volume d'Anatomia notato da Leonardo. (G. d'A.)

1495. Ll. 3–5 are written on the margin at the side of the title-line of the text given entire as No. 19.

1496. Biagio Pelacani or Biagio da Parma (died 1416), teacher of logic and philosophy at Pavia, Bologna, and Padua, author of works on Aristotle, on questions of perspective, &c. Cf. Lynn Thorndyke, 'Blasius of Parma (Biagio Pelacani)', in *Archeion*, ix. 177–90 (1928). In MS. B.N. 2038, 2*b* Leonardo quotes a passage from Pelacani's *de ponderibus* on scales and weights and criticizes it. G. Roberto Marcolongo, 'La Meccanica di L. d. V.', *Atti della R. Accademia delle Scienze Fisiche e Matematiche*, Naples, 1933, pp. 24 ff.

Giovanni di Ghiringhelli was a professor at Pavia from 1443 to 1449 when Francesco Pelacani, son of Biagio, was also a teacher there. See Solmi, *Fonti*, p. 177. The name Ghiringhello is written on fol. C. A. 205.

M. 11*a*]

1496 A

Tebit.

Tobit ben Korra.

C. A. 96*b*, 219*b*]

1496 B

Erone de acque.

Heron on water.

I.² 120*a*]

1496 C

De Moto. Dicie Alberto di Sassonia nel suo di proporzione che se una potentia move un mobile in certa velocità che moverà la metà d'esso mobile in doppio veloce, la qual cosa a me non pare. . . .

Of Motion. Albert of Saxony says in his *De Proportione* that if a force moves a body at a certain velocity, it will move half that body at double the velocity, which does not seem to me to be so. . . .

B. 8*a*]

1497

Catapulta, come dice Nonio e Plinio, è vno strumēto ritrovato da quelli ecc.

The catapult, as we are told by Nonius and Pliny, is a machine devised by those, &c.

B. N. 2037. 9*b*]

1498

Ò ritrovato nele Storie delli Spagnioli · come · nelle guerre da loro ²avute colli Inglesi fu Archimede Siracusano, il quale ī quel tēpo ³dimorava ī cōpagnia di Ecliderides, rè de' Cirodastri; Il quale nella ⁴pugnia marittima ordinò ·, che i navili fussino con lunghi arbori, ⁵e sopra le lor gaggie ⁶collocò · vna · antennetta di lūghezza di 40 piè, e ⅓ ⁷piè di grossezza; nel' una stremità era vna ancora picciola, nel' al⁸tra · vn contrapeso; a l'ancora era appiccato 12 piedi ⁹di catena · e dopo essa catena tāta corda ¹⁰che perveniua dalla catena al nascimēto della gaggia ch'era attaccata con una cordella; ¹¹da esso nascimēto mādaua ī basso īsino al nascimēto dell' arbore, ¹²dou' era collocato vn argano fortissimo, e lì era fermo ¹³il nascimēto d'essa corda; Ma per tornare all' ufitio d'essa machina ¹⁴dico che sotto a detta ācora era vno foco, il quale con sommo stre¹⁵pito gittava ī basso i sua razzi e pioggia di pegola īfocata, li qua¹⁶li piovēdo sopra alla gaggia costrignievano li omini, che lì erano, a ¹⁷abbādonare detta gaggia, ōde calato l'ancora colle acut . . . . . . ¹⁸quella cauaua ai labri della gaggia; e subito era tagliata la corda posta ¹⁹al nascimēto della gaggia a sostenere quella corda ch'ādava ²⁰da l'ācora a l'argano, e tirādo il navilio . . . .

I have found in a history of the Spaniards that in their wars with the English there was Archimedes of Syracuse who at that time was living at the court of Ecliderides, King of the Cirodastri. And in maritime warfare he ordered that the ships should have tall masts, and that on their tops there should be a spar fixed [6] 40 feet long and one-third of a foot thick. At one end of this was a small grappling-iron and at the other a counterpoise; to the grappling-iron was attached 12 feet of chain; and, at the end of this chain, as much rope as would reach from the chain to the base of the top, where it was fixed with a small rope; from this base it ran down to the bottom of the mast where a very strong spar was attached, and to this was fastened the end of the rope. But to go on to the use of this machine; I say that below this grappling-iron was a fire [14] which, with tremendous noise, threw down its rays and a shower of burning pitch; which, pouring down on the [enemy's] top, compelled the men who were in it to abandon the top to which the grappling-iron had clung. . . . This was hooked on to the edges of the top, and then suddenly the cord attached at the base of the top to support the cord which went from the grappling-iron was cut, giving way and drawing in the enemy's ship. . . .

1498. 1. chome . . guere dalloro. 2. ingilesi fu darchimede. 4. cholunghi albori. 5. essopra . . gagie. 6. chollocho . . antenetta di lūgezza. 7. grosseza. 8. vcontrapeso . . era apicato. 9. e[ttà]dopo . . chorda. 10. anassimēto . . gagia. *The following words are written on the margin* chera attaca etacata cōnuna cordella. 11. nasimēto . . nassimēto delo albore. 12. vn [albore] rgano. 13. nassimēto. 14. chon somo. 15. pido . . sua raza e piogia. 16. ala gagia chostrignieva. 17. abādonare . . gagia . . chalato lancora chole achuti rāpo (?). 18. gagia essubito. 19. [assostenere] a nascimēto dela gagia . . quela chorda. 20. navilio demi (?) essi (?) poneva (?) dancora (?).

1496 A. Arab mathematician, see G. R. Marcolongo, *La Meccanica di L. d. V.*, Naples, 1933, p. 10 f.

1496 B. *Heron of Alexandria*, see Solmi, *Fonti*, p. 143, and G. R. Marcolongo, loc. cit., p. 27 f.

1496 C. *Alberto di Sassonia*, also called Albertuccio (see No. 1421). His *Tractatus proportionum* . . . was published at Venice, 1496. Its second part is entitled *Tractatus de proportione velocitatum in motibus*. Leonardo here refers to fol. 51v.

1497. *Plinius*, see No. 946. Probably quoted from

Valturio's *De re militari*.

1498. Archimedes never visited Spain. Leonardo seems to quote here from a book, perhaps by some questionable medieval writer. Professor C. Justi writes to me from Madrid that Spanish savants have no knowledge of the sources from which this story may have been derived. Compare Solmi, *Fonti*, p. 64, note.

6. Compare No. 1115.

14. Compare No. 1128.

Leic. 16*b*]   **1499**

Teofrasto, del flusso e riflusso ²e delle vortici e de' acque.

Theophrastus on the ebb and flow of the tide, and of eddies, and on water.

B. N. 2037. 8*b*]   **1500**

Trifone Alessādrino, il quale duceua sua età in Apolonia città d'Albania (163).

Tryphon of Alexandria, who spent his life at Apollonia, a city of Albania (163).

K.³ 109*b*]   **1501**

Meser Vīcentio Aliprādo, che sta ²presso al-l'osteria dell' Orso, à il Vetru³uio di Iacomo Andrea.

Messer Vincenzio Aliprando, who lives near the Inn of the Bear, has Giacomo Andrea's Vitruvius.

L. 53*b*]   **1502**

Dice Vetruvio che i modelli piccoli ²non sono in nessuna operatione confor³mi all' effetto de' grandi; la qual co⁴sa qui disotto intendo dimostra⁵re tale conclusione · essere falsa, ⁶e massimamente allegando quelli me⁷desimi termini, coi quali lui cō⁸clude tale · sententia, cioè colla ⁹sperientia · della triuella, per la quale ¹⁰lui mostra essere fatto dalla po¹¹tentia dell'omo vno buso di cier¹²ta quantità di diametro, e che poi ¹³vn buso di dupplicato diametro nō ¹⁴sarà fatto da dupplicata potentia ¹⁵di detto uomo, ma da molto piv; all¹⁶a qual cosa si può molto ben rispō¹⁷dere, allegando che il trivello

Vitruvius says that small models are of no avail for ascertaining the effects of large ones; and I here propose to prove that this conclusion is a false one. And chiefly by bringing forward the very same argument which led him to this conclusion; that is, by an experiment with an auger. For he proves that if a man, by a certain exertion of strength, makes a hole of a given diameter, and afterwards another hole of double the diameter, this cannot be made with only double the exertion of the man's strength, but needs much more. To this it may very well be answered that an auger

L. 53*a*]   **1503**

di dupplicata figura non può ²essere mosso da dupplicata po³tentia, conciosiachè la superfitie ⁴d'ogni corpo di figura simile e di dup⁵plicata quantità alla superfitie, di ⁶quadruplicata quātità l'una ⁷all' altra, come mostrano le due ⁸figure · *a* · e · *n*.

of double the diameter cannot be moved by double the exertion because the surface of a body of the same form but twice as large has four times the extent of the surfaces of the smaller, as is shown in the two figures *a* and *n*.

G. 96*a*]   **1504**

DELLA □ᵃ DEL CIRCULO, E CHI FU IL PRIMO CHE LA ²TROVÒ A CASO

³Vetruvio, misurando le miglia colle molte intere revolutioni ⁴delle rote che movono i carri, distese nelli suoi stadi molte linie ⁵circūferētiali del circolo di tali rote; Ma lui le inparò dalli

OF SQUARING THE CIRCLE, AND WHO IT WAS THAT FIRST DISCOVERED IT BY ACCIDENT

Vitruvius, measuring miles by means of the repeated revolutions of the wheels which move vehicles, extended over many stadia the lines of the circumferences of the circles of these

---

1499. teofrassto de frusso e rifrusso. 2. vertigine.
1501. 1. aliplādo. 2. uetru.
1502. 1. picho. 2. inessuna. 3. dall effecto. 4. disocto . . dimosstra. 6. que me. 8. coe. 9. essperientia . . triuella la qua. 10. mosstra. 12. diamitro. 13. diamitro. 14. potenti"a". 15. homo. 16. si po . . rsspo. 17. trivell"o".
1503. 1. dubplichata . . non po. 3. concosia chella. 4. e di du. 6. quadruplata. 7. mosstrā le due.
1504. 1. de □ᵃ del ce chi . . chella. 2. achaso. 3. cholle. 4. movano i charri . . nelle sue stadi. 5. circhūferētiali del c. di . . mallui.

1499. See Solmi, *Fonti*, No. clxxx.

1500. Quotation from Valturio, *De re militari.* See No. 1469, note 4.

1501. *Iacomo Andrea of Ferrara*, architect, beheaded by the French in 1500. See No. 1458, l. 4, and Solmi, *Fonti*, p. 174. *Aliprando*, a Milanese nobleman, secretary of Lodovico il Moro.

1502, 1503. See Solmi, *Fonti*, cxcv, Vitruvius, *De Architectura* x 16 (22). The first Italian translation of Vitruvius appeared in 1521. Leonardo may have used the editions of Giocondo Veronese of 1511, 1513.

1504. *Vitruvius. De Architectura* x 9 (14).
10. Compare No. 1475.

ani⁶mali motori di tali carri; Ma nõ conobbe quello essere il mezzo ⁷a dare il □ᵗᵒ equale a vn circolo, il quale prima per Archimede Siragusano ⁸fu trovato: che la multiplicatione del semi-diamitro d'un circolo colla ⁹metà della sua circũferẽtia facieva vn quadrilatero rettilinio, ¹⁰equale al circolo.

wheels. He became aware of them by the animals that moved the vehicles. But he did not discern that this was a means of finding a square equal to a circle. This was first done by Archimedes of Syracuse, who by multiplying the semi-diameter of a circle by half its circumference produced a rectangular quadrilateral equal to the circle [10].

B. N. 2037. 7b]   **1505**

Virgilio dicie era lo scudo biãco e sanza laude, perchè apresso ²a li Attici le uere laude cõfermate da testimoni erano ma³teria alle pitture delli scudi ed era quale d'osso di cervi ⁴collegato e interversato e permodificato con . . . .

Virgil says that a blank shield is devoid of merit because among the people of Athens the true recognitions confirmed by testimonies were subjects for decoration of shields; they were of stag's horn inlaid and enriched with . . . .

B. 58 a]   **1506**

J̄ Vjtolone sono 805 · conclusioni in prospettiva.

In Vitolone there are 805 conclusions [problems] in perspective.

Br. M. 79b]   **1507**

Vitolone in Sã Marco.

Vitolone, at Saint Mark's.

K.² 61b]   **1508**

Come Xenofonte pro²pose il falso. ³Se a cose disequali si leuano cose ⁴disequali, le quali sieno nella mede⁵sima proportione ecc.

How this proposition of Xenophon is false. If you take away unequal quantities from unequal quantities, but in the same proportion, &c.

B. 4a]   **1509**

Inventories and accounts (1509–45)

A dì 28 d'aprile ebbi da Marchesino · lire 103 e S. 12.

On the 28th day of April I received from the Marchesino 103 lire and 12 soldi.

6. charri . . chonobbe . . mezo. 7. a vn c il quale p"a" per . . siraghusano. 8. chella . . dun c. cholla. 9. circhũferẽtia. 10. al c.
1505. 1. sanza lalde. 2. atici . . lalde chõfermate. 4. colegati ẽtraversati e per molificatiõ cõgiv̄te (?).
1506. uitolone he 805 chonclusioni in prosspettiva.   **1507.** marcho.
1508. 1. zenofonti. 3. si leua. 4. qual sieno. 6. sima pro"ne".   **1509.** addi.

1505. Verg. *Aen. ix*, v. 548. Quotation from Valturio. On the same page are notes on Plinius, Trojan arms, &c. from the same source, bearing the reference number 184. See No. 1492, note.

1506. This note was written at Pavia; comp. No. 1448, l. 26. For Witelo see C. Bäumker, *Witelo, ein Philosoph und Naturforscher des XIII. Jahrhunderts*, Beiträge zur Geschichte der Philosophie des Mittelalters, Münster, 1908. (*Witelo, Vitellion, Vitellon*), *Vitellione. È da vedersi su questo ottico prospettico del secolo XIII Luca Pacioli, Paolo Lomazzo, Leonardo da Vinci, ecc. e fra i moderni il Graesse, il Libri, il Brunet, e le Memorie pubblicate dal principe Boncompagni, e 'Sur l'orthographe du nom et sur la patrie de Witelo (Vitellion), note de Maximilien Curtze, professeur à Thorn', ove sono descritti i molti codici esistenti nelle biblioteche d'Europa. Bernardino Baldi nelle sue 'Vite de' matematici', manoscritto presso il principe Boncompagni, ha una biografia del Vitellione. Questo scritto del Baldi reca la data 25 agosto 1588. Discorsero poi di lui Federigo Risnerio e Giovanni di Monteregio nella prefazione dell' Alfagrano, Giovanni Boteone, Girolamo Cardano, 'De subtilitate', che nota gli errori di Vitellione. Visse, secondo il Baldi, intorno all' anno 1269, ma secondo il Reinoldo fioriva nel 1299, avendo dedicata la sua opera ad un frate Guglielmo di Monteca, che visse di que' tempi.*

Intorno ad un manoscritto dell' ottica di Vitellione, citato da Luca Pacioli v'ha un secondo esemplare del Kurtz, con aggiunte del principe Boncompagni, e le illustrazioni del cav. Enrico Narducci. Nel 'Catalogo di manoscritti' posseduti da D. Baldassare de' principi Boncompagni, compilato da esso Narducci, Roma, 1862, sotto al n. 358, troviamo citato: Vitellio, 'Perspectiva', manoscritto del secolo XIV. La 'Prospettiva di Vitelleone' (sic) Thuringo-poloni è citata due volte da Paolo Lomazzo nel 'Trattato dell' arte della pittura'. Vitellio o Vitello o Witelo. Il suo libro fu impresso in foglio a Norimberga nel 1535; la seconda edizione è del 1551, sempre di Norimberga, ed una terza di Basilea, 1572. (See Indagini Storiche . . . sulla Libreria Visconteo-Sforzesca del Castello di Pavia . . . per cura di G. d'A., Milano, 1879, P.I., Appendice, pp. 113, 114).

1507. *Altro codice di cotesta 'Prospettiva' del Vitolone troviamo notato nel 'Canone bibliographico di Nicolò V', conservato alla Magliabecchiana, in copia dell' originale verosimilmente inviato dal Parentucelli a Cosimo de' Medici (Magliab. cod. segn. 1 VII, 30 carte da 193 a 198). Proviene dal Convento di San Marco e lo aveva trascritto frate Leonardo Scruberti fiorentino, dell' ordine dei predicatori che fu anche bibliotecario della Medicea pubblica in San Marco. (See Indagini Storiche . . . per cura di G. d'A., P. I, p. 97.)*

1508. This Xenophon is probably a mathematician of the University of Padua; see Solmi, *Fonti*, cxcviii, and C.A. 145b, 196a, 201b.

1509. Marchesino Stanga was one of Lodovico il Moro's officials. Compare No. 1388.

B. N. 2038. 34b]　　　　　**1510**

A dì 10 di luglio 1492 ī fiorī di rē 135	l. 445
²ī dinari di 6 S	l. 112 S. 16
³ī dinari di · S 5 e ½	l. 201 S. 13
⁴ī dinari 9 d'oro e scudi 3	l. 53
⁵	l. 811 ī somma.

On the 10th day of July 1492

in 135 Rhenish florins		l. 445
in dinari of 6 soldi		l. 112 S 16
in dinari of 5½ soldi		l. 201 S 13
9 in gold	and 3 scudi	l. 53
		l. 811 in all.

S. K. M. III. 45b]　　　　　**1511**

A dì · primo · di febraio · lire 1200.

On the first day of February, lire 1,200.

S. K. M. III. 49b]　　　　　**1512**

128 passi è la sala ²di corte, larga braccia 27.

The hall towards the court is 128 paces long and 27 braccia wide.

H.³ 125a]　　　　　**1513**

La gronda stretta sopra la sala ²lire 30;
³le grōde sotto · a di questa · stimo, ciascuno ⁴quadro per sé, lire · 7, e di spesa tra azzurro, ⁵oro, biacca ·, giesso, indaco e colla · lire 3; ⁶di tēpo giornate · 3;
⁷le storie sotto a esse grōde coi suoi ⁸pilastri lire 12 per ciascuna;
⁹stimo la spesa fra smalto, azzurro e oro, ¹⁰e altri colori · lire una e ½;
¹¹le giornate stimo 3 · tralla investigatione ¹²del cōponimēto, pilastrello e altre cose.

The narrow moulding above the hall, lire 30.
The mouldings beneath that, I estimate one for each picture, lire 7, and for the cost of blue, gold, white, plaster, indigo, and glue, 3 lire; time, 3 days.
The pictures below these mouldings with their pilasters, 12 lire each.
I calculate the cost for smalt, blue and gold and other colours, at 1½ lire.
The days I calculate at 3, for the invention of the composition, pilasters, and other things.

H.³ 124b]　　　　　**1514**

Itē per ciascuna voltaiola ·	lire 7
²di spesa tra azzurro e oro ·	lire · 3½
³di · tēpo · giorni 4.	
⁴per le finestre	lire 1ªe½
⁵il cornicione sotto alle finestre	S. 6 il braccio
⁶item per 24 storie romane	lire 14 l'una
⁷i filosofi	lire 10
⁸i pilastri, vn' ōcia d'azzurro	soldi 10
⁹in oro	soldi 15
¹⁰stimo lire	2 e ½.

Item for each small vault	7 lire
outlay for blue and gold	3½
time, 4 days	
for the windows	1½
the cornice below the windows	6 soldi per braccio
item for 24 pictures of Roman history	14 lire each
the philosophers	10 lire
the pilasters, one ounce of blue	10 soldi
for gold	15 soldi
Total estimate	2½ lire.

H.³ 129b]　　　　　**1515**

Grōda di sopra	lire 30
²grōda di sotto	lire 7
³le storie l'una per l'altra	lire 13.

The moulding above	lire 30
The moulding below	lire 7
The compositions, one with another	lire 13

H.³ 142b]　　　　　**1516**

Salai lire 6 . . . ³soldi 4 . . . ⁶soldi 10 in ⁷vna ca⁸tena;
⁹14 di marzo ò avuto lire 13 ¹⁰S 4, resta lire 16.

Salai, 6 lire . . . 4 soldi . . . 10 soldi for a chain;
On the 14th of March I had 13 lire S. 4; 16 lire remain.

1510. 2. dinar. 4. ī di 9 doroesscudi. 5. soma.
1512. R. 1. ella. 2. larga br 27.
1513. 1. strecta. 3. socto a di quessta. 4. azurro. 5. oro br biache . . indacho echolla. 7. grōda chosua. 8. pilastre . . ciasschuna. 9. azuro e a oro. lire ī e ½. 11. invesstichatiō.
1514. 1. chiasschuna. 2. azuro. 5. cornicone . . il br. 6. ite. 7. i filosafi. 8. ipila vnōcia dazuro. 10. simolire.
1515. 3. perllaltra.
1516. 1–10 R. 1. 6 in vna. 2. rev (?). 3. soldi 4 nv. 4. varco eli. 5. zoni. 7. nona.

H.² 64b]   1517

Quãte braccia è alto il piã delle mvra?   How many braccia high is the level of the
                                           walls?
²123 braccia   123 braccia.
³Quãt' è larga la sala?   How large is the hall?
⁴Quãt' è larga la ghirlanda?   How large is the garland?
⁵30 ducati.   30 ducats.
⁶A dì 29 di gienaro 1494   On the 29th day of January, 1494
⁷Panno per calze   lire 4 S 3   cloth for hose   lire 4 S 3
⁸soppaño   S 16   lining   S 16
⁹fattura   S 8   making   S 8
¹⁰Salai   S 8   to Salai   S 8
¹¹anello di diaspro   S 13   a jasper ring   S 13
¹²pietra stellata   S 11   a sparkling stone   S 11
¹³Caterina   S 10   to Caterina   S 10
¹⁴Caterina   S 10   to Caterina   S 10

H.² 81a]   1518

La rota   lire 7   The wheel   lire 7
²labro   li 10   the tire   lire 10
³scudo   li 4   the shield   lire 4
⁴carello   li 8   the cushion   lire 8
⁵poli de l'albero   li 2   the ends of the axle-tree lire 2
⁶letto e telajo   li 30   bed and frame   lire 30
⁷canale   li 10   conduit   lire 10

S. K. M. II.¹ 60b]   1519

Petrosemolo   parti 10   Parsley   10 parts
²mẽta   parte 1   mint   1 part
³serpillo   parte 1   thyme   1 part
⁴aceto . . . . e sale poco;   Vinegar . . . and a little salt; two pieces of
⁵canavaccio 2 pezzi per Salai.   canvas for Salai.

S. K. M. II.² 159a]   1520

Martedì si cõprò il uino da mattina, ²venerdì   On Tuesday I bought wine for morning
a dì 4 di settẽbre il simile.   [drinking]; on Friday the 4th day of September
                                           the same.

S. K. M. II.² 65a]   1521

Piscina da Mozania all' ospedale di Brolio à   Piscin of Mozania at the hospital of Brolio
molte vene per le braccia e gambe — ²ducati   has many veins on his arms and legs— 2 ducats
2 — ³fave — ⁴melica biãca — ⁵melica rossa —   — beans — white maize — red maize —
⁶panico — ⁷miglio — ⁸fagiuoli — ⁹fave —   millet — buckwheat — kidney beans — beans
¹⁰pisegli.   — peas.

1517. 1. br e. 2. R. — 123 br. 4. girlando. 5–14 R. — 6. addi. 7. chalze. 11. di diasspis.
1518. 1–7 R. 6. ettelaro.
1519. 1. petrose milo parte. 3. srpilo pa. 4. aceto peneo essale. 5. canovacci 2 prsi.
1521. 1. piscin damozania allospedadi. 4. meliga. 5. meliga. 8. fagioli.

1520. This note enables us to fix the date of the   do not permit us to assign it to a much earlier or
MS. in which it is to be found. In 1495 the 4th of   later date (compare No. 1522, and note).
September fell on a Friday; the contents of the MS.

S. K. M. II. ²64b]   1522

<table>
<tr><td colspan="2">SPESE PER LA SOTTERATURA DI CATERINA</td><td colspan="2">FUNERAL EXPENSES OF CATERINA</td></tr>
<tr><td>²Libbre 3 di cera</td><td>S 27</td><td>For the 3 lb. of tapers</td><td>27 S</td></tr>
<tr><td>³per lo cataletto</td><td>S 8</td><td>For the bier</td><td>8 S</td></tr>
<tr><td>⁴palio sopra il cataletto</td><td>S 12</td><td>A pall over the bier</td><td>12 S</td></tr>
<tr><td>⁵portatura · e postura di croce</td><td>S 4</td><td>For bearing and placing the cross</td><td>4 S</td></tr>
<tr><td>⁶per la portatura · del morto</td><td>S 8</td><td>For bearing the body</td><td>8 S</td></tr>
<tr><td>⁷per 4 preti e 4 cherici</td><td>S 20</td><td>For 4 priests and 4 clerks</td><td>20 S</td></tr>
<tr><td>⁸canpana ·, libri, spūga</td><td>S 2</td><td>Bell, book, and sponge</td><td>2 S</td></tr>
<tr><td>⁹per li sotteratori</td><td>S 16</td><td>For the gravediggers</td><td>16 S</td></tr>
<tr><td>¹⁰all' ātiano</td><td>S 8</td><td>To the senior</td><td>8 S</td></tr>
<tr><td>¹¹per la liciētia · a li ufitiali</td><td>S 1</td><td>For a licence from the authorities</td><td>1 S</td></tr>
<tr><td></td><td>106</td><td></td><td>106 S</td></tr>
<tr><td>¹²il medico</td><td>S 5</td><td>The doctor</td><td>5 S</td></tr>
<tr><td>¹³zucchero e cādele</td><td>S 12</td><td>Sugar and candles</td><td>12 S</td></tr>
<tr><td></td><td>123</td><td></td><td>123 S</td></tr>
</table>

L. 94a]   1523

La cappa di Salai a dì 4 d'aprile 1497		Salai's cloak, the 4th of April 1497	
²4 braccia di panno argiētino	l. 15 S 4	4 braccia of silver cloth	l. 15 S 4
³velluto verde per ornare	l. 9 S	green velvet to trim it	l. 9 S —
⁴bindelli	l. S 9	binding	l. — S 9
⁵magliette	l. S 12	loops	l. — S 12
⁶manifattura	l. 1 S 5	the making	l. 1 S 5
⁷bindello · per dināzi	li · S 5	binding for the front	l. — S 5
⁸pūta		stitching	
⁹ecco di suo grossoni · 13	li 26 S 5	here are 13 grossoni of his	l. 26 S 5
¹⁰Salai ruba li soldi.		Salai steals the soldi.	

I.² 49b]   1524

Lunedì cōprai braccia 4 di tela, lire 13 S 14 ²e ½, a dì 17 di ottobre 1497.

On Monday I bought 4 braccia of cloth, lire 13 S 14½, on the 17th of October 1497.

Br. M. 229b]   1525

Ricordo come a dì 8 d'aprile 1503 io Leonardo da Vinci prestai a Vāte mi²niatore ducati 4 d'oro in oro; portògli Salai e li dette in sua propia ³mano; disse rendermeli infra lo spatio di 40 giorni;

Memorandum. That on the 8th day of April 1503, I, Leonardo da Vinci, lent to Vante, miniature-painter, 4 gold ducats, in gold. Salai carried them to him and gave them into his own hand, and he said he would repay them to me within the space of 40 days.

⁴Ricordo come nel sopradetto giorno io rēdei a Salai ducati 3 d'oro, i quali ⁵disse volersene fare vn paio di calze rosate co' sua fornimēti, e li restai a dare ⁶ducati 9 ·, posto che lui ne de' dare a me ducati 20, cioè 17 prestati a Milano e 3 a Venezia;

Memorandum. That on the same day I paid to Salai 3 gold ducats which he said he wanted for a pair of rose-coloured hose with their trimming; and there remain 9 ducats due to him —excepting that he owes me 20 ducats, that is, 17 I lent him at Milan, and 3 at Venice.

⁷Ricordo come io diedi a Salai braccia 21 di tela da fare camicie, a S. 10 il braccio, ⁸la quale li diedi a dì 20 d'aprile 1503.

Memorandum. That I gave Salai 21 braccia of cloth to make shirts, at 10 soldi the braccio which I gave him on the 20th day of April 1503.

1522. 1. socteratura. 2. In libr. 3. 3. catalecto. 4. sopra catalecto. 7. cerici. 8. libr. 9. socteratori. 10. allāziano. 12. in medico. 13. zuchero.
1523. 2. 4 br di. 9. ecci di suo. 10. P.   **1524.** 1. br 4.
1525. 1. chome. 2. innoro .. elli detti. 3. losspatio .. gorni. 4. assalai. 5. elliresstai addare. 6. duchati 9 posso chellui .. amme .. coe 1 [6] 7 prestati .. e [4] 3 a vinegia. 7. assalai br 21 .. daffare camice a S 10 il bracco. 8. la queli .. addi.

1522. See Nos. 1384 and 1517.
1525. For Vante or Attavante, the miniature-painter, see Vasari, iii. 231–5. He, like Leonardo, was one of the committee of artists who, in 1503, considered the erection and placing of Michelangelo's David. He was of the same age as Leonardo.

C. A. 71*b*]   1526

La mattina di Sc̄o Pietro a dì 29 di giugno
1504 ²tolsi ducati 10, de' quali ne diedi uno a
Tomaso, mio ³famiglio, per spēdere;
    ⁴lunedì mattina fiorino uno a Salai per spen-
    dere in casa,
    ⁵martedì tolsi soldo uno per mio spendere,

    ⁶mercoledì sera fiorino uno a Tomaso, inãti
    cena,
    ⁷sabato mattina soldo uno a Tomaso,
    ⁸lunedì mattina fiorino uno mãco S 10,
    ⁹giouedì a Salai soldo uno mãco S 10,
    ¹⁰pel giubone fiorino uno,
    ¹¹pel giubbone ⎫
    ¹²e per berretta ⎭ fr. 2,
    ¹³al calzaiolo fr. 1°,
    ¹⁴a Salai fr. 1°;
    ¹⁵Venerdì mattina a dì 19 di luglio fiorino uno
    mãco S 6, restò mi fr. 7 e 22 in cassa;
    ¹⁶martedì a dì 23 di luglio fiorino uno a
    Tomaso,
    ¹⁷lunedì mattina a Tomaso fiorino uno,
    ¹⁸[mercoledì mattina fiorino uno a Tomaso]
    ¹⁹giouedì mattina a dì p° d'agosto fiorino uno
    a Tomaso,
    ²⁰domenica 4 d'agosto fiorino uno;
    ²¹venerdì a dì 9 d'agosto 1504 ²²tolgo ducati
    10 della cassa.

On the morning of San Peter's day, June 29th,
1504, I took 10 ducats, of which I gave one to
Tommaso my servant to spend.
    On Monday morning 1 florin to Salai to
    spend on the house.
    On Tuesday I took 1 soldo for my own
    spending.
    Wednesday evening 1 florin to Tommaso,
    before supper.
    Saturday morning 1 soldo to Tommaso.
    Monday morning 1 florin less 10 soldi.
    Thursday to Salai 1 soldo less 10 soldi.
    For a jerkin, 1 florin.
    For a jerkin ⎫
    And a cap ⎭ 2 florins.
    To the hosier, 1 florin.
    To Salai, 1 florin.
    Friday morning, the 19th of July, 1 florin, less
    6 soldi. I have 7 fl. left, and 22 in the box.
    Tuesday, the 23rd day of July, 1 florin to
    Tommaso.
    Monday morning, to Tommaso 1 florin.
    [Wednesday morning 1 fl. to Tommaso.]
    Thursday morning the 1st day of August 1 fl.
    to Tommaso.
    Sunday, the 4th of August, 1 florin.
    Friday, the 9th day of August 1504, I took 10
    ducats out of the box.

Br. M. 271*b*]   1527

1504

    ²Venerdì a dì 9 d'agosto 1504 tolsi fiorini 10
d'oro ³Hanne dato venerdì a dì 9 d'agosto
grossoni quindici cioè fr. 5 S 5 ⁴Hanne dato a
me fr. 1° d'oro a dì 12 d'agosto, ⁵Hanne dato
a dì 14 d'agosto grossoni 3 a Tomaso, ⁶e a
dì 18 del detto grossoni 5 Salai, ⁷a dì 8 di
settēbre grossoni 6 al fattore ⁸per spendere cioè
il dì della donna; ⁹a dì 16 di settembre dette
grossō 4 ¹⁰a Tomaso in domenica.

1504

    On the 9th day of August, 1504, I took 10
florins in gold [2] ... [3] on Friday the 9th day
of August fifteen grossoni, that is, fl. 5 S 5 ...
given to me 1 florin in gold on the 12th day of
August [4] ... on the 14th of August, 3 grossoni
to Tommaso. On the 18th of the same 5 grossoni
to Salai. On the 8th of September 6 grossoni to
the manager to spend; that is, on the Nativity
of Our Lady. On the 16th day of September I
gave 4 grossoni to Tommaso: on a Sunday.

F.o″]   1528

    A dì d'ottobre 1508 ebbi scudi 30; ²13 ne
prestai a Salai per cōpiere la dota alla ³sorella,
e 17 ne restò a me.

    On the day of October, 1508, I had 30 scudi;
13 I lent to Salai to make up his sister's dowry,
and 17 I have left.

1526. 1–22. *Written from left to right.* 1. piero addi . . gugno. 2. ĩ attomaso. 3. isspēdere. 4. fr ĩ assalai . . isspendere in chasa. 5. s ĩ.
6. mercoledi. 6. fr ĩ attomaso . . cene. 7. s ĩ attomaso. 8. fr ĩ mãcho. 9. gouedi assalai s ĩ mãcho. 30. gubone fr ĩ. 11.
gubone. 14. assalai. 15. vene "rdi" [sabato] mattina "a di 19 di luglo" fr 1° mãcho. 16. luglo fr 1° attomaso. 17. attomaso fr
1°. 18. [mercoledi mattin fr 1° attomaso]. 19. govedi "mattina" addi . . fr 1° attomaso. 20. domenicha . . fr 1°. 21. addi
22. tolgho.
1527. *Written from left to right.* 3. anne dato [addi] venerdi . . coe. 4. anne dato ame fr ĩ doro addi 12 d'agossto. 5. an\\\\\ to addi . .
3 (?) atto maso. 6. addi . . assalai. 8. ispēdere coe. 9. addi. 10. attomaso indomenicha.
1528. 2. assalai. 3. amme.

    1527. In the original, the passage given as No. 1463
is written between ll. 2 and 3 of this text, and it is
possible that the entries in ll. 3 and 4 refer to the

payments of Jacopo Tedesco, who is there mentioned.
The first words of these lines are illegible.

C. A. 192a]   1529

Ricordo de' danari che io ho avuto dal rè per mia prouisione dal luglio 1508 insino ²aprile prossimo 1509: prima scudi 100 ·, poi 100, poi 70, e poi 50, e poi ³20, e poi 200 franchi a 48 S per l'uno.

Memorandum of the money I have had from the King as my salary from July 1508 till April next 1509. First 100 scudi, then 100, then 70, then 50, then 20, and then 200 francs at 48 soldi one franc.

C. A. 77a]   1530

Sabato a dì 5 di marzo ²ebbi da Scā Maria Nova ³ducati 50 d'oro, restò ⁴ve ne 450, de' quali 5 ne ⁵detti il medesimo dì a Salai, ⁶che me li avea prestati.

Saturday the 5th day of March I had from Santa Maria Nuova 50 gold ducats, leaving 450. Of these I gave 5 the same day to Salai, who had lent them to me.

Trn. Mz 18].   1530 A

Martedì sera addì 14 Aprile venne Lorenzo a stare con meco, disse essere d'età d'anni 17. E addì 15 del detto Aprile ebbi fiorini 25 d'oro dal camarlingo di San Maria Nova.

On Tuesday evening the 14th day of April Lorenzo came to stay with me; he said that he was 17 years of age. And on the 15th day of the said April I received 25 gold florins from the chancellor of Santa Maria Nuova.

C. A. 257b]   1531

¶ Giovedì, a dì 8 di givgnio ²tolsi grossoni 17 S 18; ¶ ³giovedì detto da mattina a Salai ⁴per spendere S 22.

Thursday, the eighth day of June, I took 17 grossoni 18 soldi; on the same Thursday in the morning I gave to Salai 22 soldi for the expenses.

W. 12352]   1532

A Salai grossoni 4, e 1 braccio ²di velluto 5 lire e ½, ³sapere S · 10, maglie d'argiēto; ⁴Salai S 14 per bindelli, ⁵fattura della cappa S 25.

To Salai 4 grossoni, and for one braccio of velvet, 5½ lire; viz. 10 soldi for loops of silver; Salai 14 soldi for binding, the making of the cloak 25 soldi.

C. A. 18b]   1533

¶ Detti a Salai lire ²93 · S 6; ³ò ne avuti lire 67, ⁴resta dare lire 26 · S 6. ¶

I gave to Salai 93 lire 6 soldi, of which I have had 67 lire, and there remain 26 lire 6 soldi.

C. A. 319b]   1534

A Salai	S 42	To Salai	S 42
²dozzine 2 di stringe	S 8	2 dozen of laces	S 8
³in fogli	S 3 d. 8	for papers	S 3 d. 8
⁴vn pajo di scarpe	S 14	a pair of shoes	S 14
⁵in veluto	S 14	for velvet	S 14
⁶spada e coltello	S 21	a sword and knife	S 21
⁷in barbiere	S 11	to the barber	S 11
⁸a Paolo per una . . .	S 20	to Paolo for a . . .	S 20
⁹per dire la uentura	S 6	for having his fortune told	S 6

1529. 1. Richordo de dinari . . da dal luglo.
1531. 1. giove. 3. assalai. 4. perispēdere.
1532. 1. assalai . . 4 e e 1 br. 2. velluto br 5 lire he ½. 3. sapr.
1533. 1. assalai. 3. one auti.
1534. 1. assalai. 2. dozine o . . string. 4. pa disscarpe 8 apagolo pr ī croetta.

1530. 5. assalai.

1529. Compare Nos. 1350 and 1561A.
1530. See *Conto corrente di L. d. V. con lo Spedale di S. Maria Nuova* [1500–7, 1513–20], published by G. Uzielli, *Ricerche intorno a L. d. V.*, Florence, 1872, pp. 164, 165, 218, and 219. The date here given by Leonardo does not occur in either of the accounts.

1530 A. For Lorenzo compare Nando de' Toni, *Fram. Vinc.*, p. 91, and (our) No. 1465. For S. Maria Nova, idem, p. 95, and the foregoing No. 1530, with footnote.
1532. Compare No. 1523.

1535

Br. M. 272b]

Venerdì mattina	in pane	S . . d		On Friday morning,	bread	S . . d
²fiorino uno a Salai	in uino	S . . d		one florin to Salai to	wine	S . . d
per spē³dere; avea	in oua	S . . d		spend; he had 3 soldi	grapes	S . . d
S 3	⁴in funghi	S . . d			mushrooms	S . . d
	⁵in frutta	S . . d			fruit	S . . d
	⁶in crusca	S . . d			[6] bran	S . . d
	⁷in barbiere	S . . d			at the barber's	S . . d
	⁸in scarpe	S . . d			for shoes	S . . d

1536

C. A. 118a]

Giovedì mattina fiorino uno.

On Thursday morning one florin.

1537

C. A. 215b]

¶Dì di Scō Ambrosio S 36 da mattina in giovedì.¶

On Saint Ambrose's day from the morning to Thursday 36 soldi.

1538

C. A. 262a]

I danari ch' io ò avuto da Ser Matteo: ²prima grossoni 20, poi in 3 volte 3 f., e di poi grossoni 61, ³e poi 3, di poi · 3 · 3.

The money I have had from Ser Matteo; first 20 grossoni, then on 3 occasions 3 f. and then 61 grossoni, then 3, and then 3 · 3.

1539

E. 0″]

Ĩ carta	S	18	For paper	S	18
²ĩ tela	S	36	for canvas	S	36
³ĩ carta	S 10 di 19		for paper	S 10 of 19	
⁴somma	73		Total	S	73

1540

Br. M. 227a]

Libbre · 20 · d'azzurro di Magnia, vn ducato la libbra	l. 80 S	d		20 pounds of German blue, at one ducat the pound	lire 80 S	d
²libbre · 60 di biacca S 60 la libbra	lire 15 S	d		60 pounds of white, S 60 the pound	lire 15 S	d
³libbre 1½ S. 4 la libbra	lire 06 S	d		1½ pound at 4 S the pound	lire 6 S	d
⁴cinabro libbre 2, S 18 la libbra	lire 01 S 16 d			2 pounds of cinnabar at S 18 the pound	lire 1 S 16 d	
⁵verde libbre 6, S 12 la libbra	lire 03 S 12 d			6 pounds of green at S 12 the pound	lire 3 S 12 d	
⁶giallo libbre 4, a S 12 la libbra	lire 02 S 08 d			4 pounds of yellow at S 12 the pound	lire 2 S 8 d	
⁷minio libbra una, a S 8 la libbra	lire 00 S 08 d			1 pound of minium at S 8 the pound	lire 0 S 8 d	
⁸aiorica libbre 4, S 2 la libbra	lire 00 S 08 d			4 pounds of . . . at S 2 the pound	lire 0 S 8 d	
⁹oguria libbre sei, a S uno la libbra	lire 00 S 06 d			6 pounds of ochre at S 1 the pound	lire 0 S 6 d	
¹⁰nero in pietra S 2 la libbra per 20	lire 02 S 00 d			black . . . at S 2 the pound for 20	lire 2 S 0 d	
¹¹ciera per fare le stelle libbre 25 a S la libbra	lire S	d		wax to make the stars 25 pounds at S—the pound	lire 0 S 0 d	
¹²olio per dipingere libbre 40 a soldi 5 la libbra	lire 10 S	d		40 pounds of oil for painting at 5 soldi the pound	lire 10 S 0 d	
¹³in somma lire 120: S 18 sanza l'oro	18			Altogether lire 120 S 18 without the gold	18	
¹⁴stagnio per appiccare l'oro	120 18			tin for putting on the gold	120 18	
	58				58	

1535. *Written from left to right.* 2. fr. ĩ assalai perispē. 3. auta — innova. 5. frutte. 6. crussca. 8 .iniscarpe.
1536. 1. govedi . . fr ĩ.   1537. abrosio.
1538. 1. chio auuto.
1540. *Written from left to right.* 1. libra, libre *throughout for* libbra; libbre dazurro. 2. biaccha. 4. libr "2" 22 "4". 7. libre ĩ a. 8. aioricha. 9. oquria libr sei a ĩ la. 12. dipigniere libre 4 0 [per] soldi. 13. insoma. 14. apichare.

1535. 6. Compare Nos. 1545, ll. 4 and 5, with similar entries for horse's fodder.

Br. M. 42b] **1541**

Due scuri grandi e vna piccina, 8 cucchiai d'ottone; [2]4 touaglie, 2 guardanappe, 14 tovagliolini, 2 tovagliole, canava 2, [3]2 invoglie, 3 paia di lenzuola, 2 paie nove e uno vechio.

Two large hatchets and one very small one, 8 brass spoons, 4 tablecloths, 2 towels, 14 small napkins, 2 coarse napkins, 2 coarse cloths, 2 wrappers, 3 pairs of sheets, 2 pairs new and 1 old.

Br. M. 212a] **1542**

	45			45
Letto	70 S.		Bed	70 S.
[2]anello	70		ring	70
[3]stovigli	25		crockery	25
[4]ortolano	12		gardener	12
[5]mainardo	28		. . . . .	28
[6]fachini	21		porters	21
[7]bichieri	10		glasses	10
[8]in ferri da foco	36		fuel	36
[9]in serratura	10		a lock	10
	327			327
	£.16, s.7			£.16, s.7

H.[3] 137b] **1543**

Peltro novo,	3 · paji di lēzuola	New tin-ware,	3 pairs of sheets,
[26]· scodellini,	di 4 teli l'uno,	6 small bowls,	each of 4 breadths,
[36] scodelle	2 lenzoli piccoli	6 bowls,	2 small sheets,
[42] piattegli grandi	2 tovaglie e ½	2 large dishes,	2 tablecloths and ½,
[52] piattegli mezzani,	16 mātili	2 dishes medium size,	16 coarse cloths,
[62] piatteletti,	8 camicie	2 small ones,	8 shirts,
[7]peltro vechio	9 pannetti	Old tin-ware,	9 napkins,
[8]3 scodellini	2 sciugatoj	3 small bowls,	2 hand-towels,
[9]4 scodelle	1 bacino	4 bowls,	1 basin,
[10]3 quadretti		3 square stones,	
[11]2 scodellini		2 small bowls,	
[12]uno scodellone		1 large bowl,	
[13]uno piatello		1 platter,	
[14]4 cādellieri		4 candlesticks,	
[15]1 candelliere piccolo		1 small candlestick.	

C. A. 134a] **1544**

Calze	S 40		Hose	S 40
[2]paglia	S 60		straw	S 60
[3]biada	S 42		wheat	S 42
[4]vino	S 54		wine	S 54
[5]pane	S 18		bread	S 18
[6]carne	S 54		meat	S 54
[7]uova	S 5		eggs	S 5
[8]salata	S 3		salad	S 3
[9]barbiere	S 2 d 6		the barber	S 2 d 6
[10]cavalli	S 1		horses	S 1

C. A. 27a] **1545**

Domenica			Sunday	
[2]carne	S 10 d		meat	S 10 d
[3]vino	S 12 d		wine	S 12 d
[4]crusca	S 5 d 4		bran	S 5 d 4
[5]erba	S 10 d		herbs	S 10 d
[6]ricotta	S 4 d 4		buttermilk	S 4 d 4
[7]melarance	S 3 d		oranges	S 3 d
[8]pane	S 3 d		bread	S 3 d 1

1541. 1. scure grande . . chuchiai. 2. tovagli . . guardanape 14 "15" tovaglolini 2 tovaglole. 3. nove e l vechio.
1542. 5. mainard"o". 8. inferi da focho.   1543. 1. para. 3. picoli. 6. piattelecti. 8. sciugatto. 12. l. 13. l. 15. picolo.
1544. 7. hova.   1545. 1–25 P. 1. domenecha S. 6. ricote. 7. melerace (?).

[9]lunedì ¶	49	8		Monday	S	49	8
[10]candele	S	6 d		candles	S	6 d	
[11]vino	S	12 d		wine	S	12 d	
[12]crusca	S	5 d 4		bran	S	5 d 4	
[13]ricotta	S	4 d 4		buttermilk	S	4 d 4	
[14]erba	S	8 d		herbs	S	8 d	
[15]martedì	S	35 d 8		Tuesday	S	35 d 8	
[16]carne	S	10 d		meat	S	10 d	
[17]vino	S	14 d		wine	S	14 d	
[18]pane	S	5 d 8		bread	S	5 d 8	
[19]crusca	S	9 d [·]		bran	S	9 d [·]	
[20]erba	S	8 d		herbs	S	8 d	
[21]mercoledì				Wednesday			
[22]vino	S	5 d		wine	S	5 d	
[23]melarance	S	2 d 7		oranges	S	2 d 7	
[24]bacelli	S	1 d		beans	S	1 d	
[25]crusca	S	5 d 4		bran	S	5 d 4	
[26]erba	S	8 d		herbs	S	8 d	
	21	11				21	11

B. N. 2038. 17a]   1546

Miseracione divina sacrosancte Romane ecclesie tituli n · cardinalis [2]vulgarit[er] nuncupatus venerabili religioso fratri Johanni Mair d'Hustorf [3]ordinis praedicatorum provintie teutonie conventus Wiennensis capellano [4]nostro commensali salutem in dño sempiternam: Religiose zelus vite ac morum [5]honestas aliarumque laudabilium probitatum et virtutum merita quibus aput nos fide [6]digno commendaris testimonio Magistri videlicet tui ordinis felicis recordacionis Leonardi de [7]Mansuetis de Perusio sigillo . . suis magisterialibus (?) dans tibi ad hujus modi (?) opera virtutum consequenda (?) [8]locum et tempus successorique ejus similiter in officio magistratus qui praedecessoris sui datum [9]confirmavit et de novo dedit aliorumque plurium [laudatis] qui opera tua laudant [10]nos inducunt ut tibi reddamus ad gratiam liberalem hinc est quod nos cupientes.

W. 12349b]   1547

Johannes · Antonius · di Johannes Ambrosius de Bolate: [2]Chi perde il tempo e' virtù non aquista; [3]Quanto più pensa l'animo più s'attrista; [4]Virtù non ha in potere lo auere, Chi lascia onore per acquistare auere; [5]Non vale fortuna a chi non s'affatica; [6]Colui si fa felice, che Christum vestiga; [7]Perfetto dono nõ s'à sanza gran pena; [8]Passano nostri triumfi, nostre pompe; [9]La gola · e 'l sonno · e l'otiose · piume Anno · dal mondo · ogni virtù sbandita, [10]Tal · che dal corso · suo · quasi · smarita, Nostra · natura · è vinta dal costume; [11]Ormai · convien · così che tu ti spoltri; Disse il maestro che segiendo · in piuma, [12]In fama · non si viene, nè sotto coltri, Sanza la qual · chi sua · vita · consuma [13]Tal · uestigia · in terra di sé lascia ·, Qual · fumo · in aria · o nell' acqua la schiuma.

Johannes Antonius di Johannes Ambrosius de Bolate. He who lets time pass does not grow in virtue: the more I think of it the more I grieve. No man has it in him to be virtuous who will give up honour for gain. Good fortune is valueless to him who knows not toil. The man becomes happy who follows Christ. There is no perfect gift without great suffering. Our glories and our triumphs pass away. Foul lust, and dreams, and luxury, and sloth have banished every virtue from the world; so that our Nature, wandering and perplexed, has almost lost the old and better track. Henceforth it were well to rouse thyself from sleep. The master said that lying in down will not bring thee to Fame; nor staying beneath the quilts. He who, without Fame, burns his life to waste, leaves no more vestige of himself on earth than wind-blown smoke, or the foam upon the sea.

13. ricote. 23. melarace. 24. crvsca.
1546–66. *All these texts are written in the ordinary way from left to right.*
1547. 1. Ambrossius. 3. pensse . . satrista. 4. lassa honore . . aquistare havere. 5. safaticha. 6. coluy . . Xstum. 7. perfecto donnõsa. 8. pasano. 9. ellotiose . . del. 10. chorso . . issmarrita . . chostume. 11. chonvien chosi chettutti spoltri . . maesstro chessiegiendo. 12. nessotto choltri. 12. chissua . . chonsuma. 13. uesstigia . . lasscia . . onnellacqua lasschiuma.

1546. A certificate given by a cardinal to the friar J. Mair of Hustorf recommending the prior of his monastery Leonardo di Mansuetis. J. Mair's model was the subject of discussion at the meeting of the Deputati del Duomo on April 26, 1490, and he was told: 'non expectet nec laudationem modeli nec aliquid aliud cum praefata fabrica'. *Annali della Fab-*

brica del Duomo di Milano, iii, p. 56; compare p. 19.
1547. 2–7. These lines are probably taken from a book of proverbs.
8. Compare Petrarca, *Trionfo del Tempo,* v. 112.
9–10. The beginning of a sonnet by Petrarca.
11–13. Compare Dante, *Inferno,* XXIV. 46–51.

Br. M. 148a]　　　　　　　1548

La mattina de santo Zanobio a dì 25 de maggio nel 1504 ²ebbi da Lionardo Vinci dvcati 15 d'oro, e cominciai a spendere; Sabato				On the morning of Santo Zanobio the 25th of May 1504, I had from Lionardo Vinci 15 gold ducats and began to spend them. Saturday			
³a mona Margarita	S	62	d 4	to Mona Margarita	S	62	d 4
⁴a rifare · l'anello	S	58	d 8	to remake the ring	S	19	d 8
⁵panni	S	13	d	clothes	S	13	
⁶barbiere	S	4		barber	S	4	
⁷uova	S	6	d	eggs	S	6	
⁸al banco debito	S	7	d	debt at the bank	S	7	
⁹velluto	S	12		velvet	S	12	
¹⁰vino	S	9	d 4	wine	S	9	d 4
pane	S	6	d 4	bread	S	6	d 4
¹¹carne	S	4	d	meat	S	4	
¹²more	S	2	d 4	mulberries	S	2	d 4
¹³funghi	S	3	d 4	mushrooms	S	3	d 4
¹⁴insalata	S	1	d	salad	S	1	
¹⁵frutta	S	1	d 4	fruit	S	1	d 4
¹⁶candele	S	3	d	candles	S	3	
¹⁷pernice (?)	S	1	d	partridge (?)	S	1	
¹⁸farina	S	2	d	flour	S	2	
¹⁹domenica	198 · 8			Sunday	198	8	
²⁰pane	S	6	d	bread	S	6	
²¹vino	S	9	d 4	wine	S	9	d 4
²²carne	S	7	d	meat	S	7	
²³minestra	S	2	d	soup	S	2	
²⁴frutta	S	3	d 4	fruit	S	3	d 4
²⁵candele	S	3	d 4	candles	S	3	d 0
²⁶Lvnedì	31			Monday	31		
²⁷pane	S	6	d 4	bread	S	6	d 4
²⁸carne	S	10	d 8	meat	S	10	d 8
²⁹vino	S	9	d 4	wine	S	9	d 4
³⁰frutta	S	4	d	fruit	S	4	
³¹minestra	S	1	d 8	soup	S	1	d 8
	32				32		

Br. M. 148b]　　　　　　　1549

Martedì			Tuesday		
²pane	S	6 d	bread	S	6
³carne	S	11 d	meat	S	11
⁴vino	S	7 d	wine	S	7
⁵frutta	S	9 d	fruit	S	9
⁶minestra	S	2 d	soup	S	2
⁷insalata	S	1 d	salad	S	1

Br. M. 149b]　　　　　　　1550

A Mona Margarita	d	5 S	5		To Mona Margarita	d	5 S	5	
²a Tomaso		S	14		to Tomaso		S	14	
³a mona Margarita	di	5 S	2		to Mona Margarita	d	5 S	2	
⁴el dì di san Zanobi					on the day of San Zanobi				
⁵resta					left . . . . . after				
⁶de pagamento	di	13 S	2 d 4		payment	d	13 S	2 d 4	
⁷di . . . . mona Margarita					of . . . . Mona Margarita				
⁸in somma	⁹d 14 S	3 · 4			altogether	d 14 S	3 d 4		

1548. 1. matina .. zanobi .. mago. 2. ebi .. cominciai. 3. magarita. 4. aresotere. 7. hove. 9. veleto. 13. fonghi. 15. frvte. 17. penice. 19. domenega. 24. frute. 25. candel. 30. frvte.
1549. 1. martedi *here Leonardo notes in his usual handwriting* a grecho ½. 5. frvte.
1550. 5. resta se mo da cord. 7. cavaljli mona malgarita. 8. soma. 10. [a mona margarita S. 7.]

1548, 1549. On the same sheet is the text No. 1015 in Leonardo's own handwriting.

Br. M. 271a]   **1551**

[Il · lvnedì a dì 13 di febraio prestai lire S 7 a Lionardo per spendere ²venerdì L 7 nel] 1502.

[On Monday, the 13th of February, I lent lire S 7 to Lionardo to spend, Friday L 7 in] 1502.

Br. M. 274a]   **1552**

¶ Stephano Iligi, Canonico di Dulcigno ³familiare del chiarissimo ⁴cardinale Grimani; ⁵a Santo Apostoli. ¶

Stephano Iligi, Canonico of Dulcigno, servant of the honorable cardinal Grimani at S. Apostoli.

C. A. 4a]   **1553**

Essendomi sollecitato; ²s'amor non è che · dvnque . . .³Bernardo · di Simone, ⁴Siluestro di Stefano ·, ⁵Bernardo · di Jacopo, ⁶Francesco di Matteo Bonciani, ⁷Francesco di Giovanni Ruberti; ⁸Antonio da Pistoia gli ha . . . diche . . . Antonio; ⁹chi tenpo à e tenpo aspetta, ¹⁰perde l'amico · e' danari non ha mai · Chi · asino è e cerbio esser si · crede, essendo.

Having become anxious; if there is no love, what then? Bernardo di Simone, Silvestro di Stefano, Bernardo di Jacopo, Francesco di Matteo Bonciani, Francis di Giovanni Ruberti, Antonio da Pistoia . . . Antonio; He who has time and waits for time will lose his friends and never has money. He who is an ass and thinks he is a stag . . . .

C. A. 35b]   **1554**

Reverendissimo Messer Don Giouañi come fratello jo parlai a maestro Zacaria di quella ²facenda et l'ho fatto esser contento di quella ordinatione ch'io ho uoluto, ³cioè in quãto alla comissione ch'io ho dalle parti, et dico che tra noi nõ ha ⁴a correre denari inquanto alli quadri della . . . .

Reverend Messer Don Giovanni, I spoke to Maestro Zacaria as a brother about this business, and I made him satisfied with the arrangement that I had wished; that is, as regards the commission that I had from the parties, and I say that between us there is no need to pay money down, as regard the pictures of the . . . .

C. A. 42b]   **1554 A**

Antonius Salvaticus debet dare scriptos in credito Innocentio Cotte in libro virido. ann. 1446 in fo. 165 a tº dì, libr. III M de XX.

Antonius Salvaticus must give what is written to the credit of Innocentio Cotte in the green book, year 1446 in fo. 165 on the third day, book III M de XX.

C. A. 76a]   **1555**

Delle cose vedute infra la nebbia quella parte che sarà più ²uicina alli estremi, sarà manco uisibile, e tanto meno ³quãto sõ più remote.

Of things seen through a mist, that which is nearest its farthest limit will be least visible, and all the more so as they are more remote.

C. A. 71a]   **1555 A**

Lionardo mio non avete d. . .
Lionardo perchè tanto penate?
Deh non m'avete a vil ch'io son povero;
Povero è quel che assai cose desidera.

Leonardo mine you have no . . .
Leonardo why do you take such pains?
Do not think ill of me because I am poor;
Poor is he who desires many things.

C. A. 78b]   **1556**

Teodoricus Rex ²semper Augustus.

Theodoricus Rex Semper Augustus.

1551. 1. el lvnedi . . prestaio . . perispende. 2. vermadi. 3. di poi mi parti di chossta nõnebbi mai senõq pochi soldi mi furõ.
1552. 2. de dul cegno. 3. k"mo". 4. Carle.
1553. 3. br bernardo. 4. saluesstro. 5. dia chopo. 6. franc"o". 8. ant"o" . . pistoia ghagha diche. 9. asspetta. 10. lamicho e danari nvna. 11. chiasmo e accierbi o esser surado (?).
1554. R "do" mstr dõ . . como frãllo . . mro. 3. dicochtra. 4. denari inquato . . guadri. *Here the text breaks off.*
1555. 1. prte. 2. extremi . . ettanto.
1556. Teodoricus R.

1551. This note is followed by an account very like the one given as No. 1549.

1552. Compare No. 674, 21–3. The will of Stefano Iligi, dated 9 Oct., 1520, is preserved in the State Archives of Venice.

1553. l. 8. Antonio da Pistoja, Antonio Cammello,

Court poet to Lodovico Sforza.

1554 A. Conte Antonio Saratico held the Castle of Milan at the death of Filippo Visconti. He was killed by a mob in 1449. Innocenzo Cotta, who played an important part in the Republica Ambrosiana was killed in 1465.

C. A. 95*b*]   1557

Πρωομιάσαι ὦ ἄνθρωπος 'Αθῆνας.
²Aut Hesperia sola dicis et significat Italiã,
³aut addis vltima et significat Ispaniã; ⁴Vmbria
pars Tuscie.

Either you say Hesperia alone, and it will mean Italy, or you add ultima, and it will mean Spain. Umbria, part of Tuscany.

C. A. 123*b*]   1558

Πάντων ἀντιαμψλίωμ δυὸ εὐθείαι ἐπισταύρονται; ²πρωομιάσαι ὦ ἄνθρωπος 'Αθῆνας τοῖς θεοῖς δέχομαι.

C. A. 132*a*]   1559

Al nome di dio a dì 5 di Luglio 1507.
²[Cara mia dileta madre e mie sorelle e mio cognato, e advisovi come ³sano per grazia di Dio e così spero di voi. per ricordarvi quello che avete a fare ⁴di una spada che io vi lasciai, portatela alla piazza delli Strozzi a Maso delle Viole, e la tegna a ogni modo perchè ela mimporta assai e rachomandovi quelle veste. E richordovi la Dianjra, fatele vezzo, acioche ella non dica chio non mi ricordi di lei. E ancora mi rachomando a patro mio chognato e ditegli che noi saremo chosta a presto (?) per tuto el mese di setembre, tuti restareno ben . . . . epoi tornereno in qua per resto, e spedirò la facenda di Pietro in modo chesso remara contento.]

In the name of God, on the 5th of July 1507.
[My dearly beloved mother, sisters, and brother-in-law, I herewith inform you that I am well, thanks to God, and I hope the same of you. To remind you what to do with the sword that I left with you—take it to the Piazza Strozzi, to Maso delle Viole for him to be sure to keep it as I set great store by it, and I recommend to you those clothes. And remember me graciously to Dianjra so that she should not say that I have forgotten her, and remember me also to my brother-in-law and tell him that I shall soon be there for the whole month of September, all will stay there . . . and then will return here for the remaining things, and I shall settle the business with Piero so that he will be satisfied.]

C. A. 167*b*]   1560

Ut bene respondet Naturae ars docta! dedisset
    Vincius, ut tribuit cetera · sic animam ·
Noluit ut similis magis haec foret: altera sic est:
    Possidet illius Maurus amans animam.

Hujus quam cernis nomen Lucretia, Divi
    Omnia cui larga contribuere manu.
Rara huic forma data est; pinxit Leonardus, amavit
    Maurus, pictorum primus hic, ille ducum.

Naturam, ac superas hac laesit imagine Divas
    Pictor: tantum hominis posse manum haec doluit,
Illae longa dari tam magnae tempora formae,
    Quae spatio fuerat deperitura brevi.

W. 12484*b*]   1560 A

Umana libertà come se' cara,
Guai a colui che vive in servitù,
E bon per chi ad altrui spese impara!

I' mi starei nel letto in dolcità
E col saccon farei dormir a paro,
Non sendo servo, chi tant' è amaro.

Human freedom how dear art thou
Woe to him who lives in servitude
It is good for one who advances at the expense of others

I should remain in bed with comfort
And with my mattress sleep in company
Not being a serf which is such bitter fate.

1557. 3. sig "cas" ispaniã.
1559. 1. la nome didio adi. 2. sorele . . chome. 4. istro"a"zi . . maso della violẽ.

1557. The Greek texts, Nos. 1557, 1558, and 1562, give no sense and are therefore not translated.
1559. Compare G. Calvi, *I manoscritti*, pp. 250, 251, note 2.
1560. These three epigrams on the portrait of

Lucrezia Crivelli, a picture by Leonardo which must have been lost at a very early date, seem to have been dedicated to Leonardo by the poet. Leonardo used the reverse of the sheet for notes on geometry.

C. A. 174b]   1561

Egidius Romanus de formatione [2]corporis humani in vtero matris.

Egidius Romanus on the formation of the human body in the mother's womb [1].

1561 A

A Mons de Vintie coll(?) des Cheveaux & [2]de lescuyer du Roy ... pour (?) ses (?) [3]laisser payement continuer (?) a messieur Lyonard fa ... paintre du Roy po [5]ses ....
A Amboise.

To Monsieur le Vinci, the horses of the king's equerry. .... Continue the payment to Ms. Lyonard, Painter to the King.
Amboise.

C. A. 178a]   1562

Πρωομιάσαι ὦ ἄνθρωπος τοῖς θεοῖς δέχομαι.

C. A. 230b]   1563

Memoria a Maestro Lionardo di havere presto la nota del [2]stato di firenze, videlicet come à tenuto le mode e stillo [3]el Reverendo patre detto frate Geronimo in ordinare el stato di forteze; [4]Item, li ordini et forma expressa di ogni luy ordinatione [5]per quel modo via ed ordine come sono servati et se [6]servano usque nunc.

Memorandum for Master Leonardo to secure quickly information on the state of Florence, *videlicet* in what condition the reverend father, called friar Girolamo, kept the fortresses. Item, the manning and armament of each command, and in what way they were equipped, and whether they are the same now.

C. A. 342b]   1564

Ricordo a Vostra Eccellentia come Ridolfo [2]Manini · condusse a Firenze una somma [3]di cristallo ... altre pietre come sono ....
Ancora ricordo a v. E.tia (che parli a) la facenda che ò cum Ser Juliano mio fratello capo de li altri fratelli, Ricordandoli come se offerse da conciar le cose mie fra noi fratelli de ... cioè de la eredità de mio Padre, e quella constringa a la expeditione qual conteneva la littera che lui me mandò.

To remind your Excellency that Ridolfo Manini brought to Florence a quantity of crystal besides other stones such as are .... I also recall to your Excellency the affair that I have with my brother Ser Juliano who is at the head of the other brothers—reminding you that if you should offer to arrange things among us brothers —namely, the inheritance of my father—and compel the dispatch of the matter, as described in the letter he sent me.

C. A. 336b.]   1565

Libro XVI[o] C. 6 de Ciuitate Dei, [2]non esse Antipodes.

Book XVI. Cp. 6 De Civitate Dei, that there are no Antipodes.

Formerly Bibl. Melzi]   1566

Leonardo's Will.

Sia manifesto ad ciaschaduna persona presente et aduenere, che nella corte del Re nostro signore in Amboysia avanti de noy personalmente con-

Be it known to all persons, present and to come, that at the court of our Lord the King at Amboise before ourselves in person, Messer

1561. 1. informatione.
1561A. 1. des cheuaux a (?). 2. de l'escuyeres (?). 4. peintre (?) du Roi P. 5. Amboyse Amboyse. 6. Amboyse amboy.
1563. 1. a m "r o" Lionardo dihavere p'sto la nolo stato.
1564. 1. vra ELL"tia". 2. Manini [porte] conduse .. som ł. 3. cristallo inporse (?) altre.
1565. 1. XVI[o] "6[o]" de Ciu"ite" Dei. 2. esse.

1561. *Magistri Aegidii Romani Tractatus aureus de formatione corporis in utero matris*, Libri IV, Paris, 1515. The following text is written on a separate sheet.

1561A. In this note addressed to Leonardo he is given the title 'Paintre du Roy'. This fact throws new light on his position in France.

1563. In November 1494 King Charles VIII entered Florence where Republican government had been proclaimed, the Medici having been banished shortly before. The terms agreed upon between the king and the heads of the Florentine government were to the effect that Florentine fortresses should be placed under the king's protectorate during his absence and until

his return from Naples, which kingdom he intended to make his by way of victory and conquest. In this connexion Leonardo appears to have been engaged to report on the state of the Florentine fortresses within the four years of Savonarola's political supremacy. According to M. Herzfeld (*Racc. Vinc.* xiii, pp. 53 f.), this memorandum refers to the arrangement with Prince Ligny. Compare No. 1379.

1565. A facsimile of part of this note is given on page 202. Reference to St. Augustine, *De Civitate Dei*, xvi. 9 (not 6).

1566. This copy of Leonardo's will was made from the original document in the archives of the Vinci family, and was sent on 15 May, 1779 by Conte stituto messer Leonardo de Vince pictore del Re, al presente comorante nello locho dicto du Cloux appresso de Amboysia, el qual considerando la certezza dela morte e l'incertezza del hora di quella, ha cognosciuto et confessato nela dicta corte nanzi de noy nela quale s'è somesso e somette circa ciò havere facto et ordinato per tenore dela presente il suo testamento et ordinanza de ultima volontà nel modo qual se seguita. Primeramente el racomanda l'anima sua ad nostro Signore Messer Domine Dio, alla gloriosa Virgine Maria, a Monsignore Sancto Michele, e a tutti li beati Angeli Santi e Sante del Paradiso.

Item el dicto Testatore vole essere seppelito drento la giesia de sancto Florentino de Amboysia et suo corpo essere portato lì per li capellani di quella.

Item che il suo corpo sia accompagnato dal dicto locho fin nela dicta giesia de sancto Florentino per il colegio de dicta giesia cioè dal Rectore et Priore, o vero dali Vicarii soy et Capellani della giesia di sancto Dionisio d'Amboysia, etiam li Fratri Minori del dicto locho, et avante de essere portato il suo corpo nela dicta chiesa, esso Testatore, vole siano celebrate ne la dicta chiesia di sancto Florentino tre grandi messe con diacono et sottodiacono, et il dì che se diranno dicte tre grandi messe che se dicano anchora trenta messe basse de Sancto Gregorio.

Item nella dicta chiesia di Sancto Dionisio simil servitio sia celebrato come di sopra.

Item nella chiesia de dicti Fratri et religiosi minori simile servitio.

Item el prefato Testatore dona et concede ad Messer Francesco da Melzo, Gentilomo da Milano, per remuneratione de' servitii ad epso grati a lui facti per il passato, tutti ei ciaschaduno li libri, che il dicto Testatore ha de presente et altri Instrumenti et Portracti circa l'arte sua et industria de Pictori.

Item epso Testatore dona et concede a sempre mai perpetuamente a Battista de Vilanis suo servitore la metà zoè medietà de uno iardino, che ha fora a le mura de Milano et l'altra metà de epso iardino ad Salay suo servitore nel qual iardino il prefato Salay ha edificata et constructa una casa, la qual sarà e resterà similmente a sempremai perpetudine al dicto Salai, soi heredi et successori, et ciò in remuneratione di boni et grati servitii, che dicti de Vilanis et Salay dicti suoi servitori lui hano facto de qui inanzi.

Item epso Testatore dona a Maturina sua

Leonardo da Vinci, painter to the King, at present staying at the place known as Cloux near Amboise, duly considering the certainty of death and the uncertainty of its time, has acknowledged and declared in the said court and before us that he has made, according to the tenor of these presents, his testament and the declaration of his last will, as follows. And first he commends his soul to our Lord, Almighty God, and to the Glorious Virgin Mary, and to our lord Saint Michael, to all the blessed Angels and Saints male and female in Paradise.

Item. The said Testator desires to be buried within the church of Saint Florentin at Amboise, and that his body shall be borne thither by the chaplains of the church.

Item. That his body may be followed from the said place to the said church of Saint Florentin by the *collegium* of the said church, that is to say, by the rector and the prior, or by their vicars and chaplains of the church of Saint Denis of Amboise, also the Minors of the place, and before his body shall be carried to the said church this Testator desires that in the said church of Saint Florentin three grand masses shall be celebrated by the deacon and sub-deacon and that on the day when these three high masses are celebrated, thirty low masses shall also be performed at Saint Gregory.

Item. That in the said church of Saint Denis similar services shall be performed, as above.

Item. That the same shall be done in the church of the said friars and lesser brethren.

Item. The aforesaid Testator gives and bequeaths to Messer Francesco da Melzo, nobleman, of Milan, in remuneration for services and favours done to him in the past, each and all of the books the Testator is at present possessed of, and the instruments and portraits appertaining to his art and calling as a painter.

Item. The same Testator gives and bequeaths henceforth for ever to Battista de Vilanis his servant one half, that is, the moiety, of his garden which is outside the walls of Milan,[1] and the other half of the same garden to Salai his servant; in which garden aforesaid Salai has built and constructed a house which shall be and remain henceforth in all perpetuity the property of the said Salai, his heirs and successors; and this is in remuneration for the good and kind services which the said de Vilanis and Salai, his servants, have done him in past times until now.

Item. The said Testator gives to Maturina

Bindo Nero Maria Peruzzi from Florence to Don Venanzio de Pagave, counsellor of the Austrian government in Lombardy. It was first published by Amoretti, *Memorie Storiche*, p. 121. Both this copy, which was preserved at the Melzi Library, and the original cannot now be traced. An older copy of the 17th century was found at Romorantin, France. See

E. Müntz, *L. d. V.*, Paris, 1899, pp. 478 f.

1. A vineyard measuring 16 pertiche outside Porta Vercellina was presented to Leonardo by Lodovico il Moro in 1498. See G. Biscaro, *La vigna di Leonardo*, Arch. Stor. Lomb. xxxvi, 1909; and L. Beltrami, *La vigna di Leonardo*, Milan, 1920. Comp. No. 1405, note.

fantescha una veste de bon pan negro foderata de pelle, una socha de panno et doy ducati per una volta solamente pagati: et ciò in remuneratione similmente de boni servitii a lui facti epsa Maturina de quì inanzi.

Item vole che ale sue exequie siano sexanta torchie, le quali seranno portate per sexanta poveri, ali quali seranno dati danari per portarle a discretione del dicto Melzo le quali torzi seranno divise nelle quattro chiesie sopradicte.

Item el dicto Testatore dona ad ciascheduna de dicte chiesie sopradicte diece libre cera in candele grosse che saranno messe nelle dicte chiesie per servire al dì che se celebreranno dicti servitii.

Item che sia dato ali poveri del ospedale di Dio alli poveri de Sancto Lazaro de Amboysia, e per ciò fare sia dato et pagato alli Tesorieri d'epsa confraternità la summa et quantità de soysante dece soldi tornesi.

Item epso Testatore dona et concede al dicto Messer Francesco Melce presente et acceptante il resto della sua pensione et summa de' danari qual a lui sono debiti del passato fino al dì della sua morte per il recevoir, ovvero, Tesaurario general M. Johan Sapin, et tutte et ciaschaduna summe de' danari che ha receputo dal p.º Sapin de la dicta sua pensione, e in caxo chel decede inanzi al prefato Melzo, e non altramente li quali danari sono al presente nella possessione del dicto Testatore nel dicto loco de Cloux como el dice. Et similmente el dona et concede al dicto de Melze tucti et ciaschaduni suoi vestimenti quali ha al presente ne lo dicto loco de Cloux tam per remuneratione de boni et grati servitii, a lui facti da qui inanzi, che per li suoi salarii vacationi et fatiche chel potrà avere circa la executione del presente Testamento, il tutto però ale spese del dicto Testatore.

Ordina et vole, che la summa de quattrocento scudi del sole che ha in deposito in man del Camarlingo de Sancta Maria de Nova nela città de Fiorenza, siano dati ali soy fratelli carnali residenti in Fiorenza con el profitto et emolumento che ne po essere debito fino al presente da prefati Camarlinghi al prefato Testatore per casone de dicti scudi quattrocento da poi el dì che furono per el prefato Testatore dati et consignati alli dicti Camarlinghi.

Item vole et ordina dicto Testatore che dicto Messer Francisco de Melzo sia et remana solo et in sol per il tutto executore del Testamento del prefato Testatore, et che questo dicto Testamento sortisca suo pleno et integro effecto, et circa ciò che è narrato et decto havere tenere guardare et observare epso Messer Leonardo de Vince Testatore constituto ha obbligato et obbliga per le presente epsi soy heredi et

his waiting-woman a cloak of good black cloth lined with fur, a . . . of cloth and two ducats paid once only; and this likewise is in remuneration for good service rendered to him in past times by the said Maturina.

Item. He desires that at his funeral sixty tapers shall be carried which shall be borne by sixty poor men, to whom shall be given money for carrying them, at the discretion of the said Melzo, and these tapers shall be distributed among the four above-mentioned churches.

Item. The said Testator gives to each of the said churches ten lb. of wax in thick tapers, which shall be placed in the said churches to be used on the day when those said services are celebrated.

Item. That alms shall be given to the poor of the Hôtel-Dieu, to the poor of Saint Lazare d'Amboise and, to that end, there shall be given and paid to the treasurers of that same fraternity the sum and amount of seventy soldi of Tours.

Item. The said Testator gives and bequeaths to the said Messer Francesco Melzo, being present and agreeing, the remainder of his pension and the sums of money which are owing to him from the past time till the day of his death by the receiver or treasurer-general M. Johan Sapin, and each and every sum of money that he has already received from the aforesaid Sapin of his said pension, and in case he should die before the said Melzo and not otherwise; which moneys are at present in the possession of the said Testator in the said place called Cloux, as he says. And he likewise gives and bequeaths to the said Melzo all and each of his clothes which he at present possesses at the said place of Cloux, and all in remuneration for the good and kind services done by him in past times till now, as well as in payment for the trouble and annoyance he may incur with regard to the execution of this present testament, which, however, shall all be at the expense of the said Testator.

And he orders and desires that the sum of four hundred scudi in his possession, which he has deposited in the hands of the treasurer of Santa Maria Nuova in the city of Florence, may be given to his brothers now living in Florence with all the interest and usufruct that may have accrued up to the present time, and be due from the aforesaid treasurers to the aforesaid Testator on account of the said four hundred crowns, since they were given and consigned by the Testator to the said treasurers.

Item. He desires and orders that the said Messer Francesco de Melzo shall be and remain the sole and only executor of the said will of the said Testator; and that the said testament shall be executed in its full and complete meaning and according to that which is here narrated and said, to have, hold, keep, and observe, the said

successori con ogni soy beni mobili et immobili presenti et advenire et ha renunciato et renuncia per la presente expressamente ad tucte et ciaschaduna le cose ad ciò contrarie. Datum nelo dicto loco de Cloux ne la presencia de magistro Spirito Fleri Vicario nela chiesia de Sancto Dionisio de Amboysia, M. Gulielmo Croysant prete et capellani, magistro Cipriane Fulchin, Fratre Francesco de Corton et Francesco da Milano religioso del convento de fratri minori de Amboysia, testimonii ad ciò ciamati et vocati ad tenire per il iudicio de la dicta Corte in presentia del prefato M. Francesco de Melze acceptante et consentiente il quale ha promesso per fede et sacramento del corpo suo per lui dati corporalmente ne le mane nostre di non mai fare venire, dire, ne andare in contrario. Et sigillato a sua requesta dal sigillo regale statuito a li contracti legali d'Amboysia, et in segno de verita.

Dat · a dì XXIII de Aprile MDXVIII avanti la Pasqua.[1]

Et a dì XXIII d'epso mese de Aprile MDXVIII ne la presentia di M. Gulielmo Borian notario regio ne la corte de Baliagio d'Amboysia il prefato M. Leonardo de Vince ha donato et concesso per il suo testamento et ordinanza de ultima voluntà supradicta al dicto M. Baptista de Vilanis presente et acceptante il dritto de laqua che qdam bone memorie Re Ludovico XII ultimo defuncto ha alias dato a epso de Vince suxo il fiume del naviglio di Sancto Cristoforo ne lo Ducato de Milano per gauderlo per epso De Vilanis a sempre mai in tal modo et forma che dicto Signore ne ha facto dono in presentia di M. Francesco da Melzo Gentilhomo de Milano et io.

Et a dì prefato nel dicto mese de Aprile ne lo dicto anno MDXVIII epso M. Leonardo de Vinci per il suo testamento et ordinanza de ultima voluntà sopradecta ha donato al prefato M. Baptista de Vilanis presente et acceptante tutti et ciaschaduni mobili et utensili de caxa soy de presente ne lo dicto loco du Cloux, in caxo però che el dicto de Vilanis surviva al dicto M. Leonardo de Vince, in presentia del prefato M. Francesco da Melzo et io Notario etc. Borean.

Messer Leonardo da Vinci, constituted Testator, has obliged and obliges by these presents the said his heirs and successors with all his goods movable and immovable, present and to come, and has renounced and expressly renounces by these presents all and each of the things which to that are contrary. Given at the said place of Cloux in the presence of Magister Spirito Fleri, vicar of the church of Saint Denis at Amboise, of M. Guglielmo Croysant, priest and chaplain, of Magister Cipriane Fulchin, Brother Francesco de Corton, and of Francesco da Milano, a brother of the Convent of the Minorites at Amboise, witnesses summoned and required to that end by the indictment of the said court in the presence of the aforesaid M. Francesco de Melze, who accepting and agreeing to the same has promised by his faith and his oath which he has administered to us personally and has sworn to us never to do nor say nor act in any way to the contrary. And it is sealed by his request with the royal seal apposed to legal contracts at Amboise, and in token of good faith.

Given on the XXIIIrd day of April MDXVIII, before Easter.

And on the XXIIIrd day of this month of April MDXVIII, in the presence of M. Guglielmo Borian, Royal notary in the court of the bailiwick of Amboise, the aforesaid M. Leonardo da Vinci gave and bequeathed, by his last will and testament, as aforesaid, to the said M. Baptista de Vilanis, being present and agreeing, the right of water which the King Louis XII of pious memory, lately deceased, gave to this same da Vinci, the stream of the canal of Santo Cristoforo in the duchy of Milan, to belong to the said Vilanis for ever in such wise and manner that the said gentleman made him this gift in the presence of M. Francesco da Melzo, gentleman of Milan, and in mine.

And on the aforesaid day in the said month of April in the said year MDXVIII the same M. Leonardo da Vinci by his last will and testament gave to the aforesaid M. Baptista de Vilanis, being present and agreeing, each and all of the articles of furniture and utensils of his house at present at the said place of Cloux, in the event of the said de Vilanis surviving the aforesaid M. Leonardo da Vinci, in the presence of the said M. Francesco Melzo and of me, Notary, &c. Borean.

[1] Date according to the French calendar. In 1518 Easter fell on 4 April, while in 1519 it fell on 24 April. The will was therefore written on 23 April, 1519.

PLATES

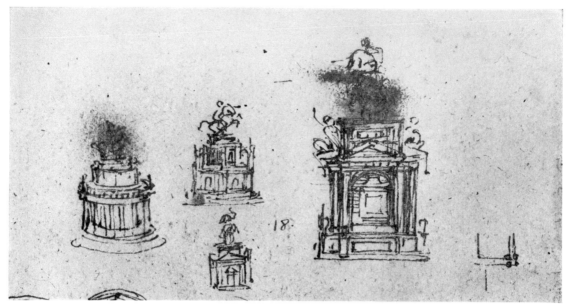

LXV, No.1. Windsor 12353 p.80

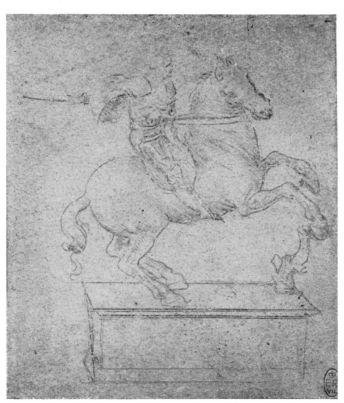

LXV, No.2. Windsor 12357

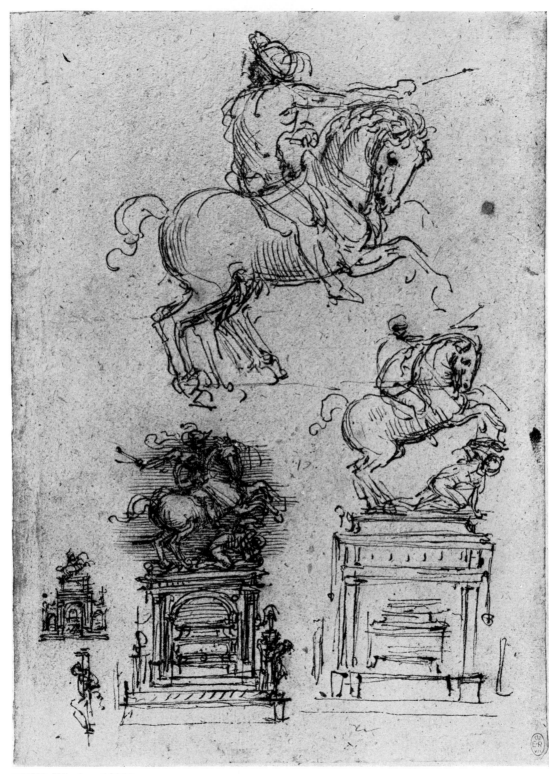

LXVI. Windsor 12355

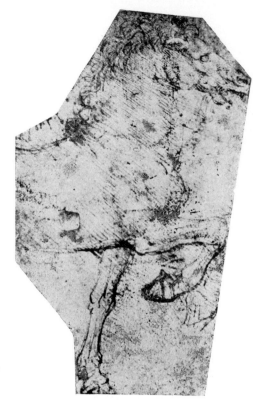

LXVIA. Ambrosiana

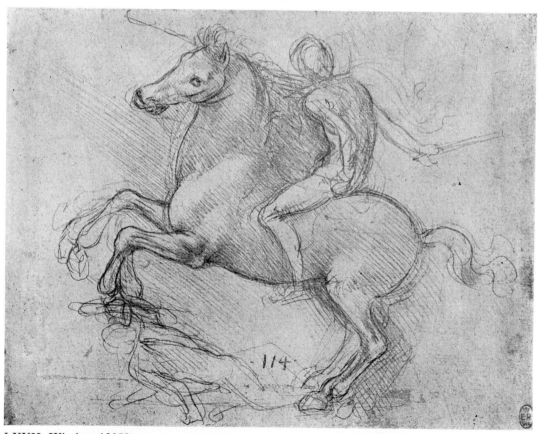

LXVII. Windsor 12358a

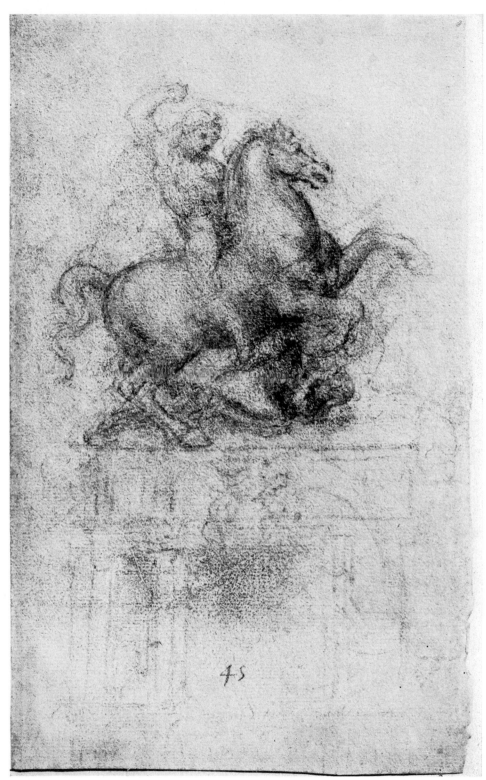

LXVIII. Windsor 12354

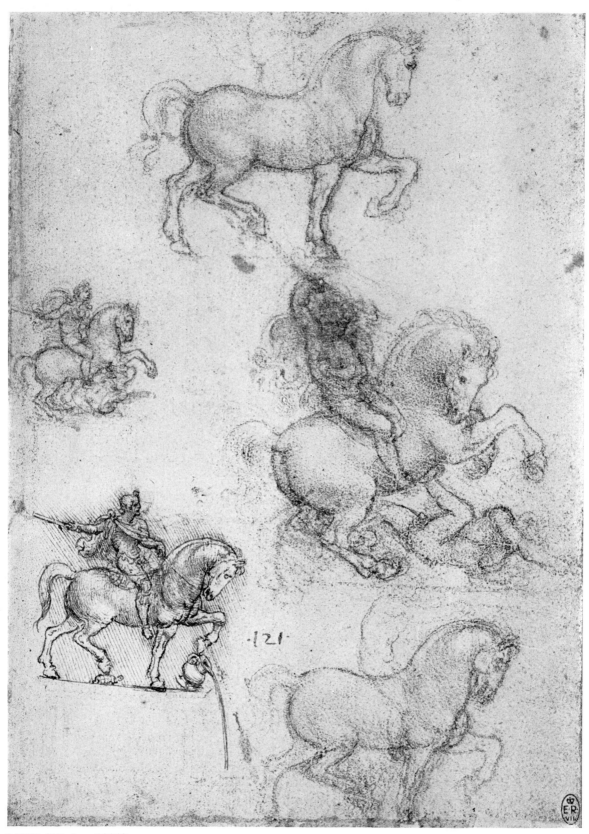

LXIX. Windsor 12360

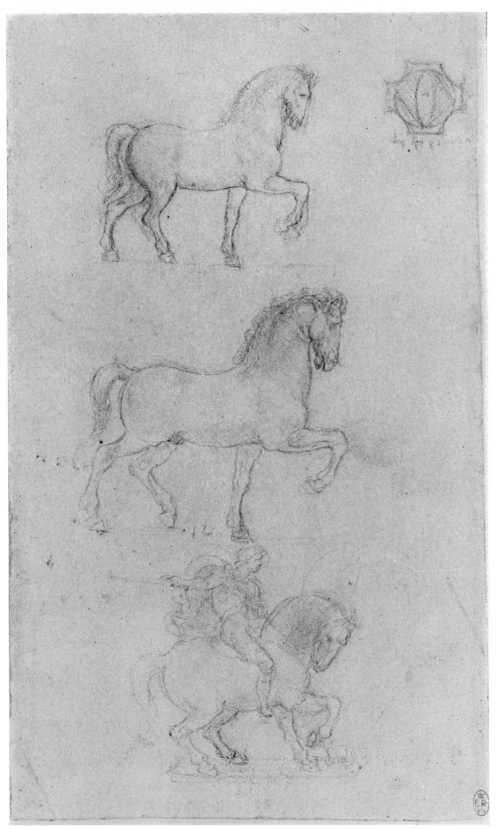

LXX. Windsor 12359

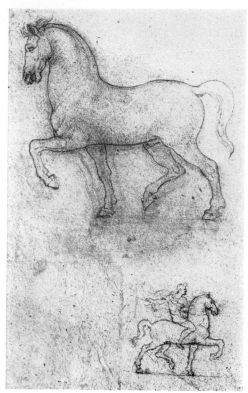

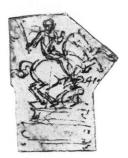

LXXII, No.1.
Windsor 12353

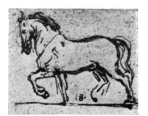

LXXI. Windsor 12344a

LXXII, No.2.
Windsor 12345a

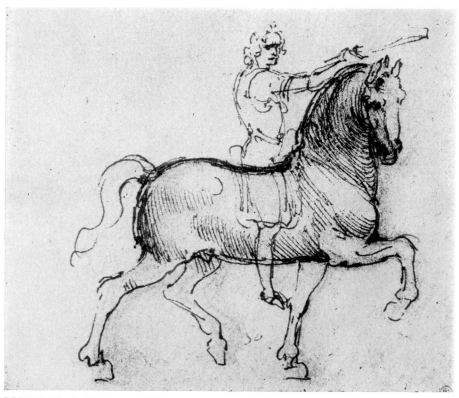

LXXII, No.3. Windsor 12343

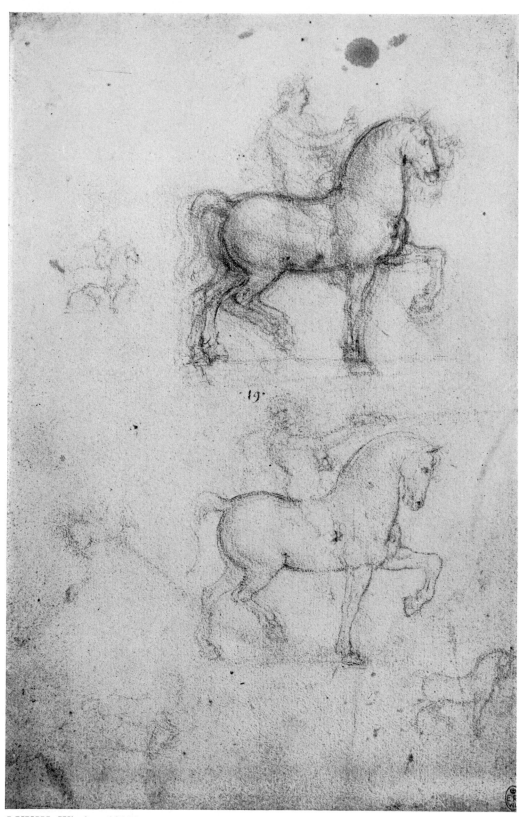

LXXIII. Windsor 12342

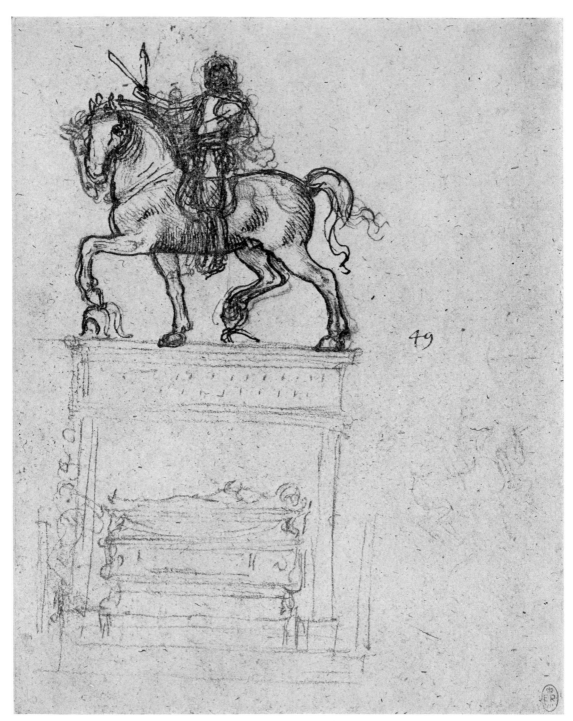

49

LXXIV. Windsor 12356a

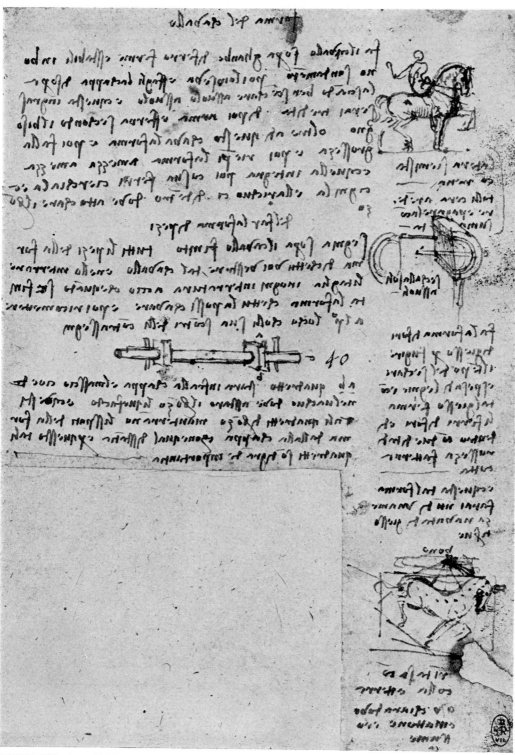

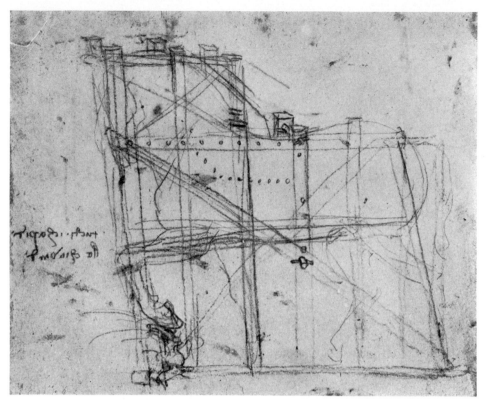

LXXVI, No.1. Cod.Atl.216v-a   712 & p.3

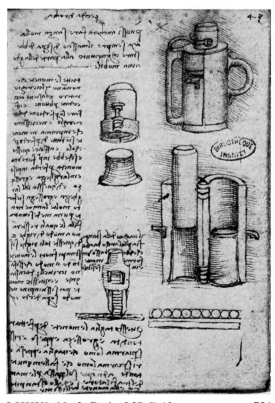

LXXVI, No.2. Paris, MS.G.43a   726

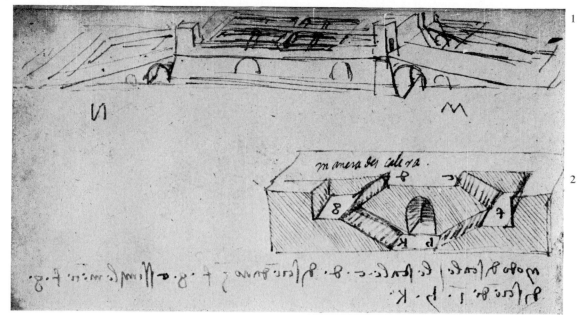

LXXVII, Nos. 1 & 2. Paris, MS.B. 15b

742, 743 & p.21

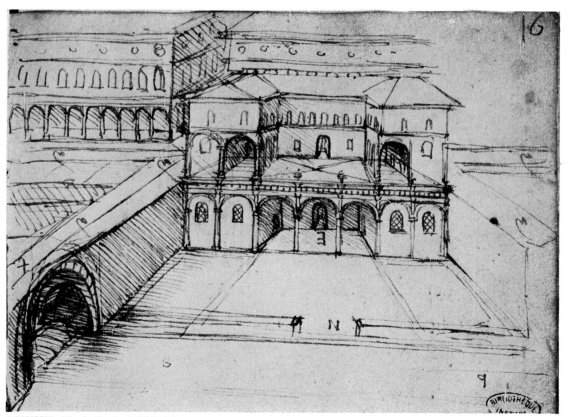

LXXVII, No.3. Paris, MS.B.16a

741 & p.21

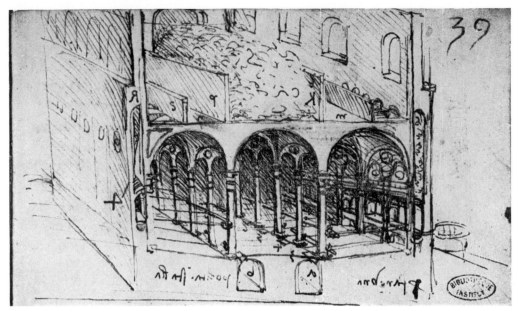

LXXVIII, No.1. Paris, MS.B.39a

761

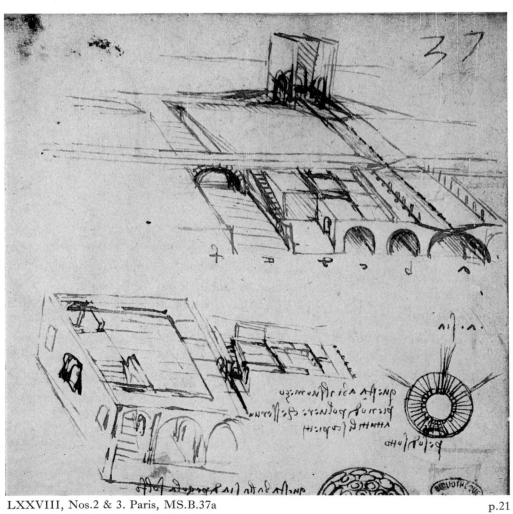

LXXVIII, Nos.2 & 3. Paris, MS.B.37a

p.21

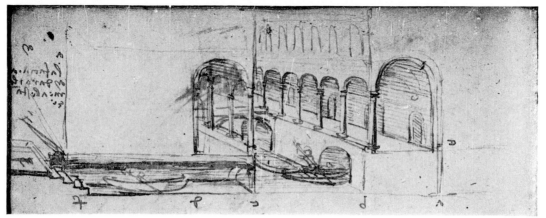

LXXIX, No.1. Paris, MS.B.37b

745 & p.23

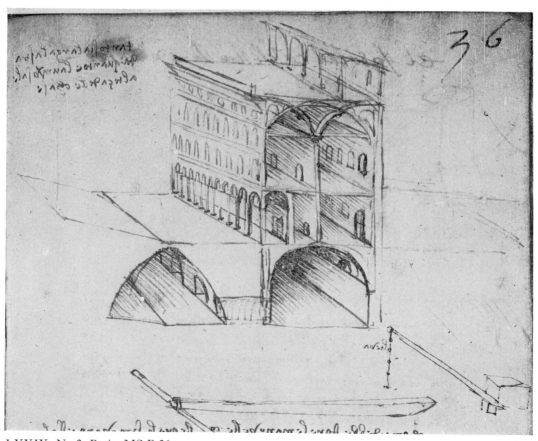

LXXIX, No.2. Paris, MS.B.36a

746

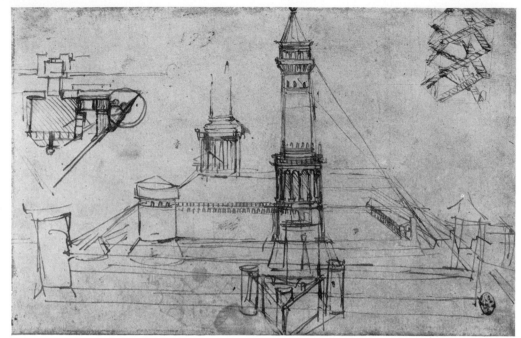

LXXX, No.1. Louvre Vallardi fol.39a(2282)　　　　　　　　　　p.24

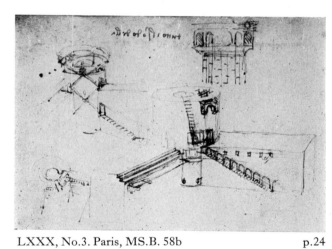

LXXX, No.3. Paris, MS.B. 58b　　　　　　　　　p.24

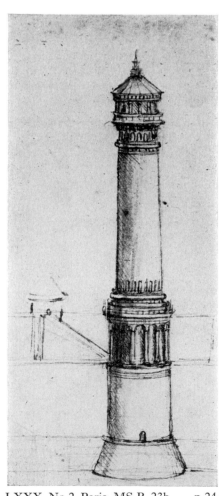

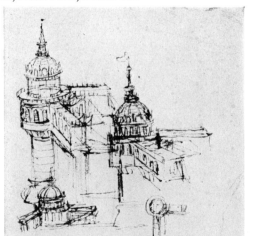

LXXX. No.2, Paris, MS.B. 23b　　　p.24

LXXX, No.4. Windsor 12552　　　　　　　p.24

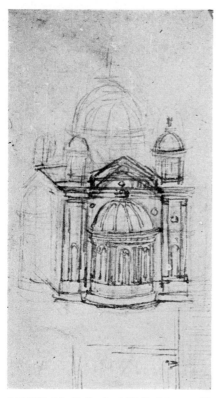

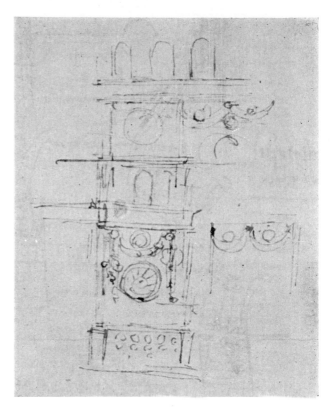

LXXX, No.5. Paris, MS.B. 25a   p.30   LXXXI, No.1. Milan, Trivulzio 22a   p.52

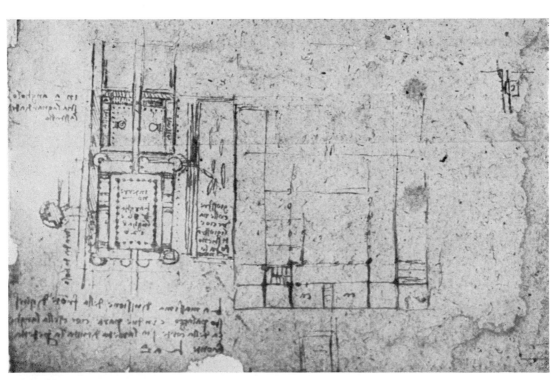

LXXXI, No.2. Cod.Atl.76v-b

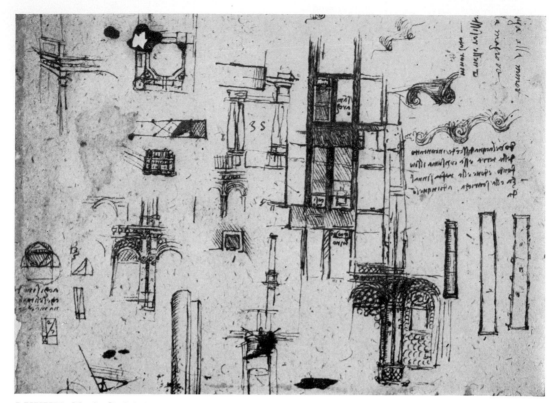

LXXXII, No.1. Cod.Atl.315r-b p.24, 57

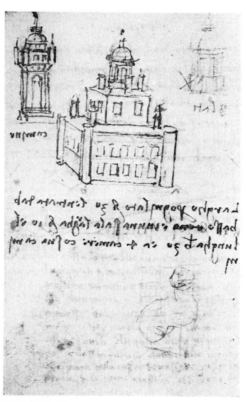

LXXXII, No.2. 749 & p.24
Paris, MS.K³.36b

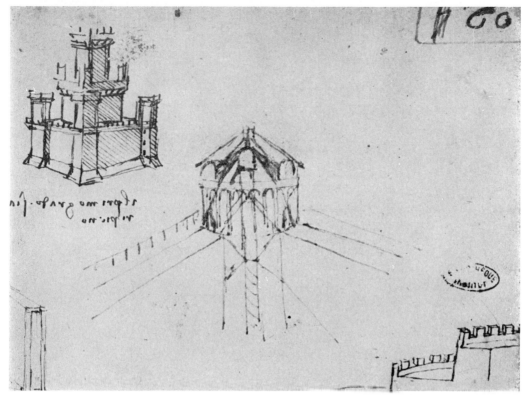

LXXXII, No.3. Paris, MS.B.60a

750 & p.24

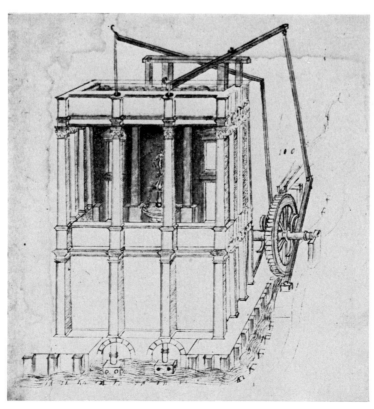

LXXXII, No.4. Cod.Atl.395v

p.24

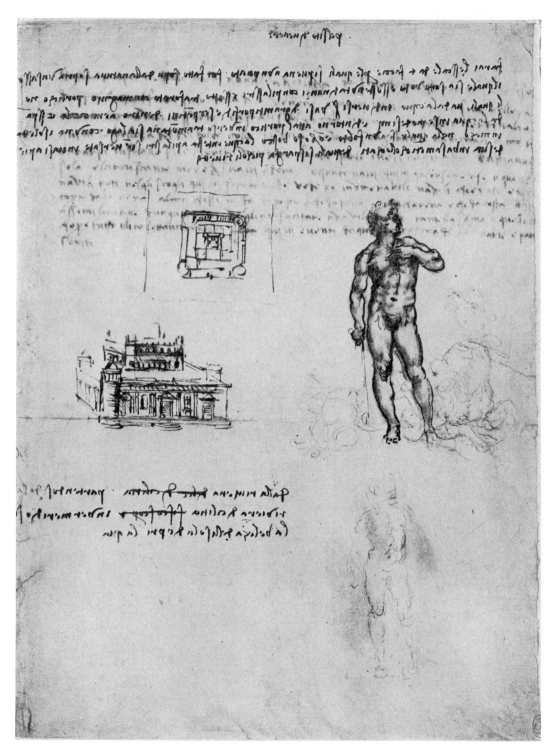

LXXXIII. Windsor 12591a   1103 & p.24

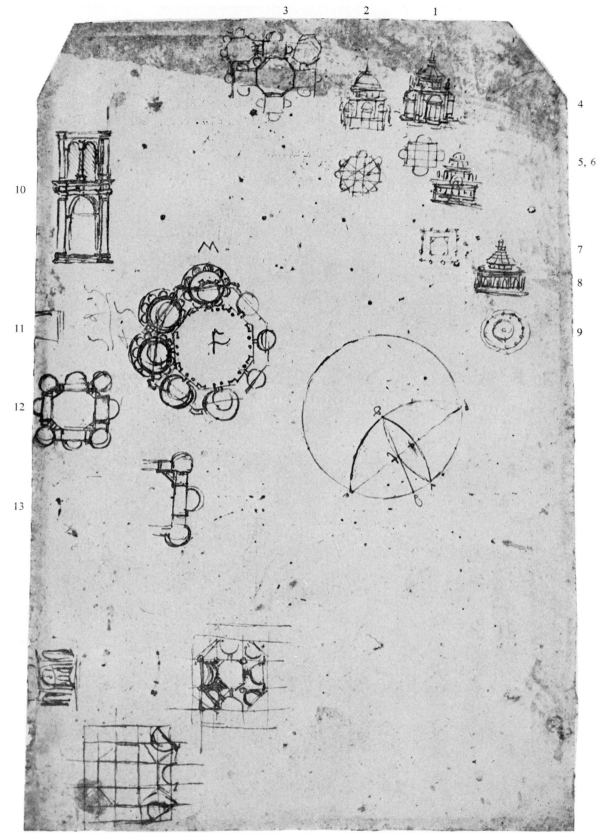

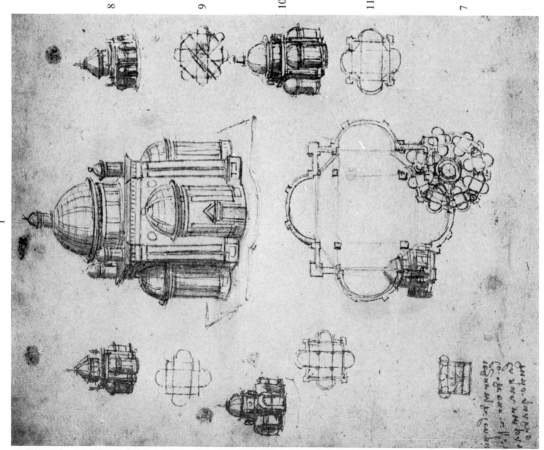

8

9

10

11

7

1

2

3

4

5

6

LXXXV, No.13. Paris, MS.I².110a

p.57

pp.29, 30, 34, 39, 57

LXXXV, Nos.1–11. Paris, MS.B.N.2037.3b

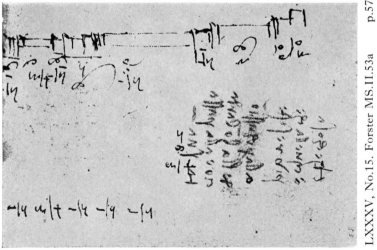

3

1

2

4

5

pp.30, 36

LXXXVI, Nos. 1–5 Cod.Atl.205b

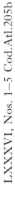

p.57

LXXXV, No.15. Forster MS.II.53a

p.52

LXXXV, No.14. Forster
MS.III.15b

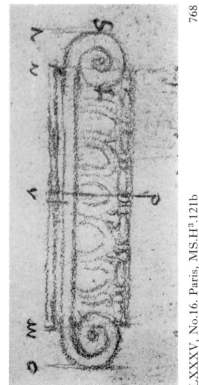

768

LXXXV, No.16. Paris, MS.H³.121b

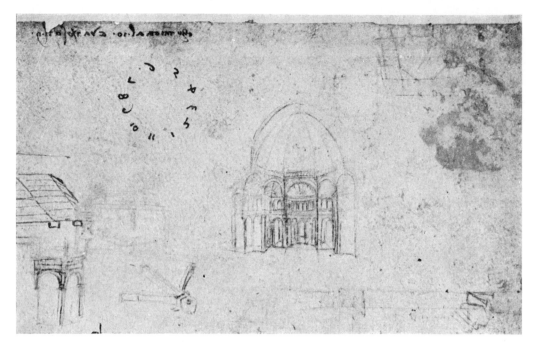

LXXXVII, No.1. Cod.Atl.7v-b

p.38

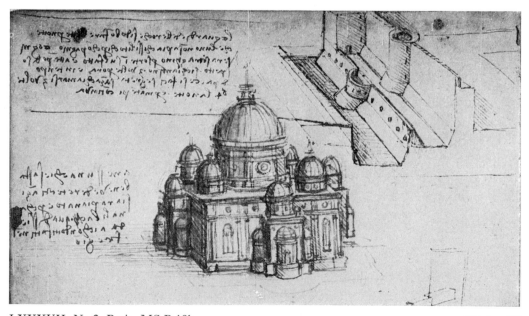

LXXXVII, No.2. Paris, MS.B.18b

755 & p.37

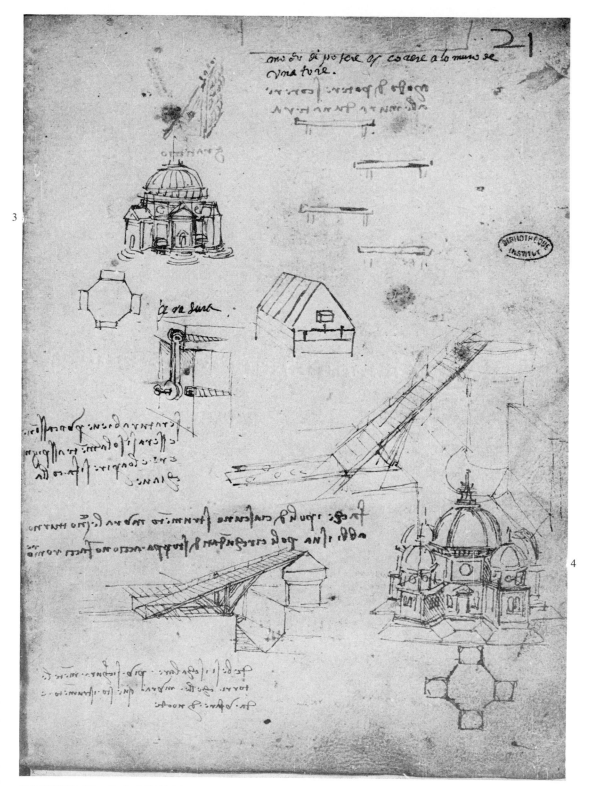

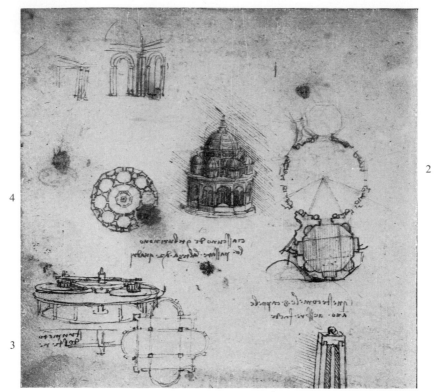

LXXXVIII, Nos.1–5. Paris, MS.B.21a pp.30, 34

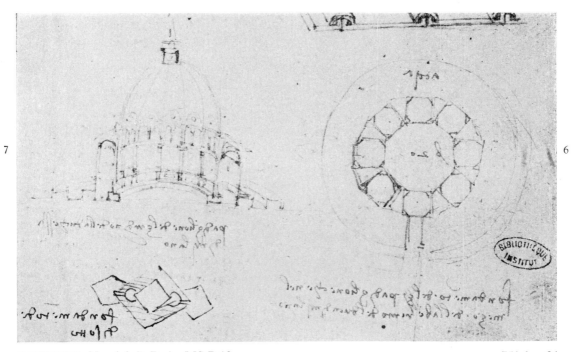

LXXXVIII, Nos.6 & 7. Paris, MS.B.12a 751 & p.24

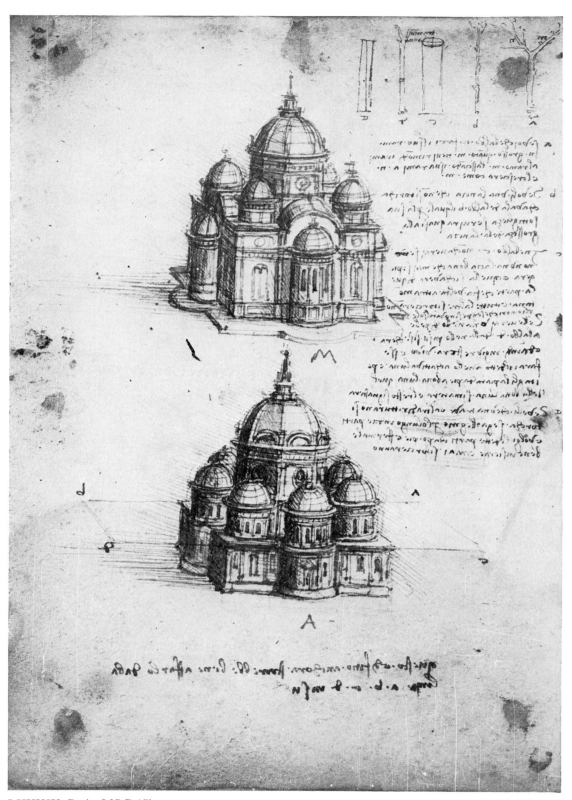

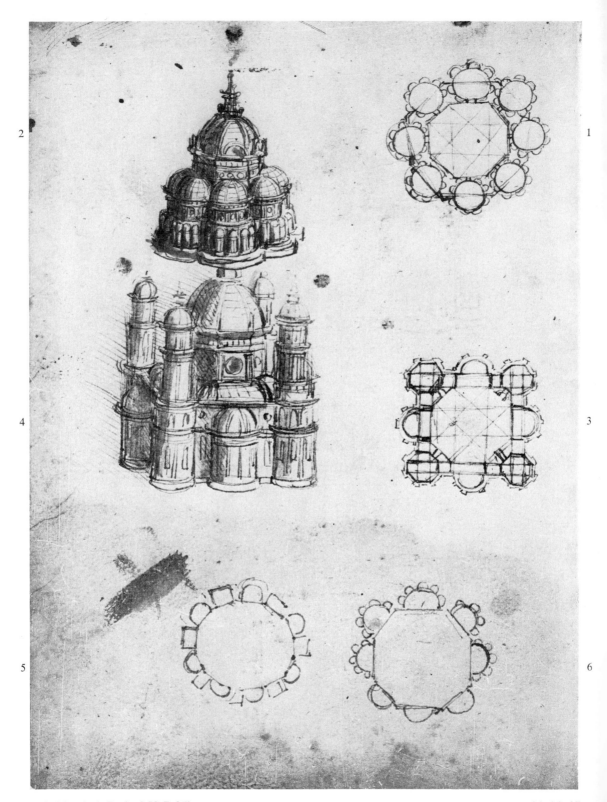

2

1

4

3

5

6

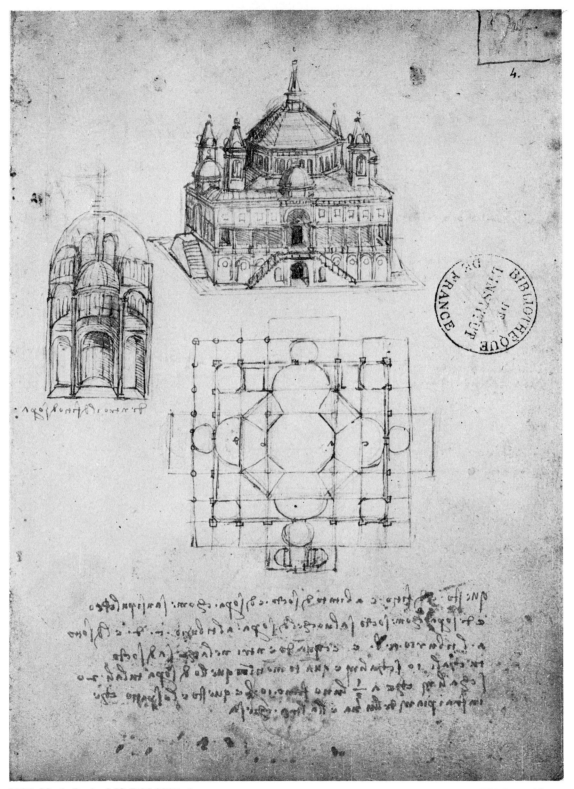

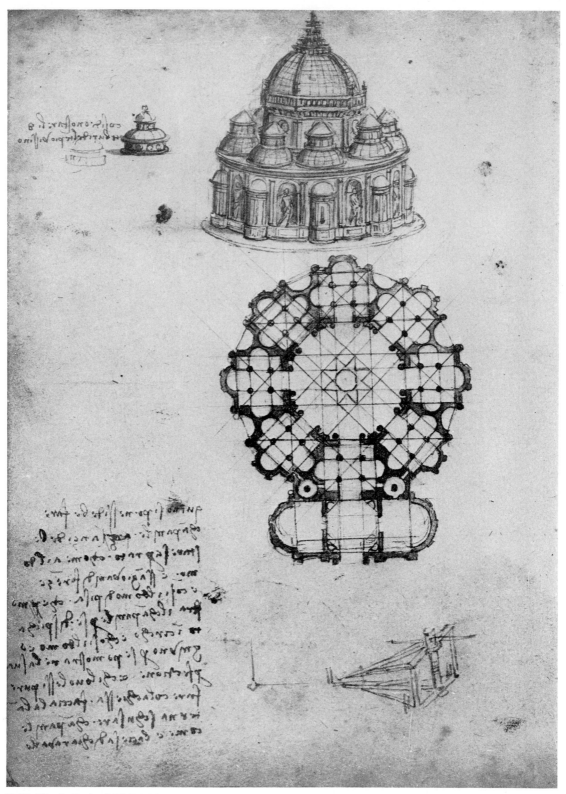

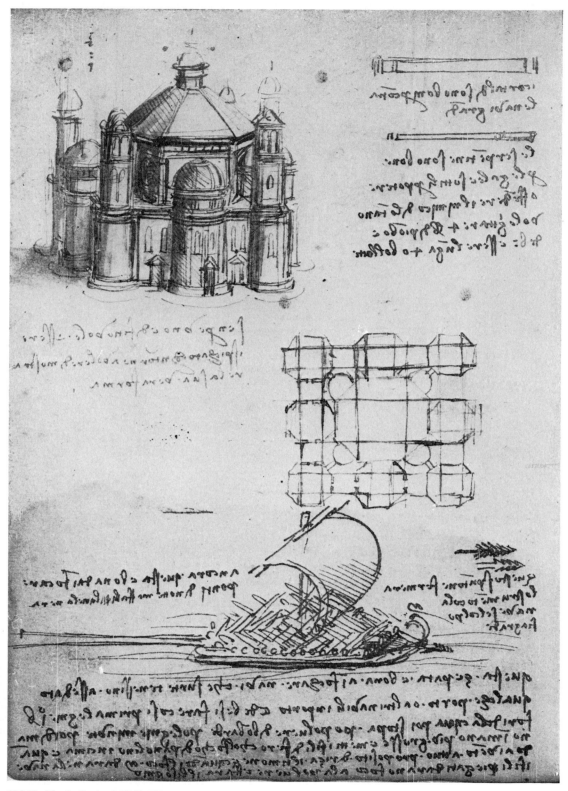

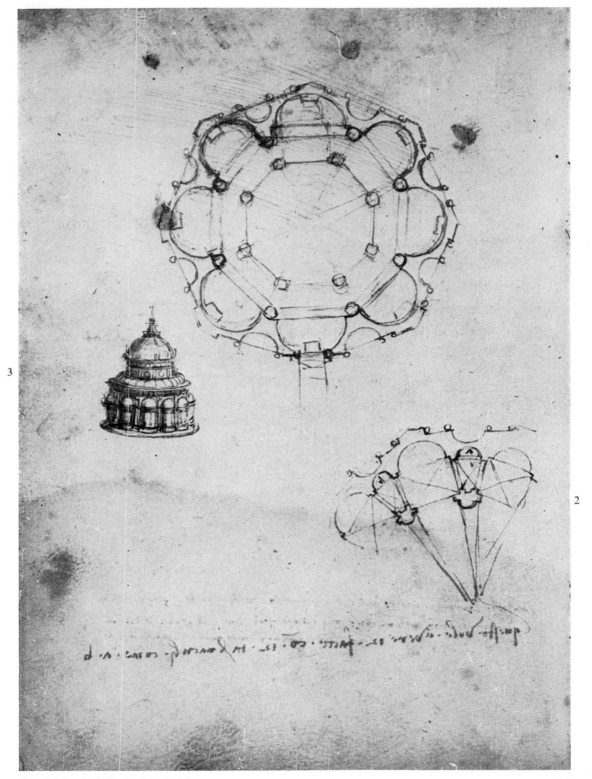

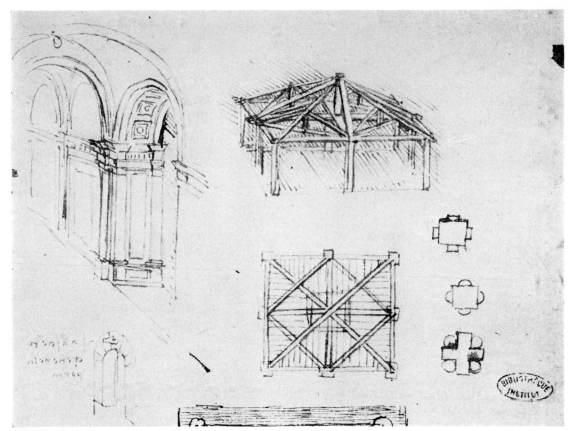

XCIII, No.1. Paris, MS.B.15a   p.57

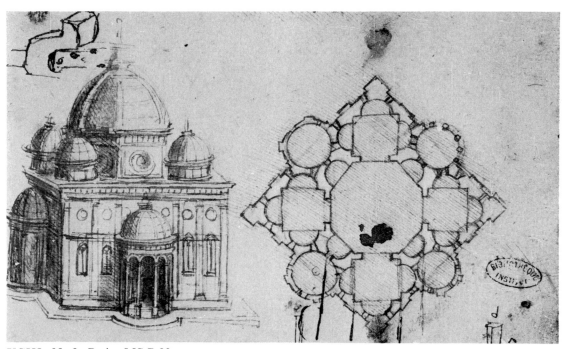

XCIII, No.2. Paris, MS.B.22a   p.37

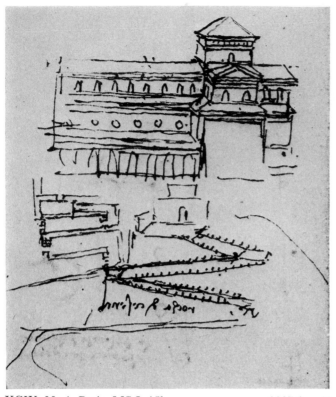

XCIV, No.4. Venice 238
(Frame 27)   p.42

XCIV, No.1. Paris, MS.L.15b   1037 & p.41

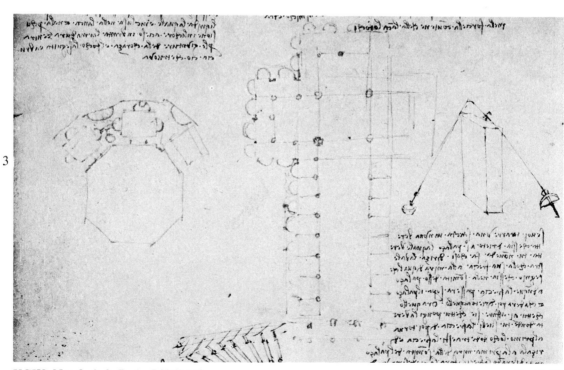

XCIV, Nos.2. & 3. Paris, MS.B.11b   pp.31, 40, 79

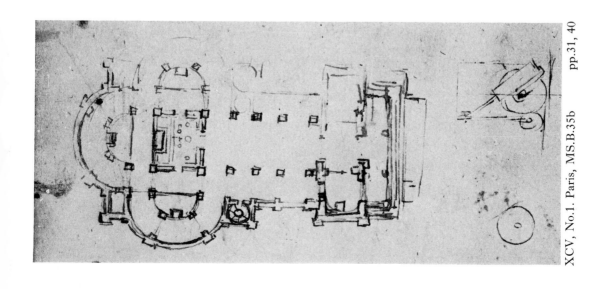

el sitio sepulcro
se p: can brçima
si se piena

A

A · el sitio sepulcro
mi can se luego se riena

el sias sepulcro se
mi can se luego se riena
B

A · el suno [...] algun [...] que [...] illustre · B · el suno [...] bo[...] logo[...]

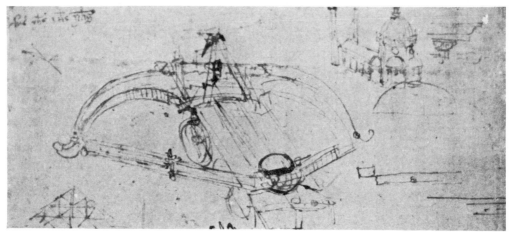

XCVI, No.1. Cod.Atl.17v-a

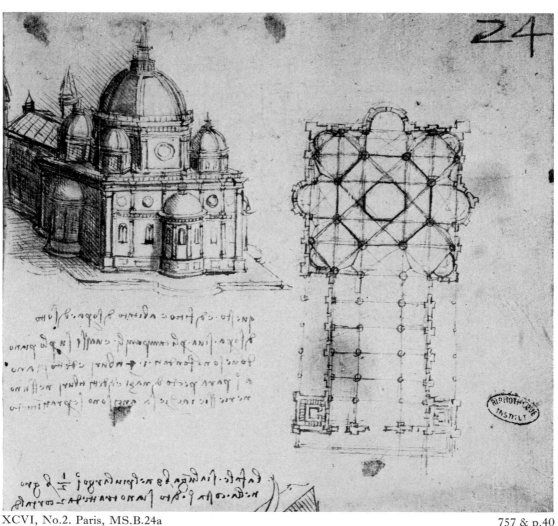

XCVI, No.2. Paris, MS.B.24a

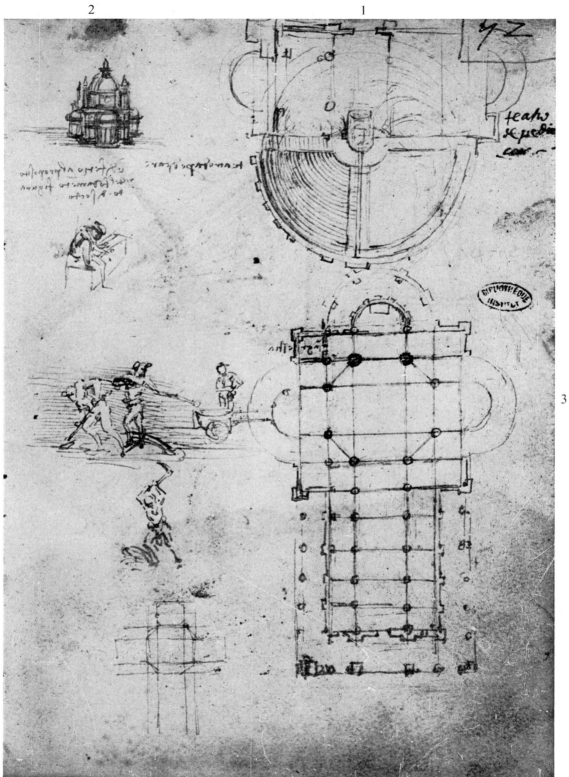

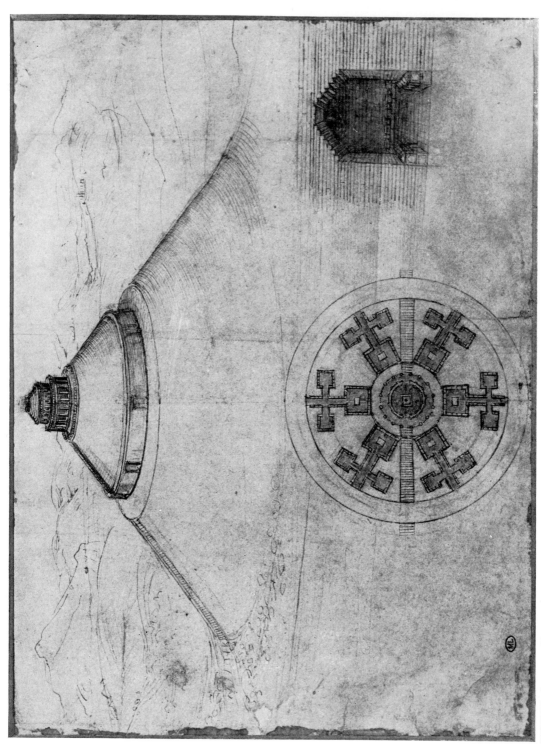

XCVIII. Louvre, Vallardi vol. 182 (2386)

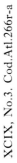

p.48

XCIX, No.3. Cod.Atl.266r-a

758

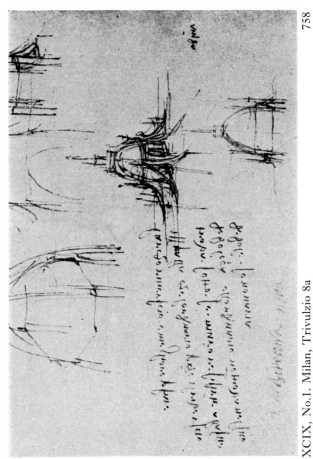

XCIX, No.1. Milan, Trivulzio 8a

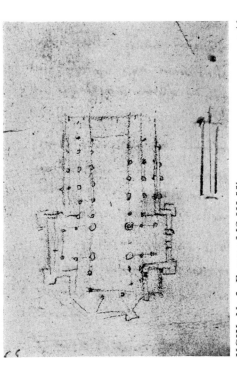

p.46

XCIX, No.2. Forster MS.III.55b

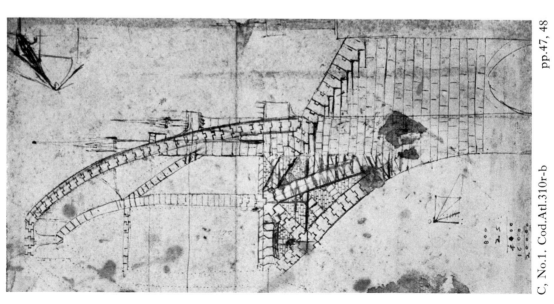

C, No.4. Milan, Trivulzio 22b

p.47

C, No.1. Cod.Atl.310r-b

pp.47, 48

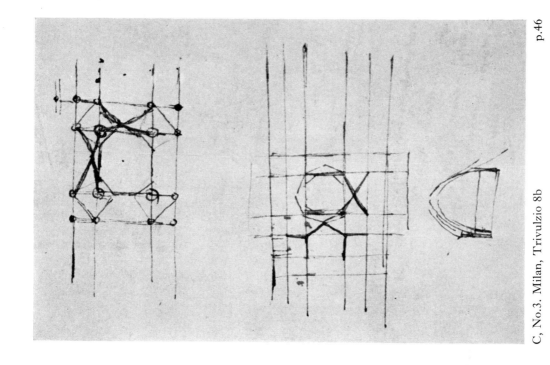

p.46

C, No.3. Milan, Trivulzio 8b

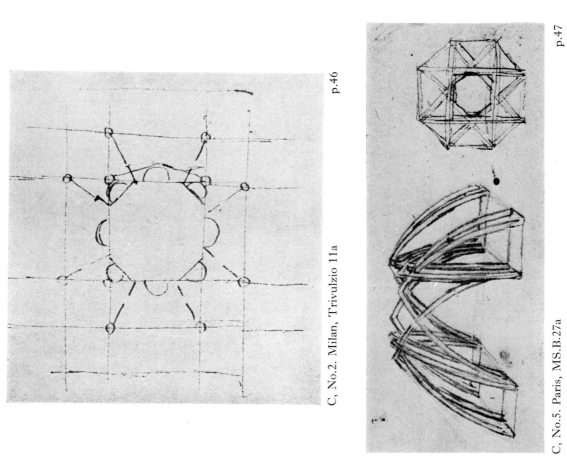

p.46

C, No.2. Milan, Trivulzio 11a

p.47

C, No.5. Paris, MS.B.27a

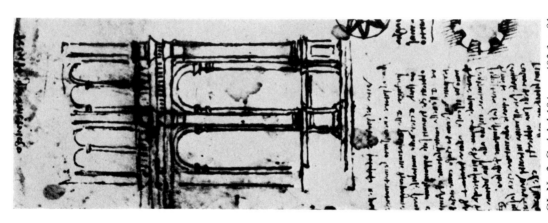

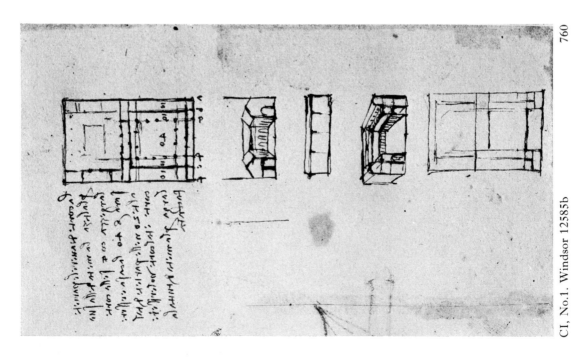

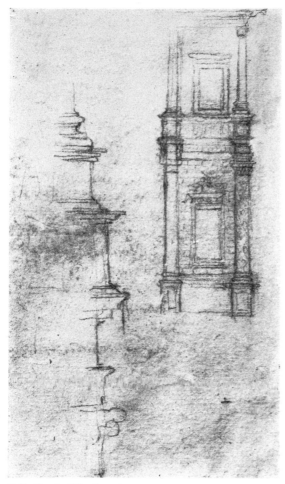

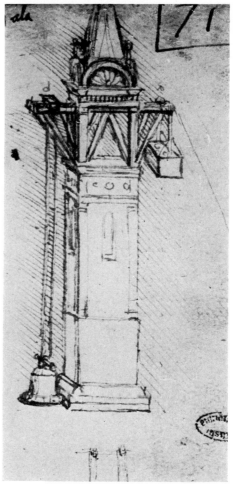

CII, No.1. Windsor 12579b p.51 CII, No.2. Paris, MS.B.71a

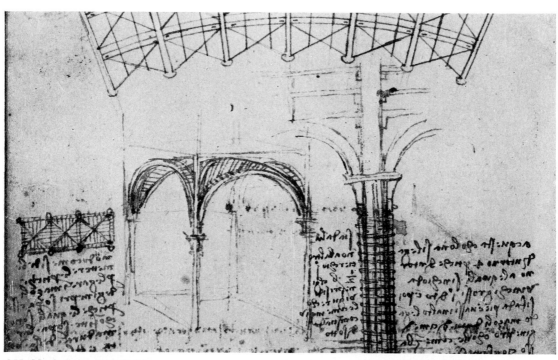

CII, No.3. Paris, MS.B.28b

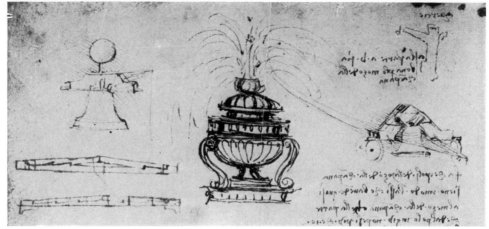

CIII, No.1. Paris, MS.B.70b   p.82

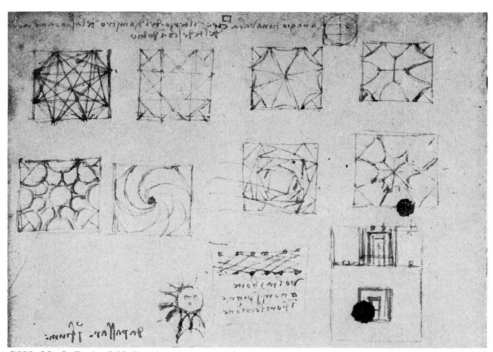

CIII, No.2. Paris, MS.B.10b   p.82

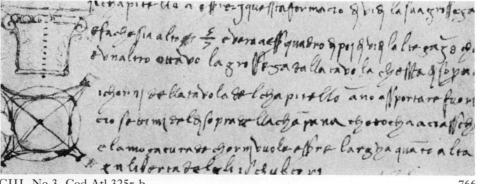

CIII, No.3. Cod.Atl.325r-b

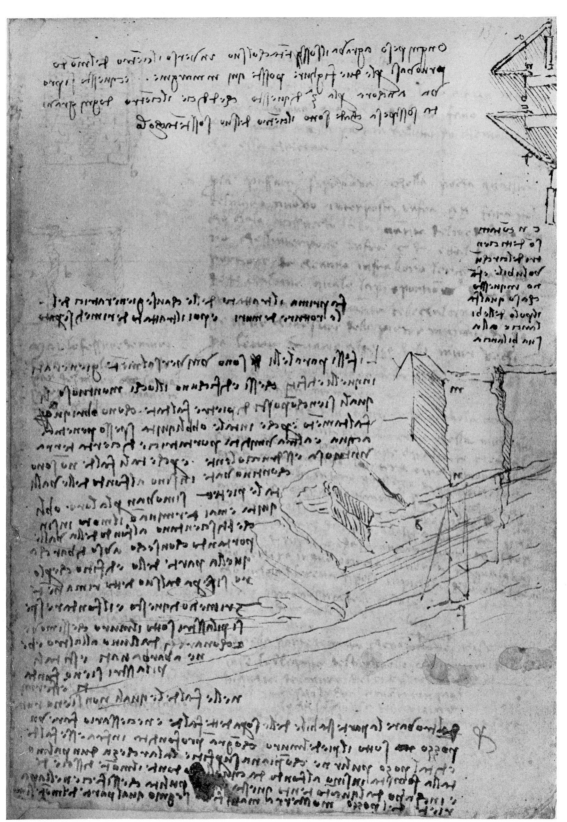

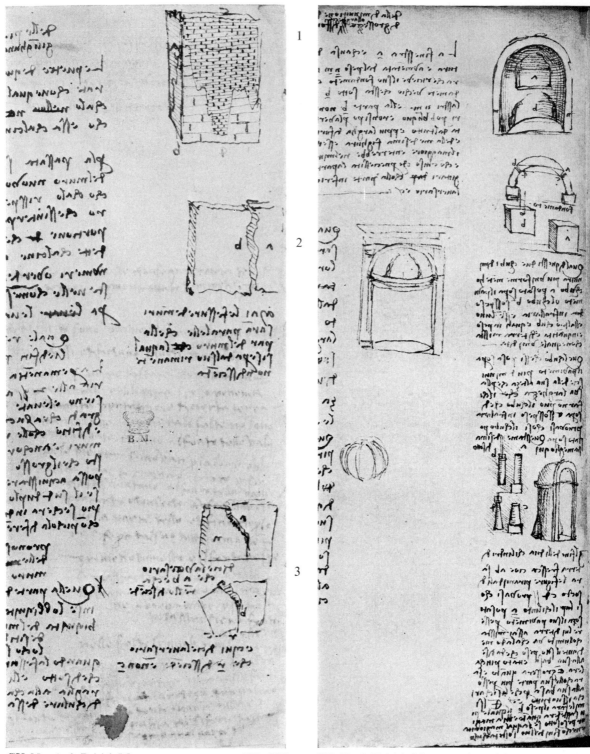

CV. Nos.1–3. British Museum,   771, 775
Arundel MS.157b

CV, No.4. British Museum, Arundel   778
MS.141b

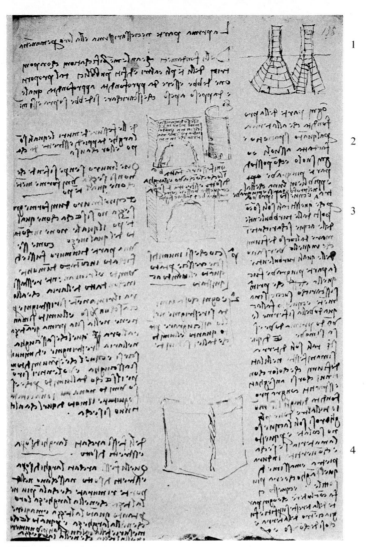

CVI. Nos.1–4. British Museum, Arundel MS.138a   772, 789

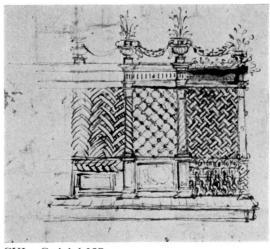

CVIA. Cod.Atl.357v-a

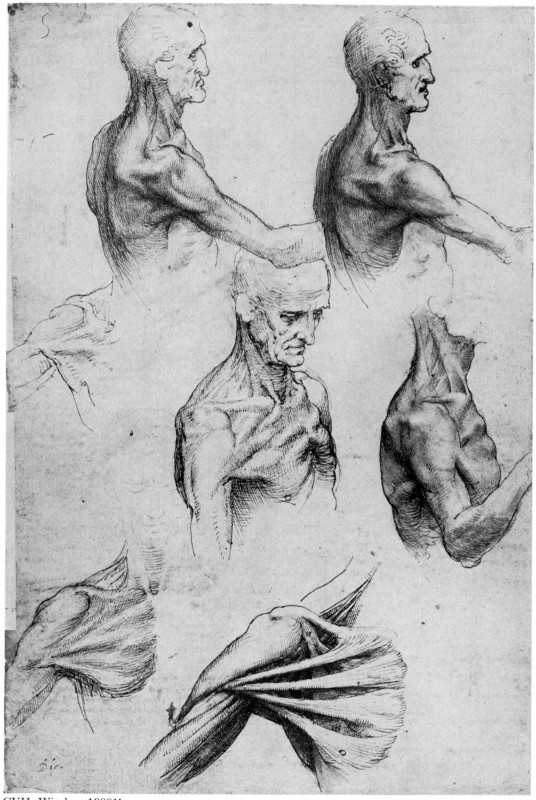

CVII. Windsor 19001b   p.88n.

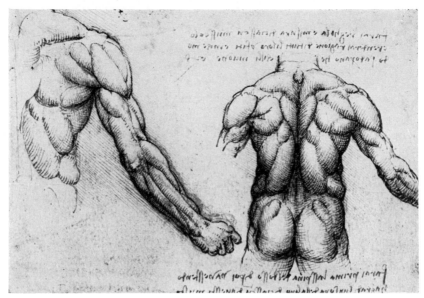

CVIII, No.1. Windsor 19044a   809

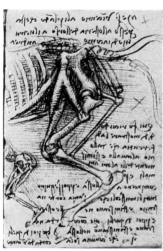

CVIII, No.2.   824
Institut MS.K³.109b

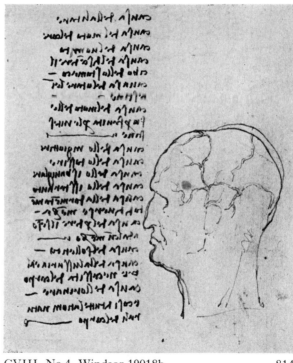

CVIII, No.4. Windsor 19018b   814

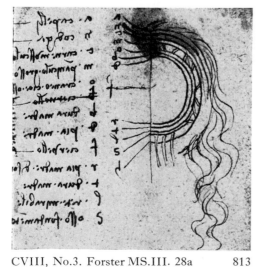

CVIII, No.3. Forster MS.III. 28a   813

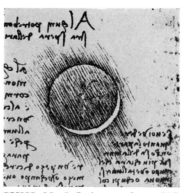

CVIII, No.5. Leicester 2a   902

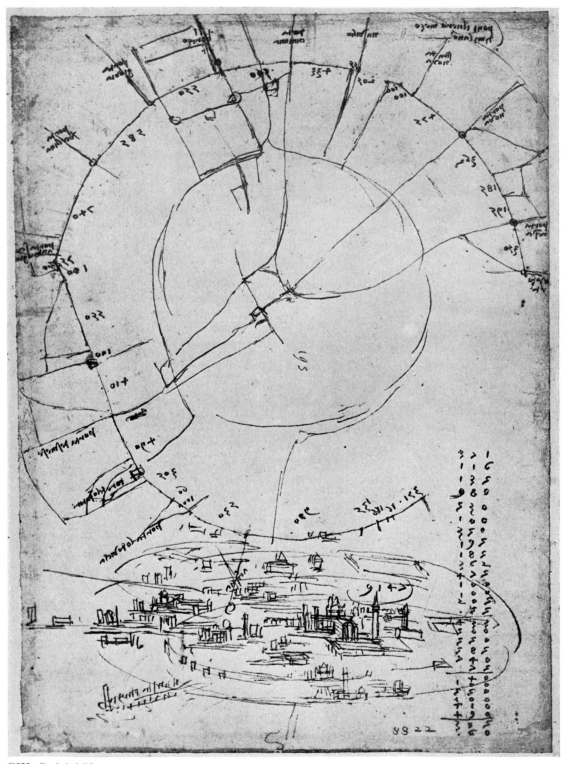

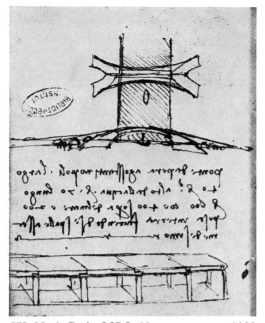

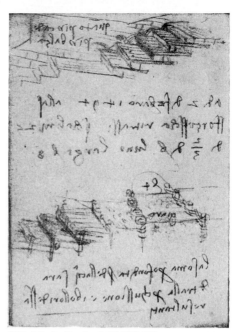

CX, No.1. Paris, MS.L.66a   1109

CX, No.2. Paris, MS.H².65b   1024

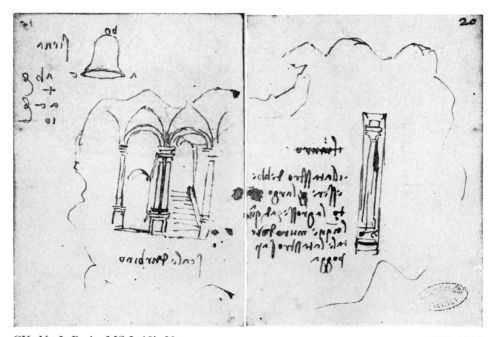

CX, No.3. Paris, MS.L.19b,20a   765, 1038

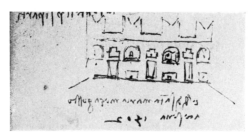

CX, No.4. Paris, MS.L.36b   1040, p.52

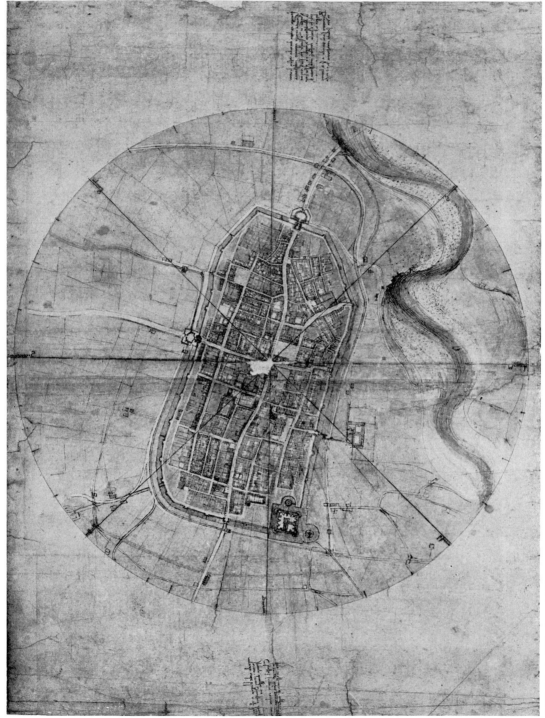

1051

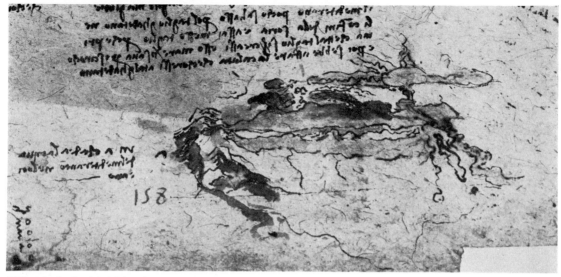

CXI, No.2. Cod.Atl.328v-b

1092

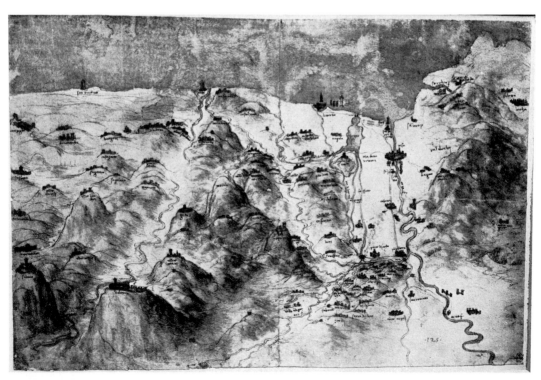

CXII. Windsor 12683

1006n.

CXIII. Windsor 12278a

1066n.

1066n.

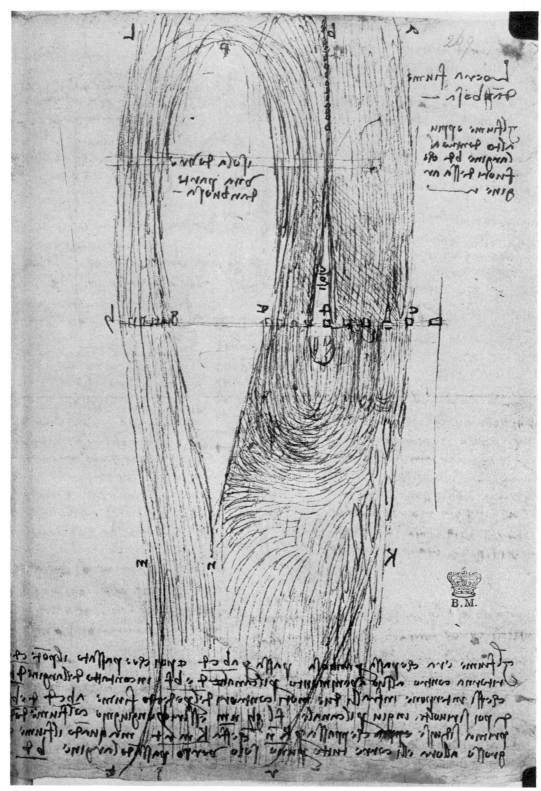

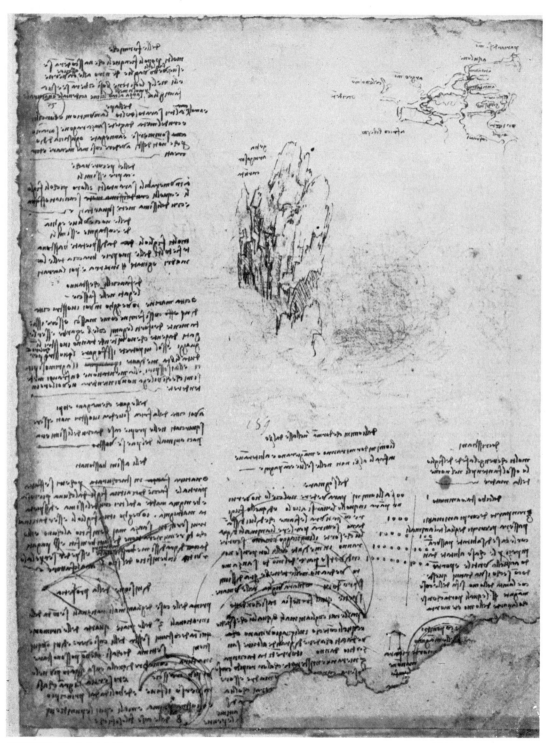

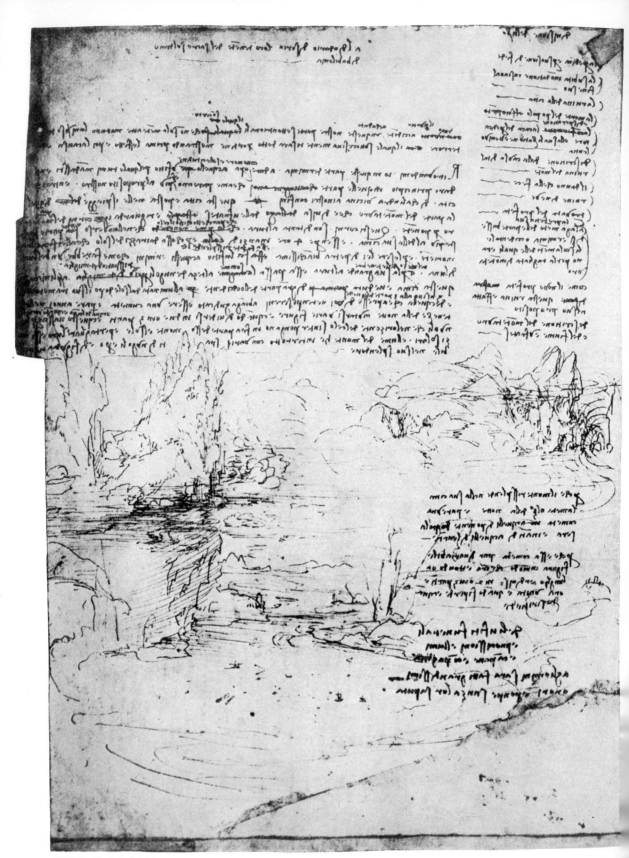

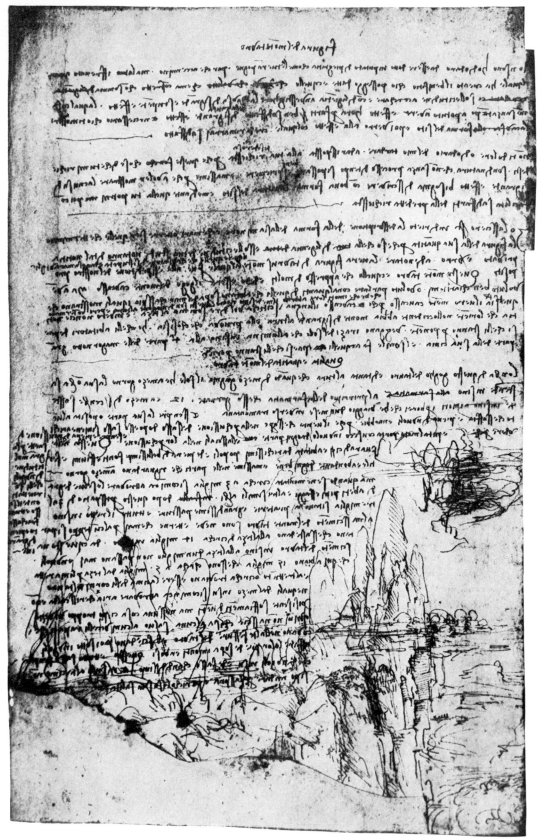

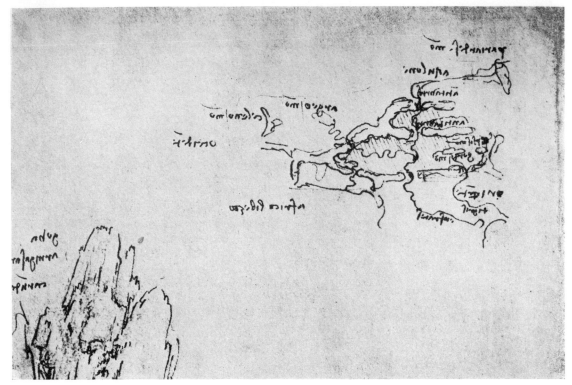

CXIX. Detail of P1.CXVIII   p.321n.

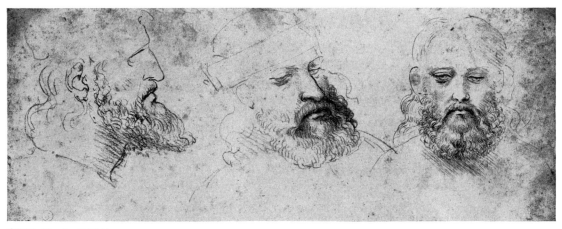

CXX. Turin 15573

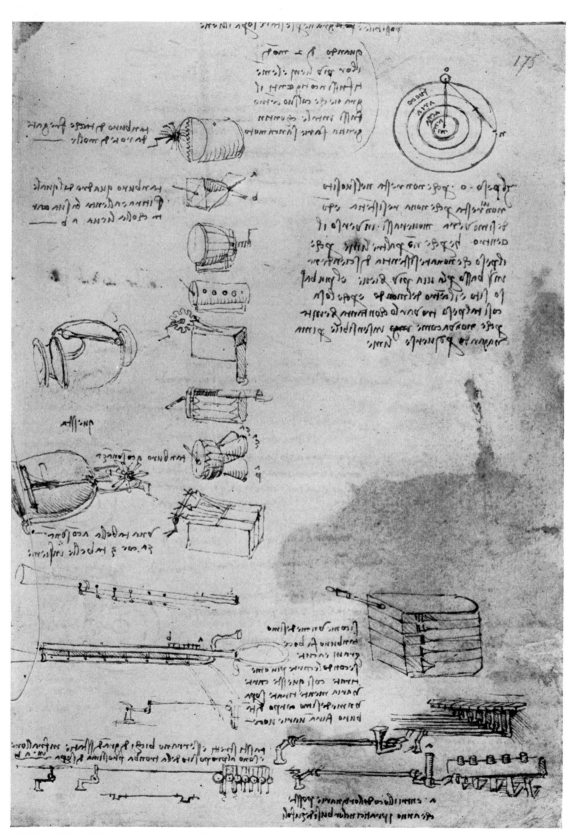

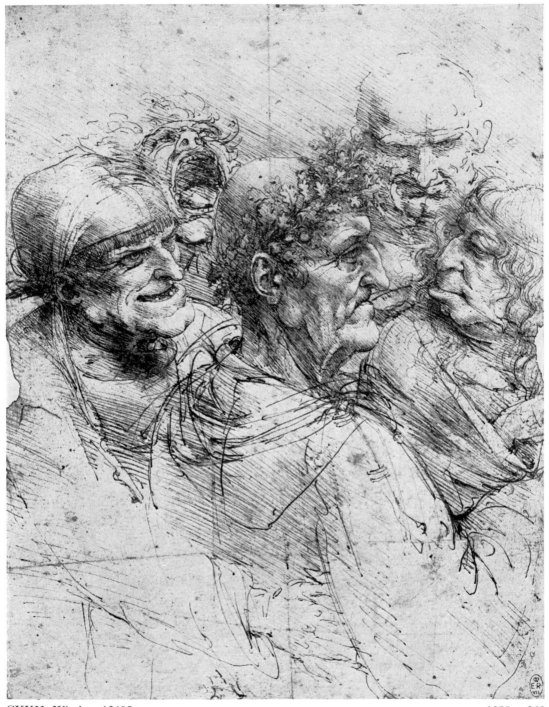

CXXII. Windsor 12495a

1355, p.260

APPENDIX

I

THE HISTORY OF THE MANUSCRIPTS

1517–1570. 1. ANTONIO DE BEATIS, who accompanied the Cardinal Luigi d'Aragona on his visit to Leonardo at Cloux on 10 October, 1517, describes the manuscripts then in his possession: 'Ha composto de notomia tanto particularmente con la demostratione de la pictura, si de membri, come de muscoli, nervi, vene, giunture, d'intestini, et di quanto si può ragionare tanto di corpi de homini, come de donne, de modo non è stato mai facto anchora da altra persona. Il che habbiamo visto oculatamente; et gia lui ne dixe haver facta notomia de più de xxx corpi tra mascoli et femine de ogni età. Ha anche composto de la natura de le acque, de diverse machine et d'altre cose, secondo ha referito lui, infinità de volumi, et tucti in lingua vulgare, quali si vengono in luce, saranno profigui et molto dilectevoli.' A publication of these manuscripts was then thought 'useful and very delightful' by these gentlemen.

Leonardo by his will expressly devised all his manuscripts and drawings to his young friend Francesco Melzi, who carried them back to Milan. Four years after Leonardo's death Alberto Bendedeo wrote from Milan to Alfonso d'Este, Duke of Ferrara: 'Et perchè ho fatto mentione de la casa de Melzi, aviso a V. Ex. che un fratello di questo che ha giostrato fù creato de Lionardo da Vinci, et herede del molti de' suoi secreti, et tutte le sue opinioni.... Credo ch'egli habbia quelli libriccini de Lionardo de la Notomia, et de molte altre belle cose.' See G. Campori, *Nuovi Documenti*, Modena, 1865, p. 10.

When Vasari visited Milan in May 1566 he mentioned Leonardo's manuscripts in Francesco Melzi's possession, and wrote as follows: 'Lionardo... di brutti caratteri scrisse lettere, che sono fatte con la mano mancina a rovescio; e chi non ha pratica a leggere, non l'intende, perchè non si leggono se non con lo specchio. Di queste carte della notomia degli uomini n'è gran parte nelle mani di messer Francesco da Melzo gentiluomo milanese, che nel tempo di Lionardo era bellissimo fanciullo e molto amato da lui, così come oggi è bello e gentile vecchio, che le ha care e tiene come per reliquie tal carte, insieme con il ritratto della felice memoria di Lionardo: e chi legge quegli scritti, par impossibile che quel divino spirito abbi così ben ragionato dell' arte e de' muscoli e nervi e vene, e con tanta

diligenza d'ogni cosa. Come anche sono nelle mani di ..., pittor milanese, alcuni scritti di Lionardo, pur di caratteri scritti con la mancina a rovescio, che trattano della pittura e de' modi del disegno e colorire. Costui non è molto che venne a Fiorenza a vedermi, desiderando stampar questa opera, e la condusse a Roma, per dargli esito; nè so poi che di ciò sia seguito.' (Ed. Milanesi, iv. 35–7).

In another place Vasari mentions that he himself possessed some drawings by Leonardo.

In the short biography of Leonardo by the so-called Anonymus Magliabechianus (best edition by C. Frey, Berlin, 1892) written before Vasari's *Vite*, the manuscripts are mentioned in these terms: '(Leonardo) tornossene a Milano et dipoi in Francia al servizio del re Francisco, dove porto assai de sua disegni, de quali ancora ne lascio in Firenze nello Spedale di S. Maria Nuova con altre masseritie et la maggior parte del cartone della sala del Consiglio, del quale il disegno del gruppo de cavalli che oggi in opera si vede rimase in Palazo ... et lascio per testamento a messer Francesco da Melzio, gentile homo milanese, tutti i danari con tutti panni, libri, scritture, disegni et instrumenti et ritratti circa la pittura et arte et industria sua che quivi si trovava, et fecelo executore del suo testamento.'

Lomazzo, the Milanese painter, writes in 1590 (*Idea del Tempio della pittura*, 2nd ed., p. 15): 'Ma sopra a tutti questi scrittori è degno di memoria Lionardo Vinci, il qual insegnò l'Anatomia dei corpi umani, e dei cavalli ch'io ho veduta appresso a Francesco Melzi, designata divinamente di sua mano. Dimostrò anco in figura tutte le proporzioni dei membri del corpo umano; scrisse della prospettiva dei lumi, del modo di tirare le figure maggior del naturale, e molti altri libri.... Ma di tante cose niuna se ne ritrova in stampa; ma solamente di mano di lui, che in buona parte sono pervenute nelle mani di Pompeo Leoni, statovaro del Cattolico Rè di Spagna, che gli ebbe dal figliuolo di Francesco Melzi, e n'è venuto di questi libri ancora nelle mani del Sig. Guido Mazenta, Dottore virtuosissimo, il quale gli tiene molto cari.'

2. After Francesco Melzi's death in 1570 his 1570–1635. son Orazio allowed Leonardo's bequest to be dispersed. We are given a detailed description of the transactions by Giovanni Ambrogio Mazzenta

II   3 E

(born in 1565, died at Rome on 23 Dec. 1635), a distinguished Milanese who held important offices in the Church. He was the brother of Guido, mentioned by Lomazzo in the passage quoted above as the owner of manuscripts by Leonardo. Ambrogio set down these recollections[1] of his youth, when he was a student of law at Pisa in 1588, for the benefit of his friend Cassiano del Pozzo in 1635 (compare Vol. I, p. 8) at a time when Leonardo's manuscripts were much sought after:

'Alcune memorie de' fatti di Leonardo da Vinci a Milano e de' suoi libri

del P. Don Gio. Ambrosio Mazzenta Cherico Reg.re Minore di S. Paolo altrimenti detti Barnabiti.

'Già quasi cinquant' anni, vennero alle mie mani libri tredici di Leonardo da Vinci, alcuni scritti in foglio, altri in quarto, alla rovescia, secondo l'uso degli Hebrei, con buoni caratteri; assai facilmente letti, mediante uno specchio grande. Io gl'hebbi per ventura, ed il caso me li portò alle mani nel seguente modo. Studiando io leggi a Pisa nella camerata di Aldo Mannucci il giovane[2] curioso assai de libri, vi fù Lelio Gauardi d'Asola,[3] preposto di S. Zeno di Pavia, ed al Mannucci stretto parente. Questi essendo stato per Maestro d'humanità con Sig.ri Melzi detti a Milano da Vauero lor villa, in differenza d'altri Melzi Nobili della medesima città, ritrouò nella villa detta in casse antiche molti disegni, libri e strumenti lasciatiui da Leonardo.' and further on in speaking of the pupils of Leonardo:

'Ma niuno l'imitò più del Louino, Cesare da Sesto, e più d'ogni altro Francesco Meltio hospite suo per molti anni, nelle cui mani, e case, quando Leonardo fu portato in Francia dal Re Francesco primo, per la più ricca preda fatta nella conquista di Milano, restorno i libri e disigni di tal Maestro. Morendo q.to S.re quale se fosse stato pouero haurebbe lauorato più opere, hoggi per essere finitissime credute del Maestro, lasciò così pretioso thesoro nella Villa di Vauero agli Heredi suoi molto diuersi di studii, e d'impieghi, e perciò molto le neglessero, e presto le dispersero: unde facile fu al detto Lelio Gauardi maestro d'humanità in quella casa, cauarne quanto

uolse, ed il portar 13 di que libri a Firenze, per donarli al Gran Duca Francesco, sperandone gran prezzo per il gusto di quel principe voglioso di simil' opere, e per il credito grande di Leonardo in Firenze sua patria, oue puoco soggiornò, e manco ui lauorò. Gionto il Gauardi a Firenze il Gran Duca vi cade malato, e morse.[4] Venne perciò egli a Pisa, con il Mannucci, oue, facendoli io scrupolo del mal acquisto, si compose, e mi pregò, che, douendo io finito li studij miei legali passar a Milano, pigliassi assonto di far hauere a Sig.ri Melzi, quanto egli toltoli hauea. Satisfeci all' officio richiestomi, bona fide, consignando il tutto al S.r Horatio Melzi dottor collegiato, e capo della casa. Si marauigliò egli ch'io hauessi preso questo fastidio, e mi fece dono de' libri, dicendomi d'hauer molt' altri disegni del medesimo Auttore, già molt' anni nelle case di Villa sotto de tetti negletti. Restorno perciò li detti libri nelle mei mani e puoi de' miei fratelli, quali facendone troppo pomposa mostra, e ridicendo a chi li uedevano il modo e la facilità dell' acquisto, molti andorno dal medesimo Dottore Melzi, e ne buscorno disegni, modelli, plastice, anatomie, con altre pretiose reliquie del studio di Leonardo. Fra questi "pescatori" ui fu Pompeo Arettino figlio del Cavaliere Leone già scuolar del Buonarotti, e famigliare del Re di Spagna Filippo II per hauerui fatti li bronzi dell' Escoriale. Promise Pompeo al Dottor Melzi officij, maggistrati, e cattedre nel senato di Milano, se, ricuperando li XIII. libri gliel' hauesse datti per donarli al Re Filippo molto curioso di simili singolarità. Mosso da tali speranze il Melzi uolò a mio fratello, e ginocchiato lo pregò a ridonarli li donatoli, come collega del collegio di Milano, degno di compassione, cortesia, e grata beneuolenza, sette de' libri li furno ridonati, sei ne restorno in casa Mazenti, de' quali uno fu donato al s.r Card. Federico[5] di gl. m. hoggi conservato nella sua bibliotheca Ambrosia, in foglio, coperto di ueluto rosso, e tratta dell' umbre e de lumi molto filosoficam.te utilm.te per li pittori, e per i prospettiui ed optici. Un altro ne donò ad Ambrosio Figgini pittor nobile di que' tempi, quale con il restante del suo studio lo lasciò all' Erede suo Ercole Bianchi.[6] Richiesto io dal Duca

---

[1] Compare D. Luigi Gramatica, *Le memorie su L. d. V. di Don Ambrogio Mazenta*, Milan, 1919. The original memorandum forms part of Codex H 227 Inf. at the Ambrosiana. There are two copies extant, one in Codex H 228 Inf. also at the Ambrosiana. The other was presented by Cassiano del Pozzo to Roland Fréart Sieur de Chambray about 1640, who gave it to his brother Sieur de Chantelou. In 1861 this copy, which was then in the possession of Firmin Didot, was translated into French by Eugène Piot in the 'Cabinet de l'Amateur'. It now belongs to the Comtesse de Béhague (see Vol. I, p. 9).

[2] Aldo Manuzio il giovane was called to Pisa by

Francesco de' Medici and taught there from May 1587 to the beginning of the year 1589.

[3] Lelio Gavardi di Asola was *rettore dello studio* at Pisa in 1588-9 and cousin to Manuzio.

[4] Francesco de' Medici died on 19 Oct. 1587.

[5] This is MS. C now at the Institut de France (Conc. 2). The Mazentas and Cardinal Federico Borromeo were on terms of friendship from their youth. See Gramatica, *Memorie*, p. 14.

[6] Lomazzo, *Trattato della pittura* (1582, p. 652), says: 'Dei quali—torchi, presepi, molini e simili— Leonardo ne disegnò trenta carte di chiaro e scuro, che sono pervenute nelle mani di Ambrogio Figino

Carlo Emanuele di Savoia procurai dal medesimo mio fratello che ne compiacesse quell' Alt. d'uno terzo.[1] Il restante, morendo mio fratello fuori di Milano, peruenne no so come nelle mani del sopranominato Pompeo Aretino.[2] E questo accogliendone altri li sfogliò, e ne fece un gran libro, lasciato puoi all' Erede suo Polidoro Calchi,[3] e uenduto al S.r Galeazzo Arconato per 300 scudi; quale, come Cavalier generosiss.mo, lo conserua nelle sue gallerie, ricche di mill' altre preziose cose, e più uolte richiestone dall' Alt. di Sauoia e da più prencipi sodisfacendo alla cortesia, ne ha ricusato più di seicento scudi.'

From this account we must conclude that none of the thirteen volumes which Gavardi took away with him from Vaprio remained the property of the Mazzentas.

Ten volumes of Gavardi's theft all came into the possession of Pompeo Leoni, who undid and rearranged them. One of the volumes thus formed out of various parts of his collection is known by the name of *Codice Atlantico*, and this **of the MSS.** Leoni's son-in-law and heir sold to Count **at Milan and Paris** Galeazzo Arconati for 300 scudi. Other Leonardo MSS. in Leoni's possession were taken by him to Spain in 1591 and we shall hear of them anon (see page 397).

3. In 1636 Count Galeazzo Arconati presented twelve MS. volumes by Leonardo to the Ambrosiana at Milan. The explicit deed of this gift is dated 21 January, 1637.[4] In it are enumerated the following twelve manuscripts:

1. The Codice Atlantico. See Concordance 30.
2. 'Un libro in foglio ordinario il qual' è coperto di corame rosso, stampato con fregi e fiori d'oro, e di dentro tutto il libro è di pergamena, e comincia in lettera rossa con queste parole, Tavola Della Presente'. . . . This manuscript is not by Leonardo but a copy of Luca Pacioli's *De Divina Proportione*.
3. 'Un libro in quarto legato in carta pergamena, nella schiena del quale si leggono le seguenti parole: DI LEONARDO DA VINCIE; è di fogli 100 in punto, ma vi manca il primo, nel secondo vi sono alcune foglie e frutti di marone colorate. Nel corpo d'esso libro a fogli 49 si trovano inserte cinque carte di disegni varii, per il più d'arme d'asta. Nel fine d'esso libro vi è un altro volumetto[5] di figure varie matematiche e uccelli di carte 18, cucito dentro

della medesima carta pergamena.' This manuscript is Cod. B (Conc. 3) in the Institut de France with No. 2037, formerly in the Bibliothèque Nationale (Conc. 4).

4. Manuscript of 114 leaves, now Cod. A, in the Institut de France (Conc. 6) with No. 2038 formerly in the Bibliothèque Nationale (Conc. 5.)
5. 'Il quinto è un altro simil libro, coperto, e in quarto, come sopra, di fogli 54, nel primo de' quali vi sono disegni di varie teste buffonesche e l'ultime quattro colonne di scrittura scritte alla rovescia, segnato nella schiena LEONARDO DA VINCI.' Now in the Trivulzi Library (Conc. 23).
6. Manuscript: see Conc. 20, E.
7. Manuscript: see Conc. 18, F.
8. Manuscript: see Conc. 21, G.
9. Three manuscripts bound in one volume; see Conc. 8–10, H[1], H[2], H[3].
10. Two small manuscripts bound in one; see Conc. 13, 14, I[1] and I[2].
11. Manuscript: see Conc. 15, L.
12. Manuscript: see Conc. 22, M.

That parts of the bequest of Arconati have been lost is shown by the list of 32 chapters of the 'Trattato' (now in MS. H 227 Inf. at the Ambrosiana) which was sent to Milan by Cavaliere Cassiano del Pozzo about 1639 with the request that these chapters should be compared with the original texts to make sure that they were correct. On this list seventeen chapters were marked with a cross to show that they had been compared with the original texts which must therefore presumably have been in Arconati's library at that time. To-day, however, several of these can no longer be traced.[6]

In 1674 Count Orazio Archinti presented to the same library a manuscript by Leonardo, consisting of three small note-books in one volume; Conc. 27–9, K[1], K[2], K[3].

In 1790 Stefano Bonsignori made a short catalogue of the manuscripts in the Ambrosian Library at Milan. It includes (1) MS. C. A., see Conc. 30; (2) MS. B and B.N. 2037, see Conc. 3, 4; (3) MS. B.N. 2038 and A, Conc. 5, 6; (4) MS. D, Conc. 26; (5) MS. E, Conc. 20; (7) MS. G, Conc. 21; (8) MSS. H[1], H[2], H[3], Conc. 8–10.

The descriptions of the others are too vague and slight to admit of our identifying by them any manuscripts now existing: (6) *Miscellanea*;

---

dove si veggono alcuni molini, che mancinano con acqua, ed altri senza, tutti fra sè diversi. . . .' These drawings were in Figino's possession as early as 1582, and cannot be the same as the book to which Mazenta refers here.

[1] This MS. is now lost.

[2] Guido Mazenta, whose name is inscribed in the MS. which he gave to Cardinal Federico Borromeo (see p. 304), died in 1613.

[3] *Calchi*. Pompeo Leoni's heir was Polidoro Calchi, his son-in-law who had married Vittoria Leoni in 1588.

[4] Published by G. Uzielli, *Ricerche*, ii, Rome, 1884, pp. 235–54.

[5] This 'Volumetto' is MS. Trn. (Conc. 25).

[6] Cf. E. Carusi, *Per il Trattato della Pittura di L.d.V. Per il IV. Centenario della Morte di L. d. V.*, Bergamo, 1919, p. 426. (See p. 398 and Vol. I, p. 8).

idrostatica, etc. È in-8 piccolo, in cartone rustico.
(9) *Miscellanea. Moto, macchine, macchinette da forar cristalli, etc. È in-16, legato in pergamena.*
(10) *Miscellanea in-16, in cartone rustico.* (11) *Miscellanea. Abbozzi informi, moto ecc. È in-16, pergamena* (see Dozio, *Degli scritti . . . di Leonardo da Vinci*, Milano 1871, pp. 21-4). It will be observed that one manuscript less is here named than in the deed of gift from Count Arconati; on the other hand, MS. *D*, not previously mentioned, is now included. The fifth manuscript of Arconati's list is evidently wanting in this list. The volume given to the Ambrosian Library by Cardinal Borromeo in 1603 (Conc. 2, C) seems also to have been omitted. It is evident then that we cannot exactly determine how many of these manuscripts were to be found in the Ambrosian Library in the year 1796.

At the suggestion of Bonaparte the Directory of the French Republic conveyed many works of art from Italy into France. This much is at any rate certain: in August 1796 the Codex Atlanticus was in the Bibliothèque Nationale: and 'Douze petits MSS. de Leonardo de Vinci, sur les sciences' were in the Institut National (Institut de France). The authors of the catalogue of the pictures and manuscripts removed from the Ambrosian Library—Peignon, *commissaire de guerre* and *le Citoyen* Tinet, *agent des Arts* (dated Milan, 24 May, 1796) either do not mention Leonardo's manuscripts at all, or may have included them under the following somewhat vague designation: 'Le Carton des ouvrages de Leonardo d'avinci'. It is certain, on the other hand, that in 1815 the commissary of the Austrian government demanded the restoration to the Ambrosian Library of thirteen (or fourteen?) manuscripts, being the number stated in G. B. Venturi's *Essai sur les ouvrages physico-mathématiques de L. d. V.*, Paris, 1797. Venturi says in his essay: 'Les Manuscrits sont au nombre de quatorze, parce que le Volume B contient un appendice de dix-huit feuillets qu'on peut séparer et considérer comme le quatorzième volume.' It was Venturi who labelled the manuscripts at the Institut by the capital letters A to M.

However, only the Codex Atlanticus found its way back again; the other twelve manuscripts remain in the possession of the Institut de France. These facts cover all that is known of the history and fate of the volumes now on the continent, that is to say, in France and Italy.

of the MSS. at Windsor and in the British Museum. 4. The history of the Leonardo MSS. at Windsor cannot be traced through all their vicissitudes, and it is not certain when and how they were acquired. The discovery of the volume at Kensington Palace in the reign of George III is thus described by Charles Rogers in *A Collection of Prints in Imitation of Drawings*, 1778, i, p. 5: 'This great curiosity . . . was deposited by King Charles himself in a large and strong chest, in which it lay unobserved and forgotten about 120 years till Mr. Dalton fortunately discovered it at the bottom of the same chest in the beginning of the reign of his present Majesty . . ., a treasure for its riches rivalling even that of Milan the Great.' Charles Rogers gives the earliest detailed description of the manuscripts: 'A large Volume of Lionardo's drawings, assembled together by the "Pompeo Leoni" so often mentioned, is happily preserved in his Majesty's inestimable Collection. . . . It is a large Volume in Folio strongly bound in calve's leather, and on its cover is this Inscription: DISEGNI . DI . LEONARDO . DA . VINCI . RESTAURATI . DA . POMPEO . LEONI . In it are contained 234 Leaves on which are pasted 779 Drawings executed in the various manners practised in designing; most of them with a Pen on common Paper; some on blue, brown or red Paper; with red or with black Chalks; or with metal Pencil on a tinted Paper; and a few of them are washed and heightened with white. Their subjects are general, as Portraits, Caricatures, single Figures, Compositions, Horsemanships, Tilting, Horses, and other Animals, Flowers, Optics, Perspective, Gunnery, Hydraulics, Mechanics, etc., and in particular very accurate Delineations with a fine Pen of a great variety of anatomical subjects, and the whole book is everywhere illustrated with his usual left-hand writing. . . .' In 1812 J. Chamberlaine published his *Original Designs of the Most Celebrated Masters in His Majesty's Collection*, engraved by Bartolozzi, with biographical and historical sketches of Leonardo da Vinci, in which he gives the following account: 'It was one of the three volumes, which became the property of Pompeo Leoni that is now in his Majesty's possession. It is rather probable than certain that this great curiosity was acquired for King Charles I by the Earl of Arundel, when he went an Ambassador to the Emperor Ferdinand II in 1636, as may indeed be inferred from an instructive inscription over the place, where the volumes are kept, which sets forth that James King of England offered three thousand pistoles for one of the volumes of Leonardo's works. And some documents in the Ambrosian Library give colour to this conjecture. This volume was happily preserved, during the civil wars of the last century, among other specimens of the fine arts, which the munificence of Charles I had amassed with a diligence equal to his taste. And it was discovered soon after his present Majesty's accession, in the same cabinet, where Queen Caroline found the fine portraits of the court of Henry VIII by Hans Holbein, which the King's liberality permitted me lately to lay before publick.'

Chamberlaine, apparently misled by the well-known inscription[1] in the Ambrosian Library, seems to assume that Lord Arundel must have derived the Leonardo MSS. in his possession from Arconati, and not from Spain; but Alfred Marks has disproved this clearly in two contributions to the Athenaeum, Nos. 2626 and 2645. John Evelyn in his *Memoirs* (vol. i, p. 213, ed. 1818) tells us that when travelling in Italy in 1646 he received from Lord Arundel, then sick at Padua, where he died in the course of that year, advice as to what he should try to see. Afterwards, visiting the Ambrosian Library, Evelyn writes: 'In this room stands the glorious (*boasting*) inscription of Cavaliero Galeazzo Arconati, valueing his gift to the librarie of severall drawings by Da Vinci, but these we could not see, the keeper of them being out of towne and he always carrying the keys with him, but my Lord Martial, who had seene them, told me all but one booke are small, that an huge folio contain'd 400 leaves full of scratches of Indians [sketches of engines?] &c., but whereas the inscription pretends that our King Charles had offer'd 1,000l. for them, my Lord himselfe told me that it was he who treated with Galeazzo for himselfe in the name and by permission of the King, and that the Duke of Feria, who was then Governor, should make the bargain: but my Lord having seen them since did not think them of so much worth.'

The leaves of the Codex Atlanticus are numbered up to 401; hence it is probable that in giving this description Lord Arundel had this single manuscript in his mind. The MS. W. at Windsor, which with the MS. C. A. formerly belonged to Pompeo Leoni, consisted of only 234 folio leaves. Arconati (see above) mentions, it is true, one collection only of manuscripts, i.e. MS. C. A, as being in the hands of Pompeo Leoni; but it can hardly be doubted that the manuscripts at Windsor were also in his possession, since Leoni's name is given in the inscription on the old binding of the two volumes in the same way. Pompeo Leoni, court sculptor to Philip II of Spain, returned to Italy in 1582 and stayed there until 1591, working most of the time in his father's studio at Milan

on the bronze altar for San Lorenzo at the Escorial. During that time he must have acquired the Leonardo MSS. The Windsor volume and others were probably taken to Spain on his return there in 1591. He died at Madrid in 1608 and his possessions were sold by auction. We learn from Carducho's *Dialogos de la Pintura*[2] (Madrid, 1633, p. 155, 6) that many of his finest things were afterwards bought by Charles, Prince of Wales, who visited Spain in 1623, but that he tried in vain to purchase two volumes of Leoni's collection which had passed into the possession of Don Juan de Espina, who planned to leave his art treasures to the King of Spain:[3] 'Allí vi dos libros dibujados y manuscritos de mano del gran Leonardo de Vinchi, de particular curiosidad . . . no los dexaria por ninguna cosa al Principe de Gales, quando estuvo en esta Corte.' . . . In Saintsbury's *Original Unpublished Papers Illustrative of the Life of Rubens* (London, 1859) we find that Lord Arundel was subsequently trying to buy these very books or one of them. On p. 294 will be found a note 'of such things as My Lord Embassador Sr Francis Cottington is to send owt of Spain for my Lord of Arondell; and not to forget the booke of drawings of Leonardo de Vinze wch is in Don Juan de Espinas hands'. This was in 1629, when Sir Francis was for the third time setting out for Spain as ambassador. His negotiations for the book were unsuccessful.

On 7 August, 1631, Arthur Hopton wrote to the Earl (M. F. S. Hervey, *The Life, Correspondence and Collections of Thomas Howard, Earl of Arundel*, Cambridge, 1921): 'The gentleman that is owner of the booke drawne by Leonardo di Vinci hath bin of late taken from his house by order from the inquisition, whoe after some time of restraint at Toledo, was permitted to goe to live at Sevill where hee now is. All the diligence that I can use therein is to procure to have advice when either by his death or otherwise his goods are to bee sould, and therein I wilbe very watchfull.' But Hopton too was unsuccessful, for on 9 January, 1637 we find Lord Arundel writing from Hampton Court to Lord Aston, then ambassador to Spain: 'I

---

[1] The following inscription is on the staircase of the Ambrosian Library.

|| LEONARDI VINCII || MANU . ET . INGENIO . CELEBERRIMI || LUCUBRATIONUM . VOLUMINA . XII || HABES . O . CIVIS || GALEAZ—ARCONATUS || INTER . OPTIMATES . TUOS || BONARUM . ARTIUM . CULTOR . OPTIMUS || REPUDIATIS . REGIO . ANIMO . || QUOS . ANGLIAE . REX . PRO . UNO . OFFEREBAT || AUREIS . TER . MILLE . HISPANICIS || NE . TIBI . TANTI . VIRI . DEESSET . ORNAMENTUM || BIBLIOTHECAE . AMBROSIANAE . CONSECRAVIT || NE . TANTI . LARGITORIS . DEESSET . MEMORIA || QUEM . SANGUIS . QUEM . MORES || MAGNO . FEDERICO . FUNDATORI || ADSTRINGUNT ||

BIBLIOTHECAE . CONSERVATORES || POSUERE || ANNO . MDCXXXVII. ||

[2] 'Muchas de las que avemos nombrado estuvieron en grande riesgo quando estuvo aqui el Principe de Gales, hoy Rei de Inglaterra, que procuró quanto pudo recoger las Pinturas y dibujos [drawings] originales que pudo aver . . . y fueron grande parte del residuo de las almonedas del Conde de Villamediana y de Pompeo Leoni' . . .

[3] Compare De Marini, *Raccolta Vinciana*, ii, p. 89. Two volumes by Leonardo were catalogued in the Royal Library at Madrid: *Tractados de meccanica y geometría escritas al revés y en los annos 1491–3*. In the year 1800 these two volumes could no longer be traced.

beseech y^{ou} be mindful of D. Jhon de Spina's booke, if his foolish humor change.' (Saintsbury, l.c., p. 299.)

It is now generally assumed that this correspondence refers to the MS. volume at Windsor which contains inscriptions in Spanish and must have come from Spain, and which it is supposed was once the property of the Earl of Arundel, since forty-three of the Windsor drawings were engraved by Hollar, who was in Arundel's service from 1636 to 1641 and probably copied Leonardo's drawings at that time. Owing to the Civil War the Earl left England for Holland in 1641, taking the larger part of his collection with him. He died at Padua in 1646. In that same year Hollar, who was then at Antwerp, signed two of the engravings he had made after Leonardo drawings with the inscription *ex Collectione Arundeliana*, and five years later he wrote the same inscription on yet another engraving.[1] But no drawings by Leonardo are mentioned in the inventory of the Arundel Collection which was drawn up at Amsterdam in 1655 after the death of the Countess. The suggestion of B. B. Woodward that Charles II at the instance of Sir Peter Lely bought the drawings and manuscripts of Leonardo da Vinci now at Windsor at the sale of the Arundel Collection in Holland in 1655 cannot therefore be substantiated.[2]

The heirs of the Arundel property after the Countess's death were her only surviving son William Viscount Stafford and her grandson Henry Howard, son of the deceased Frederick Henry, Earl of Arundel. Henry Howard was the owner of the volume now at the British Museum; John Evelyn says of him in his *Diary* (9 Jan. 1666) that he had 'so little inclination to books that in order to save them from embezzlement he persuaded him to bestow the noble library which his grandfather especially and his ancestors had collected on the Royal Society' (compare Conc. 19, Br.M.).

Although we have no record how Leonardo's manuscripts came into the possession of the

English Crown we have a written statement three times repeated, which can be dated *circa* 1639, that the King of England was then the owner of two original treatises by Leonardo. This statement was made under the following circumstances. At that time Cavaliere Cassiano dal Pozzo was having copies made of the so-called *Trattato della Pittura* (a compilation made from Leonardo's manuscripts soon after his death; compare Vol. I, p. 8), and a list of thirty-two of its chapters were sent to Conte Galeazzo Arconati in Milan for comparison with the original manuscripts, in order to make sure that they had been correctly copied.[3] On this list seventeen chapters are marked with a cross as a sign that they had been thus compared. The original texts of the remaining fifteen could not be found in Arconati's library, and it was said that they had passed into the possession of the King of England: 'Delle figure ricercate che non si mandano alcune sono pertinenti al *Trattato dell' Anatomia delle cose naturali*, et altre al *Trattato de colori, quali Trattati suono nelle mani del Re d'Inghilterra*; e perciò li capitoli in tal materia non si suon confrontati.'[4] It would seem therefore that Leonardo's anatomical MSS. were already then in Charles I's collection. The treatise on colour cannot now be traced. However, no drawings of Leonardo are mentioned in the inventory of Charles I's possessions made by the Cromwellian government.

The next reference to the Leonardo drawings in the English Royal Collections is to be found in the diary of Constantijn Huygens, secretary to William III. In 1690 he bought a volume of drawings which he supposed to be by Leonardo and reported this to his brother in a letter written from Kensington Palace (*Raccolta Vinciana*, viii, p. 176). However, this volume[5] was not by Leonardo himself, as was shown by A. W. M. Mensing (*Feest-bundel Dr. Abraham Bredius aangeboden*, Amsterdam, 1915, p. 186); and the chief interest in the incident lies in the circumstance that Queen Mary II on being informed of the purchase showed Huygens the drawings

[1] Only three of Hollar's engravings after Leonardo bear the inscription *Ex Collectione Arundeliana*: Parthey 1609, dated 1646 after a drawing now at Windsor (No. 12495); Parthey 1585, of the same date after a drawing now lost; and Parthey 1771, engraved in 1651 after No. 19002 at Windsor.

[2] B. B. Woodward, 'Drawings of Pietro Santo Bartoli in the Royal Collection', *Gentleman's Magazine*, Jan. 1866. Woodward was librarian from 1860 to 1869.

[3] There are two copies of this list extant. One is on folio 132 of the *Trattato* in the possession of the Comtesse de Béhague. The other is inserted into Codex H. 227 Inf. at the Ambrosiana. Part of the correspondence between Galeazzo Arconato and Cassiano dal Pozzo has survived and is now in the Vatican Library (Cod. Carpegna No. 160) and with Conte Lodovico Sola Cabiati at Milan. See Enrico

Carusi, *Letture di Galeazzo Arconato e C. d. Pozzo per lavori sui Manoscritti di Leonardo* in Accademie e Biblioteche d'Italia, Rome, 1929–30.

[4] This note is to be found in three different MSS. —in H. 227 and H. 229 Inf. at the Ambrosiana and in the *Trattato* belonging to the Comtesse de Béhague.

[5] This MS. volume, recently acquired by the Pierpont Morgan Library, contains 128 pages in quarto, the materials for the first five books of a treatise on the theory of art, composed by a Milanese painter about 1570. Included in these materials are 33 pages with copies from L. d. V.'s studies in human and equine proportions, about one-half of which can be connected with known originals, mostly at Windsor, but one is in Venice and another in Paris. They are shortly to be published by Dr. Erwin Panofsky, who discovered and identified them.

of Leonardo in her collection. To quote from Huygens's diary: 1 Sept. 1690 'Smorgens te 9 uren, ick noch niet op wesende, sondt de Coningin weder om mij, en sagh het boek van Leonardo da Vinci en dat van Holbeen'. (This morning at nine o'clock, I being not yet up, the Queen sent for me again and saw the book of Leonardo da Vinci and that of Holbein) ('Journal van Constantijn Huygens, den zoon', in *Werken van het Historisch benootschap*, Utrecht, Nieuwe Serie, No. 23, 1876, pp. 227, 326).

After the above account by Huygens there are no further records until the fortunate discovery of the volume by Mr. Dalton at the bottom of the chest in Kensington Palace.

In Rogers's description quoted above the volume contained 234 pages, and the number of drawings it contained are given as 779. To-day only about 600 are to be seen at Windsor. A note written in pencil at the beginning of the volume by Mr. Glover, librarian at Windsor (1836–60), may serve as explanation for this loss. It says that 64 of the pages had been cut out and were missing (see K. Clark, *Catalogue*, p. xiii). This is confirmed by the fact that among the Leonardo drawings which were engraved by Hollar several are no longer to be found (such are Parthey Nos. 1559, 1585, 1588, 1591, 1592, 1597, 1598, 1604).

The earliest inventory in which Leonardo's drawings are mentioned as being in the Royal Collection is in the manuscript department of the British Museum No. Add. 20,101 f. 28, from which the following extracts may here be quoted: *List of the Draw^gs || in ye Cabinet in || His Maj^tys Lower || Apartment || in this is marked what || has been Deliv'd for || her Maj^tys use ||* Page 28. *A list of the Books of drawings and Prints in the buroe in His Majesty's great Closet at Kensington.*

No. 3. *By Hans Holbein those fram'd & hung at Richmond.*

No. 5. *Prints by Hollar: delivered to her Maj^ty Aug. 1735 and by her lent to Lady Burlington, since put in Volumes and laid in ye Library at Kensington.*

No. 6. *Drawings by Leonardo de Vinci.*

No. 13. *Drawings by Leonardo di Vinci;— these mark^d with a cross were delivered for her Maj^tys use in ye year 1728.*

The oldest inventory in Windsor Castle, called Catalogue of Drawings and Prints, George III, is of the beginning of last century. On p. 23 we find: '*The Drawings of Leonardo da Vinci arranged by Pompeo Leoni (sculptor to Philip the Second of Spain) and interspersed with a great number of original MS. notes which being written with inverted characters are not legible unless reflected by a looking glass*'. Then follows a list of 41 pages with short descriptions of the drawings they contain. For instance: '*Page 1. Portrait of Leonardo drawn by himself as mentioned by G. Vasari—Red Chalk*' (a well-known drawing in the present collection). On p. 26 we come to '*Leonardo da Vinci, Tom. II*', which is also a list of drawings comprised on 40 pages. It begins: *page 1, the last Supper, the Architecture is varied in the painting at Millan where an open door is represented behind our Saviour, black chalk. N.B. This Drawing was not in the Vol. compiled by Pompeo Leoni, but in one of the Volumes in the Buonfiliuolo Collection bought at Venice.* (By the way I mention that the drawing in question, still at Windsor, is not an original drawing, but an old copy.) Nothing more, however, is known concerning the Buonfiliuolo collection.

On p. 29 of the Inventory we come to a catalogue of the contents of a third volume of 205 sheets, in which 549 drawings are named and shortly described, for instance:

No. 22 { *2 Heads, of Judas and one of the Apostles for the last supper at Milan.*

41 { *1 Mechanical Powers.*
{ *1 Anatomy.*

NB. All the Leaves from 41 to 142, except those few marked otherwise, are full of very copious and accurate studys in Anatomy which were done with the assistance of Marc Antonio della Torre &c.

143 { *1 Manuscript—Here ends the Anatomical study.*
{ *1 Richmond.*

Under the supervision of the Prince Consort the drawings were first cared for. A large number of them were taken out of Leoni's volume, mounted and exhibited at the Grosvenor Gallery in 1878.[1] At that time they were given inventory numbers, which have been retained in K. Clark's catalogue, and which have been adopted in the present edition.

---

[1] Grosvenor Gallery, *The Royal Collection of Drawings at Windsor*, Portfolios I and II, London, 1878.

APPENDIX

II

(1) INDEX OF MANUSCRIPTS*

	Mark of manuscript	Description of manuscript	Place	Total no. of pages	Size in centimetres	Date†
1.	W.	Sheets from Leoni's collection: originally one volume bound; some six hundred drawings	Royal Library, Windsor.	408	Various sizes	1489–1516
2.	C.	Treatise on Light and Shade, bound, marked C.	Institut de France, Paris.	56	31×22	1490
3.	B.	Bound volume, marked B.	Institut de France, Paris.	168	23·5×17	About 1488–9
4.	B.N. 2037 (Ash. II.)	Volume stitched in wrapper, marked $\frac{1875}{1}$.	Institut de France, Paris. Formerly at Ashburnham Place.	26	23×16·5	About 1488–9
5.	B.N. 2038 (Ash. I.)	Treatise on Painting marked $\frac{1875}{2}$.	Institut de France, Paris. Formerly at Ashburnham Place.	68	23×16·5	1492
6.	A.	Fragment of manuscript, treating on various matters.	Institut de France, Paris.	126	21×14	1492
7.	S.K.M.III.	Note-book, marked III.	Forster Library, Victoria and Albert Museum, London.	176	9×6·7	1490–3
8.	H.³	Note-book, forming the third portion of a bound volume, marked H.	Institut de France, Paris.	94	10·3×7·2	1493, 1494
9.	H.²	Note-book, forming the second portion of a bound volume, marked H.	Institut de France, Paris.	92	10·3×7·2	1494, January
10.	H.¹	Note-book, forming the first portion of a bound volume, marked H.	Institut de France, Paris.	96	10·3×7·2	1494, March
11.	S.K.M.II.²	Note-book, forming the second part of a bound volume, marked II.	Forster Library, Victoria and Albert Museum, London.	126	9·9×7·2	1495–7
12.	S.K.M.II.¹	Note-book, forming the first part of a bound volume, marked II.	Forster Library, Victoria and Albert Museum, London.	190	9·9×7·2	1495
13.	I.²	Note-book, forming the second part of a bound volume, marked I.	Institut de France, Paris.	182	10×7·2	1497–9
14.	I.¹	Note-book, forming the first portion of a bound volume, marked I.	Institut de France, Paris.	96	10×7·2	1497
15.	L.	Note-book, in original binding, marked L.	Institut de France, Paris.	188	10×7	1497, 1502–3
16.	S.K.M.I.¹	Treatise on Stereometry, first portion of a bound volume, marked I.	Forster Library, Victoria and Albert Museum, London.	76	14×10·5	1505
17.	S.K.M.I.²	Note-book, second portion of a bound volume, marked I.	Forster Library, Victoria and Albert Museum, London.	28	14×10·5	About 1489
18.	F.	Note-book, in original binding, marked F.	Institut de France, Paris.	192	5×10·2	1508–9
19.	Br.M.	Collection of treatises and notes, bound volume, marked: Arundel 263.	British Museum, London.	566	19×12·5	1504, 1508, after 1516
20.	E.	Note-book, in original binding, marked E.	Institut de France, Paris.	160	15·4×9·3	1513 and 1514
21.	G.	Note-book, in original binding, marked G.	Institut de France, Paris.	186	14×10	About 1510–16
22.	M.	Note-book, in original binding, marked M.	Institut de France, Paris.	188	10×7	Before 1500
23.	Triv.	Volume treating on various matters, bound, Trivulzi Bequest.	Castello Sforzesco, Milan.	102	21×14	1487–1490
24.	Leic.	Bound volume, containing chiefly scientific observations.	Leicester Library, Holkham Hall, Norfolk.	72	30×22	Between 1504 and 1506 (G. Calvi)

* A full account of the contents of the MSS. here enumerated will be found in the Concordance on pp. 402 sqq.

† Gerolamo Calvi, *I Manoscritti di Leonardo da Vinci dal Punto di Vista Cronologico Storico e Biografico*, Bologna, 1923, is fundamental for the chronology of the manuscripts.

	Mark of manuscript	Description of manuscript	Place	Total no. of pages	Size in centimetres	Date
25.	Trn.	Volume in original binding, treating on flights of birds, geometry, &c.	Turin, Royal Library.	26	21·3 × 15·5	1505
26.	D.	Treatise on the Eye, in original binding, marked D.	Institut de France, Paris.	20	25 × 16	1508
27.	K.¹	Note-book, forming the first part of a bound volume, marked K.	Institut de France, Paris.	96	10 × 6·6	After 1504
28.	K.²	Note-book, forming the second part of a bound volume, marked K.	Institut de France, Paris.	62	10 × 6·6	1504–9
29.	K.³	Note-book, forming the third part of a bound volume, marked K.	Institut de France, Paris.	96	10 × 6·6	1509 to 1512
30.	C.A.	Bound volume, commonly called Codex Atlanticus, 401 folios, each containing one or more manuscript-sheets.	Ambrosian Library, Milan.	1222	Various sizes	About 1483–1518
31.	F.U.	Two loose sheets.	Uffizi Gallery, Florence.	4	Various sizes	1473 and 1478
32.	V.	Five Loose sheets.	Academy, Venice.	10	Various sizes	1511 and other dates
33.	Mi.A.	One sheet.	Gallery in the Ambrosian Library, Milan.	2	20 × 14	Uncertain
34.	Mch.	One sheet.	Pinakothek, Munich.	2	4°	Uncertain
35.	P.	One sheet, marked N. 2260. One sheet (previously in the collection of the King of Holland). N. 2258.	Cod. Vallardi, Louvre, Paris. Collection of drawings, Louvre, Paris.	2 / 2	4° / 27·7 × 21	1485–90 ? / About 1480–1500
36.	P.A.	One sheet.	École des Beaux-Arts, Paris. Formerly collection of M. Armand.	2	26 × 18·5	About 1483–5 ?
37.	Br.M.P.	Four sheets.	British Museum, Print-room	4	8° and 4°	Uncertain
38.	B.B.	Two sheets.	Bonnat Bequest, Bayonne	4	19·5 × 7·5 / 9·6 × 9·1	1479 / 1493–4 ?
39.	Ox.	Three sheets.	Library of Christ Church, Oxford.	6	4° and 8°	Uncertain
40.	Md.	One Sheet.	Archivio Palatino, Modena.	2	18 × 13·4	1507
41.	F.L.	Treatise on Proportions, Architecture, &c., attributed to Francesco di Giorgio, with notes by Leonardo (on seven pages).	Biblioteca Laurenziana, Florence. Formerly at Ashburnham Place.	7	14·8 × 10	Uncertain
42.	Wr.	One sheet.	Schloss-Museum, Weimar.	2	19·2 × 14	1506–8
43.	N.Y.	One sheet.	Metropolitan Museum, New York.	2	10 × 13	1495
44.	P.H.N.	One sheet.	Formerly in collection of Henry, Prince of Netherlands.	2	8°	Uncertain
45.	Mo.	One sheet.	Formerly in collection of A. Morrison, London. Now in the possession of Herr Stefan Zweig.	2	8°	Uncertain
46.	G.H.	One sheet.	Autograph collection of K. Geigy-Hagenbach, Basle.	2	29·1 × 9·8	Uncertain

(2) CONCORDANCE BETWEEN THE NUMBERS OF THE MS. FOLIOS AND THE NUMBERS OF THE PARAGRAPHS IN THE PRESENT VOLUMES

The numbers of the sheets are generally not by the author, but in a more modern handwriting. The few instances when these numbers are by Leonardo will be found mentioned in the lists. The

A = Acqua (Water).
Ar = Architecture.
F = Forza (Force).
Fo = Fortezza (Fortress).
Ge = Geometry.
M = Moto, colpo (on movement, &c.).
Ma = Mathematics.

bindings are in parchment, if not otherwise stated. The following abbreviations have been introduced in the description of the contents (the Italian words are headings used by Leonardo):

Mn = Machines.
O = Optics.
P = Peso (Weight).
Ph = Physics.
V = Volatili (Flight of Birds).
+ = blank pages.

I. W.

The history of the MSS. at Windsor is given on pages 396 to 399. They were part of Pompeo Leoni's collection and were contained in a volume bound in leather inscribed with his name (compare p. 396). There, as in volume C.A., the original MSS. were fixed on the sheets of the volume.

On the first sheet of the volume is the following note, initialled IHG (*the Librarian I. H. Glover 1836–60): Pages 2 to 40 inclusive, 47, 48, 107, 121, 123?, 126, 135, 146?, 147 to 161 inclusive, 179, 186, 205 all wanting. On the reverse of sixth sheet is an inscription in Spanish:* (Este libro tiene ducientos y diçiçes ogas dibugados y setasa [*sic*] . . . . . . una con otra como en tan dibugados), *and on the upper right-hand corner of another sheet is inscribed in Spanish* (aqui faltan a esta y no se cuenta).

All the drawings contained in this volume have now been removed—a large number were mounted at the instigation of the Prince Consort and at that time they were given the inventory numbers 12275 to 12727. Under Edward VII the remainder of this series were mounted.

The majority of the anatomical drawings were not mounted and not included in this series. They were given inventory numbers 19000 to 19152 and they were bound up in 1930 in three separate volumes conforming to the following three publications under the direction of the Librarian, O. F. Morshead:

I manoscritti di Leonardo da Vinci della
Reale Biblioteca di Windsor

Volume I. Dell' Anatomia Fogli A, *published by T. Sabachnikoff and G. Piumati, Paris, 1898. The MSS. here published were bound up in one volume known as* Anatomical Manuscript A, *which includes 18 sheets with anatomical drawings*

of bones and muscles (numbers 19000 to 19017). Their size varies between 28·5 × 19·5 and 29 × 20 cm. On sheet 19016 is the note in questa vernata del mille 510 credo spedire tutta la notomia **(1376)**. *Most of the drawings of this volume are of the same date. In our concordance are given both the Windsor inventory numbers and the numbers of the Sabachnikoff publication, thus:* 19001 (A.2).

Volume II. Dell' Anatomia Fogli B, *published by T. Sabachnikoff and G. Piumati, Turin, 1901. The MSS. here published were bound up in one volume known as* Anatomical Manuscript B, *which includes 42 sheets with anatomical drawings, chiefly of nerves, blood-vessels, and internal organs (numbers 19018 to 19059). Their size is 19 × 13·5 cm. On sheet 19059 is an inscription giving the date April 1489* **(1370)**, *but this does not date the whole volume. In our concordance both the Windsor inventory numbers and the numbers of the Sabachnikoff publication are given, thus:* 19018 (B. 1).

Volume III. All the anatomical drawings not included in the above two publications and published in six volumes entitled: 'Leonardo da Vinci, Quaderni d'Anatomia, fogli della Royal Library di Windsor'; *pub. da Ove C. L. Vangensten, A. Fonahn, H. Hopstock, Christiania, 1911 to 1916.*

The MSS. thus published were bound up in one volume known as Anatomy Manuscript C. *It contains 93 sheets numbered 19060 to 19152; of various sizes and dates. The volume is divided into six sections to correspond to the six volumes of the publication. In our concordance both the Windsor inventory numbers and the numbers of the publication are given, thus:* 19061 (C. I. 2).

In the publication were included a number of

mounted drawings which had taken their place in the series of inventory numbers 12275 to 12727; these are listed thus: 12640 (C. VI. 13).

On sheet 19077b *is a note with the date 9 January 1513* (1376A) *which dates section II of the* Anatomy Manuscript C.

In Kenneth Clark's Catalogue of the Drawings of Leonardo da Vinci at Windsor Castle (*Cambridge, 1935*) *the Windsor inventory numbers were retained and the same numbers are adopted in this publication.*

12277 *map of Central Italy showing the coast from the mouth of the Magra to Corneto, in the East Rimini, Ferrara, pen and sepia—water painted blue* 31·7×44·9 *cm.* | 12278a *map* 33·8 ×48·8 *cm. reduced on* Pl. CXIII | 12279 *map of Arno west of Florence, pen and brown ink over black chalk* 33·5×48·2 *cm. Notes on left corners and to the right transliterated in* 1006. | 12280a (C. I. 11) 1475 | 12282a 682 | 12282b 683 | 12283a Pl. XXX | 12284 1051, Pl. CXI, No. 1 | 12294 717 | 12304 (C. VI. 4) Pl. VII, No. 1, 2, 310, 337 | 12319 716 | 12326 909 | 12327 868 | 12338a Pl. LVI | 12339a Pl. LVII | 12342 Pl. LXXIII | 12343 Pl. LXII, No. 3 | 12344b Pl. LXXI | 12345a Pl. LXXII, No. 2 | 12346a *drawing of a horse,* Vol. II, p. 17, *above on left* | 12347a Pl. LXXV, 711 | 12347b 642 | 12348 *drawing of section of mould for casting horse,* Vol. II, p. 17 | 12349a 713, 1175 | 12349b 1547 | 12350 710, 878, 1413 | 12351a 852, 1186 | 12351b 639, 714 | 12352 1532, Vol. II, p. 17, *sketch on right* | 12353 Pl. LXV, No. 1, Pl. LXXII, No. 1 | 12354 Pl. LXVIII | 12355 Pl. LXVI | 12356a Pl. LXXIV | 12357 Pl. LXV, No. 2 | 12358 Pl. LXVII | 12359 Pl. LXX | 12360 Pl. LXIX | 12362 *sketch of asses and ox &c.* | 12372–12375 *anatomical drawings of a bear's paw* | 12376 Pl. XXXIV | 12385 Pl. XXXIX | 12388 Pl. XXXVI, Pl. XXXVII, 477 | 12391 475 | 12404 Pl. XL, No. 2, 473 Note | 12409 Pl. XXIX | 12416 1022 | 12431b 456 | 12495a Pl. CXXI | 12484b 1560A | 12495b 1355 | 12496b Vol. I, p. 43 Note | 12497 Pl. XLVIII | 12519 Pl. XLIV | 12521 Pl. XLIII | 12542 Pl. XLV | 12546 Pl. XLIX | 12547 Pl. L | 12548 Pl. XLVII | 12551 Pl. XLVIII | 12552 Pl. LXXX | 12555a Pl. LI | 12558 Pl. XXXIII | 12566 Pl. XL, No. 2 | 12579a 389, Pl. XXV | 12579b Pl. CII, No. 1 | 12581 Pl. XXVI | 12585b 760, Pl. CI, No. 1 | 12587a 1329 | 12591a Pl. LXXXIII, 1103 | 12591b 1104 | 12601 (C. VI. 1) 316, Pl. X | 12604a 137, 575, 577, Pl. XXXII | 12605a Pl. XL, No. 1 | 12606 (C. VI. 3) 313, Pl. VII,

No. 3 | 12607 (C. VI. 2) 318, Pl. XI | 12614a (C. VI. 20) 351, Pl. XIX, No. 2 | 12625 (C. V. 22) 810 | 12631a (C. V. 23) 823 | 12639a (C. VI. 18) 297, 379, Pl. XXIII, No. 4 | 12640 (C. VI. 13) 356, Pl. XXI | 12641b Pl. XXIV, No. 1, 387 | 12642b (C. V. 24) 1133 | 12657 8F | 12665a Pl. XXXV, No. 3, 609 | 12665b Pl. XXXV, No. 2, 608 | 12668 1435 | 12669b (C. V. 25) 886 | 12671–2 *notes on the causes of the wind* | 12673–86 *maps* | 12673–4 *rivers in Brescian territory* | 12675b 1438 | 12676 *river-bed,* 1437 | 12677–8 *maps of Arno* | 12681 1004 Note, 1016 Note | 12682 *study for the map on* Pl. CXII *in pen and washes of bistre* 20·9×28·1 *cm.* | 12683 *map* 40×27 *cm.* Pl. CXII | 12684 *map* 40×27·7 *cm.* Pl. CXIV | 12685 *map of the countries north-west of Florence with Lucca, Pistoia, and the valley of the Arno* 24×36·7 *cm.* | 12690 Pl. CI, No. 3 | 12692–7 *rebuses* | 12698b Pl. LXIV, 688 | 12700a 685 | 12700b Pl. LXIII, 684 | 12701 Pl. LXII, No. 2, 681 | 12702 Pl. LII, No. 1, 594 Note, 665 Note | 12705 Pl. XXVIII, No. 7, 391 Note | 12708 Pl. XXXVIII, No. 3 | 12718a Pl. VII, No. 5.

ANATOMICAL MANUSCRIPT A

19001a (A. 2) 856, 1140 | 19001b Pl. CVII | 19002a (A. 3) 800, 833, Vol. I, p. 71, Pl. IB | 19003b (A. 4) 803 | 19016a (A. 17) 1376 | 19017a (A. 18) 804, 1494.

ANATOMICAL MANUSCRIPT B

19018b (B. 1) 814, Pl. CVIII, No. 4 | 19019a (B. 2) 838, 1412 | 19019b (B. 2) 839 | 19023b (B. 6) 801 | 19030a (B. 13) 816 | 19030b (B. 13) 827 | 19037b (B. 20) 797 | 19038a (B. 21) Pl. XXII, No. 1, 357 | 19038b (B. 21) Pl. XXIII, No. 1, 375, 1178 | 19041a (B. 24) 799 | 19044a (B. 27) Pl. CVIII, No. 1, 809 | 19044b Vol. I, p. 71 | 19045a (B. 28) 843 | 19045a, 19046a Vol. I, p. 71 | 19047b (B. 30) 1215 | 19048a (B. 31) 1214 | 19048b (B. 31) 1213 | 19050b (B. 33) Vol. I, p. 71 | 19054b (B. 37) 817 | 19055b (B. 38) Vol. I, p. 71 | 19059a (B. 42) 1370 | 19059b (B. 42) 805.

ANATOMICAL MANUSCRIPT C

19061a (C. I. 2) 798, 822 | 19064a (C. I. 5), 19068 (C. I. 9) Vol. I, p. 71 | 19070a (C. I. 13) 370 | 19070b (C. I. 13) 7, 796, 819, 1434 | 19071a (C. II. 1) Vol. I, p. 71 | 19072 (C. II. 2) Vol. I, p. 71 | 19076a (C. II. 6) 59, 121, 158, 195, 204, 209, 265, 287, 292, 1424 | 19077b (C. II. 7) 1376A, 1423 | 19082a (C. II. 12) 850 | 19084a (C. II. 14) 844, 1157, 1210, 1358 |

19088*a* (C. II. 18) **815** | 19092*b* (C. II. 22) **1436** | 19094*a* (C. II. 24) **358, Pl. XXII, No. 2** | 19097*a* (C. III. 3) **802, Vol. I, p. 88** | 19097*b* (C. III. 3) **841** | 19099 **1362** | 19101*a* (C. III. 7) **658, 1432** | 19102*a* (C. III. 8) **29, 818** | 19102*b* (C. III. 8) **1433** | 19106*b* (C. III. 12) **1411** | 19109*a* (C. IV. 3) **570** | 19114*b* (C. IV. 9) **Vol. I, p. 71** | 19115*a* (C. IV. 10) **7B, 1205A, 832, 837, Vol. I, pp. 70, 71** | 19115*b* (C. IV. 10) **1016 Note** | 19118*b* (C. IV. 14) **3** | 19129*a* (C. VI. 5) **Pl. VII, No. 4, 321, 327** | 19130*a* (C. VI. 6) **334, Pl. XIV, No. 2** | 19130*b* (C. VI. 6) **Pl. XVI, No. 1, 335** | 19131*a* (C. VI. 7) **Pl. XIX, 347** | 19131*b* (C. VI. 7) **325** | 19132*a* (C. VI. 8) **Pl. VIII, No. 2, 332** | 19132*b* (C. VI. 8) **333** | 19133*a* (C. VI. 9) **324** | 19133*b* (C. VI. 9) **322** | 19134–5*a* (C. VI. 10) **Pl. XVII, No. 2, Pl. XXXV, No. 1, 317, 336, 341, 348, 625, 707** | 19134*b* (**Vol. II, p. 32, Fig. 1, Vol. II, p. 35, Fig. 3**) | 19136–9*a* (C. VI. 11) **339, 342, 349, Pl. XVI, No. 2, Pl. XX** | **314, 326, 328, 330, 338, 1410, Pl. XIII, Pl. XIV, No. 1** | 19140*a* (C. VI. 12) **323, 331, 345, Pl. XV** | 19141*a* (C. VI. 22) **269, 365** | 19142*a* (C. VI. 22) **811** | 19143*b* (C. VI. 21 recto) **807** | 19148*b* **62, 130** | 19149*a* **77** | 19149*b* **597, 183, Pl. V** | 19150*a* **288** | 19150*b* **66, 78, 270** | 19151*a* **47, 80** | 19151*b* **276** | 19152*a* **73, 79, 81, 274** | 19152*b* **81, 120.**

2. C.

Inscribed in golden letters on the front cover: · VIDI · MAZENTÆ ‖ PATRITII · MEDIO-LANENSIS ‖ LIBERALITATE ‖ AN · M · D · C · III. *Inside the cover:* C and [O].— *On the first sheet (by an unknown hand):* Autographum Leonardi Vincii ‖ cujus in ejusdem rebus gestis meminit ‖ Raphael Trichet Fresneus ‖ agit autem de lumine et umbra.—*First sheet verso:* O.—*Second sheet marked* [,G,] *and* O. *The following sheets are numbered* 1–30, *by an unknown hand. These numbers disagree with Leonardo's own numbers, here given in brackets (). He seems to have counted the sheets backwards. They are on the back of the sheets, but some are wanting:* 1*a* **254** | 1*b* (15) **253** | 2*a* **221** | 2*b* (14) **220** | 3*a* **219** | 3*b* (13) **218** | 4*a* **217** | 4*b* (12) **216, Pl. VI, No. 3** | 5*a* **252, 215, Pl. VI, No. 2** | 5*b* (11) moto, voce, forza e moto, colpo | 6*a*

del moto dell' aria e dell' acqua, O, **Vol. I, p. 27, 77**A | 6*b* (10) forza e peso, colpo, **Vol. I, p. 72** | 7*a* colpo, peso e forza, **213, A** | 7*b* (9) 30, M, P **12** *lines*, **160, F** | 8*a* **131, O** | 8*b* **259, 180, 260** | 9*a* O, **Vol. I, p. 28, 72**A | 9*b* O | 10*a* **262, 141, Pl. II, Nos. 2, 3** | 10*a*–11*b* O | 12*a* **258, 229** | 12*b* **289** | 13*a* **290** | 13*b* **261** | 14*a* **256** | 14*b* (16) **255, 123** | 15*a* M, A | 15*b* **720, 1458, 727** | 16*a* **1130**B, **Vol. I, p. 72,** de ochio, M | 16*b* (19) O | 17*a* O | 17*b* (18) O | 18*a* **303** | 18*b*, 19*a* O | 19*b* **1334, 1380** | 20*a*, *b* O | 21*a* **174** | 21*b* (17) **257** | 22*a* A, M, O | 22*b* (8) P | 23*a* **251** | 23*b* (7) A | 24*a* **250** | 24*b* (6) A | 25*a* A, O | 25*b* (5) M, A | 26*a* A | 26*b* (4) **931**, acqua e terra | 27*a* O | 27*b* (3) **53**, O | 28*a* M | 28*b* (2) P | 29*a* *inscribed by an unknown hand:* le carte sono di n^{ro} 28 cioè Ventiotto | 29*b* [G] 30*a* O | 30*b*+

3. B.

Bound in pig-skin; marked B *inside the front-cover. On the first sheet is a short, indistinct note in Spanish, probably by P. Leoni, stating that Leonardo wrote backwards. The following sheets are numbered by very large numbers from* 3–90 (*see the facsimile Pl. LXXIX, 2).*
3*a* *drawings in water colour, fruits* | 3*b* **329, 346, 638, 675, 1188, F** | 4*a* **1509, 1131, Ph** | 4*b* A, **1212, Ma, Vol. I, p. 72** | 5*a* Fo | 5*b*, 6*a* Mn | 6*b* Mn, natura de' spechi | 7*a*, *b* Mn, Fo | 8*a* **1497** | 8*b*–10*a* arms | 10*b* da passare un fiume, Ge, **Pl. CIII, No. 2** | 11*a* Mn | 11*b* **Pl. XCIV, Nos. 2, 3,** Mn | 12*a* **Pl. LXXXVIII, Nos. 6, 7, 751** | 12*b* Ge, Ar | 13*a* Mn, *sketch of flowers* | 13*b*, 14*a*, Ge, *sketches of flowers* | 14*b* camino, Ma | 15*a* **Pl. XCIII, No. 1,** Fo | 15*b* **Pl. LXXVII, Nos. 1, 2, 742, 743** | 16*a* **Pl. LXXVII, No. 3, 741** | 16*b* Fo, Mn | 17*a* Ge | 17*b* **Pl. LXXXIX,**

481A | 18*a* **Vol. II, p. 35, Figs. 1, 2, p. 218** | 18*b* **Pl. LXXXVII, No. 2, 755,** Fo | 19*a* Fo | 19*b* **752,** Ar | 20*a* A, Mn | 20*b* A, **511** | 21*a* **Pl. LXXXVII, Nos. 3, 4,** Fo | 21*b* **Pl. LXXXVIII, Nos. 1–5** | 22*a* **Pl. XCIII, No. 2,** Mn | 23*a* *construction of bridges* | 23*b* **Pl. LXXX, No. 2** | 24*a* **Pl. XCVI, No. 2, 757** | 24*b* Mn, Fo | 25*a* Ar, Fo | 25*b* **Pl. XC** | 26*a* A, Mn | 26*b* Mn | 27*a* **Pl. C, No. 5, 788** | 27*b* *arms, drawing of a small figure* | 28*a* Ge, spechi | 28*b* **762, Pl. CII, No. 3** | 29*a* Ge, strade che vano attraverso a vno argine d'ū fiume | 29*b* Mn | 30*a* Ar, Fo | 30*b* **1128 Note** | 31*a*–32*a* *arms* | 32*b* *on passing a river* | 33*b*, 34*a* Mn | 34*b* **Vol. II, p. 32, Fig. 3** | 35*a* Mn, **Vol. II, p. 33, Fig. 1** | 35*b* **Pl. XCV, No. 1** | 36*a* **Pl. LXXIX, No. 2, 746,** Mn | 36*b* Fo | 37*a* **Pl. LXXVIII, Nos. 2, 3** | 37*b* **Pl. LXXIX, No. 1, 745** | 38*a* **745 Note** | 38*b* *canals* | 39*a*

Pl. LXXVIII, No. 1, 761 | 39*b* Pl. XCII, No. 1, 753 | 40*a* nomi d'arme da offendere, Ge | 40*b* a bresscia alla minera del fero sono mātaci d'ū pezo cioè sanza corame . . . , arms | 41*a*–46*b* arms | 47*a* Ar | 47*b* Mn | 48*a*, *b* Fo | 49*a*, *b*, Mn | 50*a* Fo | 50*b* 1381, Vol. I, p. 70, Mn | 51*a*, *b* Mn | 52*a* Pl. XCVII | 52*b* Fo, Mn | 53*a* camino | 53*b* A, Mn | 54*a* d'alzare acque, bombarda | 54*b* A, Mn | 55*a* Vol. II, p. 32, Fig. 2, p. 43, Fig. 1 | 55*b* modo di misurare alteze | 56*a* same subject, modo chome si debbe riparare a vna furia di soldati | 56*b* Pl. XCII, Nos. 2, 3, Vol. II, p. 33, Fig. 2 | 57*a* Pl. XCV, No. 2 | 57*b* rivellino | 58*a* 1506, 1023, Ar, lupanario, Fo | 58*b* Pl. LXXX, No. 3 | 59*a* Mn | 59*b* Fo | 60*a* Pl.

LXXXII, No. 3, 750 | 60*b* on passing a river | 61*a* 1080, A | 61*b* 1094, 1099 | 62*a* Pl. LXXXV, No. 13, on passing a river | 62*b* 1100 | 63*a* F, P | 63*b* 1081 | 64*a* A, Mn | 64*b* Stivali da aqua, Mn | 65*a* Vol. II, p. 218 | 66*a* walls of Pavia | 65*b*–67*a* Mn | 67*b*, 68*a* Ar | 68*b* schale docpie 1*a* per lo chastellano l'altra per i provisionati | 69*a*–70*a* Fo | 70*b* Mn, Pl. CIII, No. 1 | 71*a* Pl. CII, No. 2 | 71*b*–73*a* Mn | 73*b*–75*a* flying-machine | 75*b*–77*b* Mn | 78*a* Fo | 78*b* arms, Ar | 79*a*–80*a* flying-machine | 80*b* arms | 81*a* A | 81*b* 1117 | 82*a* Mn | 82*b* 1088 | 83*a* Mn | 84–87 wanting | 88*a* Mn | 88*b* flying-machine | 89*a* Mn | 89*b* V | 90*a* Mn | 90*b* modo di sfondare vn navilio, voce, Vol. I, p. 72.— *Inside the back cover is the mark* S.

4. B.N. 2037 (Ash. I)

The sheets of this MS. were torn out of MS. B at the Institut de France by Guglielmo Libri, author of Histoire des Sciences Mathématiques en Italie. *They then passed into the library of Lord Ashburnham (there marked 1875) and were later returned to France. The Bibliothèque Nationale had them bound, and restored the volume to the Library of the Institut (MS. N.S. 185). The volume contains 10 sheets in 8vo—formerly sheets 91–100 of MS. B, and besides, five sheets with drawings of arms and instruments (Vol. I, pp. 69, 70) not numbered, which came after sheet*

49 *in MS. B (compare G. Calvi,* I Manoscritti di L.d.V., *p. 86, Bologna, 1925).*

1*a* 1127 | 1*b* 1115 | 2*a* Fo | 2*b* 1120 | 3*a* 1116 | 3*b* Pl. LXXXV, Nos. 1–11, Vol. II, p. 33, Fig. 3, p. 57 | 4*a* 756, Pl. XCI, No. 1 | 5*a* Vol. II, p. 43, Fig. 2, p. 44, Figs. 3, 4 | 5*b* Pl. XCI, No. 2, 754 | 7*b* 1505, arms and a nude youth resting his left hand on a sword | 8*b* 1492, arms, 1500 | 9*a* carts, 1089 | 9*b* 1498 | 10*a* 1204, four columns of various words | 10*b* 1382, sketches of insects, a caricature.

5. B.N. 2038 (Ash. II)

This MS. originally formed part of MS. A at the Institut de France. It was torn out by Guglielmo Libri and passed into the library of Lord Ashburnham (there marked $\frac{1875}{2}$), and was then restored to France. The Bibliothèque Nationale had this MS. bound in a separate volume, and in 1891 presented it to the Institut de France (MS. N.S. 184). It contains sheets formerly numbered 54 and 65–114 of MS. A at the Institut.

1*a* 68 | 2*a* 506 | 4*a* 560, Pl. XXVIII, No. 6, 390 | 4*b* Pl. XXXI, No. 2, 512 | 5*a* 517, 147, 202 | 6*b* 63 | 8*b* Pl. XXXVIII, No. 2, 579 | 9*b* 171, 352 | 10*a* 293, 239, 485, 541, 537, 534 | 10*b* Pl. IV, No. 2, 169 | 11*a* Pl. IV, No. 3, 173 | 12*b* Pl. VI, No. 4, 224 | 13*a* Pl. II, No. 1, 61, 40, 546 | 13*b* Pl. III, No. 1, 275, 148 | 14*a* Pl. III, No. 2, 149 | 14*b* 48, 236, 205, 533 | 15*a* 138 | 15*b* 139, 140 | 16*a* 542, 709, 509 | 16*b* 887, 894, 565, 576, 588, 557 | 17*a* 1546 | 17*b* 483, 661, 519, 578, 392,

583 | 18*a* 582, 14, 291, 391, 299 | 18*b* 298, 145, 604 | 19*a* 535, 653 | 19*b* 654 | 20*a* 566, 659, 652, 513, 600 | 20*b* 520, 567, 176, 567, lines 13–22, 361 | 21*a* 606, 594 | 21*b* 552, 559, 122, 550 | 22*a* 119, 125, 199 | 22*b* 508, 23, 294, 591, Vol. I, p. 24 | 23*a* 99, 538, 102, 558 | 23*b* Pl. XLI, No. 1, 142, 344, 34, 92 | 24*a* 531, 523, Vol. I, p. 26 | 24*b* 656, 529 | 25*a* 501, 655 | 25*b* 295, 500, 486 | 26*a* 496, 532, 502, 285 | 26*b* 572, 507, 495 | 27*a* 497, 489, 587 | 27*b* 571, 492, 494 | 28*a* 491, 530 | 28*b* 367, 364, 555 | 29*a* 573, Pl. XXXI, No. 4, the head on the left, 368, 112, 585, 522 | 29*b* 584, 592, 164 | 30*a* 595, 182, 196 | 30*b* 602 | 31*a* 536, 504, 601 | 31*b* 568, 563, 528, 540, 561, 439 | 32*a* 574, Pl. XXXI, No. 4, the head on the right, 245, 133 | 32*b* 283, 132, 547, 203 | 33*a* 551, 484, 515, 284 | 33*b* 267, 589, 580, 516 | 34*a* 1176, knots | 34*b* 1510, 686, drawing of knots, 1183.

6. A.

Bound in parchment, marked A *outside and inside the cover. The numbers of the sheets* 1–64 *are in Leonardo's handwriting.*

1*a* **628, 190, 527, 708** | 1*b* P, M, **524, 83** | 2*a* O, **235, 518** | 2*b* O, **64**A, Pl. XVII, No. 1, P, Mn | 3*a* **50** | 3*b* M, P, O | 4*a*–5*a* P, M | 5*b* Ge | 6*a* Ge, P | 6*b* Ge | 7*a* Mn, Ge | 7*b*, 8*a* M | 8*b* **129, 624, 100, 93, 234** | 9*a* M | 9*b* **88**, Vol. I, p. 71, O, **69** | 10*a* **52** | 10*b* **94, 85** | 11*a* **98**, Ge | 11*b*, 12*a* Ge | 12*b* Ge, O | 13*a*–15*a* Ge | 15*b*, 16*a* P, Ge | 16*b*–18*b* Ge | 19*a acoustics*, **Vol. I, p. 72,** M | 19*b* **281**, O, *acoustics* | 20*a* **282**, O, Ph | 20*b*, 21*a* Ma | 21*b*–22*b* M, **Vol. I, p. 72, 1129**A | 23*a* **549, 514, 586**, M, *acoustics* | 23*b* A | 24*a* M, **1134**, A | 24*b*–25*b* A | 26*a* A, M | 26*b* O, M | 27*a* M, **58** | 27*b* M, A | 28*a* M | 28*b* Pl. XXII, No. 4, **369, 596** | 29*a* Pl. XXII, No. 3, **359** | 29*b* O, M | 30*a*–35*b* M, P | 30*b* **383** | 34*a* **Vol. I, p. 72** | 34*b* **1113**B Note | 36*a* M, P, *acoustics*, **Vol. I, p. 72** | 36*b* **55** | 37*a* O, **56** | 37*b* **57**, O | 38*a* O, **86** | 38*b* **41**, Pl. XXXI, No. 3, **526** | 39*a*–40*a* Ge | 40*b* **543** | 41*a* **544** | 41*b* **545** | 42*a* O, **527** | 42*b* **525**, P, A | 43*a acoustics*, **706**, A | 43*b*–46*b* M, P | 47*a* **1153**A | 47*b*–48*a* M, P | 48*b* **792**, P | 49*a* P | 49*b* **786** | 50*a* **790, 779** | 50*b* Ma, **780** | 51*a* **781**, Mn | 51*b*–52*b* P, M | 53*a* **795, 791, 776** | 53*b* M, P | 54 *is wanting* | 55*a* M, P, O | 55*b* **929, 967, 941** | 56*a* A, **968, 944** | 56*b* **945**, Ph | 57*a* Ph, **1083** | 57*b* M | 58*a* A | 58*b* A, **934, 940, 943** | 59–60 A | 61*a* **1130**A, **Vol. I, p. 71** | 61*b* M, O | 62*a* M, P | 62*b* **311**, *two heads of horses*, P | 63*a* **312**, Pl. VIII, No. 1 | 63*b* A | 64*a* **898, 889**, A | 64*b* O, **214, 249, 873**. *The following blank sheet has the marks* S *on the front, and* Sb *and the number* 4 *on the reverse. They are by an unknown hand.*

7. S.K.M. III

For the history of this MS. see No. 16.

1*a* bonifatio | 1*b* **1387** | 2*a* **1271** | 2*b* **1488** | 3*a* A | 3*b*, 4*a* P, Ar | 4*b* **794** | 5*a acoustics* | 5*b*, 6*a* P | 6*b* Ma | 7*a* centro del mondo | 7*b circle* | 8*a* **1470** | 8*b*–10*a sketches of costumes* | 10*b* **633, 1367** | 11*a* + | 11*b circles* | 12*a*, *b* Mn | 13*a circle* | 13*b* Ar | 14*a* **1150** | 14*b* P | 15*a* **1343** | 15*b* Pl. LXXXV, No. 14 | 16*a* Ar | 16*b* + | 17*a* forza, strumenti | 17*b* **1187** | 18*a* Mn | 18*b*, 19*a* + | 19*b* P | 20*a* passavolante | 20*b* **846** | 21*a* **1281** | 21*b* Mn | 22*a sketches of windows* | 22*b*, 23*a sketches of legs of horses* | 23*b* A | 24*a circles* | 24*b* + | 25*a sketch of a horse* | 25*b study of clouds* | 26*a* + | 26*b* Ma | 27*a* **1322** | 27*b* **812** | 28*a* **813**, Pl. CVIII, No. 3 | 28*b* Mn | 29*a* **1132** | 29*b* Ge | 30*a* A | 30*b* + | 31*a diagram* | 31*b* cavaletti da lavorare | 32*a* M | 32*b* A | 33*a* A | 33*b* Ph | 34*a* **384** | 34*b* **1283** | 35*a* Mn | 35*b* busa | 36*a* distantia | 36*b* **735** | 37*a* **734** | 37*b* **647, 1386, Vol. II, p. 55, Fig. 2** | 38*a* forma di corpo | 38*b* moto della saetta | 39*a* M | 39*b* **614, 646, 732** | 40*a* A, **629** | 40*b* M | 41*a*–42*a* Mn | 42*b* **731** | 43*a* Mn | 43*b* **1135** | 44*b* **764, 662, 1324** | 45*a* **Vol. II, p. 55, Fig. 1** | 45*b* **1511** | 46*a* **1121** | 46*b*, 47*a* P | 47*b* **1276** | 48*a* M | 48*b*, 49*a* + | 49*b* **1512** | 50*a*–52*a* P | 52*b*, 53*a* + | 53*b* M | 54*a* **208** | 54*b* Ge | 55*a* **1169** | 55*b* Pl. XCIX, No. 2 | 56*a* Ge | 56*b* Mn | 57*a* + | 57*b*, 58*a* Mn | 58*b* O | 59*a* Mn | 59*b* aquaforte | 60*a* cientro della gravità | 60*b*, 61*a* Ar | 61*b* **1385** | 62*a* Mn | 62*b* **1341** | 63*a*, *b* Ge | 64*a* + | 64*b* Mn | 65*a* Ge | 65*b* knots | 66*a* **1118** | 66*b* **498** | 67*a* + | 67*b* Mn | 68*a* **1342** | 68*b*–71*a* Ge | 71*b* P | 72*a* **651** | 72*b*–73*b* P | 74*a* Ph | 74*b* **179** | 75*a* **1491** | 75*b*, 76*a* A | 76*b* + | 77*a* + | 77*b* P | 78*a* + | 78*b*, 79*a* Mn | 79*b* **Vol. II, p. 70,** *the last two diagrams* | 80*a* + | 80*b* Ar | 81*a* Ge | 81*b*–85*b pullies* | 86*a* **1496**, del moto delle corde | 86*b*–87*b* Ph | 88*a* **1384** | 88*b* **1459** |

8. H. 3.

The three small note-books H³ H² H¹ *are bound in one volume. From the dirty state of the sheets at the beginning and at the end of each division it becomes apparent that Leonardo had used them separately. The cover is in parchment and is twice marked* H *on the outside and once inside, and* Q *on the back of the first sheet. Inside the back cover is the mark* Qᵃ, *and on the last sheet but one* N N 48, *meaning probably the number of sheets originally belonging to* H³. *MSS.* H² *and* H³ *are numbered throughout. The sheets of* H³ *are also numbered* 1–47, *below the text and in a reversed position.*

95*a* A | 95*b* **1389** | 96*a* Ma | 96*b* dimmi se mai, *profile of man's head* | 97*a*, *b* Mn | 98*a* **670** | 98*b*, 99*a allegories* | 99*b* **689** | 100*a* **999** | 100*b* **736** | 101*a* **1264, 690** | 101*b*–103*a* Mn | 103*b sketch reproduced with* **No. 1112** | 104*a*, *b* P | 105*a* P, **1462** | 105*b* M | 106*a sketch of horses and oxen drawing a cart* | 106*b* **1460** | 107*a*–108*a* Mn | 108*b drawing of compasses* | 109*a* **831**, Mn | 109*b*–116*a* Mn | 116*b*, 117*a compasses* | 117*b drawing of a cart* | 118*a* **691** | 118*b*

1191 | 119*a* **1192** | 119*b*–121*a* Mn | 121*b* **Pl. LXXXV, No. 16, 768** | 122*a* il ciĕtro dell' ochio fia for dell' abaco 1/8 di a b | 122*b*–124*a* Mn | 124*b* **1514** | 125*a* **1513** | 125*b* *drawing of cogwheel* | 126*a* + | 126*b* *terminations of Latin verbs* | 127*a*–128*a* *slight sketches* | 128*b* Mn | 129*a* *drawing of a cart* | 129*b* **1515** | 130*a* *draw-* *ing of cart drawn by horses* | 131*b* Mn, *sketch of balloon?* | 132*a, b drawing of harness* | 133*a drawing of horse in harness* | 133*b* **27** | 133*b*–136*a Latin verbs* | 136*b* **644** | 137*a* **1356**, sum, eram | 137*b* **1543** | 138*a*–140*a Latin verbs* | 140*b* P | 141*a* **1139** | 141*b Latin verbs* | 142*a Latin verbs*, legione cōtiene **6063** persone | 142*b* **1516.**

9. H. 2.

See introductory note to No. 8.—The first sixteen sheets are numbered twice, 1–16 being also written below the texts, but in reversed order.

49*a* **232** | 49*b* **692** | 50*a, b* A, Mn | 51*a sketch* | 51*b* **1265** | 52*a*–59*a* A | 59*b ornaments*, A | 60*a* **1219**A | 60*b ornaments*, **1197** | 61*a* **693** | 61*b*, 62*a* A | 62*b* **1390, 1320**, M | 63*a* M | 63*b* **694, 1316** | 64*a* A | 64*b* **1517** | 65*a* A,**1010** Note | 65*b* **Pl. CX, No. 2, 1024** | 66*a* **152** | 66*b* Mn | 67*a, b* A | 68*a* A, **464** | 68*b* A | 69*a* A, M | 69*b*, 70*a* A | 70*b* Mn | 71*a* **228**, A | 71*b* Mn | 72*a* Mn | 72*b*–73*b* A, Mn | 74*a, b* P, A | 75*a* **Pl. XXIII, No. 3, 377** | 75*b* M, Mn | 76*a* A | 76*b* **206, 105, 163** | 77*a* A | 77*b* A, **304** | 78*a* A | 78*b* A, padiglō di legni a vigievine | 79*a* M | 79*b* molino | 80*a* A | 80*b* A, P | 81*a* **91, 1518** | 81*b* M | 82*a*–83*b* A | 84*a* Mn | 84*b*–85*b* canale | 86*a* **828, 31** | 86*b* Mn | 87*a, b* A | 88*a sketch of barrel on a cart*, **32** | 88*b* **671** | 89*a* M, A | 89*b* **845** | 90*a* ricordati quādo cōmĕti lacque dallegar prima la speriĕza e poi la ragione | 90*b* **134** | 91*a* **1014** | 91*b* **33** | 92*a* P | 92*b* P, A | 93*a* A | 93*b* Ge | 94*a* **1391** | 94*b* **620**, Yhs maria **1493** *and by an unknown hand the mark* Y 46.

10. H. 1.

See introductory note to No. 8.—The text is upside down on the first 28 sheets.

1*a* amo, amas, amat, &c., **1026** | 1*b* + | 2*a* amabam, &c., A | 2*b*, 3*a* + | 3*b*, 4*a forms of* amo | 4*b* scribbles | 5*a* **1220** | 5*b* **1221** | 6*a* **1222** | 6*b* **1223** | 7*a* **1224** | 7*b* **1225** | 8*a* **1226** | 8*b* **1227** | 9*a* **1228** | 9*b* **1229** | 10*a* **1230** | 10*b* **1231** | 11*a* **1232** | 11*b* **1233** | 12*a* **1234** | 12*b* **1235** | 13*a* **1236** | 13*b* **1237** | 14*a* **1238** | 14*b* **1239** | 15*a* **1240** | 15*b*, 16*a* + | 16*b* **1194** | 17*a* **1241** | 17*b* **1242** | 18*a* **1243** | 18*b* **1244, 634** | 19*a* **1245** | 19*b* **1246** | 20*a* **1247** | 20*b* **1248** | 21*a* **1249** | 21*b* **1250** | 22*a* **1251** | 22*b* **1252** | 23*a* **1253** | 23*b* **1254** | 24*a* **1255** | 24*b* **1256** | 25*a* **1257** | 25*b* **1258** | 26*a* **1259** | 26*b* **1260** | 27*a* **1261** | 27*b* **1262** | 28*a* Mn | 28*b* tessta della viola, **Pl. I**A, **Vol. I, p. 70** | 29*a* **Vol. I, p. 70** | 29*b* Mn | 30*a*–31*a* A | 31*b* **308** | 32*a* **842**, Ge | 32*b*, 33*a knots* | 33*b* Mn, **1164** | 34*a* A | 34*b* Mn | 35*a knots* | 35*b* **782** | 36*a* **783** | 36*b* Mn | 37*a* P | 37*b* A | 38*a* **1025** | 38*b* A, Mn | 39*a, b* Mn | 40*a* **695** | 40*b* **696** | 41*a* **1461** | 41*b*–43*a* Mn | 43*b knots and sketch* | 44*a* P, **1319** | 44*b*, 45*a sketches of tents* | 45*b*, 46*a instruments*, **Pl. I**A, **Vol. I, p. 70** | 46*b*–47*b* A | 48*a* A, M | 48*b* **1263** |

11. S.K.M. II¹.

The two MSS. S.K.M. II¹ and S.K.M. II² are bound in one volume; they are placed in the binding in reversed position. The sheets of S.K.M. II³ are numbered in Leonardo's handwriting and begin with 94 going backwards to 1. The first sheet or cover sheet is not numbered. The numbers of the folios here given conform to those in the publication of these MSS. by the Reale Commissione Vinciana.

1*a knots; on the same sheet are the marks* KK. 62, 25 *by an unknown hand* | 1*b*–2*b* Ma | 3*a* **1404, 667** | 3*b*–5*b* Ge | 5*a* **154** | 6*a* **1403** | 6*b*, 7*a* + | *3 sheets missing* | 9*a* + | 9*b* **1313, 1402** | 10*a* **1401** | 10*b drawing of a bell* | 11*a*– 13*b* Mn | 14*b* Ma | 15*b* **97, 1400** | 16*a* Ge 2, 3, 5, 8, 12 | 17, 18 Ma | 19*a sketch of a head identified by Dr. A. E. Popp as being that of Francesco Nani of the Franciscan Order, cf. portrait of him in* Repertorium für Kunstwissenschaft, vol. xxxv, *p.* 257, *compare* **No. 679** | 19*b*–21*b* Ma | 22*b* + | 23*a*–24*a wheels* | 24*b* **1399** | 25*a* **1398** | 25*b* Ma | 27*a* + | 27*b sketch of a face* | 28*a* + | 28*b*, 29 *knots* | 30*a* + | 30*b* **1290** | 31*a* **1291** | 31*b* + | *4 sheets missing* | 32*a* M | 32*b acoustics* | 33*a* Ma | 33*b* M | 34*a* **1311** | 34*b* V | 35*b* P | 36*a* Ma | 37*a sketch of a woman and child* | 38*a* + | 38*b* **1397**, Ma | 39*a proportions* | 40*a* Ma | 40*b sketches* | 41*a* Ma | 41*b* **1196** | 42*a* Ge | 42*b* P |

43*a* Ge | 43*b* **1396** | 44*a* Ge | 44*b*, 45*a* P | 45*b* **1395, 376, Pl. XXIII, No. 2** | 46*a* **998** | 46*b*, 47*b* Mn | 47*a* Ge | 48*a* **103**, P | 48*b* M | 49*a* Fo | 49*b*, 50*a on weaving* | 50*b* **372** | 51*a* Mn | 51*b knots* | 52*a* Ar | 52*b* **1394, 1317**, *profile of a face* | 53*a* **Pl. LXXXV, No. 15, Vol. II,**

p. 57 | 53*b* P | 54*a* O | 54*b sketch of a flower* | 55*a* Mn | 55*b* Ge | 56*a* + | 56*b* Mn | 57*a* M, **1393** | 57*b* **1392**, Ma | 58*a* M | 58*b*, 59*a* + | 59*b* M | 60*a* + | 60*b* **1519** | 61*a* Ma | 61*b* Ma, **1312** | 62*b* **665** | 63*a* **666, 697** | 63*b* **Vol. II,** p. 48, *sketch.*

12. S.K.M. II².

Compare preliminary note to No. 11.

64*a* Mechanica potissimum in fine incipiendum. *This note is not written by Leonardo but by a later hand* | 64*b* **733, 627, 1522** | 65*a* **1521** | 65*b* **1113**A, **1118**A | 66*a*–68*a* P | 68*b*–69*b* M | 70*a bombarda* | 70*b* **793 Note** | 71*a*–72*a bombarda* | 72*b*, 73*a* P | 73*b* **Vol. I, p. 267 Note, and figure on p. 270** | 74*a*, *b* P | 75*a crossbow* | 75*b*–76 P | 77*b*–78*b screws* |

78*b*–87*a* P | 87*b* **793** | 88*a* Ar, P | 88*b*, 89*a* P | 89*b*–91*b* perpetuum mobile | 92*a* **784** | 92*b* **1206** | 93*a* P, **787** | 94–100 P | 101*a* M | 101*b* P | 102*a*, *b* A | 103–116*a* P | 116*b* **1137** | 117 A | 118–130 P | 131*a* M | 131*b*–133 De confregazione | 134–157*b* P | 158*a* Ge | 158*b* **36** | 159*a* **1520**, M, **612**.—*This is on the inside of the cover sheet.*

13. I².

This and MS. I¹ are bound in one volume. The mark I is outside and Q and Q 3 inside the cover.

49*a* Magistr M^to jachomo (*not in L's hand*) | 49*b* **1524, 704** | 50*a*–55*b Latin vocabulary* | 50*b*, 51*a* **1405 Note** | 52*a* Simon da calima tintore | 56*a* **Vol. II, p. 68, Figs. 1, 2** | 56*b dog ringing bell* | 57*a*–58*a bells* | 58*b* **1405 Note** | 59*a* **1405** | 59*b* P | 60*a*, *b* A | 61*a* M | 61*b*, 62*a* A | 62*b* Ma | 63*a* **1298** | 63*b* **1299** | 64*a* **1300** | 64*b* **1301** | 65*a* **1302** | 65*b* **1303** | 66*a* **1304** | 66*b* **1305** | 67*a* **1306** | 67*b*–72*a* A | 72*b* **932** | 73*a*–75*b* A | 76*a* M | 76*b*–79*a* A | 79*b* M | 80*a second Latin declension* | 80*b*–84*b* A | 85*a* M | 85*b crossbow*, A | 86*a* M | 86*b*–91*a* A | 91*b*–94*b* M | 95*a sketches of knots* | 95*b sketches of feathers and fish scales* | 96*a drawing*

of dog's head | 96*b* contrapeso | 97*a ornamental design of two cornucopia* | 97*b* Mn | 98*a* M | 98*b bombarda* | 99*a*–104 M | 104*b*–106*a* A | 106*b* + | 107*a* **679** | 107*b* + | 108*a*–109*b* A | 110*a* **Pl. LXXXV, No. 13** | 110*b* M | 111*a acoustics* | 111*b* + | 112*a*–114*a* M | 114*b*–118*a* A | 118*b*, 119*a* **1406** | 119*b* M | 120*a* M, **1496**C | 120*b* **1407** | 121*a* A | 121*b* M | 122*a*–123*a* A | 123*b*–126*a Latin vocabulary* | 126*b* + | 127*a*, *b* A | 128*a*–129*a bombarda* | 129*b* Voce d'echo, **Vol. I, p. 72** | 130*a* **1160** | 130*b* **1477** | 131*a*–132*a* M, P | 132*b*–134*a bombarda* | 134*b Latin declension* | 135*a* **1408** | 135*b*, 136*a Latin declension*, E | 136*b* M | 137*a*–138*a Latin conjugation* | 138*b* **672** | 139*a* **673, 1326** | 139*b* Ma, Ge.—*The two following sheets only bear the marks* Q 3 *and* Q.

14. I¹.

See No. 13 *preliminary note.*

1–12*a* Ge | 12*b* **394** | 13*a*, *b* Ge | 14*a*, *b* M | 15*a* **1140 Note** | 15*b*–17*a* Ge | 17*b* **241** | 18*a* **1151, 242** | 18*b* Ar | 19*a sketch* | 19*b* **37** | 20*a* **38** | 20*b*–23*a* Mn | 23*b da forare cristalli* | 24*a*–25*a sketches of shields* | 25*b*–27*b* Mn | 28*a* **1409** | 28*b*–32*a* Mn | 32*b* **1017** | 33*a* O | 33*b*

Ge | 34*a* **1018** | 34*b*–37*a* Mn | 37*b* **Pl. XXVIII, No. 5, 188, 452** | 38*a* O | 38*b*, 39*a* sum, es, est, &c. | 39*b* **1318** | 40*a* quis vel qui que quod ve quid, &c. | 40*b*–42*b* Mn | 43*a* O | 43*b*–46*a* Mn | 46*b sketch* | 47*a* **1092 Note** | 47*b sketch* | 48*a* **463** | 48*b* **Vol. II, p. 218**.—*The Marks* I I · 48 *and* · 20 · *are by an unknown hand.*

15. L.

This volume is in the original cover; it is a thin card of light blue colour. It is marked L on the outside and Q c inside.

o' **1414, 1323, 1102** | 1*a* **1002, 1415** | 1*b* **1416** | 2*a* **1417, 648**, *knights kneeling* | 2*b* Ma | 3*a sketch of a head* | 3*b*, 4*a knights kneeling* | 4*b* A | 5*a a note* | 5*b knots* | 6*a* **1034** | 6*b* **1035**

| 7*a*, *b* Fo | 8*a* colōbaia | 8*b* Ma | 9*a*–10*a plans* | 10*b* **1036** | 11*a* + | 11*b*–12*a* Mn | 12*b*, 13*a* + | 13*b* A, O | 14*a* O | 14*b notes* | 15*a* **1019** | 15*b* **1037, Pl. XCIV, No. 1** | 16*a* P, Ar | 16*b* Fo | 17*a* A | 17*b* P | 18*a*, *b* Mn | 19*a* Fo | 19*b* **Pl. CX, No. 3**, *left side* **1038** | 20*a* **Pl. CX, No. 3**, *right side* **765** | 20*b* Ma | 21*a* **1054** | 21*b*–23*a*

Ma | 23*b* Mn | 24*a* Fo | 24*b*–26*a* Mn | 26*b* P | 27*a* Mn | 27*b* P, **378** | 28*a* Mn | 28*b* knots | 29*a* Fo | 29*b* Mn | 30*a* A | 30*b* Mn, **1418** | 31*a*–33*a* A | 33*b* Mn, **1039** | 34*a*–35*a* Mn | 35*b* **Vol. II, p. 218** | 36*a* Mn | 36*b* **1040, Pl. CX, No. 4** | 37*a* Ar | 37*b* Ma | 38*a*–39*a* Ar | 39*b* Mn | 40*a* **1041** 40*b*, 41*a* Mn | 41*b* **35** | 42*a*–44*b* M | 45*a* Ma | 45*b* Ar | 46*a* Fo | 46*b* **1042** | 47*a* **1043** | 47*b* A | 48*a*, *b* Ar | 49*a*–52*b* Mn | 53*a* M, **1503** | 53*b* **1502** | 54*a*–60*b* V | 59*b* **1126A** | 61*a* Ar | 61*b*–62*b* V | 63*a*–65*b* Fo | 66*a* **1109, Pl. CX, No. 1** | 66*b* **1044** | 67*a* **1045** | 68*a*, *b* Ar | 69*a* P, A | 69*b*– 71*a* Mn | 71*b* sketch | 72*a* **1046** | 72*b* **1325** | | 73*a* Ge | 73*b*, 74*a* Ar | 74*b*, 75*a* Fo | 75*b* **307**,

M | 76*a* **981** | 76*b* plan | 77*a* **1047** | 77*b* **226** | 78*a* **1048**, A | 78*b* **1049** | 79*a* **488**, citadella | 79*b* Ge | 80*a* voce | 80*b* *draped figure, very like the one on Pl. XXVIII, No. 7* | 81*a* Ge | 81*b* sketch of trees | 82*a* **1047** Note | 82*b*, 83*a* **Vol. II, p. 244**, sketch | 83*b*, 84*a* outline sketch of mountains | 84*b* P | 85*a* Mn | 85*b* P | 86*a* Ge | 86*b* Mn | 87*a* **449** | 87*b* **393** | 88*a* sketch | 88*b* **1050** | 89*a* sketches | 89*b* Mn | 90*b* **1199** | 91*a* **1307** | 91*b* **1405** Note | 92*a* **623**, M | 92*b* Mn | 93*a* Ma | 93*b* vocabolo lombardo, &c. | 94*a* **1523** | 94*b* **1474, 1052** | O″ **1053, 1198, 1419**, *and, by an unknown hand*: Le carte sono 94 cioè nouāta quart.

16. S.K.M. I¹.

This is bound in one volume with MS. S.K.M. I². The three volumes in the Victoria and Albert Museum, London, were bequeathed by John Forster to the Library of the South Kensington Museum in 1876. They were given to Mr. Forster by the Earl of Lytton, who is said to have bought them at Vienna. On the first sheet is the note written in German: 'Leonardo da Vinci der grösste Maler aus der italienischen Schule 1452 zu Vinci geboren, trat 1502 als Kriegsbaumeister in die Dienste Herzogs Valentin Borgia und starb 1519.'

The subject of S.K.M. I¹ is given on sheet 3a

and transcribed in **1374** Note. *This subject is discussed on folios 3 to 40.*

3*a* Libro titolato de strasformazione cioè d'un corpo 'n un altro sanza diminuizione o acresscimento di materia | 3*b* **1374**. Jo voglio abassare la grossezza d'una tavola a data grosseza senza mutazion di sua larghezza: domando quanto cressce in sua lunghezza | 4*a* proportional compasses | 4*b* Ma | 5 *regular bodies* | 6*a* + | 7, 5 *regular bodies* | 8*a*, 13*a* + | 15, 16, 17, *and* 18 *transformation of regular bodies* | 18*b* + | 19*a*–40*b* *transformation of bodies.*

17. S.K.M. I².

The second MS. begins at folio 41; on this sheet is the mark '46'. The pages are numbered 1 to 28 and the subject dealt with is machinery for raising and moving water. At the end, on folio 54b, is the mark BB 14. The numbers of the folios given here conform to those in the publication of these MSS.

by the R. Commissione Vinciana.

41*a*–42*b* machinery for raising water | 43*a* **635, 649** | 44*a* **385** | 44*b* **650, 636** is crossed out | 45*a* –48*a* machinery for raising water | 48*b* De ponderibus. Modo di misurare un' alteza | 49 arrangement for conducting water.

18. F.

The cover of thin grey card is original. It has the mark F inside and outside.

o′ **1421, 1292, 1471A** | 1*a* **1375, 848** | 1*b* Ge | 2*a* A | 2*b* **2** | 3*a* A | 3*b*, 4*a* P | 4*b* libro 10 delle varie profondita e globbosita . . . dell' acque, **880** | 5*a* libro 9, dell' acqua che passa per un bottino, **879** | 5*b* **911, 1208** | 6*a* **881** | 6*b* flusso e reflusso | 7*a*–8*a* A | 8*b* **882** | 9*a*, *b* A | 10*a* **883** | 10*b*, 11*a* Ge | 11*b* **862**, A | 12*a*–17*b* A | 13*a* **Vol. II, p. 218** | 18*a* **302** | 18*b*–21*b* A | 22*a* **244, Pl. XLI, Nos. 3, 4** | 22*b* **861** | 23*a* **5, 277** | 23*b*–24*b* A | 25*a* ochiale di cristallo &c. | 25*b* **867** | 26*a* P | 26*b* A | 27*a* **939** | 27*b* **1422** | 28*a*–30*a* O | 30*b* A | 31*a*–34*a* O | 34*a* **81A, Vol. I, p. 27** | 34*b*

Libro 32 del moto che fa il fuoco | 35*a* Libro 42 delle pioggie | **474** | 35*b*–37*a* O | 36*a* **81B, Vol. I, p. 27** | 37*b* **1338** | 38*a* A | 38*b*–40*a* O | 39*b* **Vol. I, p. 27** | 40*b*, 41*a* A | 41*b* **858, 1123A, 8C** | 42*a* A, anatomy | 42*b*–46*b* A | 47*a* **1330** | 47*b*–48*b* A | 49*a* P | 49*b* P, O | 50*a* **1106** | 50*b*, 51*a* Ge | 51*b*, 52*a* M | 52*b*, 53*a* A | 53*b* A, **8D** | 54*a*–55*a* A | 55*b* Ge, *cells* | 56*a* **866, 617** | 56*b* acoustics | 57*a* **912** | 57*b*–59*b* Ge | 59*a* **1148C** | 60*a* **913, 870** | 60*a* M, **1087** | 61*b*–64*b* O | 65*a*–67*a* A | 67*b* dell' arco celeste | 68*a* A, **1107** | 68*b* A | 69*a* P | 69*b*–72*b* A | 73*a* **942** | 73*b* Ph | 74*a*, *b* M | 75*a* **278** | 75*b* M, A | 76*a* O | 76*b* **1010** | 77*a* A | 77*b* **877** | 78*a*, *b* A | 79*a* delli animali che an l'ossa di fori &c. | 79*b*

delle ossa de pesci che si trovā ne' pesci petrifi-
cati | 80*a* nichi e loro necessaria figura | 80*b*
de nichi ne' mōti | 81*a*–82*a* A | 82*b* prova che
la spera del' acqua è perfettamente tonda |
83*a* 371, G | 83*b* P | 84*a* 903 | 84*b* 904 | 85*a*
905 | 85*b*–86*b* O | 87*a* aria | 87*b* 922 | 88*a* 923 |

88*b*–90*a* A | 90*b* 924 | 91*a*–92*b* A | 93*a* 893 |
93*b*, 94*a* A | 94*b* 874, O | 95*a* A, O | 95*b* 806 |
96*a* *chemical materials* 613 | 96*b* 1184, 626,
chemical materials | O″ carte 96 à questo Libro
sāza la coperta, 1483, 1471, 1528, 884, 698.

19. Br. M.

Bound volume in the MSS. Department of the
British Museum, numbered Arundel 263, con-
taining 283 folios, folio 136 and 137 bound in a
separate volume.

This MS. was in the collection of Thomas
Howard, twenty-third Earl of Arundel, whose
MSS. were presented in 1681 by Mr. Henry
Howard in part to the Royal Society and in
part to the College of Arms. MSS. in the posses-
sion of the Royal Society, including this one by
Leonardo, were transferred to the British Museum
in 1831.—On the second sheet is the note: 'Soc.
Reg. Lond (ex dono Henr. Howard) Norfolcen-
sis'.—*This volume has been partly made up from*
loose sheets of unequal size and quality of paper.
Only the first sheets can be assigned to the date
indicated at the head of the volume.

1*a* 4, M | 1*b*–18*b* Ph | 19*a* 906 | 19*b*–23*b* Ge |
24*a*, *b* mantice | 25*a* A, 875 | 25*b* A, *geology* |
26*a* modo brevissimo di misurare una distan-
tia | 26*b*–27*b* Ma | 28*a* 895, 876 | 29*a*, *b* A |
30*b* 982 | 31*a*, *b* P | 32*b* 6 | 33*a*–34*b* A | 35*a*
925 | 35*b* 926 | 36*a* A | 37*a*–42*a* P, M | 42*b*
1314, 1297, 1541 | 43*a* V, M | 43*b* M | 44*a*
350 | 44*b* P | 45*a* 928 | 45*b*–47*b* Ma, Ph | 48*a*
1451 | 48*b*–56*b* Ge, Mn | 57*a* O | 57*b*–61*a* A,
O, Ge | 62*a* 109 | 62*b* Ge | 63*a* + | 63*b* Mn |
64*a* le proportioni delli archi &c. | 64*b* 830 |
65*a*–77*b* Ph, Ma | 71*b* 1484 | 72*b* centro della
gravita | 78*a* + | 78*b* 888 | 79*a* P | 79*b* 1507 |
80*a*–93*a* Ph, Ma | 93*b* 207 | 94*a* 892 | 94*b* 896 |
95*a* A | 95*b* O | 96*a* V | 96*b*–102*b* Ph, Ma | 103*a*
897 | 103*b*–112*a* Ph, O | 112*b*, 113*a* + | 113*b*
458 | 114*a* 453 | 114*b* 459, 435 | 115*a* + | 115*b*
227 | 116*a*–119*a* P | 119*b* + | 120*a* l'universo
non à cosa minor ne piv bassa che 'l suo ciētro
P | 120*b* A | 121*a* bastioni | 121*b* Ma | 122*a*
927 | 122*b* + | 123*a*–124*b* P | 125*a* + | 125*b*
sails | 126*a* P, *architectural drawing* Vol. II,
p. 52, Fig. 3 | 126*b* V, A | 127*a*–128*b* P, M |
129*a* + | 129*b* 1333, V | 130*a* A, aria | 131*a*
1216 | 131*b* 45 | 132*a* 46 | 132*b* 1452 | 133*a*,
b Ma | 134*a*, *b* V | 135*a*, *b* A, M | 136*a* 1130,
Vol. I, p. 71 | 136*b*–137*b* Mn | 138*a* 789,
772, Pl. CVI | 138*b* + | 139*a* 645 | 139*b*
fiamme | 140*a* Mn | 140*b* M | 141*a* + | 141*b*
778, Pl. CV, Nos. 4–7 | 142*a* Ge | 142*b* + |

143*a*–145*b* Mn | 146*a* V, P | 146*b* + | 147*a* A,
queste sono le cose fatte da me Simone di
Matteo Migliorotti lequali . . . (11 lines) | 147*b*
851 | 148*a* 1548 | 148*b* 1549 | 149*a* 1015 |
149*b* 1550 | 150*a* + | 150*b* 1453 | 151*a* 859 |
151*b*–154*b* M, Ma | 155*a* 1339 | 155*b* 1218 |
156*a* 1217 | 156*b* 994, 1219, 1162 | 157*a*
Pl. CIV, 770 | 157*b* Pl. CV, 775, 771 | 158*a* 777,
773 | 158*b* 785 | 159*a* Ma | 159*b* 774 | 160*a*–
166*a* Ma, Ph | 166*b* V | 167*b*, 168*b* A | 169*a* 605,
305 | 169*b* + | 170*a* *chemicals* | 170*b* 181, 165
ll. 1–5, 172, 127, 165 ll. 6–9, 167 | 171*a* 110,
136, 143, 126 | 171*b* 510, 76, O | 172*a* + |
172*b* 471, 454, 476 | 173*a* 687 | 173*b* 916 |
174*a* 615, P, M | 174*b* 871 | 175*a* 860, 1129,
Pl. CXXI, Vol. I, p. 71 | 175*b* A | 176*a*
917, 857 | 176*b*–187*b* Ph, Ma | 188*a* 231 |
188*b*–190*a* Ph, Ma | 190*b* 916 | 191*a* 918, 1156,
1454 | 191*b* Mn | 192*a* + | 192*b* 1455, 763 |
193*a* + | 193*b*–202*a* Ph, Ma | 202*b* 1420 | 203*a*–
211*a* Ph, Ma | 211*b* 266 | 212*a* 1542 | 212*b*
1310 | 213*a* + | 213*b*–219*a* Ph, Ma | 220*a* 75,
84 | 220*b*, 221*a* Ma | 221*b* 74 | 222*a* + | 222*b*–
223*b* Ge | 224*a* P, *sketches of mountains and view*
of a cavern | 224*b* + | 225*a* *decorative designs* |
225*b* + | 226*a*, *b* M | 227*a* 1540 | 227*b* P |
228*a*, *b* M | 229*a* + | 229*b* 1525 | 230*a* Mn
| 230*b* Ph | 231*a* + | 231*b* 678, *sketch with*
figures | 232*a*, *b* Ge | 233*a* A | 233*b* 964 | 234*a*–
235*a* Ph | 235*b*, 236*a* + | 236*b* 965 | 237*a*,
b + | 238*a*–242*b* Ph, Ma | 243*a* 185 | 243*b* + |
244*a*–247 Ge | 248*a* + | 248*b* 186, 124 | 249*a*,
b + | 250*a* 674 | 250*b*–251 *a* + | 251*b* 1365 |
252*a* + | 252*b* sagoma | 253*a* 1366 | 253*b*
sketch of a child's head, drawn with the silver-
point | 254*a*–255*a* + | 255*b*–262*b* Mn | 256*a* *foot*
and hand of child, silverpoint | 263*a* + | 263*b*
1079 | 264*a*–268 Ph, Mn | 269*a* 1074, Pl.
CXV | 269*b* 1076 | 270*a* *sketches* | 270*b* 744,
747, 1075, 1077 | 271*a* 1551 | 271*b* 1463,
1527, A | 272*a* 1372 | 272*b* 1535 | 273*a*
sketches | 273*b* 1004 | 274*a* 1552, 1005 | 274*b*,
275*a* + | 275*b* *canals* | 276*a*–277*a* del vēto |
277*b* 473 | 278*a* *sketch of a river* | 278*b* 1144 |
279*a* Ge | 279*b* 1476, 914 | 280*a*–282*a* Ge,
Ph | 282*b*, 283*a* + | 283*b* centro della gravita,
and sketches.

20. E.

The cover of thin grey card is the original binding. The outside bears the mark E. B is twice written inside the cover. The last sixteen pages are missing. The compiler of the treatise on painting in the Vatican library (Urbinas 1270) gives a few passages from this MS., of which he correctly notes the corresponding number of the folio, to which the mark B is added.

o′ 915, 479 | 1a 1465, 1064, 1020, P | 1b Ge, P | 2a del cognoscere la parte settentrionale della calamita, M | 2b 211 | 3a de cōdensatione, 360, 238 | 3b 117, 467 | 4a 562, Ge | 4b *acoustics*, 935, Vol. I, p. 71 | 5a A | 5b, 6a P | 6b 366, 470, 403 | 7a P | 7b, 8a Ge | 8b 1155, Ma | 9a–11a Ge | 11b Mn | 12a 930 | 12b–14a strumenti aquatici | 14b per fare l'arco | 15a 230, 156, 380 | 15b 869 | 16a 108, 825 | 16b 107 | 17a 237, 153, 268, 153, 355 | 17b 24 |

18a 286 | 18b 440, Pl. XXVIII, No. 3 *right side* | 19a 461, 441, Pl. XXVIII, No. 3 *left side* | 19b, 20a 363, 362, P | 20b, 21a P | 21b–23b V | 24a + | 24b–27a Ge | 27b Machina murale | 28a Mn, Ph | 28b–29b Ph, Ma, Vol. I, p. 26 Note | 30a Ge | 30b O, 212 | 31a 161 | 31b 135, 1190, 197, Pl. XLI, No. 5 | 32a Pl. IV, No. 1, 162, 198 | 32b 264, 159, 240, 157 | 33a Ge, del centro della gravità | 33b Da generare vento mirabile | 34a Mn | 34b, 35a Ph | 35b–51a V | 51a 8B | 51b Ma | 52a–54a V | 54a 8E, *wind* | 54b P | 55a 1148A, Vol. I, p. 24 | 55b P | 56a Ge | 56b–75a P, M | 75b, 76a Mn | 76b–79a P, M | 79b 225, 17 | 80a 222, 1065 | 80b 15, 223 | o″ le carte sono di nᵣᵒ giusto 96 cioè Nouantasei. *This note is not in Leonardo's handwriting.* 480, 1539.

21. G.

The cover of thin grey card is the original binding. Inside and outside the cover is the mark G. The numbers of the sheets are in Leonardo's handwriting.

o′ 1377, le carte sono di numero giusto 96 cioè Nouantasei eccetto che vi māca il 7 et il 18 col suo conpagno 31. *This note is by an unknown hand* | 1a 1033, li pedali delli alberi ànno superficie . . . | 1b 1057 | 2a Mn | 2b 426 | 3a 425 | 3b 118, 872, 427 | 4a 428 | 4b 429, ll. 1–11, 406, 429, ll. 12–14 | 5a 405, Mn | 5b 503, 505 | 6a 455 | 6b 607 | 7 *is wanting* | 8a 1495, 1161, 19, 421, 430 | 8b 431 | 9a 432 | 9b 442 | 10a del moto dell' aria 423 | 10b Pl. XXVIII, No. 2, 424, 433 | 11a *sketch of a horse's head and note* | 11b 556, 460 | 12a 436 | 12b 247 | 13a 399 | 13b 90, P | 14a 400, P | 14b A | 15a 437, 603 | 15b + | 16a M | 16b 415 | 17a–18b Ge | 19a 554 | 19b 465, 443 | 20a A | 20b 444 | 21a 445 | 21b 446 | 22a 447 | 22b 448, 468 | 23a 469 | 23b 564 | 24a 422 | 24b *short notes about plants* | 25a 482, 499 | 25b 450 | 26a 590* | 26b Pl. XXVIII, No. 4, 451 | 27a 413 | 27b 457, 418, Pl. XXVII, No. 3 | 28a 414, Pl. XXVII, No. 4 | 28b 434,

438 | 29a 417, Pl. XXVII, No. 5 | 29b 106 | 30a P, M | 30b 416 | 31 *is wanting* | 32a 155 | 32b 401 | 33a 412, 402, Pl. XXVII, No. 2 | 33b 419, 553 | 34a 885 | 34b 397 | 35a A, 398 | 35b 407 | 36a 408 | 36b 409 | 37a 401, 263, 49, sagoma | 37b 481, A | 38a 949, A | 38b–40a P, Ge | 40b 966 Note | 41a Mn | 41b, 42a V | 42b G | 43a 726, Pl. LXXVI, No. 2 | 43b Ge | 44a 829 | 44b de cichognola | 45a, b Mn | 46a di potentia della voce | 46b 637 | 47a Mn, 1205 | 47b sagoma | 48a 974, 966 Note | 48b 946 | 49a 1201, 947 | 49b 976, A | 50a Ge | 50b del moto de navili | 51a 410 | 51b Mn | 52a 769, Mn | 52b Ge | 53a 641 | 53b 16, 89, 306, 569 | 54a 1113 | 54b, 55a M | 55b–62a Ge | 62b M | 63a P | 63b, 64a V | 64b 820 | 65a V | 65b + | 66a–69b Ge | 70a 966 | 70b Vol. II, p. 218 | 71–72b Mn | 73a–75a V, P, M | 75b 729 | 76a–88a Mn, Ph | 88b 411 | 89a 1327, 1166 | 89b de potentia | 90a 835 | 90b A | 91a vēto | 91b *on clouds* | 92a *on the wings of the fly* | 92b vento, della velocità de' nuvoli | 93a A | 93b, 94a Mn | 94b P | 95a A | 95b P | 96a 1504, Mn | 96b 1158, Mn | o″ 1464.

22. M.

The cover of thin grey card is the original binding, marked M outside the cover.

o′ 1425 | 1a–3b Ge | 4a 699, Pl. LX, No. 2 | 4b 700, Pl. LX, No. 3 | 5a 701, Pl. LX, No. 4 | 5b Ge | 6a *on the earth* | 6b–7b Ge | 8a 1426 |

8b–36a Ma | 11 1496A | 36b–53a P, M | 53b 1427 | 54a, b bombarda, passavolanti | 55a 373 | 55b, 56a ponte | 56b Mn | 57a–58a M | 58b 1285, 1152 | 59a–61b Ph, M | 62a 1478 | 62b–66b Ph, Mn | 67a 821 | 67b–76b Ph, M |

77*a* + | 77*b* **420, Pl. XXVIII, No. 1** | 78*a*
P | 78*b* **395, Pl. XXVII, No. 1,** *left side* |
79*a* **396, Pl. XXVII, No. 1,** *right side* | 79*b*

116* | 80*a* **115** | 80*b* Ge | 81*a*–84*a* Mn | 84*b*,
85*a* + | 85*b* Ge | 86*a* camino | 86*b*–88*a* Ge |
88*b* + | 89*a*–94*b* Ph, Mn | 0″ mark Q.

23. Triv.

Marked S *inside the cover and on the first
sheet. At the beginning of the Volume is the
following note:* 1784 · 3 · Gennaro · Questo
Codicetto di Leonardo da Vinci era del Signor
Don Gaetano Caccia Cavaliere Nouarese, ma
domiciliato in Milano, morto l'anno 1782 alli
9 Gennaro sotto la Parocchia di S. Dami-
aninno La Scala. Jo Carlo Triuulzio l'acquistai
dal detto Caualiere intorno l'anno 1750 unita-
mente a un quinario d'oro di Giulio Majoriano
e a qualche altra cosa che non più mi ricordo
dandoli in cambio un orologio d'argento di
ripetizione che io due anni avanti aveva com-
perato usato per sedici gigliati ma che in verità
era ottimissimo, che però questo codicetto mi
viene a costare sei in sette gigliati.

*There are two numerations, one of the sheets
and one of pages. The older of these ennumerates
the sheets but is not consecutive. It begins with
fol. 1 and continues to fol. 13. Then comes fol. 29
to fol. 14 and then fol. 30 to fol. 55. The pagina-
tion, on the other hand, is consecutive from page 1
to 102 and is marked in red ink. Both these
numerations are given below, the numbers of the
folios are in brackets.*

2 (1*b*) **1493,** *caricatures,* **1332, 1189** | 3 (2*a*)
1469 Note, 25, *ships* | 4 (2*b*) **1486** | 5 (3*a*) Ar,
Mn | 6 (3*b*) O, P | 7 (4*a*) **853,** Ar, Mn | 8 (4*b*), 9
(5*a*) *list of words* | 10 (5*b*) + | 11 (6*a*) **1202** | 12
(6*b*) **891** | 13 (7*a*) Fo | 14 (7*b*) **840** | 15 (8*a*) **Pl.
XCIX, No. 1, 758** | 16 (8*b*) **Pl. C, No. 3** |
17 (9*a*) **Vol. II, p. 47, Figs. 1, 2** | 18 (9*b*),
19 (10*a*) + | 20 (10*b*) *list of words,* **144** | 21 (11*a*)
Pl. C, No. 2 | 22 (11*b*) *list of words,* **1429, 177** |
23 (12*a*)–26 (13*b*) *transcripts from the Latin-*
Italian vocabulary of Luigi Pulci | 27 (29*b*) Mn
| 28 (29*a*) **863, 168** | 29 (28*b*) **201, 146** | 30
(28*a*) *male figure* | 31 (27*b*) Ar, *list of words* | 32
(27*a*) **1173** | 33 (26*a*), 34 (26*b*) Mn | 35 (25*b*)–38
(24*a*) *Italian words* | 39 (23*b*) **1193,** *Italian words* |
40 (23*a*) *Italian words* | 41 (22*b*) **Pl. C, No. 4** |
42 (22*a*) **Pl. LXXXI, No. 1** | 43 (21*b*) *sketch
of a building resembling the one given on* Pl.
LXXVIII, No. 1 | 44 (21*a*) Ar | 45 (20*b*)
Vol. I, p. 24, 1147 | 46 (20*a*) Ph | 48 (19*a*)
1128, 1381 Note | 49 (18*b*) **854, 640,** *acoustics* |
50 (18*a*) *list of words* | 51 (17*b*) *list of words,* **1148**
| 52 (17*a*) **737** | 53 (16*b*) **738** | 54 (16*a*) **739** |
55 (15*b*) **740** | 56 (15*a*) bombarda | 57 (14*b*)
1487, 1181, *list of words* | 58 (14*a*) nulla puo
essere scripto per nvouo ricerchare ecquale cosa
dite a me stesso prometta, *list of words* | 59 (30*a*)
list of Italian words, drawing of a profile, fornello
| 60 (30*b*) *list of Italian words* | 61 (31*a*) A, *list
of Italian words* | 62 (31*b*) *list of Italian words* |
63 (32*a*) Mn | 64 (32*b*) *list of Italian words* |
65 (33*a*) **1145, Vol. I, p. 24** | 66 (33*b*) bombarda,
list of Italian words | 67 (34*a*) *list of Italian
words* | 68 (35*a*) **1209, 43, 1174** | 69 (36*a*)
acoustics | 70 (36*b*) **1146, 1138,** *list of Italian
words* | 71 (37*a*) M, **539** | 72 (37*b*) *list of Italian
words* | 73 (38*a*) **1321,** *sketch of male profile
with cap* | 74 (38*b*) **28** | 75 (39*a*) **1136, 296** |
76 (39*b*), 77 (40*a*) + | 78 (40*b*) Mn, **1141, 1289,
622** | 79 (42*a*) P | 80 (42*b*) + | 81 (43*a*) M, *list
of words* | 82 (43*b*)–95 (52*a*) *list of words* | 96
(52*b*) *on warfare, list of words* | 97 (53*a*) *list
of words* | 98 (53*b*) triboli | 99 (54*a*) *drawing of
crossbow* | 100 (54*b*)–102 (55*b*) *list of words.*

24. Leic.

*Bound volume in leather cover. On the first
five sheets before the beginning of the original
MS. are the following notes. On* 1*a marked in
pencil* 696: This treatise on the nature, weight
and motion of water . . . has never been printed.
On the reverse of the modern title may be found
an extract from the life of Lionardo da Vinci, by
Dufresne, in which this volume is particularly
mentioned. It appears from the title page (although the name of the possessor has been
obliterated) that it has belonged to Giuseppe
Ghezzi, an eminent painter at Rome.—W. Ros-
coe. 1*b* + | 2*a* + | 3*a* Libro Originale ‖ Della
Natura, peso, e moto delle Acque, ‖ Composto, scritto, e figurato di proprio ‖ Carattere
alla mancina ‖ Dall' Insigne Pittore e Geo-
metra ‖ Leonardo da Vinci ‖ In tempo di
Ludouico il Moro, nel condur ‖ che fece le
Acque del Nauilio della ‖ Martesana dall' Adda
a Milano. ‖ Si autentica con la precisa Mentione che ne fà Raffaelle du fresne nella Vita
di detto Leonardo, descritta nel suo Libro
stampato in Parigi da Giacomo Longlois l'Anno
1651 intitolato ‖ Trattato ‖ Della Pittura ‖ Ac-

quistato 'conla gran forza dell' Oro' (*these words cover an erasure*), per sublimare ‖ le fatigose raccolte del suo studio ‖ da ‖ Giuseppe Ghezzi Pittore in Roma ‖ 3*b* (*in another handwriting*) Soleua il Vinci scrivere Alla mancina, secondo l'uso degli Ebrei, nella qual maniera erano scritti quei sedici Volumi de quali di già abiamo fatto menzione, et esendo il carattere buono, si legeua assai facilmente mediante un spechio grande, è probabile ch'egli facessi questo, accio tutti non legessero così facilmente i suoi scritti. L'impresa dell nauiglio di Martesana gli diede ocasione di scriuere un libro della natura, peso e moto delle Aque pieno di gran numero di disegni di varie rote, Machine per molini, a regolar il corso dell' aque, e leuarle in Alto | 4*a* + | 4*b* (*in an earlier handwriting*) Libro scritto da Leonardo Vincio che tratta del sole, della luna del corso dell' acqua dei ponti e dei moti | *According to a MS. of* 1690 *in the State Archives at Milan, published by G. Bonelli in Raccolta Vinciana, ii, pp.* 91–4, *Giuseppe Ghezzi was then in possession of a Leonardo MS.*, Della natura, del peso e moto delle acque—*which he had found in a chest with other MSS. and drawings of the sculptor Guglielmo della Porta (born at Porlezza, Lake of Lugano; died at Rome in* 1577), *who, when a pupil of his uncle, the sculptor Giov. della Porta (architect of Milan Cathedral* 1524–8), *was taught drawing by copying sketches of Leonardo. This uncle had a good many Leonardo drawings, having been a pupil of C. Solari, known as 'Gobbo di Milano'. Ghezzi, it is said, felt that the Leonardo MS. in his possession should go to the Ambrosiana, but funds were lacking for its acquisition. It would follow from the above that the MS. did not form part of the Leonardo bequest to Francesco Melzi. There is no doubt that it is identical with the one now at Holkham. It was probably acquired by Thomas Coke, afterwards Lord Leicester (born* 1697) *during one of his visits to Italy between* 1713 *and* 1717 *from the above-named Giuseppe Ghezzi* (1634–1721) *painter and collector living in Rome (his correspondence with Sebastiano Resta and others is in vol. iii of G. Bottari and S. Ticozzi, Raccolta di Lettere). The arrangements of this MS. are somewhat unusual. On the head of many*

pages there are title lines here placed between ' ' giving the numbers of 'cases' (casi) or subjects treated on the page. Most of these cases are introduced by 'Come' (*how, or that*).

1*a* 864 | 1*b* 1082, 901 | 2*a* 902, Pl. CVIII, No. 5 | 2*b* Come si debbe votare vno stagno che sbochi nel mare, P, luna | 3*a* A, 985 | 3*b* A | 4*a* 300, 1060 | 4*b* A | 5*a* 957, 971, 919, 907, luna | 5*b* A | 6*a* libro 2° delle diuersità dell' onde dell' acqua | 6*b* 958, A, 977 | 7*a* dell' acqua della luna, Ar | 7*b* A, O | 8*a* A, 386, Pl. XXIV, No. 3, Ph | 8*b* '8' 987 | 9*a* 'Carte 10 e cōclusioni 853' 988, 921 | 9*b* '16' 989, 721, 1055, 1061, A | 10*a* '15' 3rd *case:* 1063, 980, 990, Mn | 10*b* '15' 991, 1056, 1101, 936, 1085, Mn | 11*a* 'casi 13' A | 11*b* 'casi 27', 4th *case* 1058, 7th 969, 9th 1029 | 12*a* 'casi,—in queste 7 carte e casi 657 d'acque e di sua fōdi' | 12*b* 'casi 24' A | 13*a* 'casi 16' 1472, 4th *and* 5th 959, 15th *and* 16th 1008 | 13*b* 'casi 16' A | 14*a* 'casi 21' A | 14*b* 'casi 24' A | 15*a* 'propositioni 26' 1st *and* 2nd 972 | 15*b* 'propositioni 38' 920 *on the margin* | 16*a* 'propositioni 23' A | 16*b* 'casi 18' 1499 *on the margin*, 973 | 17*a* 'casi 29' A | 17*b* hordine del libro delle acque, 'casi 28' 956 | 18*a* 'casi 32', 22nd 1011 | 18*b* 'casi 16' 1007 | 19*a* 'casi 17' | 19*b* 'casi 37' | 20*a* 'casi 32', 7th 992, 14th *and* 15th 953, 16th 995 | 20*b* 'casi 24', Vol. II, p. 218 | 21*a* 'propositioni 12', 2nd 1027 | 21*b* 'pro^ni 25', 4th 948, 5th, 6th 849, 963, 7th 1096, 8th 963 ll. 7, 8 | 22*a* 'casi 29', 9th 1097 | 22*b* 'casi 39', 12th *and ff.* 1114, 1, *the last* 996 | 23*a* 'casi 20', 6th 997 | 23*b* 'casi 15' A | 24*a* 'casi 20' | 24*b* A | 25*a* 'casi 12 questi son casi che ànno a stare nel principio' *on air and water* | 25*b* 'casi 15' A | 26*a* 'casi 18' A | 26*b* 'casi 15' A | 27*a* 'casi 23' A | 27*b* '19', 13th 1071, 7th 1086, 8th 954 | 28*a* '8' 1110 *on the margin*, 1021 | 28*b* '15' A | 29*a* '13' A | 29*b* aria | 30*a* 899 | 30*b* A | 31*a* '900. 5 cōclusioni 9' 962 *on the margin*, 5th 1091, 6th *and ff.* 1090, 984 *on the margin* | 31*b*, 4th 1068, 5th 1108, 8th *and* 9th 978 | 32*a* A, 1028 | 32*b* 1098 | 33*a* A | 33*b* 970 | 34*a* 1000, A | 34*b* 933, 1095, 1072, A | 35*a* 960 | 35*b* 937 | 36*a* 938, centro del mondo, 301, 993 | 36*b* 900, A.

25. Trn.

Described by Arconati in 1637 *as a 'volumetto' of* 18 *sheets forming part of MS.* B; *see p.* 395. *It was stolen by Libri from the Institut de France, refound and acquired in* 1867, *but with* 5 *sheets missing, by Giacomo Manzoni di Lugo, after*

whose death it was acquired by Sabachnikoff, who presented it to Queen Margherita. Now at Turin in the Royal Library.

The grey card cover is original, and the booklet originally contained 18 *sheets (see*

Arconati's description). The sheets are numbered in Leonardo's handwriting beginning with number 3 and ending with 17. Leonardo left out the number 5 and a later hand corrected his numbers from 5 onwards ending with 16. Sheets 1, 2, 10, 17, and 18 were missing, but have since been recovered. Extracts from folios 1 and 2 were quoted in Venturi's Essai . . ., p. 18, and in Amoretti, Memorie . . ., p. 99. A full account of the MS. is in Uzielli, Ricerche, Serie 2, *pp.* 389–412.

o' **728** | 3*a* **1154**, P | 3*b* Ge, P | 4*a* P | 4*b* V | 6 *altered into* 5 **1122, 1126**c V | 7 *altered into* 6 V | 8 *altered into* 7 V, **1124**A | 9 *altered into*

8, 10 *altered into* 9 V | 12 *altered into* 11 **1168,** V, Ge | 11*b*, 13 *altered into* 12 V | 12*b* **1124** | 14 *altered into* 13 **705** | 13*b*, 15 *altered into* 14 V | 16 *altered into* 15 **1123** | 15*b* V | 17 *altered into* 16 V, **1125, 381, 1123**B, **1374**A | 16*b* baga, V | 18*a* V | 18*b* **1530**A, **1428**A | o ʺ **1428** *and the architectural drawing,* Vol. II, p. 51.

The Royal Library at Turin has also mounted sheets of drawings: 15571 **Pl. L** | 15572 **Pl. XLII** | 15573 **Pl. CXX** | 15574 **319, Pl. XII** | 15576 **320** | 15581 **1182** | 15583 *war machines pulled by horses, with notes. Tav.* LXXX Disegni di L.d.V., R. Commissione Vinciana.

26. D.

Marked D inside and outside the cover of grey card, S inside the back cover. Four blank sheets are at the beginning. This MS. treats of the eye. The following texts are a selection of the headings.

1*a* Perchè la natura non fece equal virtu e potentia nella virtu visiva | 1*b* perchè li razzi de' corpi luminosi si fan tāto maggiori quanto son più remoti dal lor nascimēto | 2*a* se l'idolo over simulacro à terminato sito sopra dell' ochio o no . . . come la rettitudine del concorso delle spetie si piega nello entrare nell' ochio | 2*b* come le spetie di qualūche corpo che per alcuno spiraculo passano all' ochio s'inpremon sotto sopra nella sua popilla e 'l senso le vede diritte **Vol. I, p. 27** | 3*a* come le cose destre nō pajono destre alla virtù visiva, se le sue spetie non passan per due intersegationi **78**A | 3*b* come le spetie si danno alla virtù visiva con due intersegationi per neciessità | 4*a* perchè lo spechio scambia alli simulacri delli obieti li lati destri ne' sinistri e li sinistri ne' destri | 4*b* che sia vero che ogni parte della popilla abbia uirtù visiua **81**C, **Vol. I, p. 27** | 5*a* dell' ochio delli animali nocturni |

5*b* La popilla dell' ochio si muta in tante varie grandezze quante son le varietà delle chiarezze o scurità delli obbietti che dināti sé li rapresentano | 6*a* Il simulacro del sole è vnico in tutta la spera dell' acqua che vede ed è veduta da esso sole ma pare diuiso in tante parti quanti son li ochi delli animali che in diversi siti vedono la superfitie dell' acqua | 6*b* La popilla dell' ochio à virtù visiua tutta per tutto e tutta in ogni sua parte | 7*a* come la popilla piglia li simulacri delle cose antiposte all' ochio solamente dalla luce e non dallo obbietto | 7*b* perchè la cosa destra non pare sinistra nell' ochio **Vol. I, p. 27** | 8*a* **71** | 8*b* dimostrasi perchè l'ochio vede adietro a sé cose poste nelli spati laterali **79**A | 9*a* dell' ochio vmano **Vol. I, p. 27** | 9*b* perchè li corpi luminosi mostrano li lor termini pieni di diritti razzi luminosi | 10*a* delle spetie delli obbietti che passano per stretti spiracoli in loco oscuro | 10*b* delle spetie delli obbietti infuse per l'aria **Vol. I, p. 27.**—*At the end four blank sheets, two bearing the mark* S.

27. K¹.

The three MSS. K¹ K² K³ *are bound in one Volume with a leather cover inscribed* LEO-NARDI ‖ VINCI ‖ *in golden letters. The sheets of each MS. are separately numbered. Inside the cover are the marks* K *and* 13. *On the first sheet is the inscription:* Commentarii autographi ‖ Leonardi Vincii ‖ Pictoris Architecti ‖ clarissimi ‖ quos dono dedit ‖ Bibliothecae Ambros.

‖ Comes Horatius Archintus ‖ Ingenuarum Artium ‖ studiosissimus ‖ Anno MDCLXXIV ‖ *Then follow four blank sheets.*

1*a* A, *and the mark* 44 | 1*b* Ma | 2*a* **1067** | 2*b* Ge | 3*a* **8**A | 3*b*–14*a* V | 14*b* *figure for Battle of Anghiari* | 15*a*+ | 15*b*–49*a* Ge, Ma | 15*b*–16*b*, 17*b* –32*a in black chalk* | 44*b*, 46*b*, 49*b* + | 48*b has the mark* O O 47.

28. K².

See introductory note to No. 27.

50*a* P | 50*b* **1308** | 51*a* **1489** | 51*b* **1490** | 52*a* Ge | 52*b* **1481** | 53*a*–54*b* Ge | 55*a*, *b* + | 56*a* A | 56*b*–57*b* Ge | 58*a*–60*a* V | 60*b* de fiumi | 61*a*

Ma | 61*b* **1508** | 62*a* + | 62*b* P | 63*b missing* | 64*a* Ma | 64*b*, 65*a* A | 65*b* + | 66*a*–75*a* Ma, Ge | 68*a*, 71*a* + | 75*b* **1430** | 76*a*–80*b* Ma, Ge.

29. K³.

See introductory note to No. 27.

81*a* la setola del bue | 81*b*–92*a* Ge | 92*b* + | 93*a* bastion | 93*b* datietto di Porta Nova | 93*b*–96*a* A | 96*b* Ge | 97*b*–99*a* A | 99*b* porto di casscano | 100*a* **1073** | 100*b*–101*b* A | 102*a* anatomy of horse | 102*b*–105*a* A | 105*b* **113** | 106*a* **114** | 106*b*–107 A | 108*a* **808** | 108*b*, 109*a* navilio (Ticino) | 109*b* **1501, 824, Pl. CVIII,**

No. 2 | 110*a* M | 110*b* **657, Vol. I, p. 72** | 111*a* M | 111*b* **1750** | 112*a* + | 112*b* **630** | 113*a*, *b* wind | 114*a*, 115*a*, *b* calcidonio | 116*a* colla di riso | 116*b* **749, Pl. LXXXII, No. 2** | 117*a* A | 117*b* *chemicals* | 118*a* Ph | 118*b*–120*b* O | 121*a*, *b* V | 122*a*, *b* O | 123*a*–124*a* M | 124*b*–127*b* popilla | 128*a* vasi | 128*b* **1431** *and the mark* L L 48.

30. C. A.

This best-known and most voluminous volume is composed of loose sheets of various size, each folio containing one or more sheets of the original MS. The mounting is the same as in volume W. Such sheets as have notes on both sides are not fixed by their back to the folio sheets, but set into a paper frame. The numbering of sheets refers only to the folios and agrees with Piumati's publication. In the following description it seemed to me desirable to refrain from giving detailed accounts of the contents of such sheets as do not bear upon the various subjects of the present publication, the more so, as the order of the sheets, being quite accidental, throws no light whatever on the connexion of the various studies extending over about thirty years. Outside the cover is the inscription in golden letters: DISEGNI . DI MACCHINE . || DELLE . ARTI . SECRETE || ET . ALTRE . COSE || DI . LEONARDO DA VINCI || RACCOLTI DA || POMPEO LEO || NI || (*Compare A. Ratti, Il Tavolo e il cofano pel Codice Atlantico, Racc. Vinciana, iii, (1907), pp. 111–26*).

First sheet **95** | 2*a* **1370c** | 4*a* **1553** | 4*b* **631, 1359** | 7*a* **1119** | 7*b* **Pl. LXXXVII, No. 1** | 8*b*, 9*b* **Vol. II, p. 218** | 12*b* **1165A, 1439** | 13*a* **1286, Vol. II, p. 48** | 14*a* **Vol. II, p. 218** | 17*b* **Pl. XCVI** | 18*a* **1533** | 18*b* **1361** | 19*a* **Vol. II, p. 218** | 20*b* **1440** | 26*b* **Vol. II, p. 218** | 27*a* **1545** | 28*a* **1441** | 31*b* **Pl. XLI, No. 2, 200** | 34*a* **Vol. II, p. 218** | 35*b* **1554** | 37*b* **1328** | 39*b* **1360** | 42*a* **101** | 42*b* **1554A** | 45*a* **1122A** | 45*b* **272, 353** | 46*a* **1001** | 47*b* **150** | 56*b* **Vol. I, p. 218** | 59*a* **1142** | 62*b* **1373A** | 63*b* **769A** | 65*b* **1203** | 66*a* **1114B** | 66*b* **1368** | 67*a* **1268, 1277, 1278, 1282, 1279, 1273** | 67*b* **1269, 1315, 1274, 1270** | 68*a* **1466** | 68*b* **702** | 69*b* **1331** | 71*a* **1163, 619, 1442, 1555A** | 71*b* **632, 621, 1526, 1373** | 72*b* **616** | 73*a* **Pl. CIX** | 73*b* **1016** | 74*a* **669** | 76*a* **1275, 1170, 20, 1143, 1159, 1370A, 1555** | 76*b* **1288, 1165, 847, 1207, 1200, 1335, 748, Pl. LXXXI, No. 2** | 77*a* **1530** | 77*b* **Vol. I, p. 72** | 78*b* **1556, 855** | 79*a* **Pl. XXXVIII, No. 1, 472** | 83*b*

Actio et passio sunt in patiente. . . . *Quotation from Aristotle*, Physicorum auscult. viii. 2. | 84*b* **951** | 85*b* **51** | 86*a* **1149** | 87*b* **1059** | 90*a* **836, 834** | 90*b* **1353B** | 92*a* **1353A** | 93*a* **1350A** | 95*b* **1557, 1093, 1111** | 98*a* **Vol. I, p. 72** | 99*b* **354** | 101*b* **64** | 103*a* **1377A** | 104*a* **1371** | 109*b* **634, 1185** | 112*a* **1171** | 112*b* **865** | 114*a* **1443** | 116*a* **128** | 117*a* **11, 1266** | 117*b* **1195** | 118*b* **1536** | 119*a* **1267, 1280** | 119*b* **12, 9, 21, 10** | 120*a* **1440** | 123*a* **1480** | 123*b* **1558** | 125*b* **82** | 126*a* **248, 192, 246, Vol. I, p. 72** | 126*b* **243, 983** | 129*b* **1309** | 131*a* **1216A** | 132*a* **42, 1559** | 132*b* **104, 151** | 134*a* **1544** | 135*b* **70** | 138*a* **65** | 138*b* **25, 60** | 139*a* **593, 1066** | 141*a* **660** | 141*b* **210, 1012, 1485** | 144*b* **96** | 145*a* **1293, Pls. CXVIII, CXIX** | 145*b* **1294, 1336, Pls. CXVI, CXVII** | 147*a* **1148B, Vol. I, p. 28, 487, 1445** | 148*b* **194** | 149*a* **8** | 150*b* **1284** | 154*a* **1153** | 155*a* **611, 986** | 156*b* **1180** | 158*a* **1405** Note | 159*a* **1368A** | 160*a* **309, 581, 466** | 160*b* **950, 961, 979** | 161*a* **1126D** | 165*b* **955** | 167*b* **1560** | 171*a* **965A** | 172*b* **757A** | 174*b* **1561A, 1561B** | 175*b* **1272** | 176*b* **233** | 177*a* **184** | 178*a* **1562** | 178*b* M, bombarda | 179*b* **67, 725, 1446** | 181*a* **271, 374** | 182*b* **1353** | 184*b* **280, 462, 493, Pl. CI, No. 2** | 187*b* **189** | 188*b* **1447** | 190*a* **Pl. IV, No. 5, 187, 273, 910** | 190*b* **1211** | 191*b* **1368** | 192*a* **1529** | 195*b* **279** | 199*b* **490, 548, Pl. XXXI, No. 1** | 202*b* **1357A** | 203*a* **13, 39** | 204*a* **54, 179, Pl. IV, No. 4** | 205*b* **Pl. LXXXVI** | 208*a*, 209*a* astronomy | 210*a* **1469** | 211*a* **1013A** | 213*b* **Vol. I, p. 71** | 214*a* **1030, 748A** | 214*b* **1031, 1337, V** | 215*b* **1084, 1537** | 216*b* **712, Pl. LXXVI, No. 1** | 219*b* **1496B** | 220*b* Magnifico mio messer Simone (5 *lines*), V | 221*b* **18** | 224*b* *sketch map:* Pavia Milan Lodi Binasco | 225*a* **1448** | 226*b* **1172** | 230*b* **1563** | 231*b* **703** | 234*b* **1062** | 236*a* **1013** | 237*a* **890** | 241*b* **191, Pl. VI, No. 1** | 246*a* **Vol. I, p. 26** | 247*a* **1379** | 247*b* **1351** | 248*a* **Vol. II, p. 218** | 249*a* **1378** | 249*b* **Vol. II, p. 218, 1125A** | 250*a* **111** | 252*a* **1364** | 257*b* **1531** | 260*a* **1105** | 262*a* **618, 1538** | 262*b* fedelissimo amico avisoti comequi ne di passati fu uno . . . (*not continued*)| 264*a* **1467** | 266*a* **Pl. XCIX, No. 3** | 270*a* **1347**A | 271*a* **769 Note** | 275*a* **1032** | 276 *swimming belt*, V | 277*b* *sketches of hats* **724** | 283*a* **1352** | 284*a* **1468** | 285*a* **759** | 287*a* **7**A, **Vol. I, p. 71** | 289*a* **1003** | 289*b* **1177, 1479** | 291*b* **718** | 297*a* **821** | 297*b* *five lines about Rome, not by Leonardo*, **1356**A | 298*a* **Vol. II, p. 48** | 302*a, b* V, **1113** B | 303*b* *list of objects*, Ducato di Salai | 306*b* **1287** | 307–309 V | 308*b* **1126**B, **1114**A | 310*a* **Pl. C, No. 1.** | 311*a* **1354** | 312*a* **Vol. II, p. 218** | 313*a*–314*b* V | 315*a* **Pl. LXXXII, No. 1** | 315*b* **1344** | 317*a* **1349** | 317*b* V | 318*b* **1370**B | 319*b* **1534** | 320*a* Giovanni damericho bencj, **730, 1163**A | 320*b* **1449** | 323*a* **722, 1346** | 323*b* **1347** | 324*a* **680**, *eight heads in profile* | 325*a*

766, Pl. CIII, No. 3 | 328*b* **1092, Pl. CXI, No. 2** | 333*b* **Vol. II, p. 218** | 335*a* **1388**, *sketch of river Adda* | 335*b* **723, 1345** | 336*a* *map*, castiglione aretino, monterchio | 336*b* **1078, 1565**, *maps of valley of Tiber*, Corneto | 340*a* **Vol. II, p. 218** | 342*b* **1564** | 345*b* **22, 598** | 347*a* 26 | 349*a* **382, 599** | 349*b* **908** | 352*b* **388, Pl. XXIV, No. 2** | 354*a* **478** | 355*a* **Vol. I, p. 71** | 357*b* **Pl. CVI**A | 358*a* **340** | 361*b* **1069** | 362*b* **Pl. LXXXIV** | 367*b* **1070, 1450** | 370*a* **1295** | 370*b* **975, 1296** | 371*a* **193** | 372*b* **1350** | 373*b* **1167** | 375*a* **Vol. II, p. 218** | 381*b* **1126** | 382*b* **1131**A | 385*b* **1473** | 386*a* **Vol. II, p. 218** | 389*b* **1357** | 391*a* **719, 1340** | 393*a* **1405 Note** | 393*b* **1112, Vol. II, p. 218** | 395*a* **1009** | 395*b* **Pl. LXXXII, No. 4** | 397*a*, 399*a* **Vol. II, p. 218.** | 401 *last sheet* Mn.

31. F. U.

FLORENCE, UFFIZI GALLERY. Categoria i. 446. *Drawing of an old man and youth facing each other, with notes transcribed in* **663, 1383**; *on verso drawing of a machine. Reproduced by R. Commissione Vinciana*, Disegni, *Tav.* XXXIII *and* XXXVI.

Categoria v. 8 P. *Drawing of landscape with note transcribed in* **1369**, *on verso landscape,* *sketch of a nude figure, and a head in profile with note written from left to right:* Io morando dant° sono chontento. *Reproduced by R. Commissione Vinciana*, Disegni, *Tav.* I *and* II.

447. *Drawings, silverpoint on red tinted paper: Man draped, two heads in profile, head of a dragon* Mn *with notes. Reproduced by R. Commissione Vinciana*, Disegni, *Tav.* LI.

32. V.

VENICE, ACADEMY OF FINE ARTS. Frame 10 **Pl. XLVI, 668** | Frame 27 *notes and diagrams on* P; *on verso* **Pl. XCIV, No. 4** | Frame 29 **Pl. XVIII, 343** | Frame 30 **Pl. LIII** | Frame 32 **Pl. LIV**, *on verso:* motori de corpi, **Pl. LV**, *on verso, notes on proportion* | Frame 33 **Pl. IX, 315**, *on verso, drawing of a profile* | Frame 35 *drawing of cavalry charging at in-* *fantry, below lance points and notes on weapons; on verso, instruments for throwing projectiles, with notes; reproduced on Tav.* LXXII *and* LXXXII, Disegni, *R. Commissione Vinciana*.

One sheet with notes on mechanics and geometrical drawings, reproduced in Uzielli, Ricerche, Serie 2. Rome 1884, **Vol. I, p. 114 Note.**

33. Mi. A.

Among the drawings by Leonardo in the Gallery of the AMBROSIANA, MILAN, *there is an anato-* *mical study of legs with a MS. note:* **1456**; *and* **Pl. LXVI**A.

34. Mch.

Nr. 2152, *drawings of machinery in pen and ink with notes on both sides of sheet, reproduced by W. Schmidt*, Handzeichnungen alter Meister im Kgl. Kupferstichkabinett zu München, 4. Lfg. N. 74, 1887.

35. P.

PARIS LOUVRE. *No.* RF 486 (His de la Salle, 101), **Vol. I, p. 379 Note**; *reproduced on Tav.* XXXI, Disegni, *R. Commissione Vinciana*.

No. 2258. **Pl. XXXIII**B, **594 Note, 999** Note.

No. 2260. *Codex Vallardi drawings of arms and lances, &c., with notes; reproduced on Tav.* LXXI, Disegni, *R. Commissione Vinciana*.

No. 2282. **Pl. LXXX, No. 1.**

No. 2316. **Vol. I, p. 379 Note**; *reproduced on Tav.* XXXI, *Disegni di L. d. V., R. Commissione Vinciana.*

No. 2347. **Pl. LIA, Vol. I, p. 377.** Edmond de Rothschild Bequest. *Drawing of two horsemen attacking dragon; reproduced on* **Pl. XXXIII**A.

36. P. A.

PARIS, ÉCOLE DES BEAUX-ARTS, *Bibliothèque: a drawing of war-machines with seven lines of notes, reproduced in R. Commissione Vinciana,* Disegni, *Plate* LXXVII.—*Another drawing, pen-and-ink, shepherds, study for an Adoration (late Armand Collection).*

37. Br. M. P.

The BRITISH MUSEUM PRINT ROOM *has several drawings by Leonardo, some with MS. notes.*

1875–6–12–17. *A sheet* 20×26 *cm. containing a Madonna with St. Anne, in pen and ink, a study for the Royal Academy Cartoon; on it a note transcribed in* **1457.**

1860–6–16–90. *A sheet* 17·5×24·5 *cm. with a war chariot and covered chariots, also a halberd with notes on warfare reproduced on Tav.* LXXVIII, *Disegni di L.d.V., R. Commissione Vinciana, Rome.*

1886–6–9–42. *A sheet* 16·5×26·2 *cm.; allo-* *gorical drawing with inscription of names:* fortuna —invidia—ingratitudine—superbia; *silver-point partly drawn over in ink (from Breadalbane Collection, see vol. II, p. 499, No. 52 in first edition of Lit. Works) reproduced on Tav.* XCVIII, *Disegni di L.d.V., R. Commissione Vinciana, Rome.*

1886–6–9–41. *Anatomical drawing in red chalk on paper tinted red of profile view of man's left leg,* 19·8×25·2 *cm., with notes.*

1854–5–13–17. *Pen sketch* 8½×12 *cm.* **Pl. LII, No. 2.**

38. B. B.

BAYONNE, MUSÉE BONNAT, *formerly collection of A. W. Thibaudeau, London. Pen-and-ink drawing with notes,* **Pl. LXII, No. 1, 664.** *Drawing of an allegory,* **Vol. I, p. 43,** *reproduced on Tav.* LV *of Disegni di L.d.V., R. Commissione Vinciana, Rome.*

39. Ox.

CHRIST CHURCH LIBRARY, OXFORD. *Five sheets with drawings catalogued as by Leonardo. Three of these with notes written by Leonardo.*

A. 29*a, b* (29×23·4 *cm.*) *is reproduced in parts in* **Vol. I, Pl. LIX, Pl. LX, No. 1, Pl. XI, 676, 677** (*Tav.* XLIX *and* C, *Disegni di L.d.V., R. Commissione Vinciana, Rome*).

A. 32 (21×27·7 *cm.*). *Two allegories* (*Tav.* CII *and* CI, *Disegni di L.d.V., R. Commissione Vinciana, Rome*). *a. Group of two women, one* *holding a mirror and a sword, the other double-faced; to the right serpents, eagle, hounds, and satyr. b. Winged figure pursuing figure with bow and arrow, with note, transcribed in* **1183**A.

A. 30 (23·0×13 *cm.*). (*Tav.* LXXIV *and* LXXV, *Disegni di L.d.V., R. Commissione Vinciana, Rome.*) *a. A horseman attacking a fallen foe. Diagrams of a lever with notes on machinery. b. Studies of cross-bows and slings.*

40. Md.

MODENA, ARCHIVIO PALATINO, **1348.** *Letter.*

41. F. L.

FLORENCE, BIBLIOTECA LAURENZIANA (*Ashburnham* 361). Trattato *attributed to Francesco di Giorgio Martini with notes in Leonardo's handwriting on the margin: fol.* 13*b* **767**; 25*a* **952**; 27*b* **44**; *notes on mechanics, &c., on* 15*b*, 32*a*, 41*a*, 44*b. Formerly at Ashburnham Place, England.*

42. Wr.

Weimar, Schloss-museum. *Pen-and-ink draw-*
ing of dissected skulls with explanatory notes on
brain and nerves. On reverse drawing of genital
organs: Raccolta Vinciana, xiii, *Supplement.*

43. N. Y.

Metropolitan Museum of Art, New York.
Pen-and-ink drawing inside a circle, illustrating a
fable, described above in four lines of text: 1264a.
On the reverse drawing of stage scenery with notes:
705a. *Tav.* CVI, Disegni di L.d.V., *Reale Com-*
missione Vinciana, Rome; Raccolta Vinciana, x.

44. P. H. N.

Diagram and notes on Perspective at one time
in the collection of the late Prince Henry of the
Netherlands, sold by auction.

45. Mo.

Drawing of two war-machines with notes, for-
merly in the collection of the late Mr. Alfred
Morrison, London, reproduced in Sotheby's sale
catalogue, April 1918, now in the possession of
Herr Stefan Zweig.

46. G. H.

Drawing of a basilica and geometrical designs
with notes in the collection of autographs of Herr
Geigy-Hagenbach, Basle, reproduced in his cata-
logue, see p. 401.

APPENDIX
III

BIBLIOGRAPHY

(1) *Publications of Leonardo's MSS.*

I. *MS. A, B, C, &c., to M. Institut de France.*

a. Les Manuscrits de Léonard de Vinci. Manuscrit A, etc. de la Bibliothèque de l'Institut, publié par M. Charles Ravaisson-Mollien, Paris, 1881–91. (This publication includes the two MSS. formerly in the Bibliothèque Nationale (2037 and 2038).)

b. I Manoscritti e i Disegni di Leonardo da Vinci, pubblicati dalla Reale Commissione Vinciana, Vol. II. Il Codice A (2172) nell' Istituto di Francia. Danesi editore, Rome, 1936.

II. *Royal Library, Windsor.*

a. Catalogue of the Drawings of Leonardo da Vinci at Windsor Castle by Kenneth Clark. Cambridge, 1935, with reduced reproductions of Nos. 12275 to 12727.

b. Feuillets inédits de Léonard de Vinci reproduits d'après les originaux au Château de Windsor. Rouvèyre, Paris, 1901, in 22 parts.

c. Anatomical MS. A. I manoscritti di Leonardo da Vinci della Reale Biblioteca di Windsor. Dell' Anatomia, Fogli A, pubblicati da Teodoro Sabachnikoff, trascritti e annotati da Giovanni Piumati. Paris, 1898. (This volume comprises Nos. 19000 to 19017 of K. Clark's catalogue.)

d. Anatomical MS. B. I manoscritti di Leonardo da Vinci della Reale Biblioteca di Windsor. Dell' Anatomia, Fogli B, pubblicati da Teodoro Sabachnikoff, trascritti e annotati da Giovanni Piumati. Turin, 1901. (This volume comprises Nos. 19018 to 19059 of K. Clark's catalogue.)

e. Quaderni d'Anatomia. Leonardo da Vinci, Quaderni d'Anatomia, I–VI. Fogli della Royal Library di Windsor, pubblicati da Ove C. L. Vangensten, A. Fonahn, H. Hopstock, Christiania, 1911–16. (These six volumes comprise 119 folios, namely, Nos. 19060 to 19152 of K. Clark's catalogue, which are bound together in a volume known as Anatomical MS. C, and 26 other folios with anatomical drawings in the collection.)

1. Tredici Fogli . . . Respirazione, cuore, visceri addominali.
2. Ventiquatro Fogli . . . Cuore, anatomia e fisiologia.
3. Dodici Fogli . . . Organi della generazione, embrione.
4. Ventun Fogli . . . Sangue, cuore, fonetica, varie altre materie.
5. Ventisei Fogli . . . Vasi, muscoli, cervello, nervi, anatomia topografica e comparata.
6. Ventitre Fogli . . . Proporzioni, funzioni dei muscoli, anatomia della superficie del corpo umano.

III. *London, British Museum, Arundel MS. 263.*

a. Manuscrits inédits de Léonard de Vinci, reproduits d'après les originaux conservés au British Museum, London. Rouvèyre, Paris, 1901. (It was planned to publish 15 volumes with 750 facsimiles. But only 4 volumes with 100 facsimiles appeared.)

b. I manoscritti e i Disegni di Leonardo da Vinci, pubblicati dalla Reale Commissione Vinciana. Vol. I. Il Codice Arundel 263. Danesi editore, Rome, 1923–30. Parte I, fol. 1–116, 1923; Parte II, fol. 117–220, 1926; Parte III, fol. 221–82, 1928; Parte IV, Index and Notes, 1930.

IV. *Milan, Ambrosiana, Codice Atlantico.*

a. Il Codice Atlantico di Leonardo da Vinci nella Biblioteca Ambrosiana di Milano, riprodotto e pubblicato dalla R. Accademia dei Lincei da Giovanni Piumati. Milan, 1894–1904.

b. A full index is to appear shortly entitled: Dizionario Leonardesco, ossia Repertorio delle voci e cose ricorrenti nel Codice Atlantico, published by Hoepli, Milan.

c. Saggio delle Opere di L. d. V. con 24 Tavole tratte dal C.A. Milan, 1872.

V. *Turin Codex.*

a. Codice sul volo degli uccelli e varie altre materie, pubblicato da Teodoro Sabachnikoff, trascrizioni e note di Giovanni Piumati. Traduzione in lingua francese di Carlo Ravaisson-Mollien. Rouvèyre, Paris, 1893.

b. Reale Commissione Vinciana. I fogli mancanti al codice di Leonardo da Vinci nella Biblioteca Reale di Torino. A cura di Enrico Carusi. Rome, Danesi editore, 1926.

VI. *Trivulzian MS.*

Il Codice di Leonardo da Vinci, della Biblioteca del Principe Trivulzio in Milano, trascritto e annotato da Luca Beltrami. Milan, 1891.

VII. *Leicester MS.*

Il Codice di Leonardo da Vinci della Biblioteca di Lord Leicester in Holkham Hall, pubblicato sotto gli auspici del R. Instituto lombardo di scienze e lettere (premio Tomasoni) da Gerolamo Calvi. Milan, 1909.

VIII. *S.K.M. MS.*

a. I manoscritti e i Disegni di Leonardo da Vinci, pubblicati dalla Reale Commissione Vinciana, Serie minore, Codici Forster, nel Victoria and Albert Museum, London. Danesi editore, Rome, 1930–6. 5 vols. Vol. i contains MS. S.K.M. I.Vol. ii contains S.K.M. II¹. Vol. iii contains S.K.M. II². Vol. iv contains S.K.M. III. Vol. v contains Preface, Appendix, and Index by Enrico Carusi.

b. Carnets inédits de Léonard de Vinci, reproduits d'après les originaux. Forster Library, South Kensington Museum, London. Problèmes de géométrie et d'hydraulique. I. Les solides d'égal volume; II. Machines hydrauliques, Application du principe de la vie d'Archimède, Pompes, Machines d'Épuisement et de dragage. 3 vols. Rouvèyre, Paris, 1901.

IX. *New York.*

Metropolitan Museum of Art Bulletin, October 1916.

X. *Weimar, Schloss-Museum.*

One sheet published in the *Raccolta Vinciana* xiii, Supplement, Milan, 1930. Emil Möller, Abbozzi e Testi sconosciuti del Vinci sull' Anatomia.

XI.

A series of drawings by Leonardo, some with notes in his handwriting, are published in facsimile by the Reale Commissione Vinciana, sotto gli auspici del Ministero dell' Educazione Nazionale. Disegni, Fascicolo I. Plates 1–32, 1928; Fascicolo II, Plates 33–70, 1930; Fascicolo III, Plates 71—108, 1934. Fascicolo IV, Plates 109–73 (studies of horses), 1936. These include drawings at the Louvre, the École des Beaux-Arts in Paris, the Bonnat Museum at Bayonne, the British Museum, the Ashmolean Museum, the libraries at Windsor Castle and Christ Church, Oxford, the Royal Library at Turin, the Uffizi, Florence, the Reale Galleria, Venice, the Metropolitan Museum at New York, &c.

(2) *Publications of Selections from Leonardo's manuscripts made in the sixteenth and seventeenth centuries*

A. Il Trattato del Moto e Misura dell' Acqua (*Codex Vaticanus-Barberini 4332*), composed of extracts from Leonardo's writings made by the Dominican Luigi Maria Arconati in 1643 from MSS. of the Ambrosiana. For a list of passages still extant in Leonardo's original MSS., see Nando de Toni, 'L'idraulica in L.d.V:', *Frammenti Vinciani*, iii, Brescia, 1934. No extracts were included from the Leicester and Arundel Codices nor from MSS. at Windsor, but there are extracts from MSS. which are now lost. First published at Bologna in 1828 in *Raccolta d'autori italiani che* trattano del moto delle acque, vol. x, pp. 270–450.

Another edition: Del moto e misura dell' acqua, Libri nove, ordinati da F. Luigi Maria Arconati. Editi sul codice archetipo Barberiniano a cura di E. Carusi ed A. Favaro. Published by the Istituto di Studi Vinciani, Roma. Nuova serie. Testi Vinciani, Vol. I. Bologna, 1923. See A. Favaro, 'Intorno al Trattato di Leonardo da Vinci sul moto e misura dell' acqua', *Rendiconti della R. Accademia dei Lincei*, xxvii, 1918.

* * * * * * * *

B. Trattato della Pittura (see vol. I, pp. 5 sqq., for history of these manuscripts).

I

Publications based on Codex Vaticanus (Urbinas 1270)

1817. Trattato della Pittura di L.d.V., edited by Guglielmo Manzi, Rome. The illustrations were published in a separate volume: Disegni che illustrano l'opera del Trattato della pittura di L.d.V. An abbreviated edition with illustrations appeared at Milan, 1859.

1882. Leonardo da Vinci, Das Buch von der Malerei nach dem Codex Vaticanus (Urbinas 1270) übersetzt von Heinrich Ludwig. Volumes xv–xvii of Quellenschriften für Kunstgeschichte. Vienna. Second edition by Marie Herzfeld, Jena, 1909.

1890. Trattato della Pittura di L.d.V. condotto sul Codice Vaticano Urbinate 1270 con prefazione di Marco Tabbarrini.

1910. Traité de la Peinture de L.d.V. traduit sur le Codex Vaticanus (Urbinas 1270) complété par des nouveaux fragments tirés des manuscrits du Maître par S. Péladan. Paris, second edition, 1921. Traité du Paysage traduit in extenso sur le Codex Vaticanus par Péladan. Second edition, 1921. This volume contains Books VI–VIII of the Codex Vaticanus and is a continuation of the volume previously mentioned.

1914. Trattato della Pittura di L.d.V. Prefazione di Angelo Borzelli Lanciano, Carabba. 2 vols. forming part of the series *Scrittori italiani e stranieri*.

II

Publications based on abbreviated copies of the Codex Vaticanus

1651. Trattato della Pittura di Leonardo da Vinci novamente dato in luce con la Vita dell' istesso autore, scritta da Rafaelle Du Fresne, Paris. New editions: Naples, 1723, 1733, 1773; Bologna, 1786; Milan, 1804; Perugia, 1805.

The following translations were based on this edition:

1651. Traité de la Peinture de L.d.V. traduit de l'italien par R F S de C. Paris. Later editions in 1716, 1796.

1721. A Treatise of Painting by L.d.V. translated from the original Italian—done from the last edition of the French. London. Reprinted in 1796.

1724. Des vortrefflichen florentinischen Malers Lionardo da Vinci höchst nützlicher Traktat von der Malerey aus dem italienischen und französischen übersetzt von J. G. Böhm. Nürnberg. Reprinted in 1747 and 1786.

1784. El Tratado de la Pintura por L.d.V. traducido por Don Diego Antonio Riejon de Silva. Madrid. Second edition, 1827.

1802. A Treatise on Painting by L.d.V. faithfully translated and now first digested under proper heads by John Francis Rigaud, with a new Life of the author by John Sidney Hawkins. London. Later editions with the Life of the author by John William Brown in 1835 and 1877.

1827. Verhandeling over de Schilderkunst van L.d.V. vertaald naar de fransche uitgave van den jare 1716 door Juannes Vos, Amsterdam.

*   *   *   *   *

1803. Traité de la Peinture de L.d.V. par P. M. Gault de Saint Germain, Paris. Second edition, 1820. Similar to Du Fresne's, but the editor claims to have found and used in addition another MS. of the *Trattato* illustrated by Poussin.

*   *   *   *   *

1792. Trattato della Pittura di L.d.V. ridotto alla sua vera lezione sopra una copia a penna di mano di Stefano Della Bella, con le figure disegnate dal medesimo. Firenze. Edited by Francesco Fontani.

INDEX

I. NAMES AND BIBLIOGRAPHY

II. TOPOGRAPHICAL

Abila, ii. 157.
Adalia, ii. 213 *n*.
Adda, ii. 23, 23 *n*., 146, 165, 183, 184 *n*., 185, 190, 412; map, ii. 416.
Adige, ii. 165; rising and sinking of, ii. 369.
Adriatic Sea, ii. 155, 156 *n*., 157, 169, 171.
Adula mountains, ii. 204.
Aegean Sea, ii. 204, 215.
Africa, ii. 157, 162, 172, 206, 207.
Africa Minor, ii. 146, 211, 211 *n*.
Albania, ii. 204, 375.
Albanus, mountains, ii. 204.
Aleppo, ii. 319 *n*.
Alessandria della Paglia, ii. 195; petrefacts there, ii. 195.
Alexandria, ii. 317 *n*.; library of, ii. 373.
Allier, river, ii. 203 *n*.
Alps, ii. 166, 180, 195 f.; conditions in, ii. 189.
Alserio, lake of, ii. 191.
Amboise, ii. 199; court at, ii. 203 *n*.; Hôtel Dieu, ii. 390; L. at, i. 110, 374, ii. 345, 388; L.'s project for a royal residence, ii. 24, 25 *n*., 26; L.'s will, ii. 388 f.; map, Pl. LXV.
St. Denis, *see* L.'s will.
St. Florentine, *see* L.'s will.
St. Gregory, *see* L.'s will.
Anghiari, *see* Leonardo as painter.
Annone, lake of, ii. 191.
Antitaurus, ii. 321.
Antwerp, ii. 198.
Apennines, ii. 166, 171, 180, 197, 207.
Apollonia, ii. 375.
Arabia, gulf of, ii. 209.
Ararat, ii. 321 *n*.
Arbiti mountains, ii. 216.
Arezzo, ii. 171, 181, Pl. CXIII.
Armenia, ii. 151, 151 *n*., 209, 317, 318, 319, 321 *n*., Pls. CXVI–CXIX; L.'s maps of, 321 *n*.; history of, ii. 317 *n*.
Arnigasar, mountain, mentioned by L., ii. 321 *n*.
Arno, ii. 165, 169, 170, 171, 173, 181, 181 *n*., 182, 182 *n*., 183, 183 *n*., 207; map of, ii. 403, Pl. CXII; *see also* Canals, project for, in Tuscany.
Arthamis river, ii. 216.
Arve, ii. 195.
Ashburnham Place, i. 127 *n*.
Asia, ii. 157, 162 *n*., 207, 209.
Asia Minor, ii. 205, 274, 318 *n*., 320.
Atalia, sea of, ii. 213.
Atlas, Mount, ii. 207, 209, 212; giant born there, ii. 339.

Attalia, ii. 213 *n*.
Austria, ii. 198, 204.
Azov, sea of, ii. 215.

Baalbek, temple of, ii. 49 *n*.
Babylon, ii. 317.
Bactria, ii. 215.
Bagrada river, ii. 206, 207 *n*.
Balkan, ii. 204 *n*.
Barbiga, ii. 345.
Basel, Geigy-Hagenbach Collection, L.'s drawing, i. 109, ii. 401, 418.
Bavaria, ii. 204.
Bayonne, Bonnat Collection, L.'s drawings, i. 43 *n*., 109, 383 *n*., ii. 401, 418, Pl. LXII.
Bellaggio, ii. 190.
Bellinzona, ii. 190.
Belvedere, *see* Rome.
Bertinoro, ii. 193, 194.
Bethlehem, Herodium, ii. 45 *n*.
Bilaspus river, ii. 216.
Bisarno, ii. 182.
Biscay, ii. 198.
Black Sea, ii. 162, 204, 205, 209, 214, 215.
Blois, ii. 199, 201 *n*., 203 *n*.
Boccalino, measurement of, ii. 360.
Bologna, mentioned by L., ii. 193, 215; L. meeting Dürer (?), i. 27 *n*.; tower of La Magione, transport of, ii. 48 *n*.; University of, ii. 107.
Bonconvento, ii. 194.
Bordeaux, ii. 198.
Borgo San Sepolcro, i. 381, 381 *n*., ii. 354.
Bormio, ii. 190.
Bosnia, ii. 204.
Bosporus, ii. 215.
Brescia, ii. 405.
Brescian territory, L.'s map of, ii. 403.
Brivio, ii. 184, 191 *n*.
Bruges, ii. 198.
Budapest, Mathias Corvinus library, i. 65 *n*.; Museum, L.'s drawings, i. 375, 376, Pls. LB, LC.
Cairo, ii. 207 *n*., 317 *n*.
Calabria, ii. 156 *n*.
Calais, ii. 156 *n*.
Calindra, ii. 318, 318 *n*.
Calpe, ii. 157.
Candia in Lombardy, ii. 195.
Capraia, ii. 165.
Caprona, ii. 182.
Caravaggio, ii. 353.
Carpathians, ii. 204, 209.
Caruancas, ii. 204.
Carunda mountain, ii. 321 *n*.
Casa nova, ii. 194.
Casale di Monferrato, ii. 169 *n*.

Casentino, plains of, ii. 173.
Caspian Sea, ii. 214, 215, 216.
Castel Fiorentino, ii. 170; diggings at, ii. 173.
Castiglione, ii. 416.
Castille, ii. 198.
Caucasus, ii. 205, 215, 321, 321 *n*.
Ceceri, Monte, ii. 356, 357.
Celaene, mountains of, ii. 209.
Cento, clocher de, redressé, ii. 49 *n*.
Cervetri, tomb of Regolini Galassi, ii. 45.
Cesena, fair of San Lorenzo, ii. 192; grapes carried at, ii. 193; L.'s drawing made at, ii. 52, Pl. CX No. 4; rock of, ii. 192, 193.
Ceuta, ii. 170, 210.
Charolais, monts du, ii. 203 *n*.
Cher, ii. 201, 203.
Chiana, valley of, ii. 181, 197 *n*.
Chiaravalle, abbey of, ii. 27, 27 *n*.
Chiavenna, ii. 189, 190.
Chiusi, ii. 194.
Chorossan, ii. 367 *n*.
Chur, lakes of, ii. 146.
Cilicia, ii. 209, 214, 318 *n*.
Circassia, ii. 317 *n*.
Civitavecchia, L.'s visit to, ii. 58 *n*.
Cloux, ii. 83, 345, 389, 390.
Cocomeri, island of, ii. 183.
Colle Gonzoli, ii. 170.
Comedorum mounts, ii. 215.
Como, ii. 190; Duomo, ii. 28, 57; lake, *see* Lake of Como.
Constance, lake of, ii. 146.
Constantinople, ii. 215, 215 *n*.; map of, Pl. CX No. 1.
Corneto, ii. 403, 416.
Cremona, i. 75; La Colomba, ii. 351.
Cusago, i. 74.
Cyprus, ii. 24, 213, 213 *n*., 214.
Cyrenaica, ii. 273.

Dalmatia, ii. 204.
Danube, ii. 149, 197, 204, 207, 215; valley of, 204, 205.
Dardania, ii. 204, 204 *n*.
Dargados, ii. 216.
Dauphiné, ii. 198.
Dead Sea, ii. 147 *n*., 148.
Diamuna river, ii. 216.
Didyma, oracle of, ii. 237 *n*.
Digoin, ii. 203 *n*.
Don, ii. 154, 205, 207, 214, 215.
Dora, ii. 185.
Dore, ii. 203 *n*.
Dragamain river, ii. 216.
Dresden, collection, Raphael drawing, i. 376.

Egypt, ii. 317 *n*., 274. sea of, ii. 211, 212.
Elbe, ii. 165.

439

III. GENERAL INDEX

Academies of Art, i. 22; *see also* Rome, &c.

Académie de France, *see* Rome.

Académie Royale de Peinture et Sculpture, *see* Paris.

Accounts, L.'s, ii. 377 f.

Acoustics, i. 72, ii. 230, 231, 231 n.; echo, ii. 232; harmony through fall of water, ii. 193; resonance, ii. 231; shepherd's horn, ii. 197; waves of sound, ii. 231, 232; their reflection compared to optics, ii. 232.

Action of the body, i. 267 f.; classification of, ii. 86; expressive of the mind, i. 28, 55, 58, 59, 347; study from, i. 305; *see also* Human figure.

Adam and Eve, i. 389.

Adding, *see* Sculpture, Technique, and Painting.

Adoration, of an image, i. 36, 56, 64.

Advice, aphorisms on, ii. 247.

Aeolus, i. 352.

Aerial perspective, *see* Perspective, aerial.

Air, *see* Atmosphere.

Air-bags, ii. 221.

Alchemy, polemics against, ii. 85, 250; use for science, ii. 282; compared with medicine, ii. 106.

Algebra, definition of, ii. 357.

Allegory, i. 46, 47, 382 ff.; allegorical drawings, i. 42 n.; Constancy, i. 390; Disgrace, i. 390; Envy, i. 386; Falsehood, i. 388; Fame, ii. 385, 390; Fortune, i. 383, ii. 245; Ingratitude, i. 389; Pleasure and Pain, i. 385; Pls. LVIII–LXI; *see also* Symbol.

Anatomy.

  general:

    books on, mentioned by L., i. 113, 113 n., ii. 83, 353, 355, 357, 367, 371, 373. L. on his own book on, i. 261, 262, ii. 86–90; finished in 1510, ii. 345.

    plan and order for a book on, ii. 86, 87.

    difficulty of study, ii. 85.

    dissection of corpses, i. 2, 30, ii. 83, 84, 85; hindered in Rome, ii. 84, 338; Pls. I B, CVII, CVIII.

    anatomical drawings, how to begin with and to make, ii. 88, 89; dangers of, i. 261.

    L.'s studies on in 1510–16, i. 244.

    necessary for painter, i. 304.

  special:

    of the bat, ii. 226.

    bear, paw of, ii. 403, Pl. XXXIV.

    of the bird, ii. 226.

    of the bird's wing, i. 114, 114 n.

    bones, book on, ii. 360; saw for, ii. 357.

    comparative, of man and animals, ii. 94.

    corpulency and leanness, ii. 91, 92.

    elementary tissues, ii. 92.

    feet, i. 260.

    foetus, life and growth of, ii. 86; *see also* Aegidius Romanus.

    head, division of, ii. 92.

    of horses, i. 28.

    on human figure, i. 28, ii. 92.

    joints, i. 262, 263.

    limbs, i. 262, 263.

    movement of brows, eyes, lips, ii. 90; of elbows, fingers, hands, ii. 91; of feet, knees, toes, thigh, ii. 91.

    muscles, i. 259–63; shortening and stretching, i. 259; representation of, i. 261, ii. 89, 90.

    shoulder, i. 260, 261.

    tendons, i. 259–62.

    veins, i. 263; of the arms, ii. 378.

    see also Physiology, Zoology, Human figure.

Ancients originators of grammar and the sciences, ii. 356.

Ancients, primitives, ii. 373.

Angels, how to represent, i. 270.

Anghiari, battle of, description by L., i. 381, 382; *see also* Leonardo as painter.

Angle, *see* Geometry, Light, Optics.

Angry man, representation of, i. 342.

Animals deceived by painting, *see* Painting, deceptive.

Animals, imaginary, how to make, i. 342; *see also* Monstrosities.

Animals, *see* Anatomy, Bestiary, Fables, Physiology, Zoology, Symbols, Prophecies.

Anne, grandmother of Christ, *see* Leonardo as painter.

Antaeus, ii. 339 n.

Antipodes, ii. 110; Augustinus on, ii. 388.

Antique, i. 304; imitation of, ii. 359; study from, i. 303.

Apex, *see* Perspective, Pyramid of Light.

Aphrodite, ii. 213 n.

Apollo, i. 18.

Arabian philosophers and mathematicians, i. 26 n., 125, 243.

Arabs, ii. 211, 212.

Arches, *see* Architecture.

Architecture, i. 14, 20, 21, 63, 67, 72, 78 n., 90, ii. 19–82, 331; account concerning, ii. 377; L.'s ability in, ii. 326; book on, i. 113, ii. 19; designs, ii. 21 ff.; style, ii. 79 ff.; writings, ii. 59 ff.

  arches (nature of), ii. 67; abutments for, ii. 73; breaking of, ii. 67; fissures in, ii. 65–74; pointed, ii. 68; pressure on, ii. 67; stability, ii. 70; strength, ii. 68; weight of counterpoint, ii. 70.

  architraves, ii. 57.

  banquet-hall, advice for, ii. 25.

  beams, i. 113, ii. 77 f.; chaining of, ii. 77; resistance of, ii. 77; shrinking of, ii. 78.

  buildings, stability of, ii. 60–4.

  campanile, ii. 27.

  castles and villas, ii. 24 ff.

  chimney, form of at Pavia, ii. 188.

  columns, ancient, ii. 56; strength of, ii. 71; ecclesiastical, ii. 27 ff.

  foundation, laws of, geology of, ii. 75.

  moving of buildings, ii. 22.

  palace, advice for building, ii. 25.

  pillars, rules for dimensions, ii. 76.

  roofs of churches, ii. 27.

  stables, how to make clean, ii. 53.

  town, plan for ideal, ii. 21, 22, 249.

  walls, cracks and fissures, ii. 60–4.

  windows, how to place, ii. 76; *see also* Leonardo as architect.

Arithmetic, i. 14–17, 31, 34, 37, 55; *see also* Mathematics.

Arm, movements of, i. 260; proportions of, i. 251, 253, 255 f.

Art, a grandchild of God, i. 17 n., 19, 19 n., 58, 367.

  relation to nature, i. 367; *see also* Arts, Painting, Sculpture.

Artist (career), disposition for, i. 303; course of instruction for, i. 303; social position, i. 14, 16, 17, 18, 22, 91.

Artist's materials, i. 359 ff.